American Chronicle

American Chronicle

Year by Year Through the Twentieth Century

Lois Gordon and Alan Gordon

With an Introduction by Roger Rosenblatt

Yale University Press / New Haven & London

Published with assistance from the foundation established in memory of Philip Hamilton McMillan of the Class of 1894, Yale College.

Printed in the United States of America by Vail-Ballou Press, Binghamton, New York.

Library of Congress Cataloging-in-Publication Data

Gordon, Lois G.
    American chronicle : year by year through the twentieth century / Lois Gordon and Alan Gordon ; with an introduction by Roger Rosenblatt.
        p.   cm.
    Rev. ed. of: The Columbia chronicles of American life, 1910–1992. c1995.
    Includes indexes.
    ISBN 0-300-07587-1 (cloth : alk. paper)
    1. United States—Civilization—20th century—Miscellanea.
2. United States—Civilization—20th century—Chronology.
I. Gordon, Alan, 1936– . II. Gordon, Lois G.   Columbia chronicles of American life, 1910–1992.   III. Title.
E169.1.G664   1999
973.91—dc21   99-24886
                                                              CIP

A catalogue record for this book is available from the British Library.

The paper in this book meets the guidelines for permanence and durability of the Committee on Production Guidelines for Book Longevity of the Council on Library Resources.

10 9 8 7 6 5 4 3 2

To Robert

Contents

Preface

"America was designed by Providence for the theatre on which man was to make his true figure, on which science, virtue, liberty, happiness, and glory were to exist in peace." This was the hope of John Adams before the Revolution, and it remains the dream of continuing generations. We, like most Americans, feel blessed to live in this country and to share this dream, which predicates not only that liberty is the inalienable right of all people but that it grants them the greatest opportunity for fulfilling their talents.

The years covered in this book, often called "The American Century," represent in their immense richness and variety a time of great energy and productivity, as well as often fierce struggle for the ideals of human liberty. This has been the era of American ascendancy, when the United States took a leading role on the world stage and staked its claim to preeminence in the various arenas of human endeavor. The American effort during the past century to meet its forefathers' challenges is the story we seek to chronicle.

The book has two purposes. First, it documents the flowering of modern America and offers the student of American culture a useful and comprehensive reference work that is a collection of the myriad surfaces of the American scene. In many areas—music, art, theater, film, fashion, sports, science—this remains the first such extensive year-by-year compilation.

Second, the book re-creates, through the accretion of information, the essence of each particular year. Our intention has been to provide the stuff of contemporary memory—to evoke, enrich, and expand the contexts in which most people and their forebears have lived their lives. In a sense, we have hoped to furnish the reader with background material for his or her own autobiography.

"The earth did shake when I was born," proclaims Shakespeare's mighty but vain Glendower. Though we could not declare the same for ourselves, we have been fascinated, in researching this book, to discover multiple resonances and a certain inner coherence that have tended to give not just our birth years but each year a unique personality. Although at one time the span of years has tended to blur in each of our memories, we have had, through the data of this book, the pleasure of reexperiencing and imagining them with clearer definition and understanding. We have also come to better understand the lives of those who preceded us and their society's challenges, continuities, and contradictions. Our greatest wish is to give the reader a similar experience. Facts, it is our final observation, not only inform and satisfy intellectual curiosity but serve as symbols that evoke one's personal and public heritage.

Other echoes
inhabit the garden. Shall we follow?
—T. S. Eliot, *Burnt Norton*

Acknowledgments

We wish to thank the following librarians and curators for their generous assistance: Ruth Schwartz, Michelle Fanelli, Judy Barrett, Mary McMahon, Eileen McIlvaine, Rita Kecheissen, Mikki Carpenter, Maya Falaco, Franklin Riehlman, Marian Weston, Patrick Hardish, Joyce Goulet, William L. Bird, Elizabeth Lamond, May Castleberry, Anita Duquette, Beth Diefendorf, Vicky Bohm, Monica Moseley, J. J. Vissers, Charles Silver, Ron Magliozzi, Billy Kwan, Linda Seckelson, Kenneth Cooper, and Roxanna Deane. John Kelly and Eveline Overmiller, at the Library of Congress, and Ruth Dicks, at the National Archives, were of immeasurable assistance. Judy Katz and Laila Rogers deserve special thanks for their congenial and energetic willingness to track down information and verify details.

We would also like to express special thanks to a number of people who commented upon our material in the various areas of their expertise: Warren French, Bernard Dick, David Shapiro, Irwin Radezky, Christopher Boyd, Robert Coven, Oleg Kerensky, Bill Doran, Helene Fields, Danielle La Santa, Jacqueline Rettig, Michael T. Garodnitz, and especially, Gene Barnett, whose sustained interest and general knowledgeability were invaluable. And for their encouragement and assistance in any number of ways, we thank Meghan Wander, Lowell Gibbs,

Alberto Caputo, Lois Spatz, Doris Auerbach, Charlotte London, Claire Goodlin, Marvin Rechter, Daniel Fuchs, Susan Shapiro, Peggy Anderson, Hugh Johnson, David Maimin, Bill Huott, Roger Whitehouse, Josephine Manageracina, Peter Benson, Marty Feely, David Protomastro, Shepard Goldfein, and Ricardo Quintana.

For the extraordinary care, skill, and enthusiasm with which they worked on this book, along with their meticulous attention to detail, we thank Michael Sims, Carole Rollins, and Cecile Watters. To Janice Meagher, for her initial interest in this project and her ongoing support and many helpful suggestions, we owe our enduring gratitude. Finally, our admiration for Jonathan Brent at Yale University Press is impossible to express fully. His unfailing intellectual imagination and energy, as well as his warm understanding, were an everpresent source of comfort and inspiration. He offered the kind of support an author can only dream of. To Laura Jones Dooley we also express deep appreciation for the great care and amazing breadth of knowledge she brought to the book. We must, in addition, thank others at Yale, a group of unusually talented and highly affable people: Paul Royster, Lara Heimert, and Jennie Kaufman.

To our son, Robert, a very special thanks—for reasons he well knows.

To the Reader

Reference materials and photos were collected from a number of institutions, including the Library of Congress; the Smithsonian divisions of Political History, Domestic Life, Community Life, and Social and Cultural Life; the National Air and Space Museum; the National Archives; the U.S. Departments of the Army and Navy; Martin Luther King Library (Washington, D.C.); New York Public Library; Museum of the City of New York; Metropolitan Museum of Art; National Gallery; Philadelphia Museum of Art; Museum of Modern Art; Whitney Museum; Guggenheim Museum; Juilliard School of Music; Fashion Institute of Technology; Fairleigh Dickinson University; and Columbia University. Sources include a wide variety of primary and secondary materials—newspapers, magazines, government documents, and the reference texts, encyclopedias, and general and specific historical and critical studies appropriate to the subject areas and time periods.

It would be unwieldy to detail the specific sources for the many areas surveyed in this book. The broad rubric of music, for example, involved collecting data on first performances of significant works throughout the country, performers' debuts, important events (of major conductors, symphony orchestras, and virtuosos), the dating of major compositions, the openings of major concert facilities; operatic debuts and performances of major works and stars in companies throughout the country; ballet history of the major classic and modern dance companies; and popular music ranging from top songs, records, and albums (from swing to country and soul) to jazz developments and the formation of big bands, along with major awards within each category.

Our overall goals and general methodology are easier to explain. In certain areas, such as Theater, Critically Acclaimed Books, and Movies, we tried to present a spectrum of what was popular or considered important at the time, along with what has come to have retrospective significance. With Quotes, Ads, and Kaleidoscope, we tried to emphasize the preoccupations and sensibility of each year—in a manner of speaking, its unique personality. Our single imperative was to be thorough, and as we read through the extensive sources, our aim remained the collection of material of significant historical or topical importance.

Different categories required different emphases. For the Quotes, Ads, Facts and Figures, Fashion, and Kaleidoscope, we concentrated on primary materials. On the other hand, awards listings, like Pulitzer Prizes, because self-defined, involved little in the way of choice. Where

popularity was concerned, we tried to crosscheck our data with multiple sources. We consulted, for example, attendance tallies and sales charts to verify our lists of, say, plays, movies, records, and fashion. We tried similarly to validate "important," if not popular, works and events by extensive reading of critical and scholarly reviews and studies written both during the period and subsequently. Finally, we consulted experts in each field in order to minimize errors, omissions, and eccentricities in choice. Responsibility for the final content of the text, of course, remains ours. We realize that someone else studying the rich history and culture of America over the century might have designed the project differently, with other categories and other listings.

The following is intended to give further details of methodology and format relating to the various individual areas. It also includes those sources not indicated in the text from which we obtained specific awards listings.

The materials in the section **In the News** have been written in the form of headlines in an attempt to recapture their immediacy. In keeping with our overview, they include the major current events of each year that captured public interest, as well as national and international events of manifest historical significance.

Vital, economic, social, and consumer statistics are represented at the opening of each decade to provide a perspective on the country's changing demographic profile. **Facts and Figures,** given yearly, include an economic profile, followed by a list of statistics organized in a repetitive pattern according to the digit with which the year ends, such that the first entries after **Economic Profile** for 192*1*, 193*1*, 194*1*, for example, furnish similar data in each decade (except in the decade year). Prices were selected from newspapers throughout the country, and they cover a range of items from household goods to luxury products; fads and technological innovations are incorporated in the years in which they appeared. Where possible, prices were selected from familiar stores like F. W. Woolworth, Sears, or Saks Fifth Avenue. The lists of **Deaths** for each year does not include persons whose deaths are mentioned elsewhere, such as in the headlines.

Vaudeville is covered during the first decade, when it was the major form of popular entertainment. Many of its greatest stars also debuted during this period. **Radio** is covered consistently from the 1920s until the fifties, when it became more of a local medium. **TV** is listed extensively from 1946, the time of its commercial emergence. **Movies** were selected on the basis of their critical importance or popular success, either at their time of release or subsequently. Film dating is often controversial: some authorities use the date of general release; others, the New York release or the date films were screened here or abroad to qualify for a variety of awards. We have placed them according to the year they received general U.S. distribution. On occasion, the release and Academy Award dates differ—for example, for *Casablanca* (1942 and 1943). The first five films listed each year correspond to those nominated for the Academy Award as best film. Many early films listed here no longer exist, and there is no record of their actors. However, reviews at the time and film historians have identified some of the actors and the historically important films' subject matter, which are then listed in the book. The **Stars of Tomorrow** and **Top Box-Office Stars** were recorded primarily from the Quigley surveys. The former extended from 1932 to 1983; the latter began in 1941; material listed before and after these dates reflects a consensus of data reported in contemporary magazines and newspapers.

Hit Songs are listed according to copyright dates or, on rare occasions, the year the copyright was renewed and the song gained its first popularity. **Top Records** and **Top Performers,** under **Jazz and Big Bands,** include top sellers and performers reported by *Billboard, Downbeat, Cashbox,* and the various industry data sheets that tallied this information before these publications began. Because of space limitations, Top Records are not repeated under Hit Songs. **Theater** includes long runs, as well as shows of contemporary or retrospective importance. **Pulitzer Prizes** and **Tony Awards** are listed in the years they were awarded, which is, at times, the year following the production's premiere. **Classics and Revivals On and Off Broadway** also includes new Off-Broadway plays.

Other than those in New York, Washington, D.C., and Philadelphia, **Art** exhibitions are listed by city rather than museum. Unless otherwise specified, exhibitions were held at the following museums in these cities: Art Institute of Chicago, Chicago; Museum of Fine Arts, Boston; Albright Art Gallery (more recently Albright-Knox), Buffalo; Baltimore Museum of Art, Baltimore; Carnegie Institute, Pittsburgh; County Museum of Art, Los Angeles; Wadsworth Atheneum, Hartford; Cleveland Museum of Art, Cleveland; Detroit Institute of Arts, Detroit; Walker Art Center, Minneapolis; Nelson Art Gallery, Kansas City; and the Toledo Museum of Art, Toledo.

Best-Sellers lists hardcover fiction and nonfiction, as tallied by *Publisher's Weekly.* Their listing of best-selling nonfiction did not commence until 1912; during the Great War years, a best-selling war books category was added, and the nonfiction list appeared irregularly. The additional books listed under **Critics' Choice** were selected on the basis of their importance or interest at their time of publication or subsequently. Owing to space limitations, Best-Sellers are not repeated under Critics' Choice. **Pulitzer Prizes** in Letters began in 1917 in the categories of Biography and U.S. History; when the Poetry Award was added in 1918, it was funded by the Poetry Society; its official designation and funding by the Pulitzer Foundation did not occur until 1922. The prizes are listed in the year of the book's publication. Books preceded by the symbol ❧ represent the American publication of influential foreign works.

Items in **Science and Technology** preceded by the symbol ❧ are important foreign scientific events. In **Sports,** in the **Winners** section, the following data are based on selections by the indicated organizations: Baseball's MVPs: *Sporting News* (until 1929) and Baseball Writers of America thereafter; Pro football MVP: Joe F. Carr Trophy (1938–45) and Jim Thorpe Trophy (since 1955); top college football team: Citizens Savings Athletic Foundation (1920–35), Associated Press (1936–50), AP and United Press (1950–58), and AP and UPI thereafter; top college basketball team: Helms Foundation (1920–39), NCAA and NIT (1939–50), and NCAA (1950–present).

Men's **Fashion** is not included with regularity until the late fifties, since innovation tended to be less frequent until then. Italicized items in the section reflect dramatic stylistic changes that, while worn by a limited population, gained wide attention or influenced future fashion. **Kaleidoscope** highlights the events, personalities, and trends that were part of the general public awareness each year; it also amplifies or complements the material in other areas. Comparable material is placed in the particular areas of Art, Popular and Classical Music, and Sports, where it seemed that a more specialized appeal was indicated. It is in Kaleidoscope, as in **Quotes and Ads,** that we particularly attempted to convey the unique imprint of each year. **First Appearances** presents a range of entries from popular comic strips and well-known products to technological advances not mentioned in Science and Technology.

Introduction

Roger Rosenblatt

There are at least four things one can do with the sorts of facts that make up this book—one can take account of them for their own worth, draw conclusions from them, believe in them as signs, or one can dream into them, find in them Proustian moments of awakening, and embrace them as emblems of one's life and times. Of course, this requires one to trust that the facts presented are facts. In this remarkably inventive and meticulously researched *American Chronicle* by Lois and Alan Gordon are titles of books, for instance, that came out in a particular year. But every book begins years earlier than the one in which it is published, so the "fact" of *The Sun Also Rises* is that it came to public attention in 1926, and not that it meandered into existence. Similarly, the "fact" of a war occurred when some external act defined it as such, and not when it germinated in an individual mind. The beauty of facts is that they seem to avoid all consideration of process, and yet they imply process. They are at once hard and pliable, definitive and imaginative. Cole Porter's "Night and Day" was one of the hit songs of 1932, but who knows when the longing in that song became the song?

What a book like this one gives us is the best way to anchor the mind in time, as if it were a clock or a calendar—a way of ordering experience so that it seems to make sense. The fascination and fun of going through these pages, however, is the discovery of how little sense there is to anything. Here is an entire century of American production, thought, activity, and participation in the world, and one may read it as the story of a great march of progress. Or one may detect—with grim or melancholy amusement—no progress whatever.

In the late 1990s, for example, people were obsessed with fitness gyms and gizmos that would endow them with "perfect abs." An ad in 1900 reads: "Your arms can be enlarged one inch and strengthened 5 percent in one month by using the Hercules Graduated Gymnastic Club and Strength Tester 5 minutes each day." In 1900, "ladies and gentlemen" were advised to smoke Turkish Cigarets. In 1964, the attorney general advised them not to. At the end of the century, after decades of lawsuits and scientific proof linking cigarettes to death, ladies and gentlemen, and children, were smoking more than ever.

Even humor, which often changes drastically from era to era, eventually comes round again. At the beginning of the century, a popular joke ran: "I sent my wife to the Thousand Islands for a vacation. A week on each island." Which in the 1950s became Henny Youngman's "Take my wife—please." Which in the 1970s became

Rodney Dangerfield complaining that he was lying in bed when he heard his wife talking dirty: "I look over, and she's on the phone." Which in the 1990s transmogrified into Seinfeld and company's avoidance of marriage to the point of George's semiaccidental murder of his fiancée. On the grander and harsher geopolitical scale, the century progressed from Sarajevo to Sarajevo.

And yet: In 1906, a crowd of 3,000 in Ohio cheered as two African-Americans were burned to death. In 1998, a black man was dragged to death by three subhumans driving a truck in Jasper, Texas, and the town rose up in a shameful rage. Odd as it may seem, some things do get better. In the early months of 1999, a court in Brooklyn, New York, found gun manufacturers liable in a shooting incident for the marketing of handguns. One wonders what the world is coming to.

Or one may use the book to play the significance game. Take the facts of a given year, and try to determine which was the most meaningful from the perspective of the future. In 1928, arrange the following events in order of their importance: Amelia Earhart is the first woman to fly the Atlantic. America, Britain, France, Germany, and Russia sign the Kellogg-Briand Pact to outlaw war. Admiral Byrd takes off on his expedition to the Antarctic. Herbert Hoover defeats Al Smith to win the presidency, and FDR wins the New York governor's race. Georgia O'Keeffe, Charles Demuth, and Thomas Hart Benton paint major works. Proust publishes *Swann's Way,* D. H. Lawrence *Lady Chatterley's Lover,* Yeats *The Tower.* Alexander Fleming observes that a mold, penicillin, destroys bacteria. Mickey Mouse makes his debut.

The year 1928 was also significant for quotations. Hoover said, in the year before 1929: "We in America are nearer to the final triumph over poverty than ever before in the history of any land." And Charlie Chaplin said: "Moving pictures need sound as much as Beethoven's symphonies need lyrics." Question: How wrong was either of them?

Or play the ancient v. modern game. The top movies of 1994 were: *Star Trek: Generations, True Lies, Speed, Dumb and Dumber,* and *Forrest Gump* (best picture). The top movies of 1934 were *The Thin Man, Of Human Bondage, Man of Aran, The Scarlet Pimpernel, Twentieth Century, The Gay Divorcée,* and *It Happened One Night* (best picture). Now you may lay your head on your arms and weep.

To take facts for their own worth affords the simplest kind of pleasure, but even then, a fact suggests mystery. Every year chronicled offers a selection of popular advertising slogans. One mystery is that there were (are) people who believed that these slogans would actually sell products. The other mystery is that they did.

In 1917, an apparently appealing ad for Waltham watches reads: "The Czar is deposed, but under the rule of the new democracy, Waltham Watches still maintain the accuracy of Russian train schedules." Ads continued to capitalize on world events. In 1939, Dictaphone sold itself with the slogan, "How to please a Dictator." In 1945, Quaker State Motor Oil presented itself as "Something the Axis tanks don't have." In 1953, the year of the hydrogen bomb, a Salt Lake City fast food store was selling "tasty uranium burgers" for 45 cents.

Cadillacs may have shown themselves leaning toward auto-Darwinism in 1920 with their declaration: "In every field of endeavor . . . [the] 'first' must perpetually live in the white light of publicity. . . . Whistler, Wagner, Fulton . . . that which deserves to live—lives." In 1924, Packard evidently decided to stir up trouble within families: "Thousands of men are denying their wives Packard Six cars." In 1955, the makers of the movie *A Man Called Peter* overreached itself: "He was a first name kind of guy. He was everybody's kind of guy. . . . He was God's kind of guy."

Life in 1910 is revealed by the ad for the New Savage Automatic pistol: "A woman, if attacked alone in the house, will oftentimes fall in a faint. Why? The thought of utter helplessness . . . THIS GUN WILL GIVE HER NERVE." Life in 1996 is revealed by an ad by the Minnesota AIDS Project for condoms: "When you give the gift of love, make sure it's wrapped properly." In 1997, the bathroom cleanser Vanish ran the following: "If anyone doesn't believe me, ring my bell and you can small my toilet."

More profoundly and often disturbingly mysterious is the conjunction of certain facts. How can antipodal events occur in the same year, and what does their simultaneity and opposition say about human nature? In *Language and Silence,* George Steiner asked this question powerfully when he mused about a time frame during World War II. How was it possible, Steiner wondered, that at the same time people were going to the movies, shopping, and making love in New York City other people were being gassed in camps in Poland? How does one begin to understand a world in which both such things can occur in the same year, at the same hour?

American Chronicle indicates that the Oscar-winner picture of 1990 was *Dances with Wolves.* I recall watching the Oscar presentations on television that year—beautiful, perfectly formed people, dressed up in millions of dollars' worth of clothing, coming forward to the microphone to say this or that about their glittering lives. At one point in the evening, I flipped the remote to the evening news, where they were showing the stacks of bodies burned to death in the Happy Land Fire in the Bronx, New York, also noted in *American Chronicle*—the worst such incident in American history, in which 87 people, mostly low-income Latinos, were caught in a dance

hall fire set by an avenging lover. I looked at the bodies rolled like carpets in the large room, and then I flipped back to the Oscars. I asked myself: How do these events fit together? Will somebody, some day, make a movie about the Happy Land fire? Will it win an Oscar?

This is what facts do to you; they have a life of their own, which has something to do with your life. It is why a good writer of fiction or poetry will, whenever possible, make use of a fact—the name of a city, a flower, a person—because a fact is an automatic metaphor for something beyond itself. J. D. Salinger put "mules" on the feet of Seymour Glass's ditsy, self-absorbed wife in "A Perfect Day for Bananafish," and James Joyce told the Irish audience of 1918 that it was the Drumcondra tram specifically that Maria took in "Clay." The life of the fact touches the life of the person who reads it. The categories of annual facts in this book—the quotations of a year, the ad slogans, the best-sellers, hit tunes, prizewinners, political activities, fashions, et al.—provide rich material for everything from serious research to trivial pursuits, but every one of them throbs with a special pulse, derived from us as individuals and from what we bring to them.

So we come to the deepest mystery of these facts, and to the most rewarding use one can make of them. We can dream into them. Everything noted here inevitably leads to dreams, and one finds oneself flung by the merest name of a public figure or by the title of a movie into a past full of adventure. "We must learn to imagine what we know," said Shelley. Yet in some way, we already imagine what we know, and we proceed from the apprehension of a hard fact to an imagined narrative so quickly that it must be the way the brain was built to work. We are a narrative species. We make stories out of nothing, and nothing suddenly becomes everything. A stone is flung into a creek, and the ripples widen until they touch every shore of every ocean.

When I opened *American Chronicle* and turned to the year of my birth, 1940, for instance, I thought of my entrance in the world as an event like any other, and I unconsciously created a different sort of game (anyone can play) in which I saw my life predetermined or in some way affected by the other events of that year. The definition of any year is an invention, of course, but it is fun—not unlike astrology—to believe that one was destined to be born in a certain time, surrounded by other events that cooperate in one's destiny. This is an exercise in vanity, to be sure, but if one keeps it to oneself, it's fairly harmless.

So I looked at 1940 as an array of occurrences that had something to do with me. The year in which I came into the world, F. Scott Fitzgerald left it—no causality there, I hope—but Fitzgerald and *The Great Gatsby* in particular have always gone very deep with me, deeper than the objective fact that *Gatsby* is a provably great novel. Simply reading that Fitzgerald had died in the year of my birth, simply reading his name, brought me back into the novel, which is never far from my consciousness, and at once I became what I believed myself to be after first reading *Gatsby*—both Nick Carraway and Gatsby, the aware observer and the tormented dreamer who was in danger and dangerous, one who is a criminal and better than the lot of them.

No sooner had I dreamed of *The Great Gatsby* than I hauled in Alice McDermott's *Charming Billy,* a novel that has nothing to do with 1940, save that the war plays a part in the lives of the characters, yet it is about another dreamer on Long Island. The difference is that charming Billy is poor and that he does himself in with drink. Yet he has the same wistful character as Gatsby, the same faithful romanticism; he is involved with the same sort of self-centered woman goddess—even a gas station plays a part—and his story has the same heartbreaking, enduring theme of believing in the unbelievable, and trusting the untrustable, which is my theme, too, and perhaps yours.

While I'm at it, I might as well add that I live at the eastern end of Long Island myself, and I know what it means to live on a long island, that is, a configuration of land that gives the illusion of size and connectedness but is still just another thing floating in the sea. Yet all is shown to be worthwhile on a spring morning in the middle of the week, when the wet air smells of grass, the crows call out, and the sky is streaked with every blue in the book.

If a path like that is cut by one's mind by the single mention of a writer's death, imagine how far, and where, it turned when I also read that 1940 was the year of the hit songs "All or Nothing At All," "When You Wish Upon a Star," and "You Stepped Out of a Dream."

Three of what eventually turned out to be my favorite movies came out in 1940—*Rebecca, The Bank Dick,* and my very favorite, *Foreign Correspondent.* The hero, played by Joel McCrea, named Johnny Jones in the film, renamed Huntley Haverstock, is entirely unaware of everything but a story. He perceives the rise of the Third Reich as a crime story. He falls in love with Laraine Day at the drop of a hat. He is all intuition (what is there to study, ever?) and he gets the girl and he solves the crime, and he eventually learns what the story means. In the end, he is broadcasting one of his war reports from London, and the lights go out in the radio studio during a bombing raid. But he keeps on talking, even in the dark, and what he says, in 1940, is: "Hello, America, hang on to your lights: they're the only lights left in the world!" I tear up every time (fifty? a hundred?) I hear that line.

I tear up? This is only one small entry in *American Chronicle,* remember.

Now I dream of radio. When I was a kid, my dad would not allow a TV in the house, so I grew up on radio. I would come home from school and turn on *Superman, Captain Midnight,* and *Tom Mix* (that's an odd name, Mix, not that Midnight isn't), all of which began in the year 1940; so in a way every one of these characters is exactly my age. I would sit on the living room floor next to the cathedral-shaped radio and listen to my gods. I think that I liked *Captain Midnight* best, though I hated the Ovaltine that sponsored the show. I had a "de-coder ring" that I had ordered from the show, and at the end of every episode, Capt. Midnight would read aloud numbers that corresponded to letters, and the kids who had the decoder ring were able to decipher the message. Often it had something to do with buying Ovaltine.

It was at that same altar of the radio that I learned to read. On Sunday mornings, the *Journal American* was plopped at the front door along with a couple of other morning papers, and the *Journal American* contained the comics. It also ran a radio show for kids, and on every Sunday morning, long before my parents were awake, the "Comic Weekly Man" would, as he sang, "read the funnies / to you little boys and honeys." I spread out the paper and followed along as he read, until I, too, could read—Jiggs and Maggie, Dagwood and Blondie, the Little King.

The "top ten" radio shows of 1940 included "Jack Benny," "Bob Hope," the "Aldrich Family" ("Henry! Henry Aldrich!"), and the interminable "One Man's Family." I think I learned about criticism from listening to "One Man's Family." I knew that I was bored by the slow pacing, and by the pointless dialogue, and I understood why I was bored. But the program was rescued for me by the presence of Eva Marie Saint, who, when I finally saw what she looked like in the movie *On the Waterfront,* became my ideal of what a woman, my first girlfriend, ought to look like. Years later, when I started to write and publish, I received a nice note from Miss Saint. I held it in my hand not longer than twenty minutes—an hour at most.

Edward Hopper painted *Gas* in 1940. I have stared into that painting for many hours, partly for reasons already alluded to—the meaning of the gas station in America, the starting point that pumps others into motion. The African-American novelist Ann Petry wrote a novel called *Country Place* in which there is a gas jockey who fuels up the ladies of a Connecticut town. Petry would become an interest of mine in my twenties, when I was teaching Afro-American fiction at Harvard. In 1940, Richard Wright published *Native Son,* a novel I loved to teach, which forever blew the lid off race relations in America.

Other great novels came out in the year of my birth— you see the way one's dreams meander—*The Ox-Bow Incident, You Can't Go Home Again, The Power and the Glory,* and *Darkness at Noon.* Best-sellers included *For Whom the Bell Tolls, Mrs. Miniver,* and *The Grapes of Wrath.* Among these, *The Ox-Bow Incident* and *The Grapes of Wrath* stick in my mind, because they were about injustice. Ask most people what brings them to their knees with rage or sorrow, and they will answer, "injustice."

A Smattering of Ignorance, Oscar Levant's autobiography, was another best-seller of 1940. I don't know why, but even as a small child, I was always drawn to Levant. I read his name in this book, and immediately I saw his crumpled face and heard his cigarette voice. He had the odd strength that comes from enduring dissipations. Levant did a remarkable thing with his life: he openly and devotedly attached his talent to George Gershwin's genius, and when he played Gershwin's music, he seemed to show more feeling for the compositions than the composer himself. Yet Levant also gained his independent prominence through that attachment—through the unalloyed admiration of another man—by way of his wit, which was corrupt, deadly, and funny as hell. On a movie set, he once boasted that his greatest achievement was to make Joan Crawford cry. In that same movie he had the line: "Don't blame me, lady. I didn't make the world. I barely live on it."

On and on, fact upon fact, facts to dreams. The literary critic Edmund Wilson published *To the Finland Station* in 1940, his evocative account of Lenin's triumphal railroad ride into Saint Petersburg that signaled the taking of the Winter Palace and the overthrow of the czars. On my first trip to the Soviet Union in 1987, I rode the train into (then) Leningrad from the other direction, from Moscow, and my imagination re-created all that Wilson had written about. I met him once, on Cape Cod, when another great literary scholar, Harry Levin, a senior colleague at Harvard, introduced me to Wilson as someone expert in African-American literature. Wilson responded by showing me that—though the subject was only a minor interest of his—he still knew ten times more about it than I did. I remember thinking at the time that his performance was an unnecessary and unattractive act of showing off. But now I think that he simply could not perform on any level but the highest, and if that level was out of my reach, too bad for me. It was strange and a bit uncomfortable for me to realize, when I became literary editor of *The New Republic,* that Wilson had been the first ever to hold that position.

Poetry published in 1940 included E. E. Cummings's *50 Poems* and Yeats's *Last Poems and Plays.* Whenever I think of Cummings, I gratefully quote those lines of "Somewhere I have never travelled," and think of all the seductions it made possible for me and every other undergraduate male in America. I see Yeats's name and am carried back to my other, my main literary interest at Harvard, Irish literature, and the wonderful teacher who encouraged me in it, John Kelleher.

Kelleher, too, liked facts, which may have been one of the reasons he was drawn to early Irish poetry—the absence of fancy dress and of self-referral. He could not bear to read much of modern poetry (Yeats he judged an ancient) because of its self-consciousness. He preferred eighteenth-century rationality to nineteenth-century romanticism. "All romanticism," he told me, "leads to Dachau." It took me decades to understand what that meant.

More fissionable uranium 235 was isolated from the more stable uranium 238 in 1940. The listing of those significant experiments triggers a memory of a cover story I wrote for *Time* magazine in 1995 on the fortieth anniversary of the bombing of Hiroshima. I studied up on the making of the atom bomb. I visited Los Alamos and Hiroshima and even the island of Tinian, from which the *Enola Gay* took off from a long runway that had been cut into sea grass. Today the runway lies open like a gray field, grass struggles up through fissures in the concrete, and Tinian is silent.

In the same *American Chronicle* section on Science and Technology, the authors cite the work of Edwin Cohn, who separated blood plasma into globulin, albumin, and fibrin fractions, and of Robert Gross, who performed the first successful surgery for congenital defective blood vessels. Another year of killing and saving born of human ingenuity. I wandered to a passage in Walt Whitman's *Specimen Days,* in which he describes the U.S. Patent Office. During the Civil War, it stood on the site of what is now the National Portrait Gallery and was used as a hospital for the wounded and dying Union soldiers. Whitman made note of the fact that the young men were suffering from a war in the presence of models of all the bright inventions.

Bob Feller pitched his first no-hitter in 1940. Joe DiMaggio led the American League in batting with a .352 average. At the first baseball game I ever saw, in Yankee Stadium (I was six), DiMaggio hit an opposite field home run to right. Feller was knocked out of the box in the early innings. Naturally, the Yankees won. After the game, my friends and I waited outside the players' entrance to get autographs (free in 1947). When Feller emerged, we all leaned forward, and he knocked us back with an angry sweep of his arm. I was outraged that a hero of the game would treat kids that way, and when I said so to my father, he suggested, sincerely, that I write a letter of complaint to the *New York Times.* I did.

Time magazine held a lavish party to celebrate its seventy-fifth anniversary in 1997. The Clintons were there. Gorbachev was there. Tom Cruise, Sofia Loren, and lots of movie stars. But for me only DiMaggio was there. I saw him sitting by himself at a table during the cocktail hour—old, tired, and dignified. I summoned the nerve to go up and tell him about that first game I saw and his home run, and we talked baseball for a long while, which was worth a life.

Two freakish sports events of 1940: the Yankees did not get into the World Series, and the New York Rangers hockey team won the Stanley Cup.

Under women's fashions that year, I read that "air force blue" was in—short dresses, simple suits with pleated skirts, hair piled on top of the head and tied with colorful bandannas. I pictured my mother going off to work as an English teacher at a junior high school in the Delancey Street area of downtown Manhattan. She looked crisp and sharp and full of beans. Now she sits all day in a nursing home not far from the school where she taught, her body having long outlived her mind, ruined by Alzheimer's.

There were victory gardens in the 1940s—*American Chronicle* mentions them—and on many afternoons, my mother would take me downtown to be with the older children she taught and do some planting in the school victory garden. There she is in the garden now—the beloved, young, beautiful teacher, in her air force blue pleated skirt dress, her gleaming black hair done up and tied with a yellow bandanna.

The Nazis are murdering their way through Europe in 1940. There is no stopping them. No one comes to terms with the depth and the extent of their evil. Born in September of that year, I would be wheeled in my shiny black varnished perambulator by my parents on the pathways of serene Gramercy Park, while my Jewish counterparts, born the same year, in Germany, Austria, Poland, Czechoslovakia, and Hungary, would be picked up and tossed into ovens. America ambled toward a confrontation with Hitler, in spite of the efforts of Charles Lindbergh, who said in 1940: "The three most important groups which have been pushing this country toward war are the British, the Jewish and the Roosevelt administration." My parents were areligious and assimilative. It took another kid in Gramercy Park to teach me that I belonged among the Jewish.

A maple bedroom set in 1940 cost $49.88. My parents had one. An eight-room townhouse on West Seventy-seventh Street carried a purchase price of $2,600. My father turned down an opportunity to buy our eight-room apartment in Gramercy Park for $5,000—"Who'd pay that kind of money for an apartment?" A Packard cost $907. We had one, outfitted with a running board. Running boards first appeared in 1940 . . . as did McDonald's, Arnold bread, cellophane, synthetic rubber tires, commercial flights with pressurized passenger cabins, air raid shelters, "Brenda Starr," and me.

I undoubtedly have gone on too long to make the point, but you see what I mean. All one has to do with this book is turn to the year of one's birth to become lost at once in the ramiform story of one's life.

Of course, the wider value *American Chronicle* offers is the story of everybody's life, of the century of a whole—the amazing fact that one has actually lived through some, much, or most of what is recorded here. If every fact is a mystery, this compendium of facts creates something beyond our wildest dreams. One asks: "Did this all really happen?" and is astonished to acknowledge the answer: "Evidently."

Scholars will use this book to determine that the past hundred years constituted a time with a name, just as their predecessors determined "The Age of Reason" and "The Age of Romanticism." And there is much to support a case for citing the century as, say, "The Age of Invention" or "The Individual," or "Freedom." In some ways, we have not changed a great deal from the premises and attitudes of the early nineteenth century—that people are, as my professor Kelleher said, ten feet tall, that they are able to talk with God, and that God is interested in talking with them. So maybe this has been "The Age to Be Continued," which is hardly an exciting title, even if it comes close to the truth.

But the rest of us are not encumbered with the task of making an orderly construct of these years and, in our appreciation of chaos, may come even closer to an understanding of our times. Here's a final game one can play with this book. Open *American Chronicle* to any page and read something, anything, that occurred in a particular year. Then do it again and again, rapidly. Make a note of what you read, a random list. Pretty soon, you will begin to wonder if history is fantasy.

There (1977): the killer Gary Gilmore is executed by a firing squad in Utah. There (1930): Duke Ellington records "Mood Indigo." There (1904): Helen Keller is graduated from Radcliffe College. There (1951): the television opera "Amahl and the Night Visitors" has its premiere. There (1944): the mass murders at Birkenau and Auschwitz are made known to the public. There (1994): O. J. Simpson leads the Los Angeles police in a slow car chase in his white Ford Bronco. There (1931): Al Capone goes to jail. There (1974): Richard Nixon resigns. There (1945): Hiroshima. There (1985): Madonna. There (1998): Monica.

In my lifetime as a journalist, I have seen a young boy starve to death in Sudan, a car bomb explode in Beirut, a Cambodian girl terrified to silence by the Khmer Rouge, and the bodies of murdered Tutsis tumbling over a waterfall in Rwanda. I have heard Jessye Norman sing, Robert Lowell read, Roseanne tell jokes, Louis Farrakhan speak, and Billy Graham preach. I have spoken with Lewis Thomas, Chuck Close, Candice Bergen, and Yasser Arafat. I have been to the prison at Attica, Ronald Reagan's home in Pacific Palisades, a rain forest in Suriname, and the Superbowl.

Even as I write this down, I don't believe it. I do not believe any of it. If the facts of one's life seem to become dreams in retrospect, then this book is an anthology of dreams. Yet it is not. All that is recorded here, all the numbers, dates, titles, discoveries, battles, treaties, songs, killings, and births, occurred. I did not dream it. You did not dream it. The facts rise from these pages as if to assure us that we lived, and we did, once upon a time, in the twentieth century.

THE First Decade

"We think the greatest victories are yet to be won, the greatest deeds yet to be done. . . . There are yet in store for us, our people, and the grand cause we uphold, grander triumphs than have yet been scored."

—President Theodore Roosevelt.

Statistics

Vital
Population: 75,994,000
  Urban/Rural: 31/45
  Farm: 40%
Life expectancy:
  Male: 46.3
  Female: 48.3
Births/1,000: 32.3
Marriages/1,000: 17.2
Divorces/1,000: 1.6
Deaths/1,000:
  Heart: NA
  Cancer: 64
  Tuberculosis: 194
  Car accidents: NA
  Diphtheria: 40

Economic
Unemployed: 1,420,000
GNP: $18.7 billion
Federal budget: $0.52 billion
National debt: $1.2 billion
Union membership: 0.9 million
Strikes: 1,839
Car sales: 2,500
Average salary: $375

Social
Homicides/100,000: 1.2
Suicides/100,000: 10.2
Lynchings: 115
Labor force, male/female: 4.5/1
Public education: $250 million
College degrees
  Bachelors'
    Male: 22,000
    Female: 5,000
  Doctorates
    Male: 359
    Female: 23
Attendance
  Movies (weekly): NA
  Baseball (yearly): 1.6 million

Consumer
Consumer Price Index
  (1967=100): 24.3
Eggs: 21¢ (doz.)
Milk: 8¢ (qt.)
Butter: 26¢ (lb.)
Bacon: 14¢ (lb.)
Round steak: 12¢ (lb.)

In 1900, America seemed the fulfillment of the New World's promise, a land of political freedom and economic opportunity. The record number of immigrants that flooded American shores bore proof that in the world's eyes the United States offered Europe's poor and persecuted the hope that a better and freer life was available. And as the frontier closed in the 1890s and farmers suffered the vagaries of weather and interest rates, a pool of migrants from rural America also swelled the cities with additional arms for the industries that came to center in them. Although large disparities of wealth remained between the rich and "the other half," as Jacob Riis called them, Theodore Roosevelt could still say, with truth, in 1902: "The typical American is accumulating money more rapidly than any other man on earth." Horatio Alger was not just an author of bestselling dime novels of individual effort overcoming all; he provided a master guide to great achievement.

At the start of the century, America led the world in productivity, its GNP exceeding the vast colonial empires of Britain and France combined. The United States had discovered the benefits of "combination," as industry after industry merged into single corporate entities—the "trusts"—which enabled major efficiencies, even though they exposed consumers and employees to the arrogance and greed that lack of competition often breeds. The "Gay Nineties" had been a time of "conspicuous consumption" for the privileged, as Thorstein Veblen described it in 1899, but the last half of the decade had also been a good time for most, with increased income and virtual unemployment. As the sedate and stately President William McKinley put it: "The dinner pail is full," and his campaign for four more years of good fortune was thunderously propounded by his ebullient and brilliant war hero–vice presidential candidate Theodore Roosevelt.

The war, for which Roosevelt had eagerly left his post as assistant naval secretary to race headlong into gunfire up Cuba's San Juan Hill, was another indication of the multifaceted American expansion that had characterized McKinley's first term. Responding to the Cuban rebellion against Spanish rule and spurred on by the jingoism of journalists like William Randolph Hearst, the U.S. had gone to war against the Spanish empire, whose reach extended from Cuba to the Philippines. Within a short period and with few casualties, U.S. naval and ground forces vanquished the old world power, and from San Juan to Manila the American flag flew in victory. Though many, like the silver-tongued orator William Jennings Bryan, McKinley's opponent in both 1896 and 1900, claimed that imperialism was not the American way, others saw the nation's victory as an opportunity for new industrial markets, if not territorial expansion.

When McKinley fell to a lone anarchist's bullet, Roosevelt promised to continue his predecessor's policies, but many McKinleyites were rightfully skeptical, particularly the business monarchs, now in the process of completing their monopolizations. But TR wasn't the "madman" or "cowboy" some feared. He was his own person with a distinctive vision of how government could best serve the people.

Revitalizing the Monroe Doctrine, Roosevelt's "corollary" made clear that if the Caribbean required policing to keep the peace or collect debts, American—not European—troops would perform this service. And while maintaining America's "Open Door" policy of respect for Chinese integrity and equal trade rights for all, TR would also send American troops to quell the antiforeigner rebellions in China. He would continue the bloody battle in the Philippines, which was to cost thousands of American lives, in order to suppress the rebels who rejected American authority, however benignly administered. He maneuvered relentlessly for the construction of a Panama Canal under American control, which would connect the Atlantic and Pacific and ease East-West trade. Later, he would help Russia and Japan settle their war for Asian dominance, which earned him a Nobel Peace prize; he would also assist France and Germany in settling their Moroccan colonial differences. Finally, in 1907, he sent the U.S. fleet around the world to show the flag—a reminder of the value of American friendship and force, the carrot and the stick.

At home, Teddy Roosevelt demonstrated that, regardless of big business's support, he owed business only its fair due, and sought to break up many of the "trusts" that by 1904 controlled virtually every major industry. In so doing, he aimed to dismantle those that abused power by raising consumer prices and undermining workers' wages. By intervening on labor's behalf in the anthracite coal strike of 1902, staring down the "First Lord of American Finance," J. P. Morgan, and attacking his megatrust ambitions, and later seeking the dissolution of John Rockefeller's Standard Oil, TR challenged the titans of American finance.

A nature lover, Roosevelt also showed his reverence for the land he had come to know as a cowboy, a solitary young man seeking strength after the death of his first wife. Throughout his two terms, he championed "conservation" (a term coined by Gifford Pinchot, his appointee as director of the Forest Service) of the vast and beautiful American wilderness from the encroachments of industry, often through executive power. From the nation's love of the toy "teddy bear," named in his honor, to the vogue of blue gowns like the one his daughter, Alice, had worn to her White House wedding, the Roosevelts were the darlings of ordinary Americans. Yet at a time when such Reconstruction gains in civil liberties as voting and integrated facilities were being repudiated, Roosevelt's White House invitation to the renowned black educator Booker T. Washington incited deadly riots.

Since the 1890s, the would-be American aristocracy was growing, including New York's "Four Hundred"—the Astors, Vanderbilts, and Morgans. They built man-

The Wright brothers make the first heavier-than-air flight, at Kitty Hawk, N.C.

sions on Fifth Avenue and French chateaus in Newport and Palm Beach; they entertained regally on grand yachts. But their aspirations to royalty were belied by their search for true (if impoverished) European princes to marry their daughters.

The problem of the slum remained—to Jacob Riis, the archenemy of civilization—the ill-lit, overcrowded, disease-ridden tenements whose children labored through the night for three cents an hour and whose adults worked ten-hour sweatshop days for subsistence wages. So, too, did the problem of the company town, where workers lived and died at the mercy of company wages, prices, and policy. That the urban slums often stood but a stone's throw from the homes of the rich remained a dark cloud hovering near the bright sunshine of the American dream.

While some, like the Socialist Eugene V. Debs and the Western labor leader "Big Bill" Haywood, advocated the abolition of capitalism, most Americans did not favor radical solutions, hoping, like American Federation of Labor leader Samuel Gompers, for "a fair day's pay for a fair day's work." They expected—as was actually occurring—that union power, aided by enlightened government, would lead to meaningful improvement. In this struggle, they were aided by a group that many regard as the true heroes of the era, the investigative journalists: the "muckrackers," so labeled by Roosevelt, citing *Pilgrim's Progress.* These writers ferreted out for eager mass audiences, and in great detail and fiery prose, how business promoted public deceit and bought special privilege. "The History of the Standard Oil Company," "Shame of the Cities," "Treason of the Senate," and "Railroads on Trial" were vivid exposés. Most repellent was *The Jungle,* Upton Sinclair's description of meatpacking plants where vermin commingled with moldy meat to make everyone's daily breakfast sausage. Other muckrackers attacked patent-medicine makers who peddled narcotics for every infirmity from fatigue to cancer. These exposés ultimately led to the Pure Food and Drug and Meat Inspection acts of 1906.

The 1890s and 1900s were the gestation period for the technology that would define the modern world. The new century had arrived shortly after a procession of remarkable discoveries and inventions: the internal combustion engine was eight years old, movies were just six, and the magnetic recording of sounds was barely one. Nothing fascinated more than electricity, with its promise of radical improvements in communication, education, and entertainment, like the moving picture, which at first consisted primarily of news events, and radio ("wireless telegraphy"), also in its infancy.

Experimentation with the auto and airplane was also beginning. Cars, first condemned as ostentations of the rich, gradually became less exotic, as production methods and practical refinements improved. Early on, the nation learned with wonder of Graf von Zeppelin's lighter-than-air machine, which moved like a giant fish in the upper atmosphere, and in 1903, of events in a small North Carolina town, where the Wright brothers soared 850 feet in 59 seconds in their heavier-than-air machine. The world of air travel and military might had been born. By the end of the decade, both cars and planes were going more than a mile a minute, racing each other to the world's awe and delight.

With the continuation of the last century's gender roles, men—without question—ruled the day. Women could not vote and, if married, could lay no claim to their own earnings; if divorced, they were denied a share in their children's guardianship. Without the arm of a male escort, many restaurant tables and hotel rooms were off-limits to them. Men claimed as their right as much free time with their cronies as their work allowed: the wealthy on horseback, at tennis lawns, and in exclusive clubs; the less well off in barber shops, the new Rotary clubs, or their favorite saloons. In Boston and Chicago, half the male population visited drinking establishments daily, where they smoked cigars, drank whiskey, played poker, and became expert at scoring bull's-eyes in brass spitoons.

Men ruled their devoted, mostly stay-at-home wives, whose cultivated respectability was amply reflected in their dress—padded with petticoats and upheld by tight corsets. And, as expected, women dedicated themselves to pleasing their husbands, rearing their children, and caring for their homes. Wealthy women attended elegant teas, and some joined the new Junior Leagues to perform settlement house charitable work, or, like Jane Addams, Florence Kelley, and Charlotte Perkins Gilman, to lead movements for social change, including Woman Suffrage. But every aspect of culture, from stage drama to the new movies, endorsed the double standard of "Boys will be boys, but girls must be good." As the century began, "I'm Only a Bird in a Gilded Cage" topped the million sales mark.

The new century was marked by extraordinary developments in high and popular culture: prodigious growth in immigration had made America a "melting pot"—a variegated population for whom entertainment had to have a broad appeal. Its spectrum ranged from

George B. Luks,
The Spielers.
© *Addison Gallery*
of American Art,
Phillips Academy.

the first movie theater (in prosperous Pittsburgh, 1905), burlesque, and the traveling circus to virtually any form of competitive display from baby and swimming shows to sexy girl contests and hootchy-kootchy belly dancing. Of the popular entertainment forms, vaudeville remained paramount, not only because it energized the unique American genre of musical theater but because its actors—often the offspring of immigrants—performed before people of varied ethnic backgrounds, providing role models, evidence that the Horatio Alger promise was real. Vaudeville challenged the genteel values of Victorian America with a more democratic spirit and created an outlet where ethnic groups could both laugh at themselves and take pride in their center-stage compatriots.

Vaudeville was also an arena for the communal experience of laughter, tears, and wonderment. It offered something for everyone: from song-and-dance teams and ethnic and racial humor to comic cross-dressing and minidramas. "Tramp comics" ("Bananas"), in their torn clothing, were popular emblems of the lower class, victims of the Gilded Age's entrepreneurs. Stars of particular fame included Harry Houdini, Al Jolson, Eva Tanguay, Bert Williams, Lillian Russell, Lily Langtry, and Will Rogers.

The 1900s also marked a turning point in American musical theater. Composers like Victor Herbert wrote family shows like *Babes in Toyland;* Sigmund Romberg and George M. Cohan began prolific careers, and Cohan created the new patriotic show of nostalgia for all things American, from *George Washington, Jr.* to *Forty-Five Minutes from Broadway.* Many musicals' songs would become perennial favorites, typically sung from sheet music but also recorded on Columbia's and Edison's new cylinders. "Jazz" (not yet so named), in its New Orleans infancy, developed throughout the decade, largely due to "Buddy" Bolden, who played the new form everywhere, from street parades to funerals. "Jelly Roll" Morton was advancing his own "stomping" style; Scott Joplin's ragtime became a fad.

In the world of classical music, Caruso, Geraldine Farrar, Lillian Nordica, and Feodor Chaliapin were singing premieres of Wagner, Verdi, and Puccini at the Met (opened in 1883); insurance agent Charles Ives was creating innovative music that merged the folk and classical; Gustav Mahler and Arturo Toscanini began their U.S. conductorial careers; and Artur Rubinstein, Sergei Rachmaninoff, and Ignace Paderewski performed at Carnegie Hall (opened in 1891).

In architecture, a booming Chicago, rebounding from its cataclysmic 1871 fire, was rebuilt on a grander scale according to a plan that transformed the look of the modern city. Louis Sullivan, with a Whitmanesque devotion to the ideals of freedom, advanced an indigenous American style of the "proud and soaring thing" in which "form follows function." Frank Lloyd Wright, Sullivan's student and assistant, functionally integrated the material and natural in the horizontal house.

Painting also came into its own with new forms that reflected the social reality of the time. Rebeling against the technical strictures and traditional subjects of the American academy, "The Eight" or "Ash Can School" painted the urban lower class in broad new brushstrokes. Robert Henri's "revolutionary black gang" depicted the everyday life of "bedroom and barroom," "slattern and laborer," despite much censure.

In literature, Henry James, in works like *The Ambassadors,* wrote in a prose of exquisite detail and unique psychological nuance—"point of view"—as he described the cultural clash between American "innocents" and Old World sophisticates. At the same time, his brother, William, struggled to reconcile science and religion and, in *Pragmatism,* to bring experienced reality to both. Edith Wharton and Theodore Dreiser began their careers: *House of Mirth* was a best-seller, but *Sister Carrie* was deemed pornographic and withdrawn from publication. Historical tales and Horatio Alger novels were perennial best-sellers.

Other memorable events of the decade include the first World Series, the Scholastic Aptitude Tests, *The Wonderful Wizard of Oz,* the subway, Stanford White's murder, W. E. B. Du Bois's organization for racial equality, and advances in treatment of dread diseases like yellow fever and gonorrheal eye infections in infants. Albert Einstein's new theories revolutionized the understanding of the cosmos.

Honoring his pledge not to seek reelection, despite pleas for "Four—Four—Four Years More!" Teddy Roosevelt passed the baton to his longtime friend, Vice President William Howard Taft. During his last year in office, Roosevelt set forth more forcefully than ever his program for government regulation of business power. The economy, slowed by the Panic of 1907, rebounded strongly in 1909. But a new voice on the scene belonged to an idealistic academician, Woodrow Wilson, who decried financial manipulators in words much like those of William Jennings Bryan, not to mention the nation's former chief executive, TR, whose political days were far from over.

1900

In the News

ECONOMIC BOOM ENTERS FOURTH YEAR . . . HOUSE VOTES TO UNSEAT UTAH CONGRESSMAN FOR POLYGAMY . . . W. VA. COAL MINE EXPLOSION KILLS 105 . . . NEW SOCIAL DEMOCRATIC PARTY NOMINATES EUGENE V. DEBS FOR PRESIDENT . . . EXCAVATION BEGINS ON N.Y.C. SUBWAY, FIRST IN U.S. . . . ANDREW CARNEGIE FORMS WORLD'S LARGEST CORPORATION, CARNEGIE STEEL . . . BRITISH CLAIM VICTORY IN BOER WAR, 120,000 REFUGEES ARE PLACED IN CAMPS . . . PUERTO RICO, GAINED IN SPANISH AMERICAN WAR OF 1898, BECOMES U.S. TERRITORY . . . HAWAII BECOMES U.S. TERRITORY . . . CARRY NATION ATTACKS SALOONS IN KANSAS . . . CHINESE BOXERS ATTACK FOREIGN LEGATIONS IN BEIJING, 230 DIE, KAISER VOWS RUTHLESS REPRESSION . . . INTERNATIONAL LADIES' GARMENT WORKERS' UNION FORMS . . . PHILIPPINE INSURGENCY AGAINST U.S. RULE CONTINUES, U.S. CONCENTRATES TROOPS IN CITIES . . . GOP NOMINATES WILLIAM MCKINLEY AND THEODORE ROOSEVELT . . . GERMANS BEGIN 17-YEAR NAVAL BUILDUP . . . GERMAN VON ZEPPELIN'S LIGHTER-THAN-AIR SHIP MAKES MAIDEN VOYAGE . . . DEMOCRATS NOMINATE WILLIAM JENNINGS BRYAN . . . ITALIAN KING UMBERTO IS MURDERED BY ANARCHIST . . . U.S., BRITISH, GERMAN, RUSSIAN, FRENCH, JAPANESE TROOPS JOIN TO FIGHT BOXERS . . . IRISH NATIONALISTS DEMONSTRATE IN DUBLIN FOR HOME RULE . . . TIDAL WAVES DESTROY GALVESTON, TEXAS, 4,000 ARE KILLED . . . 150,000 COAL MINERS STRIKE IN PA. . . . MCKINLEY WINS WITH 7,219,530 VOTES, BRYAN GAINS 6,358,071, DEBS 87,811 . . . FLORENCE KELLEY FORMS CONSUMERS' LEAGUE TO FIGHT SUBSTANDARD GOODS, CHILD LABOR, TENEMENT SWEATSHOPS . . . U.S. NAVY BUYS FIRST SUBMARINE . . . JOHN PORTER, A BLACK, IS BURNED AT STAKE AFTER COLORADO GIRL'S MURDER.

Facts and Figures

Economic Profile
Dow-Jones: ↑ High 71– Low 55
GNP: +7.5%
Inflation: 0.1%
Unemployment: 5.0%
Bloomingdale's, N.Y.C.
Gingham baby dress, pink or blue, with ruffled neck and embroidered yoke: 67¢
Ladies' percale shirt waist, full gathered front: 59¢
Strawbridge & Clothier, Philadelphia
Men's summer bicycle suits: $2.50; all-wool winter suits: $10
Boy's all-wool suit: $2.75; all-wool sweaters: $1.50
Men's Regal patent calf shoe, with kangaroo tops, fast black eyelets, "the tabasco": $3.50
Columbia chainless bicycles: $60–$75; chain wheels: $25–$50
Olympia self-playing music box: $45
Gramophone: $10
Brass, no smoke lamp: 50¢

Above: McKinley's campaign emphasizes the nation's prosperity with a "full dinner pail" in every parade.

Deaths

Frederick Church, Stephen Crane, Roger Ingersoll, Friedrich Nietzsche, Nathaniel de Rothschild, John Ruskin, Sir Arthur Sullivan, Cornelius Vanderbilt, Oscar Wilde

Quotes

"God has marked the American people as His chosen nation to finally lead in the regeneration of the world. This is the divine mission of America. . . . We are trustees of the world's progress, guardians of its righteous peace."

—Albert J. Beveridge (R—Ind.)

"I sigh f'r' th' good ol' days before we became . . . a wurruld power. In thim days our favrite spoort was playin' solitaire, winnin' money from each other. . . . Ivry body was invious iv us. . . . Ah' now, be Hivens, we have no peace of o' mind."

—Finley Peter Dunne ("Mr. Dooley")

On the presidential campaign:
Republicans: "McKinley drinks soda water, Bryan drinks rum. McKinley is a gentleman, Bryan is a bum"; "Four more years of the full dinner pail"; "We'll stand pat!"; "William McKinley, a Western man with Eastern ideas; and Theodore Roosevelt, an Eastern man, with Western characteristics."   —for McKinley

Democrats: "No Crown of thorns. No Cross of Gold"; "We oppose militarism. It means conquest abroad and intimidation and oppression at home. It means the strong arm which has ever been fatal to free institutions. It is what millions of our citizens have fled from in Europe."   —for Bryan

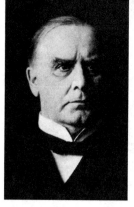

President William McKinley.

William Jennings Bryan runs again for president; he is well remembered for his 1896 remark "Thou shalt not crucify mankind upon a cross of gold."

"Lift ev'ry voice and sing / 'Til earth and heaven ring / Ring with the harmonies of Liberty; / High as the lit'ning skies / . . . Let us march on 'til victory is won."

—James Weldon and J. Rosamond Johnson, sung by a group of black Florida schoolchildren to commemorate Lincoln's birthday

"When I was a boy on the Mississippi River there was a proposition in a township there to discontinue public schools because they were too expensive. An old farmer spoke up and said if they stopped the schools, they would not save anything, because every time a school was closed, a jail had to be built."

—Mark Twain, who moves to Fifth Ave., N.Y.C., this year

"My time has not yet come either; some are born posthumously."

—Friedrich Nietzsche

Ads

An American comforts a Japanese ally during the war against China's "Society of Harmonious Fists" (the Boxer Rebellion).

Of the recent Spanish American War, Secretary of State John Hay, who was Lincoln's private secretary, says: "It has been a splendid little war, begun with the highest motive, carried out with magnificent intelligence and spirit, favored by fortune which loves the brave."

Vaudeville

Successful entrepreneurs E. F. Albee and B. F. Keith centralize vaudeville houses in powerful circuits that act as booking offices. Although critics condemn this as the establishment of "trusts," Albee and other important managers of the decade—F. F. Proctor, Alexander Pantages, and Martin Beck—promise better business practices and salary regulation. Artists rebel with a unionlike association, The White Rats ("Star" backwards), and hold meetings, or "scampers," regularly at Koster and Bial's Music Hall on 23rd Street, N.Y.C.

Of Note

George M. Cohan leaves vaudeville after a dispute with B. F. Keith over billing • Al Joelson and his brother Harry create "The Hebrew and the Cadet" sketch; the two soon join Joe Palmer and drop the "e" from their names • Smith and Dale create the New Schoolteacher sketch; they are popular for their impeccable timing and corny but funny jokes ("How could a low life like you have such high blood pressure?") • The Hungarian-born son of a rabbi Harry Houdini (Erik Weisz) is a headliner whose salary eventually jumps from $15 to $12,500 a week • Elsie Janis, invited to entertain President McKinley at the White House, impersonates Weber & Fields, Lillian Russell, and Fay Templeton • Veterans Weber & Fields, creators of knockabout comedy and author of "Who's that lady I saw you with last night?"— "She ain't no lady; she's my wife," pursue outrageous "slapstick" humor, such as breaking a violin over one partner's head or putting a finger in his eye • Because vaudeville can be a pathway out of the ghetto, parents remove their talented children from school. Francis Keaton, 5, for example, after one day of schooling, joins his parents in an acrobatics and comedy routine; the child is nicknamed "Buster" by family friend Houdini when he tumbles down the stairs • Popular joke of the year: "I sent my wife to the Thousand Islands for a vacation. A week on each island."

Movies

"Newsreel" (Edison), of Market Street, San Francisco
The Downward Path (Biograph), about streetwalker-
    daughter, with each scene listed separately
Cinderella (Méliès), with dissolve from scene to scene
Chinese Massacring Christians (Lubin), on Boxer
    Uprising
Nouvelles Lettres/Extravagantes (Méliès), women
    wrestlers becoming men with sexes rotating in
    various stages of dismemberment
Roosevelt in Minneapolis (Selig)
Maud's Naughty Little Brother (Edison/Vitagraph)
Wreckage from the Water Front (Lubin)
Beheading a Chinese Prisoner (Lubin)
Grandma's Reading Glass (G. A. Smith), eye filmed
    through magnifying glass

Movies, about five years old, are used primarily as "chasers" in vaudeville theaters; usually under five minutes long, they allow theater managers to "chase" malingerers and to sell candy. Sometimes they are shown between vaudeville acts. Audiences favor news and scenic films, as well as those with exotic dancers, parades, vaudeville acts, and onrushing trains, although most images are of fires, floods, or people performing acts like squashing a mosquito or sneezing. Some are sexually suggestive. Actors gain no screen credit; on occasion, the cameraman is listed.

Edison, American Mutoscope, and Biograph compete with foreign filmmakers, particularly the French (Pathé Frères, the Lumières, Léon Ernest Gaumont, and George Méliès); other foreign companies include Britons R. W. Paul, Cecil Hepworth, and Charles Urban, as well those in Italy, Germany, Scandinavia, and Russia. Because films are silent, foreign films are shown throughout the world: U.S. movies appear in Paris, London, St. Petersburg, Delhi, and Tokyo. Newly organized at the start of the century are Vitagraph, Selig, Lubin, Paley, and Spoor. Mrs. Sloane's Searchlight Theater in Tacoma, Washington, is the best known theater, featuring films like *Trip through Egypt, Little Red Riding Hood,* and *War Scenes.* Although other companies send cameramen to capture the vast wreckage of the Galveston tornado, Edison's Albert Smith uses a new tripod and captures sweeping panoramic scenes of the dead.

Popular Music ⎯⎯⎯⎯⎯⎯⎯⎯

Hit Songs

"A Bird in a Gilded Cage"
"Rosie, You Are My Rosie"
"He Was a Married Man"
"I'm a Respectable Working Girl"
"Give Me the Good Old Fashioned Girl"
"I Can't Tell Why I Love You, But I Do"
"Mine at Last"
"Strike Up the Band, Here Comes a Sailor"
"When the Harvest Days Are Over, Jennie"
"You Can't Keep a Good Man Down"
"Tell Me, Pretty Maiden"

Representative Recordings:

"When You Were Sweet Sixteen" (Jere Mahoney); "Mandy Lee" (Arthur Collins); "When Chloe Sings a Song" (George J. Gaskin); "Ma Tiger Lily" (Arthur Collins); "Because" (Haydn Quartet); "Absence Makes the Heart Grow Fonder" (Harry MacDonough)

Jazz

After the Civil War, many Confederate army bands left their instruments in New Orleans pawn shops. Blacks, once free to travel, bought them and found employment in saloons and dance halls throughout the city. With no knowledge of the traditional handling of slides and valves, they played by ear.

By 1900, New Orleans becomes a melting pot—the English, Italians, Germans, and Slavs joining a culture of the Spanish, French, and former American slaves. Two major populations in the city consist of the "American negroes" and "New Orleans Creoles" (descendants from the old French colonial culture). Retaining their French culture, the Creoles speak a French patois mixed with Spanish and African words; most of the great clarinetists and woodwind players—apart from "Jelly Roll" Morton (né Ferdinand Joseph La Menthe)—retain their French names: Alphonse Picou,

Sidney Bechet, Barney Bigard, Albert Nicholas, Buddy Petit, Freddie Kippard, Papa and Louis deLisle Nelson, "Kid" Ory. As the Creoles mix European forms with experimentation, American blacks like "Buddy" Bolden become prominent for their rhythmic and ornamental innovations.

Theater ⎯⎯⎯⎯⎯⎯⎯⎯

Broadway Openings

Plays

Sapho (Clyde Fitch), Olga Nethersole, John Glendinning, condemned as "immoral" and closed
Barbara Frietchie (Clyde Fitch), Julia Marlowe
Zaza (David Belasco), Mrs. Leslie Carter, Arthur Bruning
Quo Vadis (Stanislaus Stange, six acts), Joseph Haworth, Alice Fischer, Edmund D. Lyons
Arizona (Augustus Thomas), Eleanor Robson, Vincent Serrano
Hearts Are Trumps (Cecil Raleigh), Cecil B. de Mille
L'Aiglon (Edmond Rostand), Maude Adams (later replaced by Sarah Bernhardt), John S. Robertson
Richard Carvel (Robert E. Rose), John Drew
Sag Harbor (James A. Herne), Julia and Chrystal Herne, Lionel Barrymore, William T. Hodge
Madame Butterfly (David Belasco), David Bates
Kathleen ni Houlihan (W. B. Yeats), Mary E. Barker, Frank McCormack
When We Were Twenty-One (Henry V. Esmond), Maxine Elliott, Nat C. Goodwin (wife and husband)

Musicals

Florodora (Leslie Stuart, E. Boyd-Jones, Paul Rubens), Edna Wallace Hopper, Cyril Scott, Florodora Sextet of Girls
Miss Prinnt (John L. Golden, George V. Hobart), Marie Dressler, Jobyna Howland
Fiddle-Dee-Dee (John Stromberg, Edgar Smith), Lillian Russell, Fay Templeton, Weber & Fields, De Wolf Hopper
Chris and the Wonderful Lamp (John Philip Sousa, Glen MacDonough), Edna Wallace Hopper, Jerome Sykes
Whirl-A-Gig (Harry B. Smith), Joe Weber, Lew Fields, Lillian Russell, David Warwick, burlesque in two acts

Classics and Revivals On and Off Broadway

Hamlet, E. H. Sothern (first N.Y. appearance in role) and Virginia Harned; *Hamlet,* Johnston Forbes-Robertson (also first N.Y. appearance in role); *Henry V,* Richard Mansfield; *The Land of Heart's Desire,* Mr. and Mrs. John Glendinning; Modjeska Repertory: *Mary Stuart* (Schiller), *The Ladies' Battle* (Scribe, Legouver), *Macbeth,* Helena Modjeska

Sapho, with Olga Nethersole, is closed for indecency, and Nethersole is arrested; her kiss, enacted in a bedroom, gains coinage as the "sole [soul] kiss."

Maurice Barrymore, fresh from his success in *Becky Sharp,* has three successful acting children, Lionel, Ethel, and John.

Classical Music

Compositions
George Whitefield Chadwick, *Judith*
Edward MacDowell, Piano Sonata no. 3 ("Norse")
Charles Ives, *Prelude,* First Sonata for Violin and Piano
Charles Martin Loeffler, *Divertissement español for Saxophone and Orchestra*

Important Events
The Philadelphia Orchestra performs its inaugural concert under Fritz Schell with a program that includes Beethoven's Fifth Symphony and Tchaikovsky's First Piano Concerto (Ossip Gabrilowitsch, 22, soloist). Progenitor of the Minneapolis Symphony Orchestra, the Minneapolis Philharmonic Club forms, directed by Emil Oberhoffer. The Boston Symphony moves into its new home, $1 million Symphony Hall. The Pittsburgh Symphony debuts at Carnegie Hall, with Victor Herbert conducting. The Dallas Symphony presents its first concert.

Notable Performances: Hans Kriessig's N.Y.C. premiere of Bach's *B Minor Mass;* Harold Bauer's debut with the Boston Symphony, followed by an extensive tour throughout the U.S., during which he gains a reputation as a great interpreter of Beethoven.

Major Recitals: Ernst von Dohnanyi, Fritz Kriesler, Jean Gérardy

New Appointment: William Gericke, conductor of the Boston Symphony since 1884, steps down for the brief tenure of fiery Arthur Nikisch.

Debuts: Ossip Gabrilowitsch, Harold Bauer

First Performances
Frank S. Converse, *Festival of Pan* (Boston); George Whitefield Chadwick, *Adonais* (Boston); Richard Strauss, *Ein Heldenleben* (Chicago); Samuel Coleridge-Taylor, *Hiawatha's Wedding Feast* (Boston); Charles Martin Loeffler, *Tintagiles for Two Violins d'Amore and Orchestra* (Boston)

Opera
In addition to the rise of such small regional companies as Chicago's Swedish Theatre, countless troupes have traveled the U.S. since the Civil War, such as the French Opera Company of New Orleans; American groups like the Andrews, Clara Louise Kellogg, and Emma Abbott companies join predominantly English and Italian companies; about half the opera is sung in English. Operettas by Victor Herbert and John Philip Sousa are also performed. An all-black organization from Washington, D.C., inspires a Gilbert and Sullivan craze.

Metropolitan: Premieres: Nellie Melba, Giuseppe Cremonini, Marcel Journet (debut), *La Bohème;* Antonio Pini-Corsi, *Don Pasquale;* Johanna Gadski, Hans Breuer (debut), *The Flying Dutchman;* Ernestine Schumann-Heink, Milka Ternina (debut), *Lohengrin;* Antonio Scotti (debut), *Les Huguenots;* Scotti, Lillian Nordica, *Don Giovanni;* Andreas Dippel, Marcella Sembrich, *Die Zauberflöte;* Albert Alvarez (debut), *Romeo and Juliet*

Henry W. Savage Co (New York): *Aïda; The Bohemian Girl;* Grace Van Studdiford, Zelie de Lussan, *Faust*

San Francisco: *The Viceroy* (premiere, Victor Herbert); works of Gilbert and Sullivan, Victor Herbert

Chicago: *Sigurd* (Reyer); *Lohengrin; Tannhäuser; The Flying Dutchman*

New Orleans: *Salammbo; La Bohème*

Art

Painting
John Singer Sargent, *The Sitwell Family, The Wyndham Sisters*
Thomas Eakins, *The Thinker, Frank Jay St. John*
Albert Pinkham Ryder, *The Dead Bird* (1890–1900)
John Twachtman, *Round Top Road*
Henry Ossawa Tanner, *Salomé*
Cecilia Beaux, *Little Lamerche*
Maurice Prendergast, *Promenade at Nantasket*

Sculpture
Solon H. Borglum, *The Blizzard, Bulls Fighting*
Arthur Putnam, *Two Fighting Buffalo*
Charles Calverley, *Sir Walter Scott*

Important Exhibitions

Museums

New York: *Metropolitan:* Frederick E. Church; 325 Musical instruments. Acquisitions: 38 Greco-Roman terracotta masks found at Alexandria in tombs from the Roman period; six funerary stones from Palmyra; Mexican antiquities; 29 ancient Greek gold ornaments from Saldae, Haifa, Tarsus; 15 bronze objects from Abydos. Contributions of J. P. Morgan: classical Greek art objects in gold, 400–300 B.C., Henry Clay's senate chair. *Waldorf Astoria:* Watercolors; Decorative arts; *Chickering Hall:* Thomas Bonner; *Pratt Institute:* Robert F. Blum

Bert Williams, the first black in major vaudeville, receives great respect as a comedian and pantomimist as he endures racial discrimination; he is also president of the Frogs, a black social club.

Architecture
Symphony Hall, Boston (McKim, Mead & White)
Crown building, Chicago (Holabird & Roche)
Hall of Fame, New York University, N.Y.C. (Stanford White)
Field Museum of Natural History, Chicago (D. H. Burnham)
Lotus Club, New York City (Richard Howland Hund)
University Club, New York City (McKim, Mead & White)
Appelate Division, New York State Supreme Court, N.Y.C. (James Brown Lord)

Left: Augustus Saint-Gaudens, *The Puritan*, 1899–1900. *The Metropolitan Museum of Art, Bequest of Jacob Ruppert,* 1939. Right: The Gibson girl; *Life* magazine frequently advertises Charles Dana Gibson's image on plates, pillows, and dresser sets.

Boston: Japanese paintings

Chicago: James Abbott McNeill Whistler; "Artistic Photographs"; Textiles; Installation of amateur photographer Mrs. Samuel M. Nickerson's collection

New Haven: *Yale University:* James J. Jarves

Philadelphia: *Museum of Art:* Theodore Robinson; *Pennsylvania Academy of Fine Arts:* Appleton Tanagra figures

Art Briefs
For at least a decade, Robert Henri, followed by George Luks, William Glackens, John Sloan, Everett Shinn, and others, have rejected the refined "respectability" of academic art—such as idealized portraits of the wealthy—for a "soup" technique (a canvas covered with neutral tones and minimal brushstrokes) that evokes a more spontaneous form. Their interest grows in the hunger, poverty, and shabbiness of the urban world, as well as in a nude that reveals the real, not idealized, body. To Henri, the Pennsylvania Academy's domineering "respectability" in art is "appalling" • Only a handful of private galleries exist in N.Y.C., and they deal with European imports and the American old masters • Thirty paintings by Maurice Prendergast go on exhibition at the Art Institute of Chicago; only one sells, for $85; at its 11th Annual Water Color Show, 35 paintings sell for $1,899 • A journalist, Shinn publishes drawings of poverty in such magazines as *Harper's Weekly.*

Books

Fiction

Critics' Choice

Sister Carrie, Theodore Dreiser
The Man That Corrupted Hadleyburg, Mark Twain
Monsieur Beaucaire, Booth Tarkington
Whilomville Stories, Stephen Crane
The Son of the Wolf, Jack London
In Debt of Honor, Falling in with Fortune, Horatio Alger (posthumous)
The Touchstone, Edith Wharton
Fables in Slang, More Fables, George Ade
In the Palace of the King, F. Marion Crawford
A Man's Woman, Frank Norris
The Wonderful Wizard of Oz, L. Frank Baum
The Love of Parson Lord, and Other Stories, Mary E. Wilkins Freeman
The Eagle's Heart, Hamlin Garland
From Sand Hill to Pine, Bret Harte
The Web of Life, Robert Herrick
🍀 *Lord Jim*, Joseph Conrad

Best-Sellers

To Have and to Hold, Mary Johnston
Red Pottage, Mary Cholmondeley

Unleavened Bread, Robert Grant
The Reign of Law, James Lane Allen
Eben Holden, Irving Bacheller
Janice Meredith, Paul Leicester Ford
The Redemption of David Corson, Charles Frederic Goss
Richard Carvel, Winston Churchill
When Knighthood Was in Flower, Charles Major
Alice of Old Vincennes, Maurice Thompson

Nonfiction

Critics' Choice

Interpretation of Poetry and Religion, George Santayana
The Pains of Lowly Life, Mark Twain
French Portraits, Vance Thompson
Notes of an Itinerant Policeman, Josiah Flynt
America's Economic Supremacy, Brooks Adams
Mr. Dooley's Philosophy, Finley Peter Dunne
The World and the Individual, vol. 1, Josiah Royce
Literary Friends and Acquaintances, William Dean Howells
The Winning of the West, Theodore Roosevelt

Frank Merriwell is known for his last-minute heroics.

A Literary History of the United States, Barrett Wendell
🍀 *The Interpretation of Dreams*, Sigmund Freud
🍀 *Ecce Homo*, Friedrich Nietzsche (posthumous)

Poetry

James Whitcomb Riley, *Home-Folks*
William Vaughn Moody, *The Masque of Judgment*
🍀 W. B. Yeats, *The Shadowy Waters*

Science and Technology

Using human volunteers, some of whom die, Walter Reed links *Aedes aegypti* mosquito bites to yellow fever in Cuba; the disease has prevented the building of an interocean canal.

An antiserum against bacillary dysentery is created by Kiyoshi Shiga.

Reginald A. Fessenden transmits speech by wireless telegraph (radio waves).

Orville and Wilbur Wright fly their first glider; they have been experimenting since 1896.

James Keeler establishes that some nebulae contain spiral structures.

🍀 Max Planck establishes quantum theory, asserting that energy is discharged in discrete parcels, rather than continuously.

🍀 Scientists rediscover and acclaim the monk Gregor Mendel's 1860s work on the laws of heredity.

🍀 Patrick Manson identifies the *Anopheles* mosquito as the carrier of malaria.

🍀 Three blood groups that clot when mixed—A, B, and O—are identified by Karl Landsteiner.

🍀 Sigmund Freud's *The Interpretation of Dreams* postulates that dream symbolism reveals the unconscious mind.

🍀 Excavating at Knossos, Crete, Arthur Evans unearths the center of Minoan civilization.

Sports

Baseball

The National, the only major professional league, consists of Boston, Brooklyn, Chicago, Cincinnati, New York, Philadelphia, Pittsburgh, and St. Louis.

Interest in the NL continues to decline since games are rowdy, with drinking and gambling by both owners and players; umpires are often kicked and pushed.

Bancroft "Ban" Johnson, with Cornelius McGillicuddy ("Connie Mack") and Charles Comiskey, reorganizes the Western as the American League; Johnson demands NL recognition and cleaning up the game's unruliness.

After the NL's refusal, the AL raids it, offering salaries above the NL top $2,400; it attracts players like Napoleon Lajoie and John McGraw and competes in Philadelphia and Chicago.

A five-sided home plate becomes standard.

NL stars include Honus Wagner (debut), Willie ("Hit 'em where they ain't") Keeler, Cy Young, and Joe ("Iron Man") McGinnity.

Champions

Batting	Pitching
John P. "Honus" Wagner, (Pittsburgh, NL), .381	Joe McGinnity (Brooklyn, NL), 20–6
	Home runs
	Herman Long (Boston, NL), 12

Football

Yale, Harvard, Princeton, Penn, and Columbia attract the best players, but Western conference teams like Michigan and Chicago begin to challenge them. Seven of eleven All-Americans (chosen by Walter Camp) are from Yale. A touchdown and field goal are five points; an extra point, one. Athletic clubs compete for money, but there is no organized pro league.

College All-Americans: George Chadwick (HB), Yale; John Hallowell (E), Harvard; Herman Olcott (C), Yale

Basketball

Pro basketball, not organized, is widely played on dance floors surrounded by chicken wire ("cagers"); play tends to be rough; spectators poke hatpins through the wire. The best college players attend Eastern schools, although interest grows in the Midwest.

Olympics

The games, first revived in 1896, are held in Paris; 427 athletes compete. France wins most medals, 29; the U.S., 20. U.S. winners include F. W. Jarvis (100m, 10.8s), J. W. B. Tewksbury (200m, 22.2s, 400mh), J. K. Baxter (pole vault, 10'9"; high jump, 6'2.8"), Ray Ewry (standing high, broad, and hop, step, and jump), Maaxey Long (400m, 49.4s), Alvin Kraenzlein (running broad jump, 20', 9.75'), John Flanagan (hammer throw).

Other Sports

Tennis: Davis Cup play is initiated when Harvard student and player Dwight Davis donates a trophy for international competition. The U.S., led by Davis and Malcolm Whitman, defeats Great Britain 3–0 in Boston.

Winners

National League	USGA Open
Brooklyn	Harry Vardon
College Football	*Kentucky Derby*
Yale	Lieutenant Gibson (Jimmy Dolan, jockey)
U.S. Tennis Open	
Men: Malcom D. Whitman	
Women: Myrtle McAteer	

Fashion

With the Industrial Revolution spurring urban growth, woman's suffrage and "feminism" is reflected in new fashion quarters. Working women buy the new sewing machine, along with new paper patterns; great mail order houses, like Montgomery Ward (1872) and Sears, Roebuck (1894), offer ready-to-wear designs at reasonable prices. All copy the wealthy women who depend upon tailor-made clothing to rival their European counterparts abroad. A rapid expansion in the industry begins as houses of haute couture, newly opened in Paris, begin to export clothing. La Belle Epoque, with Art Nouveau designs, peaks. Designers, seeking free-flowing lines and swirling rhythmic curves, cut yards upon yards of luxurious fabrics, and dresses sweep the ground with flowing flounces of pleated chiffon and satins embellished with colorful embroidery or beads. Milady visits Paris in late February and March to select her spring and summer wardrobes; in August and September, her autumn and winter wear. At home, European styles find their way into stores like Marshall Field in Chicago. Women wear numerous outfits throughout the day: simple costumes to perform daily chores; more ornate dresses for visits and luncheons; walking frocks; and special gowns for receiving visitors at home or going out—both in the country and in town.

High-fashion note: Worth, Red Fern, Paquin, Doeuillet, Doucet, and Callot Soeurs are most sought-after designers: all create bodices with frills and flounces, a small, constricted waist, and ground-length skirts ending in pleats and extra fabric.

Kaleidoscope

- Hearing "Mrs. Bryan will be sleeping in the White House soon," a heckler replies, "Then she'll be sleeping with McKinley."
- "I find America so cheerful and so full of swagger and self-satisfaction, that I hardly know it," writes Henry Adams to a friend; the *New York Times* calls the new century "a miraculous time."
- Cities become industrial centers as they gather immigrants and rural migrants who provide unskilled and specialized labor; New York enlarges from 1 million to 3.5 million; Philadelphia, 500,000 to 1.3 million; Boston, 170,000 to 500,000; and Chicago, from "a small town" to 1.7 million (since 1880).
- The U.S. leads the world in productivity; the wealth of nations (GNP), in billions, is: the U.S., $116; Great Britain, $62.2; France, $42.8; Germany, $42; Russia, $35; and Austria-Hungary, $20.
- Marriage between whites and persons of "negro descent" is prohibited and punishable in 25 states; it is "valid and effectual" in Michigan.
- Most states require being a "citizen of the U.S." the sole qualification for voting; Mississippi adds "who can read or understand the Constitution."
- Women enjoy suffrage only in Colorado, Idaho, Utah, and Wyoming; Arizona, California, Connecticut, Illinois, Indiana, Maine, Massachusetts, Mississippi, Michigan, Oklahoma, South Dakota, Vermont, and Washington have voted against it.
- 8,000 autos (*Life* magazine's "playthings of the rich") travel a total of 144 miles of road with hard surfaces.
- Major cities have trolleys ("street railways)"; 4,000 "horseless carriages" are manufactured; 19 million horses and mules dominate the road, along with 10 million bicycles.
- A bubonic plague epidemic strikes San Francisco.
- Diarrhea and enteritis are the most frequent causes of infant mortality; contaminated water and milk are widespread.
- The Maryland state legislature decrees: "Children shall not be employed for acrobatic or similar purposes, or as beggars or street musicians."
- Illiteracy reaches a low of 10.7 percent.
- "It has been charged that our conduct of the war [in the Philippines] has been cruel. Senators, it has been the reverse. . . . We are not dealing with Americans or Europeans. We are dealing with Orientals," remarks a GOP leader on U.S. efforts to quell the rebellion in the Philippines.
- As Russia advances in Manchuria, Teddy Roosevelt calls Russia "a government for whom mendacity is a science."
- Louis Comfort Tiffany opens his glass studio in New York.
- Publisher Frank Doubleday stops the sale of Theodore Dreiser's *Sister Carrie* after his wife calls it "sordid"; Dreiser suffers a nervous illness.
- "Casey" Jones steers the *Cannonball Express* into a stalled freight train; he saves the firemen but loses his life; a ballad popularizes the incident.
- Vaudeville is the major popular entertainment, offering song and dance teams, mind-reading acts, banjoists, singers in white- or blackface, eccentric comedy (e.g., the short man with enormous feet), ethnic and racial humor, fire and fish regurgitators, dancing and drunken animal acts, comic-cross dressing, escapologists, daredevils, slapstick, and bountiful sentimentality—just to name some of its acts.
- The "colonial clap" and "boo" are born, as well as "the hook"—introduced during vaudeville's "Amateur Night" to physically remove poor performers from the stage.
- One in seven homes has a bathtub; one in 13, a telephone; the first automatic telephone exchange is installed in New Bedford, Mass.
- Postal rates are 2¢/oz.; 5¢ to foreign countries.
- Although 2 million mustangs remain on the prairie, of the millions of bison once there, only 30 are now extant.
- Smoking cigarettes is highly popular, but chewing tobacco, like cigar and pipe smoking, are considered less effete.
- The *New York Times* reports that upstate farmers have discovered that a brass band marching around orchards will kill destructive insects; they worry that a reverse effect might take place and "set in motion a desire . . . of the animal . . . to kill the performers."
- The U.S. College Entrance Examination Board is formed to screen college applicants with a Scholastic Aptitude Test; it has a scoring range of 200–800 points.
- The Brownie Box from Eastman Kodak costs $1, making photographs readily available to the masses; six exposures costs 15¢.
- The Junior League of the New York Settlement House attracts young debutantes into serving the less fortunate.
- H. J. Heinz puts up a six-story electric sign in N.Y.C. extolling "57 Good Things for the Table."
- Susan B. Anthony writes "Women in Masculine Politics"; Elizabeth Cady Stanton, "There is No Sex in Brains"; and Carrie Chapman Catt, "The Sex Line in Salaries."
- The U.S. population in 45 states has risen 21 percent since 1890 and nearly 300 percent since 1850; of 76 million, 10.6 million are foreign-born.

Fads: shirtwaists, bicycling, "The Cake Walk" (originally a black slave satire on white ballroom dancing), marriages of impoverished European aristocracy to wealthy Americans (e.g., Helena Zimmerman, daughter of iron, oil millionaire, to the Duke of Manchester, widely called "a man of dissipations and soiled reputation")

First Appearances: "hamburger" (Louis Lassen, New Haven), honeydew melon, Wesson oil, shredded wheat cereal and cracker (Triscuits), roast coffee in vacuum tins (Hills Bros.), Uneeda Biscuit, National Negro Business League (Booker T. Washington), direct primary in election (Minnesota), American Legion, "Happy Hooligan" cartoon, paper clip (patented), "Ever Ready" electric torches, steam tractors, autostage (automated bus for eight passengers), Firestone Tire and Rubber Company, drilling offshore oil wells, Cody, Wyo. (by "Buffalo Bill" Cody), Associated Press (N.Y.), Carnegie Institute of Technology (Andrew Carnegie, $1 million), *Who's Who in America,* "freedancing" (Isadora Duncan miming to music in nonclassical movements), Nobel Peace prize (Red Cross)

1901

New Yorkers stand still as a bell tolls on the day of McKinley's burial.

Facts and Figures

Economic Profile
  Dow-Jones: ↓ High 78– Low 61
  GNP: +10.6%
  Inflation: –0.8%
  Unemployment: 4.0%
Median age, first marriage:
  Male: 25.9, Female: 21.9
Average household size: 4.8
Population over 65: 4%
Population under 10: 23%
Ingersoll Dollar Watch: $1
Custom Made, U.S. Buggy & Cart Co.
  Buggies: $21.50; Buggy Top: $5.50
  Phaetons: $43.95; Surreys: $46
  Four tire wheels: $15
Storm King Whiskey (rye or bourbon):
  4 qts.: $3.50; 6: $4.50; 12: $8.75
Sears, Roebuck "Wish book" (catalog)
  Wood-burning stove: $17.48; wooden ice box: $8.52
  Turkish leather couch: $15.65
  Glass bordeaux lamp: $3.87
  Bread toaster: 20¢; iron, with snap-on handles: 75¢
  Cherry stoner: 70¢; "true-blue" enameled teapot: 58¢

Deaths

Philip D. Armour, P. T. Barnum, Duc de Broglie, Charles C. Delmonico, Benjamin Harrison, Pierre Lorillard, Clement Studebaker, Henri de Toulouse-Lautrec, Giuseppe Verdi

In the News

OIL GUSHES FROM WORLD'S GREATEST STRIKE IN TEXAS . . . BRITISH QUEEN VICTORIA, 81, DIES AFTER 64-YEAR REIGN . . . J. P. MORGAN BUYS CARNEGIE'S STEEL MILLS FOR $492 MILLION, FOUNDS U.S. STEEL, FIRST BILLION-DOLLAR CORPORATION . . . PANIC HITS WALL STREET AS MORGAN, JOHN ROCKEFELLER, EDWARD HARRIMAN FIGHT FOR CONTROL OF NORTHERN PACIFIC RAILROAD . . . MCKINLEY IS INAUGURATED . . . U.S. DECLARES END OF PHILIPPINE REVOLT WITH CAPTURE OF LEADER EMILIO AGUINALDO, FIGHTING CONTINUES . . . WALL STREET PANIC ENDS WHEN MORGAN FORMS NORTHERN SECURITIES TRUST TO CONTROL TRANSCONTINENTAL RAILROADS . . . U.S. TROOPS LEAVE CUBA, CUBA BECOMES U.S. PROTECTORATE . . . 200 DIE IN N.Y.C. HEAT WAVE . . . WHITE SETTLERS BUY 2 MILLION ACRES FROM NATIVE AMERICAN TRIBES . . . BOXER REBELLION ENDS, CHINA TO INDEMNIFY WORLD POWERS . . . MCKINLEY IS FATALLY SHOT BY ANARCHIST LEON CZOLGOSZ IN BUFFALO, ROOSEVELT BECOMES PRESIDENT . . . TR INVITES BOOKER T. WASHINGTON TO DINE AT WHITE HOUSE, RACE RIOTS FOLLOW, 34 DIE . . . STEEL WORKERS SETTLE MASSIVE STRIKE WITH WAGE AND HOUR GAINS, NO UNION RECOGNITION . . . MCKINLEY'S ASSASSIN IS EXECUTED . . . HAY-PAUNCEFORTE TREATY WITH BRITAIN GIVES U.S. SOLE RIGHT TO BUILD PANAMA CANAL . . . MARCONI TRANSMITS FIRST TRANSATLANTIC RADIO MESSAGE, THE LETTER "S" . . . SUPREME COURT GIVES PUERTO RICANS SOME RIGHTS, NOT ALL PRIVILEGES OF CITIZENS . . . RUSSIAN SOCIAL REVOLUTIONARY PARTY FORMS, CALLS FOR CLASSLESS SOCIETY AND SOCIALIZATION OF PROPERTY.

Quotes

"She has been a great Queen. . . . What she could do to make righteousness prevail on the earth has been done. . . . A simple woman she has been. [She] never lost that touch of nature that makes the whole world kin. . . . Good Queen, good faring on your long journey."
—*Life* magazine, on Queen Victoria's death

"There is a homely adage which runs, 'Speak softly and carry a big stick. You will go far.' If the American nation will speak softly and yet . . . keep a thoroughly efficient navy, the Monroe Doctrine will go far."
—Teddy Roosevelt, 43, youngest president in U.S. history

"If there is one thing more than another for which I admire *you,* Theodore, it is your original discovery of the Ten Commandments."
—Former Republican House Speaker Thomas B. Reed

"Now look! That damned cowboy is President of the United States!"
—O. Mark Hanna (R—Ohio)

On womanhood:
"One of the most important problems to be solved in the new outcry is this: 'Shall women be flowers or vegetables, ornamental or useful?'"

"Doctors tell us . . . that thousands of children will be harmed or killed before birth by the injurious effect of untimely political excitement on their mothers."

"Men want a girl who has not rubbed off the peach blossom of innocence by exposure to a rough world."
—from the *Independent* magazine

Rebel atrocities against American soldiers lead to retaliation, as the battle to subdue the Philippine Insurgency continues.

"The [Englishman] rises in the morning from his New England folding bed, shaves with American soap and a Yankee safety razor, pulls on his Boston boots over his socks from North Carolina and congratulates his wife on the way her Illinois straight-front corset sets off her Massachusetts blouse."
—London *Daily Mail*

"Step by step the Russian Empire has enlarged its area and each successive step has been marked by the crushing out of national independence and personal liberty."
—Poutney Bigelow, *The World Today*

"[In] the Kingdom of Heaven that is to be set up here on earth, there will be no patents, no railway passes, no reserved seats, no special privileges of any sort [for] a select few to live off the toil of others."
—"Golden Rule" Jones, Toledo mayor and former industrialist

"It is God's way; His will, not ours, be done."
—President McKinley's last words

Ads

Mrs. O. H. P. Belmont "takes the air" in Central Park; the wealthy vie with one another in the splendor of their carriages and dress.

Immigrants at work: ready-to-wear clothing depends on work by the piece—collars, sleeves, trousers—sewn three months in summer and three in winter for $5 a week.

Vaudeville

The first skirmish between management and labor (The Management Association and White Rats) occurs over management's insistence of a 5 percent booking commission: artists walk out of theaters and hold "sick outs"; managers retaliate by showing movies. The Rats hold a benefit at the Academy of Music; boxer James P. ("Gentleman Jim") Corbett delivers a monologue, and they net $20,000 in two performances. Due to dissension among the Rats concerning priorities, however, the Management Association regains control, along with its detested commission.

Burlesque offers unique opportunities to blacks, women, and certain ethnic groups, despite unequal salaries and discrimination from other performers. "Coon" songs are popular fare; theaters permit only one black act per show.

Of Note
Ed Wynn, 15, famed for his silly inventions like a 12-foot pole for people "you wouldn't want to touch with a 10-foot pole," makes his professional debut.

Movies

Drama at the Bottom of the Sea (Ferdinand Zecca)
The Big Swallow, Stop Thief! Fire (James Williamson)
The Conquest of the Air (Ferdinand Zecca)
Laura Comstock's Bag-Punching Dog (Edison)
A Trip Around the Pan-American Exposition (Edison), from viewpoint of spectator (as tourist)
Execution of Czolgosz (Edison)
Kansas Saloon Smasher (Edison), burlesque on Carry Nation's saloon smashing, featuring men in drag
Cutting Sugar Cane, Honolulu (Biograph)
Coaching Party, Yosemite Valley (Biograph)
New York in a Blizzard (Edison), camera is rotated to achieve panoramic effect

A common technique involves moving the camera around an area, thereby transforming the viewer into on-site inspector. So many Americans have been excited by the appearance of film at the 1900 Paris World's Fair, where the Lumière Brothers introduced the giant Lumière Cinematograph, that Sears carries a small catalogue of films, including *The Philippines and Our New Possessions, The Passing of the Indian, The*

Assassination of President McKinley, Around the World in Eighty Minutes, and *The Chicago Stockyards, or from Hoof to Market.* Filmmakers argue over the use of too many titles: "[These are] motion pictures not literature." After a U.S. court issues an injunction against Biograph for patent infringement, Thomas Edison remains the only American filmmaker to offer movies to exhibitors.

Of the beautiful Lily Langtry, whose acting is often criticized, Oscar Wilde said: "I would rather have discovered Lily Langtry than America."

Popular Music _____

Hit Songs
"Ain't Dat a Shame?"
"I Love You Truly"
"In the Great Somewhere"
"The Night We Did Not Care"
"Way Down in Old Indiana"
"When My Shakespeare Comes to Town"
"When You Loved Me in the Sweet Old Days"
"Rip Van Winkle Was a Lucky Man"
"Maiden with the Dreamy Eyes"
"She's the Flower of Mississippi"

Representative Recordings: "The Stars and Stripes Forever" (Sousa's Band); "Ma Blushin' Rose" (Albert Campbell); "When Reuben Comes to Town" (S. H. Dudley); "Good-Bye, Dolly Gray" (Big Four Quartet); "Tell Me Pretty Maiden" (Harry MacDonough and Grace Spencer); "Jim Law's Horse Trade with Deacon Witherspoon" (Cal Stewart); "Hello Central, Give Me Heaven" (Byron G. Harlan); "In the Shade of the Palm" (J. W. Myers); "The Tale of the Bumble Bee" (Harry MacDonough)

Jazz
An enormous population takes to ragtime, widely played at the many new century world fairs—in Chicago, Omaha, St. Louis, Buffalo, and elsewhere—where itinerant pianists find steady employment. With its cheerful mood, unlike that of spirituals and blues, and highly syncopated African cross-rhythms, ragtime blends West African and European musical elements. The form originates in the Midwest, with composers like Scott Joplin who have studied classical music

The only known photograph of "Buddy" Bolden.

and write down their new forms. Nevertheless, despite his unique combination of syncopated and unsyncopated rhythms, Joplin confines his music to regular tonalities and the rondo forms of the minuet and scherzo. Many, particularly in New Orleans, experiment with entirely new sounds—e.g., black banjo styles are substituted for traditional piano in ensemble playing.

Theater _____

Broadway Openings

Plays

When Knighthood Was in Flower (Paul Kester), Julia Marlowe, David Torrence
If I Were King (Justin H. McCarthy), E. H. Sothern, Cecilia Loftus
Captain Jinks of the Horse Marines (Clyde Fitch), Ethel Barrymore (debut), H. Reeves Smith
Uncle Tom's Cabin (adaptation from Harriet Beecher Stowe novel), Wilton Lackaye
To Have and To Hold (E. F. Boddington), Holbrook Blinn, Robert Lorraine, Cecil B. de Mille
A Message from Mars (Richard Ganthony), Charles Hawtrey
The Unwelcome Mrs. Hatch (Mrs. Burton Harrison), Mrs. Minnie Maddern Fiske
The Climbers (Clyde Fitch), Frank Worthing, Annie Russell
Manon Lescaut (Theodore Burt Sayre, based on Abbé Prévost novel), Herbert Kelcey
Du Barry (David Belasco), Mrs. Leslie Carter, "Egypta"
The Auctioneer (David Belasco), David Warfield
Beaucaire (Booth Tarkington), Richard Mansfield
Alice of Old Vincennes (Edward E. Rose), Virginia Harned, William Courtleigh, Cecil B. de Mille

Musicals

Hoity Toity (John Stromberg, Edgar Smith), Lillian Russell, Weber & Fields, De Wolf Hopper, Fay Templeton
The Sleeping Beauty and the Beast (J. M. Glover, Frederick Solomon, J. C. Goodwin), Joseph Cawthorn, Harry Bulger, Viola Gillette
The Girl from Up There (Gustav Kerker), Edna May, Otis Harlan, Montgomery & Stone
The King's Carnival (A. Baldwin Sloane, George V. Hobart, Sidney Rosenfeld), Marie Dressler, Charles H. Prince
The Liberty Belles (John W. Bratton, A. Baldwin Sloane, Harry B. Smith), John Slavin, Pauline Chase, Harry Davenport
The Little Duchess (Reginald DeKoven, Harry B. Smith), Anna Held, Charles A. Bigelow
My Lady (H. L. Heartz, R. A. Barnet), Charles J. Ross, Eva Tanguay, Lotta Faust
The Governor's Son (George M. Cohan), George, Jerry, and Josephine Cohan, Helen Levy

Classics and Revivals On and Off Broadway
Cyrano de Bergerac, Henry V, Richard Mansfield; *The Merchant of Venice,* Nat C. Goodwin, Maxine Elliott; *The Professor's Love Story* (James M. Barrie); *Tom Pinch* (adaptation of Dickens's *Martin Chuzzlewit*); Nazimova (her first Nora), *A Doll's House*

Classical Music

Compositions
Edward MacDowell, Sonata no. 4 ("Keltic")
Charles Ives, *From the Steeples and the Mountains*
Samuel Coleridge-Taylor, *Toussaint l'Ouverture*
Percy Grainger, *Early One Morning*
Frederick S. Converse, *Endymion's Narrative, Night and Day*

Important Events
Two San Francisco orchestras gain increased popularity, the 40-person Louis Homeier Ensemble and the Philharmonic Society Orchestra. Frederick Converse joins the Harvard music faculty. The Pittsburgh Orchestra plans a European tour.

Notable Performances: Choral Arts Society (debut, Boston); Cincinnati Music Festival; Czech violinist Jan Kubelik makes a triumphant tour of the U.S. Esteemed Russian pianist Vladimir de Pachmann concludes an extended U.S. tour to frequent poor reviews; he exhibits eccentric behavior that provokes shocked responses: he groans and shouts "Bravo!" while playing and crawls under the piano after a performance looking for the wrong notes he's played; his emotional Chopin performances are dubbed "Chopinzee."

Major Recitals: Harold Bauer, Fritz Kreisler, Josef Hofmann, Maud Powell (introducing Rimsky-Korsakov compositions), Mrs. Bloomfield Zeisler, Ignace Paderewski

Debuts: Jan Kubelik, Florence Austin

First Performances
Victor Herbert, *Hero and Leander* (Pittsburgh); Charles Martin Loeffler, *Divertissement español* (Boston); George Whitefield Chadwick, *Judith* (Worchester, Mass.), String Quartet no. 5 (Boston); Henry Hadley, Second Symphony, or *The Four Seasons* (New York, winner of 1901 Paderewski Prize); Edward MacDowell, *Six Poems after Heine* (New York).

Opera

Metropolitan: Premieres: Giuseppe Cremonini, Milka Ternina, Antonio Scotti, *Tosca;* Lillian Nordica, Ernestine Schumann-Heink, Thomas Salignac, Pol Plançon, *Messa da Requiem* (Verdi); Lucienne Bréval, Albert Saléza, *Salammbô* (Max Reger); Louise Homer (debut), Emma Eames, Emilio De Marchi, *Aïda;* Jean de Reszke, final performances, *Lohengrin, Tristan und Isolde*

Norfolk, Va.: *Priscilla, The Maid of Plymouth* (Francesco Farinelli)

Philadelphia: *Maid Marian* (Reginald DeKoven)

Music Notes
Arthur Farwell founds the Wa-Wan Press to publish Americans who incorporate American folk tunes, especially Native American compositions and country songs • Since his 1898 graduation from Yale, Charles Ives has worked at an insurance company; he begins his second year as a performing artist, an organist at Central Presbyterian Church, N.Y.C.

Lillian Russell is the toast of the town and known for her many husbands; she popularizes the plump figure.

Eugene Sandow, "the Monarch of Muscle," can lift a piano and an eight-man band.

Art

Painting

Mary Cassatt, *The Oval Mirror*
John Singer Sargent, *Study of a Nude Model*
Alfred H. Maurer, *An Arrangement*
Maurice Prendergast, *Central Park*
William J. Glackens, *Hammerstein's Roof Garden, The East River*
Childe Hassam, *Cat Boats, Newport*

Sculpture

Frederic Remington, *The Cheyenne, The Northerner*
Carl Rohl-Smith, *General William Tecumseh Sherman*
Charles M. Russell, *Chief Crawfoot, Six Reins to Kingdom Come*
A. S. Calder, *A Man Cub*
Charles Niehaus, *Mineral Wealth*

Important Exhibitions

Museums

New York: *Metropolitan:* Acquisitions: Burgy estate: 175 objects (from Henry II, Louis XIII, Louis XV, Louis XVI, in steel, bronze, lead, wood); the Jacob S. Rogers estate estimated between $5.5–$7 million; from Joseph H. Durkee: 252 Roman gold coins; 300 gold coins of East India, China, Arabia; nine ancient Etruscan vases; two bronze mirrors with Greek heads in relief; a glass goblet with two Greek inscriptions; four Greek terracotta groups (345 B.C.); a terra-cotta life-size head of Greek man; a vase of a winged boy riding a boar; a statuette of a winged boy found at Kíthira.

Chicago: Art of public schoolchildren; 45 oils; Albert Fleury; Chicago ceramics; 49 works of John Twachtman. Acquisitions: *Troilus and Cressida* (Benjamin West); 236 Japanese prints and sketches; Old laces, valuable textiles; Silver medals by Jean-Charles Cazin, Augustus Saint-Gaudens, Caudray; Four paintings by Hubert Robert.

Boston: Greek, Roman, Byzantine sculpture; Greek statuettes

Bessie O. P. Vonnoh, *Two Women (Daydreams)*
On display at the Pan-American Exposition: Charles Grafly's *Fountain of Man,* John J. Boyce's *The Savage Age in the West,* and Philip Martinez's *Fountain of Abundance*

Architecture

H. W. Poor house, New York (McKim, Mead & White, 1899–1901)
Andrew Carnegie mansion, New York City (Babb, Cook, & Willard)
Benjamin N. Duke mansion, New York City (Horace Trumbauer)
Ward Willits house, Highland Park, Ill. (Frank Lloyd Wright)

Frederic Remington, *The Bronco Buster,* 1901. *The Metropolitan Museum of Art, Bequest of Jacob Ruppert,* 1939.

Art Briefs

Frank Lloyd Wright delivers the address "The Art and Craft of the Machine" at Hull House, Jane Addams' settlement house in Chicago. Simultaneous with his new prairie style, Wright asserts that the machine can become the agent for purification and abstraction, thus saving built forms from the ravages of industrialization • At its watercolor exhibition, the Art Institute of Chicago sells 20 pictures for $1,452 • The Boston Museum of Fine Arts is given funds to purchase Velasquez's portrait *Don Baltazar and His Dwarf* • Maurice Prendergast returns from Paris after studying Paul Cézanne, becoming the first American artist to study abroad the innovative Impressionists and their explorations of process, the anatomization of the object, and sensation.

Frank Norris, author of *The Octopus,* the first book of the trilogy *Epic of Wheat,* gains fame as a novelist and social critic.

Books

Fiction

Critics' Choice
The Sacred Fount, Henry James
The Octopus, Frank Norris
The Marrow of Tradition, Charles Waddell Chesnutt
Lester's Luck, Making His Mark, Horatio Alger (posthumous)
By Bread Alone: A Novel, I. K. Friedman
Forty Modern Fables, George Ade
The Cavalier, George Washington Cable
The Fanatics, Paul Laurence Dunbar
A Pair of Patient Lovers, William Dean Howells
Under the Redwoods, Bret Harte
Spring Time and Harvest [later *King Midas*], Upton Sinclair
The Great God Success, David Graham Phillips
The Tory Lover, Sarah Orne Jewett
🐚 *Buddenbrooks,* Thomas Mann
🐚 *Kim,* Rudyard Kipling
🐚 *Erewhon Revisited,* Samuel Butler (posthumous)

Best-Sellers
The Crisis, Winston Churchill
Alice of Old Vincennes, Maurice Thompson
The Helmet of Navarre, Bertha Runkle
The Right of Way, Gilbert Parker
Eben Holden, Irving Bacheller
The Visits of Elizabeth, Elinor Glyn
The Purple Crown, Harold MacGrath
Richard Yea-and-Nay, Maurice Hewlett
Graustark, George Barr McCutcheon
D'ri and I, Irving Bacheller

Nonfiction

Critics' Choice
The Making of an American, Jacob Riis
Up from Slavery, Booker T. Washington
Heroines of Fiction, William Dean Howells
To a Person Sitting in Darkness, Mark Twain
Mr. Dooley's Opinions, Finley Peter Dunne
Understudies, Mary E. Wilkins Freeman
Lectures on Ethics, John Dewey
The World and the Individual, vol. 2, Josiah Royce
Chopin: The Man and His Music, James Huneker
The Historical Novel and Other Essays, Brander Matthews
Our National Parks, John Muir
The Mississippi Valley in the Civil War, John Fiske
🐚 *Studies in the Psychology of Sex,* Havelock Ellis
🐚 *The Psychopathology of Everyday Life,* Sigmund Freud

Poetry
Eugene Field, *A Little Book of Tribune Verse*
Edwin Markham, *London and Other Poems*
Paul Laurence Dunbar, *Candle-Lightin' Time*
George Santayana, *The Hermit of Carmel and Other Poems*
🐚 Thomas Hardy, *Poems of the Past and Present*

Science and Technology

Continuing his work on yellow fever, Walter Reed demonstrates that the disease is caused by a virus.
Neurosurgeon Harvey Cushing introduces the Italian Riva-Ricci sphygmomanometer into surgery, enabling blood pressure monitoring.
Adrenalin is isolated from the adrenal gland and purified by Jokichi Takamine.
Peter Cooper Hewitt creates the first mercury-vapor electric lamp.
G. Eineas constructs a solar-powered pump that can be used for irrigation.
🐚 Ernest Rutherford and Frederick Soddy observe that thorium spontaneously transmutes into another element.
🐚 W. H. Nerst proposes the "third law of thermodynamics."
🐚 Ilya Mechnikov's book on immunity describes how white blood cells fight disease.
🐚 The giraffe- and zebra-like okapi is discovered in Africa.
🐚 Hugo de Vries speculates that species' changes occur in leaps, which he calls "mutations."

All parts are constructed manually in the pre–assembly line auto factory.

Guglielmo Marconi, whose revolutionary idea of using electromagnetic waves, not wires, through the air gains headline success.

Sports

Baseball

A plan to make the National League a trust is exposed and then discarded when Albert Spalding, one of baseball's revered heroes, is elected to lead the NL; war between the NL and AL continues while combining them is considered.

Both leagues play a full season, with 1,920,031 attending NL games; 1,683,584, the AL.

The National Association of Minor Leagues forms.

New rules mandate that the catcher stand behind home plate at all times and not catch the first two strikes on a bounce.

Joe "Iron Man" McGinnity (Baltimore, AL) is banned for spitting on umpire Tom Connolly's face and stepping on his toes; he is later reinstated with a fine.

Honus Wagner stars for Pittsburgh (NL), and Clark Griffith for Chicago (AL),while also managing the team.

Christy Mathewson (New York, NL) pitches the first no-hitter, winning 5–0 over St. Louis.

Napoleon Lajoie (Philadelphia) is the AL's first triple crown winner.

Champions

Batting	Pitching
Honus Wagner (Pittsburgh, NL), .382	Jack Chesbro (Pittsburgh, NL), 21–9
Napoleon Lajoie (Philadelphia, AL), .405	Clark Griffith (Chicago, AL), 24–7
	Home runs
	Napoleon Lajoie (Philadelphia, AL), 13

Football

Michigan's "point-a-minute" team, coached by Fielding "Hurry Up" Yost, goes 11–0 and outscores opponents 550–0. Five of 11 All-Stars are from Harvard.

Cornell University crew team.

The first "Tournament of Roses Association Game" is played in Pasadena on Jan. 1, 1902, where Michigan beats Stanford, 49–0, gaining 1,463 yards on 142 plays.

College All-Americans: William J. Warner (G), Cornell; Robert Kernan (HB), Harvard; Harold Weekes (HB), Columbia

Other Sports

Golf: The first Open played under USGA rules is held at the Myopia Hunt Club in Hamilton, Mass.; Willie Anderson beats Alex Smith, 85–86, in the U.S. Open playoff.

Yachting: The America's Cup is defended successfully by the U.S. yacht *Columbia*.

Winners

Pennant	U.S. Tennis Open
NL—Pittsburgh	Men: William Larned
AL—Chicago	Women: Elizabeth Moore
College Football	*USGA Open*
Michigan	Willie Anderson
College Basketball	*Kentucky Derby*
Yale	His Eminence (Jimmy Winkfield, jockey)

Fashion

The "S" shaped woman is the model of fashion. Hair is puffed, padded, and piled high under hats that soar in order to emphasize the "S" curve of the mature bust and hips. Chins are held high over cumbersome serge suits trailing the ground, which make it impossible to slouch; tight skirts over the hips frequently make walking a problem. Even if one is ample in size, hip pads are added to emphasize the ideal (sometimes illusory) 18-inch waist. The day bodice extends to the face; a low evening décolletage is always softened with cascades of lace. Fabrics are soft and clinging—chiffons and crêpes de chine for evening, velveteens for daytime. A tall, elegant umbrella or parasol complements the fluffy boa that decorates the neck; it matches the feathers on the hat. A frilly petticoat with lace flowers peers out from the skirt—to ensnare the male.

High-fashion note: Girls' fashion frocks in pale pink Chinese silk with lace edging or chiffon touches for decoration; sag-green cashmere and black silk dresses with trimmings of cream lace edging—all advertised in popular media like The Delineator, McCalls, *and* Butterick.

Kaleidoscope

- McKinley, whose assassin carries his pistol in a bandaged hand, is the third president to be assassinated in 35 years.
- The *New York World* states that "the typical American is accumulating money more rapidly than any other man on earth."
- The very wealthy summer in Newport; their "cottages," such as The Elms, created for coal-magnate Edward Julius Berwind by Horace Trumbauer, are often modeled on French chateaus; city mansions, like the Carnegie, have 50 to 70 rooms and large gardens.
- Pogroms in Russia force many Jews to America; poverty in southern Italy and Central Europe also spurs immigration.
- With a population of 523 per acre, Manhattan tenements cover more than two-thirds of the city; typically six stories high, they are built end to end with little light and minimal plumbing; Cincinnati houses more than 100,000 in 5,600 tenements.
- North Carolina proposes a literacy amendment for voting; Alabama adopts a literacy test with a grandfather clause to diminish the black vote.
- U.S. citizenship is granted the "Five Civilized Tribes": the Cherokee, Creek, Choctaw, Chicasaw, and Seminole.
- West Point cadets abolish hazing.
- Since 1895, F. W. Woolworth has built more than 50 stores with bright red storefronts; shops sell items for 5¢–10¢.
- Battle Creek, Mich., is home to 42 cereal makers.
- *The Settlement Cookbook,* with its phrase "the way to a man's heart is through his stomach," is published with volunteer funds raised by Milwaukee settlement worker Lizzie Black; it is printed for immigrant women to save time in copying recipes from the blackboard.
- Defining womanhood, poet Mary Lowe Dickinson writes: "The dear little wife at home, John, / With ever so much to do, / Stitches to set and babies to pet / And so many thoughts of you— / The beautiful household fairy, / Filling your heart with light— / Whatever you meet today John, / Go cheerily home tonight."
- "Be it ever so humble, there's no place like home for wearing what you like," quips George Ade in his popular *Forty Modern Fables.*
- Four widows of Revolutionary War soldiers remain on pensions; one soldier survives from the War of 1812.
- South Dakota passes legislation making school attendance mandatory for children 8–14.
- Special moral instruction is given in schools on the nature of alcoholic drinks to "impress . . . the importance of truthfulness, temperance, public spirit, patriotism, respect for honest labor, obedience to parents, and due deference for old age."
- "Success can be measured . . . by the obstacles . . . overcome while trying to succeed," writes Booker T. Washington in *Up from Slavery.*
- Called "the richest man in the world," Andrew Carnegie retires and sets about implementing his "gospel of wealth" philosophy: the rich should be "trustees" of wealth for public use; he donates $5.2 million to the New York Public Library for its first branch libraries.
- Researchers connect obesity and heart disease.

- William Sydney Porter, after serving a two-year sentence for embezzlement in an Ohio penitentiary, comes to New York and begins writing, as O. Henry.
- During his U.S. visit, Sergei Rachmaninoff performs and dedicates his Second Piano Concerto to Dr. Nicholas Dahl for his neuropsychotherapeutic cure of the nervous tremors in his fingers.
- The first vacuum cleaner, invented by H. Brook, becomes an alternative to the Bissell Carpet Sweeper; attached to a horse-drawn cart, its long hose connects to a gasoline-driven pump.
- "Indiscriminate spitting should be suppressed," reports an International Congress.
- Spindletop oil field, Rockefeller's first competitor, produces 80,000 barrels a day, helping to make the U.S. the world's major supplier of petroleum.
- Population continues to grow in the world's major cities: in millions, N.Y.C., 3.4; London, 6.6; Paris, 2.7; Tokyo, 1.5.
- In his *World of Graft,* Josiah Flynt exposes bribe-taking in New York, Boston, and Chicago.
- The U.S. constructs a 16″ breech-loading rifle that is the most powerful in the world; it weighs 130 tons and is 48′ long.
- Of the 120,000 U.S. military on active duty, 70,000 are stationed in the Philippines fighting the insurgency.

Fads: contests (including beauty, literature, and yacht races), telepathic interviews (e.g., Horace Greeley and his granddaughter)

First Appearances: Jergens lotion, over-the-counter-drugs (Sterling Products), auto licenses (New York), travel around the world (60 days, 13 hours), Cadillac (the low "chassis"), Mercedes (Germany), Apperson car and Pierce "motorette," motor-driven bicycles, bowling club tournament (Chicago), R. H. Macy's at 34th Street, N.Y.C. (from 14th Street), mercury-vapor electric lamp, Sylvania Electric Co., Rockefeller Institute for Medical Research, administration of SATs, Texas Women's University, Idaho State University, Whittier College, U.S. Army War College (Washington, D.C.), Monsanto Chemical Co., Good Housekeeping Institute, "instant coffee," Clicquot Club ginger ale, Quaker oats, synthetic dye, electric hearing aid (M. R. Hutchinson), American Can and Asarco trusts

New Word: "tinhorn politicians" (William Allen White, *Emporia Gazette*)

Penny arcade, in the lobbies of the large vaudeville houses.

1902

Justice Oliver Wendell Holmes, son of the poet and author of *The Common Law,* is known for his liberal thinking and elegant writing.

Facts and Figures

Economic Profile
  Dow-Jones: ↑ High 64–Low 40
  GNP: +4.3%
  Inflation: +3.3%
  Unemployment: 4.0%
Households with telephones: 8%
Philippine-American War (1898–1902)
  American
    Deaths: 4,234
    Wounded: 2,818
  Philippine insurgents:
    Deaths: 16,000
Lily cream, 3 cans: 5¢
Pinkham's compound: 65¢
Allcock's plasters: 10¢
Mennen's talcum powder (lg.): 25¢
Carter's liver pills: 25¢
Bromo Quinine laxative: 10¢
Ghirardelli's chocolate: 5¢ (lb.)
Almonds: 25¢ (2 lbs.)
English or Japanese tea: 5¢ (lb.)
German prunes: 5¢ (lb.)
Oregon pure olive oil: 25¢ (1.5 pts.)
Sozodent tooth powder: 25¢
Wart remover: 10¢
Castoria: 35¢

Deaths

Albert Bierstadt, Samuel Butler, Bret Harte, Richard Krafft-Ebing, Frank Norris, Cecil Rhodes, Elizabeth Cady Stanton, Charles Tiffany, John Henry Twachtman, Emile Zola

In the News

BRITAIN ENDS "SPLENDID ISOLATION" WITH ANGLO-JAPANESE TREATY ON CHINA AND KOREA . . . RUSSIAN STUDENTS STRIKE AGAINST GOVERNMENT . . . 147,000 ANTHRACITE COAL MINERS STRIKE . . . TR BRINGS ANTITRUST SUIT AGAINST MORGAN'S NORTHERN SECURITIES CORPORATION . . . CUBA BECOMES REPUBLIC, LAST U.S. TROOPS WITHDRAW . . . BOERS ACCEPT BRITISH RULE . . . TRIPLE ALLIANCE OF GERMANY, AUSTRIA, ITALY IS EXTENDED FOR 12 YEARS . . . MT. PELEE VOLCANO KILLS 30,000 ON MARTINIQUE . . . TR ASSERTS POWER TO RETAIN PUBLIC LAND AS PARKS . . . NEWLANDS ACT PROVIDES FOR IRRIGATION DAMS TO RECLAIM ARID WESTERN LAND . . . PHILIPPINE INSURGENCY ENDS AFTER 4 YEARS, TR GRANTS AMNESTY TO POLITICAL PRISONERS . . . CONGRESS AUTHORIZES FUNDS FOR ISTHMIAN CANAL IN PANAMA, OR NICARAGUA IF NECESSARY . . . AGRICULTURE DEPARTMENT VOLUNTEERS, "POISON SQUAD," WILL TEST FOODS FOR SAFETY . . . TR NOMINATES OLIVER WENDELL HOLMES FOR SUPREME COURT . . . INTERNATIONAL HARVESTER INCORPORATES, WILL CONTROL 85% OF FARM MACHINERY . . . TR USES "BULLY PULPIT" IN NEW ENGLAND AND MIDWEST TO ATTACK MONOPOLIES . . . U.S. AND MEXICO ARE FIRST TO USE HAGUE PEACE COURT TO SETTLE INTERNATIONAL DISPUTE . . . SEC. OF STATE HAY PROTESTS ROMANIA'S TREATMENT OF JEWS . . . TR FORCES OWNERS TO ARBITRATE STEEL STRIKE, WORKERS MAKE WAGE AND WORKING CONDITION GAINS, NO UNION RECOGNITION . . . SUPREME COURT REFUSES PETITION OF DISENFRANCHISED VIRGINIA BLACKS . . . IMMIGRATION SETS RECORDS, MOST FROM ITALY, RUSSIA, EASTERN EUROPE . . . BRITAIN, GERMANY, ITALY BLOCKADE VENEZUELA OVER DEBT CLAIMS.

Quotes

"I don't pity any man who does hard work worth doing. I admire him. I pity the creature who does not work, at whichever end of the social scale he may regard himself as being."

—Theodore Roosevelt

"If you try to deprive even a savage or a barbarian of his just rights you [become] a savage or barbarian yourself. . . . You cannot maintain despotism in Asia, and a republic in America. [Let it be said of us that] the flag which we received without rent, we handed down without stain."

—Sen. George Frisbee Hoar (R—Mass.), condemning alleged U.S. atrocities in the Philippines

"When the water of Chicago is foul, the prosperous buy water bottled at distant springs; the poor have no alternative but the typhoid fever which comes from using the city's supply."

—Jane Addams

PRICES THAT STAGGER HUMANITY

—headline, Joseph Pulitzer, *New York World*, in campaign against beef trust (24¢: sirloin; 18¢: lamb, pork, ham chops)

"The rights and interests of the laboring man will be protected and cared for—not by the labor agitators, but by the Christian men to who [sic] God in His infinite wisdom has given control of the property interests of this country."

—George Baker, coal mine executive, on the United Mine Workers strike

"The God whom science recognizes must be a God of universal laws, . . . a God who does a wholesale, not a retail business. He cannot accommodate his presence to the convenience of individuals."

—William James

"[If] you let men live like pigs [or] rob a child of its childhood, its play, its freedom from toil . . . in the battle with the slum, . . . we perish."

—Jacob Riis, on the slums covering 70% of N.Y.C.

"Marriages may be made in Heaven, but most engagements are made in the back parlor with the gas so low a fellow really doesn't get a square look at what he's taking."

—George Horace Lorimer, *Letters from a Self-Made Merchant to His Son*

J. P. Morgan: "If we have done anything wrong, send your man [the attorney general] to my man and they can fix it up."
Roosevelt: "That can't be done."

—Financier to president, after government begins an action against his company

Ads

A Superb Figure!
Sent on Approval.
H.H.H. Bust Forms
take any desired shape and size and produce perfectly the full bust and slender waist. . . . Eagerly welcomed by society women.

(*Henderson & Henderson*, Buffalo)

It Puts Off Old Age
by nourishing the entire system, ... makes your blood tingle; nerves strong and steady; brain clear and active; muscles, powerful. It builds children up symmetrically into brainy and robust men and women.

(*Quaker Oats*)

Every bit of Lifebuoy Soap possesses life-saving qualities, for it is a Sanitary, Antiseptic, Disinfectant Soap.

(*Lever Bros.*)

Don't Use Matches
Use Matchless Electric Flashlights.

(*Stanley and Patterson*)

"The Samson"
Coin-operated Punching Machine, . . . Colonel Samson weighs only 200 pounds, 5'6" in height, 40" chest measurement. [He] can be punched again in the face as hard as you wish, without injury to the colonel or yourself.

(*S. M. Naflev*)

Don't Be a Robber!
Husband the Fertility of Your Farm and Everytime You Plant Seed You will Get a Paying Crop.
(The *Kemp Manure Spreader* will double and triple the value of the manure heap)

Manly Strength without Drugs
Come to Fountain of Youth, Drink Deep of the Drought of Electricity, the New Century Remedy. It Builds Up Weakened Nerves. It Gives Strength to Men Who Lack Vigor, Who Feel the Effects of Early Indiscretions.

(*Dr. Sanden Herculex Body Battery*)

"The world taught women nothing skillful and then said her work was valueless. . . . It taught her that every pleasure must come as a favor from men, and . . . when she decked herself in paint and fine feathers, as she had been taught to do, it called her vain."—Carrie Chapman Catt, National American Woman Suffrage Association

Old World traditions continue in the New World: an immigrant prepares for the Sabbath in his tenement cellar.

Vaudeville

Theaters range from opulent to modest, as a two-tier system evolves: "big" theaters have two shows a day, one show per week of eight to 12 acts; production costs are higher, as are admission fees and stars' salaries. "Low" or "small vaudeville" present two shows a week, three a day, few headliners, six acts, with lower production, admission, and salary fees. Usually 5¢–25¢ provides a seat in the balcony where one can remain all day.

Salaries similarly run the gamut—from $6 a week (for new talent) to $2,500–$3,500 a week (for stars like Eva Tanguay, Lillian Russell, and Lily Langtry).

Most lesser-known vaude-villians never complain about their unpalatable working conditions, such as sharing a dressing room with live animals (and all the attendant smells therein). Discrimination against blacks is rampant. Of enormous importance is the strict observation of superstition: whistling or passing a performer on the stairs is tantamount to the curse of failure.

Of Note

"Rah, rah, rah. Who pays my bills? / Pa and ma" is vaudevillian Ed Wynn's opening, as he razzes college students in the audience.

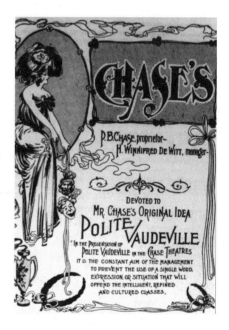

Movies

A Trip to the Moon (Méliès), science fiction and satire
Uncle Josh at the Moving Picture Show (Porter)
How They Do Things on the Bowery (Edison)
The Great Sword Combat on the Stairs (Vitagraph)
When the Cat's Away, the Mice Will Play (Biograph)
"Foxy Grandpa" series (Biograph)
La Danseuse microscopique (Méliès)
The Polite Frenchmen (Biograph)
Robinson Crusoe (Méliès)

The court rules against Edison, who wants to monopolize the industry. The Lubin group wins and begins to cut prices to compete with Edison, who follows suit. In the interim, Vitagraph has been building a distribution network. Edison competes by emphasizing strong narrative line. The owner of a Los Angeles amusement arcade removes all furnishings to install seats and a movie projector, and the Electric Theater becomes the first theater designed for the sole activity of showing films; typical are *King Edward's Coronation* and *The Martinique Disaster*. D. W. Griffith, at Biograph, and Edwin S. Porter, with Edison, begin their great pioneering work.

Popular Music

Hit Songs
"In the Good Old Summertime"
"Mister Dooley"
"On a Sunday Afternoon"
"Down on the Farm"
"Here's to the Old Folks at Home"
"If Money Talks, It Ain't on Speaking Terms with Me"
"Pinky Panky Poo"
"Pomp and Circumstance"

Representative Recordings: "Bill Bailey, Won't You Please Come Home," "Under the Bamboo Tree" (Arthur Collins); "Good Morning Carrie" (Bert Williams); "Arkansas Traveler" (Len Spencer); "On a Saturday Afternoon" (J. W. Myers); "The Mansion of Aching Hearts" (Byron G. Harlan)

Jazz
Although "Buddy" Bolden's rise to fame coincides with the rise in popularity of Storyville, the red light district at South Rampart and Perdido Streets in St. Louis, he does not play there. He plays his blues with a deeply religious quality at dance halls, carnivals, picnics—and dives. At the 601 Ranch, for example, the owner is killed in a brawl. Ragtime continues to develop in New Orleans with both black and white performers like Tom Turpin and Louis Chauvin. Four beats in the left hand replace Joplin's two beats in the same interval, with more complicated accenting in the right hand. Music becomes more danceable. "Jelly Roll" Morton announces in 1902, "I invented jazz," although in fact he plays ragtime. He does, however, stomp his foot in 4/4 time, when ragtime is traditionally two beats. White double bass player Steve Brown speaks of "bumpy music" as the "key" to 4/4 time. New rhythms are in the air.

Theater

Broadway Openings

Plays
The Darling of the Gods (David Belasco, John Luther Long), Blanche Bates, George Arliss
Iris (Arthur Wing Pinero), Virginia Harned, Oscar Asche
The Eternal City (Hall Caine), Viola Allen, E. J. Morgan
The Girl with the Green Eyes (Clyde Fitch), Lucile Watson, Edith Taliaferro
The Mummy and the Hummingbird (Isaac Henderson), John Drew, Lionel Barrymore
The Cross-Ways (Lily Langtry), Langtry, J. Hartley Manners

Musicals
Twirly Whirly (John Stromberg, Edgar and Harry B. Smith), Lillian Russell, Weber & Fields, Fay Templeton, Charles A. Bigelow
The Wild Rose (Ludwig Englander), Edwin (soon, Eddie) Foy, Junie McCree, Marguerite Clark, Evelyn Florence (later, Evelyn Nesbit)
A Chinese Honeymoon (Howard Talbot, George Dance), Thomas Q. Seabrooke, Adele Ritchie, William Pruette
Dolly Varden (Julian Edwards, Stanislaus Stange), Lulu Glaser, Van Rensselaer Wheeler
The Hall of Fame (A. Baldwin Sloane, George V. Hobart), Charles H. Prince, Ada Lewis, Marie Dressler
The Rogers Brothers in Harvard (Maurice Levi, J. C. Goodwin), Gus & Max Rogers, Pat Rooney, Pauline Frederick
The Defender (Allen Love, Charles Donnee), Lulu Glaser

Classics and Revivals On and Off Broadway
The Importance of Being Earnest, Charles Richman, William Courtney, Margaret Anglin; *As You Like It,* Henrietta Crosman, Henry Crosman; *Julius Caesar,* Richard Mansfield; Mrs. Patrick Campbell Repertory (debut): *The Second Mrs. Tanqueray,* George Arliss (debut); *Pelleas and Melisande* (Maeterlinck); *Everyman,* Edith Wynn Matthison, Charles Rann Kennedy; Eleonora Duse in *La Città Morta* and *Francesca da Rimini* (D'Annunzio, presented in Italian)

After *Floradora*'s 500 performances, each girl in the Floradora Sextette makes a wealthy marriage and retires from the stage; marriages to showgirls were the bane of Society mothers.

Classical Music

Compositions

Charles Ives, Symphony no. 2 (1897–1902), Trio for
    Violin, Clarinet, and Piano
Edward MacDowell, *Summer Wind, New England Idylls*
Frederick S. Converse, Violin Concerto
Henry Hadley, *In Bohemia*
Charles Martin Loeffler, *Deux rapsodies, Poème païen,*
    Ballade carnavalesque

Important Events

The San Francisco Symphony Orchestra is formed with
54 members. The Florida State University School of
Music and University of Minnesota music department
open. The Phoenix Symphony Orchestra begins a series
of performances.

Notable Performances: Richard Strauss conducts the
Chicago Symphony Orchestra, famed for its Beethoven
performances. Edward MacDowell, Columbia's first
professor of music, begins a sabbatical year to
concertize, frequently performing his Piano Concerto
no. 2.

New Appointments: Walter Damrosch replaces Emil
Paul at the New York Philharmonic Society,
reorganizing the repertory with his concentration on
French music (Ravel, Debussy, Berlioz); the New York
Symphony focuses on German composers.

Debut: Antonio Paoli

First Performances

Debussy, *Prelude to the Afternoon of a Faun* (Boston);
Julian Edwards, Edward MacDowell, *Fireside Tales*
(Boston); Charles Ives, *The Celestial City* (New York),
Charles Martin Loeffler, *La Villanelle du diable*
(Boston); Horatio Parker, Organ Concerto (Boston).

Pianist Ossip
Gabrilowitsch is
acclaimed for his
dazzling virtuosity.

At establishments like N.Y.C.'s Hoffman House, men gather—
dressed alike from their pommaded hair and silk cravats to
their top hats and jewelry; like women of means, they
maintain a wardrobe to suit the season, time of day, and
company they are keeping.

Opera

Metropolitan: Gala performance honoring Prince
Henry of Prussia: Andreas Dippel, Johanna Gadski,
Ernestine Schumann-Heink, Edouard de Reszke,
Lohengrin. Albert Alvarez, Lucienne Bréval, Suzanne
Adams, de Reszke, *Le Cid;* Alvarez, Emma Eames, de
Reszke, *Faust.* Premieres: Emma Calvé, *Messaline* (De
Lara); Marcella Sembrich, Thomas Salignac, *La Fille du
régiment;* Sembrich, Alexander von Bandrowski (debut),
Manru (Paderewski)

Chicago: Emilio de Marchi, *Aïda; Tannhäuser;* Calvé,
Carmen; Gadski, Schumann-Heink, de Reszke,
Lohengrin; Sembrich, Louise Homer, *Manru*
(Paderewski, premiere); Milka Ternina, Eames, *The
Ring* (first time as cycle in Chicago)

Boston: *The Prince of Pilson* (Gustav Luders)

Detroit: *When Johnny Comes Marching Home* (Julian
Edwards)

Music Notes

Oscar Sonneck is appointed to organize the Music
Division at the Library of Congress in Washington, D.C.
• In a hotel room, Enrico Caruso records "Vesti la
Giubba" from *Pagliacci* on a wax disc and sells a
million copies • Pietro Mascagni tours the U.S. with his
opera company.

Art

Painting

Everett Shinn, *London Hippodrome*

Robert Henri, *Cumulus Clouds, East River* (1901–2), *Fifty-fourth Street, Laughing Child, West 57th Street*

Arthur B. Davies, *Dancing Children*

Maurice Prendergast, *Sailboat Pond, Central Park*

Mrs. Harry Payne Whitney, *Howard G. Cushing*

John Singer Sargent, *Theodore Roosevelt*

Cecilia Beaux, *Man in White*

Thomas Eakins, *Self-Portrait*

Mary Cassatt, *Caresse Enfantine*

Edwin H. Blashfield, *Washington Laying Down His Command at the Feet of Columbia* (mural, Baltimore Courthouse)

Sculpture

Frederic Remington, *Coming through the Rye*

Robert Igersoll Aitken, Bust of President William McKinley

Albert Laessle, *Turtles and Lizards*

Augustus Saint-Gaudens, Sherman monument (*Victory*)

Architecture

Flatiron ("Fuller") building, New York (D. H. Burnham)

Arthur Heurtley house, Oak Park, Ill. (Frank Lloyd Wright)

Hillside Home School, Spring Green, Wis. (Frank Lloyd Wright)

Rosecliff mansion, Newport, R.I. (Stanford White)

White Gate, Palm Beach, Fla. (Carrère & Hastings)

N.Y.U. Hall of Fame, Gould Memorial Library, N.Y.C. (McKim, Mead, & White) (1895–1902)

Madlener house, Chicago (Richard E. Schmidt)

Richard Morris Hunt designs the central section, the Fifth Avenue facade, for the Metropolitan Museum of Art, N.Y.C.

Important Exhibitions

New York: *Metropolitan:* Jade collection; 198 musical instruments; 261 antiquities found at Abydos and the Fayum tomb; Rubens' *The Holy Family;* Frederick Edwin Church, *The Aegean Sea*

Chicago: Paintings of Russian artist Vasily Vereshchagin; Charles Walter Stetson; U.S. miniatures; Egyptian bronzes; 90 photos of architectural composition for the Ecole des Beaux Arts, Paris

Boston: Chinese and Japanese works; Etruscan vases

Detroit: "The Art of Persia and India"; Italian painting; English silver

Robert Henri, *Young Woman in Black,* 1902. Oil. 195.2 x 97.8 cm, Friends of American Art Collection, *The Art Institute of Chicago*

Art Briefs

Robert Henri holds his first one-man exhibition, and it receives little favorable critical attention • Alfred Stieglitz and Edward Steichen create the New York Photo Secession group to illustrate the "spirit" of the new art and new photography in its "honesty of revolt against the autocracy of convention" • At 72, John Quincy Adams Ward is commissioned for the pediment decoration of the N.Y. Stock Exchange • Mainstream sculptors remained obsessed with animals, American heroes, and western scenes, particularly confrontations between cowboys or Native Americans with wild animals.

After researching 25 years of court records, Ida Tarbell reveals how Standard Oil abused its power.

Books

Fiction

Critics' Choice

The Wings of the Dove, Henry James

The Battle-Ground, Ellen Glasgow

The Valley of Decision, Edith Wharton

Last Words, Stephen Crane (posthumous)

Andy Grant's Pluck, Horatio Alger (posthumous)

A Double Barrelled Detective Story, Mark Twain

The Kentons, William Dean Howells

Melomaniacs, James Huneker

The Sport of the Gods, Paul Laurence Dunbar

The Girl Proposition, George Ade

The Pothunters, P. G. Wodehouse

Brewster's Millions, George Barr McCutcheon

Grimm Tales Made Gay, Guy Wetmore Carryl

The Thirteenth District, Brand Whitlock

❧ *Heart of Darkness,* Joseph Conrad

❧ *The Immoralist,* André Gide

Best-Sellers

The Virginian, Owen Wister

Mrs. Wiggs of the Cabbage Patch, Alice Caldwell Hegan

Dorothy Vernon of Haddon Hall, Charles Major

The Mississippi Bubble, Emerson Hough

Audrey, Mary Johnston

The Right of Way, Gilbert Parker

The Hound of the Baskervilles, A. Conan Doyle

The Two Vanrevels, Booth Tarkington

The Blue Flower, Henry van Dyke

Sir Richard Calmady, Lucas Malet

Nonfiction

Critics' Choice

The Varieties of Religious Experience, William James

The Child and the Curriculum, John Dewey

Wilderness Hunter: An Account of the Big Game of the U.S.A. and Its Chase with Horse, Hound, and Rifle, Theodore Roosevelt

The Story of My Life, Helen Keller

The Service, Henry David Thoreau (posthumous)

Democracy and Social Ethics, Jane Addams

A History of the American People, 5 vols., Woodrow Wilson

Northward over the Great Ice, Adm. Robert E. Peary

A Study of Prose Fiction, Bliss Perry

Socialism and Labor, John Lancaster Spalding

Literature and Life, William Dean Howells

Observations by Mr. Dooley, Finley Peter Dunne

Wolfville Days, Alfred Henry Lewis

The New Empire, Brooks Adams

Glimpses of China and Chinese Homes, Edward Sylvester Morse

❧ *Imperialism: A Study,* John Atkinson Hobson

Poetry

Ellen Glasgow, *The Freeman and Other Verse*

E. A. Robinson, *Captain Craig*

James Whitcomb Riley, *The Book of Joyous Children*

Trumbull Stickney, *Dramatic Verses*

Science and Technology

Albert Barnes and Herman Hills develop "silver vitellin," a noncaustic antiseptic that cures eye infections—most importantly, gonorrheal infection in infants.

Harvey Cushing investigates the pituitary gland, stimulating more work on the endocrine glands.

Ross G. Harrison develops a technique for cultivating tissue cells outside the body.

The Eldorado mine in the Klondike. Gold and silver continue to be mined.

Charles W. Stiles identifies the American species of the hookworm.

In the U.S., Arthur E. Kennelly and, in England, Oliver Heaviside, hypothesize that an electrified layer in the upper atmosphere reflects radio waves.

❧ Ernest Rutherford and Frederick Soddy propose that radioactivity occurs when atoms disintegrate; particles (energy) are released in the form of radiation.

❧ During the Boer War, Almroth E. Wright develops an antityphoid vaccine.

❧ Ivan Pavlov postulates the law of conditioned reflexes: a dog repeatedly given food along with the sound of a bell will salivate with the sound alone.

❧ A process is developed to convert ammonia into nitric acid, the basis of TNT.

❧ Marcellin Boule begins his reconstruction of the skeleton of a Neanderthal man.

❧ Secretin, a substance released by the small intestine that stimulates digestion, is discovered.

Sports

Baseball

The American League outdraws the National 2,206,457 to 1,688,012, but the AL's Baltimore team is raided by the NL, which gains John McGraw, Joe McGinnity, and Roger Breshnahan; AL President Ban Johnson saves the day by restocking the Baltimore team.

After the season the two leagues finally make peace, creating "Organized Baseball," with a National Agreement that provides for protected territories, a reserve clause to bind players, and recognition of minor league rights.

Harry O'Hagen, Rochester, makes the first unassisted triple play in professional ball.

America's "Great Houdini" (Erik Weisz, 26) becomes a worldwide phenomenon with his unique escape feats; when in chains and before submerging himself in water, he says: "I must kiss my wife goodbye, perhaps for ever"; skeptics say that when she walks on stage she passes him a key.

Pittsburgh, NL, wins a record 103 of 139 games.

John ("Little Napoleon") McGraw and Joe McGinnity return to the NL with the New York Giants, whose Christy Mathewson wins 30 games.

Champions

Batting	Rube Waddell (Philadelphia,
Clarence Beaumont	AL), 23–7
(Pittsburgh, NL), .357	*Home runs*
Edward Delahanty	Ralph Seybold (Philadelphia,
(Washington, AL), .376	AL), 16
Pitching	
Jack Chesbro (Pittsburgh,	
NL), 28–9	

Football

Seven of 11 All-Americans are from Yale.

College All-Americans: Henry Holt (C), Yale; George Chadwick (HB), Yale; Paul Bunker (HB), Army

Other Sports

Running: The 6th Boston Marathon is won by Samuel Mellor, N.Y.C., in 2:43:12.

Winners

Pennant	*U.S. Tennis Open*
Pittsburgh, NL	Men: William Larned
Philadelphia, AL	Women: Marion Jones
College Football	*USGA Open*
Michigan	Laurie Auchterlonie
College Basketball	*Kentucky Derby*
Minnesota	Alan-a-Dale (Jimmy Winkfield, jockey)

Fashion

The wasp-waisted corset with curved front busk (a metal strip) is still in fashion, but medical outcry against the curved metal, causing stomach pressure, is growing. This year a straight-fronted garment appears with a rigid, perpendicular busk that lifts the stomach and throws the diaphragm and bosom up and forward, still preserving the tiny waist and round hip line. Corset covers range from cambric—and four rows of imitation lace inserted with ribbon beading—to fine-quality Nainsook with front and back Swiss embroidery panels surrounded by lace insertions. Neck and arm holes are finished with beading and an edging of real lace.

High-fashion notes: The "tempestuous tea-gown" worn before dinner; Viennese Josef Hoffmann's new clear-cut simplicity, rather than the flowery look; Mackintosh and MacNaira's Celtic design of elongated, black or stark white lines.

The glitter of the social elite is reflected in the extravagance of their dress; chinchilla is highly "fashionable."

Kaleidoscope _____

- Ragtime sweeps America.
- "The wurruld is little better than a convict's camp . . . graft everywhere," comments Mr. Dooley, who also observes of the press: "The hand that rocks th' fountain pen . . . rules the wurruld."
- *McClure* magazine sets a precedent for other magazines like *Cosmopolitan* and *Collier's* by publishing a series of exposés, including those of Josiah Flynt on graft; Lincoln Steffens, on St. Louis bossism; and Ida Tarbell, on Standard Oil; Tarbell's *History of the Standard Oil Company* reveals how Rockefeller controls 90 percent of U.S. oil refining.
- Typical boss tactics include stuffing ballot boxes with repeaters, voting names from gravestones, the "Tasmanian dodge" (pre-marked ballots), and dumping ballots into rivers.
- "I found him buying boodlers in St. Louis, defending grafters in Minneapolis . . . originating corruption in Pittsburgh [and] deploring reform in Chicago," remarks Lincoln Steffens on the businessman as a source of corruption.
- Florida makes it a misdemeanor to fire someone for voting for a particular person.
- The U.S. Army replaces blue with olive drab (blue is too easily visible).
- The Horn & Hardart Baking Company Automat opens in Philadelphia; after depositing a nickel in a slot, a door opens and people can remove their food selection.
- Savannah, Cincinnati, and San Francisco adopt an 8-mph speed limit.
- Barney Oldfield, 24, goes 5 miles in 5 minutes, 20 seconds in a 70-hp Ford "999."
- Minors can buy liquor in Arkansas; Minnesota cities of 50,000 or more limit saloons to five per block.
- The Education Act puts elementary and secondary schools under local jurisdiction; secondary schools anticipate an increase in students.
- The University of Chicago segregates the sexes during their first two college years for "educational benefits."
- Bertrand Russell's great paradox gains world attention: the set containing all sets cannot contain itself, a thesis that contradicts the assumption that math is based on logic.
- William James's *Varieties of Religious Experience* attempts a scientific study of the history of Christianity.
- A free-spirit ethos, "The Gospel of the Open Road," gains popularity: "To know the universe as a road, as many roads . . . for traveling souls [where] we are all commoners."
- The crematory industry grows: the price for an adult is $30; children under 20, $20; receptacles are free.
- N.Y.C. gets its water from the Catskills; L.A., from the Sierras; but getting water and keeping it clean remain a major health problem.
- Charles Stiles of the Public Health Service reports on the dangers of hookworm, especially in the rural South; he attacks the myth of innate laziness in Southerners.
- North Carolina Governor Aycock offers a $30,000 reward for lynchers; in Lansing, Tex., a black is burned at the stake as thousands cheer.
- Six or seven companies regularly touring with *Uncle Tom's Cabin* enjoy great commercial success.

- Chicago's Hull House, Jane Addams's "midwife in acute labor situations out of wedlock," includes a woman's club, day nursery, gymnasium, the Hull House players, and Plato Club, where guests like John Dewey and Clarence Darrow come to converse.
- New York's Lower East Side, occupied largely by Jewish immigrants, is the most densely populated square mile in the world; it is known to European Jews as "the great ghetto."
- John Dewey propounds a new method of education; it emphasizes functionality and "leaning by doing," as opposed to rote memorization; Dewey opened his first child-centered school at the University of Chicago.
- The Salvation Army enters the slums with food, shelter, camaraderie, and moral uplift; it has more than 3,000 officers across the country.
- Streetcar rails enable some of the poor to leave the city and live away from the workplace and slums.
- Trolleys can go 12 mph, twice a horse's pace.
- The Twentieth Century Limited goes from N.Y.C. to Chicago in 20 hours (24, in 1877) and includes such amenities as a library, buffet, and drawing rooms; the Broadway Limited competes on the Pennsylvania RR.
- Called "terminal madness," cities compete for the grandeur of their railroad terminals; St. Louis boasts of "the largest depot in the world" and Chicago, its clock tower, over 247 feet high.
- Whitehall, in Palm Beach, constructed by Carrère and Hastings for Henry Flagler, has 73 rooms; the *New York Herald* calls it "more wonderful than any palace in Europe."
- Roosevelt's settlement of the coal miner strike is hailed as "the greatest single event affecting capitalism and labor in the history of America."
- AFL membership surpasses 1 million; Maryland passes the first Workman's Compensation law.
- Oregon adopts the use of initiative and referendum (popular voting on laws).
- Diplomat Bunau-Varilla, who favors Panama over Nicaragua for personal economic reasons, circulates a West Indies postage stamp showing a volcano, implying a similar threat in Nicaragua for the canal.
- Allegations that orders were issued to "kill and burn" and "make a howling wilderness" of rebel areas in the Philippines feed the controversy over America's occupation there.

First Appearances: Crayola crayons, Barnum's animal crackers, Drake bakers, Fannie Farmer's School of Cookery, Limited Drug Co. (Louis K. Liggett), Texas Oil, polygraph, radio telephones on ship, International Harvester gasoline tractors, AAA, Studebaker, spark plug (Bosch), light bulbs with osmium filters, hydrogenation (hardening of liquid fats), golf ball with rubber core, *TLS, South Atlantic Quarterly,* Irish Channel crossed in balloon (J. M. Bacon), Crater Lake National Park (Oregon), Algonquin Hotel, Franklin Simon, Saks Fifth Avenue (34th Street, N.Y.C.), Philip Morris, brassiere (France)

1903

The Wright brothers, who have spent many years experimenting with kites and gliders before their major success this year.

Facts and Figures

Economic Profile
  Dow-Jones: ↓ High 65–
  Low 44
  GNP: +6.0%
  Inflation: +1.2%
  Unemployment: 3.9%
Daily newspapers: 2,452
Books published: 7,865
Postcard: 1¢
Crescent feather mattress,
  double: $15; 3/4: $11.75;
  single: $5.50
Gibson girl pillow cushions:
  57¢
Miracle whirling vaginal spray:
  $5
Women's negligee shirts: 59¢;
  underwear: mercerized,
  ribbed vests: 19¢–50¢
John Wanamaker
  Corsets: deep hip, straight
    front, low bust: 50¢;
    corset covers: 50¢–$1
  For men: balbriggan shirts
    and drawers, Japanese
    cobweb crêpe, silk or
    cotton: 39¢–75¢
Mother Hubbard dresses:
  35¢–45¢
Sears, Roebuck catalogue
  Ladies' boa: genuine thibet,
    70″, black or white: $7.50
  Double scarf (marten,
    squirrel), six tails: $15.75
  Bulgarian lamb driving coat:
    $24.85
  Fur-trimmed Monte Carlo
    jacket: $6.75
  Trousseau (cambric gown,
    skirt, drawers, corset
    cover): $5.98

Deaths

George F. Bailey, Ebenezer
  Butterick, Calamity Jane
  (Martha Jane Canary), Paul
  Gauguin, George Gissing,
  F. H. Macy, Pope Leo III,
  Camille Pissarro, Herbert
  Spencer, James A. McNeill
  Whistler

In the News

U.S. AND COLOMBIA SIGN HAY-HERRAN TREATY FOR U.S. TO BUILD PANAMA CANAL . . . U.S.-U.K. AGREEMENT ON ALASKAN BOUNDARY FAVORS U.S. . . . EX-MAYOR OF ST. LOUIS IS CONVICTED OF GRAFT . . . AFTER U.S. MEDIATES, EUROPEAN POWERS LIFT VENEZUELAN BLOCKADE . . . ELKINS ACT FORBIDS REBATES ON PUBLISHED RAILROAD FREIGHT RATES . . . DEPARTMENT OF COMMERCE AND LABOR IS CREATED WITH BUREAU TO MONITOR CORPORATIONS . . . SUPREME COURT ASSERTS PRIORITY OF FEDERAL POLICE POWER . . . TR'S MINING COMMISSION RECOMMENDS SHORTER HOURS, WAGE INCREASES, AND OPEN SHOP . . . FRENCH ARMY DOCUMENTS USED TO CONVICT ALFRED DREYFUS OF TREASON ARE EXPOSED AS FORGERIES . . . JEWS ARE MURDERED BY "BLACK HUNDREDS" IN KISHINEV, RUSSIA . . . SUPREME COURT UPHOLDS ALABAMA LAW DENYING VOTE TO BLACKS . . . ARMY OFFICERS KILL SERBIAN QUEEN AND KING . . . TR SENDS MESSAGE AROUND THE WORLD IN RECORD 12 MINUTES . . . COLOMBIAN SENATE REJECTS U.S. TREATY FOR PANAMA CANAL . . . BRITAIN OFFERS UGANDA AS NATIONAL HOMELAND FOR JEWS . . . HUNGARIANS PROTEST EMPEROR FRANZ JOSEF'S INSISTENCE ON UNITY WITH AUSTRIA . . . BOSTON RED SOX WIN FIRST WORLD SERIES . . . TYPHOID OUTBREAK IN NEW YORK IS BLAMED ON FOOD HANDLER MARY MALLON, SHE FLEES . . . PANAMA DECLARES INDEPENDENCE FROM COLOMBIA, U.S. SENDS WARSHIP *NASHVILLE* TO SUPPORT REBELS . . . RUSSIAN SOCIAL DEMOCRATS SPLIT INTO MENSHEVIKS AND BOLSHEVIKS . . . U.S. AND PANAMA SIGN TREATY PERMITTING CANAL . . . FIRE IN IROQUOIS THEATER, CHICAGO, KILLS 508 . . . WRIGHT BROTHERS MAKE FIRST FLIGHT IN HEAVIER-THAN-AIR MACHINE.

Quotes

"Aerial flight is one of that class of problems with which man can never cope."

—Simon Newcomb

"SUCCESS 4 FLIGHTS THURSDAY MORNING / ALL AGAINST 21-MILE WIND / STARTED FROM LEVEL WITH ENGINE POWER ALONE / AVERAGE SPEED THROUGH AIR 31-MILES LONG 59 SECONDS / INFORM PRESS / HOME CHRISTMAS."

—Orville Wright, telegraph to father from Kitty Hawk, N.C., Dec. 17

"Live all you can; it's a mistake not to. It doesn't so much matter what you do in particular, so long as you have your life."

—Henry James, *The Ambassadors*

"The problem of the Twentieth Century is the color line. . . . One ever feels his twoness—an American, a Negro; two souls, two thoughts, two unreconciled strivings; two warring ideals in one dark body, whose dogged strength alone keeps it from being torn asunder."

—W. E. B. Du Bois

55 HOURS OR NOTHING

—sign of striking children, Philadelphia textile mills

"Everybody is talking about Tammany men growing rich on 'graft,' but nobody [distinguishes] between honest graft and dishonest graft. There's an honest graft, and I'm an example of how it works. I would sum up by saying, 'I seen my opportunities and I took 'em.'"

—George Washington Plunkett, New York politician

TR and naturalist John Muir at Yosemite.

"We naturally associate democracy, to be sure, with freedom of action, but freedom of action without free capacity of thought behind it is only chaos."

—John Dewey

"Damn the law! I want the [Panama] Canal built!"
—attributed to Theodore Roosevelt

"When you see some girls marry, you realize how they must hate to work for a living."
—Helen Rowland, *Reflections of a Bachelor Girl*

"So blind is life, so long at last is sleep,
And none but Love to bid us laugh or weep."
—Willa Cather, "Evening Song," *April Thoughts*

Ads

Vaudeville

At the burlesque houses, a hootchy-kootchy dancer "plays" to a single male in the audience and, with increasing eroticism, finally reveals all; comedians add a titillating humor.

Vaudeville, still the most popular entertainment, provides the working class with family entertainment, unavailable in the raucous beer halls and saloons (reserved for men) and unaffordable at the concert or opera stage.

Paralleling the two-tier system during the early century is the moral tone of productions. In the "Sunday School circuit," also known as "Polite Vaudeville," "nothing offensive" is assumed, yet even here objections are raised, for example, to the popular 6-year-old "Mademoiselle Hélène," blowing kisses and pirouetting in her fluffy pink ballerina skirt. "Why isn't she home in bed?" some ask about the dimple-faced, dimple-kneed child. Other theaters touch the boundaries of burlesque, with, for example, "cooch" or hootchy-kootchy dancing and highly suggestive, near-naked performers.

Of Note

Planning a production with Annette Kellerman in a bathing suit, Edward Albee remarks: "What are we selling? We're selling backsides, aren't we? All right. If one backside is good, a hundred backsides are as many times better" • Carry Nation creates a miniplay, *Ten Nights in a Bar Room,* in which she breaks up whiskey bars and walks through the audience selling mini-hatchets; she also dares to talk back to hecklers • Called "The Queen of Burlesque," Fay Templeton is acknowledged to be the leading actress, (light opera) singer, comedienne, and parodist • Marie Dressler sings "coon songs" and performs impersonations

Movies

The Great Train Robbery (Edison, directed by Edwin S. Porter), longest, most complex dramatic narrative to date, 12 minutes

The Life of an American Fireman (Edison), nonlinear continuity, several sets

Uncle Tom's Cabin (Edison), filmed theater performance

The Gay Shoe Clerk (Edison), cut-in to close shot

The American Soldier in Love and War (Biograph)

New York Dumping Wharf (Edison), documenting the "other half" of city life

A Shocking Incident (Biograph), early "bad-boy" film, filmed under electric light

The Passion Play (Pathé-Frères), longest film to date, 30 minutes

A Search for Evidence (Biograph), keyhole shots

For the Upper Crust (Biograph)

Rube and Mandy at Coney Island (Biograph), distant and close up of same shot

Kit Carson (Biograph), early western

Interest accelerates in narrative films, but news, fashion, and scenes of boys playing pranks or women laughing from an overdose of dental laughing gas predominate. Those with more plot—melodramas, westerns, chases, comedies, and war stories—call for a "director" to work with the cameraman. The 35-mm. format becomes popular. Major vaudeville houses show fewer movies, due to boredom with repetitious content: Chase's Theater (Washington, D.C.), Keith's (Philadelphia), Cook's Opera (Rochester); only Boston's Bijou keeps movies on as a regular feature.

The Great Train Robbery is recognized for its suspenseful plotting, including a scene where a gun is fired at the audience.

Popular Music

Hit Songs
"Ida (Sweet as Apple Cider)"
"Sweet Adeline"
"Toyland"
"In the Merry Month of May"
"Congo Love Song"
"Down on the Amazon"
"Egypt"
"Always Leave Them Laughing
    When You Say Goodbye"
"Melody of Love"
"Where Are the Friends of Other
    Days"
"There Once Was an Owl"
"Since Sally Left Our Alley"

Representative Recordings:
"Down Where the Wurzburger
Flows" (Arthur Collins); "Come
Down, Ma Evening Star" (Mina
Hickman); "In the Sweet Bye and
Bye" (John Bieling); "Hiawatha"
(Harry MacDonough); "Uncle Josh
on an Automobile" (Cal Stewart)

Jazz
The new, pre-jazz forms hit New
York at Jimmie Marshall's hotel on
West 52nd Street, a gathering place
for black stars like Bert Williams,
J. Rosamond Johnson, and James
Reese Europe. Dixieland, played
primarily by whites, becomes
increasingly popular; minstrelsy,
spirituals, and ragime continue to
evolve outside New Orleans—all
paving the way for the new "jass."
Musicians gather to experiment in
Memphis, Dallas, Kansas City, and
small towns in the South and
Midwest.

Theater

Broadway Openings

Theater
Candida (George Bernard Shaw), Arnold Daly, Dorothy
    Donnelly
Her Own Way (Clyde Fitch), Maxine Elliott
The Pretty Sister of Jose (Mrs. Frances Hodgson
    Burnett), Maude Adams, Henry Ainley
Ulysses (Stephen Phillips), Tyrone Power
The County Chairman (George Ade), Miriam Nesbit
Sweet Kitty Bellairs (David Belasco), Henrietta
    Crosman
Raffles (E. W. Hornung, Eugene Presbrey), Kyrle Bellew
Merely Mary Ann (Israel Zangwill), Eleanor Robson,
    Laura Hope Crews
The Admirable Crichton (James M. Barrie), William
    Gillette

The show *The Wizard of Oz,* with Fred Stone, the straw man, and Dave Montgomery, the tin man, is an adaptation of the popular 1900 book.

Mice and Men (Madeleine Ryley), Annie Russell, Mr.
    and Mrs. John Glendinning
Glad of It (Clyde Fitch), Lucile Watson, Thomas
    Meighan, John Barrymore (N.Y. debut)
Cousin Kate (Hubert Henry Davies), Ethel Barrymore

Musicals
Babes in Toyland (Victor Herbert), De Wolf Hopper,
    Bessie Wynn
Running for Office (George M. Cohan), The Four
    Cohans, Ethel Levey
Whoop-Dee-Do (William T. Francis, Edgar Smith),
    Lillian Russell, Weber & Fields, Carter DeHaven
The Wizard of Oz (A. Baldwin Sloane, L. Frank Baum),
    Grace Kimball, Montgomery & Stone, Anna
    Laughlin
The Fisher Maiden (Harry Von Tilzer), Al Shean,
    George A. MacFarlane, Edna Bronson
The Girl from Dixie (Harry B. Smith), Evelyn Nesbit,
    Arnold Daly, Irene Bentley
Mother Goose (Frederic Solomon, George M. Cohan,
    George Hobart), Joseph Cawthorn, Clifton
    Crawford, Leila McIntyre, Pat Rooney
Mr. Bluebeard (Frederic Solomon, J. C. Goodwin),
    Eddie Foy, Dan McAvoy, Flora Parker
The Girl from Kay's (Ivan Caryll), Harry Davenport,
    Sam Bernard

Classics and Revivals On and Off Broadway
The Man from Blankley's, William Hawtrey; *Camille,*
Margaret Anglin, Henry Miller; *Romeo and Juliet; A
Midsummer Night's Dream,* Nat C. Goodwin, Lillian
Swain; *Ghosts* (Ibsen); *Hedda Gabler,* Mrs. Minnie
Maddern Fiske; *Hamlet,* E. H. Sothern; *The Merchant of
Venice,* Henry Irving; *The Light That Failed,* Johnston
Forbes-Robertson

Classical Music

Compositions
Frederick S. Converse, *Euphrosyne Overture*
Henry F. Gilbert, *Cathleen ni Houlihan Suite, Two Verlaine Moods*
Charles Ives, Symphony no. 3, *Overture and March "1776"*
Henry Hadley, *Oriental Suite*
Charles Griffes, String Quartet in B flat

Important Events
The Minneapolis Symphony, under Emil Oberhoffer, is formally organized; Modest Altschuler founds the Russian Symphony Orchestra of New York to promote Russian music in the U.S. The Seattle Symphony Orchestra gathers 24 musicians. Walter Damrosch conducts Wagner, in concert form, at the Metropolitan Opera. The Hinshaw School of Music in Chicago and Cornell music department open. The Philadelphia Orchestra performs at Carnegie Hall.

Major Recitals: Ossip Gabrilowitsch, Karl Grienauer, Arthur Hochman, Fannie Bloomfield Zeisler

Debut: Jacques Thibaud

First Performances
Victor Herbert, *Columbus* (Pittsburgh); Hugh Kaun, *Minnehaha, Hiawatha* (Chicago); Frederick S. Converse, *Endymion's Narrative* (Boston); Samuel Coleridge-Taylor, *The Song of Hiawatha* trilogy (Easton, Pa.); Edward Elgar, *Apostles* (N.Y.C.)

Opera

Metropolitan: A gala production of *La fille du régiment* honors Maurice Grau, retiring after 10 years as manager. Olive Fremsted (debut), *Die Walküre.* Premieres: Marcella Sembrich, Antonio Scotti, Emilio De Marchi, Edouard de Reszke, *Ernani* (Verdi); *Fra Diavolo* (Auber); Johanna Gadski, De Marchi, *Un ballo in*

Poet W. B. Yeats makes his first U.S. trip; like Social Darwinist Herbert Spencer, he speaks at Carnegie Hall, used until this year for lectures, as well as music.

Noted baritone Antonio Scotti sings Rigoletto the night Caruso makes his Met debut.

maschera; Albert Alvarez, *Otello;* Marcel Journet, *Philémon et Baucis;* Fritzi Scheff, *La Bohème;* Anton Van Rooy, *Siegfried;* David Bispham, *Die Meistersinger von Nürnberg.*

San Francisco: *Cavalleria rusticana, Zanetto* (Mascagni, also conducting)

Boston: *Azara* (John Knowles Paine)

St. Louis: *The New World* (Homer Moore)

Chicago: *American Kraal* (Henry Lawrence Freeman); *Babes in Toyland* (Victor Herbert); Sembrich, Thomas Salignac, Charles Gilibert, *Pagliacci;* Scheff, Sembrich, *The Magic Flute*

Washington, D.C.: *Babette* (Victor Herbert)

Music Notes
Enrico Caruso, 30, debuts November 23, at the Metropolitan Opera in *Rigoletto,* displaying his *coup de glotte* ("the Caruso sob"), where singing gives way to intermittent vocalization without tonal precision • The first complete opera is recorded, Verdi's *Ernani* • Presbyterian Churches of Chicago adopt a resolution condemning the forthcoming production of Wagner's *Parsifal* as blasphemous • Victor produces its first Red Seal recording, the Berlin Philharmonic's performance of Beethoven's Fifth Symphony • Anton Van Rooy is banned from Bayreuth for having performed in the New York *Parsifal*• The Brooklyn Academy of Music (1861) burns to the ground • Woolsey Hall is built to house the New Haven Symphony Orchestra, among the oldest U.S. orchestras in continuous operation (since 1894) • Charles Martin Loeffler resigns from the Boston Symphony to devote himself to composing and farming in Medfield, Mass.

Art

Painting

Abraham Walkowitz, *East Side Figures*

Maurice Prendergast, *Central Park in 1903*

Robert Henri, *Storm Tide*

John Singer Sargent, *Edward Robinson*

Everett Shinn, *The Laundress, Window Shopping*

Sculpture

Alma Mater figure, Low Memorial Library (1897), Columbia University, N.Y.C. (Daniel Chester French)

Bessie Potter Vonnoh, *Daydreams*

Charles M. Russell, *Smoking Up*

Henry Merwin Shrady, *Buffalo*

Adolph Weinman, *Destiny of the Red Man*

Frederic Remington, *The Mountain Man*

Augustus Saint-Gaudens, *General William Tecumseh Sherman* (1897–1903), Grand Army Plaza, N.Y.C.

Arthur Putnam, *Indian and Slain Puma*

Architecture

Church of All Souls, Evanston, Ill. (Marion Mahoney Griffin)

New York Stock Exchange, N.Y.C. (George Browne Post)

Sanborn House and Bandani House, Pasadena, Calif. (Greene & Greene)

Oelrich House, Newport, R.I. (McKim, Mead & White)

St. Louis Art Museum, St. Louis (Cass Gilbert)

Woolsey Hall and Common, Yale University, New Haven (Carrère and Hastings, 1902–3)

Important Exhibitions

New York: *Metropolitan:* 14 terra-cotta vases found in Asia Minor; seven ancient glass vases from Saida; three terra-cotta statuettes from Smyrna; six Greco-Roman statues; three bronzes from Haifa; five gold ornamental rings from Tarsus

Chicago: 15th exhibition of paintings and sculpture by Americans (524 pieces; nine sell for $2,480); *Country Children* by A. E. Albright; Will H. Low; Chicago newspaper artists. Acquisitions: *The Cliffs at Trouville* (Monet); Chinese combs; *The Pilots* (Frank Brangwyn)

Boston: Portraits by Sargent; Portraits by Rembrandt, Van Dyck, and Goya; Rembrandt, *Danaë and the Shower of Gold*

Art Briefs

Robert Henri, who joins the first cooperative artists' studio, in N.Y.C., and is an instructor at the New York School of Art, advocates, "Never mind bothering about details. The camera produces the best likenesses, but it is only the artist who can produce the temperament of

Owner of the New York *World,* Joseph Pulitzer donates $2 million to Columbia University's School of Journalism; his newspaper is noted for its hyperbolic style.

the model"; he emphasizes speed in painting, and students flock to study with him: Rockwell Kent, Glenn Coleman, Patrick Henry Bruce, Edward Hopper, Guy Pène du Bois • Alfred Stieglitz opens a gallery to exhibit photographs as an art form and founds the journal *Camera Work* • The art community follows the first exhibition of Les Fauves in Paris, led by Matisse and including André Derain, Maurice de Vlaminck, Georges Braque, Raoul Dufy, and Georges Rouault, and the exhibition of the Expressionists (Die Brücke, in Germany), including Ernst Ludwig Kirchner, Emil Nolde, Karl Schmidt-Rotluff, Fritz Bleyl, Erich Heckel, and Max Pechstein • Frank Lloyd Wright adds new metalwork, marble, and a pedestal to Burnham and Root's The Rookery (1888), in Chicago.

The 1903 Oldsmobile Curved Dash Runabout; mass production of the gas-driven car begins with the Oldsmobile.

Books

Fiction

Critics' Choice

The Ambassadors, Henry James
The Call of the Wild, Jack London
Trent's Trust and Other Stories,
  Bret Harte
Forging Ahead, Horatio Alger
  (posthumous)
The O'Ruddy, Stephen Crane
  (posthumous)
Dr. Lavendar's People, Margaret
  Deland
The Monarch Billionaire, Morrison
  I. Swift
The Bar Sinister, Richard Harding
  Davis
Man Overboard! F. Marion Crawford
In Babel, George Ade
In Old Plantation Days, Paul
  Laurence Dunbar
The Boss, Alfred Henry Lewis
🦋 *The Way of All Flesh,* Samuel
  Butler
🦋 *Tonio Kröger,* Thomas Mann

Best-Sellers

Lady Rose's Daughter, Mrs.
  Humphry Ward
Gordon Keith, Thomas Nelson Page
The Pit, Frank Norris (posthumous)
Lovey Mary, Alice Hegan Rice
The Virginian, Owen Wister
Mrs. Wiggs of the Cabbage Patch,
  Alice Hegan Rice

The Mettle of the Pasture, James
  Lane Allen
*Letter of a Self-Made Merchant to
  His Son,* George Horace Lorimer
The One Woman, Thomas Dixon
*The Little Shepherd of Kingdom
  Come,* John Fox, Jr.

Nonfiction

Critics' Choice

The Souls of Black Folk, W. E. B.
  Du Bois
People of the Abyss, Jack London
Optimism, Helen Keller
The Home: Its Work and Influence,
  Charlotte Perkins Gilman
*The Responsibility of the Novelist
  and Other Literary Essays,* Frank
  Norris
My Debut as a Literary Person,
  Mark Twain
American Masters of Sculpture,
  Charles Henry Caffin
The Log of a Cowboy, Andy Adams
*William Wetmore Story and His
  Friends,* 2 vols., Henry James
*The Impeachment and Trial of
  Andrew Jackson,* David M.
  Dewitt
🦋 G. E. Moore, *Principia Ethica*
🦋 Henri Poincaré, *Science and
  Hypothesis*
🦋 W. B. Yeats, *Ideas of Good and
  Evil*

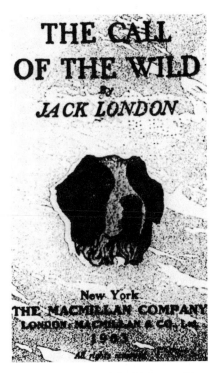

Jack London, one of the highest-paid
authors, spent time in the Alaskan gold
fields.

Poetry

Willa Cather, *April Twilights*
Paul Laurence Dunbar, *Lyrics of
  Love and Laughter*
James Whitcomb Riley, *His Pa's
  Romance*
🦋 W. B. Yeats, *In the Seven Woods*

Science and Technology

Walter Sutton argues that egg and sperm cells each
  carry chromosomes that explain inherited
  characteristics.
Atkins Thompson designs forceps that secure a patient's
  tongue to prevent choking during a surgical
  procedure.
Marconi transmits a wireless (radio) message at 17
  words-per-minute, from Wellfleet, Mass., to
  Cornwall, England.
W. F. Stearn and F. Popham produce an artificial silk,
  viscose rayon.
Cadillac introduces cars with fully replaceable parts.

Frederick Winslow Taylor applies scientific principles
  into the management of business, seeking to
  maximize machine efficiency through the optimal
  use of workers ("taylorization").
🦋 Ernst Mach questions the concepts of absolute space
  and time in Newtonian physics.
🦋 Willem Einthoven invents the string galvanometer,
  which records the heart's electrical currents.
🦋 Georg Perthes discovers that X-rays inhibit tumor
  growth.
🦋 Bertrand Russell's *Principles of Mathematics* seeks
  to show that mathematics can be derived from pure
  logic.

Sports

Baseball

"Scientific baseball" remains the order of the day: low-scoring, close games of two hours or less, with dominant pitching.

The World Series, the best of nine games between the two league champions, begins; the leagues are under a National Commission headed by chairman Garry Hermann, Cincinnati owner.

The AL outdraws the older league again (2,390,362 vs. 2,345,888), as attendance rises for both leagues; Baltimore (AL) moves to New York.

The World Series attracts modest total crowds of 100,000; the winner's share is $1,316; the loser's, $1,182.

A caught foul tip is accepted by both league's as a third strike.

The annual salary for top players is $5,000 per season.

Joe "Iron Man" McGinnity (New York, NL) pitches and wins both (full) games of a doubleheader in 3 hours, 3 minutes.

Pittsburgh (NL), led by Honus Wagner, Jack Chesbro, and Deacon Phillips, wins its third straight pennant.

Champions

Batting	Pitching
Honus Wagner (Pittsburgh, NL), .355	Sam Leever (Pittsburgh, NL), 25–7
Napoleon Lajoie (Cleveland, AL), .355	Earl Moore (Cleveland, NL), 22–7
	Home runs
	John Freeman (Boston, NL) 13

Football

Game length is reduced to 60 minutes, with two 30-minute halves. First downs are set at 10 yards. Wesleyan throws the first forward pass, though it is not yet officially legal. When Yale leads Columbia 6–0 on a forward pass, Columbia refuses to continue the game. Helping to better organize play, former Harvard player Bert Walters introduces a "neutral zone" between teams before a play.

The first World Series game is played October 1, in Boston, which loses to Pittsburgh, 7–3.

College All-Americans: William Heston (HB), Michigan; James Hogan (T), Yale; John DeWitt (G), Princeton

Other Sports

Boxing: James Corbett, who beat John O'Sullivan in 1892, loses the HW title to Jim Jeffries in 10 rounds.

Hockey: The first professional hockey league is formed in Houghton, Mich.; it consists mainly of Canadian teams.

Horse Racing: The Jamaica Race Track opens on Long Island, N.Y., and attracts celebrity gamblers like "Diamond Jim" Brady, "Bet-a-Million" Gates, and Lillian Russell.

Tennis: The U.S. loses the Davis Cup to Britain, 4–1.

Winners

World Series		U.S. Tennis Open	
Boston (AL) 5		Men: William Larned	
Pittsburgh (NL) 3		Women: Elizabeth Moore	
College Football		*USGA Open*	
Princeton		Willie Anderson	
College Basketball		*Kentucky Derby*	
Yale		Judge Himes (Hal Booker, jockey)	

Fashion

A craze begins for elaborate blouses with pouched fronts and brief collars with elaborate trim. A favorite is the shirt of white lines decorated with cherry spots and ribbons; the blue or green checkered muslin is also popular. In most styles, the straight front slopes forward at 30 degrees from the vertical; the back is severely arched with a tight fullness down the back. The stomach is virtually absent and the bosom thrown forward. Head and shoulder must be carried well to preserve one's balance. The two-part suit enters the fashion world, a gored skirt flaring to the knee with a jacket that fits smoothly on the shoulders and is tight at the waist and hips.

High-fashion note: Shirtwaists range in style from the tailored fit of crossbar lawn, with stiff laundered linen cuffs and a detachable turnover color (in white only, 98¢), to a waist of filet net in écru, navy blue, brown, smoke gray, or catawbu over Japanese silk with Bonnaz embroidery; both front and back in the latter may be decorated with lace outlined by Persian trimming.

Kaleidoscope

- The New York Society for the Suppression of Vice targets playing cards, roulette, lotto, watches with obscene pictures, and articles of rubber for immoral use.
- After TR explains to War Secretary Elihu Root how he got the canal from Panama on the same terms he proposed to Colombia, Root comments: "You have shown that you were accused of seduction, and you have proved conclusively you are guilty of rape."
- Hay defends TR's deal with Panama, saying that he had "no plainer duty [than] to preserve for the benefit of all free transit between the oceans."
- Calamity Jane (Martha Jane Canary) dies; the frontier character usually attired in men's clothing gained her nickname for her marksmanship, particularly against potential molesters.
- Composer Maurice Rosenfeld visits Harry von Tilzer on 28th Street, N.Y.C., hears rasping upright piano sounds that remind him of tin pans, and calls popular songs "Tin Pan Songs"; he calls the area "Tin Pan Alley."
- Florida gains title to the Everglades swamp, and drainage plans get under way.
- TR declares Pelican Island, Fla., a national wildlife refuge for seabirds.
- Alleged atrocities by King Leopold of Belgium, who owns the Belgian Congo, are widely reported and denounced.
- Despairing of conditions in the U.S., the National Colored Immigration Association petitions the President and Congress for $10 million to send blacks to Liberia.
- With opposing points of view, Booker T. Washington believes that blacks should accept social separation and advance by working; Du Bois, that complete equality is the first order of the day.
- The Senate rejects TR's appointment of a black, Joseph Crum, as collector at the port of Charleston; TR fights back, insisting "mere color" should never be a bar.
- Louis Sherry's on N.Y.C.'s 5th Avenue opens the New York Riding Club, where members can eat in the saddle.
- Milton Hershey plans to build a chocolate factory near Harrisburg, Pa.; its streets will have names like Chocolate Lane.
- Constructed with a reinforced concrete framework, the world's tallest skyscraper, the Ingalls Building in Cincinnati, stands 16 stories high.
- Women agitating for union rights form the National Women's Trade Union League at an AFL meeting in Boston.
- Henry Ford leaves the Detroit Auto Company to organize the Ford Motor Co.
- TR inaugurates East Room musicales in the White House with a concert by Ignace Paderewski.
- A Packard Model F goes from San Francisco to N.Y.C. in 51 days, the first authenticated transcontinental auto trip.
- At Wellfleet, Mass., Marconi sends a wireless at 17 words a minute to King Edward VII of England from TR; with the new Pacific Cable from San Francisco to Honolulu, messages can now go around the world in 12 minutes.
- The women's groups led by wealthy women fighting for better conditions for the working woman are called the "mink brigade."

- The 300,000-member Women's Christian Temperance Union (WCTU) is the largest women's organization, advocating general reform as well as temperance.
- *New York World* publisher Joseph Pulitzer donates $2 million to Columbia's school of journalism "for prizes or scholarships for the encouragement of public service, public morality, American Literature and the advancement of education."
- Lecturing at "the Hall of Carnegie [Carnegie Hall]," Yeats follows in the tradition of Boer War–hero Winston Churchill, Booker T. Washington, Mark Twain, Robert E. Peary, and TR.
- Joke in the *Harvard Lampoon* on newly popular junior year abroad: Willie: "What did you see abroad, Archie?" Archie: "I don't remember exactly, but I did three countries more than Reggie did in the same time."
- In a year in which Irish jigs, lilts, and limericks become popular, a favorite is: "There once was a man from Nantucket / Who kept all his cash in a bucket. / But his daughter called Nan / Ran away with a man / and as for the bucket Nantucket."

Fads: Chewing food 32 times a bite (advocated in Horace Fletcher's *ABC of Nutrition,* the author reducing from 217 to 152 pounds); popular games: Follow the Leader, Prisoner's Base, and King of the Hill, "Sweet Adeline" (named after Adelina Patti and sung by inebriates en route to bar from bar)

First Appearances: bottle-making machine, Caloric stoves, Springfield rifle, auto license plate (Mass.), news service (London–New York), Bankers Trust, International Mercantile and Marine Co. (J. P. Morgan), Western Pacific Park, Wind Cave National Park (S.Dak.), Williamsburg Bridge, mandatory presidential primary (Wis.), Sanka, Best Foods, Sunshine Biscuits, Steuben glassworks, Bergdorf Goodman, Western Michigan University, University of Puerto Rico, *Redbook,* electric locomotive (Siemens), Model A Ford, Cadillac, motorcycle (Harley-Davidson), silicone

Rose Schneidermann tries to organize trade union leagues, particularly in the garment industry.

1904

In the News

200 ARE KILLED IN PENNSYLVANIA MINE COLLAPSE . . . U.S. AND CHINA CONCLUDE TRADE AGREEMENT ON "OPEN DOOR" PRINCIPLES, WILL RESPECT CHINESE INTEGRITY AND U.S. TRADE RIGHTS . . . MARYLAND LEGISLATURE DISENFRANCHISES BLACKS, VIOLENCE ENSUES . . . BALTIMORE FIRE DESTROYS 26,000 BUILDINGS . . . IN SURPRISE MOVE, JAPANESE ATTACK RUSSIAN FLEET AT PORT ARTHUR, MANCHURIA . . . SOCIALISTS NOMINATE DEBS FOR PRESIDENT . . . U.S. SENATOR JOSEPH BUXTON IS CONVICTED OF BRIBE-TAKING . . . SUPREME COURT UPHOLDS DISSOLUTION OF MORGAN'S NORTHERN SECURITIES COMPANY, TR IS HAILED AS "TRUST BUSTER" . . . BRITAIN AND FRANCE SETTLE COLONIAL DIFFERENCES, SIGN "ENTENTE CORDIALE" . . . U.S. BUYS FRENCH PROPERTY IN PANAMA CANAL REGION FOR $40 MILLION . . . PADDLE STEAMER *GENERAL SLOCUM* IS DESTROYED BY FIRE IN NEW YORK HARBOR, OVER 1,000 DIE . . . REPUBLICANS NOMINATE TR . . . 45,000 MEAT PACKERS BEGIN STRIKE . . . POPULISTS NOMINATE THOMAS WATSON . . . DEMOCRATS NOMINATE JUDGE ALTON B. PARKER . . . 25,000 IN FALL RIVER, R.I., BEGIN TEXTILE STRIKE . . . YELLOW FEVER EPIDEMIC STRIKES NEW ORLEANS, 300 ARE DEAD, ANTI-MOSQUITO CAMPAIGN IS BEGUN . . . CHICAGO VOTES FOR MUNICIPAL OWNERSHIP OF STREET RAILWAYS . . . U.S. ARMY REJECTS HEAVIER-THAN-AIR FLYING MACHINES . . . DRY CREEK, COLO., BRIDGE COLLAPSES, 76 DIE . . . MOBS BURN 2 BLACKS AT STAKE IN GEORGIA . . . N.Y.C. SUBWAY OPENS, OVER 100,000 TRAVEL ON FIRST DAY . . . TR WINS LANDSLIDE VICTORY . . . TR ASSERTS RIGHT OF U.S. TO INTERVENE IN LATIN AMERICA, "ROOSEVELT COROLLARY" TO MONROE DOCTRINE.

Quotes

On the issue of big business buying Roosevelt's influence:

"[Did corporations] that are pouring money into your campaign chests assume that they are buying protection? (Joseph Pulitzer, *New York World*); "The assertion that there has been any blackmail, direct or indirect . . . is a falsehood" (Teddy Roosevelt); "We bought the son-of-a-bitch and he did not stay bought" (H. C. Frick, U.S. Steel).

"Great cases like hard cases make bad law."
—Oliver Wendell Holmes, dissent in
Northern Securities Co. vs. U.S.

"I could carve out of a banana a judge with more backbone than that!"
—Teddy Roosevelt, furious at Holmes's dissent

"Every generation has the privilege of standing on the shoulders of the generation that went before; but it has no right to pick the pockets of the first-comer."
—Brander Matthews

"I . . . protest earnestly and strongly against the lumping together of American composers. Unless we are worthy of being put on programs with other composers, to stand or fall, leave us alone. . . . You tacitly admit that we are inferior to stand comparison with composers of Europe."
—Edward MacDowell, *Juilliard Review*

Ads

"That the little brown men of Japan should in half a century have mastered all the sciences which enter into modern warfare teaches to all Western nations a new respect for the intellect and character of the Orient."
—*Current Literature*

"Chronic wrongdoing . . . in the Western Hemisphere may force the United States, however reluctantly, in flagrant cases . . . to the exercise of an international police power."
—TR, explaining the "Roosevelt corollary"

"T.R. is spanking a senator / T.R. is chasing a bear / T.R. is busting an awful Trust / And dragging it from its lair. / They're calling T.R. a lot of things / The men in the private car— / But the day-coach likes exciting folks / And the day coach likes T.R."
—*Life*

Many in TR's party question his use of presidential power; TR acknowledges: "I have caused to be done many things not previously done by the president."

The campaign "Teddy" bear decoration, also a popular children's toy, is so named after a political cartoon shows TR refusing to shoot a mother bear protecting her cub.

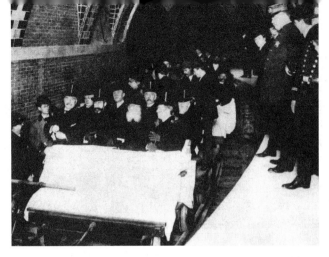

Political and business leaders vie for the opportunity to ride N.Y.C.'s first subway; it advertises "Harlem in 15 Minutes" from Wall Street.

Pittsburgh mines. Although workers could earn good wages, they often had to strike for improvements of dangerous conditions and excessive hours.

Vaudeville

Says entrepreneur Edward Franklin Albee: "See the mammoth menagerie where the wild man-eating bumbergiff is on exhibition. . . . Don't miss this greatest show, this stupendous spectacle. . . . Get your ticket here."

Oscar Hammerstein, whose earlier theater complex on 42nd Street failed, opens the Victoria Theater, which he allows his son Willie to manage. The father turns to his operatic interests, intent on building a new opera house but maintains the iron hand and high regard that Tony Pastor enjoyed during his 20-year reign from the 1880s, when he virtually created American vaudeville.

Of Note

After roping ponies in Wild West shows, including one at Madison Square Garden, Will Rogers is hired by Hammerstein; Rogers throws two ropes at one time and catches both the horse and rider separately. During the next year, with audiences laughing at his Oklahoma drawl ("A rope ain't bad . . . if it ain't around your neck"), his salary rises from $75 to $200 a week • The perennially young, tempestuous, blond Eva Tanguay debuts at Hammerstein's Victoria Theater; she is paid a record $3,500 a week • "Adgie and Her Lions" displays Adgie poking the lions as she performs a Spanish dance. At one point, she surrounds the lions with mirrors, and when they see themselves, they go berserk.

Movies

The Land beyond the Sunset (Edison), about slum youngsters taken on an outing
An Impossible Voyage ($7,500 budget, two reels)
Photographing a Female Crook (Biograph), 40-second closeup
The Strike (Pathé), concern with social conditions, inspired by Zola's *Germinal*

A Love Story (Lucien Nomguet, Pathé), great popular success
The Lost Child (Biograph), close-ups, rather than narrative, convey drama
The Suburbanite (Biograph)
Meet Me at the Fountain (Lubin)
Tramp on the Farm (Paley and Steiner)

Eva Tanguay, billed as "the Girl Who Made Vaudeville Famous" and "Mother Eve's Merriest Daughter," is well known for her fighting temperament and song "I Don't Care."

George Hale, a former fire chief, goes to the St. Louis Exposition and begins "Hale's Tours and Scenes of the World." These prove so popular that he constructs theaters like railroad cars, with ticket-sellers dressed as conductors; they are highly successful in many large cities. Adolph Zukor is a major exhibitor of Hale's tours. Biograph works under electric lights and produces multi-shot films of exotic locales, such as New York's famous "Tenderloin" district dance halls. Lubin makes films with lantern slides of songs that the audience sings, like "You Are a Soldier Boy, That's All You Know." The narrative film flourishes as the news film declines.

Popular Music

Hit Songs
"Give My Regards to Broadway"
"Meet Me in St. Louis, Louis"
"When the Bees Are in the Hive"
"In the Shade of the Pyramids"
"Absinthe Frappé"
"Teasing"
"She Went to the City"
"Please Come and Play in My Yard"
"Come Take a Trip in My Air-Ship"
"I Can't Take My Eyes Off You"

Representative Recordings:
"Bedelia" (Harry MacDonough and Haydn Quartet); "Silver Threads among the Gold" (Richard Jose); "Navajo" (Billy Murray); "Blue Bell" (Frank Stanley and Byron G. Harlan); "Toyland" (Corrine Morgan and Haydn Quartet); "All Aboard for Dreamland" (Byron G. Harlan); "Alexander" (Billy Murray); "Sweet Adeline" (Haydn Quartet)

Jazz
Clear differences mark the New Orleans sound: "Buddy" Bolden gains praise for his rhythmic drive and the emotional quality of his slow blues, in contrast with the more genteel playing of Creole bands like John Robochaux's; furthermore, Bolden does not improvise; he ornaments existing melodies. In the New Orleans resort area of West End, Abbie Brunies, Charlie Cordilla, and Emil Lacoume ("Stale Bread") play "spasm" bands with homemade instruments like cheese-box banjos and soap-box guitars. With all this variety, the first "wha-wha" sounds of jazz come from Storyville and its several environs. Even on the more lavish Mississippi showboats, which produce musical plays en route to their destination, musicians play the new music upon their return.

Theater

Broadway Openings

Theater
Leah Kleschna (C. M. S. McLellan), Mrs. Minnie Maddern Fiske, Harrison Grey Fiske
Judith of Bethulia (Thomas Bailey Aldrich), Nance O'Neill, Charles Dalton
Granny (Clyde Fitch), Mrs. G. H. Gilbert, Marie Doro
The Duke of Killicrankie (Robert Marshall), John Drew
The Dictator (Richard Harding David), John Barrymore, Lucille Watson, Thomas Meighan
Mrs. Wiggs of the Cabbage Patch (Anne Crawford Flexner), Madge Carr Cook, William T. Hodge
Olympe (Pierre Decourcelle), Henry Woodruff, Gilbert Heron
The Music Master (Charles Klein), David Warfield, Minnie Dupree, Jane Cowl
Rosmersholm (Ibsen, first U.S. production), William Morris, Florence Kahn

Musicals
The Yankee Consul (Henry Blossom, Alfred Robyn), Eva Davenport, William Danforth, John E. Hazzard
Piff! Paff! Pouf!!! (Jean Schwartz, William Jerome), Eddie Foy, Alice Fischer, John Hyams
It Happened in Nordland (Victor Herbert, Glen MacDonough), Lew Fields, Marie Cahill, Pauline Frederick
Higgledy-Piggledy (Maurice Levi, Edgar Smith), Joe Weber, Anna Held, Marie Dressler
Lady Teazle (A. Baldwin Sloane), Lillian Russell, William Carleton, John K. Bangs, Roderic C. Penfield

Little Johnny Jones (George M. Cohan), George, Jerry, and Helen Cohan, Ethel Levey
Love's Lottery (Julian Edwards, Stanislaus Stange), Madame Ernestine Schumann-Heink (only Broadway show), Louise Gunning, John Slavin
Mr. Wix of Wickham (Jerome Kern, Herbert Darnley), Julian Eltinge, Thelma Fair

Classics and Revivals On and Off Broadway
The Winter's Tale, Viola Allen; Sothern and Marlowe Repertory: each plays in *Romeo and Juliet, Much Ado about Nothing, Hamlet;* Ada Rehan Repertory: *The Taming of the Shrew, The Merchant of Venice, The School for Scandal, Twelfth Night.* Madame Gabrielle Réjane Repertory: *Amoureuse* (de Porto Riche), *La Dame aux camélias* (Dumas), *Ma cousine* (Meilhac), *Sapho* (Daudet); Robert B. Mantell Repertory: *Othello , Richard III, Richelieu; Camille* (two separate revivals), Virginia Harned, William Courtenay / Margaret Anglin, Henry Miller; *The Middleman,* E. S. Willard

E. H. Sothern and Julia Marlowe begin joint appearances in Shakespeare plays, including *Romeo and Juliet.*

Classical Music

Compositions
Charles Ives, *Ragtime Dances, Three Places in New England*

Frederick S. Converse, *The Mystic Trumpeter,* String Quartet no. 2

Henry Hadley, *Symphony Fantasia in E Flat*

Arthur Farwell, *Dawn,* Third Symphony, *Thanksgiving*

Charles Whitefield Chadwick, *Symphonic Sketches*

Important Events
The Seattle Symphony Orchestra presents its first full-length concert, conducted by Harry West. Samuel Coleridge-Taylor conducts his trilogy *The Song of Hiawatha* in Washington, D.C. Horatio Parker becomes dean of the Yale School of Music. The San Francisco Opera is reorganized under Paul Steindorf and Henry Holmes.

Notable Performances: The Boston Symphony Orchestra's opening concert, dedicated to Dvorak's memory, performs the Fifth Symphony and vocal music with Louise Homer. Another highly acclaimed concert follows: Debussy's *Prelude to the Afternoon of a Faun,* Fauré's *Pelléas et Mélisande,* and Sibelius's Symphony no 2. Richard Strauss, conducting the premiere of his *Symphonia domestica* at Carnegie Hall, receives negative reviews: the work represents a day in his family household and contains an interlude portraying the breast-feeding of a newborn child.

New Appointments: Willy Hess, Boston Symphony Orchestra; Emile Paur, Pittsburgh Symphony Orchestra

Debuts: Johannes Bishoff, Clara Clemens (Mark Twain's daughter)

First Performances
Gustav Luders, *The Sho-Gun* (New York); George Whitefield Chadwick, *Sinfonietta in D, Enterpe* (Boston); Horatio Parker, *The Eternal Feminine* (New Haven); Edward MacDowell, Prelude no. 1, *Six Idylls after Goethe* (New York)

Opera

Metropolitan: No longer leasing itself to independent impresarios, the Met establishes itself as a production company with shareholders. Heinrich Conried becomes manager; Felix Mottl, music director; the company stages its first opera by a female composer, Dame Ethel Smyth's *Der Wald*. Premieres: Milka Ternina, Alois Burgstaller, Otto Goritz (debut), Olive Fremstad (debut), *Parsifal;* Marcella Sembrich, Enrico Caruso, Antonio Scotti, *L'elisir d'amore*. Giuseppe Campanari, Sembrich, Andreas Dippel, *The Barber of Seville;* Ernst Kraus, Marion Weed (debut), *Tristan und Isolde;* Johanna Gadski, Dippel, Homer, *Cavalleria rusticana;* Ternina, Dippel, Goritz, *Fidelio;* Emma Calva, farewell performance, *Carmen;* Pasquale Amato (debut), Sembrich, Caruso, *La traviata*.

Brookline, Mass.: *Alice in Wonderland Continued* (Mabel Daniels)

Harrisburg, Pa.: *It Happened in Nordland* (Victor Herbert)

Music Notes
Carrère and Hastings redesign the Metropolitan Opera House auditorium, with an enormous sunburst chandelier, gilded waffle-structured ceiling with paintings, and ornate walls of maroon and gold; composers' names are painted on the elaborate proscenium arch • Maud Powell is the first violinist to record for Victor • The Chicago orchestra, called the Theodore Thomas Orchestra after its first president, moves into the new 2,566-seat Orchestra Hall • Chicago's Ravinia Park is built for concerts, dance, and theatrical events • Caruso's "Vesti la giubba" aria from *Pagliacci* is his first Victor recording • Edward MacDowell quarrels and resigns from Columbia University: newly appointed president Nicholas Murray Butler, unlike previous president Seth Low, takes a more conservative attitude about the role of music in the university; MacDowell moves to his Peterborough, N.H., farm, which will be established as a summer residence for U.S. artists.

Left: Sullivan and Adler's Carson, Pirie, Scott & Co. department store, in Chicago. Right: Louis Sullivan "signs" each building with intricate art nouveau decoration on the lower floors.

Art

Painting
Albert Pinkham Ryder, *Pastoral Study*
Everett Shinn, *Mouquin's, Eviction (Lower East Side)*
Edward Hopper, *Woman with Umbrella*
Robert Henri, *Portrait of George Luks, Portrait of William Glackens*
John Marin, *Weehawken Sequence 5* (1903–04)
William Merritt Chase, *An English Cod*
John Sloan, *Boy with Piccolo*
George Luks, *Closing the Café*
Alfred H. Maurer, *Evening at the Club* (ca. 1904)

Sculpture
Gutzon Borglum, *Mares of Diomedes*
Frederic Remington, *Polo, The Sergeant*
Charles Schreyvogel, *The Last Drop*
Solon Borglum, *Sioux and Indian Buffalo Dance*

Important Exhibitions

New York: *Metropolitan:* three ancient Persian panels of 112 tiles, A.D. 1586; 19 mural paintings from Pompeian villa at Boscoreale; one bronze Greco-Etruscan chariot (complete), 700–600 B.C.; two Greek terra-cotta figurines. *Brooklyn Institute of Art (opening):* 375 works from the Old Testament by James Tissot. *Grolier:* Whistler

Chicago: Impressionists: Monet, Manet, Renoir, Sisley; Portraits by Whistler, Sargent, Boldini, Zorn, and Chartran; William M. Chase; Harold Pyle; Contemporary Dutch art; British art

Minneapolis: John W. Alexander; J. Frank Currier; Charles H. Davis; Robert Henri; George Innes; Edward W. Redfield

Philadelphia: *Pennsylvania Academy of Fine Arts:* Hugh M. Breckenridge; 100th Annual Exhibition: "The

Architecture
Carson, Pirie & Scott, Chicago (Louis Sullivan)
Morton E. Plant [Cartier] building, N.Y.C. (Robert W. Gibson)
St. Regis Hotel, N.Y.C. (Trowbridge & Livingston, highest hotel in N.Y.C.)
Orchestra Hall, Chicago (D. H. Burnham)
New York Stock Exchange, N.Y.C. (George Browne Post, 1902–04)
Railway Exchange ("Santa Fe") building, Chicago (D. H. Burnham)
Darwin D. Martin house, Rochester (Frank Lloyd Wright)
Edwin H. Cheney house, Oak Park, Ill. (Frank Lloyd Wright)
Martin house, Buffalo, N.Y. (Frank Lloyd Wright)
Chicago building, Chicago (Holabird & Roche)

Frank Lloyd Wright's Martin House, Buffalo, N.Y.; as the landscape plays through the integrating indoor and outdoor worlds, houses are no longer simply objects to be placed upon the landscape.

Best of Contemporary Oil Painting Not Previously Shown in Philadelphia"

Boston: "Syracuse Coins: The Tetradrachmas of Hieron"; Velasquez, *Portrait of Philip IV of Spain;* El Greco, *Fray Feliz Hortensio Plavicino;* "French Tapestry: Two Miracles of the Eucharist"; Van der Weyden, *St. Luke Drawing the Portrait of the Virgin*

Pittsburgh: International art; Remington

Art Briefs
Louis Sullivan creates bold, artistically calculated steel constructions with multiple floors set between bold bases and cornices; pursuing his "form follows function" philosophy, his Carson, Pirie, Scott & Co. building has a horizontal design, reinforcing a department store's fluid movement • Henri, Sloan, Glackens, and Luks hold a group show to mixed reviews, several of which call their work "lugubrious" and "joyless" • Works drawing most attention at the St. Louis World's Fair are by Japanese and Germans • Harry E. Goodahue's stained glass windows for churches and universities gain special interest • A comparative exhibition of 100 American and foreign paintings at the Fine Arts Gallery, N.Y.C., draws enormous crowds • One of the year's most important auctions is that of architect Stanford White, a zealous collector of work from both the U.S. and abroad • A fire destroys Augustus Saint-Gaudens' studio in Cornish, N.H. • H. Kortwright builds a complex of 29 apartments at Sugar Hill, 1990 7th Ave., N.Y.C., for nonwhites.

Books

Fiction

Critics' Choice

The Golden Bowl, Henry James
The Sea Wolf, Jack London
Cabbages and Kings, O. Henry
The Son of Royal Langbrith,
   William Dean Howells
*Extracts from Adam's Diary, A
   Dog's Tale,* Mark Twain
Finding a Future, Horatio Alger
   (posthumous)
The Light of the Star, Hamlin
   Garland
The Givers, Mary E. Wilkins
   Freeman

Gutzon Borglum, *John Ruskin,* 1904.
*The Metropolitan Museum of Art,
Rogers Fund,* 1904.

*The Descent of Man and Other
   Stories,* Edith Wharton
Manassas: A Novel of War, Upton
   Sinclair
The Common Lot, Robert Herrick
The Cost, David Graham Phillips
🕊 *Jean Christophe,* Romain
   Rolland
🕊 *Nostromo,* Joseph Conrad

Best-Sellers

The Crossing, Winston Churchill
The Deliverance, Ellen Glasgow
The Masquerader, Anonymous
In the Bishop's Carriage, Miriam
   Michelson
Sir Mortimer, Mary Johnston
Beverly of Graustark, George Barr
   McCutcheon
*The Little Shepherd of Kingdom
   Come,* John Fox, Jr.
Rebecca of Sunnybrook Farm, Kate
   Douglas Wiggin
My Friend Prospero, Henry
   Harland
The Gold Bat, P. G. Wodehouse
The Silent Places, Stewart Edward
   White

Nonfiction

Critics' Choice

The Shame of the Cities, Lincoln
   Steffens
*The History of the Standard Oil
   Company,* Ida Tarbell

Helen Adams Keller (left), with
Alexander Graham Bell and Anne
Sullivan. "Literature is my Utopia.
Here I am not disenfranchised. No
barrier of the senses shuts me out from
the sweet, gracious discourse of my
book friends. They talk to me without
embarrassment or awkwardness."

The Theory of Business Enterprise,
   Thorstein Veblen
The Toy and the Man, Upton
   Sinclair
*The Negro: The Southerner's
   Problem,* Thomas Nelson Page
Rebels of the New South, Walter
   Marion Raymond
Overtones: A Book of Temperaments,
   James Gibbons Huneker

Poetry

Joel Chandler Harris, *The Tar-Baby
   and Other Rhymes of Uncle
   Remus*
Carl Sandburg, *In Reckless Ecstasy,
   Incidentals*
Paul Laurence Dunbar, *Li'l Gal*
James Whitcomb Riley, *A Defective
   Santa Claus*

Science and Technology

Malaria and yellow fever disappear from the Panama
   Canal zone after Army surgeon William Gorgas
   develops successful methods of disease control.
Russell Chittenden, founder of the first physiological
   chemistry lab at Yale, isolates glycogen, which is
   where the body stores carbohydrates.
George Ellery Hale sets up California's Mount Wilson
   Observatory.
The sixth moon of Jupiter is located.
B. B. Boltwood and Herbert McCoy discover that
   radium is a decay product of uranium.
A. Fasenmeyer builds the first plant to extract gasoline
   from natural gas by compressing and cooling
   techniques.

The first photoelectric cell is developed.
🕊 John Ambrose Fleming patents the diode, a radio
   wave detector that greatly facilitates radio
   communication.
🕊 David Hilbert develops a model for Euclidean
   geometry within the arithmetical system, showing
   that if there are no contradictions in arithmetics,
   there are none in geometry.
🕊 Marie Curie discovers two new radioactive elements
   in uranium ore, radium and polonium.
🕊 The barbiturate Veronal is synthesized.
🕊 Ernest Rutherford and Frederick Soddy postulate a
   general theory of radioactivity.

Sports

Baseball

The American again outdraws the National League by 3,024,028 to 2,666,271.

Rube Waddell, Philadelphia (AL), strikes out a record 343, 347, or 349.

Denton "Cy" Young (Boston, AL) pitches the first perfect game; he began his career in 1890.

Boston (AL), under playing manager Jimmie Collins, wins its 2nd straight pennant.

New York (NL) wins the pennant with Joe McGinnity, 35–8, and Christy Mathewson, 33–12.

Saying their team would be demeaned by playing "a minor league organization," John McGraw, New York (NL) manager, and owner John Brush refuse to meet the AL winner (Boston) in the scheduled World Series; AL president Ban Johnson becomes enraged, and war is almost rekindled before McGraw apologizes and agrees to a 1905 WS.

Champions

Batting
Honus Wagner (Pittsburgh, NL), .349
Napoleon Lajoie (Cleveland, NL), .381
Pitching
Joe McGinnity (New York, NL), 35–8

Jack Chesbro (New York, AL), 41–13
Home runs
Harry Davis (Philadelphia, AL) 10

Football

The field goal is reduced from 5 to 4 points; a touchdown remains at 5 and an extra point at 1. Harvard builds the first cement (oval) stadium for football.

Fashion

Hats range from the summer straw in sailor shape, trimmed with satin that twists softly to the side, to the handmade silk styles with lacy braid for the cooler seasons. The brow droops and is smartly dented and trimmed with velvet or taffeta ribbon, ostrich blooms, false fruits, stuffed birds, or floral adornments, such as two large chrysanthemums combined with silk and velvet pansies intermingled with foliage. Velvet roses in contrasting colors with clusters of forget-me-nots are also stylish. The very popular ostrich plume, both for hats and stoles, varies in color, length, and number of strands. The variety of infants' bonnets also seems unlimited—for example, of Japanese silk, dotted swiss, or lawn (Tuscan or braided), all trimmed with lace frills, embroidery, net, silk ribbon, rosettes, rose buds, chiffon ruche, and silk and ribbon streamers.

College All-Americans: Willie Heston (HB), Michigan; Walter Eckersall (E), Chicago; Thomas Shevlin (E), Yale; Frank Piekarski (G), Penn

Olympics: The games are played in St. Louis as part of the St. Louis Exposition. The U.S. leads with 21 gold medals. Winners include Archie Hahn (100m, 11s., 200m, 21.6s.), Ray Ewry (standing broad jump, high jump, and hop, step, and jump), Jim Lightbody (800m, 1:56, 1500m, 4:05.4), Jim Hick (marathon, 3:28.53), Charles Daniels, three in swimming. The U.S. demonstrates basketball.

Other Sports

Auto Racing: Henry Ford drives his 16.7-liter Hi Arrow on an ice straightaway at a world record, 91.37 mph; he remarks, "Somehow I stayed top-side up . . . making a record that went all over the world."

Winners

Baseball
NL—New York Giants
AL—Boston Red Sox
No World Series played
College Football
Penn
College Basketball
Columbia

U.S. Tennis Open
Men: Holcombe Ward
Women: May Sutton
USGA Open
Willie Anderson
Kentucky Derby
Elwood (Frankie Prior, jockey)

Victory after setting an 18-day cross-country driving record.

High-fashion note: Crêpe-de-chine evening gowns in new shades of blue, with strips of lace bound with crêpe extending over the shoulder.

Kaleidoscope

- Laura Ziegler ("Miss Laura") borrows $3,000 and opens a successful brothel in Fort Smith, Ark.; the "Social Club," the most steamy among 66 brothels, holds a grand opening, which the mayor and other dignitaries attend; trade is $3 per event, as opposed to the $1 fare at most establishments.
- Women are frequently arrested for smoking in public.
- During the campaign, TR proposes his "Square Deal": conservation, regulation of business, and friendship to labor; Democrats claim he has adopted many of William Jennings Bryan's planks.
- Having become president because of McKinley's assassination (1901), TR tells his wife this election night: "I am no longer a political accident."
- Helen Adams Keller, who lost her speech, sight, and hearing in infancy, is graduated from Radcliffe College; she writes for women's magazines about blindness, a previously forbidden subject.
- Carnegie establishes his $5 million Heroes' Fund so that society can "know the heroes of civilization" who sacrificed their lives for others rather than its "barbarians"; the funds go to widows and orphans.
- TR rules that all Civil War veterans over 62 are entitled to pensions.
- The *Ladies Home Journal* publishes an exposé of the patent medicine business.
- The *New York Times* moves to a tower at Broadway and 42nd Street (renamed "Times Square"), and a midnight celebratory fireworks display follows.
- Celebrating the centennial of the Louisiana Purchase Exposition, the St. Louis World's Fair attracts 18.7 million.
- Northerner David Decatur Emmett, the author of "Dixie," the Civil War fighting song of the South, dies at 88.
- E. H. Sothern and Julia Marlowe become virtual legends in their joint appearances in Shakespeare plays; rumors of romance accompany their partnership.
- Minnie Maddern Fiske and her husband produce *Leah Kleschna* after a 10-year battle with the Theatrical Trust and its six powerful managers—Charles Frohman, Marc Klaw, Abraham Erlanger, William Harris, Al Hayman, and J. Frederick Zimmerman.
- Isadora Duncan, successful abroad with her barefoot dancing, begins to attract attention at home.
- The drama *Madame Butterfly* by David Belasco and John Luther Long, about a tragic East-West love affair, is a great Broadway success.
- Most Americans are sympathetic to Japan in the Russo-Japanese war.
- Jujitsu becomes a fad when TR is given lessons by a Japanese teacher.
- Saks publishes a 270-page catalog featuring motoring garb.
- The free Montgomery Ward catalog mailed to 3 million rural people usually occupies a prominent position on the sitting room table; Sears & Roebuck mails out a million.
- Many foreign companies cut their steerage rates to the U.S. to $10 to compete with British lines.
- Lincoln Steffens' *Shame of the Cities* attacks the systematic purchase and sale of special privileges by business and politicians, fraud in construction, and police protection for brothels.

Lincoln Steffens' exposés of city government graft in *McClure's* are facilitated by his good-humored manner, which encourages many to speak openly with him.

- Thorstein Veblen's *Theory of Business Enterprise* is a follow-up to his *Theory of the Leisure Class* (1899), in which he coined the term "conspicuous consumption" to describe the useless spending habits of the rich.
- Said to own 100 car garages, William Vanderbilt organizes the Vanderbilt Cup Race on Long Island; 25,000 attend; the winner drives a 90-hp French Packard nearly 284 miles in 5 hours, 26 minutes.
- United Fruit puts radio equipment on all its ships; CQD is adopted as the universal wireless distress signal.
- A Yale physiologist gains attention when he recommends a low-protein diet for older people.
- Green tea outsells black tea by five-to-one.
- TR is accused of holding up statehood for Oklahoma, Arizona, and New Mexico because they are likely to vote Democratic.
- The Supreme Court rules that Puerto Ricans, while not citizens, cannot be refused U.S. admission.
- Robert La Follette campaigns on "the Wisconsin Idea" that active government can assure "a happier and better state to live in."
- When the American millionaire Ion Perdicaris is kidnapped by the Moroccan bandit Raisuli, TR sends a warship with the message "This country wants Perdicaris alive or Raisuli dead"; the prisoner is released but turns out *not* to be an American citizen.
- The Curleys of Boston are elected to top city positions on the same day their prison term for fraud begins.

First Appearances: Colgate Ribbon dental cream, Post Toasties, Campbell's Pork and Beans, ice-cream cone (Syrian pastry maker Ernest A. Hamwi), tea bags (Thomas Sullivan), iced tea (at St. Louis Exposition), Continental Can Co., Thermos, folding metal chair, stainless steel, E. F. Hutton, Maxwell and Reo (cars), Caterpillar Tractor Co., diesel engine (Rudoph Diesel), raised tire tread (Michelin), Ansonia and Astor hotels (N.Y.C.), St. Francis Hotel (San Francisco), Hotel Jefferson (St. Louis), Mount Sinai Hospital (N.Y.C.), Hispanic Society of America, United Spanish War Veterans, Camp-Fire Club, Australian crawl in U.S., American Academy of Arts and Letters (50 members), lever-filled pen (Parker), offset printing, *Musical America,* first underwater tunnel across Hudson River (Morton Street Tunnel), central heating, ultraviolet lamp, Dr. Scholl arch supports

1905

A devoted parent, TR says: "A child's hand. . . . There is nothing so beautiful"; of his own father he says: "[He] was the best man I ever knew."

Facts and Figures

Economic Profile
  Dow-Jones: ↑ High 97–Low 69
  GNP: +9.7%
  Inflation: +1.9%
  Unemployment: 4.3%
Physicians: 134,688
Dentists: 32,238
Hospital beds: 421,085
Lord & Taylor furniture
  Reed arm chairs: $2.25; settees: $4.50
  Silver birch chairs: $1.65; with arms, rockers, $2
Sanders and Staryman, Washington, D.C., Pianos Emerson, Dietz: $50
Wallach's straw hats with crown, "rather high, brim not too wide": $1.90
Power's Cameragraph projector: $140
Clothes horse, 6′, folding: 75¢
Junket tablets: 10¢
Ketchup: 3¢
Pinbone roast: 56¢ (4 lbs.)
Lion mutton chops: 14¢ (lb.)
Flounder: 10¢ (2 lbs.)

The one-room schoolhouse, which most Americans attend, is furnished with straight-back benches at desks nailed to the floor; the ruler is a popular teaching aid.

Deaths

Lyman Bloomingdale, F. A. Constable, Mary Mapes Dodge, John Hay, Sir Henry Irving, Jules Verne, Alfred Waterhouse

In the News

SUPREME COURT DECLARES BEEF TRUST ILLEGAL . . . SENATE UNDERMINES ARBITRATION TREATIES BETWEEN U.S., GREAT POWERS, AND THE HAGUE . . . SUPREME COURT RULES COMPULSORY VACCINATION LAWS CONSTITUTIONAL . . . TR IS INAUGURATED . . . SUPREME COURT RULES N.Y. STATE LAW LIMITING MAXIMUM WORKING HOURS UNCONSTITUTIONAL, A VIOLATION OF FREE CONTRACT RIGHTS . . . JAPANESE DESTROY RUSSIAN FLEET IN TSUSHIMA STRAITS . . . TR INVITES RUSSIA AND JAPAN TO PORTSMOUTH, N.H., TO NEGOTIATE END OF WAR . . . EUGENE V. DEBS AND "BIG BILL" HAYWOOD ORGANIZE INDUSTRIAL WORKERS OF THE WORLD, "WOBBLIES," IN CHICAGO . . . AFTER MUTINY ON BATTLESHIP *POTEMKIN,* CZAR PROMISES DUMA, A REPRESENTATIVE ASSEMBLY . . . GEORGIA SENATE DEFEATS BILL TO LIMIT CHILDREN'S WORKING HOURS . . . NEW ORLEANS YELLOW FEVER EPIDEMIC IS ENDED BY ANTI-MOSQUITO CAMPAIGN . . . SECRETARY OF WAR TAFT WARNS JAPAN TO STAY OUT OF PHILIPPINES . . . RUSSIA AND JAPAN SIGN PEACE TREATY, JAPAN GAINS POWER IN KOREA AND MANCHURIA, RUSSIA RECEIVES ECONOMIC COMPENSATION . . . NORWAY VOTES FOR INDEPENDENCE FROM SWEDEN . . . TR SUBMERGES ON U.S. SUBMARINE *PLUNGER* . . . CHARLES EVANS HUGHES INVESTIGATES INSURANCE FRAUD IN N.Y., CLAIMS STOCK SPECULATION WITH PREMIUMS . . . BRITISH SUFFRAGETTES EMMELINE PANKHURST AND ANNIE KENNEY ARE ARRESTED FOR ASSAULTING POLICE . . . TROTSKY ORGANIZES ST. PETERSBURG WORKERS' COUNCIL . . . 250 ARE INDICTED IN MILWAUKEE STREET RAILWAY FRAUD . . . POLES DEMONSTRATE FOR AUTONOMY FROM RUSSIA . . . OVER 1,000 JEWS ARE MURDERED IN ODESSA, 125,000 N.Y. JEWS MARCH IN SYMPATHY.

Quotes

"Those who cannot remember the past are condemned to repeat it."
—George Santayana

"The Constitution is not intended to embody a particular economic theory, whether of paternalism . . . or of *laissez-faire.*"
—Oliver Wendell Holmes' dissent on the Supreme Court's denial of N.Y.'s right to limit working hours (*Lochner v. New York*)

"O! I like my boss / He's a good friend of mine / And that's why I'm starving / Out on the picket line! / Hallelujah! What comes next / Hallelujah! I'm a bum."
—IWW song

"What was being melted away in the great melting pot, losing all form, . . . all beauty, [and] all nobility was the American nationality itself. [Immigration is] slowly, insidiously, irresistibly, eating away at the heart of America."
—Henry Pratt Fairchild

"Taft is the politest man in Washington; the other day he gave up his seat on a street-car to three ladies."
—Supreme Court Justice David Brewer, on W. H. Taft, 354 pounds

MANNERS TOWARD AUTOS
"Do not stare at another's car, nor, if at a stand still, examine the mechanism. This is the height of rudeness."
—*Everyday Etiquette*

W. E. B. Du Bois, the first black to earn a Ph.D. from Harvard, states in the Niagara Movement's "Declaration of Principles": "We believe Negroes should protest emphatically and continually [for] their political rights."

"Sensible and responsible women do not want to work. The relative positions [of] men and women [in] our civilization were assigned long ago by a higher intelligence than ours."
—Former president Grover Cleveland, *Ladies Home Journal*

"There is something mentally enervating in feminine companionship. . . . The genuine man feels that he must go off alone or with other men, out in the open air, as it were, roughing it among the rough, as a mental tonic."
—*Cosmopolitan*

"The question of transportation lies at the root of all industrial success. . . . We need to develop an orderly system . . . of efficient government control."
—TR, on the need for railroad regulation

"The more I see of the Czar, Kaiser, and the Mikado, the better I am content with democracy, even if we have to include the American newspaper as one of its assets; liability would be a better term."
—TR, on freedom of the press

Ads

The import duty on foreign champagne is 50%—
That leaves just half the price you pay to represent wine value. And because of this, duty—not the quality—makes the difference.
(Buy *Great Western Champagne*)

We are distributing fuel, . . . a prescription for the cure of the liquor habit. It can be given secretly in coffee or food.
(*Kansas Anti-Liquor Society*)

Why Don't You Have Your Own Water Works? There is no longer any reason for not having every sanitary convenience in your home.
(*C. A. Burton Machinery Co.,* Kansas City, Mo.)

A Modern Fireproof Hotel
(*Hotel Gayoso,* Memphis)

A Delightful • Palatable • Healthful Beverage for Men and Ladies, Business, Professional Students, Wheelmen, and Athletes
Relieves mental and physical exhaustion and is the favorite drink for Ladies when thirsty, weary, despondent.
(*Coca-Cola*)

Soda fountains dispensing this popular drink outnumber saloons; a new bottled version gains popularity.

Immigrant family: Many bore the hardships of tenement life as a mere obstacle that perseverance would one day overcome—when their own success arrived.

Vaudeville

Vaudeville songs, like "Sunbonnet Sue," gain increasing popularity. This year, "good-bye songs" are in vogue—"Goodbye Little Girl, Goodbye," by Cobb and Edwards ("Mr. Words" and "Mr. Music"). The first "intermission" takes place—to clear the house of people who have sat through two shows and to boost candy sales; some theaters serve tea or delicatessen.

Of Note

Bill ("Bojangles") Robinson teams up with actor George Cooper; they do a song-and-dance routine "Looking for Hannah" • Groucho Marx is the first in his family to join vaudeville, as a member of the Leroy Trio; he sings "I Wonder What's the Matter with the Mail" and is instantly successful with the timing of his gags • Already an international star of unparalleled beauty, Lillian Russell (Helen Louise Leonard) receives a salary of $100,000 for a 33-week engagement at Proctor's 23rd Street theater; "Diamond Jim" Brady buys a box for the entire run.

Family acts are popular, particularly this knockabout, acrobatic comedy team.

"Buffalo Bill" Cody becomes a vaudeville headliner at $3,000 per week.

Movies

Life of an American Policeman (Edison)
The Kleptomaniac (Porter)
The Ex-Convict (Porter), family responsibilities of two contrasting fathers, ex-convict and wealthy man
Vanderbilt Auto Races (Vitagraph), first newsreel feature
Adventures of Sherlock Holmes (Vitagraph)
The Miller's Daughter (Edison), social drama
A Policeman's Love Affair (Lubin)
Through the Matrimonial Agency (Lubin)
Escape from Sing Sing (Vitagraph)

Pathé is the largest producer and distributor of films around the world; its biggest market is the American "nickelodeon" (coined at Harry Davis's small movie theater in Pittsburgh). Within the year, hundreds of theaters open throughout the country, and attendance runs into the hundreds of thousands. Actors are hired by the week but still receive little mention. William Sorrelle is the first member of the Edison Stock Company and is paid $30 a week. Maurice Costello, a child from Brooklyn, also joins Edison. Biograph is the first studio to shift decisively to fiction "features." Edison raids the Biograph staff in an attempt to compete.

Popular Music

Hit Songs

"Wait Till the Sun Shines, Nellie"
"Starlight"
"What You Goin' to Do When the Rent Comes 'Round?"
"Forty-Five Minutes from Broadway"
"I Want What I Want When I Want It"
"Mary's a Grand Old Name"
"Daddy's Little Girl"
"Everybody Works But Father"
"How'd You Like to Spoon with Me?"
"I Don't Care"
"My Gal Sal"
"Will You Love Me in December as You Do in May?"
"A Woman Is Only a Woman But a Good Cigar Is a Good Smoke"

Representative Recordings: "Give My Regards to Broadway" (Billy Murray); "The Preacher and the Bear" (Arthur Collins); "Dearie" (Corrine Morgan and Haydn Quartet); "Where the Morning Glories Twine Around the Door" (Byron G. Harlan); "Yankee Doodle Boy" (Billy Murray); "In My Merry Oldsmobile" (Billy Murray)

Jazz

Ragtime is elaborated in New Orleans by both black and white performers like Tom Turpin and Louis Chauvin. Four beats in the left hand replace Joplin's two beats in the same interval, with more complicated accenting in the right hand. Music becomes more danceable. Typically, New Orleans musicians combine West African musical elements (instruments that are an extension of the human voice and tunes that lend themselves to endless variation), popular New Orleans march rhythms, and various European influences (the Protestant singing of psalms and hymns with free embellishments) and add to the European harmonies a blue tonality. "Buddy" Bolden is known as the New Orleans cornet "king" for his unusual tendency to "rag" melodies through rhythmic subdivision and variation. The newest music is rough and unwritten.

Theater

Broadway Openings

Plays

Mrs. Warren's Profession (George Bernard Shaw), Arnold Daly, Mary Shaw (both arrested for appearing in an "immoral" play)
John Bull's Other Island (George Bernard Shaw), Joseph Maddern, Arnold Daly
You Never Can Tell (George Bernard Shaw), Arnold Daly
Peter Pan (James M. Barrie), Maude Adams
Fedora (Victorien Sardou), Bertha Kalich (Yiddish star's English-speaking debut)
Alice-Sit-by-the-Fire (James M. Barrie), Ethel and John Barrymore
Andrea (David Belasco, John Luther Long), Mrs. Leslie Carter, Tyrone Power
The Squaw Man (Edwin Milton Royle), W. S. Hart, William Faversham
The Girl of the Golden West (David Belasco), Blanche Bates, James Kirkwood
The Lion and the Mouse (Charles Klein), Edmund Breese, Grace Elliston
The Walls of Jericho (Alfred Sutro), James K. Hackett, Mary Mannering
Monna Vanna (Maeterlinck), Bertha Kalich
Zira (J. Hartley Manners, Henry Miller), Margaret Anglin, Frank Worthing

Musicals

Mlle. Modiste (Victor Herbert, Henry Blosson), Fritzi Scheff, William Pruette, Walter Percival
The Catch of the Season (William T. Francis, Charles H. Taylor), Edna May
The Earl and the Girl (Ivan Caryll, Percy Greenbank), Eddie Foy, Templar Saxe
Fontana (Raymond Hubbell, Robert B. Smith), Julia Sanderson, Douglas Fairbanks
The Ham Tree (Jean Schwartz, William Jerome), James McIntyre, W. C. Fields (young juggler)
The Rollicking Girl (William T. Francis, Sydney Rosenfeld), Sam Bernard, Hattie Williams
Veronique (André Messager, Lillian Eldee), Kitty Gordon, Valli Valli

Classics and Revivals On and Off Broadway

The Misanthrope (Molière, first time in English), Richard Mansfield; *Man and Superman,* Robert Lorraine, Clara Bloodgood; *A Doll's House,* Ethel Barrymore; Sothern and Mansfield Repertory: *Beau Brummell* (Fitch), *Merchant of Venice, Richard III; Ivan the Terrible* (Tolstoy); *Dr. Jekyll and Mr. Hyde, A Parisian Romance* (Feuillet); *The Countess Cathleen* (W. B. Yeats), Margaret Wycherly; *She Stoops to Conquer; Carmen,* Olga Nethersole, Charles Quartermaine; *Hedda Gabler,* Nazimova; *Antony and Cleopatra,* Gertrude Elliott, Johnston Forbes-Robertson

Classical Music

Compositions
Arthur Farwell, *Symbolist Study no. 3, after Walt Whitman*
Charles Ives, *Three-Page Sonata for Piano*
George Chadwick, *Cleopatra*
Charles Griffes, *Overture*
Henry F. Gilbert, *Comedy Overture on Negro Themes*

Important Events
The first Symphony Concert for Young People is presented at Carnegie Hall with Frank Damrosch and Maud Paul; it concentrates on Beethoven. To gain a greater audience for the New York Philharmonic Orchestra, John D. Rockefeller and others engage the most eminent European conductors: Henry Wood, Felix Weingartner, Richard Strauss (1904–05).

Notable Performances: Jan Kubelik is highly lauded for performing with the New York Symphony Orchestra at Carnegie Hall the concerti of Mozart, Beethoven, Brahms, and Henryk Wieniawski, and works by Hector Berlioz, Josef Suk, Carl Maria von Weber, and Niccolò Paginini. On its 25th anniversary, the Boston Symphony gives its first pension fund concert, with Georg Henschel conducting Tchaikovsky's *Pathetic* [sic] symphony and works by Beethoven and Strauss, among others.

Major Recitals: Emma Calvé, Alfred Reisenauer, and Harold Bauer, each with the Boston Symphony; Jean Gérardy, with the Pittsburgh; Albert Spalding, 17, tours Europe to enormous acclaim. After her four-year disappearance in Europe, Alice Nielsen returns to Chicago and prepares a recital that sells out in record time.

New Appointments: Frederick Stock, Chicago Symphony Orchestra

Debuts: Marie Hall, Edward Lankow

First Performances
Frederick S. Converse, *The Mystic Trumpeter* (Philadelphia); Rachmaninoff, Piano Concerto no. 2 (New York); Rimsky-Korsakov, *The Snow Maiden* (New York, the latter two with the Russian Symphony Orchestra); Charles Martin Loeffler, *La Mort de Tintagiles* (New York)

Opera

Metropolitan: Premieres: Marcella Sembrich, Andreas Dippel, Edyth Walker, Bella Alten, *Die Fledermaus;* Maria de Macchi, Enrico Caruso, Antonio Scotti, Walker, *Lucrezia Borgia;* Caruso, Lillian Nordica, Louise Homer, Scotti, Pol Plançon, *La gioconda;* Anton Van Rooy, Alten, Heinrich Knote, Homer, *Die Meistersinger.* Sembrich, Caruso, Taurnio Paarvis, *Lucia di Lammermoor;* Sembrich, Caruso, Nordica, *Les Huguenots;* Alois Burgstaller, Nordica, Van Roy, Robert Blass, *Parsifal*

Chicago: Caruso, Sembrich, *Lucia di Lammermoor;* Nordica, Burgstaller, Von Roy, *Parsifal;* Caruso, *Pagliacci*

Dallas: *Parsifal*

Rochester: *Miss Dolly Dollars* (Victor Herbert)

Buffalo: Ottley Cranston, *Tannhäuser, Wonderland* (Victor Herbert)

Philadelphia: Walker, Caruso, Scotti, Plançon, *La favorita*

Music Notes
Vincent d'Indy visits the U.S. and conducts two concerts with the Boston Symphony • The Met's opulent gold curtain is displayed the opening night of *La gioconda;* a stage bridge collapses during *Carmen;* after eight injured people are taken to the hospital, the performance continues • Piano accompaniments to operatic areas are replaced with orchestral backgrounds in recordings • Physicians say Edward MacDowell is "completely broken down by overwork" and that "his creative career is ending" (*Musical America*) • Although physicians doubt that Ignace Paderewski will adequately recover from a stroke, after his wife's nursing, he begins work on several new projects • Engelbert Humperdinck (*Hansel and Gretel*) travels throughout the U.S. • The Institute of Musical Art (later, Juilliard) opens.

Great Wagnerian soprano Lillian Nordica commands $39,000 a season.

Art

Painting

William Glackens, *Central Park—Winter, Portrait of the Artist's Wife*

George Luks, *The Wrestlers, Hester Street*

Jerome Myers, *The Tambourine*

Otis Dozier, *Bridge for Fishing*

Childe Hassam, *Southwest Wind*

Maurice Prendergast, *Outdoor Cafe Scene* (1900–1905)

John Sloan, *Turning Out the Light, Election Night in Herald Square*

Sculpture

Charles M. Russell, *Nature's People, Scalp Dance*

Frederic Remington, *Dragoons, Troops of the Plains, 1868*

Albert Laessle, *Turning Turtle*

Paul Wayland Bartlett designs *History, Philosophy, Romance, Religion, Poetry, Drama,* the marble arch above the main entrance to the New York Public Library.

Architecture

University Club of Chicago, Chicago (Holabird & Roche)

Outdoor Art Clubhouse, Berkeley (Bernard Maybeck)

Larkin Building, Rochester, N.Y. (Frank Lloyd Wright)

G. W. Marston House, San Diego (Irving Gill, 1904–05)

W. A. Glasner House, Glencoe, Ill. (Frank Lloyd Wright)

Mandel Brothers Building, Chicago (Holabird & Roche)

Hall of Records, Centre & Chambers Streets, N.Y.C. (John R. Thomas)

College of the City of New York, 138th–140th Streets, N.Y.C. (George B. Post)

Important Exhibitions

New York: *Metropolitan:* The museum devotes more space and funding to American art. On loan: Sir Joshua Reynolds; Persian rugs from J. P. Morgan and Chinese porcelains. Acquisitions: *Portrait of William M. Chase* (Sargent); Two portraits by Gilbert Stuart and his *Washington Receiving Lafayette at Mount Vernon, Rossiter, and Mignot; Ecce Homo-Mater Dolorosa* (Jan Mostaert); *Kenyon Cox in Bas-Relief* (Augustus Saint-Gaudens); *Ariadne* (George Frederick Watts). *Astor:* Colored plates for H. T. Trigg's formal gardens in England and Scotland; Russian and Japanese caricatures. *Lenox Library:* Gifford etchings. *Knoedler:* Ten American painters; Twachtman Memorial

Chicago: Great painters of Great Britain; "Original Drawings of the Old Testament by J. James Tissot"; Van Dyke; Hals; Reynolds; Iranian portraits; Anna E. Klumke; Western drawings. Purchases: five Sargents, two Whistlers, six Zorns, five Vonnohs, 11 Chases, five Melchers

St. Louis Purchase Exhibition: grand prize: Sargent; gold medals: Hassam, Winslow Homer, J. Alden Weir, Thomas Eakins, J. J. Shann, Kenyon Cox; in sculpture: Saint-Gaudens, Gutzon Borglum, Bessie O. P. Vonnoh, Solon Borglum

Boston: Arthur B. Davies: 71st anniversary exhibition; Portraits of F. W. Benson, L. M. Genth, Frank Currier; Landscapes of Weir, W. J. Kaula, Walter Nettleton

Art Briefs

Ernest Lawson joins the New York Realists, Henri's "revolutionary black gang," who join the Academy of the Society of American Artists • The Cloisters is designed by its first curator, James J. Rorimer, in conjunction with architect Charles Collene • The Chelsea Hotel, N.Y.C., is redesigned as a cooperative (1884) • The Fraunces Tavern of 1763, in N.Y.C., is completely rebuilt by William Mersereau • Photographer Edward Steichen wins the gold medal at the Brussels Fine Arts Exhibition • Italian sculptor Ernesto Biondi sues the Metropolitan for failure to exhibit publicly his *Saturnalia*—a large group of figures representing in realistic fashion an episode of a Roman Saturnalia • Mary Cassatt wins a $500 award in Chicago, after receiving a similar award at the Pennsylvania Academy of Art last year • In Philadelphia, a painting attributed to Andrea del Sarto, *Holy Father,* brings a disappointing $200. The highest auction sale is $40,200 for Anton Mauve's *Sheep Coming Out of the Forest,* followed by Jean-François Millet's *Close of Day,* which brings $13,800.

William J. Glackens, *Chez Mouquin,* 1905, oil, 121.9 x 99.1 cm, Friends of American Art Collection, *The Art Institute of Chicago*

Books

Fiction

Critics' Choice

The Troll Garden, Willa Cather
From Farm to Fortune, Horatio Alger (posthumous)
The Line of Love, James Branch Cabell
The White Terror and the Red: A Novel of Revolutionary Russia, Abraham Cahan
Told by Uncle Remus: New Stories of the Old Plantation, Joel Chandler Harris
Visionaries, James Huneker
The Game, Jack London
The Tyranny of the Dark, Hamlin Garland
The Debtor, Mary E. Wilkins Freedom
The Memoirs of an American Citizen, Robert Herrick
The Empty Purse: A Christmas Story, Sarah Orne Jewett

Best-Sellers

The Marriage of William Ashe, Mrs. Humphrey Ward
Sandy, Alice Hegan Rice

The Garden of Allah, Robert Hichens
The Clansman, Thomas Dixon, Jr.
Nedra, George Barr McCutcheon
The Gambler, Katherine Cecil Thurston
The Masquerader, Anonymous
The House of Mirth, Edith Wharton
The Princess Passes, C. N. and A. M. Williamson
Rose o' the River, Kate Douglas Wiggin

Nonfiction

Critics' Choice

Iconoclasts: A Book of Dramatists, James Gibbons Huneker
George Bernard Shaw: His Plays, H. L. Mencken
Sir Walter Raleigh, The First and Last Journeys of Thoreau, Henry David Thoreau (posthumous)
The War of the Classes, Jack London
Our Bourgeois Literature, Upton Sinclair
Recreations of an Anthologist, Brander Matthews

Philosopher and poet George Santayana is a self-avowed "materialist" who seeks to "honor the piety and understand the poetry" of religion.

❧ *Futurist Manifesto,* F. T. Marinetti
❧ *De Profoundis,* Oscar Wilde (posthumous)
❧ *Experience and Poetry,* Wilhelm Dilthey

Poems

Paul Laurence Dunbar, *Chris'mus Is A-Comin' and Other Poems*
Edgar Lee Masters, *The Blood of the Prophets*
Eugene Field, *Hoosier Lyrics*
James Whitcomb Riley, *Riley's Songs o' Cheer*
Trumbull Stickney, *Poems*
❧ Rainer Maria Rilke, *The Book of Hours*

Science and Technology

George W. Crile performs the first direct blood transfusion.
Alexis Carrel sutures blood vessels and restores a patient's circulation.
Albert Einhorn introduces novocaine, a local anesthetic.
J. B. Murphy develops the first artificial joints, arthroplasty, for use in arthritic hip replacement.
Clarence McClung discovers that male mammals have an X-shaped chromosome paired with a Y-shaped chromosome, whereas females have two X chromosomes.
Percival Lowell predicts that a ninth planet beyond Neptune will be found.
In their *Flyer III,* the Wright brothers stay aloft over 30 minutes and circle in figure eights.
Guglielmo Marconi develops the first directional radio antenna.
❧ Albert Einstein's first paper on the special theory of relativity proposes that the speed of light is the only constant.
❧ Einstein's second paper on relativity states that energy and mass are interchangeable, according to the formula $e=mc^2$.

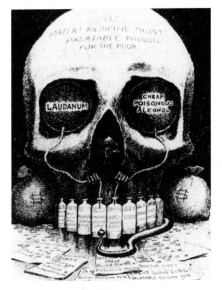

Collier's exposé of patent medicine-makers: laudanum, an opiate, was responsible for the death of a Cincinnati child whose doctor prescribed Bull's cough syrup.

❧ Alfred Binet and Théodore Simon develop an intelligence measuring test ("IQ").
❧ The cause of syphilis, *Spirocheta pallida,* is discovered.

Sports

Baseball

The World Series is renewed under National
Commission supervision; it becomes the best of 7.

Attendance continues to rise, with the AL still outpacing
the NL.

Winning the pennant again, John McGraw's Giants beat
Connie Mack's Athletics; Christy Mathewson
pitches 3 shutouts and Joe McGinnity a 4th in the
Giants' WS win.

Pitchers Chief Bender, Rube Waddell, and Eddie Plank
are the Philadelphia stars.

Ty Cobb debuts.

Baseball hero Napoleon "Larry" Lajoie ad: "Lajoie chews Red Devil Tobacco—Ask him if he don't."

Champions

Batting	Pitching
John Seymour (Cincinnati, NL), .377	Sam Leever (Pittsburgh, NL), 20–5
Elmer Flick (Cleveland, AL) .306	Rube Waddell (Philadelphia, AL) 27–10
	Home runs
	Frank Odwell (Cincinnati, NL), 9

Football

TR threatens to abolish the college game by executive
edict if rough play is not curtailed. Eighteen deaths and
over 150 serious injuries have occurred during the
season. Roosevelt has been incensed by a newspaper
photo of Swarthmore's Maxwell, a very large player
who had been attacked by the entire Penn team. A rules
committee legalizes the forward pass, to begin in 1906,
and eliminates certain dangerous scrimmage plays. The
Michigan team outscores its opponents, 501–2, but loses
its last game and the national title to Chicago, 2–0.
Coach "Hurry Up" Yost has led Michigan to a 27–1–1
record over five years, during which it outscored the
opposition 2,821 to 42. Michigan star Willie Heston is
offered $600 to play in a pro game between the Canton
Bulldogs and Massillon Tigers (Ohio) but is injured on
the first play, which ends his pro career.

College All-Americans: Walter Eckersall (Q), Chicago;
John Hubbard (HB), Amherst; Francis Burr (G), Harvard

Basketball

Christian Steinmetz, Wisconsin, scores an unheard-of 50
points in a game.

The Buffalo Germans, who gave the Olympic
demonstration of basketball in 1904, turn pro with
Forrest ("Phog") Allen as coach.

Other Sports

The first Intercollegiate Athletic Association is formed
to set standards for college athletics.

Boxing: Jim Jeffries retires as HW champ and referees
the Marvin Hart-Jack Root fight to succeed him; Hart
wins by KO in 12; Jeffries denies "giving away" the title.

Tennis: May Sutton is the first foreigner to win at
Wimbledon. Elizabeth Moore wins her 4th U.S. Open.

Golf: Willie Anderson wins his 4th U.S. Open in 5
years.

Winners

World Series	U.S. Tennis Open
New York (NL) 4	Men: Beals C. Wright
Philadelphia (AL) 1	Women: Elizabeth Moore
College Football	*USGA Open*
Chicago	Willie Anderson
College Basketball	*Kentucky Derby*
Columbia	Agile (Jack Martin, jockey)
Player of the Year	
Christian Steinmetz, Wisconsin	

Fashion

The new technology—the auto—dramatically affects
style. Large linen coats are worn over dresses; hats are
tied down with numerous oversize scarves, and
dustproof veils accompany huge goggles. Long boots
are a "must" for protection against a car mired in mud
or one totally disabled, after which the driver must walk
home. A flat tweed hat, while unbecoming, becomes
stylish, a symbol of the new motoring class. The
wealthiest women distinguish themselves with leather
coats and skirts of the same "amazingly short" length,
barely reaching the ankle; these pioneer motorists also
wear leather bloomers to below the knee. Women soon
discover gabardine as a replacement for heavier leather.

*High-fashion note: Embroidered belts that are
washable, along with elasticized, tailored French kid
belts studded with steel nail heads and a* harness *buckle;
silk, beaded, elasticized, and French kid belts are
reserved for gentler amusements.*

Kaleidoscope

- "We repudiate the monstrous doctrine that the oppressor should be the sole authority as to the rights of the oppressed. . . . Any discrimination based on color is barbarous," says W. E. B. Du Bois who, with 29 other blacks, meet at Niagara Falls (hence the Niagara Movement), to end racial discrimination in America.
- Medical researchers learn that the public fears yellow fever more than any other disease.
- Nickelodeons open in many cities, with combinations of movies and vaudeville acts; their 5¢ admission affords family entertainment for even the poor.
- "There can be no peace so long as hunger and want are found among millions of working people, and the few, who make up the employing class, have all the good things of life. . . . It is the historic mission of the working class to do away with capitalism," proclaims the IWW Preamble.
- TR reprimands American writers for overlooking their native surroundings in favor of European glamour: "The Bowery is one of the great highways of humanity, . . . of seething life, . . . of fun, of work, of sordid and terrible tragedy."
- "The accident of our finding certain opinions . . . novel or even shocking . . . [is not in] conflict with the Constitution," asserts "the great dissenter," Oliver Wendell Holmes.
- House debate continues over whether patent medicines should list their ingredients; many cures consist of cocaine, morphine, and alcohol; Massachusetts rejects the bill.
- Congress discontinues coinage of gold dollars, minted since 1849.
- The remains of John Paul Jones are placed in Annapolis.
- The last surviving soldier of the War of 1812, Hiram Cronk, 105, dies.
- A. B. Stroenger, an undertaker, invents the dial telephone.
- The Asiatic Exclusion League continues its efforts to ban Japanese immigration.
- The Chinese boycott U.S. goods to protest American treatment of upper-class Chinese tourists.
- All ships on North Atlantic routes use the Marconi radio system.
- U.S. auto production increases to 25,000 (2,500, in 1899).
- Arthur MacDonald at Daytona Beach sets a new auto speed record of 104.65 mph.
- Tiffany & Co. makes its largest sale, a $1 million pearl necklace.
- Elastic rubber replaces whalebone and lace in women's undergarments, providing greater comfort.
- Women in nonagricultural pursuits have more than doubled over the past ten years to 4.3 million (2 million, in 1880); clerical work with new machinery requires greater skills and offers better pay.
- Actress Lily Langtry asks her manager to place a carpet outside her dressing room so that she can keep her hems clean; the carpet is red.
- Theater curtains have ads painted on them.
- Willie Hoppe, 18, barnstorms as "the boy wonder" of pool.
- The Wright brothers fly a 24.5-mile circle in 3 minutes at Daytona; they tour widely in the U.S. and abroad.

- About 100 people own over 17 million acres of the Sacramento Valley, Calif., in the San Joaquin area; others own areas of at least 100,000 acres.
- The average American farmer cultivates 12 acres of land.
- Following a big oil strike, wildcat prospectors head for Tulsey Town, Okla., which becomes "the Oil capital of the World."
- The Five Tribes of the Indian Territory propose their own state, "Sequoyah," but Sen. Albert Beveridge (R—Ind.) believes that the Territory should be joined to Oklahoma in a single "American" state; TR agrees.
- Ray Stannard Baker, 35, puts "The Railroads on Trial" in *McClure's* and urges government regulation.
- Whether graft can be avoided by public ownership of utilities and public transportation becomes an issue in large cities.
- The $1,750,000 New York Hippodrome opens with the musical extravaganza *A Yankee Circus on Mars,* a new kind of spectacle.
- Arnold Daly presents a cycle of George Bernard Shaw's plays at the N.Y. Garrick: *Candida, The Man of Destiny, How He Lied to Her Husband, You Never Can Tell, John Bull's Other Island,* and *Mrs. Warren's Profession;* the last play is stopped during production, and two actors are arrested.
- "My plays advocate moral reform. I don't care what is said about me. . . or when my plays are prohibited by the police. . . . What I fight against is the immorality of the old morality," says George Bernard Shaw after *Mrs. Warren's Profession* is banned.
- Worldwide attention is given Russian musicians who sign a protest against the oppression of the Czar's government; they include Rimsky-Korsakov, Rachmaninoff, Glière, and Chaliapin.
- A talented Vachel Lindsay joins Henri's painting course at the Art Students League, but Henri advises him to follow his even more unusual poetic gift.

Fads: picture postcards in sepia, tabulating machines

First Appearances: Shaker Heights suburb (owned by the Shaker Church), cigarette testimonial by celebrity (Fatty Arbuckle, on Murads), Palmolive soap, Vicks VapoRub, Royal Crown cola, Ovomaltine ("Ovaltine"), cellophane (J. Edwin Brandenburger), non-shatter safety glass, Anchor Hocking glass, Royal typewriter, Spiegel mail order catalog, *Variety,* Institute of Musical Art, double-sided gramophone records, multiphone (71 pre-selective jukebox), Rotary Club of America, National Audubon Society, Bureau of Forestry (Gifford Pinchot, chief), Devils Tower and Petrified Forest National Parks, third rail system (LIRR), Staten Island Ferry, Carnegie Foundation for the Advancement of Teaching ($10 million), Bethlehem Steel

1906

At Germany's request and an indication of the U.S.'s importance in world affairs, Secretary of War Elihu Root mediates the French-German conflict in Morocco.

In the News

BRITAIN LAUNCHES *DREADNOUGHT,* WORLD'S MOST POWERFUL WARSHIP . . . MT. VESUVIUS ERUPTS, THOUSANDS DIE . . . EARTHQUAKE DEVASTATES SAN FRANCISCO, OVER 400 ARE DEAD . . . CHINA AGREES TO BRITISH RULE IN TIBET . . . CZAR DISSOLVES DUMA . . . TWO BLACKS ARE BURNED TO DEATH IN OHIO BEFORE CHEERING CROWD . . . SUPREME COURT RULES CORPORATION HEADS MUST TESTIFY IN ANTI-TRUST CASES . . . 3,000 IN PARIS ARE ARRESTED IN MAY DAY MARCH . . . U.S. SUPPRESSES MORO REBELLION IN PHILIPPINES, 600 ARE KILLED . . . UPTON SINCLAIR'S *JUNGLE* REVEALS SHOCKING DETAILS OF MEATPACKING INDUSTRY . . . HEPBURN ACT GIVES ICC POWER TO REGULATE RAILROAD AND PIPELINE RATES . . . PURE FOOD AND DRUG ACT REQUIRES HONEST CONTENT LABELING, PROHIBITS SALE OF ADULTERATED FOOD . . . CONGRESS PASSES MEAT INSPECTION ACT . . . MILLIONAIRE HARRY THAW IS ACCUSED OF MURDERING FAMED ARCHITECT STANFORD WHITE IN JEALOUS RAGE . . . FRENCH COURT REVERSES DREYFUS TREASON CONVICTION, HONORS HIM IN PUBLIC . . . CUBA REQUESTS U.S. INTERVENTION IN REBELLION, TR SENDS TROOPS . . . MISSIONARY'S SON IS ACCUSED OF MURDERING PREGNANT SHOPGIRL GRACE BROWN . . . 21 DIE IN ATLANTA RACE RIOT, CITY IS PLACED UNDER MARTIAL LAW . . . SAN FRANCISCO ORDERS SCHOOL SEGREGATION OF ASIAN CHILDREN . . . TR VISITS PANAMA CANAL, FIRST SITTING PRESIDENT TO GO ABROAD . . . JAPANESE LAUNCH *SATSUMA,* WORLD'S LARGEST BATTLESHIP . . . EPISCOPAL MINISTER ALGERNON CRAPSEY IS CONVICTED OF HERESY ON CHURCH CLAIM OF MARXIST INFLUENCE . . . STANDARD OIL IS CONVICTED OF ANTITRUST VIOLATIONS IN OHIO.

Quotes

"I swear upon thy white hair that I am innocent."
—Enrico Caruso's cable to his father in Italy,
after being fined $10 for molesting a woman
in the Central Park Zoo monkey house by touching
her left forearm with his right elbow

"A Word to the Wise
Why New Orleans Should Have this Directory . . .
First. Because it is the only district of its kind in the States set aside for the fast women by *law*.
Second. Because it puts the stranger in a proper path . . . secure from hold-ups, brace games and other illegal practices usually worked on the unwise in Red Light Districts."
—Preface to the *Blue Book,* a guide to the red-light
district in New Orleans

"There was not the least attention to what was cut up for sausage. . . . These rats were a nuisance, and the packers would put poisoned bread out for them. They would die, and then rats, bread, and meat would go into the hoppers together."
—Upton Sinclair, *The Jungle*

"Rubinstein is very young [and] very immature, so far as the sorrows which make the great artists are concerned. . . . Let some American girl . . . twist his heartstrings [and] Rubinstein will be the greatest of all pianists.
—*Musical America,* following the pianist's debut

"The men with the muckrackers are often indispensable to the well being of society; but only if they know when to stop raking the mud and look upward."
—TR, on investigative journalists

"Are we going to take up the question as to what a man shall eat and what a man shall drink, and put him under severe penalties if [it] is different from what the chemists of the Agricultural Department think desirable?"
—Nelson W. Aldrich (R—R.I.),
opposing the Pure Food and Drug Bill

"The moral flabbiness born of the exclusive worship of the bitch-goddess SUCCESS—that, with the squalid cash interpretation put on the word success—is our national disease."
—William James

"A human creature must do human work; and all women are no more to be contented as house servants and housekeepers than all men would be."
—Suffragette Charlotte Perkins Gilman

"Nothing has spread socialist feeling in this country more than the use of the automobile. To the countryman, they are a picture of the arrogance of wealth, with all its independence and carelessness."
—Woodrow Wilson, president of Princeton University

"We have got to support France against Germany and fortify the Atlantic system beyond attack, for if Germany breaks down England or France she becomes the center of a military world, and we are lost."
—TR, on the Moroccan crisis

Politics: "A strife of interests masquerading as a contest of principles."
Diplomacy: "The patriotic art of lying for one's country."
—Ambrose Bierce, *Devil's Dictionary*

Ads

1906

Mulberry Street pushcart peddlers, who sell virtually anything; many save enough money to open their own grocery, butcher, or hardware stores.

The San Francisco earthquake, the greatest natural disaster in American history, starts a three-day fire during which four square miles in the heart of the city are destroyed.

Vaudeville

Keith and Albee expand to merge leading U.S. and Canadian houses; with so many theaters to work with, Keith and Albee handle those in the East; Martin Beck, those in the West. The Hammerstein Victoria Theatre, N.Y.C., earns a net profit of $250,000, despite its $250,000–$300,000 maintenance costs. Keith's Orpheum theaters in Brooklyn and New York earn $200,000. An estimated 39 million people see vaudeville during the year. The Shubert brothers take over management of the Hippodrome, built in 1904–05, the block-long theater between 43rd and 44th Streets and 6th Avenue, N.Y.C.

Of Note

London actress Lily Langtry debuts in a miniplay • Irene Franklin gains increased fame for demonstrating a breadth of human emotion in her face • Particularly popular animal acts include "Fink's Mules," a multi-animal sketch, where a stereotyped black tries to ride the mule; "Swains's Birds," billed as "Feathered Thespians, featuring Jean, the Only Trained Eagle in Vaudeville"; and Ferrero's Dog Museum, where dogs play bells and perform acrobatics • Statuesque blonde

Louise Dresser debuts and is talked of as Lillian Russell's future successor • Anna Held, married to Florenz Ziegfeld, is credited both for her "I Can't Make My Eyes Behave" (in addition to an 18-inch waist) and encouraging her husband to begin the *Follies* • The first "master of ceremonies" appears, James Morton, who soon earns $2,000 a week; a former star, he now stands at the side of the stage and comments on the acts.

Anna Held, Mrs. Florenz Ziegfeld, who loves milk baths.

Movies

The Dream of a Rarebit Fiend (Edwin Porter for
    Edison), imitation of Méliès's first trick film
Automobile Thieves (Vitagraph)
The Black Hand (Biograph)
Married for Millions (Biograph), controversial, vulgar
    slapstick
Ben Hur (Kalem), spectacle, in 16 scenes and sued for
    nonacquisition rights from Lew Wallace's novel

Thomas Edison invents the cameraphone for potential sound movies, which synchronizes the phonograph and visual projection. Pathé and Vitagraph publish *Views and Film Index* magazine, a list of film selections with informative commentary; *Billboard* reports "the growth of the film business"—30 nickelodeons in Coney Island alone; 10, in Atlantic City; 100, in both Cincinnati and

Cleveland. William Swanson and Carl Laemmle open a film rental service in Chicago, which becomes the capital of the film rental market. Laemmle finds Pathé films so popular that he advertises them as "right off the reel from foreign shores." Vitagraph's narrative films, rental plans, and distribution services gain enormous power in the industry; with its own producers and story makers, it opens the first studio during the nickelodeon age. Selig gains prominence after *The Jungle* is published, and its images of the stockyards come into demand.

Popular Players

Florence Turner (the future "Vitagraph Girl" and hired at $18 a week; she doubles as an actress and a wardrobe mistress), Maurice Costello, Paul Panzer, Lawrence Trimble, John Bunny, Gladys Hulette

Popular Music

Hit Songs

"You're a Grand Old Flag"
"Hottentot Love Song"
"On San Francisco Bay"
"Chinatown, My Chinatown"
"Why Do They Call Me a Gibson Girl?"
"In Old New York"
"The Linger Longer Girl"
"Two Dirty Little Hands"
"Waiting at the Church"
"Ain't You Coming Back to Old New Hampshire, Molly?"

Representative Recordings:

"Everybody Works But Father" (Billy Murray); "How'd You Like to Spoon with Me?" (Corinne / Morgan and Haydn Quartet); "So Long, Mary" (Corinne / Morgan); "Nobody" (Bert Williams); "The Good Old U.S.A." (Byron G. Harlan); "Love Me and the World Is Mine" (Albert Campbell); "Let It Alone" (Bert Williams)

Jazz

Most of the new music has a mingling of all strains in "free counterpoint," played by three melody instruments—the trumpet (cornet), the lead; trombone, contrasting with the lead; and clarinet, intertwining with the two. Behind these is the rhythm section: bass band, banjo, drums, strings, and guitar. Rhythms follow the European marches with the stress on the first and third beat, the second and fourth not yet always accented. The word "hot" refers to the intensity of the new phrasing and the music's emotional quality. Instruments still seek to substitute for the human voice, as they communicate the performer's feelings. "Buddy" Bolden begins to show signs of mental deterioration, and his band disintegrates. His influence is deeply felt by Freddie Keppard, Bunk Johnson, and other New Orleans cornetists, who help standardize New Orleans jazz ensembles and their repertory. Ferdinand "Jelly Roll" Morton gives St. Louis rag style a heavy beat in his "King Porter Stomp."

Theater

Broadway Openings

Plays

The Clansman (Thomas Dixon), Holbrook Blinn
The Kreutzer Sonata (Jacob Gordin, two independent productions), Blanche Walsh/Berthe Kalich
The Hypocrites (Henry Arthur Jones), Richard Bennett, John Glendinning
Brewster's Millions (Winchell Smith, Byron Ongley), George Spelvin, Edward Abeles
Caesar and Cleopatra (George Bernard Shaw), Johnston Forbes-Robertson, Gertrude Elliott
Pioneer Days (Carroll Fleming), W. H. Clark, J. P. Coombs
The Man of the Hour (George Broadhurst), George Fawcett, Douglas Fairbanks
The New York Idea (Langsdon Mitchell), George Arliss, Dudley Digges
The Great Divide (William Vaughan Moody), Margaret Anglin, Henry Miller, Laura Hope Crews
The House of Mirth (Edith Wharton, Clyde Fitch), Fay Davis, Charles Bryant

W. C. Fields begins his career as a comedy juggler.

The Four Cohans, who began as vaudevillians, achieve their greatest success on Broadway, in nostalgic and patriotic shows written by son George M. (far right).

Musicals

The Red Mill (Victor Herbert), Montgomery & Stone, Augusta Greenleaf
About Town (Melville Ellis, Raymond Hubbell, Joseph Herbert), Lew Fields, Edna Wallace Hopper, Louise Dresser, Vernon Castle, Mary Murray
Forty-Five Minutes from Broadway (George M. Cohan), Fay Templeton, Lois Ewell, Donald Brian
George Washington, Jr. (George M. Cohan), The Four Cohans, Ethel Levey
The Rich Mr. Hoggenheimer (Ludwig Englander, Harry B. Smith), Sam Bernard
Twiddle-Twaddle (Maurice Levi, Edgar Smith), Joe Weber, Charles A. Bigelow, Marie Dressler
A Parisian Model (Max Hoffman, Henry B. Smith), Anna Held, Charles A. Bigelow
The Chorus Lady (James Forbes), Rose Stahl

Classics and Revivals On and Off Broadway

H. B. Irving–Dorothea Baird Repertory: *Paolo and Francesca* (Phillips); *Cymbeline,* Henry J. Hadford, Viola Ellen; *Arms and the Man; Charley's Aunt,* Arnold Daly, John Findlay

Classical Music _____

Composition

George Chadwick, Overture, *Euterpe*
Charles Ives, *The Unanswered Question, The Pond, Two Contemplations*
Frederick S. Converse, *Jeanne d'Arc*
Henry Hadley, *Salome* (1905–06), Symphony no. 3
Percy Grainger, *Green Bushes*
Henry Gilbert, *Dance in the Place Congo*

Important Events

Alexander Scriabin makes his U.S. debut as a pianist, performing his own piano concerto with the Russian Symphony Orchestra in N.Y.C. Felix Weingartner conducts the New York Symphony Orchestra. Olga Samaroff makes her first appearance with the St. Louis Choral Symphony. Following the earthquake, all activities of the San Francisco Orchestra are suspended indefinitely.

Major Recitals: Jan Kubelik, Marie Hall

New Appointments: Karl Muck, Boston Symphony Orchestra; Vassily Safonov, New York Philharmonic

Debuts: Artur Rubinstein (Camille Saint-Saëns, Concerto in G minor, Franz Liszt, *The Mephisto Waltz,* with the Philadelphia Orchestra, Carnegie Hall), Josef Lhévinne (Mozart, Chopin, and Scriabin, with the Russian Symphony Orchestra)

First Performances

Gustav Mahler, Fifth Symphony (New York); Jean Sibelius, Violin Concerto (Boston); Ernest Bloch, *Hiver-Printemps* (New York); Vása Suk, *Orchestral*

Lina Abarbanell debuts in the operetta *The Student King.*

Scherzo (New York); Charles Martin Loeffler, *A Pagan Poem* (Boston)

Opera

Metropolitan: Orchestra seats sell for $5. Premieres: Lina Abarbanell, Bella Alten, Marion Weed, Otto Goritz, *Hansel and Gretel* (Humperdinck); Andreas Dippel, Alten, Louise Homer, Goritz, *Der Zigeunerbaron* (Richard Strauss). Henrich Knote, Lillian Nordica, Homer, Goritz, *Lohengrin;* Marcella Sembrich, Enrico Caruso, Pol Plançon, *La sonnambula* (Bellini); Antonio Scotti, Nordica, Dippel, Marcel Journet, *Don Giovanni* (celebration of Mozart's 150th birthday); Sembrich, Caruso, Edyth Walker, Plançon, *Martha;* Caruso, Lina Cavalieri (debut), *Fedora;* Geraldine Farrar (debut), Charles Rousselière, Plançon, *Romeo and Juliet;* Farrar, *The Damnation of Faust;* Alessandro Boni (debut), Luisa Tetrazzini, *I Puritani* (Bellini)

Manhattan (opening): Renowned European conductor Cleofanti Campanini is brought to the U.S. as artistic director. Bonci, *I Puritani;* Maurice Renaud, *Don Giovanni;* Renaud, *Rigoletto;* Clotilde Bressler-Gianoli, *Carmen*

San Francisco: Caruso, Olive Fremsted, *Carmen* (after which the earthquake occurs)

Chicago: Edyth Walker, Marie Rappold, *The Queen of Sheba;* Emma Eames, Caruso, Scotti, Plançon, *Faust*

Cleveland: *Valdo* (Henry Lawrence Freeman)

Buffalo: *The Red Mill* (Victor Herbert)

Springfield: *The Free Lance* (John Philip Sousa)

Music Notes

German-born opera impresario Oscar Hammerstein opens a company to rival the Met, the Manhattan Opera, and gains exclusive contract rights with singers and composers; his company earns a substantial profit as the Met suffers its first deficit • Saint-Saëns visits the U.S. • Ruggiero Leoncavallo, on his first U.S. tour, conducts his own work in N.Y. and concludes with *Vivva l'America,* dedicated to Teddy Roosevelt, and variations of "Yankee Doodle" and "Dixie" • His health increasingly deteriorated after his dispute with Columbia University, a transom accident, and tertiary syphilis, Edward MacDowell elicits wide public support from Horatio Parker, Arthur Foote, Victor Herbert, George Chadwick, Frank Converse, Andrew Carnegie, J. P. Morgan, and former President Grover Cleveland, among others.

Art

Kodak's box camera enables scenes of childhood friendship to endure forever.

At Oscar Hammerstein's Manhattan Opera Company, one can buy two opera tickets for the price of one ($6); this, along with the talented company he organizes, forces the Met to buy him out and agree to never again produce opera in New York City.

Painting

John Sloan, *The Picnic Grounds* (1905–06), *Dolly with a Black Bow*
Arthur B. Davies, *Unicorns*
Glenn O. Coleman, *Street Bathers*
Albert Pinkham Ryder, *Lord Villin's Daughter*
Arthur Burnett, *Frost, Cutting Ice*
Willard Metcalf, *May Night*

Sculpture

Frederic Remington, *The Outlaw*
Solon Borglum, *Bronco Buster*
Robert Tait McKenzie, *The Competition*
Alma Hyatt Huntington, *Reaching Jaguar*

Important Exhibitions

New York: *Metropolitan:* Acquisitions: Holbein, Van Dyck. *Knoedler:* Théobald Chartran portraits

Architecture

Pierpont Morgan Library, N.Y.C. (McKim, Mead & White, 1902–06)
David Boyden house, Berkeley (Bernard Maybeck)
Madison Square Presbyterian Church, N.Y.C. (Stanford White)
Hopps house, Moss Valley, Calif. (Bernard Maybeck)
L. A. Robinson house, Pasadena, Calif. (Greene & Greene)
Second Singer building, N.Y.C. (Ernest Flagg)
DeWitt Clinton High School, 10th Avenue, N.Y.C. (C. B. J. Snyder)
Stuyvesant High School, East 15th Street, N.Y.C. (C. B. J. Snyder)
St. Thomas Church, N.Y.C. (George B. Post)

Boston: Sargent; Whistler; Monet; Women's art

Chicago: Frederick W. Freer; Belle Silveira; Herb W. Faulkner's Venetian studies; Maude I. J. Oliver; "Artists of the Glasgow School." Purchases: works of Van Dyke, Reynolds, Gainsborough; plaster cast of *Alma Mater* (Daniel Chester French), three bronze statuettes of Egyptian deities

St. Louis: Western artists; Corot; Reynolds; Lepine; Monet; Sisley

Nashville: American art

Rhode Island School of Design: Ten American printers, including H. Cyrus, Farnham, Dryer; Dudley Murphy's oils

Art Briefs

Henri, Sloan, Glackens, and Luks hold a group show, described by one critic as "overbabied" • Many of the New York Realists teach at the Art Students League, and although explicit French literature is available to all, the Purity League will not allow students to paint nudes as their instructors demonstrate • George B. Matthews works on a mammoth canvas (18′ x 9′) of Robert E. Lee surrounded by his staff, to be exhibited at the Jamestown Exhibition in 1907 • J. P. Morgan works full-time to complete and furnish his new gallery on East 36th Street, N.Y.C.; already purchased are $1 million of Oriental rugs and carpets, rare books, antiquities, and tapestries.

Books

Fiction

Critics' Choice

White Fang, Jack London
The Four Million, O. Henry
Worshippers, Henry Berman
Romance Island, Zona Gale
A Lady of Rome, F. Marion
    Crawford
Love Among the Chickens, P. G.
    Wodehouse
The Joyous Miracle, Frank Norris
    (posthumous)
Spirit of the Border, Zane Grey
In Pastures New, George Ade
Joe the Hotel Boy, Horatio Alger
    (posthumous)
*The $30,000 Bequest and Other
    Stories, Eve's Diary,* Mark Twain
Doc Gordon, Mary E. Freeman
    Wilkins
❧ *The Man of Property,* John
    Galsworthy

Best-Sellers

Coniston, Winston Churchill
Lady Baltimore, Owen Wister
The House of a Thousand Candles,
    Meredith Nicholson
Jane Cable, George Barr
    McCutcheon
The Jungle, Upton Sinclair

The Awakening of Helena Ritchie,
    Margaret Deland
The Spoilers, Rex Beach
The House of Mirth, Edith
    Wharton
The Wheel of Life, Ellen Glasgow

Nonfiction

Critics' Choice

*The Life of Reason: or The Phases
    of Human Progress,* George
    Santayana (1905–06)
Journals, Henry David Thoreau
    (posthumous), 4 vols.
What Is Man? Mark Twain
Dissertations by Mr. Dooley, Finley
    Peter Dunne
Walt Whitman at Camden, Horace
    Traubel
The Devil's Dictionary, Ambrose
    Bierce
*The Education of Black People: Ten
    Critiques,* W. E. B. Du Bois
Man, the Social Creator, Henry
    George
What Life Means to Me, Upton
    Sinclair
Dixie after the War, Myrta Lockett
    Avary
❧ *The Quest for the Historical
    Jesus,* Albert Schweitzer

O. Henry's short stories, with their
surprise endings, are best-sellers; *Four
Million* is based on his belief that
everyone in New York has "a story
worth telling."

Poems

Paul Laurence Dunbar, *Joggin'
    Erlong*
James Russell Lowell, *Four Poems*
James Whitcomb Riley, *While the
    Heart Beats Young*
George Santayana, *Sonnets and
    Other Verses*
❧ W. B. Yeats, *Poems, 1899–1905*

Science and Technology

Reginald Aubrey Fessenden invents AM radio, which
    can transmit voice and sound.
Lee De Forest invents a three-electrode vacuum tube
    amplifier that revolutionizes radio.
The tungsten filament light bulb, a vast improvement
    over earlier bulbs, is invented.

Lee De Forest, "the father
of radio," develops the
"audion" tube, which
enables a loudspeaker to
replace headphones.

Columbia University's Thomas Hunt develops the use of
    the fruit fly *Drosophila* to study the mechanisms of
    heredity.
Howard T. Ricketts discovers that spotted fever is
    transmitted through cattle ticks.
Richard Dixon Oldham's research reveals that the earth
    has a core.
❧ Paul Ehrlich develops the first synthetic drug,
    Atoxyl, to treat an infectious agent, the
    trypanosome that causes sleeping sickness.
❧ The bacterium responsible for whooping cough is
    isolated.
❧ J. J. Thomson demonstrates that a hydrogen atom has
    only one electron; Ernest Rutherford, that the alpha
    particle is a helium nucleus.
❧ Each element is found to have a characteristic effect
    on X-ray beam scattering.
❧ The Wasserman blood test for syphilis is invented.

Sports

Baseball

The Chicago Cubs, managed by "Peerless Leader" Frank Chance and led by the double-play combination of "Tinker-to-Evers-to-Chance" and pitcher Mordecai ("Three-Finger") Brown, win a record 116 games but lose to the "hitless wonders," the Chicago White Sox.

Champions

Batting
Honus Wagner (Pittsburgh, NL), .339
George Stone (St. Louis, AL), .358
Pitching
Ed Ruelbach (Chicago, NL), 19–4

Eddie Plank (Philadelphia, AL), 19–6
Home runs
Tim Jordan (Brooklyn, NL)
Henry Davis (Philadelphia, AL), 12

Football

The forward pass becomes legal, and the neutral zone is enhanced; the "first" pass is by St. Louis, from Robinson Brandburg to Jack Schneider. An attempt to fix a game by a Canton coach and Massillon players leads to a national scandal, and the pro teams disband.

College All-Americans: Walter Eckersall (Q), Chicago; Francis Burr (G), Harvard; John Mayhew (HB), Brown

Basketball: Small Midwestern schools led by Wabash take an active interest in the game.

Olympics

The games, played at Athens, Greece, are not accepted by the International Olympics Committee; the U.S. wins 12 gold, France, 15. Americans who win include Paul Pilgrim (400m, 53.3s., 800m, 2:01.2), Jim Lightbody (1500m, 4:12), Ray Ewry (standing high and broad jump), Meyer Prinztein (running broad jump, 23'7.5"). Charles Daniels wins in swimming (100m).

Other Sports

Boxing: Marvin Hart loses the HW title to Tommy Burns in 20 rounds. "Philadelphia Jack" O'Brien fights HW champ Burns to a 29-round draw in L.A.

Horse Racing: The great trotter Dan Patch does the mile in 1:55.

Winners

World Series
Chicago (AL) 4
Chicago (NL) 2
College Football
Princeton
College Basketball
Dartmouth
Player of the Year
George Grebenstein, Dartmouth

U.S. Tennis Open
Men: William Clothier
Women: Helen Homans
USGA Open
Alex Smith
Kentucky Derby
Sir Huon (Roscoe Troxlew, jockey)

Fashion

For Children: Stylishly dressed little boys from 3 to 10 wear sailor suits or Russian blouse suits in a variety of fabrics—French or English chambray, cotton, khaki, linen, English percale, and imported wool serge. Girls from 2 to 6 are presented with an enormous variety of dresses—of various fabrics with the popular high front yoke and embroidery of Vale lace. Embroidered tucks and beads may be added, as well as satin ribbon rosettes.

Lined coats are made of wool, pongee, broadcloth, Cheviot, and cashmere. A toddler's lined, short coat in cream cashmere costs $3.49.

High-fashion note: For women, a blue chiffon taffeta dress with a yoke of lighter shade in velvet; the yoke is trimmed with fancy white silk braid and cut to a pointed tab in the front.

Alice Roosevelt. "I can be president of the U.S. or Alice's father; but I can't do both," quips TR of his vivacious suffragette daughter.

A celebration dinner of wealthy businessmen adorned in laurel wreaths.

Kaleidoscope _____

- About two-thirds of San Francisco is destroyed by the earthquake on April 18; over 450 die, and 250,000 are left homeless.
- Oscar Hammerstein, with his new Manhattan Opera Company, rivals the Met, engaging leading vocalists like Luisa Tetrazzini and outstanding European and fresh U.S. talents like Mary Garden, and bringing back Nellie Melba, the most acclaimed *prima donna* of the day; his company enjoys profits as the Met loses income.
- When Alexander Scriabin makes his piano debut in New York, the scandal that he is traveling with a woman to whom he is not married forces him to cancel the remainder of his tour.
- TR's praise of E. A. Robinson's poetry introduces Robinson to a large audience.
- The *North American Review* reports that more people have died in cars over a five-month period than during the entire Spanish American War.
- Hammacher Schlemmer sells 35 tools to "fully equip your car" for $25.
- Some motorists frighten pedestrians by driving 10 mph; many anger them with their cars' gold and ruby emblems.
- After the San Francisco earthquake, Enrico Caruso and Antonio Scotti, starring in the Met's *Carmen* there, hire a wagon for $300 and retreat to the country estate of Arthur Bachman; Caruso, still shaken by the quake, sleeps outdoors under a tree in the yard.
- The widely popular *The Lion and the Mouse* by Charles Klein openly expresses hostility toward such "sanctimonious millionaires" as John D. Rockefeller.
- The show *Chorus Line* attacks middle-class values, glorifying a show girl of "loose" morals who tries to keep her sister's innocence intact.
- *The New York Idea* treats divorce lightheartedly.
- Teddy Roosevelt champions simplified spelling—e.g., thru, nite.
- En route to the North Pole, Admiral Robert E. Peary reaches the farthest northern latitude, 87°6′ to date.
- TR is the first American to win the Nobel Peace Prize ($40,000) for his work in mediating an end to the Russo-Japanese War.
- Architect Stanford White is shot by millionaire Harry K. Thaw during a performance of *Mamzelle Champagne* on the Roof Garden of Madison Square Garden; Thaw's wife, ex-chorus girl Evelyn Nesbit, was White's mistress before their marriage (and has currently been John Barrymore's).
- "Infernal fools in California," says TR, of its school segregation of Asian children.
- Two blacks in Ohio are burned to death before a cheering crowd of 3,000.
- Three distinguished companies of black soldiers are given dishonorable discharges after allegations that a black shot up Brownsville, Tex.; their guilt is not determined.
- "Accessory food factors," not proteins, fats, or carbohydrates, are said to be essentials of a good diet.
- On reading *The Jungle,* Mr. Dooley says: "[TR] suddenly rose from the table. . . . I'm poisoned," he said, and "began throwin' sausages out 'iv the window."

A former chorus girl, Evelyn Nesbit was seduced by architect Stanford White, who enjoyed placing the naked girl on a red velvet swing in his apartment; after her marriage to millionaire Harry Thaw, Thaw shoots and kills White.

- The Charles Evans Hughes' insurance company investigations lead to laws forbidding speculation with insurance premiums.
- Radio pioneer Lee De Forest, in Ireland, receives the first transatlantic radio transmission from his 40,000-watt Manhattan Beach transmitter.
- The first successful radio broadcast occurs on Christmas at Bryant Rock, Mass., and includes "O Holy Night" and a reading from St. Luke; the broadcast extends over 100 miles.
- Stuart Crawer coins the term "air conditioning" by combining his air filter with W. H. Carrier's device for cooling.
- The American Federation of Labor presents a Bill of Grievances to prevent the Sherman Antitrust Act from being used against it via prosecutions, injunctions, and yellow dog contracts.
- TR praises Wisconsin and Oregon for their use of state power for "wise experimental legislation."
- A bill to severely penalize the enforced enlistment ("shanghaiing") of citizens into commercial sailor service is passed.

Fads: picture hats with ostrich plumes, the "Alice blue gown" (worn by Miss Roosevelt at her White House wedding)

New Words: allergy, suffragettes, hot dog (from a cartoon by "Tad" Dorgen of a dachshund in a frankfurter bun)

First Appearances: Fuller Brush Co., Trolley Vac (Hoover), permanent wave, commercial cinematograph projector, regular radio broadcasts (of gramophone music, Lee De Forest), variable speed-hydraulic transmission, freeze drying (France), Mack truck (10 ton), International Hot Air Balloon Race (beginning in Paris), "S.O.S." distress call, Rolls-Royce, Grand Prix motor race, Jew in Cabinet (Oscar S. Straus, Secretary of Commerce and Labor), American Jewish Committee, *Mother Earth* (Emma Goldman, Alexander Berkman), International News Service (Hearst), Pace Institute, Forest Hills (600 acres, Queens), Mesa Verde National Park, Valencia (Calif.) oranges, Planters Nut and Chocolate Co., Battle Creek Toasted Corn Flake Co. (William Kellogg), A-1 Sauce, General Cigar Co., B. Altman (5th Avenue, 34th Street, N.Y.C.)

1907

Gifford Pinchot, head of the Inland Waterways Commission and former head forester for Agriculture, has worked diligently to preserve and cultivate forest reserves.

In the News

CONGRESS LIMITS CORPORATE CAMPAIGN CONTRIBUTIONS . . . TREATY WITH DOMINICAN REPUBLIC ALLOWS U.S. AGENTS TO COLLECT CUSTOMS FEES FOR UNPAID CREDITORS . . . TR ORDER LIMITS JAPANESE IMMIGRATION, CALIFORNIA AGREES TO ADMIT RESIDENT ASIAN SCHOOLCHILDREN . . . BRITISH SUFFRAGETTES DEMONSTRATE, 57 ARE ARRESTED . . . TR APPOINTS COMMISSION TO STUDY FOREST PRESERVATION AND COMMERCIAL WATERWAYS . . . MARINES ARE ORDERED TO HONDURAS TO RESTORE ORDER . . . GANDHI LEADS PASSIVE RESISTANCE TO ANTI-INDIAN BIAS IN SOUTH AFRICA . . . SAN FRANCISCO MAYOR IS FOUND GUILTY OF EXTORTION . . . "OPEN DOOR" AGREEMENT IS REACHED BETWEEN CHINA AND JAPAN, FRANCE, GERMANY, RUSSIA . . . AT SECOND HAGUE PEACE CONFERENCE, 46 NATIONS SET RULES OF WAR, INCLUDING GIVING NOTICE . . . TURRET EXPLOSION ON *GEORGIA* KILLS 70 . . . TRIPLE ALLIANCE OF ITALY, GERMANY, AUSTRO-HUNGARY IS RENEWED FOR 6 YEARS . . . BRITAIN AND RUSSIA ESTABLISH ENTENTE, ALIGNING THEM WITH FRANCE . . . SUN YAT-SEN ESTABLISHES NATIONALIST PARTY IN CHINA . . . BANK PANIC THREATENS TO BRING ON DEPRESSION, J. P. MORGAN QUIETS MARKETS BY ORDERING $100 MILLION IN GOLD FROM EUROPE . . . *LUSITANIA,* WORLD'S LARGEST STEAMSHIP, SETS RECORD OF 5 DAYS, 54 MIN., IRELAND–NEW YORK . . . 3,000 ELK ARE FELLED BY HEAT PROSTRATION IN PHILADELPHIA . . . OKLAHOMA BECOMES 46TH STATE . . . WEST VIRGINIA COAL MINE DISASTER KILLS 361 . . . "BIG BILL" HAYWOOD AND OTHERS ARE ACQUITTED ON CHARGES OF MURDERING FORMER IDAHO GOVERNOR, CLARENCE DARROW LEADS DEFENSE . . . TR ORGANIZES BATTLESHIP FLOTILLA FOR ROUND-THE-WORLD FRIENDSHIP MISSION.

Quotes

"A city is in theory a great business corporation but in other respects it's enlarged housekeeping. May we not say that city housekeeping has failed partly because women, as traditional housekeepers, have not been consulted as to its multiform activities?"
—Jane Addams, *Newer Ideals of Peace*

"The truth of an idea is not a stagnant property in it. Truth *happens* to an idea. It *becomes* true, is *made* true by events. Its verity *is* in fact an event, a process: the process namely of its verifying itself, its verification. Its validity is the process of its valid-*ation*."
—William James

"I [have] devoted upwards of 20 years to [a] profession that necessitates a daily intimacy with degenerates. I say after deliberation that *Salomé* [exposes] the most horrible, disgusting, revolting and unmentionable features of degeneracy that I have ever heard, read of, or imagined."
—Physician's letter to the *New York Times,* Jan. 24

"I know an old lady . . . who had heard *Salomé* 27 times, and she liked it very much. It never did her any harm."
—Unidentified statement in the *New York Times,* Jan. 25

"They tell me that there are no men in Pittsburgh but millionaires. I'm going there, and it's soon I'll be riding in my own carriage, I suppose."
—*New York World,* reporting comments of young immigrants

"I asked what it costs one of these ladies whose duty it is to shine in Newport for her gowns [for the 8–10 week season]. Ten thousand dollars a year. . . . If a woman spends only five, . . . we do not take her seriously."
—reported in *Cosmopolitan*

"To waste . . . our natural resources . . . will result in undermining in the days of our children the very prosperity which we ought by right to hand down to them amplified and developed."
—TR, on the environment

"The chief wonder of education is that it does not ruin everyone concerned in it, teacher and taught."
—Henry Adams

Depleted reserves at the Knickerbocker Bank provoke a panic.

Ads

Vaudeville

Marcus Klaw, A. L. Erlinger, and the Shuberts work with the William Morris Agency but fail in their challenge to Keith and Albee for control of advanced bookings; they are paid $250,000 to withdraw from vaudeville for 15 years.

Top vaudeville stars Arnold Daly, Lily Langtry, Cecilia Loftus, and Charles Hawtrey earn, on the average, $2,500 a week; lesser stars receive $1–$10 per minute on stage.

A popular joke: —"Did you send for the doctor when the baby swallowed the collar button?" —"You bet I did. It was the only one I had."

Of Note

Double-entendre songstress Alice Lloyd becomes the rage • Female impersonator Julian Eltinge gains instant fame after performing a "high-class" Salomé dance • Contortionist "Dracula" debuts • Traveling downtown from 188th Street in Harlem, George Jessel, 9, begins entertaining to raise money for his ailing father • Audiences applaud Harry Lauder for more than an hour; he is famed for his Scottish humor, wisdom, and songs like "I Love a Lass," "Stop Yer Tickling, Jock," and "Roamin' in the Gloamin.'"

Movies

Rescued from an Eagle's Nest (Porter), D. W. Griffith's first acting appearance
The Disintegrated Convict (Vitagraph)
Jack and the Beanstalk (Edison)
The Boy, the Bust, and the Bath (Vitagraph)
The Unwritten Law (Lubin)
Falsely Accused (Biograph), D. W. Griffith
Old Isaacs, the Pawnbroker (Biograph)
The Trainer's Daughter (Edison)
All's Well That Ends Well (Selig)
Athletic American Girls (Vitagraph)
Bargain Fiend (Vitagraph)

D. W. Griffith becomes active as an actor-writer. August Musger invents slow motion; G. M. Anderson leaves Vitagraph to join Selig. Shortly after Selig meets Spoor, they form Essanay; an expanded Kalem is joined by Samuel Long, Frank Marion, and George Kleine; they hire Robert Vignola and Sidney Olcott as actor-director.

Mary Fuller begins her career at Vitagraph. Nickelodeons begin with singalongs—songs like "Sunbonnet Sue," "Bicycle Built for Two," and patriotic anthems. Some community leaders question the "values" conveyed in film, especially for newly arrived immigrants and for women and children. *Views and Film Index* emphasizes that U.S. nickelodeons are "clean and and wholesome," and points to films like *Passion Play* and *Cinderella*. But "Fresh from Paris" and "Very Naughty" are typical nickelodeon ads. *Harper's Weekly* reports that "thousands of Bowery dwellers have learned to roar at French buffonery." About 400,000 attend nickelodeons daily in N.Y.C.; 100,000, in Chicago.

Popular Players

Viola Dana, Mary Fuller, Charles Ogle, Mabel Trunnelly, Marc McDermott, Gertrude McCoy, Herbert Prior

Notices flash frequently on the nickelodeon screen.

Boys consider *A Flirty Affliction;* empty baby carriages indicate that mothers will enjoy the show.

Popular Music

Hit Songs
"When a Fellow's on the Level with a Girl That's on the Square"
"School Days"
"Budweiser's a Friend of Mine"
"I'd Rather Be a Lobster than a Wise Guy"
"Merry Widow Waltz"
"Take Me Back to New York Town"
"There Never Was a Girl Like You"
"When We Are M-A-Double R-I-E-D"

Representative Recordings: "Let's Take an Old Fashioned Walk" (Ada Jones and Billy Murray); "Camp Meetin' Time (Arthur Collins); "He's a Cousin of Mine" (Art Williams); "I Just Can't Make My Eyes Behave" (Ada Jones); "Because You're You" (Harry MacDonough and Elise Stevenson); "Nobody's Little Girl" (Byron G. Harlan); "Harrigan" (Billy Murray).

Jazz
Typically, new groups have six instruments: a cornet, clarinet, valve trombone, guitar, drums and sometimes a violin or string bars. "Jelly Roll" Morton, Tony Jackson, and others incorporate not only the rolling rhythms of popular marching bands into their improvisations but also add a "walking" (melodic) bass and counterpoint; in the right hand, more beats are added. The music gains more of a swing quality. "Buddy" Bolden's band is taken over by trombonist Frankie Duson when Bolden has a nervous breakdown. Bolden enters a mental institution in Jackson. Originally from Sedalia—whose name is often identified with his music—Scott Joplin leaves St. Louis for New York.

Theater

The great actress Nazimova.

Broadway Openings

Plays
Captain Brassbound's Conversion (George Bernard Shaw), Ellen Terry, James Carew
Widower's Houses (George Bernard Shaw), Herbert Kelcey, Effie Shannon
When Knights Were Bold (Charles Marlowe), Francis Wilson, Pauline Frederick
Anna Karenina (Edmond Guirand, based on Tolstoy), Virginia Harned, Robert Warwick
The Thief (Henri Bernstein), Kyrle Bellew, Herbert Percy, Margaret Illington
The Warrens of Virginia (William C. de Mille), Mary Pickford (Gladys Smith, using "Pickford" for the first time), Cecil B. de Mille
The Witching Hour (Augustus Thomas), John Mason, Billie Burke
The Ranger (Augustus Thomas), Dustin Farnum, Mary Boland
Under the Greenwood Tree (H. V. Esmond), Maxine Elliott, Charles Cherry
Polly of the Circus (Margaret Mayo), Mabel Taliaferro
The Reckoning (Arthur Schnitzler), Katherine Grey, John Dean
The Truth (Clyde Fitch), Clara Bloodgood (who commits suicide during Baltimore run)

Musicals
The Merry Widow (Franz Lehar, Adrian Ross), Ethel Jackson, Donald Brian
Ziegfeld Follies of 1907 (first *Follies*, Gus Edwards, Will D. Cobb, Jean Schwartz), Mlle. Dazie, Grace LaRue, Bickel & Watson
The Girl behind the Counter (Howard Talbot, Arthur Anderson), Lew Fields, Louise Dresser, Vernon Castle
The Honeymooners (George M. Cohan), The Three Cohans, Gertrude Hoffman
The Talk of New York (George M. Cohan), Victor Moore, Emma Littlefield, Gertie Vanderbilt
The Top o' th' World (Manuel Klein, James O'Dea), Kathleen Clifford, Bessie Franklin
The Hurdy-Gurdy Girl (H. L. Heartz, Richard Carle), John E. Hazzard, Adele Rowland
The Orchid (Ivan Caryll, Adrian Ross), Eddie Foy, Amelia Stone

Classics and Revivals On and Off Broadway
Arnold Daly Repertory: *The Shirkers* (C. M. S. McLellan); *How He Lied to Her Husband* (Shaw); *Cathleen ni Houilihan* and *The Hour Glass* (Yeats); Ben Greet Repertory: Sybil Thorndike, Sydney Greenstreet, Fritz Leiber, *The Merchant of Venice, Macbeth, As You Like It, Julius Caesar, Much Ado about Nothing, Everyman,* Nazimova, *The Master Builder;* Robert Mantell's Repertory: six Shakespeare plays

Classical Music

Compositions
Charles Ives, Second Violin Concerto, *Emerson Overture*
George Chadwick, *Symphonic Sketch*
Henry Hadley, *Kunzertstück*
Arthur Foote, Suite in E

Important Events
The Cincinnati Symphony is temporarily suspended. Louisville inaugurates an annual music festival. Walter Damrosch leads the New York Philharmonic in a Grieg Memorial with Swiss Rudolph Ganz as piano soloist. Lee De Forest transmits by wireless Rossini's *William Tell Overture* from New York to Brooklyn, the first broadcast of orchestral music.

Notable Performances
Rarely heard Tchaikovsky is the focus of Josef Lhévinne's concert series. In his first conducting appearance, Edward Elgar leads his *The Apostles* (N.Y.C.). Pianist Teresa Carreño returns to Chicago from a world tour and is greeted by extraordinary praise. Vladimir de Pachmann, in his farewell performance, plays the same number of encores as scheduled pieces, including the Chopin "Butterfly" and "Black Key" études and Schumann's "Zögel als Prophet."

Major Recitals: Moriz Rosenthal, Ossip Gabrilowitsch, Ernest Schelling, Fanny Bloomfield Ziesler, Harold Bauer

New Appointments: Karl Pohlig, Philadelphia Symphony Orchestra; Max Zach, St. Louis Symphony Orchestra

Debut: Mieczyslaw Horszowski, Alice Zepilli

First Performances
Debussy, *La Mer* (Boston); Henry Hadley, *Salome* (Boston); Arthur Nevin, *Poia* (The White House, with composer at the piano); Frederick S. Converse, *Jeanne d'Arc* (Boston); Rimsky-Korsakov, Symphony no. 2 (New York); Edward MacDowell, Piano Concerto no. 2 (New York); Charles Martin Loeffler, *A Pagan Poem* (Boston)

Opera

Metropolitan: Giacomo Puccini attends the Puccini Festival; he even assists at rehearsals for the premiere of *Madama Butterfly*. Gustav Mahler is appointed conductor. Geraldine Farrar, Carl Burrian, Olive Fremsted, *Romeo and Juliet*; Katherine Fleischer-Edel, Anton Van Rooy, Carl Burran (debut), *Tannhäuser;* Johanna Gadski, Alois Burgstaller, Adolph Mühlmann, *Gotterdämmerung;* Feodor Chaliapin (debut, nearly

Geraldine Farrar in *Madama Butterfly,* becomes second only to Caruso in salary; Toscanini frequently reminds her: "The stars are all in the heavens. . . . [You,] a plain artist, must obey my direction."

nude), Farrar, Ricardo Martin, *Mefistofele* (Boito); Alessandro Bonci (debut), *Rigoletto*. Premieres: Farrar, Enrico Caruso, Louise Homer, Antonio Scotti, *Madama Butterfly;* Lina Cavalieri, Caruso, Bella Alten, Scotti, *Fedora* (Giordano); Charles Roussalière, Farrar, Pol Plançon, *The Damnation of Faust* (Berlioz); Fremstad, Burrian, Marion Weed, *Salomé* (Strauss)

Manhattan: Mary Garden (debut), *Thaïs* (Massenet, premiere); Nellie Melba, *La traviata;* Jeanne Gerville-Réache (debut), *Samson et Dalila* (Saint-Saëns); Lillian Nordica, Mario Ancona, *La gioconda* (Ponchielli); Nordica, Charles Dalmorès, *Les Contes d'Hoffmann* (Offenbach); Mario Sammarco (debut), Amedeo Bassi, Pauline Donaldo, *Pagliacci*

Italian Grand Opera of New York: *Aïda, Il trovatore, La Juive* (Halévy)

Philadelphia: Cavalieri, Caruso, Scotti, *Tosca*

Baltimore: *The Tattooed Man* (Victor Herbert)

Music Notes
Salomé, attacked for its violence and decadence, is banished after one performance at the Met • Soprano Lillian Nordica and Manhattan Opera impresario Oscar Hammerstein deny rumors of a breech between them, resulting in the absence of her name on annnouncements of future operas • Justice O'Gorman of the N.Y. State Supreme Court rules that "all musical performances on Sunday are prohibited"; the N.Y.C. public expresses outrage, and leaders plan an appeal • Violinist Maud Powell champions Western taste during her tour, including works like *The Arkansas Traveler* and *Dixie* • Composer Charles T. Griffes leaves his teaching position at the Hackley School to study the exotic works of the French Impressionists, the unusual tonalities of Asian musical style, and the Russian compositions of Mussorgsky and Scriabin.

Art

Painting

Robert Henri, *Laughing Child, Eva Green*

John Sloan, *The Haymarket, Hairdresser's Window*

Rockwell Kent, *Toilers of the Sea*

George Bellows, *Stag at Sharkey's, Forty-two Kids*

Maurice Prendergast, *April Snow, Salem*

George Luks, *Woman with Goose, The Wrestlers*

Louis M. Eilshemius, *The Flying Dutchman, The Forsaken Mill*

Ernest Lawson, *Winter in the River*

Arthur B. Davies, *Night's Overture: A Tempest*

William Glackens, *Roller Skating Rink*

Sculpture

Paul Bartlett, *Marquis de Lafayette*

Frederic Remington, *The Horse Thief*

Charles M. Russell, *Sun Worship in Montana, Indian on Horseback*

Anna V. Huntington, *Jaguar Eating*

Architecture

R. R. Blacker house, Pasadena, Calif. (Greene & Greene)

St. Paul's Episcopal Chapel, Columbia University, N.Y.C. (Howells & Stokes)

National Farmers Bank, Owatonna, Minn. (Louis Sullivan)

Pan American Union (OAS), Washington, D.C. (Paul Philippe Cret)

Plaza Hotel, N.Y.C. (Henry Hardenberg)

Colony Club (American Academy of Dramatic Arts), N.Y.C. (Stanford White)

U.S. Customs House, N.Y.C. (Cass Gilbert)

Automobile Association of America, New York City (Ernest Flagg)

Municipal Building, Centre and Chamber Streets, N.Y.C. (Carrère & Hastings)

Marshall Field & Co., Chicago (D. H. Burnham, 1892–1907)

Augustus Saint-Gaudens, "Robert Shaw Memorial"; Massachusetts-born Shaw led a black regiment during the Civil War; he was buried en masse with his troops, and his proud father refused to move him to a separate resting place.

Important Exhibitions

New York: *Metropolitan:* "Jamestown, Virginia Colonial Relics" (tercentennial exhibition, on loan). *Salmagundi:* Portraits by Joseph N. Marble; *Lotus Club:* John H. Twachtman

Chicago: Childe Hassam; Charles H. Davis; Frederic Clay Bartlett watercolors; Contemporary German artists; William P. Henderson; George F. Schultz; Anna Lynch; Chicago ceramics. Acquisitions: *El Greco's Assumption of the Virgin*

Boston: Robert Henri; Louise Kenyon Cox; Genjiro Yeto; Louis Kronbert; Louis Loeb; Henry W. Poore; "Art for the People"; Leon Dabo

St. Louis: "The Ten"

Art Briefs

Although Henri is appointed to the jury of the National Academy of Design, his colleagues' work (including Glackens, Luks, and Sloane) is accorded inferior (below eye) placement • Gertrude Vanderbilt Whitney opens the Village Studio at her home to exhibit the new painters • Several Americans, including Max Weber and Alfred Maurer, attend Matisse's painting class in Paris • The $20 ("Liberty") gold piece is designed by Augustus Saint-Gaudens • J. P. Morgan pledges $75,000 to support a photo collection of North American Indians • The Cincinnati Museum receives a $100,000 endowment with the proviso that admission be free • Surprising sales include Gainsborough's *The Woodman,* $110, and Poussin's *Classical River Scenes* (a pair), $225.

After shocking the Met audience with his half-naked appearance in *Mephistopheles,* Feodor Chaliapin finishes the 1907–08 season and then takes an extended leave from the U.S.

Books

Fiction

Critics' Choice

Hearts of the West, The Trimmed Lamp, O. Henry
Three Weeks, Elinor Glyn
The Slim Princess, George Ade
In Search of Treasure, Horatio Alger (posthumous)
Gallantry, James Branch Cabell
Uncle Remus and Brer Rabbit, Joel Chandler Harris
A Horse's Tale, Mark Twain
Through the Eye of a Needle, William Dean Howells
Encore, Margaret Deland
The Second Generation, David Graham Phillips
Toilers and Idlers: A Novel, John McMahon
The Turn of the Balance, Brand Whitlock
The Thinking Machine, Jacques Futrelle
The Red City, S. Weir Mitchell
❧ *The Secret Agent,* Joseph Conrad

Best-Sellers

The Lady of the Decoration, Francis Little
The Weavers, Gilbert Parker
The Port of Missing Men, Meredith Nicholson
The Shuttle, Frances Hodgson Burnett
The Brass Bowl, Louis J. Vance
Satan Sanderson, Hallie Erminie Rives
The Daughter of Anderson Crow, George Barr McCutcheon
The Younger Set, Robert W. Chambers
The Doctor, Ralph Connor
Half a Rogue, Harold MacGrath

Nonfiction

Critics' Choice

Pragmatism, William James
The Education of Henry Adams: An Autobiography, Henry Adams
Branchiana, James Branch Cabell
Daily Notes on a Trip Around the World, E. W. Howe
The American Scene, Henry James
The Congo and Coasts of Africa, Richard Harding Davis
Christian Science, Mark Twain
The Overman, Upton Sinclair
Good Hunting in the Pursuit of the West, Theodore Roosevelt
The Story of the Outlaw: A Study of the Western Desperado, Emerson Hough
Reed Anthony, Cowman, Andy Adams

A younger Henry Adams, a subject of *The Education of Henry Adams.*

Christianity and the Social Crisis, Walter Rauschenbusch
Jefferson Davis, William E. Dodd
Folkways, William Graham Sumner
❧ *Creative Evolution,* Henri Bergson

Poems

Richard Hovey, *To the End of the Trail*
James Whitcomb Riley, *Morning, The Boys of the Old Glee Club*
Sara Teasdale, *Sonnets to Duse and Other Poems*
❧ W. B. Yeats, *Poetical Works: Lyrical Poems, Dramatic Poems, 1906–07,* 2 vols.
❧ Rainer Maria Rilke, *New Poems*

Science and Technology

Montrose Burrows observes mitosis, cells dividing; he also isolates a heart muscle's single cell, illustrating that the heartbeat originates in the heart itself.

Surgeons discover that patients recover faster and with fewer complications if they become mobile shortly after surgery.

Ross G. Harrison, at Johns Hopkins, initiates the study of tissue culture, keeping animal tissue alive in laboratory cells.

Francis Benedict discovers how the body consumes itself in starvation after fats, carbohydrates, and finally protein are metabolized.

E. Alexander of G.E. develops a high-frequency radio alternator, which greatly broadens the range of radio transmission.

Commercial production of the five inert gases—neon, argon, xenon, helium, and krypton—is begun.

❧ Bertram Boltwood discovers the use of uranium decay to measure the age of rocks.

Nobel Prize

A. A. Michelson is the first American to win the Nobel Prize in physics for his optical precision instruments.

A. A. Michelson, the first American to win the Nobel prize in science, is renowned for his work in optics and measuring the velocity of light.

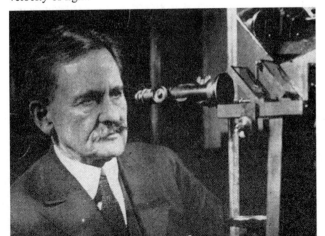

Sports

Baseball

Honus Wagner (Pittsburgh, NL) wins his 5th batting title, breaking Adrian ("Cap") Anson's record of 4.

Ty Cobb wins his first batting and stolen base titles, becoming known for his flying spikes and hard play.

Chicago wins 107 games and its 2nd straight pennant and is the first team to sweep all four WS games.

Walter Johnson (Washington, AL) arrives in August from the Idaho State League, where he struck out 20 players in one game. "No mere mortal can throw a baseball as hard. . . . I have seen him pitch, but I do not believe what I have seen," comments a reporter.

This Harvard-Yale game shows the lack of protective gear and violence that make death and serious injury the subject of national discussion.

Champions

Batting	Pitching
Honus Wagner (Pittsburgh, NL), .350	Ed Ruelbach (Chicago, NL), 17–4
Ty Cobb (Detroit, AL), .350	Bill Donovan (Detroit, AL), 25–4
	Home runs
	David Brain (Boston, AL), 10

Football

College All-Americans: Horatio Bigelow (T), Yale; T. A. Dwight Jones (Q), Yale; Edwin H. Harlan (HB), Princeton

Other Sports

Boxing: Tommy Burns defeats Gunnar Moir in London to retain his HW title.

Tennis: May Sutton wins her 2nd Wimbledon.

Winners

World Series	U.S. Tennis Open
Chicago (NL) 4	Men: William Larned
Detroit (AL) 0	Women: Evelyn Sears
College Football	*USGA Open*
Yale	Alex Ross
College Basketball	*Kentucky Derby*
Chicago	Pink Star (Andy Minder, jockey)
Player of the Year	
George Kinney, Yale	

Fashion

Women continue to change their dress and accessories five and six times a day, so that no one outfit can be seen twice during one weekend. A short trip away involves several trunks, ornate hatboxes, and, of course, an attendant. Short and long cloaks woven of broadcloth are replaced by fur, which is cut to no longer weigh down the silhouette; less expensive furs are available in addition to sable and chinchilla, such as moleskin, Hudson otter, and Siberian beaver. After British Annette Kellerman is arrested for indecent exposure in her one-piece bathing suit, she sews tights on to her swimsuit so as not to expose her thighs. But when she models this in Massachusetts, the first woman to swim across the East River in New York, she is again arrested for indecent exposure.

High-fashion note: American magazine declares that the most fashionable women are dressed by Paris couturiers

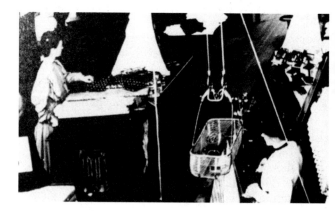

When marketing, one uses an overhead wire basket on a pulley.

Worth, Redfern, and Cadot; Parisian designer Doucet acquires Mme. Madeleine Vionnet, experimenting with the bias cut.

Kaleidoscope ———————————————

- A record 1.29 million immigrants arrive in the U.S.; Congress raises the head tax on immigration to $4.
- "We have imposed our ideals on the Irish and the Germans, as we are now imposing them on the Italians and the Russian Jew. . . . No immigrant culture has the power to resist," observes Brander Matthews, asserting the inevitability of cultural assimilation.
- Campaigns increase to help tenement immigrants gain playgrounds and parks, find work, and fight juvenile delinquency, white slave trade, and prostitution.
- Slum-dwellers often move yearly because landlords commonly offer a free month's lodging.
- Residents of N.Y.C.'s Lower East Side eagerly seek to read the news in their own language; over 50 newspapers and periodicals regularly publish in Yiddish.
- Disturbed by the dangers of unregulated big business, Woodrow Wilson decries "financial manipulators"; TR attacks "the predatory few."
- The financial panic on Wall Street, although contained, negatively affects the nation's economy.
- J. P. Morgan's decisive support for stock prices, by providing gold and his own U.S. Steel shares ("good as gold") and threatening speculators that he "would crush them," prevents a market collapse.
- A leading New York City banker commits suicide after allegations of misconduct leading to the Wall Street panic.
- TR reduces the punishment of the black soldiers given dishonorable discharges in the Brownsville incident last year; they are allowed to seek civil service employment.
- *Harper's Weekly* warns of "nickel madness"; most nickelodeons consist of long, narrow rooms, headed by a white curtain and tinny piano; the *Chicago Tribune* comments: "They cannot be defended. They are hopelessly bad . . . but their popularity is ever increasing."
- Ringling Bros. buys out Barnum & Bailey, as the circus continues to grow in popularity and size; railroad caravans carry casts of over 1,000.
- *Delineator* editor Theodore Dreiser asks H. L. Mencken for a series of articles on the care and feeding of babies and how each cry has a different meaning; both are childless.
- Privately published for select friends, Henry Adams's *Education* laments the decline in American ideals and standards.
- When the *Baltic* docks in N.Y.C., 1,002 unmarried Irish, Scottish, Welsh, English, and Scandinavian women are besieged by bachelors and a band playing "Cupid's Garden" and "I Want You Honey, Yes I Do."
- "Diamond Jim" Brady is famous not only for his showgirl companions but also for his gargantuan appetite; his dinners for 50, lasting five hours and costing $100,000, are legendary.
- With the attitude that if one has to ask the price, one can't afford the item, the Great Arrow car is advertised without its $4,500+ price tag.
- Taximeters, imported from France, appear in N.Y.C.
- J. P. Morgan calls the Broadway show *Salomé* "disgusting" and offers to pay for the entire production in order to stop it; he objects not to the dance of the seven veils but to a woman's fondling a man's head detached from the rest of his body.

With the new machinery, women gain the skilled, clerical, and better-paying jobs men find boring.

- In his lecture before an overflow audience, William James contrasts the "tender minded" rationalists who live by principles and the "tough minded" empiricists who live by facts, whom he calls "pragmatists."
- Trained Ph.D.s, the New Historians begin to challenge the work of classical historians like George Bancroft and Francis Parkman.
- Alabama and Georgia adopt Prohibition laws.
- The Protestant Episcopal Convention condemns the removal of "In God We Trust" from new gold coins.
- The Central American Peace Conference meets in Washington, seeking to establish a Central American Court of Justice.
- "A Feast, a frolic or a fight" is the commander's description of the around-the-world voyage of the Great White Fleet (named for the color of the ships); many believe it is to impress Japan with our naval prowess.
- The Jamestown Tercentenary Exposition is formally opened by the president.
- The Forest Preservation Act sets aside 16 million acres in five states.
- The U.S. has about ten times the number of railways as Great Britain, Ireland, most of Europe, and Canada.
- Pepsi-Cola sales increase to 104,000 gallons (8,000 in 1903).

Fads: Diaboo (game in which wood is tossed around by cord attached to two sticks), "peek-a-boo" shirtwaist, feather boas

New Word: conservation (Chief Forester Gifford Pinchot)

First Appearances: theater programs, "Mr. Mutt" (later "Mutt and Jeff," Bud Fisher), Klaxton (instrument), color photography (Louis Lumière), Rube Goldberg cartoons (N.Y. *Evening Journal*), self-threading sewing machine, Bendix, Gulf Oil, Willy's Overland Motors, United Press, Fairmont Hotel (San Francisco), Neiman Marcus (Dallas), Bullock's (Los Angeles), Bell & Howell, Prince Albert tobacco, Canada Dry pale ginger ale, Maytag Pastime Washer, Armstrong linoleum, American Cyanamid, sky advertising (on kites); nightclubs (vaudeville acts in eateries); spray paint gun

1908

Facts and Figures

Economic Profile
Dow-Jones: ↑ High 88–
Low 59
GNP: –6.9%
Inflation: +3.9%
Unemployment: 8.0%
Balance of international
payments: +2.0 billion
Military on duty: 128,000
Voter participation:
73% (1900)
65% (1904)
65% (1908)
Two-family block houses,
Elmira, N.Y.: $6,100 ($600
down)
Portable bungalows for
seashore or mountains:
$10–$20 mo.
Lehigh Raleigh–Valley
Railroad (round-trip)
N.Y.C. to Seattle: $87.50; to
San Francisco or L.A.: $88
Cane suitcases, 7″ deep, 24″
long: $5
Saks' auto raincoats: $4–$32.50
(men); $10–$75 (women)
Bloomingdale's women's
chamois driving gloves: 95¢
Macy's "Irontex" hosiery,
black gauze lisle, garter
tops: 33¢
Broadway theaters, N.Y.C.,
matinee: $1.00–$2.50
Steinway upright piano: $200

Above: Glenn Curtiss in his
biplane, the *June Bug,* after
winning the first U.S. aero-
nautical competition by flying
5,090 feet.

Deaths

Mrs. William Astor, Grover
Cleveland, Joel Chandler
Harris, Edward MacDowell,
Charles Eliot Norton,
Anthony ("Tony") Pastor,
Nikolai Rimsky-Korsakov

In the News

UNEMPLOYMENT REMAINS HIGH FOR FIRST TIME IN 10 YEARS . . .
SUPREME COURT APPLIES SHERMAN ANTI-TRUST ACT TO LABOR
UNIONS, RULES THAT UNION BOYCOTTS ILLEGALLY RESTRICT
INDUSTRY . . . SUPREME COURT UPHOLDS OREGON'S 10-HOUR
DAY FOR WOMEN . . . KING AND CROWN PRINCE OF PORTUGAL
ARE ASSASSINATED . . . 250,000 IN N.Y.C. WATCH START OF
N.Y.-PARIS AUTO RACE . . . FIRE KILLS 167 SCHOOLCHILDREN
NEAR CLEVELAND . . . JAPANESE AGREE TO LIMIT IMMIGRATION
TO U.S. . . . CONGRESS REGULATES CHILD LABOR IN D.C.
. . . ALDRICH-VREELAND ACT SEEKS TO REGULATE BANK
SPECULATION . . . TR REFUSES THIRD TERM, GOP NOMINATES
WILLIAM HOWARD TAFT . . . GIFFORD PINCHOT HEADS
NATIONAL COMMISSION ON CONSERVATION . . . THAW IS FOUND
NOT GUILTY OF WHITE'S 1906 MURDER BY REASON OF INSANITY,
DARROW CALLS IT "BRAIN STORM" . . . DEMOCRATS NOMINATE
BRYAN FOR THIRD TIME . . . SEVERAL BLACKS ARE LYNCHED IN
SPRINGFIELD, ILL., MARTIAL LAW IS DECLARED TO STOP RACE
RIOTS . . . OLDSMOBILE, BUICK, AND OTHERS MERGE TO FORM
GENERAL MOTORS . . . WILBUR WRIGHT CRASHES WHEN
PROPELLER BLADE BREAKS, PASSENGER LT. THOMAS SELFRIDGE
IS KILLED . . . WRIGHT SETS NEW FLIGHT RECORD FOUR DAYS
AFTER ACCIDENT . . . U.S. "GREAT WHITE FLEET" IS WELCOMED
AROUND THE WORLD . . . U.S. RETURNS BOXER INDEMNITY TO
CHINA FOR EDUCATION . . . TENNESSEE SENATOR CORMACK IS
KILLED OVER POLITICAL FEUD . . . KAISER ADMITS TO ANTI-
BRITISH SENTIMENT IN GERMANY . . . TAFT WINS WITH
7,679,006; BRYAN, 6,409,106; DEBS, 420,820 . . . BOY EMPEROR
PU YI ASCENDS CHINESE THRONE ON DEATH OF DOWAGER
EMPRESS AND EMPEROR.

Quotes

[On the presidential election:] "There are plenty of people who want me to run for a third term who, if I did run, would feel very much disappointed [and] that I had come short of the ideal they had formed of me" (TR, on keeping his 1904 promise not to run again); "Get on the Raft with Taft" (Republican campaign slogan and TR's choice); "Hit 'em hard, old man!" (TR's advice to Taft); "Shall the people rule?" (William Jennings Bryan, three-time Democratic candidate for president)

"America is God's Crucible, the great Melting-Pot where all the races of Europe are melting and reforming."
—Israel Zangwill, *The Melting Pot*

"What large and powerful body of citizens is ready to come to their aid?"
—Willing E. Walling, in the *Independent,* on the Springfield race riot

"When Love comes, it brings in its hands the keys to Paradise. . . . [To read about sex] put[s] an undue weight on the subject, making it a matter of morbid thinking. Too much analytic sex reading and sex thinking is one of the surest ways of breaking down even the strongest nerves."
—*Ladies Home Journal*

"As for America, it is the ideal fruit of all your youthful hopes and reforms. Everybody is fairly decent, respectable, domestic, bourgeois, middle-class, and tiresome. There is absolutely nothing to revile except that it's a bore."
—Henry James

"High-powered cars might with greater logic be regarded as morphine and cocaine are."
—*Independent*

"Kate Casey was baseball mad / Had the fever and had it bad / . . . On a Saturday, her young beau / Called to see if she'd like to see a show / but Miss Kate said, 'I'll tell you what you can do . . . '"
—"Take Me Out to the Ball Game," Albert Von Tilzer and Jack Norworth

"[Our mission is] to paint drunks and slatterns, pushcarts and coalmines, bedroom and barroom, [to] deliberately and consciously paint the ugly wherever it occurs."
—Robert Henri, on the New Realism (the "Ashcan School")

Ads

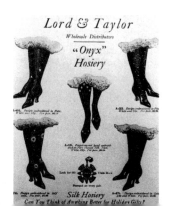

Pharmacies expand to include soda fountains.

Maude Adams, beloved for her *Peter Pan,* returns this year to triumph in another James Barrie play, *What Every Woman Knows.*

Vaudeville

Film directors begin to sign up vaudeville stars. S. L. Rothafel ("Roxy") opens his first theater, Rothafel's Family Theater, in Forest City, Pa., where he shows films accompanied by vaudeville acts.

Of Note
Eddie Cantor (Isidore Itzkowitz), 16, in borrowed trousers, makes his first stage appearance at the Miner's Bowery Theater Amateur Night and wins the $5 contest; his home is an outdoor space atop a roof • After her job of singing, washing dishes, and making knishes at a 2nd Avenue eaterie, Sophie Tucker debuts in blackface at Tony Pastor's 14th Street theater; she follows Pastor's advice and abandons blackface and then appears in Pittsburgh with the "Gay Masqueraders" • Irene Franklin wins an award as Most Popular Woman Vaudeville Artist • Eva Tanguay presents a parody of *Salomé;* creating the first Salomé to speak, her act is billed as "the sensation of the year" • (Howard) "Thurston" succeeds Harry Keller as the nation's greatest magician; he makes a car disappear, as well as a boy who has climbed a rope.

Movies

The Adventures of Dollie (D. W. Griffith's first film, less than one reel), Mrs. D. W. Griffith, Arthur Johnson
Enoch Arden (D. W. Griffith)
Romeo and Juliet (Vitagraph), Paul Panzer, Florence Lawrence
When Knights Were Bold (Biograph), Linda Arvidson, D. W. Griffith, Harry Salter
Ingobar, the Barbarian (Biograph), Florence Lawrence
Fireside Reminiscences (Edison)
The Cattle Rustlers (Selig)
A Christmas Carol (Essanay)

Edison gains patent control, and the United Film Service Protective Association forms to curb the unauthorized duplication of films. Edison and nine other major companies form a trust, the Motion Picture Patents Company; licenses are issued to those who use devices or inventions that are patented. Edison builds a new studio in the Bronx, N.Y.; Vitagraph functions in Flatbush, Brooklyn; Lubin, in Philadelphia; Selig and Essanay, in Chicago. G. M. Anderson opens a Western branch of Essanay in California and makes weekly Bronco Billy cowboy films; Biograph, in N.Y.C., produces two films a week with Lawrence Griffith and Linda Arvidson. Actor D. W. Griffith begins directing. At the end of the year, Florence Lawrence moves from Vitagraph to Biograph and becomes "the Biograph Girl," her salary raised from $15 to $25 a week. Florence Turner, "the Vitagraph Girl," and Florence Lawrence, "the Biograph Girl," become the first "movie stars." Controversy over French film morality continues.

Increasingly Familiar Screen Faces
Eddie Dillon, Harry Salter, Charles Inslee, Mack Sennett, Ruth Hart, Herbert Yost, Frank Gebhardt, John Compson, Tony O'Sullivan, Mabel Sloughton, Florence Auer, Dorothy West, Jeannie Macpherson

Most Popular Actors (still unbilled)
Florence Lawrence, Florence Turner, Kathlyn Williams, Wilfred Lucas, Owen Moore, Harold Lockwood, Hobart Bosworth, Arthur Johnson

Popular Music

Hit Songs
"Shine On, Harvest Moon"
"Take Me Out to the Ball Game"
"Golliwog's Cake Walk"
"When You First Kissed the Last
Girl You Loved"
"Consolation"
"Down among the Sugar Cane"
"If You Cared for Me"
"Love Days"
"Love Is Like a Cigarette"
"You'll Always Be Just Sweet
Sixteen to Me"

Representative Recordings:
"Cuddle Up a Little Closer, Lovey
Mine" (Ada Jones and Billy
Martin)"; "Under Any Old Flag at
All" (Billy Murray); "As Long as
the World Rolls On" (Alan Turner);
"Wouldn't You Like to Have Me as
a Sweetheart?" (Ada Jones and
Billy Murray); "The Glow-Worm"
(Victor Orchestra); "Are You
Sincere?" (Elise Stevenson);
"Sunbonnet Sue" (Harry
MacDonough and Haydn Quartet)

Jazz
The new music inflects older
forms, like ragtime, with the blues,
and undergirds two-beat marches
with a 4/4 beat. Performers then
begin to divide the new 4/4 beat
unevenly, playing eighth notes, for
example, unevenly, in terms of
duration and accent.

"Jelly Roll" Morton.

Theater

Broadway Openings

Plays
What Every Woman Knows (James M. Barrie), Maude
Adams, Richard Bennett
The Devil (Ferenc Molnár, 2 independent productions),
George Arliss, Mrs. George Arliss, Theodosia de
Cappat (later, Theda Bara)
The Fool Hath Said There Is No God (Laurence Irving,
adaptation of *Crime and Punishment),* E. H.
Sothern
The Honor of the Family (Emile Fabre), Otis Skinner
The Man from Home (Booth Tarkington, Harry Leon
Wilson), William Hodge
A Gentleman from Mississippi (Harrison Rhodes,
Thomas Wise), Wise, Douglas Fairbanks
Wildfire (George Broadhurst, George V. Hobart), Lillian
Russell, Ernest Truex
Jack Straw (W. Somerset Maugham), John Drew, Mary
Boland
Love Watches (R. De Flers, G. Caillavet), Billie Burke
Salvation Nell (Edward Sheldon), Mrs. Minnie Maddern
Fiske, Holbrook Blinn
Lady Frederick (W. Somerset Maugham), Ethel
Barrymore

Musicals
The Girls of Gottenburg (Ivan Caryll, Lionel
Monckton), Louise Dresser, Walter Percival
Little Nemo (Victor Herbert, Harry B. Smith), Florence
Tempest, Marion Sunshine, Master Gabriel
The Mimic World (Edward Madden, Ben M. Jerome),
Vernon Castle, Irene Bentley
The Queen of the Moulin Rouge (John T. Hall, Vincent
Bryan), Flora Parkman, Frank (soon, Francis) X.
Bushman
The Soul Kiss (Maurice Levi, Harry B. Smith), Adeline
Genee, Ralph Herz, Florence Holbrook
The Three Twins (Karl Hoschna, Otto Harbach), Bessie
McCoy, Clifton Crawford
Ziegfeld Follies of 1908 (Maurice Levi, Harry B. Smith),
Nora Bayes, Jack Norworth, Gertrude Vanderbilt,
Mae Murray
The Yankee Prince (George M. Cohan), The Four
Cohans, Jack Gardner, Stella Hammerstein

Classics and Revivals On and Off Broadway
The Rising of the Moon (Lady Gregory, first Irish
production in U.S.); *Electra* (Von Hoffmann-Stahl), Mrs.
Patrick Campbell; *The Flower of Yamata,* Mrs.
Campbell, Ben Webster; *The Honor of the Family*
(Emile Fabre, from Balzac's *La Robouilleuse),* Otis
Skinner; Mme. Vera F. Komisarzhevsky Repertory: *A
Doll's House, The Children of the Sun* (Gorky), *The
Master Builder, Sister Beatrice, The Miracle of St.
Anthony* (the last two, Maeterlinck); *The Old
Homestead; The Prisoner of Zenda* (Edward Rose)

Classical Music _____

Compositions

George Whitefield Chadwick, Theme, Variations, and
   Fugue for Orchestra
Charles Ives, Sonata no. 1 for Violin and Piano, *The
   Anti-Abolitionist Riots*
Henry Hadley, *The Culprit*
Arthur Foote, Piano Trio no. 2

Important Events

The Philharmonic Society of Buffalo forms. The
exchange of American and German music and
musicians continues: Henry Hadley conducts his own
work in N.Y.C. with the Berlin Philharmonic.

Notable Performances: Under Modest Altschuler, the
Russian Symphony Orchestra introduces Alexander
Scriabin's Symphony no. 4 *(Le Poème de l'extase)* in
New York. Josef Hofmann performs his own Piano
Concerto, N.Y.C., and plays five concerts in Mexico.

Major Recitals: Josef Lhévinne in Boston; Maud
Powell forms a trio, with cellist May Mukle and pianist
Anne Ford, and tours the U.S.; Albert Spalding and
Ernest Schelling, Chicago; Fritz Kreisler, Maud Powell,
Albert Rosenthal, Katharine Goodson, Richard Buhlig,
N.Y.C.

Debuts: Mischa Elman, 16 (Tchaikovsky, Violin
Concerto), with the Russian Symphony Society

First Performances

George Whitefield Chadwick, *First Symphonic Sketches*
(Boston); Emmanuel Moór, Piano Concerto in D-flat
major (Boston); Edward MacDowell, *Lamia* (Boston)

Opera

Metropolitan: Giulio Gatti-Casazza becomes director.
Premieres: Lina Cavalieri, Enrico Caruso, Josephine

Renowned Met and
Manhattan Opera company
prima donna Luisa
Tetrazzini.

Jacoby, Antonio Scotti, *Adriana Lecouvreur* (Cilea);
Emma Eames, Caruso, Scotti, *Iris* (Mascagni). Feodor
Chaliapin, *Faust, Don Giovanni;* Riccardo Stracciari,
Marcella Sembrich, Alessandro Bonci, *Rigoletto;* Lina
Cavalieri, *Fedora;* Bonci, Pasquale Amato (debut),
Caruso, Sembrich, *La traviata;* Luisa Tetrazzini,
Mignon; Heinrich Knote, *Die Meistersinger;* Herbert
Witherspoon (debut), *Parsifal;* Frances Alda (debut),
Caruso, *Rigoletto;* Emmy Destinn (debut), Caruso,
Louise Homer, Scotti, *Aïda*

Manhattan: Mary Garden, *Louise* (premiere,
Charpentier); Garden, *Pelléas et Mélisande* (Debussy,
premiere); Garden, *Hunchback of Notre Dame*
(Massenet); Eva Tetrazzini (out of retirement), *Andrea
Chénier;* John C. McCormack (debut), Tetrazzini, *La
traviata* (after exclusive contract with the Met lapses);
Florencio Constantino, Tetrazzini, Mario Sammarco,
Rigoletto; Jeanne Gerville-Réache, Charles Dalmorès,
Hector Dufranne, *Samson et Dalila*

Philadelphia (Hammerstein's third opera house):
Carmen

Chicago: *Otho Visconti* (Frederick Grant Gleason);
Eames, Scotti, *Iris* (Mascagni)

Music Notes

Arturo Toscanini makes his American debut, conducting
Aïda, the beginning of the Toscanini era at the Met •
Gustav Mahler, former director of the Vienna Court
Opera, also makes his Met debut, conducting *Tristan
and Isolde* • The New Brooklyn Academy of Music is
rebuilt on Lafayette Street • Dutch pianist Jan Sichesz
performs for TR at the White House; the president has
always manifested a strong interest in Dutch culture.

John Phillip Sousa, "the
March King," whose brass
bands and compositions are
acclaimed here and abroad;
most famous is his *Stars and
Stripes Forever.*

Art

Painting
Thomas Eakins, *William Rush's Model*
Robert Henri, *El Picador, Jessica Penn in Black*
William Glackens, *Rocks and Lighthouse, The Shoppers*
John Sloan, *South Beach Bathers*
Everett Shinn, *Revue*
Kenyon Cox, *Augustus Saint-Gaudens*
Anne Goldwaite, *4 Rue de Chevreuse, Paris*
George Bellows, *Up the Hudson*
Marsden Hartley, *Storm Clouds, Maine*

Sculpture
Frederic Remington, *The Savage, The Cowboy*
Francis Edwin Elwell, *Seventh Rhode Island Infantry*

Charles M. Russell, *When Blackfeet and Sioux Meet, The Battle*

Architecture
Coonley house, Riverside, Ill. (Frank Lloyd Wright)
Union Station, Washington, D.C. (D. H. Burnham)
David B. Gamble house, Pasadena (Greene & Greene)
Isabel Roberts house, River Forest, Ill. (Frank Lloyd Wright)
Wilson Acton Hotel, La Jolla, Calif. (Irving John Gill)
Scripps Institute for Oceanography building, La Jolla, Calif. (Irving John Gill)
Unity Temple, Oak Park, Ill. (Frank Lloyd Wright, 1905–08)

Important Exhibitions

New York: *Metropolitan:* Augustus Saint-Gaudens; John Singleton Copley. Purchases: Bronze statuette of a diskos-thrower; Greek relief of a young horseman; Armchair Greek statue of a woman; *Sekhemhathor and His Son; Lady Lilith* (Dante Gabriel Rosetti); *Girl at the Fountain* (Hunt). *Knoedler:* Paintings of the Dutch and Barbizon schools; Whistler drawings

St. Louis: Third Anniversary of American Artists

Chicago: Annual oils and sculptures by Americans (340 by 219 artists); Whistler etchings; "Six American Artist Residents in Paris," including F. C. Frieseke, H. S. Hubbell, A. H. Maurer, P. W. Bartlett. Acquisition: Plaster reproduction of bronze equestrian statue of Donatello

Toledo: American and Russian painting

Carnegie, Corcoran: *The American Salon*

Art Briefs
Sculptor Gutzon Borglum causes a controversy by calling American art "weak and imitative" • Prompted by poor treatment by the academy, indifference by

Arthur B. Davies, "A Measure of Dreams," 1908. *The Metropolitan Museum of Art, Gift of George A. Hearn, 1909.*

galleries, and increasingly poor press, Henri's group (Henri, Sloan, Luks, Glackens, Shinn, Prendergast, Davies, and Lawson) sponsors its own show at Macbeth's gallery; with mixed reviews, many calling the artists "apostles of ugliness" (N.Y. *Evening Sun),* they are finally called "The Eight" or "Ashcan School"; they collect $4,000 for seven works, four of which are bought by Gertrude Vanderbilt Whitney, but the show is welcomed in Boston, Chicago, Toledo, Detroit, and even the revered Pennsylvania Academy • Daniel Chester French oversees the first public appearance of Kenyon Cox's sculpture • Some of the year's most interesting auction prices include Corot's *On the Banks of the Seine,* $226; Gainsborough's *Portrait of John Revett, Esq.,* $40; Filippo Lippi's *Study for a Group of Figures,* $225; and Poussin's *Lake Scene,* $50.

The famed brothers, novelist Henry James, also renowned for his psychological insight, and psychologist William James, also renowned for his prose style.

Times Square, named after the *New York Times* building (1904); parking and traffic are not a problem; no white line separates directions.

Over 80 percent of all immigrants since 1900 have arrived from Central Europe, Italy, and Russia.

Books

Fiction

Critics' Choice
The Ancient Law, Ellen Glasgow
The Iron Heel, Jack London
The Voice of the City, O. Henry
The Metropolis, Upton Sinclair
The Shoulders of Atlas, Mary E. Wilkins Freeman
Wait and Win, Horatio Alger (posthumous)
Fennel and Rue, William Dean Howells
Friendship Village, Zona Gale
The Circular Staircase, Mary Roberts Rinehart
🕊 *A Room with a View,* E. M. Forster
🕊 *The Old Wives' Tale,* Arnold Bennett
🕊 *Penguin Island,* Anatole France

Best-Sellers
Mr. Crewe's Career, Winston Churchill
The Barrier, Rex Beach
The Trail of the Lonesome Pine, John Fox, Jr.
The Lure of the Mask, Harold MacGrath
The Shuttle, Frances Hodgson Burnett
Peter, F. Hopkinson Smith
Lewis Rand, Mary Johnson
The Black Bag, Louis J. Vance
The Man from Brodney's, George Barr McCutcheon
The Weavers, Gilbert Parker

Nonfiction

Critics' Choice
The Philosophy of Friedrich Nietzsche, H. L. Mencken
Robert E. Lee: The Southerner, Thomas Nelson Page
Lectures on Science, Philosophy, and Art, John Dewey
The Energies of Men, William James
The Philosophy of Loyalty, Race Questions: Provincialism and Other American Problems, Josiah Royce
"Hamlet," George Santayana
The Privileged Classes, Barrett Wendell
Viva Mexico! Charles M. Flandrau
Reminiscences, Carl Schurz
The True Story of Andersonville Prison, James Page, M. J. Haley
🕊 W. B. Yeats, *Poetry and Ireland: Essays,* with Lionel Johnson

Poems
Sidney Lanier, *Poem Outlines*
Ezra Pound, *A Lume Spento*

Science and Technology

Jacques Loeb raises an unfertilized frog egg to maturity, demonstrating parthenogenesis.
William McDougall proposes a theory of behavior based on instinct.
The 1.5-m reflecting telescope is installed at the Mount Wilson Observatory.
Helium is liquified.
George Ellery Hale observes magnetic fields in sunspots.
Howard Hughes invents a steel-toothed, rock-drilling device that penetrates hard rock.
The Holt Company develops the first tractor to use moving threads.
Thomas Edison's Amberol cylinders, with more grooves to the inch, extend a single recording from two to four minutes.

🕊 A process for extracting nitrogen from the air and making ammonia a cheap fertilizer is developed by Fritz Haber.
🕊 Ernst Zermelo revolutionizes math theory with an axiomatic treatment of set theory, using only two undefined terms and seven axioms.
🕊 The barium meal technique indicates gastric ulcers through X-ray.
🕊 Herrmann Minkowski proposes that relativity theory implies time as the fourth dimension.
🕊 The first international meeting of psychiatrists includes Sigmund Freud, Karl Jung, and Alfred Adler.

Sports

Baseball

With New York and Chicago tied 1–1 in a vital game, a single seems to score the winning run, but Fred Merkle fails to proceed to 2nd base; Johnny Evers tags him out, generating a mammoth controversy about Merkle's "bonehead play" ("a boner"). The game is ordered to be replayed as a "playoff game," and Chicago wins the game and pennant.

Chicago (NL) goes on to win its second straight WS; F. P. Adams calls "Tinkers-to-Evers-to-Chance" "the saddest words" in baseball.

Ty Cobb wins his 2nd straight batting championship; his team, its 2nd straight pennant.

Cy Young (Boston, AL) pitches his 2nd no-hitter, one of a record five during the year.

Soiling baseballs is prohibited.

Walter Johnson, 20, Washington (AL) shuts out New York 3 times in a 4-game series; Ty Cobb says: "You can't hit what you can't see," as Johnson earns the nickname "Big Train," analogizing him to a powerful locomotive.

Honus Wagner wins his 6th batting title.

Champions

Batting
　Honus Wagner (Pittsburgh, NL), .354
　Ty Cobb (Detroit, AL), .324
Pitching
　Ed Ruelbach (Chicago, NL), 24–7

　Ed Walsh (Chicago, AL), 40–15
Home runs
　Tim Jordan (Brooklyn, NL), 12

Football

College All-Americans: William Hollenbach (HB), Penn; Hamilton Fish (T), Harvard; Walter Steffen (Q), Chicago

Basketball

The 5-foul elimination rule is put into effect.

Olympics

The games are played at London, England. The U.S. is the unofficial winner with 23 gold. Ray Ewry wins 2 more gold for a record total of 10. Other winners include Mel Sheppard (800m, 1:52.8, 1500m, 4:03.4), John J. Hayes (marathon, 2:55:18.4), Martin Sheridan (discus throw, 134′2″), Frank Irons (running broad jump, 24′6.5″), Edward Cooke (pole vault, 12′2″). Charles Daniels wins another swimming gold.

Other Sports

Boxing: For a record $30,00 purse HW champion Tommy Burns meets Jack Johnson in Sydney, Australia; Johnson, who becomes the first black HW champion, is thoroughly beating Burns when the police rush to stop fight in the 14th round.

Stanley Ketchel KOs Jack ("Twin") Sullivan for the MW title in San Francisco.

Winners

World Series
　Chicago (NL) 4
　Detroit (AL) 1
College Football
　Penn
College Basketball
　Chicago
Player of the Year
　Charles Keinath, Penn

U.S. Tennis Open
　Men: William Larned
　Women: Maud Barger-Wallach
USGA Open
　Fred McLeod
Kentucky Derby
　Stone Street (Arthur Pickens, jockey)

Fashion

With Russian ballet invading Europe and Isadora Duncan enchanting American audiences, fashion follows the costume of dancers. Even Sergei Diaghilev's Oriental ballet design touches style with its jeweled fabrics, bright colors, sense of great luxury, and the wearer's sense of mobility. A certain relaxation of rigidity and solemnity is in the air: stiff satins, plush damasks, heavy tweeds, and other rigid materials are swept away—any remnant of Queen Victoria's dress— and replaced by a froth of net, faille, crêpe de chine, moire, cashmere, lace, and chiffon. Strong, emphatic or somber colors are replaced by soft, sugary tones. Nevertheless, during the summertime, the fashionable woman still endures constricting basics: chemise, corset, corset cover, drawers, flannel petticoat, one or more cotton petticoats with a silk petticoat worn over all. She also puffs her hair out and up with pads or "rats," drawing her hair over the pads that are supported by combs. Hats are worn with long, enameled hat pins, often a menacing weapon to those in close proximity. Ostrich feathers and marabou (stork) boas, as well as fur stoles and puffs, remain treasured accessories, like the pretty parasol, ubiquitous in the summertime.

High-fashion note: the Mme. de Vionnet peignoir

Kaleidoscope ———————————

- While honoring his pledge not to run again for president, TR in inundated with pleas that he reconsider.
- Cartoon caption: "That's a splendid phonograph. . . . It reproduces Roosevelt's voice better than I thought possible. What make?" "We call it the Taft"; a popular campaign slogan is: "TAFT means Take advice from Theodore."
- After catching a trolley, Bryan's daughter comments: "I seem to be the only member of the Bryan family who ever ran for anything and caught it."
- Unemployment from the 1907 panic continues; more than 2,000 men appear for free breakfast at the Bowery Mission in N.Y.C.
- Due to the highest unemployment level in 10 years, 395,000 immigrants return home.
- Movements against liquor and cigarette consumption gain momentum: a U.S. Steel subsidiary, the Henry C. Frick Co., prohibits both on its premises, as does the Baltimore and Ohio Railway.
- There are 6 million farms in the U.S.; half of all U.S. citizens live on them or in towns with fewer than 2,500 people.
- Worldwide attention is given Albert Einstein's "quantum" theory of light.
- Admiral Robert E. Peary begins his sixth and last expedition to reach the North Pole in a 184′, 600-ton steamer, *The Roosevelt.*
- Blossom Seeley, imitating black artists, tells black dialect stories, sings "Put Your Arms around Me" and dances the rag "Doing the Toledo" in San Francisco.
- "Are we going to the dogs by the ragtime route?" asks the *New York Sun,* in fear over the music's enormous popularity.
- A woman wearing a sheath gown imported from Paris (and fishnet stockings) is arrested in Chicago.
- After their show this year, the "Ashcan School" of painters ("The Eight") begin to gain recognition with their portrayals of the reality of everyday, often grim, slum reality.
- When W. C. Durant founds General Motors by organizing several auto producers, he tells the Ford company it is not worth its asking price.
- Ford introduces the Model T; it can go 45 mph and represents a new standard in value; about 25 auto companies produce 63,500 cars.
- The U.S. Army buys its first aircraft, a dirigible; because no one can fly it except its owner, T. S. Baldwin, it is never used.
- Newport, R.I., continues to be a requisite summer residence for the very rich: a "cottage" of 30 rooms can be built for about $1 million, although the William K. Vanderbilts spend $2 million (and $9 million for decorations, including an African marble ballroom paneled in gold); at one party, in search of novelty, 100 dogs and their masters appear for a feast that includes a fricassee of bones and shredded dog biscuits.
- Cornelius Vanderbilt's yacht, *North Star,* costs $250,000 and has a yearly maintenance of $20,000.
- The 47-story Singer Building in New York becomes the world's tallest skyscraper.
- Authority Kranz Kneisel states: "There are 1,000 Stradivari violins in existence," adding, "I have known of persons paying as high as $10,000 for one"; most prized are those built between 1712 and 1724, when Stradivarius was in his prime.
- Less well-off people visit Atlantic City and enjoy peep shows, the merry-go-round, and fortune tellers, or the trolley parks at the edges of the city with their Ferris wheels, band concerts, and vaudeville acts.
- Black rain from the mysterious explosion of a fireball in Siberia sends waves of fear throughout the world.
- "The danger to American democracy . . . lies in having . . . power insufficiently concentrated, so that no one can be held responsible to the people for its use," says TR to Congress, still seeking to expand federal power.
- Muir Woods and the Grand Canyon are named national monuments to be preserved.
- Wilbur Wright gets the first government contract for an airplane that flies for 60 minutes up to 40 mph; Wright wins the Michelin Cup.
- The first transatlantic wireless telegraph stations connect Canada to Ireland; the public can send messages for 15¢ a word.
- A national conference on conservation urges that we protect our forests, regulate water, improve river navigation, and retain all federal land with mineral value or waterpower.
- The fountain pen gains popularity.

First Appearances: Red-Cross Christmas seal against TB ($135,000), kinecolor (true color for film, G. A. Smith), poison gas (Carl Wheaton, Ill.), Luger pistol, Geiger counter, aviator's passenger (May Charles Furness, in Wright's plane), "Mutt and Jeff" (the same cartoon figures in a daily), *Christian Science Monitor,* Hupmobile, "limosene" (motorcar with glass-enclosed body), N.Y.C. IRT subway to the Bronx, Continental Oil, AC Spark Plug, Champion Spark Plug, professional school of journalism (U. of Missouri), Brooklyn Academy of Music, 65-note, coin-operated player piano (Wurlitzer, $700), vending machine that sells water in paper cups (1¢), oscillating fan, Brooklyn Battery Tunnel, FBI

William Jennings Bryan runs for president a third time, assailing the gluttony of business, "The Enthroned Hog."

1909

Immigrant woman showing off her balancing skills in the service of delivering goods.

Deaths

Isaac Albéniz, Francis Marion
  Crawford, Geronimo, Sarah
  Orne Jewett, Charles F.
  McKim, George Meredith,
  Prince Hirobumi Ito, Frederic
  Remington, Algernon
  Charles Swinburne, John
  Millington Synge

In the News

U.S. GIVES COLOMBIA $25 MILLION FOR RECOGNITION OF PANAMA . . . SIX "NIGHT RIDERS" ARE SENTENCED TO DEATH IN TENNESSEE . . . U.S. ENDS SECOND OCCUPATION OF CUBA, BEGUN IN 1906 . . . GREAT POWERS PERSUADE SERBIA TO ACCEPT AUSTRIAN ANNEXATION OF BOSNIA-HERZEGOVNIA, WAR IS AVERTED . . . TAFT IS INAUGURATED . . . N.Y.C. DETECTIVE IS MURDERED IN PALERMO, SICILY, WHILE INVESTIGATING "BLACK HAND" . . . TR GOES ON SCIENTIFIC EXPEDITION TO AFRICA . . . ROBERT PEARY BECOMES FIRST TO REACH NORTH POLE . . . "YOUNG TURKS" DEPOSE SULTAN ABDUL HAMID II AFTER 35-YEAR RULE . . . TAFT SIGNS CONTROVERSIAL PAYNE-ALDRICH TARIFF ACT, HIGH PROTECTIVE RATES REMAIN . . . JOAN OF ARC IS BEATIFIED AT VATICAN . . . TAFT OPENS 700,000 ACRES OF FEDERAL LAND IN NORTHWEST TO SETTLERS . . . WHITE FIREMEN AT GEORGIA RAILROAD STRIKE OVER EMPLOYMENT OF BLACKS, MOB ATTACKS BLACKS . . . BLACK LEADER W. E. B. DU BOIS CALLS FOR RENEWAL OF "ABOLITIONIST SPIRIT" . . . CONGRESS PASSES 16TH AMENDMENT TO PERMIT INCOME TAX . . . U.S. COURT ORDERS DISSOLUTION OF STANDARD OIL TRUST . . . ORVILLE WRIGHT FLIES 1 HR., 1 MIN., 40 SEC. . . . 20,000 N.Y. GARMENT WORKERS WIN FAVORABLE SETTLEMENT AFTER 3-MONTH STRIKE . . . LOUIS BLÉRIOT IS FIRST TO FLY ACROSS ENGLISH CHANNEL . . . TAFT SETS ASIDE 3 MILLION ACRES OF WESTERN LAND FOR CONSERVATION . . . CHERRY, ILL., MINE EXPLOSION KILLS 259 . . . U.S. SENDS WARSHIPS TO AID REBELLION AGAINST NICARAGUAN DICTATOR ZELAYA . . . TR RECOMMENDS PEARL HARBOR NAVAL STATION TO DEFEND U.S. FROM JAPANESE.

Quotes

Roosevelt: "I can do no further harm to the Constitution."

Taft: " 'Tis my storm. I knew it would be a cold day when I became President of the United States."
   —After the great blizzard during Taft's Inauguration

"[America] still believes that somehow and sometime something better will happen to Americans than has happened to men in any other country."
   —Herbert Croly, *The Promise of American Life*

"The Pole at last. . . . Mine at last!"
   —Admiral Robert E. Peary

"Make no little plans. Little plans have no magic to stir men's blood."
   —Architect D. H. Burnham, on rebuilding Chicago

"We want the higher marriage, . . . full-grown women of proud independence."
   —Woman's Rights' Charlotte Perkins Gilman

"The only laws women would pass . . . would prevent fathers from spoiling daughters."
   —E. O. Jones, in popular editorial opposing Woman's Suffrage

"We hear much of the divorce evil and the action of the church condemning it. Well, there is a better way, . . . homecooking."
   —Dr. H. Wiley, Chief, U.S. Bureau of Chemistry

John D. Rockefeller, the world's first billionaire, is known for his ruthlessness in business.

"There is no rule of fairness or reasonableness which regulates competition."
   —Standard Oil spokesperson, in defense of its rebate policy

"The employer puts his money into . . . business and the workman his life. The one has as much right as the other to regulate that business."
   —Clarence Darrow

"There is every reason America should attract the Italian criminal. . . . One of every three . . . is given a suspended sentence."
   —N.Y.C. detective, on the "Black Hand"

Ads

Immigrants, already under the protection of the U.S. flag at Ellis Island, must register and be examined for contagious diseases; one Russian Jew, who momentarily forgets his name, says: "Shoyn Fegessen" ("I forgot") and is registered as Sean Ferguson.

Jane Addams, who opened the first Settlement House in Chicago, with the children she loved and cared for so well.

Vaudeville

The Graumann empire of theater owners begins with Graumann's National Theater in San Francisco; it never advertises but is always filled. The family becomes associated with immortalizing actors' hand and footprints in cement, in Los Angeles.

Of Note

Eddie Cantor prepares for his major vaudeville debut by working small burlesque revues as a tramp, Jewish character, and bootblack; he then finds a job as a shill outside a big vaudeville house. At the end of the year, Roy Arthur, famed member of the juggling team "Bedini and Arthur," hires Cantor as a valet and Cantor works his way into their act • Black ventriloquist J. W. Cooper uses two kid "dummies," one black and one white • Texas Guinan ("Hello, Sucker"), a former rodeo driver, gains popularity with her well-trained soprano voice • Walter Huston and his future wife, Bayonne Whippley, create *Spoofs,* with Huston singing "I Haven't Got the Do-Re-Mi" • Charlotte Parrey, in her minidrama "Into the Light," acts as an Italian woman in court accused of murder and plays each of the witnesses • Many highly successful stars leave vaudeville (at least part-time) for the stage, movies, and even opera: Lillian Russell, Lily Langtry, W. C. Fields, George M. Cohan, Harry Houdini, Weber and Fields, Marie Dressler, and Rosa Ponselle. Some, like Sam Bernard, shuttle between musical theater and vaudeville, because the latter provides a higher salary.

Movies

Gertie the Dinosaur, first animated cartoon, 10,000 drawings

In a Lonely Villa (Griffith), Mary Pickford, Marion Leonard, Owen Moore

A Corner in Wheat (Griffith)

The Resurrection (Griffith), Florence Lawrence, Arthur Johnson

A Mender of Nets (Griffith), Mary Pickford

A Convict's Scarface (Griffith), Stephanie Longfellow, Gladys Egan, Henry B. Walthall, James Kirkwood

Oliver Twist (Vitagraph), Elita Proctor Otis

Hiawatha (Imp), Gladys Hulette

The Prince and the Pauper (Edison), Cecil Spooner (in dual role)

Regarding the U.S.-French controversy over morality, producer Carl Laemmle says: "I will make American subjects my specialty [with] virile American subjects," citing westerns as his model. About 9,000 movie theaters are tallied in the U.S. Mary Pickford, in stock since age 5, joins Biograph and is soon paired with Billy Quirk for comedy. A new Bell & Howell camera eliminates flickering from films. Newly formed studios include Laemmle, Imp, Bauman, Balshofer, Powers, and Bison. Popular actors include Henry B. Walthall, James Kirkwood, Marion Leonard, Florence La Badice at Biograph; Alice Joyce at Kalem. Maurice Costello ("the dimpled darling") moves from Edison to Vitagraph.

Popular Music

Hit Songs
"I Wonder Who's Kissing Her Now"
"By the Light of the Silvery Moon"
"Casey Jones"
"Chiribiribin"
"My Hero"
"For You Alone"
"Somebody Wants You"
"Squeeze Me Tight"

Representative Recordings:
"I'm Awfully Glad I Met You" (Victor Orchestra); "On a Monkey Honeymoon" (Arthur Collins–Byron G. Harlan); "That Mesmerizing Mendelssohn Tune" / "Cherry Rag" (Victor Orchestra);

Scott Joplin, who pioneered ragtime ("Original Rag"), sees his style continue to flourish and capture followers.

"Moonlight in Jungle Land" (Arthur Collins–Byron G. Harlan); "Shine On, Harvest Moon"/"I'm On My Way to Reno" (Billy Murray); "Good Evening Caroline" (Frank Stanley–Elise Stevenson); "The Right Church But the Wrong Pew" (Arthur Collins–Byron G. Harlan)

Jazz
W. C. Handy composes the first blues that are written down, "Memphis Blues," a campaign song for "Boss" Crump of Memphis. "Buddy" Bolden's New Orleans band, under Freddie Keppard, now includes Sidney Bechet and Joe "King" Oliver.

Theater

Broadway Openings

Plays
The Fortune Hunter (Winchell Smith), John Barrymore, Hale Hamilton
Arsene Lupin (Francis de Croisset, Maurice Leblanc), William Courtney
The Easiest Way (Eugene Walter), Frances Starr
The Girl from Rector's (Paul M. Potter), Violet Dale, J. W. Ashley, Van Rensselaer Wheeler
A Woman's Way (Thompson Buchanan), Grace George, Frank Worthing
Is Matrimony a Failure? (Leo Ditrichstein), Frank Worthing, Jane Cowl, William Morris
The City (Clyde Fitch), Frank Courtney, Mary Nash, Walter Hampden, Lucille Watson
The Melting Pot (Israel Zangwill), Walker Whiteside
The Passing of the Third Floor Back (Jerome K. Jerome), Johnston Forbes-Robertson
The Lottery Man (Rida Johnson Young), Louise Galloway

Musicals
The Chocolate Soldier (Oscar Straus, Rudolph Bernauer, Leopold Jacobson), Ida Brooks Hunt, Jack Gardner
The Dollar Princess (Leo Fall, George Grossmith, Jr.), Donald Brian, Percival Knight
Havana (Leslie Stuart, Adrian Ross), James T. Powers, Eva Davenport, William Pruette, Patsy O'Connor
The Midnight Sons (Raymond Hubbell, Glen MacDonough), Lotta Faust, Harry Fisher, Blanche Ring, Vernon Castle

Old Dutch (Victor Herbert, George V. Hobart), Lew Fields, Vernon Castle, Helen Hayes (first N.Y. appearance)
The Red Moon (J. Rosamond Johnson, Bob Cole), J. Rosamond Johnson, all-black cast
Ziegfeld Follies of 1909 (Maurice Levi, Harry B. Smith), Nora Bayes, Sophie Tucker, Eva Tanguay, Gertie Vanderbilt, Mae Murray
A Stubborn Cinderella (Will Huff, Joseph E. Howard), Sally Fisher, John Barrymore (his only musical)

Classics and Revivals On and Off Broadway
Robert B. Mantell Company: *King John;* The New Theatre opens, built by 30 wealthy men: Julia Marlowe, E. H. Sothern in *Antony and Cleopatra;* in *Strife* and *The School for Scandal,* also with Grace George, Louis Calvert; *The Master Builder*

Maxine Elliott, long recognized as one of Broadway's great actors and beauties, divorced her husband last year and now buys her own theater to manage.

Classical Music ——————

Compositions
Charles Cadman, *Four American Indian Songs*
George Whitefield Chadwick, *Everywoman's Waltz,*
    Suite Symphonique in E flat
Charles Ives, First Piano Sonata (1901–09),
    Washington's Birthday
John Alden Carpenter, Suite for Orchestra (1906–09)

Important Events
Rachmaninoff concertizes for the first time in the U.S. with
a solo recital at Smith College and his Piano Concerto
no. 2 with the Boston Symphony in Philadelphia; he also
makes conductorial premieres with the Philadelphia and
New York Symphonies (at the last, also performing his
Piano Concerto no. 3). Ignace Paderewski plays Camille
Saint-Saëns' Fourth Piano Concerto with the Boston
Symphony Orchestra, Max Fiedler conducting; the
orchestra premieres his Symphony in B minor. The
music department at Tulane University opens. Walter
Damrosch conducts the New York Symphony Orchestra
at Chautauqua, N.Y., beginning an annual music festival.

Notable Performances: Rosina and Josef Lhévinne
perform a joint recital in N.Y. that includes Anton
Arensky's *Duos for Two Pianos.* For its 100th
commemorative of Beethoven's Fifth, the Boston
Symphony performs the piece with the "Parsifal"
Prelude and works by Tchaikovsky.

Major Recitals: Misha Elman's N.Y. recital concludes
with a ten-minute standing ovation; he plays Henryk
Wieniawski's *Faust Fantasie,* Anton Rubinstein's
Melody in F, and Pablo de Sarasate's *Caprice Basque.*
British violinist Albany Ritchie receives high praise
during his U.S. tour.

New Appointments: Henry Hadley, Seattle Symphony
Orchestra; Leopold Stokowski, Cincinnati Symphony
Orchestra; Gustav Mahler, N.Y. Philharmonic Society

First Performances
Henry Hadley, Symphony (Boston); Arthur Foote, *Suite
in E Major for Strings* (Boston), *Suite symphonique*
(Philadelphia)

Opera

Metropolitan: Premieres: Emmy Destinn, Erik
Schmedes, *Tiefland* (Albert); *Le Villi* (Puccini),
conducted by Toscanini; *La Wally* (Catalani); *The
Bartered Bride* (Smetana). Adamo Didur (debut), *Faust;*
Caruso, Frances Alda (debut), *Rigoletto;* Destinn,
Caruso, *Cavalleria rusticana,* conducted by Toscanini;
Sembrich, Caruso, *La Bohème;* Caruso, Maria Gay,
Carmen; Alma Gluck (debut), *Werther* (Massenet); Leo

Gustav Mahler. The famed
composer-conductor has
left the Vienna Imperial
Opera (where he was
known as a "tyrant") to
conduct at the Met and
New York Philharmonic.

Slezak, Scotti, Frances Alda, *Otello;* Emma Eames
(farewell performance), *Tosca*

Manhattan: Mary Garden, *Salomé;* Garden, *Faust;*
Garden, *Jongleur de Notre Dame*

Chicago: Destinn, Homer, Amato, Didur, *Aïda*
(Toscanini conducting); Karl Joern, Johanna Gadski,
Die Meistersinger

Academy of Music, New York: Jane Noria, Caruso,
Amato, *Pagliacci;* Lillian Nordica, Leo Slezak, *Il
trovatore*

Boston (gala opening): under manager Henry Russell,
Nordica, Homer, Florencio Constantino, *La gioconda*
(Ponchielli); Slezak, *Otello, Aïda;* Alda (William Frank
Harling)

Philadelphia: Garden, M. Dalmorès, *Sapho;* Carmen
Melis, *Tosca;* Jeanne Gerville-Réache, Dalmorès,
Samson et Dalila; Lina Cavalieri, Emma Trentini, *The
Tales of Hoffman; Andon* (Wassili Leps); *Little Nemo*
(Victor Herbert); Garden, Charles Gilibert, Hector
Dufranne, *The Hunchback of Notre Dame;* Destinn,
Homer, Caruso, Amato, *La gioconda;* Tetrazzini, John
McCormack, *Daughter of the Regiment;* Tetrazzini,
McCormack, *La traviata*

Chicago: *The Prima Donna* (Victor Herbert)

Music Notes
Boston Mayor Hibbard bans the announced production of
Richard Strauss's *Salomé* • The first radio transmission
from the Met to the home of radio pioneer Lee De Forest
occurs; Caruso uses two microphones • At the French
Opera House in New Orleans, Léon Escalaïs hits three
high C's five times in the "Quella Pira" aria of *Il trovatore* •
Charles W. Cadman spends the summer with the Omaha
Indians • Charles Ives forms his own insurance agency in
N.Y.C. • Gustav Mahler reorganizes the Philharmonic at
Carnegie Hall, extending its season and adding musical
(e.g., Beethoven) cycles, as well as special events and
tours; he also flaunts his controversial interpretations,
adding kettledrums to Beethoven's Fifth and doubling the
flutes in Mozart's 40th; subscriptions drop.

After Emmy Destinn takes over Geraldine Farrar's role in *Madama Butterfly,* the two pass each other in silence.

Early bands choose proud names: here, the Original Superior Band, with the great cornetist Willie "Bunk" Johnson and clarinetist Louis Nelson (standing in the middle of the top row).

Art

Painting

George Bellows, *Both Members of This Club*
Rockwell Kent, *Snow Fields*
Max Weber, *Summer*
Marsden Hartley, *The Summer Camp, Blue Mountain*
John Sloan, *Three A.M., Fifth Avenue*
Arthur B. Davies, *The Flood, The Dream*
Frederic Remington, *The Stampede*
George Luks, *Roundhouses at Highbridge*

Sculpture

Frederic Remington, *Trooper of the Plains*
Edith W. Burroughs, *Edgar Allan Poe*
A. Phiminster Proctor, *Puma*
Abstemia S. Leger Eberle, *Roller Skating*
Daniel Chester French, *Mourning Victory*

Architecture

Frank Lloyd Wright home and studio, 961 Chicago Ave., Chicago (Frank Lloyd Wright)
Robie House, 5757 S. Woodlawn Avenue, Chicago (Frank Lloyd Wright, 1907–09)
Metropolitan Life Tower, N.Y.C. (Le Brun & Sons)
City National Bank Building and Hotel, Mason City, Iowa (Frank Lloyd Wright)
Avery Coonley house, River Forest, Ill. (Frank Lloyd Wright)
Meyer S. Mayhouse window, Grand Rapids, Mich. (Frank Lloyd Wright)
Carnegie Institute, Washington, D.C. (Carrère & Hastings)
Pratt house, Ojai, Calif. (Greene & Greene)
Burnham submits a highly innovative city plan, of Chicago—separating the industrial and railroad areas, parks, riverfront, and cultural and civic areas.

Important Exhibitions

New York: *Metropolitan:* Contemporary German art; Hudson-Fulton Celebration; Exhibition of drawings: Rembrandt, Jan Van Goyen, Aelbert Cuyp, Pieter Breughel, William Blake, J. M. W. Turner, Gainsborough, Arthur Davies. Acquisitions: Arms and armor; Spanish carpets; Chinese screens and carpets; Rembrandt's *Self-Portrait;* Corot's *Sleep of Diana;* 15 French tapestries; Lorenzo Monaco's *Madonna and Child;* Hans Holbein's *Portrait of Erasmus. J. P. Morgan:* "The American Midwest"

Chicago: Modern Dutch art; Henry Reinhardt; Italian Renaissance; Contemporary German Art; art of two private collections (Cyrus H. McCormick, Charles L. Hutchinson)

Met, Boston, Chicago: Edwin H. Blashfield; Frederic C. Bartlett

Boston: Alexander Robinson

Buffalo: Birge Hamilton; F. K. M. Rehm; Henry R. Poor; William Merritt Chase

Washington, D.C. (Corcoran): Dutch art at the Hudson-Fulton Exhibit

Seattle: "Notable Paintings"

Briefs

Henri resigns from the New York School of Arts and opens his own School of Art to encourage the avant-garde; it becomes a haven for young artists • Several American collectors are rumored to have leased a London gallery to display American work and introduce it to England, then Germany and Italy • Alfred Stieglitz exhibits Henri de Toulouse-Lautrec for the first time in N.Y.C.

Books

Fiction

Critics' Choice

Three Lives: Stories of the Good Anna, Melanctha, and the Gentle Lena, Gertrude Stein
Martin Eden, Jack London
The Bride of the Mistletoe, James Lane Allen
Chivalry, James Branch Cabell
Friendship Village, Zona Gale
The Romance of a Plain Man, Ellen Glasgow
Extract from Captain Stormfield's Visit to Heaven, Mark Twain
Roads of Destiny, O. Henry
The White Sister, F. Marion Crawford
The Third Circle, Frank Norris (posthumous)
Julia Bride, Henry James

Mary E. Wilkins Freeman writes of the hard life engendered by the New England Old Testament ethos; she had already achieved fame at age 50, when she married.

The Hungry Heart, David Graham Phillips
The Mills of Mammon, James Hattan Brower
🕭 *Strait Is the Gate,* André Gide

Best-Sellers

The Inner Shrine, Anonymous (Basil King)
Katrine, Elinor Macartney Lane
The Silver Horde, Rex Beach
The Man in Lower Ten, Mary Roberts Rinehart
The Trail of the Lonesome Pine, John Fox, Jr.
Truxton King, George Barr McCutcheon
54–40 or Fight, Emerson Hough
The Goose Girl, Harold MacGrath
Peter, F. Hopkinson Smith
Septimus, William J. Locke

Nonfiction

Critics' Choice

The Promise of American Life, Herbert Croly
A Pluralistic Universe, William James
The Legacy of John Brown, W. E. B. Du Bois
Stickeen: An Adventure with a Dog and a Glacier in 1880, John Muir
War: A Manifesto against It, Upton Sinclair
American Prose Masters, William C. Brownell

Geronimo, the once-feared Apache warrior who eluded capture for many years, lived out the last decades of his life peacefully; he wrote *Geronimo's Story of His Life* three years before his death.

The Wine of the Puritans, Van Wyck Brooks
Egoists: A Book of Supermen, James Gibbons Huneker
Reconstruction, Political and Economic, 1865–1877, W. A. Dunning
A Problem for Industry, William Beveridge
Italian Hours, Henry James
Modern English: Its Growth and Present Use, George Philip Krapp

Poems

Stephen Foster (posthumous), *The Melodies*
Louise Imogen Guiney, *Happy Ending: Collected Lyrics*
Edith Wharton, *Artemis to Actaeon and Other Verse*
Ezra Pound, *Personae, Exaltations*
🕭 W. B. Yeats, *Poems,* 2nd ser.
🕭 Rabindranath Tagore, *Gitanjali*

Science and Technology

The Meltzer-Auer tube, developed at the Rockefeller Institute, is inserted into the windpipe to assist patients in breathing during throat, mouth, and chest surgery.

Harvey Cushing discovers that acromegaly, the enlargement of jaws, some organs, and extremities, is due to overgrowth of the pituitary.

William McCallum, at Johns Hopkins, shows that it is fatal to remove all four small glands attached to the thyroid.

Rocky Mountain fever is shown to be transmitted by the tick louse; typhus, spread by the body louse.

Jesse L. Greenstein, studying the different elements and isotopes that comprise stars, postulates the uniqueness of every star.

The concept of pH is introduced as a measure of acidity and alkalinity.

Leo Baekeland invents Bakelite, a plastic that doesn't melt with heat.

🕭 Alpha particles are shown to bounce back from thin gold foil, confirming Ernest Rutherford's speculations.

🕭 The terms "genotype," defining genetic makeup, and "phenotype," defining the living organism produced by both environment and genes, are coined.

Sports

Baseball
Ty Cobb and "Wahoo" Sam Crawford lead Detroit to its 3rd straight pennant.

Cobb wins his 3rd straight batting title; Honus Wagner, his 7th overall.

Rookie pitcher Babe Adams wins three games, as Wagner outsteals Cobb 6 to 2, in Pittsburgh's WS victory.

Attendance has doubled since the AL and NL merged in 1903.

The cork-centered ball is introduced.

Champions

Batting	S. H. Camnitz (Pittsburgh, NL),
Honus Wagner (Pittsburgh, NL), .339	25–6
Ty Cobb (Detroit, AL), .377	George Mullin (Detroit, AL), 29–8
Pitching	*Home runs*
Christy Mathewson (New York, NL)	Ty Cobb (Detroit, AL), 9

Football
Six of eleven All-Americans are from Yale. With 33 deaths during the college season, safety concerns and controversy about playing the game heighten.

College All-Americans: W. M. Minot (HB), Harvard; John Kilpatrick (E), Yale; Edward McCoy (F), Yale

Basketball
The University of Chicago wins its 3rd consecutive national title under coach Joseph Raycroft.

Other Sports

Golf: The game becomes a fad when President Taft says it helps him regulate his weight.

Tennis: Hazel Hotchkiss raises eyebrows with her aggressive style of play.

Auto Racing: The first race is run at the Indianapolis Speedway, a brick-paved track.

Winners

World Series	U.S. Tennis Open
Pittsburgh (NL) 4	Men: William Larned
Detroit (NL) 3	Women: Hazel Hotchkiss
College Football	*USGA Open*
Yale	George Sargent
College Basketball	*Kentucky Derby*
Chicago	Wintergreen (Vincent Powers, jockey)
Player of the Year	
John Shommer, Chicago	

Fashion

For Men: According to the Haberdasher Company of New York, the proper dress code, for day weddings, afternoon calls, and matinee receptions, includes coat and overcoat (e.g., frock, chesterfield), waistcoat (pearl or white linen duck or silk), trousers (striped worsted or cheviot of dark gray), hat (high silk with broad felt band), shirts and cuffs (plain white with cuffs attached), collar (round tabbed wing), gloves (pearl glacé or white kid), cravat (either pearl or white ascot, or cravat that matches gloves), boots (patent leather—buttoned, with cloth or kid tops), and jewelry (gold links, gold studs, cravat pin).

For Women: John Forsythe's shirtwaist in Scottish madras; heightened waistlines and dresses accentuating a freer, more elongated silhouette; hats remain stylishly large, befeathered, and beribboned.

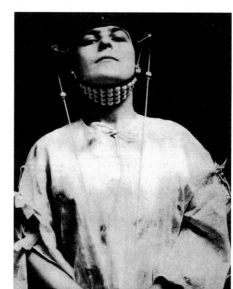

An ad for Professor E. J. Mack's chin reducer and beautifier.

Flirting in 1909; the Audubon Society makes no small protest over the fashionable hats decorated with bird feathers.

Kaleidoscope

From pushcart peddler to entrepreneur: the American Dream.

- The economy finally rebounds strongly from the Panic of 1907.
- Peary is accompanied by black aide Matthew Henson as he plants the U.S. flag at the North Pole; they reach the North Pole after a dogsled journey of 400 miles in weather so cold that Peary's flask of brandy is frozen solid on his parka.
- According to the *World Almanac and Encyclopedia:* "Rah, rah rah! rah rah rah!" is the popular cheer at both Harvard and Yale; the difference lies in delivery: Harvard's is long and deep; Yale's, quick and sharp.
- College tuitions vary from none and about $40 (Carlton, Univ. of Michigan) to $150–$250 (Harvard, Columbia, Princeton); room and board, $45–$350; other expenses, including books, $20–$75.
- Wilbur Wright designs a plane for the U.S. Army that carries two passengers, flies for an hour, and reaches 40 mph.
- The most wealthy Americans include the Vanderbilts, Goulds, Astors, Rockefellers, Morgans, Mackays, Havemeyers, Fields, Belmonts, Whitneys, Leitners, Goelets, Lorillards, Carnegies, and Armours.
- New York is the only state that allows for absolute divorce due solely to adultery; other states include such causes as desertion, abandonment, cruelty, felony, and insanity.
- Incandescent lights replace carbine flame jets on auto headlights.
- The Lincoln head penny replaces the Indian head, in circulation since 1864.
- 127,731 autos are produced, twice that of last year, with nearly 20,000 Model T's, surpassing any other car; 34 states adopt a 25-mph speed limit.
- An estimated 1 million attend various ceremonies commemorating the centennial of Lincoln's birth.
- The Rockefeller Sanitary Commission leads the fight to eradicate hookworm.
- Filtered water produces dramatic reductions in death rates, but acquiring water and keeping it clean remain a ubiquitous problem.
- A bison refuge is created near Boise, Idaho.
- Ice cream sales reach 39 million gallons (5, in 1899).
- American psychologist and Clark University president Stanley Hall invites Sigmund Freud and Carl Jung to receive honorary degrees; Freud calls it a "momentous occasion" and lectures "On Psychoanalysis."
- The largest number of fraternity members belongs to Beta Theta Pi (116,000), Delta Kappa Epson and Phi Delta Theta (about 17,500); of sororities, Kappa Alpha Theta (4,078), Kappa Kappa Gamma (15,000), and Phi Beta Phi (15,404).
- Edward Payson Weston walks from New York to San Francisco in 105 days.
- Congress bans opium import except for medicinal purposes.
- John D. Rockefeller, the world's first billionaire, gives $500 million for medical research.
- *Dr. Eliot's Five-Foot Shelf* of classic writings receives enormous advertising and success.
- "Woman Suffrage" is the subject of the first radio talk broadcast, given by Lee De Forest's mother-in-law, Harriot Stanton Blatch.
- Jane Addams worries that "thousands of young people in every industrial city [are] going to the show" so often it is becoming a daily and potentially dangerous habit.

- The National Board of Censors worries over the role models movies provide; *Motion Picture Weekly* believes movies provide more information than newspapers.
- Du Bois's Niagara Movement joins with white liberals to form a new organization for racial equality; other leaders include John Dewey, Lincoln Steffens, Clarence Darrow, and Rabbi Stephen Wise.
- The movie industry agrees to use the 35mm format (introduced by Edison in 1893) as the standard.
- Radio allows for human rescue, when it broadcasts the US *Republic*'s collision with the Italian *Florida;* only five lives are lost.
- Two of the decade's sexiest shows appear: *The Easiest Way,* about the trials and tribulations of a "kept woman," and *The Girl from Rector's,* a bedroom farce; *The Melting Pot* examines the disappearance of Jewish tradition when Jews become assimilated into the new world.
- Taft confesses that whenever he hears the words "Mr. President" he looks around for TR.

First Appearances: Kewpie doll, Elizabeth Arden beauty salon, Fifth Avenue, N.Y., Filene's Automatic Bargain Basement (Boston), *Vogue,* electric toaster (GE), Walgreen's drugstore chain with soda fountain lunch counter, J. L. Kraft Bros. and Co., gasolene cigarette lighter, smelts (planted in the Great Lakes), Walter Reed Army Medical Center (Washington, D.C.), Western Auto Supply, N.Y. Queensboro and Manhattan Bridges, *Amsterdam News,* Laguna Dam, Hudson car, gyroscopes (in aircraft, Sperry and Ford), Castrol motor oil, hydrofoil, National Conservation Association, lightweight, high-strength aluminum alloys, Silver Ghost (Rolls-Royce)

Matthew Henson is Robert E. Peary's sole companion on the final leg of their North Pole journey.

THE *Tens*

U.S. doughboys liberate a French couple from German-occupied territory. Of America's involvement in the war, President Wilson has said: "Sometimes people call me an idealist. Well that is the way I know that I am an American." *National Archives.*

Statistics

Vital
Population: 92,407,000
  Urban/Rural: 42/50
  Farm: 35%
Life expectancy:
  Male: 48.4
  Female: 51.8
Births/1,000: 30.1
Marriages/1,000: 13.2
Divorces/1,000: 1.1
Deaths/1,000
  per 100,000
    Heart: NA
    Cancer: 76
    Tuberculosis: 154
    Car accidents: 2

Economic
Unemployed: 2,150,000
GNP: $35.3 billion
Federal budget: $0.675 billion
National debt: $1.15 billion
Union membership: 2.1 million
Strikes: 1,204
Car sales: 181,000
Average salary: $750

Social
Homicides/100,000: 4.6
Suicides/100,000: 15.3
Lynchings: 76
Labor force, male/female: 3.8/1
Public education: $426 million
College degrees
  Bachelors'
    Male: 28,700
    Female: 8,400
  Doctorates
    Male: 399
    Female: 44
Attendance
  Movies (weekly): 30 million
    (est.)
  Baseball (yearly): 6.8 million

Consumer
Consumer Price Index
  (1967 = 100): 28
Eggs: 34¢ (doz.)
Milk: 8¢ (qt.)
Bread: 5¢ (loaf)
Butter: 36¢ (lb.)
Bacon: 26¢ (lb.)
Round steak: 17¢ (lb.)
Oranges: 48¢ (doz.)
Coffee: 28.2¢ (lb.)

The decade began with America's efforts to reform itself and ended with its efforts to reform the world. At home, "progressives" of both parties agreed that it was time for government to actively intervene against the industrial and financial monopolies controlled by the Morgan and Rockefeller syndicates. The ruthless striving and "special privilege" of these "malefactors of great wealth," many believed, had undermined historic democratic ideals and disempowered the ordinary citizen—despite their success in making America the world's leading industrial power. Abroad, again seeking to uphold democratic ideals and protect the vulnerable against the depredations of present (and future) aggressors, the U.S. entered the brutal worldwide clash of the European Great Powers. Notwithstanding the valorous and victorious efforts of the American doughboys abroad and the successful enactment of much of the reform domestic agenda, the "Progressive" era (1900–1919) ended in turmoil and disillusionment. Perhaps, given the grandeur of the ideals involved, this was inevitable. Nonetheless, in both domestic and foreign affairs, the beneficial potential of government in the service of humane, egalitarian ideals had been amply demonstrated.

The problems that marked the first years of the century were those of what Louis Brandeis termed "industrial democracy." A rapidly growing gross national product, in the absence of government regulation, had created marked inequities of wealth: affluence for too few and hardship for too many. The enormous expansion of industry had brought virtually full employment to both native-born Americans and the millions who continued to immigrate. However, for those in the booming factories and mine fields, unregulated working conditions often meant meager wages for long hours in dangerous work environments. Child and female worker exploitation was rampant, and militant, sometimes violent opposition to unionization was commonplace. Various public commissions also documented the deplorable living conditions both in the urban slums and in the shantytowns built around the mines.

The power of the wealthy was perpetuated by their control of the political process at every level, from the bribery of city officials to the control of state legislators, who then elected the senators who dominated the federal government. This power, given wide rein by a national tradition of "weak" government and laissez-faire economics, often relegated the ordinary person to the mercy of unscrupulous business practices and unrepresentative government. Indeed, over half the population— women and Southern blacks—was completely disenfranchised, the former constitutionally, the latter by discriminatory state legislation.

As president, Teddy Roosevelt had set out to control the trusts and regulate their abuses. In 1908, however, the charismatic former Rough Rider and Nobel Peace laureate decided to maintain tradition and honor his pledge not to seek a third term. His handpicked successor, his vice president, William Howard Taft, continued Roosevelt's antitrust suits. Nevertheless, more conservative in politics and temperament, Taft soon disappointed both his mentor and the nation by his hesitation on other reforms, such as tariff revision and conservation.

In the tumultuous election of 1912, TR reentered the presidential arena and challenged Taft for the GOP nomination. Trumpeting the "New Nationalism," a bold program of active government initiatives, Roosevelt lost the party nomination to Taft but became the candidate of the new Progressive Party. Although as a third-party candidate he came in second, the clamor for progressive change was clear; even the Socialist Eugene Debs gained nearly a million votes. With the GOP divided, victory went to a Democrat, for the first time since 1892.

A Ph.D. and distinguished academic before his Princeton presidency, Woodrow Wilson was new to politics in 1910 as New Jersey governor. Possessed of a Lincolnesque gift for oratory, he was passionately idealistic in advocating the "New Freedom," his conviction that America is "about liberty, not about money." He soon showed himself to be a master of congressional politics, working closely with progressives of both parties, committed to making America "a level playing field," where "the little man could be [as] powerful as the big." With the Federal Reserve Act, control of credit was removed from the private money trust and placed in the hands of government. With the Clayton Antitrust Act, the Federal Trade Commission was empowered to regulate anticompetitive practices. The constitutional amendments that allowed for a federal income tax and mandated the election of senators by popular vote also diminished the power of the wealthy.

Progressive ferment was evident at the local level as well. City party machines were often defeated, their leaders frequently imprisoned for practices that ranged from fraud to vote buying. At the state level, commissions investigated child labor and the exploitation of women workers, and suffragettes rallied to enfranchise women. From coast to coast, workers sought to organize, and often, of necessity, to strike—not only for better wages and conditions, but for the very right to organize.

As always, the forces of change met fierce opposition. Many women, as well as men, opposed woman suffrage. Many laborers feared the radicalism and violent methods of the unions and thus supported their suppression—by force, if necessary. While most citizens condemned the not infrequent lynchings and burnings of blacks, few actively worked to reverse segregated practices in the South or to mitigate the

Henry Ford and Thomas Edison, the inventive geniuses of the car and motion picture. *Library of Congress.*

plight of the hundreds of thousands who, in 1915, began migrating North. So, too, while immigration, mostly from Italy and Russia, continued at record levels until the war, anti-immigrant sentiment increased—from the labor unions, which feared competition for jobs, to the California governor, who feared that the 23,000 Japanese now settled in his domain would soon come to own it.

This was an age of promising new technologies. The harnessing of motor power to tractors greatly increased the productivity of the individual farmer. Electrical power found widespread use—from urban and rural trolleys (connecting places as distant as New York and Boston) to improved light bulbs, electric ranges, vacuum cleaners, and hair dryers. Wireless communication bridged Paris and New York; the telephone connected New York and San Francisco. Although, early in the decade, airplanes were novelties of stunt shows and vehicles of daring speed and distance contests, by the end of the decade, their practical uses were well documented: planes delivered mail at home and reconnaissance reports and bombs abroad. Above all, America's romance with the automobile was blossoming. Improvements like self-starters and mechanical windshield wipers in closed cars with more powerful engines promised the wealthy something better every year. At the same time, Henry Ford's Model T, the "Tin Lizzie" or "flivver"—a perennial subject of popular jokes—was falling every year in price. By 1916, the "Universal Car" cost less than half its 1908 price. The same was true for Kodak's cameras. By 1913, $2 to $6 could purchase more technological capability than $25 had just a few years earlier, enabling millions to record their lives and world—for themselves, if not for posterity.

During this period the nation's newest mass medium—movies—came to a maturity that led Vachel Lindsay to hail its pioneer, Thomas Edison, as "the new Gutenburg." Even if film's cultural status in 1910 was humble—an entertainment essentially for the poor—it was still impressive. Some twenty-five to fifty percent of the population, mostly the working class and recent immigrants, went weekly, for five to

ten cents, to nickelodeons, bare storefronts clustered in lower-class neighborhoods. By 1914, multiple-reel "feature"-length films had replaced one-reelers as program staples. As movies came to enthrall the middle and upper classes, lavish new theaters opened in fine downtown neighborhoods. When D. W. Griffith's *The Birth of a Nation* appeared, it was greeted as an artistic marvel, despite protests over its sympathetic portrayal of the Klan. The "star" system also flourished, and certain players gained such a following that by late in the decade, Charlie Chaplin ("the tramp"), Mary Pickford ("America's Sweetheart"), Douglas Fairbanks ("the American Everyman"), and William S. Hart (the "good bad man") drew salaries exceeding $1 million; the national average was $1,000.

In popular music, sheet music sold in the billions, and rag, blues, the old favorites, and Irving Berlin's and Jerome Kern's new songs decorated the pianos and pianolas that were also in vogue. The phonograph brought classical and popular music into the home; it also provided the means for people of all classes to join in the various dance crazes that captivated the nation. In 1912, Vernon and Irene Castle introduced their "Castle Walk," and for several years following, they popularized other new dances, like the respectable turkey trot and titillating tango.

Another musical art form was being born—"jass." Although black artists were virtually barred from Broadway, "the Great White Way," they composed music for Florenz Ziegfeld, Al Jolson, Nora Bayes, and the Castles. Throughout the decade, blacks like "Ma" and "Pa" Rainey, Ethel Waters, and W. C. Handy performed almost exclusively at either theaters for blacks or in touring shows for white audiences. On Broadway, Ziegfeld hired Fannie Brice, Marilyn Miller, Will Rogers, Mae West, Eddie Cantor, and W. C. Fields to complement his

Movie stars Douglas Fairbanks, Mary Pickford, and Charlie Chaplin. *D. Ouellette Collection.*

handpicked beauties (ideally, 36-26-38). George M. Cohan's dazzling virtuosity was apparent in both drama and musicals, which he often wrote, directed, staged, and starred in. Touring theater and dance companies presented foreign stars like "the divine" Sarah Bernhardt, the graceful Anna Pavlova, and the great Shakespeareans Sothern and Marlowe.

The intellectual revolt against American materialism and the "Genteel Tradition" was underway. George Eastman's *The Masses,* Herbert Croly's *The New Republic,* and H. L. Mencken's *The Smart Set* provided radical, progressive, and satirical forums for reflections on America. *The Education of Henry Adams* assailed the nation's failure to live up to its founders' ideals, while Charles Beard questioned the very motives of the Founding Fathers. Walter Lippmann and John Dewey searched for a philosophy of social improvement that would eschew both Social Darwinism and idealism in favor of a pragmatic, experimental, and scientific approach to society. Radicals like Emma Goldman and "Big Bill" Haywood held forth in New York's Greenwich Village.

Although the writers of the period represented a variety of geographic areas and styles, the greatest literary revolution occurred in poetry. Ezra Pound's exhortations to "Make it new" encouraged Harriet Monroe's *Poetry* magazine and "Imagist" experiments, including those of Pound himself, William Carlos Williams, H. D., and the cigar-smoking Amy Lowell, all of whom sought "the essence of things" in concrete, spare language. This aesthetic influenced T. S. Eliot, whose "The Lovesong of J. Alfred Prufrock" remains perhaps the era's most famous literary accomplishment. Also seeking a new but more direct form of expression, the rural New Englander Robert Frost in *North of Boston* created poems that entered the American canon, as did Carl Sandburg with his exaltation of the raw energy of the modern midwestern metropolis.

New York's upper crust produced the great novelist Edith Wharton. Her grim, realistic portrayal of the conflict of passion and convention in *Ethan Frome* would become a staple of secondary-school education, like the Nebraskan Willa Cather's evocation of America's pioneer past in *O Pioneers!* and *My Antonia.* Towering in their rude, energetic "naturalist" portrayals of the ruthless, capitalist magnate were Theodore Dreiser's *The Titan* and *The Financier.*

The most publicly renowned art event of the period was undoubtedly the 1913 Armory show, with its "Nude Descending a Staircase." While the display of European and American "modern" art inspired cries of "pathological" and "anarchism," the show drew record numbers. The photographer Alfred Stieglitz had taken the lead in exhibiting painters like Marin, Weber, O'Keeffe, and Dove at his famous "291" gallery, and he provided encouragement to the young American experimentalists.

The architecture of the period also had numerous faces. Cass Gilbert's neo-gothic Woolworth building, soaring 55 stories, dwarfed any previous structure, a harbinger of the upward thrust that would distinguish urban America. A neo-classical style characterized buildings like the New York Public Library, Washington D.C.'s many new federal buildings, and the Lincoln Memorial. Frank Lloyd Wright also pursued his unique horizontal, functionalist experiments.

Other unforgettable emblems of the decade were the *Titanic*'s sinking, Ty Cobb's batting and base-stealing records, the 1919 White Sox World Series loss, and the Native American Jim Thorpe's Olympic feats. This was also the era of Enrico Caruso and Mary Garden and the debuts of John McCormack, Jascha Heifetz, Norman Rockwell, Billy Sunday's hellfire sermons, *Pollyanna,* and *Penrod.* Of more lasting consequence, the decade was also characterized by dramatic political upheavals occurring outside the U.S.: the revolutionary overthrow of longstanding dictatorships in Mexico, China, and Russia, all of which stirred hopes and fears that would long endure.

By 1916, Wilson had essentially embraced TR's progressive vision of active government. The end of the decade was to be dominated by the Great War, where thousands in the trenches were dying over inches of territory. Wilson's neutrality had gained him reelection ("He kept us out of war"). When, however, in 1917, Germany declared a policy of unrestricted submarine warfare and the "Zimmerman telegram" was intercepted, revealing German efforts to push Mexico into war with the U.S., Wilson abandoned neutrality. Advancing the noble aim "to make the world safe for democracy," he led a militarily ill-prepared nation into full-scale, patriotic mobilization. Homefront agencies harnessed industry for massive food and material necessities and engaged leading artists to alert the citizenry to the brutal nature of the enemy. It was 1918 before significant numbers of U.S. troops were prepared to fight, but their effectiveness was decisive in repulsing the final German offensive.

Wilson went to the peace conference at Versailles a great hero. As the price of accepting certain dubious peace terms, he convinced the victors to include the League of Nations covenant in the final treaty of this "war to end all wars." On his return, however, his vision was staunchly opposed by powerful senators who feared that such a commitment might entangle America against its national interests. As the decade closed, two constitutional amendments on issues that had long excited passionate interest were finally enacted. Prohibition and woman suffrage came to pass.

1910

Library of Congress.

In the News

RUSSIA AND AUSTRIA AGREE TO MAINTAIN STATUS QUO IN BALKANS . . . HOUSE ESTABLISHES RULES COMMITTEE, REDUCING POWER OF SPEAKER "UNCLE JOE" CANNON . . . 1907 IMMIGRATION ACT IS AMENDED BARRING CRIMINALS, PAUPERS, ANARCHISTS, THE DISEASED . . . N.Y. GOVERNOR CHARLES EVANS HUGHES IS APPOINTED TO SUPREME COURT . . . KING EDWARD VII DIES, GEORGE V ASCENDS TO THRONE . . . GLENN CURTISS FLIES 137 MILES IN 2.5 HOURS . . . RUSSIA EXPELS THOUSANDS OF JEWS, U.S. DELEGATION APPEALS TO PRESIDENT TAFT . . . SENATE BILL PERMITS ARIZONA AND NEW MEXICO TO FORM STATE CONSTITUTIONS . . . MANN ACT, "WHITE SLAVE TRAFFIC" LAW, FORBIDS TRANSPORT OF WOMEN ACROSS STATE, INTERNATIONAL BORDERS FOR "IMMORAL PURPOSES" . . . MANN-ELKINS ACT EXTENDS ICC'S POWER OVER RAILROAD, TELEGRAPH, TELEPHONE, CABLE . . . 20 BLACKS AND 3 WHITES ARE KILLED IN PALESTINE, TEXAS RACE RIOT . . . JAPAN SUPPRESSES KOREAN REBELLION, ANNEXES KOREA, RENAMED "CHOSEN" . . . IN "NEW NATIONALISM" SPEECH, TEDDY ROOSEVELT ADVOCATES CONTROL OF TRUSTS, GRADUATED INCOME TAX, LABOR PROTECTION, CONSERVATION, STRONG MILITARY . . . MONTENEGRO DECLARES INDEPENDENCE FROM OTTOMAN EMPIRE . . . BRITISH SEND TROOPS TO PERSIA . . . FRANCISCO MADERO CALLS FOR REVOLUTION AGAINST MEXICAN DICTATORSHIP . . . DEMOCRATS TAKE CONTROL OF HOUSE FOR FIRST TIME SINCE 1892, REPUBLICANS HOLD SENATE . . . 43 GIRLS ARE KILLED IN N.J. FACTORY FIRE . . . STATE OF WASHINGTON ADOPTS WOMAN SUFFRAGE.

Quotes

"I stand for the square deal, . . . for fair play [and] equality of opportunity. . . . Unfair money getting has tended to create a small class of enormously wealthy and powerful men whose chief object is to hold and increase their power. . . . A policy of far more active governmental interference . . . is now necessary."
— Theodore Roosevelt, on "The New Nationalism"

"Woman's suffrage would vastly increase the ignorant and the purchasable vote, and in the mixed population of American cities would prove the strongest enemy of civic reform."
— *Life* magazine

"As a scientific achievement, . . . Wilbur Wright's flight up the Hudson . . . is memorable. But [that] this performance establishes commercial supremacy of the aeroplane is purely fantastic."
— *Engineering Magazine*

"It can safely be asserted that the chief unintentional crime of our age . . . is dirty hands."
— Dr. R. G. Eccles, on the spread of typhoid, the third most prevalent cause of death

"[Under coeducation, American boys are becoming] an inferior copy of the girls, winning a girl's gentleness and sensitiveness, but not the proper strength of either sex."
— Alexander Francis, *Americans*

"The war against war is going to be no holiday excursion. . . . We must make new energies and hardihood continue the manliness to which the military mind so faithfully clings."
— William James, "The Moral Equivalent of War"

"To the special interests, an unjust rise in the cost of living means simply higher profit, but to those who pay it, [it means] schooling, warm clothing, . . . a fair chance to make the fight for comfort, decency, and right living."
— Gifford Pinchot

"American-born children of the long-headed Sicilians and those of the round-headed East-European Hebrews have nearly the same intermediate head form. . . . Similar changes are traced in the development of the faces."
— U.S. Immigration Commission, on the "Great Melting Pot"

Ads

President Taft and his sons. *Library of Congress*.

Ellis Island. European immigrants continue to enter the U.S. in record numbers; over nine million have arrived since 1910. *Library of Congress*.

A young mill worker. Widely prevalent child labor practices become the subject of state legislation. *Library of Congress*.

Movies

Openings

Ramona (D. W. Griffith/Biograph), Mary Pickford, Francis Grandon, early film based on a novel
Ranch Life in the Great South West (Selig), Tom Mix (debut)
The Life of Moses (Charles Kent/Vitagraph), five reels, one viewed a week
Uncle Tom's Cabin (Vitagraph), three reels
A Dixie Mother (Vitagraph), Florence Turner, Carlyle Blackwell
Twelfth Night (Vitagraph), Julia Swayne Gordon, Charles Kent
The House with Closed Shutters (D. W. Griffith/ Biograph), Dorothy West, Henry B. Walthall
Frankenstein (J. Searle Dawley/Vitagraph), Charles Ogle, Augustus Phillips

Pathé weekly newsreels begin.
France and Italy still lead in film production. In the U.S., dozens of companies produce one- and two-ree films, and improvised melodramas predominate. Although actors are not given film credits, they gain followings: fan letters are addressed to "The Waif," "Bronco Billy," "The Fat Boy," and "The Man with the Sad Eyes." Florence Lawrence, known only as the "Biograph Girl," is the top box-office star.

Studios and specific directors also draw audiences—e.g., Griffith at Biograph. Production is dominated by the Motion Picture Patents Company, a trust (monopoly) formed by the merger of Vitagraph (Edison) and Biograph (Griffith). It dominates the eight leading American companies and controls the industry through patents and the licensing of theaters to show its films. Small, independent companies move to California to escape trust control; many studios remain in the New York area, like the Fort Lee-Coytesville section of New Jersey.

Ex-wife of an alcoholic, Carry Nation continues her nationwide temperance crusade by chopping up liquor crates in saloons; she carries a Bible, ax, and, frequently, souvenir hatchets (for sale). *Smithsonian Institution*.

Popular Music

Hit Songs

"Let Me Call You Sweetheart"
"Down by the Old Mill Stream"
"Ah! Sweet Mystery of Life"
"As Deep as the Deep Blue Sea"
"Some of these Days"
"The Chicken Reel"
"Come, Josephine, in My Flying Machine"
"Chinatown, My Chinatown"
"Every Little Movement"
"Plant a Watermelon on My Grave and Let the Juice Soak Through"
"Stop That Rag"
"Heaven Will Protect the Working Girl"
"I'm Awfully Glad I'm Irish"
"Italian Street Song"
"Yiddle On Your Fiddle"

Representative Recordings: Burt Shepard, "Laughing Song" (one of the earliest million-selling records, written by a former Virginia slave, George Washington Johnson); "Tramp! Tramp! Tramp!" (Harlan and Stanley); "Put Your Arms Around Me, Honey" (Arthur Collins, Byron G. Harlan); "My Wild Irish Rose" (Hayden Quartette); "You're a Grand Old Flag" (Billy Murray); "Has Anybody Here Seen Kelly?" (Nora Bayes); "That Haunting Melody" (Al Jolson)

Jazz

Almost entirely excluded from the recording industry, blacks continue to write, promote themselves, and perform ragtime, blues, and the new "jass." Most prolific songwriters to date are Bob Cole, J. Rosamond Johnson, and James Weldon Johnson. Will Marion Cook and Joe Jordan write for Ziegfeld. James R. Europe organizes the black "Europe's Society Orchestra," which tours abroad. Charles Callendar and J. H. Haverly, two white men, continue to manage touring (black) minstrel shows. Popular black vaudeville teams include Butterbeans Susie; Cool Grant and Kid Sock Wilson; George Williams and Bessie Smith (no relation to the later singer). Other leading performers include Bert Williams, W. C. Handy, "Ma" Rainey, and Sam Lucas.

Theater

Broadway Openings

Plays

Get-Rich-Quick Wallingford (George M. Cohan), J. C. Marlowe, Hale Hamilton
Your Humble Servant (Booth Tarkington, Harry Leon Wilson), Otis Skinner, Charles B. Wells
Mrs. Dot (W. Somerset Maugham), Billie Burke
Baby Mine (Margaret Mayo), Frank Glendenning, Ruth Findlay
Smith (W. Somerset Maugham), John Drew, Sybil Thorndike, Mary Boland
Rebecca of Sunnybrook Farm (Kate Douglas Wiggin, Charlotte Thompson), Marie L. Day, Ernest Truex
The Gamblers (Charles Klein), George Nash, Jane Cowl
Pomander Walk (Louis N. Parker), Dorothy Parker
Madame X (Alexander Bisson), Christine Blessing

Musicals

Tillie's Nightmare (A. Baldwin Sloane, Edgar Smith), Marie Dressler, George and John Gorman
Ziegfeld Follies of 1910 (Gus Edwards, Harry B. Smith), Fannie Brice, Bert Williams
Madame Sherry (Karl Hoschna, Otto Harbach), Lina Abarbanell, Frances Demarest
Naughty Marietta (Victor Herbert, Rida Johnson Young), Emma Trentini, Orville Harrold
The Summer Widowers (A. Baldwin Sloane, Glen MacDonough), Lew Fields, Vernon Castle, Helen Hayes

Teddy Roosevelt's African adventures, which include facing a charging lion, are closely followed by an adoring public. *Library of Congress.*

Classics and Revivals On and Off Broadway

The Bluebird (Maeterlinck); *Twelfth Night*, Louis Calvert; Ben Greet Repertory: *She Stoops to Conquer, Everyman, The Rivals, Dr. Faustus, Macbeth, The Merchant of Venice, The Tempest, A Midsummer Night's Dream;* Sothern and Marlowe Repertory: *Romeo and Juliet, The Taming of the Shrew, Hamlet; Sister Beatrice* (Maeterlinck); Madame Sarah Bernhardt and her company: *Phèdre* (Racine), *La Samaritaine* and *L'Aiglon* (Rostand), *La Dame aux Camélias* (Dumas)

Classical Music _____

Compositions

Charles Ives, Violin Sonatas, no. 1 and 2, *Adagio Sostenuto* for English Horn, Flute, Strings and Piano
George Chadwick, *Everywoman, Aphrodite*
Henry Hadley, *Lucifer*
Henry S. Gilbert, *Strife*
Arthur Foote, *Suite in E for Strings*

Important Events

Modest Altschuler conducts the Russian Symphony Orchestra in the first U.S. performance of a Stravinsky orchestral piece, *Feuerwerk* (New York). The first American opera is produced at the Metropolitan, *The Pipe of Desire,* by Frederick Converse. The MacDowell Festival opens at Peterboro, New Hampshire.

Notable Performances: Busoni has enormous success touring the U.S. with his own arrangements of Bach's *Chromatic Fantasy and Fugue* and *Choral Preludes.* When Mahler conducts a series of Beethoven concerts with the New York Philharmonic Society, his interpretations are widely criticized; his arrangements of Bach's orchestral suites, which he conducts from the piano, are more favorably received. Walter Damrosch and the New York Symphony Orchestra perform a Berlioz cycle; John McCormack gives a highly acclaimed first concert at Carnegie Hall. Mischa Elman, in his second U.S. tour, draws record audiences.

Major Recitals: Ignace Paderewski, Moriz Rosenthal, Josef Lhévinne, Fritz Kreisler, Maud Powell, Florence Austin

Boston, 1910. City streets take on a new look with motorized, rather than horse-drawn, transportation; electric autos compete with gas machines in the big cities. *National Archives.*

New Appointment: Leopold Stokowski (Cincinnati)

Debut: Anton Witek

First Performances

Mozart, Adagio and Fugue for String Orchestra (Boston); Samuel Coleridge-Taylor, *Bamboula Rhapsodic Dance* (Litchfield, Conn.); Erich Wolfgang Korngold (age 13), "Piano Trio in D Major" (New York); Henry Hadley, Symphony no. 3 (Philadelphia), *Symphonic Fantasia* (St. Louis); Glazunov, Violin Concerto (New York); Franck, *Quatre Pièces Brèves* (Boston)

Opera

Metropolitan: Enrico Caruso, Emmy Destinn, Pasquale Amato, *Girl of the Golden West* (Puccini, premiere, 47 curtain calls); Geraldine Farrar, Louise Homer, *Königskinder* (Humperdinck, premiere); John McCormack (debut), Nellie Melba, *La Traviata;* Leo Slezak, Antonio Scotto, Frances Alda, *Otello;* Slezak, Destinn, *Pique Dame* (Tchaikovsky, premiere, conducted by Mahler)

Manhattan, New York: Marietta Mazarin, *Elektra* (Strauss, premiere); *Tannhäuser,* in French; *Griselidis* (Massenet)

Boston (first season): Lillian Nordica, *La Gioconda;* Florencio Constantino (debut), *Carmen, Faust; The Miser Knight* (Rachmaninoff, premiere)

Chicago (first season, Andreas Dippel, manager): *Aïda;* Mary Garden (debut), *Pelléas and Mélisande*

Music Notes

The Indiana University and Boston schools of music open • Oscar Hammerstein retires from opera production and sells the Manhattan company's contracts, music rights, and equipment to the rival Metropolitan Opera • The Pittsburgh Symphony disbands • With music at the White House reflecting U.S. territorial expansion, the Philippine Constabulary Band and Hawaiian Quartet appear during the year • In great secrecy, Amelita Galli marries her first husband, artist Luigi Curci.

Art

Painting

William Glackens, *Nude with Apple, The Green Car*

John Marin, *Brooklyn Bridge*

Arthur G. Dove, *Abstraction Number 1*

Abraham Walkowitz, *Nude, Bathers*

John Prendergast, *Central Park* (1908–10)

Lyonel Feininger, *Uprising*

Charles Hawthorne, *The Trousseau*

Sculpture

Abestenia St. Leger Eberlie, *Windy Doorstep*

Anna V. Hyatt, *Up Hill*

Maurice Stern, *The Bomb-Thrower*

Important Exhibitions

Museums

New York: *Metropolitan:* Whistler; early Oriental rugs; "Arms and Armor"; late 18th-century silver. The Met receives singularly rare gifts: a collection of 2,546 netsukes and scarabs, and other objects of

Architecture

Pennsylvania Station, New York City (McKim, Mead and White, 1906–10), modeled on the Baths of Caracalla

Blackstone Hotel, Chicago (Benjamin Marshall)

Ritz-Carlton Hotel, New York (Charles Wetmore), 12 stories

Drummond house, River Forest, Ill. (William Drummond)

Brooks building, Chicago (Holabird and Root)

Temple of the Scottish Rite, Washington, D.C. (John Russell Pope)

Egyptian art. The wing to house the Hoentschel collection of Gothic and Renaissance art and Boller collection of early American furniture is built.

Boston: "Modern French, Italian and American Sculpture"; Prints of Dürer; Sculpture by Geoffrey Bernard; Rembrandt

Philadelphia: Small bronzes and Pennell etchings; John Sloan; George Luks; Maurice Prendergast; George Hetzel; Everett Shinn; Arthur B. Davies

Chicago: Retrospective of Chicago art; Alfred East; George Gardner Symons

Buffalo: "Spanish Art of the 16th–18th Centuries"; Childe Hassan

Art Briefs

Over 102 art schools exist, with a total registration of 31,710 • Alfred Stieglitz, at his "291" gallery, in New York, shows "Young American Artists": Gaston Lachaise, Max Weber, Joseph Stella, John Marin, Abraham Walkowitz, William Zorach, and others • Braque and Picasso receive worldwide attention with their new "analytical cubism" • The newly published *Futurist Manifesto*, signed by V. Boccioni, C. Carra, G. Balla, and G. Severini, gains great interest • Auction sales include Botticelli's *Madonna and Child, St. John and an Angel*, $1,550; Monet's *Fishing Boats*, $240; Rembrandt's *Portrait of Admiral Campbell*, $4,400; Joseph Bail's *Servants Lunching*, $5,100; and Turner's *Grand Canal*, $60,000.

Composer-pianist Ferruccio Busoni is considered the most dazzling pianist since Liszt. *D. Ouellette Collection.*

Dance

Anna Pavlova and her dance partner, Mikhail Mordkin, make their U.S. debut in *Coppelia* at the Metropolitan Opera House. Ruth Saint Denis's *Egypta* (Meyrowitz), inspired by an ad for Egyptian Deities cigarettes, debuts in New York.

Louis Comfort Tiffany lamp, about 1910. Bronze and glass. 26¼ × 14⅝ × 18½. *The Metropolitan Museum of Art,* gift of Hugh Grant, 1974.

Books

Fiction

Critics' Choice

Tales of Men and Ghosts, Edith Wharton

Robert Coverdale's Struggle: or, on the Wave of Success, Horatio Alger (posthumous)

A Doctor's Christmas Eve, James Lane Allen

Strictly Business: More Stories of the Four Million, O. Henry

Uncle Remus and the Little Boy, Joel Chandler Harris (posthumous)

The Finer Grain, Henry James

Burning Daylight, Jack London

Hopalong Cassidy, Clarence E. Mulford

🕭 *Howards End*, E. M. Forster

Best-Sellers

The Rosary, Florence Barclay

A Modern Chronicle, Winston Churchill

The Wild Olive, Anonymous (Basil King)

Max, Katherine Cecil Thurston

The Kingdom of Slender Swords, Hallie Erminie Rives

Simon the Jester, William J. Locke

Lord Loveland Discovers America, C. N. and A. M. Williamson

The Window at the White Cat, Mary Roberts Rinehart

Molly Make-Believe, Eleanor Abbott

When a Man Marries, Mary Roberts Rinehart

Nonfiction

Critics' Choice

Twenty Years at Hull-House, Jane Addams

History of the Great American Fortunes, Gustavus Meyers

My Mark Twain, William Dean Howells

Speeches, Mark Twain

Revolution and Other Essays, Jack London

Mr. Dooley Says, Finley Peter Dunne

The Spirit of Romance, Ezra Pound

The Fight for Conservation, Gifford Pinchot

The New Laokoön, Irving Babbitt

Three Philosophical Poets, George Santayana

Education in the United States, Nicholas Murray Butler

🕭 *Principia Mathematica*, Bertrand Russell, Alfred North Whitehead

Poetry

Edward Arlington Robinson, *The Town Down the River*

Carl Sandburg, *Joseffy*

Ezra Pound, *Provença: Poems Selected from Personae, Exultations, and Canzoniere*

Eugene Field, *Complete Poems*

🕭 W. B. Yeats, *The Green Helmet and Other Poems*

Science and Technology

From his work on eye color in the fruit fly, Thomas Hunt Morgan proposes that specific inherited characteristics are sex-linked.

A hereditary blood disorder that produces sickle-shaped red blood cells is discovered by James Herrick.

Major work is undertaken on the eradication of hookworm, the cause of "Idlers' Disease."

Francis Rous discovers that viruses cause some animal cancers.

Transmission of Mexican typhus by body lice is discovered by Howard Taylor Ricketts, who dies of the disease.

F. Cottrell invents an electrostatic precipitator to reduce factory air pollution.

James Angell postulates that consciousness is no longer a viable scientific concept.

The first self-propelled gas combine harvester is produced by the Holt Co., to replace horse- and tractor-pulled combines.

🕭 William Bragg discovers that X-rays and gamma rays behave like particles.

🕭 Arthur Evans completes the excavation of Knossus, Crete.

🕭 J. J. Thomson discovers neon isotopes.

Seventy percent of all bread is baked at home. *Library of Congress*.

Sports

Baseball

Top players include Christy Mathewson, Ty Cobb, Tris Speaker, Cy Young, and Honus Wagner.

The winning World Series player's share is $1,825; the losing player, $1,274.

Taft is the first president to throw out the opening-day ball.

The Philadelphia A's are the first AL team to win over 100 games.

Champions

Batting
  Sherwood Magee (Philadelphia, NL), .331
  Tyrus R. Cobb (Detroit, AL), .350
Pitching
  Leonard Cole (Chicago, NL), 20–4

Chief Bender (Philadelphia, AL), 23–5
Home Runs
  Fred Beck (Boston, NL), 10
  Frank Schulte (Chicago, NL), 10
  J. Garland Stahl (Boston, NL), 10

Football

The game is divided into 4 quarters, instead of two halves, and the return of withdrawn players in a subsequent period is permitted. College presidents debate banning football because of its many deaths and injuries; the Stanford president says: "It isn't a game; it's a battle."

College All-Americans: Percy Wendell (HB), Harvard; Talbot Pendelton (HB), Princeton; Stanfield Wells (E), Michigan

Other Sports

Boxing: Tex Rickard offers Battling Nelson $30,000 to fight Joe Gans in the mining town of Goldfield, Nevada, and $100,000 for the Johnson-Jeffries heavyweight title fight, with 60% to the winner. Johnson KOs Jeffries, "the Great White Hope," in the 15th round, to become the first black boxing champion. "He said he'd bring home the bacon, and

Fannie Brice (Borach), 18, is hired for $25 a week by Florenz Ziegfeld. *Movie Star News.*

the honey boy has gone and done it," says his mother, coining a popular phrase. The fight has grossed $101,000, caused rioting in many cities, and gained movie rights for $50,000.

Al Wolgast wins the lightweight title from Battling Nelson in the 49th round of a 45-round fight.

Auto Racing: Barney Oldfield sets a land speed record of 132 mph in a Benz at Daytona, Florida.

Winners

World Series
  Philadelphia (AL) 4
  Chicago (NL) 1
College Football
  Harvard
College Basketball
  Columbia
Player of the Year
  Harland "Pat" Page, Chicago

Stanley Cup
  Montreal
U.S. Tennis Open
  Men: William Larned
  Women: Hazel Hotchkiss
USGA Open
  Alex Smith
Kentucky Derby
  Donau (Fred Herbert, jockey)

Fashion

The "Gibson Girl," with her opulent S-shaped silhouette, enjoys her last year of fashion popularity: the large bosom extending over a tiny, pinched waistline, the pronounced and rounded derriere protruding from a long and flounced skirt. Also waning in high style are hats topped with stuffed birds or artificial fruits, feathered boas, and suede gloves and plain boots—all traditional fashion accessories. The French designer Poiret, intuiting the modern woman's growing desire for sartorial freedom, loosens the well-ribbed corsetry that scaffolded La Belle Epoque styles. Although new designs are far from functional or economical, they are lighter in

fabric, brighter in hue, and looser in fit; most important, they are less demanding of heavy steel corsetry. News arrives in America of the new French "hobble" skirt (denounced by the Pope)—a tube skirt worn with a fabric garter that ties the ankles together so that only three or four inch steps can be taken at a time. For the woman who selects this style, hopping, or mastery of the short, shuffling step, will become her only means of ambulating across the room.

High-fashion note: John Forsythe's striped shirtwaist; Poiret's walking suit in velvet and three-piece suit trimmed in skunk.

Kaleidoscope

- Despite Marie Dressler's popular song "Heaven Will Protect the Working Girl," concern mounts that low wages ($1.57/9 hours) may drive women into prostitution, "the social evil."
- J. P. Morgan is so powerful economically that *Life* proposes that he be crowned U.S. monarch; it is alternately suggested that he buy Europe.
- The Model T—the beloved "Tin Lizzie" or "Flivver Fender" —with its readily wrinkling fenders (which help drivers pull their cars out of ditches), stands over seven feet high.
- Paul Ehrlich's discovery of "salvarsan 606"—"the magic bullet" to treat syphilis—is hailed by many as a miracle; others call it an enticement to sin.
- Violence and sexuality in movies activate censorship requests; Missouri's Christian Endeavor Society tries to ban films with kissing.
- Marriage between blacks and whites is punishable in 25 states; is considered void between whites and Native Americans in four states, and void between whites and Chinese in five states.
- The return of Halley's comet stirs fear and excitement; many hide in shelters or buy "comet" pills for protection.
- Women possess full suffrage in Wyoming, Colorado, Utah, and Idaho; suffragists submit to Congress a petition of 500,000 signatures for full voting rights for all women; yellow flowers are a symbol of suffragette support.
- A beauty salon secretary borrows $6,000 to open a Fifth Avenue shop called Elizabeth Arden (after Tennyson's poem "Enoch Arden").
- The U.S. population has quadrupled since 1860; immigrants and rural migrants transform the largest cities—New York, Boston, Philadelphia, and Chicago— into industrial centers.
- The average man earns $15 for a 58-hour work week; inflation forces his family to spend 42 percent of its income ($326) on food; many blame the Swift and Armour trusts.
- Twenty-two states investigate child labor; 40 percent work seven 12-hour days for subsistence wages.
- *Colliers* reports that law enforcement is the country's worst problem with 10,000 murders and only 200 convictions.
- To stem illegal drug trafficking, a movement begins to prohibit the sale of morphine except by prescription; cocaine is already regulated.
- The new "four door," "closed in," and "torpedo" auto models attract new consumers; the American product challenges "the legend of European superiority."
- Auto safety becomes an issue: reckless driving ("joy riding," "night hawking"), highway safety, and speeding.
- To beautify Park Avenue, a New York group proposes to cover the railroad tunnel and plant a garden down the center of the street.
- The National Negro Committee, formed in 1909, becomes the NAACP; founders include Jane Addams and John Dewey; W. E. B. Du Bois is its only black officer.
- Over 10,000 nickelodeons—"democracy's theaters"— provide mass entertainment mainly for the poor; an hour of one-reel movies, vaudeville, and perhaps a dog act are featured in bare rooms with wooden seats for 5¢–10¢.
- Florenz ("Flo") Ziegfeld, whose motto is "Glorifying the American Girl," interviews over 10,000 for his annual *Follies;* his most important criterion is a woman's contour.

- With increasing sales of parlor pianos, over two billion copies of sheet music are sold; ragtime peaks in popularity.
- Stylish restaurants build dance floors for the popular afternoon "thé dansant"; the waltz remains the standard ballroom dance.
- The first Metropolitan Opera broadcast airs *Cavalleria Rusticana* and *Pagliacci* (Enrico Caruso); about 50 radio amateurs, and various ships at sea, receive it.
- The illiteracy rate drops to 7.9 percent; less than half the nation has a grade-school education; 4 percent have graduated from college.
- The Flexner report condemns U.S. medical schools as inferior to European schools (excepting Johns Hopkins); a $600 million medical education reform is initiated.
- President Taft's interest in conservation is challenged after he fires Forestry Chief Gifford Pinchot; Pinchot exposed Interior Secretary Ballinger's proposed sale of public lands to the Morgan-Guggenheim syndicate.
- The term *progressive* comes into usage to describe the reform movements battling the power and privilege of the wealthy, as well as government corruption, unsafe and unfair labor conditions, and the plight of the poor.
- Commitment to progressive causes splits the "Insurgents" and conservative "Old Guard" of the Republican party; Taft comes under fire by both parties for abandoning TR's progressive policies.

First appearances: Father's Day, Boy Scouts of America, Camp Fire Girls of America, Socialist elected to Congress (Victor Berger), seedless blueberries, Hydrox biscuit bon-bons, electric kitchen range (three settings), electric washing machines, iodine, U.S. Bureau of Mines, U.S. Postal Savings system, "Publicity Act" (requiring campaign contributions report), Gimbels and May department stores (New York), Hallmark, Fuller Brush, Salomon Brothers, Cities Service, *Pittsburgh Courier, Women's Wear Daily,* Esperanto Congress, Carnegie Endowment for International Peace, Reed, SMU, Kent State, conservation course (Minnesota), night flight, aircraft launched from a ship, radio receivers (in kits).

Fads: player-pianos, flying contests, auto races, Ford Model T jokes and jokebooks ("He named his Ford after his wife." "How funny!" "Not at all. After he got it, he found he couldn't control it").

"I came in with Halley's Comet, . . . and I expect to go out with it" was Mark Twain's accurate prediction; unfortunately, in 1910, rumors of his death were *not* "greatly exaggerated." *D. Ouellette Collection.*

1911

Facts and Figures

Economic Profile
  Dow-Jones: ↓ High 86–
    Low 73
  GNP: 0%
  Inflation: 0%
  Unemployment: 6.7%
Median age, first marriage:
  Male: 25.1, Female: 21.2
Average household size: 4.6
Population over 65: 4.4%
Population under 10: 23%
Saks Fifth Avenue, for men:
  English wool dressing
    gown: $12–$40
  Velvet housecoat: $12.50
  Hart, Schaffner & Marx
    overcoat: $22.50
  Plain and pleated bosom
    shirts: $1–$1.50
Florsheim men's shoes: $5–
  $6
Mallory derbies and soft hats:
  $3–$5
BVD union suits
  (underwear): $1–5
I. Magnin (San Francisco),
  for women:
  Dresses: velvet, $16.50–
    $35;
    serge, broadcloth:
    $17.50–$40
  Lingerie and corsets:
    $1.65–$5
Knabe "Angeles" player
  piano: $1,050; used: $295–
  $425
Knabe baby grand: $575
  (rosewood); ebony: $450

Deaths

Karl Baedecker, Alfred
  Binet, Wilhelm Dilthey,
  W. S. Gilbert, Gustav
  Mahler, Joseph Pulitzer,
  King of Siam

In the News

NATIONAL PROGRESSIVE REPUBLICAN LEAGUE FORMS, CALLS FOR INITIATIVE, REFERENDUM, AND RECALL . . . TAFT SENDS 30,000 TROOPS TO MEXICAN BORDER, U.S. SIGHTSEERS AT RIO GRANDE WATCH REBELS ATTACK . . . TRIANGLE SWEATSHOP FIRE, IN N.Y.C., KILLS 146 . . . SUPREME COURT PLACES FOREST RESERVES UNDER FEDERAL, NOT STATE, AUTHORITY . . . HOUSE OF LORDS POWER IS LIMITED BY PM'S THREAT TO CREATE NEW PEERS . . . FRANCE AND GERMANY QUARREL IN SECOND MOROCCO CRISIS . . . SAN FRANCISCO "BOSS" ABRAHAM RUEF IS CONVICTED OF BRIBERY . . . SUPREME COURT DISSOLVES ROCKEFELLER STANDARD OIL TRUST . . . MOB IN PENNSYLVANIA QUAKER TOWN BURNS BLACK, ZACH WALKER, NATIONAL OUTRAGE FOLLOWS . . . SUPREME COURT DISSOLVES AMERICAN TOBACCO TRUST . . . GUNBOAT *YORKTOWN* ENTERS NICARAGUAN WATERS TO SAFEGUARD AMERICAN INTERESTS . . . 50,000 MILITANT WOMAN SUFFRAGETTES MARCH IN LONDON . . . KING GEORGE V IS CROWNED . . . *MONA LISA* IS STOLEN FROM LOUVRE . . . ITALY DECLARES WAR AGAINST TURKEY, TAKES TRIPOLI . . . CALIFORNIA ADOPTS WOMAN SUFFRAGE . . .N.Y.C. LAW GIVES EQUAL PAY TO FEMALE TEACHERS . . . GOVERNMENT MOVES TO DISSOLVE U.S. STEEL . . . MADERO TAKES POWER IN MEXICO, ENDING 35-YEAR DIAZ RULE . . . AFTER PLEADING INNOCENT, MCNAMARA BROTHERS CONFESS TO DYNAMITING *LOS ANGELES TIMES* BUILDING . . . TR TO SEEK GOP NOMINATION IN 1912 . . . NORWEGIAN ROALD AMUNDSEN REACHES SOUTH POLE BEFORE BRITISH ROBERT F. SCOTT . . . GALBRAITH RODGERS FLIES CROSS COUNTRY IN 82 HOURS OVER 7 WEEKS . . . WIDESPREAD REVOLT THREATENS 300-YEAR CHINESE MANCHU DYNASTY.

Quotes

"Although the U.S. has only about 5% of the world's population, it produces 20% of the world's wheat; 22% of its gold; 33% of its coal; 38%, silver; 40%, pig-iron; 42%, steel; 60%, petroleum; 70%, cotton; 80%, cars. . . . Its aggregate wealth, . . . $130 billion, is as great as that of the U.K. and France, its two nearest rivals."
— *St. Louis Globe Democrat*

" 'Business must obey the law,' says Attorney General Wickersham. 'What a cruel hardship!' "
— *New York American*

"The Stanley [Senate] Committee wishes Mr. Morgan to testify in the Steel Trust inquiry, but is apparently in doubt whether to send a subpoena or an ambassador."
— *New York World*

"We cannot all be vegetarians, because there are not enough vegetables in the world."
— *Literary Review,* responding to the Worldwide Vegetarian Movement

"California believes in trying all fads at once, and being done with it."
— *Baltimore American,* on California's adoption of woman suffrage

"In reality, the open shop means the open door through which the union man goes out and the non-union man comes in to take his place."
— Clarence Darrow, "Why Men Fight For the Open Shop"

With his vast influence on hundreds of corporate boards, J. P. Morgan is widely considered the most powerful man in America. *Library of Congress.*

"The capital iv Mexico, me boy, isn't Mexico city. It's just south iv Canal Street in the city iv New York. A rivolution which isn't a good investment is only disorderhly conduck."
— Mr. Dooley

"William James's new theology [pragmatism] has broken the spell of the genteel tradition, . . . the chief foundations of [which] are Calvinism and transcendentalism."
— George Santayana, "The Genteel Tradition in American Philosophy"

"To hell with Jews, Jesuits, and steamships."
— Prescott Hall, after Taft vetoes a literacy bill for immigrants

Ads

Popular flying hero Harry Atwood takes off from the White House lawn in a Wright Type B airplane; he has flown from St. Louis to New York in 11 days, 6 hours and 3 minutes. *Library of Congress*.

A major issue for strikers is whether radical methods and revolution are justified, which the IWW maintains. *Library of Congress*.

Movies

Openings

The Lonedale Operator (D. W. Griffith), Blanche Sweet, Francis Grandon
Fighting Blood (D. W. Griffith), Blanche Sweet, Lionel Barrymore
A Tale of Two Cities (William Humphreys), Maurice Costello, Norma Talmadge
The Battle (D. W. Griffith), Blanche Sweet
Enoch Arden (D. W. Griffith), Wilfred Lucas, Robert Harron, Florence LaBadie
Vanity Fair (Vitagraph), Helen Gardner, William Ranous, John Bunny
The Poisoned Flume (Allan Dwan), J. Warren Kerrigan
The Two Orphans (Selig), Kathlyn Williams, Winnifred Greenwood, three reels, shown over three days
David Copperfield, Romeo and Juliet (Thanhouser)

D. W. Griffith, after hundreds of one-reelers, produces two-reelers that introduce more complex characterization, narrative line, and stylistic technique. His major "players" include Mae Marsh, Owen Moore, Lionel Barrymore, Mary Pickford, Robert Harron, and director Mack Sennett. Vying with the stage for quality subjects and actors, studios film plays, novels, and operas, including *The Three Musketeers, Aïda, Faust,* and *Dante's Inferno*. David Horsley, with his company of cowboys and Indians, Mutt and Jeff, and a comic villain ("Desperate Desmond"), moves from Bayonne, N.J., to a Los Angeles suburb and establishes the first studio on Sunset Boulevard, in the village of Hollywood.

Blanche Sweet is one of D. W. Griffith's regulars in the one- and two-reelers that predominate. *Movie Star News*.

Popular Music

Hit Songs
"A Ring on the Finger is Worth
Two on the 'Phone"
"I Want a Girl—Just like the Girl
that Married Dear Old Dad"
"All Alone"
"If You Talk in Your Sleep, Don't
Mention My Name"
"Child Love"
"When I Was Twenty-One and
You Were Sweet Sixteen"
"Goodnight, Ladies"
"The Spaniard that Blighted My
Life"
"Everybody's Doing It Now"
"The Oceana Roll"
"Can't You Take It Back, and
Change It for a Boy?"
"Be My Little Baby Bumble Bee"
"Come, Love, and Play Peek-a-
Boo"
"Woodman, Woodman, Spare
That Tree"

Representative Recordings:
"Alexander's Rag Time Band"
(American Quartette); "Oh, You
Beautiful Doll" (Pryor's Band);
"One O'Clock in the Morning"
(Walter Van Brunt); "Pink Lady"
(Victor Concert Orchestra);
"Life's a Funny Proposition After
All" (George M. Cohan); "Roamin'
in the Gloamin' (Harry Lauder)

Jazz
W. C. Handy writes "Memphis
Blues," assimilating black
spirituals, folk work songs, and
jazz; he sustains a melancholic
tone with flatted thirds and
sevenths and develops the "blues."

Former waiter Irving Berlin, 23,
with no formal musical education,
writes the million-copy seller "Alexander's Ragtime Band." *Smithsonian Institution.*

Theater

Broadway Openings

Plays
Mrs. Bumstead-Leigh (Harry James Smith), Mrs.
Minnie Maddern Fiske
Disraeli (Louis Parker), George Arliss
Bought and Paid For (George Broadhurst), Frank
Craven, Julia Dean
The Return of Peter Grimm (David Belasco), David
Warfield, Marie Bates
The Garden of Allah (Robert Hichens, Mary
Anderson), Mary Mannering, Alexander Salvini
Bunty Pulls the Strings (Graham Moffat), Edmond
Beresford, Molly Pearson
Kismet (Edward Knoblauch), Otis Skinner
Chantecler (Edmond Rostand), Maude Adams

Musicals
The Pink Lady (Ivan Caryll, C. M. S. McLellan),
Hazel Dawn, Frank Lalor
La Belle Paree (Jerome Kern, Edward Madden),
Kitty Gordon, Al Jolson (Asa Yoelson)

Ziegfeld Follies (Maurice Levi, Raymond Rubbell,
George V. Hobart), Fannie Brice, Bert Williams,
Dolly Sisters, Leon Errol
Around the World (Manuel Klein), Marcelaine
The Hen-Pecks (A. Baldwin Sloane, E. Ray Goetz),
Lew Fields, Vernon Castle, Blossom Seeley
The Little Millionaire (musical farce), written,
produced, staged by and starring George M.
Cohan
The Quaker Girl (Lionel Monckton), Ina Claire, Olga
Petrova, Percival Knight

Classics and Revivals On and Off Broadway
Trelawny of the Wells (Pinero); *Vanity Fair; Oedipus
Rex; The Lady from the Sea* (Ibsen); The Irish
Players (debut): *The Well of the Saints* and *The
Playboy of the Western World* (Synge), *The Rising of
the Moon* (Lady Gregory), *Cathleen ni Houlihan*
(W. B. Yeats); Robert B. Mantell's Repertory:
*Richelieu, Louis XI, Richard III, King Lear, As You
Like It, Macbeth*

Classical Music

Compositions
Charles Ives, Symphony no. 3, *Tone Roads,* no. 1
George Chadwick, Symphonic Suite
Henry F. Gilbert, *Comedy Overture on Negro Themes*
Frederick Converse, *Ormazd*
Henry Hadley, Symphony no. 4

Important Events
Josef Hofmann and Paulo Gruppa tour; the Minneapolis Symphony visits New York for the first time. Aeolian Hall opens. An all-Wagner concert is presented at the Mahler memorial at Carnegie Hall.

Major Recitals: Olga Samaroff, Mischa Elman, Maurice Renaud, Lillian Nordica, Fanny Bloomfield Ziesler

New Appointments: Josef Stransky (New York Philharmonic Society); Henry Hadley (San Francisco), the first American to lead a major symphony orchestra

Debuts: Efrem Zimbalist, Arthur Shattuck

First Performances
Edward MacDowell, Piano Concerto no. 1 (New York); Horatio Parker, *A Song of Times* (Philadelphia); Charles Martin Loeffler, *For One Who Fell in Battle* (New York); Debussy, *Iberia* (New York); Arthur Foote, Serenade in E major for Strings (St. Louis); Dvorak, Symphony (New York); Enesco, Symphony in E flat major (New York); Grieg, *Old Norwegian Romance* (Boston); Elgar, Second Symphony (Cincinnati)

Father of the future playwright, Eugene, actor James O'Neill tours the U.S. in *The Count of Monte Christo. Smithsonian Institution.*

Opera

Metropolitan: Margarete Matzenauer (debut), Enrico Caruso, Emmy Destinn, *Aïda;* Luisa Tetrazzini (debut), Florencio Constantino, *Lucia di Lammermoor;* Maurice Renaud, *Rigoletto*

Chicago-Philadelphia: Caroline White, *The Secret of Suzanne* (Ermanno Wolf-Ferrari, premiere); Caruso, *Pagliacci; Quo Vadis* (Nouguès, premiere); Jenny Dufau, *Cendrillon* (Massenet)

Philadelphia: Mary Garden, *Natoma* (Herbert); *Thaïs*

Boston: *The Sacrifice* (Frank Converse); Giovanni Zenatello, Maria Gay, *Carmen*

Music Notes
Henry Wilson Savage takes Puccini's *Girl of the Golden West,* in English, on tour across the country • Leopold Stokowski marries pianist Olga Samaroff • The Kansas City Symphony Orchestra forms under Carl Busch.

Edith Wharton, whose distinguished family goes back to colonial times, portrays the social mores of wealthy New Yorkers. *National Archives.*

Art

Painting
Robert Henri, *The Masquerade Dress: Portrait of Mrs. Robert Henri*

Max Weber, *The Geranium, Tea*

William Glackens, *Family Group*

Arthur G. Dove, *Sails of Nature Symbolized— Connecticut River*

Lyonel Feininger, *The Disparagers*

Sculpture
Janet Scudder, *Young Diana*

Herbert Adams, *Joseph Henry*

E. C. Potter, Lions, New York Public Library

Architecture
First Church of Christ, Scientist, Berkeley, Calif. (Bernard Maybeck, 1909–11)

Merchants National Bank, Winona, Minn. (Purcell Feick and Elmslie)

New York Public Library (Carrère and Hastings, 1898–1911)

Coonley Playhouse, Riverside, Ill. (Frank Lloyd Wright)

Park Avenue Christian Church, New York (Goodhue & Ferguson)

People's Savings Bank, Cedar Rapids, Iowa (Louis Sullivan)

Taliesen East, Spring Green, Wis. (Frank Lloyd Wright)

Important Exhibitions

Museums

New York: *Metropolitan:* Winslow Homer; Colonial paintings and silver; Mexican ceramics 1600–1860; "14th Century Armenian Dragon Rugs." *Public Library:* Scenes from the Old Testament by James J. Tissot. Paintings and prints formerly housed in the old Lenox Library are transferred to the new building.

Chicago: 25 paintings by Arthur B. Davies; 35 by Henry Poole; drawings and crafts by children of the public schools of Chicago

Indianapolis: Japanese and Chinese art; oils by George Hitchcock and George W. Picknell

Boston: Monet; Dürer drawings; American church silver

Art Briefs
Over 150 new art museums and societies form • The Metropolitan Museum of Art gains 10,500 new acquisitions • Museums dedicated include the Toledo and L. D. M. Sweat Memorial (Portland, Maine); under construction, New Orleans, Los Angeles, and Detroit • *Der Blaue Reiter* ("The Blue Rider," including Marc, Kandinsky, Macke, and Klee) gains a wide following in the U.S. • Auction prices cover a broad range: the Inness *Landscape and Cattle,* $120; Delacroix, *Portrait of the Artist,* $300; Fra Filippo Lippi, *Adoration of the Child,* $1,350; Joseph Bail, *Nuns Saying Grace,* $5,500; and Corot, *Landscape by the Sea,* $20,000.

Dance

Staged by Mikhail Mordkin, *Swan Lake* has its American premiere in New York. Isadora Duncan returns from Europe and gives a "free form" dance recital at Carnegie Hall; for her performance of Wagner's Bacchanale from *Tannhaüser,* she is, as one reporter puts it, "deliciously dressed in nothing but a black ta-ra-ra-boom-de-ay round her sacred head."

Underwood tries to create a noiseless typewriter. *Library of Congress.*

Books

Fiction

Critics' Choice

Ethan Frome, Edith Wharton
The Miller of Old Church, Ellen Glasgow
Jennie Gerhardt, Theodore Dreiser
Dawn O'Hara, Edna Ferber
The Iron Woman, Margaret Deland
The Secret Garden, Francis Hodgson Burnett
South Sea Tales, Jack London
The Outcry, Henry James
Members of the Family, Owen Wister
Stover at Yale, Owen McMahon Johnson
Sixes and Sevens, O. Henry
&. *Under Western Eyes*, Joseph Conrad

Best-Sellers

The Broad Highway, Jeffrey Farnol

The Little Prodigal Judge, Vaughan Kester
The Winning of Barbara Worth, Harold Bell Wright
Queed, Henry Sydnor Harrison
The Harvester, Gene Stratton Porter
The Iron Woman, Margaret Deland
The Long Roll, Mary Johnston
Molly Make-Believe, Eleanor Abbott
The Rosary, Florence Barclay
The Common Law, Robert W. Chambers

Nonfiction

Critics' Choice

The Mind of Primitive Man, Franz Boas
My First Summer in the Sierra, John Muir
The New Criticism, Joel E. Spingarn
My Story, Tom L. Johnson

New Dooley Book, Finlay Peter Dunne
The Cruise of the Snark, Jack London
The Life of George Cabot Lodge, Henry Adams
Forest Physiography, Isaiah Bowman
Some Problems of Philosophy, William James (posthumous)
The Women of Shakespeare, Frank Harris
Life of Andrew Jackson, John Spencer Bassett
&. *Cambridge Medieval History*

Poetry

Ezra Pound, *Canzoni*
Sarah Teasdale, *Helen of Troy and Other Poems*
Franklin Pierce Adams, *Tobogganing on Parnassus*
John Hall Wheelock, *The Human Fantasy*

Science and Technology

Elmer Ambrose Sperry invents the gyroscope.
The electrical automobile self-starter is devised by Charles Kettering.
Thomas Hunt Morgan begins mapping chromosome positions in the fruit fly.
The first chromosome map, indicating five sex-linked genes, is produced by Alfred Sturtevant.
Russell Hibbs devises a spinal fusion operation for scoliosis.
Thomas Addis discovers that transfusions of normal plasma help hemophiliacs.
&. Niels Bohr links atomic structure to Planck's constant.
&. Ernest Rutherford formulates a theory of atomic structure: a nucleus surrounded by a cloud of electrons.
&. Heike Kamerlingh Onnes discovers superconductivity.
&. Chaim Weizmann obtains acetone, important in munitions, through the use of bacteria.

D. W. Griffith pioneers both technical and narrative film devices. *Movie Star News.*

Sports

Baseball

Cy Young retires after 21 years, holding the record
for games pitched (906) and won (511); 516 games
were in the NL; 390, in the AL.

Honus Wagner (Pittsburgh, NL) wins his 8th batting
title, the 5th in 6 years.

Ty Cobb (Detroit, AL) wins his 5th straight batting
title with a record .420 BA, the highest since Cap
Anson in 1887, when walks counted as hits; Joe
Jackson (Cleveland, AL) hits .408.

Frank Schulte hits a major league record 21 homers.

The Philadelphia A's "$100,000" infield includes
McInnis, Collins, Barry, and Baker.

Champions

Batting
  Honus Wagner (Pittsburgh,
  NL), .334
  Tyrus R. Cobb (Detroit, AL),
  .420
Pitching
  Rube Marquard (New York,
  NL), 24–7
  S. A. Gregg (Cleveland, AL),
  23–7

Home runs
  Frank Schulte (Chicago,
  NL), 21

Football

The Carlisle Indian School, led by Jim Thorpe, upsets
Harvard 18-15.

College All-Americans: Jim Thorpe (HB), Carlisle;
Leland Devore (T), Army; Robert Fisher (G),
Harvard

Other Sports

Running: Clarence DeMar wins the Boston
Marathon in 2 hrs., 21 min., 39.6 sec.

Auto Racing: The first Indianapolis 500 is won by
Ray Harroun; his average speed is 74.59 mph.

Tennis: Hazel Hotchkiss wins her 3rd straight Open;
William Larned, his fifth. Australia defeats the U.S.,
5-0, in the Davis Cup challenge round.

Golf: Bobby Jones, 9, wins the junior title in
Atlanta.

Winners

World Series
  Philadelphia (AL) 4
  New York (NL) 2
MVP
  NL—Frank Schulte, Chicago
  AL—Tyrus Cobb, Detroit
College Football
  Princeton
College Basketball
  St. John's
Player of the Year
  Theodore Kiendl, Columbia

Stanley Cup
  Ottawa
U.S. Tennis Open
  Men: William Larned
  Women: Hazel Hotchkiss
U.S.G.A. Open
  John McDermott
Kentucky Derby
  Meridian (George Archibald,
  jockey)

Fashion

As blouses with lowered necklines are worn with
fitted and long suits, women cultivate the look of
silky and soft skin; sales of cold cream and lemon
extract escalate. (In actuality, only a fantasized
décolletage effect is simulated, as satin or silk yokes
are inserted in the bodice.) Poiret introduces a variety
of dress styles: the sack, sheath, and Hellenic tunic,
in soft fabrics for summer (chiffons, gauzes) and
lamés and damasks (rather than drapery materials) for
winter. As the youthful, thinner figure gains attention,
huge breakfasts of meats and fish are replaced by
lighter fare, like eggs and toast. A sturdy wool,
"homespun," is introduced for winter wear, along
with wools designed in stripes and small checks. This
is an important year for furs: sable, ermine, seal, and
chinchilla for the wealthy; squirrel, moleskin, and
raccoon for most others—either in full-length coats or
in the ubiquitous trim that decorates virtually every
hat, jacket, and bag. Stylish headgear includes
turbans, Grecian bandeaux, and tray-like hats that
hold ostrich feathers, flowers, or fur. Women are so
attached to their hats that they wear them at home.

*High-fashion note: Theater bonnet in silver lace with
cascading poppies.*

Smithsonian Institution.

Kaleidoscope

- The Triangle Shirtwaist factory fire, in N.Y.C., arouses nationwide demands for better working conditions; the single exit door had been locked to keep the 146 girls from absconding with thread.
- Massive European immigration continues; on April 17, a record 12,000 arrive at Ellis Island.
- South Carolina prohibits children under 16 from working between 8 p.m. and 6 a.m.; it also forbids the employment of children under 12 in a mine, factory, or textile establishment; Delaware begins to frame child labor and employers' liability laws.
- "It is getting so that an honest trust is afraid to go home in the dark," comments the *Washington Post,* as the Standard Oil and American Tobacco trusts are dissolved.
- The average salary and savings of bankers and brokers is $7,726/$2,308; of lawyers, $4,169/$1,474; physicians, $3,907/$717; railroad officials, $3,441/$628; clergymen, $3,150/$369; professors and tutors, $2,878/$543; and steamboat officials, $2,529/$603.
- Most Americans cheer the overthrow of Mexican dictator Porfirio Diaz, although some fear for the future of American investments in Mexico.
- The high divorce rate causes concern (1 in 12; 1 in 85, in 1905).
- A popular joke: He: "Were you ever in love before you met me?" She: "Yes, but not since."
- American suffragettes join worldwide protest when Marie Curie wins an unprecedented second Nobel prize but is refused admission to the French Academy of Science.
- Prohibitionists rally nationwide, although in a close vote Texas defeats a prohibition law.
- The Supreme Court condemns the use of the word "cure" in medications: a combination of arsenic and strychnine has been called "a brain, blood, and nerve food."
- Demand arises for a public parcel post system; it often costs more to mail an item to a neighboring town than another country.
- Use of fingerprinting in crime detection becomes widespread.
- Corruption scandals continue nationwide; 1,100 are indicted for vote selling in Adams county, Ohio; 210 in Danville, Illinois.
- Imprisoned former political boss Abe Reuf suggests changing prison uniforms from stripes to blue or gray, "for reasons of moral uplift."
- Jacob Riis advocates the "prevention of gang rule" by teaching children the "use of hands," not just books.
- The National Fine Arts Commission inaugurates "the greatest building project in American history," the departments of State, Commerce, and Justice in Washington D.C.
- At the fiftieth anniversary of Bull Run, Civil War veterans from both North and South mingle in friendly fashion, despite controversy over the construction of a monument to the Confederate Navy.
- Ex-Mississippi governor Vardaman raises the "black specter," as he campaigns "Vote for the White South and Uphold the White South"; he travels in a chariot drawn by 160 white oxen and is dressed in white linen.
- A New York State law forbids the representation of Jesus Christ on the stage.
- *The Masses,* founded in Greenwich Village, prints "what is too naked for the money-making press."
- An estimated 40 million attend summer "Chautauquas," which feature opera singers, orchestras, yodelers, Hawaiian crooners, magicians, American Indians, and inspirational lecturers (including William Jennings Bryan); TR calls them "the most American thing in America."
- Jean, the Vitagraph canine, becomes the first dog star.
- Sixty thousand Bibles are placed in hotel bedrooms by the Gideon Organization of Christian Commercial Travelers.
- Concern for the "deserving poor" continues; the "Self-Mastery Colony" in New Jersey and "Parting-of-the-Ways" home in Chicago are formed for "down-and-out" men.
- After two Shakers at Kissimmee, Florida, chloroform a sister dying of tuberculosis, euthanasia becomes an issue.
- "Early training is responsible for precocity," claims the prominent Dr. Boris Sidis, whose son, at 11, has entered Harvard with advanced standing.
- President Taft goes from 340 to 267 pounds.
- In the heated battle over reciprocal trade with Canada, a congressional group proposes to annex Canada.
- The U.S., Japan, Britain, and Russia sign a 15-year treaty regulating seal hunting.
- Anti-trust actions continue, as the U.S. indicts J. P. Morgan, John Rockefeller, and Andrew Carnegie in the U.S. Steel case; American steel costs more at home than in Europe.
- "How can you unscramble eggs," comments J. P. Morgan, on the impossibility of altering interlocking business interests.

First appearances: Chevrolet (Chevrolet and Durant), Crisco, Domino brand sugar, "Lee" denim work clothes, "Big Brother" movement, Skidmore and Connecticut colleges for women, collegiate ice festival (Dartmouth, with new sports skiing and tobogganning), hydro-airplane, aerial bombing (Turks by Italy), airplane tourist, tide-predicting machine, Appalachian Forest Reserve Act, licensed woman pilot (Harriet Quimby), Sante-Fe Deluxe (Chicago-Los Angeles, 63 hours), federal cemetery for both Union and Confederate soldiers (Springfield, Mo.), white line in the middle of the road, black assistant attorney general, insect electrocutor patent

Fads: fox-trot variations (crab step, Texas Tommy, Fish Walk, Kangaroo Dip, Grizzly Bear), food fasting (Upton Sinclair, *The Fasting Cure*), summer camps, summer conferences (e.g., Silver Bays, Sagamores)

New words: taylorization (scientific management of industry), phone (for "telephone," from songs "A Ring on the Finger is Worth Two on the 'Phone" and "Nora Malone [Call Me By Phone]")

1912

Facts and Figures

Economic Profile
  Dow-Jones: ↑ High 94–
    Low 80
  GNP: +10%
  Inflation: +6.3%
  Unemployment: 4.6%
Households with telephones:
  18%
Hamburg-American line,
  around-the-world cruise
  (110 days): $650
Victor, victrola: $15–$200
Hartman's Solid Oak
  (Milwaukee, Chicago):
  Writing table, 42″ × 28″:
    $7.95
  Buffet, with French plate
    mirror top: $12.50
  Bed-davenport, leather:
    $18.75
  Enamel and iron bed: $3.98
Gimbels:
  Ostrich plumed hat: 69¢
  Nemo corset: $3
  Royal Worcester Adjusto
    corset, for stout women:
    $3
  Oxford shoes: women's
    high white canvas, with
    buttons: $1.95;
    men's tan calf or gun
    metal: $2.85
McKenney Dental Company
  (Denver):
  Silver filling: 50¢; 22k gold
    crown: $3
  Plate: $5; heaviest bridge
    work, $3 per tooth

Deaths

General William Booth, King
  of Denmark Frederick
  VIII, August Strindberg,
  Vice President James
  Sherman, Wilbur Wright;
  on the *Titanic:* John Jacob
  Astor, Francis Millet,
  Benjamin Guggenheim,
  Harry Elkins Widener

In the News

SUN YAT-SEN BECOMES PRESIDENT OF CHINESE REPUBLIC, BOY EMPEROR PU YI ABDICATES, ENDING MANCHU DYNASTY . . . U.S. TROOPS OCCUPY TIENTSIN TO PROTECT AMERICAN INTERESTS . . . CLARENCE DARROW, LAWYER FOR THE MCNAMARAS, IS ACQUITTED OF JUROR BRIBING . . . JAPAN AND GERMANY LAUNCH NAVAL BUILDING PROGRAMS, BRITAIN VOWS SUPERIORITY . . . NEW MEXICO AND ARIZONA BECOME 47TH, 48TH STATES . . . TEXTILE WORKERS, LED BY IWW, WIN STRIKE IN LAWRENCE, MASS. . . . VIRGINIA MOUNTAINEERS "SHOOT UP" COURTHOUSE AT HILLSBORO, VA. . . . SS TITANIC SINKS ON MAIDEN VOYAGE AFTER COLLISION WITH ICEBERG, 1,513 DIE . . . SCOTT AND FOUR OTHERS DIE ON RETURN FROM SOUTH POLE . . . JAPANESE PROTEST CALIFORNIA ANTI-ALIEN LAND LAW . . . VIGILANTES TAR AND FEATHER ANARCHISTS IN SAN DIEGO . . . SOCIALISTS NOMINATE EUGENE V. DEBS . . . U.S. MARINES FIGHT CUBAN INSURRECTION . . . CONGRESS EXTENDS EIGHT-HOUR DAY TO FEDERAL EMPLOYEES . . . REPUBLICANS NOMINATE TAFT AND SHERMAN, DEFEATED TR BOLTS TO PROGRESSIVE PARTY . . . DEMOCRATS NOMINATE WOODROW WILSON AND THOMAS MARSHALL . . . U.S. INTERVENES IN NICARAGUAN REVOLUTION TO "RESTORE ORDER" . . . MARTIAL LAW IS PROCLAIMED IN ATLANTA DURING STREETCAR STRIKE . . . PANAMA CANAL ACT MANDATES REBATES TO U.S. SHIPS, EUROPEANS PROTEST . . . FIRST BALKAN WAR BEGINS, MONTENEGRO, SERBIA, BULGARIA DECLARE WAR ON TURKEY OVER MACEDONIA . . . NEW YORK PASSES 54-HOUR WORK WEEK LAW . . . TR SURVIVES ASSASSINATION ATTEMPT . . . WILSON IS ELECTED PRESIDENT WITH 6.3 MILLION VOTES; TR GAINS 4.1, TAFT, 3.4, DEBS, 900,000 . . . BULGARIANS THREATEN CONSTANTINOPLE.

Quotes

"Oh, they swung the lifeboats out o'er the deep and
   raging sea,
And the band struck up with 'Nearer My God to
   Thee.'
Little children wept and cried, as the waves swept
   o'er the side,
It was sad when that great ship went down."
              — popular song "The Titanic"

"Ice was in plain sight, floating ice and berg. Not only
that but Captain Smith had received at least three
warnings that icebergs were in his path."
    — *New York Times*, on Smith's obsession with speed

During the presidential election: "I feel fit as a bull
moose"; "My hat is in the ring. The fight is on and I
am stripped to the buff"; "We stand at Armageddon,
and we battle for the Lord"; "Wealth should be the
servant, not the master of people" (TR, "Declaration
of Faith"). "Such extremists are not progressives;
they are political emotionalists and neurotics" (Taft).
"Private monopoly is indefensible and intolerable"
(Wilson).

"[Suffrage] is dangerous. [Women] will play havoc
with it for themselves and society."
                — *New York Times*

"Motion Pictures are just a passing fancy and aren't
worth comment in this newspaper."
       — Arthur Brisbane, *Chicago Herald-Record*

"As we come marching, in the beauty of the day,
A million darkened kitchens, a thousand mills loft
   gray,
Are touched with all the radiance a sudden sun
   discloses,
For the people hear us singing: 'Bread and roses!
   Bread and roses!' "
           — Song of the Lawrence, Mass. strikers

"The supreme religious test of our social order is the
hideous commerce of prostitution. . . . Excessive
fatigue and underfeeding are the causes that increase
the victims of the social evil."
               — Jane Addams

"In Central America the aim has been to help such
countries as Nicaragua and Honduras to help
themselves."
       — Taft, on "substituting dollars for bullets"

Ads

Sports decks and spacious promenades, commodious
state rooms and apartments en suite; cabins deluxe
with bath; squash-raquet courts; Turkish and electric
bath establishments; glass-enclosed swimming pools;
veranda and palm courts; Louis XVI restaurants;
electric elevators.
                (The Titanic, *White Star line*)

Are you accepting steamed beans, thinking they are
baked? It's only a question of what you want,
Madam.
                (*H.J. Heinz*)

The Czar of Russia owns a Knight Motor Car. So
does the Emperor of Germany. So do the Kings of
England, Belgium, and Spain.
                (*Stearn Knight* car)

You'd never believe this closet was in the house. The
flushing of the Siwelco closet will never embarrass
you or your guests. . . . Get rid of the hoarse girgling
of the old-time closet . . . heard from parlor to garret.
       (*Siwelco Noiseless Siphon Jet Closet*)

The Automobile for Women
Electrically Started and Lighted
Controls Itself
Pumps Its Own Tires.
                (*Inter-State* automobile)

Household scraps are not fit food for the animal that
is your children's playmate and your own most
faithful friend and companion.
                (*Austin's Dog Bread*)

The suffragette movement is divided between state-by-state moderates and the more militant national amendment seekers. *Library of Congress*.

Jack Johnson flees the U.S. for Europe when he is convicted of violating the Mann Act, which prohibits transporting women across interstate lines for immoral purposes. *Library of Congress*.

Movies

Openings

The New York Hat (D. W. Griffith), Lionel Barrymore, Mary Pickford, Mae Marsh

An Unseen Enemy (D. W. Griffith), Dorothy and Lillian Gish (debut)

The Musketeers of Pig Alley (D. W. Griffith), early appearance of "the gangster," Lillian Gish, Walter Miller

Queen Elizabeth (Emile Moreau, distributed by Famous Players), Sarah Bernhardt

What Happened to Mary? (Vitagraph), Mary Fuller, forerunner of serials

War on the Plains (Thomas Ince), Ethel Grandin

A Girl and Her Trust (D. W. Griffith), Dorothy Bernard, Wilfred Lucas

From the Manger to the Cross (Sidney Olcott), R. Henderson Bland, early feature-length film

Cohen Collects a Debt (Mack Sennett), first comedy at Keystone Studios

Blazing the Trail (Thomas Ince), Ethel Grandin, Francis Ford

Imp creates the first movie star known by name: Florence Lawrence. Four- and five-reelers proliferate. Mack Sennett begins Keystone to make comedies with Mabel Normand, Ford Sterling, and Fred Mace. Adolph Zukor's Famous Players attracts stage actors Maude Adams, Julia Marlowe, David Warfield, John and Lionel Barrymore, Marie Dressler, Nazimova, and George Arliss. Carl Laemmle forms Universal; William Fox creates the Fox Company; Thanhouser, American, Reliance, and Majestic consolidate into Mutual; Universal's west coast "Ranch" opens.

Popular Stars

Alice Joyce, Carlyle Blackwell, Florence Lawrence, Kathlyn Williams, Tom Mix, J. Warren Kerrigan, Mary Fuller, King Baggot, Lillian Walker, Maurice Costello; sex symbols: Francis X. Bushman, Mabel Normand

On Teddy Roosevelt and the Bullmoose Convention: "Who can open the doors of his face?" *Library of Congress*.

Popular Music _____

Hit Songs
"Do It Again"
"I'm the Lonesomest Gal in
   Town"
"Giannina Mia"
"Hitchy Koo"
"It's a Long Way to Tipperary"
"That Old Girl of Mine"
"My Melancholy Baby"
"The Sweetheart of Sigma Chi"
"Daddy Has a Sweetheart, and
   Mother is Her Name"
"When Irish Eyes are Smiling"
"And the Green Grass Grew All
   Around"
"When I Get You Alone Tonight"

Representative Recordings: Al
Jolson, "Ragging the Baby to
Sleep" (million-selling);
"Moonlight Bay" (American
Quartette); "Row, Row, Row"
(Ada Jones); "Waiting for the
Robert E. Lee" (Heidelberg
Quartet); "In the Evening By the
Moonlight" (Hayden Quartette);
"Everything's at Home Except
Your Wife" (American Quartette);
"Ragtime Cowboy Joe" (Bob
Roberts)

Jazz
Blacks continue to find it nearly
impossible to get music published
or gain Broadway sponsorship.
James R. Europe, whose dream is
to bring black artists to the
Broadway stage, organizes the
Clef Club Orchestra, which plays
at Carnegie Hall on May 2, the
first popular music performance in
a concert auditorium. Sheldon
Brooks and Europe write music
for the dance craze that hits the
nation and is popularized by Nora
Bayes and Al Jolson. Bessie Smith
and "Ma" and "Pa" Rainey play in
Moses Stoke's *Minstrel Troupe* in
Chattanooga. Early "blues"
favorites, composed and sung by
blacks, include "Baby Seal Blues"
(Artie Matthews) and "Dallas
Blues" (Hart A. Wand).

Theater _____

Broadway Openings

Plays
A Slice of Life (J. M. Barrie), John Barrymore, Ethel
   Barrymore
The Talker (Marion Fairfax), Tully Marshall, Pauline
   Lord
The Bird of Paradise (Richard Walton Tully), Virginia
   Reynolds
A Butterfly on the Wheel (Edward G. Hemmerde,
   K. C. and Francis Neilson), Charles
   Quartermaine, Evelyn Beerbohm
Elevating a Husband (Clara Lipman, Samuel
   Shipman), Conway Tearle, Edward Everett
   Horton
Officer 666 (Augustin MacHugh), Francis D. McGinn
The "Mind-the-Paint" Girl (Arthur Pinero), Jeanne
   Eagels, Billie Burke
Within the Law (Bayard Veiller), Jane Cowl,
   Frederick Howe
Peg o' My Heart (J. Hartley Manners), Laurette
   Taylor

Musicals
A Winsome Widow (Raymond Hubbell), Elizabeth
   Brice, Leon Errol, Dolly Sisters, Mae West

The Rose Maid (Bruno Granichstaedten, Robert B.
   Smith), Edward Gallagher, Al Shean, Edith
   Decker
Over the River (John Golden), Eddie Foy, Mae
   Busch, Peggy Wood
The Whirl of Society (Louis A. Hirsch, Harold
   Atteridge), Gaby Deslys, Al Jolson, Blossom
   Seeley
The Merry Countess (Johann Strauss, Arthur
   Anderson), Jose Collins, Maurice Farkoa, Dolly
   Sisters
The Passing Show (Louis A. Hirsch, Harold
   Atteridge), Willie and Eugene Howard
The Firefly (Rudolf Friml, Otto Harbach), Emma
   Trentini, Melville Stewart
The Lady of the Slipper (Victor Herbert, James
   O'Dea), Elsie Janis, Montgomery and Stone,
   Vernon Castle, Peggy Wood

Classics and Revivals On and Off Broadway
Man and Superman; Julius Caesar (William
Faversham, Tyrone Power), *Hamlet* (John E.
Kellerd); *She Stoops to Conquer; Sumurun* (Max
Reinhardt); *Ghosts; Henry V* (Louis Waller); Sothern
and Marlow: *Hamlet, As You Like It, Romeo and
Juliet*

Classical Music ──────────

Compositions
Charles Ives, *Putnam's Camp, Lincoln, the Great Commoner*
Louis Gruenberg, Violin Sonata no. 1
Charles Wakefield Cadman, *Idealized Indian Themes*
Leo Sowerby, *Elevation*
George Chadwick, *Aphrodite*
Charles Griffes, *Bacchanale*
Erich Korngold, Sinfonietta
Arthur Farwell, *Three Indian Songs*

Important Events
The London Symphony Orchestra appears for the first time in the U.S. Conductor Josef Stransky shocks New York audiences with Bruckner's Fifth Symphony and Weingartner's Third. Eugène Ysaye returns to the stage after an eight-year absence; he performs his own work, Saint-Saën's *Rondo Capriccioso,* and the Mozart G-minor Concerto. Ysaye later joins Godowsky and Jean Gerardy in a series of chamber music recitals. The Minneapolis sponsors a Brahms festival—all the symphonies, concertos, *German Requiem,* songs, and numerous short pieces.

Major Recitals: Josef Lhévinne, Josef Hofmann, Katherine Goodson, Harold Bauer, Arthur Shattuck

New Appointments: Leopold Stokowski, Philadelphia; Ernst Kunwald, Cincinnati; Karl Muck, Boston (return)

Debut: Wilhelm Backhaus

First Performances
Schoenberg, *Five Pieces for Orchestra* (Chicago); Bruckner, Sixth Symphony (New York); Borodin, Second Symphony (Boston); *Jena Symphony,* attributed to Beethoven (Boston); Delius, *Life's Dance* (Chicago); Ravel, *Ma Mère l'Oye* (New York); Henry F. Gilbert, *Negro Rhapsody,* Coleridge-Taylor, *Negro Air* for Violin and Orchestra (Norfolk, Conn.); Frederick Converse, *Ormazd* (St. Louis); Saint-Saëns, "Hymn to Pallas Athene" (New York); Strauss, *Festival Prelude* (New York); Mary Carr Moore, *Narcissa* (Seattle)

Virtually national icons, Irene and Vernon Castle popularize new dances like the fox trot, turkey trot, and tango. *Library of Congress.*

Opera

Metropolitan: Lucrezia Bori (debut), *Manon Lescaut;* Frieda Hempel (debut), *Les Hugenots* (Meyerbeer); Louise Homer, Herbert Witherspoon, *Mona* (Horatio William Parker, recipient of $10,000 for the best English language opera by an American-born composer)

Boston: Luisa Tettrazini, Florencio Constantino, *Barber of Seville;* Mary Garden, *Pelléas and Mélisande*

Denver: Alice Zeppelli, *The Secret of Suzanne*

San Francisco: *La Bohème; Conchita*

Philadelphia: Titta Ruffo (debut), *Rigoletto*

Music Notes
The *New York World*'s $10,000 gift sponsors 61 concerts in January and February "for the masses"; over 20,000 are turned away in each of the New York City boroughs • Henry Cowell, playing with his fists and forearms, introduces his "tone-clusters" at a San Francisco recital • White New Yorkers hear the new "jass" music when James R. Europe and 115 black musicians rent Carnegie Hall for the first of several concerts.

Art

Painting

John Sloan, *Sunday, Women Drying their Hair*

John Singer Sargent, *In the General Life*

Charles Sheeler, *Chrysanthemums*

Alfred Maurer, *Autumn*

William J. Glackens, *Parade, Washington Square*

Abraham Walkowitz, *Hudson River Landscape with Figures*

Charles Demuth, *Strolling*

Maurice Sterne, *Resting at the Bazaar*

Stuart Davis, *The Front Page*

Sculpture

Daniel Chester French, *Standing Lincoln*

Gaston Lachaise, *Woman Arranging Her Hair*

Edith Woodman, *At the Threshhold*

Emil Fuchs, *La Pensierosa*

Chester Beach, *Dawn*

Frank Lloyd Wright, Multicolored lead glass

Architecture

Rice University, Houston (Ralph Adams Cram)

Bradley house, Woods Hole, Mass. (Purcell and Elmslie)

F. W. Woolworth house, 998 Fifth Avenue, New York City (McKim, Meade & White)

635 Park Avenue apartments, New York City (J. E. R. Carpenter)

Important Exhibitions

New York: *Metropolitan:* Rodin; Italian paintings from the Jarves collection; Japanese prints; Oriental wares; Chinese porcelains; "Tapestries, Lace and Other Textiles"; Musical instruments; J. Pierpont Morgan's art collections are transferred from London to the Museum.

Boston: John Singer Sargent (145 watercolors); "New Acquisitions in Chinese and Japanese Art"

Indianapolis: "Modern German Applied Arts"; Hogarth engravings; Miniatures and pencil drawings by Elsie E. Southwick

Chicago: George Inness; British and American porcelain and pottery; "Antiquarian Acquisitions: 36 costumes, 267 medals"; Awards: gold medal: Frank W. Benson, *My Daughter;* silver, J. Alden Weir, *The Plaza Nocturne*

Art Briefs

Picasso and Braque startle the art world with their experiments in "synthetic cubism" • Four museums open: in New Orleans, Toledo, Muskegan, and Rochester • Interest increases in foreign art; until this year, only the Carnegie Institute has held international exhibitions; Buffalo, Newark, and New York now sponsor major shows in French, German, and Scandinavian art • Sales include Hals' *Dutch Market Scene,* $130; Thomas Cole's *The Clove, Catskill Mountains,* $70; Fragonard's *The Lovers,* $1,800; and Anders Zorn's *The Bather,* $4,250.

Tenor John McCormack has gained meteoric fame since his debut last year. *Smithsonian Institution.*

Frank Lloyd Wright living room, Wayzata, Minnesota. *The Metropolitan Museum of Art,* bequest of Emily Crane Chadbourne, 1972.

Dance

At Ballet Arts (Studio 61, Carnegie Hall), Alys Bentley, in Grecian robes, teaches the new ballet to students Sonia and Jerome Robbins, Agnes de Mille, and Margaret D'Houbler. Ruth Saint Denis premieres *Bakawali* and her *O-Mika.*

Books

Fiction

Critics' Choice
The Financier, Theodore Dreiser
The Autobiography of an Ex-Colored Man, James Weldon Johnson
The Reef, Edith Wharton
The Butterfly House, Mary E. Wilkins Freeman
The Yates Pride, Mary E. Wilkins Freeman
Alexander's Bridge, Willa Cather
Julia France and Her Times, Gertrude Atherton
The Squirrel-Cage, Dorothy Canfield Fisher
Riders of the Purple Sage, Zane Grey

Best-Sellers
The Harvester, Gene Stratton Porter
The Street Called Straight, Basil King
Their Yesterdays, Harold Bell Wright
The Meeting of Molly, Maria Thompson Davies
A Hoosier Chronicle, Meredith Nicholson
The Winning of Barbara Worth, Harold Bell Wright
The Just and the Unjust, Vaughan Kester
The Net, Rex Beach
Tante, Anne Douglas Sedgwick
Fran, J. Breckenridge Ellis

Nonfiction

Critics' Choice
The New Democracy, Walter Weyl
Christianizing the Social Order, Walter Rauschenbusch
Ralph Waldo Emerson: Uncollected Writings, ed. Charles C. Bigelow
Lee, the American, Gamaliel Bradford
The New History, James Harvey Robinson
The Kallikak Family, Henry H. Goddard
Marcus Alonzo Hanna: His Life and Work, Herbert Croly
Essays in Radical Empiricism, William James (posthumous)
The Development of Religion and Thought in Ancient Egypt, Henry Bres;ted
Changes in the Bodily Form of Descendants of Immigrants, Franz Boas

Best-Sellers
The Promised Land, Mary Antin
The Montessori Method, Maria Montessori
A New Conscience and an Ancient Evil, Jane Addams
Three Plays, Eugène Brieux
Your United States, Arnold Bennett
Creative Evolution, Henri Bergson
How to Live on Twenty-Four Hours a Day, Arnold Bennett
Woman and Labor, Olive Schreiner
Mark Twain, Albert Bigelow Paine

Poetry
Ezra Pound, *Ripostes*
Robinson Jeffers, *Flagons and Apples*
William Vaughan Moody, *Poems*
Amy Lowell, *A Dome of Many-Colored Glass*
Vachel Lindsay, *Rhymes to be Traded for Bread*
Elinor Wylie, *Incidental Numbers*

Out for a drive in a Ford "flivver" in Boise, Idaho. *Library of Congress.*

Science and Technology

Victor Hess discovers cosmic radiation.
The detection of protons and electrons is facilitated by Charles Wilson's cloud-chamber photographs.
Henrietta Swan Leavitt discovers a method of measuring the distance of galaxies outside the Milky Way.
Serum therapy, which uses antibodies from horse serum, is the first effective therapy for pneumonia.
The "punch operation," for enlarged prostate glands, is devised at Johns Hopkins.
Casimir Funk coins the term "vitamine" for substances previously called accessory blood

factors; he proposes that they are essential to normal physiology.
Scientists demonstrate that eight essential amino acids not produced by the body can be acquired from eating meat.
The regenerative or "feedback" radio receiver is invented by de Forest and Langmuir.
🙣 The theory of continental drift is proposed by Alfred Wegener.
🙣 "Piltdown Man," 50,000 years old and with a humanlike skull and apelike jaw, is discovered by Charles Dawson.

Sports

Baseball

Rube Marquard wins a record 19 straight games.

Ty Cobb (Detroit, AL) wins his 6th straight batting title and is the first to hit over .400 in two consecutive years.

Frank ("Home Run") Baker (Philadelphia, AL) wins his 2nd straight AL home run championship with 10.

Clyde Milan (Washington, AL) steals an AL record 88 bases.

Champions

Batting
  Henry Zimmerman (Chicago, NL), .372
  Tyrus R. Cobb (Detroit, AL), .410
Pitching
  C. R. Hendrix (Pittsburgh, NL), 24–9
  Joe Wood (Boston, AL), 34–5

Home runs
  Henry Zimmerman (Chicago, NL), 14

Football

Downs to move ball 10 yards are increased from 3 to 4; the touchdown value is increased from 5 to 6 points.

College All-Americans: Jim Thorpe (HB), Carlisle; Charles Brickley (HB), Harvard; Henry Ketchem (C), Yale

Olympics

The Olympics are held at Stockholm, Sweden. The U.S. wins 23 gold medals and unofficial first place. Native American Jim Thorpe wins gold medals in the decathlon (8,413 pts.) and pentathlon. Other U.S. gold winners include Ralph Craig (100m, 10.8 s., 200m, 21.7 s.), Alma Richards (high jump, 6'3"), H. J. Babcock (pole vault, 12'11"), Duke Kahanamoko (100m, swimming), Ted Meredith (800m, 1:51.9). Thorpe is widely acclaimed as the world's greatest athlete.

Other Sports

Boxing: Johny Kilbane outpoints Abe Attell in 20 rounds for the featherweight title.

Winners

World Series
  Boston (AL) 4
  New York (NL) 3
  (one tie: second game called for darkness)
MVP
  NL—Lawrence Doyle, New York
  AL—Tris Speaker, Boston
College Football
  Harvard
College Basketball
  Wisconsin

Player of the Year
  Otto Stangel, Wisconsin
Stanley Cup
  Quebec
U.S. Tennis Open
  Men: Maurice McLoughlin
  Women: Mary K. Browne
USGA Open
  John McDermott
Kentucky Derby
  Worth (Carol Shilling, jockey)

Fashion

For Men: Like his female counterpart, the most fashion-minded gentleman changes clothing several times a day. At work, he wears striped trousers, a morning coat, starched white shirt (with the by-now institutionalized Arrow collar), and top hat—with a curve on one or both sides. The funnel-shaped hat has become passé. The frock coat, which extends to mid-calf, is reserved for more formal dress and worn with gray pants, gray hat, and tan or white shoes. Also integral to every well-dressed man's wardrobe are his informal lounge suits, tweed jackets, and striped blazers. Dinner jackets are most frequently worn in the evening, although for more formal occasions, tail coats, white waistcoats and gloves, as well as the Arrow raised and pointed collar, are absolute necessities. At a ball, or at the opera (where gray gloves replace white ones), one's gloves are never removed. Accessories for both day and evening dress remain extremely important: the hat (worn on every occasion and ranging from a variety of woolen caps to fedoras), cane of malacca with a silver or enamel top, gold watch and chain, and unpretentious cuff links, shirt studs, and tie pin; a single ring is also worn—only on the ring finger.

Fashion note: L. L. Bean hunting shoe with rubber sole.

Sarah Bernhardt's nationwide tours include a stop at San Quentin, where death row inmates get front row seats. *D. Ouellette Collection.*

Kaleidoscope _____

- On its maiden voyage, the world's largest ship, the "unsinkable" *Titanic,* hits an iceberg off the coast of Newfoundland and sinks; the band plays as the ship goes down, and the doomed sing "Nearer My God to Thee."
- "Don't harm the poor creature," says Teddy Roosevelt, holding aloft the shredded manuscript that foiled his would-be assassin's bullet; "It takes more than that to kill a Bull Moose!" he declares, and continues his speech.
- Massachusetts is the first state to establish a minimum wage for women and children.
- Attention focuses on the black smoke poisoning the air from sooty factory, office and apartment chimneys.
- James B. Herrick diagnoses a heart attack in a living patient; what was formerly considered indigestion or food poisoning is now understood to be a coronary blockage and not necessarily fatal.
- Roosevelt defeats Taft in the presidential primaries, used extensively for the first time, but Taft gains the nomination at the machine-dominated GOP convention.
- With widespread sentiment for active government leadership in combatting the power of wealth, progressives of both parties gain large victories in the national elections.
- In *The New Democracy,* Walter Weyl decries the "sensational inequalities of wealth, insane extravagances, [and] strident ostentations," which he blames for the nation's slums, poverty, crime, unsafe labor conditions, prostitution, and premature infant mortality.
- A thousand Socialists hold office in over 30 states.
- The Minsky brothers shock Winter Garden theater audiences with their new bawdy burlesques.
- Increasingly popular are "tango teas," where whiskey is served and people dance until dawn; Irene and Vernon Castle give John D. Rockefeller tango lessons for $100 an hour.
- *Variety* reports these salaries: George M. Cohan, $1,500,000; David Belasco, $1,000,000; Chauncy Olcott: $750,000; William Gillette, $300,000; Maud Adams, $225,000; and Eddie Foy, $100,000.
- J. P. Morgan says that he finds art collecting "as much fun" as stock trading; he brings art treasures valued at $60 million from London to America.
- Harriet Monroe promotes the avant-garde in *Poetry* magazine; Ezra Pound contributes and sends his wishes that "*Poetry* make the Italian Renaissance look like a tempest in a teapot."
- "Humanity shows itself in all its intellectual splendor," says Maria Montessori of childhood, on her U.S. tour.
- Military strength of the five major powers (in millions) is: Germany, 1.9; France, 1.4; Great Britain, .7; Japan, .6; the United States, .2.
- Norman Angell's influential *The Great Illusion* claims that war is outmoded due to its destructiveness.
- Concerned with their possible destitution, Andrew Carnegie provides a $25,000-a-year pension for future ex-presidents and their widows, "as long as these remain unprovided for by the nation."
- The Modern Language and National Education associations support Roosevelt's proposal for simplified spelling (e.g., "nite" for night; "thru" for through).

Ezra Pound. Imagism "presents an intellectual and emotional complex in an instant of time." *Copyright* Washington Post. *Reprinted by permission of D. C. Public Library.*

- Numerous researchers, including Jacob Loeb, investigate the chemical origins of life.
- Cherry trees, a gift to the U.S. from the Japanese royal family, are planted in Washington, D.C.
- The Beef and Bathtub trusts dissolve.
- Fifty-four labor leaders are indicted in Indianapolis for plotting over 25 dynamitings between 1906 and 1911.
- 10,000 suffragettes march in New York before 100,000 spectators; woman suffrage is passed in Arizona, Kansas, Missouri, Oregon, and Ohio; it loses in Wisconsin; prohibition passes in West Virginia.
- The American Bar Association restores the membership of three blacks with the stipulation that in the future, blacks so identify themselves on application; the ruling is widely denounced.
- Foreigners in the U.S. number 13.3 million (6.7, in 1880; 2.2, 1850); most prevalent since 1880 are immigrants from Russia and Italy.
- Widespread reports cover the Japanese claim that the U.S. welcomes as a citizen "any European" and rejects "the elite of Asia."
- Many U.S. newspapers greet the Balkan wars as the triumph of Christianity over Islam, whereas most Europeans fear a general war of the Great Powers.

First Appearances: Oreo biscuits, Lorna Doone cookies, Cracker Jack prize, Prince macaroni, Ocean Spray cranberry sauce, Seabrook Farms, Libby salmon cannery (Alaska), Morton's table salt, Morey's (New Haven), Hotels McAlpin (world's largest), Vanderbilt (New York), Beverly Hills (Los Angeles), Copley-Plaza (Boston), Rotary Club, Hadassah, Girl Scouts (Juliette Low, Savannah), laundry machine for washing money (for U.S. Treasury), heating pad, player violin, Truth in Advertising Code, Children's Bureau, *New York Times'* Neediest Cases, parcel post, train service Florida-New York, SOS as universal distress signal, "airplane" for "aeroplane," successful parachute jump, cruise ship to circumnavigate the world, municipally owned streetcars (San Francisco), doubledeck electric streetcars, motorized movie camera

Fads: electrical floor cleaners and hair dryers, Eastern swamis, "animal dances" to ragtime: fox trot, horse trot, crab step, kangaroo dip, camel walk, fish walk, chicken scratch, turkey trot, grizzly bear, bunny hug; Irene and Vernon "Castle Walk"

1913

In the News

PRESIDENT-ELECT WILSON SAYS BUSINESS MONOPOLY MUST END . . . YOUNG TURKS TAKE POWER, REJECT SETTLEMENT WITH BULGARIA, BALKAN WAR RESUMES . . . TAFT VETOES IMMIGRATION LAW MANDATING LITERACY TEST . . . SUPREME COURT UPHOLDS WHITE SLAVE ACT . . . MEXICAN PRESIDENT MADERO IS ASSASSINATED, GEN. HUERTA SEIZES POWER, TAFT REFUSES RECOGNITION . . . 16TH AMENDMENT PERMITTING INCOME TAX IS ADOPTED . . . SILK WORKERS STRIKE IN PATERSON, N.J. UNDER IWW LEADERSHIP . . . WOODROW WILSON IS INAUGURATED AS 28TH PRESIDENT . . . DEPARTMENT OF COMMERCE AND LABOR IS DIVIDED UNDER PRESSURE FROM AFL . . . BOSTON AND NEW YORK GARMENT WORKERS WIN UNION RECOGNITION AND WAGE BENEFITS . . . J. P. MORGAN DIES . . . WILSON IS FIRST SINCE JOHN ADAMS TO ADDRESS CONGRESS IN PERSON, CALLS FOR TARIFF REDUCTION . . . U.S. RECOGNIZES REPUBLIC OF CHINA . . . JAPAN THREATENS WAR AFTER CALIFORNIA PASSES ALIEN LAND-HOLDING LAW . . . JOHN D. ROCKEFELLER ESTABLISHES $100 MILLION FOUNDATION . . . FIRST BALKAN WAR ENDS, TURKEY AGREES TO ALBANIAN INDEPENDENCE . . . 17TH AMENDMENT PROVIDES FOR DIRECT ELECTION OF SENATORS . . . GREECE, SERBIA, TURKEY, AND ROMANIA REPULSE BULGARIAN ATTACK, SECOND BALKAN WAR BEGINS . . . WILSON, REFUSING TO RECOGNIZE MEXICO'S HUERTA, DECLARES ECONOMIC BOYCOTT AND POLICY OF "WATCHFUL WAITING" . . . UNDERWOOD-SIMMONS TARIFF ACT PROVIDES MAJOR REDUCTIONS . . . WILSON SETS OFF EXPLOSION OF GAMBOA DIKE, COMPLETING PANAMA CANAL . . . FEDERAL RESERVE BANK ACT PASSES.

Quotes

"I'm glad to be going. This is the loneliest place in the world."

> — Taft, on leaving the White House

"If I had my way, I would fill the penitentiaries of the U.S. so full of trust magnates that their arms and legs would stick out of the windows."

> — Champ Clark, Speaker of the House

"The great Government we loved has too often been made use of for private and selfish purposes, and those who used it had forgotten the people. . . . Our duty is to restore . . . and humanize every process of our common life. . . . Here muster not the forces of party but the forces of humanity. Men's hearts wait upon us. . . . Who shall live up to the great trust? Who dares fail to try?"

> — Woodrow Wilson, at his inauguration

"Stand up there, you bastard evolutionist. Stand up with the atheists and the infidels and the adulterers and go to hell."

> — Evangelist Billy Sunday, to the unconverted in his audience

"PICTURE ACTORS ARE ASKING FOR NAMES ON THE SCREEN"

> — Headline, *Variety*

"In this recent exhibition the lunatic fringe was fully in evidence. . . . Take the picture which for some reason is called 'A Naked Man Going Downstairs.' There is in my bathroom a really good Navajo rug

"It is a disgrace to die rich," says Andrew Carnegie, who gives $25 million to charity this year; "his gospel of wealth" asserts that those who accumulate wealth should use it for the common good. *Library of Congress*.

which, on any proper interpretation of the Cubist theory, is far more satisfactory."

> — Theodore Roosevelt, on the Armory Show

"Fast and furious becomes the scramble among the Serbs, Bulgars, Greeks, and even Italians for Turkey's compromised provinces in Europe. . . . They have made a desert and a howling waste of city and valley."

> — *Baltimore American*

"Neither snow, nor rain, nor heat, nor gloom of night stays these couriers from the swift completion of their appointed rounds."

> — Inscription on the new General Post Office, New York, taken from Herodotus

Ads

Five men opposing woman suffrage; the *New York Times* writes: "Obviously our public school system is a victim of that comparatively new and distressing malady called feminism." *Library of Congress.*

National black leader Booker T. Washington advocates black economic reform through education, rather than political change. *Library of Congress.*

Movies

Openings

Judith of Bethulia (D. W. Griffith), Blanche Sweet, Henry B. Walthall, four-reeler, 40 minutes

Traffic in Souls (George Loane Tucker), William Cavanaugh, Ethel Grandin

Quo Vadis (Enrico Guazzoni), G. Serena, C. Cattaneo, 8 reels (Italian import that spurs longer U.S. films)

The Adventures of Kathlyn (Selig), Kathlyn Williams, the first "cliffhanger" serial, 15 episodes

The Prisoner of Zenda (Edwin S. Porter), James K. Hackett, Beatrice Beckley

Tess of D'Urbervilles (Edwin S. Porter and J. Searle Dawley), Mrs. Minnie Maddern Fiske

Hamlet (Hay Plum), Johnston Forbes Robertson

Barney Oldfield's Race for Life (Mack Sennett), Sennett, Mabel Normand

The Battle of Elderbush Gulch (D. W. Griffith), Lillian Gish, Robert Harron

The Mothering Heart (D. W. Griffith), Lillian Gish

The Count of Monte Cristo (Edwin S. Porter), James O'Neill

Forty-seven companies remain in the east; sixty in California. Mack Sennett's Keystone Company makes dozens of successful one-reel comedies with Mabel Normand, Roscoe "Fatty" Arbuckle, Mack Swain, and the Keystone Cops. Charles Chaplin, newly arrived with a British touring company, signs

Mabel Normand invents Keystone Studio's madcap style when she goes to a Shriner's conference and pretends to be a lost waif in search of her father; she also originates the pie-throw. *Movie Star News.*

with Sennett for $150 a week. Universal claims the youngest of child stars, Helene ("Snookums") Rosson, 7½ months old (Allan Dwan's *Our Little Fairy*). With talk of a "new public" of "quicker-minded" audiences, movies go into legitimate theaters and into the suburbs.

Popular Stars

Henry B. Walthall, Mae Marsh, Robert Harron, Kathlyn Williams, Lillian and Dorothy Gish, Norma Talmadge, Clara Kimball Young, John Bunny, Arthur V. Johnson, Tom Moore

Popular Music

Hit Songs
"Danny Boy"
"To Have, To Hold, To Love"
"The Trail of the Lonesome Pine"
"If I Had My Way"
"The Curse of an Aching Heart"
"Something Seems Tingle-Lingeling"
"Sit Down, You're Rocking the Boat!"
"Sweethearts"
"(He'd Have to Get Under) Get Out and Get Under (To Fix Up His Automobile)"
"Panama"
"My Wife's Gone to the Country (Hurrah! Hurrah!)"

Representative Recordings: Al Jolson, "The Spaniard that Blighted My Life" (million-selling); "Peg o'My Heart" (Charles W. Harrison); "You Made Me Love You (I Didn't Want to Do It)" (Al Jolson); "Sunshine and Roses" (Edna Brown, James F. Harrison); "In My Harum" (Walter Van Brunt); "The Angelus" (Christie MacDonald)

Jazz
Black composer Joe Jordan, who sets the stage for Chicago to become the center of the jazz world, writes "Ballin' the Jack" (recorded by whites) and several other titles that become popular black dances, like the "Texas Tommy" and "Cincinnati Two-Step." James P. Johnson composes the "Charleston" for black longshoremen recently moved north from South Carolina; Johnson is the originator of the "stride" piano style.

Theater

Broadway Openings

Plays
The Seven Keys to Baldpate (George M. Cohan), Wallace Eddinger
Madam President (Jose G. Levy), Fannie Ward, Ruth Sinclair
The Philanderer (George Bernard Shaw), Charles Maude
Romance (Edward Sheldon), Doris Keane, William Courtenay
Potash and Perlmutter (Montague Glass), Louise Dressler, Alexander Carr
Today (George Broadhurst), Edwin Arden, Emily Stevens
A Good Little Devil (Rosemonde Gerard, Maurice Rostand), Lillian Gish, Ernest Truex, Mary Pickford
Joseph and His Brethren (Louis N. Parker), James O'Neill
The Poor Little Rich Girl (Eleanor Gates), Viola Dana, Alan Hale
The Things that Count (Laurence Eyre), Alice Brady

Musicals
The Sunshine Girl (Paul Rubens), Vernon Castle, Julia Sanderson
The Passing Show (Jean Schwartz, Harold Atteridge), Charlotte Greenwood, John Charles Thomas
Ziegfeld Follies (Raymond Hubbell, George V. Hobart), Leon Errol, Elizabeth Brice, Ann Pennington
Sweethearts (Victor Herbert, Robert B. Smith), Christie MacDonald

Woodrow Wilson and his family. "There has been something crude and heartless in our haste to succeed and be great. Our thought has been 'Let every man look out for himself'" (Wilson). *Library of Congress.*

High Jinks (Rudolf Friml, Otto Harbach), Elaine Hammerstein
The Honeymoon Express (Jean Schwartz, Harold Atteridge), Al Jolson, Fannie Brice

Classics and Revivals On and Off Broadway
Twelfth Night, Phyllis Neilsen-Terr; *The Merchant of Venice,* John E. Kellerd; Irish Players: *Patriots* (Lennox Robinson), *The Countess Cathleen* (W. B. Yeats), *Riders to the Sea* (Synge); Johnston Forbes-Robertson, Gertrude Elliott: *Caesar and Cleopatra, Hamlet, Othello, The Merchant of Venice; Much Ado About Nothing,* John Drew, Laura Hope Crews

Classical Music _____

Compositions

Charles Ives, *Over the Pavements,*
    Chromatimelodtune
Henry Gilbert, *Negro Rhapsody*
Leo Sowerby, Violin Concerto
John Alden Carpenter, *Gitanjali*
Charles Cadman, *Sayonara*

Important Events

At his first symphonic concert in New York (at the
Metropolitan), Toscanini conducts Beethoven's Ninth
symphony, Wagner's *A Faust Overture,* and
Strauss's *Till Eugenspiel.* The Houston Symphony
debuts, with Paul Blitz conducting Mozart,
Tchaikovsky, and Bizet.

Debuts: Max Pauer, Julia Culp, Beatrice Harrison,
Ethel Leginska

First Performances

Sibelius, Symphony no. 4 (New York); Vivaldi,
Concerto in G minor, for Violin, Organ, and
Orchestra (Boston); Elgar, *Falstaff* (New York);
Ravel, *Juon* and *Vaegtervise* (Boston); Strauss, *Der
Abend* (New York)

Opera

Metropolitan: Frieda Hempel, Otto Goritz, *Der
Rosenkavalier;* Pasquale Amato, Frances Alda,
Cyrano (Walter Damrosch, premiere); Giovanni
Martinelli (debut), *Tosca; La Bohème;* Anna Case,
Louise Homer, Paul Althouse, Adamo Didur, Sophie
Braslau (debut), *Boris Godunov* (premiere)

Century Opera, New York (opens, directed by
Milton and Sargent Aborn): Elizabeth Amsden, *Aïda*

Washington, D.C. suffragettes. *Smithsonian Institution.*

Chicago: Rosa Raisa (debut), *Aïda.* The company
tours New York, Baltimore, and Chicago with Mary
Garden and John McCormack in *Natoma.*

Boston: Mary Garden, *Monna Vanna* (Février,
premiere); Carmen Melis, *La Forêt Bleue* (Aubert)

Kansas City: Garden, *Thaïs;* Luisa Tetrazzini, *Lucia
di Lammermoor*

Baltimore: Titta Ruffo, *Rigoletto;* Raisa, *La Bohème*

Music Notes

Oscar Hammerstein reenters the opera world and
begins construction of the American National Opera
building; the new company will concentrate on
French opera • Italian futurist Luigi Russolo's
manifesto "The Art of Noises" gains wide publicity; it
urges musicians "to break out of this narrow circle of
pure musical sounds and conquer the infinite variety
of noise sounds."

George M. Cohan.
Smithsonian Institution

The growing popularity of phonographs and records expands the ease of socializing. *D. Ouellette Collection.*

Art

Painting

Maurice Prendergast, *The Promenade*

George Bellows, *Cliff Dwellers*

Joseph Stella, *Battle of Light, Coney Island*

Marsden Hartley, *Forms Abstracted, Musical Theme No. 1*

Arthur B. Davies, *Intermezzo*

Max Weber, *Tapestry No. 2, Decoration with Cloud (Motherhood)*

Edward Hopper, *Corner Saloon*

Stanton Macdonald-Wright, *Still Life Synchromy*

Ernest Lawson, *Spring Night, Harlem River*

Sculpture

Paul Manship, *Centaur and David, Dryad*

Chester Beach, *The Unveiling of Dawn*

Emil Fuchs, *Eva, Study of a Nude*

Gertrude V. Whitney, *A Caryatid Figure*

Attilio Piccirilli, National Maine Monument, Columbus Circle, New York

Architecture

Grand Central terminal New York (Reed & Stem; Warren & Wetmore, 1903–13)

Midway Gardens, Chicago (Frank Lloyd Wright)

Chick house, Berkeley, Calif. (Bernard Maybeck)

La Jolla Women's Club, La Jolla, Calif. (Irving J. Gill)

Henry Clay Frick house, 1 East 70th Street, New York City (Carrère & Hastings)

Important Exhibitions

Museums

New York: *Metropolitan:* J. P. Morgan's art (3,768 pieces); Limoges enamels; S. P. Avery's collection of spoons; Early Egyptian stone vases. *National Arts Club:* "The Applied Arts of Germany"; "Pastellists"; Hungarian peasant art. *Salmagundi:* Bellows, Henri, Sloan; Thumb-box sketches

Chicago: Contemporary German graphic art (370 works); Contemporary Scandinavian art; Retrospective: Frederick C. Frieseke, Pauline Palmer, John W. Alexander

St. Louis: Paintings of the Far West; Rare textiles; Paintings of Lockwood de Forest and Philip Little; Spanish arts; "34 Paintings by Boston Women"

Art Briefs

The February 17th "International Exhibition of Modern Art" at the Armory show in New York (1,300 works, including the Duchamp *Nude Descending a Staircase, No. 2*) becomes front page news, eliciting responses from high praise to violent displays because of its "threat to morality." At least 500,000 view it before it travels to Boston and Chicago (where Matisse is burned in effigy) • The first Paul Manship exhibition is held.

New York takes the lead in skyscraper construction, with the $13.5 million concrete-and-steel Woolworth building (55 stories). *D. Ouellette Collection.*

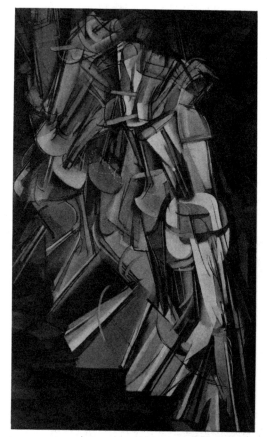

Marcel Duchamp, *Nude Descending Staircase, No. 2*, 1912. Oil on canvas. 58″ × 35″. Philadelphia Museum of Art: Louise and Walter Arensberg Collection.

Books

Fiction

Critics' Choice

Virginia, Ellen Glasgow
The Custom of the Country, Edith Wharton
O Pioneers!, Willa Cather
Rolling Stones, O. Henry (posthumous)
New Leaf Mills: A Chronicle, William Dean Howells
The Lost Road, Richard Harding Davis
The Song of Melicent, James Branch Cabell
John Barleycorn, Jack London
The Valley of the Moon, Jack London
&. *Sons and Lovers*, D. H. Lawrence

Best-Sellers

The Inside of the Cup, Winston Churchill
V. V.'s Eyes, Henry Sydnor Harrison
Laddie, Gene Stratton Porter
The Judgment House, Sir Gilbert Parker
Heart of the Hills, John Fox, Jr.
The Amateur Gentleman, Jeffrey Farnol
The Whom Thou Gavest Me, Hall Caine
Pollyanna, Eleanor H. Porter
The Valiants of Virginia, Hallie Erminie Rives
T. Tembarom, Frances Hodgson Burnett

Nonfiction

Critics' Choice

An Economic Interpretation of the Constitution, Charles Beard
A Preface to Politics, Walter Lippmann
Mont-Saint Michel and Chartres, Henry Adams
Autobiography, Robert M. La Follette
Youth and Life, Randolph Bourne
The Enjoyment of Poetry, Max Eastman
The Problem of Christianity, Josiah Royce
Winds of Doctrine, George Santayana
Interest and Effort in Education, John Dewey
Theory of Social Revolution, Brooks Adams
The Eternal Mystery, George Jean Nathan
The Drift of Romanticism, Paul Elmer More

Best-Sellers

Crowds, Gerald Stanley Lee
Germany and the Germans, Price Collier
Zone Policeman 88, Harry A. Franck
The New Freedom, Woodrow Wilson
South America, James Bryce
Your United States, Arnold Bennett
The Promised Land, Mary Antin
Auction Bridge To-Day, Milton C. Work
Three Plays, Eugène Brieux
Psychology and Industrial Efficiency, Hugo Munsterberg

Poetry

Robert Frost, *A Boy's Will*
William Carlos Williams, *The Tempers*
Vachel Lindsay, *General William Booth Enters into Heaven and Other Poems*
Paul Laurence Dunbar, *Complete Poems*
John Gould Fletcher, *The Dominant City, Fool's Gold, Visions in the Evening, The Book of Nature 1910–1912*

Brought up on a Nebraska ranch, Willa Cather captures the centrality of pioneer life in the American experience. *National Archives.*

Science and Technology

Bela Schick devises a diphtheria immunity test.
John Abel develops an artificial kidney; he also isolates amino acids from blood.
The bacterium that causes whooping cough is discovered.
Vitamins A and B are isolated.
William Coolidge revolutionizes X-ray use with the hot-cathode ray tube.
Irving Langmuir utilizes inert gas in lightbulbs and incandescent lamps.

Robert Millikan completes his "oil drop" experiment on the electron's charge.
John Watson publishes his first paper on behaviorism.
&. The ozone layer is discovered by Charles Fabry.
&. Niels Bohr formulates his quantum theory of energy.
&. Albert Schweitzer opens a hospital at Lambaréné, French Congo.

Sports

Baseball

Ty Cobb wins his 7th straight batting title.
Frank ("Home Run") Baker wins his 3rd straight AL HR title with 12.
The New York Giants, under manager John J. McGraw, win a 3rd straight pennant and lose a 3rd straight World Series.
Walter Johnson pitches a record 56 consecutive scoreless innings and posts a 1.09 ERA.

Champions

Batting
  Jacob Daubert (Brooklyn, NL), .350
  Tyrus R. Cobb (Detroit, AL), .390
Pitching
  Grover C. Alexander (Philadelphia, NL), 24–8

  Walter Johnson (Washington, AL), 36–7
Home runs
  Clifford Cravath (Philadelphia, NL), 19

Football

Little-known Notre Dame accepts $1,000 to play powerhouse Army and wins 35–13, with Gus Dorais passing to Knute Rockne and popularizing the forward pass. Coach Amos Alonzo Stagg of Chicago experiments with numbering players.

College All-Americans: Edward Mahan (F), Harvard; Stanley Pennock (G), Harvard; Paul DesJardien (C), Chicago

Other Sports

Jim Thorpe is stripped of his Olympic medals when it is discovered that he played semi-pro baseball (for $15) in 1909; he says: "I was simply an Indian boy . . . and did not know I was doing wrong."

Tennis: The U.S. beats Britain 3–2 at Wimbledon to win its first Davis Cup since 1902.

Golf: Francis Ouimet, 20, of Boston becomes a sensation when he defeats British stars Harry Vardon and Ted Ray in a 3-way USGA Open; this greatly popularizes the sport.

Winners

World Series
  Philadelphia (AL) 4
  New York (NL) 1
MVP
  NL—Jacob Daubert, Brooklyn
  Al—Walter Johnson, Washington
College Football
  Harvard
College Basketball
  Navy

Player of the Year
  Eddie Calder, St. Lawrence
Stanley Cup
  Quebec
U.S. Tennis Open
  Men: Maurice McLoughlin
  Women: Mary K. Browne
USGA Open
  Francis Ouimet
Kentucky Derby
  Donerail (Roscoe Goose, jockey)

Fashion

The Oriental influence is especially apparent: pantaloons worn under a draped overskirt (considered by Worth as "vulgar" and "wicked") and harem or Turkish trousers gathered at the ankles. The Ballet Russe influences the year's colors: clashing reds and pinks, and bright greens with purple, blue, orange, and yellow. Silk printing, formerly limited to stripes and dots, takes on wild patterns and texturing, as Raoul Dufy designs new fabrics for Poiret (the "Fauve of Fashion"). As the year ends, designers shock women by adding a slit to the side of the day skirt and the back of the evening dress. With the exposure of both the ankle and foot, the need for decorative hosiery arises. Working women find the new draped turbans (where the ever-popular bird plumage finds a new nest) very appealing after wearing a headscarf all day in the sweatshop. The first ads for maternity clothing appear.

High fashion notes: Poiret is the first couturier to substitute live models for mannequins; to create perfume for a "total, exotic" effect ("Nuit de Chine," *instead of "Rose" or "Lavender"); and to utilize fashion photography. He hires two unknown photographers: Edward Steichen and Man Ray.*

Mary Garden, whose costumes are as arresting as her voice. *Library of Congress.*

Kaleidoscope

- Americans follow the Mexican revolution with intense interest; when General Huerta murders the revolutionary Madero, Taft and Wilson refuse to recognize Huerta's "government of butchers."
- Alice Paul, 27, founds the National Woman's Party; 5,000 suffragettes march down Pennsylvania Avenue as opponents spit, curse, and attack them; 40 women are hospitalized after cavalry troops restore order.
- To placate Southern Democrats, President Wilson allows the Postmaster General to segregate black clerks.
- Anti-Semitic sentiment rises when Jewish businessman Leo Frank is convicted of murdering his employee, 13-year-old Mary Phagan.
- The B'nai B'rith founds the Anti-Defamation League to fight anti-Semitism.
- The new federal income tax will be imposed on incomes over $3,000 and affect 600,000 of the nation's 92 million; its aim is to offset revenue lost from tariff reductions.
- The "evils of narcotics" prompt vigorous newspaper editorializing.
- U.S. industrial output rises to 40 percent of the world's total production (20 percent, 1860).
- Columbia's first orchestral recordings are the "Liebestod" from *Tristan and Isolde* and Weber's *Invitation to the Dance.*
- New York's lavish new Palace Theater, which charges $2 (50¢ at most vaudeville theaters), is unsuccessful until Sarah Bernhardt opens and is joined by pantomimist-juggler W. C. Fields.
- Eugène Brieux's play *Damaged Goods* becomes the talk of New York; it deals with venereal disease.
- "Baby shows," like the "Better Baby Show," gain wide popularity; children are displayed like livestock, and problems arise over scoring methods.
- Alfred Joyce Kilmer, of the *New York Times Book Review,* publishes "Trees" in *Poetry* magazine ("I think that I shall never see / A poem as lovely as a tree").
- Camel cigarettes are first produced; the package design has been inspired by "Old Joe," a dromedary in the Barnum & Bailey circus.
- Research reveals that rabbits fed large amounts of cholesterol and fat develop hardening of the arteries.
- In response to fears that tourism and hunting will destroy forests, the National Park Service is created, and hunting limits are imposed.
- Because chocolate sales decline in the summer, Clarence Crane introduces a new candy, peppermint Life Savers, which he then sells to two salesmen who package the candy in hand-wrapped rolls.
- After teetotaler Secretary of State William Jennings Bryan serves Welch's grape juice to the British ambassador, Welch's becomes a household name.
- James E. Fraser designs the buffalo nickel, using as his models three different Indians for one side and a "Black Diamond" bison for the other.
- Teddy Roosevelt sues the *Iron Ore Weekly* for libel, for reporting that he "curses, lies, and gets drunk"; he wins but refuses damages.
- The United Mine Workers is indicted as a labor trust.
- The trial of the Jew Mendel Beilis for alleged "ritual murder" in Russia creates an uproar in the U.S.; Beilis is ultimately acquitted.
- A sheriff in Spartansburg, South Carolina, is tried for preventing a lynching; he is subsequently acquitted.
- After nineteen years of teaching, Bridget Peixico is fired by the New York Board of Education when she becomes a mother; she is reinstated as Justice Seabury rules "illness . . . caused by maternity [cannot be] construed as neglect of duty."
- Former baseball player Billy Sunday, now an evangelist, attracts a record-breaking audience at his Wyoming Valley, Pennsylvania revivals: 686,000 attend 94 services.
- Worldwide headlines report that Leonardo's *Mona Lisa,* missing since 1911, has been discovered in Florence.
- Charles Beard stirs great controversy when he contends that the Founding Fathers were motivated by economic interests rather than ideals.
- Wilson calls the Chinese revolution the "most significant event . . . of our generation."
- The public cheers the House Pujo committee's exposure of Wall Street's monopoly on credit.
- In Greenwich village, New York, many listen to the radical speeches of Emma Goldman and IWW leader "Big" Bill Haywood; the "Village's" Liberal Club includes Theodore Dreiser, Upton Sinclair, Vachel Lindsay, Sinclair Lewis, Sherwood Anderson, Louis Untermeyer, and Max Eastman.
- Socialite Mabel Dodge and her lover, John Reed, reenact in pageant form, at Madison Square Garden, the violent Paterson, New Jersey, silk workers strike; Dodge's Fifth Avenue salon gathers progressives like Carl Van Vechten, Lincoln Steffens, Walter Lippmann, and cigar-smoking poet Amy Lowell.
- Richard Hellmann moves from his small New York delicatessen to a Queens factory and produces his "Blue Ribbon" mayonnaise.
- According to *Literary Digest,* the player piano can play Beethoven but not Chopin.

First appearances: Schaeffer pen, Nedick's orange drink and hot dog stand, Jack Frost trademark, Quaker Puffed Rice and Wheat, Chesterfields, Actors' Equity, Senate whip, diesel-electric locomotives, Deusenberg, Stutz, drive-in service station (Pittsburgh), "Toonerville Trolly" comic strip, deck shuffleboard, Monthly Consumer Price Index, Keokum Dam (world's largest hydroelectric dam), dental hygienist's course (Bridgeport), occupational therapy course (Milwaukee), squad of policewomen (Chicago), conquest of Mt. McKinley, Carnegie Peace Palace (The Hague), Albania, Geiger counter, mammography (Germany), erector set (Alfred C. Gilbert)

Fads: "Fletcherism" (chewing food thoroughly), flying stunts (e.g., loops), still photography (Kodaks: $2)

1914

Economic Profile
  Dow-Jones: ↓ High 83–
    Low 53
  GNP: −3%
  Inflation: +2.5%
  Unemployment: 7.9%
Expenditures
  Recreation: $1 billion
  Bowlers: 9,000
Immigration, 1900–1914: 4.1
  million
Maxwell: $695
Overland: $950
Cadillac: $2,500–$3,250
Wrigley's spearmint-pepsin
  gum (box, 20 packages):
  85¢
Camel cigarettes (20): 10¢
Mourning pins: 5¢
Cloth opaque window
  shades: 22¢
Heavy wool blankets: $1.68
Eyelet embroidered linen
  centerpiece: 98¢
Linen, hemstitched Irish
  Huck towels: 50¢
Hot-water bottle: 59¢
Arrow shirts, red label: $1.50;
  black label: $2; blue label:
  $2.50–$10
Men's hose supporters: 4¢
Imperial "Drop Seat" Union
  suit: $1.50–$5

Deaths

Alfonse Bertillon, Ambrose
  Bierce, Adelaide Crapsey,
  Rear Admiral Alfred T.
  Mahan, Pope Pius X

In the News

HUERTA ARRESTS U.S. MARINES AT TAMPICO, U.S. DEMANDS APOLOGY, 21 GUN SALUTE . . . SECOND COXEY'S ARMY OF THE UNEMPLOYED MARCHES ON D.C. . . . STATE MILITIA ATTACKS ARMED STRIKERS AT LUDLOW, COLORADO, 25 DIE, 11 CHILDREN . . . MEXICO REFUSES DEMANDS, U.S. OCCUPIES VERA CRUZ, 4 MARINES ARE KILLED, MEXICO SEVERS RELATIONS . . . IRISH HOME RULE BILL IS PASSED, COMPROMISE EXCLUDES ULSTER . . . ARCHDUKE FRANZ FERDINAND, HEIR TO AUSTRIAN THRONE, IS ASSASSINATED BY BOSNIAN SERB ANARCHIST . . . SERBIA REJECTS AUSTRIAN DEMANDS FOR APOLOGY, GERMANY SUPPORTS AUSTRIA . . . RUSSIA STATES INTENTION TO PROTECT SERBIA, FRANCE SUPPORTS RUSSIA . . . AUSTRIA DECLARES WAR ON SERBIA . . . RUSSIA, AUSTRIA, FRANCE, GERMANY MOBILIZE . . . GERMANY DECLARES WAR ON RUSSIA . . . NEW YORK STOCK EXCHANGE CLOSES DUE TO WAR CONDITIONS . . . GERMANY DECLARES WAR ON FRANCE, INVADES BELGIUM WITHOUT FORMAL WAR DECLARATION . . . BRITAIN DECLARES WAR ON GERMANY . . . U.S. DECLARES NEUTRALITY . . . GERMANS CAPTURE BRUSSELS, ADVANCE ON PARIS, FRENCH GOVERNMENT MOVES TO BORDEAUX . . . JAPAN DECLARES WAR ON GERMANY, INVADES ITS ASIAN COLONIES . . . ALLIES COUNTERATTACK AT BATTLE OF MARNE, PARIS IS SAVED . . . RUSSIANS SUFFER HEAVY DEFEAT IN PRUSSIA . . . CLAYTON ANTITRUST ACT PASSES, FTC IS ESTABLISHED TO COMBAT MONOPOLY AND AID SMALL BUSINESS . . . COLORADO STRIKERS ACCEPT WILSON'S PROPOSALS TO SETTLE 3-YEAR STRIKE . . . GERMANS ARE HALTED AT YPRES, BOTH SIDES DIG IN FOR TRENCH WARFARE . . . "SANTA CLAUS" SHIP BRINGS 6 MILLION GIFTS TO EUROPEAN ORPHANS.

Quotes

"The lamps are going out all over Europe; we shall not see them lit again in our time."
— Foreign Secretary of Great Britain Sir E. Grey

"The United States must be neutral in fact as well as in name, during these days that are to try men's souls."
— Wilson, on the war

"If anyone had told me two years ago that the time would come when the finest looking people in town would be going to the biggest and newest theaters on Broadway for . . . motion pictures, I would have sent them down to . . . Bellevue Hospital, . . . the city's bughouse."
— Victor Watson, *New York Times*

"They have taken untold millions, / That they never toiled to earn, / But without our brain and muscle,/ Not a single wheel can turn."
— "Solidarity Forever," IWW song that becomes the labor movement anthem

"And if we want to know whether the immigrant parents are the promoters or the victims of the child labor system, we turn to the cotton mills, where forty thousand native American children between seven and sixteen years of age toil between ten and twelve hours a day."
— Mary Antin, "In Defense of the Immigrant"

"[The Federal Trade Commission is created] to make men in a small way of business as free to succeed as men in a big way and to kill monopoly in the seed."
— Wilson

"We seek to maintain the dignity and authority of the U.S. only because we wish always to keep our great influence unimpaired for the uses of liberty, . . . for the benefit of mankind."
— Wilson, on the Marine takeover of Vera Cruz

"The ideal of the Balkan warrior, be he Turk, Bulgar, Serb, Greek, or Montenegrin, is not only the defeat . . . of his enemy, but also his death, the murder of his family . . .—in short, the extinction of the race."
— Carnegie Peace Foundation Report, on the Balkan wars

Ads

The Panama Canal opens, directly connecting the Atlantic and Pacific oceans. *Library of Congress.*

The IWW (Industrial Workers of the World, or "Wobblies") continues to advocate more violent strike methods than the conservative AFL. *Smithsonian Institution.*

The movement for national prohibition gains momentum, and collecting buttons becomes a fad. *Smithsonian Institution.*

Movies

Openings

The Perils of Pauline (Louis Gasnier), Pearl White, serial

The Squaw Man (Cecil B. DeMille, Oscar Apfel), Dustin Farnum, the first full-length western

Tillie's Punctured Romance (Mack Sennett), Charles Chaplin, Marie Dressler, Mabel Normand, 6 reels

Home Sweet Home (D. W. Griffith), Henry B. Walthall, Lillian Gish

The Spoilers (Colin Campbell), William Farnum, Thomas Santschi

The Wishing Ring (Maurice Tourneur), Vivian Martin, Chester Barnett

Neptune's Daughter (Herbert Brenon), Annette Kellerman, aquatic extravanganza

Kid Auto Races at Venice ("Pathe" Lehrman), Charles Chaplin

Mabel's Strange Predicament (Mack Sennett), Chaplin's first role with derby, cane, and signature gestures

The Exploits of Elaine (Louis Gasnier, George Seitz), Pearl White, Arnold Daly

Chaplin stars in 35 Sennett pictures. Zukor's Famous Players and Lasky Feature Players form Paramount. Serials, with female stars like Florence LaBadie and Mary Fuller, become popular. President Wilson's viewing of the Italian *Cabiria* confirms the respectability of movies. Lavish and deluxe theaters grow in number. The National Committee for Better Films is formed.

Serial one-reelers of brave and vigorous heroines culminate in *The Perils of Pauline;* Pearl White performs many of her own dangerous stunts. *Movie Star News.*

Fan magazine poll of top actors

Earle Williams (Vitagraph), Clara Kimball Young (Vitagraph), Mary Pickford (Famous Players), J. Warren Kerrigan (Universal), Mary Fuller (Universal), Marguerite Clayton (Essanay), Arthur Johnson (Lubin), Alice Joyce (Kalem), Carlyle Blackwell (Alco), Francis X. Bushman (Essanay). Bushman wins "the Ladies' *World* Hero" contest over King Baggot, J. Warren Kerrigan, Maurice Costello, Carlyle Backwell, and Arthur Johnson.

Popular Music

Hit Songs

"St. Louis Blues"
"Twelfth Street Rag"
"Love's Own Sweet Song"
"The Missouri Waltz"
"They Didn't Believe Me"
"Play a Simple Melody"
"A Little Bit of Heaven—and Sure They Called It Ireland"
"By the Beautiful Sea"
"I Want to Go Back to Michigan—Down on the Farm"
"Too-Ra-Loo-Ra-Loo-Ral (That's an Irish Lullaby)"
"Fido is a Hot Dog Now"
"If You Don't Want My Peaches, You'd Better Stop Shaking My Tree"
"Shave and a Haircut, Bay Rum"
"Sister Susie's Sewing Shirts for Soldiers"

Representative Recordings: Joy Hayman Cohen, "On the Telephone" (million-selling); "Aba Daba Honeymoon" (Arthur Collins, Byron G. Harlan); "Charme d'Amour" (Olive Kline); "Mother Machree" (Charles Harrison); "California and You" (Irving Kaufman); "When You Wore a Tulip and I Wore a Big Red Rose" (American Quartette)

Jazz

Rosamund Johnson, the first black to conduct a white orchestra, and his wife, Nora, start the Music School Settlement for Colored People. Black dance-band leader Jim R. Europe leads another concert at Carnegie Hall, with a mixture of clarinets, trumpets, trombones, banjos, drums, and ten pianos; there are no oboes, basses, or second violinists.

Theater

Broadway Openings

Plays

Pygmalion (George Bernard Shaw), Mrs. Patrick Campbell, Philip Merivale
Too Many Cooks (Frank Craven), Frank Craven
On Trial (Elmer L. Reizenstein [Rice]), William Walcott
Twin Beds (Salisbury Field, Margaret Mayo), Madge Kennedy
Under Cover (Roi Cooper Megrue), Harry Crosby
Kick In (Willard Mack), John Barrymore
The Yellow Ticket (Michael Morton), John Barrymore
The Dummy (Harvey J. O'Higgins, Harriet Ford), Ernest Truex

Musicals

Watch Your Step (Irving Berlin), Elizabeth Brice, Vernon and Irene Castle
Hello Broadway (George M. Cohan), George M. Cohan, Louise Dresser
The Passing Show (Sigmund Romberg, Harold Atteridge), Marilyn Miller, Jose Collins, Willie and Eugene Howard
The Girl from Utah (Jerome Kern), Julia Sanderson, Donald Brian
Chin-Chin (Ivan Caryll, Anne Caldwell), Montgomery and Stone, Helen Falconer
The Only Girl (Victor Herbert, Henry Blossom), Adele Rowland, Ernest Torrence
The Whirl of the World (Sigmund Romberg, Harold Atteridge), Willie and Eugene Howard

"The Ice Cream Girl." *Library of Congress.*

Classics and Revivals On and Off Broadway

Margaret Anglin: *As You Like It, The Taming of the Shrew, Twelfth Night, Lady Windermere's Fan* (with Sidney Greenstreet); *Othello,* R. D. MacLean, William Faversham

Classical Music

Compositions
Louis Gruenberg, Piano Concerto no. 1
Frederick Converse, *Masque of St. Louis*
Charles Wakefield Cadman, *Thunderbird Suite*
John Alden Carpenter, *Adventures in a Perambulator*
Charles Ives, *Three Places in New England,* Sonata no. 3 for Violin and Piano
Henry Cowell, *The Tides of Manaunaun*
Daniel Mason, Symphony no. 1

Important Events
The Baltimore, Detroit, and American symphony orchestras form; the American is in Chicago.

Notable Performances: On his first visit to the U.S., Sibelius conducts his works at the 28th meeting of the Litchfield County Choral Union Festival, in Norfolk, Connecticut: *Pohjola's Daughter, Christian II, Oceanides,* and *The Swan of Tuonela;* two weeks later he receives an honorary doctorate from Yale University.

Debut: Carl Flesch

First Performances
Schoenberg, *Five Pieces for Orchestra* (Boston); Korngold, Sinfonietta (Chicago); Busoni, *Indian Fantasy* (Philadelphia); Coleridge-Taylor, *From the Prairie* (Norfolk, Conn.); Dohnanyi, Suite for Orchestra (Minneapolis); Ravel, Symphonic fragment from *Daphnis and Chloe* (New York).

Opera

Metropolitan: Lucrezia Bori, Edoardo Ferrari-Fontana, Pasquali Amato, *L'Amore dei tre rei* (premiere, Montemezzi); Elisabeth Schumann (debut), *Der Rosenkavalier;* Olive Fremstad (farewell performance), Arthur Middleton, *Lohengrin;* Geraldine Farrar, Enrico Caruso, *Julien* (Charpentier, premiere); *Madeleine* (Herbert); Caruso, Emmy Destinn, *A Masked Ball*

Century (New York): Lois Ewell, Orville Harrold, *Carmen;* Florence Macbeth (debut), *Tales of Hoffmann; Romeo and Juliet*

Chicago-Philadelphia: Rosa Raisa, *Cassandra* (Gnecchi, premiere)

St. Paul: Titta Ruffo, *Rigoletto; Macbeth;* Alice Zeppelli, Hector Dufranne, *Manon* (Massenet)

Music Notes
The International Musical Society is officially disbanded because of the war • German performers and composers scheduled for performance receive last-minute cancellation; artists who have traditionally brought new and experimental music and interpretation to the U.S. are boycotted.

Jack London, "Naturalist" novelist, former pugilist, and radical socialist. *Diana Ouellette Collection.*

Opulent theaters, like the Keith in Washington, D.C., provide elegant surroundings for the new, better-heeled moviegoer. *Copyright Washington Post. Reprinted by permission of D. C. Public Library.*

Art

Painting

Marsden Hartley, *Portrait of a German Officer*

Oscar Bluemner, *Oscar, Old Canal Port*

Stanton MacDonald-Wright, *A Synchromy, Synchromy in Orange*

Max Weber, *Maine*

Morgan Russell, *Synchromy in Orange to Form* (1913–14)

Marcel Duchamp, *Chocolate Grinder, No. 2*

Sculpture

Elie Nadelman, *Horse, Standing Form*

G. D. Pratt, *Mountain Goat*

Paul Manship, *Pauline Frances*

Alexander Proctor, *Morgan Stallion* (date approx.)

Architecture

Merchants' National Bank, Grinnell, Iowa (Louis Sullivan)

L. C. Smith building, Seattle (Gaggin & Gaggin)

St. Thomas's Episcopal Church, 5th Avenue and 53rd Street, New York (Bertram, Cram, Goodhue & Ferguson)

Municipal building, New York (McKim, Mead, White), 25-story office complex

Biltmore hotel, New York City (John McEntee Bowman)

William Gray Purcell house, Minneapolis (Purcell & Elmslie)

Chicago: Medieval and Renaissance art; Watercolors and charcoal sketches of Venice, Chartres, and Holland; One-man shows: Charles John Gollings; Leon Bakst; Paul Dougherty; Jonas Lie

Providence: Old Dutch scent bottles; Persian art; Jewelry designs; Theodore Wendel, Charles Shannon

Art Briefs

The Whitney Studio Club forms, a meeting place and gallery for artists • Marcel Duchamp begins his "readymades" • Many U.S. artists return to the U.S.: 1,741 hold shows and are added to the "Who's Who" section of the *American Art Annual* • The Minneapolis Museum and Evans wing of the Boston Museum of Fine Arts open • While Frank Lloyd Wright is in Chicago, his companion, Mamah Bothwick Cheney, her two children, and four workmen are murdered by a servant, who then sets fire to Taliesan, Wright's home (which he rebuilds in 1915) • Sales: Caravaggio's *The Cheats*, $50; Gericault's *Battle Scene*, $130; Millet's *Swedish Farm*, $50; Remington's *The Captured Deserter*, $75; Rubens' *Salome*, $1,000; B. J. Blommers' *A Cottage Interior*, $2,400; Velasquez's *Marianna of Austria*, $4,100; and Dürer's *Portrait of Sir Thomas More*, $19,700.

Important Exhibitions

Museums

New York: *Metropolitan:* Robert Henri; Roman sculpture; Vases and terracottas; Embroideries of the Near East; Chinese and Japanese paintings.

John Sloan, *Backyards, Greenwich Village*. Oil. 26″ × 21.″ *National Archives*.

Paul Manship, *Indian Hunter*. Bronze. 13.5.″ *The Metropolitan Museum of Art, bequest of George D. Pratt, 1935*.

Dance

Isadora Duncan, *Ave Maria* (Schubert), Carnegie Hall

Books

Fiction

Critics' Choice
The Titan, Theodore Dreiser
Clark's Field, Robert Herrick
Gideon's Band: A Tale of the Mississippi, George Washington Cable
Tarzan of the Apes, Edgar Rice Burroughs
Roast Beef Medium, Edna Ferber
Ade's Fables, George Ade
The Lay Anthony, Joseph Hergesheimer
Our Mr. Wrenn, Sinclair Lewis
Vandover and the Brute, Frank Norris
❧ *Dubliners*, James Joyce

Best-Sellers
The Eyes of the World, Harold Bell Wright
Pollyanna, Eleanor H. Porter
The Inside of the Cup, Winston Churchill
The Salamander, Owen Johnson
The Fortunate Youth, William J. Locke
T. Tembarom, Frances Hodgson Burnett
Penrod, Booth Tarkington
Diane of the Green Van, Leona Dalrymple
The Devil's Garden, W. B. Maxwell
The Prince of Graustark, George Barr McCutcheon

Nonfiction

Critics' Choice
Progressive Democracy, Herbert Croly
Drift and Mastery, Walter Lippmann
Insurgent Mexico, John Reed
With the Allies, Richard Harding Davis
Europe after 8:15, H. L. Mencken, with George Jean Nathan and W. H. Wright
Through the Brazilian Wilderness, Theodore Roosevelt
Behavior: An Introduction to Comparative Psychology, John B. Watson
Other People's Money, Louis Brandeis
Notes of a Son and Brother, Henry James
Notes on Novelists, Henry James
California, the Land of the Sun, Mary Austin
The Instinct of Workmanship, Thorstein Veblen
Confederate Portraits, Gamaliel Bradford

Poetry
Robert Frost, *North of Boston*
Vachel Lindsay, *The Congo and Other Poems*
Emily Dickinson, *The Single Hound: Poems of a Lifetime* (posthumous)
Gertrude Stein, *Tender Buttons: Objects, Food, Rooms*
Paul Laurence Dunbar, *Speakin' o' Christmas and Other Christmas and Special Poems*
Amy Lowell, *Sword Blades and Poppy Seed*
Conrad Aiken, *Earth Triumphant and Other Tales in Verse*
Edgar Lee Masters, *Reedy's Mirror*

Science and Technology

Thyroxin, the thyroid hormone, is isolated by Edward Kendall at the Mayo Clinic.

The first successful heart surgery (on animals) is performed by Alex Carrel.

The antiseptic chlorine compound, Dakin's solution, is developed. Sodium citrate is used to prevent blood clotting.

Stellar dust is discovered by Vesto Slipher.

Heising's vacuum-tube experiments show the importance of high-frequency radio wave modulation for the transmission of speech and music.

Irving Langmuir perfects the triode (radio) valve.

The "loaded" telephone line between New York and Denver facilitates clarity in sound.

John Watson suggests the use of animals for psychology research.

❧ Acetylcholine is proposed as a nerve transmitter.

❧ Arthur Eddington proposes that spiral nebulae are galaxies.

Nobel Prize
Theodore W. Richards wins in chemistry for his work in the determination of atomic weights.

D. Ouellette Collection.

Sports

Baseball

The United States League, a minor league, changes its name to the Federal League, seeks major status, and begins raiding the majors for players.

The "Miracle" Braves go from last place at mid-season to win the pennant and sweep the World Series.

Ty Cobb wins his 8th straight batting title.

Champions

Batting
  Jacob Daubert (Brooklyn, NL), .329
  Tyrus R. Cobb (Detroit, AL), .368
Pitching
  Bill James (Boston, NL), 26–7

Chief Bender (Philadelphia, AL), 17–3
Home runs
  Clifford Cravath (Philadelphia, NL), 19

Football

The Yale "Bowl," built on a coliseum model, seats 60,000, greatly exceeding any football stadium in size; it can be enlarged to seat 100,000. College coaches vigorously oppose professional football, claiming it will destroy the honor and honesty of the game. Five first-team All-Americans are from Harvard.

College All-Americans: Edward Mahan (F), Harvard; Harold Ballin (T), Princeton; John McEwan (C), Army; Stanley Pennock (G), Harvard

Other Sports

Tennis: Mary K. Browne wins her 3rd straight U.S. Open. The U.S. loses the Davis Cup to Australia, 3–2, at the Westside Tennis Club, Forest Hills, New York.

Boxing: Kid Williams KO's Johny Coulon in 3 for the bantamweight title.

Winners

World Series
  Boston (NL) 4
  Philadelphia (AL) 0
MVP
  NL—John J. Evers (Chicago)
  AL—Edward Collins (Philadelphia)
College Football
  Army
College Basketball
  Wisconsin
Player of the Year
  Gil Halstead, Cornell

Stanley Cup
  Toronto
U.S. Tennis Open
  Men: Norris Williams II
  Women: Mary K. Browne
USGA Open
  Walter Hagen
Kentucky Derby
  Old Rosebud (John McCabe, jockey)

Fashion

The tango dress, named for the popular new dance, has a slender line and flounced skirt and is worn with tango shoes which have ribbon straps that crisscross at the ankles; it is also worn with the new bandeau hat with osprey plumes or other jewelry or fabric decorations. Poiret designs a tango dress with split sides and a hem sewn together between the legs for the "baggy look." The new pants style ("pantaloons") suits not only the new tango dancer but every woman's need for walking ease. The lampshade tunic silhouette also revolutionizes style, with oriental pantaloons worn under a short, hooped skirt. Fabrics, influenced by Cubist designs, begin to appear in bright colors and geometric shapes. Controversy increases over the full versus slim silhouette, over wide skirts of voluminous fabric or narrower skirts, slit at the back (to enable normal walking but to also reveal more of the figure). For the former, jackets extend below the knees; for the latter, short jackets reach the top of the hip.

High-fashion note: Bergdorf Goodman's tennis outfit: a green ratine jacket, white blouse with striped batiste collar and cuffs, ankle-length white linen skirt, rubber-heeled buckskin shoes, and straw hat.

Atlanta car parade. This year, Montana and Nevada vote in suffrage. *Smithsonian Institution.*

Kaleidoscope

- "Senseless," "insane," and "utterly without cause" are typical American responses to the European war.
- A poll of 367 newspaper editors indicates that 105 favor the Allies and 20, the Germans; 242 are neutral.
- Congress votes $250,000 for relief, protection, and transportation home of 150,000 American citizens abroad.
- Whether America should lend money to the warring nations becomes a major topic of public debate.
- The nation is outraged by tales of German brutality in Belgium and the destruction of ancient cities like Louvain.
- "Contraception" is much discussed when Margaret Sanger's *Family Limitation* is published.
- In *Drift and Mastery,* Walter Lippmann advocates the use of social scientific techniques to study and remedy social problems.
- Ford gives his employees half his profits "to make twenty thousand contented and happy, rather than a . . . few millionaires"; he also raises minimum wages to $5 for an eight-hour day.
- Producing 240,700 cars, nearly as many as all other companies combined, Ford says: "Everytime I lower the price a dollar, we gain a hundred new buyers."
- The Rockefeller Foundation sends 1,200 barrels of food on a relief ship to the starving Belgians.
- Pancho Villa, previously regarded as a rebel-hero, loses favor when he executes a kidnapped American landowner.
- With virtually unrestricted drug traffic in the U.S., 4.5 percent of the population is estimated to be "addicts," the highest rate in the world; the Harrison Drug Act is passed, restricting narcotic sales.
- Chicago sets up a censorship board to shorten or cut movie scenes of beatings and dead bodies.
- Among the lavish new movie theaters with gilded columns, uniformed ushers, plush seats, and large orchestras is Roxy Rothafel's Strand in New York City.
- Songs repeatedly associated with specific silent movie scenes include "Mysterioso Pizzicato" (for the evil landlord threatening eviction of the poor widow); "Hearts and Flowers" (when the absent or sleeping husband or sheriff must be located); and the "William Tell Overture" (the chase).
- Mary Pickford becomes a household name after *Tess of the Storm Country;* her salary goes from $20,000 to $104,000, as the "star system" takes hold.
- The dance craze peaks as *Ladies Home Journal* features "The Castle Gavotte," with the Castles illustrating their various steps.
- Pope Pius X condemns the tango as a "new paganism."
- President Wilson urges the public to display the flag on the newly created "Mother's Day," as a sign "of our love and reverence for the mothers of our country."
- Mrs. Wilson is told on her deathbed that the Senate has passed her beloved bill for the destruction of Washington slums.

- The president agrees to segregation among federal employees but promises to retain the current level of blacks in government posts.
- Charles Dawes opens a Chicago hotel for men "searching for employment," rather than "idlers."
- Grossinger's Hotel, in Ferndale, N.Y., opens as a boarding house for sweatshop workers.
- Virginia becomes the 10th state to adopt prohibition; 1,478 prisoners in a Pennsylvania penitentiary appeal for prohibition, pleading that drinking caused their problems.
- *Modern Sanitation* questions whether the new fad of frequent bathing may be injurious to the body.
- A controversy arises over whether American girls studying abroad will inevitably be "stripped of their health, their jewels, their innocence, even their belief in God."
- Tuition, room, and board at Harvard cost $700; at Columbia and Wesleyan, $500; room and board constitutes two-thirds of college fees.
- J. P. Morgan, Jr.'s resignation from the directorates of thirty corporations is dubbed the final "surrender of the Money Trust."
- The Triangle fire litigation is settled; families of twenty-three victims receive $75.
- Major urban populations, in millions, include: New York, 5.3; Chicago, 2.4; Philadelphia, 1.7; Dallas, .1; San Francisco, .5; Los Angeles, .5.
- A gold strike in Alaska draws huge numbers; in the first 24 hours, $1.7 million in gold arrives in Seattle.
- Teddy Roosevelt returns from South America with 1,500 bird and 500 mammal specimens; he claims to have discovered a new river, the "River of Doubt."
- The outbreak of war increases U.S. production of pasta, which until now, has been mostly imported.

First appearances: *The New Republic,* passport photo requirement, Van Camp Sea Food, Kelvinator, Doublemint gum patent, Stutz Bearcat (racing car), railroad operated by the federal government (Alaska Railroad), ASCAP, auction bridge championship (Lake Placid, N.Y.), figure skating international tournament, nonskid tire, automobile road map (Gulf Co.), red-green electric traffic signal (Cleveland), woman chief of police (Milford, Ohio), liquid-fuel rocket patent (Robert Goddard), anti-aircraft gun (Britain), Big Bertha (artillery, Germany), "political fast" (Gandhi), *The Fatherland* (pro-German newspaper), rotogravure section (brown-tinted photojournalism, *New York Times*)

New words and usages: "birth control" (Margaret Sanger, *The Woman Rebel*), "Buy a bale of cotton" (to help Southern planters)

1915

Economic Profile
 Dow-Jones: ↑ High 95–
  Low 54
 GNP: +2.6%
 Inflation: −0.6%
 Unemployment: 8.5%
Physicians: 142,432
Dentists: 42,606
Hospital beds: 532,481
Monogram Private Stock
 whiskey, 8 qts.: $5
Monogram Plain City
 whiskey, gallon: $3.50
Coffee percolator: $2–$5
For Men:
 Bernard Hewitt (Chicago),
  custom tailored suit: $15
 T. T. Lewis (Denver, New
  York, Paris): suits
  (brown, green, wistaria,
  blue, black), all fabrics,
  jackets lined in silk:
  $13.95
 Boys' norfolk suits, with
  extra knickers: $5
Little girls' coats in
 balmacaan: $15
Doll outfits, stamped to
 embroider (with complete
 set of underwear): 10¢
Piano rental, any type: $2.50–
 $3.50 monthly
Sunshine ("Revelation Box")
 biscuits (14 kinds): 10¢

In the News

WILSON VETOES BILL REQUIRING LITERACY TESTS FOR IMMIGRANTS . . . U.S. AND PANCHO VILLA SIGN TREATY ENDING BORDER WAR . . . GERMANS BOMB ENGLAND FROM ZEPPELINS . . . GERMANY ANNOUNCES U-BOAT BLOCKADE OF BRITAIN, BRITAIN ORDERS ALL GOODS FOR GERMANY SEIZED . . . WILSON WARNS GERMANY THAT ATTACKS ON U.S. SHIPS BREACH NEUTRALITY, PROTESTS BRITISH USE OF U.S. FLAGS TO DECEIVE GERMANS . . . BRITISH SUSTAIN MASSIVE CASUALTIES FROM CHLORINE GAS AT YPRES . . . U-BOAT SINKS BRITISH PASSENGER SHIP LUSITANIA, 1,198 DIE, 114 AMERICANS . . . U.S. SENDS PROTEST NOTE, GERMANS CLAIM SHIP CARRIED ARMS . . . SECOND NOTE WARNS GERMANY AGAINST ATTACK ON UNARMED SHIPS . . . U.S. STEEL FOUND NOT GUILTY OF ANTITRUST VIOLATION . . . EXCURSION STEAMER *EASTLAND* CAPSIZES AT CHICAGO PIER, 852 DIE . . . NEW YORK COURT UPHOLDS N.Y. WORKINGMEN'S COMPENSATION LAW . . . GERMANS AGREE NOT TO ATTACK PROPERLY MARKED SHIPS, WILSON WARNS VIOLATIONS WILL BE TAKEN AS "DELIBERATELY UNFRIENDLY" . . . *NEW YORK WORLD* EXPOSES GERMAN SPY AND PROPAGANDA RING . . . J. P. MORGAN, JR. ARRANGES $500 MILLION CREDIT TO ENGLAND AND FRANCE . . . U.S. MARINES OCCUPY HAITI AFTER PRESIDENT'S ASSASSINATION, HAITI BECOMES 10-YEAR PROTECTORATE . . . "GREAT OFFENSIVE" TO DISLODGE GERMANS FROM FRANCE FAILS AT CHAMPAGNE AND ARTOIS . . . REPORTS INDICATE TURKS HAVE KILLED ONE MILLION ARMENIANS . . . WILSON ASKS FOR ENLARGED STANDING ARMY OF 142,000 . . . ONE MILLIONTH FORD ROLLS OFF ASSEMBLY LINE.

Quotes

"American citizens have come to the assistance of my country, which the German invasion has plunged into untold misery. . . . Once again the great American people . . . have undertaken a work of humanity and brotherly love and have reasserted before the whole world their ideals of justice and of liberty."
— Albert, King of the Belgians, on American aid

"There is such a thing as being too proud to fight."
— Wilson, defending neutrality and "preparedness"

"Records of old wars mean more or less nothing to me. History is more or less bunk."
— Henry Ford

"What this country really needs is a good five-cent cigar."
— Vice President Thomas R. Marshall, during a Senate debate

"[Family limitation is] contrary not only to the law of the state, but to the law of God."
— Obscenity ruling in the conviction of Margaret Sanger

"[It is a] high-class, mystic, social, patriotic, benevolent association."
— William Joseph Simmons, on seeking the KKK charter in Georgia

"Don't waste time mourning. Organize!" says songwriter and IWW leader Joe Hill, on the eve of his controversial execution. *Diana Ouellette Collection.*

"A large part of our industrial population are . . . living in a condition of actual poverty . . . with one-third to one-half the wage earners living below a decent level. In large cities, up to 20% of children are undernourished and poor children die at three times the rate of the middle class; only one-third of children finish elementary school, and less than 10% graduate public high school."
— U.S. Commission on Industrial Relations

"Mr. Watson, come here, I want you."
— Alexander Graham Bell to Thomas Watson, during the first transcontinental telephone call

Ads

Bad roads have no terrors for the motorist with a PULL-U-OUT in his tool box. . . . If the auto turns over and someone is hurt, he doesn't have to spend precious time going for help. . . . In ten minutes one man and a PULL-U-OUT can pull a big machine out of mud or a ditch, or right an over-turned car.
(*PULL-U-OUT,* St. Louis, Mo.)

The world's Greatest Ball Player smokes the World's Best Tobacco. Ty Cobb says, "Tuxedo makes a wonderfully pleasant pipe-smoke."
(*Tuxedo* tobacco)

China's Perfect Girl: Miss Yarlock Lowe, a Chinese student at the University of California, enjoys the distinction of being the only physically perfect girl among 500 female students. She underwent a careful examination and was declared to be perfect not only in health, but to be the most symmetrical of the entire class. The examining physicians were amazed at this, since, they say, a Chinese woman who even approached physical perfection has never before been recorded.
(*Read* Leslie's Illustrated Weekly Newspaper)

"Yes, drive over right away. I'll be ready. My housework? Oh that's all done? How do I do it? I just let electricity do my work nowadays. I have an electric dish washer, . . . electric clothes washer, . . . electric iron, . . . electric vacuum, . . . toaster stove, . . . coffee percolator . . ."
(*Western Electric Co.*)

William S. Hart directs and often writes the complex "good-bad" character he portrays in westerns. *Library of Congress*.

"The vamp[ire]," Theda Bara (Theodosia Goodman) seduces rich men and "sucks them dry"; many believe her film image is her real-life personality. *Movie Star News*.

Movies

Openings

The Birth of a Nation (D. W. Griffith), Lillian Gish, Mae Marsh, Henry B. Walthall, Miriam Cooper, Robert Harron, 12 reels

The Champion (Charles Chaplin), Edna Purviance

The Tramp (Charles Chaplin), Chaplin

A Fool There Was (Frank Powell), Theda Bara, Eduard Jose

The Coward (Thomas Ince), Charles Ray

Phunphhilms (Hal Roach), Harold Lloyd (as Lonesome Luke)

Carmen (Cecil B. DeMille), Geraldine Farrar, Wallace Reid

Cinderella (James Kirkwood), Mary Pickford, Owen Moore

The Eternal City (Edwin S. Porter, Hugh Ford), Pauline Frederick

Enoch Arden (William Christy Cabanne), Lillian Gish, Alfred Paget

The Lamb (D. W. Griffith, William Christy Cabanne), Douglas Fairbanks

Regeneration (Raoul Walsh), Rockcliffe Fellowes, Anna Q. Nilsson

The Battle Cry of Peace, a preparedness film

Southern California, producing 125 reels a week, becomes the "Mecca of the Motion Picture"; studios run from Santa Monica to San Francisco but center around Los Angeles. *The Birth of a Nation* establishes the financial potential of long films, which can now command higher admission prices ($2). Carl Laemmle opens Universal City; Ince, Griffith, and Sennett form Triangle ("Clean Pictures for Clean People"). Chaplin writes, directs, and acts in his own films at Essanay.

Top Film Stars from Theater and Opera

Geraldine Farrar, John Barrymore, Hope Dawn, Marguerite Clark, Pauline Frederick, Florence Reed, Marie Doro, Gaby Deslys, Henry Ainley

Top Box-Office Stars

Charles Chaplin, Mary Pickford, Wallace Reid, Theda Bara, Pearl White, Charles Ray, J. Warren Kerrigan, Marguerite Clark

Popular Music _____

Hit Songs
"I Didn't Raise My Boy to be a
    Soldier"
"The Sunshine of Your Smile"
"Pack Up Your Troubles in Your
    Old Kit Bag"
"Don't Bite the Hand That's
    Feeding You"
"How'd You Like to Spoon with
    Me?"
"Hello, Broadway!"
"She's the Daughter of Mother
    Machree"
"You Know and I Know"
"Fascination"
"Jelly Roll Blues"
"There's a Broken Heart for Every
    Light on Broadway"

Representative Recordings: Alma
Cluck, "Carry Me Back to Old
Virginny/Old Black Joe" (million-
selling); "M-O-T-H-E-R" (Henry
Burr); "Auf Wiedersehn" (Alice
Green, Edward Hamilton);
"Araby" (Harry MacDonough);
"My Tango Girl" (Victor Military
Band); "Keep the Home-Fires
Burning" (Frederick Wheeler)

Jazz
Entrepreneurs on Tin Pan Alley—
the white, popular music industry
on 28th Street, New York—add
the word "jazz" or "blues" to
dozens of songs and publish sheet
music with blacks on the cover;
the songs are recorded, almost
entirely, by whites. Black shows
and leading black actors have yet
to break into Broadway's "Great
White Way." Some of the leading
black entertainers performing in
their own theaters include
Hamtree Harrington, Dusty
Fletcher, Sammy Lewis, Billy
King, Tom Fletcher, the
Whiteman Sisters, Ethel Waters
("Sweet Mama Stringbean"), and
Bessie Smith. Gertrude Pridgett
marries William "Pa" Rainey; they
become a successful minstral
dance team and create "Rainey &
Rainey: Assassination of the
Blues." Composer Sheldon Brooks
leads a large black orchestra in
Chicago's Grand Theatre; Chicago
becomes associated with the best
black bands; New York, with the
best black piano and drum
performers. Noble Sissle and
Eubie Blake publish their first song
together: "It's All Your Fault."
Clarence Williams starts "NO"
music publishing company and
advertises himself as the originator
of jazz and boogie-woogie.

Theater _____

Broadway Openings

Plays
The Doctor's Dilemma (George Bernard Shaw),
    Walter Geer, Ian Maclaren
Androcles and the Lion (George Bernard Shaw),
    O. P. Heggie, Walter Creighton
Major Barbara (George Bernard Shaw), Grace
    George, Louis Calvert, Conway Tearle
Our Mrs. McChesney (George Hobart, Edna Ferber),
    Ethel Barrymore
Hit-the-Trail-Holiday (George M. Cohan), Fred Niblo
Fair and Warmer (Avery Hopwood), Ralph Morgan,
    Madge Kennedy
The Unchastened Woman (Louis K. Anspacher),
    Emily Stevens, H. Reeves-Smith
Marie-Odile (Edward Knoblauch), Ada Neville
The White Feather (Lechmere Worrall, J. E. Harold
    Terry), Arthur Elliot

Musicals
Nobody Home (Jerome Kern, Schuyler Green),
    Adele Rowland, George Lydecker
The Passing Show (Leo Edwards, W. F. Peters, J.
    Leubrie Hill, Harold Atteridge), Marilyn Miller,
    Willie and Eugene Howard
Ziegfeld Follies (Louis A. Hirsch, David Stamper,
    Channing Pollock), W. C. Fields, Ed Wynn, Bert
    Williams, Leon Errol, Ina Claire
Katinka (Rudolf Friml, Otto Harbach), Adele
    Rowland, Edith Decker
The Princess Pat (Victor Herbert, Henry Blossom),
    Al Shean
Very Good, Eddie (Jerome Kern, Schuyler Green),
    Ernest Truex, Alice Dovey
Stop! Look! Listen! (Irving Berlin), Gaby Deslys,
    Marion Davies

Classics and Revivals On and Off Broadway
Peter Pan, Maud Adams, Ruth Gordon; *John Gabriel
Borkman, Ghosts* (Ibsen); *You Never Can Tell, Arms
and the Man, Candida* (Shaw); Robert B. Mantell
Repertoire: *King John, Macbeth, Hamlet, Great
Catherine, The Inca of Jerusalem.* Founded: The
Washington Square Players, New York; Drama
League of America, Chicago.

Classical Music

Compositions
Charles Ives, Violin Sonata no 4, Orchestral Set no.
    2, *Concord Sonata* (piano), *Tone Roads,* no. 3
Frederick Converse, *The Peace Pipe*
George Whitefield Chadwick, *Tam O'Shanter* (1914–
    15)
Louis Gruenberg, *Puppet Suite*

Important Events
Visits by international musicians are severely
curtailed, due to the war, although Pablo Casals
returns to New York for the first time since 1904 and
performs a series of recitals with Harold Bauer. The
Russian Symphony introduces Scriabin's *Prometheus*
with a color organ. At the Panama-Pacific
International Exposition, Saint-Saëns conducts the
premiere of his *Hail California!* Karl Muck also
conducts the Boston Symphony in a series of thirteen
concerts, including works from all countries.

New Appointments: Frederick Stock (Chicago
Symphony), Alfred Hertz (San Francisco)

Debuts: Percy Grainger, Guiomar Novaes

First Performances
Schoenberg, *Kammer Symphonie* (Philadelphia);
John Alden Carpenter, *Adventures in a Perambulator*
(Chicago); Reger, first of the *Four Tone Poems*
(Boston); Stock, Violin Concerto (Norfolk, Conn.);
Delius, *A Dance Rhapsody* (Minneapolis); Scriabin,
Symphony no. 3 (Philadelphia)

Opera

Metropolitan: Geraldine Farrar, Giovanni
Martinelli, *Madame Sans Gêne* (Umberto Giordano);
Pasquale Amato, Giuseppe De Luca (debut), *The
Barber of Seville;* Margarete Matzenauer, *Fidelio;*
Frances Alda, Pasquale Amato, Andrès de Segurola,
Adamo Didur, *Prince Igor* (Borodin, premiere);
Emmy Destinn, Arthur Middleton, Paul Althouse,
Carl Braum, Albert Reiss, Mme. Melanie Kurt,
Margarete Ober, *The Ring*

Boston: *Der Rosenkavalier*

Chicago: Carmen Melis, *Dejanire* (Saint-Saëns,
premiere)

Los Angeles: *Fairyland* (Horatio Parker, awarded
$10,000 prize by the National Federation of Music
Clubs)

Music Notes
Arturo Toscanini resigns from the Met and returns to
Italy; Austrian conductor Artur Bodanzky debuts
there with *Götterdämmerung* • Lewisohn Stadium of
the College of the City of New York is dedicated, a
gift of Adolph Lewisohn • With a rise in community
concert participation, Frederick Stock conducts
Schubert songs with the audience as chorus •
Carnegie Hall becomes a center for political causes.
Nobel laureate Rabindranath Tagore speaks to a full
house against the dangers of nationalism. Paderewski
hosts a series of concerts for Polish Children's Relief;
after his first hour-long speech, "The Martyrdom of
Poland," his wife auctions her antique doll collection
for $16,000.

The expensive Pierce Arrow car is popular with
well-to-do Ivy League students. *Diana Ouellette
Collection.*

"Ma" Rainey and the new "syncopation," or "jass." *Diana Ouellette Collection.*

Art

Painting
Max Weber, *Chinese Restaurant, Rush Hour New York*

Stanton MacDonald-Wright, *'Conception' Synchromy*

Marsden Hartley, *Painting, Number 5, E*

Morgan Russell, *Synchromy, No. 7*

Arthur B. Davies, "Intermezzo"

Marcel Duchamp begins "The Bride Stripped Bare by her Bachelors, Even" (1915–23)

Sculpture
James Earle Fraser, *The End of the Trail*

A. A. Weinman, *Descending Night, Rising Day*

Arthur Lee, *Volupté*

Elie Nadelman, *Man in the Open Air, Standing Bull*

Gaston Lachaise, *Dancing Woman*

Mahonri M. Young, *Man with a Wheelbarrow*

Daniel Chester French, *The Melvin Memorial (Mourning Victory)*

Malvina Hoffman, *Pavlova Dancing the Gavotte, Boy and Panther Cub*

Paul Manship, *Wrestlers*

Architecture
Palace of Fine Arts, Panama-Pacific Exposition, San Francisco (Bernard Maybeck)

Cathedral of St. Paul, Minn. (Emmanuel L. Masqueray)

Ghirardelli Square, San Francisco (Wurster, Bernardi & Emmons)

Public Library, Indianapolis (Paul Phillippe Cret)

Despite its unprecedented popularity, *The Birth of a Nation* stirs vigorous protest against its positive portrayal of the KKK. *Movie Star News.*

Important Exhibitions

Museums

New York: *Metropolitan:* The tomb of Perneb, 2650 B.C., is installed, transported to N.Y.C. stone by stone; the museum acquires Raphael's *Ansidei Madonna* from J. P. Morgan and 18 Sargent watercolors; Loan collection of textiles; Early Chinese pottery and sculpture. *Brooklyn:* Swedish art from the Panama-Pacific exhibit

Buffalo: Japanese and Chinese brocades; Far West paintings; Charles Caryl Coleman; Stephen Parrish

Boston: Sargent; Japanese Noh drama costumes; Chinese painting; work by children from settlement houses

Chicago: Sargent, Copley; Western and contemporary American painters; 28th Annual awards: J. Alden Weir, Joseph T. Pearson, Bellows, Joseph Pennell, Helen Hyde

Minneapolis: Egyptian collection; "Swedish and Franco Belgian Art from the Panama-Pacific Exposition"

Cincinnati: 250 Sculptures by Frank Duveneck

Art Briefs
Many artists contribute funds from exhibitions and sales to war relief funds • Highest sales: Luini's *Madonna Enthroned,* $33,500; Andrea del Sarto's *The Holy Family,* $27,000; Botticelli's *Madonna and Child,* $20,000; highest American sale: Blakelock's *Moonlight,* $20,000.

Dance

Metropolitan: Isadora Duncan, *Dionysian*

San Francisco: *The Garden of Kama* (Ruth Saint Denis, Ted Shawn)

Books

Fiction

Critics' Choice

The "Genius", Theodore Dreiser
The Book of Repulsive Women, Djuna Barnes
The Song of the Lark, Willa Cather
The Star Rover, Jack London
Emma McChesney & Co., Edna Ferber
Old Judge Priest, Irvin S. Cobb
Ruggles of Red Gap, Harry Leon Wilson
🙠 *The Rainbow*, D. H. Lawrence
🙠 *The Good Soldier*, Ford Madox Ford
🙠 *Of Human Bondage*, W. Somerset Maugham

Best-Sellers

The Turmoil, Booth Tarkington
A Far Country, Winston Churchill
Michael O'Halloran, Gene Stratton Porter
Pollyanna Grows Up, Eleanor H. Porter
K, Mary Roberts Rinehart
Jaffery, William J. Locke
Felix O'Day, F. Hopkinson Smith
The Harbor, Ernest Poole
The Lone Star Ranger, Zane Grey
Angela's Business, Henry Sydnor Harrison

Nonfiction

Critics' Choice

America's Coming-of-Age, Van Wyck Brooks
The Negro, W. E. B. Du Bois
Fighting France, Edith Wharton
Aristocracy and Justice, Paul Elmer More
My Year of the Great War, Frederick Palmer
Ivory, Apes, and Peacocks, James Huneker
A Hilltop on the Marne, Mildred Aldrich
The Modern Drama, Ludwig Lewisohn
The Pentecost of Calamity, Owen Wister
Travels in Alaska, John Muir
Reminiscences, Lyman Abbott
The Art of the Moving Picture, Vachel Lindsay
Greek Genius and Other Essays, John Jay Chapman

Poetry

Edgar Lee Masters, *Spoon River Anthology*
Amy Lowell, ed., *Some Imagist Poets*
Sarah Teasdale, *Rivers to the Sea*
James Gould Fletcher, *Irradiations: Sand and Spray*
Edwin Markham, *The Shoes of Happiness and Other Poems*
Don Marquis, *Dreams and Dust*
Adelaide Crapsey (posthumous), *Verse*
🙠 Rupert Brooke, *1914 and Other Poems*

Science and Technology

Scopolamine, a preoperative medication prior to anaesthesia, is pioneered by George Crile at the Cleveland Clinic.

An AB-2 flying boat is catapulted into the air from the *USS North Carolina*.

AT&T demonstrates the single sideband radio, which facilitates multichannel transmission.

Manson Benedict discovers that a germanium crystal can convert AC to DC, facilitating circuit integration.

AT&T effects the first transatlantic radio-telegraph communication.

Heat and chemical resistant "pyrex" glass is devised by Corning Glass Works.

🙠 Albert Einstein formulates the general theory of relativity.

T. S. Eliot publishes "The Love Song of J. Alfred Prufrock" in *Poetry* magazine. D. Ouellette Collection.

Sports

Baseball

Ty Cobb steals a record 96 bases, while winning his 9th straight batting title.

Clifford Cravath sets a major league record with 24 HRs.

The Federal League disbands at the end of the season.

The Chalmer MVP award is discontinued.

Champions

Batting	Pitching
Lawrence Doyle (New York, NL), .320	Grover C. Alexander (Philadelphia, NL), 31–10
Tyrus R. Cobb (Detroit, AL), .369	E. G. Shore (Boston, AL), 19–7
	Home runs
	Clifford Cravath (Philadelphia, AL), 24

Football

Pittsburgh begins numbering players. The second Tournament of Roses game is scheduled (the first, 1902).

College All-Americans: Charles Barrett (Q), Cornell; Bert Baston (E), Minnesota; Robert Peck (C), Pittsburgh

Rose Bowl (Jan. 1, 1916): Washington State 14-Brown 0

Other Sports

Boxing: Jess Willard, "the Great White Hope," beats Jack Johnson in 23 rounds in Havana, Cuba, for the heavyweight title. Johnson, a Mann Act fugitive, is guaranteed $30,000 for the fight. Johny Ertle defeats Kid Williams on a disputed foul in the 5th round, leaving the title in doubt.

Running: Norman Taber breaks the world record by 2 sec. with a 4:12.6 mile.

Tennis: The U.S. Open is moved to Forest Hills. The Davis Cup is suspended because of the war.

Golf: Due to Ouimet's 1914 triumph, many teachers from abroad come to the U.S., and many amateurs turn professional, leading to the need for professional organization.

Winners

World Series	Stanley Cup
Boston (AL) 4	Vancouver
Philadelphia (NL) 1	*U.S. Tennis Open*
College Football	Men: William Johnston
Cornell	Women: Molla Bjurstedt
College Basketball	*USGA Open*
Illinois	Jerome Travers
Player of the Year	*Kentucky Derby*
Ernest Houghton, Union	Regret (Joe Notter, jockey)

Fashion

With war in Europe, fashion design and export come to a standstill. Jean Patou and Edward Molyneux, among many other couturiers, enlist. The sinking of the *Lusitania* and increased difficulties in transatlantic travel also limit imports. A "Made in America" fad begins (although the very wealthy continue to import from Paris). A small group of designers gathers at the San Francisco Exhibition to show conservative designs: dresses and skirts with natural waistlines, broader and shorter skirts, hems falling a few inches above the ankles. At fundraising balls for the Allies, stylish gowns are both décolleté and lengthened; they have added trains and the skirts, on some, are stiffened with hoops. Most women on both sides of the Atlantic buy less and wear older costumes—not only because of the paucity of new designs but for patriotic reasons.

High fashion note: Worth's pale mauve and white, high-waisted dress with train and a crossover bodice and low, square neckline.

Anna Pavlova, whose graceful and original classical dance performances attract audiences nationwide. *D. Ouellette Collection.*

Kaleidoscope

- "Look abroad upon the troubled world. Only America at peace!" proclaims President Wilson, amid controversy over America's entry into the war and the country's state of readiness.
- Roosevelt condemns Wilson's "supine inaction" and "milk and water" diplomacy, accusing him of standing for "every soft creature, every coward and weakling, every man who can't look more than six inches ahead."
- Testing the navy's potential to protect the eastern seaboard from enemy attack, the president orders naval war games; he concludes that the nation needs a larger naval force and more efficient equipment.
- The public is outraged after German submarines attack U.S. passenger liners (e.g., *Arabic*) and merchant ships (*William Frye*), resulting in American deaths.
- A German espionage ring is exposed when the government acquires a portfolio belonging to Dr. Heinrich F. Albert; its contents are published in the press.
- The Senate reception chamber is destroyed by a bomb planted by Cornell German instructor Erich Muenter, alias Frank Holt, who later shoots J. P. Morgan, Jr. and then commits suicide.
- Carrie Chapman Catt becomes head of the National American Woman Suffrage Association, which seeks to lobby for a federal constitutional amendment ("Susan B."), rather than proceed state by state; over 40,000 march for suffrage in Washington D.C., including a contingent from The Men's League for Woman Suffrage.
- Jane Addams leads eighty women to The Hague to protest the war.
- Over 40,000 march in Chicago, protesting the closing of saloons on Sunday.
- South Dakota abolishes the death penalty.
- Leo Frank, found guilty of murdering a young girl, is lynched by a Georgia mob after the governor commutes his death sentence to life imprisonment.
- The Harrison Law regulating the sale of opium and its derivatives takes effect.
- The "taxicab" appears: travelers pay a nickel for a short ride from "hackers" (or "hackies," in the east; "cabbies," in the midwest); intercity bus lines also begin.
- Two fairs celebrating the Panama Canal open in California—the Panama-Pacific International Exposition (San Francisco) and Panama-California Exposition (San Diego); the former attracts 18.9 million visitors.
- After the public is informed that one in 20 New York children (37,776) lack the penny to pay for a "square meal" luncheon, a fund is established to underwrite these costs.
- A New York law provides funding that would otherwise be paid state institutions to widowed mothers so they may keep their children at home.
- Paul Whiteman leaves the world of symphonic music in order to organize an orchestra for the new "syncopation" ("jazz").
- After publishing *Family Limitation,* Margaret Sanger is arrested and imprisoned on obscenity charges.
- Kiss me, my fool," says "the vamp" Theda Bara, in an ad for *A Fool There Was;* she is an overnight success.
- President Wilson marries a second wife, Edith Bolling Galt, widow of a Washington jeweler.

Popular poster. *D. Ouellette Collection.*

- The U.S. and Britain argue over the British blockade of noncontraband, especially food, to neutral nations like Holland and Italy; trade with Germany and Austria declines, while trade with the Allies dramatically increases.
- In response to war needs and high market prices, U.S. farmers produce a record one billion bushels of wheat.
- The Supreme Court rules unconstitutional both a Kansas law that forbids hiring only nonunion employees and an Arizona anti-alien law requiring that 80 percent of employees be native born.
- An "easy divorce" bill requiring six months' residency becomes law in Nevada.

First appearances: Disposable scalpel, gas mask, fighter plane (Germany), U.S. Naval Reserve, Coast Guard, Dixie Highway (covering 4,206 miles), telephone service between New York and San Francisco ($20.70), transatlantic call (Arlington-Paris), direct wireless between U.S.-Japan and U.S.-Prussia, Rocky Mountain National Park (Colorado), motor scooter (Auto-Ped), tractor trailer (Ford), doubledecker bus (Fifth Avenue Coach, N.Y.C.), General Tire and Rubber, Carrier Corp., Widener Library (Harvard), Emory University (A. G. Candler, owner of Coca-Cola formula), Brooks Brothers (on Madison Avenue, N.Y.C.), J. W. Robinson (Los Angeles), Muehlbach Hotel (Kansas City), barless zoological garden (Denver), Kiwannis, Protestant church for lepers (Carville, La.), Jewish governor (Moses Alexander), 50-dollar gold piece, Kraft processed cheese, Kellogg's 40%-Bran Flakes, International Fingerprint Society (Oakland, Calif.)

1916

Jeanette Rankin, 36, the first woman elected to Congress. *U.S. Senate.*

Deaths

Thomas Eakins, Emperor Franz Joseph, Henry James, Jack London, Ernst Mach, Franz Marc, Ilya Mechnikov, Rasputin, Odilon Redon, Max Reger

In the News

SUPREME COURT RULES FEDERAL INCOME TAX CONSTITUTIONAL . . . VILLA LEADS RAID ON COLUS, N.M., KILLS 17 AMERICANS, PERSHING LEADS EXPEDITION TO CAPTURE VILLA . . . GERMANY ACCEPTS *LUSITANIA* RESPONSIBILITY AND PROMISES FUTURE RESTRAINT; WILSON WARNS THAT FURTHER PASSENGER SHIP ATTACKS WILL FORCE DIPLOMATIC BREAK . . . MARINES INVADE NICARAGUA TO QUELL CIVIL WAR . . . I.R.B. ATTACKS DUBLIN POST OFFICE, LEADERS PEARSE AND CONNOLLY ARE CAPTURED . . . FRENCH COUNTERATTACK AT VERDUN, LOSSES ON BOTH SIDES NEAR 700,000 . . . NATIONAL DEFENSE ACT ENLARGES STANDING ARMY AND RESERVE . . . REPUBLICANS NOMINATE CHARLES EVANS HUGHES AND CHARLES FAIRBANKS . . . DEMOCRATS RENOMINATE WILSON AND MARSHALL . . . U.S. REJECTS MEXICAN REQUEST TO REMOVE TROOPS, 17 AMERICANS, 38 MEXICANS DIE IN CLASH . . . FEDERAL LAND BANK SYSTEM IS CREATED TO HELP FARMERS . . . U.S. ACCUSES BRITAIN OF VIOLATING NEUTRALS' RIGHTS IN BLOCKADE . . . BRITISH MOUNT OFFENSIVE ON SOMME, 30,000 ARE KILLED IN FIRST HALF-HOUR . . . U.S. AND MEXICO NEGOTIATE SETTLEMENT . . . GERMAN SABOTEURS ARE BLAMED IN N.J. MUNITIONS DUMP EXPLOSION . . . U.S. BUYS VIRGIN ISLANDS FROM DENMARK FOR $25 MILLION . . . WORKMEN'S COMPENSATION ACT PROVIDES FOR FEDERAL EMPLOYEES . . . ADAMSON EIGHT-HOUR ACT FOR RAILROAD WORKERS IS PASSED . . . KEATING-OWENS ACT REGULATES CHILD LABOR . . . WILSON WINS NARROW ELECTORAL VICTORY, VOTE IS 9.1 TO 8.5 MILLION . . . GERMANY ASKS WILSON TO NEGOTIATE PEACE, ALLIES REJECT OFFER, FEARING GERMANY'S ADVANTAGE.

Quotes

"My mother and my wife."
— Navy Secretary Josephus Daniels,
on why he supports woman suffrage

"The vampire I play is the vengeance of my sex upon its exploiters. I have the face of a vampire, but the heart of a *feministe*."
— The "vamp" Theda Bara

"I do not know how to deal with the fiendish lies that are being . . . circulated about my personal character. . . . Poison of this sort is hard to find an antidote for."
— Wilson, on rumors of infidelity to his first wife

"All I know is what I read in the papers."
— Will Rogers

On the presidential election: "What did we do? What did we do? We didn't go to war" (Democratic party campaign slogan). "America first and America efficient" (Hughes campaign slogan). "You tell that to the marines" (Wilson, when his daughter reports that the election is still "unsettled"). "THE PRESIDENT-ELECT—CHARLES EVANS HUGHES" (newspaper headlines, on election day).

"It is a grave conclusion . . . that a great democracy . . . must teach all its young men how to fight."
— Charles Eliot, "Shall We Adopt Universal Military Service?"

"Once lead this people into war, and they'll forget there ever was such a thing as tolerance. To fight you must be ruthlessly brutal."
— Woodrow Wilson

Louis D. Brandeis, the first Jew appointed to the Supreme Court. *U.S. Senate.*

"His burdens are heavier than any president's since Lincoln."
— Col. Edward House, on Wilson

"The European war . . . has entirely upset preconceived notions of war. . . . The test has gotten down to which country can fastest and longest supply the munitions of war to men on the fighting line. . . . The skilled mechanic . . . is going to win the wars for this country."
— Howard Coffin, chairman, Committee of Industrial Preparedness

Ads

Once considered a populist rebel hero, Pancho Villa now organizes lethal raids on New Mexico; the U.S. invades Mexico to capture him. *National Archives*.

Suffragettes in New York, bearing the names of their successes to date. *Smithsonian Institution*.

Movies

Openings

Intolerance (D. W. Griffith), Dorothy Gish, Mae Marsh, Robert Harron, Constance Talmadge

Civilization (Thomas Ince), Howard Hickman, Hershell Mayall

Hell's Hinges (William S. Hart), Hart, Clara Williams

War Brides (Herbert Brenon), Alla Nazimova

The Floorwalker (Charles Chaplin), Chaplin, Lloyd Bacon

The Pawnshop (Charles Chaplin), Chaplin, Edna Purviance

Manhattan Madness (John Emerson), Douglas Fairbanks

A Daughter of the Gods (Herbert Brenon), Annette Kellerman

Joan the Woman (Cecil B. DeMille), Geraldine Farrar

The Fireman (Charles Chaplin), Chaplin, Edna Purviance, Albert Austin

Hoodoo Ann (Lloyd Ingraham), Mae Marsh, Robert Harron

The Aryan, written, directed, and starring William S. Hart

The Dumb Girl of Portici (Lois Weber-Smalley), Anna Pavlova, first feature

The Battle of the Somme (Geoffrey Malins, J. B. McDowell), first significant documentary of World War I

Chaplin signs with Mutual for a record salary, $675,000. Samuel Goldwyn (Goldfish) and Archibald Selwyn found Goldwyn Picture Company. Famous

Dressed in dude ranch costumes and performing his own riding stunts, Tom Mix popularizes the straightforward, good-guy western. *Library of Congress*.

Players-Lasky-Paramount is formed under Adolph Zukor as a production-distribution combine, "the U.S. Steel Corporation" of the motion picture industry.

Top Box-Office Stars

Blanche Sweet, Wallace Reid, Marguerite Clark, Mary Pickford, Francis X. Bushman, Douglas Fairbanks, William S. Hart, Norma Talmadge, Robert Harron

Popular Music

Hit Songs
"If You Were the Only Girl in the World"
"Beale Street (Blues)"
"Roses of Picardy"
"I Ain't Got Nobody"
"M-I-S-S-I-S-S-I-P-P-I"
"You Belong to Me"
"Ireland Must Be Heaven for My Mother Came from There"
"It's the Irish in Your Eye, It's the Irish in Your Smile"
"He May Be Old, But He's Got Young Ideas"
"Rolling Stones"
"I Can Dance with Everyone but My Wife"
"There's a Little Bit of Bad in Every Good Little Girl"
"Oh, How She Could Yacki Hacki Wicki Wacki Woo"

Representative Recordings:
Henry Burr, "Just a Baby's Prayer at Twilight" (million-selling); "Where Did Robinson Crusoe Go with Friday on Saturday Night?" (Al Jolson); "Evelyn" (Mitzi Hajos); "Pretty Baby" (Billy Murphy); "Goodbye, Good Luck, God Bless You" (Henry Burr, Ernest Ball); "Ziegfeld Follies of 1916 Medley" (Conway's Band)

Jazz
The Dixieland Jass Band [sic], which opens at Schiller's Cafe in Chicago, includes Dominique La Rocca, Alcide "Yellow" Nunez, Eddie Edwards, Tony Sbarbaro, and Henry Ragas.

Theater

Broadway Openings

Plays
Getting Married (George Bernard Shaw), William Faversham
Good Gracious Anabelle (Clare Krummer), Lola Fisher, Walter Hampden, Ruth Harding, Roland Young
Turn to the Right! (Winchell Smith, John Hazzard), Forrest Winant, Alice Hastings
Erstwhile Susan (Marian de Forest), Mrs. Minnie Maddern Fiske
Justice (John Galsworthy), John Barrymore, Cathleen Nesbitt
Seven Chances (Roi Cooper Megrue), Frank Craven, Otto Kruger
A Kiss for Cinderella (J. M. Barrie), Maude Adams
Cheating Cheaters (Max Marcin), Marjorie Rambeau
The Man Who Came Back (Jules Eckert Goodman), Henry Hull, Edward Emery
Upstairs and Down (Frederic and Fannie Hatton), Leo Carrillo
Come Out of the Kitchen (A. E. Thomas), Ruth Chatterton, Walter Connolly, William Boyd

Musicals
The Century Girl (Irving Berlin, Victor Herbert), Hazel Dawn, Elsie Janis, Leon Errol, Van and Schenck
Ziegfeld Follies (Louis Hirsch, Jerome Kern, Dave Stamper), W. C. Fields, Will Rogers, Fannie Brice, Bert Williams, Ina Claire
The Passing Show (Sigmund Romberg, Harold Atteridge), Ed Wynn
The Big Show (Raymond Hubbell, John Golden), Anna Pavlova, Alexandre Volinine

"If You Want WAR, Vote for HUGHES! If You Want Peace with Honor VOTE FOR WILSON!"—Wilson supporters. *Smithsonian Institution.*

Robinson Crusoe, Jr. (Sigmund Romberg, Harold Atteridge), Al Jolson
The Show of Wonders (Sigmund Romberg, Harold Atteridge), Marilyn Miller, Willie and Eugene Howard

Classics and Revivals On and Off Broadway
Macbeth, James K. Hackett; *The Merchant of Venice*, Sir Herbert Tree, Lyn Harding; *The Tempest*, Louis Calvert; *A Woman of No Importance* (Wilde), Margaret Anglin, Holbrook Blinn; Washington Square Players: *The Seagull, Ghosts, Trifles* (Glaspell); Mme. Sarah Bernhardt: scenes from *La Dame aux Camélias, The Merchant of Venice, L'Aiglon*; Stuart Walker's Portmanteau Theatre: *The Gods of the Mountain, The Golden Doom*

Classical Music

Compositions
Charles Ives, *At the River,* Fourth Symphony,
    Second String Quartet
Frederick Converse, *Ave atque vale*
Howard Hanson, *Symphonic Prelude*
Leo Sowerby, *Serenade,* Wind Quartet
Charles Griffes, *Four Roman Sketches*
Henry Hadley, *The Ocean*

Important Events
The Russian Symphony Orchestra premieres
Stravinsky's First Symphony (E flat) in New York.
After leaving the French army, Pierre Monteux tours
the U.S. as conductor of the Ballet Russe. Fritz
Kreisler introduces Ernest Schelling's Violin
Concerto with the Boston Symphony in Providence,
R.I.; he plays his revision of Schumann's Fantasia in
C major for Violin and Orchestra in New York.

Notable Performances: D'Indy's prize-winning *Le
Chant de la Cloche,* Boston; Grainger's *In a
Nutshell,* Norfolk, Conn. (conducted by the
composer); Cadman's symphonic fantasy, *To a
Vanishing Rose,* Seattle.

New Appointment: Gustav Strube (Baltimore
Symphony Orchestra)

Debut: Mischa Levitzki

First Performances
Mahler's *Giant [Eighth] Symphony* (New York, with
over 1,000 performers); Strauss, *Alpine Symphony*
(Cincinnati); John Alden Carpenter, Piano Concertino
(Chicago); Charles Martin Loeffler, *Hora Mystica*
(Norfolk, Conn.); Schelling, Violin Concerto
(Boston); Ravel, *Valses Nobles et Sentimentales*
(New York); Skilton, *Two Indian Dances*
(Minneapolis); Ravel, *Introduction and Allegro* for
Harp, Strings, Quartet, Flute, and Clarinet (New
York); Daniel Gregory Mason, Symphony in C
(Philadelphia); Bruch, Concerto for Two Pianos
(Chicago)

Opera

Metropolitan: Claudia Muzio (debut), Enrico
Caruso, Antonio Scotto, *Tosca;* Anna Fitziu (debut),
Giovanni Martinelli, *Goyescas* (Granados, first opera
sung in Spanish); *The Pearl Fishers* (Bizet, first U.S.
complete production); *Francesca di Rimini*
(Zandonai); Melanie Kurt, Marie Rappold, *Iphigenia
in Tauris* (Gluck, premiere); *Lakmé;* centennial
anniversary performance of *The Barber of Seville*

Lewisohn Stadium, N.Y.:   *Cavalleria Rusticana,
Pagliacci*

Chicago: Amelita Galli-Curci (debut), *Rigoletto;*
Conchita Supervia (debut), *Carmen*

Music Notes
Noted statesmen continue to speak at music centers
like Carnegie Hall on America's entrance into the war
• William Damrosch pleads with the New York
Symphony Society to play Bach, Beethoven, and
Brahms • After Pierre Monteux refuses to conduct
Strauss's *Till Eulenspiegel* in a New York
performance, he is replaced by German conductor
Anselm Goetz; Monteux conducts the rest of the
program • Despite the boycott of German and
Austrian conductors, composers, and performers,
little financial support is given young American
musicians for their experiments toward a unique
American idiom • Ernst Bloch visits the U.S. for the
first time as accompanist to singer Maud Allen • The
Mannes College of Music opens in New York.

Subject of many retrospectives, John Singer Sargent, *Madame X.* Oil on canvas. 82½″ × 43¼. *The Metropolitan Museum of Art, Arthur H. Hearn Fund, 1916.*

Art

Painting
Man Ray, *The Rope Dancer Accompanies Herself with Her Shadows*
Marsden Hartley, *Movement #2*
Morton L. Shamberg, *Machine*
Charles Burchfield, *Rogue's Gallery, The City*
Charles Demuth, *The Shine, Nana, Seated Left, and Satin at Laure's Restaurant*
John R. Covert, *Temptation of St. Anthony*

Sculpture
Paul Manship, *Dancer and Gazelles*
Leo Friedlander, *A Bacchante*
E. B. Parsons, *Turtle Baby* (1910–16)
Paul Bartlett, *Preparedness*
Henry Clews, *Frederick Delius*
Thomas Hastings, Statue at Pulitzer Fountain, Fifth Avenue at 58th Street, N.Y.C.

Architecture
Vizcaya, Miami (Paul Chalfin, F. Burrel Hoffman, Jr.)
Ellen Scripps house, La Jolla, Calif. (Irving Gill)

Important Exhibitions

Museums

New York: *Metropolitan:* Print department opens with an exhibition; 18th-century English paintings; British portraits and landscapes; art of local high school students. *Brooklyn:* Early American portraits and furniture; Engravings of Alfred and Fanny Prunaire; Paintings of Ignacio Zuloauga; Watercolors of Dougherty, Coleman, Homer, Blum, and Sargent. *Columbia University:* Architectural designs by James Whistler and Carrère and Hastings; Typical French war hospital plans

San Francisco: War posters and etchings by Frank Brangwyn; Development of Greek sculpture (lent by the Greek government); 400 examples of contemporary Dutch graphic art

Cleveland: American Colonial art; Bronzes and marbles by Carpeaux, Rivière

Dance

New York: Diaghilev's Ballets Russes (debut), Leonide Massine, Xenia Maclezova, *The Firebird;* Massine, Lydia Lopokova, *Petroushka; Les Sylphides* (premiere)

Art Briefs
Posters for recruiting, Liberty Bond sales, and the Red Cross drive are mounted indoors and outdoors throughout the country • Women organize Art War Relief headquarters, and profits go to the war effort • Disruption of trade relations with Germany throws the U.S. on to its own resources for the development of industrial arts; progress is made in textiles; craft societies increase both for cultural value and as a trade for disabled men.

To combat criticism of racism in *Birth of a Nation*, D. W. Griffith makes the even more costly *Intolerance;* it fails at the box office. *Movie Star News.*

Lincoln Memorial, with Daniel Chester French's sculpture of the president. *Copyright Washington Post. Reprinted by permission of D. C. Public Library.*

Books

Fiction

Critics' Choice

Xingu and Other Stories, Edith Wharton

The Certain Hour, James Branch Cabell

The Leatherwood God, William Dean Howells

Windy McPherson's Sons, Sherwood Anderson

The Mysterious Stranger, Mark Twain (posthumous)

Mrs. Balfame, Gertrude Atherton

The Rising Tide, Margaret Deland

You Know Me Al: A Busher's Letters, Ring Lardner

Novels and Stories (12 vols.), Richard Harding Davis

❧ *A Portrait of the Artist as a Young Man*, James Joyce

Best-Sellers

Seventeen, Booth Tarkington

When A Man's a Man, Harold Bell Wright

Just David, Eleanor H. Porter

Mr. Britling Sees It Through, H. G. Wells

Life and Gabriella, Ellen Glasgow

The Real Adventure, Henry Kitchell Webster

Bars of Iron, Ethel M. Dell

Nan of Music Mountain, Frank H. Spearman

Dear Enemy, Jean Webster

The Heart of Rachael, Kathleen Norris

Nonfiction

Critics' Choice

The Hope of the Great Community, Josiah Royce

Democracy and Education, John Dewey

"Noh" or Accomplishment: A Study of the Classical Stage of Japan, Ezra Pound, with Ernest Fenallosa

A Book of Burlesques, H. L. Mencken

Life of John Marshall, Albert Beveridge

Oscar Wilde, Frank Harris

Life in the War Zone, Gertrude Atherton

The Gary Schools, Randolph Bourne

Venetian Paintings in America, Bernard Berenson

Shakespeare, George Lyman Kittredge

Henry David Thoreau, Mark Van Doren

Egotism in German Philosophy, George Santayana

Poetry

Robert Frost, *Mountain Interval*

Carl Sandburg, *Chicago Poems*

Edward Arlington Robinson, *The Man Against the Sky*

Robinson Jeffers, *Californians*

H. D., *Sea Garden*

Conrad Aiken, *The Jig of Forslin*

John Gould Fletcher, *Goblins and Pagodas*

Alan Seeger, *I Have a Rendezvous with Death*

Ezra Pound, *Lustra*

Pulitzer Prizes

With Americans of Past and Present Days, J. J. Jusserand (U.S. history)

Julia Ward Howe, Laura E. Richards, Maude Howe Elliott, assisted by Florence Howe Hall (biography)

Science and Technology

Pellagra is shown to be a deficiency disease, not an infection, by Joseph Goldberger.

Elmer McCollum and Marguerite Davis declare vitamins A and B essential for growth.

Blood is refrigerated for safe storage.

Planck's constant and Einstein's work on the photoelectric effect are confirmed by Robert A. Millikan.

A small, rapidly moving star is discovered by Edward Barnard.

❧ The theory of shell shock is proposed by F. W. Mott.

❧ Powder crystallography, using X-rays, is pioneered by Peter Debye.

Although the lower-priced Model T dominates the market, the wealthy seek faster, sleeker, and more sophisticated machines; here, a woman and her pet on a Stutz. *Library of Congress.*

Sports

Baseball

The New York Giants set a modern record with 26 consecutive wins; the Boston Braves break the streak. Grover Cleveland Alexander (Philadelphia, NL) pitches a record 15 shutouts.

Champions

Batting
Harold Chase (Cincinnati, NL), .339
Tristram Speaker (Cleveland, AL), .386
Pitching
Thomas Hughes (Boston, NL), 16–3
Harry Covaleskie (Detroit, AL), 23–10

Home runs
Davis Robertson (New York, NL), 12
Frederick Williams (Chicago, NL), 12
Walter Pipp (New York, AL), 12

Football

Georgia Tech beats Cumberland (Tenn.) 222–0.

College All-Americans: Elmer Oliphant (F), Army; Clinton Black (G), Yale; Robert Peck (C), Pittsburgh

Rose Bowl (Jan. 1, 1917): Oregon 14-Penn 0

Basketball

The NCAA and the AAU (Amateur Athletic Union) form the Joint Basketball Rules Committee to standardize rules and reduce regional variations.

Olympics

The Olympics are not held, due to the war.

Other Sports

Golf: Multimillionaire businessman Rodman Wanamaker organizes the Professional Golfers Association of America (PGA), and James Barnes wins its first tournament at Siwanoy (Bronxville, NY); Bobby Jones, 14, wins four tournaments and debuts in the U.S. Open.

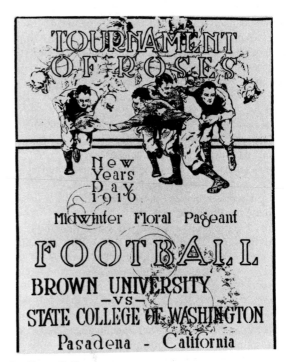

D. Ouellette Collection.

Boxing: "Battling" Levinsky outpoints Joe Dillon for the light heavyweight title, reinvigorating the weight class when "ballyhoo" manager Dan Morgan touts "the champion."

Winners

World Series
Boston (AL) 4
Brooklyn (NL) 1
College Football
Pittsburgh
College Basketball
Wisconsin
Player of the Year
George Levis, Wisconsin

Stanley Cup
Montreal
U.S. Tennis Open
Men: R. Norris Williams II
Women: Molla Bjurstedt
USGA Open
Charles Evans, Jr.
Kentucky Derby
George Smith (Johny Loftus, jockey)

Fashion

For Women: Marching suffragettes model the new styles, which have pockets everywhere—on dresses, suits, and even coats. They also carry a walking cane, traditionally reserved for male fashion. The hobble skirt is entirely rejected for full skirts, which permit greater freedom of movement. Hosiery need no longer match footwear and dress (in color and design); a single decoration, a clock, remains on the instep of each stocking.

For Men: Now accompanying slimmer and more natural-looking women, men adopt an equivalent "natural" look—the "natty" style, with unpadded shoulders, narrow jacket sleeve, and slim pants (with a cuff and crease). The five-button waistcoat and jacket is also shortened, and lapels are lengthened; the waist is lifted. Due to war shortages in fabric, pleats disappear, and slash pockets replace patched pockets.

High-fashion notes: Coco Chanel's use of jersey in dresswear (formerly used only for underclothing); Erté's fashion covers for Harper's Bazaar.

Kaleidoscope

- Republicans Roosevelt and Taft unite behind an "Anyone but Wilson" for president policy; Charles Evans Hughes resigns from the Supreme Court to run on the GOP ticket.
- Hughes retires on election eve, expecting to awaken as president-elect; he loses thirteen electoral votes in California, decisive in Wilson's 277–254 electoral college victory.
- Hughes's loss by 4,000 of California's 928,000 votes is widely attributed to his snubbing of Governor Hiram Johnson ("the forgotten handshake").
- American investors buy over $2 billion in bonds from the Allies.
- Wilson makes repeated but unsuccessful efforts to mediate the European war.
- Henry Ford charters the *Oscar II,* or "Peace Ship," to stop the war in Europe, caused, he says, by international Jews and Wall Street; the ship reaches Europe and returns.
- A polio epidemic strikes 28,767 in the summer and fall; 6,000 die.
- "Father Divine" organizes the Peace Mission Movement, advocating racial equality and renouncing tobacco, sex, liquor, movies, and personal property.
- South Carolina raises the minimum working age of children from twelve to fourteen.
- Labor leader "Tom" Mooney and his wife are convicted of murder after a bomb at the Preparedness Day parade kills ten and wounds forty; the president commutes the sentence on their controversial conviction to life imprisonment.
- Margaret Sanger opens the first birth control clinic in the country (in Brooklyn) and distributes information in English, Italian, and Yiddish; she is jailed for thirty days, after which she founds the New York Birth Control League.
- Stanford Terman introduces the first test for measuring intelligence and coins the term *IQ* (intelligent quotient).
- The Ford factory has a sociological department that monitors the working habits of Ford's employees.
- Educator John Dewey castigates parents who "look with impatience upon immaturity, regarding it as something to be got over as rapidly as possible."
- The average seating capacity of the nation's 21,000 movie theaters is 502; the average charge is 5¢–10¢ (up to $2, for specials).
- Interest in ballet increases, and foreign dancers like Vaslav Nijinsky draw enormous audiences; Serge Diaghilev brings the Ballet Russe to New York; Americans gaining in popularity include Ted Shawn and Ruth St. Denis.
- Anna Pavlova dances two shows daily in "The Big Show" at the Hippodrome and earns an estimated $8,500 a week.
- Norman Rockwell publishes his first illustration in *The Saturday Evening Post;* Rockwell, a high school dropout, has been art director of the Boy Scouts' magazine *Boy's Life* since 1913.
- The Mercury dime (Mrs. Wallace Stevens) and Liberty fifty-cent piece go into circulation; both are designed by A. A. Weinman.

- The revised New York building code allows for skyscraper construction of unlimited height.
- Although the average cost of a new car is over $600, the Model T costs $360 ($850, 1908); about 3.5 million cars are on the nation's roads.
- The Shackleford Good Roads Bill authorizes $5 million for state road-building programs; states must contribute equal amounts.
- Enamel bathtubs begin to replace claw-footed cast-iron tubs.
- At $900, the new mechanized home refrigerator exceeds the price of the average car.
- Woodrow Wilson, a child violinist and later a tenor with the Princeton and Johns Hopkins University glee clubs, thrills listeners by holding the high note near the end of "The Star-Spangled Banner."
- The rage for ukuleles and Hawaiian music is apparent in several popular songs like "They're Wearing 'Em Higher in Hawaii" and "Yaacka Hula Hickey Dula."
- Hetty Green, the world's wealthiest woman, dies at age 82; she leaves $100 million.

First appearances: Piggly-Wiggly (Memphis), Orange Crush, Coco-Cola bottle shape, Nathan's hotdogs (5¢), Rialto Theater ("the temple of the Motion Picture," N.Y.C.), Lincoln Logs (toy), Nash, mechanical windshield wipers, agitator washing machine, camera with coupled range finder (Kodak), loudspeaker public address system, National Research Council, ROTC, Ecological Society of America, Boeing, airplane to fly over 500 miles (Chicago-Hornell, N.Y.), sonar (France), automobile all-steel body (Dodge), Clift Hotel (San Francisco), American Indian Day (May 13), municipal orchestra supported by taxes (Baltimore), Reynolds Metals (foil wrappings), Lucky Strike, Planters' "Mr. Peanut" logo

John Dewey proposes that early education emphasize thinking skills rather than rote memorization; he also advocates a social engineering approach to social problems. *Library of Congress.*

1917

Bernard Baruch heads the War Industries' Board, overseeing America's war preparedness in industry and resources. *Library of Congress.*

Deaths

Johann von Baeyer, Emil von Behring, "Diamond" Jim Brady, W. F. ("Buffalo Bill") Cody, Edgar Degas, François Auguste Rodin, Albert Pinkham Ryder, Ferdinand Count Zeppelin

In the News

WILSON ASKS FOR WORLD FEDERATION, "PEACE WITHOUT VICTORY" . . . GERMANS ANNOUNCE UNRESTRICTED SUBMARINE WARFARE, U.S. SEVERS RELATIONS . . . IMMIGRATION LAW WITH LITERACY TESTING BARS MOST ASIANS . . . MERCHANT MARINE SHIPS ARE ARMED . . . SAILORS MUTINY AT PETROGRAD, CZAR NICHOLS II ABDICATES, REFORM GOVERNMENT IS ESTABLISHED . . . U.S. IS FIRST TO RECOGNIZE NEW RUSSIAN GOVERNMENT . . . LIBERTY LOAN ACT OFFERS $2 BILLION IN BONDS . . . SELECTIVE SERVICE ACT AUTHORIZES CONSCRIPTION, MALES 21–30 MUST REGISTER . . . ESPIONAGE ACT FORBIDS INTERFERENCE WITH WAR EFFORT . . . ZIMMERMAN NOTE URGING MEXICO TO WAR ON U.S. IS REVEALED, U.S. DECLARES WAR ON GERMANY . . . V.I. LENIN IS TRANSPORTED BY GERMANS FROM ZURICH TO PETROGRAD, DEMANDS POWER FOR WORKERS . . . BRITISH GAIN 5 MILES AT PASSCHENDALE, 400,000 DIE . . . BOLSHEVIK COUP IS REPULSED, MODERATE ALEXANDER KERENSKY BECOMES GOVERNMENT LEADER . . . SERBIA, CROATIA, SLOVENIA AGREE TO FORM NEW COUNTRY . . . LAWRENCE OF ARABIA LEADS ARABS AGAINST TURKS . . . GOVERNMENT RAIDS IWW HEADQUARTERS IN 24 CITIES . . . GERMAN SPY MATA HARI IS EXECUTED BY FRENCH . . . U.S. TROOPS HAVE FIRST ENGAGEMENT IN FRANCE, REPULSE GERMAN ATTACK . . . BOLSHEVIKS UNDER LENIN AND TROTSKY REVOLT AND TAKE FULL POWER . . . BALFOUR DECLARATION FAVORS "NATIONAL HOME" FOR JEWS IN PALESTINE . . . BOLSHEVIKS CONCLUDE ARMISTICE ON EASTERN FRONT . . . BRITISH TAKE JERUSALEM . . . CONGRESS PASSES PROHIBITION AMENDMENT.

Quotes

During the Great War:
"We [Germany] make Mexico a proposal of alliance
. . . to recover the lost territory in Texas, New
Mexico, and Arizona."
> — The intercepted Zimmerman note,
> preceding America's declaration of war

"The equality of nations must be an equality . . .
between those who are powerful and those who are
weak."
> — Wilson, "Peace without Victory"

"The world must be made safe for democracy. . . .
We have no selfish ends. We desire no conquest, no
dominion. We seek no indemnities . . . for the
sacrifices we shall freely make."
— Woodrow Wilson, asking Congress to declare war

"America has joined forces with the Allied powers,
and what we have of treasure and blood are
yours. . . . Lafayette, we are here."
> — Col. Charles E. Stanton at
> Lafayette's tomb in Paris

"Over there, over there,
Send the word, send the word, over there,
That the Yanks are coming, The Yanks are coming,
The drums, rum-tumming everywhere.
> — "Over There," the AEF's favorite
> marching song, for which George M.
> Cohan receives the Congressional Medal

"This Russian boy . . . is a divinely inspired marvel,
. . . the supremest genius of the violin . . . perchance
evermore."
> — on Jascha Heifetz's debut, *New York Times*

"The American . . . casts up all ponderable values,
even the values of beauty, in terms of right or wrong.
He is above all things else a judge and a policeman.
. . . This is the essential fact of the new Puritanism;
its recognition of the moral expert—the professional
sinhound, the virtuouso of virtue."
> — H. L. Mencken, *A Book of Prefaces*

"Americans believe happiness not merely desirable,
but possible. . . . It has become a national ideal.
Consequently, American art . . . must be happy art.
Good must triumph over evil. Love must find a way.
Hence—the happy ending."
> — *Photoplay*

Ads

General Pershing insists that soldiers be given academy-level training before being sent into battle; many believe the U.S.'s lack of preparedness has emboldened the Germans into unrestricted submarine warfare. *National Archives.*

In the first draft since the Civil War, 9.8 million men are registered; 2.8 million are drafted without resistance. *National Archives.*

Movies

Openings

The Woman God Forgot (Cecil B. DeMille), Geraldine Farrar, Wallace Reid
Easy Street (Charles Chaplin), Chaplin, Edna Purviance, Albert Austin
The Immigrant (Charles Chaplin), Chaplin, Edna Purviance
A Tale of Two Cities (Frank Lloyd), William Farnum, Jewel Carmen
The Butcher Boy (Roscoe Arbuckle), Arbuckle, Buster Keaton
A Poor Little Rich Girl (Maurice Tourneur), Mary Pickford
Rebecca of Sunnybrook Farm (Marshall Neilan), Mary Pickford
The Fall of the Romanoffs (Herbert Brenon), Edward Connelly, Conway Tearle
Straight Shooting (John Ford, debut), Harry Carey
The Adventurer (Charles Chaplin), Chaplin, Edna Purviance
Les Miserables (Frank Lloyd), William Farnum, Hardee Kirkland
Wild and Woolly (John Emerson), Douglas Fairbanks
Polly of the Circus (Charles Horan), Mae Marsh, Matt Moore, Bartlett's circus
Panthea (Allan Dwan), Norma Talmadge, Earle Fox

First National acquires Chaplin by offering him his own studio in Hollywood at Sunset and La Brea, and $1,075,000 for eight two-reel films. Universal employs

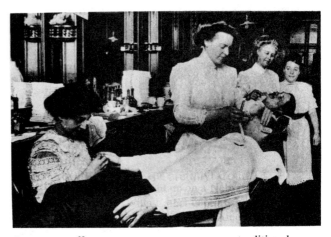

As men go off to war, women assume many traditional male roles. *D. Ouellette Collection.*

numerous women directors: Lois Weber, Cleo Madison, Ruth Stonehouse, Grace Cunard, Ruth Ann Baldwin. The U.S. Signal Corps establishes a training school for medical and historical films; student instructors include Joseph von Sternberg, Ernest Shoedsack, Alan Crosland, and Lewis Milestone.

Top Box-Office Stars

Charles Chaplin, Mary Pickford, Douglas Fairbanks, Marguerite Clark, William S. Hart, William Farnum, Theda Bara, Wallace Reid, Pauline Frederick, Norma Talmadge

Popular Music

Hit Songs
" 'Till the Clouds Roll By"
"Will You Remember (Sweetheart)"
"Hail, Hail, The Gang's All Here"
"Smiles"
"Nobody Knows de Trouble I've Seen"
"Go Down Moses"
"Sweet Little Buttercup"
"The Bells of St. Mary's"
"Bring Back My Daddy to Me"
"Goodbye Broadway, Hello France"
" 'Round Her Neck She Wore a Yellow Ribbon"
"(Back Home in) Indiana"
"Thine Alone"

Representative Recordings:
"Love Will Find a Way" (Reed Miller); "Oh Johnny, Oh Johnny, Oh" (American Quartette); "For Me and My Gal" (Van & Schenck); "The Magic of Your Eyes" (Henry Burr); "Let's All Be Americans Now" (Knickerbocker Quartette); "Over There" (American Quartette)

Jazz
With patent rights held by Victor, Edison, and Columbia expiring, the record industry opens to new companies like Okeh, Vocation, Emerson, and Brunswick. Bradford Perry is the first black entrepreneur to convince companies to record black songs by black vocalists, backed by black jazz musicians. Rosamund Johnson directs a "singing orchestra"—"The Coloured Players"—in a series of ground-breaking performances at Madison Square Garden. "Ma" Rainey forms her own touring company, "Madame Gertrude Rainey and the George Smart Set," a female chorus line with a small string band. The Original Dixieland Jass Band opens at Reisenweber's Cafe, in New York. Million-selling "Darktown Strutters Ball," by Sheldon Brooks—with the native folk sound of New Orleans transformed into the new jazz— revolutionizes popular music. Other important jazz records include "One-Step" and "Fuzzy Wuzzy Blues" (W. C. Handy), "Tiger Rag," "Barnyard Blues," "Reisenweber Rag," "Bluin' the Blues," "Ostrich Walk" (Original Dixieland Jass Band).

Theater

Broadway Openings

Plays
Why Marry? (Jesse Lynch Williams), Estelle Winwood
A Successful Calamity (Clare Kummer), William Gillette, Roland Young
Peter Ibbetson (John Raphael), John Barrymore, Lionel Barrymore
Business before Pleasure (Montague Glass, Jules Eckert Goodman), Edward Mordant
Tiger Rose (Willard Mack), Willard Mack, Pedro de Cordoba
A Tailor Made Man (Harry James Smith), Frank G. Harley
The Country Cousin (Booth Tarkington, Julian Street), Julia Stuart
Polly with a Past (George Middleton, Guy Bolton), Ina Claire
Lombardi, Ltd. (Frederic and Fanny Hatton), Leo Carillo, Warner Baxter
Eyes of Youth (Charles Guernon, Max Marcin), Marjorie Rambeau

Musicals
Have a Heart (Jerome Kern, P. G. Wodehouse), Louise Dresser, Thurston Hall
Chu Chin Chow (Frederick Norton, Oscar Asche), Tyrone Power
Love o' Mike (Jerome Kern, Harry B. Smith), Peggy Wood, Clifton Webb
Oh, Boy! (Jerome Kern, P. G. Wodehouse), Tom Powers, Marion Davies, Edna May Oliver
The Passing Show (Sigmund Romberg, Harold Atteridge), Chick Sale, De Wolf Hopper
Ziegfeld Follies (Raymond Hubbell, Dave Stamper, Victor Herbert), W. C. Fields, Eddie Cantor, Will Rogers, Fannie Brice
Maytime (Sigmund Romberg, Rida Johnson Young), Peggy Wood, Charles Purcell
Over the Top (Sigmund Romberg, Charles Manning), Justine Johnstone, Fred and Adele Astaire
Going Up (Louis A. Hirsch, Otto Harbach), Frank Craven, Donald Meek
Cheer Up (Raymond Hubbell, John Golden), Nat M. Wills, Harry Houdini
Leave It to Jane (Jerome Kern, P. G. Wodehouse), Georgia O'Ramey, Oscar Shaw

Classics and Revivals On and Off Broadway
Salome (Wilde), Mme. Yorska, Louis Calvert, Walter Hampden; *In the Zone* (O'Neill); Robert B. Mantell Repertoire: *The Merchant of Venice, Hamlet, Macbeth*

Classical Music ─────────────────

Compositions
Charles Ives, *The Things Our Fathers Loved*
Howard Hanson, *Symphonic Legend*
Leo Sowerby, Woodwind Quintet, *Comes Autumn
    Time for Organ*, Piano Concertos, no. 1 and 2
Charles Cadman, *Oriental Rhapsody*
John Alden Carpenter, Concertino, Symphony

Important Events
The New York Philharmonic celebrates its 75th anniversary. The Boston Symphony hosts highly acclaimed recitals by Eugène Ysaye, Jascha Heifetz, and the Flonzaley Quartet. The San Francisco Symphony, conducted by Alfred Hertz, travels to several cities; the Minneapolis visits San Francisco. The New York Society of Friends of Music sponsors a concert of music composed and conducted by Ernest Bloch.

New Appointments: Arthur Dunham (Chicago), Pierre Monteux, Metropolitan Opera (*Faust*); Gabrilowitch debuts as a conductor, with New York's two major orchestras.

Debut: Jascha Heifetz, 16 (Vitali, *Chaconne,* Paganini-Auer Capriccio no. 24, Wieniawski, Second Concerto)

First Performances
Bloch, *Trois poèmes juifs* (Boston); *Schelomo* (New York); John Alden Carpenter, Symphony no. 1 (Norfolk); Sibelius, *Polyola's Daughter* (Boston); Debussy, *Gigues* (Boston); Converse, *Ave atque Vale* (Boston); Bruch, Concerto for Two Pianofortes (New York); Liszt, *Twenty-Third Psalm* (New York)

Opera

Metropolitan: Margaret Ober, Edith Mason, Johannes Sembach, *The Canterbury Pilgrims* (Reginald De Koven, premiere); Frances Alda, Guiseppe de Luca, Andres de Segurola, *Marouf* (Rabaud, premiere); Johanna Gadski gives her farewell performance.

Chicago: Anna Fitziu, *Azora* (Hadley); *Isabeau* (Mascagni, premiere); Genevieve Vix, *Manon*

Music Notes
After Heifetz's extraordinary debut, Fritz Kreisler and Efrem Zimbalist's earlier comment is much repeated: "You and I might as well take our fiddles and break them across our knees" • Geraldine Farrar and Johanna Gadski defend themselves against rumors that they are pro-German • The New York Board of Education prohibits discussion of German opera in class; throughout the country, German music titles are translated into English • Opera stars raise money for the war effort • The Manhattan School of Music and San Francisco Convervatory of Music are founded • Leopold Stokowski and the Philadelphia begin recording for Victor (the Brahms Hungarian Dance no. 1) • Without clear cause, the Cincinnati Orchestra's Ernst Kunwald is arrested and deported as an enemy alien; Karl Muck, at the Boston Symphony, is badgered for not playing "The Star-Spangled Banner" • German and Austrian composers are almost entirely overlooked in programming.

8,000 blacks from Harlem march down Fifth Avenue to protest wartime race riots in East St. Louis, Waco, Texas, and Memphis. *D. Ouellette Collection.*

College students challenge Wilson, who still favors a state-by-state approach to suffrage, rather than a constitutional amendment. *Smithsonian Institution.*

Art

Painting
Georgia O'Keeffe, *Light Coming Over the Plains III, Evening Star, III*
Arthur Dove, *Sentimental Music*
Charles Demuth, *Trees and Barns, Bermuda*
Max Weber, *The Two Musicians*
Abraham Walkowitz, *New York*
Charles Burchfield, *Garden of Memories, Noontide in Late May*
Thomas Hart Benton, *Constructivist Still Life*
Lyonel Feininger, *Markwippack*
John S. Sargent creates *The Church* and *The Synagogue* murals for the Boston Public Library.

Sculpture
Malvina Hoffman, *Bacchanale Russe*
Mario Korbel, *Andante*

Robert Laurent, *The Flame*
Elie Nadelman, *Woman at the Piano, Seated Woman*
Mahonri Young, *Man with a Pick* (1912–17)
Hunt Diederich, *Fighting Goats*

Architecture
MIT, Cambridge, Mass. (William Wells Bosworth)
"Everist house," Sioux City, Iowa (Richard Guy Wilson)
Swedenborgian Cathedral, Bryn Athyn, Pa. (Ralph Adams Cram)
Annex, Treasury building, Washington, D.C. (Cass Gilbert)
Marion County Public Library, Indianapolis (Paul P. Cret)
AT&T building, New York City (William Welles Bosworth)

Important Exhibitions
Sculpture and paintings of war scenes are displayed throughout the country, including the work of George Bellows, Childe Hassam, S. J. Woolf, George Luks, and John C. Jonansen.

Museums

New York: *Metropolitan:* 3,000 items from the J. P. Morgan collection (Byzantine and medieval enamels); Commercial and war posters. *Brooklyn:* first children's museum opens.

Boston: George Hallowell; Millet; Liberty Loan posters by Charles L. Woodbury, Ernest Major, Arthur Speare, Gertrude Fiske

Toledo: Paintings by Zuloaga, Frederic C. Frieseke, Gardner Symons, Leon Gaspard

Art Briefs
Several memorials are given to Thomas Eakins, Albert Ryder, and J. Carroll Beckwith • Highest sales: Gainsborough's *Blue Boy,* $38,800;

A Howard Chandler Christy poster. *National Archives.*

As workers receive massive appeals to increase productivity, labor and wages rise dramatically. *National Archives.*

Rembrandt's *Balaam and the Angels,* $10,549; for an American, Inness's *The Wood Gatherers,* $30,800. Also: Pieter Bruegel's *Betrothal Festivity,* $1,700; John La Fargue's *Landscape,* $450; Rubens's *Minerva and Thesis,* $2,700; Albert Pinkham Ryder's *Sheep and Landscape,* $80.

Books

Fiction

Critics' Choice
One Man's Initiation, John Dos Passos
King Coal, Upton Sinclair
Susan Lenox: Her Rise and Fall, David Graham Phillips
Marching Men, Sherwood Anderson
The Rise of David Levinsky, Abraham Cahan
Waifs and Strays, O. Henry (posthumous)
The Innocents, Sinclair Lewis
Summer, Edith Wharton
Gullible's Travels, Ring Lardner

Best-Sellers
Mr. Britling Sees It Through, H. G. Wells
The Light in the Clearing, Irving Bacheller
The Red Planet, William J. Locke
The Road to Understanding, Eleanor H. Porter
Wildfire, Zane Grey

Nonfiction

Critics' Choice
A Son of the Middle Border, Hamlin Garland
Interpreters and Interpretations, Carl Van Vechten
A Book of Prefaces, H. L. Mencken
The Middle Years, Henry James (posthumous)
Mrs. Fiske, Alexander Woollcott

Best-Sellers
Rhymes of a Red Cross Man, Robert W. Service
The Plattsburg Manual, O. O. Ellis and E. B. Garey
Poems of Alan Seeger, Alan Seeger
God the Invisible King, H. G. Wells
Laugh and Live, Douglas Fairbanks

Best-Sellers: War Books
The First Hundred Thousand, Ian Hay
My Home in the Field of Honor, Frances W. Huard
A Student in Arms, Donald Hankey
Over the Top, Arthur Guy Empey
Carry On, Coningsby Dawson
Getting Together, Ian Hay

Poetry
T. S. Eliot, *Prufrock and Other Observations*
Edna St. Vincent Millay, *Renascence and Other Poems*
Edward Arlington Robinson, *Merlin*
James Weldon Johnson, *Fifty Years and Other Poems*
Conrad Aiken, *Nocturne of Remembered Spring*
H. D., *The Tribute, and Circe*
William Carlos Williams, *Al Que Quiere!*

Pulitzer Prizes
His Family, Ernest Poole (novel)
A History of the Civil War, 1861–1865, James Ford Rhodes (U.S. history)
Benjamin Franklin, Self-Revealed, William Cabell Bruce (biography)
Love Songs, Sara Teasdale (poetry)

Science and Technology

The use of air contrast X-rays during brain surgery is pioneered by Johns Hopkins's Walter Dandy.

"Twilight sleep," from a scopolamin-morphine mixture, gains wide usage for childbirth; it causes amnesia for the childbirth experience.

A vaccine against Rocky Mountain spotted fever is developed.

Heparin, a natural anticoagulant, is discovered.

Graham Lusk and R. J. Anderson demonstrate that body energy relates to total intake of calories, regardless of their source.

The connection between food freezing and freshness is discovered by Clarence Birdseye when he observes that frozen fish remains edible.

The world's largest refracting telescope (100 inches) is installed at Mt. Wilson, California.

Edwin Armstrong invents a superheterodyne circuit, which increases sensitivity and selectivity of radio receivers.

🍃 C. G. Jung publishes *Psychology of the Unconscious*.

🍃 Freud publishes *Introduction to Psychoanalysis*.

Joseph Stella, *Brooklyn Bridge*. Oil. 84″ × 76″. *National Archives.*

Sports

Baseball

Ty Cobb wins his 10th batting title.

Jim Vaughn (Chicago) and Fred Toney pitch the first 9-inning double no-hit game; Cincinnati wins 1–0 in the 10th.

Ernie Shore (Boston, AL) pitches a perfect game, beating Washington 4–0.

Managers John J. McGraw (New York) and Christy Mathewson (Cincinnati) are arrested in the first game at New York's Polo Grounds for violating the Sunday ball-playing prohibition.

Champions

Batting	
Edd Roush (Cincinnati, NL), .341	Carl Mays (Boston, AL), 22–9
Ty Cobb (Detroit, AL), .383	*Home runs*
Pitching	Davis Robertson (New York, NL), 12
Ferdie Schupp (New York, NL), 21–7	Clifford Cravath (Philadelphia, NL), 12

Football

College All-Americans: The usual selections are not made due to the war.

Rose Bowl (Jan. 1, 1918): Mare Island Marines 19–Camp Lewis Army 7

Other Sports

Boxing: Benny Leonard wins the lightweight title with a 9th round TKO of Freddie Welsh.

Horse racing: Two-year-old Exterminator begins his career.

Hockey: The National Hockey Association disbands; the National Hockey League is formed (Frank Calder, president); first games are played on Dec. 19.

Winners

World Series	*U.S. Tennis ("Patriotic") Open*
Chicago (AL) 4	Men: R. Lindley Murray
New York (NL) 2	Women: Molla Bjursted
College Football	*USGA Open*
Georgia Tech	No competition, due to war
College Basketball	*Kentucky Derby*
Washington State	Omar Khayyam (C. Borel, jockey)
Player of the Year	
Ray Woods, Illinois	
Stanley Cup	
Seattle Metropolitans	

Fashion

With America involved in the war, many women become indifferent to fashion. Functional and comfortable attire becomes the fashion requirement for people of all classes, along with simple design and practical colors, such as "hopeful" green. Popular day outfits include navy suits and coats, adorned with only military epaulettes or gauntlet cuffs. The narrow chemise seems particularly appropriate for wartime dress: it calls for less fabric and permits easier movement for the woman working in the war effort. Corsets remain long but are more comfortable. As preferences increase for the slender, not voluptuous, figure, the bosom is disguised in loose bodices, both in day and evening wear. Men's styles are also incorporated into day fashions—waistcoats, mannish hats, and ties. The "barrel look" is new, in a variety of fabrics, such as the sturdy new corduroy and velveteen.

High-fashion note: Burberry's tailored brown tweed suit with a broad cape.

Opponents to the war, anarchists Emma Goldman and Alexander Berkman are convicted under the Sedition Act and sentenced to two years in jail and a $10,000 fine. *National Archives.*

Kaleidoscope

- On August 2, the Senate votes 90–6 and the House 373–50 to declare war.
- Financier Bernard Baruch hires a hundred leading businessmen to reorganize the War Industries Board to mobilize and control the economy: food and fuel is rationed; taxes, increased; the government takes control of the railroads.
- Herbert Hoover ("Hooverizing") institutes wheatless Mondays and Wednesdays, meatless Tuesdays, porkless Thursdays and Saturdays ("for the starving children in Belgium"), and four lightless nights a week in July (to conserve fuel for the next winter).
- "Victory gardens" are planted; Walter Camp's "Daily Dozen" fitness exercises become popular; mothers and girlfriends knit for the boys "over there."
- Churches, business firms, and schools erect tablets with names of the fighting men; home windows display flags starred with the number of men in the service.
- To meet war expenses, Congress authorizes the first War Savings certificates and Liberty Loans, $2 billion to be sold at 3 percent interest.
- When only 32,000 enlist, it becomes evident that a draft will be necessary; some predict draft riots.
- After the draft law, nearly 10 million draftees line up for examination without incident.
- Artists, including James Montgomery Flagg and Howard Christy Chandler, create a variety of poster ads; Flagg uses himself as the model for the "I Want You" recruitment poster.
- "The enormous majority of our men . . . were drilling with broomsticks or else rudely whittled guns," comments TR, after visiting a training camp.
- The Shipping Board assembles a merchant marine of over 3.5 million tons by building, buying, and renting ships; a convoy system is devised to protect against submarines.
- The cartoon "Katzenjammer Kids" is renamed "The Captain and the Kids" because of anti-German sentiment.
- Over 400,000 blacks have come North in search of work; many settle on railroad trunk line cities, and their first jobs are on the railroads; some later work in steel mills and war plants; they receive lower wages and pay higher rents.
- Parisian jeweler Pierre Cartier buys a building at Fifth Avenue at 52nd Street from financier Morton Plant for a two-strand oriental pearl necklace.
- A record 11 billion ride 80,000 electric trolleys for 5¢; one could travel from New York to Boston by trolley.
- For the first time, tax revenues from income taxes surpass those from custom taxes.
- Cotton prices soar to 21.25¢ a pound on the New York Exchange, the highest since the Civil War.
- Alleged IWW antiwar activities lead to federal raids on union headquarters in twenty-four cities; "Big Bill" Haywood is arrested; over 1,000 Arizona miners are left without food and water in the New Mexican desert.

- Thirty-nine are killed, and hundreds injured, in an East St. Louis, Illinois, race riot.
- A second Liberty Loan drive sells out immediately—$3 billion at 4 percent interest.
- Twenty-five-cent Liberty Stamp books for children advise: "Lick a stamp and Lick the Kaiser."
- Trench Warfare is a popular child's game; many women learn to shoot rifles; over 11,000 females enlist in the navy as clerks and stenographers.
- The Committee on Public Information, headed by George Creel, enlists over 100,000 "four-minute men" to give speeches and write literature stirring pro-war and anti-German sentiment.
- Fear of sabotage becomes pervasive—e.g., in poisoned bandages and medicines.
- Suspicion of "hyphenated-Americans" increases; Roosevelt exhorts "America for Americans" and disregard for anyone's country of origin.
- Courses in the German language are outlawed; Henry Ford teaches non-English speakers to say "I am a good American."
- Olga Samaroff, Leopold Stokowski's pianist-wife, and Mrs. Ossip Gabrilowitsch, Mark Twain's daughter, visit Wilson to discuss the widespread banning of German music; he assures them that war need not extend to dead composers.
- Tons of fruit pits, especially from peaches, are saved to make charcoal filters for gas masks.
- Patriotic songs include "We're Going to Take the Germ Out of Germany" and "We're Going to Show the Kaiser the Way to Cut Up Sauerkraut."

First appearances: "Liberty-standing" quarter, electric voting machine (Madison, Wis.), army camp for training black officers (Des Moines), Block Buster (British bomb), Travelers Aid Society, "Stop-Look-Listen" sign at railroad crossings, regular air mail (New York-Washington), American Anthropological Society, woman lawyer in American Bar Association (M. F. Lathrop), woman petty officer (Loretta Walsh), woman electrician in the navy, Jewish navy chaplain, "Cloture" rule in Senate, Phillips Petroleum, Humble Oil, Union Carbide and Carbon, Union Station (Kansas City), Acme markets, electric food mixer and beater, "The Gumps" cartoon, Rivoli theater (N.Y.C.), *World Book*

Fads: Trench Warfare game, toy dirigibles and airplanes

New words: liberty steak, liberty cabbage (sauerkraut), liberty pups (dachshunds)

1918

In the News

WILSON ANNOUNCES 14-POINT PEACE PLAN . . . WOMAN'S SUFFRAGE AMENDMENT PASSES HOUSE, IS DEFEATED IN SENATE . . . SEDITION ACT FORBIDS SPEECH AGAINST AMERICA OR WAR . . . TREATY OF BREST-LITOVSK ENDS WAR IN EAST, RUSSIA GIVES UP BALTICS AND UKRAINE . . . GERMAN ATTACK THREATENS PARIS . . . ALLIED TROOPS LAND IN VLADIVOSTOK, RUSSIA . . . U.S. TROOPS HALT GERMAN ADVANCE ON PARIS AT CHATEAU THIERRY . . . U.S. TROOPS RETAKE LOST TERRITORY AT BELLEAU WOOD, 7,870 ARE KILLED . . . ALLIES REPULSE GERMAN ATTACK IN SECOND BATTLE OF MARNE, 85,000 U.S. TROOPS ARE ENGAGED . . . SUPREME COURT DECLARES 1916 FEDERAL CHILD LABOR LAW UNCONSTITUTIONAL . . . 250,000 U.S. TROOPS, WITH FRENCH, LAUNCH AISNE-MARNE OFFENSIVE, GERMANS ARE FORCED BACK OVER HINDENBURG LINE . . . CZAR AND FAMILY ARE MURDERED AT YEKATERINBURG . . . BRITISH AND ARAB FORCES TAKE DAMASCUS AND BEIRUT, TURKS SIGN ARMISTICE . . . SOVIET CONSTITUTION PROCLAIMS "DICTATORSHIP OF PROLETARIAT" UNDER LENIN . . . U.S. FORCES WIN MAJOR VICTORY AT ST. MIHIEL SALIENT . . . SOCIALIST DEBS IS SENTENCED TO TEN YEARS UNDER ESPIONAGE ACT . . . 1.2 MILLION U.S. TROOPS FIGHT AT MEUSE-ARGONNE, CUT GERMAN SUPPLY LINES AT SEDAN-MEZIERES . . . HUNGARY DECLARES INDEPENDENCE FROM AUSTRIA . . . GOP TAKES CONGRESS FROM DEMOCRATS . . . KAISER WILHELM ABDICATES, FLEES TO HOLLAND . . . AUSTRIAN EMPEROR KARL ABDICATES . . . U.S. AND BRITISH TROOPS OCCUPY GERMANY . . . GERMANY AND ALLIES SIGN ARMISTICE IN RAILROAD CAR AT COMPIEGNES . . . WILSON ANNOUNCES HE WILL ATTEND PEACE CONFERENCE

Quotes

"Would you rather be a colonel with an eagle on your shoulder, or a private with a chicken on your knee?"
— popular war song

"Mademoiselle from Armentiers, parlay-voo,
Madmoiselle from Armentieres, parlay-voo,
Mademoiselle from Armentiers,
She never did hear of underwear.
Hinky-dinky parlay voo."
— popular war song

"This is a people's war. . . . We have made partners of women in this war; shall we admit them only to a partnership of suffering and sacrifice and toil and not to a partnership of privilege and right?"
— Helen Gardner

"A general association of nations must be formed . . . for the purpose of affording mutual guarantees of political independence and territorial integrity to great and small [states] alike. It is the foundation of the whole diplomatic structure of a permanent peace."
— Frank Cobb and Walter Lippmann, explaining the 14th point of Wilson's peace policy

"The good Lord had only ten!"
— Georges Clemenceau, on hearing that Wilson's peace proposal has 14 points.

" 'Americans, you are surrounded on all sides. Surrender and you will be well treated.' Major Whittlesly did not hesitate a fraction of a second. 'Go to hell!' he shouted."
— Report on the "Lost Battalion," trapped by the Germans

"Save Her from the Hun" poster. "Force, Force to the utmost . . . righteous and triumphant Force . . . shall make Right the law of the world," says Wilson. *National Archives*.

"There is . . . a voice calling for . . . principle . . . which is . . . thrilling and . . . compelling. . . . It is the voice of the Russian people."
— Wilson, on the overthrow of Czar Nicholas

"The American people, who . . . [waged] a revolutionary war against feudal slavery, now find themselves . . . playing the role of hired thugs. . . . The workers of the world . . . applaud us for breaking the iron ring of imperialist chains."
— Lenin, "An Open Letter to American Workers"

Ads

For most of the war, fixed lines of trenches enclose a no-man's land where millions die and little ground is gained–or lost. *National Archives*.

New medical techniques, such as chest wound closure, help reduce mortality and morbidity, although new infections, like influenza, add to the death rate. *National Archives*.

Movies

Openings

Shoulder Arms (Charles Chaplin), Chaplin, Edna Purviance

Hearts of the World (D. W. Griffith), Lillian and Dorothy Gish, Robert Harron

Stella Maris (Marshall Neilan), Mary Pickford, Conway Tearle

A Dog's Life (Charles Chaplin), Chaplin, Albert Austin, Edna Purviance

A Modern Musketeer (Allan Dwan), Douglas Fairbanks

Men Who Have Made Love to Me (Arthur Berthelet), Mary MacLane

Old Wives for New (Cecil B. DeMille), Elliott Dexter, Wanda Hawley

Tarzan of the Apes (Scott Sidney), Elmo Lincoln, Enid Markey

The Kaiser, the Beast of Berlin (E. J. Clawson), Rupert Julian

Whispering Chorus (Cecil B. DeMille), Raymond Hatton, Kathlyn Williams

Carmen (Ernst Lubitsch), Pola Negri

A Dog's Life (Charles Chaplin), Chaplin, Edna Purviance

The Heart of Humanity (Allen Holobard), Dorothy Phillips, Erich von Stroheim

Prunella (Maurice Tourneur), Marguerite Clark

Blue Blazes Rawden (Thomas Ince), William S. Hart

First National gets Chaplin from Mutual and Pickford from Paramount; each negotiates a $1 million contract and a $150,000 signing bonus.

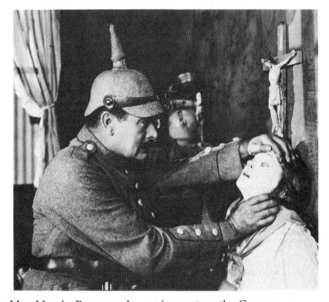

Mae Marsh. Propaganda movies portray the Germans as brutal and barbaric Huns. *National Archives*.

Motion Picture Hall of Fame contest winners

Douglas Fairbanks, Harold Lockwood, William S. Hart, Wallace Reid, Francis X. Bushman

Motion Picture magazine poll

Mary Pickford, Marguerite Clark, Douglas Fairbanks, Harold Lockwood, William S. Hart, Wallace Reid, Pearl White, Anita Stewart, Theda Bara, Francis X. Bushman

Popular Music ━━━━━━━━━━━━━━━━━━━━━━━━━

Hit Songs
"'Till Me Meet Again"
"I'd Like to See the Kaiser with a
    Lily in His Hand"
"Oh! How I Wish I Could Sleep
    until My Daddy Comes Home"
"If He Can Fight Like He Can
    Love, Good Night Germany!"
"Rose of No Man's Land"
"Singapore"
"I Found the End of the Rainbow"
"The Daughter of Rosie O'Grady"
"Ja-da"
"They Were All Out of Step but
    Jim"

"My Mammy"
"There's Life in the Old Dog Yet"

Representative Recordings:
"Rock-a-bye Your Baby with a
Dixie Melody" (Al Jolson); "I'm
Always Chasing Rainbows"
(Charles Harrison); "Oh! How I
Hate to Get Up in the Morning"
(Arthur Fields); "K-K-K-K-Ka-ty"
(Charles Hart); "After You've
Gone"/"A Good Man is Hard to
Find" (Marion Harris); "Ostrich
Walk" (Original Dixieland Jazz
Band)

Jazz
The Beale Street Palace Theater,
in Memphis, continues its Friday
night "Midnight Rambles,"
showcasing the best-known black
blues singers and jazz bands.
Three of the most popular singers,
Henry Burr, Albert Campbell, and
Marian Harris, gain enormous
popularity in the black community
with songs by Henry Creamer and
Turner Layton.

Theater ━━━━━━━━━━━━━━━━━━━━━━━━━━━━━

Broadway Openings

Plays
Misalliance (George Bernard Shaw), Mrs. Edmund
    Gurney
Lightnin' (Winchell Smith, Frank Bacon), Frank
    Bacon
Friendly Enemies (Samuel Shipman, Aaron
    Hoffman), Mathilde Cottrelly
Three Faces East (Anthony Paul Kelly), Frank
    Westerton
Daddies (John Hobble), Jeanne Eagels, George
    Abbott
Forever After (Owen Davis), Alice Brady, Conrad
    Nagel
Redemption (Leo Tolstoy), John Barrymore, Thomas
    Mitchell
Sleeping Partners (Sacha Guitry), H. B. Warner,
    Irene Bordoni
The Better 'Ole (Capt. Bruce Bairnsfather, Capt.
    Arthur Elliott), Charles Coburn, Mrs. Charles
    Coburn
Three Wise Fools (Austin Strong), Harry Davenport
The Betrothal (Maurice Maeterlinck), Reggie
    Sheffield
Dear Brutus (J. M. Barrie), William Gillette, Helen
    Hayes
East is West (Samuel Shipman, John B. Hymer), Fay
    Bainter, Frank Kemble Cooper

Musicals
O, Lady! O, Lady! (Jerome Kern, P. G. Wodehouse),
    Vivienne Segal

Sinbad (Sigmund Romberg, Harold Atteridge), Al
    Jolson
The Passing Show (Sigmund Romberg, Harold
    Atteridge), Willie and Eugene Howard, Fred and
    Adele Astaire, Charles Ruggles, Frank Fay
Ziegfeld Follies (Louis A. Hirsch, Gene Buck), Eddie
    Cantor, Will Rogers, Marilyn Miller, W. C.
    Fields
Yip Yip Yaphank (Irving Berlin), 350 soldiers from
    Camp Upton, N.Y.
Sometime (Rudolf Friml, Rida Johnson Young), Mae
    West, Ed Wynn
Everything (Irving Berlin, John Philip Sousa, John
    Golden), Belle Story, Houdini, De Wolf Hopper

Classics On and Off Broadway
Hamlet, Macbeth, Walter Hampden; *Julius Caesar,*
Tyrone Power, Hampden; *Elektra,* Margaret Anglin;
The Moon of the Caribees (O'Neill); *As You Like It;*
Laurette Taylor in Scenes from Shakespeare;
Nazimova, Lionel Atwill: *A Doll's House, Hedda
Gabler; 'Ile* (O'Neill); *A Woman's Honor* (Glaspell);
An Ideal Husband (Wilde)

Pulitzer Prize
Why Marry?, Jesse Lynch Williams

Classical Music

Compositions
Charles Ruggles, *Mood*
Charles Griffes, *Poem for Flute and Orchestra*, Piano Sonata
Henry Hadley, *Silhouettes*, Suite in E Flat
Henry Cowell, Symphony no. 1
Deems Taylor, *Through the Looking Glass*

Important Events
Prokofiev makes his American debut in Chicago; he plays his first Piano Concerto and conducts his Scythian suite *Ala and Lilli*. In New York, he plays his Sonata for Piano, no. 2. Caruso, Heifetz, and Rachmaninoff give a concert for the Red Cross at Carnegie Hall. The Cleveland Symphony Orchestra forms; the Paris Conservatory Orchestra, with conductor André Messager, tours.

New Appointments [Major Conductors]: Eugène Ysaye (Cincinnati), Henry Rabaud (Boston), Ossip Gabrilowitsch (Detroit), Nicolai Sokoloff (Cleveland)

Debut: Alfred Cortot. Refugee Leopold Auer, 72, makes his U.S. debut at Carnegie Hall; in the audience are his former students Heifetz, Zimbalist, and Elman.

First Performances
Charles Tomlinson Griffes, *Notturno, The White Peacock, Clouds, Bacchanale* (Philadelphia); John Powell, *Black Rhapsody* (New York); Henry Gilbert, *Dance in Place Congo* (New York); Stravinsky, *The Faun and the Shepherdess* (New York); Glière, Third Symphony (Chicago); Sowerby, *Set of Four* (Chicago); Bloch, Symphony in C sharp minor (New York); Henry Hadley, *Othello Overture* (Philadelphia)

Opera

Metropolitan: Enrico Caruso, Giuseppe De Luca, Rosa Ponselle (debut), *La Forza del Destino;* Luigi Montesanto, Giulio Crimi, Geraldine Farrar, Claudia Muzio, *Il Trittico: Il Tabarro, Suor Angelica, Gianni Schicchi* (Puccini, premiere); Maria Barrientos, Adamo Didur, *Le Coq d'Or* (premiere); Sophie Braslau, Marie Sundelius, Paul Althouse, *Shanewis* (premiere, Charles Wakefield Cadman); Hipolito Lazaro (debut), *Rigoletto*

Chicago: Alexandro Dolci, *La Gioconda*

Music Notes
Rachmaninoff, 45, arrives in the U.S. nearly penniless, his money and property confiscated by the Russian revolutionists; he rejects three conductorial offers to pursue the career of a virtuoso; • Patriotic lectures and benefits continue at Carnegie Hall: Margarete Matzenauer sings with the hall decorated inside and out with banners, posters, and photos of soldiers in battle; one sign says: "These boys are giving their lives. Will you lend your quarters?" • Sensing the deep anti-German sentiment in the country, Fritz Kreisler voluntarily cancels all engagements and remains in isolation at his home • Stokowski ("Stokie"), already known for his aggressive programming (Stravinsky, Varèse, Mahler), initiates a new conductorial style to draw attention to the podium—with new lighting techniques and his own stage flair • The Boston Symphony Orchestra performs in New York, despite demonstrations to remove conductor Karl Muck; Muck is later arrested as an enemy alien and interned at Fort Oglethorp, in Georgia.

General Pershing (left), leader of the American Expeditionary Force; Eddie Rickenbacher (right), who shoots down 26 planes in 7 months. *National Archives.*

Major entertainers like Douglas Fairbanks lead huge Liberty Loan rallies; they collect $23 billion to fund the war effort. *National Archives.*

Art

Painting

Stanton Macdonald Wright, *Synchromy in Blue-Green*

Charles Sheeler, *Barn Abstraction*

Charles Demuth, *Acrobats*

Max Weber, *Interior with Figure*

Katherine S. Dreier, *Abstract Portrait of Marcel Duchamp*

Charles Burchfield, *The First Hepaticas*

Arthur B. Davies, *The Wine Press*

Sculpture

Elie Nadelman, *Hostess*

Morton L. Schamberg, *God*

Gaston Lachaise, *The Peacocks, Dancing Figure*

William Zorach, *Child Learning to Walk*

Attilo Piccirilli, *Study of a Head*

Albert Laessle, *Victory*

Architecture

People's Savings and Loan Association Bank, Sidney, Ohio (Louis Sullivan)

Bush Terminal building, New York (Helmle & Corbett)

Woodbury County Courthouse, Sioux City, Iowa (Purcell & Elmslie)

St. Bartholomew's Church, New York (Cram, Goodhue & Ferguson)

Boston seamstresses demonstrate their patriotic pride. *Smithsonian Institution.*

Important Exhibitions

Museums

New York: *Metropolitan:* Czechoslovakian art; Drawings of the Venetian and Bolognese schools; Modern manufactured objects; American silver; Ryder. *Art Alliance:* "Handicrafts of Many Nations"

Washington, D.C.: "Twenty-four New European Masterpieces," including works by Titian, Rubens, Gainsborough, and Hogarth

Chicago: "Paintings and Sculpture by Foreign Born Citizens and their Children"

Cleveland: "Homelands Exhibition" of foreign-born residents of Cleveland

Toledo: Winslow Homer, John Singer Sargent; oils by Elizabeth W. Roberts; sculpture by Gertrude V. Whitney

Art Briefs

After the war, New York artists Arthur Crisp, Frederick Waugh, and Charles S. Chapman paint "Victory Way," a block-long frieze, to mark the starting point of victory parades • Louis Comfort Tiffany establishes a foundation-retreat at his Oyster Bay, New York, home for artists "to find themselves" • Museums begin to sponsor weekend concerts.

The Red Cross, Nobel Peace laureate of 1917. *National Archives.*

Books

Fiction

Critics' Choice
My Antonia, Willa Cather
Edgewater People, Mary E. Wilkins Freeman
The Flower of the Chapdelaines, George Washington Cable
Lovers of Louisiana (Today), George Washington Cable
Free and Other Stories, Theodore Dreiser
Birth, Zona Gale
Treat 'Em Rough, Ring Lardner

Best-Sellers
The U.P. Trail, Zane Grey
The Tree of Heaven, Mary Sinclair
The Amazing Interlude, Mary Roberts Rinehart
Dere Mable, Edward Streeter
Oh Money! Money! Edward H. Porter
Greatheart, Ethel M. Dell
The Major, Ralph Connor

Nonfiction

Critics' Choice
The Profits of Religion, Upton Sinclair
The Changing Status of Negro Labor, James Weldon Johnson
In Defense of Women, H. L. Mencken
Pavannes and Divisions, Ezra Pound
And They Thought We Wouldn't Fight, Floyd Gibbons
In Our First Year of War, Woodrow Wilson
Leaders and Leadership, Van Wyck Brooks
🔊 *Eminent Victorians*, Lytton Strachey
🔊 *Gravitation and the Principle of Relativity*, A. S. Eddington

Best-Sellers
Rhymes of a Red Cross Man, Robert W. Service
Treasury of War Poetry, G. H. Clark
With the Colors, Everard J. Appleton
Recollections, Viscount Morley
Laugh and Live, Douglas Fairbanks
Mark Twain's Letters, ed. Albert Bigelow Paine
Adventures and Letters of Richard Harding Davis, Richard Harding Davis
Over Here, Edward Guest

Best-Sellers: War Books
My Four Years in Germany, James W. Gerard
The Glory of the Trenches, Coningsby Dawson
Over the Top, Arthur Guy Empey
A Minstrel in France, Harry Lauder
Private Peat, Harold R. Peat
Outwitting the Hun, Lieut. Pat O'Brien
Face to Face with Kaiserism, James W. Gerard

Poetry
Stephen Vincent Benét, *Young Adventure*
Amy Lowell, *Can Grande's Castle*
Edgar Lee Masters, *Toward the Gulf*
Conrad Aiken, *The Charnal Rose, Senlin: A Biography, and Other Poems*
🔊 Gerard Manley Hopkins (posthumous), *Poems*

Pulitzer Prizes
The Magnificent Ambersons, Booth Tarkington (novel)
Old Road to Paradise, Margaret Widdemer (U.S. history)
The Education of Henry Adams, Henry Adams (biography)
Corn Huskers, Carl Sandburg (poetry)

Science and Technology

Excavations in Babylonia are begun by Leonard Woolley.

Harlow Shapley discovers the size of the Milky Way; he places the solar system near its edge.

Alcohol is distilled from cactus for munitions.

Closing chest wounds is found to reduce mortality rates by 48 percent.

H. Abraham and E. Bloch invent the "electronic swing," or multibrator circuit, which induces the bouncing of waves between two unstable points.

The radio crystal oscillator is developed.

🔊 The first mass spectrograph, built by Francis Aston, indicates that certain atomic elements exist in different forms with different masses.

🔊 Emmy Noether proposes that every symmetry in physics implies a conservation principle and vice versa.

The improved machine gun becomes a major weapon in causing massive loss of life. *National Archives.*

Sports

Baseball

Babe Ruth wins two World Series games for Boston, including a 1–0 shutout in the opener. He pitches 16 consecutive scoreless innings to extend his World Series record to 29 (13 in 1916). He also ties the AL homer lead with 11.

Due to the war, play ends on Sept. 1.

The players' request for the World Series winner's minimum of $1,800 and of the loser's of $1,200 is turned down. The former is $1,102, an all-time low.

Champions

Batting	
Zachary Wheat (Brooklyn, NL), .335	Walter Johnson (Washington), 23–13
Tyrus R. Cobb (Detroit, AL), .382	*Home runs* Clifford Cravath (Philadelphia, NL), 12
Pitching C. R. Hendrix (Chicago, NL), 20–7	

Football

Knute Rockne becomes coach at Notre Dame.

College All-Americans: Paul Robeson (E), Rutgers; Thomas Davies (H), Pittsburgh; Ashel Day (C), Georgia Tech

Rose Bowl (Jan. 1, 1919): Great Lakes Naval Training Station 17–Mare Island Marines 0

Other Sports

Boxing: Heavyweight contender Jack Dempsey KOs Carl Morris in 14 seconds; Fred Fulton in 18 seconds.

Golf: Bobby Jones, 15, wins the Southern Amateur championship.

Winners

World Series Boston (AL) 4 Chicago (NL) 2	*Stanley Cup* Toronto
College Football Pittsburgh	*U.S. Tennis Open* Men: R. Lindley Murray Women: Molla Bjurstedt
College Basketball Syracuse	*USGA Open* No competition, due to war
Player of the Year William Chandler, Wisconsin	*Kentucky Derby* Exterminator (Willie Knapp, jockey)

Fashion

The last vestiges of fashion preoccupation end with the increased activism of the suffragettes, women's increased voluntarism during the war, and the suspension of traditional social life (with men in the military). The inevitable mourning for the injured and dead that accompanies war has no small effect on the current indifference to fashion. Clothing becomes strikingly plain and austere. With the ban on German imports and Germany the chief exporter of clothing dyes, styles are limited to blue, black, and brown. To save leather, shorter boots are worn with skirts that are once again lengthened. Fabric shortages still permit 4.5 yards of cloth for a suit, dress, or coat, but wool is scarce. A new standardization of attire becomes noticeable, as women recycle their outfits and begin mixing separates. The once very stylish woman changes her dress only once or twice a day.

High-fashion notes: Cartier's "tank" watch (a tribute to the American Tank Corps); Jean Patou's innovative designer labels on the exterior of his clothing—a "J" or "P" on his pants pocket.

Continuing traditions—even in time of war.
Smithsonian Institution.

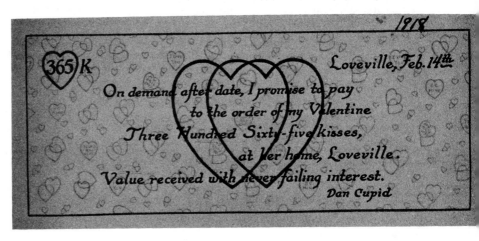

Kaleidoscope

- Americans march into battle bedecked with flowers strewn by the French.
- An American soldier gives the Marne front its name when he tells a frightened peasant "Pas finie."
- Taxes are raised 250 percent to meet war costs; 80 percent of tax revenue comes from large incomes, taxed at a 77 percent rate.
- New techniques of mine-laying are devised by Americans to help combat German submarine warfare.
- The "convoy system"—groups of ships protected by destroyers—carries 911,047 soldiers to France; transport of material increases from 94,000 pounds to 3.25 tons.
- The third Liberty Loan campaign ends with $4.2 billion from 17 million subscribers; a fourth campaign for $6 billion begins.
- Secretary of War Newton Baker orders that conscientious objectors be given leave from the service; they must work on farms without pay.
- Daylight Savings Time is instituted to permit more day light for war production.
- Women are increasingly employed in the manufacture of shells and explosives; railroad employment of women triples to over 100,000.
- Of the 240 American flyers in the Lafayette Esquadrille, 60 die in action.
- TR's youngest son, Quentin, is shot down and killed during the war; Germans bury him with full honors.
- The worldwide "Spanish" flu strikes 21.64 million; 25 percent of all Americans fall ill; 500,000 die, as emergency tents go up through the nation after hospitals are filled; store workers and ordinary citizens wear masks to avoid contagion.
- Dancer Vernon Castle, who served in the Royal Air Force, is killed in a wartime plane crash in Fort Worth, Texas.
- The U.S. Post Office burns issues of the *Little Review* containing installments of James Joyce's *Ulysses.*
- Walter Hampden is hailed as the best Hamlet since Edward Booth.
- Vaudeville peaks with 25,000 performances at 4,000 theaters.
- A popular parody of "K-K-K-Ka-ty" in the Army is directed to the typhoid carrier: "C-C-C-Coo-Tie, Horrible Cootie, You're the Only B-B-B-Bug that I Abhor."
- Camels are the soldiers' favorite cigarette.
- N.J. passes an "Anti-Loafing Law," requiring that all able-bodied males be regularly employed.
- After local draft boards are told to enforce the "Work or Fight" laws, 653 are arrested in a "slacker" and alien roundup at Coney Island, New York.
- The Wisconsin State Senate condemns Robert La Follette's antiwar attitude.
- Loans to Allies in the first year of war total $5.2 billion.
- The president declares May 30th (Decoration Day) a day of public humiliation, prayer, and fasting.
- The Post Office announces that that 5.5 tons of letter mail have been delivered during the first month of air mail service between New York, Philadelphia, and Washington D.C.; the average plane speed is 70 mph.

Thousands cheer in Philadelphia when the armistice is announced, at the eleventh hour, on the eleventh day of the eleventh month. *National Archives.*

- A German-owned steel plant near Pittsburgh is seized; 11 officers are arrested as enemy aliens.
- Movie producer Robert Goldstein is sentenced to three years in prison for portraying British soldiers in an attack against Americans during the American Revolution.
- Under the new war rules, restaurants exclude toast as garniture, additional bread after the first course, and double cream or creme deluxe; all food waste is saved to feed animals.
- Citizens of Berlin, N.H. vote to rename their city.
- Ohio, Florida, Minnesota, Wyoming, and Virginia vote for prohibition; California, Missouri, and Minnesota vote against it.
- Mississippi is the last state to pass a mandatory school attendance law.
- In Madison Square Garden 12,000 Reds send fraternal greetings to German socialists and are attacked by groups of soldiers and sailors who beat anyone wearing the Red emblem.
- The death sentence of Thomas Mooney for the killing of ten during a Preparedness Day parade in San Francisco is commuted from hanging to life.
- More than 5,000 Wobblies (IWW) are arrested by the end of the year.
- After the Armistice, 150 tons of paper and ticker tape decorate the New York City parade; shops are posted with signs like "Closed for the Kaiser's Funeral."
- Sailing to Europe to represent America at the Versailles Peace Conference, Wilson states his hope to prevent "a peace of loot or spoliation" and notes: "The plot is thickening."

First Appearances: pop-up toaster, three-color traffic lights (N.Y.), Ronzoni, Contadina canned tomato soup, *New York Times* home delivery, "Ripley's Believe It Or Not" *(New York Globe), Stars and Stripes,* Raggedy Ann doll, Celanese Corp., Rinso, Kotex ("Celucotton"), Berkshire Music Festival (Pittsfield, Mass.), woman district attorney (Annette Adams)

1919

Above: Alvin York, originally
denied conscientious objector
status, captures 132 Gemans
virtually singlehandedly. *National Archives.*

Deaths

Andrew Carnegie, Henry
Clay Frick, Ernst Haeckel,
A. D. Juilliard, Sir William
Osler, Auguste Renoir,
Theodore Roosevelt, F. W.
Woolworth

In the News

PARIS PEACE CONFERENCE OPENS AT VERSAILLES, WILSON
PRESENTS LEAGUE OF NATIONS CONVENANT . . . PROHIBITION
AMENDMENT IS RATIFIED BY STATES . . . 37,000 METAL
WORKERS STRIKE IN SEATTLE . . . COMMUNIST REVOLTS
OCCUR IN NUMEROUS GERMAN CITIES . . . COMMUNIST THIRD
INTERNATIONAL PROCLAIMS DOCTRINE OF WORLD
REVOLUTION . . . COMMUNIST DICTATORSHIP TAKES OVER
HUNGARY, RUMANIANS INVADE TRANSYLVANIA, HUNGARY . . .
SUPREME COURT UPHOLDS DEBS'S CONVICTION . . . GENEVA IS
SELECTED FOR LEAGUE OF NATIONS HEADQUARTERS . . .
150,000 STRIKE IN CLEVELAND . . . GURKA TROOPS FIRE ON
UNARMED PROTESTERS LED BY GANDHI AT AMRITSAR, INDIA,
379 ARE KILLED . . . GREEKS INVADE TURKEY AT SMYRNA,
ALLIES CONCUR, MUSTAFA KEMAL ORGANIZES RESISTANCE
. . . NEW GERMAN CABINET AGREES TO ALLIED PEACE
DEMANDS . . . 500,000 STRIKE IN CHICAGO, TROOPS SUPPRESS
RIOTING, 36 DIE . . . GERMANY ACCEPTS "WAR GUILT" AND
REPARATIONS, DEMILITARIZES RHINELAND, CEDES ALSACE-
LORRAINE, SAAR, POSEN, WEST PRUSSIA . . . 300,000 WORKERS
STRIKE IN N.Y.C. . . . VERSAILLES TREATY GOES TO SENATE
FOR RATIFICATION, SEN. HENRY CABOT LODGE (R-MASS.)
LEADS RESISTANCE TO LEAGUE . . . GOV. CALVIN COOLIDGE
SUPPRESSES POLICE STRIKE IN BOSTON . . . WILSON SUFFERS
STROKE WHILE ON TOUR PROMOTING LEAGUE . . . AUSTRIA-
HUNGARY DIVIDES INTO SEPARATE NATIONS . . . SEVERE
FAMINE AFFLICTS GERMANY AND CENTRAL EUROPE . . .
ITALIAN POET GABRIELLE D'ANNUNZIO SEIZES FIUME, SETS
UP GOVERNMENT . . . VOLSTEAD ACT TO ENFORCE
PROHIBITION AMENDMENT PASSES OVER WILSON VETO . . .
SENATE FAILS TO RATIFY PEACE TREATY, 55–39.

Quotes

"My clients are the children; my clients are the next generation."
— Wilson, in his Pueblo, Colorado speech advocating the League, during which he suffers a stroke

"Who is to control this tribunal? . . . Are Costa Rica, Nicaragua, and Bulgaria to . . . determine the size of our Army and Navy?"
— Sen. Hiram Borah (R-Idaho), on the League

"I have been over into the future, and it works."
— Lincoln Steffens, after his trip to Russia

"On diplomatic matters, we may assume the president knows more than ordinary persons, but on the question of the saloon, a mother of a drunken son knows more than he does."
— William Jennings Bryan, on Wilson's veto of the Volstead Act

"When a nation is at war, many things that might be said in time of peace are such a hindrance to its effort that their utterance will not be endured so long as men fight and no court could regard them as protected by Constitutional right."
— Justice Oliver Wendell Holmes, upholding the Sedition Act

"There is no right to strike against the public safety by anybody, anywhere, anytime."
— Calvin Coolidge to Samuel Gompers, on the Boston police strike

Q: "Have there been any revolutions in this country?
A: "Yes."
Q: "When?"
A: "1812."
Q: "Any other time?"
A: "I don't know of any others."
Q: "Do you know of any traitors?"
A: "No."
Q: "Who was Benedict Arnold?"
A: "He was a writer, I guess."
Q: "You must be thinking of Arnold Bennett."
— Henry Ford, testimony in a libel suit when accused of being an "ignorant idealist"

Ads

400,000 blacks served in the war; above, a group decorated with the Croix de Guerre. *National Archives.*

The Council of Four at the Versailles Peace Conference: David Lloyd George, Georges Clemenceau, Vittorio Orlando, Woodrow Wilson. *Library of Congress.*

Movies

Openings

Broken Blossoms (D. W. Griffin), Lillian Gish,
    Richard Barthelmess
Blind Husbands (Erich von Stroheim), von Stroheim
His Majesty the American (Joseph Henaberry),
    Douglas Fairbanks
Miracle Man (George Loane Tucker), Tom Meighan,
    Lon Chaney
True Heart Susie (D. W. Griffith), Lillian Gish,
    Robert Harron
Anne of Green Gables (William Desmond Taylor),
    Mary Miles Minter
Daddy Long Legs (Marshall Neilan), Mary Pickford
Don't Change Your Husband (Cecil B. DeMille),
    Gloria Swanson
The Turn in the Road (King Vidor), Lloyd Hughes,
    Helen Eddy
Male and Female (Cecil B. DeMille), Gloria Swanson
The Red Lantern (June Mathis), Alla Nazimova
A Romance of Happy Valley (D. W. Griffith), Lillian
    Gish, Robert Harron

D. W. Griffith, Mary Pickford, Douglas Fairbanks, and Charles Chaplin form United Artists for complete artistic freedom and higher profits. Older studios such as Biograph, Edison, Lubin, Triangle, Essanay, and Thanhouser cease to exist. Famous Players-Lasky builds major studios in Astoria, Long Island. W. H. Hearst founds Cosmopolitan Pictures.

Top Box-Office Stars

Douglas Fairbanks, Mary Pickford, Constance and Norma Talmadge, Mary Fuller, Blanche Sweet, Billy Quirk, Clara Kimball Young, Maurice Costello

After the war, massive inflation destroys the nation's sense of shared sacrifice; workers everywhere strike for higher wages to counter rapidly rising prices. *Courtesy Amalgamated Clothing and Textile Workers Union.*

Popular Music

Hit Songs
"Swanee"
"Baby, Won't You Please Come Home?"
"Indian Summer"
"My Buddies"
"In My Sweet Little Alice Blue Gown"
"Dear Old Sue"
"Daddy Long-Legs"
"Rose of Washington Square"
"When My Baby Smiles at Me"
"Oh, What a Pal Was Mary"
"The World is Waiting for the Sunrise"
"Let the Rest of the World Go By"
"When the Moon Shines on the Moonshine"
"That Revolutionary Rag"

Representative Recordings: "A Pretty Girl is Like a Melody" (John Steel); "I'm Forever Blowing Bubbles" (Selvin's Novelty Orchestra); "How Ya Gonna Keep 'Em Down on the Farm?" (Nora Bayes); "You Ain't Heard Nothing Yet" (Al Jolson); "Mandy" (Van & Schenck); "The Alcoholic Blues" (Lousiana Five); "Dardanella" (Ben Selvin Orchestra)

Jazz and Other Notes
Chris Smith, who is black, and Jimmy Durante, who is white, collaborate in a vaudeville routine. Noble Sissle and Eubie Blake form an act for the vaudeville circuit; since only one black set is permitted per show, they turn their attention to Broadway. Several black-owned publishing and recording companies are launched.

Theater

Broadway Openings

Plays
John Ferguson (St. John Ervine), Augustin Duncan, Dudley Digges
Mis' Nelly of N'Orleans (Laurence Eyre), Mrs. Minnie Maddern Fiske
Hobohemia (Sinclair Lewis), Helen Westley
Up in Mabel's Room (Wilson Collison, Otto Harbach), Hazel Dawn, Enid Markey
The Jest (Sem Benelli), John Barrymore, Lionel Barrymore, Gilda Varesi
Augustus Does His Bit (George Bernard Shaw), Norman Trevor
Abraham Lincoln (John Drinkwater), Frank McGlynn
Déclassée (Zoe Atkins), Ethel Barrymore
The Fall and Rise of Susan Lenox (George V. Hobart), Alma Tell
Adam and Eva (Guy Bolton, George Middleton), Ruth Shepley, Otto Kruger
The Gold Diggers (Avery Hopwood), Ina Clare, Ruth Terry
Clarence (Booth Tarkington), Alfred Lunt

Musicals
The Velvet Lady (Victor Herbert, Henry Blossom), Fay Marbe, Alfred Gerrard, Ernest Torrence
[George White's] Scandals (Richard Whiting, Arthur Jackson), Ann Pennington, George White
Ziegfeld Follies (Irving Berlin), Marilyn Miller, Eddie Cantor, Bert Williams, Eddie Dowling, Van and Schenck
Ziegfeld's Midnight Frolics (Dave Stamper, Gene Buck), Fannie Brice, Ted Lewis, W. C. Fields, Chick Sale
Apple Blossoms (Victor Jacobi, Fritz Kreisler, William Le Baron), Fred and Adele Astaire
The Passing Show (Jean Schwartz, Sigmund Romberg, Harold Atteridge), Blanche Ring, Avon Comedy Four, Charles Winninger
Buddies (B. C. Hilliam), Donald Brian, Peggy Wood, Roland Young
Irene (Harry Tierney, Joseph McCarthy), Edith Day
La, La, Lucille (George Gershwin, Arthur Jackson), Janet Velie, Jack E. Hazzard

Classics and Revivals On and Off Broadway
Ghosts; Aria Da Capo (Edna St. Vincent Millay); *The Rise of Silas Lapham* (Lillian Sakine); E. H. Sothern, Julia Marlowe: *Hamlet, The Taming of the Shrew, Twelfth Night*

Pulitzer Prize
No prize is awarded.

Classical Music

Compositions
Louis Gruenberg, *Hill of Dreams for Orchestra, The Enchanted Isle*

Daniel Gregory Mason, *String Quartet on Negro Themes*, Prelude and Fugue for Piano and Orchestra

Leo Sowerby, Trio for Flute, Viola, and Piano

Frederick Converse, Symphony no. 2, *The Answer of the Stars*

Howard Hanson, *Symphonic Rhapsody*

Important Events
The New Symphony, under Edgard Varèse, debuts with a concert of Debussy and Bartok. The Los Angeles Philharmonic forms under Walter Henry Rothwell. The Eastman and University of Iowa schools of music are founded.

Notable Performances: Rachmaninoff plays the first performance of his First Piano Concerto with the Russian Symphony Orchestra. The orchestra also premieres Prokofieff's *Classical Symphony* from manuscript. Artur Rubinstein is once again rejected by New York audiences as a pianist of "charm and technical finesse," yet "a minimalist."

New Appointment: Pierre Monteux (Boston Symphony)

Debuts: Benno Moiseiwitsch, Winifred Christie

First Performances
Chadwick, *The Angel of Death* (New York, concert in memory of Theodore Roosevelt); Rubin Goldmark, *Requiem* (New York, for the anniversary of the *Gettysburg Address*); Dvorak, Third Symphony (New York); Respighi, *Fountains of Rome* (New York); Stock, *March and Hymn to Democracy* (Chicago); Charles T. Griffes, *The White Peacock* (Philadelphia), *The Pleasure Dome of Kubla Khan* (Boston); *Poems for Flute and Orchestra* (New York); John Alden Carpenter, *The Birthday of the Infanta* (Chicago); Arthur Farwell, *Chant of Victory* (Berkeley, Calif.); D'Indy, Third Symphony (New York); Turina, *La Procession del Racio* (New York)

Opera

Metropolitan: Rosa Ponselle, *The Legend* (J. C. Breil, premiere); Florence Easton, Morgan Kingston, *The Temple Dancer* (John Adam Hugo); Geraldine Farrar, *La Reine Fiamette* (Leroux)

St. Louis Municipal Opera (*debut*): Robin Hood

Chicago: Mary Garden, *Gismonda* (Henri Février, premiere); Rosa Raisa, Virgilio Lazzari, *La Nava* (Montemezzi, premiere, with the composer conducting)

Music Notes
With German influence declining and Franco-Russian influence increasing, Tchaikovsky dominates as much as 20% of concert programming; Stravinsky, Debussy, D'Indy, and Franck also gain more concert exposure • While recuperating from a heart attack, Charles Ives resolves that despite public indifference to his work, it should be published; he prints and distributes *The Concord Sonata* • Wanda Landowska opens a school in Paris for the study of early music.

A Victory Liberty Loan poster displaying a list of "Americans All." *National Archives.*

Art _____

Painting

Charles Demuth, *Acrobats*

John Covert, *Ex Act, Brass Band*

John Marin, *Tree Forms, Stonington, Maine*

Man Ray, *Admiration of the Orchestrelle for the Cinematograph*

Marcel Duchamp, *L.H.O.O.Q*

Georgia O'Keeffe, *Red and Orange Streak, Black Spot, No. 2*

Sculpture

Elie Nadelman, *Orchestra Conductor*

Edward Clark Potter, *Sleeping Infant Faun*

Daniel Chester French, *Memory*

John Storrs, *Study for Walt Whitman Monument*

Gertrude Vanderbilt Whitney, bas relief for Thomas Hastings' Victory Arch, Madison Square Garden, New York

Architecture

Hallidie building, San Francisco (Willis Polk)

Broad Street Station, Richmond, Virginia (John Russell Pope)

Gillette Castle, near East Haddam, Conn. (William Hooker Gillette)

[Farmer's Merchant] Union Bank, Columbus, Wis. (Louis H. Sullivan)

The Lower East Side, New York City. Home to thousands of Jewish immigrants, its street boundaries often correspond to national origins. *Smithsonian Institution.*

Important Exhibitions

Museums

New York: *Metropolitan:* Courbet centenary; "Plants and Objects Showing Plant Motifs"; Chinese ancestral portraits; Ingres; Drawings of children in the elementary schools of Paris during the war; Modern French art: Renoir, Monet, Besnard, Cottet, Roussel, Bonnard, Vallotton

Washington: *National:* Titian, Reynolds, Hogarth, Raeburn, Rommney. *Smithsonian:* Charles J. Taylor, A. F. Bunner, Paul Manship, Charles H. Woodbury, Anders Zorn, Charles A. Platt

Boston: Semi-centennial celebration: Modern French Art; "Laces and Tapestries" (on loan)

Providence: "Portraits of Distinctive Young Americans Who Sacrificed their Lives in the War"; Photos of war memorials

Cincinnati: Silverwork by Elizabeth Copeland; Frank Brangwyn; Modern Chinese paintings and calligraphy; Robert Henri, J. Alden Weir, John Twachtman

Art Briefs

"The Bauhaus," directed by Walter Gropius, attracts wide interest; its emphasis is on design in the arts utilizing industrial age materials • Major sales include Renoir's *Female Portrait Sketches,* $40–$50; *Woman Bathing,* $165; *Woman Glancing over her Shoulder,* $200; and *La Seine à Argenteuil,* $11,700.

Dance _____

Los Angeles: *Juinar of the Sea* (Louis Horst, Ted Shawn)

Books

Fiction

Critics' Choice
Winesburg, Ohio, Sherwood Anderson
Jurgen, James Branch Cabell
Java Head, Joseph Hergesheimer
On the Makaloa Mat, Jack London (posthumous)
Free Air, Sinclair Lewis
All the Brothers Were Valiant, Ben Ames Williams
Linda Condon, Joseph Hergesheimer

Best-Sellers
The Four Horsemen of the Apocalypse, V. Blasco Ibanez
The Arrow of Gold, Joseph Conrad
The Desert of Wheat, Zane Grey
Dangerous Days, Mary Roberts Rinehart
The Sky Pilot in No Man's Land, Ralph Connor
The Re-Creation of Brian Kent, Harold Bell Wright
Dawn, Gene Stratton Porter
The Tin Soldier, Temple Bailey
Christopher and Columbus, "Elizabeth"
In Secret, Robert W. Chambers

Nonfiction

Critics' Choice
Ten Days that Shook the World, John Reed
Rousseau and Romanticism, Irving Babbitt
Our America, Waldo Frank
Untimely Papers, Randolph Bourne
The Degradation of the Democratic Dogma, Brooks Adams and Henry Adams
The American Language, H. L. Mencken
The Chicago Race Riots, July 1919, Carl Sandburg
Stabilizing the Dollar in Purchasing Power, Irving Fisher
Prejudices, H. L. Mencken
Africa in the World Democracy, James Weldon Johnson, with Horace M. Kallen
🔊 *The Economic Consequences of the Peace*, J. M. Keynes

Best-Sellers
The Education of Henry Adams, Henry Adams
The Years Between, Rudyard Kipling

Belgium, Brand Whitlock
The Seven Purposes, Margaret Cameron
In Flanders Fields, John McCrae
Bolshevism, John Spargo

Poetry
T. S. Eliot, *Poems*
Ezra Pound, *Quia Pauper Amavi, The Fourth Canto*
Sara Teasdale, *Vignettes of Italy*
John Crowe Ransom, *Poems about God*
Amy Lowell, *Pictures of the Floating World*
Louis Untermeyer, ed., *Modern American Poetry*
🔊 W. B. Yeats, *The Wild Swans at Coole*

Pulitzer Prizes
The War with Mexico, Justin H. Smith (U.S. history)
The Life of John Marshall, Albert J. Beveridge (biography)

Science and Technology

Robert Goddard proposes using rockets to send a vehicle to the moon.
Irving Langmuir postulates the theory of atomic covalent bonding.
The first nonstop transatlantic flight is made by J. W. Alcock and A. Whitten (Newfoundland to Ireland) in 16 hours, 27 minutes.
W. H. Eccles and F. W. Jordan invent the "flip-flop" electronic switching circuit, which aids rapid electronic counting.

The crystal microphone, using the peizo-electric principle and permitting high-quality sound at low cost, is produced.
John Watson's *Psychology From the Standpoint of a Behaviorist* advocates behavioral conditioning research and application.
🔊 A. S. Eddington confirms Einstein's theory of relativity during a total solar eclipse.
🔊 Ernest Rutherford reports the first man-made atomic fission.

Sports

Baseball

Ty Cobb wins his 12th batting title.

The World Series is changed to 5 of 9.

Poor play by the heavily favored Chicago White Sox leads to rumors of a "fix," but no proof emerges during the year.

Babe Ruth hits a major league record of 29 homers.

Champions

Batting	Pitching
Edd Roush (Cincinnati, NL), .321	Dutch Reuther (Cincinnati, NL), 19–6
Tyrus R. Cobb (Detroit, AL), .384	Ed Cicotte (Chicago, AL), 29–7
	Home runs
	Babe Ruth (Boston, AL) 29

Football

College All-Americans: Edward Casey (H), Harvard; L. A. Alexander (G), Syracuse; Charles Harley (H), Ohio State

Rose Bowl (Jan. 1, 1920): Harvard 7-Oregon 6

Other Sports

Boxing: Jack Dempsey, "the Manassa Mauler," knocks down champion Jess Willard 7 times in the 1st, and wins on a TKO in the 3rd at Toledo to gain the heavyweight title. Dempsey wins four more title bouts and one non-title fight, grossing over $1 million from each.

Hockey: The Stanley Cup is called off after one player dies and many are stricken by the flu; Seattle and Montreal were tied 2 games each.

Horse Racing: Sir Barton, ridden by Johny Loftus, is the first to win the Triple Crown (Kentucky Derby, Preakness, Belmont).

Ty Cobb (left) and Shoeless Joe Jackson, the decade's two greatest hitters. *Library of Congress.*

Golf: The PGA tournament is resumed and won by James Barnes. Hagen beats Brady in a playoff at the U.S. Open.

Winners

World Series	*U.S. Tennis Open*
Cincinnati (NL) 5	Men: William Johnston
Chicago (AL) 3	Women: Hazel Hotchkiss
College Football	Wightman
Harvard	*USGA Open*
College Basketball	Walter Hagen
Minnesota	*Kentucky Derby*
Player of the Year	Sir Barton (Johny Loftus,
Erling Platou, Minnesota	jockey)
Stanley Cup	
Not awarded	

Fashion

Variety describes the fashion year as unclear, as lengths, widths, and colors—and even the manners ordinarily associated with "proper dress" for "proper occasions"—remain undefined. Waistlines, for example, vary: Oriental styles now drop the blouse below the hips, yet the Empire style gains popularity; in some dresses, the waist is higher in the front than in the back; other fashions rely on the normal waistline. Since the victory, colors and patterns have become less sober, and feathers, ribbons, fringes, and cut-outs return as dress and accessory decorations.

With their sons home from war, matrons resume traditional styles (along with their traditional underpinnings), and they also resume their prewar social schedules.

High-fashion notes: Jean Patou's dresses with bell-shaped skirts, high waists, and Russian embroidery; Lanvin's slouch back black satin dress; pants and dresses with harem-like hems that fall over silver and green brocade dancing shoes with French heels and rhinestone buttons, designed by the American Bob.

Kaleidoscope _____

- After a triumphant reception in London, Rome, and Paris, Wilson goes to the peace conference at Versailles proclaiming America's idealism: "Tell me what's right and I'll fight for it."
- When Wilson returns to the U.S., greeted by hundreds of thousands, he speaks repeatedly of both his homesickness for and pride in the "clean young men America sent to war."
- Labor unrest is most severe since the 1890s; unemployment rises to 3 million; inflation prompts 2,665 strikes, involving over 4 million workers; almost all are successful in gaining wage benefits and improved hours.
- Prices are up 79 percent since 1914; adjusting for inflation, wages have risen 14 percent in industry and 25 percent in agriculture.
- A poll of newspaper editors indicates that 77 percent favor the ratification of the peace treaty, including the League of Nations provision.
- While in Colorado promoting the league, Wilson suffers a paralyzing stroke on his left side that physically incapacitates him; the nation awaits daily bulletins on Wilson's condition; from his sick bed he refuses compromise on the League.
- Wilson wins the Nobel Peace Prize.
- Henry Ford repurchases full control of the Ford Motor Company for $105 million.
- After suing the *Chicago Tribune* for portraying him as "an anarchist" and "ugly ignorant idealist," Ford wins 6¢ in damages.
- Conrad Hilton, 31, spends his $5,000 life savings on the Mobley Hotel in Crisco, Texas.
- States rapidly ratify the Eighteenth Amendment, prohibiting the sale of alcoholic beverages (the minimum, 0.5% alcohol), to take effect in 1920.
- New York's black troops march down Fifth Avenue to large ovations.
- Race riots occur in 26 cities, with scores killed and hundreds seriously injured; in Chicago thirty-one die, and 500 are injured.
- Seventy lynchings occur in the South (34 in 1917); the Klan grows to 100,000 in 27 states.
- After 110 days of striking, steelworkers in Gary, Indiana return to work, unsuccessful in gaining union recognition from U.S. Steel.
- The attorney general brings an injunction to halt a United Mine Workers strike.
- An actors' strike for recognition of Actors' Equity closes numerous theaters in New York, Philadelphia, Boston, and Chicago.
- A nationwide Red plot to mark May Day with mail bomb assassinations is disclosed when sixteen packages are held at various post offices for insufficient postage; intended victims included Rockefeller, Morgan, and Justice Holmes.
- Herbert Hoover is named director of the relief organization for liberated countries, both neutral and enemy.
- At the Victory Liberty Loan concert at the Metropolitan Opera, $7.8 million is raised; Jascha Heifetz encores for $500,000; Rachmaninoff, for $1.2 million.
- The Senate rejects (50–21) disloyalty charges against Senator La Follette, stemming from a 1917 speech.
- When 45,000 strikers threaten to paralyze Seattle, the mayor sets up machine guns and threatens anyone attempting to take over municipal functions.
- Anticipating Prohibition are the songs: "You Cannot Make Your Shimmy Shake on Tea" and "What'll We Do on a Saturday Night When the Town Goes Dry?"
- Paul Magge, a Casevill, Michigan farmer, kills his mother and three children as a religious sacrifice.
- Eugene Debs goes to jail for sedition, calling Lenin and Trotsky the "foremost statesmen of the age" and the Supreme Court "begowned, bewhiskered, bepowdered old fossils."
- A study reveals that the public condemns saloons but resents the prohibition amendment.
- Over 30,000 Jews march in Baltimore to protest pogroms in Poland and elsewhere.
- Hoarding and black-market profiteering of items in short supply (e.g., food, fuel, clothing) become widespread.
- An official report in August tallies 300,000 strikers, including actors, painters, waiters, machinists, cigar makers, and gravediggers.
- 1,250 American troops leave Vladivostok.
- Attorney General Mitchell Palmer organizes the FBI to round up 249 known communists, who are then deported on the "Soviet Ark" to Finland; 34 states enact statutes outlawing the display of the Red flag.
- The Senate orders a nationwide investigation into Bolshevism.

First Appearances: nonstop flight: New York-Chicago, airplane wedding, American Legion convention, purple 3¢ Victory postage stamp, Communist Party of America, Roseland (New York), RCA, Peter Paul's Konobar (coconut, fruit, nuts, chocolate), mechanical rabbit (for greyhound racing), Drake Hotel (Chicago), armored commercial car (Minneapolis), KLM, Bentley, Citroen, $1 billion-assets bank (National City, New York), GMAC, state gas tax (Oregon), UCLA, dial telephone (AT&T, Norfolk), illustrated tabloid (*New York Daily News*), Harcourt Brace, Distinguished Service Medal awarded to a woman (Evangeline Booth), American-born woman to become member of Parliament (Lady Astor), woman editor-in-chief of a law review (M. Donlon, Cornell)

THE Twenties

Women registering to vote in Los Angeles. *General Research Division. The New York Public Library. Astor, Lenox and Tilden Foundations.*

Statistics

Vital
Population: 106,491,000
  Urban/Rural: 54/52
  Farm: 30%
Life expectancy
  Male: 53.6
  Female: 54.6
Births/1,000: 27.7
Marriages/1,000: 12.0
Divorces/1,000: 1.6
Deaths/1,000: 13.0
  per 100,000
    Heart: 370
    Cancer: 83
    Tuberculosis: 113
    Car accidents: 11

Economic
Unemployed: 2,132,000
GNP: $91.5 billion
Federal budget: $6.4 billion
National debt: $23.7 billion
Union membership: 5 million
Strikes: 3,411
Prime rate: 5.4%
Car sales: 1,905,500
Average salary: $1,236

Social
Homicides/100,000: 6.8
Suicides/100,000: 10.2
Lynchings: 61
Labor force, male/female: 4/1
Public education: $1.04 billion
College degrees
  Bachelors'
    Male: 32,000
    Female: 17,000
  Doctorates
    Male: 522
    Female: 93
Attendance
  Movies (weekly): 33 million
  Baseball (yearly): 9.3
    million

Consumer
Consumer Price Index
  (1967 = 100): 60
Eggs: 68¢ (doz.)
Milk: 17¢ (qt.)
Bread: 12¢ (loaf)
Butter: 70¢ (lb.)
Bacon: 52¢ (lb.)
Round steak: 42¢ (lb.)
Oranges: 63¢ (doz.)
Coffee: 47¢ (lb.)

When America entered the Great War in 1917, it became, as British prime minister Lloyd George said, "a world power in a sense [it] never was before." Led by the idealism of Woodrow Wilson, the United States sent troops into battle for the first time on European soil in an effort to aid England and France in their bloody stalemate with the German Empire. This was the war "to make the world safe for democracy," and with American assistance, the war finally ended. When Wilson went to the Peace Conference at Versailles, the French greeted him as a savior. America had moved to the forefront of the world stage, its ideals and might triumphant. In the same year that America entered the war, a sealed train sped Lenin across Germany to the Finland Station. Within a few months, the Bolsheviks seized control of the Russian Revolution, and Marxism-Leninism found its first national home.

Profound changes were also taking place in science and technology. Max Planck and Albert Einstein were formulating discoveries that challenged the divine order of Newtonian physics. Sigmund Freud was proposing theories that questioned the prim rectitude and proud self-mastery of Victorian society. Technology was rapidly advancing with the advent of wireless communication, the airplane, auto, movie, and phonograph; indeed, airplanes were used as a military weapon for the first time during World War I, and truck transport played a role at the Battle of the Marne. As the new technology and ideas of time, space, matter, energy, and human behavior were harbingers of modernity, the immense carnage of World War I appeared to many a Last Judgment on nineteenth-century positivism.

The immediate postwar period was a time of disappointment for Wilson and America. Widespread strikes, along with fears of "Reds" and terrorist bombs, frightened the public and gave rise to stern police action. Inflation, unemployment, and the Prohibition Amendment, passed in 1918, further unsettled a triumphant America. As the contentiousness and disarray of the postwar world become apparent, many questioned whether the noble aims for which the war had been fought and for which so many had died could be achieved. The final blow was the Peace Conference in France, where it soon became clear that the European victors wanted their material spoils more than a just, international order.

Feeling betrayed, America recoiled from Europe and from Wilson's League of Nations and, in 1920, elected a little-known, handsome, and well-spoken Ohio senator, Warren Harding, who promised "not revolution but restoration." Politically, the subsequent decade was marked by a turning away from the activism of Teddy Roosevelt (1900–1908) and Woodrow Wilson (1912–20), both of whom had

sought a powerful role for government. Elected by wide margins, the laissez-faire Republican presidents and Congresses of the twenties legislated less, taxed less, and reduced armaments. Although the United States was not a member of the league, its leaders nonetheless convened disarmament conferences, mediated when necessary for the hopelessly combative Europeans, and supported international treaties settling boundaries and outlawing war. The active leadership in the world that Wilson had sought was thus restricted to a more ceremonial role.

In 1920, America turned from the world into itself with unparalleled economic, social, and intellectual energy, and until the Crash in 1929, public excitement soared. During this time, many of the bold features of the face of modern America were drawn, and many of the heroes of the American pantheon were born. The economy underwent a transformation that was virtually an industrial revolution. Henry Ford's ideas—the mass production of lower cost luxuries and the payment of higher wages to workers which increased their buying power—became the model for industry. Simultaneously, aggressive new advertising methods accelerated sales and enlarged markets. The economy took off in 1921 on eight years of sustained flight, during which the GNP grew 40 percent with little inflation. As wages rose and working hours moderated, consumers had more leisure time for recreational pursuits, as well as more income for self-indulgence, self-improvement, and invidious consumption. The upwardly mobile consumer society developed. A forthright spiritual glorification of business took place. Calvin Coolidge likened factories to places of worship, and Bruce Barton, an advertising pioneer, wrote best-sellers that portrayed Christ as the archetypal entrepreneur in a scheme that compared business to salvation, advertising to the Gospel, and salesmen to the apostles. Universities, in growing numbers, sought to develop a more scientific, if no less enthusiastic, approach to business.

While not a time of social reform, the booming economy, combined with the new technology, both enlarged the middle class and had a democratizing effect. Radio gave everyone a common reservoir of diverse entertainment (varying from "Amos 'n' Andy" to live theater, from sporting events to concerts, jazz, and popular evangelists), as well as a common and immediate awareness of important events (from presidential speeches, like Harding's inaugural, to first flights, like those of the Graf Zeppelin and Lindbergh); the global village was in its inception. Recordings similarly exposed everyone to the same music—the Ipana Troubadours, the New York Philharmonic-Symphony Orchestra, Enrico Caruso, Paul Whiteman, Al Jolson, and Bessie

191

Smith. Movies provided common fantasies and idols, from the Sheik, Rudolph Valentino, and the "It Girl," Clara Bow, to the innocent Mary Pickford and vamp Theda Bara. Charlie Chaplin, Buster Keaton, and Harold Lloyd provided a shared comic imagery. The new advertising industry, in its mission to reach the largest possible audience, presented role models often based on common culture heroes; the pleasures, conveniences, and status symbols of the wealthy were also presented as attainable in some version to everyone. The well-to-do and less well-off began to look more alike.

Stirred by competition from the new media and aided by improved communications and the rapidly growing appetite for news, excitement, and heroes, journalists were on the spot everywhere, producing mountains of type to fill tabloid front pages. They covered everything from news of sports figures and trials to movie stars, divorces, and natural disasters. Adultery-murder trials like the Hall-Mills and Snyder-Gray cases received greater coverage than the Great War. The nation waited with bated breath to learn the fate of Floyd Collins, trapped in a mine for 18 days, the delivery of diphtheria vaccine in Alaska by the husky dog Baltho, and the whereabouts of the sexy evangelist Aimee Semple McPherson. Figures like Charles Atlas, the new Miss America, Texas Guinan, and Helen Morgan, and events like the Teapot Dome scandal and St. Valentine's Day Massacre, along with new modifications in manners, such as Emily Post's *Etiquette* and Trojan contraceptives, also received great attention.

Some of the heroes matched the mountains of type—the sports figures Babe Ruth, Red Grange, Jack Dempsey, Gene Tunney, Bill Tilden, Bobby Jones, Helen Wills, Johnny Weismuller, and Gertrude Ederle; public figures Clarence Darrow, William Jennings Bryan, Margaret Sanger, Billy Mitchell, and Adm. Richard Byrd; and performing and creative artists Isadora Duncan, Bessie Smith, and George Gershwin. Most honored of the twenties' heroes was Charles Lindbergh, the modest, courageous farm boy who flew solo across the Atlantic.

Extensive coverage was also given to the most unusual and colorful of the decade's businesses, those created in response to the Eighteenth Amendment—bootlegging and speakeasies. Prohibition, the "noble" experiment in moral betterment, by edict, was widely ignored, and for the first time, a vast mass of Americans of all classes openly and knowingly patronized crime. This made gangsters into public servants of sorts, and Al Capone, the most enterprising of all, was a popular and oft-quoted personality.

The interplay of economic and social forces produced other dramatic changes. As economic opportunities drew people to the cities, urban dwelling became the increasingly predominant mode of American life. Bigger office and apartment buildings were constructed, including the many art deco masterpieces of the late twenties. The car became an achievable staple in everyman's American dream; more roads were paved, and as congestion increased, more traffic lights and no-parking signs appeared. The city began to take on the look of today, as did the countryside, where gas stations and motels multipled.

In the freedom of the city, in the atmosphere of the speakeasy, in the wake of postwar disillusion and the advent of popular Freudianism, the music of the Jazz Age and the dancing of the Charleston flourished. Victorian manners and morals were shed, along with their cumbersome over- and undergarments, and the flapper appeared. There was a thrust for female emancipation sartorially, sexually, and intellectually. Business also contributed to the new liberation, as it sought customers for everything from baked bread to vacuum cleaners, all of which were promoted as emancipators from household drudgery. Women, first allowed to vote nationally in 1920, were thus encouraged to the higher life, which could and did include, in increasing numbers, college and employment and, in unknown numbers, free love.

All these social changes were not without powerful resistance. Intense controversy developed over women smoking, skirt and hair lengths, contraception, and "loose" morals in films; the latter culminated in a film code limiting sexual material. Early in the decade there was strong political reaction. Alleged radicals were incarcerated without evidence, strikes were brutally suppressed, the KKK was revived, and immigration was restricted on ethnically discriminatory lines. In the two great and closely followed trials of the decade, a Tennessee teacher (Scopes) was convicted of teaching scientific material that conflicted with religious fundamentalism, and two Italian immigrant anarchists (Sacco and Vanzetti) were convicted and executed for murder, although many thought their "crime" was their political ideology and foreign origin.

Reaction came as well from the intellectuals, as many despaired of hollow materialism, forsaken idealism, and small-town provincialism. F. Scott Fitzgerald's *The Great Gatsby* portrayed the "meretricious [American] dream"; Ernest Hemingway's *The Sun Also Rises* told of the "lost generation"; William Faulkner's *The Sound and the Fury* detailed the moral decay of the South; Sinclair Lewis indicted the bourgeoise of midwestern America, and H. L. Mencken relentlessly assailed the "booboisie." His focus less social than

As the sale of alcohol becomes illegal, prohibitionists in Norfolk, Virginia, gleefully bury the bottle. *D. Ouellette Collection.*

psychological, Eugene O'Neill devised experimental forms to portray the perennial conflicts that arise from the disparity between dream and reality. T. S. Eliot's *The Waste Land* remains the ultimate indictment of the modern world's loss of personal, moral, and spiritual values.

But the hope and excitement of the new predominated. America seemed to be acting on the motto of Emil Coué's best-selling self-help book, "Every day, in every way, I am getting better and better." As the decade progressed, the possibilities for everyone seemed boundless, and get-rich-quick schemes proliferated. The Florida land rush of the mid-twenties drew large numbers eager for instant profit, and although latecomers bought swamp, the speculative spirit remained undampened. The greatest and most surefire possibility of rapid wealth

was provided by the Great Bull Market of the late twenties. As a *New York Times* headline of 1929 reported, a "speculative fever" gripped the nation.

In 1928, American elected yet another rugged individualist to the White House; by far the best qualified of the three presidents of the decade, Herbert Hoover foresaw the end of poverty in America. Then, just two months before the end of the decade, the Great Bull Market expired. A shock of disbelief met the Crash. Those in power attempted to deny its reality or importance—it was just another swing in the boom-depression cycle. But the "up" in American life had lasted so long that people had forgotten the "downs"; the Great Depression that followed was to equal in magnitude that great sweeping exaltation that was the twenties.

1920

Facts and Figures

Economic Profile
Dow-Jones: ↓
High 100–Low 67
GNP: +9%
Inflation: +8.2%
Unemployment: 5.2%
Maxwell: $885
Chandler: $1,895
Cadillac: $2,885
Russian pony coat: $169.50
Tweed coat (Hart Schaffner
& Marx): $37.50
Jackal mink coat: $1,750–
$2,750
E-Z ladies' garters: 40¢–60¢
Waltham wristwatch: $5
Women's silk stockings:
$1.65–$3.65
Sloane's vacuum cleaner: $48
Grafonola: $300–$2,100
Phonograph (Sears &
Roebuck): $115
Player piano: $475
Baby stroller: $12.50–$25
Miloviolet scented, gold-
tipped cigarettes: 10¢
(pack)

In the News _____

ATTORNEY GENERAL A. MITCHELL PALMER DIRECTS NEW YEAR'S
DAY RAIDS ON REDS . . . PROHIBITION AMENDMENT TAKES EFFECT
. . . SECRETARY OF STATE ROBERT LANSING IS FORCED TO RESIGN FOR
HOLDING UNAUTHORIZED CABINET MEETINGS . . . FIVE ELECTED
SOCIALISTS ARE BARRED FROM N.Y. ASSEMBLY . . . LEAGUE OF
NATIONS OPENS IN PARIS . . . WOODROW WILSON REFUSES SENATE
COMPROMISE ON LEAGUE, SENATE DEFEATS U.S. MEMBERSHIP . . .
POLES UNDER JOSEF PILSUDSKI INVADE RUSSIA . . . DEMOCRATS
NOMINATE W. W. COX FOR PRESIDENT ON 44TH BALLOT, FRANKLIN
D. ROOSEVELT FOR VICE PRESIDENT . . . WARREN HARDING IS
CHOSEN BY GOP, CALVIN COOLIDGE IS POPULAR CHOICE AS RUNNING
MATE . . . EUGENE V. DEBS, IN PRISON, IS SOCIALIST CANDIDATE . . .
NICOLA SACCO AND BARTOLOMEO VANZETTI, ANARCHIST LABORERS,
ARE ARRESTED FOR PAYROLL MURDERS IN BRAINTREE, MASS. . . .
MARCUS GARVEY'S UNIVERSAL NEGRO IMPROVEMENT ASSOCIATION
MEETS IN NEW YORK, 25,000 ATTEND . . . FAMINE SWEEPS RUSSIA,
LENIN ASKS AMERICAN COMMUNIST PARTY FOR INFORMATION ON
U.S. AGRICULTURAL METHODS . . . BRITAIN GETS LEAGUE MANDATE
FOR PALESTINE . . . EIGHT CHICAGO WHITE SOX ARE INDICTED FOR
1919 WORLD SERIES FIX . . . BOMB EXPLODES ON WALL STREET
KILLING 20 . . . WOMEN VOTE FOR FIRST TIME IN NATIONAL
ELECTION . . . HARDING WINS WITH 16 MILLION VOTES, COX GAINS
9 MILLION, DEBS, 919 THOUSAND . . . ENGLAND GRANTS NORTH AND
SOUTH IRELAND SEPARATE PARLIAMENTS . . . CALIFORNIA PASSES
LAW LIMITING JAPANESE LAND HOLDINGS.

Deaths

Reginald DeKoven, William
C. Gorgas, William Dean
Howells, Amedeo
Modigliani, Robert E.
Peary, John Reed.

Quotes

"The great creators of the government . . . thought of America as a light to the world, as created to lead the world in the assertion of the right of peoples and the rights of free nations."
— Woodrow Wilson, in defense of the League of Nations

"America's present need is not heroics but healing; not nostrums but normalcy; not revolution but restoration; not surgery but serenity."
— Warren G. Harding

"The Department of Justice has undertaken to tear out the radical seeds that have entangled American ideas, . . . the IWW's, the most radical socialists, the misguided anarchists, . . . the moral perverts and the hysterical neurasthenic women who abound in communism."
— Attorney General A. Mitchell Palmer

"My candle burns at both ends; / It will not last the night; / But ah, my foes, and, oh, my friends— / It gives a lovely light."   — Edna St. Vincent Millay

"If our world is ever . . . to be destroyed, the problems are that its destruction will come from outside of our own solar system. Accordingly, we should probably have plenty of time to await such a possible disaster."   — *Munsey's* magazine

"If Mr. Einstein doesn't like the natural laws of this universe, let him go back to where he came from."
— Robert Benchley

"Here was a new generation, . . . dedicated more than the last to the fear of poverty and the worship of success; grown up to find all gods dead, all wars fought, all faiths in man shaken."
— F. Scott Fitzgerald, *This Side of Paradise*

Ads

Bathing beauties with a Columbia Six sportscar. The decade begins with more cars and less body covering. *Library of Congress.*

1920

Radio _____

Dr. Frank Conrad, director of Westinghouse's
station, KDKA, Pittsburgh, plays music records for
radio hams; he terms these events *broadcasts* • On
November 2, KDKA makes the first scheduled
broadcast, the Harding-Cox election • Thirty radio
licenses are issued.

Fourth of July parade in Boise, Idaho. While Woodrow
Wilson tours the country proseletyzing for the League of
Nations, America is busy cultivating its own traditions.
Library of Congress.

Movies _____

Campaign song for the candidates of "Law and Order" and
"America First." *La Salle Collection. Smithsonian
Institution.*

Openings

Dr. Jekyll and Mr. Hyde (John S. Robertson), John
  Barrymore, Nita Naldi
The Idol Dancer (D. W. Griffith), Clarine Seymour,
  Richard Barthelmess
Copperhead (Charles Maigne), Lionel Barrymore
The Golem (Paul Wegener), Paul Wegener, Albert
  Steinruck
Huckleberry Finn (William Desmond Taylor), Gordon
  Griffith
Humoresque (Frank Borzage), Vera Gordon, Dore
  Davidson
The Love Flower (D. W. Griffith), Carol Dempster,
  Richard Barthelmess
Way Down East (D. W. Griffith), Lillian Gish,
  Richard Barthelmess
Madame X (Frank Lloyd), Pauline Frederick,
  William Courtleigh
Mark of Zorro (Fred Niblo), Douglas Fairbanks,
  Noah Beery
One Week (Buster Keaton), Buster Keaton
Passion (Ernst Lubitsch), Pola Negri
Pollyanna (Paul Powell), Mary Pickford
The Cabinet of Dr. Caligari (Robert Wiene), Conrad
  Veidt

Top Box-Office Stars

Wallace Reid, Marguerite Clark, Roscoe ("Fatty")
Arbuckle, Douglas Fairbanks, Mary Pickford,
Charles Chaplin, Tom Mix, William S. Hart, Alla
Nazimova, Gloria Swanson, Dorothy Gish, Lillian
Gish, Constance Talmadge, Norma Talmadge, Mary
Miles Minter, Mabel Normand, Thomas Meighan,
Charles Ray

Popular Music

Hit Songs
"Avalon"
"I'll Be with You in Apple
Blossom Time"
"When My Baby Smiles at Me"
"Whispering"
"Look for the Silver Lining"
"I Never Knew I Could Love
Anyone Like You"
"My Mammy"
"Daddy, You've Been a Mother to
Me"
"Hiawatha's Melody of Love"

"When the Moon Shines on the
Moonshine"
"Who Ate Napoleons with
Josephine when Bonaparte Was
Away?"

Top Records
Crazy Blues (Mamie Smith), first
blues recording; *Wang Wang Blues*
(Harry Busse); *Dardanella* (Ben
Selvin Orchestra); *Japanese
Sandman* (Paul Whiteman); *I'll*

See You in C-U-B-A (Ted Lewis
Orchestra); *After You Get What
You Want, You Don't Want It* (Van
and Schenck); *Margie* (Original
Dixieland Jazz Band)

Jazz and Big Bands
Paul Whiteman tours Europe, and
interest in jazz booms. Louis
Armstrong, 20, plays cornet on a
Mississippi River steamboat.

Theater

Broadway Openings

Plays
The Emperor Jones (Eugene O'Neill), Charles S.
Gilpin
Beyond the Horizon (Eugene O'Neill), Richard
Bennett
Miss Lulu Bett (Zona Gale), Carroll McComas
The Bat (Mary Roberts Rinehart, Avery Hopwood),
Effie Ellsler
Enter Madame (Gilda Varesi, Dolly Byrne), Gilda
Varesi
Rollo's Wild Oat (Clare Kummer), Roland Young
Bab (Edward Childs Carpenter), Helen Hayes
Ladies Night (Avery Hopwood, Charlton Andrews),
John Cumberland, Judith Vosselli, Charles
Ruggles
The First Year (Frank Craven), Frank Craven
Heartbreak House (George Bernard Shaw), Effie
Shannon, Lucile Watson, Dudley Digges
The Wonderful Thing (Lillian Trimble Bradley),
Jeanne Eagels
The Skin Game (John Galsworthy), Marsh Allen
Poldekin (Booth Tarkington), George Arliss

Musicals
Sally (Jerome Kern, Victor Herbert, Clifford Grey),
Marilyn Miller, Leon Errol
Ziegfeld Follies of 1920 (Victor Herbert, Irving
Berlin), Fannie Brice, W. C. Fields
The Night Boat (Jerome Kern, Anne Caldwell),
Louise Groody, John E. Hazzard
Tickle Me (Herbert Stothart, Otto Harbach, Oscar
Hammerstein II), Frank Tinney

John Barrymore, "the
great profile," stars on
stage in *Richard III*
(left) and in the movie
*Dr. Jekyll and Mr.
Hyde. Billy Rose
Theatre Collection. The
New York Public
Library at Lincoln
Center. Astor, Lenox,
and Tilden
Foundations.*

The Passing Show (Jean Schwartz, Harold
Atteridge), Janet Adair, Marie Dressler, Willie
Howard, Eugene Howard
Honeydew (Efrem Zimbalist, Joseph Herbert),
Ethelind Terry, Mlle. Marguerite, Hal Forde
Mary (Lou Hirsch, Otto Harbach, Frank Mandel),
Jack McGowan, Janet Velie
George White Scandals (George Gershwin, Arthur
Jackson), Ann Pennington, Lou Holtz
Poor Little Ritz Girl (Sigmund Romberg, Richard
Rodgers, Alex Gerber, Lorenz Hart), Lulu
McConnell, Charles Purcell

Classics and Revivals On and Off Broadway
Richard III (John Barrymore, Shakespeare debut);
Medea (Euripides), Ellen Von Volkenberg; *The
Power of Darkness* (Tolstoy); *Deirdre of the Sorrows,
Cathleen ni Houlihan* (William Butler Yeats); *The
Beggar's Opera* (John Gay); *An Enemy of the People*
(Ibsen)

Pulitzer Prize
Beyond the Horizon, Eugene O'Neill

Classical Music _____

Compositions

Edgard Varèse, *Amériques*
Aaron Copland, Keyboard Sonatas 1–3
Carl Ruggles, *Men and Angels*

Important Events

The Cleveland Institute and Juilliard are founded.

Notable Performances: Damrosch Series (History of the Symphony); Harold Bauer, Ossip Gabrilowitsch, Olga Samarov, Concerto for Three Pianos (Bach-Stokowski); Festivals: 71st Armory Regiment, New York, the largest musical event in 40 years; London String Quartet, complete Beethoven Quartets (New York); Efrem Zimbalist and Henry Cowell, Beethoven, opus 96, Brahms, opus 108, and works of Cowell (Berkshire Festival)

Major Recitals: Sergei Rachmaninoff, Josef Hofmann, Josef Lhévinne, Guiomar Novaes, Jascha Heifetz, Pablo Casals, Fritz Kreisler, Alfred Cortot, Luisa Tetrazzini, Mrs. Ernestine Schumann-Heink

Major Conductors: Walter Damrosch (New York Symphony); Joseph Stransky (Philharmonic, New York); Artur Bodanzky (National, New York); Pierre Monteux (Boston); Leopold Stokowski (Philadelphia); Eugène Ysaye (Cincinnati); Ossip Gabrilowitsch (Detroit)

Debuts: Louis Kentner, Joseph Fuchs

First Performances

Edward Elgar, *Enigma Variations* (Philadelphia); Jean Sibelius, *Finlandia* (New York); Gustav Holst, *The Planets* (Chicago); Rachmaninoff, *The Bells* (Philadelphia); Ralph Vaughan Williams, *London Symphony* (New York); John Alden Carpenter, *A Pilgrim Vision* (Mayflower Centennial, Philadelphia); Sergei Prokofiev, *Overture on Hebrew Themes* (New York); Frank S. Converse, Symphony no. 1 (Chicago), Symphony no. 4 (Boston); Ernest Bloch, Suite for Viola and Orchestra (New York)

Opera

Metropolitan: 172 performances of 36 works by 25 composers. Most frequently performed: Geraldine Farrar, *Zaza* (Ruggiero Leoncavallo). Most popular: *Monsieur Beaucaire* (André Messager). Premieres: Madame Chrysanthème (Messager); *Cleopatra's*

Sergei Rachmaninoff, premiering his own works in America. *Library of Congress.*

Night (Henry Hadley); *Parsifal* (in English); *Eugene Onègin* (in Italian). Debuts: Beniamino Gigli, Frances Peralta (*Mefistofele*); Ann Roselle (*La bohème*); Giusseppe Danise (*Aïda*); Mario Chamlee (*Tosca*); Florence Easton (*Madama Butterfly*).

Chicago: Mary Garden, *L'amore dei tre re* (Italo Montemezzi). Premieres: *L'heure espagnole* (Ravel); *Edipo ré* (Leoncavallo); *Rip Van Winkle* (Henry De Koven)

San Diego: *The Sunset Trail* (Charles Wakefield Cadman, premiere)

Cincinnati: *Martha* (company's inaugural performance)

Music Notes

New York replaces Berlin as the mecca for musical hopefuls • Three orchestras compete with Beethoven performances (for the 150th anniversary) and experimental pieces like Francesco Malipiero's *Impressions* • Visiting Willem Mengelberg tries to convert hostile New York audiences to Gustav Mahler • The New York Symphony is the first American orchestra to tour Europe • Arturo Toscanini brings the La Scala Orchestra to New York • Enrico Caruso collapses on stage in *I pagliacci;* he bursts a blood vessel in *L'elisir d'amore;* his last performance is *La Juive.*

Art

Painting

John Marin, *Lower Manhattan*

Marsden Hartley, *Lilies in a Vase*

Charles Demuth, *Stairs, Providence, Machinery, End of the Parade, Box of Tricks, The Tower*

Georgia O'Keeffe, *Red Cannas*

Thomas Hart Benton, *Portrait of Josie West*

Lyonel Feininger, *Church, Viaduct*

Charles Burchfield, *February Thaw, The Interurban Line, Railroad Gantry, Peppin House*

George Bellows, *Elinor, Jean and Anna*

Joseph Stella, *Flowers, Portrait of Walt Whitman*

Sculpture

Jo Davidson, *Gertrude Stein*

Paul Manship, *J. Pierpont Morgan Memorial* (cornerstone tablet in the Great Hall, Metropolitan Museum of Art, New York)

Lorado Taft, *Fountain of Time* (Chicago Art Institute)

Architecture

Field Museum, Chicago (Graham, Anderson, Probst, and White)

Amphitheater, U.S. National Cemetery, Arlington, Virginia (Carrère and Hastings)

Barnsdall House, Hollywood (Frank Lloyd Wright)

Important Exhibitions

Museums

New York: *Metropolitan:* Fiftieth anniversary exhibition (the most important in American history) includes loans from private collections of arms, Byzantine ivories, glass, modern masters; other shows: Renoir, van Gogh, Gauguin, Dürer; Flemish tapestries of the sixteenth century

Philadelphia: Italian paintings of the fourteenth and sixteenth centuries

Boston: Colonial objects; Japanese prints

Chicago: Thirty-third annual exhibit of American art: Frederick Frieseke and George Luks win top prizes. Museum purchases Redon prints and etchings.

Pittsburgh: Carnegie International resumes after the war years.

Individual shows

New York: Maurice Prendergast, James A. MacNeill Whistler, William Glackens, Frederick Detwiller, Mary Cassatt, George Bellows, Winslow Homer; Jo Davidson and Mahonri Young (war sculptures)

Art Briefs

Marcel Duchamp, Man Ray, and Katherine Dreier found the N.Y. Société Anonyme to promote modern art • Man Ray photographs Duchamp in his female disguise as Rrose Sélavy • Duchamp builds his first motor-driven constructions • Joseph Pennell's widely discussed letter to the *New York Times* urges that the Metropolitan Museum of Art exhibit works of living artists.

Dance

The Pavley-Oukrainsky Ballet debuts. It is the first American ballet company and the official ballet of the Chicago Civic Opera.

The innovative Isadora Duncan, shortly before departing for Moscow to open a school of dance. *Library of Congress.*

Books ───────────────────────────

Fiction

Critics' Choice

Main Street, Sinclair Lewis
Poor White, Sherwood Anderson
This Side of Paradise, F. Scott Fitzgerald
Flappers and Philosophers, F. Scott Fitzgerald
Youth and the Bright Medusa, Willa Cather
Master Eustace, Henry James (posthumous)
The Vacation of the Kelwyns, William Dean Howells
Miss Lulu Bett, Zona Gale
One Man's Initiation, John Dos Passos
Moon-Calf, Floyd Dell
🙚 *Women in Love*, D. H. Lawrence
🙚 *Guermantes' Way*, Marcel Proust

Best-Sellers

The Man of the Forest, Zane Grey
Kindred of the Dust, Peter B. Kyne
The Re-Creation of Brian Kent, Harold Bell Wright
The River's End, James Oliver Curwood
A Man for the Ages, Irving Bacheller
Mary-Marie, Eleanor H. Porter
The Great Impersonation, E. Phillips Oppenheim

Harriet and the Piper, Kathleen Norris
The Lamp in the Desert, Ethel M. Dell
The Portygee, Joseph C. Lincoln

Nonfiction

Critics' Choice

Character and Opinion in the U.S., George Santayana
Ancient Man, Hendrik Willem Van Loon
Darkwater, W. E. B. Du Bois
The Ordeal of Mark Twain, Van Wyck Brooks
Recreations of a Psychologist, G. S. Hall
Autobiography, Andrew Carnegie
Reconstruction in Philosophy, John Dewey
🙚 *The Concept of Nature*, Alfred North Whitehead
🙚 *Relativity*, Albert Einstein
🙚 *A General Introduction to Psychoanalysis*, Sigmund Freud

Best-Sellers

Now It Can Be Told, Philip Gibbs
The Economic Consequences of the Peace, J. M. Keynes
Roosevelt's Letters to His Children, ed. Joseph B. Bishop
Theodore Roosevelt, William Roscoe Thayer

White Shadows in the South Seas, Frederick O'Brien
An American Idyll, Cornelia Stratton Parker
The Years Between, Rudyard Kipling
Bolshevism, John Spargo
Belgium, Brand Whitlock

Poetry

T. S. Eliot, *Poems*
Ezra Pound, *Umbra, Hugh Selwyn Mauberley*
William Carlos Williams, *Kora in Hell*
Edna St. Vincent Millay, *A Few Figs from Thistles*
Edwin Arlington Robinson, *Lancelot, The Three Taverns*
Conrad Aiken, *The House of Dust*
Carl Sandburg, *Smoke and Steel*
H. D., *Poems by a Little Girl*
Edgar Lee Masters, *Domesday Book*

Pulitzer Prizes

The Age of Innocence, Edith Wharton (novel)
The Victory at Sea, William S. Sims, with Burton J. Hendrick (U.S. history)
The Americanization of Edward Bok, Edward Bok (biography)
No prize is awarded in poetry.

Science and Technology ───────────────

A. A. Michelson and Francis Pease, at the Mt. Wilson Observatory, California, measure the diameter of a star, Betelgeuse, at 240 million miles.

Public radio begins with Pittsburgh's KDKA broadcast of the Harding-Cox election returns.

The first regular commercial airline service in the United States begins; it connects Key West and Havana and takes approximately one hour.

William G. Harkins, of the University of Chicago, postulates the existence of a subatomic particle, the neutron, a heavy particle of no electric charge.

The Smithsonian Institution announces Robert Goddard's work with rockets, which, it says, will eventually fly people to the moon.

The tommy gun is patented by retired army officer John T. Thompson.

The Duesenberg car introduces hydraulic brakes.

Specialized scientific journals begin to flourish.

Sports

Baseball

The Boston Red Sox sell Babe Ruth to the New York
    Yankees for $100,000, plus a $385,000 loan. Ruth
    hits 54 home runs and asks that his salary be
    doubled to $20,000. The Yankees draw a record
    1,289,422. Ruth's slugging percentage is .847.

A young boy approaches Shoeless Joe Jackson, one
    of the eight White Sox players accused of
    throwing the 1919 World Series, and pleads:
    "Say it ain't so, Joe."

In the longest game ever, 26 innings, the Brooklyn
    Dodgers and Boston Braves tie, 1–1.

Bill Wambsganss, Cleveland second baseman, makes
    the first unassisted triple play in a World Series.

Babe Ruth's
54 home runs
break the
previous
record by 25.
*Library of
Congress.*

Rose Bowl (Jan. 1, 1921): California 28–Ohio State 0

Champions

Batting	Pitching
Rogers Hornsby (St. Louis, NL), .370	Burleigh Grimes (Brooklyn, NL), 23–11
George Sisler (St. Louis, AL), .407	Jim Bagby (Cleveland, AL), 31–12
	Home Runs
	Babe Ruth (New York, AL), 54

Football

The American Professional Football Association, the
first organized pro league, is formed in Canton, Ohio,
with Jim Thorpe as president. Franchises are $100.
George Halas buys the Decatur Staleys and moves
them to Chicago. Games are poorly attended.

Pro Stars: Paddy Driscoll (Racine), Joe Guyon
(Canton)

College All-Americans: George Gipp (FB), Notre
Dame; Donald Lourie (QB), Princeton; Timothy
Callahan (C), Yale

Olympics

The Olympics are held at Antwerp, Belgium.
American gold medal winners include Charles
Paddock (100m, 10.8 s.), Alan Woodring (200m,
22.0s), Dick Landon (high jump, 6′3″), Frank Foss
(pole vault, 13′5″), John Kelly (single and double
skulls), Duke Kahanamoku (100m, swimming),
Ethelda Bleibtrey (100m, 200m, and relay swimming).

Other Sports

Tennis: Bill Tilden is the first American to win at
Wimbledon.

Horse Racing: Man O'War wins in all his 11 races,
including the Preakness and Belmont, and is retired
after the season.

Winners

World Series	Stanley Cup
Cleveland (AL) 5	Ottawa
Brooklyn (NL) 2	*U.S. Tennis Open*
American Professional	Men: William Tilden II
Football Association	Women: Molla Mallory
Akron Pros	*U.S. Golf Association Open*
College Football	Ted Ray
California	*Kentucky Derby*
College Basketball	Paul Jones (T. Rice, jockey)
Penn	
Player of the Year	
Howard McCann, N.Y.U.	

Fashion

For Women: Release of war tensions and the new
emancipation liberate "bachelor girls" from heavy
corsetry, hoops, and bustles (the hourglass look) for
loose, easy-fitting, casual clothes. Hand-embroidered
silk or crepe de chine lingerie flattens the bosom,
waist, and hips into a body cylinder. The flapper age,
in its infancy, introduces barrel-shaped skirts above
the ankle with the waistline dropped to the hip.
Bobbed and waved hair is brought forward to the
cheeks; the bun is discarded. Edwardian feathers and
flowers begin to disappear; black stockings and high-
laced shoes give way to natural-colored hose that
exposes the well-turned leg in low pumps. The
increasing emphasis on the flat, boyish look and
greater angularity is paralleled through the decade by
shorter hair and skirts. Soon to appear are ready-
made clothes and the fashion industry, "style"
(clothing obsolescence), and fashion magazines.

*High-fashion notes: The caftan; Chanel's transparent
overdresses.*

Kaleidoscope

- "Good-bye, John. You were God's worst enemy," chant 10,000 Virginia Prohibitionists, as they bury a 20-foot, horse-drawn coffin symbolizing John Barleycorn.
- Speakeasies open almost as fast as saloons close.
- As women enter speakeasies, many check their old-fashioned corsets in the powder room, order the new "cocktail" ("Between the Sheets"), smoke, and discuss current topics like sex and the new psychology.
- Places to hide the "hooch" or "giggle water" include canes, hot-water bottles, and satin garters.
- Margaret Sanger campaigns for birth control and advocates women's personal and economic freedom.
- The General Federation of Women's Clubs attempts to stamp out popular songs because of their "influence on our young people"; it will endorse only old standards like "Keep the Home Fires Burning" and "The Long, Long Trail."
- A large whiskey still is found on the farm of Texas senator Morris Sheppard, a leading proponent of the Eighteenth Amendment.
- Portable stills are available in hardware stores for $6.
- The high cost of living is a predominant national complaint as a result of postwar inflation.
- Financier Charles Ponzi receives $15 million from 40,000 people by claiming rapid profits from foreign exchange manipulations; after the pyramid scheme fails and his arrest, investors recover 12 cents on the dollar.
- Advertising expands, and the public is warned about acid teeth, B.O., cigarette throat, and wallflowerism. Aiming as well at children, advertisers market Santa Claus, in low favor over the past five years.
- Installment buying gains popularity; a vacuum cleaner costs $40—$2 down, $4 monthly.
- Cars on the market include the Templar, Stanley Steamer, Stephens, Salient, Overland, Stutz, Hupmobile, Maxwell, Pierce-Arrow, Milburn Electric, Chalmers, Franklin, Liberty, Peerless, Ford, Chevrolet, Hudson, Packard, Cadillac, Mercedes, and Rolls-Royce.
- Women are urged by the Fleischmann Company to buy, not bake, bread.
- Sales of coffee, tea, soft drinks, and ice-cream sodas increase with the advent of Prohibition.
- A postwar interest develops in nutrition, caloric consumption, and physical vitality.
- Coco Chanel introduces a new perfume, Chanel No. 5.
- The Algonquin Hotel in New York hosts "Round Table" gatherings with writers such as Dorothy Parker, Robert Benchley, George S. Kaufman, Alexander Woollcott, Heywood Broun, and Robert E. Sherwood. They meet in the Rose Room and call themselves the "Vicious Circle."
- Mary Pickford and Douglas Fairbanks marry, and their home, Pickfair, becomes a center of Hollywood social life.

- Newly married Scott and Zelda Fitzgerald achieve renown as uninhibited New York partygoers whose escapades include riding taxitops down Fifth Avenue and diving into fountains at Union Square and in front of the Plaza Hotel.
- Six thousand people are arrested on January 1, as alleged Communists; 2,000 are arrested the next day; few charges are substantiated.
- After Chicago gangster and restaurateur Big Jim Colossimo is shot to death, his gangland funeral, the first of its kind, is attended by movie and opera stars, judges, aldermen, and his suspected assassin, Johnny Torrio ("We was like brothers").
- The illiteracy rate reaches a new low of 6 percent.
- Of nearly 3 million miles of rural highways, over 90 percent are for horse travel.
- Two-thirds of the world's oil originates in the United States.
- The greatest national celebration of the year is the Tercentenary of the Pilgrim landing at Plymouth.

New Words and Usages: Pep, jazz, profiteer, addict, fabricated, sundae, tank, repression, Freudian slip, nonmonogamous love, fetish, and fixation

First Appearances: Trojan contraceptives, two-pants suits, Hilton Hotel Corporation, pogo sticks, Sunkist trademark, Frigidaire, Kellogg's All-Bran, La Choy, Hercule Poirot (in *The Mysterious Affair at Styles,* Agatha Christie), Pitney Bowes postage meter, ITT, water skiing, boysenberries (a cross between blackberries, raspberries, loganberries), Brillo, Assorted Charms candy, Campfire marshmallows, Underwood sardines, Baby Ruth (named after Grover Cleveland's daughter), "Call for Philip Morris . . ."

Gangster Big Jim Colossimo and his girlfriend, Dale Winter. *Library of Congress.*

1921

A divided public considered Sacco and Vanzetti (*center*) either red anarchists or victims of official persecution. *Library of Congress.*

Facts and Figures

Economic Profile
  Dow-Jones: ↓ High 81–
    Low 65
  GNP: −24%
  Inflation: −6.4%
  Unemployment: 11.7%
Median age, first marriage:
  Male: 24.6, Female: 21.2
Average household size: 4.6
Population over 65: 4.6%
Population under 10: 23%
Beaver teddy bear: $5
Shah of Persia soap: 3/$1
Scotch linen knickers: $11
Alaskan seal coat: $600–$750
Dress oxford shoes (Saks):
  $7.75
Meat prices per pound
  leg of lamb: 38¢
  chicken: 47¢
  salmon steak: 35¢
  butterfish: 22¢
Chocolate bonbons: 2/$1

Enrico Caruso. *Library of Congress.*

Deaths

Enrico Caruso, Engelbert
  Humperdinck, Camille
  Saint-Saëns, Barrett
  Wendell.

In the News

U.S. Steel Reduces Wages for the Third Time as Economy Falters . . . Warren Harding Is Inaugurated, His Speech Is Broadcast on Radio . . . U.S. Rejects Soviet Plea for Trade . . . Nebraska Law Forbids Aliens from Holding Land . . . Emergency Quota Act Restricts Immigration to 3% of 1910 Census . . . Samuel Gompers Defeats John L. Lewis for AFL Presidency . . . Former President W. H. Taft Is Appointed Chief Justice, Supreme Court . . . Unemployment Conference Begins under Herbert Hoover, 3.5 Million Are out of Work . . . Famine Relief Act Authorizes $20 Million in Grain, Corn, Milk, for Russia . . . Britain Grants South Ireland Dominion Status . . . Billy Mitchell Destroys German Battleship with Air Bombs . . . General Accounting Office Is Created to Monitor Federal Spending . . . Congress Passes Oil Depletion Allowance . . . Hoover Organizes Relief for Russian Famine . . . Sacco and Vanzetti Are Sentenced to Death . . . Arkansas River Overflows, Killing 1,500 . . . Eugene Debs's Prison Sentence Is Commuted by Harding . . . Congress Declares Official End to War with Germany . . . Fatty Arbuckle Is Accused of Starlet Murder . . . Greeks Defy League of Nations and Declare War with Turkey . . . Fascists Gain First Seats in Italian Parliament . . . Armistice Day Is Proclaimed, the First Ceremony Held for the Unknown Soldier . . . Washington Arms Limitation Conference Begins, Britain, France, Italy, Japan Attend . . . Persia Expels Russians . . . Klan Burnings Multiply in South and Midwest.

Quotes _____

"We seek no part in directing the destinies of the world."

— Warren G. Harding

"Since the Crusades I do not know of any enterprise which has done more honor to men than the intervention of America in the War."

— C. de Wiert, prime minister of Belgium

"The cost of modern warfare is so colossal that wars can no longer be waged at a profit."

— Hudson Maxim, "Shall America Disarm?"
Current Opinion

"The future of the white race relies on driving out the twin evils of liquor and prostitution."

— Charles W. Eliot, president emeritus, Harvard

"Fads run their course through the mob like the measles. . . . One of the latest is psychoanalysis."

— Dr. Frank Crane, *Current Opinion*

"An economist asks what England gets out of Ireland. The question isn't what, but when."

— *Cleveland News*

"The future work of the business man is to teach the

The handsome and genial Warren Harding was fond of White House gatherings in order to meet his constituents. *Library of Congress.*

teacher, preach to the preacher, admonish the parent, advise the doctor, justify the lawyer, superintend the statesman, fructify the farmer, stabilize the banker, harness the dreamer, and reform the reformer."

— Edward E. Purinton, *Independent*

"From drugstore to drugstore is the shortest distance between two pints."

— *Life*

Ads _____

Radio

Firsts

Church broadcast (Calvary Episcopalian Church, Pittsburgh)
Band concert (T. J. Vastine)
Farm news (Sioux City, Ia.)
Stock report (New York)
Boxing match (Johnny Ray vs. Johnny Dundee, with Florent Gibson as announcer)
World Series (New York Giants vs. New York Yankees)

Of Note

President Harding delivers the Armistice Day address from the Tomb of the Unknown Soldier at Arlington National Cemetery • Vincent Lopez, radio's first bandleader, starts his broadcast from the Hotel Taft, New York, with "Lopez speaking . . ." • WWJ, Detroit, begins with the first news broadcast • WJZ originates from the Westinghouse factory roof, Newark, with announcer Thomas H. Cowan • Westinghouse produces the first popular-priced home receiver; it sells for $60.

Movies

Openings

The Kid (Charles Chaplin), Charles Chaplin, Jackie Coogan (debut)
Dream Street (D. W. Griffith), Carol Dempster, Ralph Graves
The Sheik (George Melford), Rudolph Valentino, Patsy Ruth Miller
Tol'able David (Henry King), Richard Barthelmess, Lassie
The Saphead (Buster Keaton), Buster Keaton, Beula Booker
The Four Horsemen of the Apocalpyse (Rex Ingram), Rudolph Valentino, Alice Terry
Deception (Ernst Lubitsch), Henry Porten
Gypsy Blood (Ernst Lubitsch), Pola Negri
One Arabian Night (Ernst Lubitsch), Pola Negri, Ernst Lubitsch

Little Lord Fauntleroy (Alfred E. Green), Mary Pickford
Peck's Bad Boy (Sam Wood), Jackie Cooper, Charles Hatton, Queenie (a dog)
The Passion Flower (Herbert Brenon), Norma Talmadge
Miss Lulu Bett (William de Mille), Lois Wilson, Milton Sills

Top Box-Office Stars

Mary Pickford, Douglas Fairbanks, Wallace Reid, Charles Ray, Norma Talmadge, Constance Talmadge, Thomas Meighan, Eugene O'Brien, Anita Stewart, Dorothy Gish, William S. Hart, William Faversham, Clara Kimball Young, Gloria Swanson

Far left: Rudolph Valentino, as the exotic lover in *The Sheik*, drove women to faint in the aisles and men to slick down their hair. *Movie Star News*.

Left: Charles Chaplin with Jackie Coogan in *The Kid*. By this time, Chaplin's portrayal of "the little fellow" or "the tramp" has made him the world's most famous movie star. *Movie Star News*.

Popular Music

Hit Songs

"Second Hand Rose"
"Make Believe"
"I'm Nobody's Baby"
"Ain't We Got Fun?"
"I'm Just Wild about Harry"
"The Sheik of Araby"
"Ma—He's Making Eyes at Me"
"Shuffle Along"
"Whip-poor-will"
"Say It with Music"
"Eve Cost Adam Just One Bone"
"When Buddha Smiles"

"Don't Send Your Wife to the Country"
"Big Chief Wally Ho Woo (He'd Wiggle His Way to Her Wigwam)"

Top Records

Wabash Blues (Isham Jones); *Make Believe* (Nora Bayes); *Bandana Days* (Eubie Blake); *April Showers* (Al Jolson); *I Love You Sunday* (Ted Lewis); *Aunt*

Hagar's Blues (Ladd's Black Aces); *The Harlem Strut* (James P. Johnson)

Jazz and Big Bands

The New Orleans Rhythm Kings play at the Friars' Inn, Chicago. James P. Johnson makes his first solo jazz piano session for Okeh records.

Theater

Broadway Openings

Plays

Anna Christie (Eugene O'Neill), Pauline Lord
Diff'rent (Eugene O'Neill), Mary Blair, James Light
Gold (Eugene O'Neill), Willard Mack
The Straw (Eugene O'Neill), Margola Gilmore, Otto Kruger
Liliom (Ferenc Molnár), Eva Le Gallienne, Joseph Schildkraut
A Bill of Divorcement (Clemence Dane), Katharine Cornell
Dulcy (George S. Kaufman, Marc Connolly), Lynn Fontanne, Elliott Nugent
The Green Goddess (William Archer), George Arliss
Getting Gerty's Garter (Wilson Collison, Avery Hopwood), Hazel Dawn
The Wren (Booth Tarkington), Helen Hayes, Leslie Howard
Blood and Sand (Tom Cushing), Otis Skinner, Cornelia Skinner
Bluebeard's Eighth Wife (Alfred Savoir), Ina Claire
The Circle (Somerset Maugham), Mrs. Leslie Carter, John Drew
The Intimate Strangers (Booth Tarkington), Billie Burke, Alfred Lunt
The Playboy of the Western World (John Synge), Thomas Mitchell
The Trial of Joan of Arc (Emile Moreau), Margaret Anglin

Musicals

Shuffle Along (Noble Sissle, Eubie Blake), Josephine Baker, Noble Sissle (first Broadway musical acted, directed, and written by blacks)
Blossom Time (Sigmund Romberg, Dorothy Donnelly), Bertram Peacock, Olga Cook
Bombo (Sigmund Romberg, Harold Atteridge), Al Jolson, Janet Adair
Music Box Review (Irving Berlin), Ethelind Terry, Joseph Santley
The Perfect Fool (Ed Wynn), Ed Wynn, Janet Velie
Tangerine (Carlo Sanders, Howard Johnston), Julia Sanderson, Joseph Cawthorn
Greenwich Village Follies (Carey Morgan, Arthur Swanstron), Irene Franklin, Joe E. Brown
Two Little Girls in Blue (Vincent Youmans, Arthur Francis), Fairbanks Twins, Oscar Shaw

Classics and Revivals On and Off Broadway

Macbeth, Lionel Barrymore, Walter Hampden; *The Taming of the Shrew*, E. H. Sothern; *Twelfth Night*, Julia Marlowe; *Iphigenia in Aulis* (Euripides), Margaret Anglin

Regional

Cleveland Playhouse, begun in 1915, becomes the first resident professional theater in the United States.

Pulitzer Prize

Miss Lulu Bett, Zona Gale

Classical Music _____

Compositions
Carlos Salzedo, *Four Preludes to the Afternoon of a Telephone*
George Antheil, *Zingareska*
Arthur Farwell, *Music for the Pilgrimage Play*
Charles Ives, Thirty-four Songs for Voice and Piano
John Powell, *Virginia*
Percy Grainger, *Molly on the Shore*
Howard Hanson, Concerto for Organ, Strings, and Harp

Important Events
The New York National and Philharmonic symphonies merge into the Philharmonic-Symphony Orchestra of New York. The Cleveland Orchestra, under Nikolai Sokoloff, tours Washington, Boston, and New York. The Eastman School opens, Rochester, N.Y. Isadora Duncan opens her Moscow school for the dance. Edgard Varèse founds the International Composers Guild to champion contemporary music.

Debuts: Artur Schnabel, Erica Morini

First Performances
John Alden Carpenter, *Krazy Kat* (Chicago); Sergei Prokofiev, pianist, Piano Concerto no. 3 (Chicago); Henry F. Gilbert, *Indian Sketches* (Boston); Henry Hadley, conducting, *The Ocean* (New York)

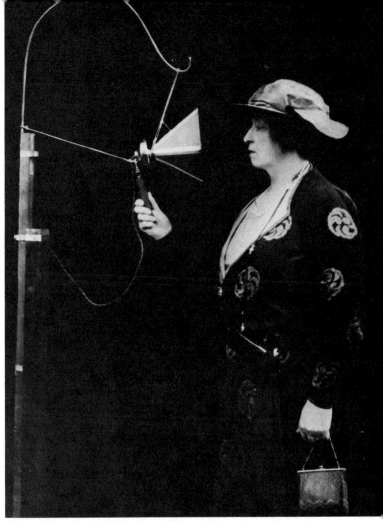

Nellie Melba's broadcasts over the wireless contribute to the popular interest in opera and classical music. *Library of Congress.*

Teenage Josephine Baker and Noble Sissle (*center*) in *Shuffle Along.* Billy Rose Theatre Collection. *The New York Public Library at Lincoln Center. Astor, Lenox, and Tilden Foundations.*

Opera

Metropolitan: Amelita Galli-Curci, *La traviata;* Maria Jeritza, *Die tote Stadt, Tosca;* Feodor Chaliapin, *Boris Godunov;* Leon Rothier, *Louise; L'oracolo, Mefistofele*

Chicago: Mary Garden: *Le jongleur de Notre-Dame; The Love for Three Oranges* (Prokofiev, also conducting, world premiere)

Music Notes
Aaron Copland studies in Paris with the famed Nadia Boulanger • Howard Hanson wins the Prix de Rome • "Organized audience plans" (music series) begin • Antheil provokes an international scandal with his violent compositions and piano performances • The futurists play concerts of noise instruments to reproduce the machine age • Mary Garden's realistic performance of *Salomé* creates a scandal in Chicago • Radio and record sales spur a great interest in classical music.

Art

Painting

Stuart Davis, *Lucky Strike, Bull Durham*
Niles Spencer, *City Walls*
Charles Demuth, *Business, Assassin and Nicolette, Incense of a New Church, Roofs and Steeples*
Arthur G. Dove, *Thunderstorm*
John Marin, *Off Stonington*
Joseph Stella, *Collage #11*
Max Weber, *Still Life*
Lyonel Feininger, *Gelmeroda, VIII*

Sculpture

Alexander Archipenko, *Turning Torso*
Robert Laurent, *Flirtation*
William Zorach, *Figure of a Child*
Elie Nadelman, *Dancer*
Man Ray, *Cadeau*

Architecture

Wrigley Building, Chicago (Graham, Anderson, Probst, and White)
Harkness Quadrangle, New York (James Gamble Rogers)

Important Exhibitions

Museums

New York: *Metropolitan:* "Paintings of the Peace Conference: American and Allied Leaders on View"; early Oriental rugs and carpets; modern Japanese paintings; "Impressionism and Postimpressionism"; children's art. *Public Library:* Manet prints. *Société Anonyme:* Alexander Archipenko

Individual Shows

Alfred Stieglitz, art photos; Stuart Davis, John Sloan, Robert Henri, Reynolds Peal (Society of Independent Artists)

Art Briefs

The Phillips Gallery in Washington, D.C., opens, the first American modern art museum • George Bellows and Franklin DeHaven win national art prizes • The Impressionism and Postimpressionism show at the Metropolitan begins a controversy: an anonymous pamphlet that attacks the show is called KKK propaganda; a long debate follows on the virtues of showing living American artists rather than older foreign masters • Henry E. Huntington buys Gainsborough's *The Blue Boy* and Reynolds's *Portrait of Mrs. Siddons* for $1 million • Raibolini's *Virgin and Child,* discovered in a New York restaurant and wrapped in a newspaper, is returned to the Bologna Museum.

Lyonel Feininger, *Gelmeroda VIII*, 1921. Oil. 39 1/4 × 31 1/4". *Collection of Whitney Museum of American Art. Purchase.*

The fascination with flight continues, and interest grows in using the plane for mail service. Right: "The Goddess of Flight." *Library of Congress.*

Books

Fiction

Critics' Choice

Three Soldiers, John Dos Passos
The Triumph of the Egg, Sherwood Anderson
Carter and Other People, Don Marquis
Erik Dorn, Ben Hecht
Figures of Earth, James Branch Cabell
The Big Town, Ring Lardner

Best-Sellers

Main Street, Sinclair Lewis
The Brimming Cup, Dorothy Canfield
The Mysterious Rider, Zane Grey
The Age of Innocence, Edith Wharton
The Valley of Silent Men, James Oliver Curwood
The Sheik, Edith M. Hull
A Poor Wise Man, Mary Roberts Rinehart
Her Father's Daughter, Gene Stratton Porter
The Sisters-in-Law, Gertrude Atherton
The Kingdom Round the Corner, Coningsby Dawson

Nonfiction

Critics' Choice

The American Novel, Carl Van Doren
Notes and Reviews, Henry James (posthumous)
Symptoms of Being Thirty-Five, Ring Lardner
Representative Government, William H. Taft
Our Common Country, Warren Harding
America and the Young Intellectual, Harold Stearns
The Engineers and the Price System, Thorstein Veblen
Of All Things, Robert Benchley
⮞ *Dream Psychology*, Sigmund Freud
⮞ *Tractatus Logico-Philosophicus*, Ludwig Wittgenstein

Best-Sellers

The Outline of History, H. G. Wells
The Mirrors of Downing Street, by a Gentleman with a Duster (Harold Begbie)
Mystic Isles of the South Seas, Frederick O'Brien
White Shadows in the South Seas, Frederick O'Brien
Peace Negotiations, Robert Lansing

The Theater, the Drama, the Girls, George Jean Nathan
Miracle Mongers and Their Methods, Harry Houdini
The Story of Mankind, Hendrik Willem Van Loon
Queen Victoria, Lytton Strachey
The Autobiography of Margot Asquith, Margot Asquith

Poetry

Ezra Pound, *Poems 1918–1921, Cantos I–IV*
Edwin Arlington Robinson, *Avon's Harvest*
Edna St. Vincent Millay, *Second April, Renascence, The Lamp and the Bell*
Amy Lowell, *Legends*
Marianne Moore, *Poems*
William Carlos Williams, *Sour Grapes*

Pulitzer Prizes

Alice Adams, Booth Tarkington (novel)
The Founding of New England, James Truslow Adams (U.S. history)
A Daughter of the Middle Border, Hamlin Garland (biography)
Collected Poems, Edwin Arlington Robinson (poetry)

Science and Technology

The antiknock properties of tetraethyl lead, which facilitate premium gasoline, are discovered by Thomas Midgeley.

Newly developed quartz crystals stabilize fluctuating radio signals.

Herbert McLean Evans discovers vitamin E, an antisterility substance.

Elmer V. McCollum discovers vitamin D, a substance in cod liver oil, which prevents rickets.

The Mayo Clinic pioneers dye techniques to outline the kidneys on X rays.

Ear microsurgery is introduced.

Edward Murray East and George Harrison Schull develop a hybrid corn for higher crop yields.

Theories of atomic structure and absorption are proposed by Irving Langmuir.

⮞ The "ink-blot" test is devised by Hermann Rorschach.

Sports

Baseball

Kenesaw Mountain Landis is appointed commissioner of baseball following the "Black Sox Scandal," with a mandate to maintain the integrity of the game.

Babe Ruth (New York, AL) hits 59 home runs, bats .378, and drives in 170 runs.

Eight Chicago White Sox are found not guilty when grand jury testimony disappears; Commissioner Landis bans them from baseball.

Champions

Batting	Pitching
Rogers Hornsby (St. Louis, NL), .397	Art Nehf (New York, NL), 20–10
Harry Heilmann (Detroit, AL), .394	Carl Mays (New York, AL), 27–9
	Home runs
	Babe Ruth (New York, AL), 59

Football

Joseph Carr takes over the American Professional Fooball League; franchises are reduced to $50; the Chicago–New York game draws 80 people.

Pro Stars: George Halas (Chicago), Jim Thorpe (Cleveland)

College All-Americans: Glenn Killinger (HB), Penn State; Malcolm Aldridge (HB), Yale

Rose Bowl (Jan. 1, 1922): Washington & Jefferson 0–California 0

Basketball

The New York Whirlwinds, with Nat Holman, play the New York Original Celtics with Pete Barry and Johnny Whitty in a "World Series." Holman later joins the Original Celtics.

Other Sports

Boxing: Jack Dempsey KO's Georges Carpentier in the fourth round for the heavyweight title; this is the first fight gate of over $1 million.

Winners

World Series
New York (NL) 5
New York (AL) 3
American Professional Football Association
Chicago Staleys
College Football
Cornell
College Basketball
Penn
Player of the Year
George Williams, Mo.
Stanley Cup
Ottawa
U.S. Tennis Open
Men: William Tilden II
Women: Molla Mallory
U.S. Golf Association Open
James M. Barnes
Kentucky Derby
Behave Yourself (C. Thompson, jockey)

Fashion

For Men: The Prince of Wales style is popular: padded shoulders, narrow lapels, a tight fit over the hips, "working-class" brown shoes, bright red ties, colored pocket handkerchiefs. Dress becomes less formal—for example, with butterfly bow ties or long ties with sailor knots. Oxford shoes replace high-buttoned styles; wristwatches replace the pocket watch and fob. The new sports look focuses on the belted Norfolk jacket with knickers or Oxford "bags" (pants with unusually wide trousers, sometimes 25 inches around the knees). Formal wear is also more relaxed, the matching frock coat and cutaway now challenged by the single- or double-breasted dark jacket with striped trousers and soft, medium-wing collars. Shirts are white, with silver gray, black, or white ties. High hats, if worn, are placed at a rakish angle. Spats are linen or canvas in white, biscuit, or gray. Accessories consist of chesterfield coats with mufflers knotted at the neck, and crooked-handle or straight-shaft malacca canes.

High-fashion note: Reboux's straw hats

Kaleidoscope

- A bill is proposed in Utah to imprison any woman who wears her skirt higher than three inches above the ankle.
- The American Medical Association continues to endorse whiskey prescriptions; 2.5-gallon quantities of beer are prescribed for a variety of complaints.
- President Harding pleads for a "Ban by Civilization on War."
- Harding pardons the ailing socialist Eugene Debs and invites him to the White House: "I have heard so damned much about you, Mr. Debs, that I am very glad to meet you personally."
- "Here rests in honored glory an American soldier, known but to God" is inscribed on the Tomb of the Unknown Soldier at Arlington National Cemetery.
- A silver quarter is minted with "Peace" under the figure of an eagle and the liberty head on the reverse side.
- A *New York Times* editorial speculates that Robert Goddard's rockets will not work, since there is nothing in outer space for a rocket's exhaust to push against.
- Prof. Albert Einstein arrives in New York, delivers a lecture at Columbia University on relativity, and introduces "time as the fourth dimension."
- Literature dealing with contraception is banned; a New York physician is convicted of selling *Married Love.*
- Conditions of work for children under 14 are regulated by the Education Act.

- Cigarette consumption rises to 43 billion annually, despite its illegality in 14 states; college girls are often expelled if caught smoking; Iowa legalizes cigarette sales to adults.
- Disillusioned with American values, Ernest Hemingway, William Carlos Williams, Ezra Pound, Glenway Wescott, Katherine Anne Porter, and F. Scott Fitzgerald, among many others, depart for Europe.
- The Chicago Crime Commission records that during the year 10,000 criminals have stolen $12 million.
- Universities whose business schools expand include California, Chicago, Dartmouth, New York, Boston, Harvard, Northwestern, Cincinnati, Syracuse, Ohio State, Michigan, Wisconsin, and Stanford.
- Boston bans *Birth of a Nation.*
- Because threats have been made to people who propose to produce German opera in its original language, the Metropolitan and Chicago opera companies boldly advertise all operas "IN ENGLISH."
- A rage to visit Harlem and see black entertainment is stimulated by the show *Shuffle Along.*
- Plastic surgery becomes heavily advertised in trade union journals in terms of the "WONDERS" it has performed on actors' faces.
- Rudolph Valentino skyrockets to fame in *The Four Horsemen of the Apocalpyse.*
- Hollywood star types include the sweet, innocent girl (Mary Pickford); strong, silent cowboy (William S. Hart); exuberant, boyish athlete (Douglas Fairbanks); lonely, funny tramp (Charles Chaplin); vamp (Theda Bara); and exotic, foreign lover (Rudolph Valentino).
- For the first time, heart disease ranks as the number one cause of death.
- Former U.S. secretary of the navy Franklin D. Roosevelt, 39, is stricken with poliomyelitis.

First Appearances: Mounds bar, Eskimo Pie (replacing I-Scream bar), Betty Crocker, Bel Paese cheese, Wise potato chips, Wrigley's chewing gum, iodized salt, Band-Aids, table tennis, Miss America pageant in Atlantic City (and one-piece form-fitting bathing suits), Sardi's, Lindy's, Arrow shirts and the "Sanforizing Process," starchless but stiff collars (Van Heusen), artificial or "cultured" pearls, "Tillie the Toiler," "Smitty," American Birth Control League (Margaret Sanger), Emmett Kelley's career with Barnum and Bailey, Austin 7, Lincoln auto, Electrolux vacuum cleaner, Drano, coin bearing a living person's portrait (Alabama centennial commemorative half-dollar with image of Governor T. E. Kilby), helium-filled balloons, coast-to-coast telephone service

The well-dressed man wearing knickers, oxford shoes, and a hip-hugging coat. *D. Ouellette Collection.*

1922

Secretary of Interior Albert P. Fall, whose secret leases of oil on public lands have come under investigation. *Library of Congress.*

In the News

FIRST IRISH GOVERNMENT IS FORMED UNDER MICHAEL COLLINS, THE SINN FEIN REBEL . . . U.S., BRITAIN, JAPAN, FRANCE, ITALY AGREE ON NAVAL LIMITATIONS TREATY AND AFFIRM CHINESE "OPEN DOOR" . . . MAHATMA GANDHI IS SENTENCED TO SIX YEARS FOR CIVIL DISOBEDIENCE . . . HARDING ORDERS U.S. TROOPS HOME FROM RHINELAND . . . OIL IS DISCOVERED IN VENEZUELA . . . COAL MINERS AND STRIKE BREAKERS CLASH AT HERRIN, ILLINOIS, 26 DIE . . . SECRETARY OF INTERIOR ALBERT FALL IS QUESTIONED ON TEAPOT DOME LAND LEASES . . . U.S. REFUSES TO FORGIVE EUROPEAN ALLIES' DEBT . . . WASHINGTON, D.C., KNICKERBOCKER THEATER ROOF COLLAPSES, 98 ARE KILLED . . . REBECCA L. FELTON, GEORGIA, IS FIRST WOMAN APPOINTED TO THE SENATE . . . MUSSOLINI LEADS MARCH ON ROME . . . MICHAEL COLLINS IS ASSASSINATED BY I.R.A. . . . KEMAL PASHA PROCLAIMS TURKISH REPUBLIC, ENDING SULTANATE . . . ECONOMY REVIVES, AUTOS LEAD THE WAY . . . JAMES DOOLITTLE MAKES FIRST ONE-DAY TRANSCONTINENTAL FLIGHT, 21 HOURS, 28 MINUTES . . . TOMB OF KING TUTANKHAMEN IS OPENED BY AMERICAN HOWARD CARTER AND BRITISH LORD CARNARVON . . . CONGRESS PASSES RESOLUTION FAVORING PALESTINE AS JEWISH HOMELAND . . . CLERGYMAN EDWARD HALL AND CHOIR MEMBER ELEANOR MILLS ARE FOUND SHOT TO DEATH IN N.Y. SUBURB, HALL IS HUSBAND OF JOHNSON & JOHNSON HEIRESS . . . INDEPENDENT MONARCHY IS PROCLAIMED IN EGYPT, BRITISH PROTECTORATE ENDS.

Quotes

"I do not like women who know too much."
— Rudolph Valentino

"[There has been] a change for the worse during the past year in feminine dress, dancing, manners, and general moral standards. [One should] realize the serious ethical consequences of immodesty in girls' dress."
— *Pittsburgh Observer*

"Day by day, in every way, I am getting better and better."
— Coué motto for widely successful self-improvement course

"The real hope of the world lies in putting as painstaking thought into the business of mating as we do into other big businesses."
— Margaret Sanger

"His motor car was poetry, tragedy, love and heroism."
— Sinclair Lewis, *Babbitt*

"An imposed peace was made at Paris. There was left out every element of justice and hope for brotherhood which [Woodrow] Wilson had. . . . The allies thought vengeance was theirs. . . . The fruits are bitter."
— Frank A. Vanderlip

"Eugenics [is] the science of race betterment, . . . the segregation of the insane and feeble-minded, . . . the prevention of all obvious degenerates from having children."
— Essay on Lothrop Stoddard's *The Revolt against Civilization,* in *Current Opinion*

"The picture is so essentially Spanish that I want everyone in the theater . . . to eat garlic during the performance."
— Fred Niblo, discussing his film *Blood and Sand*

Margaret Sanger, founder of the American Birth Control League, persuades an American manufacturer to produce diaphragms. *Library of Congress.*

Ads

Radio

Premieres
"Broadway Broadcasting," Miss Bertha Brainard
  (play reviews)
"Lucky Strike Radio Show"
"New York Philharmonic-Orchestra"
"Paul Whiteman"

Specials
Warren Harding's opening speech to Congress; "The Perfect Fool," Ed Wynn (first comedic play); first presidential news conference; "The Great Commoner" (sermon by William Jennings Bryan); "Will Rogers and the Ziegfeld Follies Girls"

Of Note
The first radio commercial is for apartments in Jackson Heights, N.Y. • With 314 stations, a federal legislative authority is established.

Movies

Openings
Orphans of the Storm (D. W. Griffith), Lillian Gish,
  Dorothy Gish, Joseph Schildkraut
Foolish Wives (Erich von Stroheim), Eric von
  Stroheim, Miss Dupont
Prisoner of Zenda (Rex Ingram), Lewis Stone, Alice
  Terry
Blood and Sand (Fred Niblo), Rudolph Valentino,
  Lila Lee, Nita Naldi
Grandma's Boy (Fred Newmeyer), Harold Lloyd
Robin Hood (Allan Dwan), Douglas Fairbanks,
  Wallace Beery
When Knighthood Was in Flower (Robert G.
  Vignola), Marion Davies, Ernest Glendinning
Sherlock Holmes (Albert Parker), John Barrymore,
  Carol Dempster, Hedda Hopper, Roland Young
One Glorious Day (James Cruze), Will Rogers, Lila
  Lee, Alan Hale
Oliver Twist (Frank Lloyd), Jackie Coogan, Lon
  Chaney
A Doll's House (Charles Bryant), Alla Nazimova
Nanook of the North (Robert Flaherty) (first
  documentary)
Salomé (Charles Bryant), Alla Nazimova
Nosferatu (F. W. Murnau), Max Schreck

Top Box-Office Stars
Mary Pickford, Douglas Fairbanks. *Also popular:* Norma Talmadge, Constance Talmadge, Tom Mix, Buck Jones, John Gilbert, Ramon Novarro, Charles Chaplin, Ben Turpin, Lon Chaney

Far left: after two hung juries, a third trial exonerates "Fatty" Arbuckle of murder. *Movie Star News.*

Lillian and Dorothy Gish play endangered innocents in *Orphans of the Storm,* D. W. Griffith's epic of the French Revolution. *Movie Star News.*

Popular Music

Hit Songs
"I Wish I Could Shimmy Like My
  Sister Kate"
"Georgia"
"Ain't It a Shame"
"Chicago—That Toddling Town"
" 'Way Down Yonder in New
  Orleans"
"L'Amour—Toujours—L'Amour"
"Rose of the Rio Grande"
"Do It Again"
"Somebody Stole My Gal"
"Lovin' Sam, the Sheik of
  Alabam' "
"Ooo Ernest—Are You Earnest
  with Me?"

"You Remind Me of My Mother"

Top Records
Dreamy Melody (Art Landry and
Call of the North Orchestra); *Sing
Song Man* (Nora Bayes); *I Love
Her, She Loves Me* (Eddie
Cantor); *Mister Gallagher and
Mister Shean* (Gallagher and
Shean); *Hot Lips* (Cotton
Pickers); *Lonesome Mama Blues*
(Mamie Smith); *Birmingham Blues*
(Fats Waller)

Jazz and Big Bands
Paul Whiteman plays at the Palais
Royale. Louis Armstrong joins
King Oliver's Creole Jazz Band in
Chicago.

First Recordings: Coleman
Hawkins with Mamie Smith; Kid
Ory with Spike's Seven Pods of
Pepper Orchestra in Los Angeles

New Bands: Red Nichols, New
York; Miff Mole, with the Original
Memphis Five.

Theater

Broadway Openings

Plays
Rain (John Colton, Clemence Randolph), Jeanne
  Eagels
Merton of the Movies (George Kaufman, Marc
  Connelly), Glenn Hunter
Abie's Irish Rose (Anne Nichols), Robert Williams,
  Marie Carroll, John Cope
Loyalties (John Galsworthy), James Dale
Back to Methusela (George Bernard Shaw), George
  Gaul, Margaret Wycherly
The Hairy Ape (Eugene O'Neill), Louis Wolheim
R.U.R. (Karel Čapek), Basil Sydney
The World We Live In (Joseph and Karel Čapek),
  May Hopkins, Kenneth MacKenna
The Cat and the Canary (John Willard), Florence
  Eldridge, Henry Hull
The Old Soak (Don Marquis), Harry Beresford
Seventh Heaven (Austin Strong), Helen Menken,
  George Gaul
The Tidings Brought to Mary (Paul Claudel), Jeanne
  de Casalis
Six Characters in Search of an Author (Luigi
  Pirandello), Margaret Wycherly, Florence
  Eldridge
He Who Gets Slapped (Leonid Andreyev), Richard
  Bennett
Fashions for Men (Ferenc Molnár), Helen Gahagan

Musicals
Ziegfeld Follies (Louis A. Hirsch, Ring Lardner),
  Will Rogers, Gallagher and Shean, Olsen and
  Johnson

The Gingham Girl (Albert Von Tilzer, Neville
  Fleeson), Eddie Buzzell, Helen Ford
Sally, Irene and Mary (J. Fred Coots, Raymond
  Klages), Eddie Dowling, Hal Van Rensselaer
Greenwich Village Follies (George V. Hobart, Louis
  A. Hirsch), John E. Hazzard, Savoy and
  Brennan
Little Nellie Kelly (George M. Cohan), Elizabeth
  Hines, Robert Pitkin
The Blushing Bride (Sigmund Romberg, Cyrus
  Wood), Cleo Mayfield
The Blue Kitten (Rudolph Friml, Otto Harbach),
  Joseph Cawthorn, Lillian Lorraine
Orange Blossoms (Victor Herbert, B. G. DeSylva),
  Queenie Smith, Edith Day, Hal Skelly
Make It Snappy (Jean Schwartz, Harold Atteridge),
  Eddie Cantor, Lew Hearn
Chauve-Souris, Nikita Baliuff's revue of Russian folk
  songs, dances, and burlesque skits.

Classics and Revivals On and Off Broadway
Hamlet, John Barrymore; *The Merchant of Venice,*
David Warfield, Glenn Hunter; *Julius Caesar,* Fritz
Lieber; *Macbeth, Romeo and Juliet,* both with Ethel
Barrymore; *The Rivals* (Sheridan), Robert Warwick

Pulitzer Prize
Anna Christie, Eugene O'Neill

Classical Music _____

Compositions

Douglas Moore, *Four Museum Pieces*
George Antheil, *Airplane Sonata* for Piano, *Sonata
Sauvage, Death of the Machines,* Jazz Sonata,
Symphony no. 1
Howard Hanson, Symphony no. 1
Edgard Varèse, *Offrandes*
Aaron Copland, Passacaglia for Piano
Edward Hill, *Stevensoniana* Suite
Arthur Farwell, *Symbolistic Study* no. 3

Important Events

A record $7 million is earned in an extraordinary
New York season; four orchestras give 100 concerts
at Carnegie Hall. At an unusual benefit in New York,
five conductors in a single concert lead their
specialties for the Damrosch Fellows in Rome
(conductors: Joseph Stranksy, Artur Bodanzky,
Albert Coates, Willem Mengelberg, Leopold
Stokowski). In another benefit, 15 pianists perform in
unison to raise $15,000 for Moritz Moszkowski
(pianists include Harold Bauer, Ossip Gabrilowitsch,
Percy Grainger, Josef Lhévinne). 108 music festivals
include the Berkshire, Sing Sing Prison, and
Columbia University festivals, the visiting Berlin
State Opera *Ring,* the Philadelphia Orchestra's 80th
anniversary celebration, and the New York String
Quartet Festival.

Notable Performances: Richard Strauss, Sergei
Rachmaninoff, Geraldine Farrar, Pablo Casals, Josef
Hofmann, Vincent d'Indy, Fritz Kreisler, Albert
Coates

Debut: Myra Hess

First Performances

Ernest Schelling, *A Victory Ball* (Philadelphia);
Ernest Bloch, Quintet for Piano and String Quartet
(New York); Leo Sowerby, Symphony no. 1 (New
York)

Opera

Metropolitan: Titta Ruffo, Amelita Galli-Curci, *Il
barbiere di Siviglia;* Elisabeth Rethberg (debut),
Aïda; premiere: *Cosi fan tutte; Le roi d'Ys*

Chicago: Mary Garden, *Thaïs*

San Francisco: Premieres, in Russian: *Boris
Godunov, Eugene Onègin; The Czar's Bride* (Nikolai
Rimsky-Korsakov)

Los Angeles: *Snegourotchka* (Rimsky-Korsakov)

Music Notes

Richard Strauss hires the Philadelphia Orchestra to
play four concerts of his work in New York, one in
Philadelphia • George Antheil goes to Paris to join
Ezra Pound, James Joyce, Sylvia Beach, and Virgil
Thomson • The New York Philharmonic Orchestra,
with Willem Mengelberg conducting, records the
Coriolan Overture on two 12-inch, single-faced discs
for Victor Company, the orchestra's first recording.

Gertrude Stein, one of the leading Americans abroad,
entertained Hemingway, William Carlos Williams, and
Sherwood Anderson, among others, at her Paris home.
Library of Congress.

Art

Painting

George Bellows, *The White House*

Maurice Prendergast, *Acadia*

John Marin, *Lower Manhattan II, Maine Islands*

William Zorach, *Sailing by Moonlight*

Joseph Stella, *Skyscrapers*

Arthur G. Dove, *Gear*

Charles Demuth, *Still Life, No. 1*

Sculpture

Gaston Lachaise, *Walking Woman*

John Storrs, *Male Nude*

William Zorach, *Floating Figure*

Saul Baizerman, *Road Builder's Horse*

Architecture

Institute of Fine Arts, Detroit (Paul Phillippe Cret)

Lincoln Memorial, Washington, D.C. (Henry Bacon)

William Randolph Hearst's San Simeon, Calif., house (Julia Morgan).

Important Exhibitions

Museums

New York: *Metropolitan:* Duncan Phyfe furniture; Japanese sword fittings; Chinese funerary portraits

Milwaukee: Wisconsin painters and sculptures

Chicago: Second international watercolor show

Cleveland: Renaissance art

Pittsburgh: Carnegie International First Prize: George Bellows's *Elinor, Jean, and Anna*

Art Briefs

The Baltimore Museum of Art opens • William Jennings Bryan learns that his so-called copy of Gilbert Stuart's *George Washington* is an original • Public debate occurs over the exhibition of George Bellows's *Nude Girl with a Shawl*.

The World We Live In (or *The Insect Comedy*) and *R. U. R.* (which introduces the term "robot") express the Capeks' fear of the dehumanizing effects of technological advances. *Billy Rose Theatre Collection. The New York Public Library at Lincoln Center. Astor, Lenox, and Tilden Foundations.*

Left: popular brother-and-sister dance team Fred and Adele Astaire. *Movie Star News.*

Books

Fiction

Critics' Choice

The Beautiful and Damned, F. Scott Fitzgerald
Tales of the Jazz Age, F. Scott Fitzgerald
Babbitt, Sinclair Lewis
The Enormous Room, E. E. Cummings
The Glimpses of the Moon, Edith Wharton
One Man in His Time, Ellen Glasgow
ᴥ *Ulysses,* James Joyce
ᴥ *The Garden Party,* Katherine Mansfield
ᴥ *The Forsythe Saga* (completed), John Galsworthy

Best-Sellers

If Winter Comes, A. S. M. Hutchinson
The Sheik, Edith M. Hull
Gentle Julia, Booth Tarkington
The Head of the House of Coombe, F. H. Burnett
Simon Called Peter, Robert Keable
The Breaking Point, Mary Roberts Rinehart
This Freedom, A. S. M. Hutchinson
Maria Chapdelaine, Louis Hémon
To the Last Man, Zane Grey

Nonfiction

Critics' Choice

The Economic Basis of Politics. Charles and Mary Beard
Public Opinion, Walter Lippmann
The Argument about Co-Education, C. Pestalozzi
Human Nature and Conduct, John Dewey
Peter Wiffle, Carl Van Vechten
American Individualism, Herbert Hoover
Geography and Plays, Gertrude Stein
All in a Life-Time, Henry Morgenthau
Prejudices, H. L. Mencken
ᴥ *Methodology of the Social Sciences,* Max Weber
ᴥ *Decline of the West,* Oswald Spengler

Best-Sellers

The Outline of History, H. G. Wells
The Story of Mankind Hendrik Willem Van Loon
The Americanization of Edward Bok, Edward Bok
Diet and Health, Lulu Hunt Peters
The Mind in the Making, James Harvey Robinson
The Outline of Science, J. Arthur Thomson
Outwitting Our Nerves, Josephine A. Jackson, Helen M. Salisbury
Queen Victoria, Lytton Strachey
Mirrors of Washington, Anonymous (Clinton W. Gilbert)
In Defense of Woman, H. L. Mencken

Poetry

T. S. Eliot, *The Waste Land*
Conrad Aiken, *Priapus and the Pool*
Carl Sandburg, *Slabs of the Sunburnt West*
John Hall Wheelock, *The Black Panther*
ᴥ W. B. Yeats, *Later Poems*

Pulitzer Prizes

One of Ours, Willa Cather (novel)
The Supreme Court in United States History, Charles Warren (U.S. history)
The Life and Letters of Walter H. Page, Burton J. Hendrick (biography)
The Ballad of the Harp-Weaver, A Few Figs from Thistles, 8 Sonnets in American Poetry, 1922, A Miscellany, Edna St. Vincent Millay (poetry)

Science and Technology

Ur, the ancient Sumerian city on the Euphrates, 2600 B.C., is unearthed by Charles Woolley of the British Museum and a University of Pennsylvania team.

Numerous well-preserved artifacts are discovered in the 1350 B.C. tomb of King Tutankhamen, in the Valley of the Kings, at Luxor, Egypt.

New devices are developed for chiseling vibrations into wax that improve the quality of records.

The first mechanical telephone switchboard is installed, in New York (its exchange is Pennsylvania).

The beneficial effect of calves' liver on hemoglobin production is demonstrated by George Hoyt Whipple.

Herbert McLean Evans discovers the substance that promotes human growth, a hormone from the anterior lobe of the pituitary gland.

A converted cargo ship becomes the first U.S. aircraft carrier, the U.S.S. *Langley.*

ᴥ Insulin, which regulates the use of sugar by cells, is extracted and first used to treat diabetes by Frederick Banting and Herbert Best.

Sports

Jim Thorpe. *Pro Football Hall of Fame.*

Baseball

Babe Ruth is suspended by Commissioner Landis for 40 days for barnstorming; Ruth's salary increases to $56,000.

A record 49 runs is scored in one game: Chicago 26–Philadelphia 23 (NL).

Champions

Batting	Pitching
Rogers Hornsby (St. Louis, NL), .401	Pete Donohue (Cincinnati, NL), 18–9
George Sisler (St. Louis, AL), .420	Joe Bush (New York, AL), 26–7
(Ty Cobb, Detroit, AL, also bats over .400, at .401)	*Home Runs*
	Rogers Hornsby (St. Louis, AL), 42

Football

The American Professional Football Association is renamed the National Football League; Green Bay joins the league. Jim Thorpe organizes an all-Indian pro team, the Oorang Indians.

Pro Stars: Pete Henry (Canton), Curly Lambeau (Green Bay)

College All-Americans: Harold Kipke (HB), Michigan; Edward Kaw (HB), Cornell; Cal Hubbard (G), Harvard

Rose Bowl (Jan. 1, 1923): Southern California 0–Penn State 0

Basketball

Jim Furey reorganizes the Original Celtics to play in the New York Armory, with salaries instead of per-game pay; Celtics include Johnny Beckman, Tom Furey, Dutch Dehnert, Johnny Witte, and Joe Lapchik, most from New York's Hell's Kitchen. They win 194 of 204 games. The Renaissance Rens, a black team, is organized.

Other Sports

Golf: Gene Sarazen wins the PGA title.

Winners

World Series		Player of the Year
New York (NL) 4		Charles Carney, Ill.
New York (AL) 0		*Stanley Cup*
MVP		Toronto
NL–Not chosen		*U.S. Tennis Open*
AL–George Sisler, St. Louis		Men: William Tilden II
		Women: Molla Mallory
NFL		*USGA Open*
Canton Bulldogs		Gene Sarazen
College Football		*Kentucky Derby*
Cornell		Morvich (A. Johnson, jockey)
College Basketball		
Kansas		

Fashion

For Women: Edwardian laces and feathers are rejected for epicene fashions: "men's" lounging robes and blazers, shirts with ties and cuff links, fitted suits. Hair is cropped short at the ears with waves. Antoine de Paris's mannish shingle bob appears, despite Irene Castle's lingering 1914 bob. With the emphasis on youth, little makeup is worn. The focus is on the flat, angular look; every curve of the body is suppressed by long, cylindrical corsets or hip belts and bust bodices (the "foundation garment") to create the hipless and bosomless appearance. Underwear, now called "undies," is more practical and hygienic: cotton replaces silk in cream, beige, soft pastels, and "ivory" (surplus khaki dye added to white). The "thin voman" of Greenwich Village, like her Left Bank counterpart, gains attention in harem pantaloons and skirts above the ankle (in black hose), Dutch-boy hairdos, berets, asexual smocks, unconventional colors (chartreuse, henna, puce, magenta), and African jewelry of bangles and bone, wood, shell, mock jade (by Chanel).

High-fashion notes: Silk, velvet masks for the flirtatious vamp to peek through; gauntlet gloves with art deco lines; onyx and crystal hat pins; low-strapped pumps with chunky heels and perforated detailing; Chanel's Balkan embroideries; Vuitton luggage.

Kaleidoscope _____

- Clara Bow, 17, wins a fan magazine contest for "The Most Beautiful Girl in the World"; Charles Atlas wins the "World's Most Perfectly Developed Man" contest.
- Describing the new "flapper," *Vanity Fair* reports: "[She] will never . . . knit you a necktie, but she'll go skiing with you. . . . She may quote poetry to you, not Indian love lyrics but something about the peace conference or theology."
- Radio becomes a national obsession, and many stay up half the night listening to concerts, sermons, "Red Menace" news, and sports. Those without home radios gather around crystal sets in public places like the post office.
- $5,000-a-week star Roscoe "Fatty" Arbuckle, exonerated of starlet Virginia Rappe's murder following an alleged sexual episode, changes his name to William Goodrich but is still blacklisted.
- Actresses Mabel Normand, Mary Miles Minter, and Mary Pickford are romantically linked with murdered actor-director William Desmond Taylor; only Pickford's career remains unharmed.
- One-time actor-idol Wallace Reid, addicted to rum and morphine, dies in a sanitarium; Hollywood has recently placed his name first on a blacklist of 117 "unsafe" persons.
- Although the Hollywood morals code is established with William H. Hays as its chief enforcer, studios continue to advertise films with "red kisses," "white kisses," and "pleasure-mad daughters [and] sensation-craving mothers."
- The two-year ban on James Branch Cabell's *Jurgen* is lifted.
- Protestant Episcopal bishops vote to erase *obey* from the marriage ceremony.

- Women married to aliens are no longer required to relinquish their citizenship.
- *Reader's Digest* starts a wave of magazine book digests.
- Attorney General Harry Daugherty persuades Harding that government control of railroads would be "a conspiracy worthy of Lenin" and then obtains an injunction barring all union activity.
- H. L. Mencken defends the American husband against current charges of infidelity, calling him "fundamentally moral," if only because he "lacks . . . courage . . . [and] money."
- Boston mayor Curley bans Isadora Duncan from the stage when she wears a transparent Greek dress and publicly praises the Soviet regime.
- Syracuse University bans dancing.
- Florenz Ziegfeld forbids his stars to work on radio because it "cheapens them."
- The manager of radio station WEAF rejects the first toothpaste commercial because "care of the teeth" is too delicate a subject for the air.
- At the Washington Arms Limitation Conference presided over by Secretary of State Charles Evans Hughes, the first agreement in history is made to reduce already existing armaments of major powers.
- The U.S. Post Office burns 500 copies of James Joyce's *Ulysses*.
- Henry Ford, who earns over $264,000 a day, is declared a "billionaire" by the Associated Press.

Fads: Radio, college football, Eskimo Pies, the three o'clock raisin break, collecting tabloids

First Appearances: Self-winding wristwatch, Checker Cab, State Farm Mutual auto insurance, commercially prepared baby food (Clapp's vegetable soup), Canada Dry ginger ale, cruise ship circumnavigating the world, Federal Narcotics Board, New York City curfew (2 A.M.) on dancing, skywriting, push-button elevators, Maytag Gyrofoam washing machine, soybean processing plant, Thom McAn, microfilm machine, *New York Daily Mirror, Better Homes and Gardens, True Confessions, New York Times Book Review* (as a separate section), transcontinental dirigible flight, parachuting from a disabled flight, the expression "Pike's Peak or Bust," woman automotive engineer, Strongheart (first leading dog movie star)

Commercial flights, like the "Highball Express" to Bimini, are frequently short hops between small cities. *Library of Congress.*

1923

Facts and Figures

Economic Profile
  Dow-Jones: ↑ High 105–
    Low 86
  GNP: +14%
  Inflation: +0.9%
  Unemployment: 2.4%
Daily newspapers: 2,038
Books published: 8,863
Airmail postage: 8¢
Postcard: 1¢
IRS collections: $2.6 billion
Movie (Apollo, New York):
  50¢–$1
Broadway, top seat: $2.50
Metropolitan Opera matinee:
  $1–$5
Four-month around-the-world
  cruise: $1,000
Willoughby folding camera:
  $24
Mark Cross attaché case:
  $40–$50
Dinner, Hotel Vanderbilt,
  New York: $2.50 (p.p.)
Stephens car: $1,295
Packard: $2,485
Rolls-Royce: $10,900

Deaths

Sarah Bernhardt, Lord
  Carnarvon, Eleonora Duse,
  Gustave Eiffel, William
  Holabird, Katherine
  Mansfield, Wilhelm Conrad
  Roentgen, Charles
  Steinmetz.

In the News

PRESIDENT HARDING SHAKES 10,000 SHRINER HANDS AT WHITE HOUSE . . . SECRETARY OF STATE CHARLES EVANS HUGHES REJECTS U.S. RECOGNITION OF U.S.S.R. UNTIL FOREIGN DEBTS ARE HONORED . . . FRANCE AND BELGIUM OCCUPY THE RUHR TO FORCE GERMAN REPARATIONS PAYMENT, GERMANY ORGANIZES PASSIVE RESISTANCE . . . WASHINGTON, D.C., MINIMUM WAGE FOR WOMEN AND CHILDREN IS DECLARED UNCONSTITUTIONAL . . . WARREN HARDING DIES OF CEREBRAL APOPLEXY IN SAN FRANCISCO AFTER HECTIC ALASKAN JOURNEY . . . CALVIN COOLIDGE TAKES OFFICE, SWORN IN BY FATHER, VERMONT JUSTICE OF THE PEACE . . . ECONOMY SOARS, UNEMPLOYMENT FALLS . . . U.S. OFFERS TO MEDIATE GERMAN DEBT PROBLEM, FRANCE REFUSES . . . OKLAHOMA GOVERNOR DECLARES MARTIAL LAW TO COMBAT KKK OUTRAGES, STATE SENATE MOVES TO IMPEACH HIM . . . FEDERAL TAX DISCLOSURE LAW IS PASSED, JOHN D. ROCKEFELLER, SR., PAYS $124,000, ROCKEFELLER, JR., $7.4 MILLION . . . U.S. STEEL FIGHTS REDUCTION OF 12-HOUR DAY . . . EARTHQUAKE DESTROYS TOKYO AND YOKAHAMA, U.S. OFFERS AID . . . KKK CONVENTION AT KOKOMO, IND., DRAWS 200,000 . . . HUNG JURY FREES COMMUNIST WILLIAM Z. FOSTER, TRIED FOR PREACHING VIOLENT REVOLUTION . . . OILMAN HARRY SINCLAIR PLANS TO VISIT RUSSIA TO BUY SIBERIAN OIL FIELDS . . . PANCHO VILLA IS ASSASSINATED . . . LAST-MINUTE SETTLEMENT AVERTS COAL STRIKE . . . GERMAN CURRENCY GOES TO ONE TRILLION MARKS PER DOLLAR . . . ADOLF HITLER FAILS IN ATTEMPT TO OVERTHROW GERMAN GOVERNMENT FROM MUNICH BEER GARDEN . . . SENATE WALSH COMMITTEE STARTS TEAPOT DOME INVESTIGATION . . . U.S. STEEL AGREES TO 8-HOUR DAY.

221

Quotes _____

"My soul yearns for peace. My passion is for justice over force. My hope is in the Great Court. If in our search for everlasting peace, we . . . follow humbly but dauntlessly the 'kindly light' of divine inspiration, . . . God will not let us fail."
— President Warren G. Harding, on the World Court

"My God, this is a hell of a job! I have no trouble with my enemies. I can take care of my enemies all right. But my damn friends, my God-damn friends. . . . They're the ones that keep me walking the floor nights!"
    — President Warren G. Harding (quoted in William Allen White, *Autobiography*)

"Men nowadays are tired of liberty. . . . These masses like rule by the few. . . . Fascismo . . . will pass again without the slightest hesitation over the more or less decomposed body of the goddess of liberty."
    — Benito Mussolini

"[It is resolved] that war between nations should be outlawed as an instrument of settlement of international controversies by making it a public crime."
    — Senator Hiram Borah, Senate resolution

"The height of folly is to imagine that the cutting of armaments would ensure peace. World peace is best maintained when nations are armed to the hilt."
    — Japanese general Kenichi Oshimi

"If this nation is to obtain its destiny, there will have to be a harmonious assimilation [which] three powerful elements will defy: . . . the Negro, . . . alarmingly vitiated by venereal infection, . . . the Jew, . . . not American, . . . [and] the illiterate Catholic."
— Imperial Wizard H. W. Evans, keynote speaker, KKK State Fair, Texas

"[Evolution theory is a] program of infidelity masquerading under the name of science."
    — William Jennings Bryan

"No woman is justified in being supported in idleness by any man. The most womanly woman today is the woman who works."
    — Mrs. Carrie Chapman Catt, suffragist

Library of Congress.

Ads _____

One Year Married and All Talked Out . . .
Is there anything that would brighten their evenings? . . . How can they turn their silent, lonely hours into real human companionship?
    (Dr. Eliot's Five-Foot Shelf of Books)

The truth is—the Playboy was built for her. Built for the lass whose face is brown with the sun when the day is done of revel and romp and race.
    (Car named after Synge's The Playboy of the Western World)

She Who Prizes Beauty Must Obey Nature's Law!
    Faulty Elimination is the greatest enemy that beauty knows. It plays havoc with the complexion, brings sallow skin, dull and listless eyes.
Everybody / Everyday / Eat POST's Bran Flakes, as an ounce of Prevention.
    (Post's Bran Flakes)

The King and Queen Might Eat Thereof / And Noblemen Besides.
    (JELL-O)

At thirty every woman reaches a crossroads. Will she develop—or merely age?
    (Boncilla Beautifier, the Clasmic Clay)

Try the "Daily Dozen" Muscle Build to Music.
    (Daily Dozen)

What is the great story of the War? Is it . . . Joffre at the first Marne or . . . Foch at the second? Or . . . "They shall not pass" at Verdun? Is it . . . the first gas attack at Ypres? . . . Or . . . the Lost Battalion? . . . A different sort of story stands comparison with these . . . of a fight by the soldiers . . . against a countless and implacable foe.
    (Zonite Antiseptic)

Radio

Premieres
"Eveready Hour" (variety)
"The Happiness Boys," Billy Jones, Ernie Hare
  (first comedy series)
"Roxy and His Gang"
"Dr. Walter Damrosch" (lecture-recital)
"Joseph M. White, 'The Silver-Masked Tenor' "
"A & P Gypsies," Harry Orlich Orchestra

Specials
"The Laughing Lady" (Ethel Barrymore, first radio
  drama)

Of Note
Sponsors take over the air waves: Cliquot Club
Eskimos, Ipana Troubadours, A & P Gypsies,
Rheingold Quartet, Lucky Strike Show • Announcer
Graham McNamee gains wide popularity with news
"editorializing."

Movies

Openings
The Ten Commandments (Cecil B. DeMille), Richard
  Dix, Rod La Rocque
Anna Christie (John Griffith Wray), Blanche Sweet,
  William Russell
The Covered Wagon (James Cruze), Lois Wilson, J.
  Warren Kerrigan
Peg O'My Heart (King Vidor), Laurette Taylor
The Green Goddess (Sidney Olcott), George Arliss,
  Alice Joyce
The Hunchback of Notre Dame (Wallace Worsley),
  Lon Chaney, Ernest Torrence
Our Hospitality (Buster Keaton), Buster Keaton
Main Street (Harry Beaumont), Monte Blue, Noah
  Beery, Robert Gordon
Peter the Great (Dimitri Buchowetzski), Dagni
  Servais, Emil Jannings
The Pilgrim (Charles Chaplin), Charles Chaplin,
  Edna Purviance

Rosita (Ernst Lubitsch), Mary Pickford, Holbrook
  Blinn
Safety Last (Fred Newmeyer), Harold Lloyd,
  Mildred Davis
Scaramouche (Rex Ingram), Ramon Novarro, Alice
  Terry
White Sister (Henry King), Lillian Gish, Ronald
  Colman
A Woman of Paris (Charles Chaplin), Edna
  Purviance, Adolphe Menjou

Top Box-Office Stars
Norma Talmadge, Thomas Meighan

Stars of Tomorrow
Jean Arthur, Clara Bow, Norma Shearer, Ronald
Colman

Rin Tin Tin, a German
shepherd saved by an
American soldier in
World War I, becomes
a film star. *Movie Star
News.*

Far left: the shy Harold
Lloyd character
performs daredevil
stunts in *Safety Last* in
order to win his girl.
Movie Star News.

Popular Music ──────────────

Hit Songs
"Yes! We Have No Bananas"
"Who's Sorry Now?"
"Charleston"
"Mexicali Rose"
"It Ain't Gonna Rain No Mo' "
"That Old Gang of Mine"
"You've Got to See Mamma Ev'ry
    Night—or You Can't See
    Mamma at All"

Top Records
Three O'Clock in the Morning
(Paul Whiteman); *Somebody Stole*
My Gal (Ted Williams); *Barney*
Google (Jones and Hare); *I Won't*
Say I Will (Irene Bordoni); *Linger*
Awhile (Paul Whiteman); *Twelve*
O'Clock at Night (Sophie Tucker)

Jazz and Big Bands
Roseland replaces society dance
orchestras with Fletcher
Henderson's jazz band.
Henderson also brings a ten-piece
band to the Club Alabam, New
York. Newly organized bands
include Bix Beiderbecke, King
Oliver (with Louis Armstrong),
Jelly Roll Morton's Red Hot
Peppers, Jabbo Smith's Rhythm
Aces, and the Reuben Reeves
River Boys. Bessie Smith's
Downhearted Blues sells a record
2 million copies. Other popular
blues singers include Ma Rainey
and Ida Cox.

Other New Bands: Horace Heidt,
Oakland; Ted Weems, Philadelphia

Theater ──────────────

Broadway Openings

Plays
St. Joan (George Bernard Shaw), Winifred Lenihan
The Swan (Ferenc Molnár), Eva Le Gallienne, Basil
    Rathbone
Icebound (Owen Davis), Edna May Oliver, Willard
    Robertson
The Shame Woman (Lula Vollmer), Florence
    Rittenhouse
The Adding Machine (Elmer Rice), Dudley Digges,
    Margaret Wycherly
White Cargo (Leon Gordon), Richard Stevenson
Tweedles (Booth Tarkington, Harry Wilson), Ruth
    Gordon
Spring Cleaning (Frederick Lonsdale), Violet
    Heming, Estelle Winwood
Meet the Wife (Lynn Starling), Mary Boland, Clifton
    Webb
Laugh, Clown, Laugh (David Belasco, Tom
    Cushing), Lionel Barrymore

Musicals
Kid Boots (Harry Tierney, Joseph McArthur), Eddie
    Cantor, Mary Eaton
Wildflower (Herbert Stothart, Vincent Youmans,
    Oscar Hammerstein II), Edith Day, Guy
    Robertson
Ziegfeld Follies (Victor Herbert et al., Gene Buck),
    Fannie Brice, Eddie Cantor, Ann Pennington
Poppy (Stephen Jones, Arthur Samuels), W. C.
    Fields, Madge Kennedy

Battling Butler (Walter Rosemont), Charles Ruggles,
    Marie Saxon, William Kent
Earl Carroll's Vanities (Earl Carroll), Joe Cook,
    Peggy Hopkins Joyce
Runnin' Wild (James Johnson, Cecil Mack), Miller
    and Lyles, all-black cast

Classics and Revivals On and Off Broadway
The Devil's Disciple (George Bernard Shaw), Basil
Sydney, Roland Young; *The Lady from the Sea,*
Ghosts (Ibsen), Eleonora Duse; *Romeo and Juliet,*
Jane Cowl; *Pelleas and Melisande* (Maeterlinck),
Jane Cowl; *Cymbeline,* E. H. Sothern, Julia
Marlowe; *The School for Scandal* (Sheridan), John
Drew, Ethel Barrymore; *Oedipus Rex* (Sophocles),
John Martin Harvey; *Cyrano de Bergerac* (Rostand),
Walter Hampton; *Hamlet,* John Barrymore

Regional

Founded: Hedgerow Theatre, near Philadelphia, by
Jasper Deeter

Pulitzer Prize
Icebound, Owen Davis

Classical Music

Compositions

Ernest Schelling, *A Victory Ball*
George Antheil, Violin Sonata no. 1
Wallingford Riegger, *La belle Dame sans merci*
Howard Hanson, *North and West, Lux Aeterna*
Roger Sessions, *The Black Maskers*
Aaron Copland, *As It Fell upon a Day*
Arthur Farwell, Symphonic Song on "Old Black Joe"
Charles Loeffler, *Music for Four String Instruments*

Important Events

Notable Concerts: Darius Milhaud conducts and plays the piano with the City Symphony (New York); George Enesco conducts the New York Philharmonic; Fritz Kreisler gives a farewell concert in Hollywood; the San Francisco Orchestra features the new English school of composers: Eugene Goossens, Ralph Vaughan Williams, Arthur Bliss, Frederick Delius, Gustav Holst

Major Recitals: Ignace Paderewski, Efrem Zimbalist, Pierre Monteux, Artur Rubinstein, Mrs. Ernestine Schumann-Heink, Ossip Gabrilowitsch, Mr. and Mrs. Pablo Casals, Mr. and Mrs. Josef Lhévinne, Myra Hess, Alexander Cortot, Moriz Rosenthal, Josef Hofmann, Jascha Heifetz

Guest Conductors Visiting the United States: Willem Mengelberg, Eugene Goossens, Albert Coates, Bruno Walter, Darius Milhaud

Debuts: Wanda Landowska, Claudio Arrau

First Performances

Edgard Varèse, *Hyperprism* (New York); Frank S. Converse, *Scarecrow Sketches* (Boston)

Opera

Metropolitan: The company enjoys the largest subscription to date; audiences also expand as the company travels to Brooklyn and Philadelphia. Productions: Maria Jeritza, Feodor Chaliapin, *Boris Godunov;* Lucrezia Bori, *Anima allegra* (Franco Vittadini, premiere); Richard Crooks, *Manon;* Beniamino Gigli, Frances Alda, *Martha;* Lawrence Tibbett (debut), *Faust.* Six major revivals include *Don Carlo, Roméo et Juliette, Faust, Tannhaüser, Der Rosenkavalier* (in German for the first time since the war)

Chicago: Claudia Muzio, Alexander Kipnis, *La forza del destino*

Los Angeles: Inaugural productions: Giovanni Martinelli, *La bohème;* and *I pagliacci.* First full production: *Il trittico* (Giacomo Puccini)

Music Notes

Josef Hofmann gives a benefit recital for Robert Schumann's daughters • Arnold Schoenberg's *Kammersymphonie* is met with public hissing • John McCormack sings in darkness as his audience demands more encores • 3,256 people perform in Cincinnati's golden jubilee production of *Elijah* • Geraldine Farrar is banned from singing in two Atlanta churches • Boston bans Richard Strauss's *Salomé* • Richard Wagner's wife, in a state of poverty, sells her late husband's artifacts.

The comedy hit *Abie's Irish Rose* deals with religious intermarriage. Billy Rose Theatre Collection. *The New York Public Library of Lincoln Center. Astor, Lenox and Tilden Foundations.*

Art

Painting

George Bellows,
Between Rounds
John Marin, *Ship, Sea
and Sky Forms,
Impression*
Marsden Hartley, *New
Mexico Recollections,
Color Analogy*
Charles Sheeler, *Bucks
County Barn, Self-
Portrait*
Rockwell Kent, *Shadows
of Evening* (1921–23),
The Kathleen
Preston Dickinson,
Industry

Sculpture

James Earle Fraser,
Head of a Faun
Lorado Taft, *Mask from
the Fountain of Time*
Gertrude V. Whitney,
Chinoise

Important Exhibitions

Museums

New York: *Metropolitan:* "Tut-ankh-Amen
Discoveries"; American handicrafts; art of the Italian
Renaissance; George Fuller centennial; women
painters and sculptors; John Singer Sargent, Winslow
Homer, Childe Hassam, John Marin, Paul
Dougherty. *Public Library:* James A. McNeill
Whistler

**Boston, Washington, Pittsburgh,
Minneapolis:** Spanish art

Boston: Indian art

Chicago: Artists of Chicago and vicinity

Cleveland: Cleveland arts and craftsmen

Gallery Shows

New York: Naum Gabo constructions; Jacob
Epstein's female portraits and bust of Joseph Conrad;
Gaston Lachaise's *Egyptian Head.* Bellows's

Architecture

St. Bartholomew's
Church, New York
(Bertram Goodhue)
Millard House,
Pasadena, Calif.
(Frank Lloyd Wright)
Bowery Savings Bank,
New York (York and
Sawyer)
Standard Oil Building,
New York (Carrère
and Hastings)
Skyscraper in Black
Glass and Aluminum
project, Los Angeles
(Rudolph Schindler)

Crucifixion of Christ dominates the fifth New York
Society of Artists Annual Exhibition. The Grand
Central Palace opens with a Russian art show.

Art Briefs

Gainsborough's *The Blue Boy* tours • National
attention is given to Alfred Stieglitz's photographs •
Interest grows in war subjects—Sargent's *Marching
Soldiers, The Duke of York, Death and Victory*—and
in animal sculpture—Robert Laurent, Herbert
Haseltine • Dr. A. C. Barnes plans a gallery in
Merion, Pa., to house his $3 million collection.

Sherwood Anderson. *D. Ouellette Collection.*

Dance

Mikhail Mordkin, formerly with the Bolshoi and
partner of Pavlova, forms a dance company that
performs in the *Greenwich Village Follies;* Martha
Graham joins.

Books

Fiction

Critics' Choice

A Lost Lady, Willa Cather
The Shadowy Third and Other Stories, Ellen Glasgow
Streets of Night, John Dos Passos
Three Stories and Ten Poems, Ernest Hemingway
Many Marriages, Sherwood Anderson
Four of a Kind, John Marquand
Cane, Jean Toomer
The High Place, James Branch Cabell
🐚 *Antic Hay*, Aldous Huxley
🐚 *The Good Soldier Schweik*, Jaroslav Hašek

Best-Sellers

Black Oxen, Gertrude Atherton
His Children's Children, Arthur Train
The Enchanted April, "Elizabeth"
Babbitt, Sinclair Lewis
The Dim Lantern, Temple Bailey
The Sea-Hawk, Rafael Sabatini
This Freedom, A. S. M. Hutchinson
The Mine with the Iron Door, Harold Bell Wright
The Wanderer of the Wasteland, Zane Grey
Flaming Youth, Warner Fabian

Nonfiction

Critics' Choice

Money, Credit and Commerce, Alfred Marshall
Unemployment, W. A. Appleton
My Life and Loves, Frank Harris
Indiscretions, Ezra Pound
Science and Life, Robert Millikan
Skepticism and Animal Faith, George Santayana
Absentee Ownership and Business Enterprise in Recent Times, Thorstein Veblen
🐚 *The Ego and the Id*, Sigmund Freud
🐚 *Psychological Types*, Carl Jung
🐚 *I and Thou*, Martin Buber

Best-Sellers

Etiquette, Emily Post
The Life of Christ, Giovanni Papini
The Life and Letters of Walter H. Page, ed. Burton J. Hendrick
The Mind in the Making, James Harvey Robinson
The Outline of History, H. G. Wells
Diet and Health, Lulu Hunt Peters
Self-Mastery through Conscious Auto-Suggestion, Emile Coué
The Americanization of Edward Bok, Edward Bok
The Story of Mankind, Hendrik Willem Van Loon
A Man from Maine, Edward Bok

Poetry

Wallace Stevens, *Harmonium*
E. E. Cummings, *Tulips and Chimneys*
William Carlos Williams, *Spring and All*
Vachel Lindsay, *Collected Poems*
Elinor Wylie, *Black Armour*
Louise Bogan, *Body of This Death*
🐚 Kahil Gibran, *The Prophet*

Pulitzer Prizes

The Able McLaughlins, Margaret Wilson (novel)
The American Revolution—A Constitutional Interpretation, Charles Howard McIlwain (U.S. history)
From Immigrant to Inventor, Michael I. Pupin (biography)
New Hampshire: A Poem with Notes and Grace Notes, Robert Frost (poetry)

Science and Technology

Astronomers' measurements of the bending of the sun's rays during an eclipse are in accord with Einstein's theory of relativity.

Lee De Forest devises a method of recording sound directly on film—fonofilm.

The iconoscope, the first electronic television camera, is patented by Vladimir Zworykin.

The first American helium-filled rigid airship, the *Shenandoah*, is launched at Lakehurst, N.J.

Harry Steenbock, at the University of Wisconsin, discovers that radiating food with ultraviolet light adds vitamin D.

A whooping cough (pertussis) vaccine is developed.

Scopolamine, previously used as a childbirth anesthetic, is reported to be a "truth" serum after tests on convicts at San Quentin Prison.

Surgeons debate the virtues of the Steinach sex-gland rejuvenation transplants.

🐚 Tetanus toxoid is developed by Gaston Ramon.

Nobel Prize

Robert A. Millikan wins the prize in physics for his work on photoelectric phenomena.

Sports _____

Baseball

Yankee Stadium opens, the "house that Ruth built." Ruth hits .398 with 41 home runs. Casey Stengel's home runs win two World Series games, 1–0.

Champions _____

Batting
    Rogers Hornsby (St. Louis, NL), .403
    Harry Heilmann (Detroit, AL), .401
Pitching
    Adolfo Luque (Cincinnati, NL), 27–8
    Herb Pennock (New York, AL), 19–6

Home runs
    Babe Ruth (New York, AL), 41
    Fred Williams (Philadelphia, NL), 41

Football

Red Grange begins his college career at Illinois.

Pro Stars: Guy Chamberlin (Canton), Jim Conzelman (Rock Island).

College All-Americans: Red Grange (HB), Illinois; Cal Hubbard (G), Harvard.

Rose Bowl (Jan. 1, 1924): Navy 14–Washington 14

Basketball

The Original Celtics' game at Cleveland draws a record 22,000.

Other Sports

Tennis: Helen Wills, 17 ("Little Miss Poker Face"), wins the U.S. Open Singles. Bill Tilden wins his third straight U.S. Open Singles.

Golf: Gene Sarazen wins his second straight PGA title. Bobby Jones wins his first USGA Open.

Boxing: Jack Dempsey KO's "Wild Bull of the Pampas" Luis Firpo in the second round, after being knocked out of the ring in the first.

Swimming: Johnny Weismuller swims 200 yards free style in a record 1 minute, 59 ⅕ seconds.

Amateur Bobby Jones, who won the National Open on the 18th hole. *Library of Congress.*

Winners _____

World Series
    New York (AL) 4
    New York (NL) 2
MVP
    NL–Not chosen
    AL–Babe Ruth (New York)
NFL
    Canton Bulldogs
College Football
    Illinois
College Basketball
    Kansas

Player of the Year
    Paul Endacott, Kansas
Stanley Cup
    Ottawa
U.S. Tennis Open
    Men: William Tilden II
    Women: Helen Wills
USGA Open
    Robert T. Jones, Jr.
Kentucky Derby
    Zev (E. Sande, jockey)

Fashion _____

For Women: Boyish bobbed hair transforms into the shingle cut, flat and close to the head, with a center or side part. A single curl at each ear is pulled forward onto the face. New felt cloche (helmet-shaped) hats appear with little or no decoration in colors that match the day's dress. Hats are pulled down to the eyes, and their brims are turned up in the front or back. Eccentric hairstyles also gain popularity, for example, curled and brushed to a peak resembling a rooster's comb. In clothing, the straight line still emphasizes the boyish look, but fabrics are now embroidered, striped, printed, and painted, influenced by Chinese, Russian, Japanese, and Egyptian art. The Tutankhamen discoveries set off a rage for oriental fringed scarves, slave bangles, and long earrings. Artificial silk stockings, later called rayon, are stronger and less expensive than real silk ones, although they are shiny. The new seamless stocking, despite its wrinkling, also makes the leg look naked. At bedtime, girls wear boyish pajama bottoms, halter tops, and boudoir caps to protect their new hairdos.

High-fashion notes: Poirot's oriental dress; Lanvin's "robe de style"

Kaleidoscope _____

- The nation mourns President Harding as his cortege travels from San Francisco to Washington; the public's response is "the most remarkable expression of affection, respect and reverence in U.S. history" *(New York Times)*.
- Prescription liquor remains unlimited.
- Secretary of Interior Albert Fall's affluence comes under scrutiny during the Senate Walsh committee's investigation of federal oil leases; Fall has purchased a costly ranch in New Mexico with hundred-dollar bills.
- Marcus Garvey, leader of the Universal Negro Improvement Association, is convicted of mail fraud in raising money for his Black Star shipping line.
- Two of Harding's appointees suspected of graft commit suicide.
- An interest in psychology and self-healing continues to capture the nation; Emile Coué's mind-over-matter prescriptions attract thousands.
- Evangelist Aimee Semple McPherson opens a $1.5 million Angelus Temple in Los Angeles; it includes a "miracle room" for discarded crutches and wheelchairs and a rotating, illuminated cross visible for 50 miles.
- Clarence Darrow and William Jennings Bryan debate evolution versus fundamentalism in the *Chicago Tribune*.
- "It won't be Long now" becomes the popular slogan directed against Huey Long in the Louisiana gubernatorial race.
- Nicola Sacco goes on a 30-day hunger strike.
- President Coolidge, as a matter of budget and character, sleeps in a train berth rather than a Pullman.
- After the public's hostile response toward his 6 A.M. "matutinal" exercises, Coolidge turns to horseback riding.
- When his daughter is mailed *Women in Love,* Boston justice Ford prosecutes the offending circulating library; a "Clean Books League" forms to judge new and old books, and a long debate over D. H. Lawrence begins.
- Arthur Schwartz's Broadway show *Artists and Models,* with its bare-breasted chorus, sets off a censorship drive.
- Ida Rosenthal introduces Maidenform bras by giving them away to unshapely flappers who patronize her dress shop.
- In a record-setting dance marathon—90 hours, 10 minutes—Homer Morehouse, 27, drops dead in the 87th hour.
- Tennessee flappers are banned from public schools until they roll their stockings back up over their knees.
- Chicago racketeer Johnny Torrio goes into the bootleg business and makes $25,000 a week.
- Rudolph Valentino attacks Adolph Zukor on the radio with "language waves so hot" he is cut off the air. Valentino pans the motion picture "trust" for producing "nothing but cheap trash."

- The vast improvement in recording electronics eradicates screeches and howls.
- ASCAP wins a court decision requiring broadcasters to pay for the right to play copyrighted music on the air.
- Montana and Nevada are the first states to introduce old-age pensions.
- A HOLLYWOODLAND sign (now HOLLYWOOD) is erected in Los Angeles, each letter measuring 30 by 50 feet.
- A German Shepherd, Rin Tin Tin, becomes a top movie star.
- An air speed record of 243.67 m.p.h. is set in a Curtiss monoplane by former New York Giants pitcher Lt. A. I. Williams.
- Montana grasshoppers devour all plants in an area 300 miles long, 100 miles wide, and a half mile in altitude.
- $250 million is invested in the construction of 300 hotels; the largest is the $8 million Shelton in New York with 1,200 rooms.

Fads: Marathon dancing; flagpole sitting; spiritualism; ouija boards; mah-jongg (1.5 million sets sold); and the King Tut craze, extending to hats, rings, home decorations, jewelry, dress patterns, hair accessories, and newborn babies' names

First Appearances: Rubber diaphragm, Pan American World Airlines, Zenith, Milky Way, Butterfinger, Sanka, *Time, American Mercury,* Pet milk, Libby's tomato soup, Welch's grape jelly, Russell Stover, the name *Popsicle (changed from epsicle)*, Birds Eye, "Moon Mullins," neon tube advertising sign, chinchilla farm, "Junior Year Abroad," oven thermostat, photoelectric eye, Schick electric razor patent, Du Pont cellophane, Hertz Drive-Ur-Self, eggbeater and wooden bowl patent, 2¢ commemorative stamp of President Harding, White House Christmas tree lights, birth control clinic (New York)

Easter-egg rolling at the White House. *Library of Congress.*

1924

Facts and Figures

Economic Profile
  Dow-Jones:—High 120–
    Low 89
  GNP: 0%
  Inflation: +0.1%
  Unemployment: 5.0%
Expenditures
  Recreation: $2.7 billion
  Spectator sports: $47
    million
  European travel: $2.3
    million
Golf courses: 131
Bowlers: 60,000
Willys-Knight: $1,450
Chrysler: $1,395
Steinway: $875 (upright),
  $1,425 (grand)
Mah-jongg set: $3
Ouiji board: 87¢
Gorham silver spoon: $8.50
Hand-tailored wool tuxedo:
  $55
Man's collar pin, 14k gold,
  1¾": $1
Sulka silk cravat: $6

Deaths

Frances Hodgson Burnett,
  Ferruccio Busoni, Joseph
  Conrad, Gabriel Fauré,
  Anatole France, Victor
  Herbert, Franz Kafka,
  Maurice Prendergast,
  Giacomo Puccini, Louis
  Sullivan, Woodrow Wilson.

In the News

CONGRESS PASSES SOLDIERS' BONUS BILL OVER COOLIDGE VETO . . . LENIN DIES, JOSEPH STALIN, LEV KAMENEV, GRIGORY ZINOVIEV TAKE OVER . . . U.S. MARINES LEAVE NICARAGUA . . . SECRETARY OF INTERIOR ALBERT FALL, NAVY SECRETARY EDWIN DENBY, AND ATTORNEY GENERAL HARRY DAUGHERTY RESIGN IN TEAPOT DOME SCANDAL . . . 171 ARE KILLED IN CASTLE GATE, UTAH, COAL MINE DISASTER . . . NEW IMMIGRATION LAW TAKES EFFECT: 2% OF 1890 CENSUS AND NO JAPANESE . . . BRITAIN RECOGNIZES U.S.S.R. . . . U.S. BANKER CHARLES DAWES PROPOSES PLAN FOR GERMAN REPARATIONS . . . GOP NOMINATES COOLIDGE, DEMOCRATS NOMINATE JOHN DAVIS ON 103RD BALLOT . . . CONGRESS DECLARES NATIVE-BORN INDIANS CITIZENS . . . N.Y. REPEALS ITS STATE PROHIBITION ENFORCEMENT LAW . . . ITALIAN SOCIALIST DEPUTY GIACOMO MATTEOTI IS MURDERED, FASCISTS DENY RESPONSIBILITY . . . TWO WELL-TO-DO YOUTHS, NATHAN LEOPOLD AND RICHARD LOEB, ARE ACCUSED OF MURDERING 14-YEAR-OLD BOBBY FRANKS . . . ADOLF HITLER IS SENTENCED TO FIVE YEARS FOR MUNICH PUTSCH . . . JAPANESE CONDEMN IMMIGRATION HUMILIATION IN "HATE AMERICA" RALLIES . . . DAWES'S PLAN FOR GERMAN REPARATIONS IS ACCEPTED . . . FRANCE AGREES TO LEAVE RUHR . . . GERMAN MARK STABILIZES . . . J. EDGAR HOOVER IS APPOINTED HEAD OF BUREAU OF INVESTIGATION . . . ZINOVIEV LETTER URGING COMMUNIST INFILTRATION HELPS BRITISH CONSERVATIVES RECAPTURE GOVERNMENT . . . COOLIDGE WINS LARGE VICTORY FOR PRESIDENT, ROBERT M. LA FOLLETTE, THIRD-PARTY CANDIDATE, RECEIVES 17% . . . CLARENCE DARROW PLEA AVERTS DEATH PENALTY FOR LEOPOLD AND LOEB.

Quotes

"I can picture them awakened in the gray light of morning, furnished a suit of clothes by the State, led to the scaffold, . . . black caps down over their heads, . . . the hangman pressing a spring. . . . I can see them fall through space."
> — Clarence Darrow's courtroom appeal against the death penalty for Leopold and Loeb

"The United States once went on the notion that all men are created equal, and admitted everybody. . . . But we found we were becoming an insane asylum. . . . Unless the U.S. adopts this biologic principle [of racial differences] they will be flooded over by people of inferior stock because of their greater fecundity."
> — Dr. Harry H. Laughlin for the secretary of labor, on the new exclusionary immigration law

"He would be a national advertiser today, I am sure, as He was a great advertiser in His own day. He thought of His life as business."
> — Bruce Barton, speaking of Christ

"Ford has saved America from a social crisis. . . . When alcohol was taken [away], . . . the flivver was needed to replace it."
> — Samuel M. Vaudain, labor leader

"I am making this statement of my own free will and spending my own money . . . to assure well-meaning friends, who have been incessantly telephoning me and expressing their condolences, . . . that I'm satisfied."
> — Fannie Brice, in defense of the plastic surgeon who reconstructed her nose

"We are leaning too much on government. If our forefathers did not make enough money, they worked harder, and did not run to the government for a bonus. The American stock is changing."
> — Sen. David Reed (R-Pa.)

An ad for mineral water in which the tastes of the upper class appear accessible to all. *Library of Congress.*

Ads

Calvin Coolidge and his sons. "This is a business country, and it wants a business government," affirmed the president during a campaign speech. *Library of Congress.*

Radio

Premieres
"Spike Shannon" (early-morning physical culture)
Political convention coverage (Republican, Cleveland; Democratic, New York)

Of Note
Many actresses, like Olga Petrova, stand before a microphone in full costume • Debates continue over whether industry, government, or voluntary contributions should subsidize radio • Questions of licensing are also raised, as well as whether performers should be salaried • News and sports stations begin to expand • Radio sales rise from $60 million (1923) to $350 million.

Movies

Openings
America (D. W. Griffith), Carol Dempster, Lionel Barrymore

Babbitt (Harry Beaumont), Willard Louis, Mary Alden

Beau Brummel (Harry Beaumont), John Barrymore, Mary Astor

The Eternal City (George Fitzmaurice), Barbara La Marr, Bert Lytell

Girl Shy (Fred Newmeyer, Sam Taylor), Harold Lloyd, Jobyna Ralston

Greed (Erich von Stroheim), ZaSu Pitts, Gibson Gowland, Jean Hersholt (42 reels)

He Who Gets Slapped (Victor Seastrom), Lon Chaney

The Last Laugh (F. W. Murnau), Emil Jannings

The Iron Horse (John Ford), George O'Brien, Madge Bellamy

The Marriage Circle (Ernst Lubitsch), Marie Prevost, Florence Vidor, Adolphe Menjou

Merton of the Movies (James Cruze), Glenn Hunter, Charles Sellon

Monsieur Beaucaire (Sidney Olcott), Rudolph Valentino, Bebe Daniels

Isn't Life Wonderful? (D. W. Griffith), Carol Dempster, Neil Hamilton

The Thief of Bagdad (Raoul Walsh), Douglas Fairbanks, Anna May Wong

Sherlock Holmes (Buster Keaton), Buster Keaton, Kathryn McGuire

Le ballet mécanique (Fernand Léger, designer)

Top Box-Office Stars
Norma Talmadge, Rudolph Valentino. *Also popular:* Thomas Meighan, Lionel Barrymore, Jackie Coogan, Harold Lloyd, Tom Mix, Pola Negri, Mary Pickford, Rin Tin Tin

The dashing acrobatic Douglas Fairbanks in *The Thief of Bagdad,* which he also wrote under the pseudonym Elton Thomas. *Movie Star News.*

Popular Music

Hit Songs

"Somebody Loves Me"
"Lady, Be Good"
"Indian Love Call"
"Rose Marie"
"I'll See You in My Dreams"
"Deep in My Heart, Dear"
"I Want to Be Happy"
"California, Here I Come"
"All Alone"
"The Drinking Song"
"Mandalay"
"Fascinating Rhythm"
"The Man I Love"

"Does the Spearmint Lose Its Flavor on the Bedpost over Night?"

Top Records

The Prisoner's Song (Vernon Dalhart); *The Sinking of the "Titanic"* (Ernest Van "Pop" Stoneman); *Charley My Boy* (Eddie Cantor); *What'll I Do?* (Lewis Hames), *June Night* (Waring's Pennsylvanians); *There's Yes Yes in Your Eyes* (Paul Whiteman); *Tea Pot Dome Blues* (Fletcher Henderson)

Jazz and Big Bands

Paul Whiteman introduces *Rhapsody in Blue* at Aeolian Hall, New York. Fletcher Henderson lures Louis Armstrong away from King Oliver. Bix Beiderbecke records with the First Wolverine Orchestra.

New Band: Earl Hines, Chicago

Theater

Broadway Openings

Plays

Desire under the Elms (Eugene O'Neill), Walter Huston, Mary Morris, Walter Abel
S. S. Glencairn (Eugene O'Neill), Walter Abel, James Meighan
All God's Chillun Got Wings (Eugene O'Neill), Paul Robeson
Hell-Bent fer Heaven (Hatcher Hughes), Glenn Anders
They Knew What They Wanted (Sidney Howard), Pauline Lord, Richard Bennett, Glenn Anders
What Price Glory? (Maxwell Anderson, Laurence Stallings), Louis Wolheim, William Boyd
The Show-Off (George Kelly), Louis John Bartels
Minick (George S. Kaufman, Edna Ferber), Phyllis Povah, O. P. Heggie
Outward Bound (Sutton Vane), Alfred Lunt, Leslie Howard
Beggar on Horseback (George S. Kaufman, Marc Connelly), Roland Young, Osgood Perkins, Spring Byington
Dancing Mothers (Edgar Selwyn, Edmund Goulding), Helen Hayes
A Right to Dream (Irving Kaye Davis), Ralph Shirley, Bertha Broad
The Guardsman (Ferenc Molnár), Alfred Lunt, Lynn Fontanne
The Firebrand (Edwin Justus Mayer), Joseph Schildkraut, Edward G. Robinson
Old English (John Galsworthy), George Arliss
The Miracle (Max Reinhardt, Karl Vollmoeller), Lady Diana Manners

Musicals

The Student Prince (Sigmund Romberg, Dorothy Donnelly), Ilse Marvenga, Howard Marsh (biggest money-maker in history)
Rose Marie (Rudolph Friml, Otto Harbach), Dennis King, Mary Ellis, William Kent
Ziegfeld Follies (Victor Herbert et al., Gene Buck), Will Rogers, Ann Pennington, W. C. Fields
Lady Be Good (George Gershwin, Ira Gershwin), Fred and Adele Astaire
I'll Say She Is (Tom Johnstone, Will Johnstone), Marx Brothers, Lotta Miles
George White's Scandals (George Gershwin, B. G. DeSylva), Winnie Lightner, Lester Allen
Music Box Review of 1924 (Irving Berlin), Fannie Brice, Clark and McCullough, Grace Moore, Claire Luce
André Charlot Review of 1924 (Noel Coward), Beatrice Lillie, Gertrude Lawrence

Classics and Revivals On and Off Broadway

Antony and Cleopatra, Jane Cowl, Rollo Peters; *The Second Mrs. Tanqueray* (Pinero), Ethel Barrymore; *Hedda Gabler* (Ibsen), Clare Eames; *Peter Pan* (James M. Barrie), Marilyn Miller

Pulitzer Prize

Hell-Bent fer Heaven, Hatcher Hughes

Classical Music _____

Compositions
George Antheil, *Ballet mécanique*
George Gershwin, *Rhapsody in Blue*
Ferde Grofé, *Mississippi Suite*
Charles Wakefield Cadman, *The Witch of Salem*
Edgard Varèse, *Octandre*
Carl Ruggles, *Men and Mountains*
Henry Cowell, *Vestiges*
Charles Ives, Three Pieces for Two Pianos
Aaron Copland, Symphony for Organ and Orchestra
John Alden Carpenter, *Skyscrapers*

Important Events
The Piano Festival at the Metropolitan for the
Association for Improving the Condition of the Poor
includes Harold Bauer, Alexander Brailowsky, Ossip
Gabrilowitsch, Myra Hess, Josef Lhévinne, Guiomar
Novaes, and Ernest Schelling.

Major Recitals: Efrem Zimbalist, Wanda
Landowska, Moritz Rosenthal, Siegfried Wagner,
Maria Jeritza

New Appointments: Howard Hanson becomes
director of the Eastman Symphony, Serge
Koussevitsky, of the Boston Symphony.

Debut: Alexander Brailowsky

First Performances
Ralph Vaughan Williams, Violin Concerto
(Minneapolis); Deems Taylor, *Alice through the*

Looking Glass (Philadelphia); Henry Hadley, *Ocean
Symphony* (Boston); Igor Stravinsky, *Histoire du
Soldat* (League of Composers, New York); *Le chant
du rossignol* (New York); Frederick Jacobi,
Symphony No. 1 (San Francisco); Arthur Honegger,
Pacific 231 (New York)

Opera

Metropolitan: Antonio Scotti celebrates his twenty-
fifth anniversary with *Tosca;* Giacomo Lauri-Volpi,
Le roi de Lahore; Karin Branzell, *Die Walküre;*
Friedrich Schorr (debut), *Tannhaüser;* premiere: *I
compagnacci* (Primo Riccitelli); *Le coq d'or; La
habanera* (Raoul Laparra)

Chicago: *The White Bird* (Ernest Carter, premiere)

San Francisco: Beniamino Gigli, Giuseppe De Luca,
Claudia Muzio, *Andrea Chenier*

Dallas: Mary Garden, *Salomé*

Music Notes
The St. Louis and Curtis Institutes open • Siegfried
Wagner makes his first U.S. visit to raise $200,000
for the Bayreuth Festival • Nellie Melba bids one of
many farewells • Ernest Schelling begins the
Children's Concerts with the New York
Philharmonic.

George Bellows, *Dempsey and Firpo*.
1924. Oil. 51 × 63 1/4 inches. *Collection
of Whitney Museum of American Art.*

Art

Painting

Arthur G. Dove, *Portrait of Ralph Dusenberry*
George Bellows, *Dempsey and Firpo*
Georgia O'Keeffe, *Dark Abstraction*
Max Weber, *Still Life with Chinese Teapot*
Peter Blume, *Fruit*
Yasuo Kuniyoshi, *Sleeping Beauty*

Sculpture

Malvina Hoffman, *Mask of Anna Pavlova*
Alexander Calder, *The Horse*
Gaston Lachaise, *Dolphin Fountain*
Alexander Archipenko, *Archipenturo*

Architecture

American Radiator Building, New York (Hood, Godley, and Fouilhoux)
National Academy of Science and Research Council, Washington, D.C. (Bertram C. Goodhue)
Cathedral of St. John the Divine, New York, renewed construction (Heins and LaFargue, Cram)
Federal Reserve Building, Cleveland (Walker and Weeks)

Arthur G. Dove, *Portrait of Ralph Dusenberry*, 1924. Oil. 22 × 18″. *The Metropolitan Museum of Art, The Alfred Steiglitz Collection.*

Art Briefs

The third traveling exhibit leaves the Metropolitan Museum of Art to tour the United States with works by Chase, Colman, Dabo, J. G. Brown, Hicks, Hopner, Nicol, Wyant, and Van der Velde • Stanford White's Madison Square Garden is razed; its Saint-Gaudens tower, "Diana," is to be reerected at University Heights, New York University.

Important Exhibitions

Museums

New York: *Metropolitan:* Arts of the book; J. Alden Weir; Chinese color prints; European drawings; Art of the American home (displayed in the new American wing). *Société Anonyme:* Paul Klee's first U.S. show. *Whitney:* American folk art: Kuniyoshi, Sheeler, Demuth

Cleveland: Winslow Homer

Detroit: American art, featuring Maurice Prendergast's *Landscape with Figures*

Chicago: Works by Chicago artists

Buffalo: Selected American paintings and sculpture

Washington: *Corcoran:* Contemporary American painting, featuring Childe Hassam and Charles Webster Hawthorne

Individual and Group Shows: Wassily Kandinsky, Aristide Maillol, Jo Davidson, John Marin, George Bellows, Dürer, Matisse, and Sargent; Whistler and Alfred Stieglitz continue to draw much attention; Russian lapidary work is popular.

Dance

Michel Fokine, with Vera Fokina, organizes the American Ballet.

Books

Fiction

Critics' Choice
In Our Time, Ernest Hemingway
Old New York, Edith Wharton
How To Write Short Stories (with Samples), Ring Lardner
The Apple of the Eye, Glenway Wescott
The Green Bay Tree, Louis Bromfield
Balisand, Joseph Hergesheimer
🍃 *Strait Is the Gate*, André Gide
🍃 *Death in Venice*, Thomas Mann
🍃 *A Passage to India*, E. M. Forster

Best-Sellers
So Big, Edna Ferber
The Plastic Age, Percy Marks
The Little French Girl, Anne Douglas Sedgwick
The Heirs Apparent, Philip Gibbs
A Gentleman of Courage, James Oliver Curwood
The Call of the Canyon, Zane Grey
The Midlander, Booth Tarkington
The Coast of Folly, Coningsby Dawson
Mistress Wilding, Rafael Sabatini
Hopalong Cassidy Returns, Clarence Mulford

Nonfiction

Critics' Choice
A Story Teller's Story, Sherwood Anderson
The Seven Lively Arts, Gilbert Seldes
Antheil and the Treatise on Harmony, Ezra Pound
Sticks and Stones, Louis Mumford
State of the Nation, A. J. Beveridge
Democracy and Leadership, Irving Babbitt
Lawrence in Arabia, Lowell J. Thomas
The Gift of Black Folk, W. E. B. Du Bois
🍃 *Manifesto of Surrealism*, André Breton
🍃 *Beyond the Pleasure Principle*, Sigmund Freud

Best-Sellers
Diet and Health, Lulu Hunt Peters
The Life of Christ, Giovanni Papini
The Boston Cooking School Cookbook, new ed., Fannie Farmer
Etiquette, Emily Post

Ariel, André Maurois
The Cross Word Puzzle Books, Prosper Buranelli et al.
Mark Twain's Autobiography, Mark Twain
Saint Joan, George Bernard Shaw
The New Decalogue of Science, Albert E. Wiggam
The Americanization of Edward Bok, Edward Bok

Poetry
John Crowe Ransom, *Chills and Fever*
Marianne Moore, *Observations*
Edgar Lee Masters, *The New Spoon River Anthology*
Robinson Jeffers, *Tamar and Other Poems*

Pulitzer Prizes
So Big, Edna Ferber (novel)
A History of the American Frontier, Frederic L. Paxson (U.S. history)
Barrett Wendell and His Letters, M. A. DeWolfe Howe (biography)
The Man Who Died Twice, Edwin Arlington Robinson (poetry)

Science and Technology

Edwin Hubble, at Mt. Wilson Observatory, California, demonstrates that spiral nebulae are composed of stars like our own galaxy; this is the first indication of the immense size of the universe; Hubble also begins measuring the distances of stars from the earth.

Two Douglas world cruisers—the *Chicago*, piloted by Lowell Smith and Alva Harvey, and the *New Orleans*, by Erick Nelson and John Harding—complete round-the-world flights.

RCA transmits a wireless photo from London to New York in 25 minutes.

A radio message is transmitted to and from Japan in 1 minute, 45 seconds.

Liver is shown to prevent pernicious anemia by Boston physicians George Minot and William Murphy.

George and Gladys Dick demonstrate that streptococcus is the cause of scarlet fever.

Dye techniques for gall bladder X rays are devised by Ewart Graham and Lewis Cole.

Malaria, or "fever therapy," shows promise as a treatment for third-stage syphilis.

🍃 Hans Berger develops the electroencephalogram (EEG) for recording brain waves.

Sports

Baseball

Bucky Harris, 24, becomes the "boy wonder" manager of the Washington Senators (AL); the team wins the pennant and the World Series.

Champions

Batting	Pitching
Rogers Hornsby (St. Louis, NL), .424	Dazzy Vance (Brooklyn, NL), 28–6
Babe Ruth (New York, AL), .378	Walter Johnson (Washington, AL), 28–7
	Home runs
	Babe Ruth (New York, AL), 46

Football

Red Grange, Illinois, runs 95, 67, 56, and 44 yards the first four times he handles the ball against Michigan. Sportswriter Grantland Rice calls him the "Galloping Ghost." Notre Dame upsets Army 13–7; Rice calls the ND backfield the "Four Horsemen of the Apocalypse": Stuldreyer, Miller, Crowley, and Layden.

Pro Stars: Jim Thorpe (Rock Island), Ernie Hamer (Frankford)

College All-Americans: Red Grange (HB), Illinois; Walter Koppisch (HB), Columbia

Rose Bowl (Jan. 1, 1925): Notre Dame 27–Stanford 10

Olympics

In the summer games at Paris U.S. winners include Jackson Scholz (200m, 21.6s), D. C. Kinsey (100 mh, 15.0s), F. Morgan Taylor (400 mh, 52.6s), Harold Osborn (high jump, 6'5 5/16"), Delfort Hubbard (broad jump, 24'5 1/8" and decathlon), Johnny Weismuller (swimming, 100m and 400m), A. C. White (2 in diving), Ethel Lackie (swimming, 100m), Martha Norelius (swimming, 400m). Harold Abrahams and Eric Liddell of Great Britain and Paavo Nurmi of Finland are other gold medal winners.

Other Sports

Horse Racing: Exterminator retires with a record 50 wins and $252,996 earnings.

Tennis: The Forest Hills Tennis Stadium opens.

Winners

World Series	Player of the Year
Washington (AL), 4–New York (NL), 3	Charles Black, Kansas
MVP	*Stanley Cup*
NL–Arthur Vance, Brooklyn	Montreal
AL–Walter Johnson, Washington	*U.S. Tennis Open*
	Men: William Tilden II
NFL	Women: Helen Wills
Cleveland Bulldogs	*USGA Open*
College Football	Cyril Walker
Notre Dame	*Kentucky Derby*
College Basketball	Black Gold (J. D. Mahoney, jockey)
North Carolina	

Fashion

For Women: Still stylish is the straight, knee-length skirt, gathered slightly or cut with two front pleats, and long sleeveless tops, middies, or Peter Pan blouses. Coats, broadly cut at the shoulder and tapered to the knee, are fastened with a single button at the hip and have honey beige or dyed ermine fur on the collar and cuffs. The cloche hat covers the eyes. Enormous interest grows in masklike makeup (orange lips and rouge are also popular) and accessories (strings of pearls trail from the shoulder or are knotted at the neck and thrown over the right shoulder and under the arm). Silver bracelets are worn on the upper arm.

High-fashion notes: The chinchilla wraparound; Lanvin's black georgette crepe dress with steel discs and slashed sleeves.

For Men: Interest grows in the F. Scott Fitzgerald look and narrower torso: the blue blazer with sport or school badge and shorter and less padded jacket and Oxford bags—high-waisted and pleated but loose in the hips. Shoes have round toes and laces; socks are patterned. Top coats, with loose raglan sleeves and wide collars, fall well below the knee. More formal dress includes bow ties in striped, paisley, and spotted patterns, bowlers, spats, double-breasted suits, and vests.

Kaleidoscope _____

- In his two-day plea against the death penalty for Leopold and Loeb, Clarence Darrow introduces into the courtroom the concept of mental illness, quotes poetry, and weeps as he begs for mercy.
- "Galloping Ghost" Red Grange is so popular that college football surpasses boxing as a national pastime; Grange is wooed by Hollywood, big business, and a variety of political groups.
- The Charleston, carried north from Charleston, South Carolina and incorporated into the all-black show *Shuffle Along,* is picked up by white dancers at Texas Guinan's El Fey Club and Silver Slipper.
- Newest places to hide liquor include shoe heels, flasks form-fitted to women's thighs, folds of coats, and perfume bottles.
- Whether a woman should work outside the home becomes a major topic of discussion.
- Commercial laundry use increases 57 percent (since 1914); bakery production, 60 percent; 90 percent of all homes have electric irons.
- The Methodist Episcopal General Conference lifts its ban on theatergoing and dancing.
- "America's Most Beautiful Suburb" is the catchphrase of the Florida get-rich-quick ads, and thousands flock south to buy land with small down payments (binders), which they can then quickly sell for profit.
- Gangland king Dion O'Banion is buried in a $10,000 bronze casket; 40,000 call at the funeral chapel and 20,000 attend the funeral. Although Catholic rites are denied him, a priest-friend says three Hail Marys and the Lord's Prayer.
- Former Rutgers football player Paul Robeson, acting as a black man married to a white woman in *All God's Chillun Got Wings,* is threatened by the KKK; police officers stand guard in the theater.
- Whether or not to specifically condemn the KKK is a major concern at both presidential conventions; neither issues an outright condemnation.
- News takes a prominent position on radio, challenging the popularity of dance music.
- The U.S. Supreme Court declares unconstitutional an Oregon law requiring all grammar school children to attend school.
- A popular GOP convention drink is the "Keep Cool with Coolidge" highball, consisting of raw eggs and fruit juice.
- Alvin "Shipwreck" Kelly sits on top of a flagpole for 13 hours and 13 minutes.
- Henry Ford pays $2,467,946 in income tax.
- Half a million people write Henry Ford begging for money.
- Pulps—dime magazines of 150 pages like *Detective Story* and *Western Story*—increase in circulation to half a million.
- Five violinists at one of Herbert Bayard Swope's famous Long Island parties engage in an endurance contest by repeating Paganini's *Moto Perpetuo;* Josef Fuchs lasts 21 minutes, defeating Jascha Heifetz,

Efrem Zimbalist, Paul Kochaniski, and Albert Spalding.
- John Barrymore earns from Warner's $76,250 per picture, plus $7,625 over seven weeks and all expenses.
- Walt Disney begins creating cartoons with "Alice's Wonderland."
- Lillian Leitzel, Ringling Brothers and Barnum and Bailey star, sets a record of 239 planges (swinging in circular revolutions by throwing the lower part of her body over her shoulder while hanging from a rope).
- Ernest Hemingway leads fellow writers Donald Ogden Stewart and John Dos Passos in a running of the bulls at Pamplona, Spain, and gains esteem at home and abroad.

Fads: Richard L. Simon and Max L. Schuster begin the Plaza Publishing Company with the *Cross Word Puzzle Book* (pencils are attached). Crossword puzzles and mah-jongg are the year's most popular fads. The B & O Railroad stocks dictionaries for its passengers.

First Appearances: Ice-cream-cone rolling machine, chrome-plating process, the permanent wave, contact lenses (imported), MGM, Columbia Pictures, two perfect games rolled by a bowler, U.S. Foreign Service, Chrysler, IBM, Kleenex ("Celluwipes"), airmail service (New York to San Francisco), spiral-bound notebook, spin dryer, deadbolt lock, college marriage course (University of North Carolina, Chapel Hill), Beech-Nut Coffee, Wheaties, Stouffer's chain, corn-husking championship, "Little Orphan Annie," Barney's, Macy's Thanksgiving Day Parade down Central Park West, New York

The Mack Sennett girls from the studio of the "King of Comedy," whose movies include *Boobs in the Woods* and *The Wild Goose Chasers. Movie Star News.*

1925

Above: Clarence Darrow and Williams Jennings Bryan, opposing lawyers at the Monkey Trial. *Library of Congress.*

In the News

NELLIE ROSS, WYOMING, BECOMES FIRST WOMAN GOVERNOR . . . "MA" FERGUSON, TEXAS, BECOMES SECOND WOMAN GOVERNOR . . . LEON TROTSKY IS DEMOTED, JOSEPH STALIN EXTENDS HIS POWER . . . CORRUPT PRACTICES ACT OUTLAWS DIRECT CORPORATE CONTRIBUTIONS IN ELECTIONS . . . FRENCH TROOPS BEGIN RUHR EVACUATION . . . FLOYD COLLINS, TRAPPED IN COAL MINE, DIES AFTER 18 DAYS . . . COLONEL BILLY MITCHELL ACCUSES NATIONAL AIR BOARD OF INCOMPETENCE . . . COOLIDGE ARBITRATES PERU-CHILE BORDER DISPUTE . . . DRUZES REVOLT IN SYRIA, THE FRENCH BOMB DAMASCUS . . . WORLD POWERS SIGN TREATY TO OUTLAW POISON GAS . . . MASSIVE COAL STRIKE HITS W. VA. . . . FLA. PASSES LAW REQUIRING DAILY BIBLE READING . . . DIRIGIBLE SHENANDOAH IS TORN BY STORM, 14 DIE . . . LOCARNO TREATIES BETWEEN WORLD WAR FOES SETTLE GERMAN BOUNDARIES . . . JOHN SCOPES GOES ON TRIAL IN DAYTON, TENN., FOR TEACHING EVOLUTION, CLARENCE DARROW DEFENDS SCOPES . . . BRITISH SOLDIERS KILL CHINESE STUDENTS IN SHANGHAI RIOT . . . 40,000 KKK MARCH IN WASHINGTON, D.C. . . . CARL ROGERS FLIES SEAPLANE NONSTOP FROM SAN FRANCISCO TO HONOLULU . . . JOHN SCOPES IS CONVICTED AND FINED $100, WILLIAM JENNINGS BRYAN, PROSECUTOR, DIES OF HEART ATTACK . . . GREECE INVADES BULGARIA, LEAGUE OF NATIONS SETTLES DISPUTE . . . BILLY MITCHELL IS COURT-MARTIALED FOR INSUBORDINATION . . . FLORIDA LAND SCAMS ARE EXPOSED, UNDERWATER LOTS WERE SOLD.

Deaths

George Bellows, William Jennings Bryan, Walter Camp, Robert M. La Follette, Amy Lowell, John Singer Sargent, Erik Satie, Sun Yat-sen.

Quotes

"Our defense planes are the worst of any country I know. . . . Our pilots know they are going to be killed in the old floating coffins that we are still flying."

— Col. Billy Mitchell

"The business of America is business."

— Calvin Coolidge

"This is the way the world ends
Not with a bang but a whimper."
— T. S. Eliot, "The Hollow Men"

"[In New York] I saw 7,000,000 two-legged animals penned in an evil smelling cage, . . . streets as unkempt as a Russian steppe, . . . rubbish, waste paper, cigar butts. . . . One glance and you know no master hand directs."

— Article in *Pravda*

"Shoot them in the head,
Shoot them in the feet,
Shoot them in the dinner bucket;
How are they going to eat?"
— Coal miners' song during West Virginia strike

Bryan: I believe that everything in the Bible should be accepted as it is given there.
Darrow: But when you read that Jonah swallowed the whale—or that the whale swallowed Jonah—do you literally interpret it?
Bryan: Yes sir. . . . If the Bible said so.
— Clarence Darrow's cross-examination of William Jennings Bryan in the Scopes trial

"If a young man at the age of twenty-three can write a symphony like that, in five years he will be ready to commit murder."
— Walter Damrosch, conducting Aaron Copland's Symphony for Organ and Orchestra

Ads

Why gamble with bootleg gasoline?

(Tydol)

AND THEN HE KNEW . . .
This was the second dance in a month, and both times the girls seemed to avoid him. . . . Nearly all young men are inclined to have a grimy-looking skin, spotted with blackheads. Few men realize that this hinders their success in life.

(Pompeiian Massage Cream)

Betrayed. . . .
Their first conversation
Betrayed the fact that
She was not fastidious.
(Listerine Toothpaste)

WHY ENVY THE LIVE-WIRE?
Mucus when present in large quantities prevents the nerves from assimilating their due nutriment. It is a cause of undue fatigue.
Stop using mucus-making foods and learn to take brain-and-nerve foods, etc. Build yourself into a go-getter, a live-wire, an untiring person, internally clean.

(Drinkler School of Eating)

New scientific discoveries like radium are marketed for commercial use. *Library of Congress.*

Packard luxury is mental no less than physical. . . . Nothing the world can offer is finer. That knowledge, perhaps, is the greatest luxury of all.

(Packard Automobiles)

Radio

Premieres

"Atwater Kent Audition," Graham McNamee
"Gold Dust Twins"
"Goodrich Silvertown Orchestra"
"EWSM Barn Dance" ("Grand Ole Opry")
"Sam and Henry" ("Amos 'n' Andy"), Freeman
    Gosden, Charles Correll

Of Note

NBC, the first nationwide network, is established •
New catchphrase: "I'm goin' back to the wagon,
boys. These shoes are killin' me" ("Grand Ole
Opry") • "NEAF Grand Opera Company" begins
weekly opera performances.

The radio audience is estimated at 50 million. *Library of
Congress.*

Movies

Openings

The Gold Rush (Charles Chaplin), Charles Chaplin,
    Mack Swain
The Big Parade (King Vidor), John Gilbert
The Merry Widow (Erich von Stroheim), Mae
    Murray, John Gilbert
The Dark Angel (George Fitzmaurice), Ronald
    Colman, Vilma Banky
Stella Dallas (Henry King), Ronald Colman, Belle
    Bennett
Ben-Hur (Fred Niblo), Ramon Novarro, Francis X.
    Bushman

Potemkin (Sergei Eisenstein), A. Antonov
The Salvation Hunters (Josef von Sternberg), George
    K. Arthur
Lord Jim (Victor Fleming), Percy Marmont, Noah
    Beery
The Golden Bed (Cecil B. DeMille), Lillian Rich,
    Rod La Rocque
Madame Sans-Gene (Léonce Perret), Gloria
    Swanson, Charles De Roche
The Phantom of the Opera (Rupert Julian), Lon
    Chaney
The Freshman (Fred Newmeyer), Harold Lloyd,
    Jobyna Ralston
The Vanishing American (George B. Seitz), Noah
    Beery, Richard Dix
The Eagle (Clarence Brown), Rudolph Valentino,
    Vilma Banky

Top Box-Office Stars

Rudolph Valentino, Norma Talmadge. *Also popular:*
Douglas Fairbanks, Mary Pickford, Charles Chaplin,
Harold Lloyd, Gloria Swanson, Pola Negri,
Constance Talmadge, Dorothy Gish, Lillian Gish

"Stoneface" Buster Keaton in *Go West. Movie Star News.*

Popular Music _____

Hit Songs
"If You Knew Suzy"
"I'm Sitting on Top of the World"
"Sweet Georgia Brown"
"Sleepy Time Gal"
"Dinah"
"Manhattan"
"If You Were the Only Girl"
"Keep Your Skirts Down, Mary
    Ann"
"Always"

Top Records
Yes Sir, That's My Baby (Gene
Austin); *Poor Little Rich Girl*
(Gertrude Lawrence); *Carolina*
Shout (James P. Johnson); *Sleepy-
Time Gal* (Jesse Crawford); *Five
Foot Two* (Art Landry); *Sugar
Foot Stomp* (Fletcher Henderson);
Death of Floyd Collins (Vernon
Dalhart); *Song of the Vagabonds*
(Vincent Lopez)

Jazz and Big Bands
Popular stars include Louis
Armstrong, Tennessee Tooters,
Cotton Pickers, Halfway House
Orchestra, Bix Beiderbecke and
his Rhythms Jugglers, Lanin's
Redheads

First Recordings: Louis
Armstrong Five; Duke Ellington
Washingtonians

Blues Singers: Bessie Smith,
Edith Wilson, Ethel Waters,
Lucille Hegamin, Alberta Hunter,
Mary Stafford

Jazz Piano: Hersal Thomas,
Meade Lux Lewis, Clarence
"Pinetop" Smith, Charles "Cow
Cow" Davenport

New Band: Lawrence Welk,
North Dakota

Theater _____

Broadway Openings

Plays
The Vortex (Noel Coward), Noel Coward, Lillian
    Braithwaite
Hay Fever (Noel Coward), Laura Hope Crews
Easy Virtue (Noel Coward), Jane Cowl
Craig's Wife (George Kelly), Josephine Hull
The Enemy (Channing Pollock), Fay Bainter
The Green Hat (Michael Arlen), Katharine Cornell,
    Leslie Howard
The Jazz Singer (Samson Raphaelson), George Jessel
The Cradle Snatchers (Russell Medcroft, Norma
    Mitchell), Mary Boland, Edna May Oliver,
    Humphrey Bogart
The Last of Mrs. Cheyney (Frederick Lonsdale), Ina
    Claire, Roland Young
The Butter and Egg Man (George S. Kaufman),
    Gregory Kelly
The Dove (Djuna Barnes), Judith Anderson

Musicals
Sunny (Jerome Kern, Otto Harbach, Oscar
    Hammerstein II), Marilyn Miller, Clifton Webb,
    Jack Donahue
The Vagabond King (Rudolf Friml, Brian Hooker),
    Dennis King
Artists and Models (J. Fred Coots, Clifford Grey),
    Walter Woolf, Lulu McConnell
Earl Carroll's Vanities (Clarence Gaskill, William A.
    Grew), Julius Tannen, Ted and Betty Healy

Garrick Gaieties (Richard Rodgers, Lorenz Hart),
    Sterling Holloway, Libby Holman
The Cocoanuts (Irving Berlin), Marx Brothers,
    Frances Williams
George White's Scandals (Ray Henderson, B. G.
    DeSylva), Helen Morgan, Tom Patricola
Ziegfeld Follies (Sigmund Romberg et al.), W. C.
    Fields, Ray Dooley

Classics and Revivals On and Off Broadway
Caesar and Cleopatra, Helen Hayes, Lionel Atwill;
Candida, Peggy Wood, *Androcles and the Lion,*
Henry Travers, and *Arms and the Man* (George
Bernard Shaw), Alfred Lunt, Lynn Fontanne;
Merchant of Venice, (Walter Hampden, Ethel
Barrymore; *Hamlet,* Basil Sydney, in modern dress;
Othello, Walter Hampden; *The Wild Duck* (Ibsen),
Blanche Yurka; *Lysistrata* (Aristophanes; music by
Glière), Moscow Art Theatre

Regional

Founded: Goodman Theatre, Chicago, by the
Kenneth Sawyer Goodman family

Pulitzer Prize
They Knew What They Wanted, Sidney Howard

Classical Music

Compositions

Aaron Copland, *Music for the Theater, Grogh, Dance Symphony*
Howard Hanson, *The Lament of Beowulf*
Edgard Varèse, *Intégrales*
John Powell, *At the Fair*
Wallingford Riegger, Rhapsody for Orchestra
Henry Cowell, *The Banshee*
John Alden Carpenter, Jazz Orchestra Pieces
Ernest Bloch, Concerto Grosso

Important Events

Ignace Paderewski, Fritz Kreisler, and Igor Stravinsky triumph in their U.S. appearances. Stravinsky plays *Song of the Volga Boatmen* with the New York Philharmonic and Concerto for Piano and Winds with the Boston Symphony.
Paul Whiteman performs George Gershwin's *Twenty Minute Grand Opera* and *135th Street* and Deems Taylor's *Circus Day* at Carnegie Hall.
The New York Philharmonic celebrates its 2,000th concert with a portion of its first, December 1842, program: Beethoven's Symphony no. 5 and Johann Kalliwoda's New Overture in D.

Debut: Paul Robeson

First Performances

George Gershwin, playing, Concerto in F for Piano and Orchestra (New York); Leo Sowerby, *Monotony, Syncopation* (Chicago); Aaron Copland, Symphony for Organ and Orchestra (New York)

Opera

Metropolitan: Rosa Ponselle, *La Gioconda;* Giovanni Martinelli, *Tosca;* Maria Jeritza, Beniamino Gigli, *Fedora;* Jeritza, *Turandot;* Lucrezia Bori, *L'heure espagnole;* Lawrence Tibbett, *Falstaff*

Chicago: Mary Garden, *Resurrection* (Franco Alfano); *Carmen*

San Francisco: Tito Schipa, *Manon*

Music Notes

For the first Festival of Chamber Music, at the Library of Congress, work is commissioned from Charles Loeffler, Frederick Stock, and Frederick Jacobi • In honor of Leopold Auer, 80, celebrated violin teacher, a benefit concert is given in New York by Efrem Zimbalist, Jascha Heifetz, Josef Hofmann, Sergei Rachmaninoff, and Ossip Gabrilowitsch; $25,000 is raised for Auer • Copland wins the first Guggenheim Fellowship.

Exercising on the beach—part of the national trend toward slimness and physical fitness. *Library of Congress.*

Art

Painting

Edward Hopper, *House by the Railroad*
Stuart Davis, *Italian Landscape*
Charles Demuth, *Apples and Bananas*
Lyonel Feininger, *Tower*
Arthur G. Dove, *Portrait of Alfred Stieglitz*
Yasuo Kuniyoshi, *Waitresses from Sparhawk*
Man Ray, *Sugar Loaves*

Sculpture

Malvina Hoffman, *England*
Herbert Haseltine, *Percheron Mare and Foal*
John Storrs, *Seated Gendarme*
Paul Manship, *Flight of Europa*

Architecture

Chicago Tribune Tower, Chicago (Hood and Howells)
New York Telephone Building, New York City (McKenzie, Vorhees, and Gmelin)
Powell Symphony Hall, St. Louis (Rapp and Rapp)
Warren and Wetmore receive the Fifth Avenue Association Gold Award for Steinway Hall.
Horace Trumbauer completes the Gothic design plan for Duke University.

Important Exhibitions

Museums

New York: *Metropolitan:* Greek athletes; objects from the International Exposition of Modern Decorative Art; telephotographs; George Bellows memorial; American historical portraits

Boston: Mural decorations by John Singer Sargent; Eleanor Norcross memorial

St. Louis: 100 paintings by 100 American artists; Ivan Mestrovic

Philadelphia: American Sculpture Prizes are awarded to Walker Hancock, William James, and George Bellows

Art Briefs

"The Blue Four" gain a following after their New York show: Alexei Von Jawlensky, Wassily Kandinsky, Paul Klee, and Lyonel Feininger • John D. Rockefeller makes possible the purchase of medieval art and property for what will become the

F. Scott Fitzgerald's *The Great Gatsby* portrays the "Jazz Age" and the problematical nature of the American dream. *Scribners.*

Cloisters • Henry E. Huntington bequeaths 188 paintings to the Metropolitan, which also records the largest attendance in its history—1,156,102 visitors.

Dance

Mikhail Mordkin organizes his Russian Ballet Company with Vera Nemchinova, Hilda Butsova, and Pierre Vladimiroff.

Books

Fiction

Critics' Choice

The Great Gatsby, F. Scott Fitzgerald
In Our Time (revised), Ernest Hemingway
The Professor's House, Willa Cather
An American Tragedy, Theodore Dreiser
Manhattan Transfer, John Dos Passos
Drums, James Boyd
Barren Ground, Ellen Glasgow
Porgy, DuBose Heyward
🍂 *Mrs. Dalloway*, Virginia Woolf
🍂 *No More Parades*, Ford Madox Ford

Best-Sellers

Soundings, A. Hamilton Gibbs
The Constant Nymph, Margaret Kennedy
The Keeper of the Bees, Gene Stratton Porter
Glorious Apollo, E. Barrington
The Perennial Bachelor, Anne Parish
Arrowsmith, Sinclair Lewis
Gentlemen Prefer Blondes, Anita Loos
The Green Hat, Michael Arlen
One Increasing Purpose, A. S. M. Hutchinson
The Carolinian, Rafael Sabatini

Nonfiction

Critics' Choice

The Tragedy of Waste, Stuart Chase
In the American Grain, William Carlos Williams
The New Negro: An Interpretation, Alain Locke
Seventy Years of Life and Labor, Samuel Gompers
Experience and Nature, John Dewey
The Phantom Public, Walter Lippmann
The Book of American Negro Spirituals, ed. James Weldon Johnson
The Diaries of George Washington, ed. John C. Fitzpatrick
Our Debt and Duty to the Farmer, Henry Wallace
Calvin Coolidge, William Allen White
My Disillusionment in Russia, Emma Goldman
🍂 *Mein Kampf*, Adolph Hitler
🍂 *Science and the Modern World*, Alfred North Whitehead

Best-Sellers

Diet and Health, Lulu Hunt Peters
The Boston Cooking School Cook Book, new ed., Fannie Farmer

When We Were Very Young, A. A. Milne
The Man Nobody Knows, Bruce Barton
Twice Thirty, Edward Bok
Twenty-Five Years, Lord Grey
Jungle Days, William Beebe
Anatole France Himself, J. J. Brousson
The Life of Christ, Giovanni Papini
Ariel, André Maurois

Poetry

T. S. Eliot, *Poems, 1909–1925*
Ezra Pound, *A Draft of XVI Cantos*
H. D., *Collected Poems*
E. E. Cummings, *XLI Poems, &*
Robinson Jeffers, *Roan Stallion*
Edwin Arlington Robinson, *Dionysus in Doubt*
Countee Cullen, *Color*

Pulitzer Prizes

Arrowsmith, Sinclair Lewis (novel)
The History of the United States, Edward Channing (U.S. history)
The Life of Sir William Osler, Harvey Cushing (biography)
What's O'Clock, Amy Lowell (poetry)

Science and Technology

An all-electric radio mechanism is developed that eliminates the need for bulky batteries and crystal sets with earphones.
Charles David Jenkins produces a working television set.
The all-electric phonograph is developed.
The Menninger Clinic, which emphasizes a "total environment approach," opens on a farm in Topeka, Kansas.
James B. Collip isolates the parathyroid hormone.

Alfred Sturdevant, Columbia University, demonstrates that developmental effects of genes are influenced by neighboring genes.
John Abel isolates insulin.
Vitamin A deficiency is shown to cause night blindness.
W. W. Coblentz's measurements of temperature conditions on Mars indicate it may be suitable for life.
🍂 John Baird, in London, transmits the first television image, a ventriloquist's dummy named Bill.

Sports

Baseball

Lou Gehrig (New York, AL), former Columbia University star, takes over first base from Wally Pipp. Rogers Hornsby wins the triple crown and leads the majors with 39 home runs.

Champions

Batting	Pitching
Rogers Hornsby (St. Louis, NL), .403	Dazzy Vance (Brooklyn, NL), 22–9
Harry Heilmann (Detroit, AL), .393	Stan Covaleskie (Washington, AL), 23–7
	Home runs
	Rogers Hornsby (St. Louis, NL), 39

Football

Red Grange, Illinois, gains 363 yards against Pennsylvania, quits college, and tours with an all-star team organized by C.C. ("Cash and Carry") Pyle; he earns $80,000 on tour and then joins the Chicago Bears; 73,000 attend in New York to see Grange. Tim Mara buys the N.Y. Giants for $500; Jim Thorpe plays for the Giants.

Pro Stars: George Trafton (Chicago), Walter French (Pottsville)

College All-Americans: Red Grange (HB), Illinois; Ernie Nevers (F), Stanford

Rose Bowl (Jan. 1, 1926): Alabama 20–Washington 19

Basketball

The American Basketball League is organized, the first "national" pro league with teams from Fort Wayne to New York.

Other Sports

Tennis: Bill Tilden wins his fifth straight U.S. Open Singles; Helen Wills wins her third straight U.S. Open Singles

Golf: Bobby Jones wins his second straight USGA Open.

Red Grange brings his college fame to pro football, drawing unprecedented crowds as he plays 10 games in 17 days. *Pro Football Hall of Fame.*

Winners

World Series	*Player of the Year*
Pittsburgh (NL) 4	Earl Mueller, Colorado
Washington (AL) 3	College
MVP	*Stanley Cup*
NL–Rogers Hornsby, St. Louis	Victoria
AL–Roger Peckinpaugh, Washington	*U.S. Tennis Open*
	Men: William Tilden II
	Women: Helen Wills
NFL	*USGA Open*
Chicago Cardinals	Willie Macfarlane
College Football	*Kentucky Derby*
Alabama	Flying Ebony (E. Sande, jockey)
College Basketball	
Princeton	

Fashion

For Women: Fashion turns to the "little girl look" in "little girl frocks": curled or shingled hair, saucer eyes, the turned-up nose, bee-stung mouth, and obliterated eyebrows, which emphasize facial beauty; shirt dresses have huge Peter Pan collars or floppy bow ties and are worn with ankle-strap shoes with Cuban heels and an occasional buckle. Underwear is fashionable in both light colors and black, and is decorated with flowers and butterflies. With the cult of youth and the new spirit of equality come the camisole knickers and the cami-knickers; also fashionable is no underwear at all. Along with the rage for drastic slimming, women still strive to flatten their breasts and obliterate their hips; the waistline remains ignored. The cult of the tan begins; lotions to prevent burning and promote tanning appear on the market; skin stains are also manufactured, along with Elizabeth Arden and Helena Rubinstein moisturizers, tonics, cream rouges, eye shadows, and more varied lipstick shades. Women use two pounds of powder yearly.

High-fashion note: Vionnet's shimmy dress

Kaleidoscope

- President Coolidge cuts the White House budget $12,500; he replaces paper cups with glasses, reduces the number of towels supplied in the lavatories from 175 to 88, orders that manila envelopes be reused, and rations food in the kitchen.
- Bootleg prices appear regularly at the end of the "Talk of the Town" section of the *New Yorker*.
- Cars appear for the first time in such colors as Florentine cream and Versailles violet; bodies are lower with balloon tires; a new interest in line and style appears.
- As prosperity increases with 40 percent of the population earning at least $2,000 a year, the mass market increases for items like cars, radios, refrigerators, and vacuum cleaners.
- Bruce Barton's best-selling *The Man Nobody Knows* insists that "selling" continues Christ's mission: "Jesus . . . picked up twelve men from the bottom ranks of business and forged them into an organization that conquered the world."
- John Scopes reads to his class Hunter's *Civil Biology:* "We have now learned that animal forms may be arranged so as to begin with the simple one-celled forms and culminate with a group which includes man himself."
- The nation's press and numerous evangelists gather in rural Tennessee to watch Clarence Darrow "show up fundamentalism" and William Jennings Bryan "protect the word of God against the greatest atheist and agnostic in the United States."
- The credibility of the KKK is greatly impaired when Grand Dragon Davis Stevenson, convicted of his secretary's murder, makes revelations that damage the reputations of major pro-Klan Indiana politicians.
- Chicago mayor William Hale ("Big Bill") Thompson is the congenial associate of gangsters Johnny Torrio and Al Capone.
- Prohibition agents Izzy Einstein and Moe Smith—who, through various disguises, confiscated an estimated 5 million bottles of bootleg liquor in five years—are fired. Many speculate that their superiors were jealous of their fame.
- Delaware sheriffs and deputy constables are permitted to whip criminals: 60 lashes for poisoning attempts, 30 for wife beating, and 6 for setting fire to the courthouse.
- The nightclub business booms with stars like Paul Whiteman, Roger Wolfe, Texas Guinan, and Joe E. Lewis.
- The top burlesque star is Carrie Finnel, who twirls tassels from her breasts and buttocks.
- Detroit wages for a bartender average $75 a week, with $50 additional for each arrest; if the arrest occurs over a Sunday and no bail can be arranged, a $75 bonus is added.
- "Yellow-Drive-It-Yourself-Systems" become popular: 12¢ a mile for a Ford and 22¢ for a 6-cylinder car.
- Courtship trends change, as the car replaces the parlor.

- The last fire engine drawn by a span of three horses, in Washington, D.C., is retired.
- President Coolidge buys a mechanical hobbyhorse to exercise on in the White House.
- After surviving an attempt on his life, Chicago gangland boss John Torrio turns his entire crime empire over to his former bodyguard Al Capone and retires to Italy with $10–$30 million.
- Floyd Collins's entrapment and death in a Kentucky cave is much publicized as an example of man's fight against nature.
- One of the year's best-covered events involves the half-breed malamute dog Balto, as it leads a team to Nome, Alaska, with life-saving antidiphtheria serum.
- The police dog becomes a house pet after the film success of Rin Tin Tin.
- Joseph Schenck, of United Artists, hires Lucille LeSueur, who is then named Joan Crawford by a fan-magazine contest.
- The top-grossing film to date is *The Big Parade* ($22 million), the most expensive, *Ben-Hur* ($3.95 million).
- In a Metropolitan performance of *Siegfried*, tenor Curt Taucher plunges 25 feet through a trap door, breaks his finger, staggers back on stage, and finishes his performance.
- Of the New York season's new plays (244 productions: 194 plays, 50 musicals), 75 percent fail.
- Blacks continue to move North as manufacturers tour the South and promise good jobs and pay. Black Harlem, with its "Negro Renaissance," joins midtown Manhattan and Greenwich Village as a major cultural center.
- Trinity College changes its name to Duke University when James B. Duke contributes $40 million.
- Earl Wise's potato chips are so successful that he moves his business from a remodeled garage to a concrete plant in Berwick, Pa.
- While on a Caribbean tour, Harold S. Vanderbilt invents contract bridge.

Fads: Limerick contests, baseball cards, athlete hero worship (Babe Ruth, Dempsey, Tunney, Bobby Jones, Helen Wills, Weismuller, Grange), marathons (flagpole sitting, dancing, talking, eating, drinking)

First Appearances: National Spelling Bee (organized by a Louisville newspaper), the motel, dry ice, covered vacuum flasks, automatic potato-peeling machine, Wesson oil, Caterpillar tractors, automatic and self-lubricating GE refrigerator, Lux soap, Woman's world's fair, compulsory auto insurance, embossed and inlaid linoleum, outdoor museum (Tuxedo Park, N.Y.), University of Miami, Charlie Chan (*The House without a Key*, Der Biggers), *New Yorker, Cosmopolitan, Parents'* magazine, Simmons Beautyrest mattress, high-vacuum radio tube patent, electrical records, Lucky Strike, Old Gold

1926

Facts and Figures

Economic Profile
  Dow-Jones: ↑ High 162–
    Low 145
  GNP: +4%
  Inflation: 0.0%
  Unemployment: 1.8%
Male/female ratio: 53/51
High school graduates
  entering college: 12%
Four-year colleges: 1,224
Public/private school ratio:
  10/1
Cunard four-month around-
  the-world cruise, $1,250
  and up
Tripler linen jacket, knickers:
  $18
Linenlike collars: 3/$1
Rayon-pigskin garters: 50¢
Mon Boudoir (Houbigant)
  perfume: $12–$20 (oz.)
Kent toothbrush: 75¢
Cocker spaniel (from kennel):
  $35
Toy Pomeranian (from
  kennel): $50
Marlboro cigarettes: 20¢
  (pack)
Cocoa chocolate (Huyler's):
  $1.50 (lb.)

In the News

BILLY MITCHELL IS CONVICTED OF INSUBORDINATION AND SUSPENDED FROM SERVICE . . . U.S. ACCEPTS WORLD COURT, WITH CONDITIONS . . . CAPONE HEADQUARTERS ARE MACHINE-GUNNED FROM A FILE OF CARS . . . FIRST TRANSATLANTIC PHONE CALL IS MADE . . . PEACHES, 16, SUES MILLIONAIRE "DADDY" BROWNING, 53, FOR DIVORCE . . . ARMY AIR CORPS IS ESTABLISHED . . . GERTRUDE EDERLE SWIMS ENGLISH CHANNEL IN RECORD TIME . . . CHIANG KAI-SHEK BECOMES HEAD OF CHINESE REVOLUTIONARY PARTY, KUOMINTANG . . . ADM. RICHARD BYRD AND FLOYD BENNETT MAKE FIRST FLIGHT OVER NORTH POLE . . . RUDOLPH VALENTINO DIES, 100,000 ATTEND FUNERAL . . . HIROHITO BECOMES JAPANESE EMPEROR . . . U.S. TROOPS RETURN TO NICARAGUA TO QUELL REVOLT . . . SUPREME COURT OVERRULES 1878 LAW AND DECLARES PRESIDENT CAN REMOVE CABINET OFFICERS . . . HEIRESS FRANCES STEPHENS HALL IS ACQUITTED IN MURDER OF HUSBAND AND CHOIR-GIRL MISTRESS . . . GENE TUNNEY BEATS JACK DEMPSEY FOR HEAVYWEIGHT TITLE . . . LEON TROTSKY AND GRIGORY ZINOVIEV ARE EXPELLED FROM POLITBURO, STALIN RULES ALONE . . . HARRY HOUDINI DIES FROM STOMACH PUNCH LEADING TO PERITONITIS . . . FRANCE PROCLAIMS LEBANON A REPUBLIC . . . WORLD COURT REJECTS U.S. CONDITIONS . . . NEW YORKERS CHALLENGE LAW ALLOWING RELIGIOUS INSTRUCTION IN SCHOOLS.

Deaths

Luther Burbank, Mary
  Cassatt, Emile Coué,
  Eugene V. Debs, Charles
  Eliot, Claude Monet,
  Annie Oakley, Joseph
  Pennell, Rainer Maria
  Rilke.

Col. Billy Mitchell, convicted of insubordination, after accusing the army of negligence in the care of its aircraft. *Library of Congress.*

FIVE DEFINITIONS OF "THE IDEAL WOMAN"

"When in my company, she never admires other men."—Charles Chaplin

"(1) Lockjaw, (2) Hereditary obesity, (3) Absolutely fireproof, (4) Day and night elevator service."
—Ring Lardner

"Fidelity . . . [and] courage."   —Rudolph Valentino

"Native refinement . . . the quality of glory, . . . as definite yet intangible as the perfume of flowers."
—Florenz Ziegfeld

"She may weigh four hundred pounds, if her heart is of gold. [Also] the gift of stretching a can of sardines into a banquet."—Al Jolson
— *Vanity Fair*

Quotes

"Applesauce" / "So's your anchovie" / "banana oil"/ "Chew to the line" / "Let the hips fall where they will"
— A "lady's" retorts to "uncouth" advances, quoted in *Life* magazine

"The very thing that made us stands in the way of our development as a civilized people. . . . The machine [has caused] the herding of men into towns and cities, the age of the factory. . . . Men all began to dress alike, eat the same foods, read the same kind of newspapers and books. Minds began to be standardized as were the clothes men wore."
— Sherwood Anderson, on America's 150th birthday

"The smell of money in Florida attracts men as the smell of blood attracts a wild animal."
— G. M. Shelby, on the "Florida Frenzy," *Harper's*

"You are all a lost generation."
— Gertrude Stein, quoted in Ernest Hemingway's *The Sun Also Rises*

"The restlessness approached hysteria. The parties were bigger. The shows were bigger. The pace was faster, . . . the buildings higher, the morals looser."
— F. Scott Fitzgerald

Ads

Radio _____

Premieres
"Allen's Alley"
"Betty Crocker" (recipes)

Of Note
New voices on the air include Alice Brady, Father Charles E. Coughlin, Eddie Cantor, George Burns and Gracie Allen, Al Jolson, Jack Benny, Groucho Marx, Bing Crosby, and Jimmy Durante.

Movies _____

Openings
Don Juan (Alan Crosland), John Barrymore, Mary Astor

Beau Geste (Herbert Brenon), Ronald Colman, Noah Beery

What Price Glory? (Raoul Walsh), Victor McLaglen, Edmund Lowe

Metropolis (Fritz Lang), Alfred Abel, Gustav Froelich

The Scarlet Letter (Victor Seastrom), Lillian Gish, Lars Hanson

Moana (Robert Flaherty), documentary

So This Is Paris (Ernst Lubitsch), Monte Blue

The Black Pirate (Albert Parker), Douglas Fairbanks, Billie Dove

Tramp, Tramp, Tramp (Harry Edwards), Harry Langdon, Joan Crawford

Up in Mabel's Room (E. Mason Hopper), Marie Prevost

Kid Boots (Frank Tuttle), Eddie Cantor, Clara Bow

The Son of the Sheik (George Fitzmaurice), Rudolph Valentino, Vilma Banky

The Torrent (Monta Bell), Greta Garbo (American debut), Ricardo Cortez

The Great Gatsby (Herbert Brenon), Warner Baxter, Lois Wilson

The Sorrows of Satan (D. W. Griffith), Adolphe Menjou, Lya de Putti

Top Box-Office Stars
Colleen Moore, Tom Mix

New Faces
Greta Garbo, Janet Gaynor, Charles "Buddy" Rogers, Delores Del Rio, Walter Pidgeon, Myrna Loy, James Hall, Ralph Forbes, Basil Rathbone, Fay Wray

Helen Morgan, the original torch singer. *Movie Star News.*

Sex symbol Clara Bow, the "It" girl. *Movie Star News.*

Popular Music

Hit Songs
"One Alone"
"The Blue Room"
"If I Could Be with You One Hour To-Night"
"Bye Bye Blackbird"
"After I Say I'm Sorry"
"Breezin' Along with the Breeze"
"The Birth of the Blues"
"Baby Face"
"La Cumparsita"
"In a Little Spanish Town"
"Someone to Watch over Me"
"When the Red, Red Robin Comes Bob, Bob, Bobbin' Along"
"There's a New Star in Heaven Tonight" (written for Valentino's death)

Top Records
Some of These Days (Sophie Tucker); *Two Black Crows* (Moran and Mack); *You Made Me Love You* and *Heebie Jeebies* (Louis Armstrong); *I Wonder What's Become of Joe* (Goofus Five); *Black Bottom Stomp* (Morton's Red Hot Peppers); *Tootin' in Tennessee* (Ipana Troubadours)

Jazz and Big Bands
Duke Ellington plays at the Kentucky Club, New York

First Recordings: Jelly Roll Morton's Red Hot Peppers on Victor; Red Nichols's Five Pennies; Jean Goldkette

New Bands: Gus Arnheim, Los Angeles; Ben Pollack, Los Angeles (with Benny Goodman, age 16)

Theater

Broadway Openings

Plays
The Great God Brown (Eugene O'Neill), William Harrigan
Caponsacchi (Arthur Goodrich, Rose A. Palmer), Walter Hampden
The Play's the Thing (Ferenc Molnár), Holbrook Blinn, Reginald Owen
The Silver Cord (Sidney Howard), Laura Hope Crews, Vernon Steele
In Abraham's Bosom (Paul Green), Rose McClendon
Gentlemen Prefer Blondes (Anita Loos, John Emerson), June Walker, Frank Morgan
An American Tragedy (Philip Dunning, George Abbott), Miriam Hopkins, Morgan Farley
The Noose (Willard Mack), Barbara Stanwyck
The Constant Wife (W. Somerset Maugham), Ethel Barrymore
The Goat Song (Franz Werfel), Alfred Lunt, Lynn Fontanne, Edward G. Robinson
The Great Gatsby (Owen Davis), James Rennie
Yellow (Margaret Vernon), Spencer Tracy, Chester Morris
Sex (Jane Mast), Mae West (who goes to jail for one day when it is closed down)
Juno and the Paycock (Sean O'Casey), Augustan Duncan, Louise Randolph

Musicals
The Desert Song (Sigmund Romberg, Otto Harbach, Oscar Hammerstein II), Robert Halliday, Vivienne Segal
Oh Kay! (George Gershwin, Ira Gershwin), Victor Moore, Gertrude Lawrence
Countess Maritza (Emmerich Kalman, Julius Brammer), Yvonne D'Arle, Odette Myrtil, Walter Woolf
Great Temptations (Maurice Rubens, Clifford Grey), Hazel Dawn, Jack Benny
Earl Carroll's Vanities (Morris Hamilton, Grace Henry), Julius Tannen, Moran and Mack, Smith and Dale
Americana (Con Conrad, Ira Gershwin, George Gershwin), Helen Morgan
Honeymoon Lane (Eddie Dowling, James Hanley), Eddie Dowling, Kate Smith
Tip Toes (George Gershwin, Ira Gershwin), Queenie Smith, Jeanette MacDonald

Classics and Revivals On and Off Broadway
Pygmalion (George Bernard Shaw), Lynn Fontanne; *What Every Woman Knows* (James M. Barry), Helen Hayes; *Ghosts* (Ibsen), Lucile Watson. *Founded:* The Civic Repertory Theater by Eva Le Gallienne

Regional
Goodman Theatre, Chicago: *The Game of Love and Death* (Romain Rolland), premiere

Pulitzer Prize
Craig's Wife, George Kelly

Classical Music

Compositions
Aaron Copland, Piano Concerto, Jazz Symphoniette
    for 22 Instruments
Carl Ruggles, *Portals*
Edgard Varèse, *American Arcana*
George Gershwin, Three Preludes for Piano
Ernest Bloch, *America*
Virgil Thomson, *Sonata da Chiesa*
William Grant Still, *From the Black Belt*
Howard Hanson, *Pan and the Priest,* Concerto for
    Organ and Orchestra
Roy Harris, *Impressions of a Rainy Day*

Important Events
The United States continues to lead the world in the magnitude of orchestral events. A renewed interest in the old masters is marked by numerous performances of Bach's *Brandenburg Concertos* and Mozart's *Eine kleine Nachtmusik.* Also much performed are Sibelius's Symphony no. 7 and *Tapiola,* Respighi's *Pines of Rome,* Stravinsky's Two Suites for Orchestra, and Ralph Vaughan Williams's *Fantasia on a Theme by Thomas Tallis.*

For the American sesquicentennial, the Philadelphia Orchestra plays two concerts a week for 16 weeks with conductors Willem Van Hoogstraten, Nikolai Sokoloff, Artur Rodzinski, and Leopold Stokowski.

Major Recitals: violinists Albert Spalding, Josef Szigeti, Paul Kochanski, Efrem Zimbalist, Fritz Kreisler; pianists Ossip Gabrilowitsch, Harold Bauer, Alexander Cortot, Alfredo Casella, Darius Milhaud; harpsichordist Wanda Landowska; cellists Pablo Casals, Felix Salmont; and joint artists Josef and Rosina Lhévinne, Albert Spalding and Efrem Zimbalist

Guest Conductors: Arturo Toscanini (premiering Respighi's *Pines of Rome,* New York Philharmonic Society), Otto Klemperer (New York Symphonic Society), Georges Enesco (New York Philharmonic)

Debut: Walter Gieseking

First Performances
Darius Milhaud, playing *Carnival d'Aix* (New York); George Antheil, *Amériques* (Philadelphia); Douglas Moore, *Pageant of P. T. Barnum* (Cleveland); Louis Gruenberg, *The Creation* (New York); William Grant Still, *Darker Avenue* (New York); Emerson Whitehorne, *New York Days and Nights* (Philadelphia)

Opera
Twenty cities actively produce opera; especially popular are *The Witch of Salem* (Charles Wakefield Cadman) and *Hansel and Gretel* (Englebert Humperdinck). The 100th anniversary of Italian opera and 25th anniversary of Verdi's death are widely celebrated.

Metropolitan: Ezio Pinza (debut), Rosa Ponselle, *La vestale;* Lauritz Melchior (debut), *Tannhäuser.* Premieres: *Skyscraper* (John Alden Carpenter); *La vida breve* (Manuel de Falla); Maria Jeritza, *Le rossignol* and *Turandot* (American premieres); Mrs. Ernestine Schumann-Heink returns. Free opera is performed at the Polo Grounds and Starlight Park (Coney Island).

Chicago: *A Light from St. Agnes* (W. Franke Harling); *Judith* (Arthur Honegger)

Philadelphia: *Deep River* (W. Franke Harling); *Tannhäuser* (in English)

Northampton, Mass.: *L'incoronazione di Poppea*

San Francisco: *Pique dame* (Tchaikovsky); *Fra Diavolo* (Auber)

Music Notes
The Pittsburgh Symphony Orchestra, disbanded in 1910, reorganizes under Richard Hageman • Plans continue to construct a new Metropolitan Opera House • Leopold Stokowski tries the daring experiment of conducting in a dark hall with the podium alone lighted; his performance raises great indignation.

Art

Painting

Thomas Hart Benton, *The Lord Is My Shepherd, The Path Finder*
Charles Demuth, *Eggplant and Tomatoes*
Edward Hopper, *Mrs. Acorn's Parlor*
Georgia O'Keeffe, *Black Iris, Abstraction*
Raphael Soyer, *Reading from Left to Right*
Walt Kuhn, *Dressing Room*
John Marin, *Fir Tree, Deer Isle, Maine*
Glenn O. Coleman, *Downtown Street*
Guy Pène du Bois, *Opera Box*

Sculpture

William Zorach, *Child with Cat*
Mahonri M. Young, *Groggy*
Paul Manship, *Indian Hunter*

Architecture

Sunnyside Gardens, New York City (Clarence Stein, Henry Wright)
Philip Lovell Beach House, Newport Beach, Calif. (Rudolph Schindler)
Liberty Memorial, Kansas City, Mo. (H. Van Buren Magonigle)

Important Exhibitions

Museums

New York: *Metropolitan:* John Singer Sargent; Joseph Pennell; modern decorative arts; the K Wing opens to house the Altman Collection. *Brooklyn:* "International Exhibition of Modern Art" (307 works from 23 countries)

Chicago: Modern painting, with prizes to George Luks, Charles Hopkinson, Eugene Speicher

Washington: *Corcoran:* Tenth exhibit of contemporary paintings, with awards to Charles W. Hawthorne and W. Elmer Schofield

Los Angeles: Painters of the West

Hispanic Society of America: Paintings of the provinces of Spain by Joachim Sorolla y Bastida (opening show)

Traveling Exhibitions: The American Federation of Arts sponsors 40 to 50 shows that reach all but four states.

Art Briefs

The Toledo Museum receives a $14 million endowment, and Kansas City receives $8 million for the Nelson Gallery • Also expanding are museums in St. Louis, Cincinnati, Baltimore, Newark, Houston, and Providence; Des Moines purchases land for a museum site • Alexander Calder holds his first exhibition of paintings at the Artist's Gallery in New York.

Dance

Martha Graham debuts in New York as a choreographer and dancer in *Three Gopi Maidens* and *A Study in Lacquer.*

Miriam Hopkins and Morgan Farley in *An American Tragedy* (adapted from Theodore Dreiser's novel), an attack on contemporary social and business morality. *Billy Rose Theatre Collection. The New York Public Library at Lincoln Center. Astor, Lenox and Tilden Foundations.*

Books

Fiction

Critics' Choice

The Sun Also Rises, Ernest Hemingway
The Torrents of Spring, Ernest Hemingway
Soldier's Pay, William Faulkner
The Silver Stallion, James Branch Cabell
My Mortal Enemy, Willa Cather
The Love Nest, Ring Lardner
All the Sad Young Men, F. Scott Fitzgerald
The Cabala, Thornton Wilder
Preface to a Life, Zona Gale

Best Sellers

The Private Life of Helen of Troy, John Erskine
Gentlemen Prefer Blondes, Anita Loos
Sorrell and Son, Warwick Deeping
The Hounds of Spring, Sylvia Thompson
Beau Sabreur, P. C. Wren
The Silver Spoon, John Galsworthy
Beau Geste, P. C. Wren
Show Boat, Edna Ferber
After Noon, Susan Ertz
The Blue Window, Temple Bailey

Nonfiction

Critics' Choice

Dictionary of American Usage, H. W. Fowler
The Physical Significance of the Quantum Theory, F. Lindemann
The Outlook for American Prose, Joseph Warren Beach
Art through the Ages, Helen Gardner
The Making of the Modern Mind, Herman Randall
Microbe Hunters, Paul de Kruif
Notes on Democracy, H. L. Mencken
The Mauve Decade, Thomas Beer
Abraham Lincoln: The Prairie Years, Carl Sandburg
Tar: A Midwest Childhood, Sherwood Anderson
🔊 *Religion and the Rise of Capitalism*, R. H. Tawney
🔊 *The End of Laissez-Faire*, J. M. Keynes

Best-Sellers

The Man Nobody Knows, Bruce Barton
Why We Behave Like Human Beings, George A. Dorsey
Diet and Health, Lulu Hunt Peters
Our Times, vol. I, Mark Sullivan
The Boston Cooking School Cook Book, new ed., Fannie Farmer
Auction Bridge Complete, Milton C. Work
The Book Nobody Knows, Bruce Barton

Ernest Hemingway, whose *The Sun Also Rises* portrays the "lost generation" of American expatriates in postwar Europe. *Library of Congress.*

The Story of Philosophy, Will Durant
The Light of Faith, Edgar A. Guest
Jefferson and Hamilton, Claude G. Bowers

Poetry

E. E. Cummings, *Is 5*
Hart Crane, *White Buildings*
Langston Hughes, *The Weary Blues*
Laura Riding, *The Close Couplet*
Sara Teasdale, *Dark of the Moon*

Pulitzer Prizes

Early Autumn, Louis Bromfield (novel)
Pinckney's Treaty, Samuel Flagg Bemis (U.S. history)
Whitman, Emory Holloway (biography)
Fiddler's Farewell, Leonora Speyer

Science and Technology

Robert Goddard fires the first liquid fuel–propelled rocket, and it rises 41 feet at 60 m.p.h.
The first movie with sound is demonstrated, a comedy short with Chic Sale.
A three-engine, all-metal Stout airplane is developed by Henry Ford for the purpose of improved passenger service.
Thomas Hunt Morgan, in *Theory of the Gene*, presents his theories of heredity developed at his Drosophila (fruit fly) workshop, Columbia University.

Thomas M. Rivers defines distinctions between viruses and bacteria, establishing virology as a separate discipline.
James B. Sumner isolates the metabolic enzyme urease.
The semiautomatic .30 MI rifle is patented by John Garand.
Auto antifreeze for radiators permits year-round motoring.
🔊 Oscar Barnack develops the 35mm camera.

Sports

Baseball

Babe Ruth hits three home runs in a World Series game. Aging Grover Alexander (St. Louis, NL), in relief, strikes out Tony Lazzeri (New York, AL) with the bases loaded to save the seventh game.

Champions

Batting	Pitching
Eugene Hargrave (Cincinnati, NL), .353	Ray Kremer (Pittsburgh, NL), 20–6
Heinie Manush (Detroit, AL), .378	George Uhke (Cleveland, AL), 27–11
	Home runs
	Babe Ruth (New York, AL), 47

Football

"Cash and Carry" Pyle starts the American Football League with Red Grange; the league is a financial failure. The NFL rules that college players are ineligible until their classes graduate.

Pro Stars: Elbert Bloodgood (Kansas City), Ernie Nevers (Duluth).

College All-Americans: Bennie Friedman (Q), Michigan; Victor Hanson (E), Syracuse.

Rose Bowl (Jan. 1, 1927): Alabama 7–Stanford 7.

Basketball

New York's Original Celtics are broken up to keep the ABL competitive; their overall record is 1,320–66.

Gertrude (Trudy) Ederle, during her record-breaking swim from Dover, England, to Gris-Nez, France. *Library of Congress.*

Other Sports

Swimming: Bronx-born Gertrude Ederle swims the English Channel in 14 hours and 31 minutes, breaking the previous record by 2 hours.

Boxing: Gene Tunney, a Shakespeare fan ("I worship at his shrine"), beats Jack Dempsey by a decision for the heavyweight title in Philadelphia; the gate is a record $1.9 million.

Tennis: Suzanne Lenglen beats Helen Wills in the "Match of the Century" at Cannes. Wills suffers appendicitis after the match. C. C. Pyle tours the United States with Lenglen, pays her $50,000, and draws large crowds.

Winners

World Series	*Player of the Year*
St. Louis (NL) 4	John Cobb, North Carolina
New York (AL) 3	*Stanley Cup*
MVP	Montreal Maroons
NL–Robert O'Farrell, St. Louis	*U.S. Tennis Open*
AL–George Burns, Cleveland	Men: René Lacoste
	Women: Molla Mallory
NFL	*USGA Open*
Frankford Yellow Jackets	Robert T. Jones, Jr.
College Football	*Kentucky Derby*
Stanford	Bubbling Over (A. Johnson, jockey)
College Basketball	
Syracuse	

Fashion

For Women: Skirts, shortest of the decade, stop just below the knee with flounces, pleats, and circular gores that extend from the hip; they are worn with horizontal-striped sweaters and long necklaces. Short and colorful evening dresses have elaborate embroidery, fringes, futuristic designs, beads, and appliques. The cocktail dress is born, and Clara Bow's "look" replaces Mary Pickford's. The new sex appeal extends from the bee-stung mouth and touseled hair to a new focus on legs, with silk stockings rolled around garters at rouged knees. The "debutante slouch" emerges: hips thrown forward, as the woman grips a cigarette holder between her teeth. Mothers and daughters are flappers, many nearly nude beneath the new, lighter clothing. Epicene fashions peak in a final statement of emancipation; also stylish is the odd earring, a pearl stud in one ear and dangling paste from the other.

High-fashion notes: Callot's beaded sheath; Chanel's simple two-piece jersey; gold and silver baguette bracelets; Premet's "garçonne dress"

Kaleidoscope

- Elinor Glyn uses the term "It Girl" to describe Clara Bow and the new sex appeal: the "same as before but more of it showing" and "a little more available." "Flaming youth" is coined for the younger generation.
- The popular "Charleston flare dress" sells at Gimbels for $1.58.
- Stars like Pola Negri and Marion Kay compete at Rudolph Valentino's funeral to show their devotion to him; a widely publicized photo of Valentino meeting Caruso in heaven appears in the *Evening Graphic*.
- The Supreme Court upholds the law limiting the medical prescription of whiskey to one pint every ten days.
- 2,000 people die of poisoned liquor; the illegal liquor trade nets $3.5 billion a year; prices for bootleg Scotch are $48 a case; rye, $85; champagne, $95; beer, $30.
- Over 14,500 movie houses show 400 films a year, as movies become America's favorite entertainment. *The Black Pirate* is the first in technicolor.
- Many top movie stars—John Gilbert, Greta Garbo, Emile Jannings, Pola Negri, Conrad Veidt—are forced to learn English with the advent of the Vitaphone sound system; some will retire because of the poor quality of their recorded voices.
- Greta Garbo's salary goes from $350 to $5,000 a week at MGM. Football star Red Grange is paid $300,000 for a film *(One Minute to Play)*.

- The U.S. sesquicentennial is celebrated.
- Gertrude Ederle loses her hearing after swimming the English Channel.
- After his victory over Dempsey, Gene Tunney lectures on Shakespeare at Yale and then visits Europe with Thornton Wilder.
- Evangelist Aimee Semple McPherson's fame turns to notoriety as her so-called kidnapping is suspected by some to have been a romantic interlude with her radio operator.
- After "Daddy" Browning divorces her, Peaches loses 40 pounds and earns $8,000 a week in vaudeville.
- New faces on the Broadway stage include Barbara Stanwyck, Paul Muni, Spencer Tracy, Chester Morris, and Claudette Colbert.
- In one of his last feats, Houdini stays underwater 91 minutes with only 5 to 6 minutes of air.
- The New York Public Library starts its "Ten Worst Books Contest."
- The public eagerly follows the Hall-Mills murder case and is especially interested in their love letters: "I just want to crush you for two hours" (Hall).
- *Vanities'* producer Earl Carroll offers 17-year-old Joyce Hawley $1,000 to sit naked in a bathtub of champagne at a party he is hosting; she begins to cry when the guests appear.
- The tabloid market expands; Bernarr Macfadden's *True Story* gains a circulation of 2 million with stories such as "The Diamond Bracelet She Thought Her Husband Didn't Know About"; many call the *Evening Graphic* the "Porno-Graphic."
- Sinclair Lewis refuses the Pulitzer Prize because it makes the writer "safe, polite, obedient, and sterile."
- To fight the depression in the auto industry, Henry Ford introduces the eight-hour day and five-day week.
- Advocated by Secretary of the Treasury Andrew Mellon, a bill to reduce taxes on incomes of $1 million or more from 66 percent to 20 percent is passed by Congress.

First Appearances: Distinguished Flying Cross, Scotch tape, zippers, pop-up electric toaster, John Powers model agency, Hotel Carlyle (New York), Mark Hopkins hotel (San Francisco), Inter-Greyhound Racing Association, plastic surgery professorship, coin bearing the portrait of a living president (Calvin Coolidge), Chrysler Imperial, Prestone, safety glass and windshields, Pontiac, Du Pont waterproof cellophane, Safeway stores, First National, Trans World Airways, flavored yogurt, Book-of-the-Month Club (40,000 subscribers), Long Island University, Sarah Lawrence College, senator unseated after a recount (S. W. Brookhart), 16mm film (Kodak)

High School basketball team, Englewood, New Jersey. *I. Goldfein.*

1927

Facts and Figures

Economic Profile
  Dow-Jones: ↑ High 202–
    Low 152
  GNP: −2%
  Inflation: −0.5%
  Unemployment: 3.3%
Average salary: $1,312
  Teacher: $1,277
  Lawyer: $5,205
  Physician: $5,150
  Factory worker: $1,502
Pillowcases, sheets: $1
Wool blankets, 70″ by 80″:
  $9.95
Face towels: $7.50–$10.50
  (doz.)
Liggett's Drugs
  Phillips milk of magnesia:
    50¢
  Listerine, Lavoris: $1
  Kolynos, Pepsodent: 50¢
  Odorona: 60¢; Mum: 25¢
  Wampole's cod liver oil: $1
  Ivory soap: 8¢

In the News

COOLIDGE CALLS FOR NAVAL DISARMAMENT CONFERENCE, BRITAIN AND JAPAN ATTEND, FRANCE AND ITALY DECLINE . . . FRENCH MINISTER ARISTIDE BRIAND SUGGESTS OUTLAWING WAR, SECRETARY OF STATE FRANK KELLOGG ENDORSES BRIAND . . . TEAPOT DOME LEASE IS INVALIDATED BY SUPREME COURT . . . CHIANG KAI-SHEK AND COMMUNIST FORCES DEFEAT WARLORDS IN SHANGHAI, CANTON, NANKING . . . REGULAR TRANSATLANTIC PHONE SERVICE BEGINS . . . GERMAN ECONOMY COLLAPSES ON "BLACK FRIDAY" . . . GIANT FEDERAL RELIEF EFFORT UNDER HERBERT HOOVER AIDS FLOODED MISSISSIPPI VALLEY . . . LAST APPEALS FAIL, SACCO AND VANZETTI ARE EXECUTED, WORLDWIDE PROTESTS OCCUR . . . CHARLES LINDBERGH FLIES SOLO, NONSTOP, FROM NEW YORK TO PARIS, 3,610 MILES IN 33 ⅓ HOURS, 100,000 FRENCH CHEER LINDBERGH'S ARRIVAL . . . COOLIDGE SAYS: "I CHOOSE NOT TO RUN" IN '28 . . . HOUSEWIFE RUTH SNYDER AND ART DIRECTOR HENRY GRAY ARE CONVICTED OF HUSBAND'S MURDER . . . GENE TUNNEY, DOWN FOR THE "LONG COUNT," RISES TO DECISION JACK DEMPSEY BEFORE 104,943 IN CHICAGO . . . BRITAIN BREAKS DIPLOMATIC RELATIONS WITH RUSSIA, CLAIMING SOVIET INTRIGUE . . . SUPREME COURT RULES ILLEGAL INCOME IS TAXABLE . . . 40 MEN DIE IN SUB S-4 AFTER RESCUE EFFORTS FAIL.

Deaths

Lizzie Borden, Georg Brandes, John Dillon, John Drew.

Quotes _____

"Isn't it nice that Calvin is President? You know we really never had room before for a dog."
— Mrs. Coolidge

"I am going to St. Petersburg, Florida, tomorrow. Let the worthy citizens of Chicago get their liquor the best they can. I'm sick of the job—it's a thankless one and full of grief. I've been spending the best years of my life as a public benefactor."
— Al Capone

Question: In other words, you want the jury to believe that you were a perfect lady? . . . You did nothing to make your husband unhappy?
Reply: Not that he knew about.
— Testimony of housewife Ruth Snyder, accused of murder

"I am innocent. I am suffering because I am a radical . . . an Italian . . . more for my family and for my beloved than for myself, but I am so convinced to be right that if you could execute me two times, and I could be reborn two other times, I would live again to do what I have done already."
— Bartolomeo Vanzetti

"This man [Vanzetti], although he may not actually have committed the crime . . . is . . . the enemy of our existing institutions. . . . The defendant's ideals are cognate with crime."
— Webster Thayer, presiding judge at the Sacco-Vanzetti trial

"I am Charles A. Lindbergh," he said, when he arrived in Paris. *Library of Congress.*

"There was a closet in the anteroom, evidently a place for hats and coats. . . . We repaired there many times in the course of my visits to the White House . . . and there the President [Harding] and his adoring sweetheart made love."
— Nan Britton's autobiography, *The President's Daughter*

"Lindbergh . . . has shown us that we are *not* rotten at the core, but morally sound and sweet and good!"
— Mary B. Mullet, "The Biggest Thing that Lindbergh Has Done," *American* magazine

Ads _____

Radio

Premieres

"The Two Black Crows," George Moran, Charles Mack

"The Cities Service Concert" (opera from the Chicago Civic Auditorium)

"Ida Bailey Allen and Her Cooking School"

"The Palmolive Hour"

"Duke Ellington" (from the Cotton Club)

"Rose Bowl" (first coast-to-coast program)

Specials

Lindbergh's landing, announced by Graham McNamee; Dempsey-Tunney fight; Floyd Bennett's funeral service from Arlington; Herbert Hoover accepting the Republican nomination in Palo Alto; Ted Husing announcing the arrival of the Graf Zeppelin at Lakehurst, N.J.

Of Note

The Federal Radio Commission is appointed.

Movies

Openings

The Jazz Singer (Alan Crosland), Al Jolson (first successful full-length talkie)

Wings (William A. Wellman), Clara Bow, Buddy Rogers, Gary Cooper

Napoleon (Abel Gance), Albert Dieudonne

The King of Kings (Cecil B. DeMille), Joseph Schildkraut, Rudolph Schildkraut, H. B. Warner

Flesh and the Devil (Clarence Brown), Greta Garbo, John Gilbert

Underworld (Josef von Sternberg), Evelyn Brent, George Bancroft

The Night of Love (George Fitzmaurice), Ronald Colman, Vilma Banky, Montagu Love

Camille (Fred Niblo), Gilbert Roland, Norma Talmadge

The Way of All Flesh (Victor Fleming), Emil Jannings

The Ten Days that Shook the World (Sergei Eisenstein), V. Nikandrov, N. Popov

Sunrise (F. W. Murnau), Janet Gaynor, George Brien

Seventh Heaven (Frank Borzage), Janet Gaynor, Charles Farrell

Love (Edmund Goulding), Greta Garbo, John Gilbert

The Unknown (Tod Browning), Lon Chaney, Joan Crawford

The General (Buster Keaton, Clyde Bruckman), Buster Keaton

Top Box-Office Stars

Tom Mix, Colleen Moore, John Gilbert, Greta Garbo

Al Jolson's limited dialogue in *The Jazz Singer* includes "You ain't seen nothin' yet." *Movie Star News.*

Popular Music

Hit Songs
"Ol' Man River"
"Bill"
"Can't Help Lovin' Dat Man"
"Why Do I Love You?"
"I'm Looking over a Four-Leaf
   Clover"
"S'Wonderful"
"Let a Smile Be Your Umbrella"
"Blue Skies"
"My Heart Stood Still"
"The Best Things in Life Are
   Free"
"East of the Moon, West of the
   Stars"
"Jealousy"
"Me and My Shadow"

"Ramona"
"Thou Swell"
"Henry's Made a Lady out of
   Lizzie"

Top Records
*The Song Is Ended, It All
Depends on You* (Ruth Etting);
Side by Side (Ipana Troubadours);
Rio Rita (The Knickerbockers);
Highways Are Happy Ways (Ted
Weems); *Hear My Prayer* (Ernest
Lough); *Ida, Sweet as Apple Cider*
(Red Nichols); *The Soldier's
Sweetheart* (Jimmie Rodgers); *My
Blue Heaven* (Gene Austin)

Jazz and Big Bands
Earl Hines joins Louis Armstrong.
Duke Ellington opens at the
Cotton Club, New York, where he
begins radio broadcasting. Wayne
King plays at Chicago's Aragon
Ballroom.

First Recordings: Adelaide Hall's
Creole Love Call with Duke
Ellington (the first use of voice as
orchestral instrument); Red
McKenzie and Eddie Condon (the
first classic Chicago jazz session)

New Bands: Jack Teagarden,
New York; Jimmy Lunceford,
Memphis

Theater

Broadway Openings

Plays
Paris Bound (Philip Barry), Madge Kennedy
The Royal Family (George S. Kaufman, Edna
   Ferber), Otto Kruger
Saturday's Children (Maxwell Anderson), Ruth
   Gordon, Roger Pryer
The Road to Rome (Robert E. Sherwood), Jane Cowl
Coquette (George Abbott, Anna Preston Bridges),
   Helen Hayes
The Barker (Kenyon Nicholson), Claudette Colbert
Her Cardboard Lover (Jacques Deval), Jeanne
   Eagels, Leslie Howard
Burlesque (Arthur Hopkins), Barbara Stanwyck,
   Oscar Levant
The Trial of Mary Dugan (Bayard Veiller), Ann
   Harding, Rex Cherryman, Robert Cummings
The Letter (W. Somerset Maugham), Katharine
   Cornell
Crime (Samuel Shipman, John B. Hymer), Sylvia
   Sidney, Chester Morris
Dracula (Hamilton Deane, John Balderston), Bela
   Lugosi
Porgy (Dorothy Heyward, DuBose Heyward), Rose
   McClendon, Frank Wilson
Baby Mine (Margaret Mayo), Roscoe Arbuckle,
   Humphrey Bogart

Musicals
Good News (Ray Henderson, B. G. DeSylva), John
   Price Jones, Mary Lawlor

Ziegfeld Follies (Irving Berlin), Eddie Cantor, Ruth
   Etting, Claire Luce
A Connecticut Yankee (Richard Rodgers, Lorenz
   Hart), William Gaxton, Constance Carpenter
Show Boat (Jerome Kern, Oscar Hammerstein II),
   Helen Morgan, Charles Winninger, Edna May
   Oliver
Hit the Deck (Vincent Youmans, Leo Robin), Louise
   Groody, Charles King, Brian Donlevy
Funny Face (George Gershwin, Ira Gershwin), Fred
   and Adele Astaire
The Merry Malones (George M. Cohan), George M.
   Cohan, Polly Walker
Padlocks of 1927 (Henry H. Tobias, Billy Rose),
   Texas Guinan, Lillian Roth
Sidewalks of New York (Eddie Dowling, Jimmy
   Hanley), Ruby Keeler, Ray Dooley

Classics and Revivals On and Off Broadway
Electra (Sophocles), Margaret Anglin; *The Doctor's
Dilemma* (George Bernard Shaw), Alfred Lunt, Lynn
Fontanne; *Trelawney of the Wells* (Pinero), John
Drew, Pauline Lord; *An Enemy of the People* (Ibsen),
Walter Hampden; *A Midsummer Night's Dream*, Lili
Darvis; *The Plough and the Stars* (Sean O'Casey),
Arthur Sinclair; *Escape* (John Galsworthy), Leslie
Howard

Pulitzer Prize
In Abraham's Bosom, Paul Green

Classical Music

Compositions

Virgil Thomson, *La valse grégorienne*
Roy Harris, Concerto for Piano, Clarinet and String
  Quartet
Wallingford Riegger, Study in Sonority for Nineteen
  Violins and Any Multiple of Ten

Important Events

An unusual amount of modern music is performed,
and works of Gershwin, Copland, Varèse, and
Antheil receive wide acclaim. Bartók's and Antheil's
appearances in New York receive unprecedented
publicity.

New Appointment: Georg Schneevoight becomes
conductor of the Los Angeles Philharmonic.

Debut: Yehudi Menuhin, age 10

First Performances

Igor Stravinsky, Octet (International Composers
League, New York); Carlos Salzedo, Concerto for
Harp and Seven Woodwinds (New York); Aaron
Copland, playing, Concerto for Piano and Orchestra
(Boston); Roger Sessions, Symphony in E minor
(Boston); George Antheil, *Ballet mécanique* (New
York); Sergei Rachmaninoff, playing, Piano Concerto
no. 4 (Philadelphia); Frank S. Converse, *Flivver
10,000,000* (Boston); Edgard Varèse, *Arcane* (New
York); Leoš Janáček, *Sinfonietta* (New York); Ruth
Crawford, Violin Sonata (New York); James Dunn,
WE (celebrating Lindbergh's flight, New York); Béla
Bartók, *The Miraculous Mandarin* (Cincinnati);
Albert Roussel, Suite (Boston); Alfredo Casella,
Scarlattiana (New York); Charles Ives, Symphony
no. 4 (New York); Emerson Whitehorne, *Aeroplane*
(Cleveland)

Opera

Metropolitan: Rosa Ponselle, *Norma;* Edward
Johnson, *Roméo et Juliette;* Richard Mayr, Grete
Stückgold, *Die Meistersinger.* Premieres: *The King's
Henchman* (Deems Taylor, Edna St. Vincent Millay);
Violanta (Erich Korngold)

Chicago: *Judith* (Arthur Honegger, premiere)

Philadelphia: *Boris Godunov* (original score)

San Francisco: Antonio Scotti, *Falstaff; La cena
della Beffe* (Giordano)

Music Notes

Ernest Bloch's *America* wins the $3,000 "Musical
America" prize • The Pittsburgh Symphony is
founded • During Hungarian Week in New York,
Zoltán Kodály performs Béla Bartók and Imre
Weisshaus • Cleveland audiences are shocked by the
orchestra's performances of Bax and Scriabin • Radio
scheduling begins to include contemporary music, as
well as the old masters.

Ziegfeld Follies' star Ruth Etting. *Movie Star News.*

Art

Painting

Alfred Maurer, *Self-Portrait*

Lyonel Feininger, *The Steamer Odin, Village*

Guy Pène du Bois, *Americans in Paris*

Edward Hopper, *Manhattan Bridge, Lighthouse Hill*

Georgia O'Keeffe, *Radiator Building, New York*

Charles Demuth, *My Egypt, Eggplant and Squash*

Thomas Hart Benton, *Lonesome Road*

Stuart Davis, *Egg Beater, No. 2*

Arthur G. Dove, *Hand Sewing Machine*

Gerald Murphy, *Wasp and Pear*

Sculpture

Mahonri Young, *Right with the Jaw*

Gaston Lachaise, *Georgia O'Keeffe, Floating Figure, Standing Woman* (also called *Elevation*)

John Storrs, *Study in Form #1*

Reuben Nakian, *The Lap Dog, Young Calf*

Elie Nadelman, *Man in a Top Hat*

Architecture

Dymaxion House, 4-D house model (Buckminster Fuller)

Heath House, Los Angeles (Richard Neutra)

Ocotillo Camp design (Frank Lloyd Wright)

Grauman's Chinese Theatre, Hollywood, Calif. (Meyer and Holler)

Important Exhibitions

Museums

New York: *Metropolitan:* American miniatures, 1720–1850; Swedish contemporary decorative arts; painted and printed fabrics

Chicago: Chinese Buddhist art of the Wei Dynasty

Boston: Claude Monet; Tricentennial exhibition of the Society of Arts and Crafts

Art Briefs

Highlights of the Alexander Archipenko show in New York include *Two Women, Woman Walking,* and *Torso* • Gutzon Borglum begins a five-year, $437,500 project on Mt. Rushmore in South Dakota: 465-foot figures of Washington, Jefferson, Lincoln, and Roosevelt • An estimated 10,000 professional artists live in the United States • The influx of European art dealers gains public attention • The Fogg Museum at Harvard opens.

Dance

Martha Graham founds the Martha Graham School of Contemporary Dance.

John Storrs, *Forms in Space*, 1927. Stainless steel and copper. 20½ × 25″. *The Metropolitan Museum of Art, Bequest Fund, 1967.*

Books

Fiction

Critics' Choice
Mosquitos, William Faulkner
Death Comes for the Archbishop, Willa Cather
The Grandmothers, Glenway Wescott
Men without Women, Ernest Hemingway
Blue Voyage, Conrad Aiken
Giants in the Earth, Ole Rölvaag
Oil! Upton Sinclair
ം *To the Lighthouse*, Virginia Woolf
ം *The Magic Mountain*, Thomas Mann

Best-Sellers
Elmer Gantry, Sinclair Lewis
The Plutocrat, Booth Tarkington
Doomsday, Warwick Deeping
Sorrell and Son, Warwick Deeping
Jalna, Mazo de la Roche
Lost Ecstasy, Mary Roberts Rinehart
Twilight Sleep, Edith Wharton
Tomorrow Morning, Anne Parrish
The Old Countess, Anne Douglas Sedgwick
A Good Woman, Louis Bromfield

Nonfiction

Critics' Choice
The Story of a Wonder Man, Ring Lardner
The Main Stream, Stuart Pratt Sherman
The American Songbag, Carl Sandburg
The Rise of American Civilization, Charles Beard, Mary Beard
The Emergence of Modern America, Allan Nevins
Platonism and the Spiritual Life, George Santayana
Evolution in Science and Religion, Robert Millikan
My Religion, Helen Keller
What about Advertising? Kenneth Goode, Harford Powel, Jr.

Best-Sellers
The Story of Philosophy, Will Durant
Napoleon, Emil Ludwig
Revolt in the Desert, T. E. Lawrence
Trader Horn, vol. 1, Alfred Aloysius Horn, Ethelreda Lewis
We, Charles A. Lindbergh
Ask Me Another, Julian Spafford, Lucien Esty

The Royal Road to Romance, Richard Halliburton
Why We Behave Like Human Beings, George A. Dorsey
Mother India, Katherine Mayo
The Glorious Adventure, Richard Halliburton

Poetry
Laura Riding, *Voltaire*
Robinson Jeffers, *The Women at Point Sur*
John Crowe Ransom, *Two Gentlemen in Bonds*
Amy Lowell (posthumous), *Ballads for Sale*
Countee Cullen, *Copper Sun, The Ballad of the Brown Girl*
Don Marquis, *archy and mehitabel*

Pulitzer Prizes
The Bridge of San Luis Rey, Thornton Wilder (novel)
Main Currents in American Thought, Vernon Louis Parrington (U.S. history)
The American Orchestra and Theodore Thomas, Charles Edward Russell (biography)
Tristram, Edwin Arlington Robinson

Science and Technology

Physicists Clinton Davisson and Lester Germer, of Bell Telephone Laboratories, confirm de Broglie's theory that electrons behave as "matter waves."

A. A. Michelson, at Mt. Wilson Observatory in California, begins experiments to measure the speed of light.

Philo T. Farnsworth constructs the first all-electronic television set.

The first national radio beacon to inform pilots when they are off course is implemented.

Philip Drinker, at Harvard, devises the iron lung, a respirator for people who cannot breathe on their own.

Thyroxine, a thyroid hormone, is prepared synthetically, enabling cretinism to be treated.

An adrenal cortical extract, cortin, prepared by F. A. Hartman, is used to treat once-fatal Addison's disease.

Karl Landsteiner and Philip Levine, of the Rockefeller Institute, discover blood groups M, N, and P.

The Holland Tunnel is the first vehicular route across the Hudson River between New York and New Jersey.

ം Fossil remains of Pithecanthropus pekinensis, "Peking man," 300,000–400,000 B.C., are discovered by Davidson Black.

ം Werner Heisenberg propounds the Uncertainty Principle.

Nobel Prize
Arthur H. Compton wins the prize in physics for his discovery of wave-length change in diffused X rays.

Sports

Baseball

Babe Ruth (New York, AL) hits a record 60 home
   runs. Lou Gehrig (New York, AL) bats .378 with
   175 runs batted in and 47 home runs. The
   Yankees win a record 110 games with
   "Murderers' Row"—Ruth; Gehrig; Earle
   Coombs, .356; Bob Meusel, .336; and Tony
   Lazzeri, .309.
Walter Johnson retires with a record 113 shutouts and
   3,497 strikeouts.

Champions

Batting	Pitching
Paul Waner (Pittsburgh, NL), .380	Jessie Haynes (St. Louis, NL), 24–10
Harry Heilmann (Detroit, AL), .398	Waite Hoyt (New York, AL), 22–7
	Home runs
	Babe Ruth (New York, AL), 60

Football

The NFL goes from 32 to 12 teams.

Pro Stars: Steve Owens, Cal Hubbard (New York)

College All-Americans: Bennie Oosterban (Q),
Michigan; Chris Cagle (H), Army

Rose Bowl (Jan. 1, 1928):   Alabama 7–Pittsburgh 6

Basketball

The Harlem Globetrotters, a black team, is organized
by Abe Saperstein.
Brooklyn, with most of the Original Celtics, wins the
ABL.

The Rens, a black team, splits an exhibition series
with Brooklyn.

Other Sports

Boxing: Jack Dempsey fails to go to a neutral
corner when he knocks Gene Tunney down; the
length of the count is disputed; the gate at Soldier's
Field, Chicago, is a record $2.65 million. The Golden
Gloves is inaugurated by the *New York Daily News*.

Swimming: Johnny Weismuller swims 100 yards in a
record 51 seconds.

Tennis: Helen Wills returns and wins the
Wimbledon Singles.

Golf: Walter Hagen wins his fourth straight PGA
title.

Winners

World Series		*Player of the Year*	
New York (AL) 4		Victor Hanson, Syracuse	
Pittsburgh (NL) 0		*Stanley Cup*	
MVP		Ottawa	
NL–Paul Waner, Pittsburgh		*U.S. Tennis Open*	
AL–Lou Gehrig, New York		Men: Rene Lacoste	
NFL		Women: Helen Wills	
New York Giants		*USGA Open*	
College Football		Tommy Armour	
Illinois		*Kentucky Derby*	
College Basketball		Whiskery (L. McAtee,	
Notre Dame		jockey)	

Fashion

For Men: September *Vanity Fair* reports the
"sartorial practices" of "a certain flamboyant
youth," the Harvard, Yale, or Princeton collegian
who moves "like a darting elephant": he wears gray
sagging Oxford pants, drooping socks over square-
toed, barely visible saddle shoes with crepe or rubber
soles, and a single-breasted, gray Oxford overcoat. A
felt hat, battered, bent, twisted, or folded, falls over
his nose, or a cap is pushed to the back of his head.

Knickers or white denims, overalls, and jackets are
sometimes worn, as well as the double-breasted
lounge jacket and soft white shirt with attached collar
(inserted with a simple pin), tweed worsteds, and
chemises. Two- or three-button single-breasted sack
coats are most stylish; ties are knitted. Clothes are
made only by local, New York, or London tailors;
they appear better pressed at Yale.

U.S. delegates at the Geneva Disarmament Conference. Left to right: George V. Strong, H. C. Train, J. N. Greely, Frank B. Kellogg, J. T. Marriner, A. T. Long. *Library of Congress.*

- Eighteen hundred tons of ticker tape and shredded newspaper and phone books contribute to the Lindbergh parade in New York; it costs the city $16,000 to sweep up.
- Lindbergh receives 3.5 million letters containing $100,000 in return postage, 100,000 wires, and 7,000 job offers; a dance, the "Lindy Hop" is named for him.
- Edna St. Vincent Millay is arrested outside the Boston courthouse during the deathwatch for Sacco and Vanzetti. Others defending them include three-fourths of the Harvard Law School graduating class, Felix Frankfurter, Heywood Broun, Dorothy Parker, Robert Benchley, John Dos Passos, Albert Einstein, G. B. Shaw, H. G. Wells, Anatole France, Rabbi Stephen Wise, Jane Addams, Romain Rolland, and John Galsworthy.
- The bootleg best-seller *The President's Daughter* by Nan Britton tells of Britton's love affair with President Harding and their illegitimate daughter.
- Babe Ruth's record home run pace elicits such epithets as the Sultan of Swat, Behemoth of Swing, and Colossus of Clout.
- Film producers add sound sequences to silent films and call them "part-talkies."
- The Ford Model A appears in four colors (including Arabian Sand) with a self-starter and other gadgetry, a rumble seat, and shatterproof windshield. Ford has sold 15 million Model Ts since 1908.
- The Hays list of do's and don'ts for Hollywood films prohibits "any licentious or suggestive nudity," "miscegenation," "ridicule of clergy," and "inference of sexual perversion"; it also urges care on themes such as "the sale of women."
- A survey reports a "loosening" in manners and morals. Mrs. Bertrand Russell defends "free love," and Judge Lindsay advocates "companionate [trial] marriage."
- Restaurants hire detective-waiters to search customers for hip flasks and bottles before serving ice and ginger ale; Prohibition agents can arrest clients on the basis of "a good smell."
- Because lethal ingredients are added to industrial alcohol, the wets accuse the government of murder.
- Since diguised government agents are allowed to shoot to kill, a number of innocent people die.
- The Al Capone gang nets $100 million in the liquor trade, $30 million in protection money, $25 million in gambling, $10 million in vice, and $10 million in the "rackets" (a new word).

Kaleidoscope _____

- The influence of the *American Mercury* is so powerful that *Harper's, Forum, Atlantic,* and *Scribner's* begin to similarly attack the "Christian" glorification of business, moral conformity, and the "booboisie" (Mencken's word).
- The Scripps-Howard and Hearst news empires expand as public interest increases in scandals and gossip.
- Henry Ford publicly apologizes for his *Dearborn Independent* newspaper remarks against Jews.
- The latest topics in Bernarr Macfadden's confessional magazines include feminism and the various ways of carousing.
- Alexander Kerensky, head of the provisional government during the 1917 Russian Revolution, settles in New York.
- Black leader Marcus Garvey, convicted of mail fraud in 1923, has his sentence commuted and is deported to the West Indies by President Coolidge.
- Isadora Duncan dies of a broken neck when her scarf is tangled in the wheel of a moving car.
- President Coolidge urges that the nation pray more.
- Strong language, like *lousy, damn,* and *hell,* enters the popular arts and replaces words like *grand* and *swell.*
- Broadway presents a record 268 plays. Florenz Ziegfeld opens a theater with his name and presents *Show Boat* and *Rio Rita.*
- The "clean book" bill is defeated in the Senate; forty leading authors form the Committee for the Suppression of Irresponsible Censorship.
- The postwar education boom peaks, along with a variety of outline and how-to books.
- Fifteen million Sears & Roebuck catalogs are distributed to U.S. homes.
- One of the nation's best-dressed men, President Coolidge wears $125–$140 suits, which are double-breasted and cuffless; he dislikes soft collars, prefers black to brown shoes, and wears only one ring; he always carries three cigars, even in his formal wear, and never wears a fob.

First Appearances: All-electric juke box, cyclone rollercoaster (Coney Island), lightweight brick, electric sign flasher, car radio, Federal Radio Commission, commercial armored car hold-up, pilot license granted a woman, phonograph with automatic record changer, drive-up mailbox (Houston), Yeshiva College, Super Suds, Borden's homogenized milk, the slow fox-trot, the "Varsity Drag," Volvo, carbonated grape Welch-Ade, wall-mounted can opener, B&M Brick Oven baked beans, Literary Guild of America, Remington Rand, Hostess cakes, Sherry Netherland Hotel (New York), Delmonico's, A & W root beer, Lender bagel factory, Gerber baby food, *Ile de France,* GE refrigerator with "monitor top," simultaneous television-phone transmission, Movietone News

1928

Library of Congress.

In the News

COOLIDGE OPENS INTER-AMERICAN CONFERENCE IN HAVANA . . .
25TH ANNIVERSARY OF KITTY HAWK IS CELEBRATED, LINDBERGH
RECEIVES AWARD . . . SOCIALIST PARTY NOMINATES NORMAN
THOMAS FOR PRESIDENT, COMMUNISTS NOMINATE WILLIAM Z. FOSTER
. . . TURKEY DECLARES ISLAM NO LONGER STATE RELIGION . . . ST.
FRANCIS DAM, IN CALIFORNIA, COLLAPSES, 450 ARE KILLED . . .
GOP NOMINATES HERBERT HOOVER, DEMOCRATS NOMINATE AL
SMITH . . . CHIANG KAI-SHEK BECOMES CHINESE PRESIDENT . . .
AMELIA EARHART IS FIRST WOMAN TO FLY ATLANTIC . . . U.S.
SIGNS KELLOGG-BRIAND PACT TO OUTLAW WAR, BRITAIN, FRANCE,
GERMANY, AND RUSSIA ALSO SIGN . . . ALBANIA BECOMES KINGDOM
UNDER ZOG I . . . ADMIRAL RICHARD BYRD DEPARTS ON ANTARCTIC
EXPEDITION . . . BRITISH WOMEN GAIN THE VOTE . . . U.S. AND
CHINA AGREE TO COMMERCE TREATY . . . INTERNATIONAL
CONFERENCE ON ECONOMIC STATISTICS MEETS IN GENEVA . . . RUSSIA
ANNOUNCES FIVE-YEAR PLAN TO COLLECTIVIZE AGRICULTURE . . .
PAN-AMERICAN CONFERENCE MEETS TO PROVIDE FOR ARBITRATION IN
INTERNATIONAL DISPUTES . . . MEXICAN PRESIDENT ALVARO
OBREGON IS ASSASSINATED . . . HOOVER DEFEATS SMITH 21 TO 15
MILLION, THOMAS RECEIVES 260,000 VOTES, FOSTER, 21,000 . . .
FDR WINS N.Y. GUBERNATORIAL RACE . . . CLARK MEMO STATES
U.S. WILL NOT PLAY "COP" IN LATIN DISPUTES . . . BOULDER DAM
ACT PASSES, GOVERNMENT WILL PARTICIPATE IN HYDROELECTRIC
POWER.

Deaths

Roald Amundsen, Vicente
Blasco-Ibáñez, Holbrook
Blinn, William Du Pont,
Henry F. Gilbert, George
Goethals, Thomas Hardy,
Leoš Janáček, Robert
Lansing, Ellen Terry.

Quotes

"We in America today are nearer to the final triumph over poverty than ever before in the history of any land. The poor-house is vanishing from among us."

— Herbert Hoover

"Here were the imponderable processes and forces of the cosmos, harmonious and soundless. Harmony, that was it! . . . The universe was a cosmos, not a chaos; man was as rightfully a part of that cosmos as were the day and night."

— Adm. Richard E. Byrd, on flying over the North Pole

"It is very difficult and expensive to undo after you are married the things that your mother and father did to you while you were putting your first six birthdays behind you."

— from a study prepared by the Bureau of Social Hygiene

"Moving pictures need sound as much as Beethoven symphonies need lyrics."

— Charles Chaplin

"After twenty years of being only in its infancy, the moving picture which gave some promise of an interesting adult life has suddenly gone senile—and garrulous. It is talking at the top of its voice, talking to itself, talking in its sleep. Terrified of . . . radio broadcasting, it has incorporated radio itself."

— Gilbert Seldes, "The Movies Commit Suicide," *Vanity Fair*

"Wall Street's brokerages were overflowing with a new type of speculator, . . . the inexperienced—the "suckers," . . . men who had been attracted by newspaper stories of the big, easy profits to be made in a tremendous bull market."

— *Nation*

"I say it's spinach and I say the hell with it."

— *New Yorker* cartoon of child refusing to eat the "new" Italian vegetable, broccoli

Ads

An ad demonstrating both fashion and art deco design.

Radio

Premieres

"Real Folks, Main Street" (first drama series)
"Chase and Sanborn Hour," Maurice Chevalier
"The Voice of Firestone"
"National Farm and Home Hour," Don Ameche
"Music Appreciation Hour," Walter Damrosch
"True Story with Mary and Bob"
"National Radio Pulpit"
"Shell Chateau," Al Jolson
"Uncle Don," Don Carney

Of Note

Maurice Chevalier is paid $5,000 a week by Chase and Sanborn • Al Smith's pronunciation of "raddio" is much parodied • NBC is organized into two semi-independent networks, the Red and Blue • Popular singer Vaughn de Leath, "the Radio Girl," develops the new style of singing called "crooning" to deal with the limitations of radio technology.

Movies

Openings

The Last Command (Josef von Sternberg), Emil Jannings, Evelyn Brent, William Powell
The Racket (Lewis Milestone), Thomas Meighan, Marie Prevost
The Crowd (King Vidor), Emil Jannings, Marlene Dietrich
Sadie Thompson (Raoul Walsh), Gloria Swanson, Lionel Barrymore
Abie's Irish Rose (Victor Fleming), Charles Rogers
Our Dancing Daughters (Harry Beaumont), Joan Crawford
Steamboat Bill, Jr. (Charles F. Reisner), Buster Keaton
Street Angel (Frank Borzage), Janet Gaynor, Charles Farrell
The Singing Fool (Lloyd Bacon), Al Jolson
The Mysterious Lady (Fred Niblo), Greta Garbo
The Passion of Joan of Arc (Carl Dreyer), Marie Falconetti, Antonin Artaud
The Circus (Charles Chaplin), Charles Chaplin, Merna Kennedy
The Docks of New York (Josef von Sternberg), George Bancroft, Betty Compson
Sorrell and Son (Herbert Brenon), H. B. Warner

Academy Awards (1927–28)

First year of presentations.

Best Picture: *Wings*
Best Director: Frank Borzage (*Seventh Heaven*)
Best Comedy Director: Lewis Milestone (*Two Arabian Knights*)
Best Actress: Janet Gaynor (*Street Angel, Seventh Heaven, Sunrise*)

Best Actor: Emil Jannings (*The Way of All Flesh, The Last Command*)
Special Awards: Charles Chaplin (*The Circus*), Warner Brothers (*The Jazz Singer*)

Top Box-Office Stars

Clara Bow, Lon Chaney. *Also popular:* Greta Garbo, Emil Jannings, Harold Lloyd, John Gilbert

Joan Crawford, Clara Bow's rival as the prototype of flaming youth, in *Our Dancing Daughters. Movie Star News.*

Popular Music

Rudy Vallee, "the Vagabond Lover," with his famous megaphone. *D. Ouellette Collection.*

Hit Songs

"She's Funny That Way"
"Lover, Come Back to Me"
"You're the Cream in My Coffee"
"Crazy Rhythm"
"Button Up Your Overcoat"
"Love Me or Leave Me"
"Makin' Whoopee!"
"Sweet Lorraine"
"I'll Get By"
"I Can't Give You Anything but Love"
"Short'nin' Bread"
"Stout-Hearted Men"

Top Records

Sonny Boy (Al Jolson); *Ramona* (Gene Austin); *My Yiddishe Momme* (Sophie Tucker); *Was It a Dream?* (Dorsey Brothers Orchestra); *Laugh Clown, Laugh* (Ted Lewis); *Maybe My Maybe Don't Mean Maybe* (Paul Whiteman); *The Mooche* (Duke Ellington); *Blue Yodel* (Jimmie Rodgers)

Jazz and Big Bands

Soloists gain importance: Coleman Hawkins, Benny Goodman, Gene Krupa, Fats Waller, Teddy Wilson, Johnny Hodges, Roy Eldridge, Bunny Berigan. Johnny Hodges joins Duke Ellington; Count Basie joins Walter Page's Blue Devils. Luis Russell plays at the Savoy Ballroom, Harlem.

First Recordings: Benny Goodman, as leader; Pinetop Smith's *Boogie Woogie,* Chicago

New Bands: Cab Calloway, Chicago; Rudy Vallee, New York

Theater

Broadway Openings

Plays

Strange Interlude (Eugene O'Neill), Lynn Fontanne, Glenn Anders, Tom Powers
Holiday (Philip Barry), Hope Williams
Marco Millions (Eugene O'Neill), Alfred Lunt, Morris Carnovsky, Dudley Digges
The Front Page (Ben Hecht, Charles MacArthur), Lee Tracy, Osgood Perkins, Dorothy Stickney
Machinal (Sophie Treadwell), Clark Gable
The Age of Innocence (Margaret Ayer Barnes), Katharine Cornell, Franchot Tone, Rollo Peters
The Kingdom of God (G. Martinez Sierra), Ethel Barrymore
The Big Fight (Milton Herbert Gropper), Estelle Taylor, Jack Dempsey (Mr. and Mrs. Dempsey)
The Patriot (Alfred Neumann), Lyn Harding, John Gielgud (U.S. debut)
Brothers (Herbert Ashton, Jr.), Bert Lytell (dual role)
Diamond Lil (Mae West), Mae West (closed by police)
Maya (Simon Gantillon), Aline MacMahon (closed by police)

Musicals

The New Moon (Sigmund Romberg, Oscar Hammerstein II), Evelyn Herbert, Robert Halliday
Blackbirds of 1928 (Jimmy McHugh, Dorothy Fields), Bill Robinson, Adelaide Hall, The Plantation Orchestra
Animal Crackers (Harry Ruby, Bert Kalmar), Marx Brothers, Margaret Dumont
Whoopee (Walter Donaldson, Gus Kahn), Eddie Cantor, Ruth Etting
The Three Musketeers (Rudolph Friml, P. G. Wodehouse, Clifford Grey), Dennis King, Vivienne Segal
Rosalie (George Gershwin, Sigmund Romberg, P. G. Wodehouse, Ira Gershwin), Marilyn Miller, Frank Morgan, Jack Donahue
Earl Carroll's Vanities (Morris Hamilton), W. C. Fields, Lillian Roth, Vincent Lopez Orchestra
Present Arms (Richard Rodgers, Lorenz Hart), Charles King, Busby Berkeley, Flora LeBreton

Classics and Revivals On and Off Broadway

Volpone (Ben Jonson), Alfred Lunt, Dudley Digges; *The Cherry Orchard* (Chekhov), Alla Nazimova; *The Merry Wives of Windsor,* Mrs. Fiske, Otis Skinner; *The Merchant of Venice,* George Arliss, Peggy Wood; *She Stoops to Conquer* (Goldsmith), Fay Bainter

Pulitzer Prize

Strange Interlude, Eugene O'Neill

Classical Music

Compositions
Virgil Thomson, *Symphony on a Hymn Tune, Four
  Saints in Three Acts*
Frank S. Converse, *California*
Douglas Moore, *Moby Dick*
Roy Harris, Piano Sonata
John Alden Carpenter, String Quartet

Important Events
Albert Stoessel and the Oratorio Society debut at
Carnegie Hall with the Bach B minor Mass.
The New York and Philharmonic Symphonies merge;
Arturo Toscanini become director of the New York
Philharmonic. Béla Bartók is soloist in the first New
York performance of his Piano Concerto no. 1.
Frequently performed are works by Carlos Chávez
(New York, San Francisco, Chicago); Adolph Weiss
and Charles Ives (New York, San Francisco); Nicolas
Slonimsky (Boston): Igor Stravinsky (*Oedipus Rex,*
Boston, New York); Bloch's *America* is performed
by 20 orchestras.

Theodore Dreiser. *Library of Congress.*

Guest conductors at the Philadelphia Orchestra: Fritz
Reiner, Ossip Gabrilowitch, Willem Mengelberg,
Frederick Stock, Thomas Beecham, Pierre Monteux.
Under Reiner, Bartók performs his Rhapsody for
Piano and Orchestra.

Debuts: Thomas Beecham, Andrés Segovia,
Maurice Ravel, José Iturbi, Ruggiero Ricci. Vladimir
Horowitz, 23, debuts at Carnegie Hall; he and Sir
Thomas Beecham perform the Tchaikovsky B-flat
minor concerto at tempos different from each other.

First Performances
Walter Piston, *Symphonic Piece* (Boston); George
Gershwin, playing, *An American in Paris* (New
York); Randall Thompson, *Jazz Poem* (Rochester,
N.Y.); David Mason, *Chanticleer Overture*
(Cincinnati)

Opera

Metropolitan: Lucrezia Bori, *La rondine* (Puccini,
premiere); Maria Jeritza, *Die aegyptische Helena*
(Richard Strauss, premiere); *Carmen*; Elisabeth
Rethberg, Giovanni Martinelli, *La campana
sommersa* (Respighi, premiere); Beniamino Gigli,
Manon; Grace Moore, *La Bohème*

Jolson Theater, New York: *L'histoire du soldat* (Igor
Stravinsky, premiere)

Chicago, Ravinia: *Marouf* (Henri Rabaud, premiere)

Philadelphia: *Ariadne auf Naxos* (Richard Strauss,
American premiere)

San Francisco: Ezio Pinza, *L'amore dei tre re*

Music Notes
The "Leaderless Orchestra" in New York debuts, in
which each member "can express himself" • The
Beethoven Symphony disbands • Artur Bodanzky
resigns • Percy Grainger marries a Swedish woman in
a public ceremony at the Hollywood Bowl. They
stand at a lighted cross atop the mountain, and then
he conducts "To a Nordic Princess" before 22,000
people.

Art

Painting

Charles Demuth, *I Saw the Figure Five in Gold*

Charles Sheeler, *River Rouge Industrial Plant*

Thomas Hart Benton, *Loading Louisiana Rice Fields*

Kenneth Hayes Miller, *Shopper*

John Steuart Curry, *Baptism in Kansas*

Edward Hopper, *From Williamsburg Bridge*

John Sloan, *Sixth Avenue Elevated at Third Street*

Max Weber, *Tranquility*

John Kane, *Fourth of July Parade*

Georgia O'Keeffe, *New York Night*

Arshile Gorky, *Composition, Horse and Figures*

Edwin Dickinson, *The Fossil Hunters*

Marsden Hartley, *The Window*

Sculpture

Gaston Lachaise, *Dancer, John Marin*

Alexander Calder, *The Horse, Sow, The Hostess, Elephant Chain with Lamp, Soda Fountain*

Architecture

New York Life Insurance Company, New York (Cass Gilbert)

Radburn, N.J., plan (Clarence Stein and Henry Wright)

House of 2089 project (William Lescaze)

Merchandise Mart, Chicago (Graham, Anderson, Probst, and White)

Fisher Building, Detroit (Albert Kahn)

333 North Michigan Building, Chicago (Holabird and Root)

Grant's Tomb, New York, design (Duncan and Pope)

Charles Demuth, *I Saw the Figure Five in Gold*, 1928. Oil. 36 × 29¾″. *The Metropolitan Museum of Art, The Alfred Stieglitz Collection.*

Important Exhibitions

Museums

New York: *Metropolitan:* French Gothic tapestries; Spanish paintings from El Greco to Goya; international ceramic arts

Chicago: George Inness

Philadelphia: Portraits of the seventeenth through the nineteenth centuries

Washington: *Corcoran:* Contemporary American art, including Bernard Karfiol, Henry Lee McFee, Frederick C. Frieseke, Eugene Speicher

San Francisco: Comprehensive sculpture exhibit with 1,500 works

Boston: Decorative arts of Europe and America (on display in its new wing)

San Antonio: Texas wild flowers, ranch life

Pittsburgh: Carnegie International First Prize: Henri Matisse

Art Briefs

Giorgio de Chirico holds his first American one-man show in New York • Alexander Calder has his first one-man show of wire animals and caricatures in New York • Department stores, such as New York's Macy's, Abraham and Strauss, and Lord and Taylor, hold public exhibits of modernist art • After a long trial, a customs court determines that Constantin Brancusi's *Bird in Space* can enter the United States as a duty-free work of art rather than a manufactured object, despite its nonrepresentational nature.

Dance

Le sacre du printemps (Léonide Massine, Stravinsky) is staged in Philadelphia and New York with the Philadelphia Symphony Orchestra and Martha Graham in the lead role.

Books

Fiction

Critics' Choice

The Children, Edith Wharton
Good-bye, Wisconsin, Glenway Wescott
The Island Within, Ludwig Lewisohn
The Bishop's Wife, Robert Nathan
Nothing Is Sacred, Josephine Herbst
Strange Fugitive, Morley Callaghan
⬧ *Lady Chatterley's Lover,* D. H. Lawrence, expurgated ed.
⬧ *Swann's Way, The Past Regained,* Marcel Proust
⬧ *Point Counterpoint,* Aldous Huxley

Best-Sellers

The Bridge of San Luis Rey, Thornton Wilder
Wintersmoon, Hugh Walpole
Swan Song, John Galsworthy
The Greene Murder Case, S. S. Van Dine
Bad Girl, Viña Delmar
Claire Ambler, Booth Tarkington
Old Pybus, Warwick Deeping
All Kneeling, Anne Parrish
Jalna, Mazo de la Roche
The Strange Case of Miss Annie Spragg, Louis Bromfield
Strange Interlude (play), Eugene O'Neill

Nonfiction

Critics' Choice

Coming of Age in Samoa, Margaret Mead
The Happy Warrior, Alfred E. Smith
The New Russia, Theodore Dreiser
The Rediscovery of America, Waldo Frank
Anthropology and Modern Life, Franz Boaz
Life of Lincoln, Albert J. Beveridge
The Art of the Dance, Isadora Duncan (posthumous)
Psychological Care of Infant and Child, John B. Watson
⬧ *The Nature of the Physical World,* A. S. Eddington

Best-Sellers

Disraeli, André Maurois
Mother India, Katherine Mayo
Trader Horn, vol I, Alfred Aloysius Horn, Ethelreda Lewis
Napoleon, Emil Ludwig
We, Charles A. Lindbergh
Count Luckner, the Sea Devil, Lowell Thomas
Goethe, Emil Ludwig
Skyward, Richard E. Byrd

The Intelligent Woman's Guide to Socialism and Capitalism, George Bernard Shaw

Poetry

Edwin Arlington Robinson, *Sonnets 1889–1927*
Robert Frost, *West-Running Brook*
Archibald MacLeish, *The Hamlet of A. MacLeish*
Allen Tate, *Mr. Pope and Other Poems*
Ezra Pound, *A Draft of Cantos XVII to XXVII*
Robinson Jeffers, *Cawdor and Other Poems*
Edna St. Vincent Millay, *The Buck in the Snow*
⬧ W. B. Yeats, *The Tower*

Pulitzer Prizes

Scarlet Sister Mary, Julia Peterkin (novel)
The Organization and Administration of the Union Army, 1861–1865, Fred A. Shannon (U.S. history)
The Training of an American, The Earlier Life and Letters of Walter H. Page, Burton J. Hendrick (biography)
John Brown's Body, Stephen Vincent Benét (poetry)

Science-Technology

Milton Humason begins to measure the speed of stars, at the 100-inch Mt. Palomar telescope.

Margaret Mead's anthropological study of Samoans indicates that more tolerant attitudes about sex among the islanders have beneficial social effects.

E. Herzfeld discovers Pagarsardae, the Persian capital prior to Persepolis.

George Papanicolau develops a test for early detection of uterine cancer, the "Pap" test.

Oscar Riddle discovers the pituitary (postpartum) milk-releasing hormone.

GE and RCA hold the first public demonstration of home television sets in Schenectady, N.Y.;

W2XCW, Schenectady, becomes the first regularly broadcasting station.

Vladimir Zworykin perfects the kinescope, a television receiver.

The first animated electric sign, on the *New York Times* building, begins operation.

⬧ Alexander Fleming observes a mold, penicillin, that destroys bacteria.

⬧ Albert Szent-Györgi isolates vitamin C.

⬧ The Ascheim-Zondek urine pregnancy test is developed.

Meetings between heroes of different sports captivate the public. Johnny Weismuller, right, gives swimming advice to Jack Dempsey. *Library of Congress.*

Baseball

Ty Cobb retires with lifetime records of 4,191 hits, .367 BA, and 892 stolen bases. Babe Ruth bats a record .625 in the World Series.

Champions

Batting	Pitching
Rogers Hornsby (St. Louis, NL), .387	L. Benton (New York, NL), 25–9
Goose Goslin (Washington, AL), .379	Lefty Grove (Philadelphia, AL), 20–6
	Alvin Crowder (St. Louis, AL), 21–5
	Home runs
	Babe Ruth (New York, AL), 54

Football

Pro Stars: Jim Conzelman (Providence), Ben Friedman (Detroit)

College All-Americans: Ken Strong (F), New York University; Chris Cagle (H), Army

Rose Bowl (Jan. 1, 1929): Georgia Tech 8– California 7

Basketball

The Brooklyn Celtics win the ABL for the second year.

Sports

Olympics

The Olympics are held in Amsterdam. U.S. winners include Ray Barbuti (400m, 47.8s), Edward Hamm (broad jump, 25′4 ¾″), Sabin Carr (pole vault, 13′9 ¾″), John Kuck (shot put, 52′ ¹¹/₁₆″), Clarence Howser (discus, 155′ 2 ⅘″), Elizabeth Robinson (100m, 12.2s), Johnny Weismuller (swimming, 400m), Albina Osipowich (swimming, 100m), Martha Norelius (swimming, 400m).

Other Sports

Boxing: Gene Tunney beats Tom Heeney in a title defense, gains a $525,000 purse, retires, and marries an heiress.

Swimming: Johnny Weismuller retires, having set 67 world records and won three Olympic gold medals.

Hockey: Les Patrick, 44-year-old New York Rangers coach, plays goalie in one Stanley Cup game.

Winners

World Series	*Player of the Year*
New York (AL) 4	Vic Holt, Oklahoma
St. Louis (NL) 0	*Stanley Cup*
MVP	New York Rangers
NL–Jim Bottomly, St. Louis	*U.S. Tennis Open*
AL–Gordon Cochrane, Philadelphia	Men: Henri Cochet
	Women: Helen Wills
NFL	*USGA Open*
Providence Steamrollers	Johnny Farrell
College Football	*Kentucky Derby*
Georgia Tech	Reigh Count (E. Lang, jockey)
College Basketball	
Pittsburgh	

Fashion

For Men: The Chaplin mustache is replaced by the John Gilbert pencil-line style with waxed tips. Valentino sideburns are now rarely seen as men part their hair in the middle and apply pomades. The more mature man, in his square-cut jacket, wears bold, checked patterns, and his silhouette complements that of his escort, whose loose, shapeless chemise emphasizes the broad-shouldered, slim-hipped line. The gentleman's formal dress consists of an Oxford gray morning coat with squared collar of natural width, notched lapels, and one button. For slightly less formal occasions he wears a morning coat with ribbed silk and silk-covered buttons, and pleatless trousers with a slight break over the instep. The well-dressed man has at least six pairs of shoes (*Esquire*), including two-tone saddles for the active sports look; blue, dark gray, or lightweight brown shoes for country wear; plain brown shoes for informal business and travel; dark reddish brown, patterned shoes for conservative suits; and spectators for flannels and washable fabrics.

High-fashion note: Worth tweeds

Kaleidoscope _____

- The continuing veneration of business is apparent in the noticeable growth of college business courses and service clubs, such as Rotary and Kiwanis.
- Speakeasies host a new mix of people: women in the carriage trade, alongside women in the skin trade.
- By the end of the year, 78 percent of the world's motor vehicles—21,630,000 cars and 3,120,000 trucks—are on U.S. roads.
- Real wages (adjusted for inflation) are up 33 percent from 1914.
- The Methodist Board of Temperance, Prohibition, and Public Morals reports that high school and college students are drinking at parties and dances and in hotels and parked cars.
- Various devices that provide entrance to speakeasies include ringing bells, sliding door panels, cabalistic signatures, and passwords like "Joe sent me."
- Al Smith's wet attitudes and Catholicism are major election issues.
- Hoover, "the great engineer," promises a chicken in every pot and two cars in every garage.
- Five states of the solid South vote Republican.
- Of the 231 members of the Academy Awards selection body, only Mary Pickford, Douglas Fairbanks, Louis B. Mayer, Sid Grauman, and Joe Schenck vote. "Oscar" is designed by Cedric Gibbons.
- Broadway stars who leave for Hollywood include Claudette Colbert, Clark Gable, Barbara Stanwyck, Cary Grant, Paul Muni, Chester Morris, Lee Tracy, and Miriam Hopkins.
- Walt Disney produces *Galloping Gaucho* and *Steamboat Willie*, the first cartoons with sound.
- Personal loans are initiated by National City Bank of New York.
- Brokers' loans to stock market margin investors reach a record $4 billion.
- Three car mergers take place: Chrysler and Dodge, Studebaker and Pierce-Arrow, Chandler and Cleveland.

Walt Disney's popular rodent debuts in *Steamboat Willie,* with Disney himself recording Mickey's voice. *Movie Star News.*

- Five women employed in a New Jersey factory are poisoned by radium and are awarded $10,000, medical costs, and their pension.
- Dutch Schultz gives up bartending to join the mob in beer running; he begins his association with the Maddens, Costellos, and "Legs" Diamond.
- The Feds and Coast Guard arrest 75,000 people a year for Prohibition violations.
- The Treasury Department fires 706 Prohibition agents and prosecutes 257 for taking bribes.
- Speakeasies, like Texas Guinan's and Helen Morgan's, feature torch singers who sit on top of pianos; Helen Morgan popularizes "Can't Help Lovin' Dat Man" and "Why Was I Born?"
- Al Jolson's "Sonny Boy" sells 12 million copies in four weeks.
- Eleven-year-old Yehudi Menuhin goes East from California and astonishes audiences with his performances of the Beethoven and Tchaikovsky violin concertos.
- *Abie's Irish Rose,* the most popular play in Broadway history, closes after 2,400 performances.
- Crooner Rudy Vallee opens at New York's Heigh-Ho Club with a megaphone to amplify his voice.
- North Carolina governor May O. Gardner blames dieting women for the drop in farm prices.
- A thousand crew members gather on the USS *Utah* and sing "Let Me Call You Sweetheart," as President-Elect and Mrs. Hoover return from a Christmas cruise.
- An Ohio University study catalogs undergraduate words that refer to an unpopular girl; expressions include *pill, pickle, priss, drag, rag, oilcan, flat tire,* and *nutcracker.* A popular girl is a *peach, whiz, sweet patootie, pippin, choice bit of calico,* and *snappy piece of work.*

Fads: Ninety-one couples last three weeks in the $5,000 "Dance Derby of the Century"; after 482 hours, it is closed down. Other fads include talkathons and travel. Steeplejack and flagpole sitter Howard Williams ties for first place in a talk marathon, a "Noun and Verb Rodeo" that lasts 81 hours and 45 minutes.

First Appearances: Peter Pan peanut butter, peanut butter cracker sandwiches, Rice Krispies, Nehi, adhesive tape, *Modern Mechanics,* Barricini candy, shredded wheat, Philco radios, quartz clock, Frog-Jumping Jubilee, Mickey Mouse, diesel electric freight locomotives, night coaches (Yelloway), someone going over Niagara Falls in a rubber ball, fully automated film developing machinery, *Oxford English Dictionary,* Bryce Canyon National Park, Newark airport, Plymouth, DeSoto, Marcel Breuer chair

1929

Facts and Figures

Economic Profile
  Dow-Jones: ↑↓ High
    381–Low 198
  GNP: +6%
  Inflation: 0.0%
  Unemployment: 3.2%
Police expenditures, federal,
  state, and local: $320
  million
Prisoners, federal and state:
  120,000
Executions: 155
Paroles, federal and state:
  24,008
Furniture (W&J Sloane):
  Upholstered armchair:
    $24.50–$50
  Martha Washington serving
    table: $19.50
  Windsor chair: $7.75–$40
  Persian rug: $44–$55
Furniture (Wanamaker):
  Dining room suite: $110–
    $330
  Lounging chair: $200–$333
Isphahan rug (Stern's): $289
Flower bulbs, hyacinths: 68¢
  (doz.)

Deaths

David Buick, Georges
  Clemenceau, Sergei
  Diaghilev, Jeanne Eagels,
  Joseph Goldberger, Robert
  Henri, Hugo von
  Hofmannsthal, Lillie
  Langtry, Thorstein Veblen.

In the News

FEDERAL RESERVE HALTS LOANS FOR MARGIN SPECULATION . . .
CRUISER ACT AUTHORIZES NEW WARSHIPS . . . SEVEN "BUGS"
MORAN ASSOCIATES ARE MACHINE-GUNNED TO DEATH ON ST.
VALENTINE'S DAY . . . CONGRESS PASSES SEVERE PENALTIES FOR
VOLSTEAD VIOLATIONS . . . ALBERT FALL, FORMER SECRETARY OF
INTERIOR, IS CONVICTED FOR TEAPOT DOME FRAUD . . . LEON
TROTSKY IS EXPELLED FROM U.S.S.R. . . . AGRICULTURAL
MARKETING ACT ALLOCATES $500 MILLION FOR PRICE SUPPORTS . . .
KELLOGG-BRIAND PACT IS RATIFIED BY SENATE, OUTLAWRY OF WAR
IS PROCLAIMED . . . MISSISSIPPI LYNCH MOB OF 2,000 BURNS
ACCUSED NEGRO . . . CHARLES LINDBERGH MARRIES DIPLOMAT'S
DAUGHTER, ANNE MORROW . . . THREE DIE IN STRIKE AT GASTONIA
MILLS, SOUTH CAROLINA . . . STOCK MARKET REACHES ALL-TIME
HIGH, 381 . . . CHARLES MITCHELL, OF FIRST NATIONAL CITY BANK,
DECLARES ECONOMY SOUND . . . STOCK MARKET PLUMMETS, 19
MILLION SHARES ARE SOLD . . . MARKET CRASHES, SELLING PANIC
CONTINUES, BILLIONS ARE LOST OVERNIGHT . . . HOOVER AFFIRMS
CONFIDENCE IN AMERICAN BUSINESS . . . ADMIRAL BYRD FLIES OVER
SOUTH POLE.

Wall Street
hysteria began on
Black Thursday,
October 24th
(*left*), and peaked
on Black
Tuesday, October
29th. *Library of
Congress.*

Quotes

Before the Crash

"[This] has been a twelvemonth of unprecedented advance, of wonderful prosperity. . . . If there is any way of judging the future by the past, this new year may well be one of felicitation and hopefulness."

— Herbert Hoover

"If a man saves $15 a week and invests in good common stocks, . . . at the end of 20 years, he will have at least $80,000 and . . . $400 a month. He will be rich. And because income can do that, I am firm in my belief that anyone not only can be rich, but ought to be rich."

— John T. Raskob, former top executive, General Motors, and chairman, Democratic National Committee

After the Crash

"Any lack of confidence in the economic future of the basic strength of business in the United States is foolish."

— Herbert Hoover

"[There is just] a little distress selling on the Stock Exchange."

— Financier Thomas Lamont, after leaving the offices of J. P. Morgan

John D. Rockefeller says, during the Crash: "[I see] nothing to warrant the destruction of values. . . . My son and I have . . . been purchasing sound common stocks." *Library of Congress.*

*

"Nobody shot me."
  — Dying Moran gang member, St. Valentine's Day

"[Women] must pay for everything. . . . They do get more glory than men for comparable feats. But, also, women get more notoriety when they crash."

— Amelia Earhart

"The report has gotten out that Miss [Marion] Davies has a pronounced lisp, which may have caused the scrapping of the talkie version."

— *Photoplay,* discussing *The Five O'Clock Girl*

"The hope [college students] . . . cherish is not that of ingesting in culture, but that of increasing in efficiency."

— Editorial, *American Mercury*

"The legitimate theatre is in a panic . . . [with] talking pictures . . . [and] all their seats at the same price. . . . Get it? The rich man stands in line with the poor."

— Lloyd Lewis, *New Republic*

Ads

Radio

Premieres
"The Back Home Hour" (Billy Sunday)
"Fleischmann Hour," Rudy Vallee (first radio variety)
"La Palma Smokers' Program" (with leading entertainers)
"H. V. Kaltenborn News"
"The Rise of the Goldbergs," Gertrude Berg
"Headline Hunters," Floyd Gibbons, Lowell Thomas
"The Hour of Charm," Phil Spitalny and His All-Girl Orchestra, Arlene Frances (emcee)
"Blackstone Plantation," Frank Crumit, Julia Sanderson
"First Nighter," Charles P. Hughes (host), Don Ameche, June Meredith (drama)
"Amos 'n' Andy," Freeman Gosden, Charles Correll (network)

Specials
"Symphonic Music from Queen's Hall" (first shortwave broadcast from London); "Over and Under New York" (airplane broadcast, parachutist describing his descent); "Leopold Stokowski conducts *Sacre du printemps*" (Philadelphia Orchestra).

Of Note
CBS is founded by William S. Paley, age 27 • Rudy Vallee, the "Vagabond Lover," opens each show with "Heigh-Ho, everybody" and closes with "Your Time Is My Time" • Arthur Godfrey debuts on a Baltimore amateur hour.

New Catchphrases: "I'se regusted!" "Holy mackerel, Andy!" "Now ain't that sumpin'!" (Amos 'n' Andy, of the Mystic Knights of the Sea Lodge)

Movies

Openings
The Broadway Melody (Harry Beaumont), Anita Page, Bessie Love, Charles King
In Old Arizona (Raoul Walsh), Warner Baxter, Edmund Lowe
Pandora's Box (G. W. Pabst), Louise Brooks
Blackmail (Alfred Hitchcock), Anny Ondra, Sara Allgood
Coquette (Sam Taylor), Mary Pickford
The Last of Mrs. Cheyney (Sidney Franklin), Norma Shearer, Basil Rathbone, Hedda Hopper
Madame X (Lionel Barrymore), Ruth Chatterton, Lewis Stone, Sidney Toler
Rio Rita (Luther Reed), John Boles, Bebe Daniels
Sunny Side Up (David Butler), Janet Gaynor, Charles Farrell, Joe Brown
The Four Feathers (Merian C. Cooper, Ernest Schoedsack), Richard Arlen, Fay Wray, William Powell
The Love Parade (Ernst Lubitsch), Maurice Chevalier, Jeanette MacDonald, Lillian Roth
Hallelujah! (King Vidor), Daniel L. Haynes
The Taming of the Shrew (Sam Taylor), Douglas Fairbanks, Mary Pickford
Bulldog Drummond (F. Richard Jones), Ronald Colman, Joan Bennett
The Virginian (Victor Fleming), Gary Cooper, Walter Huston
The Letter (Jean De Limur), Jeanne Eagels, Reginald Owen, Herbert Marshall

Academy Awards (1928–29)
Best Picture: *The Broadway Melody*
Best Director: Frank Lloyd (*The Divine Lady*)
Best Actor: Warner Baxter (*In Old Arizona*)
Best Actress: Mary Pickford (*Coquette*)

Top Box-Office Stars
Clara Bow, Lon Chaney

The Marx Brothers—Zeppo, Groucho, Chico, and Harpo—film their first movie, *The Cocoanuts* (*above*), while starring on Broadway in *Animal Crackers*. *Movie Star News.*

Popular Music

Hit Songs
"Tiptoe through the Tulips"
"Singin' in the Rain"
"Honeysuckle Rose"
"Am I Blue?"
"More than You Know"
"Happy Days Are Here Again"
"I'm Just a Vagabond Lover"
"With a Song in My Heart"
"Ain't Misbehavin' "
"You Do Something to Me"
"Without a Song"
"Stardust"
"That Old Gang of Mine"

Top Records
Piccolo Pete (Ted Weems); *I Get the Blues When It Rains* (Guy Lombardo); *Why Was I Born?* and *Don't Ever Leave Me* (Helen Morgan); *My Kinda Love* and *Till We Meet Again* (Bing Crosby); *I'll Always Be in Love with You* (Morton Downey)

Jazz and Big Bands
The "golden era" of recording includes Armstrong's Hot Five and Hot Seven; Jelly Roll Morton and his Red Hot Peppers; Nichols and the Pennies; Bix and Trumbauer; Venuti and Lang.

New Bands: Shep Fields, New York; Glen Gray and the Casa Loma Orchestra

Popular Bands: Austin High Gang, Chicago; Duke Ellington, New York; Andy Kirk, Kansas City: Earl Hines, Chicago; Jimmy Lunceford, Memphis

Theater

Broadway Openings

Plays
Street Scene (Elmer Rice), Erin O'Brien-Moore, Mary Servoss, Beulah Bondi
Murder on the Second Floor (Frank Vasper), Laurence Olivier (first American role)
Journey's End (R. C. Sherriff), Leon Quartermaine, Colin Keith-Johnstone, Derek Williams
The First Mrs. Fraser (St. John Ervine), Grace George, A. E. Matthews
Young Sinners (Elmer Harris), Raymon Guion (Gene Raymond)
Death Takes a Holiday (Alberto Casella), Philip Merivale, Rose Hobart
Meteor (S. N. Behrman), Alfred Lunt, Lynn Fontanne
Candle Light (Siegfried Geyer), Leslie Howard, Gertrude Lawrence, Reginald Owen
Broken Dishes (Martin Flavin), Bette Davis
Serena Blandish (S. N. Behrman), Ruth Gordon
Dynamo (Eugene O'Neill), Claudette Colbert
Gypsy (Maxwell Anderson), Louis Calhern
Berkeley Square (John Balderston), Leslie Howard
June Moon (Ring Lardner, George S. Kaufman), Frank Otto, Jean Dixon

Musicals
Earl Carroll's Sketch Book (E. Y. Harburg, Jay Gorney), Will Mahoney, Patsy Kelly, William Demarest
Sons-O-Guns (J. Fred Coots, Arthur Swanstrom, Benny Davis), Jack Donahue, Lily Damita, William Frawley
Fifty Million Frenchmen (Cole Porter), William Gaxton, Genevieve Tobin, Betty Compton
Sweet Adeline (Jerome Kern, Oscar Hammerstein II), Helen Morgan, Irene Franklin, Charles Butterworth
Hot Chocolates (Thomas Waller, Harry Brooks), Jazz Lips Richardson, Jimmy Baskette, Louis Armstrong
The Street Singer (John Gilbert, Graham Johns), Queenie Smith, Guy Robertson
The Show Girl (George Gershwin, Ira Gershwin), Ruby Keeler, Jimmy Durante, Duke Ellington Orchestra

Classics and Revivals On and Off Broadway
Mrs. Bumpstead-Leigh (Henry James Smith), Mrs. Fiske; *The Lady from the Sea* (Ibsen), Blanche Yurka; *The Seagull* (Chekhov), Jacob Ben-Ami

Pulitzer Prize
Street Scene, Elmer Rice

Speakeasy queen Texas Guinan (*center*), who starred in Hollywood westerns before coming to New York. *Movie Star News.*

President Herbert Hoover. *Library of Congress.*

Classical Music

Compositions
Aaron Copland, *Dance Symphony, Vitebsk, Symphonic Ode*
Frank S. Converse, *American Sketches*
Samuel Barber, Serenade for String Quartet
Walter Piston, Viola Concerto
Roy Harris, Piano Sonata, *American Portraits*
George Antheil, *Transatlantic*

Important Events
Alexander Glazunov, on his first U.S. visit, conducts his symphony no. 6 in Detroit. Twenty-four perform at Carnegie Hall in the "Musicians' Gambol" for the MacDowell Colony.

Major Recitals: Andrés Segovia, José Iturbi, Walter Gieseking, Paul Robeson, Arthur Honneger, Alexander Glazunov, Vladimir Horowitz

Debuts: Nathan Milstein, Gregor Piatigorsky

First Performances
Leo Sowerby, Symphony no. 2 (Chicago, Alexander Glazunov conducting); Symphony no. 6 (Detroit); Anton Webern, *Symphonie* (New York); Frederick Stock, Cello Concerto (Chicago); Arnold Bax, Symphony No. 2 (Boston); Louis Gruenberg, *Jazz Suite* (Cincinnati)

Opera

Metropolitan: Gladys Swarthout (debut), *La Gioconda, Carmen;* return of Ernestine Schumann-Heink, 68, *Das Rheingold;* Ezio Pinza and Elisabeth Rethberg, *Don Giovanni;* Lauritz Melchior, *Tristan und Isolde*

Chicago: In new Opera House, Edith Mason, *Iris* (Mascagni); Rosa Raisa, *Otello*

Music Notes
Stravinsky's *Les noces* draws a $25,000 audience at the Met • Eugene Goossens leads the Rochester Civic Orchestra.

Art

Painting

Edward Hopper, *The Lighthouse at Two Lights*

Georgia O'Keeffe, *Blue Cross, Late George Window*

John Kane, *Self-Portrait*

Charles Sheeler, *Upper Deck*

Arshile Gorky, *The Artist and His Mother*

Charles Demuth, *Poppies, Corn and Peaches*

Grant Wood, *Woman with Plants, John B. Turner, Pioneer*

Lyonel Feininger, *Sailing Boats*

Thomas Hart Benton, *Georgia Cotton Pickers*

Guy Pène du Bois, *Woman with Cigarette*

Arthur G. Dove, *Distraction, Foghorns*

Sculpture

Alexander Calder, *Circus* (1927–29), *The Cow, The Brass Family, Josephine Baker*

Saul Baizerman, *Hod Carrier*

Isamu Noguchi, *Head of Martha Graham*

Paul Manship is commissioned to do an equestrian statue of General Grant.

Architecture

Lovell (Heath) House, Los Angeles (Richard Neutra)

Williamsburgh Savings Bank, New York (Halsey, McCormack, and Helmer)

Folger Shakespeare Library, Washington, D.C. (Paul Phillippe Cret)

Palmolive Building, Chicago (Holabird and Root)

Important Exhibitions

Museums

New York: *Metropolitan:* Chinese paintings of the Sung and Ming periods; the print collection; art deco; the architect and the industrial arts. *Museum of Modern Art:* A loan exhibit of the works of Cézanne, Seurat, Gauguin, van Gogh, and 19 living Americans (opening show)

Washington, Chicago, UCLA: Stuart Davis

Philadelphia, Minneapolis: American modernist art

San Francisco: American sculpture show (1,300 works)

Art Briefs

Modigliani has his first one-man show in New York • Gertrude Vanderbilt announces the founding of her museum, the Whitney Museum of American Art, which will be temporarily housed at 8 and 10 West 8th Street, New York • The American Artists' Professional League tries unsuccessfully to legislate a protective tariff on contemporary foreign art.

Dance

Atlanta Ballet starts as the Dorothy Alexander Concert Group. Martha Graham dances in *Heretic*.

Edward Hopper, *The Lighthouse at Two Lights*, 1929. Oil on canvas. 29½ × 43¼". *The Metropolitan Museum of Art Purchase, Hugo Rastor Fund, 1962.*

Horn and Hardart cafeteria in art deco style, Philadelphia. *Smithsonian Institution.*

Books

Fiction

Critics' Choice

The Sound and the Fury, William Faulkner
Sartoris, William Faulkner
A Farewell to Arms, Ernest Hemingway
Look Homeward, Angel, Thomas Wolfe
Hudson River Bracketed, Edith Wharton
The Way of Ecben, James Branch Cabell
Round Up, Ring Lardner
Cup of Gold, John Steinbeck
I Thought of Daisy, Edmund Wilson
Bottom Dogs, Edward Dahlberg
🙠 *Lady Chatterley's Lover,* D. H. Lawrence, unabridged ed.

Best-Sellers

All Quiet on the Western Front, Erich Maria Remarque
Dodsworth, Sinclair Lewis
Dark Hester, Anne Douglas Sedgwick
The Bishop Murder Case, S. S. Van Dine
Roper's Row, Warwick Deeping
Peder Victorious, O. E. Rölvaag
Mamba's Daughters, DuBose Heyward
The Galaxy, Susan Ertz

Scarlet Sister Mary, Julia Peterkin
Joseph and His Brethren, H. W. Freeman

Nonfiction

Critics' Choice

The Modern Temper, Joseph Wood Krutch
Midstream: My Later Life, Helen Keller
The International Jurisdiction, Henry Morgenthau
Middletown, Robert Lynd, Helen Lynd
Is Sex Necessary? E. B. White, James Thurber
A Quest for Certainty, John Dewey
Men and Machines, Stuart Chase
Are We Civilized? R. H. Lowie
🙠 *What Is Philosophy?* Martin Heidegger
🙠 *Marriage and Morals,* Bertrand Russell

Best-Sellers

The Art of Thinking, Ernest Dimnet
Henry the Eighth, Francis Hackett
The Cradle of the Deep, Joan Lowell
Elizabeth and Essex, Lytton Strachey
The Specialist, Chic Sale

A Preface to Morals, Walter Lippmann
Believe It or Not, Robert L. Ripley
John Brown's Body (poetry), Stephen Vincent Benét
The Mansions of Philosophy, Will Durant
The Tragic Era, Claude G. Bowers

Poetry

Vachel Lindsay, *Every Soul Is a Circus*
Robinson Jeffers, *Dear Judas*
Edgar Lee Masters, *The Fate of the Jury*
Louise Bogan, *Dark Summer*
Countée Cullen, *The Black Christ*
Eleanor Wylie, *Angels and Earthly Creatures*
Edwin Arlington Robinson, *Cavender's House, The Prodigal Son*
Emily Dickinson, *Further Poems* (posthumous)

Pulitzer Prizes

Laughing Boy, Oliver La Farge (novel)
The War of Independence, Claude H. Van Tyne (U.S. history)
The Raven, Marquis James (biography)
Selected Poems, Conrad Aiken (poetry)

Science and Technology

Robert and Helen Lynd apply anthropological methods to the study of a small American city, Muncie, Indiana, in *Middletown.*
Edward Doisy isolates the female sex hormone estrogen in pure form.
George W. Corner, Rochester, isolates the female hormone progesterone.
Hypertension and heart disease are shown to be related by Samuel Levine, Harvard.
Manfred Sakel reports that overdoses of insulin in order to produce coma are successful in the treatment of schizophrenia.

Lt. James Doolittle pilots a plane solely on instruments.
Dunlop Rubber Company produces foam rubber—latex whipped with liquid soap.
🙠 Alexander Fleming treats a skin infection successfully with penicillin, its first clinical trial; the absence of a pure, concentrated form makes use of the substance limited.
🙠 Albert Einstein proposes the unified field theory.

Sports

Baseball

Babe Ruth (New York, AL) hits his 500th home run. Lefty O'Doul (Philadelphia, NL) gets a record 254 hits.

Champions

Batting	Pitching
Lefty O'Doul (Philadelphia, NL), .398	Charles Root (Chicago, NL), 19–6
Lew Fonseca (Cleveland, AL), .369	Lefty Grove (Philadelphia, AL), 20–6
	Home runs
	Babe Ruth (New York, AL), 46

Football

Ernie Nevers (FB) scores all 40 points in the Chicago Cardinal 40–0 defeat of the Chicago Bears.
The Rose Bowl at Pasadena draws 101,000. Roy Riegels, California center, runs 60 yards the wrong way with a fumble.

Pro Stars: Blood McNally, Verne Lewellen (Green Bay)

College All-Americans: Frank Carideo (Q), Notre Dame; Bronko Nagurski (T), Minnesota

Rose Bowl (Jan. 1, 1930):   Southern California 47– Pittsburgh 7

Basketball

The Cleveland Rosenblums win the ABL with the Original Celtics' Joe Lapchik, Pete Barry, and Dutch Dehnert on the team.

Tennis star Bill Tilden wins his seventh U.S. Open. *Movie Star News.*

Other Sports

Tennis: Helen Wills wins the U.S. Open and Wimbledon, each for the third consecutive time.

Winners

World Series	*Player of the Year*
Philadelphia (AL) 4	J. A. Thompson, Montana
Chicago (NL) 1	State
MVP	*Stanley Cup*
NL–Rogers Hornsby, St. Louis	Boston
AL–Al Simmons, Philadelphia	*U.S. Tennis Open*
	Men: William Tilden II
NFL	Women: Helen Wills
Green Bay Packers	*USGA Open*
College Football	Robert T. Jones, Jr.
Notre Dame	*Kentucky Derby*
College Basketball	Clyde Van Dusen (L.
Montana State	McAtee, jockey)

Fashion

For Women: The flapper look passes as hems begin to fall and more body curves appear. Jean Patou drops the evening hem to the floor; backless, sleeveless frocks with panels or drapes lengthen to the ankle; all have a V neck. Undergarments change: flowery slips with bra tops appear, some with a shaped band at the waist and attached knickers. The bosom also makes its reappearance in the corset with "breast pockets." In addition to the unisex "sun tan bathing suits" (black, one piece, with buttons up the back), women buy the new backless style, cut in front with an X halter, or the racy white or orange jersey-top suit with black taffeta trunks. Beauty shops open for facials and pomades; face lifting is popularized. Women use, yearly, one pound of powder, eight rouge compacts, and countless face creams and lipsticks, like Mme. Rubinstein's crushed rose leaves (geranium) "for the convervative woman" and "Georgine Lachtee" if "muscles droop."

High-fashion note: Boulanger chiffon evening dress.

For Men: The ice-cream suit in husky diagonal tweeds for Ivy Leaguers.

Kaleidoscope _____

- On September 3, the big bull market peaks; on November 13, it reaches bottom; within a few weeks of "Black Tuesday," unemployment rises from 700,000 to 3.1 million.
- An estimated 4.5 million people put money into "investment trusts," brokerage offerings that speculate for them; there are 70,950 stockbrokers in the United States (26,609 in 1920).
- Frank Billings Kellogg receives the Nobel Peace Prize for the Kellogg-Briand Pact outlawing war.
- Commenting on contemporary mores, two prominent authors write: "If love has come to be less often a sin, it has also come to be less often a supreme privilege" (Joseph Wood Krutch, *The Modern Temper*), and "If you start with the belief that love is a pleasure of a moment, is it really surprising that it yields only a momentary pleasure?" (Walter Lippmann, *A Preface to Morals*).
- "Come on, suckers," begins Texas Guinan's famous invitation, "open up and spend some jack."
- At least 32,000 speakeasies thrive in New York City; especially popular are Jack and Charlie's, Texas Guinan's Three Hundred, and Belle Livingston's Country Club, all of which promise no danger from "jake foot," the disguised authorities. The Midwest has corresponding "beer flats," blind pigs," and "shock houses."
- Calvin Coolidge is elected director of the New York Life Insurance Company.
- The "Age of the Car" is manifest throughout the country in the marked increase in red and green lights, one-way streets, stop signs, parking regulations, and traffic.
- Several men, dressed like police, tell the Bugs Moran gang to "put your noses to the wall," then they spray them with bullets (St. Valentine's Day Massacre).
- Al Capone serves a year in Philadelphia on a weapons-carrying charge; it is widely believed that he governs his crime empire from his cell.
- The sister of Charles Lindbergh's fiancée, Constance Morrow, like others prominent in the news, is threatened with kidnapping; Lindbergh flies the family to Maine.
- "Air Way Limited" provides coast-to-coast commercial travel in only 48 hours by a combination of plane and overnight train.
- The Museum of Modern Art is founded by Abby Aldrich Rockefeller, Lizzie P. Bliss, and Mary Sullivan at 730 Fifth Avenue, New York.
- Because of the zeppelin's success, plans for the Empire State Building include a mooring mast as a dirigible way station 1,300 feet above the ground.
- Commander Richard E. Byrd plants a U.S. flag on the South Pole.
- President Hoover becomes a Tenderfoot Boy Scout; he also dresses like a cowboy and an Indian.
- "Amos 'n' Andy" is so popular that at resorts like Atlantic City, loudspeakers broadcast the show.
- Of the 20,500 movie theaters in the United States, the

With typical public charm, Al Capone (*left*) greets the respected Chicago chief of detectives, John Stege. *Library of Congress.*

number with sound facilities increases during the year from 1,300 to 9,000.
- Following the Crash, New York mayor Jimmy Walker urges movie houses to show cheerful pictures.
- Al Jolson tries to help his wife, Ruby Keeler, in her first role in *Show Girl* by appearing nightly in the aisle and singing "Liza" as she tap dances.
- Admission to New York theaters ranges from 35¢ to $2.50.
- Movie musicals are in vogue, such as *Broadway Melody, The Golddiggers of Broadway, Desert Song,* and *The Singing Fool.*
- Archie Leach (Cary Grant) stars in two Broadway musicals, *A Wonder Night* and *Boom Boom.* Guy Lombardo and the Royal Canadians open at the Hotel Roosevelt, New York.
- German Kurt Barthel sets up in New Jersey the first American nudist colony with three married couples.
- Goucher College girls are permitted to smoke.
- Robert Maynard Hutchins, 30, becomes president of the University of Chicago.
- A Baltimore survey discovers rickets in 30 percent of its children.

First Appearances: Paper money of the present size, American League for Physical Culture (nudist organization), automatic electric stock-quotation board, high-speed telegraph ticker, John Reed Club, Blue Cross Health Insurance (Dallas), Convention Hall in Atlantic City, New York Central, Bendix, Chicago Union Carbide, Riverside Church (New York), Temple Emanuel (New York), Temple Rodeph Sholom (New York), Herblock, "Popeye," Oscar Meyer wieners trademark, auto sun roof, Delta, Chevrolet 6 cylinder, Ford station wagon with boxed wood panels, mobile home trailer (Hudson), aluminum furniture, front-wheel drive (Auburn), gas range, electric food disposal, *Business Week,* 7-Up ("Lithiated Lemon"), Nestlé Colorinse in ten shades, auto radio (Motorola), Federated Department Stores, Conoco

THE *Thirties*

"Hoovervilles" in New York's Central Park, shantytowns built in the shadow of luxury. *Museum of the City of New York.*

Statistics ———————————————————————

Vital

Population: 123,188,000
  Urban/Rural: 69/54
  Farm: 24.9%
Life expectancy
  Male: 58.1
  Female: 61.6
Births/1,000: 21.3
Marriages/1,000: 9.2
Divorces/1,000: 1.6
Deaths/1,000: 11.3
  per 100,000
    Heart: 414
    Cancer: 97
    Tuberculosis: 71
    Car accidents: 26.7

Economic

Unemployed: 4,340,000
GNP: $90.4 billion
Federal budget: $5.46 billion
National debt: $16.9 billion
Union membership: 3.6
  million
Strikes: 637
Prime rate: 3.6%
Car sales: 2,787,400
Average salary: $1,368

Social

Homicides/100,000: 8.8
Suicides/100,000: 15.6
Lynchings: 21
Labor force, male/female:
  3.7/1
Social welfare: $4.09 billion
Public education: $2.32 billion
College degrees
  Bachelors'
    Male: 73,600
    Female: 48,800
  Doctorates
    Male: 1,946
    Female: 353
Attendance
  Movies (weekly): 90 million
  Baseball (yearly): 10.2
    million

Consumer

Consumer Price Index
  (1967 = 100): 50.0
Eggs: 44¢ (doz.)
Milk: 14¢ (qt.)
Bread: 9¢ (loaf)
Butter: 46¢ (lb.)
Bacon: 42¢ (lb.)
Round steak: 42¢ (lb.)
Oranges: 57¢ (doz.)
Coffee: 39¢ (lb.)

The thirties, with the Great Depression and rise of fascism in Europe and Asia, were a period of profound trial in American life—not just of personal and material survival but of democracy and capitalism, the fundamental systems of the American way. The beginning of the decade was a time of increasing hardship and despair. After a brief rise in the market in 1930, the economic decline returned. Everything was falling: industrial output, employment, wages, prices, and, not least of all, human spirits. Banks began to fail and cities to default. Apple sellers appeared on street corners, breadlines at soup kitchens lengthened, and people slept on park benches. Large numbers of the homeless began to wander to the edges of towns, to other cities—anywhere—only to find more of the same. The farmer, beset by his unsellable produce and mortgage foreclosure, and the city dweller, unable to find work at retrenching factories and fearful that even his savings were not safe, shared the woe.

The government, as usual, depended on private charity and public optimism while it waited for the invisible hand of the free market to lift the economy. In some intellectual circles, the fulfillment of Marxist prophecy was thought to be at hand: the inevitable demise of capitalism had arrived. For most, a sense of numb shock, fear, and perhaps self-failure pervaded. There was remarkably little agitation. The most noted example of protest, the Bonus March of 1932, was comprised of 12,000 veterans who sought early payment of a promised bonus—nothing more. Since the twenties, people had believed in the endless potential of the system and of themselves. They could not just blame the system when all fell down.

Franklin Delano Roosevelt, the Democratic nominee in 1932, seemed to understand what the nation needed—recognition of its despair and a determined active government. An optimistic and gregarious patrician, FDR lifted the nation's spirits as he spoke of the "forgotten man." The country gave him a landslide victory over a somber Herbert Hoover, who warned that grass would grow in the streets of the cities if FDR won. In his inaugural address, Roosevelt pledged "a new deal," and then, using radio in an innovative manner to directly communicate with the people, he began his widely listened-to fireside chats.

The rest of the decade is the story of the New Deal with its three Rs: relief, recovery, and reform. With an overwhelming public mandate, Roosevelt kept Congress in session for a hundred days after his inauguration and enacted an encompassing legislative program affecting major areas of the American economic polity. Measures were passed concerning banking, securities, industry, and agriculture. To meet the immediate crisis, federal relief was provided

in unprecedented amounts, and vast government work projects were authorized. The National Recovery Administration (NRA) was created to coordinate and regulate activities in all industries. Its emblem, the Blue Eagle, appeared in shops and factories everywhere as a symbol of labor and management's willingness to cooperate for the general well-being. A litany of initials for other new agencies multiplied, and the nation recited them with hope, as government took on a unique role in the direct regulation of the economy and provision of its people. Many of the early regulatory reforms were clearly necessary and beneficial. Those such as the Federal Deposit Insurance Corporation (FDIC) and the Securities Exchange Commission remain today, as does government responsibility to intervene in times of economic crisis and to directly aid the needy. Later legislation, such as Social Security, the minimum wage, and labor's right to collective bargaining, have also become part of American life.

Recovery proceeded more slowly. Industrial output and the market rose during the remainder of Roosevelt's first term, although unemployment remained high, and direct and work relief remained a necessity for millions. Opposition to FDR grew. Business leaders initially supportive of the president now took a public beating in congressional hearings, as their dubious twenties' business practices were exposed; by 1935 they had regrouped in such forums as the Liberty League and attacked "that man," FDR, as a dangerous radical. Charismatic demagogues and one-time supporters, like the radio priest Father Coughlin and Louisiana senator Huey Long, also denounced the president. Still others portrayed him as the kind of fascist now taking over in Europe. The Supreme Court began overturning major legislation, most notably the National Industrial Recovery Act.

In 1936, the nation gave Roosevelt the largest electoral majority in history, but early in his second term, his attempt to "pack" the Supreme Court in order to circumvent its opposition alienated many supporters. In 1937–38, the economy fell again; large-scale unemployment ended only with World War II. During the last half of the decade, nonetheless, many of the roads, bridges, public buildings, dams, and trees that cover the nation were set in place by federally employed workers. Other WPA projects included the arts, and these provided a remarkable opportunity for expression and acculturation for artists and public alike. The Federal Music Project, for example, presented thousands of low-cost or free concerts and premieres of such composers as Samuel Barber and Walter Piston. The Federal Theatre Project employed 1,300 and reached 25 million people with over 1,200 productions. The Federal Writers' Program hired such writers as Saul Bellow, Ralph

Ellison, and Nelson Algren. The Federal Art Project produced tens of thousands of paintings, along with hundreds of murals that still decorate post offices, statehouses, and other public buildings throughout the country. One of the most important art forms to emerge from these projects was the great photographic documentary of Walker Evans, Dorothea Lange, and Margaret Bourke-White.

In their hour of trial, the American people were entertained, of necessity, inexpensively. In the popular arts, escape was the order of the day. People sang "Life Is Just a Bowl of Cherries" and "I've Got My Love to Keep Me Warm." Radio matured as a mass medium. Comedians Jack Benny and Fred Allen carried on a decade-long feud over the quality of Benny's violin playing. Fibber McGee and Molly, Burns and Allen, and Bob Hope also gathered faithful audiences. Soap opera—serial melodrama sponsored by detergent makers—captured large followings with heroines such as "Oxydol's own Ma Perkins," "Backstage Wife" Mary Noble, and Helen Trent. The Lone Ranger, Buck Rogers in the 25th Century, and Jack Armstrong (the "All-American Boy") provided male heroes. Commentators like Gabriel Heatter, H. V. Kaltenborn, and Walter Winchell offered hard and soft news in breathless tones. Sales of magazines like *True Story* and *Screenland* skyrocketed. Media gave extensive coverage to the "G-men" tracking of "Public Enemies" such as John Dillinger, Bonnie and Clyde, and Ma Barker and her sons.

Movies also provided escape. Sound had dramatically enhanced the medium's possibilities, and Hollywood drew many talents from Broadway. There were Busby Berkeley extravaganzas, Cary Grant screwball comedies, and James Cagney and Edward G. Robinson gangster epics. Stalwart, confident heroes, like Clark Gable, Errol Flynn, James Stewart, and Gary Cooper, made love and war triumphantly. Blondes like Mae West and Jean Harlow were the popular sex symbols. Jeanette MacDonald and Nelson Eddy, and Fred Astaire and Ginger Rogers, sang and danced their way into everyone's heart, as did child stars like Shirley Temple and Mickey Rooney. Donald Duck and Snow White debuted. The casting of Rhett Butler and Scarlett O'Hara in the film version of Margaret Mitchell's best-selling *Gone with the Wind* was of major public interest.

Big bands played the land, and swing was king. Jazz, for the first time, became the predominant popular musical form, with Duke Ellington, Benny Goodman, and later Glenn Miller, among the popular bandleaders. Sidemen, like Count Basie, were also stars, and their moves from band to band were closely followed. The Italian musician Arturo Toscanini was recruited by NBC to lead a new symphony orchestra, and, like another classical conductor, Leopold Stokowski, he too became a star of radio and film.

Although spectator sports declined, softball became a popular hobby, and many people played golf when private links went public. Night baseball and the NFL championship began. A black athlete, Jesse Owens, won four gold medals at Berlin (with Hitler in attendance), and the "Brown Bomber," Joe Louis, beat another Aryan for the heavyweight title. Candid photography, backgammon, and contract bridge gained many enthusiasts, and fads included bingo and marathon dancing; the Charleston gave way to the jitterbug, big apple, shag, rhumba, samba, and congo.

Elsewhere, others sought to portray and confront the problems of the depression. James Farrell wrote of the hard times in the city. Steinbeck immortalized the farmer's plight through the decade of droughts, floods, and dust storms in his tale of the Okies' migration westward. John Dos Passos continued his moral dissection of America, and Clifford Odets, who sought to politically engage his audience, questioned the viability of capitalism and the validity of the American dream. Lillian Hellman portrayed the venality of the apparently proper, and *Tobacco Road,* the long-running hit of the decade, drew laughter from the encroachment of the modern world on the rural South. In the visual arts, controversial left-wing murals portrayed the plight of the masses, ironically, in such capitalist palaces as Rockefeller Center and Dartmouth College. It is interesting that some of the nation's greatest landmarks and skyscrapers, like the Empire State Building, the Chrysler Building, and Rockefeller Center, were built in the early 1930s; they had been planned in better times.

Needless to say, personal commitments and ideologies accommodated to the troubled times. On the one hand, the viability of capitalism and representative government came into question. There were those who thought that the age of rugged individualism was over and that a new ideology was needed. As militaristic, fascist governments grew more powerful abroad and the Western democracies struggled with economic problems and pacifist sentiments, Russia and its system appeared to some the only viable alternative. Many of the writers, intellectuals, and entertainers who became fellow travelers or Communists and, in some instances, spies were recruited in this atmosphere. On the other hand, populist movements gained a less educated but more substantial following. Leaders like Huey Long and Father Coughlin expressed a more fascistic ideology.

Most Americans, however, while disillusioned with the worship of business and eager to see a

John Barrymore and Greta Garbo in *Grand Hotel. Movie Star News.*

Russell Lee, *Daughter of Sharecropper; New Madrid County, Mo. Library of Congress.*

larger, more caring government role, retained their faith in the American system. During these difficult times, they shared a remarkable solidarity and sense of community with their fellow Americans; their accommodations to the troubled times were less political than practical. They married later, had fewer children, and divorced less. Extended families lived under one roof; college students were in no hurry to graduate. Whenever possible, women worked, and civil service jobs, looked upon as limited opportunities in prosperous times, became highly prized for the security they provided. If moving upward (affluence) was the common goal of the twenties, maintaining one's position (survival) was the main hope of the thirties.

It was thus only with aloof concern that America, preoccupied with its own troubles, heard the news of Japan's invasion of China, Hitler's remilitarization of the Rhine, and Italy's conquest of Ethiopia. While condemning aggressive conquest, the United States maintained an official policy of neutrality. The Spanish Civil War, nevertheless, stirred intense feelings in many who saw it as a test of democracy's will to resist fascism, and some, such

as the Lincoln Brigade, went illegally to fight with the Loyalists.

America's awareness of the fascist menace crystallized with Hitler's territorial threats against the Czechs. The nation listened closely to radio reports from the Munich Conference, which ended with Czechoslovakia's dismemberment and Chamberlain's improbable prediction of "peace for our time." America watched, still torn between its natural, emotional support of Britain and its strong fear of involvement in foreign war. FDR offered moral and, later, material support to the European democracies, but isolationist sentiment remained strong among the people and the Congress. Respected figures, such as Charles Lindbergh and Herbert Hoover, warned against American entanglement. By February 1939, Franco had won the Spanish Civil War, and in May, the world was stunned by the announcement of Germany's nonaggression pact with Russia. As the twenties had ended in a cataclysm foreshadowing prolonged suffering, so did the thirties. In September 1939, Hitler's armies invaded Poland, and Europe went to war.

1930

Facts and Figures

Economic Profile

Dow-Jones: ↓ High 294–
Low 157
GNP: −13%
Inflation: −1.3%
Unemployment: 8.7%

Ford: $495

Studebaker: $1,395

Chrysler: $1,695

Pierce-Arrow: $2,595

Duesenberg: $8,500

Man's wool overcoat
(Stern's): $38–$46

Walkover saddle shoes: $10

Man's wool suit (B. Altman):
$65–$95

Solid jackets and trousers:
$45

Hamilton watches: $48 and
up

Women's clothing (Best &
Co.):
Pleated spring skirts:
$12.50
Matching cotton blouses:
$5

Roger's five-piece tea set:
$100

Sunkist electric orange juice
extractor: $15

Gillette razors: 10 for $1; 14k
gold-plated razor and case:
$1

Deaths

Edward W. Bok, Robert
Bridges, Lon Chaney,
Glenn Curtiss, Arthur
Conan Doyle, D. H.
Lawrence, William
Howard Taft.

In the News

GRAIN, COTTON, COPPER PRICES FALL . . . UNEMPLOYMENT RISES
SHARPLY . . . MAHATMA GANDHI REJECTS DOMINION STATUS AND
DEMANDS INDEPENDENCE . . . HAILE SELASSIE BECOMES EMPEROR OF
ETHIOPIA . . . U.S. JOINS FRANCE, BRITAIN, JAPAN, GERMANY, AND
ITALY AT LONDON DISARMAMENT CONFERENCE . . . SMOOT-HAWLEY
LAW RAISES IMPORT DUTIES, 1,000 ECONOMISTS PETITION AGAINST
NEW TARIFFS . . . UNEMPLOYMENT PASSES FOUR MILLION . . . LAST
ALLIED TROOPS LEAVE RHINELAND AND SAAR . . . BRITISH WHITE
PAPER CALLS FOR HALT TO JEWISH IMMIGRATION TO PALESTINE . . .
$230 MILLION PUBLIC BUILDINGS ACT IS PASSED . . . DOW-JONES
RISES, UP NEARLY 30% SINCE '29 DROP . . . HOOVER APPOINTS
COMMISSION FOR UNEMPLOYMENT RELIEF . . . N.Y. JUDGE CRATER
DISAPPEARS, LAST SEEN HAILING TAXI . . . SUPREME COURT RULES
PURCHASE OF LIQUOR IS NOT VIOLATION OF 18TH AMENDMENT . . .
POLL SHOWS MAJORITY FAVOR REPEAL OF PROHIBITION . . .
DROUGHT DEVASTATES WESTERN U.S. . . . CONGRESS PASSES RELIEF
LAW . . . FIRE IN OHIO STATE PENITENTIARY KILLS 320 INMATES . . .
EMERGENCY PUBLIC WORKS ACT PROVIDES $116 MILLION . . .
MILITARY LEADS REVOLUTION IN ARGENTINA . . . POLICE RAID
MARGARET SANGER CLINIC IN N.Y.C. . . . GETÚLIO VARGAS LEADS
REVOLUTION IN BRAZIL . . . CHICAGO BOOTLEG CRACKDOWN INDICTS
31 CORPORATIONS AND 158 MEN . . . DEMOCRATS WIN FIRST
CONTROL IN CONGRESS SINCE 1916 . . . BANK OF U.S. CLOSES ALL
60 BRANCHES . . . ONE MILLION ON RADIO HEAR KING GEORGE
PROCLAIM SUCCESS OF LONDON DISARMAMENT CONFERENCE . . .
FRANCE BEGINS CONSTRUCTION OF MAGINOT LINE.

Quotes

"I see nothing in the present situation that is either menacing or warrants pessimism. During the winter months there may be some slackness or unemployment, but hardly more than at this season each year."
— Secretary of Treasury Andrew W. Mellon

"While the crash only took place six months ago, I am convinced we have passed the worst."
— Herbert Hoover

"These really are good times but only a few know it."
— Henry Ford

"Probably no nation in modern times has suffered so frequently or so greatly as the United States from recurrent periods of exaggerated optimism and unrealistic interpretation of its economic situation."
— Virgil Jordan, *North American Review*

"This year, when we all needed something to take our minds off our troubles, miniature golf did it. . . . If we cannot find bread, we are satisfied with the circus."
— Elmer Davis, *Harper's*

"The woman who doesn't want to make a home is undermining our nation."
— Mrs. Thomas A. Edison (radio talk show)

Making, rather than buying, becomes popular. *Library of Congress.*

Far left: Al Capone's free soup kitchen in Chicago. *Library of Congress.*

Ads

Exhibition of Old Spanish Painting from the Collection of Count Contini Bonacossi
In Aid of the Fascist Institute of Culture . . .
to be held from April to June, 1930 at
The Royal Gallery of Modern Art, Rome
under the Patronage of
His Excellency BENITO MUSSOLINI
(in Art News, *May 3*)

—It's Playtime in Havana Now.
(El Encanto, *"Cuba's largest and smartest Department Store"*)

GARBO TALKS!
(Anna Christie)

Today the discriminating family finds it absolutely necessary to own two or more motor cars.
(Buick)

To give is to flatter, to excite and to leave all of a flutter! and to flatter, do not forget that in all the world there is nothing so close to the heart of a woman as her opinion of her own good taste. Then when that opinion is an opinion justified there is no gift like a Guerlain perfume!
(Guerlain)

If SIDNEY CARTON were alive to-day he could, on trying "King George IV," truthfully say—"It is a far, far better thing I do, than I have ever done before."
(King George IV Old Scotch Whiskey)

Participating in almost anything for an excessive period of time—and for money—remains in vogue. Left: a dance marathon in Chicago. *Library of Congress.*

"Walter Winchell"
"Town Crier," Alexander Woollcott (mixture of gossip and literature)
"Father Charles E. Coughlin"

Specials

Two-way conversations between Adm. Richard E. Byrd in New Zealand and NBC; first broadcast from ship at sea; arrival of Albert Einstein in New York.

Of Note

Most popular shows include "Amos 'n' Andy," "Headline Hunters," "The Goldbergs," "Cities Service Concert," "The National Farm and Home Hour," "The Fleischmann Hour."

New Catchphrases: "So long . . . until tomorrow" (Lowell Thomas); "There will be a brief pause . . . while we throw at you Mrs. Pennyfeather's Personal Service for Perturbed People . . ." ("The Cuckoo Hour").

Radio

Premieres

"The Adventures of Helen and Mary" ("Let's Pretend"), Bill Adams
"Lum and Abner," Chester Lauck, Norris Goff
"Singin' Sam, the Barbasol Man," Harry Frankel
"Tony Wons' Scrapbook" (poetry reading to women)
"Easy Aces," Goodman Ace
"Lady Esther Serenade," Wayne King Orchestra
"Believe It or Not" (Robert L. Ripley)
"Death Valley Days" (Tim Frawley)
"American School of the Air," Dr. Lyman Bryson

TV

W2XBS, the CBS pioneer experimental station, begins operation. First telecast: "Felix the Cat."

Movies

Openings

All Quiet on the Western Front (Lewis Milestone), Lew Ayres, Louis Wolheim
The Big House (George Hill), Robert Montgomery, Chester Morris
The Divorcee (Robert Z. Leonard), Norma Shearer, Chester Morris, Robert Montgomery
Disraeli (Alfred E. Green), George Arliss, Joan Bennett
Animal Crackers (Victor Heerman), Marx Brothers, Margaret Dumont
Abraham Lincoln (D. W. Griffith), Walter Huston, Una Merkel
The Blue Angel (Josef von Sternberg), Marlene Dietrich, Emil Jannings
Liliom (Frank Borzage), Charles Farrell, Rose Hobart
Monte Carlo (Ernst Lubitsch), Jeanette MacDonald, Jack Buchanan
Hell's Angels (Howard Hughes), Jean Harlow, Ben Lyon
Morocco (Josef von Sternberg), Marlene Dietrich, Adolphe Menjou

The Big Trail (Raoul Walsh), John Wayne, Marguerite Churchill
Little Caesar (Mervyn Leroy), Edward G. Robinson, Douglas Fairbanks, Jr., Glenda Farrell
Min and Bill (George Hill), Marie Dressler, Wallace Beery
Brats (James Parrott), Stan Laurel, Oliver Hardy
Dawn Patrol (Howard Hawks), Richard Barthelmess, Douglass Fairbanks, Jr.
Anna Christie (Clarence Brown), Greta Garbo, Charles Bickford, Marie Dressler

Academy Awards (1929–30)

Best Picture: *All Quiet on the Western Front*
Best Director: Lewis Milestone (*All Quiet on the Western Front*)
Best Actress: Norma Shearer (*The Divorcee*)
Best Actor: George Arliss (*Disraeli*)

Top Box-Office Stars

Joan Crawford, William Haines

Popular Music _____

Hit Songs
"Body and Soul"
"Georgia on My Mind"
"The Battle of Jericho"
"Beyond the Blue Horizon"
"What Is This Thing Called
　Love?"
"Walkin' My Baby Back Home"
"Embraceable You"
"I Got Rhythm"
"Bidin' My Time"
"Little White Lies"
"On the Sunny Side of the Street"
"Love for Sale"
"St. James Infirmary"

Top Records
Tiger Rag (Mills Brothers); *You Brought a New Kind of Love to Me* (Maurice Chevalier); *Ten Cents a Dance* (Ruth Etting); *Let Me Sing and I'm Happy* (Al Jolson); *Three Little Words* (Ipana Troubadours); *Puttin' on the Ritz* (Leo Reisman); *Kansas City Kitty* (Rudy Vallee); *Sing You Sinners* (Smith Ballew)

Jazz and Big Bands
Duke Ellington records *Mood Indigo.* Paul Whiteman is still called the "King of Jazz"; also popular is the Nichols Band with Benny Goodman, Gene Krupa, Tommy Dorsey, Glenn Miller, and Jack Teagarden.

First Recordings:　Lionel Hampton, with Louis Armstrong

Theater _____

Broadway Openings

Plays
The Green Pastures (Marc Connelly), Richard B. Harrison, all-black cast
Hotel Universe (Philip Barry), Ruth Gordon, Franchot Tone, Morris Carnovsky
Elizabeth the Queen (Maxwell Anderson), Alfred Lunt, Lynn Fontanne
Bad Girl (Vina Delmar), Sylvia Sidney, Paul Kelly
Grand Hotel (Vicki Baum), Eugenie Leontovich, Henry Hull, Sam Jaffe
Once in a Lifetime (Moss Hart, George S. Kaufman), Spring Byington, Hugh O'Connell, Jean Dixon
A Farewell to Arms (Laurence Stallings), Elissa Landi, Glenn Anders
Courtesan (Irving Kaye Davis), Elsa Shelley
Tonight or Never (Lili Hatvany), Helen Gahagan, Melvyn Douglas
Penny Arcade (Marie Baumer), James Cagney, Joan Blondell
Scarlet Sister Mary (Daniel Reed), Ethel Barrymore, Estelle Winwood (in black face)
The Vinegar Tree (Paul Osborn), Mary Boland
Alison's House (Susan Glaspell), Eva Le Gallienne, Howard da Silva
Art and Mrs. Bottle (Benn W. Levy), Katharine Hepburn, Jane Cowl

Musicals
Brown Buddies (Joe Jordan, Millard Thomas), Bill Robinson, Adelaide Hall, all-black cast

Flying High (Ray Henderson, B. G. DeSylva), Oscar Shaw, Bert Lahr, Kate Smith
Garrick Gaieties of 1930 (Vernon Duke et al.), Edith Meiser, Sterling Holloway, Imogene Coca
Girl Crazy (George Gershwin, Ira Gershwin), Allen Kearns, Willie Howard, Ethel Merman, Ginger Rogers
The New Yorkers (Cole Porter), Clayton, Jackson, and Durante, Hope Williams
Simple Simon (Richard Rodgers, Lorenz Hart), Ed Wynn, Ruth Etting
Smiles (Vincent Youmans, Clifford Grey), Marilyn Miller, Fred and Adele Astaire, Eddie Foy, Jr., Bob Hope
Strike Up the Band (George Gershwin, Ira Gershwin), Clark and McCullough, Blanche Ring
Sweet and Low (Billy Rose), Fannie Brice, George Jessel, James Barton, Arthur Treacher

Classics and Revivals On and Off Broadway
A Month in the Country (Turgenev), Nazimova; *Uncle Vanya* (Chekhov), Lillian Gish, Osgood Perkins; *The Inspector General* (Gogol), Dorothy Gish; *Twelfth Night,* Jane Cowl. *Founded:* Group Theatre by Harold Clurman, Lee Strasberg, Morris Carnovsky, Stella Adler, and Sanford Meisner

Pulitzer Prize
The Green Pastures, Marc Connelly

Classical Music _____

Compositions

Ferde Grofé, *Grand Canyon Suite*
Walter Piston, Flute Sonata
Henry Cowell, *Synchrony*
Roy Harris, String Quartet no. 1
Aaron Copland, Piano Variations
Roger Sessions, Piano Sonata no. 1
Sergei Rachmaninoff (in U.S.), Three Russian Folk-
    Songs

Important Events

Jacques Thiabaud, Pablo Casals, and Alexander
Cortot form a trio. Arthur Fiedler becomes
conductor of the Boston Pops. Ferdinand Schaefer
leads the Indianapolis Symphony Orchestra in its
first program. Bach's unknown Clavier Concerto in C
minor is discovered. CBS begins to broadcast Sunday
performances of the New York Philharmonic. *Fidelio*
is broadcast to the United States from Dresden.

First Performances

Roger Sessions, *Black Maskers* (Cincinnati); Charles
Sanford Skilton, *The Sun Bride* (New York); E. B.
Hill, Symphony no. 2 (Boston); Daniel Gregory
Mason, Symphony no. 2 (Cincinnati). For the fiftieth
anniversary of the Boston Symphony: Ottorino
Respighi's *Metamorphosis;* Sergei Prokofiev's
Symphony no. 4; Howard Hanson's Symphony no. 2;
Stravinsky's *Symphony of Psalms;* Albert Roussel's

Symphony in G minor; Walter Piston's Suite for
Orchestra (he conducts), and Paul Hindemith's
Concerto for Viola

Opera

Metropolitan: Rosa Ponselle, *Don Giovanni;*
Frederick Jagel, *Norma;* Friedrich Schorr, *Die
Meistersinger;* Ezio Pinza, *Il barbiere di Siviglia;*
Sadko (Nicolai Rimsky-Korsakov, American
premiere); Elisabeth Ohms (debut),
Götterdämmerung.

Chicago: Mary Garden, *Camille* (Hamilton Forrest,
premiere); Lotte Lehmann, *Die Walküre;* John
Charles Thomas, *I pagliacci*

San Francisco: Maria Jeritza, *The Girl of the
Golden West; L'enfant et les sortilèges*

Music Notes

The Society of Contemporary Musicians names as
the "Most Important Works of the Year": Edgard
Varèse's *Arcane;* Aaron Copland's Concerto; Louis
Gruenberg's *Jazz Suite;* and Carl Ruggles's *Portraits*
• The League of Composers' "Greatest Works of the
Year" include Wallingford Riegger's *Sonarities* and
Carlos Salzedo's Harp and Chamber Concerto • The
Conductorless Symphony of New York is disbanded.

William Faulkner. *Library of Congress.*

Philip Barry's *Hotel Universe. Billy Rose Theatre
Collection. The New York Public Library at Lincoln Center.
Astor, Lenox and Tilden Foundations.*

Art _____

Painting
Grant Wood, *American Gothic*
Edward Hopper, *Early Sunday Morning*
Thomas Hart Benton, *The Old South, City Scenes*
Stuart Davis, *Egg Beater V*
Reginald Marsh, *Why Not Use the "L"?*
John Kane, *Creek Valley, No. 1*
Peter Blume, *Parade*
Charles Sheeler, *American Landscape*
Ivan Le Lorraine Albright, *Into the World There Came a Soul Called Ida*
George Luks, *Mrs. Gamley*
Georgia O'Keeffe, *Horse's Skull*
John Marin, *Storm over Taos*
Lyonel Feininger, *Ruin by the Sea*
Patrick Henry Bruce, *Painting*

Sculpture
William Zorach, *Mother and Child*
John B. Flannagan, *Elephant*
Alexander Calder, *Little Ball with Counterweight*
Chaim Gross, *Offspring*
Gaston Lachaise, *Torso*

Important Exhibitions

Museums

New York: *Metropolitan:* Egyptian wall paintings from tombs and palaces of the eighteenth and nineteenth dynasties, 1600–1200 B.C.; the Henry Havemeyer collection. *Museum of Modern Art:*

Architecture
Daily News Building, New York (Hood and Howells)
Chrysler Building, New York (William Van Alen)
Constitution Hall, Philadelphia (John Russell Pope)
Shopping center, Michigan Square Building, Chicago (Holabird and Root)
A "Radio City" is planned to cover three New York city blocks; it will include underground bus terminals, subterranean boulevards, surface fountains, sculpture, and broadcasting facilities; its estimated cost is $250 million.

Reginald Marsh, *Why Not Use the 'L'?*, 1930. Egg tempera. 36 × 48". Collection of Whitney Museum of American Art. Geoffrey Clements.

Early watercolors of Charles Burchfield; "46 Artists under 35 Years Old"; Corot and Daumier; Weber, Klee, Lehmbruck, Maillol, Homer, Eakins

Boston: Russian icons; Boston painters

Philadelphia, Washington (Corcoran): American moderns

Pittsburgh: Carnegie international prizes to Picasso (for *Madame Picasso*), Henry Lee McFee, Niles Spencer, Maurice Sterne

Chicago: Sculpture prize to Heinz Warneke; Delacroix

Art Briefs
Walker Evans's *Lehmbruck: Head of Man* is the first photo acquired for the Museum of Modern Art's photo collection • Diego Rivera completes the San Francisco Stock Exchange mural • The construction of period rooms peaks throughout U.S. museums • Interest grows in prints, especially lithographs and woodcuts • The director of the Detroit Institute pays $400 for an overpainted Titian valued at $150,000 • Arguments continue over whether U.S. dealers should sell European art.

Books

Fiction

Critics' Choice

As I Lay Dying, William Faulkner
The 42nd Parallel, John Dos Passos
Flowering Judas, Katherine Anne Porter
The Babe's Bed, Glenway Wescott
Arundel, Kenneth Roberts
Laments for the Living, Dorothy Parker
Mirthful Haven, Booth Tarkington
The Maltese Falcon, Dashiell Hammett
Pure Gold, O. E. Rölvaag
🐾 *The Castle,* Franz Kafka

Best Sellers

Cimarron, Edna Ferber
The Door, Mary Roberts Rinehart
Exile, Warwick Deeping
Years of Grace, Margaret Ayer Barnes
The Woman of Andros, Thornton Wilder
Angel Payment, J. B. Priestley
Rogue Herries, Hugh Walpole
Chances, A. Hamilton Gibbs
Twenty-Four Hours, Louis Bromfield
Young Man of Manhattan, Katharine Brush

Nonfiction

Critics' Choice

The American Leviathan, Charles and Mary Beard
The Realm of Matter, George Santayana
I'll Take My Stand, Robert Penn Warren
The Human Mind, Karl Menninger
The Second Twenty Years at Hull House, Jane Addams
Little America, Adm. Richard E. Byrd
Pre-War America, Mark Sullivan
The Crusades: Iron Men and Saints, Harold Lamb
The Story of a Friendship, Owen Wister
🐾 *Civilization and Its Discontents,* Sigmund Freud
🐾 *The Revolt of the Masses,* Ortega y Gasset

Best-Sellers

The Story of San Michele, Axel Munthe
The Strange Death of President Harding, Gaston B. Means, May Dixon Thacker
Byron, André Maurois
The Adams Family, James Truslow Adams
Lone Cowboy, Will James
The Story of Philosophy, Will Durant

The Outline of History, H. G. Wells
The Rise of American Civilization, Charles Beard, Mary Beard
Lincoln, Emil Ludwig
The Art of Thinking, Ernest Dimnet

Poetry

T. S. Eliot, *Ash-Wednesday*
Hart Crane, *The Bridge*
Ezra Pound, *The Cantos,* vol. 3
Archibald MacLeish, *New Found Land*
Richard Eberhart, *A Bravery of Earth*
Edgar Lee Masters, *Lichee Nuts*
Edwin Arlington Robinson, *The Glory of the Nightingales*
🐾 W. H. Auden, *Poems*

Pulitzer Prizes

Years of Grace, Margaret Ayer Barnes (novel)
The Coming of the War, Bernadotte E. Schmitt (U.S. history)
Henry James, Charles W. Eliot (biography)
Collected Poems, Robert Frost (poetry)

Nobel Prize

Sinclair Lewis

Science and Technology

Ernest O. Lawrence devises the cyclotron, a means of accelerating particles by magnetic resonance for the purpose of splitting atoms.

Pluto is identified by photos taken at Lowell Observatory, Arizona, by C. W. Tombaugh; its discovery confirms mathematical predictions.

Robert R. Williams determines the chemical structure of the vitamin thiamine.

John H. Northrup isolates the enzyme pepsin in crystalline form.

W. C. Rose, University of Illinois, shows that ten amino acids are "essential" for rats.

The first psychoanalytic institute for training analysts opens in Boston.

The first all-air commercial New York–Los Angeles transport is begun by Transcontinental and West Airlines.

Dr. William Beebe, in his bathysphere, descends to a record 1,426 feet underwater.

Artificial fabrics are made from an acetylene base by biochemist J. Walter Reppe.

Nobel Prize

Karl Landsteiner wins the prize in physiology and medicine for the discovery of human blood groups.

Sports

Baseball

Babe Ruth's salary is increased to $80,000; when told it exceeds the president's, he quips, "Well, I had a better year than he did." Ruth hit 49 home runs.

Champions

Batting	Pitching
Bill Terry (New York, NL), .401	Fred Fitzsimmons (New York, NL) 19–2
Al Simmons (Philadelphia, AL), .380	Lefty Grove (Philadelphia, AL) 28–5
	Home runs
	Hack Wilson (Chicago, NL), 56, NL record

Football

The New York Giants beat Notre Dame in a benefit game for the Unemployment Fund.

Pro Stars: Bronko Nagurski (Chicago Bears), Ernie Nevers (Chicago Cards).

College All-Americans: Frank Carideo (Q), Notre Dame; Leonard Macaluso (B), Colgate.

Rose Bowl (Jan. 1, 1931): Alabama 24–Washington State 0

Other Sports

Golf: Bobby Jones, still an amateur, wins the Grand Slam and retires; 18,000 attend the U.S. Open at Marion, Ohio.

Horse Racing: Gallant Fox, ridden by jockey Earl Sande, wins the Triple Crown. The Irish Sweepstakes are organized.

Boxing: Max Schmeling beats Jack Sharkey for the heavyweight title on a foul before 75,000 spectators.

Winners

World Series	*Player of the Year*
Philadelphia (AL) 4	Charles Hyatt, Pittsburgh
St. Louis (NL) 3	*Stanley Cup*
MVP	Montreal
NL–William Terry, New York	*U.S. Tennis Open*
AL–Joseph Cronin, Washington	Men: John Doeg
	Women: Betty Nuthall
NFL	*USGA Open*
Green Bay Packers	Robert T. Jones, Jr.
College Football	*Kentucky Derby*
Notre Dame	Gallant Fox (E. Sande, jockey)
College Basketball	
Pittsburgh	

A high school science teacher in Cleveland exhibits models of atomic structure, a subject of intense investigation in the scientific world. *Library of Congress.*

Fashion

For Women: With the Clara Bow flapper passé, the rage is for the sophisticated Garbo look. The silhouette is tall and slender, emphasizing broad shoulders, a small bosom, streamlined hips, and the normal waistline. Both hair and hems are longer; narrower skirts widen softly below the hip and then reach mid-calf. Several screen stars actually set the styles: Garbo and the windblown look (with hair parted at the side or middle); Crawford and puffed sleeves, which emphasize the small waist; Harlow's slinky halter tops and satin evening gowns; and Garbo and Dietrich's slacks. Thick, clinging fabrics are enormously popular. The gradual broadening and squaring of the shoulders leads to three-inch shoulder pads, even in nightgowns. Evening fashion consists of backless dresses with slightly bloused bodices and fox furs with heads and tails. Makeup emphasizes angularity. Every woman owns a magnifying mirror to pencil in well-plucked eyebrows and apply black mascara and eye shadow. Curling irons are popular.

Kaleidoscope

- Joke: "Have you heard the one about the two men who jumped hand in hand because they had a joint account?"
- The International Apple Shippers Association gives 6,000 jobless men surplus apples on credit to sell for 5¢ on street corners.
- More than 1,300 banks close by the end of the year.
- Early in the year, a Little Bull Market sees giants like U.S. Steel, General Motors, and General Electric regain ground, which leads to a wave of optimism among political and business leaders.
- The first federal census of unemployment appears in April and reports 3 million unemployed.
- William Randolph Hearst owns 33 newspapers with a total circulation of 11 million.
- In the last ten years the mileage of paved roads has doubled to 695,000; gas consumption rises to 16 billion gallons.
- The illiteracy rate falls to 4.3 percent.
- Ellen Church becomes the first airline stewardess (United Airlines). The job is created to allay passengers' fear of flying; requirements are that the applicant be female, single, at least 21 years old, no taller than 5'4", and under 115 pounds; she must also have a "pleasant personality."
- Operatic films are in vogue, such as *New Moon* with Grace Moore and Lawrence Tibbett.
- "The Lone Ranger," in Detroit, starts with the *William Tell* overture and "A fiery horse with the speed of light, a cloud of dust, and a hearty 'Hi-yo Silver'—the Lone Ranger Rides Again."
- The following want ad appears in the *New York Times:* "Bookkeeper and typist: Thoroughly experienced. Prefer someone with silk underwear."

- A well-publicized study reports that bright children are prone to bullying, perseverance, cruelty, and argumentativeness.
- A *Literary Digest* poll indicates that 40 percent favor Prohibition repeal, 29 percent favor modification.
- The new Institute for Advanced Studies at Princeton University is dedicated to the "usefulness of useless knowledge."
- Howard Hunt buys his first wildcat oil well for $40,000 in cash.
- "Gif me a viskey . . . and don't be stingy, baby," is Garbo's first line in *Anna Christie,* her first talkie.
- Jean Harlow becomes blonde for *Hell's Angels.*
- Busby Berkeley introduces his dizzying camera angle techniques into the filming of musical sequences.
- With the new, smaller and improved German cameras, spontaneous candid photography becomes popular.
- A federal law is passed requiring the labeling of substandard foods.
- Lloyd's of London begins to sell civilian commotion insurance in the U.S.
- *I'll Take My Stand,* a manifesto by Southern agrarian writers, supports the "Southern way of life against . . . the American or prevailing way."

New Words and Usages: *Hoovervilles* (slums), *Hoover blankets* (newspapers covering park-bench indigents), *Hoover flags* (pockets emptied and inside out), and *Hoover wagons* (mule-pulled trucks).

Fads: Tree sitting, contract bridge (overtaking whist), backgammon, "Sorry," and knitting

First Appearances: Hostess Twinkies, Snickers, sliced bread (Wonder), French's Worcestershire sauce, Mott's applesauce, Jiffy biscuits, supermarket (King Kullen), broiler chickens, dry ice, Birds Eye frozen vegetables, "freewheeling" drive (Studebaker), house trailers, windshield wipers, photoflash bulbs, plexiglass, "candid camera" (term), El Dorado (art deco apartment building, New York), Braniff, National, United, TWA, and American airlines, Brooklyn College, *Fortune, Daily Worker,* "Blondie," "Death Valley Days," Breck shampoo, Merthiolate, St. Moritz Hotel, Carlsbad Caverns National Park, mechanical operator for coal mines, windowless factory, Medical Rogues' Gallery, pinball machine, planetarium open to the public (Chicago), president buried in the National Cemetery at Arlington (Taft), benzedrine inhaler

With difficulties in prohibition enforcement and the decline in the economy, the "wet" movement gathers force.
Library of Congress.

1931

Facts and Figures

Economic Profile
  Dow-Jones: ↓ High 194–
    Low 74
  GNP: −16%
  Inflation: −4.4%
  Unemployment: 15.9%
Median age, first marriage:
  Male: 24.3, Female: 21.3
Average household size: 4.11
Population over 65: 5%
Population under 10: 19%
Automobiles:
  Pierce-Arrow: $810
  Auburn: $945
  Buick: $1,025
  Cadillac: $2,695
Steinway: $875–$1,375
Lady's seal or caracul coat:
  $188
I. Miller shoes: $5.85
Rogers Peet wool coat: $20
Hart Schaffner & Marx suit:
  $29.50
Reading glasses: $3.50;
  bifocals: $4.95

Deaths

David Belasco, Arnold
  Bennett, Thomas Alva
  Edison, Daniel Chester
  French, Frank Harris,
  Vincent d'Indy, Vachel
  Lindsay, Nellie Melba,
  A. A. Michelson, Dwight
  Morrow, Anna Pavlova,
  Eugene Ysaye.

In the News

MASSACHUSETTS SENATE MAKES FIRST RESOLUTION TO REPEAL PROHIBITION . . . UNEMPLOYMENT NEARS 16% . . . BRITISH FREE GANDHI, ON HUNGER STRIKE, AND AGREE TO DISCUSS HIS DEMANDS . . . HOOVER'S WICKERSHAM COMMISSION FINDS PROHIBITION INEFFECTIVE . . . LARGEST VIENNA BANK GOES BANKRUPT . . . "LEGS" DIAMOND IS AMBUSHED OUTSIDE ALBANY ROOMING HOUSE . . . FEDERAL COUNCIL OF CHURCHES OF CHRIST AFFIRMS BIRTH CONTROL . . . JAPANESE INVADE MANCHURIA, CLAIM PROVOCATION AT MUKDEN . . . HOOVER PROPOSES MORATORIUM ON INTERNATIONAL DEBTS AND REPARATIONS . . . SPANISH KING ALFONSO IS DEPOSED, A REPUBLIC DECLARED . . . GRASSHOPPER PLAGUE HITS THE MIDWEST . . . MUSCLE SHOALS GOVERNMENT POWER PLANT IS VETOED BY HOOVER . . . STAR FAITHFULL, 25-YEAR-OLD BEAUTY, WASHES ASHORE ON LONG ISLAND, N.Y. . . . WILEY POST AND HAROLD GATTO FLY "WINNIE MAE" AROUND THE WORLD IN 8 DAYS . . . CHIANG KAI-SHEK'S NATIONALISTS CLASH WITH MAO TSE-TUNG'S COMMUNISTS . . . NINE NEGRO BOYS FROM SCOTTSBORO, CHARGED WITH RAPING TWO WHITE WOMEN ON A TRAIN, ARE SENTENCED TO DEATH . . . AMERICAN BAR ASSOCIATION APPROVES ELIHU ROOT FORMULA FOR U.S. TO ENTER WORLD COURT . . . BRITAIN LEAVES THE GOLD STANDARD, AMERICA AND FRANCE REMAIN . . . TWO OUT OF THREE WORKERS IN DETROIT ARE UNEMPLOYED . . . HUNGER MARCHERS ARE TURNED AWAY FROM WHITE HOUSE . . . AL CAPONE, GUILTY OF TAX EVASION, IS SENTENCED TO 11 YEARS . . . HOOVER ASKS FOR EMERGENCY RECONSTRUCTION FINANCE AND PUBLIC WORKS BILLS . . . STRIKING COAL MINERS BATTLE GUARDS IN HARLAN, KY., FOUR ARE KILLED . . . LEAGUE OF NATIONS ASKS U.S. TO SIT IN ON MANCHURIA MEETINGS, U.S. AGREES.

Quotes

"I should like to find out at what stage of your poverty other people realize or sense it, and pass you by as one no longer interesting or useful to them. . . . You realize that for the first time in your rather carefree, indifferent life you are worth more dead than alive—a good deal more."

— Frank G. Moorhead, *Nation*

"MIDDLETON, N.Y., Dec. 24—Attracted by smoke from the chimney of a supposedly empty summer cottage . . . in Sullivan County, [the] constable . . . found a young couple starving. Three days without food, the wife, who is 23 years old, was hardly able to walk. They went into the cottage, preferring to starve rather than beg."

— *Buffalo Evening News*

"More than 100,000 applications have been received at the [Soviet] Ambassador's . . . for the 6,000 jobs. . . . Because of the general knowledge that Russia is 'industrializing,' applicants usually are skilled workers."

— *New York Times*

"We are the first nation in the history of the world to go to the poorhouse in an automobile."

— Will Rogers

"I'm a small fish here in Washington. But I'm the Kingfish to the folks down in Louisiana."

— Huey Long

Ads

Commercial airlines provide new passenger comfort. *Library of Congress.*

Radio

Premieres

"The Ed Sullivan Show"
"The March of Time," Ted Husing
"The Eddie Cantor Show"
"Singing Lady," Irene Wicker
"Buck Rogers"
"Skippy," Franklin Adams, Jr.
"Little Orphan Annie," Shirley Bell
"Myrt and Marge," Myrtle Vail, Donna Damerel
    Fick
"Metropolitan Opera Broadcasts," Milton Cross
"The American Album of Familiar Music," Donald
    Dame

Specials

Mussolini broadcasts his peace goals; Pope Pius XI
makes the first worldwide broadcast; Gertrude
Ederle speaks from an aquaplane, William Beebe,
from a bathysphere 2,200 feet below the sea.

Of Note

The longest running comedy is "Smith Brothers";
music, "Atwater Kent" and "Midweek Hymn Sing";
news, Frederick William Wile; religious-talk,
"National Radio Pulpit"; and miscellaneous-talk,
"Cook's Travelogue" and "Auction Bridge" • "The
University of Chicago Round Table," with John
Howe and George Probst, sends out transcripts of
meetings; 21,000 subscribe • "Buck Rogers" fans can
exchange Cocomalt box strips for "interplanetary
maps" to become "solar scouts."

New Catchphrases: "Who's that little chatterbox? /
The one with pretty auburn locks? / Who can it be?
It's 'Little Orphan Annie'"; "Time . . . marches on!
As it must to all men, death came this week to . . ."
("The March of Time"); "How *do* you *do?*" ("The
Eddie Cantor Show" with Bert Gordon as the Mad
Russian)

Laurel and Hardy
are enormously
successful in their
displays of
monumental
ineptitude. Left:
*Brats. Movie Star
News.*

Movies

Openings

The Struggle (D. W. Griffith, last film), Hal Skelly,
    Zita Johann
Cimarron (Wesley Ruggles), Richard Dix, Irene
    Dunne
The Front Page (Lewis Milestone), Pat O'Brien,
    Adolphe Menjou
Trader Horn (W. S. Van Dyke), Harry Carey
The Public Enemy (William A. Wellman), James
    Cagney, Jean Harlow
Monkey Business (Norman Z. McLeod), Marx
    Brothers
An American Tragedy (Josef von Sternberg), Sylvia
    Sidney, Phillips Holmes
A Nous la Liberté (René Clair), Raymond Cordy,
    Henri Marchand
The Champ (King Vidor), Wallace Beery, Jackie
    Cooper
City Lights (Charles Chaplin), Charles Chaplin,
    Virginia Cherrill
Dishonored (Josef von Sternberg), Marlene Dietrich,
    Victor McLaglen
Dracula (Tod Browning), Bela Lugosi
Frankenstein (James Whale), Boris Karloff, Colin
    Clive
Platinum Blonde (Frank Capra), Jean Harlow,
    Loretta Young
Street Scene (King Vidor), Sylvia Sidney
Tabu (F. W. Murnau, Robert Flaherty), Matahi, Reri,
    Hitu
A Free Soul (Clarence Brown), Norma Shearer,
    Lionel Barrymore, Clark Gable, Leslie Howard
The Guardsman (Sidney Franklin), Alfred Lunt,
    Lynn Fontanne
The Sin of Madelon Claudet (Edgar Selwyn), Helen
    Hayes, Lewis Stone, Robert Young
Skippy (Norman Taurog), Jackie Cooper

Academy Awards (1930–31)

Best Picture: *Cimarron*
Best Director: Norman Taurog (*Skippy*)
Best Actress: Marie Dressler (*Min and Bill*)
Best Actor: Lionel Barrymore (*A Free Soul*)

Top Box-Office Stars

Janet Gaynor, Charles Farrell

Popular Music _____

Hit Songs

"Life Is Just a Bowl of Cherries"
"Minnie, the Moocher"
"Mood Indigo"
"All of Me"
"Between the Devil and the Deep
    Blue Sea"
"Dancing in the Dark"
"Dream a Little Dream of Me"
"Of Thee I Sing"
"The Thrill Is Gone"
"Lady of Spain"
"Love Is Sweeping the Country"

Top Records

The Peanut Vendor (Don
Azpiazu); *Where the Blue of the
Night* (Bing Crosby); *Goodnight,
Sweetheart* (Ruth Etting); *When
the Moon Comes over the
Mountain* (Kate Smith); *You
Rascal You* (Jack Teagarden); *Just
a Gigolo* (Bing Crosby); *I Found a
Million-Dollar Baby* (Ben Pollack)

Jazz and Big Bands

Freddie Martin performs at the
Bossert Hotel in Brooklyn, N.Y.

First Recordings: Mildred Bailey;
Duke Ellington's extended *Creole
Rhapsody*

New Bands: Eddie Duchin, New
Jersey; Don Redman; Henry
Busse

Theater _____

Broadway Openings

Plays

Mourning Becomes Electra (Eugene O'Neill),
    Nazimova, Alice Brady
Tomorrow and Tomorrow (Philip Barry), Herbert
    Marshall, Osgood Perkins
Private Lives (Noel Coward), Noel Coward,
    Gertrude Lawrence
The Barretts of Wimpole Street (Rudolf Beiser),
    Katharine Cornell, Brian Aherne
Counsellor-at-Law (Elmer Rice), Paul Muni
Reunion in Vienna (Robert E. Sherwood), Alfred
    Lunt, Lynn Fontanne
Springtime for Henry (Benn W. Levy), Leslie Banks
The House of Connelly (Paul Green), Franchot Tone,
    Luther Adler, Stella Adler, Clifford Odets,
    Morris Carnovsky
As You Desire Me (Luigi Pirandello), Judith
    Anderson
The Left Bank (Elmer Rice), Katherine Alexander,
    Horace Braham

Musicals

America's Sweetheart (Richard Rodgers, Lorenz
    Hart), Harriette Lake (Ann Sothern), Jack
    Whiting
The Bandwagon (Arthur Schwartz, Howard Dietz),
    Fred and Adele Astaire, Frank Morgan
The Cat and the Fiddle (Jerome Kern, Otto
    Harbach), Eddie Foy, Jr., Bettina Hall
Earl Carroll's Vanities of 1931 (Harold Adamson,
    Burton Lane), William Demarest, Lillian Roth
George White's Scandals (Ray Henderson), Ethel
    Merman, Rudy Vallee, Alice Faye
Rhapsody in Black (Jimmy McHugh, Dorothy
    Fields), Ethel Waters, all-black cast

Stage and screen star Alla Nazimova (seated), in *Mourning
Becomes Electra*, Eugene O'Neill's retelling of Aeschylus's
Oresteia in a Civil War setting. *Billy Rose Theatre
Collection. The New York Public Library at Lincoln Center.
Astor, Lenox and Tilden Foundations.*

Of Thee I Sing (George Gershwin, Ira Gershwin),
    Victor Moore, William Gaxton, Lois Moran

Classics and Revivals On and Off Broadway

The Merchant of Venice, Otis Skinner, Maude
Adams; *Hamlet,* Raymond Massey, Celia Johnson;
The School for Scandal (Sheridan), Ethel Barrymore;
The Father (Strindberg), Robert Loraine; *Camille*
(Dumas), Eva Le Gallienne

Pulitzer Prize

Alison's House, Susan Glaspell

Auto Show in Detroit: handsome machines without buyers. *Library of Congress.*

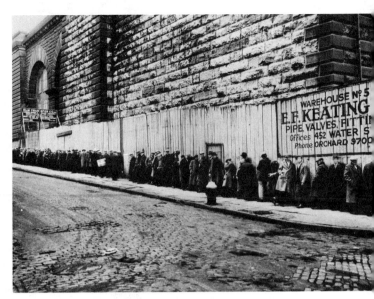

With government relief limited, bread lines, like this one beneath the Brooklyn Bridge, form throughout the nation. *Library of Congress.*

Classical Music

Compositions

Samuel Barber, *School for Scandal, Dover Beach*
Virgil Thomson, Symphony no. 2, Serenade for Flute and Violin, *Stabat Mater*
John Powell, *Natchez on the Hill*
Henry Cowell, *Two Appositions*
Douglas Moore, *Overtures on an American Tune*
Walter Piston, Suite for Oboe and Piano
Gian Carlo Menotti, *Variation on a Theme of Schumann*

Important Events

The National and St. Louis symphonies are organized. Interest in American music grows abroad. Nicolas Slonimsky travels to Paris, Berlin, Vienna, Prague, and Stockholm, and plays Gershwin, Sessions, Copland, Gruenberg, and Ruggles. European publishers begin to publish living American composers.

Debuts: Isaac Stern, Milstein-Piatigorsky-Horowitz Trio

First Performances

Roy Harris, Andante (Los Angeles); Charles Ives, *Three Places in New England* (New York); Igor Stravinsky, *Symphony of Psalms* (Boston); Ferde Grofé, *Grand Canyon Suite* (Chicago); Arthur Honegger, Symphony no. 1 (Boston); Paul Hindemith, *Konzertmusik* (Boston); William Grant Still, *Afro-American Symphony* (Rochester); Ottorino Respighi, *Five Picture Studies* (Boston)

Opera

Metropolitan: Lucrezia Bori, Edward Johnson, *Peter Ibbetson* (premiere); Lily Pons (debut), *Lucia di Lammermoor, Rigoletto;* Elisabeth Rethberg, *Iris.* Premieres: *Schwanda* (Jaromir Weinberger); *La notte di Zoraima* (Montemezzi)

Philadelphia: *Oedipus Rex, Wozzeck* (premieres)

Chicago: René Maison, *Parsifal*

Music Notes

The Bruckner Society is organized "to develop in the public an appreciation of the music of Bruckner, Mahler, and other moderns" • "The Star Spangled Banner," written by lawyer Francis Scott Key (1814) and based on an English drinking tune, officially becomes the national anthem • Severence Hall in Cleveland opens • The first full-length opera from the Metropolitan is broadcast (*Hansel and Gretel*).

Art _____

Painting

Georgia O'Keeffe, *The White Flower, Cow's Skull, Red, White and Blue*

Walt Kuhn, *The Blue Clown*

Charles Sheeler, *Classic Landscape (River Rouge Plant)*

Edward Hopper, *Route 6, Eastham*

Arthur G. Dove, *Ferry Boat Wreck*

John Kane, *Panther Hollow*

Willem de Kooning, *Untitled*

Stuart Davis, *Salt Shaker, House and Street, Trees and El*

Reginald Marsh, *Swinging Carousel*

John Steuart Curry, *Spring Shower*

Grant Wood, *Midnight Ride of Paul Revere*

Charles Demuth, *Buildings Abstraction*

Sculpture

Isamu Noguchi, *The Queen*

Gloria Vanderbilt Whitney, *Titanic Memorial*

Ibram Lassaw, *Torso*

Architecture

McGraw-Hill Building, New York (Hood and Fouilhoux)

George Washington Bridge, New York and New Jersey (Othmar Ammann)

Arthur Peck house, Paoli, Pa. (William Lescaze)

Rockefeller Center construction begins (Reinhard & Hofmeister, Hood, Godley, and Fouilhoux, Corbett, Harrison, and MacMurray).

The Empire State Building (Shreve, Lamb, and Harmon) is completed, 102 stories and 1,250 feet high, the tallest building to date.

Georgia O'Keeffe, *The White Calico Flower*, 1931. Oil. 30 × 36". *Collection of Whitney Museum of American Art. Geoffrey Clements.*

Important Exhibitions

Museums

New York: *Metropolitan:* European arms and armor; Russian icons from the twelfth to the nineteenth centuries; early New York silver; Chinese court robes and accessories; ceramic art of the Near East; Robert Henri memorial; contemporary industrial art. *Museum of Modern Art:* Murals of Diego Rivera; German art—Beckmann, Grosz; Redon, Toulouse-Lautrec, Matisse retrospective. *Whitney:* George Bellows, Arthur B. Davies, William Glackens, George Luks, Maurice Prendergast, Robert Henri

Pittsburgh: Franklin C. Watkins receives the Carnegie International first prize for *Suicide in Costume.*

Hartford: *Wadsworth Atheneum:* "Newer Super-Realism: Ernst, Masson, Miró, Picasso, de Chirico, Dali"

Art Briefs

The Whitney opens with a permanent collection of 500 works, the first museum of American art • New galleries include the Addison (Andover, Mass.) and Jocelyn (Omaha) • Arshile Gorky holds his first one-man show in Philadelphia.

Dance _____

Martha Graham dances in *Primitive Mysteries*.

Books

Fiction

Critics' Choice

Sanctuary, William Faulkner
These Thirteen: Stories, William Faulkner
The Dream Life of Balso Snell, Nathanael West
S.S. San Pedro, James Gould Cozzens
Sparks Fly Upward, Oliver La Farge
Their Father's God, Ole Rölvaag
The Harbourmaster, William McFee
The Forge, T. S. Stribling
❧ *The Son Avenger*, Sigrid Undset

Best-Sellers

The Good Earth, Pearl S. Buck
Grand Hotel, Vicki Baum
Shadows on the Rock, Willa Cather
The Road Back, E. M. Remarque
Back Street, Fannie Hurst
Maid in Waiting, John Galsworthy
The Bridge of Desire, Warwick Deeping
A White Bird Flying, Bess Streeter Aldrich
Years of Grace, Margaret Ayer Barnes
Finch's Fortune, Mazo de la Roche

Nonfiction

Critics' Choice

Axel's Castle, Edmund Wilson
Autobiography, Lincoln Steffens
Philosophy and Civilization, John Dewey
Only Yesterday, William Lewis Allen
The Brown Decades, Louis Mumford
The Genteel Tradition at Bay, George Santayana
The Owl in the Attic and Other Perplexities, James Thurber
Can Europe Keep the Peace? Frank Simonds
Tragic America, Theodore Dreiser
Living My Life, Emma Goldman
The Literary Mind, Max Eastman

Best-Sellers

Education of a Princess, Grand Duchess Marie
Washington Merry-Go-Round, Anonymous (Drew Pearson and Robert S. Allen)
Fatal Interview (poetry), Edna St. Vincent Millay
Culbertson's Summary, Ely Culbertson
The Story of San Michele, Axel Munthe

Contract Bridge Blue Book, Ely Culbertson
The Epic of America, James Truslow Adams
New Russia's Primer, M. Ilin
Mexico, Stuart Chase
Boners

Poetry

Conrad Aiken, *Preludes for Memnon*
Edwin Arlington Robinson, *Matthias at the Door*
Edgar Lee Masters, *Godbey*
Robinson Jeffers, *Descent to the Dead*
Langston Hughes, *Dear Lovely Death*
H. D., *Red Roses for Bronze*

Pulitzer Prizes

The Good Earth, Pearl S. Buck (novel)
My Experiences in the World War, John J. Pershing (U.S. history)
Theodore Roosevelt, Henry F. Pringle (biography)
The Flowering Stone, George Dillon (poetry)

Science and Technology

Karl Jansky, at Bell Telephone Laboratories, begins the science of radio astronomy as he observes interference in the form of hissing sounds coming from beyond the earth's atmosphere.

Harold Urey, Columbia University, discovers heavy water, water that contains deuterium, a rare hydrogen isotope.

Robert J. de Graaff constructs a subatomic particle accelerator that uses static electricity.

Lt. Robert Hyland, Washington, D.C., observes that planes can be detected by means of their reflection of radio beams.

Growth hormone is used clinically for the first time.

An electron microscope is developed by Vladimir Zworykin and James Hillier.

The enzyme trypsin is isolated in crystalline form by John H. Northrup and Moses Kunitz.

Clyde Pangborn and Hugh Herndon make the first nonstop flight across the Pacific, 4,860 miles in 41 hours.

The George Washington Bridge, the longest suspension bridge in the world, is built.

Sports

Baseball

Pepper Martin (St. Louis, NL) bats .500 as he leads the "Gashouse Gang" to a World Series victory; Herbert Hoover throws out the first ball and is booed.

Champions

Batting
Chuck Hafey (St. Louis, NL), .349
Al Simmons (Philadelphia, AL), .390

Pitching
Paul Derringer (St. Louis, NL), 18–8
Lefty Grove (Philadelphia, AL), 31–4

Home runs
Babe Ruth (New York, AL), 46
Lou Gehrig (New York, AL), 46

Football

Knute Rockne, Notre Dame coach, dies in a plane crash. He had coached Notre Dame since 1918; his record was 105 wins, 12 losses, and 5 ties.
Chicago, Green Bay, and Portsmouth are fined $1,000 for using players whose college class has not graduated.

Pro Stars: Bronko Nagurski, Link Lyman (Chicago Bears)

College All-Americans: Marchmont Schwartz (B), Notre Dame; Paul Schwegler (T), Washington

Rose Bowl (Jan. 1, 1932): Southern California 21– Tulane 12

Basketball

The ABL disbands because of financial problems.

Walter Hagen (left) demonstrating a sport that is growing more and more egalitarian. *Library of Congress.*

Other Sports

Boxing: Max Schmeling is stripped of his heavyweight crown by New York officials for his refusal to fight Jack Sharkey.

Winners

World Series
St. Louis (NL) 4
Philadelphia (AL) 3

MVP
NL–Frank Frisch, St. Louis
AL–Robert Grove, Philadelphia

NFL
Green Bay Packers

College Football
USC

College Basketball
Northwestern

Player of the Year
Bart Carlton, Ada Teachers

Stanley Cup
Montreal

U.S. Tennis Open
Men: Ellsworth Vines, Jr.
Women: Helen Wills Moody

USGA Open
Billy Burke

Kentucky Derby
Twenty Grand (C. Kurtsinger, jockey)

Fashion

For Women: New accessories include suede gloves with matching bag and shoes, a red or gray fox fur flung over one shoulder, batik or fine silk scarves, heavy finger rings, and watches set with gems. Hats are deep and close-fitting with large and small brims, and they dip over one eye. Hair is longer and loosely waved with a side part; a roll is sometimes combed in the back. Fashionable shoes include the black silk style with ankle strap and the white suede style with T strap.

High-fashion note: Reveillon's white satin pajama suit.

For Men: Hair is short and natural, parted on the side; water replaces pomade for the Charles Farrell or Buddy Rogers look; mustaches remain on the older sophisticate, whose "essential accessories" include cigarette case, wallet, signet ring, cuff links, and two handkerchiefs, one in the breast pocket, the other, for use, tucked up the coat sleeve. The hearty, "tough" look appears with the double-breasted darker suit and the hat brought down over the face.

Kaleidoscope _____

- National income is down 33 percent since 1929; payrolls drop 40 percent; department store clerks earn $5–$10 a week and secretaries, $15; many working women earn 25¢ an hour.
- Hundreds of the unemployed dig clams in New England and sell them door to door for 25¢ a peck.
- Double features begin; they provide a place for the unemployed to go.
- Gangster and horror films increase in popularity.
- Lectures and books on Russia become more popular as interest in the "Soviet experiment" increases.
- John Reed clubs, named after the American Communist who died in Moscow, form in many cities.
- For the first time, emigration exceeds immigration.
- Sales of glass jars increase dramatically, while sales of canned goods decline.
- The National Education Association reports that 75 percent of all cities ban the employment of wives.
- The rate of admissions to state mental hospitals for 1930–31 is triple that of 1922–30.
- To generate income, Nevada legalizes both gambling and the six-month divorce.
- The remains of Miles Standish, leader of the Mayflower, are transported and buried at Duxbury, Mass.
- Hattie T. Caraway (Arkansas) becomes the first woman elected to the U.S. Senate.
- Nearly 6,000 cases of infantile paralysis strike New York, which is placed in a state of partial quarantine.
- Farmers, to no avail, use electrified fences and other devices to inhibit the horde of grasshoppers that destroys 160,000 miles of America's finest farmlands.
- Lucky Luciano organizes the Mafia into federated families.
- Animal trainer Clyde Beatty debuts with Ringling Brothers and Barnum and Bailey.
- A popular joke: "But surely," cried Jean, "you didn't tell him straight out that you loved him?" "Goodness, no," Mary said calmly, "he had to squeeze it out of me" (Buffalo News).
- Ethel Merman steals the show in George White's Scandals with "Life Is Just a Bowl of Cherries."
- Ethel Waters, in Rufus Jones for President, is upstaged by five-year-old Sammy Davis, Jr.

Catching bank robbers in N.Y.C. with machine guns and tear gas. General Research Division. The New York Public Library. Astor, Lenox and Tilden Foundations.

Gangster films, like *The Public Enemy,* with Jean Harlow and James Cagney, surpass westerns at the box office; this is one of the first to portray gangsters as the spawn of social problems. *Movie Star News.*

- Silent film extra Clark Gable appears in *A Free Soul,* slaps Norma Shearer, and wins instant stardom; Bing Crosby croons in his debut in Max Sennett shorts.
- Universal recruits Bette Davis who, one agent reports, has "as much sex appeal as Slim Summerville."
- Kate Smith sets a record run of eleven weeks at the Palace.
- When the *New York World* ceases publication, Walter Lippmann goes to the *New York Herald Tribune,* becomes nationally syndicated, and achieves great popularity.
- Offended by his political remarks, Theodore Dreiser slaps Sinclair Lewis's face twice at a dinner of American writers at the Metropolitan Club, New York.
- Lucky Strike outsells its rival, Camel, for the first time.
- Charles Lindbergh builds a house, widely called a "Nest for the Lone Eagle," in a secluded area of New Jersey.
- Investigations into the death of Star Faithfull indicate that she was sexually abused as a teenager by a member of a distinguished Back Bay Boston family.
- *Oh, Yeah,* a series of optimistic statements by bankers and politicians about the depression, is a popular source of grim humor.
- Jane Addams and Nicholas Murray Butler win the Nobel Peace Prize.

First Appearances: Bahai House of Worship (Wilmette, Ill.), coaxial cable, moving picture of a grand opera (*I pagliacci),* Nobel Prize to an American woman (Addams), photoelectric cell installed commercially, infrared photograph, air conditioner, electric dry shaver (Schick), absolute monarch visiting the United States (King Prajadhipok, Siam), stockings in transparent mesh, Beech-Nut baby food, Hotel Bar butter, Wyler's bouillon cubes, Bisquick biscuit mix, Clairol hair dye, Black Muslims, Jehovah's Witnesses (the name), Starch Rating (public polling method), "Dick Tracy," Alka Seltzer (from Dr. Miles' Nervine Tonic), New School for Social Research, Waldorf Astoria, *New York World Telegram*

1932

Facts and Figures

Economic Profile
  Dow-Jones: ↓ High 88–
    Low 41
  GNP: −23%
  Inflation: −4.7%
  Unemployment: 23.6%
Radios produced: 2,446,000
AM stations: 604
Household telephones: 31%
Toll rate, New York–San
  Francisco: $7.50
Advertising expenditures:
  $1.5 billion
Mattress, box spring: $19.75
Gimbel's glider sofa: $8.94
Macy's coffee table: $9.94
Cut crystal stemware
  (dozen): $3.95
Eight-piece enameled pot set:
  $1
Dental filling: $1
Cigarettes: 15¢
Loft's candy, per pound:
  Chocolates: 49¢
  Chocolate, vanilla kisses,
    peanut brittle: 19¢

Above: Aviatrix Amelia
Earhart. *Library of
Congress.*

Deaths

Aristide Briand, William
  Burns, Hart Crane, George
  Eastman, Alfred Maurer,
  John Philip Sousa, G.
  Lytton Strachey, William
  Wrigley, Jr., Florenz
  Ziegfeld.

In the News

UNEMPLOYMENT REACHES 24% . . . SECRETARY OF STATE HENRY STIMSON SAYS U.S. WILL RECOGNIZE NO TERRITORIAL ACQUISITIONS BY AGGRESSION . . . JAPANESE PROCLAIM NEW STATE IN FORMER MANCHURIA AND ATTACK SHANGHAI . . . RECONSTRUCTION FINANCE CORPORATION LAW IS PASSED TO AID AGRICULTURE AND INDUSTRY . . . AUTO SALES ARE DOWN 80% FROM 1929 . . . GERMANS AGREE TO FINAL REPARATIONS PAYMENT . . . GLASS-STEAGALL BILL INCREASES FEDERAL RESERVE CREDIT . . . ADOLF HITLER GETS 32% OF GERMAN VOTE FOR PRESIDENT . . . NORRIS-LAGUARDIA BILL PROHIBITS EASY INJUNCTIONS AGAINST UNIONS . . . LINDBERGH BABY IS KIDNAPPED, ABDUCTED FROM N.J. HOME . . . LINDBERGH BABY IS FOUND DEAD . . . HOOVER IS RENOMINATED BY GOP, FRANKLIN DELANO ROOSEVELT, N.Y. GOVERNOR, IS NOMINATED BY THE DEMOCRATS ON FOURTH BALLOT . . . FDR TALKS TO THE "FORGOTTEN MAN" . . . SCOTTSBORO BOYS GAIN RETRIAL BASED ON ABSENCE OF COUNSEL . . . EMERGENCY RELIEF CONSTRUCTION ACT IS PASSED . . . HOUSE PASSES BUT SENATE DEFEATS BONUS BILL FOR VETERANS . . . RED CROSS DISTRIBUTES WHEAT GIVEN BY FEDERAL FARM BUREAU . . . AMELIA EARHART IS FIRST WOMAN TO FLY TRANSATLANTIC SOLO . . . NEW YORK MAYOR JIMMY WALKER RESIGNS IN CORRUPTION SCANDAL . . . 12,000 VETERANS PROTEST DEFEAT OF BONUS BILL AND MARCH ON WASHINGTON, D.C. . . . TROOPS UNDER GEN. DOUGLAS MACARTHUR DRIVE OUT BONUS MARCHERS . . . TWO STATES DECLARE MORATORIUM ON FIRST MORTGAGE FORECLOSURES . . . FDR IS ELECTED WITH 22 MILLION VOTES, HOOVER RECEIVES 15 MILLION, SOCIALIST NORMAN THOMAS, 880,000 . . . HITLER REJECTS CHANCELLORSHIP IN COALITION . . . JAPAN IS BRANDED AGGRESSOR IN CHINA BY LEAGUE OF NATIONS.

Quotes

"Brother, Can You Spare a Dime?"
— Gorney and Harburg song

"Men who lost their jobs dropped out of sight. They were quiet, and you had to know just when and where to find them: at night, for instance, on the edge of town huddling for warmth around a bonfire, or even the municipal incinerator; at dawn, picking over the garbage dump for scraps of food or salvageable clothing."
— *Fortune*

"It is obvious that relief is of the scantiest kind and in some districts entirely nonexistent. In one camp the women talked brokenheartedly of a bowel disease which they called 'Flux' that had proved fatal to some of the children and was the result of prolonged underfeeding and efforts to stay the pangs of hunger by devouring chunks of raw cabbage or anything at all which they could lay hands on."
— Jennie Lee, describing a Kentucky mine camp

"Chicago, June 18— . . . A check-up of the city schools revealed today that 11,000 hungry children are being fed by teachers . . . [who themselves] are seriously handicapped by the failure of the Board of Education to pay them."
— Report by the chief of the Children's Bureau, Department of Labor, in the *New York Times*

"[A] descent from respectability . . . must be numbered in the millions. This is what we have accomplished with our bread lines and soup kitchens, . . . defeated, discouraged, hopeless men and women cringing and bowing as they come to ask for public

On President Hoover's orders, General Douglas MacArthur commands his troops and tanks to disperse the Bonus Marchers. *Library of Congress.*

aid. . . . It is a spectacle of national degeneration. That is the fundamental tragedy for America."
— Joseph L. Heffernan, *Atlantic Monthly*

"The breakdown in which we are living is the breakdown of the particular romance known as business, . . . the revelation that the elated excitement of the romantic adventure has to be paid for with an equal depression."
— John Dewey

"Very well, we strike hands with our true comrades, the Communist Party."
— Edmund Wilson

"Ever since I could remember I'd wished I'd been lucky enough to be alive at a great time—when something big was going on, like the crucifixion. And suddenly I realized I was."
— Ben Shahn

"I pledge you, I pledge myself, to a new deal, for the American people. Let us all here assembled constitute ourselves prophets of a new order of competence and courage. This is more than a political campaign; it is a call to arms."
— FDR's acceptance of the presidential nomination

Ads

Radio

Premieres

"Music That Satisfies," Ruth Etting, Boswell Sisters,
 Arthur Tracy ("The Street Singer")
"Kaltenmeyer's Kindergarten," Bruce Kamman
"The George Burns and Gracie Allen Show"
"Just Plain Bill," Arthur Hughes
"Yours for a Song," Jane Froman
"One Man's Family," J. Anthony Smythe
"Clara Lu'n" (first daytime serial)
"Today's Children," Helen Kane
"National Barn Dance"
"The Jack Benny Program," Jack Benny (age 38)
"The Fred Allen Show"
"Tom Mix," Artells Dickson
"The Fire Chief" (Ed Wynn)

Specials

"Tosca" (San Francisco Opera); Floyd Gibbons from
the Manchurian battlefields; the World Disarmament
Conference, Geneva

Of Note

Jack Benny debuts on "The Ed Sullivan Show" •
Hourly bulletins follow the Lindbergh baby
kidnapping • Ed Wynn insists upon a live audience
for his "Fire Chief" program • The first broadcast
from Radio City, November 11, includes a 400-piece
symphony orchestra, Jane Cowl, Jessica Dragonette,
John McCormack, Maria Jeritza, Rudy Vallee, Will
Rogers, "Amos 'n' Andy," Paul Whiteman, and the
Schola Cantorum Choir • Segments on "The Fred
Allen Show" include the Mighty Allen Art Players,
the Average Man's Round Table, and Allen's Alley,
with Senator Claghorn, Titus Moody, and Ajax
Cassidy.

New Catchphrases: "Good evening, Mr. and Mrs.
America, and all the ships at sea" (Walter Winchell);
"Now, cut that out," "Wait a minute," "Anaheim,
Azusa, and Cu-ca-monga" (Jack Benny)

Movies

Openings

Grand Hotel (Edmund Goulding), John Barrymore
 Lionel Barrymore, Wallace Beery, Joan
 Crawford, Greta Garbo
Shanghai Express (Josef von Sternberg), Clive
 Brook, Marlene Dietrich
I Am a Fugitive from a Chain Gang (Mervyn
 LeRoy), Paul Muni
M (Fritz Lang), Peter Lorre
What Price Hollywood? (George Cukor), Constance
 Bennett (original of *A Star Is Born*)
The Sign of the Cross (Cecil B. DeMille), Claudette
 Colbert, Fredric March
Tarzan, the Ape Man (W. S. Van Dyke), Johnny
 Weismuller, Maureen O'Sullivan
A Farewell to Arms (Frank Borzage), Gary Cooper,
 Helen Hayes
Dr. Jekyll and Mr. Hyde (Rouben Mamoulian),
 Fredric March, Miriam Hopkins
Rain (Lewis Milestone), Joan Crawford, Walter
 Huston
Red-Headed Woman (Jack Conway), Jean Harlow,
 Charles Boyer
Blonde Venus (Josef von Sternberg), Marlene
 Dietrich, Cary Grant

Bill of Divorcement (George Cukor), John
 Barrymore, Katharine Hepburn
Trouble in Paradise (Ernst Lubitsch), Miriam
 Hopkins, Herbert Marshall
Mata Hari (George Fitzmaurice), Greta Garbo,
 Ramon Novarro
Scarface (Howard Hawks), Paul Muni, George Raft
Freaks (Tod Browning), Leila Hyams, Olga
 Baclanova

Academy Awards (1931–32)

Best Picture: *Grand Hotel*
Best Director: Frank Borzage (*Bad Girl*)
Best Actress: Helen Hayes (*The Sin of Madelon
 Claudet*)
Best Actor: Wallace Beery (*The Champ*), Fredric
 March (*Dr. Jekyll and Mr. Hyde*)
Special Award: Mickey Mouse

Top Box-Office Stars

Marie Dressler, Janet Gaynor, Joan Crawford,
Charles Farrell, Greta Garbo, Norma Shearer,
Wallace Beery, Clark Gable, Will Rogers, Joe E.
Brown

Popular Music

Composer-performer Duke Ellington.

Hit Songs
"Night and Day"
"April in Paris"
"I'm Getting Sentimental over You"
"In a Shanty in Old Shanty Town"
"Shuffle Off to Buffalo"
"I Told Every Little Star"
"How Deep Is the Ocean?"
"Granada"
"You're an Old Smoothie"
"Forty-Second Street"
"You're Getting to Be a Habit with Me"

Top Records
New Tiger Rag (Louis Armstrong); *Reefer Man* and *The Man from Harlem* (Cab Calloway); *If You Were the Only Girl* (Rudy Vallee); *It Don't Mean a Thing If It Ain't Got That Swing* (Duke Ellington)

Jazz and Big Bands
Louis Armstrong makes his first trip abroad. Fats Waller performs at Adelaide Hall, New York.

New Band: Fats Waller, New York

Theater

Broadway Openings

Plays
Another Language (Rose Franken), Glenn Anders, Margaret Wycherly
Autumn Crocus (C. L. Anthony), Dorothy Gish, Francis Lederer, Patricia Collinge
The Animal Kingdon (Philip Barry), Leslie Howard
The Late Christopher Bean (Sidney Howard), Pauline Lord, Walter Connolly
Criminal at Large (Edgar Wallace), Emlyn Williams, William Harrigan
Dangerous Corner (J. B. Priestley), Jean Dixon, Colin Keith-Johnston
When Ladies Meet (Rachel Crothers), Frieda Inescort, Walter Abel, Spring Byington
Dinner at Eight (George S. Kaufman, Edna Ferber), Ann Andrews, Cesar Romero, Sam Levene
Too True to Be Good (George Bernard Shaw), Beatrice Lillie, Leo G. Carroll
Biography (S. N. Behrman), Ina Claire
Twentieth Century (Ben Hecht, Charles MacArthur), Eugenie Leontovich

Musicals
Earl Carroll's Vanities of 1932 (Harold Arlen, Ted Koehler), Milton Berle, Lillian Roth
Flying Colors (Arthur Schwartz, Howard Dietz), Clifton Webb, Patsy Kelly, Buddy and Velma Ebsen, Imogene Coca, Larry Adler
Gay Divorce (Cole Porter), Fred Astaire, Luella Gear, Claire Luce
Hot-Cha (Ray Henderson, Lew Brown), Lupe Velez, Bert Lahr, Eleanor Powell
Music in the Air (Jerome Kern, Oscar Hammerstein II), Al Shean, Walter Slezak, Katherine Carrington
Take a Chance (Herb Brown, B. G. DeSylva), Ethel Merman, Jack Haley
Face the Music (Irving Berlin, Moss Hart), Andrew Tombes, Mary Boland

Classics and Revivals On and Off Broadway
Liliom (Molnár), Joseph Schildkraut; *Oedipus Rex, The Rising of the Moon* (Lady Gregory), Abbey Players

Regional

Founded: Barter Theatre, Abingdon, Va., by Robert Porterfield

Pulitzer Prize
Of Thee I Sing, George S. Kaufman, Morrie Ryskind, and Ira Gershwin

Classical Music

Compositions
Virgil Thomson, *Americana*
Samuel Barber, Sonata for Violoncello and Piano
Wallingford Riegger, *Dichotomy*
John Alden Carpenter, *Song of Faith*
Roy Harris, *From the Gayety and Sadness of the American Scene,* String Sextet, Fantasy, Chorale for Strings

Important Events
Because of the depression, many events are canceled, numerous musical organizations go bankrupt, and seasons are divided in half; sporadic concerts of the unemployed take place; "monster" concerts are played at the Roxy Theater, New York City; composers organize in protective organizations, such as ASCAP, the American Composers Alliance, and AGMA.

Guest Conductors: Ottorino Respighi and Bruno Walter, the New York Philharmonic

Debut: E. Power Biggs

First Performances
Respighi, conducting, *Maria Egiziaca* (New York); Ernest Bloch, *Helvetia* (Chicago); Arnold Bax, Symphony no. 4 (San Francisco); Aaron Copland, Symphonic Ode (Boston); George Gershwin, playing, *Second Rhapsody* (Boston); John Alden Carpenter, playing, *Patterns* (Boston)

Opera

Metropolitan: Lawrence Tibbett, *Simon Boccanegra* (Giuseppe Verdi, American premiere); Tito Schipa, *L'elisir d'amore, Don Giovanni;* Rose Bampton (debut), *La Gioconda;* Richard Bonelli, *Faust.* Premiere: *Il Signor Bruschino* (Gioacchino Rossini)

San Francisco: Lily Pons, Alfredo Gandolfi, *Tosca* (nationally broadcast); *The Fairy Queen* (Purcell, premiere)

Music Notes
The League of Composers performs Arnold Schoenberg's *Gurrelieder* • Aaron Copland organizes Yaddo (its name derived from a child's pronunciation of *shadow*) and the first Festival of Contemporary American music. Composer-performers include Copland, Piston, Thomson, Ives, Bowles, Bennett, Harris, Chávez, Riegger, Gruenberg, and Blitzstein • Leopold Stokowski publicly asks for compositions for radio performance and receives 400; he performs Powell, Gruenberg, Copland, Bennett, Piston, Cowell, and Cubensky • The Pan American Association of Composers continues to bring American music to European capitals. Most performed are Ives, Ruggles, Riegger, Harris, Crawford, and Cowell.

Ben Shahn, *The Passion of Sacco and Vanzetti,* 1931–32. Tempera. 84½ × 48″. *Collection of Whitney Museum of American Art. Geoffrey Clements.*

Art

Painting
Raphael Soyer, *Mina*

Paul Cadmus, *Sailors and Floosies*

Georgia O'Keeffe, *Cross by the Sea*

Charles Sheeler, *Buck's County Barn, River Rouge Plant*

Grant Wood, *Daughters of the American Revolution*

Ben Shahn, *The Passion of Sacco and Vanzetti*

Clyfford Still, *Spring Landscape*

Peter Blume, *Light of the World*

Arshile Gorky, *Organization*

Reginald Marsh, *Tattoo and Haircut, Locomotive Watering*

Isabel Bishop, *On the Street*

John Marin, *Region of Brooklyn Bridge Fantasy*

John Kane, *From My Studio*

Sculpture
John Storrs, *Composition around Two Voids*

David Smith, *Head, Construction*

Theodore Roszak, *Airport Structure*

Gaston Lachaise, *Standing Woman*

William Zorach, *Torso*

Alexander Calder, *Motorized Mobile, Construction*

Elie Nadelman, *Construction Workers*, at the Fuller Building, New York

Architecture
Philadelphia Savings Fund Society, Philadelphia (Howe and Lescaze)

Travel and Transport Building, Century of Progress Exhibit, Chicago (Joseph Urban)

Pennsylvania Station, Philadelphia (Graham, Anderson, Probst and White)

Nebraska State Capitol Building, Lincoln (Bertram Goodhue)

U.S. Forest Products Laboratory, Madison, Wisc. (Holabird and Root)

Broadacre City model (Frank Lloyd Wright)

Raphael Soyer, *Mina,* 1932. Oil on canvas. 28 × 26³/₁₆". *The Metropolitan Museum of Art, Bequest of Margaret S. Lewisohn, 1954.*

Important Exhibitions

Museums

New York: *Metropolitan:* "Favorite paintings of the Younger Generation: The Taste of Today in Masterpieces before 1900," Leonardo, Rembrandt, and Raphael, among others; the Washington Bicentennial; Costumes, 1750–1850; Samuel French Morse. *Museum of Modern Art:* American folk art, 1750–1900; "Art of the Common Man"; American painting and sculpture, 1862–1932; "Modern Architecture: International Exhibition"

Chicago: Drawings; modern paintings and watercolors; loan exhibit of Islamic bookbindings

Boston: Contemporary art

Pittsburgh: The Carnegie International is canceled because of the depression.

Art Briefs
Mural commissions are given to Diego Rivera, José Orozco, David Alfaro Siqueiros, and Frank Brangwyn for Rockefeller Center; to Dean Cornwall for the Los Angeles Public Library; to Thomas Hart Benton for the Whitney Museum; and to José Sert for the Waldorf Astoria • Max Ernst holds his first American show in New York • Depression arts are displayed in open-air marts, the first held in Washington Square, New York, where 970 of 1,700 works are sold; Chicago, Dallas, Cleveland, and Detroit also sponsor outdoor shows • Dealers hold shows where any painting costs $100 • Duchamp names Calder's mechanized constructions *mobiles.*

Books

Fiction

Critics' Choice

Light in August, William Faulkner
From Flushing to Calvary, Edward Dahlberg
The Unvanquished, Howard Fast
1919, John Dos Passos
The Gods Arrive, Edith Wharton
Year before Last, Kay Boyle
Young Lonigan, James Farrell
Tobacco Road, Erskine Caldwell
⁂ *Brave New World*, Aldous Huxley

Best-Sellers

The Good Earth, Pearl S. Buck
Sons, Pearl S. Buck
The Fountain, Charles Morgan
The Sheltered Life, Ellen Glasgow
Magnolia Street, Louis Golding
Old Wine and New, Warwick Deeping
Mary's Neck, Booth Tarkington
Inheritance, Phyllis Bentley
Magnificent Obsession, Lloyd Douglas
Three Loves, A. J. Cronin

Nonfiction

Critics' Choice

Death in the Afternoon, Ernest Hemingway
The Life of Emerson, Van Wyck Brooks
Mark Twain's America, Bernard De Voto
20,000 Years in Sing Sing, Warden Lewis E. Lawes
I Am a Fugitive from a Georgia Chain Gang, Robert E. Burns
Frank Lloyd Wright's Autobiography, Frank Lloyd Wright
The U.S. in World Affairs, Walter Lippmann
Moral Man and Immoral Society, Reinhold Niebuhr
A New Deal, Stuart Chase
The Age of Technocracy, Howard Scott
On Being Creative, Irving Babbitt
Anthropology and Modern Life, Franz Boaz

Best-Sellers

The Epic of America, James Truslow Adams
Only Yesterday, Frederick Lewis Allen
A Fortune to Share, Vash Young
Culbertson's Summary, Ely Culbertson
Van Loon's Geography, Hendrik Willem Van Loon
What We Live By, Ernest Dimnet
The March of Democracy, James Truslow Adams
Washington Merry-Go-Round, Anonymous (Drew Pearson, Robert S. Allen)
The Story of My Life, Clarence Darrow
More Merry-Go-Round, Anonymous (Drew Pearson, Robert S. Allen)

Poetry

T. S. Eliot, *Sweeney Agonistes*
Eleanor Wylie, *Collected Poems*
Robinson Jeffers, *Thurso's Landing*
Edwin Arlington Robinson, *Nicodemus*
Stephen Vincent Benét, *Rip Tide*
Allen Tate, *Poems 1928–1931*
⁂ W. H. Auden, *The Orators*

Pulitzer Prizes

The Store, T. S. Stribling (novel)
The Significance of Sections in American History, Frederick J. Turner (U.S. history)
Grover Cleveland, Allan Nevins (biography)
Conquistador, Archibald MacLeish (poetry)

Science and Technology

Carl David Anderson discovers the positron, a subatomic particle.
Edwin Land devises the first synthetic sheet light polarizer.
Dr. Arthur Holly Compton concludes that cosmic rays are electrons from the earth's upper atmosphere.
Adrenal cortex stimulating hormone, ACTH, is prepared by James C. Collip.
Dr. William Beebe, in his bathysphere, descends to a record 2,200 feet underwater.
The semiflexible gastroscope is introduced for internal viewing of the stomach.
James Chadwick discovers the neutron.
Ernest O. Lawrence constructs the first practical cyclotron. He splits the atom artificially two to three weeks after John Cockcroft and Ernest Walton in England use a beam of protons to split it; theirs is the first atomic transformation accomplished without a radioactive substance.
⁂ Prontosil, a sulfa red dye, is developed by Gerhard Domagk.
⁂ Albert Butenandt isolates the male sex hormone, testosterone.

Nobel Prizes

Edgar D. Adrian wins the prize in physiology and medicine for work on the function of the neuron.
Irving Langmuir wins in chemistry for research on surface chemistry.

Sports

Baseball

Babe Ruth (New York, AL), after being heckled from the Cubs' dugout, points "to the spot" and hits a home run off Charlie Root (Chicago, NL) in the World Series.

Lou Gehrig (New York, AL) hits four home runs in a nine-inning game.

Champions

Batting	Pitching
Lefty O'Doul (Philadelphia, NL), .368	Lon Warneke (Chicago, NL), 22–6
D. D. Alexander (Detroit-Boston, AL), .367	John Allen (New York, AL), 17–4
	Home runs
	James Foxx (Philadelphia, AL), 58

Football

NFL Season Leaders: Arnie Herber (Green Bay), passing; Bob Campiglio (Stapleton), rushing; Luke Johnsos (Chicago Bears), receiving.

College All-Americans: Harry Newman (Q), Michigan; William Corbus (G), Stanford

Bowls (Jan. 1, 1933)

Rose: Southern California 35–Pittsburgh 0
Orange: Miami 7–Manhattan 0

Basketball

A new college rule requires the ball to be brought over the midcourt line in 10 seconds.

Johnny Wooden, the "Indiana Rubber Man," is All-American, at Purdue, for the third time.

Olympics

The first Winter Games to be held in the United States are at Lake Placid, N.Y. John Shea (500m, 1500m) and Irving Jaffee (5000m, 10,000m) win gold medals in speed skating. In the Summer Games at Los Angeles, U.S. winners include Babe Didrikson (javelin, 143'4", and 80m hurdles, 11.7s), Eddie Tolan (100m, 10.3s and 200m, 21.1s), Edward Gordon (broad jump, 25' 4¾"), William Miller (pole vault, 14' 1⅞"), James Bausch (decathlon), Clarence "Buster" Crabbe (swimming, 400m), Helen Madison (100m and 400m), Eleanor Holm (100m backstroke).

Other Sports

Boxing: Jack Sharkey beats Max Schmeling to regain the heavyweight crown.

Tennis: Helen Wills Moody wins at Wimbledon.

Winners

World Series	Player of the Year
New York (AL) 4	John Wooden, Purdue
Chicago (NL) 0	*Stanley Cup*
MVP	Toronto
NL–Charles Klein, Philadelphia	*U.S. Tennis Open*
AL–James Foxx, Philadelphia	Men: Ellsworth Vines, Jr.
	Women: Helen Hull Jacobs
NFL	*USGA Open*
Chicago Bears	Gene Sarazen
College Football	*Kentucky Derby*
USC	Burgoo King (E. James, jockey)
College Basketball	
Purdue	

Fashion

For Women: With the growing vogue in slinky silks popularized through the movies, undergarments change dramatically. Though still embroidered and generally of one piece—in chemises, camisoles, vests, drawers, and slips—there is a new absence of seams, since they show through the tight or clinging clothing. Heavy corsetry soon appears on the market "to hold up the muscles," and a new interest emerges in the "uplift," provided by darts and hidden circular stitching. Artificial silks and zippers make clothing less expensive. A blue and white plaid rayon dress with sashed belt and bow collar is virtually ubiquitous. Fashionable hats range from the pillbox, toque, trimmed turban, and Basque beret (worn on the side like Dietrich), to summer styles trimmed with flowers, ribbons, and quills.

High-fashion notes: Mainbocher's molded sheath; Chanel's cotton evening dress

For Men: For the first time, wool, not silk, ties appear in solids, foulards, and stripes, or with small (often sports) figures.

Kaleidoscope _____

- Wages drop 60 percent since 1929; white-collar salaries are down 40 percent. Unemployment is over three times that of 1930. The suicide rate rises to 17.4 per 100,000 people, up 30 percent from 1920s levels; homicide levels remain stable.
- The Federal Reserve Board's index of production is down 55 percent from 1929.
- Indigents are barred from voting in Lewiston, Maine; a million nomads wander America with no voting rights in ten other states.
- Wages for picking figs are 10¢ per 50-pound box, $1.50 a day for 15 boxes; for picking peas, 14¢ a pound, $1.25 a day, $30 for the season.
- Twelve-thousand veterans encamp in Washington to demand their World War I bonus (due in 1945); Hoover calls out the army, headed by Douglas MacArthur and junior officers Dwight Eisenhower and George Patton, and the marchers are disbanded with tear gas and force of arms.
- On May 28, the Detroit Welfare Department announces that it owes $800,000 and has on hand only $8,000.
- News columnists assume great popular importance; joining Walter Lippmann are Westbrook Pegler, David Lawrence, Frank Kent, and Dorothy Thompson.
- Enormous public response to the Lindbergh kidnapping includes the AFL's offer of membership assistance and prayer by major religious figures.
- A new crime epidemic begins with Dillinger, "Baby Face" Nelson, "Machine Gun" Kelly, "Pretty Boy" Floyd, "Ma" Barker, and Bonnie and Clyde.
- The FBI publicizes a list of "Public Enemies."
- Sam Insull, the utilities magnate, escapes to Greece when he faces indictment for questionable business practices.
- Ivan Kreuger, the Swedish "match king" industrialist extensively financed by American banks, commits suicide as he faces charges of fraud.
- With depression audiences noticeably decreasing, theaters lower admissions and present low-budget productions.
- Radio City Music Hall, with 6,200 seats, opens, the world's largest movie theater.
- Nude statues by William Zorach, Gwen Lux, and Robert Laurent are barred from Radio City, creating a furor; after the ban is lifted, the situation is questioned as a publicity hoax.
- In Los Angeles, a David Siqueiros mural depicting a peasant's crucifixion under an American eagle is whitewashed.
- Two-a-day vaudeville closes on Broadway.
- In response to "Goodness, what beautiful diamonds!" Mae West, in her movie debut, *Night after Night,* replies, "Goodness had nothing to do with it."
- Ad executive Elmer Zilch is a featured character of *Ballyhoo,* a new satire magazine which soars to 2 million in circulation.
- New foreign actors in Hollywood include George Arliss, David Niven, Charles Laughton, Basil

Economically pressed veterans seek "bonus" payment for past service. *Library of Congress.*

Rathbone, Laurence Olivier, Maurice Chevalier, and Marlene Dietrich.
- Howard Scott gains a wide following with his "technocracy," which proposes the substitution of energy units, like ergs, for dollars and cents.
- The "Great I Am" movement, a mystic faith promising its followers wealth and power, gains 300,000 followers.
- New York physician Thomas Parran's attempt to fight venereal disease leads to the permissible use of the word *syphilis* in newspapers and other public media.
- In response to the depression, Hoover reduces his salary by 20 percent and asks the same of his vice president and nine cabinet members.
- On being questioned about a $26,000 stock gift, New York mayor Jimmy Walker replies that he has "many kind friends."
- Herbert Hoover declares that "grass will grow in the streets of 100 cities" if FDR is elected.
- Franklin Roosevelt breaks tradition and flies to address the Democratic National Convention immediately after he is nominated; "Happy Days Are Here Again" is the party's theme.
- FDR is aided by his brains trust, Columbia University Professors Raymond Moley, Rexford Tugwell, and Adolph Berle, Jr.
- With the recent discovery of the male hormone testosterone, animal gonad transplants provoke a great deal of interest.
- An interest in skiing is stimulated by the Winter Olympics at Lake Placid, N.Y.

Fads: New dances include the jitterbug and swing ("It don't mean a thing if it ain't got that swing," coined by Duke Ellington), the big apple, shag, boogie-woogie, Susie-Q, Lindy hop, and truckin'; Rudy Vallee becomes "the rage"; astrology.

First Appearances: Zippo lighter, Mounds (twin bars), Frito corn chips, Skippy peanut butter, Teachers College (Columbia), Folger Library (Washington), Revlon, Johnson Glo-Coat wax, International Experiment in Living, the name Saudi Arabia *(Hejas Nejd),* tax on gasoline, wooden money (Tacoma, Wash.), Route 66

1933

Facts and Figures

Economic Profile
Dow-Jones: ↑ High 108–
  Low 50
GNP: −4%
Inflation: +1.3%
Unemployment: 24.9%
Daily newspapers: 1,903
Books published: 8,092
Airmail postage: 8¢/oz.
Postcard: 1¢
IRS collections: $1.6 billion
Tuxedo (Saks Fifth Avenue):
  $39.50
Trousers (Brooks Brothers):
  $15–$18
Mark Cross gloves: $2.75
Four-course dinner: 60¢–
  $1.50 (Hotel Taft)
  Breakfast: 25¢
  Lunch: 40¢–50¢
Air fares:
  Chicago to Los Angeles:
    $207 (round trip)
  New York to Chicago:
    $86.31 (round trip)
Around-the-world cruise, 85
  days, 14 countries: $749
Kodak Brownie camera:
  $2.50

Above: FDR, at his
inauguration, asks for "broad
executive powers to wage a
war against the emergency."
Library of Congress.

Deaths

Roscoe "Fatty" Arbuckle,
  Irving Babbitt, Earl Derr
  Biggers, Calvin Coolidge,
  John Galsworthy, Stefan
  George, Ring Lardner,
  George B. Luks, George
  Moore, Frederick Henry
  Royce, Louis Comfort
  Tiffany.

In the News

HITLER BECOMES GERMAN CHANCELLOR . . . U.S. MARINES LEAVE
NICARAGUA . . . GERMAN REICHSTAG BURNS DOWN, HITLER ASSUMES
DICTATORIAL POWERS . . . ROOSEVELT ESCAPES FLORIDA
ASSASSINATION ATTEMPT, CHICAGO MAYOR ANTON CERMAK IS SHOT
TO DEATH . . . MICHIGAN GOVERNOR DECLARES EIGHT-DAY BANK
HOLIDAY . . . N.Y. GOVERNOR DECLARES BANK HOLIDAY . . . FDR
IS INAUGURATED . . . FDR DECLARES NATIONAL BANK HOLIDAY . . .
3.2% BEER AND WINE ARE AUTHORIZED BY CONGRESS . . .
AGRICULTURAL ADJUSTMENT ACT IS PASSED TO RESTORE FARM PRICES
. . . EMERGENCY BANK ACT GIVES PRESIDENT CONTROL OVER
BANKING AND GOLD . . . FEDERAL DOLE BEGINS . . . ECONOMY ACT
REDUCES VETERANS' PAY AND FEDERAL SALARIES . . .
UNEMPLOYMENT RELIEF ACT CREATES CIVILIAN CONSERVATION
CORPS . . . U.S. LEAVES GOLD STANDARD . . . SECURITIES ACT
PROVIDES FOR CAREFUL REGULATION OF NEW SECURITIES . . . BANKS
GIVE UP GOLD, GOLD CLAUSES IN CONTRACTS ARE VOIDED . . .
TENNESSEE VALLEY AUTHORITY BILL IS PASSED ALLOWING
GOVERNMENT TO PRODUCE ELECTRIC POWER . . . OIL IS STRUCK IN
SAUDI ARABIA, SO-CAL OIL GETS CONCESSION . . . U.S.
EMPLOYMENT AGENCY WILL COORDINATE UNEMPLOYMENT
ACTIVITIES . . . JAPAN WITHDRAWS FROM LEAGUE OF NATIONS . . .
NATIONAL INDUSTRIAL RECOVERY ACT PROVIDES CODES OF FAIR
COMPETITION . . . FARM CREDIT ACT WILL CONSOLIDATE RURAL
CREDIT AGENCIES . . . GLASS-STEAGALL BANK REFORM IS PASSED TO
PROTECT DEPOSITS . . . GERMANY WITHDRAWS FROM LEAGUE OF
NATIONS . . . CIVIL WORKS ADMINISTRATION WILL PROVIDE 400,000
EMERGENCY JOBS . . . ANTONIO SALAZAR BECOMES PORTUGUESE
DICTATOR . . . U.S. RESUMES DIPLOMATIC TIES WITH U.S.S.R. . . .
PROHIBITION REPEAL TAKES EFFECT.

Quotes _____

"We are at the end of our string. There is nothing more we can do."
— Herbert Hoover, on the eve of FDR's inauguration

"The only thing we have to fear is fear itself."
— FDR, inauguration speech

"I shall ask the Congress for the remaining instruments to meet the crisis—broad executive power to wage a war against the emergency, as great as the power that would be given me if we were invaded by a foreign foe."
— FDR

"In war in the gloom of night attack, soldiers wear a bright badge on their shoulders to be sure that comrades do not fire on comrades. On that principle, . . . we have provided a badge of honor [the blue eagle]. . . . It is essential to our purpose."
— FDR, fireside chat

"I can assure you that it is safer to keep your money in a reopened bank than under the mattress."
— FDR

"Professors are one of the chief curses of the country. They talk too much. Most professors are a bunch of cowards and meddlers. The sooner we get away from their influence the better."
— Frederick Henry Price, owner of 46 railroads

The blue eagle, emblem of the National Recovery Administration (NRA). *Smithsonian Institution.*

"Surely some professors are meddlers and busybodies, just as some financiers are crooks."
— Dean Ralph Emerson Heilman, Northwestern University

"There is no rule so sure as that one that the same mill that grinds out fortunes above a certain size at the top grinds out paupers at the bottom."
— Huey Long

"I will say one thing for this administration. It is the only time when the fellow with money is worrying more than the one without it."
— Will Rogers

Ads _____

Radio

Radio stars Eddie Cantor, Al Jolson, Gracie Allen, and George Burns, all of whom began in vaudeville. *Movie Star News.*

Premieres

"The Romance of Helen Trent," Virginia Clark
"Jack Armstrong, the All-American Boy," St. John Terrell
"Don McNeill's Breakfast Club"
"The Lone Ranger," George Seaton, John Todd
"Ma Perkins," Virginia Payne
"The Jimmy Durante Show"

Specials

"Eleanor Roosevelt"; "Vatican City" (Pope Pius opens the Holy Door of St. Peter's Basilica); "George Bernard Shaw"

Of Note

Music offerings in a typical week might include the Metropolitan Opera, New York Philharmonic, Boston Symphony, Lily Pons, Lawrence Tibbett, and Josef Hoffmann • Premiums offered for Wheaties' boxtops include Jack Armstrong whistling rings, secret decoders, and Norden "bombsights" • FDR begins his fireside chats • The largest radio audience to date listens to FDR's plans to reopen the national banks • The Federal Radio Commission becomes the FCC.

New Catchphrases: ". . . dedicated to the mothers and fathers of the younger generation and their bewildering offspring" ("One Man's Family"); ". . . [the story of a woman] who sets out to prove . . . romance can live . . . at thirty-five" ("The Romance of Helen Trent"); "Be good to yourself!" ("Breakfast Club")

Movies

Openings

Cavalcade (Frank Lloyd), Diana Wynward, Clive Brook
Forty-second Street (Lloyd Bacon), Ruby Keeler, Dick Powell, Ginger Rogers, Bebe Daniels
The Private Life of Henry VIII (Alexander Korda), Charles Laughton, Elsa Lanchester
She Done Him Wrong (Lowell Sherman), Mae West, Cary Grant, Gilbert Roland
State Fair (Henry King), Janet Gaynor, Will Rogers, Lew Ayres
Dinner at Eight (George Cukor), John Barrymore, Lionel Barrymore, Marie Dressler, Jean Harlow
Little Women (George Cukor), Katharine Hepburn, Joan Bennett
The Invisible Man (James Whale), Claude Rains, Henry Travers
Gold Diggers of 1933 (Mervyn LeRoy), Dick Powell, Ruby Keeler, Joan Blondell, Aline MacMahon
Queen Christina (Rouben Mamoulian), Greta Garbo, John Gilbert
King Kong (Merian C. Cooper, Ernest Schoedsack), Fay Wray, Bruce Cabot
Flying Down to Rio (Thornton Freeland), Fred Astaire, Ginger Rogers, Dolores del Rio
Rasputin and the Empress (Richard Boleslawski), John Barrymore, Ethel Barrymore, Lionel Barrymore (only time all together on the screen)
Design for Living (Ernst Lubitsch), Gary Cooper, Fredric March, Miriam Hopkins
Duck Soup (Leo McCarey), Marx Brothers
Footlight Parade (Lloyd Bacon), James Cagney, Joan Blondell, Dick Powell, Ruby Keeler
Morning Glory (Lowell Sherman), Katharine Hepburn, Douglas Fairbanks, Sr.
Thunder over Mexico (Sergei Eisenstein, not completed)

Academy Awards

Best Picture: *Cavalcade*
Best Director: Frank Lloyd *(Cavalcade)*
Best Actress: Katharine Hepburn *(Morning Glory)*
Best Actor: Charles Laughton *(The Private Life of Henry VIII)*

Top Box-Office Stars

Marie Dressler, Will Rogers, Janet Gaynor, Eddie Cantor, Wallace Beery, Jean Harlow, Clark Gable, Mae West, Norma Shearer, Joan Crawford

Popular Music

Hit Songs
"It's Only a Paper Moon"
"Smoke Gets in Your Eyes"
"Lazy Bones"
"Easter Parade"
"Who's Afraid of the Big Bad
   Wolf?"
"Everything I Have Is Yours"
"Inka Dinka Doo"
"Lover"
"Let's Fall in Love"
"Temptation"

Top Records
Stormy Weather (Ethel Waters); *I
Cover the Waterfront* (Eddy
Duchin); *Forty-second Street* (Hal
Kemp); *Gold Diggers' Song* (Dick
Powell); *Honeymoon Hotel*
(Freddy Martin); *Heartaches* (Ted
Weems, with Elmo Tanner
whistling); *Sophisticated Lady*
(Duke Ellington)

Jazz and Big Bands
Duke Ellington and his band visit
Europe. Charlie Barnet plays at
the Paramount Grill, New York.

First Recordings: Billie Holiday,
with Benny Goodman

New Band: Nemmu Carter (and
Teddy Wilson)

Theater

Broadway Openings

Plays
Ah, Wilderness! (Eugene O'Neill), George M. Cohan,
   Gene Lockhart, Walter Vonnegut, Jr.
Tobacco Road (Jack Kirkland), Henry Hull,
   Margaret Wycherly, Dean Jagger
Both Your Houses (Maxwell Anderson), Walter C.
   Kelly, Sheppard Strudwick, Mary Philips
Men in White (Sidney S. Kingsley), Alexander
   Kirkland
Design for Living (Noel Coward), Alfred Lunt, Lynn
   Fontanne, Noel Coward
Alien Corn (Sidney Howard), Katharine Cornell,
   Luther Adler, James Rennie
The Lake (Dorothy Massingham, Murray
   MacDonald), Katharine Hepburn
Jezebel (Owen Davis), Miriam Hopkins, Joseph
   Cotten
The Green Bay Tree (Mordaunt Shairp), Laurence
   Olivier
Mary of Scotland (Maxwell Anderson), Helen Hayes

Musicals
As Thousands Cheer (Irving Berlin), Marilyn Miller,
   Clifton Webb, Ethel Waters
Champagne, Sec (Johann Strauss, Robert Simon),
   George Meader, Helen Ford, Peggy Wood, Kitty
   Carlisle
Let 'Em Eat Cake (George Gershwin, Ira Gershwin),
   William Gaxton, Victor Moore, Lois Moran
Murder at the Vanities (Herman Hupfield et al.),
   James Rennie, Bela Lugosi, Olga Baclanova
Roberta (Jerome Kern, Otto Harbach), Tamara, Ray
   Middleton, Bob Hope, Sydney Greenstreet, Fred
   MacMurray

The Golddiggers of 1933. Busby Berkeley's extravagant
dance routines revolutionize the film musical. *Movie Star
News.*

Strike Me Pink (Ray Henderson, Lew Brown),
   Jimmy Durante, Lupe Velez, Hope Williams

Classics and Revivals On and Off Broadway
Romeo and Juliet, Eva Le Gallienne; *The Cherry
Orchard* (Chekhov), Nazimova, Eva Le Gallienne

Pulitzer Prize
Both Your Houses, Maxwell Anderson

Classical Music _____

Compositions
Roy Harris, Symphony no. 1, String Quartet no. 2
Walter Piston, Concerto for Orchestra, String
    Quartet no. 1
Howard Hanson, *Merry Mount*
Samuel Barber, *Music for a Scene from Shelley*
Aaron Copland, Short Symphony no. 2
John Cage, Sonata for Clarinet
Frank S. Converse, *American Sketches*
Henry Cowell, *Irish Suite*

Important Events
After Goebbels cancels Bruno Walter and forbids
Negro jazz, Jewish music, and Jewish musicians,
American musicians mail protest cables to Hitler.
Arnold Schoenberg, Walter, and Otto Klemperer
arrive in the United States. Nationalism increases
throughout the musical world. Societies of American
musicians form, and American music is performed
everywhere with a program that includes, typically,
Harris, Wallingford Riegger, Adolph Weiss, Edgard
Varèse, Piston, and Robert Russell Bennett.

New Appointment: Otto Klemperer becomes
conductor of the Los Angeles Philharmonic.

Debut: Rudolf Serkin

First Performances
Varèse, *Ionization* (New York); Leoš Janáček, *Taras
Bulba* (New York); William Walton, *Belshazzar's
Feast* (Boston); Werner Josten, *Concerto Sacro no. 1*
(Philadelphia); John Alden Carpenter, *Sea-Drift*
(Chicago); Rudolf Ganz, *Animal Pictures* (Chicago)

Opera
Metropolitan: Lawrence Tibbett, *The Emperor
Jones* (Louis Gruenberg, premiere); Frida Leider,
Tristan und Isolde; Richard Crooks, *Manon Lescaut;*
farewell: Antonio Scotti, *L'oracolo*

Chicago: Rosa Raisa, *Turandot*

Central City, Colo.: Gladys Swarthout, *The Merry
Widow*

Music Notes
Yehudi Menuhin, 15, tours.

Benny Goodman. *Movie Star News.*

Mae West in *I'm No Angel. Movie Star News.*

Art

Painting

Edward Hopper, *Cottages at Wellfleet*

William Gropper, *Farmers' Revolt*

Reginald Marsh, *The Park Bench, Belmont Hotel*

Niles Spencer, *Near Avenue A*

Florine Stettheimer, *Family Portrait*

Morris Kantor, *Skyrocket*

Thomas Hart Benton, *Civil War, Industry, and Agriculture*

John Steuart Curry, *Kansas Cornfield*

Sculpture

Gaston Lachaise, *Knees, The Conquest of Time and Space, Knowledge Combating Ignorance*

Paul Manship, Rainey Memorial Gate, New York Zoological Society

David Smith, *Chain Head*

John B. Flannagan, *Figure of Dignity—Irish Mountain Goat*

Malvina Hoffman's bronzes are placed in the Museum of Natural History, Chicago.

Architecture

Union Terminal, Cincinnati (Fellheimer and Wagner)

Oakland Bay Bridge, San Francisco (Pfleuger, Brown, and Donovan)

Seattle Art Museum (Bebb and Gould)

William Rockhill Nelson Gallery, Kansas City, Mo. (Wight and Kech)

Plans are completed for the U.S. Post Office and Court House, Philadelphia (Sternfeld).

Important Exhibitions

Museums

New York: *Metropolitan:* Plant forms in ornament; Islamic paintings and book illuminations; American japanned furniture. *Museum of Modern Art:* Sources of modern art; Edward Hopper; Maurice Sterne; photographs by Walker Evans. *Whitney:* Thomas Eakins

Pittsburgh: Carnegie Institute prizes: André Dunoyer, John Steuart Curry

Washington: Negro art

Chicago: *World's Fair:* "A Century of Progress," organized by the Art Institute, which simultaneously presents "Recent Art"

Portland: Mark Rothko

Philadelphia: European and American sculpture

Art Briefs

Salvador Dali has his first American one-man show in New York • José Orozco paints the largest mural to date, 3,000 square feet, at Dartmouth College • Ben Shahn joins the Diego Rivera group of artists working on the Rockefeller Center murals • Henri Cartier-Bresson has his first photo exhibit in New York.

Dance

Dancers in Colonel de Basil's Ballet Russe de Monte Carlo visit the United States and include teenagers Irina Baronova, Tamara Toumanova, and Tatiana Riabouchinska; choreographers include Léonide Massine, George Balanchine, and Mikhail Fokine. Balletomane Lincoln Kirstein meets ex-Diaghilev choreographer George Balanchine in Paris and invites him to New York.

The San Francisco Ballet is founded with Adolph Bolm as chief choreographer.

Prof. Albert Einstein, "the father of the theory of relativity," and Mrs. Einstein remain in the limelight. *Library of Congress.*

Books

Fiction

Critics' Choice

Miss Lonelyhearts, Nathanael West
God's Little Acre, Erskine Caldwell
Presenting Lily Mars, Booth Tarkington
The Disinherited, Jack Conroy
In Tragic Life, Vardis Fisher
Winner Take Nothing, Ernest Hemingway
To a God Unknown, John Steinbeck
&⋅ *Man's Fate*, André Malraux

Best-Sellers

Anthony Adverse, Hervey Allen
As the Earth Turns, Gladys Hasty Carroll
Ann Vickers, Sinclair Lewis
Magnificent Obsession, Lloyd C. Douglas
One More River, John Galsworthy
Forgive Us Our Trespasses, Lloyd C. Douglas
The Master of Jalna, Mazo de la Roche
Miss Bishop, Bess Streeter Aldrich
The Farm, Louis Bromfield
Litle Man, What Now? Hans Fallada

Nonfiction

Critics' Choice

The Autobiography of Alice B. Toklas, Gertrude Stein
Mellon's Millions, Harvey O'Conner
Along This Way, James Weldon Johnson
The Brown Book of the Hitler Terror
Industrial Discipline, Rexford G. Tugwell
Principles of Harmonic Analysis, Walter Piston
Alice through the Cellophane, E. B. White
My Life and Hard Times, James Thurber
The Great Tradition, Granville Hicks
The Use of Poetry and the Use of Criticism, T. S. Eliot
Seeds of Revolt, Mauritz A. Hallgren
&⋅ *The Expanding Universe*, A. S. Eddington

Best-Sellers

Life Begins at Forty, Walter B. Pitkin
Marie Antoinette, Stefan Zweig
British Agent, R. H. Bruce Lockhart
100,000,000 Guinea Pigs, Arthur Kellet, F. J. Schlink
The House of Exile, Nora Waln
Van Loon's Geography, Hendrik Willem Van Loon
Looking Forward, Franklin D. Roosevelt
The March of Democracy, vol. 2, James Truslow Adams
Contract Bridge Blue Book of 1933, Ely Culbertson
The Arches of the Years, Halliday Sutherland

Poetry

Edwin Arlington Robinson, *Talifer*
Robinson Jeffers, *Give Your Heart to the Hawks*
Archibald MacLeish, *Frescoes for Mr. Rockefeller's City*
Sara Teasdale, *Last Poems*
Hart Crane, *Collected Poems*

Pulitzer Prizes

Lamb in His Bosom, Caroline Miller (novel)
The People's Choice, Herbert Agar (U.S. history)
John Hay, Tyler Dennett (biography)
Selected Verse, Robert Hillyer (poetry)

Science and Technology

Frequency modulation (FM) radio transmission is devised by Edwin Armstrong.

A. A. Michelson's work on the speed of light is completed posthumously by his coworkers; their finding is that light travels 186,264 miles per second.

Biochemist Roger J. Williams isolates pantothenic acid, an antiberiberi substance.

Theophilus S. Painter describes a new method of mapping out details of chromosome structure.

Maud Sly's research on rats indicates a genetic predisposition to cancer.

The use of electric shock to the heart to reverse potentially fatal ventricular fibrillation is developed by William Kouwenhoven and O. R. Langeworthy.

H. Trendley Dean begins studies relating fluoride and tooth decay.

Vitamin D-fortified milk is marketed.

The Douglas DC-1, which carries 12 passengers and travels 150 m.p.h., is introduced.

&⋅ The structure of vitamin C is determined by Albert Szent-Györgyi to be ascorbic acid.

Nobel Prize

Thomas H. Morgan wins the prize in physiology and medicine for work on the hereditary function of chromosomes.

Sports

Baseball

The first All-Star game is played in Comiskey Park, Chicago: AL 4–NL 2; Babe Ruth hits a home run.

Champions

Batting
- Chuck Klein (Philadelphia, NL), .368
- James Foxx (Philadelphia, AL), .356

Pitching
- Lyle Tinning (Chicago, NL), 13–6
- Lefty Grove (Philadelphia, AL), 24–8

Home runs
- James Foxx (Philadelphia, AL), 48

Football

The first NFL championship game is played at Chicago: Chicago (Bears) 23–New York 21.
NFL franchises cost $10,000.
The Philadelphia Eagles, owned by Bert Bell, and the Pittsburgh Steelers, owned by Art Rooney, enter the NFL.
Goal posts in the pros are moved to the goal line.

NFL Season Leaders: Harry Newman (New York), passing; Cliff Battles (Boston), rushing; John Kelley (Brooklyn), receiving

College All-Americans: Beattie Feathers (B), Tennessee; Cotton Warburton (Q), USC.

Bowls (Jan. 1, 1934)

Rose: Columbia 7–Stanford 0
Orange: Duquesne 33–Miami 7

Basketball

The New York Renaissance (Rens), a black team, defeats the Celtics, 7–1, in a series. Rens' stars are Pappy Ricks, Fats Jenkins, Bruiser Saitch, Tarzan Cooper. Admission to the series is $1.
The ABL reopens, consisting of eastern teams within short distances of each other.

Other Sports

Boxing: Primo Carnera, "the Italian Alp," 6'7", KO's Jack Sharkey in the sixth for the heavyweight title.

Tennis: Helen Wills Moody wins her second straight Wimbledon title, her sixth Wimbledon to date.

Winners

World Series
- New York (NL) 4
- Washington (AL) 1

MVP
- NL–Carl Hubbell, New York
- AL–James Foxx, Philadelphia

NFL
- Chicago (Bears) 23
- New York 21

College Football
- USC

College Basketball
- Kentucky

Player of the Year
- Forest Sale, Kentucky

Stanley Cup
- New York Rangers

U.S. Tennis Open
- Men: Fred Perry
- Women: Helen Hull Jacobs

USGA Open
- Johnny Goodman

Kentucky Derby
- Broker's Tip (D. Meade, jockey)

Fashion

For Women: The stylish V shape, from wide shoulders to a small waist and flared skirt, places a new emphasis on corsetry—the two-way stretch and the new, all-in-one, full-length corset with Lastex bra and six suspenders to hold stockings. Bolero jackets and puff sleeves are also fashion news, as are short, fitted sweaters (sometimes in stripes) and buttons decorating pockets and belts. In the evening, necklines are frequently high in the front, and backs are bare; large brimmed hats reinforce the long, statuesque look. Women follow both Garbo in the new "man's" evening suit and Crawford in their makeup—bright lips, eye shadow, and artificial eyelashes (applied only in beauty salons; time: two hours).

High-fashion notes: Chanel's satin suit, Schiaparelli's exotic buttons; hair dusted with phosphorescent powder in bright colors; an evening shell-pink satin blouse wrapped and tied around a high-waisted black satin skirt (Lanvin).

Kaleidoscope ———————

- Unemployment reaches 15 million, five times that in 1931. The marriage rate is down 40 percent from 1920s levels.
- During the week FDR declares that all banks must remain closed, the nation functions without readily available cash.
- *Esquire,* the first magazine for men, begins publication; it features women in scanty dress.
- Mae West's profile: she is from Brooklyn, N.Y., seldom drinks, smokes denicotinized cigarettes and is 5'5", 120 pounds, 36–26–36; she likes diamonds, rare beefsteaks, and racehorses, and develops her body by lifting weights. The Central Association for Obstetricians and Gynecologists in Milwaukee congratulates her for popularizing the plump figure, "a boon to motherhood."
- Jack Benny becomes a radio sensation as a perpetual 39-year-old miser who owns an old Maxwell and keeps his money in a basement vault. His audience laughs longer than any in radio history when he replies to a gangster's "Your money or your life" with "I'm thinking it over."
- Movie star Baby LeRoy, 19 months old, works two hours a day in seven-minute periods; he especially likes baked potatoes, spinach, zweibach, and butter.
- Paul Getty earns $1,000 his first year in the oil business.
- The reputation of business falls with revelations such as First National City bank chairman Charles Mitchell's admission that he sold stocks at a loss to his family to cut his taxes and then bought them back the next year.
- The Federal Bureau of Investigation is expanded to become a "national Scotland Yard" in response to the "public enemies" threatening the nation.
- A survey estimates that illness is 40 percent higher among the jobless.
- To help raise farm prices by cutting supply, 6 million young pigs are killed and thousands of acres of cotton are plowed under.
- As part of the bargaining for American diplomatic recognition, Russia informally agrees not to interfere in American politics.
- "Don't shoot, G-Men," cries "Machine Gun" Kelly, who gives the FBI agents their nickname.
- A kidnapping wave strikes the United States; when two confessed kidnappers are lynched in San Francisco, California governor James Rolph praises the action as "the best lesson California ever had"; *rolphing* becomes a synonym for *lynching.*
- Diego Rivera is dismissed from the Rockefeller Center murals project when he refuses to erase a small head of Lenin; the mural is destroyed.
- Major attention is given Grant Wood's *American Gothic* at the Chicago World's Fair.
- In Judge Woolsey's opinion in favor of James Joyce's *Ulysses,* Woolsey comments: "[It is] in many places . . . emetic . . . nowhere aphrodisic."
- Frances Perkins becomes the first female cabinet

The end of prohibition, like its beginning 13 years ago, is widely celebrated. General Research Division. *The New York Public Library. Astor, Lenox and Tilden Foundations.*

member when FDR appoints her secretary of labor.
- Sally Rand is the star of the Chicago World's Fair in her fan dance with ostrich feathers.
- Mussolini sends 25 seaplanes to the Century of Progress Exposition at the fair.
- Calvin Coolidge leaves a $400,000 estate to his wife in a hand-written, 75-word will.
- The Federal Emergency Relief Administration (FERA) is set up under Harry Hopkins to distribute relief funds; Hopkins favors paid public work over a dole.
- The Public Works Administration (PWA), under Harold Ickes, utilizes private contractors for major public works, such as dams and bridges.
- The Civil Works Administration (CWA) authorizes employment for civic purposes, such as building and maintaining parks, roads, and schoolhouses.
- The National Industrial Recovery Act (NIRA) enables industry to regulate prices in return for guarantees on wages and hours; Section 7A affirms the right to collective bargaining.
- Eight states remain dry despite the repeal of Prohibition; all are southern except North Dakota and Kansas; 50 to 60 percent of the liquor consumed is still bootleg because it is readily available and less expensive.
- "The smallest woman in the world wants to meet the richest man in the world," says a circus midget, who sits in J. P. Morgan's lap during Senate hearings on banking practices.

First Appearances: Lame duck constitutional amendment, Sunsweet prune juice, Tree-sweet canned orange juice, blood banks, Sanka, Food-Fair margarine made from soybeans, Campbell's cream of mushroom and chicken noodle soup, Ritz crackers, "Liederkranz" cheese, mandatory death penalty for kidnapping (Kansas City, Mo.), drive-in (Camden, N.J.), Dy-Dee-Doll, Dreft, Windex, White House swimming pool, singing telegram, patent for invisible glass, walkie-talkies, *Newsweek, Catholic Worker,* "Smilin' Jack," Sheraton Corporation, Perry Mason (Erle Stanley Gardner)

1934

Facts and Figures

Economic Profile
  Dow-Jones:—High 110–
    Low 85
  GNP: +17%
  Inflation: 4.5%
  Unemployment: 21.7%
Expenditures:
  Recreation: $2.4 billion
  Spectator sports: $65
    million
  European travel: $1.78
    million
Golf courses: 343
Bowlers: 168,000
Original, signed etchings
  (including Curry, Hoffman,
  Ryder): $5
Elgin 17-jewel watch: $35
Barbizon Plaza Hotel, New
  York (1–2 rooms): $68 per
  month
Dinner:
  75¢ (Rosoff's, New York)
  $1.50 (Cavanaugh's)
Met opera (Saturday
  evening): $1.50–$4
Movie: 35¢–50¢
Madison Square Garden
  rodeo: $1
Fifty tulip bulbs: $2.19; ten
  daffodils: 79¢

Deaths

Marie Curie, Frederick
  Delius, Marie Dressler,
  Edward Elgar, Roger Fry,
  Cass Gilbert, Gustav
  Holst, Arthur Wing Pinero,
  Raymond Poincaré.

In the News

STORM TROOPER ERNST ROEHM AND 77 FOLLOWERS ARE KILLED BY HITLER . . . GOLD RESERVE ACT SETS VALUE OF GOLD TO DOLLAR . . . CIVIL WORKS EMERGENCY RELIEF AUTHORIZES $950 MILLION FOR WORK AND DIRECT RELIEF . . . RIOTS OCCUR IN FRANCE OVER STAVISKY STOCK FRAUD . . . CROP LOAN ACT WILL AID 4.7 MILLION ON RELIEF . . . COTTON CONTROL ACT PASSES . . . BONNIE PARKER AND CLYDE BARROW ARE GUNNED DOWN IN POLICE AMBUSH IN TEXAS . . . SUGAR IMPORT QUOTA ACT IS PASSED . . . DUST STORMS DENUDE LARGE PORTIONS OF MIDWEST . . . AUSTRIAN CHIEF DOLLFUSS IS ASSASSINATED BY LOCAL NAZIS . . . SECURITIES EXCHANGE COMMISSION IS ESTABLISHED . . . NATIONAL LABOR RELATIONS BOARD IS CREATED . . . CHINESE COMMUNISTS UNDER MAO TSE-TUNG BEGIN LONG RETREAT . . . PRESIDENT IS AUTHORIZED TO NATIONALIZE SILVER . . . FEDERAL COMMUNICATIONS COMMISSION IS CREATED . . . FRAZIER-LEMKE FARM BANKRUPTCY ACT RELIEVES FORECLOSURES . . . G-MEN KILL JOHN DILLINGER OUTSIDE CHICAGO THEATER . . . TAYLOR GRAZING ACT ENSURES SOIL CARE . . . RECIPROCAL TRADE ACT GIVES PRESIDENT SWEEPING POWER OVER TARIFFS . . . BRUNO HAUPTMANN IS ARRESTED FOR LINDBERGH KIDNAPPING . . . MIRONOVICH KIROV, STALIN ASSOCIATE, IS ASSASSINATED IN LENINGRAD . . . RUSSIA ENTERS LEAGUE OF NATIONS . . . JAPAN RENOUNCES WASHINGTON AND LONDON NAVAL LIMITATION TREATIES . . . FIRE ON CRUISE BOAT "MORRO CASTLE" OFF N.J. KILLS 130 . . . FIRST GENERAL STRIKE IN U.S. SLOWS SAN FRANCISCO . . . ITALY AND ETHIOPIA CLASH AT SOMALI BORDER.

Political cartoon. *Library of Congress.*

"The present depression is one of abundance, not of scarcity. . . . The cause of the trouble is that a small class has the wealth, while the rest have the debts. . . . The remedy is to give the workers access to the means of production, and let them produce for themselves, not for others, . . . the American way."
— Upton Sinclair, "The Epic Plan for California," *Nation*

Quotes

"She was sitting on the stoop. When I walked by, she crossed her legs showing her thighs and winked. I walked over to her. She said: 'How about it, hon?' I said: 'Christ, kid, if I had any dough I'd rather eat.'"
— M. Shulimson, quoted in Albert Maltz, *New Masses*

"I am ready to concede that the capitalistic system is not fool-proof."
— John W. Davis of the Liberty League

"Puzzler: The average cost of a new automobile—$600—is almost as much as the average income."
— *Life*

"President Roosevelt is getting more like Huey P. Long every day."
— Huey P. Long

"I'm just dumb enough not to want to be a Tarzan all my life."
— Johnny Weismuller

"Everybody has a chance to become President of the United States. I'll sell mine for a quarter."
— Lawrence Lee

Ads

Fashion model.

Radio

Premieres
"Bob Becker: Talk about Paintings"
"Kraft Music Hall," Bing Crosby (host)
"The Bob Hope Show"
"Hollywood Hotel," Dick Powell, Louella Parsons (hosts)
"The Palmolive Beauty Box Theatre," Jessica Dragonette, Fannie Brice ("Baby Snooks")
"Heart Throbs of the Hills" (Mary Pickford drama)
"Major Bowes and His Original Amateur Hour"

Of Note
Popular comedian Joe Penner's "Wanna buy a duck?" and "You *nasty* man" become part of American lingo.

New Catchphrases: "The wheel of fortune goes 'round and 'round and where she stops nobody knows" ("Major Bowes"); "Who's Yehoodi?" "Greetings, Gate!" "Put something in the pot, boy" ("The Bob Hope Show," with Jerry Colonna)

Gossip columnist Louella Parsons and Dick Powell, hosts of "Hollywood Hotel," which features movie stars in radio dramas. *Movie Star News.*

Movies

Openings
It Happened One Night (Frank Capra), Claudette Colbert, Clark Gable
The Thin Man (W. S. Van Dyke), William Powell, Myrna Loy
Twentieth Century (Howard Hawks), John Barrymore, Carole Lombard
The Gay Divorcée (Mark Sandrich), Ginger Rogers, Fred Astaire
The House of Rothschild (Alfred L. Werker), George Arliss, Loretta Young
Imitation of Life (John M. Stahl), Claudette Colbert, Warren William
One Night of Love (Victor Shertzinger), Grace Moore, Tullio Carminati
Viva Villa! (Jack Conway, Howard Hawks), Wallace Beery, Stuart Erwin
The Lost Patrol (John Ford), Victor McLaglen, Boris Karloff
Of Human Bondage (John Cromwell), Leslie Howard, Bette Davis
Man of Aran (Robert Flaherty), Colman King (documentary)
The Scarlet Pimpernel (Harold Young), Leslie Howard, Merle Oberon
The Count of Monte Cristo (Rowland V. Lee), Robert Donat, Elissa Landi
Cleopatra (Cecil B. DeMille), Claudette Colbert, Henry Wilcox
Stand Up and Cheer (Hamilton MacFadden), Shirley Temple, 6, Warner Baxter
It's a Gift (Norman Z. McLeod), W. C. Fields
The Scarlet Empress (Josef von Sternberg), Marlene Dietrich, John Lodge (later governor of Connecticut)
Treasure Island (Victor Fleming), Wallace Beery, Freddie Bartholomew

Academy Awards
Best Picture: *It Happened One Night*
Best Director: Frank Capra (*It Happened One Night*)
Best Actress: Claudette Colbert (*It Happened One Night*)
Best Actor: Clark Gable (*It Happened One Night*)

Top Box-Office Stars
Will Rogers, Clark Gable, Janet Gaynor, Wallace Beery, Mae West, Joan Crawford, Bing Crosby, Shirley Temple, Marie Dressler, Norma Shearer

Popular Music

Hit Songs
"Blue Moon"
"Anything Goes"
"Blow, Gabriel, Blow"
"I Only Have Eyes for You"
"Cocktails for Two"
"The Continental"
"What a Diff'rence a Day Made"
"Tumbling Tumbleweeds"
"On the Good Ship Lollipop"
"You and the Night and the Music"
"You're the Top"
"I Get a Kick out of You"
"Isle of Capri"
"The Very Thought of You"

Top Records
Honeysuckle Rose (Dorsey Brothers); *Moonglow* (Duke Ellington, Benny Goodman); *Limehouse Blues* (Fletcher Henderson); *Sweet Georgia Brown* (Earl Hines); *Stars Fell on Alabama* (Jack Teagarden); *Down Yonder* (Gil Tanner); *The Darktown Strutter's Ball* (Luis Russell); *Let's Fall in Love* (Eddy Duchin)

Jazz and Big Bands
Benny Goodman, 24, brings swing to big audiences on his National Biscuit radio series, "Let's Dance." His band includes Bunny Berigan, Jess Stacy, and Gene Krupa, with arrangements by Fletcher Henderson. *Downbeat* is founded.

First Recordings: Jimmy Lunceford

New Band: Dorsey Brothers

Theater

Broadway Openings

Plays
The Children's Hour (Lillian Hellman), Ann Revere, Katherine Emery
No More Ladies (A. E. Thomas), Melvyn Douglas, Lucile Watson, Ruth Weston
Dodsworth (Sidney Howard), Walter Huston, Fay Bainter
The Distaff Side (John Van Druten), Sybil Thorndike, Estelle Winwood
Personal Appearance (Lawrence Riley), Gladys George
Accent on Youth (Samson Raphaelson), Constance Cummings, Irene Purcell
They Shall Not Die (John Wexley), Ruth Gordon, Claude Rains
The Shining Hour (Keith Winter), Raymond Massey, Gladys Cooper
The Wind and the Rain (Merton Hodge), Mildred Natwick, Frank Lawton
The Farmer Takes a Wife (Frank B. Elser, Marc Connelly), Henry Fonda, June Walker
Dark Victory (George Brewer, Bertram Bloch), Tallulah Bankhead
Divided by Three (Margaret Leech, Beatrice Kaufman), Judith Anderson, James Stewart, Hedda Hopper
The Bride of Torozko (Otto Indig), Jean Arthur, Van Heflin
Within the Gates (Sean O'Casey), Moffat Johnston
Days without End (Eugene O'Neill), Earle Larrimore, Stanley Ridges
Yellow Jack (Sidney Howard), Robert Shayne, Geoffrey Kerr

Musicals
Anything Goes (Cole Porter), Ethel Merman, William Gaxton, Victor Moore
The Great Waltz (Johann Strauss, Sr. and Jr., Desmond Carter), Guy Robertson, Marian Clare
Life Begins at 8:40 (Harold Arlen, Ira Gershwin), Bert Lahr, Ray Bolger, Brian Donlevy
New Faces of 1934 (Warburton Guilbert, Viola Shore), Hildegarde Halliday, Henry Fonda, Imogene Coca
Revenge with Music (Arthur Schwartz, Howard Dietz), Libby Holman, Georges Metaxa, Charles Winninger
Ziegfeld Follies of 1934 (Vernon Duke et al., E. Y. Yarburg), Fannie Brice, Willie Howard, Eugene Howard, Eve Arden, Jane Froman

Classics and Revivals On and Off Broadway
Romeo and Juliet, Katharine Cornell, Basil Rathbone, Brian Aherne, Edith Evans; *L'Aiglon* (Clemence Dane, Rostand), Eva Le Gallienne, Ethel Barrymore; *The Plough and the Stars* (Sean O'Casey), Barry Fitzgerald and *Playboy of the Western World* (O'Casey), Abbey Players

Pulitzer Prize
Men in White, Sidney Kingsley

Classical Music

Compositions
Henry Cowell, *Four Continuations*
George Antheil, Symphony no. 3
Roy Harris, Symphony no. 2
Walter Piston, Prelude and Fugue
Ernest Bloch, *A Voice in the Wilderness*
William Schuman, *Choreographic Poem*
John Cage, Six Short Inventions for Seven
    Instruments
Arnold Schoenberg (in America), Suite in G for
    Strings

Important Events
Arnold Schoenberg makes his first appearance as a
conductor, with the Boston Symphony Orchestra, in
a concert of his early works.

Debut: Eugene List, Oscar Shumsky, Beveridge
Webster

First Performances
Rachmaninoff, playing, *Rhapsody on a Theme by
Paganini* (Philadelphia); Piston, Concerto for
Orchestra (Boston); Harris, Symphony no. 5
(Boston); Louis Gruenberg, Symphony no. 1
(Boston); Ernest Toch, *Big Ben* (Boston); Edgard
Varèse, *Ecuatorial* (New York)

Clark Gable, "the King," and Claudette Colbert in *It
Happened One Night*. Gable, at odds with MGM, was
"demoted" to Columbia for this film, which won five major
Academy Awards. *Movie Star News*.

Leading lady of the American stage Katharine Cornell and
Basil Rathbone in *Romeo and Juliet*. Billy Rose Theatre
Collection. The New York Public Library at Lincoln Center.
Astor, Lenox and Tilden Foundations.

Opera

Metropolitan: Elisabeth Rethberg, *Tannhaüser;*
Rosa Ponselle, *La Gioconda;* Lotte Lehmann (debut)
Die Walküre; Paul Althouse, *Tristan und Isolde;*
return of Claudia Muzio, *La traviata; Merry Mount*
(Harold Hanson, premiere)

Chicago: Giovanni Martinelli, *La forza del destino;*
Ezio Pinza, *Don Giovanni*

Philadelphia: *Mavra* (Igor Stravinsky, premiere)

Hartford, Conn.: *Four Saints in Three Acts* (Virgil
Thomson, Gertrude Stein, premiere, all black cast)

Music Notes
Albert Einstein makes his violin debut at the home of
Adolph Lewisohn; for this benefit for Scientists in
Nazified Berlin, Einstein plays the second violin in
Bach's Concerto for Two Violins; he also plays in a
Mozart quintet.

Art

Painting

Charles Burchfield, *November Evening*

Thomas Hart Benton, *Ploughing It Under*

Lyonel Feininger, *The Glassy Sea, Negroes on Rockaway Beach*

George Grosz, *Couple*

William Palmer, *Dust, Drought, and Destruction*

Ernest Lawson, *High Bridge*

Paul Cadmus, *Greenwich Village Cafeteria*

Jack Levine, *String Quartet*

Isabel Bishop, *Nude*

Sculpture

Joseph Cornell, *Object, Beehive*

Gaston Lachaise, *Torso*

Alexander Calder, *A Universe, Constellation with Red Object*

John Storrs, *Abstract Figure*

Architecture

Customs House, Philadelphia (Ritter and Shay)

Shusham Airport, New Orleans (Weiss, Dreyfous, and Seifforth)

North Dakota State Capitol Building, Bismarck (De Remer and Kurt, Holabird and Root)

Yale University School of Architecture plan, New Haven (Eero Saarinen)

Important Exhibitions

Museums

New York: *Metropolitan:* 300 Years of landscape painters, New York State furniture; Pennsylvania crafts; Lace and embroidered aprons. *Museum of Modern Art:* "Machine Art"; Otto Dix's war etchings; Whistler. *National Academy of Design:* Jo Davidson, Herbert Haseltine

Chicago: "A Century of Progress" (721 paintings from the Century of Progress Exhibit)

Pennsylvania Academy of Fine Arts: Henry Gottlieb, Yasuo Kuniyoshi; Raphael Soyer

Pittsburgh: Awards are given to Peter Blume *(South of Scranton),* Édouard Vuillard, André Derain, and Salvador Dali

Art Briefs

Alberto Giacometti has his first American one-man show in New York • FDR suggests remodeling the gingerbread ornamentation of the Library of Congress in a $1 million project.

Dance

School of American Ballet begins, with George Balanchine and Lincoln Kirstein; their first performance is a workshop of the new Balanchine *Serenade*. Ruth Page becomes principal dancer and director of the Chicago Grand Opera Company.

Charles Burchfield. *November Evening,* 1934. Oil. 32⅛ × 52". *The Metropolitan Museum of Art, George A. Hearn Fund, 1934.*

Books _____

Fiction

Critics' Choice

Tender Is the Night, F. Scott
  Fitzgerald
A Cool Million, Nathanael West
Hacienda: A Story of Mexico,
  Katherine Anne Porter
*The Daring Young Man on the
  Flying Trapeze*, William Saroyan
Tropic of Cancer, Henry Miller
Appointment in Samarra, John
  O'Hara
*The Young Manhood of Studs
  Lonigan*, James T. Farrell
Call It Sleep, Henry Roth
The Postman Always Rings Twice,
  James M. Cain
ੋੋ *Joseph and His Brothers*,
  Thomas Mann
ੋੋ *I, Claudius*, Robert Graves

Best-Sellers

Anthony Adverse, Hervey Allen
Lamb in His Bosom, Caroline
  Miller
So Red the Rose, Stark Young
Good-Bye Mr. Chips, James
  Hilton
Within This Present, Margaret
  Ayer Barnes
Seven Gothic Tales, Isak Dinesen
Work of Art, Sinclair Lewis
Private Worlds, Phyllis Bottome
Mary Peters, Mary Ellen Chase
Oil for the Lamps of China, Alice
  Tisdale Hobart

Nonfiction

Critics' Choice

*U.S. History: The People's
  Choice*, Herbert Agar
Exile's Return, Malcolm Cowley
Art as Experience, John Dewey
Patterns of Culture, Ruth
  Benedict
The Ways of White Folks,
  Langston Hughes
*The Robber Barons: The Great
  American Capitalists*, Matthew
  Josephson
Hitler over Europe, Ernst Henry
Merchants of Death, H. C.
  Englebrecht
American Ballads and Folk Songs,
  J. Lomax

Best-Sellers

While Rome Burns, Alexander
  Woollcott
Life Begins at Forty, Walter B.
  Pitkin
Nijinsky, Romola Nijinsky
100,000,000 Guinea Pigs, A.
  Kallett, F. J. Schlink
The Native's Return, Louis
  Adamic
You Must Relax, Edmund
  Jacobson
The Life of Our Lord, Charles
  Dickens

Edna St. Vincent Millay. *D. Ouellette
Collection.*

Brazilian Adventure, Peter
  Fleming
*Forty-two Years in the White
  House*, Ike Hoover

Poetry

Ezra Pound, *Eleven New Cantos,
  XXXI–XLI*
Edna St. Vincent Millay, *Wine
  from These Grapes*
Edwin Arlington Robinson,
  Amaranth
Laura Riding, *The Life of the
  Dead*
William Carlos Williams,
  Collected Poems, 1921–1931
ੋੋ W. H. Auden, *Poems*

Pulitzer Prizes

Now in November, Josephine
  Winslow Johnson (novel)
*The Colonial Period of American
  History*, Charles M. Andrews
  (U.S. history)
R. E. Lee, Douglas S. Freeman
  (biography)
Bright Ambush, Audrey
  Wurdemann (poetry)

Science and Technology _____

Ruth Benedict's *Patterns of Culture* explores the
  impact of culture as a cohesive ideological
  substrate.
Ladislas Von Meduna initiates chemical (Metrazol)
  convulsions as a treatment for schizophrenia.
Sodium pentothal, intravenous anesthesia, becomes
  widely used.
Dicumarol, an anticoagulant, is developed from
  clover.
ੋੋ Enrico Fermi pursues his work in Italy on the
  creation of new elements through the
  bombardment of uranium with neutrons.

ੋੋ Irène and Frédéric Joliot-Curie create the first
  man-made radioactive substance by bombarding
  aluminum with alpha particles that create
  radioactive phosphorus.

Nobel Prize

G. H. Whipple, George R. Minot, and W. P. Murphy
win in physiology and medicine for work on liver
therapy against anemia. Harold C. Urey wins in
chemistry for the discovery of heavy hydrogen.

Sports

Baseball

Dizzy Dean (St. Louis, NL) predicts: "Me and Paul [his brother] will win 40–45 games"; they win 49; Dizzy wins 30.

In the All-Star game, Carl Hubbell (New York, NL) strikes out in succession Babe Ruth, Lou Gehrig, Jimmy Foxx, Al Simmons, and Joe Cronin.

Champions

Batting	*Pitching*
Paul Waner (Pittsburgh, NL), .362	Dizzy Dean (St. Louis, NL), 30–7
Lou Gehrig (New York, AL), .363	Lefty Gomez (New York, AL), 26–5
	Home runs
	Lou Gehrig (New York, AL), 49

Football

Beattie Feathers (Chicago Bears) is the first pro to rush for over 1,000 yards in a season. Other NFL season leaders are Arnie Herber (Green Bay), passing; Joe Carter (Philadelphia), receiving. Steve Owens, New York Giant coach, has his players wear sneakers on the icy turf in their upset championship win.

College All-Americans: Pug Lund (F), Minnesota; Don Hutson (E), Alabama. The Sugar Bowl is inaugurated on New Year's Day, 1935.

Bowls (Jan. 1, 1935)

Rose: Alabama 29–Stanford 13
Orange: Bucknell 26–Miami 0
Sugar: Tulane 20–Temple 14

Basketball

Ned Irish arranges a college doubleheader in Madison Square Garden between national and local powers, which popularizes the college game.

Other Sports

Golf: Babe Didrickson takes up golf; when asked, "Is there anything you don't play?" she replies, "Yeah, dolls."

Boxing: Maxie Baer KO's Primo Carnera in the eleventh for the heavyweight title; Carnera is down twelve times in eleven rounds.

Winners

World Series	*Player of the Year*
St. Louis (NL) 4	John Moir, Notre Dame
Detroit (AL) 3	*Stanley Cup*
MVP	Chicago
NL–Jerome Dean, St. Louis	*U.S. Tennis Open*
AL–Gordon Cochrane, Detroit	Men: Fred Perry
NFL	Women: Helen Hull Jacobs
New York 30–Chicago (Bears) 13	*USGA Open*
College Football	Olin Dutra
Michigan	*Kentucky Derby*
College Basketball	Cavalcade (M. Garner, jockey)
Wyoming	

Fashion

For Women: Hair is pushed back across the head at a sharp angle, and hats, worn on one side of the head, look like record discs. Many women color and curl their hair like Harlow, wear red lipstick, rouge, and nail polish, and pencil in their brows. A new passion for hiking, sports, sunbathing, and even nudism, invites briefer sportswear. Bathing suits are slashed and backless, made of linen and Lastex yarn; described as "corset bathing suits," they mold the body as the woman walks out of the water. Designer news fills the magazines: the tailored look, Chanel's ready-to-wear collection, and the new surrealism in design. Chanel retains the easy skirt and jersey jacket for "understated" elegance (her term); Schiaparelli pursues "hard-edge chic" and fantasy, with prints designed by Dali and Cocteau, and buttons of huge fish, circus horses, and stars. Padded shoulders are even wider and covered with gold embroidery. The "little black dress" is new for the evening, as well as the long dinner suit in "shocking" colors: Patou's citron yellow, Schiaparelli's "shocking" blue and pink. New color combinations redefine day attire: brown and pink; prune and turquoise.

Other high-fashion notes: Silver fox broadtail, with muskrat for the more modest; Schiaparelli's and Mainbocher's box jackets.

Kaleidoscope

- The NRA banner of a bird and "We do our Part" is eventually displayed by 2.25 million firms with 22 million employees.
- The Civil Works Administration provides employment for 4 million people.
- The birth of the Dionne quintuplets in Ontario stirs international interest.
- The army takes over airmail delivery for a period, but numerous crashes lead to its return to private contractors.
- Food shopping patterns shift as consumers buy more red meats, fruits, green vegetables, and dairy products.
- Coca-Cola sales drop with the repeal of Prohibition. Wine companies, like Frank Schoonmaker's, begin operation but do poorly; Ernest and Julio Gallo invest $5,900 in a wine company.
- Cocktail lounges, most furnished with jukeboxes, are the only type of major new construction.
- Doubling up becomes prevalent, as grown children, in-laws, and parents share living space.
- Owing to the shortage of work, the five-day week becomes increasingly common.
- Many private golf courses are sold and become public links, as golf becomes less exclusively a sport of the wealthy.
- Estimates place Walter Lippmann's readership at 10 million in 200 newspapers.
- A *Literary Digest* poll reports that of six occupational groups (clergymen, businessmen, educators, lawyers, physicians, and bankers), all are pro-FDR except the bankers, where 52.4 percent are against the New Deal.
- Members of the Liberty League who oppose "that man" in the White House include Alfred Sloan of General Motors, the Du Ponts, Sewell Avery of Montgomery Ward, and Alfred E. Smith.
- Since the government pays high prices for gold, vast amounts accumulate at Fort Knox.
- A rocky island in San Francisco Bay becomes a maximum security prison, Alcatraz.
- Dillinger, "Baby Face" Nelson, "Pretty Boy" Floyd, Bonnie Parker and Clyde Barrows are all shot and killed during the year.

- After Clark Gable removes his shirt and reveals a naked chest in *It Happened One Night,* the male underwear business slumps.
- According to *Photoplay,* "Unmarried [Hollywood] Husbands and Wives" include Clark Gable and Carole Lombard, Paulette Goddard and Charles Chaplin, Gilbert Roland and Constance Bennett, Virginia Pine and George Raft, Barbara Stanwyck and Robert Taylor.
- The Hays Office, under pressure from the Catholic Legion of Decency, prescribes a code for motion pictures: no long kisses, double beds, naked babies, exposure of breasts, or suggestion of seduction or cohabitation; wrongdoing is not to be treated sympathetically.
- The Sears & Roebuck catalog begins to list contraceptive devices.
- "Little Orphan Annie," the comic strip, and its various spinoff products (e.g., rings) and endorsements (Ovaltine), gross $100,000.
- José Orozco's murals at Dartmouth College depicting capitalist persecution of the masses are not destroyed, despite a great deal of controversy.
- Within two months, 5 million people sign up for Father Coughlin's National Union for Social Justice, which advocates nationalization of banks.
- Huey Long presents his plan to the Senate to heavily tax the wealthy and distribute tax monies to the poor in order to make "Every Man a King."
- Francis Townsend, a California physician, proposes an old-age revolving pension plan based on a 2 percent tax that would provide $200 a month to all Americans over 60; they would be required to spend their stipend within the month, thus benefiting the economy.
- Novelist Upton Sinclair runs for governor in California on his End Poverty in California plan (EPIC).
- The migration to the West continues.
- In the Plains States, 300 million tons of soil blow away in the "black blizzard."

First Appearances: Snow goosebirds hatched, Eskimo chicken hatched, Mother-in-Law Day celebration (March 5, Amarillo, Texas), U.S. Information Service, pipeless organ, talking book for the blind, theater school offering a Ph.D. (Yale), washing machine for public use (Fort Worth, Texas), X ray of entire body in one-second exposure, paper underwear, launching of SS *Queen Mary,* Donald Duck, "Martha Dean," "Terry and the Pirates," "Li'l Abner," "Flash Gordon," "Jungle Jim," *Partisan Review,* Walgreen drugstores, Carvel, Seagram's Seven Royal Crown, Bard College, Black Mountain College, Hi-Fi (term for marketing records)

John Dillinger is killed by federal agents after seeing *Manhattan Melody* at the Biograph Theatre in Chicago. *D. Oulette Collection.*

1935

Facts and Figures

Economic Profile
  Dow-Jones: ↑ High 144–
    Low 96
  GNP: +9%
  Inflation: +1.0%
  Unemployment: 20.7%
Infant mortality/1,000: 57.1
Maternal mortality/1,000:
  56.8
Physicians in U.S.: 161,359
Hospital beds: 1,014,000
Used cars:
  1932 Pontiac: $325
  1932 Ford: $275
  1928 Buick: $65
Toys:
  Carpet sweeper: 24¢
  Typewriter: 98¢
  Doll in cradle: 98¢
Liquor:
  Cariola rum: $1.19 (pt.)
  Rock and Rye: 99¢ (pt.)
  Jameson Irish: $3.99 (⅘)
  Old Grand Dad: $2.99 (⅘)
  White Horse: $2.77 (pt.)

Deaths

Jane Addams, Alban Berg,
  Charles Demuth, Childe
  Hassam, Gaston Lachaise,
  T. E. Lawrence, Billy
  Mitchell, Wiley Post,
  Edwin Arlington Robinson,
  Will Rogers

In the News _____

SAAR VOTES 10–1 FOR UNION WITH GERMANY . . . FRED AND "MA" BARKER ARE KILLED BY G-MEN IN FLORIDA . . . GRIGORY ZINOVIEV, FORMER STALIN ASSOCIATE, IS FOUND GUILTY OF TREASON . . . SOIL CONSERVATION ACT IS PASSED . . . NATIONAL LABOR RELATIONS ACT PROVIDES FOR COLLECTIVE BARGAINING . . . WORKS PROGRESS ADMINISTRATION IS ORGANIZED . . . RURAL ELECTRIFICATION ACT IS PASSED . . . NATIONAL INDUSTRIAL RECOVERY ACT IS VOIDED BY SUPREME COURT . . . ADOLF HITLER DENOUNCES VERSAILLES TREATY AND DISARMAMENT . . . EMPLOYMENT RELIEF ACT ALLOWS GOVERNMENT TO PROVIDE JOBS . . . FEDERAL DOLE IS DISCONTINUED . . . INHERITANCE AND GIFT TAXES ARE ENACTED . . . THIRD COMMUNIST INTERNATIONAL SUPPORTS POPULAR FRONT GOVERNMENTS . . . BANKING ACT REORGANIZES FEDERAL RESERVE, FDIC IS CREATED . . . SHAH REZA PAHLAVI RENAMES PERSIA "IRAN" . . . HEINRICH HIMMLER BEGINS STATE BREEDING PROGRAM TO PRODUCE PERFECT ARYANS . . . HURRICANE KILLS 400 IN FLORIDA KEYS . . . FRANCE AND U.S.S.R. SIGN MUTUAL ASSISTANCE PACT . . . SOCIAL SECURITY ACT IS PASSED TO PROVIDE FOR THE AGED . . . HUEY LONG IS ASSASSINATED BY LOUISIANA PHYSICIAN . . . ITALY INVADES ETHIOPIA, LEAGUE OF NATIONS IMPOSES SANCTIONS . . . NUREMBERG LAWS ARE PASSED WITH DEATH PENALTY FOR INTERMARRIAGE . . . NEUTRALITY ACT PERMITS EMBARGO OF FOREIGN ARMS SHIPMENTS . . . JOHN L. LEWIS ORGANIZES CIO . . . DUTCH SCHULTZ IS VICTIM OF GANGLAND SLAYING . . . LEON BLUM, POPULAR FRONT CANDIDATE, IS ELECTED IN FRANCE.

333

Quotes —————

"The doctor says i hev got me thet sickness like Tom Prescott and thet is the reeson wy i am coughin sometime. . . . It is a terrible plague. . . . the doctor says i will be dead in about fore months."
— a West Virginia miner, a silicosis victim, quoted in Albert Maltz, *New Masses*

"The New Deal will bring them [the Communist party] within striking distance of the overthrow of the American form of government and the substitution therefore of a communist state."
— Arthur Sears Henning, *Chicago Tribune*

"Oh, I'm glad I've seen my Father—face to face!"
— Song at Harlem rally for Father Divine

"This may be the last presidential election America will have. The New Deal is to America what the early phase of Nazism was to Germany and the early phase of fascism to Italy."
— Mark Sullivan, *Buffalo Evening News*

"The editors of *Partisan Review* endorse this [Writer's] Congress . . . to accelerate the . . . establishment of a workers' government, [and] a new literature rooted in the dynamics of social development."
— *Partisan Review*

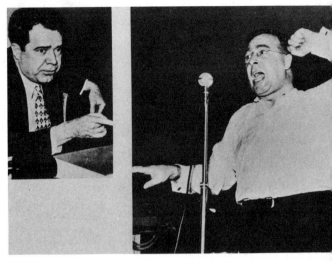

The "Kingfish," Senator Huey Long, and the "Radio Priest" Father Charles Coughlin, new opponents of President Roosevelt. *D. Ouellette Collection.*

"Four centuries of oppression, . . . hopes, . . . [and] bitterness . . . were rising to the surface. Yes, unconsciously [the young] . . . imputed to the brawny image of Joe Louis all the balked dreams of revenge . . . AND HE HAD WON! . . . Here's the real dynamite that Joe Louis uncovered!"
— Richard Wright

"The last temptation is the greatest treason: to do the right deed for the wrong reason."
— T. S. Eliot, *Murder in the Cathedral*

Ads —————

One fiddler you won't have to pay.
(Sanka Coffee)

Watch for your beer in this new container. You ought to have it soon. We're trying hard to catch up with the tremendous demand.
(Continental Can Co.)

All trails lead to ice-cold Coca-Cola.
(Coca-Cola)

Some Like It Cold.
(Heinz Consommé)

What makes the common cold so common?—Colds are no respecters of rank.
(Dixie Cups)

Museum of the City of New York.

Tortured in bed! Milly made a serious mistake. . . . She bought her husband pajamas with drawstrings, . . . "the rope" that ruins sleep.
(Faultless No-Belt Pajamas, Wilson Bros.)

Radio

Premieres
"Your Hit Parade"
"Backstage Wife," Vivian Fridell
"Vox Pop," Parks Johnson, Jerry Belcher
"Fibber McGee and Molly," Jim and Marian Jordan
"Dick Tracy," Matt Crowley
"Flash Gordon," Gale Gordon
"America's Town Meeting," George V. Denny, Jr.
"Cavalcade of America"
"The Helen Hayes Theatre"

Specials
Haile Selassie's plea for assistance against the invading Italians; Silver Jubilee celebration of King George V and Queen Mary's reign; first birthday party of the Dionne quintuplets

Of Note
Longest running shows include "Cities Service," "Concert" (Jessica Dragonette); "Major Bowes," "Midweek Hymn Sing," "A & P Gypsies," "Breen and DeRose," "H. V. Kaltenborn," "Betty Crocker Cooking Talk," "Cheerio" (inspirational talk with organ music).

New Catchphrases: ". . . the story of . . . what it means to be the wife of a famous Broadway star— dream sweetheart of a million other women ("Backstage Wife"); "You're a hard man, McGee [sound of crashing items from closet]" ("Fibber McGee and Molly")

Ginger Rogers and Fred Astaire in *Top Hat*. "Can't act. Slightly bald. Can dance a little" was the verdict of Astaire's 1933 Hollywood screen test. *Movie Star News*.

Movies

Openings
Mutiny on the Bounty (Frank Lloyd), Clark Gable, Charles Laughton
Captain Blood (Michael Curtiz), Errol Flynn, Olivia de Havilland
The Informer (John Ford), Victor McLaglen, Preston Foster
Lives of a Bengal Lancer (Henry Hathaway), Gary Cooper, Franchot Tone
Les Miserables (Richard Boleslawski), Fredric March, Charles Laughton
A Midsummer Night's Dream (Max Reinhardt, William Dieterle), James Cagney, Mickey Rooney, Joe E. Brown
Naughty Marietta (W. S. Van Dyke), Nelson Eddy, Jeanette MacDonald
Ruggles of Red Gap (Leo McCarey), Charles Ruggles, Charles Laughton
Top Hat (Mark Sandrich), Fred Astaire, Ginger Rogers
Dangerous (Alfred E. Green), Bette Davis, Franchot Tone
Anna Karenina (Clarence Brown), Greta Garbo, Fredric March, Freddie Bartholomew, Maureen O'Sullivan
A Night at the Opera (Sam Wood), Marx Brothers
Bride of Frankenstein (James Whale), Elsa Lanchester, Boris Karloff
Becky Sharp (Rouben Mamoulian), Miriam Hopkins, Cedric Hardwicke, Pat Nixon

The 39 Steps (Alfred Hitchcock), Robert Donat, Madeleine Carroll
She (Irving Pichel), Helen Gahagan, Randolph Scott
Magnificent Obsession (John M. Stahl), Irene Dunne, Robert Taylor
Crime and Punishment (Josef von Sternberg), Peter Lorre, Edward Arnold
Gold Diggers of 1935 (Busby Berkeley), Dick Powell, Alice Brady

Academy Awards
Best Picture: *Mutiny on the Bounty*
Best Director: John Ford (*The Informer*)
Best Actress: Bette Davis (*Dangerous*)
Best Actor: Victor McLaglen (*The Informer*)

Top Box-Office Stars
Shirley Temple, Will Rogers, Clark Gable, Fred Astaire and Ginger Rogers, Joan Crawford, Claudette Colbert, Dick Powell, Wallace Beery, Joe E. Brown, James Cagney

Popular Music _____

Hit Songs
"Begin the Beguine"
"The Music Goes 'Round and
  'Round"
"East of the Sun and West of the
  Moon"
"It Ain't Necessarily So"
"I Got Plenty o' Nuthin' "
"Lovely to Look At"
"Red Sails in the Sunset"
"Stairway to the Stars"
"Summertime"
"These Foolish Things Remind
  Me of You"
"I Loves You, Porgy"
"You Are My Lucky Star"
"When I Grow Too Old to
  Dream"

Top Records
Cheek to Cheek (Fred Astaire);
I'm in the Mood for Love (Frances
Langford); *It's You I Adore* (Russ
Morgan); *The Oregon Trail* (Ozzie
Nelson); *Lullaby of Broadway*
(Dick Powell); *Zing! Went the
Strings of My Heart"* (Victor
Young); *June in January* (Bing
Crosby); *Footloose and Fancy
Free* (Dorsey Brothers)

Jazz and Big Bands
The Savoy Ballroom, "the home
of happy feet," in Harlem,
presents Chick Webb and Teddy
Hill. Benny Goodman, the "King
of Swing," opens at the Palomar
Ballroom, Los Angeles; his band
includes Lionel Hampton, Gene
Krupa, and Teddy Wilson. "Sweet
bands," like Guy Lombardo's,
compete with Goodman, the
Dorseys, and Artie Shaw. Tommy
and Jimmy Dorsey split up and
form their own bands.

First recordings: Ella Fitzgerald,
with Chick Webb; Billie Holiday,
with Teddy Wilson

New Bands: Russ Morgan, Bob
Crosby, New York; Count Basie,
Kansas City

Theater _____

Broadway Openings

Plays
The Petrified Forest (Robert E. Sherwood), Leslie
  Howard, Humphrey Bogart, Peggy Conklin
Winterset (Maxwell Anderson), Margo, Burgess
  Meredith
Awake and Sing (Clifford Odets), Morris Carnovsky,
  Luther Adler, Stella Adler, John Garfield
The Old Maid (Zoe Akins), Judith Anderson, Helen
  Menken
Waiting for Lefty (Clifford Odets), Elia Kazan,
  Herbert Rattner, Paula Miller, Abner Bibberman
Till the Day I Die (Clifford Odets), Walter Coy, Elia
  Kazan, Alexander Kirkland, Lee J. Cobb
Paradise Lost (Clifford Odets), Morris Carnovsky,
  Stella Adler
Three Men on a Horse (John Cecil Holm, George
  Abbott), Shirley Booth, Sam Levene
Night of January 16 (Ayn Rand), Doris Nolan
Mulatto (Langston Hughes), Rose McClendon
Dead End (Sidney Kingsley), Marjorie Main, Dan
  Duryea, Martin Gabel, Sidney Lumet, Leo
  Gorcey
Victoria Regina (Laurence Housman), Helen Hayes

Musicals
At Home Abroad (Arthur Schwartz, Howard Dietz),
  Beatrice Lillie, Ethel Waters, Eleanor Powell,
  Reginald Gardner

Jubilee (Cole Porter), Mary Boland, Charles Walters,
  Montgomery Clift
Jumbo (Richard Rodgers, Lorenz Hart), Jimmy
  Durante, Bob Lawrence, Gloria Grafton
May Wine (Sigmund Romberg, Oscar Hammerstein
  II), Walter Slezak, Leo G. Carroll, Nancy
  McCord
Porgy and Bess (George Gershwin, Ira Gershwin),
  Todd Duncan, Anne Brown

Classics and Revivals On and Off Broadway
The Taming of the Shrew, Alfred Lunt, Lynn
Fontanne; *Romeo and Juliet,* Katharine Cornell,
Maurice Evans (U.S. debut), Ralph Richardson,
Tyrone Power, Jr.; *Ghosts* (Ibsen), Nazimova; *Rain*
(John Colton, Clemence Randolph), Tallulah
Bankhead. *Founded:* American National Theatre and
Academy (ANTA) by presidential charter (FDR)

Regional

Founded: Oregon Shakespeare Festival Association,
Ashland, by Angus Bowmer; Federal Theatre Project
organized under Hallie Flanagan

Pulitzer Prize
The Old Maid, Zoe Akins

Classical Music _____

Compositions
Roger Sessions, Violin Concerto
Edgard Varèse, Chamber Pieces
John Alden Carpenter, *Danza*
Walter Piston, Trio for Violin, Cello, and Piano;
    String Quartet no. 2
John Powell, *A Set of Three*
George Antheil, *Dreams*
Roy Harris, *Farewell to Pioneers*
Henry Cowell, *Sinister Resonance*
David Diamond, Partita for Oboe, Bassoon, and
    Piano
William Schuman, *Symphony no. 1 for Eighteen*
    Instruments

Important Events
18,000 musicians of all ranks are hired by the
government; the Federal Music Project also sponsors
thousands of concerts. The Composers Forum Lab
(organized by the Federal Music Project) opens in
New York with a program of Roy Harris's music.
Owing to the depression, the San Francisco
Orchestra almost goes bankrupt; Pierre Monteux is
appointed as musical director to attract larger
audiences. Arthur Schnabel, in seven consecutive
concerts at Carnegie Hall, plays all 32 Beethoven
sonatas.

Debuts: Emanuel Feuermann, Rosalyn Tureck

First Performances
Leo Sowerby, Concerto no. 2 for Violoncello and
Orchestra (New York); Roy Harris, *When Johnny
Comes Marching Home* (Minneapolis)

Opera

Metropolitan: Marjorie Lawrence, Kirsten Flagstad,
Die Walküre; Lotte Lehmann, Emmanuel List, *Der
Rosenkavalier;* Lotte Lehmann, *Tosca;* Lauritz
Melchior, Kirsten Flagstad, *Tristan und Isolde;*
Lawrence Tibbett, *Rigoletto.* Premieres: *In the
Pasha's Garden* (J. K. Seymour); *La serva padrona*
(G. B. Pergolesi, in Italian); gala farewell for Giulio
Gatti-Casazza

Chicago: Rosa Raisa, *La fiamma* (Respighi,
premiere); Lily Pons, *Lakmé*

Boston: *Porgy and Bess* (George Gershwin,
premiere)

Cleveland: *Lady Macbeth of the District of Mzensk*
(Shostakovitch, premiere)

San Francisco: Complete *Ring* (Kirsten Flagstad,
Elisabeth Rethberg, Friedrich Schorr, Emmanuel
List)

Philadelphia: *Iphigenie en Aulide* (C. W. Gluck,
premiere)

Music Notes
Pierre Monteux revives the San Francisco Orchestra
with $55,000 from municipal taxes and then concen-
trates on performing European music • Leopold
Stokowski retires • Otto Klemperer guest conducts
the New York Philharmonic • Igor Stravinsky leads
the Chicago • The Metropolitan Opera bans singers
from hiring claqueurs and hissers • Herbert
Witherspoon takes over management of the Met but
dies of a heart attack after six months; he is
succeeded by Edward Johnson.

Porgy and Bess, George Gershwin's transformation of
DuBose Heyward's novel. *Billy Rose Collection. The New
York Public Library at Lincoln Center. Astor, Lenox and
Tilden Foundations.*

Art _____

Painting

Joe Jones, *Threshing*
Arthur G. Dove, *Moon*
George Biddle, *Georgia Sweatshop*
Philip Evergood, *Railroad Men*
William Glackens, *The Soda Fountain*
William Gropper, *Senators*
Niles Spencer, *The Bird, Workmen*
Willem de Kooning, *Study of a Mural for a Project*
Paul Cadmus, *To the Lynching*
Frank A. Mechau paints *Dangers of the Mail* for the Post Office Department Building, Washington, D.C.

Sculpture

Chaim Gross, *Handlebar Riders, Strong Woman (Acrobat)*
Robert Laurent, *Kneeling Figure*
Alexander Archipenko, *Boxing*
Jo Davidson, *Dr. Albert Einstein*
Ibram Lassaw, *Sculpture*
Paul Manship, *Prometheus,* Rockefeller Center Fountain

Important Exhibitions

Museums

New York: *Metropolitan:* "Artistic Work of the Employees"; Bryson Burroughs memorial; Hogarth; Japanese costumes. *Museum of Modern Art:* African Negro art; Gaston Lachaise retrospective; George Caleb Bingham; Léger; Le Corbusier. *Whitney:* Abstract painting in America; genre painting from the nineteenth and twentieth centuries

Chicago: Rembrandt and his circle; Boudin, Léger

Architecture

Carl MacKley Public Housing Projects, Philadelphia (W. Pope Barney)
Triborough Bridge, New York (Aymar Embury II)
National Archives, Washington, D.C. (Cass Gilbert)
Corona Elementary School, Los Angeles (Richard Neutra)
Restoration of Williamsburg, Va. (Perry, Shaw, and Hepburn)

Threshing, Joe Jones, 1935. Oil on board. 36 × 48″. *The Metropolitan Museum of Art, George A. Hearn Fund,* 1937.

Dallas: Survey of the great masters

Toledo: French and Flemish primitives

Pittsburgh: Prizes are awarded to Hipolito Hidalgo de Caviedes, Burchfield, Vlaminck

Boston: Independent painters of nineteenth-century Paris

Art Briefs

Andrew Mellon donates $10 million and his $25 million art collection for the construction of the National Art Gallery in Washington, D.C., with the proviso that no gallery be named for him • John D. Rockefeller contributes $2.5 million for the construction of the Cloisters, the medieval branch of the Metropolitan Museum of Art • The Frick Gallery (New York) and the Wichita Museum open • The Federal Art project, under Holger Cahill, sponsors such artists as Jackson Pollock, Willem de Kooning, Arshile Gorky, and Raphael Soyer • Jacques Lipchitz has his first major show, in New York • "The Ten," a group of artists interested in abstractionism and expressionism, is founded.

Dance _____

George Balanchine and Lincoln Kirstein organize a touring company, the American Ballet. In two weeks at Adelphi College, New York, they perform seven Balanchine works; principal dancers include Tamara Geva, Eugene Loring, William Dollar, Leda Anchutina, and Ruthanna Boris. The Metropolitan Opera invites the ballet to be its permanent company.

Books

Fiction

Critics' Choice
Pylon, William Faulkner
Taps at Reveille, F. Scott Fitzgerald
Tortilla Flat, John Steinbeck
It Can't Happen Here, Sinclair Lewis
Somebody in Boots, Nelson Algren
Studs Lonigan (complete version), James T. Farrell
They Shoot Horses, Don't They, Horace McCoy
Paths of Glory, Humphrey Cobb
The Last Puritan, George Santayana
Bury the Dead, Irwin Shaw
Butterfield 8, John O'Hara

Best-Sellers
Green Light, Lloyd C. Douglas
Vein of Iron, Ellen Glasgow
Of Time and the River, Thomas Wolfe
Time Out of Mind, Rachel Field
Good-Bye, Mr. Chips, James Hilton
The Forty Days of Musa Dagh, Franz Werfel
Heaven's My Destination, Thornton Wilder
Lost Horizon, James Hilton
Come and Get It, Edna Ferber
Europa, Robert Briffault

Nonfiction

Critics' Choice
America Faces the Barricades, John L. Spivak
The Road to War, Walter Millis
The U.S., 1830–1850, Frederick Jackson Turner
Gay Reformer: Profits before Plenty under F.D.R., Mauritz A. Hallgren
The Green Hills of Africa, Ernest Hemingway
Jefferson and/or Mussolini, Ezra Pound
Black Reconstruction, W. E. B. Du Bois
Growing Up in New Guinea, Margaret Mead
My Country and My People, Lin Yutang
Proletarian Literature in the U.S., Granville Hicks
My Ten Years in a Quandary and How They Grew Up, Robert Benchley
Enjoyment of Laughter, Max Eastman
ᕗ *The Two Sources of Morality and Religion*, Henri Bergson

Best-Sellers
North to the Orient, Anne Morrow Lindbergh
While Rome Burns, Alexander Woollcott

Life with Father, Clarence Day
Personal History, Vincent Sheean
Seven Pillars of Wisdom, T. E. Lawrence
Francis the First, Francis Hackett
Mary Queen of Scotland and the Isles, Stefan Zweig
Rats, Lice and History, Hans Zinsser
R. E. Lee, Douglas Southall Freeman
Skin Deep, M. C. Phillips

Poetry
Wallace Stevens, *Ideas of Order*
Lincoln Kirstein, *Low Ceiling*
Muriel Rukeyser, *Theory of Flight*
Marianne Moore, *Selected Poems*
Kenneth Fearing, *Poems*

Pulitzer Prizes
Honey in the Horn, Harold L. Davis (novel)
The Constitutional History of the U.S., Andrew C. McLaughlin (U.S. history)
The Thought and Character of William James, Ralph B. Perry (biography)
Strange Holiness, Robert P. Tristram Coffin (poetry)

Science and Technology

Du Pont chemist Wallace Hume Carothers creates nylon, the first completely synthetic fabric.
Wendell Stanley, at the Rockefeller Institute, isolates a virus (tobacco mosaic) in pure crystalline form, which demonstrates its proteinaceous nature.
Alcoholics Anonymous is organized in New York.
A federal hospital for narcotics addicts is opened in Lexington, Ky.
John Northrup isolates chymotrypsin from pancreatic juice.

The first wearable hearing aid, weighing 2½ pounds, is produced by A. Edwin Stevens.
Ergonovine is developed for obstetric use.
Robert Goddard continues his rocket experiments in New Mexico, achieving heights of 8,000 feet and supersonic speeds.
ᕗ Aircraft-detecting radar is pioneered by Robert Watson Watt in England.
ᕗ Clinical application of sulfa therapy, using Prontosil, takes place in Germany.
ᕗ Henrik Dam discovers vitamin K.

Sports

Baseball

The first night baseball game is played in Cincinnati against Philadelphia; 22,422 attend.

Babe Ruth, traded to Boston (NL), hits three home runs in his last game and retires with lifetime records of 714 home runs, 5,793 total bases, and a .342 BA.

Rookie Wally Berger (Cincinnati, NL) leads his league with 38 home runs.

Champions

Batting	Home runs
Arky Vaughan (Pittsburgh, NL), .385	Jimmy Foxx (Philadelphia, AL), 36
Charles Myer (Washington, AL), .349	Hank Greenberg (Detroit, AL), 36
Pitching	
Bill Lee (Chicago, NL), 20–6	
Eldon Auker (Detroit, AL), 18–7	

Football

The NFL college draft begins. Jay Berwanger, Chicago, is the first selection, by Philadelphia; Berwanger decides not to play pro ball.

Red Grange retires; Don Hutson (E), Green Bay, debuts.

The Heisman Trophy begins; Berwanger is the first winner.

NFL Season Leaders: Ed Danowski (New York), passing; Doug Russell (Chicago Cards), rushing; Todd Goodwin (New York), receiving.

College All-Americans: Sammy Baugh (Q), Texas Christian; Gaynell Tinsley (F), Louisiana State

Bowls (Jan. 1, 1936)

Rose: Stanford 7–Southern Methodist 0
Orange: Catholic 20–Mississippi 19
Sugar: Texas Christian 3–Louisiana State 2

Basketball

Hank Luisetti, Stanford star, originates the one-handed shot and breaks scoring records.

Other Sports

Horse Racing: Omaha, ridden by W. Saunders, wins the Triple Crown.

Boxing: James Braddock beats Maxie Baer for the heavyweight crown.

Tennis: Helen Hull Jacobs wins her third straight U.S. Open.

Winners

World Series	Player of the Year
Detroit (AL) 4	Leroy Edwards, Kentucky
Chicago (NL) 2	*Stanley Cup*
MVP	Montreal (Maroons)
NL–Gabby Harnett, Chicago	*U.S. Tennis Open*
AL–Henry Greenberg, Detroit	Men: Wilmer Allison
NFL	Women: Helen Hull Jacobs
Detroit 26–New York 17	*USGA Open*
College Football	Sam Parks, Jr.
Minnesota	*Kentucky Derby*
Heisman Trophy	Omaha (W. Saunders, jockey)
Jay Berwanger, Chicago	
College Basketball	
New York University	

Fashion

For Women: A severe, though eclectic, military look is introduced with square, epaulette shoulders, low heels, plumed hats, and gauntlet gloves. Even Schiaparelli designs suits with a "tidy look" in his drummer-boy jackets. Evening wear contrasts: Greek or Indian dresses with heavy jewelry, extraordinary prints (of pigs, radishes, newspaper print). Hair is brushed to the top of the head in a mass of curls. Makeup emphasizes bone structure in a bold way. A red pencil lines the lips for very bright red shades; rouge is applied to earlobes and cheeks and over the eyes. Eyebrows are plucked to their thinnest, if not completely; false eyelashes are worn. Fingernails are scarlet and long; toenails, fashionable pink. Bra cup sizes (A–D) are introduced; net, woven fabrics, and zippers enter corsetry.

High-fashion note: Mainbocher's two-piece navy wool dress with lace cuffs and collar.

Kaleidoscope ────────────

- One out of four households is on relief; 750,000 farms have been foreclosed since 1930.
- The Civilian Conservation Corps (CCC) employs half a million young men in conservation projects for which they earn $40 a month.
- Direct relief is returned to the states as the WPA takes over work relief. A total of 8 million people build schools, libraries, bridges, roads, hospitals, and sewage systems.
- On the New Deal's "Black Monday," May 27, the Supreme Court voids the NIRA and condemns the president in the "Sick Chicken Case" begun by the Schechter brothers of Brooklyn.
- *Boondoggling* enters the national vocabulary when some critics call relief work busy work for the unemployed.
- Oklahoma, Texas, and Missouri are the leading places of origin of migrant families.
- FDR announces IRS figures: 0.1 percent of U.S. corporations own 52 percent of total corporate assets and earn 50 percent of all profits.
- William Randolph Hearst earns the highest salary in America, and Mae West, the second highest.
- Participation in group sports in public areas increases—swimming, golfing, and ice skating; there is also a marked increase in bicycling, skiing, and softball.
- The rhumba becomes popular.
- Bingo begins in movie houses and soon becomes popular with charity organizations.
- The 10¢ chain letter craze begins. Denver post office employees work into the night sorting hundreds of thousands of letters.
- Americans still spend $1,000 each day on buggy whips.
- The DC-3, with heated cabins and soundproofing, is the first reliable passenger plane able to go cross-country nonstop, in 15 hours.
- The Russian tourist agency, Intourist, advertises: "Travel dollars have not shrunk in the Soviet Union"; an estimated 30,000 travel to Russia.
- The average cost of advertising on radio is $360.80 per minute (NBC); the reduced rate is $262.91 per minute for a full hour.
- Instead of mailing Christmas cards, a Chicago printing salesman sends out a list of his favorite restaurants; he receives so many requests for copies, he goes into business: "Recommended by Duncan Hines."
- The Massachusetts Department of Mental Health reports that children from small families have a greater tendency to steal, and children from large families have a greater tendency to lie.
- Americans consume 50 million chickens a year and pay more for poultry than red meat.
- Theater audiences cry "Strike!" at the highly successful Clifford Odets's *Waiting for Lefty,* which asks that they pretend to be union members.
- The Federal Theatre Project under Hallie Flanagan

The administration completes Hoover Dam (formerly Boulder Dam) for flood control, irrigation, and electric power. *Library of Congress.*

presents 924 productions to more than 20 million people.
- Documentary prose-photography thrives, including the work of Margaret Bourke-White, Walker Evans, James Agee, Dorothea Lange, and Archibald MacLeish. The Rural Resettlement Administration (later, the Farm Security Administration), under Rexford G. Tugwell, photographs America's blighted land.
- WPA writers include Saul Bellow, John Cheever, Ralph Ellison, Chester Himes, Richard Wright, and Kenneth Rexroth.
- A senate committee investigates the munitions industry and its role in instigating American involvement in World War I; several popular books, like Walter Millis's *The Road to War,* indict the arms makers.
- New York attorney general Thomas Dewey convicts Lucky Luciano and 70 others of racketeering.
- Counterfeiting has increased 400 percent since the depression began.
- Huey Long's assassin is shot with 61 bullets by Long's bodyguards.
- With the enormous growth of Bernarr Macfadden's magazine empire (*True Confessions* sells 7,355,000 copies, an even greater number than *Collier's),* Macfadden considers running for president.

Fads: Monopoly (20 million sets sold in one week), the Irish Sweepstakes, pinball, bridge, bingo (in churches), gambling

First Appearances: Auto exceeding 300 m.p.h., woman stock exchange member, beer in cans, lie detector used in court, book series microfilmed, roller derby (Chicago), national skeet tournament (Indianapolis), Toyota, Richter scale for measuring earthquakes, Kodachrome for 16mm camera, RealLemon, Jolly Green Giant, Hayden Planetarium, Gallup Poll, hot meals served in the air, Shenandoah National Park (Virginia), SS *Normandie* in service crossing Atlantic

1936

Facts and Figures

Economic Profile
  Dow-Jones: ↑ High 182–
    Low 143
  GNP: +14%
  Inflation: +0.4%
  Unemployment: 16.9%
Urban/rural population ratio:
  69/54
Male/female ratio: 62/61
High school graduates
  entering college: 12.9%
Four-year colleges: 1,213
Public/private schools ratio:
  10/1
Hepplewhite bedroom set
  (four-piece): $179
Living room suite (Abraham
  and Strauss): $129
Altman's gold-hued butter
  knives: 6 for $5
Walgreen's cod liver oil: 39¢
Dr. Scholl's Zino pads: 19¢
Anacin (12): 14¢
Calox toothpowder (large):
  29¢
Zee toilet tissue: 2 for 9¢
Libby's baby food: 3 for 25¢
Silver King dog food: 2 for
  15¢

Deaths

Louis Blériot, G. K.
  Chesterton, Federico
  García Lorca, John
  Gilbert, Maxim Gorky,
  A. E. Housman, Rudyard
  Kipling, Luigi Pirandello,
  Ottorino Respighi, Oswald
  Spengler, Miguel de
  Unamuno.

In the News

DUST STORMS SWEEP THE MIDWEST . . . AGRICULTURAL ADJUSTMENT ACT IS STRUCK DOWN BY SUPREME COURT . . . GEORGE V OF BRITAIN DIES, EDWARD, PRINCE OF WALES, SUCCEEDS TO THE THRONE . . . SUPREME COURT UPHOLDS TENNESSEE VALLEY AUTHORITY . . . HITLER REPUDIATES LOCARNO TREATY, GERMAN TROOPS REENTER RHINELAND . . . MAJOR FLOODS HIT NORTHEAST U.S., MANY PEOPLE ARE HOMELESS OR DEAD . . . DEMOCRATS RENOMINATE FDR, GOP CHOOSES ALF LANDON . . . PANAMA TREATY ENDS U.S. PROTECTORATE . . . MINIMUM WAGE FOR WOMEN IS FOUND UNCONSTITUTIONAL . . . MUSSOLINI'S TROOPS TRIUMPH OVER ILL-EQUIPPED ETHIOPIANS . . . BRUNO HAUPTMANN IS ELECTROCUTED FOR LINDBERGH KIDNAPPING . . . 16-YEAR-OLD FAROUK BECOMES KING OF EGYPT . . . CIVIL WAR BEGINS IN SPAIN, FRANCISCO FRANCO AND EMILIO MOLA LEAD ARMY AGAINST THE REPUBLIC . . . GERMANY AND ITALY AID FRANCO . . . THOMAS DEWEY CONVICTS LUCKY LUCIANO, SENTENCED TO 30–50 YEARS . . . ANASTASIO SOMOZA LEADS COUP IN NICARAGUA . . . CHARLES LINDBERGH TOURS GERMANY ON HERMAN GOERING INVITATION . . . U.S. DECLARES NONINTERVENTION POLICY FOR SPAIN . . . STALIN BEGINS LARGE GOVERNMENT PURGE . . . ROME-BERLIN AXIS IS PROCLAIMED . . . SUPREME COURT INVALIDATES BITUMINOUS COAL CONSERVATION ACT . . . FDR IS REELECTED BY LANDSLIDE, ELECTORAL VOTE IS 523–8 . . . JAPAN AND GERMANY ANNOUNCE ANTI-COMINTERN PACT . . . PLANT WORKERS STAGE "SIT-DOWN" AT GENERAL MOTORS . . . EDWARD VIII ABDICATES FOR LOVE OF AMERICAN DIVORCÉE WALLIS WARFIELD SIMPSON.

Quotes

"The hand of Moscow backs the Communist leaders in America . . . [and] aims to support FDR. . . . I ask you to purge the man who claims to be a Democrat from the Democratic Party, and I mean Franklin Double-Crossing Roosevelt."
— Father Charles Coughlin

"For twelve years this nation was afflicted with hear-nothing, see-nothing, do-nothing government. Never before in our history have these forces been so united against one candidate as they stand today. They are unanimous in their hatred for me—and I welcome their hatred."
— FDR, final campaign speech

"This generation of Americans has a rendezvous with destiny."
— FDR

"Withering heat, rushing out of the furnace of the prairie dust bowl, blasted crops, sucked up rivers and lakes, and transformed the nation—from the Rockies to the Atlantic—into a vast simmering cauldron."
— *Newsweek*

"God and history will remember your judgment. It is us today. It will be you tomorrow."
— Ethiopian emperor Haile Selassie, appealing to the League of Nations for assistance

Despite his cheery campaign button, Alf Landon loses every state but Maine and Vermont. *Smithsonian Institution.*

"The Fifth Column will take Madrid."
— Gen. Emilio Mola

"They shall not pass."
— Spanish loyalist La Pasionara, Dolores Ibarruri

"I wanted to see New York . . . so I tried to see how fast I could do it in."
— Howard Hughes, on breaking cross-country flight record

"Suppose I'm not so cute when I grow up as I am now?"
— Shirley Temple

"I have found it impossible to carry the heavy burden of responsibility and to discharge my duties as King as I should wish to do, without the help and support of the woman I love."
— Edward VIII, abdication speech

"I regret that I have but one wife to lay down for my country."
— Apocryphal remark attributed to Ernest Simpson, as he and Wallis Warfield Simpson separate

Ads

Radio

Premieres

"The Kate Smith Show"
"John's Other Wife," Jimmy Scribner
"The Shadow," Robert Hardy Andrews
"Gangbusters," Phillips H. Lord
"Lux Radio Theatre," Cecil B. DeMille (host)
"We, the People," Gabriel Heatter
"Columbia Workshops" (experimental theater)
"Chase and Sanborn Hour," Edgar Bergen, Charlie McCarthy
"Professor Quiz," Craig Earl (first giveaway and quiz program)
"Pepper Young's Family," Curtis Arnall

Specials

Radio pickup from Nanking, China, on the kidnapping of Chiang Kai-shek.

Of Note

The first question on "Professor Quiz" is "What is the difference between a llama and lama?" • Favorite programs include "Kate Smith," "Easy Aces," "Boake Carter," "Frances Langford and Dick Powell," "Burns and Allen," "Helen Trent," "One Man's Family," "Just Plain Bill," "Lux Radio Theater" • Jack Benny and Fred Allen begin their "feud"—a running gag on both shows—when Allen insults Benny's violin playing.

New Catchphrases: "I'll clip ya! So help me, I'll mow ya down" (Edgar Bergen and Charlie McCarthy); "*(Marching feet, machine-gun fire, siren wail)* . . . Calling all Americans to war on the underworld!" ("Gangbusters"); "You have a friend and adviser in John J. Anthony" ("The Goodwill Hour"); "Several years ago in the Orient, [Lamont] Cranston learned . . . the hypnotic power to cloud men's minds so they cannot see him. . . . Who knows what evil lurks in the hearts of men? The Shadow knows! *(Laugh)*" ("The Shadow")

Movies

Openings

The Great Ziegfeld (Robert Z. Leonard), Luise Rainer, William Powell, Myrna Loy
Anthony Adverse (Mervyn LeRoy), Fredric March, Olivia de Havilland
Dodsworth (William Wyler), Walter Huston, Ruth Chatterton, David Niven
Romeo and Juliet (George Cukor), Leslie Howard, Norma Shearer, Basil Rathbone, John Barrymore
Libeled Lady (Jack Conway), Spencer Tracy, Myrna Loy, William Powell, Jean Harlow
Mr. Deeds Goes to Town (Frank Capra), Gary Cooper, Jean Arthur
San Francisco (W. S. Van Dyke), Clark Gable, Jeanette MacDonald, Spencer Tracy
A Tale of Two Cities (Jack Conway), Ronald Colman, Elizabeth Allan
The Story of Louis Pasteur (William Dieterle), Paul Muni
Three Smart Girls (Henry Koster), Deanna Durbin, Ray Milland
Modern Times (Charles Chaplin), Charles Chaplin, Paulette Goddard
Fury (Fritz Lang, U.S. debut), Spencer Tracy, Sylvia Sidney

Camille (George Cukor), Greta Garbo, Robert Taylor
These Three (William Wyler), Miriam Hopkins, Merle Oberon, Joel McCrea
The Ghost Goes West (René Clair), Robert Donat, Jean Parker
My Man Godfrey (Gregory La Cava), Carole Lombard, William Powell
Swingtime (George Stevens), Ginger Rogers, Fred Astaire

Academy Awards

Best Picture: *The Great Ziegfeld*
Best Director: Frank Capra (*Mr. Deeds Goes to Town*)
Best Actress: Luise Rainer (*The Great Ziegfeld*)
Best Actor: Paul Muni (*The Story of Louis Pasteur*)

Top Box-Office Stars

Shirley Temple, Clark Gable, Fred Astaire and Ginger Rogers, Robert Taylor, Joe E. Brown, Dick Powell, Joan Crawford, Claudette Colbert, Jeanette MacDonald, Gary Cooper

Popular Music

Hit Songs

"I'm an Old Cow Hand"
"Is It True What They Say about Dixie?"
"I've Got You under My Skin"
"The Night Is Young and You're So Beautiful"
"Sing, Sing, Sing"
"Stompin' at the Savoy"
"There's a Small Hotel"
"W.P.A. Blues"
"Wiffenpoof Song"
"You've Gotta Eat Your Spinach, Baby"

Top Records

Let's Face the Music and Dance, Let Yourself Go, The Way You Look Tonight, and *Pick Yourself Up* (Fred Astaire); *Pennies from Heaven* (Bing Crosby); *In the Chapel in the Moonlight* (Ruth Etting) (Shep Fields); *No Regrets* (Billie Holiday); *Love Is Like a Cigarette* and *Welcome Stranger* (Eddy Duchin); *Indian Love Call* (Nelson Eddy, Jeanette MacDonald)

Jazz and Big Bands

Jo Jones and Buck Clayton join Count Basie; Mildred Bailey sings with the new Red Norvo band. Popular boogie-woogie piano includes Meade Lux Lewis, Pete Johnson, Albert Ammons, and Bob Zurke. Lester Young plays with the Count Basie combo in Chicago.

New Bands: Red Norvo; Woody Herman

Top Performers *(Downbeat):* Benny Goodman (soloist, big band); Ray Noble (sweet band); Eddie Lang, Pops Foster, Teddy Wilson, Gene Krupa, Tommy Dorsey, Bix Biederbecke (instrumentalists)

Theater

Broadway Openings

Plays

Idiot's Delight (Robert E. Sherwood), Alfred Lunt, Lynn Fontanne
Call It a Day (Dodie Smith), Gladys Cooper, Philip Merivale
Tovarich (Jacques Deval), John Halliday, Marta Abba
Stage Door (George S. Kaufman, Edna Ferber), Margaret Sullavan
You Can't Take It with You (Moss Hart, George S. Kaufman), Josephine Hull, Frank Conlan
Brother Rat (John Monks, Jr., Fred Finklehoff), Eddie Albert, Frank Albertson, José Ferrer
The Women (Clare Booth), Margalo Gillmore, Ilka Chase, Audrey Christie
Johnny Johnson (Paul Green), John Garfield, Elia Kazan, Luther Adler
The Postman Always Rings Twice (James M. Cain), Richard Barthelmess, Mary Philips
Ethan Frome (Owen Davis, Donald Davis), Pauline Lord, Ruth Gordon, Raymond Massey
The Wingless Victory (Maxwell Anderson), Katharine Cornell, Effie Shannon, Walter Abel
Tonight at 8:30 (Noel Coward), Noel Coward, Gertrude Lawrence
St. Helena (R. C. Sherriff, Jeanne de Casalis), Maurice Evans, Barry Sullivan
Night Must Fall (Emlyn Williams), May Whitty, Emlyn Williams

Musicals

George White's Scandals of 1936 (Ray Henderson, Jack Yellen), Rudy Vallee, Bert Lahr, Willie and Eugene Howard
On Your Toes (Richard Rodgers, Lorenz Hart), Tamara Geva, Ray Bolger, Monty Woolley, choreographed by George Balanchine
Red, Hot and Blue (Cole Porter), Ethel Merman, Jimmy Durante, Bob Hope
White Horse Inn (Ralph Benatsky, Irving Caesar), William Gaxton, Kitty Carlisle, Robert Halliday
Ziegfeld Follies of 1936 (Vernon Duke, Ira Gershwin), Fannie Brice, Bob Hope, Eve Arden, Josephine Baker

Classics and Revivals On and Off Broadway

St. Joan (George Bernard Shaw), Katharine Cornell, Maurice Evans, Tyrone Power, Jr.; *The Country Wife* (Wycherley), Ruth Gordon; *Cyrano de Bergerac* (Rostand), Walter Hampton; *Hamlet,* John Gielgud, Judith Anderson, Lillian Gish. *Founded:* The WPA, with *Chalk Dust, The Living Newspaper, Class of 1929, Macbeth,* Orson Welles; *Murder in the Cathedral* (T. S. Eliot), Harry Irvine

Regional

Cleveland: *Not for Children* (Elmer Rice), premiere

Pulitzer Prize

Idiot's Delight, Robert E. Sherwood

Classical Music

Compositions

Edgard Varèse, *Densité*
Aaron Copland, *El salon México*
Samuel Barber, Symphony no. 1, Adagio for Strings,
    String Quartet no. 1
Roy Harris, Quintet for Piano and Strings
Roger Sessions, String Quartet no. 1
Virgil Thomson, *The Plough that Broke the Plains*
John Alden Carpenter, Violin Concerto
Howard Hanson, Symphony no. 3
David Diamond, Psalm
William Schuman, String Quartet no. 1
Arnold Schoenberg (in U.S.), Violin Concerto

Important Events

The WPA Federal Music Program broadens to
support concert bands, chamber groups, and opera.
Lajos Shuk conducts the Buffalo Philharmonic in its
first concert, with Mischa Elman. Most frequently
performed international composers are Francesco
Malipiero, Georges Enesco, and Paul Hindemith. A
controversy is raised over whether orchestras should
have single or multiple conductors; the New York
Philharmonic has invited Arturo Toscanini, Wilhelm
Fürtwängler, Igor Stravinsky, Carlos Chávez, and
John Barbirolli, who becomes its permanent
conductor.

Debut: Gary Graffman, Robert Casadesus

First Performances

Chávez (conducting), *Sinfonia India* (New York);
Sergei Rachmaninoff, Symphony no. 3 (Philadelphia);
Roy Harris, Symphony no. 3 (Boston); Prelude and
Fugue for String Orchestra (Philadelphia); William
Schuman, Symphony no. 1 (New York); Samuel
Barber, Symphony no. 1 (Cleveland)

Opera

Metropolitan: Widespread efforts to popularize
opera include 25¢ to $3 tickets; the Opera Guild is
established to sponsor public talks and opera
publications; companies travel widely. Kerstin
Thorborg (debut), *Die Walküre; Tristan und Isolde;*
Bruna Castagna, *Il trovatore;* Dusolina Giannini,
Aïda; Gianni Schicchi (in English); Florence Easton's
farewell, *Die Walküre*

Chicago: *Jack and the Beanstalk* (Louis Gruenberg,
premiere); Helen Jepson, *Louise*

San Francisco: Mozart is introduced into the
repertory: *The Marriage of Figaro* (Elisabeth
Rethberg, Ezio Pinza); Fritz Reiner joins the
company to continue Wagner's *Ring* cycle from last
year.

Walker Evans's *Georgia* is
part of the pictorial record of
America gathered by the
Resettlement Administration
(RA) under Roy Stryker.
Library of Congress.

Art

Painting

Lyonel Feininger,
Church at Gelmeroda

Arshile Gorky, *Aviation,
Self-Portrait*

Adolph Gottlieb, *Sun
Deck*

William Gropper,
*Suburban Post in
Winter*

Reginald Marsh, *Twenty-
Cent Movie, End of
the Fourteenth Street
Crosstown Line*

Joe Jones, *American
Farm*

John Steuart Curry,
*Westward Migration,
The Mississippi*

Raphael Soyer, *Office
Girls, Artists on WPA*

Mark Tobey, *Broadway*

Ernest Leonard
Blumenschein, *Jury
for Trial of a
Sheepherder for
Murder*

Marsden Hartley, *The
Old Bars*

Ben Shahn, *East Side
Soap Box*

Sculpture

Alexander Calder,
Gibraltar

Anna Hyatt Huntington,
Greyhounds Playing

David Smith, *Head as
Still Life, Growing
Forms*

Alexander Archipenko,
Torso in Space

Architecture

Hoover Dam, Boulder
City, Nev. (U.S.
Bureau of
Reclamation)

Barclay-Vesey Building,
New York (McKenzie,
Vorhees, and Gmelin)

U.S. Supreme Court,
Washington, D.C.
(Cass Gilbert)

Designs are approved for
the Jefferson
Memorial,
Washington, D.C.
(John Russell Pope)
and National Gallery,
Washington, D.C.
(Pope).

Dorothea Lange, *Migrant Mother. Library of Congress.*

Important Exhibitions

Museums

New York: *Metropolitan:* "Benjamin Franklin and his Circle"; Goya's drawings, Copley, La Farge. *Museum of Modern Art:* New horizons in American Art; Architecture of H. H. Richardson and his times; Cubism and abstract art; John Marin; "Fantastic Art, Dada and Surrealism" show includes Duchamp, Grosz, Moholy-Nagy, Seligmann, Tanguy. *Whitney:* "American Scene: WPA"

Chicago: Rembrandt; Mexican arts and crafts

Philadelphia: Degas

Boston: Art treasures of Japan

Art Briefs

Regional shows attract large audiences in Kansas City, Dallas, Buffalo, Syracuse, the Cumberland Valley, Pittsburgh, Chicago, Iowa, and Indiana; sales also revive • FDR publicly supports native art. • Government payments are $23.86 for a 15-hour week; 5,300 artists in 44 states paint 600 to 700 murals. William Baziotes and Mark Rothko join the WPA project • The influx of French art stirs little public interest, although Picasso, Matisse, Cézanne, Derain, and Vlaminck are widely shown in commercial galleries • American Abstract Artists is formed by Ilya Bolotowsky, Giorgio Cavallon, and Ibram Lassaw.

Dance

Lincoln Kirstein organizes a touring company, Ballet Caravan; Catherine Littlefield begins the Philadelphia Ballet Company.

Books

Fiction

Critics' Choice
The Crack-Up, F. Scott Fitzgerald
Absalom, Absalom! William Faulkner
The Big Money, John Dos Passos
Black Spring, Henry Miller
In Dubious Battle, John Steinbeck
House of Incest, Anaïs Nin
A World I Never Made, James T. Farrell
No Villain Need Be, Vardis Fisher
🙣 *Stories of Three Decades*, Thomas Mann

Best-Sellers
Gone with the Wind, Margaret Mitchell
The Last Puritan, George Santayana
Sparkenbroke, Charles Morgan
Drums along the Mohawk, Walter D. Edmonds
It Can't Happen Here, Sinclair Lewis
White Banners, Lloyd C. Douglas
Eyeless in Gaza, Aldous Huxley
The Thinking Reed, Rebecca West
The Hurricane, Charles Nordhoff, J. N. Hall
The Doctor, Mary Roberts Rinehart

Nonfiction

Critics' Choice
The Interpretation of History, Paul Tillich
The Geographical History of America, Gertrude Stein
The Higher Learning in America, Richard M. Hutchins
The Living Jefferson, James T. Adams
Hitler, Konrad Heiden
Hearst: Lord of San Simeon, O. Carlson, E. Sutherland Bates
Rich Land, Poor Land, Stuart Chase
The Family Encounters the Depression, Robert C. Angell
Homeless Men, Thomas Menchen
Mathematics for the Million, Lancelot Hogben
🙣 *General Theory of Employment, Interest and Money*, J. M. Keynes

Best-Sellers
Man the Unknown, Alexis Carrel
The Way of a Transgressor, Negley Farson
North to the Orient, Anne Morrow Lindbergh
Wake Up and Live! Dorothea Brande
Around the World in Eleven Years, Patience Abbe, Richard Abbe, Johnny Abbe

Live Alone and Like It, Marjorie Hills
I Write as I Please, Walter Duranty
An American Doctor's Odyssey, Victor Heiser
Life with Father, Clarence Day
Inside Europe, John Gunther

Poetry
T. S. Eliot, *Collected Poems*
Dorothy Parker, *Not So Deep as a Well*
Carl Sandburg, *The People, Yes*
Wallace Stevens, *Owl's Clover*
Marianne Moore, *The Pangolin and Other Verse*
Robert Penn Warren, *Thirty-Six Poems*
🙣 A. E. Housman, *More Poems*

Pulitzer Prizes
Gone with the Wind, Margaret Mitchell (novel)
The Flowering of New England, Van Wyck Brooks (U.S. history)
Hamilton Fish, Allan Nevins (biography)
A Further Range, Robert Frost (poetry)

Nobel Prize
Eugene O'Neill

Science and Technology

Dehydro-cortisone is the first adrenal cortex hormone to be isolated, by Edward C. Kendall.

Vitamin B, thiamine, is synthesized by Robert R. Williams.

Vitamin E is isolated by Herbert McLean Evans and Gladys Emerson.

Pharmaceutical firms develop sulfa drugs.

Alexis Carrel and Charles Lindbergh develop the first artificial heart.

Ernest O. Lawrence transmutes platinum into gold in the cyclotron.

The Douglas twin-engine DC-3, which can carry 21 passengers over 1,500 miles, begins production.

Boulder Dam, on the Colorado River, is completed; it creates the largest artificial reservoir in the world, 246 square miles, and provides power to 1.5 million people.

The cheap "baby" combine harvester is marketed by Allis Chalmers, facilitating small farm mechanization.

🙣 The first jet-powered flight is made by a Heinkel aircraft, based on Hans von Ohain's work.

🙣 The first successful helicopter flight is made.

Sports _____

Baseball
The first players elected to the Hall of Fame are Ty Cobb, Honus Wagner, Babe Ruth, Christy Mathewson, and Walter Johnson.

Joe DiMaggio (New York, AL) and Bob Feller (Cleveland, AL) debut; Feller strikes out 15 in his first game.

Champions _____

Batting	*Pitching*
Paul Waner (Pittsburgh, NL), .373	Carl Hubbell (New York, NL), 26–6
Luke Appling (Chicago, AL), .388	Monte Pearson (New York, AL), 19–7
	Home runs
	Lou Gehrig (New York, AL) 49

Football

NFL Season Leaders: Arnie Herber (Green Bay), passing; Tuffy Leemans (N.Y.), rushing; Don Hutson (Green Bay), receiving.

College All-Americans: Sammy Baugh (Q), Texas Christian; Clint Frank (B), Yale.
The Cotton Bowl, played at Dallas, Texas, is inaugurated on New Year's Day, 1937.

Bowls (Jan. 1, 1937)
Rose: Pittsburgh 21–Washington 0
Orange: Duquesne 13–Mississippi State 12
Cotton: Texas Christian 16–Marquette 6
Sugar: Santa Clara 21–Louisiana State 14

Basketball
The entire Renaissance Rens team is voted into the Basketball Hall of Fame; their overall record is 473–49.

Jesse Owens setting the broad jump record in the Berlin Olympics. *D. Ouellette Collection.*

Olympics
In the Berlin Olympics, the "Ebony Antelope," Jesse Owens, wins four gold medals (100m, 10.3s; 200m, 23.7s; broad jump, 26' $31/64''$, a record; and 400m relay). Nine out of ten American blacks win gold medals. Hitler leaves the stadium before the awards are given. Other U.S. winners include Archie Williams (400m, 46.5s), John Woodruff (800m, 1:52.9s), Forest Towns (110m, 14.2s), Glenn Hardin (400 m.h., 52.4s), Cornelius Johnson (high jump, 6' $7^{15}/_{16}''$), Earle Meadows (pole vault, 14' $3¼''$), Ken Carpenter (discus, 65' $7^{29}/_{64}''$), Glenn Morris (decathlon), Helen Stephens (100m, 11.5s).

Other Sports

Boxing: Max Schmeling defeats Joe Louis in 12 rounds; he says of Louis: "He fought like an amateur. This is no man who could ever be champion."

Winners _____

World Series	*Player of the Year*
New York (AL) 4	John Moir, Notre Dame
New York (NL) 2	*Stanley Cup*
MVP	Detroit
NL–Carl Hubbell, New York	*U.S. Tennis Open*
AL–Lou Gehrig, New York	Men: Fred Perry
NFL	Women: Alice Marble
Green Bay 21–Boston 6	*USGA Open*
College Football	Tony Manero
Minnesota	*Kentucky Derby*
Heisman Trophy	Bold Venture (I. Hanford, jockey)
Larry Kelley, Yale	
College Basketball	
Notre Dame	

Fashion _____

For Women: Enormously popular in the day is a plum or dark green wool tailored dress with long, tight sleeves and slightly bloused bodice; the dress gently flares to midcalf, has side pleats, and is worn with a wide leather belt. For evening, the black silk crepe with white silk overjacket is fashionable, along with the shiny, brown satin with its matching jacket and feather-trimmed sleeves. Formal wear ranges from short dresses in bright colors to gold lamé frocks with pressed pleats and short jackets.

Ferragamo designs the first evening wedge shoe in gold kid and red satin, but ankle boots of gold kid or embroidered velvet are also shown. The "bra" becomes a separate garment for the high and pointed look; falsies are marketed.

High-fashion notes: Schiaparelli's square bag and collarless coat with high sleeves; Molyneux's crescent brown calf pouch bag.

Kaleidoscope _____

- Dust storms denude large portions of the farmlands of Kansas, Oklahoma, Colorado, Nebraska, and the Dakotas.
- A Colorado farmland survey indicates that half of 6,000 farmhouses in one area have been abandoned.
- An ad for California's "All-Year Club" reads: "Warning! Come to California for a glorious vacation. Advise anyone not to come seeking employment."
- At its peak, the WPA Federal Art Project employs 3,500 artists, who in the next six years produce 4,500 murals, 19,000 sculptures, and 450,000 paintings. The WPA Federal Writers' Project employs 6,500; the Federal Music Project, 15,000 who, in 30 orchestras, play 225,000 programs.
- Joke: "St. Peter: We're a bit behind schedule today. God has an appointment with His psychiatrist. Recently He's started behaving like Franklin D. Roosevelt."
- Numerous federal parks and fish and game sanctuaries are set up by the National Park Service; 600,000 acres are added to state preserves.
- The Institute for Propaganda Analysis is set up in New York with a board that includes Charles Beard, Paul Douglas, and Robert Lynd.
- A *Fortune* article notes: "As for sex . . . the campus takes it more casually than it did ten years ago. . . . It is news that it is no longer news."
- A *Fortune* poll indicates that 67 percent favor birth control.
- Molly Dewson of the National Consumers League leads the fight for female federal patronage. More women postmasters are appointed.
- Josephine Baker introduces the conga to Broadway.
- According to *Life* magazine, one out of ten Americans is tattooed in whole or in part.
- At a premiere of *New Faces,* New York mayor S. Wilson Davis leaps out of his seat to demand the removal of a skit that caricatures Eleanor Roosevelt.
- David Sarnoff coaxes Arturo Toscanini out of retirement in Italy to lead a symphony orchestra for NBC; the finest musicians are gathered and perform in a special studio, 8H, at Rockefeller Center, New York.
- The Swing Music Concert in New York includes Bob Crosby, Tommy Dorsey, Stuff Smith, Red Norvo, Bunny Berigan, Glen Gray's Casa Loma Orchestra, groups from Paul Whiteman and Louis Armstrong, and Arthur (*sic*) Shaw's String Ensemble.
- Small jazz clubs spring up on 52nd Street, New York, with Stuff Smith and Jonah Jones at the Onyx and Wingy Malone at the Famous Door.
- Celebrity marriages include Paulette Goddard and Charles Chaplin, John Barrymore and Elaine Barrie, Mary Pickford and Buddy Rogers, Lily Pons and André Kostelanetz.
- Margaret Mitchell's *Gone with the Wind* sells a record 1 million copies in six months.

Works Progress Administration site. During the year the WPA, under Harry Hopkins, provided employment to over 3 million. *Museum of the City of New York.*

- Herbert LeRoy Hechler runs a trained flea circus on West 42nd Street, New York, where, for 30¢, spectators can watch, through magnifying glasses, fleas dance, juggle, walk a tightrope, stage a chariot race, and operate a carousel.
- Photography-related sales increase, owing to recent advances like the exposure meter and 35mm camera.
- Trailer sales peak; tourist camps for vacationing motorists are also popular.
- Seven million women pay more than $2 billion for 35,000,000 permanents.
- Ferdinand the Bull, Munro Leaf's fantasy about a pacifistic flower-loving bull, is a popular success.
- Sunflower buttons (the Kansas flower) appear throughout the counry in Alf Landon's campaign against FDR. Tiffany and Co. advertises a gold 19-petal sunflower pin with yellow diamonds for $815.
- German pro-Nazi Bund societies form as "Amerika-deutscher Volkbund," ostensibly devoted to social and athletic pursuits.
- Commemorative half-dollars are issued with the heads of P. T. Barnum, Stephen Foster, and Moses Cleveland (the city founder); three-cent Susan B. Anthony and Boulder Dam stamps are also issued.
- A revolt against progressive education is led by Robert M. Hutchins, president of the University of Chicago.
- The popular *Literary Digest* poll, correct since 1920, forecasts a Landon victory of 54 percent; the newer Gallup poll predicts that FDR will win.
- A sleeper berth from Newark to Los Angeles costs $150; the New York Fifth Avenue double-decker bus fare goes from 5¢ to 10¢.

First Appearances: Giant panda in U.S. (San Francisco), art course in fresco painting (Louisiana State University), newspaper microfilming current issues *(New York Herald Tribune),* old-age colony (Melville, N.Y.), photo-finish camera (electric eye) at racetrack, bicycle traffic court (Racine, Wisc.), screw-cap bottle with pour lip, sheet of postage stamps containing more than one variety, Presbyterian Church of America, Penguin books, Ford Foundation, *Life,* Chunky, knock-knock jokes, Goren point-counting system, Vitamin Plus (first vitamin pill), fluorescent tube, Tampax

1937

Economic Profile
  Dow-Jones: ↓ High 190–
    Low 118
  GNP: +9%
  Inflation: +1.5%
  Unemployment: 14.3%
Average salary: $1,250
  Teacher: $1,367
  Lawyer: $4,485
  Physician: $4,285
  Factory Worker: $1,376
I. Miller straparound sandal:
  $14.75
Tailored Woman wool and
  lamb coat: $95
Russek's velvet wraparound:
  $35
McCreery's fur coats, black
  pony, dyed lamb, leopard:
  $119
Bloomingdale's cashmere
  dress: $12.95
Mark Cross bag: $5–$16.50
Cocktails, double
  (Rockefeller Center): 25¢
Name-imprinted Christmas
  cards: $9.75 (for 100)
China porcelains: $1–$12

Deaths

J. M. Barrie, John
  Drinkwater, George
  Gershwin, Jean Harlow,
  Frank Billings Kellogg,
  Guglielmo Marconi,
  Maurice Ravel, John D.
  Rockefeller, Ernest
  Rutherford, Irving
  Thalberg, Edith Wharton.

In the News

SIT-DOWN STRIKES CLOSE 15 GENERAL MOTORS PLANTS . . . LEON TROTSKY ARRIVES IN MEXICO . . . HOWARD HUGHES FLIES FROM LOS ANGELES TO NEWARK IN RECORD 7 HOURS, 28 MINUTES, 5 SECONDS . . . NEVILLE CHAMBERLAIN APPEALS TO HITLER FOR COOPERATION IN PEACEKEEPING . . . HITLER REPUDIATES GERMAN WORLD WAR I GUILT . . . 13 PROMINENT DEFENDANTS ARE SENTENCED TO DEATH IN MOSCOW FOR TREASON . . . FDR ASKS CONGRESS FOR POWER TO REORGANIZE THE SUPREME COURT . . . NEW LAW ALLOWS SUPREME COURT JUSTICES TO RETIRE AT 70 WITH FULL PAY . . . U.S. STEEL AND WORKERS SETTLE FOR $5/DAY MINIMUM WAGE AND 40-HOUR WEEK . . . DIRIGIBLE "HINDENBERG" CRASHES AT LAKEHURST, N.J., 38 DIE . . . GERMAN EMBASSY PROTESTS FIORELLO LAGUARDIA'S ATTACKS ON HITLER . . . AMELIA EARHART, ON ROUND-THE-WORLD FLIGHT, VANISHES OVER PACIFIC . . . AFL LEADER WILLIAM GREEN CONDEMNS SIT-DOWN STRIKES, JOHN L. LEWIS ASSAILS GREEN . . . SUPREME COURT UPHOLDS MINIMUM WAGE LAW . . . WAGNER LABOR ACT IS DECLARED CONSTITUTIONAL . . . JOINT NEUTRALITY RESOLUTION OF CONGRESS FORBIDS WAR MATERIAL TRANSPORT TO BELLIGERENTS . . . DIVORCED WALLIS WARFIELD SIMPSON TO WED DUKE OF WINDSOR . . . SUPREME COURT UPHOLDS THE SOCIAL SECURITY ACT . . . FDR ASKS INVESTIGATION OF "IMMORAL" TAX EVASION BY THE WEALTHY . . . 7 SOVIET GENERALS, INCLUDING HERO TUKHACHEVSKY, ARE EXECUTED . . . CLARENCE NORRIS, SCOTTSBORO DEFENDANT, IS SENTENCED TO DEATH FOR THE THIRD TIME . . . SENATE VOTES DOWN COURT REORGANIZATION BILL . . . HUGO BLACK IS NOMINATED TO THE SUPREME COURT FOR THE WILLIS VAN DEVANTER SEAT . . . STOCK MARKET DECLINES SHARPLY.

Quotes _____

"I see one-third of a nation ill-housed, ill-clothed, ill-nourished."

— FDR, second inauguration

"No tin-hat brigade of goose-stepping vigilantes or Bible-babbling mob of blackguarding corporation-scoundrels will prevent the onward march of labor."

— John L. Lewis

"We'll never recognize the United Auto Workers Union or any other union."

— Henry Ford

"The major development in the General Motors strike is the sitdown. . . . It is a tactic which permits workers to halt production with a minimum of effort and a maximum of initial success—and it has management of all industry wondering how to stop it."

— Business Week

"Berlin does not hide its contempt for the democracies: 'stupid cows' Goebbels calls them. . . . Today it is Madrid. Tomorrow it will be Prague. How long before it knocks at our own doors?"

— I. F. Stone, Nation

"I am the law."

— Frank Hague, mayor of Jersey City

The Federal Arts Project strives to integrate "the arts with the daily life of the community." Above: a gas station in the Northeast U.S. *Library of Congress.*

"It is the people of Spain who have won already one of the great victories against fascism. How then can we, who profit by that victory, not claim the war as ours? How then can we refuse our help?"

— Archibald MacLeish

"When an epidemic of physical disease starts to spread, the community . . . joins in a quarantine . . . to protect the health of the community against the spread of the disease."

— FDR, on the fascist countries

"There are worse things than war. Cowardice, . . . treachery, . . . and simple selfishness."

— Ernest Hemingway

Ads _____

Radio

Premieres

"Stella Dallas," Anne Elstner
"The Guiding Light," Ed Prentiss, Sarajane Wells
"NBC Symphony," Arturo Toscanini
"Our Gal Sunday," Dorothy Lowell
"Grand Central Station," Jack Arthur
"Big Town," Edward G. Robinson
"Dr. Christian," Jean Hersholt
"Mr. Keen, Tracer of Lost Persons," Bennett Kilpack

Specials

John Barrymore in six Shakespeare plays; "Hamlet" (Burgess Meredith, Walter Abel, Grace George)

Of Note

Mae West's sexy repartee with Charlie McCarthy on the "Chase and Sanborn Hour" leads to an FCC investigation • Popular quiz programs include "Melody Puzzles," "Professor Quiz," "Spelling Bee," and "Uncle Jim's Question Bee" • Most popular comedians include Jack Benny, Edgar Bergen and Charlie McCarthy, Burns and Allen, Eddie Cantor, Fred Allen, Fibber McGee and Molly, Joe Penner, Fannie Brice, George Jessel, Jack Oakie, Jack Haley, Phil Baker, and Al Pearse and his gang.

New Catchphrases: "Can this girl from a mining town in the West find happiness as the wife of a wealthy and titled Englishman?" ("Our Gal Sunday"); "Drawn by the magnetic force of the fantastic metropolis, . . . great trains rush towards . . . [the] gigantic stage on which are played a thousand dramas daily!" ("Grand Central Station")

Movies

Openings

The Life of Emile Zola (William Dieterle), Paul Muni
The Awful Truth (Leo McCarey), Irene Dunne, Cary Grant
Captains Courageous (Victor Fleming), Freddie Bartholomew, Spencer Tracy, Lionel Barrymore
Dead End (William Wyler), Sylvia Sidney, Joel McCrea, Humphrey Bogart
The Good Earth (Sidney Franklin), Luise Rainer, Paul Muni
In Old Chicago (Henry King), Tyrone Power, Alice Faye, Don Ameche
Lost Horizon (Frank Capra), Ronald Colman, Sam Jaffe, Margo
Stage Door (Gregory LaCava), Katharine Hepburn, Ginger Rogers
A Star Is Born (William A. Wellman), Janet Gaynor, Fredric March
Nothing Sacred (William A. Wellman), Carole Lombard, Fredric March
Stella Dallas (King Vidor), Barbara Stanwyck, John Boles
Topper (Norman Z. McLeod), Cary Grant, Roland Young, Constance Bennett
Elephant Boy (Robert Flaherty, Zoltan Korda), Sabu, W. E. Holloway
One Hundred Men and a Girl (Henry Koster), Deanna Durbin, Leopold Stokowski and large orchestra

Warner Oland, in his 16th role as the B-film detective-hero Charlie Chan. *Movie Star News.*

They Won't Forget (Mervyn LeRoy), Claude Rains, Allyn Joselyn, Lana Turner
You Only Live Once (Fritz Lang), Henry Fonda, Sylvia Sidney
La grande illusion (Jean Renoir), Jean Gabin, Eric von Stroheim

Academy Awards

Best Picture: *The Life of Emile Zola*
Best Director: Leo McCarey (*The Awful Truth*)
Best Actress: Luise Rainer (*The Good Earth*)
Best Actor: Spencer Tracy (*Captains Courageous*)

Top Box-Office Stars

Shirley Temple, Clark Gable, Robert Taylor, Bing Crosby, William Powell, Jane Withers, Fred Astaire and Ginger Rogers, Sonja Henie, Gary Cooper, Myrna Loy

Popular Music

Hit Songs
"A Foggy Day"
"The Donkey Serenade"
"Harbor Lights"
"Nice Work if You Can Get It"
"Whistle while You Work"
"I've Got My Love to Keep Me Warm"
"Johnny One Note"
"The Lady Is a Tramp"
"My Funny Valentine"
"September in the Rain"
"Thanks for the Memory"
"In the Still of the Night"
"Where or When"

Top Records
Bei mir bist du Schoen (Andrew Sisters); *They Can't Take that Away from Me, They All Laughed, Let's Call the Whole Thing Off,* and *Shall We Dance?* (Fred Astaire); *Someone to Care for Me* (Deanna Durbin); *Ebb Tide* (Bunny Berigan); *Have You Met Miss Jones?* (Sammy Kaye); *Sweet Leilani* (Bing Crosby and Lani McIntire and His Hawaiians)

Jazz and Big Bands
Benny Goodman records *Sing, Sing, Sing.* Charlie Parker joins the Jay McShann Band. Mary Lou Williams plays with Andy Kirk's Kansas City Band in New York. Harry James plays with Benny Goodman.

First Recordings: George Shearing

New Bands: Glenn Miller, New York

Top Performers *(Downbeat):* Benny Goodman (soloist, big band); Hal Kemp (sweet band); Ella Fitzgerald (vocalist); Carmen Mastren, Bob Haggert, Teddy Wilson, Gene Krupa, Tommy Dorsey, Chu Berry, Harry James (instrumentalists)

Theater

Broadway Openings

Plays
High Tor (Maxwell Anderson), Burgess Meredith
Golden Boy (Clifford Odets), Luther Adler, Art Smith
Yes, My Darling Daughter (Mark Reed), Lucile Watson, Peggy Conklin
Having Wonderful Time (Arthur Rober), John Garfield
Room Service (John Murray, Allen Boretz), Eddie Albert, Betty Field, Sam Levene
The Star-Wagon (Maxwell Anderson), Lillian Gish, Burgess Meredith
Susan and God (Rachel Crothers), Gertrude Lawrence, Nancy Kelly
Amphitryon 38 (Jean Giraudoux), Alfred Lunt, Lynn Fontanne
Of Mice and Men (John Steinbeck), Broderick Crawford, Wallace Ford
French without Tears (Terence Rattigan), Frank Lawton
The Ghost of Yankee Doodle (Sidney Howard), Ethel Barrymore

Musicals
Babes in Arms (Richard Rodgers, Lorenz Hart), Mitzi Green, Ray Heatherton, Alfred Drake

Frederika (Franz Lehár), Helen Gleason, Dennis King, Ernest Truex
Horray for What! (Richard Arlen, E. Y. Harburg), Ed Wynn, Vivian Vance
I'd Rather Be Right (Richard Rodgers, Lorenz Hart), George M. Cohan
Pins and Needles (Harold Rome), International Ladies Garment Workers' Union (ILGWU), Millie Weitz, Ruth Rubinstein, Hy Goldstein
The Show Is On (Vernon Duke et al.), Bert Lahr, Beatrice Lillie, Reginald Gardner

Classics and Revivals On and Off Broadway
Julius Caesar, Orson Welles, Joseph Cotten, Martin Gabel; *Dr. Faustus* (Marlowe), Orson Welles; *Richard II,* (Maurice Evans); *Candida* (George Bernard Shaw), Katharine Cornell; *A Doll's House* (Ibsen), Ruth Gordon, Walter Slezak; *Othello,* Walter Huston. *Founded:* Playwrights' Company by Maxwell Anderson, S. N. Behrman, Sidney Howard, Elmer Rice, and Robert E. Sherwood.

Pulitzer Prize
You Can't Take It with You, George S. Kaufman and Moss Hart

Classical Music

Compositions

Roy Harris, *Time Suite*, Symphony no. 3, String Quartet no. 3
Virgil Thomson, *The River, Filling Station*
Aaron Copland, *The Second Hurricane*
Ferde Grofé, *Broadway at Night, Symphony in Steel*
John Cage, *Construction in Metal*
Walter Piston, Symphony no. 1
William Schuman, Symphony no. 2, String Quartet no. 2, Choral Etude
John Powell, Symphony in A
Samuel Barber, First Essay for Orchestra
Arnold Schoenberg (in U.S.), String Quartet no. 4

Important Events

Robert Whitney conducts the first concert of the Louisville Symphony Orchestra. Paul Hindemith makes his first U.S. appearance, playing his Viola Sonata at the Library of Congress. Artur Rubinstein, at Carnegie Hall, premieres Stravinsky's *Petroushka's Suite,* dedicated to Rubinstein. Well-known composers writing for radio include Aaron Copland ("Music for Radio"); Harris ("Time Suite"); William Grant Still ("Lenox Avenue"); Piston ("Concertino"); Howard Hanson (Symphony no. 3); Henry Gruenberg ("Three Mansions"). Toscanini signs with NBC to conduct the orchestra created for him.

Guest Conductors: Pierre Monteux, Artur Rodzinsky, and Arturo Toscanini, the New York Philharmonic

Debut: Jorge Bolet, Julius Katchen

First Performances

Ernest Bloch, *A Voice in the Wilderness* (Los Angeles); E. B. Hill, Symphony no. 3 (Boston); John Alden Carpenter, Violin Concerto (Chicago); Daniel Gregory Mason, *A Lincoln Symphony* (New York); Marc Blitzstein, *The Cradle Will Rock* (New York)

Opera

Metropolitan: Bidú Sayão (debut), *Manon;* Sayão, Helen Traubel (debut), *The Man without a Country* (Walter Damrosch, premiere); Giovanni Martinelli, *Otello* (first time since 1913); Kirsten Flagstad, *Elektra, Der Rosenkavalier;* Zinka Milanov, *Il trovatore*

Chicago: Jussi Bjoerling (American debut), *Rigoletto;* Kirsten Flagstad, Lauritz Melchior, *Tristan und Isolde;* Grace Moore, *Manon*

Philadelphia: Premieres: *Amelia Goes to the Ball* (Gian Carlo Menotti); *Le pauvre Metelot* (Darius Milhaud)

Music Notes

At the first outdoor concert at Tanglewood, Lenox, Mass., rain pours during the first piece ("The Ride of the Valkyries"); arrangements are made to build a "shed." • A typical concert program consists of Beethoven, Brahms, Wagner, or Strauss, with the moderns Sibelius and Stravinsky; virtually no unfamiliar compositions are played.

Already a legend as past conductor of La Scala and the New York Philharmonic (and a passionate antifascist), Arturo Toscanini is 70 when he begins his career with the NBC Symphony Orchestra. *Library of Congress.*

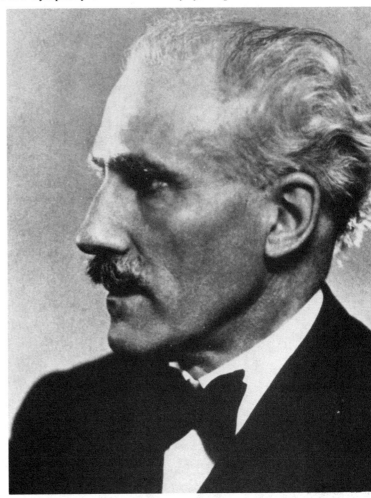

Art

Painting
Arnold Friedman, *Unemployable*

Peter Blume, *The Eternal City*

John Sloan, *Nude and Nine Apples*

Charles Burchfield, *Ice Glare, November Evening*

Ben Shahn, *West Virginia, 1937*

Willem de Kooning, *Untitled*

Jackson Pollock, *Untitled*

Arthur G. Dove, *Rise at the Full Moon*

Jack Levine, *The Feast of Pure Reason*

Philip Evergood, *The Story of Richmond*

Edwin Dickinson, *Composition with Still Life*

Sculpture
Paul Manship, *Night, Day, Time*

James Earle Fraser, *George Washington*

William Zorach, *Ben Franklin*

Lee Lawrie, *Atlas* (Rockefeller Center)

Naum Gabo, *Spheric Theme*

Alexander Archipenko, *Walking Woman*

John B. Flannagan, *Triumph of the Egg*

Architecture
Golden Gate Bridge, Oakland-San Francisco (Strauss, Ammann, Moisseff, and Derleth)

Kaufman House ("Falling Water"), Bear Run, Pa. (Frank Lloyd Wright)

Keck-Gottschalk-Keck Coop Apartment Building, Chicago (George F. Keck)

Trowbridge and Livingston win the design competition for the Oregon State Capitol Building, Salem.

Important Exhibitions

Museums

New York: *Metropolitan:* Renoir; "Sporting Prints and Painting"; Italian Renaissance prints and illustrative books; *Museum of Modern Art:* Van Gogh; Photography 1839–1937. *Whitney:* Gaston Lachaise memorial; Cleveland artists; "The Realists"

Philadelphia: French art; William Rush

Washington: *Corcoran:* Bicentennial prizes to Edward Hopper, Guy Pène du Bois, Francis Speight

Boston: Lithographs 1799–1937

Pittsburgh: Carnegie International First Prize won by Georges Braque

Art Briefs
Regional shows expand in Kansas City, Chicago, Cleveland, San Francisco, Pittsburgh, Denver, St. Louis, Milwaukee, and Seattle • The Washington Museum of Modern Art opens • The Solomon R. Guggenheim Museum for nonobjective art is planned • Gropius, Archipenko, Moholy-Nagy, and others open a new Bauhaus in a 25-room mansion in Chicago, donated by Marshall Field III • Major sales include Gauguin's *Tahiti* ($1,700), Corot's *Landscape with Bathers* ($9,000), Millet's *Shepherdess* ($3,700), Rembrandt's etching *Christ Healing the Sick* ($10,500), and Cézanne's *Bathers* ($110,000), purchased by the Philadelphia Museum.

Dance

The Mordkin Ballet opens in New York. Stravinsky visits the United States for the premiere of *Jeu de cartes* at the Metropolitan (Balanchine), with Lew Christensen and William Dollar.

Other Premieres
American Ballet: *La baiser de la fée* (Balanchine), Dollar; *Apollo* (Balanchine), Christensen. Martha Graham: *Letter to the World, Deep Song*

Dreams on a Washington, D.C., street. *Library of Congress.*

Books

Fiction
Critics' Choice
To Have and Have Not, Ernest Hemingway

Noon Wine, Katherine Anne Porter

The Sea of Grass, Conrad Richter

Their Eyes Were Watching God, Zora Neale Hurston

The Red Pony, John Steinbeck

Remembering Laughter, Wallace Stegner

They Came Like Swallows, William Maxwell

The Grandmothers, Glenway Westcott

The Seven Who Fled, Frederic Prokosch

Serenade, James M. Cain

❧ *Bread and Wine*, Ignazio Silone

Best-Sellers
Gone with the Wind, Margaret Mitchell

Northwest Passage, Kenneth Roberts

The Citadel, A. J. Cronin

And So—Victoria, Vaughan Wilkins

Drums along the Mohawk, Walter D. Edmonds

The Years, Virginia Woolf

Theatre, W. Somerset Maugham

Of Mice and Men, John Steinbeck

The Rains Came, Louis Bromfield

We Are Not Alone, James Hilton

The Education of Hyman Kaplan, Leonard Q. Ross

Nonfiction
Critics' Choice
Bulwark of the Republic, Burton J. Kendrick

The Ultimate Power, Morris Ernst

Middletown in Transition, Robert S. and Mary M. Lynd

The Life and Death of a Spanish Town, Elliott Paul

The Realm of Truth, George Santayana

The Folklore of Capitalism, Thurman Arnold

An Artist in America, Thomas Hart Benton

You Have Seen Their Faces, Margaret Bourke-White, Erskine Caldwell

Beloved Friend, Catherine Drinker Bowen

In the American Jungle, 1925–1937, Waldo Frank

The Neurotic Personality of Our Time, Karen Horney

Let Your Mind Alone, James Thurber

Best-Sellers
How to Win Friends and Influence People, Dale Carnegie

An American Doctor's Odyssey, Victor Heiser

The Return to Religion, Henry C. Link

The Arts, Hendrik Willem Van Loon

Orchids on Your Budget, Marjorie Hollis

Present Indicative, Noel Coward

Life with Mother, Clarence Day

The Nile, Emil Ludwig

The Flowering of New England, Van Wyck Brooks

Mathematics for the Million, Lancelot Hogben

Poetry
Edna St. Vincent Millay, *Conversation at Midnight*

Robinson Jeffers, *Such Counsels You Gave to Me*

Ezra Pound, *The Fifth Decade of Cantos*

Wallace Stevens, *The Man with the Blue Guitar*

Louise Bogan, *The Sleeping Fury*

Richard Eberhart, *Reading the Spirit*

Sara Teasdale, *Collected Poems*

Archibald MacLeish, *The Fall of the City*

Allen Tate, *The Mediterranean*

Pulitzer Prizes
The Late George Apley, John P. Marquand (novel)

The Road to Reunion, 1865–1900, Paul H. Buck

Pedlar's Progress, Odell Shepard (U.S. history)

Andrew Jackson, Marquis James (history)

Cold Morning Sky, Marya Zaturenska (poetry)

Science and Technology

Johns Hopkins researchers release the first American report of successful treatment of bacterial infection with sulfanilamide.

Vitamin B is found to cure alcoholic neuritis.

Vitamin B_2 is isolated and analyzed and found to be nicotinic acid, an already known substance.

C. Bradley introduces amphetamines for the treatment of hyperactive children.

The structure of vitamin E is determined by Donald Fernholz.

Corticosterone, a second adrenal cortex hormonal substance, is isolated by Edward Kendall.

A prototype "antihistamine" is produced to treat allergic, or histamine, response to outward stimuli.

James Hillier and Albert Prebus build the first practical electron microscope.

AT&T completes the first coaxial cable for television hookups between New York and Philadelphia.

❧ Hans Krebs postulates his "cycle" of oxidative phosphorylation, the basic process of cellular metabolism.

Nobel Prize
Clinton J. Davisson wins the prize in physics for work on the diffraction of electrons by crystals.

Sports

Baseball

Carl Hubbell is beaten after a record 24-game streak extending over two seasons.

Cy Young, Nap Lajoie, and Tris Speaker are added to the Hall of Fame.

Champions

Batting	Pitching
Ducky Medwick (St. Louis, NL), .374	Carl Hubbell (New York, NL), 22–8
Chuck Gehringer (Detroit, AL), .371	John Allen (New York, AL), 15–1
	Home runs
	Joe DiMaggio (New York, AL), 46

Football

Sammy Baugh (QB), Washington, debuts.

NFL Season Leaders: Sammy Baugh (Washington), passing; Cliff Battles (Washington), rushing; Don Hutson (Green Bay), receiving.

College All-Americans: Byron "Whizzer" White (B), Colorado; Marshall Goldberg (B), Pittsburgh; Clark Hinckle (G), Vanderbilt

Bowls (Jan. 1, 1938)
Rose: California 13– Alabama 0
Orange: Auburn 6– Michigan State 0
Cotton: Rice 28– Colorado 0
Sugar: Santa Clara 6– Louisiana State 0

Basketball

The National Basketball League, composed of neighboring midwestern teams, begins.

Hank Luisetti, Stanford, scores a record 50 points in one game.

Other Sports

Boxing: Joe Louis, 23, the "Brown Bomber," defeats James Braddock for the heavyweight title.

Winners

World Series	*College Basketball*
New York (AL) 4	Stanford
New York (NL) 1	*Player of the Year*
MVP	Hank Luisetti, Stanford
NL–Joe Medwick, St. Louis	*Stanley Cup*
AL–Charles Gehringer, Detroit	Detroit
NFL	*U.S. Tennis Open*
Washington 28	Men: Donald Budge
Chicago 21	Women: Anita Lizana
College Football	*USGA Open*
Pittsburgh	Ralph Guldahl
Heisman Trophy	*Kentucky Derby*
Clint Frank, Yale	War Admiral (C. Kurtsinger, jockey)

Fashion

For Women: The hourglass silhouette, with padded shoulders and small waist, gives way to a more tubular, natural shape with the new "uplift." Evening lengths remain long in wool fabrics; jewels are bulky and immense; Cartier clips of blackamoors' heads are copied everywhere. Bulky blue fox and silk jersey are also new. Veils return on hats. In makeup, Christian Berard introduces cyclamen rouge and deep blue lashes for blondes, and brown suntan rouge and pomegranate lips for brunettes.

High-fashion note: Strassner's white pullover, white wool slacks.

For men: For spring and summer: the single-breasted gabardine suit with patch pockets and

An ad displaying current fashion.

panama hat; for fall: the double-breasted dark blue suit with wide-cuffed trousers, padded square shoulders, double-pleated, high-waisted trousers. Vertical stripe suits, in two tones or with windowpane checks, are also new, as well as fabric blends of cotton and wool, nylon and silk, silk and wool. Neckwear is in deep tones, regimentals, polka dots, and tartans; socks are elasticized and have circular stripes.

Kaleidoscope _____

- The *Hindenburg,* the world's largest dirigible, carries 98 people and has 50 private cabins; its crash is witnessed by hundreds who have come to watch its triumphant landing.
- The massive Ohio River flood leaves 500,000 homeless.
- Despite torrential rains, the Tennessee River, with its TVA dams, does not overflow.
- A Gallup poll shows that 80 percent approve of relief through paid public work, as opposed to a dole.
- Controversy follows Hugo L. Black's appointment to the Supreme Court because of his youthful membership in the KKK.
- The United States is the world's greatest producer and consumer of spirits, with gin most in demand, followed by whiskey and rum.
- The AMA recognizes birth control advice as a legitimate professional concern.
- A *Fortune* poll reports that 50 percent of all college men and 25 percent of all college women have had premarital sexual relations; two-thirds of the women "would for true love."
- The Marijuana Taxation Act prohibits importation, sale, or possession, with heavy penalties for violators.
- The Miller-Tydings fair trade law is passed, allowing resale prices to be fixed by brand-name manufacturers.
- The UAW is recognized by General Motors as sole bargaining agent for its workers.
- Pierce-Arrow autos go out of business.
- Spinach growers erect a statue to Popeye in Wisconsin.
- Companies like American Radiator, Celotex, and Sears & Roebuck attempt prefabricated housing.
- According to *Vogue,* "It is no longer smart to be sleek, slick, and sexy but smart to be feminine . . . in a new calm way showing the body as a superb piece of sculpture."
- New writers in Hollywood include F. Scott Fitzgerald, Sidney Howard, Robert Sherwood, and Ernest Hemingway.
- Of the great silent movie comedians, only Charles Chaplin remains in Hollywood; others find that sound slows them up and retire (Buster Keaton, Harold Lloyd, and Harry Langdon).
- Among the many films on social themes are *They Won't Forget* (anti–mob violence), *Black Legion* (anti-KKK), *White Bondage* (on sharecroppers), *Make Way for Tomorrow* (on old age), and *Dead End* (about slums).
- Three thousand teenagers line up outside the Paramount Theater to see Benny Goodman.
- According to a Paramount poll, the top bands include Benny Goodman, Guy Lombardo, Shep Fields, Eddy Duchin, Tommy Dorsey, Horace Heidt, Fred Waring, and Sammy Kaye.
- A study indicates that people spend 4.5 hours daily listening to the radio.
- An Old Gold radio contest leads to greatly increased

FDR presenting the Harmon Trophy for outstanding aviator to the flamboyant industrialist-Hollywood playboy Howard Hughes. *Copyright* Washington Post. *Reprinted by permission of D.C. Public Library.*

usage of the New York Public Library.
- Bauhaus architect Walter Gropius becomes head of Harvard's Graduate School of Design; Marcel Breuer, also from Germany, joins him.
- Frank Lloyd Wright tells the International Congress of Architects in Moscow: "Vertical is vertigo in human life. The horizontal line is the lifeline of human kind."
- The restoration of Colonial Williamsburg, Va., is completed.
- Satin programs are distributed at the first NBC Symphony concert under Toscanini so that the rattling of paper will not disturb the maestro.
- John D. Rockefeller, dead at 98, leaves an estate estimated at $1 billion.
- Several thousand Americans join the Abraham Lincoln Brigade to fight with the Loyalists against the fascist-supported Franco forces; about 50 percent die in battle. Among the writers who go to Spain to report on the war are Dorothy Parker, Lillian Hellman, John Dos Passos, Ernest Hemingway, Malcolm Cowley, Josephine Herbst, and Upton Sinclair.
- United Steel agrees to terms with John L. Lewis without a strike, which greatly enhances Lewis's prestige.
- From September 1, 1936, to June 1, 1937, 484,711 workers have been involved in sit-down strikes.

First Appearances: Nylon, okapis (animals) imported in New York, National Cancer Institute, children's church (Milton, Mass.), Flag Day (June 14), Santa Claus school (Albion, N.Y.), trampoline, skywriting at night, Pepperidge Farm, Spam, sodium cyclamate, shopping cart, franchising (Howard Johnson), Lincoln Tunnel, Harlem River House

1938

In the News

FDR ASKS FOR BUILDUP OF ARMY AND NAVY . . . SECOND AGRICULTURAL ADJUSTMENT ACT IS PASSED AND PROVIDES FOR EVER-NORMAL GRANARY . . . WINSTON CHURCHILL PROTESTS NEVILLE CHAMBERLAIN'S POLICIES OF APPEASEMENT . . . MUD SLIDES IN SOUTHERN CALIFORNIA KILL 144 . . . GERMANY INVADES AUSTRIA, PROCLAIMS ANSCHLUSS . . . SUDETEN GERMANS IN CZECHOSLOVAKIA "DEMAND" AUTONOMY . . . HERBERT HOOVER ADVISES AGAINST EUROPEAN ALLIANCES . . . HITLER VISITS MUSSOLINI IN ROME . . . NAVAL EXPANSION ACT OF 1938 IS PASSED, $1 BILLION ALLOCATED . . . HOUSE UN-AMERICAN ACTIVITIES COMMITTEE IS FORMED . . . WHEELER-LEA ACT PROVIDES CLOSER FOOD AND DRUG REGULATION . . . HOWARD HUGHES SETS ROUND-THE-WORLD FLYING RECORD, 3 DAYS, 19 HOURS, 8 MINUTES . . . "WRONG-WAY" CORRIGAN HEADS FOR CALIFORNIA, LANDS IN DUBLIN . . . FAIR LABOR STANDARDS ACT REGULATES MAXIMUM HOURS AND MINIMUM WAGES . . . FDR URGES ARBITRATION OF CZECH CRISIS . . . HITLER, CHAMBERLAIN, DALADIER, MUSSOLINI MEET IN MUNICH AND AGREE TO CEDE PART OF CZECHOSLOVAKIA TO GERMANY . . . POLES TAKE TESCHEN AREA FROM CZECHS . . . JAPANESE ADVANCE AND CAPTURE CANTON, MOVE ON HANKOW . . . MUSSOLINI PROCLAIMS LIBYA PART OF ITALY . . . HUNGARY ANNEXES SLOVAKIA FROM CZECHOSLOVAKIA . . . JEWISH SHOPS ARE SMASHED AND LOOTED THROUGHOUT GERMANY ON KRISTALNACHT, U.S. AMBASSADOR IS RECALLED FOR CONSULTATION . . . ANTHONY EDEN, ON NEW YORK RADIO, WARNS AMERICA OF FASCIST PERIL . . . FRANCO BEGINS MAJOR ASSAULT ON CATALONIA.

Quotes

"I sense a deep happiness that, despite the depression, Americans are happy at surviving under a democratic form of government."

— FDR

"It is intolerable at this moment to think of a large portion of our people exposed to the democratic hoards who threaten our people. I refer to Czechoslovakia!

— Adolf Hitler

"[This declaration] is symbolic of the desire of our two peoples never to go to war again."

— Joint document signed by Hitler and Chamberlain at Munich

"My friends, . . . there has come back from Germany peace with honor. I believe it is peace for our time."

— Neville Chamberlain

"It took the Big Four just five hours and twenty-five minutes here in Munich today to dispel the clouds of war and come to an agreement over the partition of Czechoslovakia. There is to be no European war, after all."

— William Shirer, CBS

Farmers with a recent loan from the Tenant Purchase Program. *Library of Congress.*

"[Let us be warned] against war or against alliances against fascists."

— Herbert Hoover

"The American people surely want to stay out of the next world war. . . . It may cost the blood of countless American boys."

— Charles A. Beard, defining *isolationism*

"I'm speaking from the roof of the Broadcasting Building, New York City. The bells you hear are ringing to warn the people to evacuate the city as the Martians approach."

— Announcer, "The War of the Worlds," Mercury Radio Theatre

Ads

Radio

Premieres

"World News Roundup," William Shirer (London); Ansel Mowrer (Paris); Ed Murrow (Vienna); Bob Trout (Washington)

"Information, Please!" Clifton Fadiman (host), Oscar Levant, John Kieran, Franklin P. Adams

"Young Widder Brown," Florence Freeman

"The Green Hornet," Al Hodge

"The Mercury Theatre on the Air," Orson Welles

"Kay Kyser's Kollege of Musical Knowledge"

"Joyce Jordan, Girl Interne," Rita Johnson

Specials

"Air Raid" (Archibald MacLeish, with Orson Welles, Ray Collins)

Of Note

Most popular light, homey, or love-interest dramas include "Aunt Fanny," "Brent House," "County Seat," "Curtain Time," "Dog Heroes," "Dr. Christian" (Jean Hersholt), "First Nighter," "Grand Central Station," "Irene Rich," "Mary and Bob," "One Man's Family," "Princess Pat Players," "Second Husband" (Helen Mencken), "Those We Love," and "Wings for the Martins"

New Catchphrases: "Wake Up, America! It's time to stump the experts" ("Information Please!"); "Britt Reid, daring young publisher, matches wits with [the] underworld. . . . He hunts the biggest . . . of all game. Public enemies who try to destroy our America" ("The Green Hornet")

TV

Programs

Sidewalk interviews with passersby, Rockefeller Center, New York

Coverage of the suicide of John Warde, "the man on the ledge," who leaped from the seventeenth floor of the Hotel Gotham in N.Y.C. after 11 hours.

Movies

Openings

You Can't Take It with You (Frank Capra), James Stewart, Jean Arthur

The Adventures of Robin Hood (Michael Curtiz, William Keighley), Errol Flynn, Olivia de Havilland

Boys' Town (Norman Taurog), Spencer Tracy, Mickey Rooney

Jezebel (William Wyler), Bette Davis, Henry Fonda

Pygmalion (Anthony Asquith, Leslie Howard), Leslie Howard, Wendy Hiller

Test Pilot (Victor Fleming), Clark Gable, Myrna Loy, Spencer Tracy

Angels with Dirty Faces (Michael Curtiz), James Cagney, Pat O'Brien

Love Finds Andy Hardy (George B. Seitz), Mickey Rooney, Judy Garland

Algiers (John Cromwell), Charles Boyer, Hedy Lamarr (debut)

Marie Antoinette (W. S. Van Dyke), Norma Shearer, Tyrone Power

Blockade (William Dieterle), Madeleine Carroll, Henry Fonda

Bringing Up Baby (Howard Hawks), Katharine Hepburn, Cary Grant

Snow White and the Seven Dwarfs (Walt Disney)

The Baker's Wife (Marcel Pagnol), Raimu

The Lady Vanishes (Alfred Hitchcock), Michael Redgrave, Margaret Lockwood

Alexander Nevsky (Sergei Eisenstein), Nikolai Cherkassov

Academy Awards

Best Picture: *You Can't Take It with You*

Best Director: Frank Capra (*You Can't Take It with You*)

Best Actress: Bette Davis (*Jezebel*)

Best Actor: Spencer Tracy (*Boys' Town*)

Top Box-Office Stars

Shirley Temple, Clark Gable, Sonja Henie, Mickey Rooney, Spencer Tracy, Robert Taylor, Myrna Loy, Jane Withers, Alice Faye, Tyrone Power

Popular Music

Hit Songs
"Chiquita Banana"
"Falling in Love with Love"
"This Can't Be Love"
"They Say"
"You Must Have Been a Beautiful Baby"
"Get Out of Town"
"My Heart Belongs to Daddy"
"September Song"
"Jeepers Creepers"
"My Reverie"
"Spring Is Here"

Top Records
Love Walked In (Kenny Baker); *I Married an Angel* (Larry Clinton); *It's Wonderful* (Shep Fields); *Thanks for the Memory* and *Two Sleepy People* (Bob Hope

and Shirley Ross); *You Go to My Head* (Kay Kyser); *Love in the Starlight* (Dorothy Lamour); *One O'Clock Jump* (Harry James); *Begin the Beguine* (Artie Shaw); *Jalousie* (Boston Pops, Arthur Fiedler); *Beer Barrel Polka* (Will Glahe); *A-Tisket, A-Tasket* (Chick Webb, Ella Fitzgerald); *Boogie Woogie* (Jimmy Dorsey)

Jazz and Big Bands
Benny Goodman gives his first Carnegie Hall concert.
The first John Hammond "From Spirituals to Swing" concert is given at Carnegie Hall with Count

Basie and Joe Turner.
Billie Holiday joins Artie Shaw's band.

New Bands: Larry Clinton, Les Brown, Gene Krupa, all in New York

Top Performers *(Downbeat):* Benny Goodman (soloist); Artie Shaw (big band); Casa Loma (sweet band); Ella Fitzgerald (vocalist); Benny Heller, Bob Haggart, Bob Zurke, Jimmy Dorsey, Bud Freeman, Tommy Dorsey, Harry James (instrumentalists)

Theater

Broadway Openings

Plays
Our Town (Thornton Wilder), Frank Craven, John Craven, Martha Scott
Bachelor Born (Ian Hay), Frederick Leister or Philip Tonge (alternating roles)
Shadow and Substance (Paul Vincent Carroll), Cedric Hardwicke, Sara Allgood
On Borrowed Time (Paul Osborn), Dudley Digges, Frank Conroy
Kiss the Boys Good-Bye (Clare Boothe), Helen Claire, Hugh Marlowe, Benay Venuta
Abe Lincoln in Illinois (Robert E. Sherwood), Raymond Massey, Muriel Kirkland
Missouri Legend (E. B. Ginty), Dorothy Gish, Dean Jagger, José Ferrer, Dan Duryea
Here Come the Clowns (Philip Barry), Eddie Dowling
Rocket to the Moon (Clifford Odets), Morris Carnovsky, Luther Adler

Musicals
The Boys from Syracuse (Richard Rodgers, Lorenz Hart), Teddy Hart, Jimmy Savo, Eddie Albert, Burl Ives
Hellzapoppin' (Sammy Fain), Olson and Johnson, Barte and Mann, Radio Rogues

Raymond Massey. *Billy Rose Theatre Collection. The New York Public Library at Lincoln Center. Astor, Lenox and Tilden Foundations.*

I Married an Angel (Richard Rodgers, Lorenz Hart), Vera Zorina, Dennis King, Vivienne Segal
Knickerbocker Holiday (Kurt Weill), Walter Huston, Ray Middleton, Jeanne Madden
Leave It to Me (Cole Porter), William Gaxton, Victor Moore, Mary Martin, Sophie Tucker, Gene Kelly
The Three Waltzes (Johann Strauss, Sr. and Jr.), Kitty Carlisle, Michael Bartlett, Glenn Anders
The Cradle Will Rock (Marc Blitzstein), Will Geer

Classics and Revivals On and Off Broadway
Outward Bound (Sutton Vane), Laurette Taylor; *Hamlet* (Maurice Evans, in first full-length performance); *The Seagull* (Chekhov), Alfred Lunt, Lynn Fontanne. *Mercury Theatre: Heartbreak House* (George Bernard Shaw), Orson Welles, Vincent Price, Geraldine Fitzgerald; *Danton's Death* (Georg Buchner), Martin Gabel; *The Shoemaker's Holiday* (Dekker), Vincent Price, Joseph Cotten

Pulitzer Prize
Our Town, Thornton Wilder

Classical Music _____

Compositions

Aaron Copland, *An Outdoor Overture*
Arthur Shepherd, Symphony no. 2
Ernest Bloch, Violin Concerto
Elliott Carter, *Prelude, Fanfare, and Polka*
David Diamond, Elegy, Cello Concerto
Roy Harris, Symphony no. 3 in One Movement,
   Soliloquy and Dance
John Cage, *Bacchanale, Metamorphosis*

Important Events

The Federal Music Project employs 2,642 musicians in 38 orchestras. The Philadelphia Orchestra's Roy Harris concert is widely acclaimed. Eleanor Roosevelt heads the committee that sponsors Carnegie Hall's celebration concert for Moriz Rosenthal.

Major Recitals: Harold Bauer, Moriz Rosenthal, Josef Hofmann, Ignace Jan Paderewski

Debut: Rudolf Firkusny

First Performances

Stravinsky, *Dumbarton Oaks* (Washington, D.C.); Samuel Barber, Adagio for Strings (NBC); Bloch, Violin Concerto (Cleveland); Copland, *Billy the Kid* (Chicago); Walter Piston, Symphony no. 1, *The Incredible Flutist* (Boston); Samuel Barber, Essay for Orchestra (New York); William Schuman, Symphony no. 2 (New York); Milhaud, conducting and playing, Piano Concerto no. 1 (Minneapolis); Virgil Thomson, *Filling Station* (Hartford)

Shirley Temple, *Movie Star News.*

Opera

Metropolitan: Debuts: Risë Stevens, *Mignon;* Jussi Bjoerling, *La bohème;* Erich Leinsdorf, *Die Walküre.* Premieres: *Amelia Goes to the Ball* (Gian Carlo Menotti); *Beauty and the Beast* (Vittorio Giannini, on CBS)

Hartford, Conn.:   *Knickerbocker Holiday* (Kurt Weill)

Chicago: Beniamino Gigli, Helen Jepson, *Martha;* Ezio Pinza, Jepson, *Faust*

San Francisco: Ebe Stignani (debut), Janine Micheau, *Pelléas et Mélisande;* Kerstin Thorborg, *Elektra;* Salvatore Baccaloni, *Don Pasquale*

Music Notes

Arturo Toscanini receives $4,000 per concert with the newly formed NBC Symphony • Harvard University awards Marian Anderson an honorary doctorate • Copland chairs the American Composers Alliance to promote "serious music" • The WPA sponsors a successful jazz *Mikado* • Serge Koussevitzy conducts Bach and Beethoven at the inaugural concert of the music shed, Tanglewood (Berkshire Festival).

Snow White and the Seven Dwarfs, Walt Disney's first feature length film, is an enormous success. "It made the nation smile," said critic Bosley Crowther. *Movie Star News.*

Art _____

Painting

Thomas Hart Benton, *Cradling Wheat, I Got a Gal on Sourwood Mountain, Rainy Day*

Willem de Kooning, *Pink Landscape*

Reginald Marsh, *Human Pool Tables*

Stuart Davis, *Swing Landscape*

Arshile Gorky, *Argula*

Peter Hurd, *Dry River*

John Steuart Curry, *Oklahoma Land Rush, Our Good Earth*

Joseph Stella, *Song of Barbados, Machina Naturale No. 13*

Jackson Pollock, *Composition with Figures and Banners, The Flame*

Yasuo Kuniyoshi, *I'm Tired*

Sculpture

Ibram Lassaw, *Sculpture in Steel*

José de Rivera, *Black and Red (Double Element)*

Burgoyne Diller, *Construction #16*

Heinz Warneke, *Mother and Child*

Isamu Noguchi, *News,* Associated Press Building, Rockefeller Center.

David Smith, *Amusement Park, Leda*

Placed at the N.Y. World's Fair: James Earle Fraser's *George Washington,* Paul Manship's *Time Groups,* and Leo Friedlander's *Four Freedoms*

Architecture

N.Y. World's Fair, Central Mall (William and Geoffrey Platt)

Kleinhan's Music Hall, Buffalo, N.Y. (Saarinen and Saarinen)

Taliesen West, near Scottsdale, Ariz. (Frank Lloyd Wright)

Resor House, Jackson Hole, Wyo. (Mies van der Rohe)

Gropius House, Lincoln, Mass. (Gropius and Breuer)

Important Exhibitions

Museums

New York: *Metropolitan:* 500 Years of Chinese bronzes; Egyptian styles in the Eastern Mediterranean; Tiepolo and his contemporaries. *Morgan:* French Art of ten centuries. *Museum of Modern Art:* Bauhaus art, U.S.A.; Frank Lloyd Wright; prints of Rouault; primitive art. *Whitney:* Art west of the Mississippi; memorials for Charles Demuth, William Glackens

Chicago: The two Tiepolos; Chicago artists; Giacometti

San Francisco: Fifteenth- and sixteenth-century Venetian painting

Philadelphia: Nineteenth-century art; Renoir; Benjamin West

Virginia: Inauguration of "American Painting Today" biennial, with prizes to Eugene Speicher and Henry Lee McFee

Boston: John Benson; Edmund Charles Tarbell; John Singleton Copley

Detroit: Italian Gothic and early Renaissance art

Buffalo: Artists of the Great Lakes

Traveling Show: "American Retrospective"—from Thomas Eakins to Thomas Hart Benton—through the United States and then Paris and London

Art Briefs

The Bauhaus group, transplanted from Germany to Chicago, disbands for lack of funds • The Cloisters opens • Arshile Gorky holds his first one-man show in New York • The Federal Art project employs 5,000; many decorate new federal buildings; John Steuart Curry is commissioned for the Topeka Capitol Building murals, Reginald Marsh for the N.Y. Customs House.

Dance _____

The National Ballet with the Ballet Caravan is organized, and the company makes a transcontinental tour. Willam Christensen becomes choreographer of the San Francisco Ballet and increases its repertoire to include full-length works, such as *Swan Lake*. The association of the American Ballet and Metropolitan Opera ends in acrimony and public controversy over artistic differences.

Premieres

Ballet Caravan: *Billy the Kid* (Eugene Loring), Loring, Lew Christensen, Todd Bolender; *Filling Station* (Christensen), Bolender

Chicago Grand Opera Ballet: *Frankie and Johnny* (Ruth Page, Bentley Stone)

Books ───────────────────────────

Fiction

Critics' Choice

The Fifth Column and the First Forty-nine Stories, Ernest Hemingway
The Unvanquished, William Faulkner
Uncle Tom's Children, Richard Wright
The Long Valley, John Steinbeck
No Star is Lost, James Farrell
The Fathers, Allan Tate
The King Was in His Counting House, James Branch Cabell
Laughter in the Dark, Vladimir Nabokov (trans. by author)
ᵅ *Homage to Catalonia*, George Orwell
ᵅ *Murphy*, Samuel Beckett

Best-Sellers

The Yearling, Marjorie Kinnan Rawlings
The Citadel, A. J. Cronin
My Son, My Son! Howard Spring
Rebecca, Daphne Du Maurier
Northwest Passage, Kenneth Roberts
All This, and Heaven Too, Rachel Field
The Rains Came, Louis Bromfield
And Tell of Time, Laura Krey
The Mortal Storm, Phyllis Bottome
Action at Aquila, Hervey Allen

Nonfiction

Critics' Choice

The World's Body, John Crowe Ransom
Understanding Poetry, Cleanth Brooks, Robert Penn Warren
Journey between Wars, John Dos Passos
The Tyranny of Words, Stuart Chase
The Culture of Cities, Lewis Mumford
Logic and the Theory of Inquiry, John Dewey
Tom Watson, Agrarian Rebel, C. Vann Woodward
Beyond Dark Hills, Jesse Stuart
The House That Hitler Built, Stephen H. Roberts
Red Star over China, Edgar Snow
Save America First, Jerome Frank
Man against Himself, Karl Menninger
Guide to Kulchur, Ezra Pound

Best-Sellers

The Importance of Living, Lin Yutang
How to Win Friends and Influence People, Dale Carnegie
Madame Curie, Eve Curie
Alone, Adm. Richard E. Byrd
Listen! The Wind, Anne Morrow Lindbergh
I'm a Stranger Here Myself, Ogden Nash

With Malice toward Some, Margaret Halsey
The Horse and Buggy Doctor, Arthur E. Hertzler
Benjamin Franklin, Carl Van Doren
Fanny Kemble, Margaret Armstrong

Poetry

William Carlos Williams, *Complete Collected Poems*
Archibald MacLeish, *Land of the Free—U.S.A.*
E. E. Cummings, *Collected Poems*
Kenneth Fearing, *Dead Reckoning*
Robinson Jeffers, *The Selected Poetry*
Delmore Schwartz, *In Dreams Begin Responsibilities*
Laura Riding, *Collected Poems*
ᵅ W. B. Yeats, *New Poems*

Pulitzer Prizes

The Yearling, Marjorie Kinnan Rawlings
A History of American Magazines, Frank Luther Mott (U.S. history)
Benjamin Franklin, Carl Van Doren (biography)
Selected Poems, John Gould Fletcher (poetry)

Nobel Prize

Pearl S. Buck

Science and Technology ──────────────

Carl David Anderson discovers the meson—a particle 200 times the mass of an electron.
Chester F. Carlson produces the first xerographic print.
Teflon is developed by Joseph Plunkett at Du Pont.
Albert Doisy and Sidney Thayer isolate pure vitamin K.
Julius Lempert develops the fenestration operation to treat otosclerosis, a cause of deafness.
Reports indicate that Dilantin benefits epilepsy, eliminating the need for toxic bromide therapy.
Sulfonilamide is found to cure bruccellosis, a severe febrile illness.
Harold Cox grows typhus bacilli suitable for vaccine development in chick embryo yolk sacs.
ᵅ The Biro brothers, George and Ladislav, invent the ballpoint pen.
ᵅ U. Cerletti and L. Bini introduce electroconvulsive therapy, ECT or "shock," for the treatment of mental illness.

Sports

Baseball

Johnny Vandermeer (Cincinnati, NL) pitches back-to-back no-hitters against Boston and Brooklyn.
Bob Feller (Cleveland, AL) strikes out a record 18 in one game.

Champions

Batting	Pitching
Ernie Lombardi (Cincinnati, NL), .342	Bill Lee (Chicago, NL), 22–9
Jimmy Foxx (Boston, AL), .349	Red Ruffing (New York, AL), 21–7
	Home runs
	Hank Greenberg (Detroit, AL), 58

Football

NFL Season Leaders: Ed Danowski (New York), passing; Byron White (Pittsburgh), rushing; Gaynell Tinsley (Chicago Cards), receiving.

College All-Americans: Parker Hall (B), Mississippi; Marshall Goldberg (B), Pittsburgh

Bowls (Jan. 1, 1939)

Rose: Southern California 7–Duke 3
Orange: Tennessee 17–Oklahoma 0
Cotton: St. Mary's (California) 20–Texas Tech 13
Sugar: Texas Christian 15–Carnegie Tech 7

Basketball

The Akron Goodyear Tires win the ABL title.
The National Invitation Tournament, at Madison Square Garden, is organized; it is the first national postseason tournament.

Other Sports

Boxing: Joe Louis knocks out Max Schmeling in the first round. Louis is hailed as "the first American to KO a Nazi."

Tennis: Ellsworth Vines and Fred Perry tour as pros and earn $34,000 each; Vines wins 48, and Perry 35. Helen Wills Moody wins her eighth Wimbledon title.

Winners

World Series	*College Basketball*
New York (AL) 4	Temple
Chicago (NL) 0	*Player of the Year*
MVP	Hank Luisetti, Stanford
NL–Ernest Lombardi, Cincinatti	*Stanley Cup*
AL–James Foxx, Boston	Chicago
NFL	*U.S. Tennis Open*
New York 23–Green Bay 17	Men: Donald Budge
MVP	Women: Alice Marble
Mel Hein, New York	*USGA Open*
College Football	Ralph Guldahl
Texas Christian	*Kentucky Derby*
Heisman Trophy	Lawrin (E. Arcaro, jockey)
Davey O'Brien, Texas Christian	

Fashion

For Women: A varied elegance marks the year. The popular look is the modern pencil-thin silhouette—the black outfit and skunk jacket, hair piled on top of the head, an extravagant hat, and enormous amounts of artificial jewelry. In the evening, skin-tight molded dresses and short tailored jackets with paillettes or embroidery are worn. By spring, romantic styles are shown: full skirts in gay and sentimental patterns, tiny sailor hats trimmed with feathers and flowers, and clogs. Also new are the more formal strapless evening gowns. Hair is worn in a pageboy with side combs and bobby pins, or it is pushed off the ears or tied back in George Washington bows. Styles of 1890 and 1900 are revived for day and evening: big muffs, hoopskirts, leg-of-mutton sleeves. The smart color is cyclamen. Lipsticks and rouges have a bluish tint. Yellow red is out.

High-fashion note: Schiaparelli's print crepe dress

Bette Davis received her second Academy Award this year. *Movie Star News.*

Kaleidoscope ─────────

- H. V. Kaltenborn covers the Munich crisis with 85 broadcasts in 18 days, as intense interest is paid to the possibility of war in Europe.
- A Gallup poll indicates that 65 percent of the population approves of the Munich agreement with Germany.
- Orson Welles's radio show "The War of the Worlds" is so lifelike that people rush into the streets and cry out in fear of an extraterrestrial invasion.
- The newly formed House Un-American Activities Committee, under Martin Dies, receives more coverage than any other domestic news event; its investigations of the ACLU, Campfire Girls, and the WPA Federal Theatre Project raise great protests.
- The Ludlow Amendment, requiring a referendum before Congress can declare war except in the case of invasion, is defeated in the House by a narrow margin.
- Ten million are unemployed as the "second depression" worsens.
- The Fair Labor Standards law provides a 25¢-an-hour minimum wage, 44-hour work week, and time and a half for overtime; it abolishes child labor.
- The Civil Aeronautics Authority is created to regulate air traffic.
- Mae West's name is banned from mention on 130 licensed radio stations.
- The expensive search for stars for *Gone with the Wind* continues at a cost of $96,000.
- Foreign dances, such as the rhumba, tango, conga, and Lambeth walk, as well as community and group dances, gain in popularity.
- Elsa Maxwell becomes prominent as a Washington party hostess.
- Former New York speakeasies that become chic include the supper clubs El Morocco, Stork Club, and 21.
- Heiress Brenda Frazier makes her society debut, and the strapless gown becomes a national fad.
- As a promotional strategy, airlines offer wives free passage with their husbands, as female fear of flying is thought to be keeping air traffic down.

- Salvador Dali offers Harpo Marx a role in a surrealistic ballet.
- A container made of indestructible metal and containing photographic records and other examples of contemporary culture is buried in the New York World's Fair grounds; it is to be opened in 5,000 years.
- The Carnival of Swing at Randall's Island attracts 25,000 jitterbugs for five and three-quarters hours.
- To celebrate the 20th anniversary of the Armistice, Kate Smith revives "God Bless America," and it becomes a second national anthem.
- The Jefferson-head nickel goes into circulation.
- Thomas Mann settles in the United States.
- A "Thirty Dollars Every Thursday" movement is proposed that promises "ham and eggs" to all; it gains 1 million votes in a California referendum.
- The Oxford Movement promotes moral rearmament: "If men will be good, there will be no more wars."
- North Carolina initiates the first state-sponsored birth control clinics.
- As a result of federal activity, numerous highways are built, which in turn facilitate suburban expansion.
- The United States leads the world in candy production, which ranks sixth among food industries; 2 billion pounds are manufactured a year; 16 pounds are consumed per capita.
- "Wrong-Way Corrigan," refused a permit to fly across the Atlantic to Dublin, announces that he will fly to California; afterwards, he intentionally flies to Dublin and remarks, "Sorry, I flew the wrong way."

First Appearances: Society for the Preservation and Encouragement of Barber Shop Quartet Singing in America (Tulsa), cartoon school, chlorophyll (patent), Euthanasia Society, law requiring marriage license applicants to undergo medical tests, law requiring serological blood tests of pregnant women, nylon bristle filament for toothbrushes, woman of American descent to become a queen (King Zog of Albania's wife), March of Dimes

Russell Lee, *Travelling Evangelists. Library of Congress.*

FDR and his sons at Marblehead, Mass. *Smithsonian Institute*

1939

Economic Profile
Dow-Jones: − High 155–
Low 121
GNP: +7%
Inflation: −0.6%
Unemployment: 17.2%
Police expenditures, federal,
state, local: $378 million
Persons arrested: 577,000
Executions: 160
Prisoners, federal, state:
179,000
Juvenile court appearances:
40,365
Average wages:
62¢/hour
$22.30/week
$1,230/year
$26/week (male)
$15/week (female)
Billy Rose's Cafe Mañana,
New York (dinner,
entertainment): $1–$2.50
Yacht Club, New York
(featuring Fats Waller):
$1.50
Schiaparelli "grasshopper
dress": $1.98
Horn and Hardart mince pie:
35¢ (whole pie)
Glass coffee maker: $2.95

Deaths

Artur Bodanzky, Heywood
Broun, Harvey Cushing,
Havelock Ellis, Douglas
Fairbanks, Sr., Ford
Madox Ford, Sigmund
Freud, William Butler
Yeats.

In the News

FDR Asks $535 Million for Defense . . . Golden Gate International Exposition Begins in San Francisco . . . Germany Invades Czechoslovakia . . . U.S. Recalls Ambassador to Germany . . . Franco Takes Madrid, Loyalists Surrender . . . U.S. Recognizes Franco Government . . . Hatch Act Prohibits Government Employees from Politicking . . . New York World's Fair Opens . . . Hitler and Mussolini Sign 10-Year "Pact of Steel" . . . King George VI Visits U.S., Is Treated to Hot Dogs . . . Pan-Am Dixie Clipper Begins First Regular Transatlantic Flights to Lisbon . . . House Un-American Activities Committee Continues to Investigate Federal Theater Project . . . Germany and U.S.S.R. Agree to Commerce Treaty . . . Germany and U.S.S.R. Sign Nonaggression Pact . . . German Armies Invade Poland in Land and Air Assault . . . Britain and France Declare War on Germany . . . Poland Surrenders to Nazi Armies . . . Charles Lindbergh Speaks Out against Intervention . . . Britain Sends 150,000 Troops to France . . . Germany and U.S.S.R. Divide Poland at Oder-Nesse Line . . . FDR Orders U.S. Ports and Waters Closed to Foreign Submarines . . . Congress Amends Neutrality Act, Britain and France Can Buy Arms "Cash and Carry" . . . Germans Scuttle Battleship "Graf Spee" in Montevideo . . . U.S.S.R. Invades Finland.

Edward R. Murrow helps inform America about the European situation; his broadcast ends nightly with "Good night and good luck." *Billy Rose Theatre Collection. The New York Public Library at Lincoln Center. Astor, Lenox and Tilden Foundations.*

Quotes _____

"We are prepared to defend it [freedom]. Men are not prisoners of fate but prisoners of their own minds. They have within them the power to be free at any moment."

— FDR

"[Germany stands with Italy] against all hateful and incomprehensible attempts to restrict the justified will for living of our two peoples."

— Adolf Hitler

"Hitler and Mussolini jes' need a good whippin'."
— World War I hero Sgt. Alvin York

"It may be possible to set up a nuclear reaction in uranium by which vast amounts of power could be released. . . . This new phenomenon would also lead to the construction of . . . extremely powerful bombs of a new type."

— Albert Einstein, in a letter to FDR

"Force is the only language they understand, like bullies."

— FDR

"This nation will remain a neutral nation. . . . I have seen war and . . . I hate war. . . . I hope the United States will keep out of this war. I believe that is wise."

— FDR, fireside chat

"I cannot forecast to you the action of Russia. It is a riddle wrapped in a mystery inside an enigma."
— Winston Churchill

Clark Gable and Vivien Leigh in David O. Selznick's *Gone with the Wind,* the longest (3 hours, 42 minutes) and most expensive ($4.2 million) movie yet made and winner of 10 Academy Awards. *Movie Star News.*

"They were not farm men any more, but migrant men. . . . [Thought] and worry were not any more with rainfall, with wind and dust, with the thrust of the crops. Eyes watched tires, ears listened to clattering motors, and minds struggled with oil, with gasoline, with the thinning rubber between air and road. . . . A broken gear was a tragedy."
— John Steinbeck, *The Grapes of Wrath*

Ads _____

Radio

Premieres

"Kate Smith's Bandwagon"
"The Aldrich Family," Ezra Stone
"I Love a Mystery," Michael Raffetto
"The Colgate Sports Newsreel," Bill Stern
"Dr. I.Q. (the Mental Banker)," Lew Valentine
"The Milton Berle Show"
"Lil' Abner," John Hodiak
"Mr. District Attorney," Dwight Weist
"Young Doctor Malone," Alan Bunce

Specials

Edward R. Murrow broadcasts nightly from London.

Of Note

Popular journalists include Lowell Thomas, H. V. Kaltenborn, Drew Pearson, and Fulton Lewis, Jr.

New Catchphrases: Mrs. Aldrich: "Henry! Hen-ry Aldrich!" Henry: "Coming, Mother!" ("The Aldrich Family"); ". . . strange and fantastic stories . . . some legend, some hearsay, . . . but all so interesting" ("The Colgate Sports Newsreel"); "And it shall be my duty . . . not only to prosecute to the limit of the law all persons accused . . . but to defend with equal vigor the rights and privileges of all . . . citizens" ("Mr. District Attorney")

TV

Opening ceremonies of the New York World's Fair with FDR; the king and queen of England's arrival at the fair
First major league baseball game (Brooklyn Dodgers versus Cincinnati Reds)
Opening of *Gone with the Wind*

Dramas: "Mamba's Daughter," "Stage Door," "Dulcy"

Movies

Openings

Gone with the Wind (Victor Fleming), Clark Gable, Vivien Leigh, Leslie Howard, Olivia de Havilland
Dark Victory (Edmund Goulding), Bette Davis, George Brent, Humphrey Bogart, Ronald Reagan
Goodbye, Mr. Chips (Sam Wood), Robert Donat, Greer Garson
Mr. Smith Goes to Washington (Frank Capra), James Stewart, Jean Arthur
Ninotchka (Ernst Lubitsch), Greta Garbo, Melvyn Douglas
Destry Rides Again (George Marshall), Marlene Dietrich, Gary Cooper
Stagecoach (John Ford), John Wayne, Claire Trevor
The Wizard of Oz (Victor Fleming), Judy Garland, Frank Morgan, Ray Bolger, Bert Lahr, Jack Haley
Wuthering Heights (William Wyler), Laurence Olivier, Merle Oberon, David Niven
Babes in Arms (Busby Berkeley), Judy Garland, Mickey Rooney
The Women (George Cukor), Norma Shearer, Joan Crawford, Joan Fontaine, Rosalind Russell
The Hunchback of Notre Dame (William Dieterle), Maureen O'Hara, Charles Laughton
The Roaring Twenties (Raoul Walsh), James Cagney, Priscilla Lane, Humphrey Bogart
Gunga Din (George Stevens), Cary Grant, Douglas Fairbanks, Jr.
Jesse James (Henry King), Tyrone Power, Henry Fonda
Confessions of a Nazi Spy (Anatole Litvak), Edward G. Robinson, Francis Lederer
Pinocchio (Walt Disney)
Rules of the Game (Jean Renoir), Marcel Dalio, Nora Gregor

Academy Awards

Best Picture: *Gone with the Wind*
Best Director: Victor Fleming (*Gone with the Wind*)
Best Actress: Vivien Leigh (*Gone with the Wind*)
Best Actor: Robert Donat (*Goodbye, Mr. Chips*)
Special Award: Judy Garland (outstanding performance of a screen juvenile)

Top Box-Office Stars

Mickey Rooney, Tyrone Power, Spencer Tracy, Clark Gable, Shirley Temple, Bette Davis, Alice Faye, Errol Flynn, James Cagney, Sonja Henie

Popular Music ────────────────

Hit Songs
"All the Things You Are"
"South of the Border"
"Frenesi"
"I Concentrate on You"
"I Didn't Know What Time It
    Was"
"I'll Never Smile Again"
"If I Didn't Care"
"My Prayer"
"Brazil"
"Ding-Dong! The Witch Is Dead"
"Tara's Theme"

Top Records
Oh Johnny, Oh (Orrin Tucker,
with Bonnie Baker); *Miss Thing*
(Count Basie): *Jazz Me Blues,*
Bunny Berigan; *It Don't Mean a
Thing* (Lionel Hampton); *Body
and Soul* (Coleman Hawkins);
Indiana (Earl Hines); *Some Like
It Hot* (Gene Krupa); *Little Brown
Jug, In the Mood,* and *Sunrise
Serenade* (Glenn Miller); *That
Silver-Haired Daddy of Mine*
(Gene Autry); *Ciribiribin* (Harry
James); *Over the Rainbow* (Judy
Garland); *Strange Fruit* (Billie
Holiday); *Tuxedo Junction*
(Erskine Hawkins); *Cherokee*
(Charlie Parker)

Jazz and Big Bands
Charlie Parker goes to New York
and plays at Monroe's Uptown
House. Charlie Christian joins
Benny Goodman. Jimmy Blanton,
Billy Strayhorn, and Ben Webster
join Duke Ellington. Sy Oliver
leaves Jimmy Lunceford to join
Tommy Dorsey; Billy Eckstine
joins Earl Hines.

New Bands: Teddy Wilson,
Harry James, Tony Pastor, Jack
Teagarden (all in New York)

Top Performers *(Downbeat):* Benny
Goodman (soloist, big band);
Tommy Dorsey (sweet band); Ella
Fitzgerald, Bing Crosby
(vocalists); Charlie Christian, Jess
Stacy, Gene Krupa, Coleman
Hawkins, Benny Goodman, Harry
James (instrumentalists)

Theater ────────────────

Broadway Openings

Plays
Life with Father (Howard Lindsay, Russel Crouse),
    Howard Lindsay, Dorothy Stickney
The Little Foxes (Lillian Hellman), Tallulah
    Bankhead, Patricia Collinge, Charles Dingle,
    Dan Duryea
The Philadelphia Story (Philip Barry), Katharine
    Hepburn, Joseph Cotten, Van Heflin
No Time for Comedy (S. N. Behrman), Laurence
    Olivier, Katharine Cornell
The Man Who Came to Dinner (Moss Hart, George
    Kaufman), Monty Woolley, David Burns
The Time of Your Life (William Saroyan), Julie
    Hayden, Eddie Dowling
Skylark (Samson Raphaelson), Gertrude Lawrence
Mamba's Daughters (Dorothy and DuBose
    Heyward), Ethel Waters
The Gentle People (Irwin Shaw), Franchot Tone, Elia
    Kazan, Sylvia Sidney
Key Largo (Maxwell Anderson), Paul Muni
The White Steed (Paul Vincent Carroll), Barry
    Fitzgerald, Jessica Tandy
Mornings at Seven (Paul Osborn), Dorothy Gish,
    Effie Shannon

Musicals
Dubarry Was a Lady (Cole Porter, B. G. DeSylva),
    Ethel Merman, Bert Lahr, Betty Grable
George White's Scandals of 1939 (Sammy Fain, Jack
    Yellin) Willie and Eugene Howard, The Three
    Stooges, Ann Miller
One for the Money (Morgan Lewis), Nancy
    Hamilton, Alfred Drake, Gene Kelly, Keenan
    Wynn
Set to Music (Noel Coward), Beatrice Lillie, Richard
    Haydn
Stars in Your Eyes (Arthur Schwartz, Dorothy
    Fields), Ethel Merman, Jimmy Durante, Richard
    Carlson, Tamara Toumanova, Dan Dailey,
    Mildred Natwick
Too Many Girls (Richard Rodgers, Lorenz Hart),
    Marcy Wescott, Hal LeRoy, Eddie Bracken,
    Desi Arnaz, Van Johnson

Classics and Revivals On and Off Broadway
The Importance of Being Earnest (Oscar Wilde),
Clifton Webb, Estelle Winwood; *Henry IV, Part I,*
Maurice Evans

Pulitzer Prize
Abe Lincoln in Illinois, Robert E. Sherwood

Classical Music _____

Compositions
Roy Harris, Symphony no. 4
Walter Piston, Violin Concerto, Sonata for Violin and
    Piano
John Cage, *Imaginary Landscape*
Howard Hanson, Fantasy for String Orchestra
Aaron Copland, *The City, Sorcery and Science*
Elliott Carter, *Pocahontas*
Henry Cowell, *A Celtic Symphony*
William Schuman, *Prelude for Voices*
Roger Sessions, *Pages from a Diary*
Samuel Barber, Violin Concerto

Important Events
The World's Fair Festivals communicate the
"Brotherhood of Music" with numerous unusual
events, including the festivals of Norway, the Balkan
states, and Brazil (Heitor Villa-Lobos is a great
success); also of great interest is Arnold Bax's
Symphony no. 7; Georges Enesco as conductor of his
work at the Rumanian Pavilion, and Piston's Prelude
and Fugue, the only American work presented.
Boston holds a Festival of American Music with
Arthur Foote, George Gershwin, Virgil Thomson,
Hanson, Harris, and Schuman.
Béla Bartók plays *Contrasts* with Josef Szigeti and
Benny Goodman in New York.
Budget cuts reduce WPA programs; New York mayor
Fiorello La Guardia sponsors a symphony series of
single-composer concerts.

Major Recital: Josef and Rosina Lhévinne celebrate
40 years of piano partnership in a Carnegie Hall
program.

Marian Anderson at the Lincoln Memorial. She stays in Washington, D.C., at a private home because no hotel will accommodate her. *Library of Congress.*

Debuts: Leonard Rose, Gyorgy Sandor, Leonard
Pennario, William Masselos, Clifford Curzon

First Performances
Harris, Symphony no. 3 (Boston); Copland, Sextet
(New York); Schuman, *American Festival Overture*
(Boston); William Walton, Violin Concerto
(Cleveland); Ralph Vaughan Williams, *Five Variants
on Dives and Lazarus* (New York); Charles Ives,
Second Pianoforte Sonata (New York)

Opera

Metropolitan: Grace Moore, *Louise;* Herbert
Janssen, *Tannhäuser;* John Brownlee, Elisabeth
Rethberg, Ezio Pinza, Licia Albanese, *Der
Rosenkavalier;* John Charles Thomas, Helen Jepson,
Thaïs; Leonard Warren (debut), *Simon Boccanegra;*
44 of its 123 performances are of Wagner.

Martin Beck Theater, New York: *The Devil and
Daniel Webster* (Douglas Moore)

Dallas: Grace Moore, *Manon*

Chicago: Ezio Pinza, Rose Bampton, *Boris
Godunov;* Grace Moore, *Louise*

San Francisco: Marjorie Lawrence, Kirsten
Flagstad, *Die Walküre;* Jarmila Novotna, Lawrence
Tibbett, *La traviata*

Music Notes
Leopold Stokowski shocks audiences as he
rearranges the placement of the instruments.

Kate Smith, "the Songbird of the South." *Movie Star
News.*

Art

Painting

Edward Hopper, *Cape Cod Evening*

Thomas Hart Benton, *Threshing Wheat, Little Brown Jug*

Ben Shahn, *Jesus Exalted in Song, Handball*

John Steuart Curry, *The Tragic Prelude, The Homesteading*

Milton Avery, *The Dessert*

Philip Evergood, *Lily and the Sparrows*

Joseph Stella, *The Brooklyn Bridge*

Willem de Kooning, *Elegy, Portrait of Rudolph Burckhardt*

Lyonel Feininger, *San Francisco*

Grant Wood, *Parson Weems' Fable*

William Gropper's mural *Construction of the Dam* and Edgar Britton's *The Story of Petroleum* are placed in the Department of Interior, Washington, D.C.

Sculpture

Alexander Archipenko, *Moses*

José de Creeft, *The Cloud, Saturnia*

Isamu Noguchi, *Capital*

David Smith, *Medals for Dishonor: Bombing Civilian Populations*

Alexander Calder, *Lobster Trap and Fish Tail*

Important Exhibitions

Museums

New York: *Metropolitan:* "Life in America for 300 Years" (held concurrently with the fair); American pewterers; Augustan art; American daguerrotypes.

Calder's *Stabile* wins a major prize at the World's Fair.

Heinz Warneke's *Lewis and Clark* is placed at the Department of the Interior, Washington, D.C.

The last of Gutzon Borglum's presidents, Teddy Roosevelt, is unveiled on Mt. Rushmore.

Architecture

Johnson Wax Administration Building, Racine, Wisc. (Frank Lloyd Wright)

Hert Jacobs House, Middleton, Wisc. (Frank Lloyd Wright)

Black Mountain College project, North Carolina (Walter Gropius and Marcel Breuer)

The new Museum of Modern Art, on 53rd Street, New York, is completed (P. Goodwin and E. Stone).

Eliel and Eero Saarinen and Robert Swanson win the competition for the new Smithsonian Gallery of Art.

Mies van der Rohe begins work on the Illinois Institute of Technology, Chicago campus.

New York World's Fair: "Masterpieces of America and the World." *Museum of Modern Art:* Forty years of Picasso; "Art in Our Time"; Sheeler.

Chicago: Paintings of Bonnard, Vuillard; Picasso; ten best American watercolorists; San Francisco Golden Gate exhibit

Detroit: Pre-Columbian Art

Philadelphia: Blake; Flemish Art

Boston: Maillol, Despiau

San Francisco Golden Gate Exposition: Pacific cultures; contemporary art; masterworks of five centuries, including Botticelli's *Birth of Venus,* Raphael's *Madonna of the Chair,* and work by Michelangelo

Art Briefs

For the first time, European masterpieces travel on loan (for the New York World's Fair and San Francisco Exposition) • The Kress collection is added to the Mellon at the National Gallery, Washington, D.C. • 30 million people view art exhibitions at the World's Fair • The curtailment of the WPA Art Project is offset by commissions for the fair, the exposition, and new construction of public buildings in Washington, D.C. • After Hitler brands modern art "degenerate" and sells museum works at a Lucerne auction, many masterpieces pass into American museums and private collections • Important sales include Reynolds's *Lady Frances Warren* ($10,500); van Gogh's *Mlle. Ravoux* ($19,000); Cézanne's *Mme. Cézanne* ($27,500); Rouault's *The Clown* ($2,500); and Toulouse-Lautrec's *Femme dans le jardin* ($5,700).

Dance

Companies and stars emigrate to the United States: Massine's Ballet Russe with Alexandra Danilova, Alicia Markova, David Lichine, and Tamara Toumanova.

Premieres

Every Soul Is a Circus (Martha Graham); *Eight-Column Line* (Alwin Nikolais); the first American full-length *Coppelia* (Willam Christensen, San Francisco)

Books

Fiction

Critics' Choice
Wild Palms, William Faulkner
The Web and the Rock, Thomas Wolfe (posthumous)
Night Rider, Robert Penn Warren
Tommy Gallagher's Crusade, James T. Farrell
Adventures of a Young Man, John Dos Passos
Pale Horse, Pale Rider, Katherine Anne Porter
Tropic of Capricorn, Henry Miller
The Day of the Locust, Nathanael West
Children of God, Vardis Fisher
ꝰ *Finnegans Wake*, James Joyce

Best-Sellers
The Grapes of Wrath, John Steinbeck
All This, and Heaven Too, Rachel Field
Rebecca, Daphne Du Maurier
Wickford Point, John P. Marquand
Disputed Passage, Lloyd C. Douglas
The Yearling, Marjorie Kinnan Rawlings
Kitty Foyle, Christopher Morley
The Nazarene, Sholem Asch

Nonfiction

Critics' Choice
Thoreau, Henry Seidel Canby
Freedom and Culture, John Dewey
Heritage of America, Henry Steele Commager, Allan Nevins
Incredible Era, Samuel Hopkins Adams
After Seven Years, Raymond Moley
The Living Tradition: Change and America, Simeon Stransky
America in Mid-Passage, Charles and Mary Beard
Hereditary Fortunes, Gustavus Myers
Propaganda for War: The Campaign against American Neutrality, 1914–1917, H. C. Peterson et al.
ꝰ *The Knowledge of God and the Service of God*, Karl Barth

Best-Sellers
Days of Our Years, Pierre van Paassen
Reaching for the Stars, Nora Waln
Inside Asia, John Gunther
Autobiography with Letters, William Lyon Phelps

Wind, Sand, and Stars, Antoine de Saint-Exupéry
Mein Kampf, Adolf Hitler
A Peculiar Treasure, Edna Ferber
Not Peace But a Sword, Vincent Sheean
Listen! The Wind, Anne Morrow Lindbergh

Poetry
Robert Frost, *Collected Poems*
Edna St. Vincent Millay, *Huntsman, What Quarry?*
Robert P. Tristram Coffin, *Collected Poems*
Archibald MacLeish, *America Was Promises*
T. S. Eliot, *Old Possum's Book of Practical Cats*
Muriel Rukeyser, *A Turning Wind*

Pulitzer Prizes
The Grapes of Wrath, John Steinbeck (novel)
Abraham Lincoln: The War Years, Carl Sandburg (U.S. history)
Woodrow Wilson, Life and Letters, Vols. VII and VIII, Ray Stannard Baker (biography)
Collected Poems, Mark Van Doren (poetry)

Science and Technology

Newly emigrated Enrico Fermi and John R. Dunning, Columbia University, use the cyclotron to split uranium and obtain a huge energy release; Fermi suggests the idea of a "chain reaction."

Utilizing quantum theory, Linus Pauling postulates a resonance theory of chemical valence.

Karl Landsteiner and Alexander Weiner discover the Rh factor in blood.

Edward Doisy determines the chemical formula of vitamin K.

Studies accumulate indicating that sulfanilamide can treat many forms of coccal infection (for example, streptoccocal and gonococcal infections).

Heinz Hartmann's *Ego Psychology and the Problem of Adaptation* develops the importance of the ego, as opposed to the id, the previous emphasis of Freudian psychology.

Igor Sikorsky constructs and flies the first single rotor helicopter.

ꝰ Howard Florey and Ernest Chain concentrate penicillin and test it with success.

ꝰ Ernst Strassman and Otto Hahn set off a nuclear fission reaction by bombarding uranium with neutrons.

ꝰ Paul Miller develops DDT.

Nobel Prize
E. O. Lawrence wins the prize in physics for the development of the cyclotron.

Sports

Baseball

"You've been reading about my tough breaks for weeks now. But today I think I'm the luckiest man alive," says Lou Gehrig at his retirement ceremony at Yankee Stadium. Gehrig played 2,130 consecutive games since 1925, before becoming ill with amyotrophic lateral sclerosis.

Ted Williams (Boston, AL) debuts.

Cooperstown is established as the site of the Baseball Hall of Fame.

Champions

Batting	Pitching
John Mize (St. Louis, NL), .349	Paul Derringer (Cincinnati, NL), 25–7
Joe DiMaggio (New York, AL), .381	Lefty Grove (Boston, AL), 15–4
	Home runs
	Jimmy Foxx (Boston, AL), 35

Football

NFL Season Leaders: Parker Hall (Cleveland Rams), passing; Bill Osmanski (Chicago Bears), rushing; Don Hutson (Green Bay), receiving

College All-Americans: Ken Kavanaugh (E), Louisiana State; John Kimbrough (Q), Texas A&M; Tom Harmon (B), Michigan

Bowls (Jan. 1, 1940)
Rose: Southern California 14– Tennessee 0
Orange: Georgia Tech 21–Missouri 7
Cotton: Clemson 6– Boston College 3
Sugar: Texas A&M 14– Tulane 13

Fashion

For Women: Suits become more "feminine"— pleated, flared, or straight—with tightly fitted jackets and gay blouses. Prime Minister Chamberlain's famous umbrella and hat become motifs in accessories and prints; snoods are popular. Hair is "Edwardian" or worn up in front, with the back hanging in a long mane of curls; the first permanent waves appear. In the summer, bare midriffs, flat sports sandals, Indian moccasins, and Carmen Miranda turbans are everywhere. Many winter dresses have fitted bodices for Mainbocher's new corset, which, laced up the back, makes front-page headlines. Smaller bras with circular seamed cups and stiffened inserts achieve the high-bosomed look. From Europe come "black-out" fashions: tailored suits, white hats and accesories, flashlights, and containers for gas masks.

High-fashion notes: Schiaparelli's patterned cardigan; Pinguet's reemphasis of the square shoulder ("the look" until Dior).

Basketball

The first NCAA postseason championship tournament is played with teams from all over the country.

Other Sports

Tennis: Don Budge beats both Ellsworth Vines and Fred Perry on a pro tour.

Winners

World Series		College Basketball	
New York (AL) 4		Oregon (NCAA)	
Cincinnati (AL) 0		Long Island University (NIT)	
MVP		*Player of the Year*	
NL–William Walters, Cincinnati		Chester Jaworski, Rhode Island State	
AL–Joe DiMaggio, New York		*Stanley Cup*	
NFL		Boston	
Green Bay 27–New York 0		*US Tennis Open*	
MVP		Men: Robert L. Riggs	
Parker Hall, Cleveland		Women: Alice Marble	
College Football		*USGA Open*	
Texas A&M		Byron Nelson	
Heisman Trophy		*Kentucky Derby*	
Niles Kinnick, Iowa		Johnstown (J. Stout, jockey)	

Fashion model.

Kaleidoscope

- Eight million are unemployed.
- Newsreels, like the *March of Time,* gain in importance as worldwide events are documented.
- A Gallup poll indicates that 58 percent believe the United States will be drawn into war; 65 percent favor boycotting Germany.
- After the German attack on Poland and subsequent declarations of war, there is a quiet on the front, widely called the "Phony War."
- Barred from DAR-owned Constitution Hall, Marian Anderson gives an open-air concert before 75,000 people in Lincoln Memorial Park; the concert is sponsored, in part, by Secretary of State Harold Ickes and Eleanor Roosevelt.
- Two major expositions take place: (1) the New York World's Fair, "The World of Tomorrow," which holds exhibitions from almost every country (Germany does not participate) and is visited by 25 million, and (2) the Golden Gate Exposition, whose theme is "Recreation: Man's Gift from a Machine Age," built on a 400-acre man-made island in the center of San Francisco Bay.
- The sounds of King Tutankhamen's 22½″ trumpet of silver and gold, as well as his 19½″ copper trumpet, are heard on a world radio broadcast after their 3,297-year silence.
- Fifty percent of those polled select radio as the most reliable news media, 17 percent choose newspapers.
- *Reader's Digest,* whose circulation was 250,000 in 1930, is up to 8 million.
- Al Capone is released from prison but is severely ill with third-stage syphilis.
- Gangster Louis Lepke surrenders to columnist Walter Winchell, who hands him over to J. Edgar Hoover (whom Lepke prefers to New York district attorney Tom Dewey).
- Clara Adams is the first woman to fly around the world.
- The Social Security Act is amended to allow extended benefits to the aged and the widows, minors, and parents of a deceased person.
- Controversy arises over FDR's decision to appoint an envoy to the Vatican.

- Because of the war abroad, the Finns cease shipping cheese to the United States; Swiss production takes over.
- Sixty thousand German immigrants have arrived since 1933.
- Movie box-office receipts reach an all-time high and average out to $25 per family per year.
- Hollywood production code restrictions are lifted to enable Clark Gable, in *Gone with the Wind,* to say: "Frankly, my dear, I don't give a damn."
- The Federal Theatre Project is disbanded after accusations of Communist influence.
- In 1938, Columbia College seniors chose Madeleine Carroll as the woman with whom they would most like to be shipwrecked; their reason: her ability to speak French. This year they choose Hedy Lamarr and offer no reason.
- The largest production of chickens and turkeys in U.S. farm history is recorded.

College Fads: Swallowing goldfish (the record is 210), beetles, white mice, angleworms, phonograph records with salt and pepper—each followed by milk or soda; roller skating; knock-knock jokes; Chinese checkers; "skatarinas" (matching bloomers and circular skirts) and unisex clothes (baggy sweaters, saddle shoes, shirttails, jeans); the dances: chicken scratch, howdy-do, American promenade, palais glide, chestnut tree, boomps-a-daisy

Jive Language (from Gene Krupa): "Blowin' his plumbin'," "beating his skins," "spank the skin"

First Appearances: Billy Rose Aquacade, commercial manufacture of nylon yarn, anti–pinball machine legislation (Atlanta), air-conditioned auto (Packard), electric slicing knife, disposable can for dispensing under pressure (patent), transatlantic airmail service, marketing of nylon stockings

Far left: "George Washington" (James Farmer) and "The Mood of Time" (Paul Manship), at the New York World's Fair. *General Research Division. The New York Public Library. Astor, Lenox and Tilden Foundations.*

The king and queen of England visiting the U.S. *Manny Warman, Columbia University.*

THE *Forties*

Sailors decorating graves at Pearl Harbor. *Copyright* Washington Post. *Reprinted by permission of D.C. Public Library.*

Statistics

Vital

Population: 132,122,000
   Urban/Rural: 74/57
   Farm: 23.2%
Life expectancy
   Male: 60.8
   Female: 68.2
Births/1,000: 19.4
Marriages/1,000: 12.1
Divorces/1,000: 2.0
Deaths/1,000: 12.1
   per 100,000
      Heart: 485
      Cancer: 120
      Tuberculosis: 40
      Car accidents: 26.2

Economic

Unemployed: 8,120,000
GNP: $99.7 billion
Federal budget: $13.2 billion
National debt: $43.0 billion
Union membership: 8.1
   million
Strikes: 2,508
Prime rate: 0.6%
Car sales: 3,767,300
Average salary: $1,299

Social

Homicides/100,000: 6.3
Suicides/100,000: 14.4
Lynchings: 5
Labor force, male/female: 3/1
Social welfare: $8.80 billion
Public education: $2.34 billion
College degrees
   Bachelors'
      Male: 109,000
      Female: 77,000
   Doctorates
      Male: 2,861
      Female: 429
Attendance
   Movies (weekly): 80 million
   Baseball (yearly): 10.0
   million

Consumer

Consumer Price Index
   (1967 = 100): 42
Eggs: 33¢ (doz.)
Milk: 13¢ (qt.)
Bread: 8¢ (loaf)
Butter: 36¢ (lb.)
Bacon: 27¢ (lb.)
Round steak: 36¢ (lb.)
Oranges: 29¢ (doz.)
Coffee: 21¢ (lb.)

The first years of the decade were the darkest in modern times. A savage and militarily awesome German dictatorship conquered most of Western Europe and put England under furious aerial bombardment. Russia was invaded, and Moscow and Leningrad came under siege. A militarist government came to power in Japan, and on the infamous day of December 7, 1941, the Japanese launched a surprise air attack on the American naval base at Pearl Harbor, Hawaii, and then mounted swift, massive invasions throughout Southeast Asia, including the Philippines. Congress declared war, and U.S. "isolation" ended. As it turned out, the "bullies," as FDR called them, were no match for someone their own size, but proving this involved a great four-year struggle that required all the men and material that America, harnessed to her full capacity, could produce.

Both at home and on the fronts, the war became a calling—loud, clear, and pure—and with the vast needs for swift production and manpower, employment ceased to be a problem. Large numbers enlisted: women worked in factories; dollar-a-year men went to Washington; baseball players, actors, and entertainers—people from every social stratum— signed up; labor and management agreed to keep peace; and even children, doing their share, collected scrap and helped plant the Victory Gardens that sprouted everywhere. With austerity a wartime necessity, consumer deprivation afforded a badge of honor. The desperate plight of the world, the malignant nature of the enemy, and the sneak attack had stirred a universal, idealistic commitment.

In 1942 came the first moments of victory, in North Africa and at Midway. Gigantic bombing raids began, and in 1943, the tide turned. The Russians beat the Germans into retreat. American and British forces took Sicily and began their way up the Italian peninsula. Guadalcanal was retaken. In 1944, the "great crusade" on the Continent fought ashore at Normandy, and the emancipation of Europe began. In the East, the Russians proceeded with equal speed. MacArthur returned to the Philippines, as he had promised, and the bloody Pacific island-hopping continued. All along, in both theaters, bombers from the great American arsenal filled the enemy skies.

Roosevelt, elected for a fourth time in 1944, did not live to see the final victory. In April 1945, the beloved president died, and when Arthur Godfrey, describing the funeral procession on radio, broke into tears, he echoed the sorrow of millions of his countrymen at the passing of a man who had led and comforted them through their most difficult trials.

Harry Truman, the feisty Missourian who succeeded FDR, accepted Germany's unconditional surrender in June 1945, before facing one of history's epochal decisions. On August 6, he deployed a weapon secretly developed during the war at Roosevelt's directive; an atomic bomb was dropped on Hiroshima, Japan. Three days later, a second bomb was dropped on Nagasaki. Japan surrendered unconditionally, averting the possibility of a bloody invasion. A force of apocalyptic destructiveness had been demonstrated.

The postwar period was frenzied. Demobilization was rapid; in 1946, there were 35,000 discharges a day. Personal savings accumulated during wartime austerity sought an outlet, and a peacetime ethos of the pursuit of personal happiness replaced the wartime one of sacrifice. A mania developed for such consumer items as beef, ice cream, alcohol, cars, and toys; tickets for sporting events, theater, and travel were in short supply; housing was at a premium.

As workers sought higher wages and business higher profits, the relations between labor and management were strained. Massive strikes and inflation followed, and black markets developed; consumer goods remained in short supply while factories retooled for peacetime production. In the meantime, millions of veterans took advantage of the GI bill to educate themselves, start businesses, buy homes, and have families. Despite all the frenzy, fears that the depression would return proved unfounded, and the economy stabilized.

Throughout the decade, radio remained an important news and entertainment medium; some of its most popular shows included "Red Skelton," "Abbott and Costello," and "Lux Radio Theater." After the war, a new medium developed. Television, for twenty years an experimental toy, went into mass production, and large-scale programming began. Top programs starred ex-vaudevillian Uncle Miltie (Milton Berle), solemn Ed Sullivan, and congenial Arthur Godfrey, his friends and talent scouts. Popular "personalities" ranged from wrestler Gorgeous George to puppet Howdy Doody. At the end of the decade, Sid Caesar and Imogene Coca, as well as original drama showcases like "Studio One," explored the medium's potential.

Sports attendance soared beyond 1920s' levels. In football, the T-formation, validated by Sid Luckman in Chicago's 73–0 victory against Washington (1940), moved into prominence. The National Basketball Association (NBA) was formed, and George Mikan became the first of the dominating "big men." In baseball, Joe DiMaggio, Ted Williams, and Stan Musial returned from the service to stardom. The great baseball story of the decade, however, went beyond sports when Jackie Robinson became the first black in organized baseball. Robinson was subjected to abuse from bigots on and

Bob Hope and Bing Crosby ham it up on the golf course. Their "Road" pictures with Dorothy Lamour have been enormously successful. *Movie Star News.*

off the field, but his courage and dazzling talent gained him wide admiration, as it highlighted on a national stage the injustice of racial discrimination.

Among the great movies of the decade—and perhaps of all time—were *Citizen Kane, The Grapes of Wrath,* and *Casablanca,* as well as the revival favorites *The Maltese Falcon* and *Mildred Pierce.* Many patriotic war movies appeared, such as *Mrs. Miniver, The Purple Heart,* and *Guadalcanal Diary.* Betty Grable and Rita Hayworth were the sex symbols of the early decade, and their pinups were GI favorites; later on, Jane Russell, in a special undergarment designed by aircraft tycoon Howard Hughes, became prominent. Acting teams were also popular: in comedy, Abbott and Costello, and Hope and Crosby; for tough romance, Bogart and Bacall. After the war, a number of films explored social and previously taboo themes—*The Lost Weekend* (alcoholism), *Gentleman's Agreement* (anti-Semitism), *The Snake Pit* (mental illness), *Pinky* (racism), and *All the King's Men* (the abuse of political power). Perhaps the idealistic nature of the war encouraged a more open and urgent examination of moral problems on the home front.

This was the era when many big bands broke up and lead singers went out on their own. Frank Sinatra became a phenomenon as a bobby-sox idol. Bing Crosby's mellow voice and manner made him a top singer, as well as leading movie star. Other popular singers included Bob Eberle, Helen O'Connell, Ella Fitzgerald, Sarah Vaughan, and the Andrews sisters. War songs like "Praise the Lord and Pass the Ammunition" were hits, along with ballads like "As Time Goes By" and "My Foolish Heart," most of which told of the precariousness of love in wartime. "Bop" and "cool" succeeded swing in the forefront of jazz, and instrumentalists like Miles Davis and Thelonius Monk pursued their

experiments with harmony and improvisation.

In 1946, Dr. Spock's *The Common Sense Book of Baby and Child Care* appeared, to advise the many newcomers to the booming baby business. Dale Carnegie taught *How to Stop Worrying and Start Living,* and Rabbi Joshua Liebman advised on *Peace of Mind. Forever Amber,* a blockbuster in most cities, was banned in Boston, while Lloyd Douglas's tale of Christ's *Robe* sold out everywhere. Richard Wright's *Native Son* symbolically prophesied the fire to come; Saul Bellow debuted with *Dangling Man* and *The Victim,* both in his characteristic existential vein. French existentialism had a vogue in America, and writers like Jean-Paul Sartre and Albert Camus were much discussed in literary circles. Norman Mailer debuted with his realistic war novel *The Naked and the Dead.*

In the late forties, two American classics appeared on Broadway, Tennessee Williams's *A Streetcar Named Desire* and Arthur Miller's *Death of a Salesman.* Williams portrayed the fragility of romantic illusion, and Miller the tragic illusion of the American dream. For the musical stage, the new team of Rodgers and Hammerstein wrote *Oklahoma* and *South Pacific.* Painters like Jackson Pollock, Willem de Kooning, and Arshile Gorky worked in the new form of abstract expressionism. The music world saw the debuts of Leonard Bernstein, Richard Tucker, Jan Peerce, and Lorin Maazel (age 11), and premieres of Paul Hindemith, Béla Bartók, Arnold Schoenberg, and Igor Stravinsky, all now residing in the United States.

On the international scene, America determined not to isolate itself again, and the United States led in the formation of the United Nations, based on principles similar to the forsaken League of Nations. The Second World War had changed the order of

Victory gardening in New York City. *Library of Congress*

Supreme Allied Commander Dwight D. Eisenhower speaking to a soldier prior to Operation Overlord, the invasion of Nazi Europe. *Smithsonian Institution.*

Code name Trinity, the first atomic bomb, was exploded at Alamogordo Air Force Base, New Mexico, July 16, 1945. *Library of Congress.*

world power, and the former dominance of Western Europe was ended. When Britain turned out Winston Churchill in 1946 and gave independence to India, it was apparently ready to relinquish its world role. Once again, however, victory in a world war had not brought an easy peace, and the two remaining great powers, the United States and the USSR, though wartime allies, soon clashed over the fate of Berlin and West Germany, Poland and Czechoslovakia, China and Greece. Thus began, in Bernard Baruch's words, the "cold war."

America's involvement in world affairs went further. With severe economic conditions on the Continent and widespread food shortages, America took a number of steps. Large amounts of money and food were sent abroad. (Meatless Tuesdays and Eggless Thursdays were observed at home, because "children are starving in Europe.") Truman, now aided by previous isolationist leaders, also implemented Point Four, providing economic and arms assistance to rebellion-torn countries like Greece. This was followed by the Marshall Plan, which gave economic aid to Western Europe, including Germany. America thus became deeply committed to helping the "Free World" stay free from poverty and totalitarian forces.

At home, in 1946, the Republicans took Congress and then united against Truman's efforts to extend the New Deal reformation. Civil rights and housing legislation was vetoed; the Taft-Hartley Act

restricted labor. By 1948, everyone was certain that the Republicans would take the White House and that the president, opposed within his own party by Strom Thurmond's States' Righters and Henry Wallace's Progressive party, was headed for certain defeat. Truman's victory will undoubtedly remain one of the nation's great political upsets.

Conservative forces were, nevertheless, gaining in support, and with the advance of Communism abroad came fears of internal subversion. Loyalty became an issue, and President Truman ordered that federal employees be subjected to a loyalty check. Hollywood was investigated by the House Un-American Activities Committee (HUAC), and the clandestine blacklisting of entertainment and media figures began. A motif of the thirties, that the New Deal was merely a subterfuge for Communism, grew in credence. By the end of the decade, Czechoslovakia and China had fallen to Communist forces, and Russia had the bomb.

The decade closed with a trial that was viewed by many as a measure of the extent of Communist conspiracy, although others saw it as a right-wing persecution. Distinguished former New Dealer Alger Hiss was tried for perjury, for having denied under oath that he was a Russian spy; in January 1950, the jury convicted Hiss. Thus, while the nation was prosperous and at peace, its factories and families expanding, the forties closed on a disturbing and, to some, a menacing note.

1940

Economic Profile
  Dow-Jones: ↑ High 152–
    Low 113
  GNP: +10%
  Inflation: +0.4%
  Unemployment: 14.6%
Nash: $780
Packard: $907
Three-room apartment, New
  York City, E. 63d St.: $82
  (monthly)
Eight-room townhouse, W.
  77th St.: $2,600 (purchase
  price)
Gas range: $44.50
Chrome breakfast set: $25
Voss washing machine: $38
Noritake dinner set, 105-
  piece, gold encrusted: $54
Maple bedroom set: $49.88
Carpeting, wool: $3.88 (sq.
  yd.)
Wet mop: 89¢; dry mop:
  $1.49
Jumbo clothes hamper: $2.99
Ping-pong table: $18.98
Floor lamp: $9

Deaths

Mrs. Patrick Campbell,
  Neville Chamberlain, F.
  Scott Fitzgerald, Hamlin
  Garland, Emma Goldman,
  Paul Klee, Luisa
  Tetrazzini, Édouard
  Vuillard, Nathanael West.

In the News

FDR ASKS RECORD $1.8 BILLION FOR DEFENSE . . . WINSTON CHURCHILL REPLACES NEVILLE CHAMBERLAIN AS BRITISH P.M. . . . FINLAND AND USSR MAKE PEACE, FINNS CEDE TERRITORY . . . NAZIS INVADE DENMARK AND NORWAY, VIDKUN QUISLING IS INSTALLED AS HEAD OF NORWAY. . . . FDR APPEALS TO MUSSOLINI FOR HELP WITH PEACE . . . GERMAN ARMIES INVADE HOLLAND, BELGIUM, AND LUXEMBOURG IN LIGHTNING ATTACK . . . OFFICE OF EMERGENCY MANAGEMENT IS ESTABLISHED . . . AFL AND CIO PLEDGE WAR AID . . . 350,000 BRITISH TROOPS EVACUATE DUNKIRK IN SMALL BOATS . . . ITALY DECLARES WAR ON BRITAIN AND FRANCE, FDR DECRIES "STAB IN THE BACK" AND PLEDGES MATERIAL AID TO "OPPONENTS OF FORCE" . . . NAVAL SUPPLY ACT PROVIDES $1.5 BILLION, MILITARY SUPPLY ACT, $1.8 BILLION . . . GERMANS ENTER PARIS UNOPPOSED . . . FDR REJECTS GERMAN TERRITORIAL TRANSFERS . . . FRENCH SIGN ARMISTICE AT COMPIÈGNE, SITE OF WORLD WAR I TRIUMPH . . . JAPAN, ITALY, GERMANY SIGN 10-YEAR AXIS PACT . . . GERMANS COMMENCE DAILY AERIAL BOMBARDMENT OF ENGLAND, RAF FIGHTS BACK . . . FDR IS RENOMINATED FOR THIRD TERM, WENDELL WILLKIE IS GOP CANDIDATE . . . LEON TROTSKY IS ASSASSINATED BY RUSSIAN AGENT IN MEXICO . . . BRITISH NAVY SINKS FRENCH FLEET AT ORAN . . . U.S. GIVES BRITAIN 50 DESTROYERS UNDER LEND-LEASE BILL . . . FIRST PEACETIME DRAFT BEGINS . . . RUSSIA INVADES RUMANIA . . . TAX INCREASE IS VOTED . . . MILITARIST KONOYE BECOMES JAPANESE PREMIER, TOJO BECOMES WAR MINISTER . . . FDR WINS THIRD TERM WITH 27 MILLION, WILLKIE GAINS 22 MILLION . . . BRITISH DRIVE BACK ITALIANS IN NORTH AFRICA.

Quotes

"The three most important groups which have been pressing this country toward war are the British, the Jewish, and the Roosevelt administration."
— Charles Lindbergh

"I have said this before, but I shall say it again and again and again. Your boys are not going to be sent into any foreign wars."
— FDR

"France has been conquered and the sea power of Britain seems to be trembling in the balance. We may be next."
— Secretary of State Henry Stimson

"Never . . . was so much owed by so many to so few."
— Winston Churchill, on the RAF

"I have nothing to offer but blood, toil, tears and sweat."
— Winston Churchill

John Vachon, *Ozark Mountains, Missouri. Library of Congress.*

ON THE PRESIDENTIAL ELECTION
"The record of the New Deal is one of broken promises, contempt for free institutions and abuse of power" (Thomas Dewey). "Given four years more, the third-term candidate will lead you over the hills to the poorhouse" (Alfred E. Smith). "The reelection of [FDR] . . . will result in . . . war" (John L. Lewis). "I'm the cockiest fellow you ever saw. If you want to vote for me, fine. If you don't, go jump in the lake, and I'm still for you" (Wendell Willkie).

"Roosevelt will beat this Willkie just as bad as I'll beat Joe Louis the next time I catch up with the bum" (Boxer Tony Galento).

"I have a great stake in this country. My wife and I have given nine hostages to fortune. Our children and your children are more important than anything else in the world. . . . I believe Franklin Delano Roosevelt should be reelected president of the United States."
— Joseph P. Kennedy

Ads

Which [caricature] is Adolf? —There's a rumor that Hitler has a number of "doubles" all exactly like him—and all equally nasty! But it's a fact that FLAG margarine is exactly like butter—equally NICE and equally NOURISHING.
(Flag Margarine)

[They're] hunting the biggest game in the universe— the invisible atom. When the scientists successfully track it down and burst it wide open—they may be able to give us gold, . . . a cancer cure, or a rocket ship. . . . In man's long climb up from savagery, copper has been his best metal friend.
(Revere Copper and Brass)

Who is this man? He looks like an American. He dresses like an American. . . . But . . . he hates American democracy. He is a fifth columnist! Don't trust him!
(The League of Human Rights, Freedom and Democracy)

Their churches suffer pillage and burning. Our churches offer worship and learning.
("Appreciate America Day," Sunday, September 8)

PEACE OR WAR? Which will you choose? Should we fight for England? . . . Let's stop the Rush toward War! Let's make America Impregnable.
(America First Committee)

Radio

Premieres

"Quiz Kids," Joe Kelly and panelists under sixteen years old
"Truth or Consequences," Ralph Edwards
"Beat the Band," The Incomparable Hildegarde
"Captain Midnight," Ed Prentiss
"Gene Autry's Melody Ranch"
"Portia Faces Life," Lucille Wall
"Crime Doctor," Ray Collins
"Superman," Clayton "Bud" Collyer

Top Ten

"Jack Benny," "Chase and Sanborn Hour," "Fibber McGee and Molly," "Lux Radio Theater," "Bob Hope," "Kate Smith Hour," "Major Bowes," "Kay Kyser," "Aldrich Family," "One Man's Family"

Top Thriller Dramas: "Big Town" (Edward G. Robinson), "Bishop and the Gargoyle," "City Desk," "Crime Doctor," "Death Valley Days," "Famous Jury Trials," "Gangbusters," "I Love a Mystery," "The Lone Ranger," "Mr. District Attorney," "Mr. Keen," "The Shadow," and "Sherlock Holmes"

Of Note

"Take It or Leave It," with Phil Baker and a top prize of $64, popularizes the phrase, "the $64 question" • The first question on the "Quiz Kids" is: "What would I be carrying home if I bought an antimacassar, a dinghy, a sarong, and an apteryx?"

New Catchphrases: "Give me a little traveling music, Harry" (Hildegarde); "Doctor Ordway will be back in exactly forty-seven seconds with the solution to tonight's case" ("Crime Doctor"); ". . . able to leap tall buildings at a single bound! . . . It's a bird! It's a plane! It's . . ." ("Superman").

TV

The first color broadcast takes place from the CBS transmitter on the Chrysler Building, New York, August 27.
The FCC grants the first state TV license to DuMont.
The Republican National Convention is telecast from Philadelphia.

Movies

Openings

The Grapes of Wrath (John Ford), Henry Fonda, Jane Darwell, John Carradine
Rebecca (Alfred Hitchcock), Joan Fontaine, Laurence Olivier
The Great Dictator (Charles Chaplin), Charles Chaplin, Jack Oakie, Paulette Goddard
The Letter (William Wyler), Bette Davis, Herbert Marshall
The Philadelphia Story (George Cukor), Katharine Hepburn, Cary Grant, James Stewart
Abe Lincoln in Illinois (John Cromwell), Raymond Massey, Ruth Gordon
Fantasia, (Walt Disney)
Boom Town (Jack Conway), Spencer Tracy, Clark Gable, Hedy Lamarr
The Bank Dick (Edward Cline), W. C. Fields
My Little Chickadee (Edward Cline), Mae West, W. C. Fields
They Drive by Night (Raoul Walsh), George Raft, Ida Lupino, Pat O'Brien
Waterloo Bridge (Mervyn LeRoy), Robert Taylor, Vivien Leigh
The Great McGinty (Preston Sturges), Brian Donlevy, Akim Tamiroff
The Thief of Bagdad (Michael Powell, Tim Whelan, Ludwig Berger), Sabu, Conrad Veidt
Pride and Prejudice (Robert Z. Leonard), Laurence Olivier, Greer Garson
Foreign Correspondent (Alfred Hitchcock), Joel McCrea, Laraine Day
Road to Singapore (Victor Schertzinger), Bob Hope, Bing Crosby, Dorothy Lamour

Academy Awards

Best Picture: *Rebecca*
Best Director: John Ford *(The Grapes of Wrath)*
Best Actress: Ginger Rogers *(Kitty Foyle)*
Best Actor: James Stewart *(The Philadelphia Story)*

Top Box-Office Stars

Mickey Rooney, Spencer Tracy, Clark Gable, Gene Autry, Tyrone Power, James Cagney, Bing Crosby, Wallace Beery, Bette Davis, Judy Garland

Popular Music

Hit Songs
"You Are My Sunshine"
"The Last Time I Saw Paris"
"When You Wish upon a Star"
"It's a Big, Wide Wonderful World"
"You Stepped out of a Dream"
"Cabin in the Sky"
"All or Nothing at All"
"Back in the Saddle Again"
"Pennsylvania 6–5000"
"Taking a Chance on Love"

Top Records
I'll Never Smile Again (Tommy Dorsey, Pied Pipers); *Beat Me, Daddy, Eight to the Bar* (Andrews Sisters); *Fools Rush In* (Mildred Bailey); *The Breeze and I* (Charlie Barnet); *I Hear a Rhapsody* (Jimmy Dorsey, Tommy Dorsey); *The Starlit Hour* (Ella Fitzgerald); *How High the Moon* (Benny Goodman); *Frenesi* (Artie Shaw); *The Nearness of You* (Dinah Shore); *Come Down to Earth, My Darling* (Fats Waller, Lawrence Welk); *Stardust* (Artie Shaw); *Concerto for Cootie* (Duke Ellington); *Perfidia* (Jimmy Dorsey); *Limehouse Blues* (Larry Clinton); *High Society* (Roy Eldridge); *Swing Time up in Harlem* (Tommy Dorsey)

Jazz and Big Bands
Harry James forms his own band and hires Frank Sinatra. *Bebop,* an onomatopoetic description of the new music, is coined. Lionel Hampton leaves Benny Goodman to form his own band. Minton's Playhouse, New York, introduces Dizzy Gillespie, Thelonious Monk, and Kenny Clark. Charlie Christian plays the electric guitar in Oklahoma City.

First Recording: King Cole Trio

Top Performers *(Downbeat):* Benny Goodman (soloist, big band); Glenn Miller (sweet band); Charlie Christian, Jess Stacy, Irving Fazola, Ziggy Elman, Ray Bauduc (instrumentalists); Helen O'Connell, Bing Crosby (vocalists)

Theater

Broadway Openings

Plays
The Corn Is Green (Emlyn Williams), Ethel Barrymore
My Sister Eileen (Joseph Fields, Jerome Chodorov), Shirley Booth, Morris Carnovsky, Jo Ann Sayers
The Male Animal (James Thurber, Elliott Nugent), Gene Tierney, Elliott Nugent
Ladies in Retirement (Reginald Denham, Edward Percy), Flora Robson
Love's Old Sweet Song (William Saroyan), Walter Huston, Jessie Royce Landis
My Dear Children (Catherine Turney, Jerry Horwin), John Barrymore
There Shall Be No Night (Robert E. Sherwood), Alfred Lunt, Lynn Fontanne, Montgomery Clift
The Fifth Column (Ernest Hemingway), Franchot Tone, Lenore Ulric
George Washington Slept Here (George S. Kaufman, Moss Hart), Ernest Truex, Dudley Digges

Musicals
Cabin in the Sky (Vernon Duke, John Latouche), Ethel Waters, Dooley Wilson, Rex Ingram, Todd Duncan
Hold on to Your Hats (Burton Lane, E. Y. Harburg), Al Jolson, Martha Raye, Jinx Falkenburg
Louisiana Purchase (Irving Berlin), Victor Moore, William Gaxton, Vera Zorina, Irene Bordoni
Panama Hattie (Cole Porter, B. G. DeSylva), Ethel Merman, James Dunn, Betty Hutton, June Allyson
Two for the Show (Morgan Lewis), Betty Hutton, Richard Haydn, Alfred Drake
Keep Off the Grass (James McHugh, Howard Dietz), Jimmy Durante, Ray Bolger, José Limón, Larry Adler, choreographed by George Balanchine
Pal Joey (Richard Rodgers, Lorenz Hart), Gene Kelly, June Havoc, Van Johnson

Classics and Revivals On and Off Broadway
Charley's Aunt (Brandon Thomas), José Ferrer, *Romeo and Juliet,* Laurence Olivier, Vivien Leigh; *Twelfth Night,* Helen Hayes, Maurice Evans; *Liliom* (Molnár), Ingrid Bergman, Burgess Meredith; *Juno and the Paycock* (Sean O'Casey), Barry Fitzgerald, Sara Allgood. *Founded:* The American Negro Company

Pulitzer Prize
The Time of Your Life, William Saroyan

Classical Music

Compositions

Samuel Barber, *A Stop Watch and an Ordnance Map*
Aaron Copland, *Quiet City, Of Mice and Men*
Paul Creston, Symphony no. 1
David Diamond, Concerto for Small Orchestra
Ulysses Kay, Ten Essays
Roy Harris, *Western Landscape, American Creed,*
    Ode to Truth, Challenge. String Quartet
Walter Piston, Chromatic Study for Organ
William Schuman, Secular Cantata no. 1

Important Events

An extraordinary amount of American music is performed throughout the country. In Rochester, José Iturbi conducts the Rochester Symphony in 40 American works. Also premiering contemporary and American work are John Barbirolli (Philadelphia), Leopold Stokowski and Eugene Ormandy (Philadelphia), Serge Koussevitsky (Boston), Frederick Stock (Chicago), Artur Rodzinsky (Cleveland), and Eugene Goossens (Cincinnati).
For the 50th anniversary of the Chicago Symphony, work is commissioned from Frederick Stock, John Carpenter, Roy Harris, Igor Stravinsky, and Darius Milhaud.
At the MoMA Carlos Chávez conducts the Mexican Orchestra in a concert of modern work, including *Xochipili-Macuilxochitl.*
Milhaud conducts for CBS *La cortège funèbre,* written shortly before the German occupation of France.
European refugees settle in the United States: Bruno Walter, Ignace Jan Paderewski, Fritz Kreisler, Paul Hindemith, Béla Bartók, Darius Milhaud, Arnold Schoenberg, Mario Castelnuovo-Tedesco, Igor Stravinsky, Kurt Weill; Sergei Rachmaninoff writes Piano Concerto no. 4, Stravinsky, Symphony in C major, Hindemith, *The Four Temperaments,* Symphony in E-flat Major, Harp Sonata, and Cello Concerto.
Stokowski forms the All-American Youth Orchestra with members from every state. One hundred are selected from 15,000 tryouts. Formed to acknowledge "native American talent," the orchestra travels through South America and performs at Carnegie Hall.
Toscanini tours South America; NBC Symphony radio broadcasts also resume during the year.

Debuts: Abbey Simon, Joseph Szigeti

First Performances

Roger Sessions, Violin Concerto (Chicago); Arnold Schoenberg, Violin Concerto (Philadelphia); Chamber Symphony no. 2 (New York); Roy Harris, *Folk Song Symphony* (Cleveland); Walter Piston, Violin Concerto (Boston); Paul Creston, Concerto for Marimba and Orchestra (New York); William Grant Still, *And They Lynched Him on a Tree* (New York); John Carpenter, Symphony in C (Chicago); Béla Bartók, First Rhapsody (Washington, D.C.)

Opera

Metropolitan: Public donations exceed the necessary $1 million to purchase the company's new home. Performances include Kirsten Flagstad, Lauritz Melchior, Helen Traubel, *Siegfried;* Alexander Kipnis, *Parsifal;* Licia Albanese (debut) *La bohème;* Zinka Milanov, *Tosca;* Jennie Tourel, *Carmen;* Risë Stevens, *Der Rosenkavalier;* Lily Pons, Salvatore Baccaloni, *La fille du regiment;* Elisabeth Rethberg, John Brownlee, Ezio Pinza, Licia Albanese, *Figaro*

Chicago: Zinka Milanov, Giovanni Martinelli, *Aïda;* Kirsten Flagstad, Lauritz Melchior, *Tristan und Isolde*

San Francisco: Lotte Lehmann, Robert Weede, *Der Rosenkavalier;* John Brownlee, *La bohème*

Central City, Colo.:   *The Bartered Bride*

Henry Fonda and Jane Darwell in *The Grapes of Wrath,* the highly acclaimed film version of John Steinbeck's novel about migrant farmers. *Movie Star News.*

Music Notes

Toscanini performs the original overture to *Aïda,* cut by Verdi from the opera • The appointment of the conductor Erich Leinsdorf, 27, to the Metropolitan Opera Company provokes threats from Kirsten Flagstad and Lauritz Melchior; publicity draws large audiences • Nervous Melchior puts on a warrior's helmet backwards in *Götterdämmerung.*

Katharine Hepburn, in *The Philadelphia Story. Movie Star News.*

Art _____

Painting
Edward Hopper, *Gas*
Marsden Hartley, *Log Jam, Fishermen's Last Supper*
Loren MacIver, *Hopscotch*
Reginald Marsh, *New Dodgem, Swimming off West Washington Market*
Morris Graves, *Blind Bird*
Stuart Davis, *Hot Still-Scape for Six Colors*
Willem de Kooning, *Seated Woman*
Lyonel Feininger, *The River, Manhattan I*
Paul Cadmus, *Sailors and Floozies*
Ben Shahn, *Willis Avenue Bridge*
Edmund Archer, *Howard Patterson of the "Harlem Yankees"*
Morris Hirschfield, *Tiger*
Edward Laning paints four murals that trace the history of printing for the New York Public Library.

Sculpture
William Zorach, *Head of Christ*
Hugo Robus, *Girl Washing Her Hair*
Jacques Lipchitz, *Flight*
Alexander Calder, *Thirteen Spines, Black Beast*
Carl Milles, Aloe Fountain Plaza, St. Louis, Mo.

Architecture
Berkshire Music Shed, Tanglewood, Lenox, Mass. (Joseph Franz)
Workers' Village, New Kensington, Pa. (Gropius, Breuer)
Rockefeller Center is completed (Reinhard and Hofmeister, Hood and Fouilhoux, Corbett, Harrison and MacMurray)
Museum of Science and Industry, Chicago (Burnham)

Important Exhibitions

Museums
Latin American art travels across the United States.

New York: *Metropolitan:* The Art of the Jeweler; "Heads in Sculpture"; American watercolors. *Museum of Modern Art:* Visual and Nonvisual expressionism: "War Comes to the People"; Designs of Frank Lloyd Wright; Mexican art. *Iranian Institute:* 6,000 years of Iranian art

Chicago: 50 years of American art; Picasso; Amédée Ozenfant

San Francisco: Paintings of France since the Revolution

Boston: Arts of the Middle Ages, 1000–1400 A.D.; Giovanni Martino; Art of Argentina

Detroit: "The Age of Impressionism and Objective Realism"

Toledo: Four centuries of Venetian Art

Los Angeles: Pre-Columbian Art

Individual Shows
John Marin, O'Keeffe (20 paintings of Hawaiian flora commissioned by the Dole Pineapple Company), Levi, Sheeler, Calder, Marc, MacIver, Avery, Davis, Moholy-Nagy, Feininger, Klee, Ozenfant, Kokoschka, Epstein, Vlaminck.

Art Briefs
Piet Mondrian joins the American Abstract Artists in New York • American artists boycott the Venice Biennale because of Italy's war declaration • More than 200 artists auction their work to provide bread for Finnish children • The Federal Art Project produces 1,125 murals, although the WPA is curtailed at the end of the year • Mrs. John D. Rockefeller donates 36 works to the Museum of Modern Art, including Maillol, Zorach, and Despiau sculptures for the museum garden • Charles Eames and Eero Saarinen win the Museum of Modern Art competition for "Organic Design in Home Furnishings" • The Department of Photography is established at the Museum of Modern Art.

Dance _____

Ballet Theatre, an outgrowth of the Mordkin Ballet, is founded by Lucia Chase and Richard Pleasant; its first season includes *Les sylphides, La fille mal gardée,* and *Jardin aux lilas* (Anthony Tudor). Dancers include Nora Kaye, Lucia Chase, Anton Dolin, William Dollar, Jerome Robbins, Alicia Alonso, Alicia Markova, Irina Baronova and Tudor.

Martha Graham: *El Penitente*

Books ━━━━━━━━━━━━━━━━━━━━━━━

Fiction

Critics' Choice
The Hamlet, William Faulkner
Sapphira and the Slave Girl, Willa Cather
You Can't Go Home Again, Thomas Wolfe (posthumous)
The Man Who Loved Children, Christina Stead
My Name Is Aram, William Saroyan
The Pilgrim Hawk, Glenway Wescott
The Heart Is a Lonely Hunter, Carson McCullers
Native Son, Richard Wright
The Ox-Bow Incident, Walter van Tilburg Clark
Darkness at Noon, Arthur Koestler
ᶽ *The Power and the Glory*, Graham Greene

Best-Sellers
How Green Was My Valley, Richard Llewellyn
Kitty Foyle, Christopher Morley
Mrs. Miniver, Jan Struther
For Whom the Bell Tolls, Ernest Hemingway
The Nazarene, Sholem Asch
Stars on the Sea, F. van Wyck Mason
Oliver Wiswell, Kenneth Roberts
The Grapes of Wrath, John Steinbeck

Night in Bombay, Louis Bromfield
The Family, Nina Fedorova

Nonfiction

Critics' Choice
The Realm of Spirit, George Santayana
Since Yesterday, Frederick Lewis Allen
Race, Language and Culture, Franz Boas
Education for a Classless Society, James Bryant Conant
Dusk of Dawn, W. E. B. Du Bois
America Learns to Play, Foster Rhea Dulles
The President Makers, Matthew Josephson
John D. Rockefeller, Allan Nevins
To the Finland Station, Edmund Wilson
ᶽ *How to Pay for the War*, J. M. Keynes
ᶽ *The Interpretation of Personality*, C. G. Jung

Best-Sellers
I Married Adventure, Osa Johnson
How to Read a Book, Mortimer Adler
A Smattering of Ignorance, Oscar Levant
Country Squire in the White House, John T. Flynn

American White Paper, Joseph W. Alsop, Jr., and Robert Kintnor
New England: Indian Summer, Van Wyck Brooks
Land Below the Wind, Agnes Newton Keith
As I Remember Him, Hans Zinsser
Days of Our Years, Pierre van Paassen
Bet It's a Boy, Betty B. Blunt

Poetry
Robert Hayden, *Heartshape in the Dust*
E. E. Cummings, *50 Poems*
Edna St. Vincent Millay, *Make Bright the Arrows*
H. D., *Collected Poems*
Kenneth Rexroth, *In What Hour*
Muriel Rukeyser, *The Soul and Body of John Brown*
John Ciardi, *Homeward to America*
ᶽ W. B. Yeats, *Last Poems and Plays* (posthumous)

Pulitzer Prizes
The Atlantic Migration, 1607–1860, Marcus Lee Hansen (U.S. history)
Jonathan Edwards, Ola Elizabeth Winslow (biography)
Sunderland Capture, Leonard Bacon (poetry)
No prize is awarded for the novel.

Science and Technology ━━━━━━━━━

More fissionable uranium 235 is isolated from the more stable uranium 238.

The University of California begins construction of a 4,900-ton cyclotron that produces mesons from atomic nuclei.

A new method of converting coal into organic chemicals useful for dyes, explosives, and medicines is developed at the California Institute of Technology.

The U.S. Air Force P-51 Mustang is designed.

Freeze drying is adapted for food preservation.

Hans Zinsser, at Harvard, announces a method to mass produce an antityphus vaccine.

Edwin Cohn separates blood plasma into globulin, albumin, and fibrin fractions.

Plasma is discovered to be a substitute for whole blood in transfusions.

Robert Gross performs the first successful surgery for congenital major blood vessel defect.

Karl Pabst designs the jeep.

Joe Louis, the youngest heavyweight champion in history, defends his title four times during the year. *Library of Congress.*

Baseball

Bob Feller (Cleveland, AL) pitches his first no-hitter, on opening day.

Champions

Batting
Debs Garms (Pittsburgh, NL), .355
Joe DiMaggio (New York, AL), .352

Pitching
Fred Fitzsimmons (Brooklyn, NL), 15–2
Lyn Rowe (Detroit, AL), 16–3
Home runs
John Mize (St. Louis, NL), 43

Football

"Students derive no special benefit from intercollegiate football," says the University of Chicago, as it withdraws from the Big Ten.

NFL Season Leaders: Sammy Baugh (Washington), passing; Don Looney (Philadelphia), rushing; and Don Hutson (Green Bay), passing.

College All-Americans: Frankie Albert (Q), Stanford; John Kimbrough (B), Texas A & M

College Bowls (Jan. 1, 1941)
Rose: Stanford 21–Nebraska 13
Orange: Mississippi State 14–Georgetown 7
Cotton: Texas A & M 13–Fordham 12
Sugar: Boston College 19–Tennessee 13

Sports

Other Sports

Horse Racing: Eight-year-old Seabiscuit becomes racing's all-time moneywinner. Gallahadion, the Kentucky Derby winner, goes off at 35–1.

Track and Field: Connie Warmerdam is the first to pole vault over 15 feet.

Boxing: Joe Louis KO's Arturo Godoy, who crouches in the ring like an ape and kisses him.

Car Racing: George Shaw wins his third Indianapolis 500.

Wimbledon, the Olympics, and Davis and Wightman Cups are called off because of the war.

Winners

World Series
Cincinnati (NL) 4
Detroit (AL) 3
MVP
NL–Frank McCormick, Cincinnati
AL–Henry Greenberg, Detroit
NFL
Chicago (Bears) 73–Washington 0
MVP
Ace Parker, Brooklyn
College Football
Minnesota
Heisman Trophy
Tom Harmon, Michigan

College Basketball
Indiana (NCAA)
Colorado (NIT)
Player of the Year
George Glamack, North Carolina
Stanley Cup
New York
US Tennis Open
Men: Donald McNeill
Women: Alice Marble
USGA Open
W. Lawson Little, Jr.
Kentucky Derby
Gallahadion (C. Bierman, jockey)

Fashion

For Women: With the occupation of France, the fashion center moves to New York. French "air force blue" becomes the popular color. Suit lapels are decorated with enamel shields in Ally colors; eagles appear on hatbands and purses. The times demand an emphasis on simplicity, economy, and practicality: short dresses, simple suits with pleated skirts; day dresses that can be worn at night with a muff or fur. New fashions include day dresses with aprons and pinafores and, at the other extreme, South Sea sarongs (after Dorothy Lamour) in colorful slinky crepes that expose the bare midriff and uplift bosom. Hair is worn to the shoulder with big curls, piled on top of the head with curls and pompadours, or curled into a sausage in the back. Lips are modeled like Crawford's "bow tie," in shades like "Regimented Red" (with matching polish); powder and rouge are applied over pancake makeup.

For Men: Fashions are marked by a new conservatism: the granite gray or blue striped suit; solid or red, blue, and white striped ties worn in Windsor knots; and spread-collared white, blue, or blue-white striped shirts. Rayon is introduced for wrinkleproof ties.

Kaleidoscope _____

- The speed and efficiency of the Nazi blitzkrieg, a sudden, combined air and tank assault, stuns America.
- The American movies *You Can't Take It with You* and *Going Places* are playing on the Champs Élysées as the Germans march through the Arc de Triomphe.
- FDR announces the buildup of a peacetime army; the Selective Service Training Act is passed, and 16,313,240 men receive registration cards for the first peacetime draft.
- Defense plants spring up throughout the United States with seven-day, round-the-clock workweeks.
- The Statue of Liberty stamp is issued with "For Defense" inscribed near the uplifted torch.
- Sheboygan, Wisconsin, votes to commence all concerts with "America" and "The Stars and Stripes Forever"; the second half will begin with "God Bless America" and "The Star Spangled Banner."
- Nickel jukeboxes appear in taverns, tearooms, variety stores, gas stations, restaurants, and barber shops; 16 records cost 50 cents; three minutes of silence is available for 5 cents.
- A *Downbeat* top singers poll includes Bing Crosby, Bob Eberle, Frank Sinatra, and James Rushing; "top girl singers" include Helen O'Connell, Dinah Shore, Billie Holiday, Mildred Bailey, Helen Forrest, and Martha Tilton.
- The popular Lindy Hop generates Saturday night social clubs; new dances include La Varsonviana; the rhumba peaks in popularity; Arthur Murray creates the "Americonga" and "Rhumba Reel."
- Artie Shaw, thought to be engaged to Betty Grable, marries Lana Turner, thought to be engaged to a Los Angeles attorney. Al Jolson and Ruby Keeler divorce.
- Newfangled supermarkets merchandise food differently; vegetables, for example, are available in bunches, rather than by the pound (carrots, 5 cents the bunch).
- McDonald's is started by Pasadena movie owners Richard and Maurice McDonald.
- The consumption of vermouth reaches a record high, 1,650,000 gallons.
- Radio news commentators include Boake Carter, Walter Winchell, Lowell Thomas, Fulton Lewis, Jr., Edward Morgan, Edward R. Murrow, and H. V. Kaltenborn (whose rolling *r*'s become an announcing style).
- In one of the auto industry's best years, the average car costs $1,200, a luxury car, $1,400; gasoline is 14 to 19 cents a gallon.
- John L. Lewis becomes a Republican.
- Albert Einstein becomes a U.S. citizen.
- The Pan American Yankee Clipper flies from New York to Lisbon in a record 18½ hours.
- When the New York El is torn down, the scrap is sold to Japan.
- The suspension bridge Galloping Gertie falls into Puget Sound.
- Bugs Bunny debuts in *O'Hare*.
- Procter and Gamble sues Lever Brothers for stealing

The Andrews Sisters popularize "Beat Me, Daddy (Eight to the Bar)." *Movie Star News*.

the "Ivory secret"; they settle for $10 million.
- The first Social Security checks total $75,844; the first recipient receives $22.54.
- A New York bill is signed that permits children to be absent from school for religious reasons.
- The NAACP denounces the army's policies of separate units for blacks and whites.
- A Syracuse University study reports that the word *I* is used every 53 words by Hitler, every 83 by Mussolini, and every 100 by FDR.
- The wartime shortage of Indian monkeys hinders medical research.
- FDR's gastronomic outline is as follows: he prefers seafood (terrapin), cheese, ice cream, and hot dogs; he enjoys one Scotch every afternoon and four old-fashioneds at banquets, and is a heavy smoker, his cigarette brand, Camels.
- News item: Hitler's Christmas cards are a photo of the *Winged Victory of Samothrace,* which the Germans took from the Louvre. His greeting is "Our Winged Victory."

First Appearances: Arnold bread, Morton salt, "Brenda Starr," cellophane wrap, cars with built-in running boards, safety wheel rims, fully air-conditioned store (Tiffany), commercial flight with pressurized cabins, photo of an albatross on U.S. coastal waters, photos of a sneeze, nonreflecting glass, odor absorber, chicken-feather plucker, cars with "torpedo" bodies, parachute wedding (New York, August 25), air raid shelter, synthetic rubber tire, public demonstration of stereo, synthetic tooth fillings. Patented: cigarettes with ads in invisible ink, ice bag shaped like a hat for headache sufferers, window alarm that catches a burglar at the window

1941

Facts and Figures

Economic Profile
  Dow-Jones:—High 133–
    Low 106
  GNP: +25%
  Inflation: +2.1%
  Unemployment: 9.9%
Median age, first marriage:
  Male: 24, Female: 21.5
Average household size: 3.16
Population over 65: 7%
Population under 10: 13%
Beer: 5¢
Soda: 49¢ (case)
Bokar coffee: 33¢ (2 lbs.)
Silver Crow gin: $1.14 (qt.)
Kentucky Straight whiskey:
  $1.59 (qt.)
Hiram Walker whiskey: $1.59
  (qt.)
Veal: 13¢ (lb.)
Shrimp, frozen: 15¢ (lb.)
Chicken: 23¢ (lb.)
A&P salad dressing: 25¢ (qt.)

Above: FDR asking Congress
to declare war, to which it
assents 410 to 1 (Rep.
Jeanette Rankin). *Library of
Congress.*

Deaths

Sherwood Anderson,
  Frederick Banting, Henri
  Bergson, James Frazer,
  Charles Evans Hughes,
  James Joyce, Ignace Jan
  Paderewski, Joe Penner,
  Kaiser William II, Virginia
  Woolf.

In the News

OFFICE OF PRODUCTION MANAGEMENT IS CREATED . . . USO BEGINS
. . . BRITISH ADVANCE IN AFRICA, GERMANS SEND ARMY UNDER
ROMMEL . . . NATIONAL DEFENSE MEDIATION BOARD IS CREATED TO
HANDLE STRIKES . . . NAZIS INVADE YUGOSLAVIA . . . NAZIS INVADE
GREECE . . . 60,000 BRITISH TROOPS ARE SENT TO GREECE . . .
OFFICE OF CIVIL DEFENSE IS CREATED . . . U.S. MERCHANT SHIP
"ROBIN MOOR" IS SUNK BY NAZI SUB . . . FDR DECLARES STATE OF
"LIMITED NATIONAL EMERGENCY" . . . FDR FREEZES AXIS FUNDS IN
U.S. AND CLOSES CONSULATES . . . GERMANY INVADES RUSSIA . . .
U.S. WILL GIVE RUSSIA $1 BILLION FOR LEND-LEASE . . . BRITAIN
AND RUSSIA INVADE IRAN . . . FDR EMBARGOES OIL AND SCRAP
METAL TO JAPAN . . . FDR AND CHURCHILL MEET IN NORTH
ATLANTIC, DECLARE 8-POINT CHARTER FOR POSTWAR WORLD . . .
SELECTIVE SERVICE IS EXTENDED TO 30 MONTHS . . . JAPANESE
PREMIER KONOYE SAYS JAPAN WANTS PEACE . . . 100 DIE AS U.S.
DESTROYER "REUBEN JAMES" IS SUNK OFF ICELAND . . . GERMANS
REACH OUTSKIRTS OF LENINGRAD AND THREATEN MOSCOW . . . TOJO
BECOMES JAPANESE PREMIER . . . JOHN L. LEWIS THREATENS COAL
STRIKE, FDR INTERVENES . . . CALIFORNIA ANTI-OKIE LAW IS
DECLARED UNCONSTITUTIONAL . . . FDR APPEALS TO HIROHITO FOR
PEACE . . . JAPANESE ATTACK PEARL HARBOR, HAWAII, IN SURPRISE
AIR ASSAULT, MASSIVE SHIP AND PLANE DAMAGE IS INFLICTED,
JAPANESE ALSO ATTACK MANILA, SINGAPORE, AND HONG KONG . . .
U.S. DECLARES WAR ON JAPAN . . . GERMANY AND ITALY DECLARE
WAR ON U.S. . . . WAKE ISLAND AND GUAM FALL TO THE JAPANESE
. . . DRAFT IS EXTENDED, MEN 18–65 MUST REGISTER, THOSE 20–44
MAY SERVE . . . $10 BILLION IS APPROPRIATED FOR DEFENSE . . .
HONG KONG FALLS.

Quotes

"In the future days, which we seek to make secure, we look forward to a world grounded upon four essential freedoms: . . . speech . . . worship . . . freedom from want [and] . . . fear."

— FDR

"This decision [to aid Britain] is the end of any attempts at appeasement, . . . the end of compromise with tyranny and the forces of oppression."

— FDR

"This is a war warning. An aggressive move by Japan is expected within the next few days."
— Adm. Harold "Betty" Stark to Pacific Command, November 1941

"Yesterday, December 7, 1941—a date which will live in infamy—the United States of America was suddenly and deliberately attacked by naval and air forces of the Empire of Japan. . . . Very many American lives have been lost. Always will our whole nation remember the character of the onslaught against us. . . . No matter how long it may take to overcome this premeditated invasion, the American people in their righteous might will win through to absolute victory. We will not only defend ourselves to the uttermost but will make it very certain that this form of treachery shall never again endanger us. We will gain the inevitable triumph—so help us God. I ask that the Congress declare . . . a state of war."

— FDR

"[The final solution] will be killing with showers of carbon monoxide while bathing."

— Adolf Eichmann

Naval air station at Pearl Harbor, December 7, 1941. Three hours after the surprise attack, the Japanese declared war. *Official Navy Photograph. By permission of D.C. Public Library.*

Ads

Radio

Premieres
"Spirit of '41," John Charles Daly
"The Red Skelton Show"
"Armstrong Theater of Today"
"Inner Sanctum," Raymond Edward Johnson
"The Great Gildersleeve," Hal Peary
"Duffy's Tavern," Ed Gardner, Shirley Booth
"The Thin Man," Lester Damon

Most Popular Soap Operas: "Guiding Light,"
"Woman in White," "Road of Life," "Right to
Happiness" (all written by Irma Philips)

Of Note
An estimated world audience of 90 million people
listen to FDR on December 9 declare "We are going
to win the war and . . . the peace that follows" •
Popular reporters include Edward R. Murrow,
William L. Shirer, Albert Warner, and Bill Henry •
"Gangbusters" is canceled for fear it may instigate
crime.

New Catchphrases: "If I dood it, I gets a whipping"
(Red Skelton); ". . . where the elite meet to eat.
Archie, the manager, speaking" ("Duffy's Tavern";
Duffy never appeared); "Now it's time to close the
door of the Inner Sanctum. . . . *(Door squeaks shut)*
("Inner Sanctum")

TV

A 90-minute documentary on Pearl Harbor and the
national reaction reaches a record audience.
The first commercial: the Bulova Time Signal

Movies

Openings
How Green Was My Valley (John Ford), Walter
Pidgeon, Maureen O'Hara
Citizen Kane (Orson Welles), Orson Welles, Joseph
Cotten
Hold Back the Dawn (Mitchell Leisen), Charles
Boyer, Olivia de Havilland
The Little Foxes (William Wyler), Bette Davis,
Herbert Marshall
The Maltese Falcon (John Huston), Humphrey
Bogart, Mary Astor, Peter Lorre
Sergeant York (Howard Hawks), Gary Cooper,
Walter Brennan, Joan Leslie
Suspicion (Alfred Hitchcock), Cary Grant, Joan
Fontaine
The Lady Eve (Preston Sturges), Barbara Stanwyck,
Henry Fonda
Major Barbara (Gabriel Pascal), Wendy Hiller, Rex
Harrison
The Shanghai Gesture (Josef von Sternberg), Gene
Tierney, Victor Mature
Dumbo (Ben Springsteen)
Blood and Sand (Rouben Mamoulian), Tyrone
Power, Nazimova, Linda Darnell
Dr. Jekyll and Mr. Hyde (Victor Fleming), Spencer
Tracy, Ingrid Bergman
High Sierra (Raoul Walsh), Ida Lupino, Humphrey
Bogart
Meet John Doe (Frank Capra), Gary Cooper,
Barbara Stanwyck
Two-Faced Woman (George Cukor), Greta Garbo
(her last film), Melvyn Douglas

Academy Awards
Best Picture: *How Green Was My Valley*
Best Director: John Ford (*How Green Was My
Valley*)
Best Actress: Joan Fontaine (*Suspicion*)
Best Actor: Gary Cooper (*Sergeant York*)

Top Box-Office Stars
Mickey Rooney, Clark Gable, Abbott and Costello,
Bob Hope, Spencer Tracy, Gene Autry, Gary
Cooper, Bette Davis, James Cagney, Judy Garland

Stars of Tomorrow
Laraine Day, Rita Hayworth, Ruth Hussey, Robert
Preston, Ronald Reagan, John Payne, Jeffrey Lynn,
Ann Rutherford, Dennis Morgan, Jackie Cooper

Popular Music

Hit Songs
"Deep in the Heart of Texas"
"You Don't Know What Love Is"
"God Bless the Child"
"I'll Remember April"
"There! I've Said It Again"
"Jersey Bounce"
"How about You?"
"Waltzing Matilda"
"The Anniversary Waltz"

Top Records
Green Eyes (Jimmy Dorsey); *You Made Me Love You* (Harry James); *Racing with the Moon* (Vaughn Monroe); *By the Light of the Silvery Moon* (Ray Noble); *Blues in the Night* (Dinah Shore); *Dancing in the Dark* (Artie Shaw); *Flamingo* (Duke Ellington); *Buckle Down, Winsocki* (Benny Goodman); *This Love of Mine* (Stan Kenton); *Chattanooga Choo Choo* (Glenn Miller)

Jazz and Big Bands
Stan Kenton opens at the Rendezvous Ballroom, Balboa, California. Gil Evans joins the Claude Thornhill Orchestra. Peggy Lee, Cootie Williams, and Big Sid Catlett perform with Benny Goodman.

First Recording: Charlie Parker, with Jay McShann

Top Performers *(Downbeat):* Harry James (soloist); Benny Goodman (big band); Glenn Miller (sweet band); Tex Beneke, Irving Fazola, J. C. Higginbotham, Ziggy Elman (instrumentalists); Helen O'Connell, Frank Sinatra (vocalists)

Theater

Broadway Openings

Plays
Watch on the Rhine (Lillian Hellman), Lucile Watson, Paul Lukas, Ann Blythe
Blithe Spirit (Noel Coward), Peggy Wood, Clifton Webb, Mildred Natwick
Arsenic and Old Lace (Joseph Kesselring), Josephine Hull, Boris Karloff
Native Son (Paul Green, Richard Wright), Canada Lee
Angel Street (Patrick Hamilton), Judith Evelyn, Vincent Price
Junior Miss (Jerome Chodorov, Joseph Fields), Francesca Bruning
Candle in the Wind (Maxwell Anderson), Helen Hayes
Clash by Night (Clifford Odets), Tallulah Bankhead, Joseph Schildkraut, Robert Ryan
Claudia (Rose Franken), Dorothy McGuire

Musicals
Best Foot Forward (Hugh Martin, Ralph Blane), June Allyson, Nancy Walker
Lady in the Dark (Kurt Weill, Ira Gershwin), Gertrude Lawrence, Victor Mature
Let's Face It (Cole Porter), Danny Kaye, Eve Arden, Vivian Vance, Nanette Fabray
Sons o' Fun (Sam E. Fain, Jack Yellen), Olsen and Johnson, Carmen Miranda, Ella Logan
Banjo Eyes (Vernon Duke, John Latouche), Eddie Cantor, June Clyde, Virginia Mayo

Classics and Revivals On and Off Broadway
Macbeth, Maurice Evans, Judith Anderson; *As You Like It,* Alfred Drake, Helen Craig; *Twelfth Night,* Beatrice Straight, Hurd Hatfield; *The Doctor's Dilemma* (George Bernard Shaw), Katharine Cornell, Raymond Massey; *Ah, Wilderness!* (Eugene O'Neill), Harry Carey. *Founded:* The Experimental Theatre of Dramatists by Antoinette Perry

Pulitzer Prize
There Shall Be No Night, Robert E. Sherwood

Clark Gable and Carole Lombard attend a Hollywood wedding shortly before her death. *Movie Star News.*

Classical Music

Compositions

Aaron Copland, Piano Sonata
Douglas Moore, *Village Music*
Walter Piston, *Sinfonietta*
William Schuman, Symphony no. 3, Symphony no. 4
John Alden Carpenter, *Song of Freedom*
Roy Harris, *Railroad Man's Ballad, From This Earth, Accelerator,* Violin Sonata
Leonard Bernstein, Symphony no. 1, Clarinet Sonata
Roger Sessions, *Montezuma*
Samuel Barber, Violin Concerto
David Diamond, Symphony no. 1
John Cage, *Double Music*

Important Events

For the conclusion of the Chicago Symphony's 50th anniversary, music performed includes Stravinsky's Symphony in C Major and Leo Sowerby's Symphony no. 3. Guest conductors are Leopold Stokowski, Bruno Walter, Artur Rodzinsky, Dimitri Mitropoulos, Eugene Goossens, Serge Koussevitzky, John Barbirolli, Walter Damrosch, Arturo Toscanini, and Fritz Busch, each for two weeks.

The League of Composers presents the work of the younger John Ayres Lessard, Emil Koehler, Donald Fuller, Norman Dello Joio, and Lukas Foss.

Debuts: Malcolm Frager, William Kapell

First Performances

Béla Bartók, Quartet no. 6, *Music for Strings, Percussion, and Celeste* (New York); Rachmaninoff, Symphonic Dances (Philadelphia); William Schuman, Symphony no. 3 (Boston); Aaron Copland, *Quiet City* (New York); Paul Hindemith, Cello Concerto (Boston); Symphony in E-flat (Seattle); Benjamin Britten, Sinfonia da Requiem (New York); Stravinsky, *Tango* (Philadelphia, Benny Goodman conducting); Ernest Bloch, *Baal Shem* (WPA Orchestra, New York); Virgil Thomson, Symphony no. 2 (Seattle); Samuel Barber, Concerto for Violin (Philadelphia); Robert Russell Bennett, *A Symphony in D for the Dodgers* (New York); Leo Sowerby, Symphony no. 3 (Chicago); Alfredo Casella, Symphony no. 3 (Chicago)

Opera

Metropolitan: Jan Peerce (debut), *La traviata, Rigoletto;* Astrid Varnay, *Siegfried;* Grace Moore, Ezio Pinza, *L'amore dei tre re;* Stella Roman, *Aïda;*

Joseph Cotten and Orson Welles in *Citizen Kane,* "boy wonder" Welles's first film, based on the life of William Randolph Hearst. Hearst tried to suppress the film. *Movie Star News.*

Helen Traubel, *Die Walküre;* Salvatore Baccaloni, *Il barbiere di Siviglia;* Elisabeth Rethberg, Lawrence Tibbett, Giovanni Martinelli, *Fidelio*

New Opera of New York: Organized to perform at modest costs and in English; *Così fan tutte* (premiere performance); scores commissioned are *Solomon and Balkis* (Randall Thompson); *No for an Answer* (Marc Blitzstein)

Boston: *Orfeo* (Claudio Monteverdi, the Malipiero version, premiere)

Chicago: Licia Albanese, Gladys Swarthout, *Carmen, Madama Butterfly*

San Francisco: *Simon Boccanegra;* Lily Pons, Salvatore Baccaloni, *La fille du regiment*

Music Notes

Albert Einstein plays the violin in a benefit concert for Refugee Children in England, in Princeton, N.J.

Art _____

Painting

Jackson Pollock, *Naked Man with Knife, Man, Bull, Bird, Birth*

Lyonel Feininger, *Tug*

Max Weber, *The Night Class*

Robert Motherwell, *The Little Spanish Prison*

Willem de Kooning, *The Wave*

Andrew Wyeth, *Farm at Broad Cove, Cushing, Maine*

Edward Hopper, *Nighthawks*

Stuart Davis, *New York under Gaslight*

Hyman Bloom, *The Bride*

Arshile Gorky, *Garden in Sochi*

Louis Guglielmi, *Terror in Brooklyn*

Morris Graves, *Bird in the Spirit*

Sculpture

Alexander Calder, *Mobile*

Peter Grippe, *The City #1, 1941*

Isamu Noguchi, *Contoured Playground*

Joseph Cornell, *Swiss Shoot-the-Chutes*

Carl Milles's figures are placed at the Cranbrook Academy Fountain, Bloomfield Hills, Mich.

Architecture

Federal housing communities, California, Texas (Richard Neutra)

Platt House, Portland, Oreg. (Pietro Belluschi)

Cranbrook Academy of Art, Bloomfield Hills, Mich. (Saarinen and Saarinen)

West Building, National Gallery of Art, Washington, D.C. (Pope, Eggers, and Higgins)

Important Exhibitions

Museums

New York: *Metropolitan:* "China Trade and Its Influences" (tours United States); Prints by six masters from the Warburg Collection; French prints after 1800; WPA exhibitions; Pages from early Korans; The art of Australia; French Painters from David to Toulouse-Lautrec. *Museum of Modern Art:* Miró, Dali, Grosz. *Brooklyn:* Paganism and Christianity in Egypt

Chicago: The first century of printmaking; 52nd exhibition of American paintings and sculpture; French paintings from David to Toulouse-Lautrec; Goya

Boston: Modern Mexican painters

Toledo: Spanish art

Niles Spencer, *Waterfront Mill*, 1941. Oil. 30 × 36″. *The Metropolitan Museum of Art, Arthur H. Hearn Fund, 1942.*

San Francisco: Baroque Italian painting

Individual Shows

Goya (Chicago); Cassatt (Baltimore); Gorky (San Francisco); Grosz, Miró, Dali, Myers (New York); Grosz (Minneapolis); Weber (New York, Philadelphia, Washington, Chicago)

Art Briefs

Because of the war, the art capital moves from Paris to New York. Refugee artists in the United States include Léger, Lipchitz, Kisling, Mondrian, Tanguy, Masson, Tchelitchew, Chagall, Berman, Ozenfant, Zadkine, Moholy-Nagy, Dali, and Ernst • Kokoschka, called "most degenerate" by Hitler, holds the largest one-man show in the United States • The National Gallery in Washington, D.C., opens, the largest marble building in the world; it contains the Mellon, Kress, and Widener collections valued at $50 million.

Dance _____

At Nelson Rockefeller's request, Lincoln Kirstein and George Balanchine organize the American Ballet Caravan for a goodwill tour of Latin America; they premiere *Concerto Barocco* and *Ballet Imperial* (Balanchine), with Nicholas Magallanes and William Dollar. Alicia Markova and Anton Dolin organize the Jacob's Pillow International Dance Festival near Lee, Mass.

Other Premieres

Ballet Theatre: *Three Virgins and a Devil* (Agnes de Mille), de Mille, Lucia Chase; *Pas de Quatre* (Anton Dolin)

Martha Graham: *Letter to the World*

Doris Humphrey: *Song of the West*

Books

Fiction

Critics' Choice

The Last Tycoon, F. Scott Fitzgerald (posthumous)
Reflections in a Golden Eye, Carson McCullers
The Real Life of Sebastian Knight, Vladimir Nabokov
Fables, William Saroyan
The Hills Beyond, Thomas Wolfe (posthumous)
What Makes Sammy Run? Budd Schulberg
I'll Never Go There Any More, Jerome Weidman
Mildred Pierce, James Cain

Best-Sellers

The Keys of the Kingdom, A. J. Cronin
Random Harvest, James Hilton
This Above All, Eric Knight
The Sun Is My Undoing, Marguerite Steen
For Whom the Bell Tolls, Ernest Hemingway
Oliver Wiswell, Kenneth Roberts
H. M. Pulham, Esquire, John P. Marquand
Mr. and Mrs. Cugat, Isabel Scott Rorick
Windswept, Mary Ellen Chase
Saratoga Trunk, Edna Ferber

Nonfiction

Critics' Choice

Two-Way Passage, Louis Adamic
Twelve Million Black Voices, Richard Wright et al.
The New Critic, John Crowe Ransom
Let Us Now Praise Famous Men, James Agee, Walker Evans
A Philosophy of Literary Form, Kenneth Burke
The Mind of the South, C. F. Cash
Escape from Freedom, Erich Fromm
The Wound and the Bow, Edmund Wilson
Mythology, Edith Hamilton

Best-Sellers

Berlin Diary, William L. Shirer
The White Cliffs, Alice Duer Miller
Out of the Night, Jan Valtin
Inside Latin America, John Gunther
Blood, Sweat and Tears, Winston S. Churchill
You Can't Do Business with Hitler, Douglas Miller
Reading I've Liked, ed. Clifton Fadiman
Reveille in Washington, Margaret Leech

My Sister and I, Dirk van der Heide
Exit Laughing, Irvin S. Cobb

Poetry

Theodore Roethke, *Open House*
William Carlos Williams, *The Broken Span*
Edna St. Vincent Millay, *Collected Sonnets*
Louis Zukofsky, *55 Poems*
E. E. Cummings, *50 Poems*
Horace Gregory, *Poems 1930–1940*
Louise Bogan, *Poems and New Poems*
Robinson Jeffers, *Be Angry at the Sun*
Josephine Miles, *Poems on Several Occasions*

Pulitzer Prizes

In This Our Life, Ellen Glasgow (novel)
Reveille in Washington, Margaret Leech (U.S. history)
Crusader in Crinoline, Forrest Wilson (biography)
The Dust Which Is God, William Rose Benét

Science and Technology

Uranium and thorium are split into equal parts in the cyclotron at the University of California, Berkeley, by Glenn Seaborg and Emilio Segre.

At Berkeley, Glenn Seaborg and E. McMillan isolate plutonium, a fuel preferable to uranium for nuclear reactors.

The Manhattan Engineering District, a project to develop atomic energy for military purposes, is secretly authorized by FDR; scientists include Enrico Fermi, Leo Szilard, and Edward Teller.

RCA demonstrates a new simplified electron microscope that magnifies up to 100,000 times.

Successful treatment of pneumonia with sulfanilamide is reported by Dr. Norman Plummer.

The U.S. Indian Service reports that trachoma, a sight-destroying disease, can be cured by sulfanilamide.

Cardiac catheterization is developed by Dickinson Richards and André Cournaud.

Prevention of hemorrhage by vitamin K is announced by Dr. Henry Poncer, University of Illinois.

Standard Oil announces a new, simpler, and cheaper process of cracking oil.

The *American Medical Association Journal* describes the Sister Kenny massage method for treating infantile paralysis.

Sports

Baseball

Ted Williams (Boston, AL) bats .400 until the last day of the season, plays despite this, and goes 6 for 9.

Joe DiMaggio (New York, AL) hits safely in 56 consecutive games; he gets 91 hits during a streak that ends in Cleveland.

Champions

Batting	Pitching
Pete Reiser (Brooklyn, NL), .343	Elmer Riddle (Cincinnati, NL), 19–4
Ted Williams (Boston, AL), .406	Lefty Gomez (New York, AL), 15–5
	Home runs
	Ted Williams (Boston, AL), 37

Football

Elmer Layden is named NFL high commissioner.

NFL Season Leaders: Cecil Isbell (Green Bay), passing; Clarence Manders (Brooklyn), rushing; Don Hutson (Green Bay), receiving

College All-Americans: Frankie Albert (Q), Stanford; Bill Dudley (B), Virginia; Frank Sinkwich (B), Georgia

Bowls (Jan. 1, 1942)

Rose: Oregon 20–Duke 15
Orange: Georgia 40–Texas Christian 26
Cotton: Alabama 29–Texas A & M 21
Sugar: Fordham 2–Missouri 0

Other Sports

Horse Racing: Whirlaway, ridden by Eddie Arcaro, wins the Triple Crown.

Golf: Sam Snead wins the PGA tournament.

Winners

World Series	*College Basketball*
New York (AL) 4	Wisconsin (NCAA)
Brooklyn (NL) 1	Long Island University (NIT)
MVP	*Player of the Year*
NL–Adolph Camilli, Brooklyn	George Glamack, North Carolina
AL–Joe DiMaggio, New York	*Stanley Cup*
NFL	Boston
Chicago (Bears) 37–New York 9	*US Tennis Open*
MVP	Men: Robert L. Riggs
Don Hutson, Green Bay	Women: Sarah Palfrey Cooke
College Football	*USGA Open*
Minnesota	Craig Wood
Heisman Trophy	*Kentucky Derby*
Bruce Smith, Minnesota	Whirlaway (E. Arcaro, jockey)

Fashion

For Women: Government regulations limit fabric lengths and banish pleats, more than one pocket, and trim. Civilian women follow the look of servicewomen with gray flannel suits, low-heeled shoes in polished leathers, the shoulder strap bag, and the beret or felt cloche hat. Hair is swept up and off the face, though sometimes decorated with bright little ribbon bows attached to combs and clips. At night, frilly dresses appear, along with short skirts of black crepe and long-sleeved blouses with deep décolletages. The satin evening suit is also worn with high-heeled ankle straps. With wool shortages, new fabrics are developed for new purposes: rayon and cotton stockings, cotton dresses for winter, trench and peacoats.

High-fashion note: Albouys's duster hats; the rayon crepe Molyneux dress with fuchsia sequined yoke and cyclamen sash

Joe DiMaggio, "the Yankee Clipper." *Library of Congress.*

Current fashion in clothing and cars. *Library of Congress.*

- In his fifteenth fireside chat, FDR informs the nation that rationing will be necessary for full defense productivity; he adds: "Never before . . . has our American civilization been in such danger. . . . We must be the great arsenal of democracy."
- Thousands join the nation's industries that call for more workers; because of rising rents and the unavailability of building materials, many are forced to live in tents and tarpaper cities, raw-wood shacks, unused barns, garages, warehouses, and chicken coops.
- Major networks cancel broadcasts of their Berlin correspondents because of Nazi censorship.
- "Rosie the Riveter" (named after Rosina Bonavita) becomes the emblem of the American woman working in defense industries.
- After the opening of the Russian front, the peacetime draft is accelerated; "Uncle Sam Needs You" signs are posted in all public places.
- A Gallup Poll reveals that 60 percent of the public wants to aid Britain even if it risks war; 12 percent would go to war immediately.
- Goods shipped to England include Spam, a new kind of canned and processed meat, dehydrated meats, vegetables, and fruits; similar products begin to appear at home.
- With the shortage of certain metals, use of plastics increases; Philip Wrigley, in gum packaging, introduces cellophane in place of tinfoil; Lucky Strike substitutes a white and red bullseye logo for its green and red one, since green ink contains metal.
- With prices rising, FDR establishes the Office of Price Administration (OPA); priorities are set on civilian supplies: for example, spices, wine, palm oil, burlap, and tea are labeled nonessential.
- With the improvement in the economy, car sales soar; alcohol consumption also rises.
- Henry Ford, for the first time, agrees to negotiate with a union.
- Chrysler begins building the M-3 tank; GM, the B-25 bomber; Ford, Pratt Whitney engines.
- With soaring box office receipts Hollywood can barely produce films fast enough, and many westerns and grade B and C films are released.
- Greta Garbo, 36, retires after *Two-Faced Woman;* the film is banned in Rhode Island as "immoral."
- Charles Chaplin rejects the New York Film Critics' best male actor award because it implies competition.
- Cary Grant donates his entire salary, $137,500, from *The Man Who Came to Dinner* to British war relief.
- A *Photoplay* poll reports that the best figures in Hollywood belong to Betty Grable and Errol Flynn.

Kaleidoscope

- "Gentleman" Joe Louis, who defeats a contender a month, becomes a national hero.
- Eleven-year-old Lorin Maazel, who knows 22 symphonies by heart, leads the NBC Summer Symphony.
- "I'd have people buy the paintings and hang them in privies or anywhere anybody had time to look at 'em," says Thomas Hart Benton.
- St. John the Divine, the largest Gothic church in the world, opens in New York City; the Hoover Library on War, Peace and Revolution opens in Palo Alto, Calif.
- William Bishop, University of Michigan librarian, says the highly perishable nature of wood pulp threatens the preservation of documents; he suggests microfilm.
- Stalin toasts FDR at a ten-hour, seven-course dinner after the German invasion; there are 32 bottoms-up toasts in vodka and cognac.
- The Andrews sisters earn $5,000 a week—2 cents for each play of 8 million Decca records on jukeboxes.
- Liquidating some assets, William Randolph Hearst offers Gimbels and Saks part of his $50 million art collection for sale over their bargain counters; most works are bought by browsing housewives.
- The FDA seizes all heatless permanent wave preparations because they contain poisonous ammonia hydrogen sulfide.
- Pope Pius XII authorizes Roman Catholic bishops throughout the world to allow meat on Friday and omit certain fast days during the war.
- Yale, Harvard, and Princeton decide to cut their programs from four to three years by staying in session all year round.
- Claire Chennault organizes a group of American volunteers to fight in China, the Flying Tigers.
- Navy Secretary Frank Knox says that U.S. services were not "on the alert against the surprise air attack on Hawaii" and calls for a formal investigation.
- Pearl Harbor statistics: 1,500 civilians killed, 1,500 injured; 5 battleships sunk or beached *(Arizona, Oklahoma, California, Nevada, West Virginia),* 11 smaller ships destroyed, 3 ships damaged so as to be unusable; 177 planes destroyed; 91 navy officers killed, 20 wounded; 2,638 enlisted men dead, 636 wounded; 168 army men killed, 223 wounded, 26 missing.

Fads: The saying "Kilroy was here," the congo, Lindy hop, and kangaroo jump

First Appearances: Rationing of silk stockings, Quonset huts, Merrill, Lynch, Pierce, Fenner, and Beane, furniture with plastic vinylite, Cheerios, Spice Island, Buitoni foods, paprika mill, municipally owned parking, Chemex coffee maker, "Sad Sack," health insurance clause in labor contract (ILGWU), heredity clinic, motion picture professorship (New York University)

1942

Ration coupon. *Smithsonian Institution.*

Deaths

John Barrymore, George M.
  Cohan, Michel Fokine,
  Condé Nast, Otis Skinner,
  Grant Wood.

In the News

MANILA FALLS, MACARTHUR RETREATS TO BATAAN . . . BURMA IS INVADED . . . SINGAPORE AND RANGOON FALL . . . FDR ASKS FOR 60,000 PLANES AND 45,000 TANKS . . . $58 BILLION BUDGET ALLOTS $52 BILLION FOR DEFENSE . . . WAR PRODUCTION BOARD IS ESTABLISHED . . . LATIN-AMERICAN TIES TO GERMANY AND ITALY ARE SEVERED . . . U.S. TROOPS LAND IN NORTHERN IRELAND . . . EMERGENCY PRICE CONTROL ACT IS PASSED . . . U.S. AND BRITAIN COMBINE CHIEFS OF STAFF . . . PRESIDENTIAL ORDER RELOCATES WEST COAST JAPANESE . . . JAPANESE WIN IN BATTLE OF JAVA SEA . . . MACARTHUR LEAVES PHILIPPINES FOR AUSTRALIA . . . WAR PRODUCTION BOARD STOPS ALL NONESSENTIAL BUILDING . . . JAPANESE TAKE SOLOMONS . . . BATAAN FALLS, WAINWRIGHT SURRENDERS . . . DOOLITTLE LEADS AIR RAID ON TOKYO . . . NAZIS BURN LIDICE IN REPRISAL FOR HEYDRICH ASSASSINATION . . . RAF RAIDS COLOGNE . . . JAPANESE SUFFER FIRST LOSSES IN CORAL SEA BATTLE . . . ROMMEL TAKES TOBRUK . . . WILLKIE RETURNS FROM OVERSEAS MISSION . . . COFFEE, SUGAR, AND GAS RATIONING BEGINS . . . GERMANS REACH STALINGRAD . . . NAVY WINS MAJOR BATTLE AT MIDWAY . . . JAPANESE OCCUPY ALEUTIANS . . . OFFICE OF STRATEGIC SERVICES FORMS . . . FDR AND CHURCHILL CONFER IN D.C. . . . SCRAP RUBBER DRIVE BEGINS . . . WACS, WAVES, SPARS RECRUIT . . . $25,000 SALARY CEILING IS INSTITUTED . . . MARINES LAND ON GUADALCANAL . . . ALLIES RAID DIEPPE AND SUFFER HEAVY LOSSES . . . MONTGOMERY'S TANKS SHATTER ROMMEL'S FORCES AT EL ALAMEIN . . . HALSEY DEFEATS JAPANESE IN SOLOMONS . . . WPA ENDS, GIVEN "HONORABLE DISCHARGE" . . . 400,000 U.S.-BRITISH FORCES UNDER EISENHOWER LAND IN NORTH AFRICA . . . 492 DIE IN COCOANUT GROVE FIRE, BOSTON.

Quotes ————————

"This is a civilians' war—and as civilians, we must face the fury of our enemies, who have no respect for an 'open city' nor an unarmed opponent."
— N. Y. State Council of Defense

"Hard work isn't hard—it's a badge of courage. That 'old clothes look' doesn't matter. It's smart to be mended. . . . Conservation is a war weapon in the hands of every man, woman, and child."
— Office of Civilian Defense

"When we are dealing with the Caucasian race [in America], we have methods that will test . . . loyalty. But when we deal with the Japanese, we are in an entirely different field."
— California attorney general Earl Warren, on evacuating the Japanese to relocation camps

"Has the Gestapo come to America? Have we not risen in righteous anger at Hitler's mistreatment of the Jews? Then, is it not incongruous that citizen Americans of Japanese descent should be similarly mistreated and persecuted?"
— Miki Masoka, before the Tolan Committee, National Defense Migration Hearings

Library of Congress.

"We come among you to repulse the cruel invaders. . . . Help us where you are able. *Viva la France éternelle!*
— FDR, as U.S. troops invade French North Africa

"The President of the United States ordered me to break through the Japanese lines and proceed from Corregidor to Australia for the purpose of organizing the American offense against Japan. . . . I came through and I shall return."
— Gen. Douglas MacArthur

Smithsonian Institution.

Ads ————————

"I'm fighting for my right to boo the Dodgers!"
(Texaco)

An American Privilege—Dutch Master Cigars.
(Dutch Master Cigars)

Victory won't wait for the nation that's late.
(Big Ben Clocks)

Will victory catch you unprepared? . . . There is every indication that the post-war world will offer rich opportunities for alert manufacturers who see ahead and make the most of the knowledge, techniques, and skills developed by war production.
(Bryant Chucking Grinder Co.)

Fighting Red—new brave lipstick color by Tussey.
(Tussey Cosmetics)

Radio

Premieres
"Suspense," Joe Kearns
"Stage Door Canteen," Bert Lytell
"People Are Funny," Art Baker, Art Linkletter
"It Pays to be Ignorant," Tom Howard
"This Is War," Fredric March

Specials
"America Speaks to China," with Chinese journalist Yen Ying Yen (eight dramas by Pearl Buck translated and shortwaved to China)

Top Ten
"Chase and Sanborn Hour," "Jack Benny," "Fibber McGee and Molly," "Lux Radio Theater," "Aldrich Family," "Bob Hope," "Maxwell House Coffee Time," "Walter Winchell," "Kate Smith Hour," and "Fitch Bandwagon"

Of Note
Frances Langford, on "Command Performance," broadcasts, via 13 shortwave stations, song requests to U.S. troops throughout the world • "This Is War," written by famous authors and performed with extensive sound effects, is broadcast on the four major networks.

New Catchphrases: "Hey Abbott! I'm a ba-a-a-d boy" (Abbott and Costello); "It pays to be ignorant, To be dumb, to be dense, to be ignorant. / It pays to be ignorant, / Just like me!" ("It Pays to Be Ignorant" theme song)

TV

Training programs for air-raid wardens are televised.

Movies

Openings
Mrs. Miniver (William Wyler), Greer Garson, Walter Pidgeon
Casablanca (Michael Curtiz), Ingrid Bergman, Humphrey Bogart
The Magnificent Ambersons (Orson Welles), Tim Holt, Joseph Cotten, Anne Baxter, Dolores Costello Barrymore
Pride of the Yankees (Sam Wood), Gary Cooper, Teresa Wright
Random Harvest (Mervyn LeRoy), Ronald Colman, Greer Garson
Wake Island (John Farrow), Brian Donlevy, William Bendix
Yankee Doodle Dandy (Michael Curtiz), James Cagney, Walter Huston
Now, Voyager (Irving Rapper), Bette Davis, Paul Henreid
Tortilla Flat (Victor Fleming), Spencer Tracy, John Garfield, Hedy Lamarr
Woman of the Year (George Stevens), Spencer Tracy, Katharine Hepburn
In Which We Serve (Noel Coward, David Lean), Noel Coward, John Mills
To Be or Not to Be (Ernst Lubitsch), Jack Benny, Carole Lombard

Sullivan's Travels (Preston Sturges), Joel McCrea, Veronica Lake
Road to Morocco (David Butler), Bob Hope, Bing Crosby, Dorothy Lamour
The Battle of Midway (John Ford), documentary
Cat People (Jacques Tourneur), Simone Simon

Academy Awards
Best Picture: *Mrs. Miniver*
Best Director: William Wyler (*Mrs. Miniver*)
Best Actress: Greer Garson (*Mrs. Miniver*)
Best Actor: James Cagney (*Yankee Doodle Dandy*)

Top Box-Office Stars
Abbott and Costello, Clark Gable, Gary Cooper, Mickey Rooney, Bob Hope, James Cagney, Gene Autry, Betty Grable, Greer Garson, Spencer Tracy

Stars of Tomorrow
Van Heflin, Eddie Bracken, Jane Wyman, John Carroll, Alan Ladd, Lynn Bari, Nancy Kelly, Donna Reed, Betty Hutton, Teresa Wright

Popular Music

Hit Songs
"Don't Get Around Much
  Anymore"
"Praise the Lord and Pass the
  Ammunition!"
"Rosie, the Riveter"
"Serenade in Blue"
"Happiness Is a Thing Called Joe"
"In the Blue of Evening"
"I Left My Heart at the Stage
  Door Canteen"
"A String of Pearls"
"When the Lights Go on Again"
"We'll Meet Again"
"That Old Black Magic"
"You'd Be So Nice to Come
  Home To"
"This Is the Army, Mr. Jones"

Jitterbugging at a Washington, D.C., Elks' Club dance. *Library of Congress.*

Top Records
Don't Sit under the Apple Tree
(Andrews Sisters); *White
Christmas, Moonlight Becomes
You* (Bing Crosby); *Sleepy Lagoon*
(Xavier Cugat); *He Wears a Pair
of Silver Wings* (Kate Smith);
Strip Polka (Kay Kyser); *Why
Don't You Do Right?* (Peggy Lee,
Benny Goodman); *I've Got a Gal
in Kalamazoo* (Glenn Miller);
Paper Doll (Mills Brothers); *I Had
the Craziest Dream* (Helen
Forrest); *Der Fuehrer's Face*
(Spike Jones)

Jazz and Big Bands
Max Roach joins Charlie Parker at
Monroe's, New York. Swing
bands become service bands.

Top Performers (*Downbeat*): Benny
Goodman (soloist); Duke Ellington
(big band); Tommy Dorsey (sweet
band); Eddie Condon, Buddy
Rich, Johnny Hodges, Tex
Beneke, Pee Wee Russell, Roy
Eldridge (instrumentalists); Helen
Forrest, Frank Sinatra (vocalists)

Theater

Broadway Openings

Plays
The Skin of Our Teeth (Thornton Wilder), Tallulah
  Bankhead, Fredric March, Florence Eldridge,
  Montgomery Clift
The Eve of St. Mark (Maxwell Anderson), William
  Prince
Without Love (Philip Barry), Katharine Hepburn,
  Elliott Nugent
The Pirate (S. N. Behrman), Alfred Lunt, Lynn
  Fontanne, Estelle Winwood
Flare Path (Terence Rattigan), Alec Guinness, Nancy
  Kelly
The Morning Star (Emlyn Williams), Gregory Peck,
  Gladys Cooper

Musicals
By Jupiter (Richard Rodgers, Lorenz Hart), Benay
  Venuta, Ray Bolger, Constance Moore
Rosalinda (Johann Strauss, Paul Kerby), Dorothy
  Sarnoff, Gene Barry
Star and Garter (Irving Berlin et al., burlesque),
  Bobby Clark, Gypsy Rose Lee
This Is the Army (Irving Berlin), Ezra Stone, Irving
  Berlin, all-soldier cast

Irving Berlin's musical *This Is the Army*, with its all-army
cast. *Billy Rose Theatre Collection. The New York Public
Library at Lincoln Center. Astor, Lenox and Tilden
Foundations.*

Classics and Revivals On and Off Broadway
The Three Sisters (Chekhov), Katharine Cornell,
Judith Anderson, Ruth Gordon, Kirk Douglas;
Candida (George Bernard Shaw), Katharine Cornell,
Burgess Meredith, Raymond Massey, Mildred
Natwick; *The Rivals* (Sheridan), Mary Boland,
Walter Hampden

Pulitzer Prize
No prize is awarded.

Classical Music

Compositions

George Antheil, Symphony no. 4
Samuel Barber, Essay for Orchestra, no. 2
William Schuman, Secular Cantata no. 2, *A Free Song*
Roy Harris, Symphony no. 5, *American Ballads, Piano Concerto with Band,* Violin Sonata
Douglas Moore, Wind Quintet
Walter Piston, Quintet for Flute and Strings
Roger Sessions, Duo for Violin and Piano
Igor Stravinsky (in U.S.), *Dances Concertantes*

Important Events

The United States becomes the world music center and shelter for foreign musicians Bruno Walter, George Szell, Béla Bartók (Columbia University), Darius Milhaud (Mills College), Ernst Krenek (Vassar), Arnold Schoenberg (University of South Carolina), Paul Hindemith (Yale), Kurt Weill, and Ernest Toch.

Toscanini conducts the New York Philharmonic in six all-Beethoven concerts.

At NBC, Toscanini plays the music of American composers Paul Creston (*Choric Dance),* Morton Gould (*Lincoln Legend),* Charles Martin Loeffler (*Memories of My Childhood),* and George Gershwin (*Rhapsody in Blue,* with Earl Wild and Benny Goodman).

Shostakovitch's Symphony no. 7 gains world attention; it is sent to the United States on microfilm through enemy lines before its performance by Toscanini and the NBC Symphony.

American works to gain most attention during the year are William Schuman's Symphony no. 3 (Boston) and Symphony no. 4 (Cleveland).

Debut: Earl Wild

First Performances

Samuel Barber, Violin Concerto (Boston); Carlos Chávez, Piano Concerto (New York); John Cage, *Imaginary Landscape no. 3* (Chicago); Harl McDonald, *Bataan* (tribute to Douglas MacArthur, Washington); Paul Creston, *A Fanfare for Paratroopers* (Cincinnati); Darius Milhaud, *Fanfare de la liberté;* also commissioned by Cincinnati: *Lincoln Portrait* (Copland); *The Mayor La Guardia Waltzes* (Virgil Thomson); *Mark Twain* (Jerome Kern); Oscar Levant, playing his Concerto in One Movement (NBC radio); David Diamond, Symphony no. 1 (New York); Copland, *Statements* for Orchestra (New York)

Opera

Metropolitan: Helen Traubel, *Tristan und Isolde;* Eleanor Steber, *Le nozze di Figaro;* Leonard Warren, Astrid Varnay, Raoul Jobin, *The Island God* (Gian Carlo Menotti, George Szell, conducting, premiere); Lily Djanel, *Carmen*

New Opera Company, New York: *Solomon and Balkis* (Randall Thompson, premiere and on radio)

Chicago: *A Tree on the Plains* (Ernest Bacon); all-black *Aïda* (Chicago Negro Opera Guild)

Philadelphia: *Ramuntcho* (Deems Taylor, premiere)

Music Note

E. Power Biggs begins his Sunday morning organ recitals in Cambridge, Mass.; they are broadcast nationally and internationally by shortwave.

Weekend pass at the United Service Organization (USO). *Library of Congress.*

Art

Painting

Thomas Hart Benton, *July Hay* and *Negro Soldier, Invasion*

Marsden Hartley, *Evening Storm, Schoodic, Maine*

Ralston Crawford, *Elevators for the Bridge*

Edward Hopper, *Cobb's House, South Truro*

Isabel Bishop, *Card Game*

Stuart Davis, *Ursine Park*

Mark Tobey, *Threading Light, The Void Devouring the Gadget Era*

Arshile Gorky, *Bull in the Sun*

Yves Tanguy, *Slowly toward the North*

Pavel Tchelitchew, *Hide and Seek*

Jackson Pollock, *Moon Woman*

John Steuart Curry paints murals for the University of Wisconsin Law School and Kansas State Capitol Building.

Sculpture

Chaim Gross, *Acrobatic Dancers*

Theodore Roszak, *Vertical Composition*

Alexander Calder, *Constellation with Red Object*

Joseph Cornell, *Homage to the Romantic Ballet, A Pantry Ballet (for Jacques Offenbach)*

Jo Davidson, *Bust of Vice-President Wallace*

José de Creeft, *Himalaya*

Architecture

The Saarinens and Robert Swanson win the design competition for Wayne University, Detroit.

Church of Saints Peter and Paul, Pierre, S.D. (Barry Byrne)

Kramer Homes, Center Line, Mich. (Eliel and Eero Saarinen)

Packaged House System for General Panel Corporation (Gropius, Wachsmann)

Important Exhibitions

Numerous shows benefit war causes: "Dutch Masters" (for the Queen Wilhelmina Fund); El Greco (for Greek relief); Cézanne (for the Fighting French); Yasuo Kuniyoshi (United Chinese Relief); at the Metropolitan Museum of Art, "Artists for Victory"; at the Museum of Modern Art, the poster exhibit,

Corset display at R. H. Macy's. *Library of Congress.*

"Road to Victory (text by Carl Sandburg, photos by Lt. Comm. Edward Steichen).

Museums

New York: *Metropolitan:* Rembrandt; Gallatin posters of the nineties; "As Russia Saw Us in 1812"; "Originals of Renaissance in Fashion 1942." *Museum of Modern Art:* Eighteen artists from nine states; John Flannagan; Pavel Tchelitchew

Boston: Paul Revere

Chicago: Henri Rousseau; Grant Wood; "Hudson River School"

Baltimore: Age of the icon

Art Briefs

An important one-man show is held in New York by the little-known Marc Chagall • Yves Tanguy and others present "Artists in Exile" in New York • The "First Papers of Surrealism," with Robert Motherwell, David Hare, and William Baziotes, are exhibited at the Whitelaw Reid Mansion, New York • The Metropolitan Museum of Art leases a concrete and steel vault in which to store its treasures during wartime • Wendell Willkie brings 80 paintings and drawings from China to the Metropolitan for display • The Tennessee National Gallery of Art and Santa Barbara Museum of American Art open.

Dance

Michel Fokine restages *Petrouchka* for Ballet Theatre; he dies while working on *Helen of Troy.* George Balanchine stages an elephant ballet to Stravinsky for Ringling Brothers and Barnum and Bailey.

Ballet Theatre: *Pillar of Fire* (Antony Tudor, Arnold Schoenberg), Harold Laing, Nora Kaye; *Helen of Troy* (Fokine, David Lichine)

Ballet Russe de Monte Carlo: *Rodeo* (Agnes de Mille), de Mille

Books

Fiction

Critics' Choice
Go Down Moses, William Faulkner
Never Come Morning, Nelson Algren
The Just and the Unjust, James Gould Cozzens
Until the Day Break, Louis Bromfield
The Robber Bridegroom, Eudora Welty
The Unvanquished, Howard Fast
Valley of Decision, Marcia Davenport

Best-Sellers
The Song of Bernadette, Franz Werfel
The Moon Is Down, John Steinbeck

Dragon Seed, Pearl S. Buck
And Now Tomorrow, Rachel Field
Drivin' Woman, Elizabeth Pickett
Windswept, Mary Ellen Chase
The Robe, Lloyd C. Douglas
The Keys of the Kingdom, A. J. Cronin
Kings Row, Henry Bellamann
The Sun Is My Undoing, Marguerite Steen

Nonfiction

Critics' Choice
Lee's Lieutenants, D. S. Freeman
Men on Bataan, John Hersey
The Managerial Revolution, James Burnham
Our Fighting Faith, James B. Conant
Storm over the Land, Carl Sandburg
Willard Gibbs, Muriel Rukeyser
On Native Grounds, Alfred Kazin
Generation of Vipers, Philip Wylie
Last Train from Berlin, Howard K. Smith
No Day of Triumph, J. Saunders Redding

Best-Sellers
See Here, Private Hargrove, Marion Hargrove
Mission to Moscow, Joseph E. Davies

Cross Creek, Marjorie Kinnan Rawlings
Victory through Air Power, Maj. Alexander O. de Seversky
Past Imperfect, Ilka Chase
They Were Expendable, W. L. White
Flight to Arras, Antoine de Saint-Exupéry
Washington Is Like That, W. M. Kiplinger
The Last Time I Saw Paris, Elliot Paul
Inside Latin America, John Gunther

Poetry
Wallace Stevens, *Parts of a World, Notes toward a Supreme Fiction*
John Berryman, *Poems*
Randall Jarrell, *Blood for a Stranger*
Kenneth Patchen, *The Teeth of the Lion*
J. V. Cunningham, *The Helmsman*

Pulitzer Prizes
Dragon's Teeth, Upton Sinclair (novel)
Paul Revere and the World He Lived In, Esther Forbes (U.S. history)
Admiral of the Ocean Sea, Samuel Eliot Morison (biography)
The Witness Tree, Robert Frost (poetry)

GI favorite pinup Betty Grable, whose legs are insured with Lloyds of London. *Movie Star News*.

Science and Technology

The first safe self-sustaining nuclear chain reaction is accomplished by Enrico Fermi, Edward Teller, and Leo Szilard, at the University of Chicago.

Louis Fieser, at Harvard, develops napalm, a jellylike mixture of gasoline and palm oils that sticks to its target until it burns out.

Bazookas, shoulder-held rocket containers used as antitank weapons, are developed.

Radar comes into operational use.

A jet-propelled plane is tested by Bell Aircraft.

A synthetic morphinelike substance, demerol, said to be nonaddictive, is developed by Dr. David Climento, at Winthop Laboratories.

The vagotomy operation for the treatment of ulcers is introduced.

Radioactive iodine therapy is developed as an alternative to surgery for overactive thyroid.

Tubeless tires are successfully tested.

LORAN (Long-Range Air Navigation) goes into operation; it diagrams the air and sea like streets.

Sports _____

Baseball
Stan Musial (St. Louis, NL) hits .315 in his first full
season.

Champions _____

Batting
Ernie Lombardi (Cincinnati,
NL), .330
Ted Williams (Boston, AL),
.356

Pitching
John Beasley (St. Louis,
NL), 21–6
Ernie Bonham (New York,
AL), 21–5
Home runs
Ted Williams (Boston, AL),
36

Football
Don Hutson (E), Green Bay, sets an NFL season
scoring record, 138 points on 17 touchdowns.
Cecil Isbell (QB), Green Bay, is the first to pass for
2,000 yards in a season.

NFL Season Leaders: Cecil Isbell (Green Bay),
passing; Bill Dudley (Pittsburgh), rushing; Don
Hutson (Green Bay), receiving.

College All-Americans: Paul Governali (Q),
Columbia; Mike Holovak (B), Boston College.

Bowls (Jan. 1, 1943)
Rose: Georgia 9–UCLA 0
Orange: Alabama 37–Boston College 21
Cotton: Texas 14–Georgia Tech 7
Sugar: Tennessee 14–Tulsa 7

More than 350 colleges abandon football "for the
duration."

Hitler toilet paper. *Smithsonian Institution.*

Other Sports

Boxing: The heavyweight title is frozen as Joe Louis
enters the service.

Winners _____

World Series
  St. Louis (NL) 4
  New York (AL) 1
MVP
  NL–Morton Cooper, St.
  Louis
  AL–Joe Gordon, New York
NFL
  Washington 14-Chicago
  (Bears) 6
MVP
  Don Hutson, Green Bay

College Football
  Ohio State
Heisman Trophy
  Frank Sinkwich, Georgia
College Basketball
  West Virginia (NIT)
  Stanford (NCAA)
Player of the Year
  Stan Modzelewski, Rhode
  Island State
Stanley Cup
  Toronto
US Tennis Open
  Men: Ted Shroeder
  Women: Pauline Betz
Kentucky Derby
  Shut Out (W. D. Wright,
  jockey)

Fashion _____

For Women: Emphasis remains on practical,
inconspicuous styles: wartime regulations allow for
little difference between high-style and inexpensive
clothing, apart from fabric. Suit jackets are cut with
peplums and with short, straight skirts. Striped wool
jersey middies appear over pleated wools; shirtwaists
are popular. What clothes lack in innovation they
gain in color, especially greens, pinks, and reds;
blouses, skirts, jackets, and snoods contrast in
brilliant color. Also new are ballet slippers with
winding ribbons, strapped and platform shoes, and
the enormously successful sling-back platform pump
with open toe. Jet is worn with everything, and short
satin evening skirts appear with lace blouses in a
variety of colors. The official regulations for
women's dress: no more than a two-inch hem, no
skirt more than 22 inches around, no more than one
patch pocket, no attached hoods or shawls, no coat
cuffs, no zippers or metal fastenings (wraparounds
instead), no silk stockings (cotton or rayon instead).
(Eyebrow pencil lines the naked leg to give the
illusion of hose.)

Kaleidoscope _____

110,000 Japanese Americans are sent to "relocation" centers by executive order. *Library of Congress.*

- New Year's Day is proclaimed a National Day of Prayer; the president leads the nation "asking God's help in the days to come."
- Eligible for the draft are single men 18 to 35 and married men 18 to 26.
- Service flags hang in millions of windows, a star for each of the nation's 8 million sons in the service.
- The face of New York's Time Square changes: lights on Roseland, the Astor, and all high places are dimmed so that ships at sea are not betrayed to U-boats.
- Sales of women's trousers are five to ten times greater than last year.
- Willow Run, Detroit, becomes the fastest growing city in the United States, as thousands move there for defense work.
- The OPA stops all car and truck production; sugar, tire, and gas rationing begins: "A" stickers for cars used only for pleasure; "B," to drive to work; "C," to drive at work; "E," emergency vehicles.
- Boy Scouts salvage 150,000 tons of wastepaper; children receive 50 cents a pound per aluminum foil ball; Los Angeles contributes 6 tons of car tires to the nationwide rubber drive; Victory Book rallies are held throughout the country; 600,000 books are donated to the armed services through a New York Public Library two-week drive.
- One billion pounds of plastics are produced for use in everything from airplanes to hose nozzles; metal is replaced in every possible way.
- Of the vegetables consumed in the United States, 40 percent is grown in Victory Gardens; two-thirds of the crop had been grown by the Japanese-Americans now detained in camps.
- Over 900 translator-censors work in the New York Post Office examining foreign mail.
- Winston Churchill receives from his American admirers an extraordinary number of letters and gifts, including corncob pipes, a Shriner's hat, a set of Indian arrowheads, a turkey wishbone (the V-symbol), and a copy of George Washington's will.
- Soldiers at California's Camp Callan vote Rita Hayworth "proxy mother" for Mother's Day.
- Among those in the armed forces are Gene Autry, Richard Barthelmess, Jackie Coogan, Broderick Crawford, Douglas Fairbanks, Raymond Massey, Burgess Meredith, Robert Montgomery, Cesar Romero, James Stewart, Robert Stack, Spencer Tracy, Darryl Zanuck, Frank Capra, John Ford, and Hal Roach. Clark Gable enlists at 41.
- Eighty war movies are made.
- Carole Lombard and 20 others die in a TWA transport crash; she was on a tour selling War Bonds.
- The first open-air base hospital opens in Bataan.
- Songwriter Frank Loesser reads about a chaplain at Pearl Harbor who tells his congregation to "Praise the Lord and pass the ammunition. . . ."
- Billy Mitchell is posthumously restored to the rank of major general.

- The Nobel Prize ceremonies, discontinued in Stockholm since 1939, take place at a dinner at the Waldorf Astoria, New York.
- Blacks complain of discrimination in the services, especially the navy.
- Thomas Mann joins the staff of the Library of Congress.
- Lew Ayres leaves Hollywood for a conscientious objectors' camp after his refusal to bear arms; his films are banned in 100 Chicago theaters; he later joins the army as a noncombatant.
- Dooley Wilson sings "As Time Goes By" in *Casablanca,* from the 1931 Broadway flop *Everybody's Welcome.*
- RCA Victor sprays gold over a recording of Glenn Miller's *Chattanooga Choo Choo* for having sold more than 1 million copies, the first "gold record."
- After the musicians' strike against the major record companies, Frank Sinatra leaves Tommy Dorsey to take his first club date at the Rio Bomba in New York and is highly successful.
- Hedda Hopper's contract with the *Chicago Tribune* and *New York News* syndicate challenges the queen of the gossipers, Louella Parsons.
- The romances of Mickey Rooney and Ava Gardner and Barbara Hutton and Cary Grant are highly publicized.
- Enrico Fermi secretly accomplishes a controlled nuclear fission reaction at the University of Chicago gym; in a coded message he informs FDR: "The Italian navigator has entered the new world."
- FDR has four sons on the front lines.
- A Japanese submarine fires about 25 shells at an oil refinery near Santa Barbara, California, the first attack on the American mainland.
- Reports of the deportation of Jews from Occupied Western Europe reach the United States.
- The Japanese execute three fliers captured during General Doolittle's raid on Tokyo.

First Appearances: Daylight Savings Time, three-cent "Win the War" stamp, nylon parachute, K rations packed by Wrigley Company, air raids and sirens, periodic blackout drills, zinc-coated pennies, Hunt Foods, Paine Webber, Jackson and Curtis, Dannon yogurt, Kellogg's Raisin Bran, *Yank* magazine

1943

Facts and Figures

Economic Profile
Dow-Jones: ↑ High 146–
    Low 119
GNP: +21%
Inflation: +3.0%
Unemployment: 1.9%
Daily newspapers: 2,043
Books published: 8,035
IRS collections: $22.5 billion
Airmail postage: 8¢
Postcard: 1¢
Rogers Peet boys' shoes:
    $5.45
Wanamaker men's shoes:
    $6.45
Tailored Woman alligator
    purse: $25
Dude ranch, New York State:
    $29 (week)
Maine resort: $6 (daily)
Two-gallon fish tank: 49¢
Guppies, snails: 5¢
Angel fish, tetras: 12¢
Talking doll: $5.95
Nelly Bee weaving set: $1.59

Deaths

Stephen Vincent Benét,
  George Washington
  Carver, Lorenz Hart,
  Marsden Hartley, Leslie
  Howard, Karl Landsteiner,
  Sergei Rachmaninoff,
  W. S. Van Dyke, Conrad
  Veidt, Beatrice Webb,
  Alexander Woollcott.

In the News

FDR AND CHURCHILL MEET AT CASABLANCA AND SET GOAL OF UNCONDITIONAL SURRENDER . . . DAYLIGHT BOMBING OF GERMANY BEGINS . . . JAPANESE COLLAPSE ON GUADALCANAL . . . FORCES UNDER PATTON RECAPTURE KASSERINE PASS, TUNISIA . . . FLYING FORTRESSES DESTROY 21 JAPANESE SHIPS IN BISMARCK SEA . . . POINT RATIONING SYSTEM IS SET . . . FREE FRENCH FORM UNDER DE GAULLE . . . AMERICAN FORCES TAKE TUNIS . . . U.S. RETAKES ATTU IN ALEUTIANS . . . GERMAN ARMIES IN NORTH AFRICA SURRENDER . . . NAZIS MASSACRE THOUSANDS IN WARSAW GHETTO UPRISING . . . "PAY AS YOU GO" INCOME TAX BEGINS, 20% IS WITHHELD . . . TROOPS QUELL DETROIT RACE RIOT, 34 DIE . . . RUSSIANS DESTROY GERMAN ARMY AT STALINGRAD . . . FDR ORDERS ICKES TO TAKE OVER MINES DURING STRIKE THREAT . . . ALLIES UNDER PATTON INVADE SICILY . . . SUPREME COURT RULES FLAG SALUTE OPTIONAL IN SCHOOL . . . ASSAULT ON SALERNO ESTABLISHES ITALIAN BEACHHEAD . . . NAPLES FALLS TO ALLIES . . . ITALY SURRENDERS UNCONDITIONALLY, MUSSOLINI ABDICATES . . . GERMANS RETREAT FROM CAUCASUS . . . CONGRESS FAVORS U.S. IN WORLD ORGANIZATION 360–29 . . . UNITED NATIONS RESCUE RELIEF ASSOCIATION IS FORMED . . . JAPANESE SUFFER WORST LOSSES TO DATE AT RABAUL . . . TARAWA IS TAKEN . . . AMERICANS LAND IN BOUGAINVILLE . . . STALIN AND FDR MEET AT TEHERAN . . . USSR AND CZECH EXILE GOVERNMENTS AGREE ON POSTWAR COLLABORATION . . . QUOTAS REPLACE CHINESE EXCLUSION IMMIGRATION LAW . . . IKE IS NAMED COMMANDER, ALLIED EUROPEAN FORCES . . . ALLIES POUND PAS DE CALAIS IN GIANT AIR RAID . . . GOVERNMENT SEIZES RAILROADS TO FORESTALL STRIKE.

Quotes _____

Yes, we have no Cassino
We have no Cassino today.
We have Aversa, Caserta, Mignano, Minturno
And dear old Napolii,
But, yes, we have no Cassino
We have no Cassino today.

      — Popular GI song in Italy

STAMP OUT
Black Markets with your ration stamps.
Pay no more than legal prices.

      — OPA

"Wear it up, wear it out, make it do, or do without."
      — Home front saying

FIRST THING I SEE—in a MAN
 "His mouth" (Ellen Drew)
 "His dignity" (Dorothy Lamour)
 "His speaking voice" (Mary Martin)
 "His eyes" (Joan Fontaine)

—in a WOMAN
 "The general stance" (Tyrone Power)
 "The face" (Gary Cooper)
 "Her hands" (Brian Aherne)
 "It depends on the woman" (Bob Hope)
      — *Photoplay*

U.S. Flying Fortresses bomb Stuttgart, Germany, one of many massive air raids on Axis military and industrial targets. *Library of Congress.*

"To American productivity, without which this war would have been lost."

      — Joseph Stalin's toast at Teheran

"I know how easy it is . . . for a girl to be tempted to foresake her chastity . . . especially in these times when human life is uncertain, . . . especially still if the boy is in uniform. Our salvation . . . lies within us, in a hard-boiled code of wartime morals."

      — Actress Bonita Granville

Ads _____

Radio

Premieres
"The Dunninger Show," Joseph Dunninger
"Nick Carter, Master Detective," Lon Clark
"Perry Mason," Bartlett Robinson
"A Date with Judy," Dellie Ellis
"Meet Corliss Archer," Janet Waldo
"Theatre Guild on the Air," Lawrence Langner
"Blind Date," Arlene Francis
"The Buster Brown Gang," Ed McConnell
"Cisco Kid," Jackson Beck
"The Judy Canova Show"

Most Popular Variety Shows: "Army Hour" (from army camps), "Basin Street Chamber Music Society," "Bing Crosby," "Broadway Showtime," "Ed Sullivan Entertains," "Gay Nineties Revue," "Kate Smith Variety Show," "Meet Your Navy," "Paul Whiteman," "Stage Door Canteen," "This Is Fort Dix"

Most Popular Music Programs: "Cities Service," "Boston Symphony," "Cleveland Symphony," "Metropolitan Opera Auditions," "NBC Symphony Orchestra," "New York Philharmonic," "Salt Lake Tabernacle Choir, Stradivarius Orchestra," "Telephone Hour," "Voice of Firestone"

Of Note
Arguments intensify over the value of soap opera and of news editorializing • NBC is forced to sell its blue network, which later becomes ABC.

New Catchphrases: Pancho: "Cisco, the sheriff and hees posse . . . they are comeeng closer." Cisco: "This way, Pancho, *Vamonos*" ("Cisco Kid"); "Pardon me for talking in your face, Señorita" ("The Judy Canova Show").

Movies

Openings
The Ox-Bow Incident (William A. Wellman), Henry
   Fonda, Dana Andrews
For Whom the Bell Tolls (Sam Wood), Gary Cooper,
   Ingrid Bergman
The Human Comedy (Clarence Brown), Mickey
   Rooney, Frank Morgan
Madame Curie (Mervyn LeRoy), Greer Garson,
   Walter Pidgeon
The More the Merrier (Geroge Stevens), Jean Arthur,
   Joel McCrea
Stage Door Canteen (Frank Borzage), all-star cast
The Song of Bernadette (Henry King), Jennifer
   Jones, Charles Bickford
Watch on the Rhine (Herman Shumlin), Paul Lukas,
   Bette Davis
Five Graves to Cairo (Billy Wilder), Franchot Tone,
   Anne Baxter
Lassie Come Home (Fred M. Wilcox), Roddy
   McDowall, Donald Crisp
The Phantom of the Opera (Arthur Lubin), Nelson
   Eddy, Claude Rains
Air Force (Howard Hawks), John Garfield, Arthur
   Kennedy
I Walked with a Zombie (Jacques Tourneur), Frances
   Dee, Tim Conway
Guadalcanal Diary (Lewis Seiler), William Bendix,
   Lloyd Nolan, Preston Foster
Shadow of a Doubt (Alfred Hitchcock), Joseph
   Cotten, Teresa Wright
Ivan the Terrible (Sergei Eisenstein), N. Cherkassov

Whether Humphrey Bogart and Ingrid Bergman would go off together in the last scene of *Casablanca* was decided in the final shooting. *Movie Star News.*

Academy Awards
Best Picture: *Casablanca*
Best Director: Michael Curtiz (*Casablanca*)
Best Actress: Jennifer Jones (*The Song of
   Bernadette*)
Best Actor: Paul Lukas (*Watch on the Rhine*)

Top Box-Office Stars
Betty Grable, Bob Hope, Abbott and Costello, Bing Crosby, Gary Cooper, Greer Garson, Humphrey Bogart, James Cagney, Mickey Rooney, Clark Gable

Stars of Tomorrow
William Bendix, Philip Dorn, Susan Peters, Donald O'Connor, Anne Baxter, Van Johnson, Gene Kelly, Diana Barrymore, Gig Young, Alexis Smith

Popular Music _____

Hit Songs

"I Couldn't Sleep a Wink Last
    Night"
"Oh What a Beautiful Mornin' "
"Oklahoma"
"People Will Say We're in Love"
"Speak Low"
"The Surrey with the Fringe on
    Top"
"G.I. Jive"
"One for My Baby"
"As Time Goes By"

Top Records

You'll Never Know (Dick
Haymes); *All or Nothing at All*

(Harry James, Frank Sinatra);
Besamé Mucho (Jimmy Dorsey,
Kitty Kallen and Bob Eberle);
Pistol Packin' Mama (Bing
Crosby, Andrews Sisters); *I'll Be
Home for Christmas* (Bing
Crosby); *Boogie Woogie* (Tommy
Dorsey); *Harlem Folk* (Stan
Kenton); *Cross Your Heart* (Artie
Shaw); *Furlough Fling* (Freddie
Slack)

Jazz and Big Bands

The Earl Hines Bop Band includes
Charlie Parker, Dizzie Gillespie,
and Sarah Vaughan.

Duke Ellington gives his first
Carnegie Hall concert, "Black,
Brown, and Beige."
Art Tatum forms a trio with Tiny
Grimes and Slam Stewart.
Dinah Washington joins Lionel
Hampton's band.

Top Performers *(Downbeat):*

Benny Goodman (soloist, big
band); Tommy Dorsey (sweet
band); Eddie Condon, Artie
Bernstein, Mel Powell, Gene
Krupa, Vido Musso
(instrumentalists); Jo Stafford,
Frank Sinatra (vocalists)

Theater _____

Broadway Openings

Plays

The Voice of the Turtle (John Van Druten), Margaret
    Sullavan, Elliott Nugent, Audrey Christie
The Patriots (Sidney Kingsley), Raymond Edward
    Johnson, Cecil Humphreys, Madge Evans
Harriet (Florence Ryerson, Colin Clements), Helen
    Hayes
Kiss and Tell (F. Hugh Herbert), Joan Caulfield,
    Richard Widmark, Jessie Royce Landis
Tomorrow the World (James Gow, Arnaud d'Usseau),
    Ralph Bellamy, Shirley Booth
Get Away Old Man (William Saroyan), Richard
    Widmark, Glenn Anders

Musicals

Carmen Jones (Georges Bizet, Oscar Hammerstein
    II), Muriel Smith and Muriel Rohn alternating as
    Carmen; Luther Saxon and Napoleon Reed
    alternating as Joe; all-black cast
Oklahoma (Richard Rodgers, Oscar Hammerstein II),
    Alfred Drake, Joan Roberts, Celeste Holm,
    choreographed by Agnes de Mille
Something for the Boys (Cole Porter), Ethel
    Merman, Bill Johnson
Winged Victory (Sgt. David Rose, Moss Hart), all-
    soldier cast: Don Taylor, Barry Nelson, Peter
    Lind Hayes, Richard Travis, Ray Middleton

Ziegfeld Follies of 1943 (Ray Henderson, Jack
    Yellen), Milton Berle, Ilona Massey
One Touch of Venus (Kurt Weill, Ogden Nash), John
    Boles, Mary Martin

Classics and Revivals On and Off Broadway

Othello, Paul Robeson, José Ferrer, Uta Hagen,
Margaret Webster; *Richard III*, George Coulouris,
Uta Hagen. *Founded:* The New York City Center of
Music and Drama by Jean Dalrymple

Regional

Cleveland: *You Touched Me* (Tennessee Williams
and Donal Windham), premiere

Pulitzer Prize

The Skin of Our Teeth, Thornton Wilder

Classical Music ────────────────

Compositions
Aaron Copland, Violin Sonata
Roy Harris, Cantata for Choir,
    Organ, and Brass, Mass
Douglas Moore, *In Memoriam*
Walter Piston, Symphony no. 2
Howard Hanson, Symphony no. 4
Ross Lee Finney, *Hymn, Fuguing
    and Holiday*
John Cage, *Amores*
William Schuman, *William Billings
    Overture,* Symphony for
    Strings, *Three Score Strings,*
    Symphony no. 5
Paul Hindemith (in U.S.),
    Symphonic Metamorphoses
Béla Bartók (in U.S.), Concerto
    for Orchestra

Important Events
Nineteen major orchestras give 1,398 performances
of 710 works by 242 composers. Most performed are
Tchaikovsky's Symphony no. 5, Wagner's *Die
Meistersinger* overture, and works by Beethoven,
Strauss, and Gershwin.

Othello, with Paul Robeson and Uta Hagen, has the longest
Broadway run of any Shakespeare play to date. *Billy Rose
Theatre Collection. The New York Public Library at
Lincoln Center. Astor, Lenox and Tilden Foundations.*

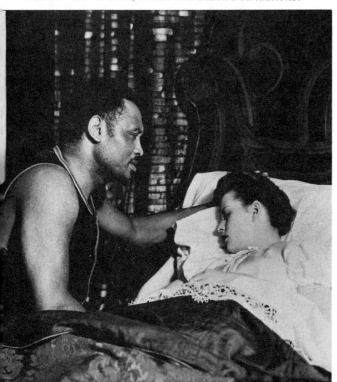

Bruno Walter conducts the uncut Bach *Passion
according to St. Matthew* at Carnegie Hall.
Eugene Istomin wins the Leventritt Award with the
Brahms Piano Concerto no. 2.

New Conductors: Karl Krueger at Detroit; Alfred
Wallenstein at Los Angeles; Erich Leinsdorf at
Cleveland

Premieres of Patriotic Music: Aaron Copland,
Fanfare for the Common Man; Robert Russell
Bennett, *The Four Freedoms* (based on FDR's
speech); Daniel Gregory Mason, *A Lincoln
Symphony;* Robert Palmer, *Lincoln Walks at
Midnight;* Bernard Rogers, *Invasion;* Samuel Barber,
Commando; William Schuman, *A Free Song and
Prayer in Time of War;* William Grant Still, *Plain
Song on America;* Ross Lee Finney, *Pole Star*

Debut: John Browning

First Performances
Roy Harris, Symphony no. 5 (Boston); Roger
Sessions, A Duo for Violin and Piano (Boston);
William Schuman, Symphony for Strings (Boston);
Concerto for Piano and Small Orchestra (New York);
Howard Hanson, Symphony no. 4 (Boston); Aaron
Copland, Sonata for Viola and Piano (New York);
Igor Stravinsky, *Dances Concertantes* (New York),
Ode (Boston)

Opera

Metropolitan: Alexander Kipnis, *Boris Godunov;*
Donald Dame, Patrice Munsel, *Mignon;* Zinka
Milanov, *Norma;* Farewell: Friedrich Schorr,
Siegfried; revivals: *Les contes d'Hoffmann; La forza
del destino*

Los Angeles: Kurt Baum, *Il trovatore*

Music Notes
Music is played regularly in U.S. factories to
stimulate war production • Shostakovich sells the
U.S. first performance rights to Symphony no. 8
(based on the Russian offensive) for $10,000 • With
news of Mussolini's fall, Toscanini conducts a gala
concert called *Victory Act I,* saving Acts II and III
for the downfall of the other Axis partners.

Art

Painting

Thomas Hart Benton, *Picnic*

Mark Rothko, *Sacrifice*

Arshile Gorky, *Virginia Landscape, Waterfall*

Robert Motherwell, *Pancho Villa, Dead and Alive, Surprise and Inspiration*

Jackson Pollock, *Pasiphaë, Search for a Symbol, The She-Wolf*

Mark Tobey, *Pacific Transition*

Loren MacIver, *Red Votive Lights*

Clyfford Still, *1943-A*

Bradley Walker Tomlin, *Burial*

Anna Mary ("Grandma") Moses, *The Thanksgiving Turkey*

Reginald Marsh, *Coney Island Beach, Number 1*

Piet Mondrian (in N.Y.), *Broadway Boogie Woogie*

Sculpture

Reuben Nakian, *Head of Marcel Duchamp*

Isamu Noguchi, *Monument to Heroes, Noodle, This Tortured Earth*

Theodore Roszak, *Vertical Construction*

Alexander Calder, *Morning Star*

Architecture

Willow Run Housing, Willow Run, Mich. (Eliel and Eero Saarinen, Robert F. Swanson)

Ford Motor Company Factory, Ypsilanti, Mich. (Albert Kahn)

John B. Nesbitt House, Brentwood, Calif. (Richard Neutra)

Important Exhibitions

Transportation difficulties created by the war curtail international exhibitions, with a resulting emphasis in the United States on native art and patriotic themes.

Museums

New York: *Metropolitan:* "Artists for Victory" continues; Contemporary American paintings from the University of Arizona; Modern Chinese paintings; "War Art"; "American Industry at War." *Metropolitan, Whitney:* "Front Line Paintings by War Correspondents." *Museum of Modern Art:* "Airways to Peace"; "Realistic and Magic Realists"; American Romantic painters. *Guggenheim:* Jackson Pollock. *Brooklyn:* Revival of "The Eight." *Whitney:* Gloria Vanderbilt Whitney Sculpture Memorial; Pollock; Calder Retrospective

Worcester: Eighteenth-century New England portraits

San Francisco: "Meet the Artist" (self-portraits)

Chicago: O'Keeffe, Hopper, Hartley, Watkins, Sheeler

Individual Shows

Pollock, I. Rice Pereira, Matta, Ruffino Tamayo

Art Briefs

Julius Rosenwald donates his rare print and drawing collection to the National Gallery • Forty-two paintings of J. P. Morgan are sold for $2 million.

Jackson Pollock, *Pasiphaë*, 1943. Oil. 56⅛ × 96″. *The Metropolitan Museum of Art, Purchase, 1982.*

Dance

Premieres

Ballet Theatre: *The Judgment of Paris* (Antony Tudor), Maria Karnilova, Hugh Laing, Tudor; *Dark Elegies* (Tudor), Laing, Nora Kaye, Tudor; *Romeo and Juliet* (Tudor), Alicia Markova, Laing; *Dim Lustre* (Tudor); Kaye, Laing

American Concert Ballet: *Mother Goose Suite* (Todd Bolender); *Concerto Barocco* (George Balanchine)

Martha Graham: *Deaths and Entrances*

Books

Fiction

Critics' Choice

The Way Some People Live, John Cheever
Gideon Planish, Sinclair Lewis
At Heaven's Gate, Robert Penn Warren
The Wide Net, Eudora Welty
Number One, John Dos Passos
The Big Rock Candy Mountain, Wallace Stegner
Wide Is the Gate, Upton Sinclair
Georgia Boy, Erskine Caldwell

Best-Sellers

The Robe, Lloyd C. Douglas
The Valley of Decision, Marcia Davenport
So Little Time, John P. Marquand
A Tree Grows in Brooklyn, Betty Smith
The Human Comedy, William Saroyan
Mrs. Parkington, Louis Bromfield
The Apostle, Sholem Asch
Hungry Hill, Daphne Du Maurier
The Forest and the Fort, Hervey Allen
The Song of Bernadette, Franz Werfel

Nonfiction

Critics' Choice

The Nature and Destiny of Man, Reinhold Niebuhr
Bound for Glory, Woody Guthrie
The Century of the Common Man, Henry Wallace
Thirty Seconds over Tokyo, Capt. Ted Lawson
My Native Land, Louis Adamic
The Infant and Child in the Culture of Today, Arnold L. Gesell
History of Bigotry in the United States, Gustavus Myers
God Is My Co-Pilot, Col. Robert L. Scott, Jr.
Seven Came Through, Capt. Eddie Rickenbacker
Total Peace, Ely Culbertson
➤ *Being and Nothingness*, Jean-Paul Sartre
➤ *Christianity and Democracy*, Jacques Maritain

Best-Sellers

Under Cover, John Roy Carlson
One World, Wendell L. Willkie
Journey among Warriors, Eve Curie
On Being a Real Person, Harry Emerson Fosdick

Guadalcanal Diary, Richard Tregaskis
Burma Surgeon, Lt. Col. Gordon Seagrave
Our Hearts Were Young and Gay, Cornelia Otis Skinner and Emily Kimbrough
U.S. Foreign Policy, Walter Lippmann
Here Is Your War, Ernie Pyle
See Here, Private Hargrove, Marion Hargrove

Poetry

T. S. Eliot, *Four Quartets*
Delmore Schwartz, *Genesis*
Kenneth Fearing, *Afternoon of a Pawnbroker*
Kenneth Patchen, *Cloth of the Tempest*
Weldon Kees, *The Last Man*

Pulitzer Prizes

Journey in the Dark, Martin Flavin (novel)
The Growth of American Thought, Merle Curti (U.S. history)
The American Leonardo: The Life of Samuel F. B. Morse, Carlton Mabee (biography)
Western Star, Stephen Vincent Benét (poetry)

Science and Technology

Selman Waksman discovers streptomycin and coins the term *antibiotic* for the actinomycete streptomyces griseus.

Sulfa is credited with an extraordinary reduction of U.S. Army fatalities.

Sulfathiazole is reported to prevent the venereal diseases gonorrhea and chancroid by army doctors James Loveless and William Denton.

A new painless method of childbirth, continuous caudal anesthesia, is described by Drs. Robert Hingson and Waldo Edwards.

Xylocaine, for local anesthesia, is developed.

Hepatitis is differentiated into two strains, A (short incubation) and B (long).

DDT is introduced in the United States and hailed as a boon to farmers.

The Lockheed Constellation becomes a military transport, the C-29; manufacture begins on the B-29 Superfortress.

Nobel Prize

Edward Doisy receives the prize in physiology and medicine for the discovery of the chemical structure of vitamin K. Otto Stern receives the prize in physics for the detection of the magnetic momentum of protons.

Sports

Baseball

Because of the war, spring training is held in the North for the first time.

Champions

Batting	Pitching
Stan Musial (St. Louis, NL), .357	Mort Cooper (St. Louis, NL), 21–8
Luke Appling (Chicago, AL), .328	Spud Chandler (New York, AL), 21–8
	Home runs
	Rudy York (Boston, AL), 34

Football

Sid Luckman, Chicago Bears, passes for 7 touchdowns against the New York Giants.

NFL Season Leaders: Sammy Baugh (Washington), passing; Bill Paschal (New York), running; Don Hutson (Green Bay), receiving.

College All-Americans: Otto Graham (Q), Northwestern; Alex Agase (G), Purdue

Bowls (Jan. 1, 1944)

Rose: Southern California 29–Washington 0
Orange: Louisiana State 19–Texas A & M 14
Cotton: Randolph Field 7–Texas 7
Sugar: Georgia Tech 20–Tulsa 18

Other Sports

Horse Racing: Count Fleet, ridden by Johnny Longden, wins the Triple Crown.

Winners

World Series	*Heisman Trophy*
New York (AL) 4	Angelo Bertelli, Notre Dame
St. Louis (NL) 1	*College Basketball*
MVP	Wyoming (NCAA)
NL–Stan Musial, St. Louis	St. John's (NIT)
AL–Spud Chandler, New York	*Player of the Year*
NFL	George Senesky, St. Joseph
Chicago (Bears) 41–Washington 21	*Stanley Cup*
MVP	Detroit
Sid Luckman, Chicago Bears	*US Tennis Open*
College Football	Men: Joseph Hunt
Notre Dame	Women: Pauline Betz
	Kentucky Derby
	Count Fleet (J. Longdon, jockey)

Fashion

For Women: Two silhouettes predominate: the slim, tubular look in knitted dresses or chemises with cinch belts, and the bulky look in box suits and coats with heavy, loose fabrics. Hair is neat, folded at the ear, netted at the back, twisted into braids, or pinned on top of the head. Small tight hats and snoods remain fashionable. Later, the "versatile suit," with nipped-in waist, short jacket, back hiked or pleated skirt, is popular. Women wear suits everywhere. Coats are long (the "officer's" style), or short (the "seaman's"). The fur-lined wool or canvas coat is new. Lounging teenage girls wear rolled-up jeans, sloppy shirttails, mixed shoes, and rag curlers.

For Men: Male teens are offered the "zoot suit," a long, one-button jacket with large padded shoulders, peaked lapels, and high-waisted trousers ballooning at the knees and gripping at the ankels, worn with knee-length key chains, broad-brimmed hats, and wide silk ties against striped or colored shirts. Older men reject mustaches because of their current, fascist associations.

Training women marines. The first, Oveta Culp Hobby, was sworn in by FDR. *Library of Congress.*

Kaleidoscope

- American planes make 64,000 sorties and drop 55,000 tons of bombs during the year.
- The American Jewish Congress reports that over 3 million Jews have been killed by the Nazis.
- Gen. George Patton strikes a GI being treated for shell shock; Patton is reprimanded and apologizes.
- Rubber, metal, tin, nylon, silk, and paper are collected for recycling. Kitchen fats are exchanged for ration points. Despite the 28-ounce allowance per week, meat consumption rises to 128.9 pounds per year. Butter is rationed at 4 ounces per week; cheese, 4 pounds per week; the sale of sliced bread is banned; flour, fish, canned goods, and coffee are rationed. Shoes are rationed at 3 pairs a year; new sneakers are unavailable because of the rubber shortage.
- With meat increasingly unavailable, Tuesdays and Fridays become "meatless days"; casseroles, fish, omelets, and soufflés become popular.
- Because alarm clock manufacture has ceased, thousands are late to work; 1.75 million "Victory model" clocks are ordered.
- With the paper shortage, few Christmas cards are available; women recycle their brown grocery bags.
- With the combined goods scarcity and improved economy, long lines develop at groceries, movies, bars, and restaurants; cabs are obliged to take as many passengers as they can carry; long-distance calls are limited to five minutes.
- The manpower shortage stimulates "pampering" of employees; music is piped into factories, and coffee breaks and suggestion boxes are instituted, as well as awards and fringe benefits. FDR orders a minimum 48-hour work week in war plants.
- Sonja Henie applies for $250,000 insurance on her remaining five pairs of ice skates, since skates are not being produced during wartime.
- An estimated 30,000 people riot at the Paramount Theater when Frank Sinatra appears.
- New pastimes for teens include the "slumber party," jalopies, the Saturday night soda shop (with jukebox and "messing around"), and "smooching" jargon; also popular are BMOC's, pep rallies, beach parties, and roller rinks; girls wear their boyfriends' parkas, knit argyles, and meet their dates at hamburger "joints."
- Dance tempos are either very fast or slow, for the fox trot, polka, rhumba, samba, waltz, jitterbug, and Lindy hop, along with their variations, the Jersey jump, flea hop, job walk, victory walk, and "Praise the Lord and Pass the Ammunition" dance.
- "Amos 'n' Andy" is canceled after 15 years and 4,000 consecutive radio shows. Campbell Soup, whose sales are cut in half by the tin shortage, can no longer afford to sponsor the show.
- One thousand special radio programs are sent to the troops, including Ann Sheridan preparing a steak dinner and Rita Hayworth singing in Spanish.
- The opening of Beethoven's Fifth Symphony becomes the Victory theme of the Allies; it is also the Morse code (. . .—) for the letter *V,* for *Victory.*

With her dedicated and vigorous public life, including a newspaper column, radio program, and tireless efforts for social reform, Eleanor Roosevelt sets a new style for the First Lady. Here she entertains Madame Chiang Kai-shek at the White House. *Library of Congress.*

- At a War Bond rally at Gimbels' basement, in New York, Jack Benny's $75 violin is bought for $1 million by Julius Klorten, president of Garcia Grande cigars, who shuns publicity following the purchase.
- Orson Welles marries Rita Hayworth, thought to be engaged to Victor Mature.
- Leslie Howard and 16 others are lost in an overseas airliner en route from Lisbon to England after being attacked by an enemy plane.
- A series of flag stamps is issued, honoring the countries overrun by Axis forces.
- Second-class mailings of *Esquire* are prohibited when the magazine is charged with being "lewd and lascivious."
- Ernie Pyle is the most widely read war correspondent, as he describes the ordinary GI's experiences in the war.
- As blacks move into the Detroit plants, racial tensions heighten; a riot develops when a black is killed for using a white swimming area.
- The AMA is found guilty of violating antitrust laws by preventing the activities of cooperative health groups.
- Marian Anderson's performance, January 7th, at Constitution Hall, Washington, D.C., breaks the DAR segregation policy.
- Bible sales increase 25 percent, and books on religious themes, like *The Robe* and *Song of Bernadette,* are popular.

First Appearances: Rent control, "converted" rice (Uncle Ben, Gordon Hariwell), women's fire department (Asheville, N.Y.), election law permitting 18-year-olds to vote (Georgia), Chicago subway

1944

Facts and Figures

Economic Profile
  Dow-Jones: ↑ High 152–
    Low 135
  GNP: + 10%
  Inflation: +0.9%
  Unemployment: 1.2%
Expenditures:
  Recreation: $5.4 billion
  Spectator sports: $80
    million
Golf courses: 409
Bowlers: 910,000
Arthur Rubinstein concert,
  Carnegie Hall: $1.20–$3.60
Ice show: 75¢–$1.00
Ballet International: $1–$3.50
New York City Center: 90¢–
  $2.40
Broadway show, top price: $3
Tabu: $18.50 (oz.)
Lily of France:
  girdles: $9
  bras: $1.85–$2.00

Deaths

Jean Giraudoux, Wassily
  Kandinsky, Josef
  Lhévinne, Aristide Maillol,
  Edvard Munch, Lucien
  Pissaro, Antoine de Saint-
  Exupéry, Al Smith,
  William Allen White,
  Wendell Willkie.

In the News

EISENHOWER GOES TO ENGLAND . . . ALLIES LAND AT ANZIO, NEAR ROME . . . LENINGRAD IS RELIEVED . . . MARINES LAND ON KWAJALEIN . . . MASSIVE AIR ATTACK HITS JAPANESE BASE AT TRUK, 201 PLANES ARE DESTROYED, 17 U.S. AIRCRAFT LOST . . . ROUND THE CLOCK MASS AIR RAIDS STRIKE BERLIN . . . SUPREME COURT RULES COLOR CANNOT BE BAR TO PRIMARY VOTING . . . CASSINO IS CAPTURED . . . ROME IS TAKEN . . . D-DAY ALLIES LAUNCH A MASSIVE ASSAULT ON NORMANDY AND ESTABLISH BEACHHEAD . . . THOMAS DEWEY IS NOMINATED BY GOP, FDR IS NOMINATED FOR THE FOURTH TIME . . . U.S. SUPERFORTS BOMB JAPAN FOR THE FIRST TIME . . . 100,000 GERMAN SOLDIERS ARE CAPTURED AT MINSK . . . 402 JAPANESE PLANES ARE DOWNED IN BATTLE OF THE PHILIPPINE SEA . . . GI BILL OF RIGHTS IS PASSED . . . WORLD BANK IS CREATED AT BRETTON WOODS, N.H., CONFERENCE . . . OFFICERS' ATTEMPT TO ASSASSINATE HITLER FAILS . . . GUAM IS RECAPTURED . . . ALLIES BREAK OUT PAST ST. LO IN NORMANDY, GERMANS RETREAT . . . THIRD ARMY UNDER PATTON REACHES THE SEINE . . . ALLIES LAND IN SOUTH FRANCE . . . UN IS ESTABLISHED AT DUMBARTON OAKS, D.C. . . . RUMANIA SURRENDERS TO RUSSIA . . . PARIS IS LIBERATED . . . BRUSSELS IS LIBERATED . . . FDR AND CHURCHILL MEET AT QUEBEC . . . FIRST ARMY BREAKS THROUGH SIEGFRIED LINE . . . V-2 ROCKETS FALL ON LONDON . . . RUSSIA ENTERS HUNGARY AND YUGOSLAVIA . . . 300 JAPANESE PLANES ON FORMOSA ARE DESTROYED BY CARRIER-BASED PLANES . . . GENERAL MACARTHUR RETURNS, LANDS AT LEYTE GULF, PHILIPPINES, LARGE NAVAL VICTORY IS WON . . . FDR IS REELECTED, 25 MILLION TO 22 MILLION . . . GERMANS COUNTERATTACK, ARE DEFEATED AT BATTLE OF THE BULGE AS PATTON'S THIRD ARMY BRINGS RELIEF.

Quotes

"You are about to embark upon the Great Crusade, toward which we have striven these many months. The eyes of the world are upon you. The hopes and prayers of liberty-loving people everywhere march with you. . . . You will bring about the destruction of the German war machine, the elimination of Nazi tyranny over the oppressed peoples of Europe, and security for ourselves in a free world.

Your task will not be an easy one. Your enemy . . . will fight savagely.

But this is the year 1944! . . . The tide has turned! The free men of the world are marching together to Victory! . . . Let us beseech the blessing of Almighty God upon this great and noble undertaking."

> — Dwight D. Eisenhower
> to the Allied Expeditionary
> Forces, before Normandy

"Men were sleeping on the sand, some of them sleeping forever. Men were floating in the water, but they didn't know they were in the water, for they were dead.

> — Ernie Pyle, *Brave Men*

"I have returned. By the grace of Almighty God, our forces stand again on Philippine soil."

> — Gen. Douglas MacArthur

"Good evening again to all the all-forgetting and forgotten men, the American fighting men of the South Pacific."

> — Tokyo Rose

D-Day, June 6: Allied troops landing at Normandy. *Library of Congress.*

"We cannot have jobs and opportunities if we surrender our freedom to Government control. . . . We can have both opportunity and security within the framework of a free society."
— Thomas E. Dewey, presidential campaign address

"Truman? I never can remember that name."
> — John W. Bricker, Dewey's running mate

"I've always voted for Roosevelt as President. My father always voted for Roosevelt as President."
> — Bob Hope

Ads

Caught in machine gun crossfire when his tank was hit . . . Private Jim Thornbro was severely wounded. . . . [But] Jim Thornbro isn't the kind that quits. Today, after months in hospitals, he's fighting again— fighting in the production line at PACKARD.
> *(Packard Automobiles)*

When they [the enemy] find the Pepsi-Cola bottles are empty, their morale will go down another 10 points.
> *(Pepsi-Cola)*

Through ancient Iran, U.S. weapons and goods flow to Russian fronts in paper packages.
> *(Container Corp. of America)*

It costs a lot to bring a hero home.
Get ready to buy Victory Bonds.
> *(Public service ad)*

WANTED! a pint of your blood to save a fighter's life. The appeal for your red blood is contributed to the American Red Cross by HART SCHAFFNER & MARX.
> *(Hart Schaffner & Marx Apparel)*

The More Women at War
The Sooner We'll Win
> *(Public service ad)*

You're Somebody when you're a WAC—
Join Now!
> *(Public service ad)*

Radio

Premieres
"Roy Rogers"
"Chesterfield Supper Club," Perry Como
"The Adventures of Ozzie and Harriet [Nelson]"
"The Danny Kaye Show"
"Ethel and Albert," Peg Lynch, Richard Widmark
"The FBI," Martin Blaine
"House Party," Art Linkletter
"Columbia Presents Corwin" (plays written,
    produced, directed by Norman Corwin)

Top Ten
"Bob Hope," "Fibber McGee and Molly," "Bing
Crosby," "Edgar Bergen and Charlie McCarthy,"
"Joan Davis/Jack Haley," "Walter Winchell,"
"Radio Theatre," "Abbott and Costello," "Mr.
District Attorney," "Eddie Cantor," "Jack Benny"

Most Popular Daytime Programs: "When a Girl
Marries," "Aunt Jenny," "Life Can Be Beautiful,"
"Ma Perkins," "Romance of Helen Trent," "Kate
Smith Show," "Big Sister," "Portia Faces Life,"
"Stella Dallas," "Young Widder Brown"

Of Note
"The FBI" begins with the march from *The Love of
Three Oranges* • Evening programs consist of serial
dramas (27.8 percent), audience participation shows
(13.2 percent), news and talk shows (17.5 percent),
popular and familiar music (18.2 percent), classical
and semiclassical music (3.0 percent), and children's
programs (2.1 percent).

TV

Premieres
"Missus Goes A'Shopping," Reed King
"At Home Show," Pacquito Anderson, Yul Brynner
"CBS News"

Movies

Openings
Going My Way (Leo McCarey), Bing Crosby, Barry
    Fitzgerald
Double Indemnity (Billy Wilder), Barbara Stanwyck,
    Fred MacMurray, Edward G. Robinson
Gaslight (George Cukor), Charles Boyer, Ingrid
    Bergman
The Purple Heart (Lewis Milestone), Dana Andrews,
    Richard Conte
Since You Went Away (John Cromwell), Claudette
    Colbert, Jennifer Jones, Joseph Cotten
Lifeboat (Alfred Hitchcock), Tallulah Bankhead,
    Walter Slezak, John Hodiak
Laura (Otto Preminger), Gene Tierney, Dana
    Andrews, Clifton Webb
None but the Lonely Heart (Clifford Odets), Cary
    Grant, Ethel Barrymore
Mr. Skeffington (Vincent Sherman), Bette Davis,
    Claude Rains
The Seventh Cross (Fred Zinnemann), Spencer
    Tracy, Signe Hasso
Dragon Seed (Jack Conway, Harold S. Bucquet),
    Katharine Hepburn, Walter Huston
Hail the Conquering Hero (Preston Sturges), Eddie
    Bracken, Ella Raines
Meet Me in St. Louis (Vincente Minnelli), Judy
    Garland, Margaret O'Brien
Destination Tokyo (Delmer Daves), Cary Grant, John
    Garfield
The Miracle of Morgan's Creek (Preston Sturges),
    Betty Hutton, Eddie Bracken
Up in Arms (Elliott Nugent), Danny Kaye, Dinah
    Shore
Cover Girl (Charles Vidor), Rita Hayworth, Gene
    Kelly

Academy Awards
Best Picture: *Going My Way*
Best Director: Leo McCarey (*Going My Way*)
Best Actress: Ingrid Bergman (*Gaslight*)
Best Actor: Bing Crosby (*Going My Way*)
Special Award: Margaret O'Brien (outstanding child
    actress)

Top Box-Office Stars
Bing Crosby, Gary Cooper, Bob Hope, Betty Grable,
Spencer Tracy, Greer Garson, Humphrey Bogart,
Abbott and Costello, Cary Grant, Bette Davis

Stars of Tomorrow
Sonny Tufts, James Craig, Gloria DeHaven, Roddy
McDowall, June Allyson, Barry Fitzgerald, Marsha
Hunt, Sydney Greenstreet, Turhan Bey, Helmut
Dantine

Popular Music

Hit Songs
"Don't Fence Me In"
"Acc-cent-tchu-ate the Positive"
"I Should Care"
"I'll Walk Alone"
"Irresistible You"
"Long Ago and Far Away"
"Put the Blame on Mame"
"Spring Will Be a Little Late This
  Year"
"Dream"

Top Records
Tico-Tico (Andrews Sisters); *In the Middle of Nowhere* (Carmen Cavallaro); *Time Waits for No One* (Helen Forrest); *A Lovely Way to Spend an Evening* (Ink Spots); *This Heart of Mine* (Vaughn Monroe); *I Couldn't Sleep a Wink Last Night* (Frank Sinatra); *Tumbling Tumbleweeds* (Jo Stafford); *Rum and Coca-Cola* (Andrews Sisters); *Too-Ra-Loo-Ra-Loo-Rah* (Bing Crosby); *Cocktails for Two* (Spike Jones); *Moonlight in Vermont* (Billy Butterfield, Margaret Whiting). Country: *Smoke on the Water* (Red Foley); *I'm Wastin' My Tears on You* (Tex Ritter)

Jazz and Big Bands
Thelonious Monk's *Round Midnight* and Billie Holiday's *Record Man* gain wide attention.

First Recordings: Billy Eckstine's bop session with Dizzy Gillespie and Budd Johnson; Sarah Vaughan

Top Performers (*Downbeat*): Benny Goodman (soloist); Duke Ellington (big band); Charlie Spivak (sweet band); Bob Haggart, Lester Young, Harry Carney, Buddy Rich, Mel Powell (instrumentalists); Dinah Shore, Bing Crosby (vocalists); Pied Pipers (vocal group)

Theater

Broadway Openings

Plays
Harvey (Mary Chase), Josephine Hull, Frank Fay
Anna Lucasta (Philip Yordan), Hilda Simms, Canada Lee
I Remember Mama (John Van Druten), Mady Christians, Oscar Homolka, Marlon Brando
Ten Little Indians (Agatha Christie), Estelle Winwood, Halliwell Hobbes
Jacobowsky and the Colonel (S. N. Behrman), Louis Calhern
The Late George Apley (John P. Marquand, George S. Kaufman), Leo G. Carroll, Janet Beecher
Over 21 (Ruth Gordon), Ruth Gordon
Catherine Was Great (Mae West), Mae West
The Searching Wind (Lillian Hellman), Cornelia Otis Skinner, Dennis King, Montgomery Clift
Pick-up Girl (Elsa Shelley), William Harrigan
A Bell for Adano (Paul Osborn), Margo, Fredric March
The Two Mrs. Carrolls (Martin Vale), Elisabeth Bergner

Musicals
Bloomer Girl (Harold Arlen, E. Y. Harburg), Celeste Holm, Joan McCracken, David Brooks, Dooley Wilson
Follow the Girls (Phil Charig et al.), Gertrude Niesen, Jackie Gleason
Mexican Hayride (Cole Porter), Bobby Clark, June Havoc
The Seven Lively Arts (Cole Porter), Beatrice Lillie, Bert Lahr, Dolores Gray, Benny Goodman Quintet
Song of Norway (Edvard Grieg, Robert Wright), Lawrence Brooks, Irra Petina
On the Town (Leonard Bernstein, Betty Comden, Adolph Green), Sono Osato, Nancy Walker, Betty Comden, Adolph Green
Sing Out, Sweet Land (many authors), Alfred Drake, Burl Ives

Classics and Revivals On and Off Broadway
The Cherry Orchard (Chekhov), Eva Le Gallienne, Joseph Schildkraut; *Othello,* Paul Robeson, José Ferrer. *Founded:* Equity Library Theatre by Sam Jaffe and George Freedley

Pulitzer Prize
No prize is awarded.

Classical Music

Compositions
John Cage, A Book of Music for Two Prepared
    Pianos
Aaron Copland, *Appalachian Spring*
Roger Sessions, Symphony no. 2
Samuel Barber, Symphony no. 2, *Capricorn*
    Concerto
Walter Piston, Fugue on a Victory Tune
Don Gilles, Symphony no. 5
Igor Stravinsky (in U.S.), Sonata for Two Pianos
Paul Hindemith (in U.S.), *Hérodiade*
Béla Bártok (in U.S.), Sonata for Unaccompanied
    Violin

Important Events
Serge Koussevitzky is reengaged at the Boston
Symphony; Artur Rodzinski takes over the New
York Philharmonic for two-thirds of the season,
followed by Bruno Walter, William Steinberg, and
Steinberg's assistant, Leonard Bernstein, 25, who
conducts on a few hours' notice to standing ovations.
Bernstein begins conducting the New York
Philharmonic and other orchestras regularly and
plays 14 world premieres, including his *Jeremiah
Symphony* and *Fancy Free*. George Szell receives
enormous acclamation as he conducts the Cleveland
Symphony Orchestra.

Debut: Leon Fleischer, Byron Janis

First Performances
Dmitri Shostakovich, Symphony no. 8 (New York);
Roy Harris, Symphony no. 6 (Boston); Paul
Hindemith, *Symphonic Metamorphoses on Themes
by Carl Maria von Weber* (New York); Arnold
Schoenberg, *Ode to Napoleon Buonaparte* (New
York), Piano Concerto no. 4 (NBC), Theme and
Variations in G minor (Boston); Samuel Barber,
Symphony no. 2 (Washington); Stravinsky
(conducting), *Four Norwegian Moods* (Boston);
William Schuman, *William Billings Overture* (New
York); Louis Gruenberg, Violin Concerto (New York,
for and with Jascha Heifetz).

Opera

Metropolitan: Celebration of Diamond Jubilee. Of
165 performances, most frequently produced are
*Mignon, La bohème, Carmen, La traviata, Tristan
und Isolde*. "Auditions of the Air" award ($1,000 and
Met contract): Regina Resnik. Performances: Resnik,
Il trovatore; Kerstin Thorborg, *Die Walküre;* Martial
Singher, *Pelléas et Mélisande, Aïda;* Emercy Darcy,
Parsifal; Patrice Munsel (debut), *Mignon*

National Negro Opera Co.: *La traviata,* Madison
Square Garden, New York, which then tours
Chicago, Pittsburgh, and Washington, D.C.

City Center, New York (first performance): *Tosca*

Chicago: Zinka Milanov, Kurt Baum, *Il trovatore;*
Jan Peerce, *Rigoletto;* Gladys Swarthout, Kurt
Baum, *Carmen*

San Francisco: Lily Djanel, Frederick Jagel,
Salomé; Salvatore Baccaloni, Vivian Della Chiesa,
Falstaff

Music Notes
After a year of inactivity, the Chicago Opera and
Detroit symphonies resume • William Grant Still wins
the $1,000 War Bond prize for *Jubilee Overture,*
which celebrates the Cincinnati Symphony
Orchestra's fiftieth anniversary.

Glenn Miller. Since 1939, everyone knew the "Miller
sound," with its penetrating tutti sax-section and lead
clarinet. *Movie Star News*.

Art

Painting

Milton Avery, *Mother and Child, Seated Girl with Dog*
Abraham Rattner, *The Emperor*
Arshile Gorky, *The Liver Is the Cock's Comb, Water of the Flowery Mill*
Reginald Marsh, *Bowery and Mell Street—Looking North*
Clyfford Still, *Jamais*
Lyonel Feininger, *Steamboat on the Yukon*
Mark Tobey, *Tundra*
I. Rice Pereira, *Green Depth*
Edward Hopper, *Morning in a City*
Jackson Pollock, *Gothic*
Robert Motherwell, *Mallarmé's Swan-C*
William Baziotes, *Cyclops*

Sculpture

Isamu Noguchi, *Bird's Nest*
William Zorach, *The Future Generation* (1942–44)
Peter Grippe, *Growth after Destruction*
David Hare, *The Magician's Game*

Architecture

Carver Court, Coatesville, Pa. (Howe, Stonorov, Kahn)
Municipal Asphalt Plant, New York (Kahn, Jacobs)

Arshile Gorky, *Water of the Flowery Mill,* 1944. Oil. 42½ × 48¾". *The Metropolitan Museum of Art, George A. Hearn Fund, 1956.*

Important Exhibitions

Museums

New York: *Metropolitan:* "Naval Aviation in the Pacific"; Four masters of the Renaissance; 600 paintings (stored during the war); American battle paintings, 1776–1918. *Museum of Modern Art:* Hartley; Feininger; Renoir to the present: Modern Cuban painters; American snapshots; Twentieth-century Italian art. *Brooklyn:* One hundred paintings of Abraham Walkowitz (done by fellow artists). *Whitney:* Winslow Homer

Washington: American battle paintings, 1776–1918

Philadelphia: Thomas Eakins centennial

Cincinnati: Reconstructed 1913 Armory Show

Chicago: Art in the United Nations; "The Art of Posada"; Advertising art

Detroit: Romantic art

Cleveland: Islamic art

Boston: Sporting art

Dayton: "The Church Tradition"

Art Briefs

Samuel Kress gives 90 more works to the National Gallery • Felix M. Warburg donates a house to the Jewish Theological Seminary for the Museum of Jewish Art, New York.

Dance

Premieres

Ballet Theatre: *Tally-Ho* (Agnes de Mille), Janet Reed, Anton Dolin; *Fancy Free* (Jerome Robbins, Leonard Bernstein), John Kriza, Erik Bruhn, Robbins; *Appalachian Spring* (Martha Graham, Aaron Copland), Graham (with designs by Isamu Noguchi); *Danses Concertantes* (George Balanchine)

San Francisco Ballet: The first full-length American *Nutcracker.*

Books

Fiction

Critics' Choice

The Dangling Man, Saul Bellow
The Leaning Tower, Katherine Anne Porter
Boston Adventure, Jean Stafford
The Lost Weekend, Charles Jackson
The Women on the Porch, Caroline Gordon
Avalanche, Kay Boyle
Under a Glass Bell, Anaïs Nin
Angels Can't Do Better, Peter de Vries
🞜 *Winter Tales*, Isak Dinesen

Best-Sellers

Strange Fruit, Lillian Smith
The Robe, Lloyd C. Douglas
A Tree Grows in Brooklyn, Betty Smith
Forever Amber, Kathleen Winsor
The Razor's Edge, W. Somerset Maugham
The Green Years, A. J. Cronin
Leave Her to Heaven, Ben Ames Williams
Green Dolphin Street, Elizabeth Goudge
A Bell for Adano, John Hersey
The Apostle, Sholem Asch

Nonfiction

Critics Choice

A Walk in the Sun, Harry P. M. Brown
U.S. War Aims, Walter Lippmann
The Road to Serfdom, Frederick A. Hayek
Invasion Diary, Richard Tregaskis
Bataan, Allison Ind
Many a Watchful Night, John Mason Brown
Air Gunner, Sgt. Bud Hutton, Sgt. Andy Rooney
An American Dilemma, Gunnar Myrdal
A Basic History of the United States, Charles and Mary Beard
The Public Schools and Spiritual Values, John Dewey
Social Darwinism in American Thought, Richard Hofstadter

Best-Sellers

I Never Left Home, Bob Hope
Brave Men, Ernie Pyle
Good Night, Sweet Prince, Gene Fowler
Under Cover, John Roy Carlson
Yankee from Olympus, Catherine Drinker Bowen
The Time for Decision, Sumner Welles

Here Is Your War, Ernie Pyle
Anna and the King of Siam, Margaret Landon
The Curtain Rises, Quentin Reynolds
Ten Years in Japan, Joseph C. Grew

Poetry

Robert Lowell, *Land of Unlikeness*
Kenneth Rexroth, *The Phoenix and the Turtle*
Muriel Rukeyser, *Beast in View*
E. E. Cummings, *1 × 1*
Allen Tate, *Winter Sea*
Stanley Kunitz, *Passport to War*
Maturya Zaturenska, *Golden Mirror*
🞜 W. H. Auden, *For the Time Being*

Pulitzer Prizes

A Bell for Adano, John Hersey (novel)
Unfinished Business, Stephen Bonsal (U.S. history)
George Bancroft: Brahmin Rebel, Russel Blaine Nye (biography)
V-Letter and Other Poems, Karl Shapiro (poetry)

Science and Technology

A mathematical "robot," a giant, automatic, sequence-controlled computer with a 50-foot panel of knobs, gears, and switches, is created at Harvard by Howard Aiken and IBM engineers.

Manufacturers of penicillin agree to pool their knowledge in order to speed production.

William Doering produces synthetic quinine from coal tar products.

Sister Kenny's methods of infantile paralysis treatment come under considerable debate.

DNA, the basic material of heredity, is isolated by Oswald Avery, Rockefeller Institute.

Aureomycin, the first broad-spectrum antibiotic, is extracted from soil.

The U.S. Army announces the development of a jet-propelled, propless plane.

The second atomic pile is built at Clinton, Tennessee, for the manufacture of plutonium for the atomic bomb.

🞜 The Germans develop the first true missile, the 1,600-pound V-2, with a 200-mile range; they also introduce the first operational jet fighter.

Nobel Prize

Joseph Erlanger and Herbert Gasser share the prize in physiology and medicine for work on nerve transmission. I. I. Rabi receives the prize in physics for work on the magnetic movements of atomic particles.

Sports ──────────────────

Baseball

Many retired major leaguers return to active play, since many young players are now in the service.

Champions ──────────────

Batting	Pitching
Dixie Walker (Brooklyn, NL), .357	Ted Wilks (St. Louis, NL), 17–4
Lou Boudreau (Cleveland, AL), .327	Cecil Hughson (Boston, AL), 18–5
	Home runs
	Bill Nicholson (Chicago, NL), 33

Football

NFL Season Leaders: Frank Filchok (Washington), passing; Bill Paschal (New York), rushing; Don Hutson (Green Bay), receiving

College All-Americans: Felix "Doc" Blanchard (B), Glenn Davis (B), Army ("Mr. Inside and Mr. Outside"); Les Horvath (QB), Ohio State

Bowls (Jan. 1, 1945)

Rose: Southern California 25–Tennessee 0
Orange: Tulsa 26–Georgia Tech 12
Cotton: Oklahoma A & M 34–Texas Christian 0
Sugar: Duke 29–Alabama 26

Basketball

The NIT semifinal matches De Paul, with 6′9″ George Mikan, and Oklahoma State, with 7′ Bob Kurland, in a "Battle of the Giants." De Paul wins 41–38, but loses to St. Johns in the final.

Other Sports

Hockey: Maurice Richard (Montreal Canadiens) scores a record 50 goals in the 50-game season.

Winners ──────────────

World Series	*College Basketball*
St. Louis (NL) 4	Utah (NCAA)
St. Louis (AL) 2	St. John's (NIT)
MVP	*Player of the Year*
NL–Martin Marion, St. Louis	George Mikan, De Paul
AL–Hal Newhouser, Detroit	*Stanley Cup*
NFL	Montreal
Green Bay 14–New York 7	*US Tennis Open*
MVP	Men: Sgt. Frank Parker
Frank Sinkwich, Detroit	Women: Pauline Betz
College Football	*Kentucky Derby*
Army	Pensive (C. McCreary, jockey)
Heisman Trophy	
Les Horvath, Ohio State	

Fashion ──────────────────

For Women: With fabrics still limited, three-quarter-length box coats and suits have false fronts; sleeveless dresses expose wide shoulders or have small shoulder caps. Chignons, as well as small pillbox hats and berets, draw attention to the face and makeup; the earring industry expands. Décolletage returns for both day and evening wear. The concept of "separates," or interchangeable clothes, enters the fashion world.

High-fashion note: Schiaparelli's hourglass black fur-lined wool coat with fur-trimmed buttons

For Men: War Production Board specifications, since 1942: 23¾″ length for size 37 jacket; no waistcoat; trousers, 22″ at the knee, 18½″ at the bottom, 35″ inseam for 32″ waist; no cuffs, pleats, tucks, or overlapping waistbands.

World War II poster. *Smithsonian Institution.*

Kaleidoscope ─────────────────────────

- On D day, June 6, Operation Overlord, the Normandy invasion, is mounted by 6,939 naval vessels, 15,040 aircraft, and 156,000 troops. After two months, Normandy casualties number 16,434 dead, 76,535 wounded, 19,704 missing.
- Within five months of D day, the Allies take 637,544 prisoners.
- The War Refugee Board reveals the first details of mass murder at Birkenau and Auschwitz, estimating that 1.7 million have been killed there.
- With 3.5 million women working alongside 6 million men on assembly lines, production capacities change. Cargo ships are completed in 17 days, bombers in 13 days. For the working woman, slacks become, as Max Lerner puts it, a "badge of honor."
- Nearly half the steel, tin, and paper needed for the war are provided by people salvaging goods.
- Paper shortages stimulate publishers' experiments with soft-cover books.
- Because of a shortage of cheese and tomato sauce, pasta sales fall. Jello becomes a dessert substitute for canned fruit; baking powder sales fall with so many women on the work force; neighborhood groceries, rather than supermarkets, proliferate because of gas rationing and the consumer's greater spending power. Camel cigarettes, a GI favorite, are scarce.
- Seven laboratories refine and improve DDT, invaluable in reducing typhus and malaria; 350,000 pounds a month are sent to the military.
- Both women and men's fashions feature broad shoulders and pointed lapels, what many call the "football player" look.
- Horse racing is banned because of the war.
- Hollywood personalities still in the service include Clark Gable, James Stewart, Robert Taylor, Robert Montgomery, Mickey Rooney, Frank Capra, John Ford, William Wyler, and John Huston.
- "Stars for Dewey" include Ginger Rogers, Hedda Hopper, Cecil B. De Mille, Anne Baxter, Adolphe Menjou, and Leo G. Carroll. "For FDR" are Rita Hayworth, Olivia de Havilland, Katharine Hepburn, Orson Welles, Harpo Marx, Lana Turner, Walter Huston, and Fannie Brice.
- Some gossip columnists attribute Humphrey Bogart and Mayo "Sluggy" Methot's break up to his FDR support and her Dewey support.
- Paulette Goddard, the "Cheesecake Girl" of 1944, marries Air Force captain Burgess "Buzz" Meredith.
- Boston bans *Forever Amber* and *Strange Fruit,* the latter about the love between a white man and black woman.
- A New York judge finds *Lady Chatterley's Lover* obscene and orders to trial the publisher, Dial Press; a higher court reverses the decision.
- Bill Mauldin's cartoon "Willie & Joe," originally in *Yank* and *Stars and Stripes,* is picked up by the domestic press and achieves great acclaim.
- Hit song "Mairzy Doats" is written by Milton Drake after he listens to his small daughter's baby talk.

- The first jazz concert at the Metropolitan Opera House, New York, takes place, sponsored by *Esquire;* it features Coleman Hawkins, Louis Armstrong, Roy Eldridge, Jack Teagarden, Art Tatum, Lionel Hampton, Billie Holiday, and Mildred Bailey, among others.
- With many baseball players still in the service, college football becomes the number one sporting event.
- "Kilroy was here" graffiti moves out of public bathrooms to billboards, buildings, phone booths, and construction fences, mythologizing the valor of the GI.
- The worst disaster in theatrical history occurs in Hartford, Connecticut when, with the Barnum and Bailey Wallendas on a high wire, a fire begins and 168 people are killed.
- Maj. Glenn Miller is lost on a flight from England to Paris.
- Lt. John F. Kennedy receives the Navy and Marine Corps Medal for "extreme heroism" in rescuing two sailors after a Japanese destroyer cuts his PT boat in half.
- Richard Bong, 25, surpasses Eddie Rickenbacker's 26-year-old record by destroying his 27th Japanese aircraft.
- Maj. James Stewart, Eighth Air Force squadron commander and pilot leader of more than 20 B-24s on 11 missions over Germany, receives the Distinguished Flying Cross.
- Congress approves the appointment of the first five-star generals and five-star admirals.

First Appearances: Seabrook farms, Chiquita bananas, quadruplets delivered by cesarean section

Following the News on D-Day, Times Square, New York City. *Library of Congress.*

1945

Facts and Figures

Economic Profile
Dow-Jones: ↑ High 195–
    Low 155
GNP: 0%
Inflation: +1.2%
Unemployment: 1.9%
World War II Casualty
    Figures
    Americans
        16,354,000 in arms
        291,557 battle deaths
        113,842 other deaths
        670,846 wounded
    Russians: 7,500,000
    Germans: 2,900,000
    Chinese: 2,200,000
    Japanese: 1,500,000
    British: 398,000
    Italians: 300,000
    Jews: 6,000,000
Total Deaths: 54,800,000

Above: Churchill, FDR, and
Stalin meet at Yalta, a resort
on the Russian Black Sea, to
plan the postwar world.
Library of Congress.

Deaths

Béla Bartók, Theodore
    Dreiser, Jerome Kern,
    David Lloyd George,
    Pietro Mascagni, John
    McCormack, Alla
    Nazimova, George Patton,
    Ernie Pyle, Paul Valéry,

In the News

RUSSIANS TAKE WARSAW, HUNGARY SURRENDERS . . . BATAAN IS
RETAKEN, 500 POWS ARE FREED . . . 1,000-PLANE ARMADA BOMBS
GERMANY . . . FDR, CHURCHILL, STALIN MEET AT YALTA TO MAKE
POSTWAR PLANS . . . PRO-RUSSIAN GOVERNMENT IS INSTALLED IN
RUMANIA . . . IWO JIMA IS CAPTURED, U.S. FLAG IS RAISED ON MT.
SURIBACHI, 4,189 U.S. ARE DEAD, 20,000 JAPANESE . . . U.S. ARMY
REACHES RHINE . . . BENEŠ FORMS CZECH GOVERNMENT . . . N.Y.
PASSES ANTIDISCRIMINATION LAW . . . 325,000 GERMAN SOLDIERS
SURRENDER IN RUHR . . . FDR DIES OF CEREBRAL HEMORRHAGE AT
WARM SPRINGS, GEORGIA, THE NATION MOURNS . . . TRUMAN TAKES
OFFICE . . . BUCHENWALD IS LIBERATED . . . RUSSIANS REACH
BERLIN . . . MUSSOLINI AND MISTRESS ARE EXECUTED IN MILAN . . .
GERMAN ARMIES IN ITALY SURRENDER . . . DOENITZ REPORTS
HITLER'S SUICIDE . . . GERMANY SURRENDERS UNCONDITIONALLY . . .
GERMANY IS DIVIDED INTO FOUR ZONES . . . OKINAWA IS TAKEN,
13,000 U.S. DEAD, 100,000 JAPANESE DEAD . . . FIRST ATOM BOMB
IS TESTED IN NEW MEXICO . . . TRUMAN, CHURCHILL, STALIN MEET
IN POTSDAM . . . RUSSIA DECLARES WAR ON JAPAN AND ENTERS
MANCHURIA . . . LEAFLETS WARN JAPAN OF TERRIBLE DESTRUCTION
. . . ATOM BOMB IS DROPPED ON HIROSHIMA, 189,000 CASUALTIES
. . . ATOM BOMB IS DROPPED ON NAGASAKI . . . JAPANESE
SURRENDER UNCONDITIONALLY . . . B-25 BOMBER CRASHES INTO
EMPIRE STATE BUILDING, 13 DIE . . . BITUMINOUS COAL WORKERS
STRIKE . . . GM AND FORD STRIKE . . . U.S., USSR OCCUPY KOREA
. . . GANDHI AND NEHRU ASK BRITISH TO LEAVE INDIA . . . HO CHI
MINH PUSHES FOR INDOCHINA INDEPENDENCE . . . ZIONISTS ASK
THAT 1 MILLION JEWS GO TO PALESTINE . . . CHIANG KAI-SHEK AND
MAO TSE-TUNG FORCES BEGIN FIGHTING . . . $6 BILLION IS VOTED
IN TAX RELIEF . . . RATIONING ENDS.

Quotes

"I want a prayer to stop this rain. If we got a couple of clear days we could get in there and kill a couple of hundred thousand of those krauts."
— Gen. George Patton to his chaplain

"You begin to feel that you can't go on forever without being hurt. I feel that I have used up all my chances. And I hate it. I don't want to be killed."
— Ernie Pyle

"When he says he loves me he takes it about as seriously as his promises which he never keeps. . . . The weather is gorgeous and I, mistress of Germany's greatest man, have to sit at home and look at it through a window. If only I had a dog."
— from Eva Braun's diary

"We have learned lessons—at a fearful cost—and we shall profit by them. We have learned that we cannot live alone, at peace. . . . As Emerson said, . . . 'the only way to have a friend is to be one.'"   — FDR

"Have you ever seen stacks and piles of human bodies—200 to 300 in each pile, sprawled out, starved, beaten, and gassed to death?"
— Anonymous GI, on the liberation of Dachau

"Here were three greedy nations eager for loot and seeking greedily to advance their own self-interests by war, yet unable to agree on a strategic over-all plan for accomplishing a common objective."
— The Marshall Report

"Your city will be obliterated unless your government surrenders."
— Leaflets dropped on Hiroshima, August 5

Fierce battles on land and Kamikaze attacks at sea are occurring at Okinawa May 7th, as these GIs hear the news of V-E Day. *Copyright* Washington Post. *Reprinted by permission of D.C. Public Library.*

"Sixteen hours ago an American airplane dropped one bomb on Hiroshima . . . [with] more power than 20,000 tons of TNT. It is an atomic bomb. . . . If they do not now accept our terms, they may expect a rain of ruin from the sky the likes of which has never been seen on this earth."   — Harry S Truman

"A lightning flash covered the whole sky. . . . All green . . . perished."   — Witness, Hiroshima

Ads

Know what it's like to lie in a foxhole and hear the unearthly scream of "Banzai" in the night? How it feels to have your guts torn out by shrapnel? How you'd face the future with aluminum where a leg used to be? Or with your sight in the head of a dog? For God's sake, get back to work. . . . Buy more bonds. . . . Give more blood. Every little bit you do *is* important. *Remember, the shorter the war, the fewer American boys killed.*
(*Jones and Lamson Machine Co.*)

Something the Axis tanks don't have.
(*Quaker State Motor Oil*)

FREEDOM! Paper packages carried weapons to the Philippines.   (*Container Corp. of America*)

Home must be the greatest rehabilitation center of them all!
Vets—Belong to the 5220 Club: Unemployment pay, $20 for 52 Weeks.   (*Public service ad*)

—What You Can Do to Help the Returning Veteran
—Will He Be Changed?
—After two or three weeks he should be finished with talking, with oppressive remembering. If he still goes over the same stories, reveals the same emotions, you had best consult a psychiatrist. This condition is neurotic.   (*Good Housekeeping*)

Winged Victory—a new lipstick with matching nail polish.   (*Elizabeth Arden*)

Radio

Premieres
"Queen for a Day," Jack Bailey
"Arthur Godfrey Time"
"The Adventures of Topper," Roland Young
"Beulah," Marlin Hurt
"The Fat Man," Ed Begley, J. Scott Smart
"Meet Met at Parky's," Harry Einstein
"Bride and Groom" live weddings
"The Andrews Sisters Eight-to-the-Bar Ranch"
"The Second Mrs. Burton"
"This Is Your FBI," Frank Lovejoy, Stacy Harris

Favorite Programs: "One Man's Family" (soap opera), "Information Please!" (quiz), "Bob Hope" (entertainment/comedy), "Bing Crosby," "Dinah Shore" (singers), "Lowell Thomas" (commentator), "New York Philharmonic-Symphony"

Most Popular Serials: "Young Widder Brown," "Backstage Wife," "Guiding Light," "Helen Trent," "Ma Perkins," "Our Gal Sunday," "Portia Faces Life," "Right to Happiness," "Stella Dallas"

Of Note
During a newspaper deliverers' strike, New York mayor Fiorello La Guardia broadcasts the funnies.

TV

Premieres
"Here's [Henry] Morgan"
"The Singing Lady," Irene Wicker
"Ladies Be Seated," Johnny Olsen

Specials
Documentaries on V-E and V-J days; "Ring on Her Finger," unsponsored drama, 1 hour, 40 minutes (John Baragrey); Macy's first Thanksgiving Day Parade

Of Note
William Paley becomes chairman of the board at CBS • RCA's new camera, the image orthicon, has 100 times the sensitivity of the previous camera, developed in the 1920s.

Movies

Openings
The Lost Weekend (Billy Wilder), Ray Milland, Jane Wyman
Anchors Aweigh (George Sidney), Frank Sinatra, Gene Kelly
The Bells of St. Mary (Leo McCarey), Bing Crosby, Ingrid Bergman
Mildred Pierce (Michael Curtiz), Joan Crawford, Zachary Scott
Spellbound (Alfred Hitchcock), Ingrid Bergman, Gregory Peck
National Velvet (Clarence Brown), Mickey Rooney, Elizabeth Taylor
The Southerner (Jean Renoir), Zachary Scott
A Tree Grows in Brooklyn (Elia Kazan), Dorothy McGuire, James Dunn
The Story of GI Joe (William A. Wellman), Burgess Meredith, Robert Mitchum
The Picture of Dorian Gray (Albert Lewin), George Sanders, Hurd Hatfield
The House on 92nd Street (Henry Hathaway), William Eythe, Lloyd Nolan
They Were Expendable (John Ford), John Wayne, Robert Montgomery
The Body Snatcher (Robert Wise), Boris Karloff, Bela Lugosi
The Woman in the Window (Fritz Lang), Joan Bennett, Edward G. Robinson
Open City (Roberto Rossellini), A. Fabrizzi, Anna Magnani
Children of Paradise (Marcel Carne), Jean-Louis Barrault, Arletty

Academy Awards
Best Picture: *The Lost Weekend*
Best Director: Billy Wilder (*The Lost Weekend*)
Best Actress: Joan Crawford (*Mildred Pierce*)
Best Actor: Ray Milland (*The Lost Weekend*)
Special Award: Peggy Ann Garner (outstanding child actress)

Top Box-Office Stars
Bing Crosby, Van Johnson, Greer Garson, Betty Grable, Spencer Tracy, Humphrey Bogart, Gary Cooper, Bob Hope, Judy Garland, Margaret O'Brien, Roy Rogers

Stars of Tomorrow
Dane Clark, Jeanne Crain, Keenan Wynn, Peggy Ann Garner, Cornel Wilde, Tom Drake, Lon McCallister, Diana Lynn, Marilyn Maxwell, William Eythe

Popular Music

Hit Songs
"Cruising down the River"
"Autumn Serenade"
"I Love You for Sentimental Reasons"
"On the Atchison, Topeka and the Sante Fe"
"If I Loved You"
"It Might as Well Be Spring"
"Laura"
"Let It Snow!"
"June Is Bustin' Out All Over"
"Dig You Later-A-Hubba-Hubba-Hubba"
"It's a Grand Night for Singing"

Top Records

Albums: *The King Cole Trio* (King Cole Trio); *Songs of Norway* (original cast); *Glenn Miller* (Glenn Miller); *Carousel* (original cast); *Boogie Woogie* (Freddie Slack)

Singles: *I Fall in Love Too Easily, Am I Blue?* (Eugenie Bard with Mel Torme's Meltones); *The More I See You* (Carmen Cavallaro); *It's Been a Long, Long Time* (DeMarco Sisters); *This Heart of Mine* (Judy Garland); *Aren't You Glad You're You?* (Bing Crosby); *Put Your Dreams Away* (Frank Sinatra); *Sentimental Journey* (Les Brown, Doris Day); *Temptation* (Perry Como); *There, I've Said It Again* (Vaughn Monroe); *Cottage for Sale* (Billy Eckstine); *April Showers* (Al Jolson). Country: *At Mail Call Today* (Gene Autry); *Oklahoma Hills* (Jack Guthrie)

Jazz and Big Bands
Dizzy Gillespie tours with his first big band. Bop is at its peak. Miles Davis goes to New York to study at Juilliard. June Christy joins Stan Kenton; Charlie Shavers joins Tommy Dorsey.

First Recording: Dizzy Gillespie with Charlie Parker

New Bands: Ray Baudac, Billy Butterfield, Les Elgart, Dizzy Gillespie, Ted Heath

Top Performers (*Downbeat*): Benny Goodman (soloist); Woody Herman (big band); Tommy Dorsey (sweet band); Oscar Moore, Chubby Jackson, Dave Tough, Charlie Ventura, Buddy De Franco, Bill Harris (instrumentalists); Jo Stafford, Anita O'Day, Bing Crosby, Stuart Foster (vocalists); Pied Pipers (vocal group)

Theater

Broadway Openings

Plays
The Glass Menagerie (Tennessee Williams), Laurette Taylor, Julie Haydon, Eddie Dowling
State of the Union (Howard Lindsay, Russel Crouse), Ralph Bellamy, Ruth Hussey
The Hasty Heart (John Patrick), John Lund, Richard Basehart
Deep Are the Roots (Arnaud d'Usseau, James Gow), Barbara Bel Geddes
Dream Girl (Elmer Rice), Betty Field, Wendell Corey
He Touched Me (Tennessee Williams, Donald Windham), Montgomery Clift, Edmund Gwenn
Home of the Brave (Arthur Laurents), Eduard Franz
Foolish Notion (Philip Barry), Tallulah Bankhead, Donald Cook

Musicals
Are You with It? (Harry Revel, Arnold Horwitt), Joan Roberts, Johnny Downs, Dolores Gray
Carousel (Richard Rodgers, Oscar Hammerstein II), Jan Clayton, John Raitt
Laffing Room Only (Burton Lane), Olsen and Johnson, Betty Garrett
Up in Central Park (Sigmund Romberg, Dorothy Fields), Wilbur Evans, Maureen Cannon, Noah Beery
Dark of the Moon (Walter Hendl), Carol Stone, Richard Hart
The Day before Spring (Alan Jay Lerner, Frederick Loewe), Irene Manning, Bill Johnson

Classics and Revivals On and Off Broadway
Hamlet, Maurice Evans (GI version); *The Tempest*, Vera Zorina; *Pygmalion* (George Bernard Shaw), Gertrude Lawrence, Raymond Massey

Pulitzer Prize
Harvey, Mary Chase

Classical Music _____

Compositions

Walter Piston, Sonata for Violin and Harpsichord
Roy Harris, Piano Concerto no. 1
Samuel Barber, Cello Concerto
Norman Dello Joio, *Diversion of Angels*
Ross Lee Finney, *Pilgrim Psalms*
Béla Bartók (in U.S.), Piano Concerto no. 3, Viola Concerto
Arnold Schoenberg (in U.S.), *Prelude to a Genesis Suite*
Paul Hindemith (in U.S.), Piano Concerto
Igor Stravinsky (in U.S.), Symphony in Three Movements

First Performances

Stravinsky (conducting), *Scenes de Ballet* (New York); Bohuslav Martinů, Symphony no. 7 (Philadelphia); Leo Sowerby, *The Canticle of the Sun* (New York); Paul Creston, Symphony no. 2 (New York); Darius Milhaud (conducting), *La bal martiniquais* (New York). In Los Angeles, *Genesis for Narrator and Orchestra: Seven Pieces by Seven Composers* includes Arnold Schoenberg, Nathaniel Shilkret, Alexander Tansman, Darius Milhaud, Mario Castelnuovo-Tedesco, Ernest Toch, and Igor Stravinsky.

Opera

Metropolitan: Of 29 operas performed, most popular are *Die Meistersinger, Aïda, La bohème,* *Lucia di Lammermoor, Manon,* and *Don Giovanni.* Performances include Mimi Benzell, *Die Zauberflöte;* Jennie Tourel, *Il barbiere di Siviglia;* Richard Tucker (debut), *La Gioconda;* Risë Stevens, *Carmen;* Nadine Conner, *Faust.* Robert Merrill wins the radio auditions contest.

Chicago: Bidú Sayão, *La bohème;* in the company: Sayão, Zinka Milanov, Kerstin Thorborg, Helen Traubel, Jan Peerce

San Antonio: Grace Moore, *La bohème*

San Francisco: Licia Albanese, Salvatore Baccaloni, *L'heure espagnole;* Helen Traubel, Lauritz Melchior, *Tristan und Isolde, Die Walküre;* Lily Djanel, *Salomé*

Music Notes

The liberation of Europe is followed by the immediate restoration of musical activity • As a token of "global friendship," the State Symphony of Moscow performs a concert of Roy Harris, Wallingford Riegger, Samuel Barber, Élie Siegmeister, and George Gershwin • Numerous persons are investigated for suspected Nazi collaboration • War losses leave many orchestras with vacancies • William Schuman becomes president of Juilliard • The first Annual Festival of Contemporary American Music, at Columbia University, features David Diamond, Howard Hanson, Henry Brant, and Walter Piston.

Tommy Dorsey. *Movie Star News.*

Tennessee Williams's *The Glass Menagerie. Billy Rose Theatre Collection. The New York Library at Lincoln Center. Astor, Lenox and Tilden Foundations.*

Art _____

Paintings

William Baziotes, *The Room*

Clyfford Still, *Number 6 (1945–46)*, *Self-Portrait*

Walt Kuhn, *Young Clown*

Jackson Pollock, *Moon Woman Cuts the Circle, Totem Lesson II*

Arshile Gorky, *Diary of a Seducer*

Mark Rothko, *Baptismal Scene*

Reginald Marsh, *White Tower Hamburger*

Willem de Kooning, *Pink Angels*

Charles Sheeler, *Water*

Philip Guston, *Sentimental Moment*

Charles Burchfield, *Autumnal Fantasy*

Sculpture

Isamu Noguchi, *Kouros*

José de Creeft, *Rachmaninoff*

Alexander Calder, *Red Pyramid*

Herbert Ferber, *Three Legged Woman I*

David Smith, *Cockfight—Variation*, *The Rape*

Jacques Lipchitz, *Joy of Orpheus*

Architecture

Graduate Center, Harvard University, Cambridge (Walter Gropius)

Case Study, House 8, Pacific Palisades, Calif. (Charles Eames)

Frank Lloyd Wright completes the model for the Guggenheim Museum.

Important Exhibitions

Museums

New York: *Metropolitan*: Goya's prints and drawings; "The War against Japan"; "The Living Past of China"; "Costumes from the Forbidden City: Peking"; William Sidney Mount and his circle; Greek art (in the new permanent installation). *Museum of Modern Art:* Rouault, Stuart Davis. *Whitney:* Early American art

Chicago: Hudson River School

Boston: A thousand years of landscape art

Philadelphia: "The Philadelphia Story as Told by Philadelphia Press Artists": William Glackens, George Luks, Everett Shinn, John Sloan

Pittsburgh: "Painting in the U.S.," Philip Guston, first prize

Washington: *Corcoran:* Prizes are awarded to Reginald Marsh for *Strip Tease in New Jersey,*

Smithsonian Institution.

Malvin A. Zsissley for *Deer Isle, Maine,* and Isabel Bishop for *Two Girls Outdoors.*

Individual Shows

Klee, Kandinsky, Mondrian, Stuart Davis, Rouault, Miró (his first in the United States), Picasso, Matisse, and Bonnard.

Art Briefs

Auction rooms record the largest business in history; Parke-Bernet in New York sells $6 million of art; the top painting, Hals's *The Merry Lute Player,* brings $127,000 • Robert Niles wins first prize at the National Army Artists' Contest for *Between Trains* • Corporations like IBM, Pepsi-Cola, Encyclopædia Britannica, and Upjohn continue to support the arts.

Dance _____

Lucia Chase and Oliver Smith become codirectors of Ballet Theatre. Martha Graham signs for a world tour.

Premieres

Ballet Theatre: *Interplay* (Jerome Robbins), Janet Reed, Michael Kidd, John Kriza, Robbins; *Elegie* (George Balanchine); *Undertow* (Anthony Tudor), Hugh Laing, Nana Gollner; *The Firebird* (Adolf Bolm)

Ballet Russe de Monte Carlo: *Mozartiana* (Balanchine)

Books

Fiction

Critics' Choice
Cannery Row, John Steinbeck
The Friendly Persuasion, Jessamyn West
Apartment in Athens, Glenway Wescott
If He Hollers Let Him Go, Chester Himes
The Crack-Up, with Other Uncollected Pieces, F. Scott Fitzgerald (posthumous)
🐾 *Animal Farm*, George Orwell
🐾 *The Dwarf*, Pär Lagerkvist

Best-Sellers
Forever Amber, Kathleen Winsor
The Robe, Lloyd C. Douglas
The Black Rose, Thomas B. Costain
The White Tower, James Ramsey Ullman
Cass Timberlane, Sinclair Lewis
A Lion Is in the Streets, Adria Locke Langley
So Well Remembered, James Hilton
Captain from Castile, Samuel Shellabarger
Immortal Wife, Irving Stone
Earth and High Heaven, Gwethalyn Graham

Nonfiction

Critics' Choice
Atomic Energy for Military Purposes, Henry DeWolf Smyth
Race and Democratic Society, Franz Boaz (posthumous)
The American Language, (suppl. I), H. L. Mencken
Wars I Have Seen, Gertrude Stein
Japan and the Son of Heaven, Willard Price
Big Business in Democracy, James Truslow Adams
The Winning of the War in Europe and the Pacific, Gen. George C. Marshall
American Guerrilla in the Philippines, Ira Wolfert
Men under Stress, Lt. Col. Roy R. Grinker, Maj. John P. Spiegel
The Big Three: The United States, Britain and Russia, David J. Dallin
The Pattern of Soviet Power, Edgar Snow

Best-Sellers
Brave Men, Ernie Pyle
Dear Sir, Juliet Lowell
Up Front, Bill Mauldin
Black Boy, Richard Wright
Try and Stop Me, Bennett Cerf

Anything Can Happen, George and Helen Papashvily
General Marshall's Report, Gen. George C. Marshall
The Egg and I, Betty MacDonald
The Thurber Carnival, James Thurber
Pleasant Valley, Louis Bromfield

Poetry
Gwendolyn Brooks, *A Street in Bronzeville*
H. D., *Tribute to Angels*
Robert Frost, *A Masque of Reason*
Randall Jarrell, *Little Friend, Little Friend*
Kenneth Patchen, *An Astonishing Eye Looks Out of the Air*
John Crowe Ransom, *Selected Poems*
🐾 W. H. Auden, *The Collected Poems*

Pulitzer Prizes
The Age of Jackson, Arthur M. Schlesinger, Jr. (U.S. history)
Son of the Wilderness, Linnie Marsh Wolfe (biography)
No prizes are awarded for poetry or the novel.

Science and Technology

The first atomic bomb exploded in the Alamogordo, New Mexico, desert is a plutonium bomb; its power (equal to 20,000 tons of TNT) exceeds expectations.

Glenn Seaborg announces the discovery of two new elements, atomic numbers 95 and 96.

The method of administering penicillin orally is developed by Raymond Libby.

Successful treatment of scarlet fever with penicillin is reported.

The vitamin folic acid is discovered by American Cyanimid.

The navy reports a "complete cure" for cholera.

Dr. William Robbins reports the development of six new antibiotics: pleurotin, grisic acid, pleurin, irpexin, obtusin, and corticin; streptomycin, corticin, and pleurotin are marketed.

Helen Taussig and Alfred Blalock pioneer "blue baby" surgery.

A C-54 Douglas Skymaster goes around the world in a record 149 hours, 44 minutes.

A TWA Lockheed Constellation sets a New York–Paris record of 12 hours, 57 minutes.

Samuel Kramer, from the Pennsylvania Museum, discovers evidence of the 3000 B.C. Heroic Age of Sumer.

Sports

Baseball

A. B. "Happy" Chandler, former Kentucky senator, succeeds Kenesaw Landis as baseball commissioner with a seven-year contract at $50,000 a year.

Champions

Batting	Pitching
Phil Cavaretta (Chicago, NL), .355	Harry Brecheen (St. Louis, NL), 15–4
Snuffy Stirnweiss (New York, AL), .309	Hal Newhouser (Detroit, AL), 25–9
	Home runs
	Tommy Holmes (Boston, NL), 28

Football

Bob Waterfield (QB), Los Angeles, debuts.

NFL Season Leaders: Sammy Baugh (Washington), passing; Steve Van Buren (Philadelphia), rushing; Don Hutson (Green Bay), receiving.

College All-Americans: Herman Wedemeyer (QB), St. Mary's; Bob Fenimore (B), Oklahoma A & M; Glenn Davis (B), Army; Felix "Doc" Blanchard (B), Army.

Bowls (Jan. 1, 1946)

Rose: Alabama 34–Southern California 13
Orange: Miami 13–Holy Cross 6
Sugar: Oklahoma A & M 33–St. Mary's 13
Cotton: Texas 40–Missouri 27

Basketball

In the NIT semifinal, Ernie Calverly, Rhode Island, ties the game at the buzzer with a 3/4 court shot; Rhode Island wins in overtime.

Winners

World Series	*College Basketball*
Detroit (AL) 4–Chicago (NL) 3	Oklahoma A & M (NCAA) De Paul (NIT)
MVP	*Player of the Year*
NL–Phil Cavaretta, Chicago	George Mikan, De Paul
AL–Hal Newhouser, Detroit	*Stanley Cup*
NFL	Toronto
Cleveland 15–Washington 14	*US Tennis Open*
MVP	Men: Sgt. Frank Parker
Bob Waterfield, Los Angeles	Women: Sarah Palfrey Cooke
College Football	*Kentucky Derby*
Army	Hoop Jr. (E. Arcaro, jockey)
Heisman Trophy	
Felix Blanchard, Army	

Fashion

For Women: Ingenious designers deal with war regulations and the industry's need for change and style with "the rounded look." Dresses and suits are fitted at the midriff, neck, waist, and wrist; skirts bell over the stomach and thighs; large, felt, globe hats envelop the hair so the face and throat are again emphasized. Hair is worn in top and back knots with ribbons and bands of intertwined metal. Beachwear also gives the rounded look, especially bloomer shorts worn with breast bands. The new loose, shoulder-to-thigh cotton coat, the "cholo," appears. Flat shoes, like the new ballet slipper, and the low suede sandal with soft ankle band, are more popular than heeled styles. Also popular are gold neck bands, Zulu-like metal rings, gold chains, and the new belt with decals and a variety of decorative shapes. Cropped jeans and pants with stockings in the same rib (foreshadowing tights) are shown.

High-fashion note: Joffé's lampshade suit

Current fashion model. *Movie Star News.*

Kaleidoscope

- The East Coast is alerted to the possibility of robot bomb attacks, and blackouts and brownouts intensify.
- Children continue to buy Defense Stamps weekly; schools give air raid drills; toys are scarce (there are no tricycles, bikes, sleds, skates, toy cars, mechanical or electric trains); girls write service boys whose names have been supplied by the USO.
- Thousands weep beside the train tracks and pay their last respects to FDR, as a train carries his body from Warm Springs, Georgia, to Washington.
- The 7th Army counterintelligence unit discovers Goering's $200 million art collection; the 101st Airborne Division puts it on display in the Bavarian village of Berchtesgaden.
- Ezra Pound, arrested near Geneva, is committed to a mental hospital in Washington, rather than tried for treason.
- William L. Laurence, *New York Times* science reporter, is permitted to join bombardier Maj. Thomas Ferebee and pilot Col. Paul Warfield Tibbets on the *Enola Gay* when the A-bomb is dropped on Hiroshima. Laurence's commentary is released a month later: "A giant ball of fire rose from the bowels of the earth. Then . . . a pillar of purple fire, 10,000 feet high, shooting skyward. . . . There came shooting out of the top a giant mushroom."
- The first Japanese envoys to Gen. Douglas MacArthur and Richard K. Sutherland in Manila arrive with half a dozen cartons of American cigarettes; the gifts are refused.
- Pablo Picasso welcomes GIs who tour Paris at the end of the war.
- Gas fuel rationing ends in August; by November, all items are available but sugar; the midnight curfew is lifted; the nationwide dimout is lifted; President Truman lights the National Community Christmas Tree at the White House for the first time since 1941.
- Penicillin, previously distributed to the armed forces, becomes more available to the civilian population.
- Former secretary of state Cordell Hull receives the Nobel Peace Prize.
- Audie Murphy returns home from North Africa, Italy, and France, the most decorated World War II hero; he is awarded 15 citations, including the Congressional Medal of Honor and high awards from both Belgium and France.
- Many families take their first vacations since Pearl Harbor; cabaret shows open in cities like Las Vegas, a by-product, in part, of the USO troop shows; motel construction increases.
- According to a Gallup poll, Greer Garson is America's most popular star.
- Gene Kelly and Fred Astaire dance together (the only time) in the film *Ziegfeld Follies*.
- Princess Elizabeth, 19, names Bing Crosby her favorite crooner.
- Frank Sinatra earns $13,500 a week, almost $1 million a year.
- Shirley Temple, 17, marries Air Force physical

V-E Day in an elementary school. *Copyright* Washington Post. *Reprinted permission D.C. Public Library.*

instructor John Agar; Judy Garland, 23, marries Vincente Minnelli, 38.
- The New York police commissioner resigns to preside over the radio show "Gangbusters."
- The bebop craze continues; the saying "Kilroy was here" remains popular.
- Truman is widely quoted for his sayings "The buck stops here" and "If you can't stand the heat, get out of the kitchen."
- The shortage of an estimated 4,660,000 homes forces many into makeshift arrangements that range from "doubling up" to living in autos.
- Women auto workers in Detroit, laid off because of returning war veterans, stage a march with posters such as "Stop Discrimination because of Sex."
- When Truman proposes his plan for peace and prosperity, some say it "out-Deals the New Deal."
- The Department of Agriculture reports that 20 million tons of food are needed to feed Europe.
- Nobel Laureate Irving Langmuir urges the establishment of a National Science Foundation in order to stay ahead of Russia in scientific progress.
- The Supreme Court affirms the right of each state to recognize or reject the Nevada divorce decree.
- The governor of Massachusetts signs a bill to end unofficial book censorship.
- A New York Court of Appeals voids the ban on *Esquire*'s second-class mail privileges.

First Appearances: Frozen orange juice, Flying Tiger airline; ballpoint pens on sale, aerosol spray insecticides, CARE (Cooperative for American Remittances to Europe), butane cigarette lighter, Tupperware, trademark "Coke" registered, long-lasting strawberry (University of California), Swanson and Sons' frozen chicken and turkey, an actor elected to Congress (Helen Gahagan Douglas), wax pencils, nonpictorial stamp (United Nations)

1946

Facts and Figures

Economic Profile
    Dow-Jones:—High 212–
        Low 165
    GNP: −2%
    Inflation: +4.6%
    Unemployment: 3.9%
High school graduates
    entering college: 39%
4-year colleges: 1,304
Public/private schools: 10/1
Cartier victory pin, flag of
    rubies, diamonds,
    sapphires: $270–$750
Bergdorf Goodman or
    Bloomingdale's crepe and
    chiffon gown: $110
    Beaver or Persian lamb
        coat: $600
    Mink coat: $2,250
Neiman Marcus, Harzfeld, or
    Saks navy jersey bra: $7
Lily of France bra: $2 and up
I. Magnin fuchsia and purple
    robe: $29.75
Real-hair chignon: $18
Blue Grass perfume: $3.75
    and up
Tabu set of two lipsticks and
    vial: $2.50

Deaths

George Arliss, Robert
    Benchley, W. C. Fields,
    William S. Hart, Harry
    Hopkins, Damon Runyon,
    Gertrude Stein, Alfred
    Stieglitz, Booth
    Tarkington, H. G. Wells.

In the News

CIVIL WAR RAGES IN CHINA . . . SENATE ESTABLISHES ATOMIC ENERGY COMMISSION, DEAN ACHESON CHAIRMAN . . . AT FIRST UN MEETING, IN LONDON, NORWAY'S TRYGVE LIE IS ELECTED SECRETARY-GENERAL . . . 200,000 STRIKE AT GENERAL ELECTRIC . . . 750,000 STEELWORKERS STRIKE . . . JUAN PERON IS ELECTED PRESIDENT OF ARGENTINA . . . FAIR EMPLOYMENT PRACTICES ACT IS DEFEATED IN SENATE . . . BRITAIN AND FRANCE EVACUATE LEBANON . . . KOREAN PROVISIONAL GOVERNMENT IS SET UP, USSR TO CONTROL NORTH, U.S. TO CONTROL SOUTH . . . SECRETARY OF STATE JAMES BYRNES ADVISES TOUGH POLICY ON RUSSIAN AGGRESSION OR INFILTRATION . . . 400,000 COAL WORKERS STRIKE . . . TRUMAN ORDERS RAILROADS SEIZED IF WORKERS STRIKE . . . TRUMAN SEIZES COAL MINES . . . ATOM BOMB TEST IS HELD AT BIKINI ATOLL IN THE PACIFIC . . . PHILIPPINES ARE DECLARED INDEPENDENT . . . CONGRESSIONAL COMMITTEE ABSOLVES FDR OF BLAME FOR PEARL HARBOR . . . YUGOSLOVIA SHOOTS DOWN TWO U.S. PLANES, 5 ARE KILLED . . . U.S. AND USSR DISAGREE ON GERMANY AT PARIS PEACE CONFERENCE . . . 12 NAZIS ARE SENTENCED TO DEATH AT NUREMBERG, HERMAN GOERING COMMITS SUICIDE . . . HENRY WALLACE ATTACKS BYRNES ON HARSH POLICY TO USSR . . . TRUMAN ASKS WALLACE TO RESIGN . . . ALL WAGE AND PRICE CONTROLS, EXCEPT RENT AND SUGAR, ARE ABOLISHED, PRICES SOAR . . . REPUBLICANS MAKE MAJOR SENATE AND HOUSE GAINS . . . COMMUNIST PARTY GAINS PLURALITY IN FRENCH PARLIAMENT . . . U.N. ATOMIC ENERGY COMMISSION OUTLAWS A-BOMB . . . MACARTHUR PURGES JAPANESE ULTRANATIONALISTS, ORDERS WAR CRIMES TRIBUNAL.

Eisenhower travels briefly with his wartime comrade Winston Churchill, who tours the U.S. warning of world communism. *Library of Congress.*

"Across the motion picture screen moved, in light and shadow, what veteran war correspondents called the most terrible pictures of mass slaughter and torture they had ever seen—single corpses and small mountains of them, corpses lying still and corpses being carted away . . . corpses shrunk by starvation and . . . battered by boots or clubs."
— *Time,* on films of concentration camps shown during the Nuremberg trials

Subsequent reports . . . confirmed fears that this . . . election would not be free. . . . [The provisional government] employed widespread measures of coercion and intimidation. . . . The provisions of Yalta and Potsdam have not been fulfilled."
— State Department report on Poland

Quotes

"The general treaty known as the Kellogg-Briand Pact was binding on 63 nations, including Germany, Italy, Japan. After 1928, war was an illegal thing."
— Nuremberg Tribunal

Judge: For what reason were children murdered?
S.S. Officer Ohlendorf: The order was that the Jewish population should be totally exterminated.
Judge: Including the children?
Ohlendorf: Yes.
— Nuremberg trial testimony

"From Stettin in the Baltic to Trieste in the Adriatic, an iron curtain has descended across the Continent. . . . I am convinced there is nothing they so much admire as strength, and there is nothing for which they have less respect than weakness, especially military weakness."
— Former prime minister Winston Churchill, at Fulton, Mo.

"The danger of war is much less from communism than imperialism, whether it be of the U.S. or England."
— Secretary of Agriculture Henry Wallace, at Madison Square Garden

"If it is not possible . . . to keep Mr. Wallace . . . from speaking out on foreign affairs, then it would be a grave mistake . . . for me to continue in my office."
— Secretary of State James Byrnes

Ads

Radio

Premieres
"Winner Take All," Bill Cullen
"Sam Spade," Howard Duff
"Meet the Press," Martha Rountree, Lawrence Spivak
"The Bing Crosby Show"
"Arthur Godfrey's Talent Scouts"
"Twenty Questions," Bill Slater

Most Popular Programs: "Jack Benny," "Fibber McGee and Molly," "Bob Hope," "Fred Allen," "Radio Theater," "Amos 'n' Andy," "Walter Winchell," "Red Skelton" "Screen Guild Players"

New Catchphrases: "[Is it] animal, vegetable, or mineral? . . . larger or smaller than a breadbox?" ("Twenty Questions")

Movies

Openings
The Best Years of Our Lives (William Wyler), Fredric March, Myrna Loy, Dana Andrews, Harold Russell
The Big Sleep (Howard Hawks), Humphrey Bogart, Lauren Bacall
The Postman Always Rings Twice (Tay Garnett), John Garfield, Lana Turner
It's a Wonderful Life (Frank Capra), James Stewart, Donna Reed
The Razor's Edge (Edmund Goulding), Tyrone Power, Gene Tierney
The Yearling (Clarence Brown), Gregory Peck, Jane Wyman, Claude Jarman, Jr.
Brief Encounter (David Lean), Celia Johnson, Trevor Howard
Henry V (Laurence Olivier), Laurence Olivier, Robert Newton
The Killers (Robert Siodmak), Burt Lancaster, Ava Gardner
The Jolson Story (Alfred E. Green), Larry Parks, Evelyn Keyes
Gilda (Charles Vidor), Rita Hayworth, Glenn Ford
Duel in the Sun (King Vidor), Jennifer Jones, Gregory Peck
Song of the South (Harve Foster), Ruth Warrick, Bobby Driscoll
Notorious (Alfred Hitchcock), Cary Grant, Ingrid Bergman
The Blue Dahlia (George Marshall), Alan Ladd, Veronica Lake, William Bendix

TV

Premieres
"Small Fry Club," Bob Emery
"At Home with Tex [McCrary] and Jinx [Falkenburg]"
"Faraway Hill" (first TV soap opera), Flora Campbell
"You Are an Artist," John Gnagy
"See What You Know," Bennett Cerf
"Hour Glass," Helen Parris, first program with major sponsor (Standard Brands)

Of Note
The Joe Lewis versus Billy Conn fight is telecast on June 19 • In September, large numbers of TV sets become commercially available • Wrestling (with Dennis James) airs three times weekly from Jamaica Arena, N.Y.; popular wrestlers include Gorgeous George, Haystack Calhoun, and Antonino Rocca, who frequently wins with his "airplane spin."

Road to Utopia (Hal Walker), Bing Crosby, Bob Hope, Dorothy Lamour
My Darling Clementine (John Ford), Henry Fonda, Victor Mature, Linda Darnell
Shoeshine (Vittorio De Sica), Franco Interlenghi, Rinaldo Smordini

Academy Awards
Best Picture: *The Best Years of Our Lives*
Best Director: William Wyler (*The Best Years of Our Lives*)
Best Actress: Olivia de Havilland (*To Each His Own*)
Best Actor: Fredric March (*The Best Years of Our Lives*)
Special Awards: Laurence Olivier (actor, director, producer, *Henry V*); Claude Jarman, Jr. (outstanding child actor)

Top Box-Office Stars
Bing Crosby, Ingrid Bergman, Van Johnson, Gary Cooper, Bob Hope, Humphrey Bogart, Greer Garson, Margaret O'Brien, Betty Grable, Roy Rogers

Stars of Tomorrow
Joan Leslie, Butch Jenkins, Zachary Scott, Don DeFore, Mark Stevens, Eve Arden, Lizabeth Scott, Dan Duryea, Yvonne DeCarlo, Robert Mitchum

Lana Turner, in *The Postman Always Rings Twice. Movie Star News.*

Popular Music

Top Records

Albums: *State Fair* (Dick Haymes); *Merry Christmas* (Bing Crosby); *The Voice of Frank Sinatra* (Frank Sinatra); *Dancing in the Dark* (Carmen Cavallaro); *The Ink Spots Album* (Ink Spots)

Singles: *Prisoner of Love* (Perry Como); *South America, Take It Away* (Bing Crosby, Andrews Sisters, Vic Schoen Orchestra); *Shoo-Fly Pie and Apple Pan Dowdy* (Stan Kenton, June Christy); *Hey! Ba-Ba-Re-Bop* (Tex Beneke); *Hampton's Sal* (Lionel Hampton); *Say It Isn't So* (Coleman Hawkins); *A Night in Tunisia* (Charlie Parker). Country: *You Will Have to Pay* (Tex Ritter); *Sioux City Sue* (Louis Jordan)

Jazz and Big Bands

Kai Winding and Shelly Manne join Stan Kenton. Red Norvo, with Woody Herman, introduces Stravinsky's *Ebony Concerto.* Eddie Condon opens a club in Greenwich Village, N.Y.

Top Performers *(Downbeat):* Benny Goodman (soloist); Duke Ellington (band); Eddie Safranski, Vido Musso, Roy Eldridge, Bill Harris (instrumentalists); Peggy Lee, Frank Sinatra (vocalists)

Hit Songs

"Chiquita Banana"
"To Each His Own"
"Come Rain or Come Shine"
"Doin' What Comes Natur'lly"
"Full Moon and Empty Arms"
"I Got the Sun in the Morning"
"Zip-a-Dee-Do-Dah"
"Ole Buttermilk Sky"
"Now Is the Hour"
"Golden Earrings"
"Tenderly"
"There's No Business Like Show Business"
"They Say It's Wonderful"

Theater

Broadway Openings

Plays

The Iceman Cometh (Eugene O'Neill), James Barton, Dudley Digges
Joan of Lorraine (Maxwell Anderson), Ingrid Bergman
Another Part of the Forest (Lillian Hellman), Patricia Neal, Mildred Dunnock, Leo Genn
Born Yesterday (Garson Kanin), Judy Holliday (replacing Jean Arthur), Paul Douglas, Gary Merrill
O Mistress Mine (Terence Rattigan), Alfred Lunt, Lynn Fontanne
Present Laughter (Noel Coward), Clifton Webb
Years Ago (Ruth Gordon), Fredric March, Florence Eldridge
Antigone (Jean Anouilh), Katharine Cornell, Cedric Hardwicke
No Exit (Jean-Paul Sartre), Claude Dauphin, Annabella
Christopher Blake (Moss Hart), Richard Tyler, Shepperd Strudwick

Musicals

Annie Get Your Gun (Irving Berlin), Ethel Merman, Ray Middleton
Around the World in 80 Days (Cole Porter), Orson Welles

Call Me Mister (Harold Rome), Betty Garrett, Jules Munshin
Lute Song (Raymond Scott, Bernard Hanighen), Mary Martin
St. Louis Woman (Harold Arlen, Johnny Mercer), Ruby Hill, Rex Ingram, Pearl Bailey; all-black cast
Beggar's Holiday (Duke Ellington, John Latouche), Zero Mostel, Alfred Drake

Classics and Revivals On and Off Broadway

Candida (George Bernard Shaw), Marlon Brando, Katharine Cornell; *Lady Windermere's Fan* (Oscar Wilde), Cornelia Otis Skinner, Estelle Winwood; *The Playboy of the Western World* (John Synge), Burgess Meredith, Mildred Natwick; *The Duchess of Malfi* (Webster), Elisabeth Bergner, Canada Lee; Old Vic: *Oedipus, Henry IV, Parts I, II, Uncle Vanya* (Chekhov), *The Critic* (Sheridan), Laurence Olivier, Ralph Richardson, Margaret Leighton, Joyce Redman. *Founded:* American Repertory Theatre by Eva Le Gallienne, Margaret Webster, and Cheryl Crawford

Pulitzer Prize

State of the Union, Howard Lindsay and Russel Crouse

Classical Music ━━━━━━━━━━━━━━━━━━

Compositions

Roy Harris, Concerto for Two Pianos
Roger Sessions, Piano Sonata no. 2
Samuel Barber, *Medea*
Don Gillis, Symphony no. 5½, *Symphony for Fun*
Peter Mennin, Symphony no. 3
Ned Rorem, *Alleluia*
Ulysses Kay, Inventions for Piano
Walter Piston, Divertimento for Nine Instruments
John Cage, Sonatas and Interludes for Prepared
    Pianos
Robert Ward, *Jubilation*

Important Events

Postwar attendance at musical events breaks all records.
Beethoven is most frequently performed by the 21 major U.S. orchestras, followed by Tchaikovsky, Wagner, Mozart, Bach, and Mendelssohn, and, among the contemporaries, Richard Strauss and Aaron Copland.
Leonard Bernstein becomes director of symphony programs at New York City Center and conducts the New York City Symphony Orchestra without pay (1946–48). Artur Rodzinski returns to the New York Philharmonic Symphonic Society. Charles Munch conducts the Boston Symphony Orchestra.
Festivals resume throughout the country. The Berkshire premieres Benjamin Britten's *Peter Grimes* and Shostakovich's Symphony no. 9.

First Performances

Charles Ives, Symphony no. 3 (New York); Stravinsky, *Ebony Concerto* (New York); Stravinsky, conducting, Symphony in Three Movements (New York); Béla Bartók, Piano Concerto no. 3 (New York); Samuel Barber, Cello Concerto (Boston); Aaron Copland, Symphony no. 3 (Boston); Paul Hindemith, *When Lilacs Last in the Dooryard Bloom'd* (New York); Ernst Krenek, Piano Concerto no. 3 (Minneapolis); Darius Milhaud, Concerto for Clarinet and Orchestra (Washington); Arnold Schoenberg, *Genesis* (Los Angeles)

Opera

Metropolitan: Joel Berglund, *Tristan und Isolde, Die Meistersinger;* Raoul Jobin, *Lakmé;* Stella Roman, *La bohème;* Set Svanholm (debut) *Siegfried;* Ramon Vinay, *Otello;* premiere: *The Medium* (Gian Carlo Menotti); revival: *Il tabarro* (Puccini); company makes extensive tour of twelve countries.

City Center, New York: *Ariadne auf Naxos* (Richard Strauss, American premiere)

Chicago: Zinka Milanov, Kurt Baum, Leonard Warren, Italo Tajo, *Aïda;* Patrice Munsel, Richard Tucker, *Lucia di Lammermoor;* Helen Traubel, Set Svanholm, Blanche Thebom, *Tristan und Isolde;* premieres: *Amelia Goes to the Ball* (Gian Carlo Menotti) and *Emperor Jones* (Louis Gruenberg)

San Francisco: Risë Stevens, Eleanor Steber, *Carmen;* Set Svanholm, Astrid Varnay, *Lohengrin*

Dallas: *Bluebeard's Castle* (Béla Bartók, premiere, in English)

Nathan Milstein, Vladimir Horowitz, and Gregor Piatigorsky. *D. Ouellette Collection.*

Art _____

Paintings

Jackson Pollock, *Sounds in the Grass, Shimmering Substance*
Jack Levine, *Welcome Home*
Adolph Gottlieb, *Voyager's Return*
Mark Rothko, *Prehistoric Memories*
Dong Kingman, *The El and Snow*
Paul Cadmus, *Fantasia on a Theme by Dr. S.*
George Grosz, *Peace, II*
Willem de Kooning, *Queen of Hearts, Light in August*

Sculpture

Isamu Noguchi, glass and wood table

José de Rivera, *Yellow Block*
David Smith, *Spectre of Profit*
William Zorach, *The Artist's Daughter* (1930–46)
Chaim Gross, *Sisters*
Louise Nevelson, *Lovers II*

Architecture

Solar House, Kalamazoo, Mich. (George Fred Keck)
Plans are drawn for the Opera Pavillion, Cincinnati (William H. Tunke) and the UN Building (Wallace K. Harrison).

Important Exhibitions

Loans travel throughout the U.S.: from King George VI and the London Museum, Hogarth, Constable, Turner; from Standard Oil, "The Visual Story of Oil" (Joe Jones, Thomas Hart Benton).

Disabled veteran Harold Russell, with Dana Andrews and Fredric March, in *The Best Years of Our Lives,* which wins 8 Academy Awards. *Movie Star News.*

Museums

New York: *Metropolitan:* Diamond Jubilee displays include Michelangelo's *Madonna and Child* and Delacroix's *La Barricade* (from the Louvre); "The Taste of the '70s." *Museum of Modern Art:* Art of the South Seas; Fourteen Americans; Henry Moore and Marc Chagall retrospectives. *Whitney:* Pioneers of modern art (34 artists, including Marin, Stella, Weber, Hartley, Man Ray, Maurer); Current U.S. sculpture

Chicago: Chinese bronzes; George Bellows; Constable and Turner

Pittsburgh: Carnegie prizes are awarded to Karl Knath *(Gear),* Jack Levine *(Welcome Home),* and William Gropper *(Don Quixote, No. 1).*

Individual Shows

Inness, Robinson, Still

Art Briefs

A survey of museum directors on their favorite painters reports Hartley, first, followed by Kuniyoshi, Franklin C. Watkins, Marsh, Alexander Brook, Mattson, Burchfield, and Hopper • Billy Rose pays a record price ($75,000) for Rembrandt's *A Pilgrim at Prayer;* also sold this year are Cézanne's *Portrait of Mme. Cézanne* ($34,500); and Ryder's *Siegfried and the Rhine Maidens* ($23,500).

Dance _____

Ballet Society is organized by George Balanchine and Lincoln Kirstein to give subscription performances of new works.

Premieres

Ballet Theatre: *Facsimile* (Jerome Robbins), Nora Kaye, John Kriza

Ballet Society: *The Four Temperaments* (Balanchine, Hindemith), Tanaquil Le Clercq

Martha Graham: *Cave of the Heart*

Books

Fiction

Critics' Choice
The Bulwark, Theodore Dreiser
Thirty Stories, Kay Boyle
The Member of the Wedding, Carson McCullers
Delta Wedding, Eudora Welty
Focus, Arthur Miller
Mister Roberts, Thomas Heggen
The American, Howard Fast
Brewsie and Willie, Gertrude Stein
๑ *The Stranger*, Albert Camus

Best-Sellers
The King's General, Daphne Du Maurier
This Side of Innocence, Taylor Caldwell
The River Road, Frances Parkinson Keyes
The Miracle of the Bells, Russell Janney
The Hucksters, Frederic Wakeman
The Foxes of Harrow, Frank Yerby
Arch of Triumph, Erich Maria Remarque
The Snake Pit, Mary Jane Ward
B. F.'s Daughter, John P. Marquand

Nonfiction

Critics' Choice
Atomic Energy in Cosmic and Human Life, George Gamow
Manifesto for the Atomic Age, Virgil Jordan
Touched with Fire, ed. Mark De Wolfe
The Chrysanthemum and the Sword, Ruth Benedict
The Common Sense Book of Baby and Child Care, Benjamin Spock
Hiroshima, John Hersey
Problems of Men, John Dewey
War Reports, Henry Arnold, George Marshall, Ernest King
Thunder Out of China, Theodore White, Annalee Jacoby

Best-Sellers
The Egg and I, Betty MacDonald
Peace of Mind, Joshua L. Liebman
As He Saw It, Elliott Roosevelt
The Roosevelt I Knew, Frances Perkins
Last Chapter, Ernie Pyle
I Chose Freedom, Victor Kravchenko
The Anatomy of Peace, Emery Reves

Top Secret, Ralph Ingersoll

Poetry
Elizabeth Bishop, *North and South*
H. D., *Flowering of the Rod*
Robinson Jeffers, *Medea*
Kenneth Patchen, *Sleepers Awake*
William Carlos Williams, *Paterson, Book One*
Denise Levertov, *The Double Image*
Wallace Stevens, *Esthétique du Mal*
May Sarton, *The Bridge of Years*
๑ Dylan Thomas, *Deaths and Entrances*

Pulitzer Prizes
All the King's Men, Robert Penn Warren (novel)
Scientists against Time, James Phinney Baxter III (U.S. history)
The Autobiography of William Allen White, William Allen White (biography)
Lord Weary's Castle, Robert Lowell (poetry)

Science and Technology

"Printing" wiring circuits on ceramic furthers miniaturization of radios and other electronic equipment.

Eniac, the giant automated electronic computer, is further developed at Harvard to perform 1,000 times faster than humans.

The army makes the first radar contact with the moon, bouncing back a signal in 2.4 seconds.

Ernest O. Lawrence reports that the synchrotron, the new atom smasher, produces 300 million volts.

The first atomic pile for peaceful purposes is set up at Oak Ridge, Tennessee; plans for other facilities in Illinois and New York are announced.

The Mayo Clinic reports that streptomycin can check the advance of tuberculosis.

The University of Pennsylvania experiments with carbon 14, the first manmade radioactive substance to be used in medical research.

RCA markets an unbreakable disc of vinylite on which *Til Eulenspiegel* is recorded.

Harry Stack Sullivan, in *Conceptions of Modern Psychiatry*, develops his theory of the importance of interpersonal relations.

Nobel Prizes
The prize in chemistry is shared by James B. Sumner, for his research on enzymes, and Wendell Stanley and John Northrop, for their work on viruses. Percy W. Bridgman wins the award in physics, for his work on atmospheric pressure. Hermann J. Muller wins in physiology and medicine, for work on the effect of X rays on genes.

Sports _____

Baseball

Many stars return from the war.

Jackie Robinson, the first black player in organized baseball, stars for Montreal, a Brooklyn (NL) farm team.

Bob Feller (Cleveland) strikes out a record 348.

Warren Spahn (Boston, NL) and Yogi Berra (New York, AL) debut.

St. Louis (NL) beats Brooklyn (NL) in two out of three in the first pennant playoff.

Ted Williams goes four for four with two home runs in the All-Star game.

Champions _____

Batting	Pitching
Stan Musial (St. Louis, NL), .365	Howie Pollet (St. Louis, NL), 21–10
Mickey Vernon (Washington, AL), .353	Dave Ferris (Boston, AL), 25–6
	Home runs
	Hank Greenberg (Detroit, AL), 44

Football

The All-America Conference begins competition with the NFL. The Cleveland Browns beat the New York Yanks 14–7.

NFL Season Leaders: Bob Waterfield (Los Angeles), passing; Bill Dudley (Pittsburgh), rushing; Jim Benton (Los Angeles), receiving.

College All-Americans: John Lujack (QB), Notre Dame; Charles Trippi (B), Georgia; Glenn Davis (B), Army; Felix "Doc" Blanchard (B), Army

Bowls (Jan. 1, 1947)

Rose: Illinois 45–UCLA 14
Orange: Rice 9–Tennessee 8
Cotton: Arkansas 0–Louisiana 0
Sugar: Georgia 20–North Carolina 10

Basketball

The NBA is formed with 11 teams in major cities; Maurice Podoloff is president.

Other Sports

Boxing: Joe Louis knocks out Billy Conn in the eighth round at Yankee Stadium, New York; ringside seats are a record $100.

Golf: Ben Hogan, the top pro golfer, wins five tournaments and $42,566.

Horse Racing: Assault, ridden by W. Mehrtens, wins the Triple Crown.

Winners _____

World Series	College Basketball
St. Louis (NL) 4	Oklahoma A & M (NCAA)
Boston (AL) 3	Kentucky (NIT)
MVP	Player of the Year
NL–Stan Musial, St. Louis	Bob Kurland, Oklahoma
AL–Ted Williams, Boston	A & M
NFL	Stanley Cup
Chicago (Bears) 24–New York 14	Montreal
MVP	US Tennis Open
Bill Dudley, Chicago	Men: John Kramer
College Football	Women: Pauline Betz
Notre Dame	USGA Open
Heisman Trophy	Lloyd Mangrum
Glenn Davis, Army	Kentucky Derby
	Assault (W. Mehrtens, jockey)

Fashion _____

For Women: *Harper's Bazaar* reports five casual fashion trends: (1) shirtwaists worn with Civil War Phelps bags, (2) ginghams, which recall the frontier, (3) ballerina-length skirts, (4) overalls, (5) wool tights, hoods, and tightly belted coats. Most noticeable is the postwar trend toward femininity with emphasis on the natural, slightly idealized figure with no padding. Pastel day dresses have Peter Pan collars, full-gathered skirts, sashes, and ruffles. The "bellhop" suit is neat, tailored, buttoned, and tight. Wide-neck dinner dresses, which expose the shoulders and part of the back and chest, are willowy, in yards of fabric. Some have only one strap and an uneven hemline. Colors are faded pink, ice blue, yellow, and mauve. Hats are pleated or turbaned and trimmed with fine feathers; some match striped or patterned bags, blouses, and umbrellas. With nylons back again, shoes draw attention to the ankle and the arch and have slender high heels and ankle straps; cutouts above the toe expose even more foot to emphasize femininity.

High-fashion note: Hartnell's purple sheath; the Capezio ballet slipper

Kaleidoscope _____

- John D. Rockefeller, Jr. donates $8.5 million for the construction of the UN headquarters along the East River, New York.
- Albert Einstein and a group of other nuclear scientists form the Emergency Committee of Atomic Science to advance the peaceful use of atomic energy.
- The August 31 issue of the *New Yorker* publishes John Hersey's *Hiroshima*.
- German physicists Otto Hahn and Werner Heisenberg claim they completed an "atomic energy machine" in Leipzig at the end of 1941, but lack of funds and facilities prohibited production of a bomb.
- Within a year of V-J Day, the American military goes from 11 to 1 million.
- A *New York Daily News* headline "PRICES SOAR, BUYERS SORE / STEERS JUMP OVER THE MOON" reflects the large accumulation of wartime capital and insufficient production of consumer goods; the cost of living is up 33 percent over 1941.
- Buying and vacation sprees occur; money is frequently paid under the counter for cars, apartments, and theater and sports tickets.
- The birth rate increases 20 percent over 1945.
- With sugar rationing over, ice-cream consumption takes on fad proportions.
- Bread consumption drops as flour and wheat are exported to Europe; flour whiteners are added for American consumers who dislike dark bread.
- The "Moscow mule" (vodka and ginger ale) is invented, and vodka sales increase.
- Fashion columnists report Louis Reard's "bikini" sensation in Paris.
- Auto innovations include the single unit of welded steel (Nash 600), wide windows (Studebaker Champion), and combined wood station wagon and passenger car (Chrysler Town and Country).
- The RCA 10-inch TV sells for $374, the Model T of television sets.
- More than half the top bands dissolve (Tommy Dorsey, Benny Goodman, Woody Herman, Les Brown, Benny Carter), and band vocalists strike out on their own (Dick Haymes, Doris Day, Perry Como).
- The DAR bars Eddie Condon's jazz band from Constitution Hall because of "the type of audience" it will attract.
- Mobster Bugsy Siegel and his gang open the Flamingo in Las Vegas, and building is widespread at the "entertainment capital of America."
- A syndicate that includes Bob Hope buys the Cleveland Indians.
- Ads for the movie *The Outlaw* read: "The Music Hall gets the Big Ones. What are the two great reasons for Jane Russell's rise to stardom?" Miss Russell wears a special uplift bra designed by Howard Hughes.
- Bing Crosby introduces transcribed, rather than live, programs on ABC; he earns $30,000 a week on the Philco radio show.
- Blacks vote for the first time in the Mississippi Democratic primary.

- The auction of FDR's stamp collection brings $211,000.
- Former secretary of state Henry Wallace becomes editor of the *New Republic*.
- Dr. Benjamin Spock's *The Common Sense Book of Baby and Child Care* is published; it was written while Spock was in the Navy Medical Corps in charge of severe disciplinary cases.
- Oklahoma City offers the first rapid public treatment of venereal diseases.
- United Airlines announces it has ordered jet planes for commercial purposes.
- The *AMA Journal* reports that the primary results of radiation disease suffered by Hiroshima and Nagasaki victims are disturbed liver function and suppression of the blood-formation system.
- A C-45 crashes into the 58th floor of a New York bank building; five are killed.
- *Life* reports (January 17) on the growing popularity of Jean-Paul Sartre's existentialism.

First Appearances: Estée Lauder, "Beautiful Hair" Breck ads, Sunshine biscuits, French's instant potatoes, electric blankets, FDR dime instead of the 1916 Mercury dime, DC-6 (Douglas Aircraft) for 70 passengers, 300 m.p.h., with cargo, Crosby compact car, autobank service, Lewyt vacuum cleaner, artificial snow, mobile telephone service, coin-operated TV, Fulbright awards, Tide, Timex watches, telephones on trains, automatic clothes dryers, *Family Circle, Scientific American, Holiday,* ektachrome color film, J. L. Hudson store (world's second largest, Detroit)

Jane Russell in *The Outlaw*. The film, first released in 1943 but withdrawn because of censorship controversy, is now released in defiance of the production code. *Movie Star News*.

1947

Facts and Figures

Economic Profile
  Dow-Jones:—High 184–
    Low 166
  GNP: +11%
  Inflation: +8.4%
  Unemployment: 3.9%
Average salary: $2,589
  Teacher: $2,261
  Lawyer: $7,437
  Physician: $10,700
  Factory Worker: $2,793
Samson folding table: $3.95
Bendix automatic washer:
  $239.50
Emerson AC-DC battery-
  operated, portable radio:
  $29.95
GE vacuum cleaner: $27.95
San Moritz Hotel, New York:
  $4.50 up
Hotel Commodore, San
  Francisco: $3 up
Copacabana, New York, Joe
  E. Lewis, star; three-
  course dinner: $2.50
Broadway theater: $1.20–
  $4.30
Pop records, Victor: 4/99¢

Above: Admiral Byrd, having
already explored the North
Pole, departs for Antarctica.
Copyright Washington Post.
*Reprinted by permission of
D.C. Public Library.*

Deaths

Henry Ford, Mark Hellinger,
  Fiorello La Guardia, Ernst
  Lubitsch, Grace Moore,
  Max Planck, Damon
  Runyan, Laurette Taylor,
  Alfred North Whitehead.

In the News

GENERAL GEORGE MARSHALL BECOMES SECRETARY OF STATE . . .
U.S. CEASES MEDIATION OF CHINESE CIVIL WAR . . . COUNCIL OF
FOREIGN MINISTERS MEETS IN MOSCOW BUT FAILS TO AGREE . . .
TRUMAN ORDERS LOYALTY INVESTIGATION OF ALL FEDERAL
EMPLOYEES . . . BRITAIN PROPOSES PARTITION OF PALESTINE, ARABS
AND JEWS PROTEST . . . TELEPHONE COMPANY STRIKES NATIONWIDE
. . . TRUMAN ASSERTS DOCTRINE OF SUPPORT TO FREE PEOPLES, $400
MILLION IN AID TO GREECE AND TURKEY . . . FREIGHTER IN TEXAS
GULF EXPLODES, 500 ARE KILLED . . . SELECTIVE SERVICE ACT
EXPIRES . . . HENRY WALLACE ATTACKS U.S. "IMPERIALIST" POLICY
. . . MARSHALL PROPOSES PLAN TO HELP REBUILD EUROPE . . . $350
MILLION IS ALLOCATED TO WAR-RAVAGED COUNTRIES . . . $4
BILLION TAX REDUCTION IS PASSED . . . COAL MINES RETURN TO
PRIVATE OPERATION WITH LARGE WAGE HIKE . . . CONGRESS PASSES
TAFT-HARTLEY "EMPLOYER RIGHTS" ACT OVER TRUMAN VETO . . .
INDEPENDENCE OF INDIA IS PROCLAIMED WITH SEPARATE STATES FOR
HINDUS AND MOSLEMS, MASSIVE FIGHTING OCCURS . . . WILLIAM
ODUM SETS ROUND-THE-WORLD FLYING RECORD OF 73 HOURS IN
"REYNOLD'S BOMBSHELL" . . . PALESTINE QUESTION GOES TO UN
. . . HOUSE UN-AMERICAN ACTIVITIES COMMITTEE BEGINS HEARINGS
ON HOLLYWOOD COMMUNISTS . . . $540 MILLION FOR FRANCE,
HOLLAND, AND AUSTRIA IS APPROPRIATED . . . COMMUNISTS WIN IN
HUNGARIAN ELECTION . . . HUAC INDICTS 10 HOLLYWOOD FIGURES
FOR CONTEMPT . . . TAYLOR ACT PROHIBITS PUBLIC EMPLOYEE
STRIKES . . . JOHN L. LEWIS WITHDRAWS UNITED MINE WORKERS
FROM THE AFL . . . WALLACE ANNOUNCES CANDIDACY FOR
PRESIDENT.

Marlon Brando, as the brute Stanley Kowalski, alternately caresses and bellows for his "Stella," played by Kim Hunter (center) in *A Streetcar Named Desire*. Jessica Tandy, right, plays Blanche DuBois. *Billy Rose Theatre Collection. The New York Public Library at Lincoln Center. Astor, Lenox and Tilden Foundations.*

"[A woman must] accept herself fully as a woman [and] know . . . she is dependent on a man. There is no fantasy in her mind about being an independent woman, a contradiction in terms."
> — Marynia Farnham and Ferdinand Lundberg, *Modern Woman*

"I have always depended on the kindness of strangers."
> — Blanche DuBois, *A Streetcar Named Desire* (Tennessee Williams)

Quotes

"I believe that it must be the policy of the United States to support free peoples who are resisting attempted subjugation by armed minorities or by outside pressures."
> — Truman Doctrine

"The people of America are highly concerned about whether . . . this is the opening wedge in taking over the job that Britain has done so well in the last 150 years."
> — Sen. Arthur Vandenberg, on the Truman Doctrine

"Our policy is not directed against any country or doctrine, but against hunger, poverty, desperation and chaos. We of the United States are deeply conscious of our responsibilities in the world."
> — George Marshall, in Harvard speech

ON THE IMPENDING HUAC MEETINGS:
"Before every free conscience in America is subpoenaed, please speak up."
> —Judy Garland

"Are they going to scare us into silence?"
> —Fredric March

"Once they get movies throttled, how long before we're told what we can say . . . into a radio microphone?"
> —Frank Sinatra

"I'd like to see them all in Russia. . . . A taste of Russia would cure them [the Reds]."
> —Adolphe Menjou

"You can't help smelling them [the Reds]."
> —Rupert Hughes, novelist-screenwriter

Ads

TV

Premieres
"Kraft Television Theater" ("Double Door")
"World Series," New York Yankees–Brooklyn
    Dodgers
"Meet the Press," Larry Spivak, Martha Rountree
"Howdy Doody," "Buffalo Bob" Smith
"Juvenile Jury," Jack Barry
"Party Line"
"Mary Kay and Johnny," first situation comedy
"U.S. Congress," first coverage

Specials
"The Late George Apley" (Leo G. Carroll); Ilona
Massey entertaining the veterans at St. Albans Naval
Hospital on Christmas Day

Of Note
Newsletters and magazines such as *Counterattack*
list American entertainers with alleged Communist
ties • The dramatic rise in Kraft's Imperial Cheese
sales, advertised on the "Kraft Television Theater,"
demonstrates TV's marketing potential.

Radio

Premieres
"You Bet Your Life," Groucho Marx
"The Jack Paar Show"
"Lassie," Marvin Miller
"Strike It Rich," Todd Russell
"Candid Microphone," Allen Funt
"My Friend Irma," Marie Wilson
"Stop Me if You've Heard This One," Roger Bower
"You Are There," Don Hollenbeck

Movies

Openings
Gentleman's Agreement (Elia Kazan), Gregory Peck,
    Dorothy McGuire, John Garfield
Crossfire (Edward Dmytryk), Robert Ryan, Robert
    Mitchum
Great Expectations (David Lean), John Mills, Valerie
    Hobson, Alec Guinness
Miracle on 34th Street (George Seaton), Edmund
    Gwenn, John Payne, Maureen O'Hara
Body and Soul (Richard Rossen), John Garfield, Lilli
    Palmer
Life with Father (Michael Curtiz), William Powell,
    Irene Dunne
Mourning Becomes Electra (Dudley Nichols),
    Rosalind Russell, Leo Genn
Kiss of Death (Henry Hathaway), Victor Mature,
    Richard Widmark
The Egg and I (Chester Erskine), Claudette Colbert,
    Fred MacMurray, Marjorie Main
The Bachelor and the Bobbysoxer (Irving Reis), Cary
    Grant, Myrna Loy, Shirley Temple
Monsieur Verdoux (Charles Chaplin), Charles
    Chaplin, Martha Raye
The Ghost and Mrs. Muir (Joseph L. Mankiewicz),
    Gene Tierney, Rex Harrison
Black Narcissus (Michael Powell, Emeric
    Pressburger), Deborah Kerr, Flora Robson
Odd Man Out (Carol Reed), James Mason, Kathleen
    Ryan
Brute Force (Jules Dassin), Burt Lancaster, Hume
    Cronyn, Howard Duff

Academy Awards
Best Picture: *Gentleman's Agreement*
Best Director: Elia Kazan (*Gentleman's Agreement*)
Best Actress: Loretta Young (*The Farmer's
    Daughter*)
Best Actor: Ronald Colman (*A Double Life*)

Top Box-Office Stars
Bing Crosby, Betty Grable, Ingrid Bergman, Gary
Cooper, Humphrey Bogart, Bob Hope, Clark Gable,
Gregory Peck, Claudette Colbert, Alan Ladd

Stars of Tomorrow
Evelyn Keyes, Billy De Wolfe, Peter Lawford, Janis
Paige, Elizabeth Taylor, Claude Jarman, Jr., Janet
Blair, MacDonald Cary, Gail Russell, Richard Conte

Popular Music

Hit Songs
"Almost Like Being in Love"
"Chi-Baba Chi-Baba"
"Civilization (Bongo, Bongo, Bongo)"
"Mam'selle"
"Papa, Won't You Dance with Me?"
"Woody Woodpecker"
"Ballerina"
"A Fellow Needs a Girl"
"I'll Dance at Your Wedding"
"Open the Door, Richard"

Top Records

Albums: *Al Jolson Album* (Al Jolson); *All Time Favorites* (Harry James); *Dorothy Shay Sings* (Dorothy Shay); *Al Jolson Album—Vol. 2* (Al Jolson); *Glenn Miller Masterpieces—Vol. 2* (Glenn Miller)

Singles: *How Are Things in Glocca Morra / Treasure of Sierra Madre* (Buddy Clark); *That's My Desire* (Frankie Laine); *Peg o' My Heart / Fantasy Impromptu* (The Harmonicats); *But Beautiful You* (Tex Beneke); *Near You* (Francis Craig); *Confess* (Doris Day); *Everything I Have Is Yours* (Billy Eckstine); *I'm Looking over a Four-Leaf Clover* (Art Moonie); *Temptation* (Jo Stafford). Country: *It's a Sin* (Eddy Arnold); *Divorce Me C.O.D.* (Merle Travis)

Jazz and Big Bands
Louis Armstrong breaks up his big band and forms a sextet that includes Jack Teagarden and Barney Bigard; Woody Herman organizes the second "Herd."

Top Performers *(Downbeat):* Benny Goodman (soloist); Duke Ellington (band); Shelly Manne, Johnny Hodges, Oscar Moore, Eddie Safranski (instrumentalists); Nat "King" Cole (jazz group); Sarah Vaughan, Frank Sinatra (soloists)

Theater

Broadway Openings

Plays
A Streetcar Named Desire (Tennessee Williams), Marlon Brando, Jessica Tandy, Kim Hunter, Karl Malden
All My Sons (Arthur Miller), Ed Begley, Arthur Kennedy
The Heiress (Ruth Augustus Goetz), Wendy Hiller, Basil Rathbone
For Love or Money (F. Hugh Herbert), June Lockhart, Vicki Cummings
Command Decision (William Wister Haines), Paul Kelly, James Whitmore
The Winslow Boy (Terence Rattigan), Frank Allenby, Valerie White
John Loves Mary (Norman Krasna), William Prince, Nina Foch, Tom Ewell
An Inspector Calls (J. B. Priestley), Thomas Mitchell

Musicals
Allegro (Richard Rodgers, Oscar Hammerstein II), John Battles, Roberta Jonay
Barefoot Boy with Cheek (Sidney Lippman, Sylvia Dee), Nancy Walker, William Redfield, Red Buttons
Brigadoon (Alan Jay Lerner, Frederick Loewe), Marion Bell, David Brooks
Finian's Rainbow (Burton Lane, E. Y. Harburg), Ella Logan, David Wayne
High Button Shoes (Jule Styne, Sammy Cahn), Phil Silvers, Nanette Fabray, Helen Gallagher, Joey Faye
Street Scene (Kurt Weill, Langston Hughes), Norman Cordon, Anne Jeffreys, Hope Emerson

Classics and Revivals On and Off Broadway
Medea (Robinson Jeffers adaptation), Judith Anderson, Florence Reed, John Gielgud; *Man and Superman* (George Bernard Shaw), Maurice Evans; *Crime and Punishment* (Rodney Ackland), John Gielgud, Lillian Gish; *The Importance of Being Earnest* (Oscar Wilde), John Gielgud; *Antony and Cleopatra,* Katharine Cornell, Godfrey Tearle; *King Lear,* Donald Wolfit and Company. *Founded:* Actors Studio by Elia Kazan, Cheryl Crawford, and Robert Lewis

Regional

Founded: Theatre '47 (Margo Jones Theatre), Dallas, by Margot Jones: *Farther Off from Heaven [Dark at the Top of the Stairs]*, William Inge, premiere; Alley Theatre, Houston, by Nina Vance

Pulitzer Prize
No prize is awarded.

Classical Music _____

Compositions
Henry Cowell, *Hymn and Fuguing Tune*
Walter Piston, Symphony no. 3, String Quartet no. 3
Leonard Bernstein, Symphony no. 2 *(Age of Anxiety)*
George Antheil, Symphony no. 5
Roy Harris, *Quest*
Samuel Barber, *Knoxville: Summer of 1915*
William Schuman, Violin Concerto
Milton Babbitt, Three Compositions for Piano
Alan Hovhaness, Symphony no. 8

Important Events
Widespread interest in music grows, as orchestras travel. The New York Philharmonic gives 28 concerts in 24 cities; the San Francisco Symphony tours with 56 concerts. Fritz Reiner takes the Pittsburgh to Mexico City, the first major U.S. orchestra in Mexico. The Metropolitan Opera gives 57 performances in 14 cities.
Artur Rodzinski resigns from the New York Philharmonic and signs with the Chicago.

Debut: Michael Rabin

First Performances
Roger Sessions, Symphony no. 2 (San Francisco); Paul Hindemith, *Symphonia Serena* (Dallas), Concerto for Piano and Orchestra (Cleveland); George Antheil, Concerto in D (Dallas); Erich Korngold, Violin Concerto (St. Louis); Heitor Villa-Lobos, conducting, *Bachianas Brasileiras* (New York); Don Gillis, Symphony no. 5½ (Boston).

Opera
Metropolitan: Ferruccio Tagliavini (debut), *La bohème;* Robert Merrill, *Il barbiere di Siviglia;* Astrid Varnay, *Die Walküre;* Jussi Bjoerling, *Roméo et Juliette;* Regina Resnik, *The Warrior* (Barnard Rogers, premiere)

New York: *The Medium, The Telephone* (Gian Carlo Menotti); *Street Scene* (Kurt Weill); *Trial of Lucullus* (Roger Sessions). Max Leavitt directs the Lemonade Opera Company in its first performance, *The Mother of Us All* (Virgil Thomson, Gertrude Stein); *The Cradle Will Rock* (Marc Blitzstein) is performed on Broadway.

Philadelphia: *Street Scene* (Kurt Weill, premiere)

Lenox, Mass.: *Idomeneo* (Mozart, premiere)

Jascha Heifetz, who first gained recognition as a child prodigy. *Movie Star News.*

Chicago: *Amelia Goes to the Ball* (Gian Carlo Menotti); *The Emperor Jones* (Henry Gruenberg); Kirsten Flagstad, *Tristan und Isolde*

Central City, Colo.: Regina Resnik, *Fidelio;* Leopold Simoneau, *Martha*

Music Notes
Margaret Truman makes her debut with the Detroit Symphony Orchestra • Pablo Casals vows to give no more public performances as long as Franco is in power • The National Symphony gives a series of "Hit Parade" concerts in Washington, and polls are held in hotel lobbies, groceries, and drugstores to determine public taste • $70,000 is raised in New York for the Palestine Philharmonic Symphony.

Art _____

Painting

Charles Sheeler, *Classic Still Life*
Stuart Davis, *Iris*
William Baziotes, *Dwarf*
Jackson Pollock, *War, Full Fathom Five*
Arshile Gorky, *The Betrothal II, Agony*
Stephen Greene, *The Deposition, The Burial*
Willem de Kooning, *Noon*
Robert Motherwell, *Western Air* (1946–47), *The Red Skirt*
Barnett Newman, *The Euclidean Abyss*
Hans Hofmann, *Ecstasy*

Sculpture

Theodore Roszak, *The Specter of Kitty Hawk*

Alexander Calder, *Little Red under Blue*
Mahonri Young, Mormon Memorial, Salt Lake City
Isamu Noguchi, *Kouros, Night Land*
José de Rivera, *Yellow Black*
William Zorach, *The Future Generation*

Architecture

Kauffmann House, Palm Springs, Calif. (Richard Neutra)
Robinson House, Williamstown, Mass. (Marcel Breuer)
Architect's House, New Canaan, Conn. (Philip Johnson)

Important Exhibitions

Museums

New York: *Metropolitan:* Costumes 1830–1912; Egyptian art; Far Eastern art; Survey of American art. *Museum of Modern Art:* Ben Shahn retrospective; Alfred Stieglitz memorial. *Whitney:* Painting in France 1939–47; Braque's "The Studio";

French contemporary paintings of artists under 49 years old

Chicago: Stieglitz collection of porcelain; Survey of abstract and surreal art

Baltimore: 1,000 Byzantine objects

Cleveland: Degas; Gold objects

Major Prizes: Zoltan Sapeshy (Carnegie); Steumpfig (Corcoran); Guston (National Academy of Design); Baziotes (Chicago Art Institute); Kallem (Pepsi-Cola)

Art Briefs

Jean Dubuffet holds his first New York one-man show • Chrysler joins the Encyclopædia Britannica, Pepsi-Cola, and Gimbels in the industrial patronage of the arts • The State Department recalls from Czechoslovakia 79 American paintings sent on a goodwill tour but used for Communist propaganda • The Bay Psalm Book of 1640, the first book printed in America, sells for $151,000.

Dance _____

Premieres

Ballet Theater: *Theme and Variations* (George Balanchine), Alicia Markova, Igor Youskevitch

Ballet Society: *The Seasons* (Merce Cunningham), Tanaquil Le Clercq

Gregory Peck and John Garfield in *Gentleman's Agreement,* with Peck posing as a Jew in order to investigate upper middle class anti-Semitism. *Movie Star News.*

Books

Fiction

Critics' Choice
The Victim, Saul Bellow
Bend Sinister, Vladimir Nabokov
The Harder They Fall, Budd Schulberg
Reflections in a Golden Eye, Carson McCullers
The Big Sky, A. B. Guthrie
End as a Man, Calder Willingham
Knock on Any Door, Willard Motley
The Middle of the Journey, Lionel Trilling
ᴥ *The Diary of Anne Frank*, Anne Frank
ᴥ *Dr. Faustus*, Thomas Mann

Best-Sellers
The Miracle of the Bells, Russell Janney
The Moneyman, Thomas B. Costain
Gentleman's Agreement, Laura Z. Hobson
Lydia Bailey, Kenneth Roberts
The Vixens, Frank Yerby
The Wayward Bus, John Steinbeck
House Divided, Ben Ames Williams
Kingsblood Royal, Sinclair Lewis
East Side, West Side, Marcia Davenport
Prince of Foxes, Samuel Shellabarger

Nonfiction

Critics' Choice
Ordeal of the Union, Allan Nevins
On Understanding Science, J. B. Conant
The Cold War, Walter Lippmann
American Memoir, Henry Seidel Canby
The Nuremberg Case, Robert H. Jackson
Command Decision, William Wister Haines
The Times of Melville and Whitman, Van Wyck Brooks
End of a Berlin Diary, William Shirer
The Well-Wrought Urn, Cleanth Brooks
Essay on Morals, Philip Wylie
History of Naval Operations in World War II, ed. Samuel Eliot Morison
Philosopher's Quest, Irwin Edman
Modern Woman: The Lost Sex, Ferdinand Lundberg, Marynia Farnham
ᴥ *Existentialism*, Jean-Paul Sartre

Best-Sellers
Peace of Mind, Joshua L. Liebman
Information Please Almanac, 1947, ed. John Kieran
Inside U.S.A., John Gunther

A Study of History, Arnold J. Toynbee
Speaking Frankly, James F. Byrnes
Human Destiny, Pierre Lecomte du Noüy
The Egg and I, Betty MacDonald
The American Past, Roger Butterfield
Together, Katharine T. Marshall
The Fireside Book of Folk Songs, ed. Margaret Boni

Poetry
Wallace Stevens, *Transport to Summer*
Richard Wilbur, *The Beautiful Changes*
Conrad Aiken, *The Kid*
Robert Frost, *A Masque of Mercy*
Karl Shapiro, *Trials of a Poet*
Robert Duncan, *Heavenly City, Earthly City*

Pulitzer Prizes
Tales of the South Pacific, James A. Michener (fiction)
Across the Wide Missouri, Bernard De Voto (U.S. history)
Forgotten First Citizen: John Bigelow, Margaret Clapp (biography)
Age of Anxiety, W. H. Auden (poetry)

Science and Technology

Naval expeditions under Adm. Richard Byrd and Comdr. Finn Ronne explore Antarctica.

A United Airlines plane over Idaho reports "flying discs," "flat and round" and "larger than aircraft."

The Atomic Bomb Commission reports abnormalities in the offspring of bomb survivors.

Edwin Land announces the invention of a camera that develops and prints a picture in one minute.

A cure for schizophrenia through prefrontal lobotomy is announced by Spring Grove Hospital, Maryland.

The discovery of the anticoagulant heparin is reported.

ᴥ Thor Heyerdal sets sail on a raft, the *Kon Tiki*, from Peru toward Tahiti.

Nobel Prize
Carl F. and Gerty Cori win the prize in physiology and medicine for the discovery of the catalytic metabolism of glycogen.

Sports

Baseball

Jackie Robinson (Brooklyn, NL) becomes the first black major league player and wins the Rookie of the Year Award.

Ralph Kiner (Pittsburgh, NL) hits eight home runs in four games.

In the World Series, Cookie Lavagetto (Brooklyn, NL) hits a double ending the no-hitter of Floyd Bevan (New York, AL) after 8⅔ innings and beats him 3–2.

Champions

Batting	Home runs
Harry Walker (St. Louis, Philadelphia, NL), .363	Ralph Kiner (Pittsburgh, NL), 51
Ted Williams (Boston, AL), .343	John Mize (New York, NL), 51
Pitching	
Larry Jansen (New York, NL), 21–5	
Allie Reynolds (New York, AL), 19–8	

Football

Charlie Trippi, Georgia tailback, signs with the NFL's Chicago Cardinals for a record $100,000 for four years.

NFL Season Leaders: Sammy Baugh (Washington), passing; Steve Van Buren (Philadelphia), rushing; Jim Keane (Chicago Bears), receiving.

College All-Americans: Chuck Bednarik (C), Pennsylvania; Doak Walker (B), Southern Methodist; John Lujack (QB), Notre Dame; Bob Chappuis (B), Michigan.

Bowls (Jan. 1, 1948)

Rose: Michigan 49–Southern California 0
Orange: Georgia Tech 20–Kansas 14
Cotton: Southern Methodist 13–Pennsylvania State 13
Sugar: Texas 27–Alabama 7

Other Sports

Boxing: Rocky Graziano KO's Tony Zale in the sixth for the middleweight title before a record indoor gate of $422,918. Sugar Ray Robinson wins the welterweight title.

Tennis: Jack Kramer and Bobby Riggs tour as pros and draw $248,000 for 89 appearances.

Winners

World Series	College Basketball
New York (AL) 4	Holy Cross (NCAA)
Brooklyn (NL) 3	Utah (NIT)
MVP	*Player of the Year*
NL–Robert Elliott, Boston	Gerald Tucker, Oklahoma
AL–Joe DiMaggio, New York	*Stanley Cup*
	Toronto
NFL	*US Tennis Open*
Chicago (Cards) 28–Philadelphia 21	Men: John Kramer
	Women: Louise Brough
College Football	*USGA Open*
Notre Dame	Lou Worsham
Heisman Trophy	*Kentucky Derby*
John Lujack, Notre Dame	Jet Pilot (E. Guerin, jockey)

Fashion

For Women: Dior's "New Look" revolutionizes fashion history. The squarish straight skirt and flat hip look, popular for nearly a decade, is replaced by the swirling "feminine" dress, 12 inches from the floor with a natural shoulder and an entirely rounded look. Emphasis is on the hips, tiny waist, and pointed bosom. Some 450 Dior silks are copied by the thousands in $20 rayons. "New" also are suits and coats lengthened to the ankle, fitted jackets, and circle, often pegged, skirts. Complementing the round hips and small waists are spike heels with straps and "naked" sandals, all designed to emphasize the leg. To help accomplish the new look are boned girdles with waistbands and padded bras that flatten the midriff, cinch the waist, and point the breasts. Other innovations include the pillbox hat and beret, worn over one ear; fezzes with veils and feathers; V-neck and frothy blouses; the evening dress in pale blue, burgundy, green, cocoa, and brown taffeta or satin (although the strapless ball dress remains, worn with a tiara and long gloves above the elbow), espadrilles, long pearl chains, short pearl dog collars, and rhinestones. Flat ballet shoes remain very popular.

High-fashion note: Dior's first collection, February 12

Jackie Robinson, the first black in organized baseball. *Movie Star News.*

Kaleidoscope

- Oral Roberts gains a following as he claims healing through prayer and assistance from God.
- Publishing events include Mickey Spillane's sexy detective fiction, *I, the Jury,* Dr. Eustace Chesser's sexual manual *Love without Fear,* and Arnold Toynbee's study of the rise and fall of civilizations, *A Study of History.*
- The U.S. Motion Picture Association votes for stronger regulations against the glorification of crime on the screen; Communists are barred from holding office by the Screen Directors Guild.
- Gillette and Ford pay $65,000 to sponsor the first TV World Series; an estimated 3.7 million watch the Dodgers and Yankees on all three networks.
- Fleer's bubble gum blowing contests reach fad proportions.
- A fire destroys the $5 million Grace Lines pier 57 in New York; 144 firemen are injured.
- The United States is urged to study bacteriological warfare by the American Association of Scientific Workers.
- Kaiser-Frazier manufactures the first new make of car in more than 20 years, the 1947 Frazier.
- The GM-UAW settlement agrees to a cost-of-living raise for its workers, the first of its kind.
- The American Friends Service Committee wins the Nobel Peace Prize.
- Four million returning GI veterans take advantage of the GI bill and its broad opportunities for education, housing, and business.
- College enrollment rises to an all-time high of 6.1 million students.
- The first Pan American world service costs $1,700.
- A 25.8-inch snowfall paralyzes New York City for 16 hours.
- The KKK charter is revoked by the Georgia Supreme Court.
- New York bans Howard Fast's *Citizen Thomas Paine* from school libraries. Massachusetts rules *Forever Amber* not obscene.
- Soviets use repeated vetoes and boycott the UN Trusteeship Council with claims of "barbarous American imperialism."
- A new member is added to the president's cabinet to unify the army and navy commands—the "Secretary of Defense."
- Tax is reduced 10 percent on incomes of $10,000, 48 to 65 percent on incomes over $100,000.

First Appearances: Transit fares up from 5¢ to 10¢ (New York City), end of street cars (New York City), camera zoom lens demonstration, UN flag, Almond Joy, Redi Whip, Minute Maid Corp., Chun King, MSG as "Accent," Ajax, continuous coal-cutting machine, Everglades National Park, commercial tubeless auto tires, Sony, Cannes Film Festival, Edinburgh Festival, "Steve Canyon," Tony awards

- The Freedom Train, with 100 of the United States' greatest documents, tours America; the Friendship Train donates 200 carloads of food to France and Italy.
- "Let us not be deceived. Today we are in the midst of a *cold* war," says Bernard Baruch, in Columbia, South Carolina. Walter Lippmann publicizes the phrase.
- In an article signed "X" in *Foreign Affairs,* George Kennan proposes a policy of "containment" of Russia, which becomes the basis of U.S. policy.
- The CIA is authorized by Congress to counter Soviet espionage.
- A Hollywood blacklist of alleged Communist sympathizers includes 300 writers, directors, and actors.
- Jackie Robinson is refused hotel rooms in numerous cities and is abused verbally both on and off the field; he remarks: "I've got two cheeks."
- Seventeen children die from an overdose of Anabis, a tonsillitis treatment, now banned.
- "A sleeping sickness is spreading among the women of the land," remarks Fannie Hurst. "They are retrogressing into . . . that thing called Home."
- The American Meat Institute reports a turn from wartime casseroles to meat five nights a week.
- Pittsburgh begins a program to clean the smoky air.

1948

Economic Profile
  Dow-Jones: − High 193–
    Low 165
  GNP: +11%
  Inflation: +5.2%
  Unemployment: 3.8%
Balance of international
  payments: +$5.4 billion
Military on duty: 1,445,000
Voter participation: 63%
  (1940); 53% (1948)
Population with religious
  affiliation: 79 million
Buick Roadmaster: $2,900
DeSoto convertible: $2,500
Packard: $4,300
Rolls-Royce convertible:
  $18,500
Nash convertible: $3,100
Krum chocolate assortment:
  92¢ (lb.)
Schenley whiskey: $4.05 (⅘)
Margaret O'Brien "Memory
  Book" dress: $5
Best & Co. girls' shoes: $5

Deaths

Charles Beard, Ruth
  Benedict, Sergei
  Eisenstein, D. W. Griffith,
  Charles Evans Hughes,
  Rabbi Joshua Liebman,
  Fred Niblo, George
  Herman ("Babe") Ruth,
  Dame May Whitty, Orville
  Wright

In the News

TRUMAN ASKS VOLUNTARY RESTRAINT OF GAS AND OIL USE . . .
MUNDT ACT AUTHORIZES VOICE OF AMERICA . . . MAHATMA GANDHI
IS ASSASSINATED BY HINDU EXTREMIST . . . SUPREME COURT RULES
THAT STATE MONEY CANNOT BE USED FOR RELIGIOUS SCHOOLS . . .
COMMUNISTS GAIN ON CHIANG KAI-SHEK . . . 350,000 COAL MINERS
STRIKE, PENSION IS MAJOR ISSUE . . . TAX REDUCTION IS VOTED
OVER TRUMAN VETO . . . EUROPEAN RECOVERY PROGRAM
IMPLEMENTS MARSHALL PROGRAM, $5.3 BILLION IS APPROPRIATED
. . . RUSSIA CONDEMNS MARSHALL PLAN . . . RUSSIA BANS ALL
LAND TRAFFIC TO BERLIN, WEST AIRLIFTS SUPPLIES . . . UN PASSES
PALESTINE PARTITION PLAN, ISRAEL IS CREATED . . . EGYPT, SYRIA
AND TRANSJORDAN ATTACK ISRAEL . . . U.S. RECOGNIZES ISRAEL . . .
YUGOSLOVIA IS EXPELLED FROM COMINFORM . . . TRUMAN IS
NOMINATED BY DEMOCRATS, THOMAS DEWEY BY GOP, PROGRESSIVES
NOMINATE HENRY WALLACE . . . DIXIECRATS BOLT DEMOCRATIC
CONVENTION ON STATES' RIGHTS ISSUE AND NOMINATE STROM
THURMOND . . . HUAC FINDS SPY MICROFILM HIDDEN IN PUMPKIN
. . . DISPLACED PERSONS BILL IS PASSED, 205,000 ARE ADMITTED . . .
CHINESE COMMUNISTS DECLARE REPUBLIC IN NORTH CHINA . . .
TRUMAN CALLS SPECIAL SESSION OF CONGRESS AS COST OF LIVING
HITS ALL-TIME HIGH . . . 12 COMMUNIST PARTY LEADERS ARE
INDICTED FOR SMITH ACT VIOLATION . . . FEDERAL RESERVE IMPOSES
INSTALLMENT CURBS . . . RUSSIAN TEACHER JUMPS FROM SOVIET
EMBASSY WINDOW TO U.S. . . . SOVIETS CLOSE U.S. CONSULATES IN
MOSCOW, U.S. RECIPROCATES . . . 4 POWERS DISAGREE IN MOSCOW
OVER GERMAN ISSUE . . . TOJO AND 5 OTHERS HANG FOR WAR
CRIMES . . . TRUMAN DEFEATS DEWEY IN GIANT UPSET . . .
CARDINAL MINDSZENTY IS ARRESTED IN HUNGARY . . .

Quotes

Dewey's presidential victory was considered so certain that premature reports went to press. *Smithsonian Institution.*

President Harry S Truman. *Library of Congress.*

"Government will remain big, active, and expensive under President Thomas E. Dewey."
— *Wall Street Journal* (October)

"[The Truman civil rights plan] wants to reduce us to the status of a mongrel, inferior race, mixed in blood, our Anglo-Saxon heritage a mockery."
— Alabama governor F. Dixon, keynote speech, Dixiecrat convention

"I'll mow'em down, Alben. I'll give 'em Hell."
— Truman to Vice-President Barkley (overheard)

"Republicans are . . . bloodsuckers with offices in Wall Street, princes of privilege, plunderers."
— Harry S Truman, "whistlestop" speech

"We're about as much in favor of Communism as J. Edgar Hoover."
— Bogart and Bacall

"I love your pictures and your directions. So if there's ever a small part for a little Swedish actress, please think of me."
— Letter to Roberto Rossellini from Ingrid Bergman

"A smart teenager thinks about how to start a conversation . . . [and] looks over . . . conversation starters, . . . like animals. [He might say] 'My dog has fleas—what'll I do?' "
— Edith Heal, *Teen Age Manual*

Ads

You can't baby a baby too much—whether she's 1, 21, or simply not telling.
—Give her Yolande Handmades.
(Yolande Lingerie)

Air Power is Peace Power—Lockheed
(Lockheed Aircraft)

One of America's Greatest Success Stories—Kaiser-Frazier
(Kaiser-Frazier Automobile)

High Blood Pressure . . . a fortunate warning.
(Upjohn Pharmaceuticals)

Railroads can't afford *not* to modernize!
(Chesapeake and Ohio Lines)

Which twin has the Toni?
(Toni Permanents)

Is fish really brain food?
(American Cyanimid Corp.)

It's in the bag.
(Ballantine Beer)

TV

Premieres

"The Morey Amsterdam Show," Art Carney,
Jacqueline Susann
"Douglas Edwards and the News"
"Candid Camera," Allen Funt
"The Toast of the Town," Ed Sullivan
"Arthur Godfrey's Talent Scouts"
"The Milton Berle Show [Texaco Star Theater]"
"Studio One" ("The Storm," Margaret Sullavan)
"The Chesterfield Supper Club," Perry Como
"Philco Television Playhouse"
"The Bigelow Show," Paul Winchell and Jerry
Mahoney
"Camel Newsreel Theater," John Cameron Swayze,
first nightly news show

Specials

"Julius Caesar" (in modern dress, "Studio One");
"The NFL" (first regular pro sports event)

Emmy Awards

"Pantomine Quiz Time" (most popular); Shirley
Dinsdale (personality); "The Necklace" on "Your
Show Time" (TV-made film)

Radio

Premieres

"Life with Luigi," J. Carrol Naish
"Stop the Music," Bert Parks
"This Is Your Life," Ralph Edwards
"Our Miss Brooks," Eve Arden, Jeff Chandler
"My Favorite Husband," Lucille Ball, Gale Gordon

Most Popular Programs: "Walter Winchell," "Lux
Radio Theater," "Arthur Godfrey," "Duffy's
Tavern," "Phil Harris–Alice Faye"

Most Popular Comedy/Variety Shows: "Bing
Crosby," "Dorothy Lamour," "Duffy's Tavern,"
"Jack Benny," "Fred Allen," "Fibber McGee and
Molly," "George Burns and Gracie Allen"

Movies

Openings

Hamlet (Laurence Olivier), Laurence Olivier, Jean
Simmons
Johnny Belinda (Jean Negulesco), Jane Wyman, Lew
Ayres
The Red Shoes (Michael Powell, Emeric
Pressburger), Moira Shearer, Marius Goring
The Snake Pit (Anatole Litvak), Olivia de Havilland
The Treasure of Sierre Madre (John Huston),
Humphrey Bogart, Walter Huston
Sitting Pretty (Walter Lang), Clifton Webb, Robert
Young, Maureen O'Hara
I Remember Mama (George Stevens), Irene Dunne,
Barbara Bel Geddes
Sorry, Wrong Number (Anatole Litvak), Barbara
Stanwyck, Burt Lancaster
Key Largo (John Huston), Humphrey Bogart, Lauren
Bacall, Edward G. Robinson
The Naked City (Jules Dassin), Barry Fitzgerald,
Howard Duff
Red River (Howard Hawks), John Wayne,
Montgomery Clift, Joanne Dru
The Three Musketeers (George Sidney), Lana Turner,
Gene Kelly
A Foreign Affair (Billy Wilder), Marlene Dietrich,
Jean Arthur

Letter from an Unknown Woman (Max Ophuls), Joan
Fontaine, Louis Jourdan
The Pirate (Vincente Minnelli), Judy Garland, Gene
Kelly
Easter Parade (Charles Walters), Fred Astaire, Ann
Miller, Judy Garland

Academy Awards

Best Picture: *Hamlet*
Best Director: John Huston (*The Treasure of Sierra
Madre*)
Best Actress: Jane Wyman (*Johnny Belinda*)
Best Actor: Laurence Olivier (*Hamlet*)

Top Box-Office Stars

Bing Crosby, Betty Grable, Abbott and Costello,
Gary Cooper, Bob Hope, Humphrey Bogart, Clark
Gable, Cary Grant, Spencer Tracy, Ingrid Bergman

Stars of Tomorrow

Jane Powell, Cyd Charisse, Ann Blyth, Celeste
Holm, Robert Ryan, Angela Lansbury, Jean Peters,
Mona Freeman, Eleanor Parker, Doris Day

Popular Music

Hit Songs
"Buttons and Bows"
"It's a Most Unusual Day"
"A—You're Adorable"
"Cuanto le Gusta"
"So in Love"
"Mañana"
"Enjoy Yourself—It's Later than You Think"
"If I Had a Hammer"
"Baby, It's Cold Outside"
"On a Slow Boat to China"

Top Records

Albums: *Al Jolson, Vol. III* (Al Jolson); *Merry Christmas* (Bing Crosby); *A Sentimental Date with Perry Como* (Perry Como); *Down Memory Lane* (Vaughn Monroe); *A Presentation of Progressive Jazz* (Stan Kenton); *Busy Fingers* (Three Sons)

Singles: *Twelfth Street Rag* (Pee Wee Hunt); *Once in Love with Amy* (Ray Bolger); *Nature Boy* (Nat "King" Cole); *It's Magic* (Doris Day); *The Streets of Laredo* (Dennis Day); *My Happiness* (Ella Fitzgerald); *My Darling, My Darling* (Jo Stafford); *It's Too Soon to Know* (Dinah Washington); *Now Is the Hour* (Bing Crosby); *Lazy River* (Mills Brothers); *Because* (Perry Como); *The Fat Man* (Fats Domino). *Early Autumn* (Stan Getz);

Country: *Bouquet of Roses,* (Eddy Arnold); *Smoke, Smoke, Smoke that Cigarette* (Tex Williams)

Jazz and Big Bands
Stan Kenton gives a concert at the Hollywood Bowl. Earl Hines joins Louis Armstrong. Many of the 52d Street, New York, jazz clubs close.

Top Performers *(Downbeat):*
Benny Goodman (soloist); Duke Ellington (band); Errol Garner, Shelly Manne, Flip Phillips, Charlie Shavers (instrumentalists); Charlie Ventura (jazz group); Sarah Vaughan, Billy Eckstine (vocalists)

Theater

Broadway Openings

Plays
Mister Roberts (Thomas Heggen, Joshua Logan), Henry Fonda, David Wayne, William Harrigan, Robert Keith
Anne of the Thousand Days (Maxwell Anderson), Rex Harrison, Joyce Redman
Edward, My Son (Robert Morley, Noel Langley), Robert Morley
The Madwoman of Chaillot (Jean Giraudoux), Estelle Winwood, Nydia Westman
Summer and Smoke (Tennessee Williams), Margaret Phillips, Tod Andrews
The Respectful Prostitute (Jean-Paul Sartre), Meg Mundy
Life with Mother (Howard Lindsay, Russel Crouse), Dorothy Stickney
Red Gloves (Jean-Paul Sartre), Charles Boyer
Goodbye, My Fancy (Fay Kanin), Madeleine Carroll, Conrad Nagel, Sam Wanamaker
The Silver Whistle (Robert McEnroe), José Ferrer

Musicals
Inside U.S.A. (Arthur Schwartz, Howard Dietz), Beatrice Lillie, Jack Haley
Look, Ma, I'm Dancin' (Hugh Martin), Nancy Walker, Harold Lang
Love Life (Kurt Weill, Alan Jay Lerner), Nanette Fabray, Ray Middleton
Magdalena (Heitor Villa-Lobos, Robert Wright, George Forrest), John Raitt, Irra Petina
Where's Charley? (Frank Loesser), Ray Bolger
Kiss Me, Kate (Cole Porter), Alfred Drake, Patricia Morison
Lend an Ear (Charles Gaynor), William Eythe, Carol Channing

Classics and Revivals On and Off Broadway
Private Lives (Noel Coward), Tallulah Bankhead; *The Play's the Thing* (Molnár), Faye Emerson, Louis Calhern; *Ghosts, Hedda Gabler* (Ibsen), Eva Le Gallienne; *Macbeth,* Michael Redgrave, Flora Robson; *John Bull's Other Island* (George Bernard Shaw), Michael MacLiammoir, Dublin Gate Theater

Pulitzer Prize
A Streetcar Named Desire, Tennessee Williams

Classical Music

Compositions

John Cage, Sonatas and Interludes
Howard Hanson, Piano Concerto
Walter Piston, Toccata for Orchestra, Suite no. 2
Milton Babbitt, Three Compositions for Piano,
    Composition for Twelve Instruments
Elliott Carter, Sonata for Cello
Roy Harris, Elegy and Paean for Viola and Orchestra
William Schuman, Symphony no. 6
Aaron Copland, Concerto for Clarinet and Strings,
    with harp and piano
Virgil Thomson, *Louisiana Story*

Important Events

A record number of festivals occur during the year,
as well as TV music specials (Toscanini and the NBC
Symphony performing Wagner; Eugene Ormandy
and the Philadelphia Symphony with "The
Classics").

Debuts: Alfred Brendel, Paul Badura-Skoda,
Raymond Lewenthal

First Performances

Rachmaninoff, Symphony in D minor (Philadelphia);
Samuel Barber, James Agee, *Knoxville: Summer of
1915;* Walter Piston, Symphony no. 3 (Boston);
David Diamond, Symphony no. 4 (Boston); Heitor
Villa-Lobos, *Mandu-Carara* (New York); Paul
Creston, Fantasy for Trombone and Orchestra (Los
Angeles); Wallingford Riegger, Symphony no. 3
(New York); Virgil Thomson, *The Seine at Night*
(Kansas City); George Antheil, Symphony no. 4
(Philadelphia); Norman Dello Joio, Three Symphonic
Dances (Pittsburgh); Harold Shapero, Symphony for
Classical Orchestra (Boston).

Opera

Metropolitan: Ferruccio Tagliavini, *L'elisir
d'amore; Peter Grimes* (Benjamin Britten)

New York City: *The Old Maid and the Thief* (Gian
Carlo Menotti, premiere)

Central City, Colo.: Regina Resnik, *Die Fledermaus*

San Francisco: Ezio Pinza, *Boris Godunov* (Pinza's
last Boris); Tito Gobbi (debut) *Il barbiere di Siviglia*

Music Notes

As a promotional activity, the Buffalo Philharmonic
provides babysitters for season ticket holders •
Vincenzo Bellini's grandson, Ferruccio Burco, age 9,
makes his Carnegie Hall debut and conducts Wagner
and Beethoven.

Far left: Milton
Berle, "Mr.
Television." *Movie
Star News*.

The great
Shakespearean
Laurence Olivier
starred in and
directed *Hamlet*.
Movie Star News.

Art

Painting

Andrew Wyeth,
Christina's World
Hans Hofmann,
Construction
Willem de Kooning,
Woman
Clyfford Still, *1948-D,
World Tablet, Stamos*
Jackson Pollock,
*Composition No. 1,
November 1, 1948*
Mark Tobey, *Tropicalism*
Ben Shahn, *Miners'
Wives*
Edward Hopper,
Seven A.M.
Thomas Hart Benton,
Poker Night
Arshile Gorky, *The
Betrothed*
Lyonel Feininger, *The
Lake*
Barnett Newman, *Two
Edges*

Sculpture

Jacques Lipchitz,
Primordial Figure
(1947–48)

Alexander Calder,
Aspen, Snow Flurry
Richard Lippold,
Primordial Figure
Joseph Cornell, *Multiple
Cubes*
Seymour Lipton,
Imprisoned Figure

Architecture

Baker House,
Massachusetts
Institute of
Technology,
Cambridge (Alvar
Aalto)
Container Corporation of
America, Greensboro,
N.C. (Walter Gropius)
Graduate Housing Unit,
Harvard University,
Cambridge, Mass.
(Gropius)
The Saarinen design for
the Jefferson National
Expansion Memorial
in St. Louis wins
$40,000.

Important Exhibitions

Museums

New York: *Metropolitan:* French tapestries; World-famous masterpieces of painting from the Berlin museums; "From Casablanca to Calcutta" (costumes, fabrics). *Whitney:* Yasuo Kuniyoshi. *Museum of Modern Art:* Cole, Nadelman, Gabo-Pevsner

Boston: Japanese art; English watercolors; Kokoschka

Philadelphia: Matisse retrospective

Cleveland, Museum of Modern Art: Bonnard

Washington: Dutch Art

St. Louis: Max Beckmann

Art Briefs

The Des Moines Art Center (Saarinen) is built, the first museum construction since Pearl Harbor • Motherwell, Rothko, Hare, Baziotes, and Still found the Subjects of the Artist School in New York • Major sales include van der Weyden's *View of Delft* ($15,000) and Degas's pastel of Mary Cassatt ($4,000) • German masterpieces found by the U.S. Third Army in a salt mine near Merkers are sent on a tour of the United States; proceeds go to German children in the American zone.

Andrew Wyeth, *Christina's World*, 1948. Tempera. 32¼ × 47¾". *Collection, The Museum of Modern Art, New York.*

Dance

Ballet Society accepts New York City Center's offer of a home and becomes the New York City Ballet. In the company are Maria Tallchief, Tanaquil Le Clercq, Nicholas Magallanes, Francisco Moncion, Herbert Bliss, and Todd Bolender. Its first program consists of *Serenade, Orpheus,* and *Symphony in C,* all by Balanchine.
Alwin Nikolais becomes director of the New York Henry Street Playhouse.

Ballet Theater: *Fall River Legend* (Agnes de Mille), Nora Kaye, Lucia Chase, Sallie Wilson

Books

Fiction

Critics' Choice

Other Voices, Other Rooms, Truman Capote
Intruder in the Dust, William Faulkner
Remembrance Rock, Carl Sandburg
The City and the Pillar, Gore Vidal
Act of Love, Ira Wolfert
The Ides of March, Thornton Wilder
The World Is a Wedding, Delmore Schwartz
Circus in the Attic, Robert Penn Warren
🕭 *The Plague*, Albert Camus
🕭 *Cry, the Beloved Country*, Alan Paton

Best-Sellers

The Big Fisherman, Lloyd C. Douglas
The Naked and the Dead, Norman Mailer
Dinner at Antoine's, Frances Parkinson Keyes
The Bishop's Mantle, Agnes Sligh Turnbull
Tomorrow Will Be Better, Betty Smith
The Golden Hawk, Frank Yerby
Raintree County, Ross Lockridge, Jr.

Shannon's Way, A. J. Cronin
Pilgrim's Inn, Elizabeth Goudge
The Young Lions, Irwin Shaw

Nonfiction

Critics' Choice

The American Political Tradition, Richard Hofstadter
The Protestant Era, Paul Tillich
Jefferson, the Virginian, vol. 1, Dumas Malone
Our Plundered Planet, Fairfield Osborn
No Place to Hide, David Bradley
The Early Tales of the Atomic Age, Daniel Lang
The Price of Power, Hanson W. Baldwin
The United States and China, John King Fairbank
World Communism, Martin Ebon
The Nightmare of American Foreign Policy, Edgar Ansel Mowrer

Best-Sellers

Crusade in Europe, Dwight D. Eisenhower
How to Stop Worrying and Start Living, Dale Carnegie
Peace of Mind, Joshua L. Liebman
Sexual Behavior in the Human Male, A. C. Kinsey

Wine, Women and Words, Billy Rose
The Life and Times of the Shmoo, Al Capp
The Gathering Storm, Winston Churchill
Roosevelt and Hopkins, Robert E. Sherwood
A Guide to Confident Living, Norman Vincent Peale
The Plague and I, Betty MacDonald

Poetry

John Berryman, *The Dispossessed*
Theodore Roethke, *The Lost Sun*
Allen Tate, *Poems, 1922–1947*
Ezra Pound, *The Pisan Cantos*
Robinson Jeffers, *The Double Axe*
Randall Jarrell, *Losses*
William Carlos Williams, *Paterson*, Book Two

Pulitzer Prizes

Guard of Honor, James Gould Cozzens (fiction)
The Disruption of American Democracy, Roy F. Nichols (U.S. history)
Roosevelt and Hopkins, Robert E. Sherwood (biography)
Terror and Decorum, Peter Viereck (poetry)

Science and Technology

Captain Charles Yaeger breaks the sound barrier in a rocket-powered Bell X-1 at 35,000 feet.
Cmdr. Finn Ronne reports that Antarctica is a single continent, not two islands.
The world's largest reflector telescope, 200 inches, is dedicated at Mt. Palomar Observatory, California.
The University of Chicago and seven major corporations announce plans for cooperative atomic research for industrial use.
John Bardeen, William Shockley, and Walter Brattain of Bell Telephone Laboratories develop the transistor.

A new liquid hydrogen fuel for rockets is announced by H. L. Johnson, who says it will "send men to the moon."
Immunologist Bettina Carver, Pittsburgh, develops Rh hapten to save "Rh" babies.
The human poliomyelitis virus in concentrated form is isolated at the University of Minnesota.
Antibiotics aureomycin and chloromycetin are developed; vitamin B_{12}, the cure for pernicious anemia, is isolated.
Success with radiocobalt treatment of cancer is reported by the AEC.

Sports _____

Baseball

"Spahn and Sain and two days of rain" is the pennant-winning Boston Braves' motto. Cleveland beats Boston, 8–3, in the first American League pennant playoff tie.

Champions _____

Batting	Home runs
Stan Musial (St. Louis, NL), .376	Ralph Kiner (Pittsburgh, NL), 40
Ted Williams (Boston, AL), .369	John Mize (New York, NL), 40
Pitching	
Harry Brecheen (St. Louis, NL), 20–9	
Jack Kramer (Boston, AL), 18–5	

Football

NFL Season Leaders: Tommy Thompson (Philadelphia), passing; Steve Van Buren (Philadelphia) rushing; Tom Fears (Los Angeles), receiving.

College All-Americans: Charlie Justice (B), North Carolina; Chuck Bednarik (C), Pennsylvania; Jackie Jensen (B), California; Johnny Rauch (Q), Georgia.

Bowls (Jan. 1, 1949)	Cotton: Southern
Rose: Northwestern 20–California 14	Methodist 21–Oregon 13
Orange: Texas 41–Georgia 28	Sugar: Oklahoma 14–North Carolina 6

Basketball

NBL star George Mikan signs with the BAA; four NBL teams then merge with the BAA, forming the NBA. The BAA champion is Baltimore, with Max Zaslofsky. The Harlem Globetrotters beat the NBL champs 61–59.

Olympics

In the 1948 Olympics at London, U.S. gold medal winners include Harrison Dillard (100m, 10.3s), Mel Patton (200m, 21.1s), Mal Whitfield (800m, 1:49.2), Willie Steele (broadjump, 25'8"), Guinn Smith (pole vault, 14', 1¼"), Wilbur Thompson (16 lb. shot put, 56'2"), Bob Matthias (decathlon), Walter Ris (100m, swim, 57.3s). In the Winter Games at St. Moritz, Switzerland, Richard Button wins figure skating.

Other Sports

Horse Racing: Citation, ridden by Eddie Arcaro, wins the Triple Crown.

Golf: Ben Hogan wins the U.S. Open with a record 5 under par and is the top PGA money winner with $36,000.

Winners _____

World Series	College Basketball
Cleveland (AL) 4	Kentucky (NCAA)
Boston (NL) 2	St. Louis (NIT)
MVP	Player of the Year
NL–Stan Musial, St. Louis	Ed McCauley, St. Louis
AL–Lou Boudreau, Cleveland	Stanley Cup
	Toronto
NFL	US Tennis Open
Philadelphia 7–Chicago (Cards) 0	Men: Pancho Gonzales
	Women: Margaret Osborne DuPont
College Football	
Michigan	USGA Open
Heisman Trophy	Ben Hogan
Doak Walker, Southern Methodist	Kentucky Derby
	Citation (E. Arcaro, jockey)

Fashion _____

For Women: Dior's "New Look" continues, and jackets are even shorter and more fitted until they are rib tight; skirts are straight, except at the back. The tank coat is replaced by either the belted greatcoat or the fitted one with back fullness or pleats. Shoulder capes on coats are also fashionable. Many styles seem more interesting from the back and are called "going-away styles." At the end of the year, the empire gains attention, as well as the "lampshade" dress, with its body-glove-fit and immense flair at mid-thigh. Patent leather reappears in belts and bags; hair is shorter; gloves are wrist-length.

High-fashion note: Balenciaga's grass-green faille hat with black wings

For men: *Esquire* salutes the man of "self-confidence and good taste" with the "bold look." He initiates a revival of interest in men's fashion accessories: wide tie clasps, heavy gold key chains, bold striped ties, big buttons, and the coordination of hair coloring and clothing (brown hair with grey clothing, for example).

Kaleidoscope _____

- Inflation statistics include the following: a house costing $4,440 in 1939 is now $9,060; clothing is up 93 percent; food, 129 percent; home furnishings, 93.6 percent; rent, 12.2 percent; only gas and electricity are down, 4.8 percent.
- A Spokane butcher shop, responding to the meat shortage, advertises: "Choice Meats. The Management Will Accept Cash, First Mortgages, Bonds, and Good Jewelry."
- The bikini arrives on American beaches.
- Newly published Alfred Kinsey's *Sexual Behavior in the Human Male* reports the prevalence of sexual problems and indicates that 85 percent of those married have had premarital sex and 50 percent have been unfaithful.
- Isolationist Arthur Vandenberg defends the Marshall Plan as seeking "peace and stability . . . in a free world, . . . by economic rather than military means."
- McDonald's is franchised; the Baskin-Robbins chain begins.
- Fifty cities ban comic books dealing with crime or sex.
- A Nevada court declares prostitution legal in Reno.
- A Gallup poll reports the highest rate of belief in God in Brazil (96 percent); the lowest in France (66 percent); the American figure is 94 percent.

Hollywood beefcake. *Movie Star News.*

- *Cybernetics,* the study of information theory, is coined by MIT's Norbert Wiener.
- Five scientists are reported to be going blind as a result of their work with cyclotrons.
- To gain new literary perspectives, John Hopkins holds a symposium on criticism with John Crowe Ransom, Allen Tate, Herbert Read, André Gide, Benedetto Croce, and Richard Blackmur.
- Peter Goldmark of CBS invents a high-fidelity long-playing record that plays up to 45 minutes.
- The Supreme Court upholds the obscenity ban on Edmund Wilson's *Hecate County.*
- New York begins a fluoridation program for 50,000 children.
- With government supporting the well-balanced lunch, North Carolina children receive, for 5 cents, black-eyed peas, eggs, cheese, potatoes, a biscuit, milk, and a tangerine.
- Despite the financial success of his song "Nature Boy," Eben Ahbez continues to live in a Hollywood vacant lot on nuts and berries.
- Jack Benny sells his NBC radio program to CBS for a reported $2 to $3 million; the IRS then forces Benny to pay a 75 percent personal income tax, instead of 25 percent capital gains tax from the sale.
- Milton Berle's "Texaco Star Theatre" scores an 86.7 percent rating. The show's "Tell ya' what I'm gonna do" and Berle's "Duhh" gain popular usage.
- Truman orders racial equality in the armed forces; he also proposes antilynching and FEPC legislation, which Congress declines to act on.
- Eisenhower rejects Democratic efforts to draft him for president.
- Alger Hiss sues Whittaker Chambers for $75,000 for libel when Chambers accuses him of Communist party membership from 1934 to 1938; Hiss loses and is subsequently tried for perjury; the entire affair is dismissed by the president as a "red herring."
- On election eve, the Roper, Gallup, and Crossley polls predict a 5 to 15 percent Dewey victory.
- Patents are acquired for the vacuum leaf raker, fountain safety razor, suction ear muffs, metallic shoes, and "Adventure" bra with plastic prop-up snap-ins and uplift that won't wash out.

Fads: frozen foods, and chlorophyll gum, candies, and toothpaste

First Appearances: Garbage disposals, street lamp plastic lenses, nonglare headlights, heat-conducting windshields, Land Rover, Porsche sports car, Honda motorcycle, car air conditioner (for under dash), Salton Hottray, Nestlés Quik, Michelin radial tires, completely solar-heated house (Dover, Maine), Franklin 50¢ piece, World Health Organization, color newsreels, Scrabble, Dial soap, Nikon 35mm.

1949

Facts and Figures

Economic Profile

  Dow-Jones: ↑ High 200–
    Low 161
  GNP: 0%
  Inflation: −0.7%
  Unemployment: 5.9%
Police expenditures, federal,
    state, local: $724 million
Persons arrested: 792,000
Executions: 119
Prisoners, federal, state:
    163,700
Juvenile court cases: 45,775
Arnold Constable black or
    gray Persian lamb coat:
    $350
Boys' storm coat with
    mouton collar: $15.95
Zenith portable "tip top" dial
    radio: $39.95
Gladiolas: $1 (for 50)
Roses: $1.98 (for 25)
Red salmon: 59¢ (1 lb. can)
Del Monte asparagus: 35¢ (19
    oz.)
Cottage cheese: 13¢ (8 oz.)
Kraft's Velveeta: 30¢ (8 oz.)
Rib veal chops: 69¢ (lb.)

Deaths

Wallace Beery, Richard Dix,
    James Forrestal, Maurice
    Maeterlinck, Rev. Peter
    Marshall, Bill Robinson,
    Edward Stettinius, Richard
    Strauss.

In the News

U.S. Recognizes Republic of Korea Headed by Syngman Rhee . . . Truman Announces Point Four . . . George Marshall Resigns, Dean Acheson Becomes Secretary of State . . . Nationalist Chinese Suffer Severe Defeats, Chiang Kai-Shek Resigns . . . French Send Gratitude Train to U.S. . . . U.S. Recognizes Israel and Transjordan . . . Whittaker Chambers Accuses Alger Hiss of Spying . . . XB-4 Plane Goes Cross-Country in 3 Hours, 46 Minutes . . . $16 Million Is Appropriated for Palestinian Refugees . . . N.Y. Legislature Orders Communists Dismissed from Schools . . . North Atlantic Pact Is Signed, NATO Created . . . Three Western Zones of Germany Merge . . . France Recognizes Bao Dai as Head of Noncommunist Vietnam . . . Berlin Blockade Is Lifted . . . Siam Becomes Thailand . . . Britain Recognizes Eire as Independent, Northern Ireland Remains in United Kingdom . . . Last U.S. Troops Leave Korea . . . Apartheid Begins in South Africa . . . Housing Act Is Passed, Providing Federal Aid . . . Communists Drive Nationalists off Mainland to Formosa . . . Stratocruiser Goes Coast to Coast in 9 Hours . . . U.S. White Paper Concludes That Nationalists Lost China . . . 500,000 Steelworkers Strike . . . $29 Million Is Voted for Yugoslovia . . . 11 Communist Party Members Are Convicted of Smith Act Violation . . . Greek Civil War Ends with Communist Rebels Defeated . . . Mutual Defense Assistance Act Provides Funds for Nato . . . India Adopts Constitution, Nehru Visits U.S. and Addresses Congress . . . U.S. Embassy in Manchuria Is Attacked . . .

Quotes

"In some crude sense, which no vulgarity, no humor, no overstatement can quite extinguish, the physicists have known sin, and this is a knowledge which they cannot lose."

— J. Robert Oppenheimer

Examiner: The Commission's information is also to the effect that you were attending Communist meetings at the time. Do you have any explanation?
Scientist: No, none. This just can't be true. May I ask, can it be found out who the person [accuser] is?
Examiner: I do not know at this time.

— Atomic Energy Commission hearing

"I believe the American people are entitled to be informed of all developments in the field of atomic energy. We have evidence that within recent weeks an atomic explosion occurred within the USSR."

— Charles Ross, presidential press secretary

"Here's the thing that is top secret. Our scientists . . . [since] Hiroshima and Nagasaki have been trying to make what is known as a superbomb, . . . a thousand times the effect of that terrible bomb. That's the secret, the big secret.

— Secretary of Defense Louis Johnson

"Past events . . . have no objective existence. . . . The past is whatever the records and memories agree upon. . . . The Party is in full control of all the records."

— George Orwell, *1984*

"Attention must be paid. . . . A small man can be just as exhausted as a great man."

— Arthur Miller, *Death of a Salesman*

"You eat it, usually sitting in a booth in a bare, plain restaurant, with a mural of Vesuvio on the wall, a jukebox, and a crowded bar. The customers are Italian families, Bohemians, lovers, and—if a college is nearby—students and faculty members."

— About the new "pizza," *Atlantic Monthly*

Ads

I dreamed I went shopping in my Maidenform bra.
(Maidenform Bras)

Darling, you don't need reins to be a dear.
(Warner's Foundations)

Escape from Seams! Nylon Nudes by Hanes.
(Hanes Hoisery)

Over three million Americans are heavy "social" drinkers—many are on their way to becoming confirmed alcoholics—helpless and lost. But this tragic fate can be largely averted if the sound practical advice given here reaches enough of them in time.

(Woman's Home Companion)

What chance TWINS?
    If you are expecting the stork, the chances that he'll bring you twins may be greater than you think. One in eighty-nine. In any event, twins—or any new arrival . . . make it virtually important to see your PRUDENTIAL representative.

(Prudential Life Insurance)

Fervent Femininity in Four Fragrances—Plaintive, Tabu, Emir, 20 Carats

(Dana)

For your enchanted moment (and it may come any moment) only one lipstick will do!

(Tangee)

New! A lighter-bodied *cream* tonic . . . gives your hair that "clean-groomed look."

— *Vitalis*

Double protection against Under-Arm Perspiration and Odor!—Veto

(Veto Deodorant)

Model room in Bloomingdale's, New York. *Library of Congress.*

Radio

Premieres
"Martin Kane, Private Eye," William Gargan
"Dragnet," Jack Webb

TV

Premieres
"Mr. I. Magination," Paul Tripp
"Quiz Kids," Joe Kelly
"Original Amateur Hour," Ted Mack
"Arthur Godfrey and His Friends"
"Captain Video and His Video Rangers," Al Hodge
"The Fred Waring Show"
"Cavalcade of Stars," Jack Carter
"Hopalong Cassidy," William Boyd
"Mama," Peggy Wood
"The Goldbergs," Gertrude Berg
"Pantomime Quiz," Mike Stokey
"Kukla, Fran and Ollie," Fran Allison
"The Lone Ranger," Clayton Moore, Jay Silverheels

"Blind Date," Arlene Francis
"Crusade in Europe," first documentary
"These Are My Children," first daytime soap opera

Specials
"Kathy Fiscus Rescue [from a well]," "Nuremburg Trials," "Teleforum," "Crusade in Europe"

Emmy Awards
"Ed Wynn Show" (live); "Texaco Star Theatre" (kinescope): "Time for Beany" (children); "Life of Riley" (film for TV); "Wrestling, KTLA" (sports)

Of Note
Charlton Heston plays his first major role in "Battleship Bismarck" ("Studio One") • Milton Berle hosts the first telethon, 14 hours, for cancer research and raises $1 million • TV's first major weekly situation comedies begin with ". . . but most of all, I remember Mama" ("Mama") and "Yoo-hoo, Mrs. Bloom" ("The Goldbergs").

Movies

Openings
All the King's Men (Richard Rossen), Broderick Crawford, John Ireland, Mercedes McCambridge
Battleground (William A. Wellman), Van Johnson, John Hodiak
The Heiress (William Wyler), Olivia de Havilland, Montgomery Clift
A Letter to Three Wives (Joseph L. Mankiewicz), Linda Darnell, Ann Sothern, Kirk Douglas
Home of the Brave (Mark Robson), Lloyd Bridges, Frank Lovejoy, James Edwards
Twelve O'Clock High (Henry King), Gregory Peck, Dean Jagger, Gary Merrill
Champion (Stanley Kramer), Kirk Douglas, Arthur Kennedy
Sands of Iwo Jima (Allan Dwan), John Wayne, John Agar
Pinky (Elia Kazan), Jeanne Crain, Ethel Barrymore, Ethel Waters
My Foolish Heart (Mark Robson), Susan Hayward, Dana Andrews
White Heat (Raoul Walsh), James Cagney, Virginia Mayo
On the Town (Gene Kelly, Stanley Donen), Gene Kelly, Frank Sinatra, Betty Garrett
She Wore a Yellow Ribbon (John Ford), John Wayne, Joanne Dru
Little Women (Mervyn LeRoy), June Allyson, Elizabeth Taylor, Janet Leigh, Margaret O'Brien

Lost Boundaries (Alfred L. Werker), Mel Ferrer, Beatrice Pearson
Intruder in the Dust (Clarence Brown), David Brian
The Bicycle Thief (Vittorio De Sica), Lamberto Maggiorani
The Third Man (Carol Reed), Joseph Cotten, Trevor Howard, Orson Welles, Alida Valli

Academy Awards
Best Picture: *All the King's Men*
Best Director: Joseph L. Mankiewicz (*A Letter to Three Wives*)
Best Actress: Olivia de Havilland (*The Heiress*)
Best Actor: Broderick Crawford (*All the King's Men*)

Top Box-Office Stars
Bob Hope, Bing Crosby, Abbott and Costello, John Wayne, Gary Cooper, Cary Grant, Betty Grable, Esther Williams, Humphrey Bogart, Clark Gable

Stars of Tomorrow
Montgomery Clift, Kirk Douglas, Betty Garrett, Paul Douglas, Howard Duff, Pedro Armendariz, Dean Stockwell, Wanda Hendrix, Wendell Corey, Barbara Bel Geddes

Popular Music _____

Hit Songs
"Mona Lisa"
"Rudolph, the Red-Nosed
  Reindeer"
"Mule Train"
"Let's Take an Old-Fashioned
  Walk"
"Some Enchanted Evening"
"My Foolish Heart"
"Diamonds Are a Girl's Best
  Friend"
"The Cry of the Wild Goose"
"Ghost Riders in the Sky"
"Huckle-Buck"

Top Records

Albums: *Vaughn Monroe Sings*
(Vaughn Monroe); *Roses in
Rhythm* (Frankie Carle); *Words
and Music* (Soundtrack); *Kiss Me
Kate* (original cast); *South Pacific*
(original cast)

Singles: *Dear Hearts and Gentle
People* (Bing Crosby); *You're
Breaking My Heart* (Vic Damone);
That Lucky Old Sun (Frankie
Laine); *Baby, It's Cold Outside*
(Esther Williams, Ricardo
Montalban); *September in the
Rain* (George Shearing); Country:
Candy Kisses (George Morgan);
Lovesick Blues (Hank Williams)

Jazz and Big Bands
"Cool jazz" ("cultivated chamber
jazz") includes Miles Davis, Bill
Evans, Lee Konitz, Gerry
Mulligan, Modern Jazz Quartet
(John Lewis), Dave Brubeck, and
Lenny Tristano.
Miles Davis's nine-piece band
includes a tuba and French horn,
and soloists John Lewis, Gunther
Schuller, Max Roach, Gerry
Mulligan, Lee Konitz, and J. J.
Johnson.
The George Shearing Quintet is
organized; Milt Jackson joins
Woody Herman; Canadian Oscar
Peterson debuts in the United
States at Carnegie Hall; Birdland
opens in New York.

First Recordings: Lennie Tristano
with Lee Konitz; Dave Brubeck

Top Performers *(Downbeat):*
Woody Herman (band); George
Shearing (jazz group); Billy Bauer,
Oscar Peterson, Shelly Manne,
Charlie Parker, Serge Chaloff,
Howard McGhee
(instrumentalists); Sarah Vaughan,
Billy Eckstine (vocalists); Pied
Pipers (vocal group)

Theater _____

Broadway Openings

Plays
Death of a Salesman (Arthur Miller), Lee J. Cobb,
  Mildred Dunnock, Arthur Kennedy
Detective Story (Sidney Kingsley), Ralph Bellamy,
  Lee Grant
I Know My Love (S. N. Behrman), Alfred Lunt,
  Lynn Fontanne
Two Blind Mice (Samuel Spewack), Melvyn Douglas
Harlequinade (Terence Rattigan), Maurice Evans
The Browning Version (Terence Rattigan), Maurice
  Evans, Edna Best
The Big Knife (Clifford Odets), John Garfield

Musicals
South Pacific (Richard Rodgers, Oscar Hammerstein
  II), Mary Martin, Ezio Pinza, Juanita Hall
Gentlemen Prefer Blondes (Jule Styne, Leo Robin),
  Carol Channing
Lost in the Stars (Kurt Weill, Maxwell Anderson),
  Todd Duncan
Miss Liberty (Irving Berlin), Eddie Albert
Touch and Go (Jay Gorney, Jean and Walter Kerr),
  Kyle MacDonnell

Texas, Li'l Darlin' (Robert Dolan, Johnny Mercer),
  Kenny Delmar, Loring Smith

Classics and Revivals On and Off Broadway
Diamond Lil (Mae West), Mae West; *Caesar and
Cleopatra* (George Bernard Shaw), Cedric
Hardwicke, Lilli Palmer; *The Father* (Strindberg),
Raymond Massey, Grace Kelly; *Medea* (Euripides),
Judith Anderson; *Richard II,* Richard Whorf.
Founded: The Loft Players (Circle in the Square) by
Theodore Mann, José Quintero, Emile Stevens, and
Jason Wingreen; League of Off-Broadway Theatres
and Producers

Regional

Founded: Mummer's Theatre, Oklahoma City, by
Mack Scism

Pulitzer Prize
Death of a Salesman, Arthur Miller

Classical Music _____

Compositions
Samuel Barber, Piano Sonata
Wallingford Riegger, Music for Brass Choir
Walter Piston, Piano Quintet, Duo for Violin and
　　Cello
Virgil Thomson, Cello Concerto
Ernest Bloch, *Scherzo Fantasque*

Important Events
Antal Dorati succeeds Dimitri Mitropoulos at
Minnesota; Charles Munch, Serge Koussevitzky in
Boston; Howard Mitchell, Hans Kindler, at the
National, in Washington. Leopold Stokowski and
Mitropoulos are appointed principal conductors of
the New York Philharmonic.
Musical organizations proliferate throughout the
United States. Texas has three major orchestras:
Dallas, Houston, and San Antonio.
Two hundred works are premiered at 500 concerts in
New York; the Chopin 100th anniversary is
celebrated throughout the country.

Debuts:　Aldo Ciccolini, Gina Bachauer

First Performances
William Schuman, Symphony no. 6 (Dallas); Roy
Harris (conducting), *Kentucky Spring* (Louisville);
Leonard Bernstein (playing), Symphony no. 2 *(The
Age of Anxiety)* (Boston); Béla Bartók, Viola

For the second year Billy Eckstine is named "most popular
singer" by *Downbeat. Movie Star News.*

Bruno Walter's interpretations of Mozart and Mahler with
the New York Philharmonic gain wide critical and popular
success. *Movie Star News.*

Concerto (Minneapolis); David Diamond, *The
Enormous Room* (Cincinnati); Douglas Moore, *The
Emperor's New Clothes* (New York); Darius Milhaud,
Concerto for Marimba, Vibraphone (St. Louis);
Arnold Schoenberg, Phantasy for Violin (Los
Angeles); Paul Hindemith, Concerto for Organ,
Brass, Woodwinds (Boston)

Opera

Metropolitan:　*Otello* is televised with backstage
interviews. Ljuba Welitsch (debut), *Salomé;* Bidú
Sayão, Giuseppe Di Stefano (debuts), *La traviata;*
Giuseppe Valdengo, *Simon Boccanegra;* Cloë Elmo,
Gianni Schicchi

City Opera, City Center, New York: *Troubled Island*
(William Grant Still, premiere); *The Love for Three
Oranges*

New Haven:　*Regina* (Marc Blitzstein, premiere)

San Francisco:　Kirsten Flagstad, Set Svanholm, *Die
Meistersinger;* Jussi Bjoerling and Licia Albanese,
Manon Lescaut

Music Notes
The Detroit Symphony calls off its season because its
members refuse a pay cut • Public protests continue
against many Germans as undesirables or aliens.

Art

Painting
Barnett Newman,
*Abraham, Covenant,
Concord, Onement III*
Stuart Davis, *The Paris
Bit*
Willem de Kooning,
Ashville, Attic
Robert Motherwell, *At
Five in the Afternoon,
The Voyage*
Robert Gwathmey,
Sowing
Mark Rothko, *Number
24, Number 18*
Bradley Walker Tomlin,
Number 20, Number 5
Clyfford Still, *Number 2*
Jackson Pollock,
Number 2
Loren MacIver, *Venice*
Mark Tobey, *Universal
Field*

Sculpture
Richard Lippold,
*Variation No. 7: Full
Moon*
Alexander Calder,
Pomegranate
Herbert Ferber, *Portrait
of Jackson Pollock II*
Isamu Noguchi,
Unknown Bird

Ibram Lassaw, *Star
Cradle*
Louise Bourgeois, *The
Blind Leading the
Blind, Installation*
The Lincoln Memorial
Circle, at the approach
to the Arlington
Memorial Bridge,
Washington, D.C.
(Fraser, Friedlander)

Architecture
Glass House, New
Canaan, Conn. (Philip
Johnson)
Warren Tremaine House,
Montecito, Calif.
(Richard Neutra)
140 Maiden Lane
project, San Francisco
(Frank Lloyd Wright)
Promontory Apartments,
Chicago (Mies van der
Rohe)
Laboratory Tower for
S. C. Johnson and
Son, Racine, Wisc.
(Frank Lloyd Wright)
Case Study House, Santa
Monica, Calif.
(Charles Eames)

Important Exhibitions
International exchanges of old and modern masters
increases: 116 American artists are displayed in three
Israeli museums; paintings from major Italian
museums and eighteenth-century art from the Louvre
visit various U.S. galleries.

Museums

New York: *Metropolitan:* Van Gogh, Michelangelo,
Donatello; Art treasures of Iran; Nine Worthies
tapestries and the Hunt of the Unicorn (Cloisters);
Italian art. *Museum of Modern Art:* Braque
retrospective; "Modern Art in the Modern World."
Whitney: Juliana Force and American Art; Weber

Chicago: The woodcut through six centuries;
Toulouse-Lautrec; "From Colony to Nation, 1650–
1815"

Willem de Kooning, *Attic*, 1949. Oil, enamel, newspaper
transfer on paper. 61⅞ × 81". *The Metropolitan Museum
of Art, jointly owned by the Metropolitan Museum of Art
and Muriel Kallis Newman, in honor of her son, Glen
David Steinberg. The Muriel Kallis Steinberg Newman
Collection, 1982.*

Washington: *National:* Michelangelo's "David,"
Donatello's "San Lodovico"; Art Treasures from
Vienna. *Corcoran:* "De Gustibus" (History of
American taste)

Boston: Forty years of Canadian painting; Third
National Ceramic Exhibition; Pompeiian silver (from
the Louvre)

St. Louis: Mississippi panorama

Philadelphia: Third International Exhibit of
Sculpture; Antique, engraved and Steuben glass

Pittsburgh: Carnegie International first prize to Max
Beckmann *(Fisher Women);* second prize to Philip
Evergood *(Leda)*

Art Briefs
Jean Arp has his first American show in New York •
Because of the postwar European currency
devaluation, U.S. sales accelerate: Degas's *L'école
de ballet* ($25,000); Homer's *The Voice from the
Cliffs* ($12,000); Renoir's *Young Bather* ($10,500).

Dance

Premieres
New York City Ballet: *The Firebird* (George
Balanchine, Stravinsky), Maria Tallchief, Francisco
Moncion, Patricia McBride

Of Interest
Sadler's Wells is acclaimed on its first visit to the
Metropolitan with *Swan Lake* and *The Sleeping
Beauty.* In the company are Margot Fonteyn,
Frederick Ashton, Robert Helpmann, Moira Shearer,
and Beryl Grey • Erik Bruhn joins Ballet Theatre.

Books

Fiction

Critics' Choice

Golden Apples, Eudora Welty
The Man with the Golden Arm, Nelson Algren
The Journey of Simon McKiever, Albert Maltz
The Sheltering Sky, Paul Bowles
The Track of the Cat, Walter Van Tilburg Clark
Knight's Gambit, William Faulkner
The Lottery, Shirley Jackson
The Cannibal, John Hawkes
&· *1984*, George Orwell

Best-Sellers

The Egyptian, Mika Waltari
The Big Fisherman, Lloyd C. Douglas
Mary, Sholem Asch
A Rage to Live, John O'Hara
Point of No Return, John P. Marquand
Dinner at Antoine's, Frances Parkinson Keyes
High Towers, Thomas B. Costain
Cutlass Empire, Van Wyck Mason
Pride's Castle, Frank Yerby
Father of the Bride, Edward Streeter

Nonfiction

Critics' Choice

American Freedom and Catholic Power, Paul Blanshard
Modern Arms and Free Men, Vannevar Bush
Situation in Asia, Owen Lattimore
The Negro in the United States, E. Franklin Frazier
Killers of the Dream, Lillian Smith
Mirror for Man, Clyde Kluckhohn
The Universe and Dr. Einstein, Lincoln Barnett
This I Remember, Eleanor Roosevelt
Theory of Literature, Rene Wellek, Austin Warren
Faith and History, Reinhold Niebuhr
Ralph Waldo Emerson, Ralph L. Rusk

Best-Sellers

White Collar Zoo, Clare Barnes, Jr.
How to Win at Canasta, Oswald Jacoby
The Seven Storey Mountain, Thomas Merton
Home Sweet Zoo, Clare Barnes, Jr.
Cheaper by the Dozen, Frank B. Gilbreth, Jr., Ernestine G. Carey

The Greatest Story Ever Told, Fulton Oursler
Canasta, the Argentine Rummy Game, Ottilie H. Reilly
Canasta, Josephine Artayeta de Viel, Ralph Michael
Peace of Soul, Fulton J. Sheen
A Guide to Confident Living, Norman Vincent Peale

Poetry

Robert Frost, *Complete Poems*
Kenneth Fearing, *Stranger at Coney Island*
Louis Simpson, *The Arrivistes*
Muriel Rukeyser, *Orpheus*
Conrad Aiken, *Skylight One*
William Carlos Williams, *Paterson*, Book Three, *Selected Poems*

Pulitzer Prizes

The Way West, A. B. Guthrie, Jr. (fiction)
Art and Life in America, Oliver W. Larkin (U.S. history)
John Quincy Adams and the Foundations of American Foreign Policy, Samuel Flagg Bemis (biography)
Annie Allen, Gwendolyn Brooks (poetry)

Science and Technology

In his condensation theory of the solar system, Gérard Kuiper, University of Chicago, postulates that the planets were formed from a nebula of gas and dust rotating around the sun 3 billion years ago.

The U.S. Air Force ends its two-year investigation of flying saucer reports by denying the authenticity of UFOs.

A two-stage rocket soars to a record 250 miles at 5,000 m.p.h. above the White Sands Proving Grounds, N.M.

Willard Libby, University of Chicago, reports the use of carbon-14 to determine the age of objects.

The "breeder reactor," an atomic reactor that produces more energy than it uses, is developed.

"Binac" is demonstrated by John Mauch and J. Presper Eckert; it computes at 12,000 times the speed of the human brain.

Eight essential amino acids for humans are described.

The commercial production of ACTH, which stimulates the body to produce cortisone, begins.

The first use of the betatron to treat cancer occurs at the University of Illinois, Chicago.

&· The first atomic bomb tests begin in the USSR.

Nobel Prize

William Giauque wins the prize in chemistry for work in thermodynamics.

Sports

Baseball

Casey Stengel becomes New York Yankee manager.
Happy Chandler declares amnesty for Mexican
  League jumpers; Danny Gardella sues and wins
  out of court.

Champions

Batting	Pitching
Jackie Robinson (Brooklyn, NL), .342	Preacher Roe (Brooklyn, NL), 15–6
George Kell (Detroit, AL), .343	Ellis Kinder (Boston, AL), 23–6
	Home runs
	Ralph Kiner (Pittsburgh, NL), 54

Football

The flanker is introduced by Clark Shaughnessy.
The AAC and NFL merge, with Baltimore,
Cleveland, and San Francisco joining 10 NFL teams.

NFL Season Leaders: Sammy Baugh (Washington),
passing; Steve Van Buren (Philadelphia), rushing;
Tom Fears (Los Angeles), receiver

College All-Americans: Doak Walker (B), Southern
Methodist; Charlie Justice (B), North Carolina; Leon
Hart (E), Notre Dame

Bowls (Jan. 1, 1950)

Rose: Ohio State 17–California 14	Cotton: Rice 27–North Carolina 13
Orange: Santa Clara 21–Kentucky 13	Sugar: Oklahoma 35–Louisiana State 0

Basketball

NBA All-Pro first team: George Mikan
(Minneapolis), Joe Fulks (Philadelphia), Bob Davies
(Rochester), Jim Pollard (Minneapolis), Max
Zaslofsky (Chicago)
Kentucky wins its second straight NCAA title; its
stars include Alex Groza, Ralph Beard, Wah Wah
Jones.

Other Sports

Golf: Ben Hogan is seriously injured in a car
accident.

Boxing: Jake La Motta KO's Marcel Cerdan for the
middleweight title; Cerdan is killed in a plane crash
while flying to America for a return match. Joe Louis
retires. Ezzard Charles outpoints Joe Walcott for the
heavyweight title.

Tennis: Pancho Gonzales turns pro and tours with
Jack Kramer; they earn $250,000.

Winners

World Series	College Basketball
New York (AL) 4	Kentucky (NCAA)
Brooklyn (NL) 1	San Francisco (NIT)
MVP	*Player of the Year*
NL–Jackie Robinson, Brooklyn	Dante Lavelli, Yale
AL–Ted Williams, Boston	*Stanley Cup*
NFL	Toronto
Philadelphia 14–Los Angeles (Rams) 0	*US Tennis Open*
	Men: Pancho Gonzales
College Football	Women: Margaret Osborne DuPont
Notre Dame	*USGA Open*
Heisman Trophy	Cary Middlecoff
Leon Hart, Notre Dame	*Kentucky Derby*
	Ponder (S. Brooks, jockey)

Fashion

For Women: Dior, Schiaparelli, Fath, and others
commute to New York and design for mass
production. For evening, the chemise, beaded and
fringed, is either strapless or has a slender shoulder
strap. Day fashions include shirtwaists, tight skirts
with panels of matching or contrasting fabrics, hip
bows, tunic effects, overblouses, oval necklines, and
the dropped shoulder line with large sleeves. Fabrics
range from thick fleeces, tweeds, and chinchilla cloth
to ribbed wools and silks. Nylon is increasingly
popular. Accessories include long pearl ropes,
dangling earrings, and pigskin, alligator, and even fur
textures for bags, belts, gloves, and shoes.

*High-fashion note: Hardy Amies's "princess" coat;
McCardell's "monastic dress" with string criss-
crossing at the midriff; mutation minks in colors like
gold*

For Men: A carryover from the military are light
suits that hold their shape; also popular are the new
nylon cord suits, seersuckers, and cotton, nylon, and
rayon blends, which also permit a new boldness in
dress and informality. Two-trouser suits in variations
of gray, blue, tan, and brown are also stylish.

Kaleidoscope _____

- William Levitt converts a Long Island potato field into a prefabricated, "carbon copy," suburban community. For $60 a month and no down payment, one can buy a $7,990, four-room house with attic, outdoor barbecue, washing machine, and 12½-inch built-in TV set.
- For the first time, blacks are invited to the important social events at the Presidential Inaugural and stay at the same hotels as whites.
- Pro– and con–Alger Hiss factions provoke intense rivalries that frequently center on New and Fair Deal loyalties.
- Comedy teams in films are very popular: Hope and Crosby, Martin and Lewis, Abbott and Costello.
- Vaudeville returns to the Palace Theatre after 14 years.
- An enormous controversy occurs over the FBI loyalty checks of Atomic Energy Commission scientists; Enrico Fermi and the California Institute of Technology president question the FBI investigations of AEC researchers as a step toward a police state.
- A test tube with one ounce of uranium oxide, which is missing from an Illinois lab, sets off an intensive search; it is later recovered from wastes sent to Oak Ridge, Tennessee.
- San Diego experiences its first snowfall.
- Because of a water shortage, New Yorkers have bathless and shaveless days.
- The postwar baby boom levels off with 3.58 million live births.
- The AMA advocates voluntary medical care plans.
- The minimum wage rises from 40 cents to 75 cents an hour.
- A sharp decline in prices occurs until the fall: 5 cents for beer in New York, pie à la mode for a penny in Los Angeles.
- Because of the Communist takeover of China and Russia's development of the A-bomb, many fear an impending war with Russia.
- Rita Hayworth marries Prince Ali Khan.
- Phonograph records in three different speeds (33⅓, 45, 78) baffle listeners and cause sales to fall.

Alger Hiss, Harvard '29, a member of the Washington social register and former New Deal administrator. Was he a Soviet spy? *Library of Congress.*

"I Remember Mama" (*above*) and "The Goldbergs" are TV's first two successful sitcoms. *Movie Star News.*

- The Polaroid Land camera, which produces a picture in 60 seconds, goes on sale for $89.75.
- The FCC ends an eight-year ban on radio editorializing but warns that stations must present all sides of controversial questions.
- The Nobel Prize for literature is withheld when the academy fails to choose among Winston Churchill, William Faulkner, Carl Sandburg, and Benedetto Croce.
- Dr. Ralph J. Bunche successfully guides negotiations for a truce in war-torn Palestine after UN mediator Folke Bernadotte is assassinated.
- Travel restrictions are relaxed with visas no longer necessary for many countries outside the Iron Curtain; travelers ship their cars to Europe for $375 and pay high gas prices of 60 cents a liter; hotel rates in Capri are $2.50 a day, including meals.
- In order to prove that growing old is nonsense, Bernarr Macfadden, 81, parachutes from a plane and, greeting his wife, 43, remarks that anyone using white flour could probably do it.

Fads: Gorgeous George, lady wrestlers, roller derbies, pyramid clubs, Canasta, décolletage and boned bras, bikinis, short straight hair, matching sweaters, mother-daughter matching playsuits, cowboy and Indian suits and toys, plastic erector sets, Toni permanents, Caesar salads

First Appearances: LP record catalog (by record shop owner William Schwann), bicycle rider crossing the continent in less than three weeks, lightweight plastic foam, inflatable vinyl products (boats), ripping needle for sewing machine, midget microphone, scented bras (by Love-E of Hollywood), O'Hare Airport (named), Volkswagen (in the United States), Radio Free Europe's news broadcasts behind the Iron Curtain, airmail post card, prepared cake mixes, Pillsbury "Bake-Offs," Sara Lee cheesecake, Revlon's "Fire and Ice," Silly Putty, vice president to marry in office (Alben Barkley)

THE *Fifties*

President Eisenhower and his grandson. *Library of Congress.*

Statistics

Vital
Population: 149,188,000
  Urban/rural: 16/9
  Farm: 15.3%
Life expectancy
  Male: 65.6
  Female: 71.1
Births/1,000: 24.1
Marriages/1,000: 11.1
Divorces/1,000: 2.6
Deaths/1,000: 9.6
  per 100,000
    Heart: 502
    Cancer: 139
    Tuberculosis: 22
    Car accidents: 21.3

Economic
Unemployed: 3,288,000
GNP: $364.8 billion
Federal budget: $39.6 billion
National debt: $257.4 billion
Union membership: 14.8
  million
Strikes: 4,843
Prime rate: 1.5%
Car sales: 6,665,800
Average salary: $2,992

Social
Homicides/100,000: 5.3
Suicides/100,000: 11.4
Lynchings: 2
Labor force male/female: 5/2
Social welfare: $23.51 billion
Public education: $5.84 billion
College degrees
  Bachelors'
    Male: 328,000
    Female: 103,000
  Doctorates
    Male: 6,969
    Female: 714
Attendance
  Movies (weekly): 60 million
  Baseball (yearly): 17.6
  million

Consumer
Consumer Price Index
  (1967 = 100): 77.1
Eggs: 72¢ (doz.)
Milk: 21¢ (qt.)
Bread: 14¢ (loaf)
Butter: 60¢ (lb.)
Bacon: 64¢ (lb.)
Round steak: 94¢ (lb.)
Oranges: 52¢ (doz.)
Coffee: 55¢ (lb.)

The fifties were a time of conservative politics, economic prosperity, and above all, social conformity. From the tidy lawns of spreading split-level suburbs to the tidy minds of board rooms, club rooms, and bedrooms, "neat and trim" and "proper and prim" were "in." These attitudes, invariably associated with the period, may perhaps be explained as a response to the unsettling events at the beginning of the decade.

Czechoslovakia and China had just come under Communist rule and Russia had recently announced its A-bomb when Truman revealed in 1950 that the United States was developing an even more powerful nuclear weapon, the H-bomb. Such a disclosure exacerbated an already palpable fear about the cold war, and it became clear that a race for annihilating weapons was underway. Three other events of the same year further intensified national anxiety: Senator Joseph McCarthy claimed knowledge of Communists in the State Department, the Kefauver Committee exposed a widespread and powerful underworld, and North Korea invaded South Korea.

Truman was widely supported in his decision to send troops to Korea, and MacArthur's Inchon landings and subsequent campaign promised a quick victory. But Communist China entered the war in massive numbers, and a long, bloody, and disheartening stalemate developed. South Korea was largely under control, but the war continued alongside tortuous peace negotiations. When Truman dismissed MacArthur, who was eager to attack China proper, regardless of the risks, the nation rallied around the general, who later returned to the largest hero's welcome since Lindbergh.

Capitalizing on the nation's fear of Communist aggression at home and abroad, Joseph McCarthy moved the threat of Communist infiltration into everyone's backyard. In a time of relative helplessness against an alarming enemy abroad, combined with "egghead" thinking at home from "bleeding hearts," "do-gooders," and "fellow travelers," McCarthy claimed to know the enemies. His accusations, though never proved, mounted, and his general thesis of widespread Communist influence in government gained wide credibility. A suspiciousness enveloped American life, and scientists, diplomats, academics, and entertainers came under scrutiny, along with movies, television, and even classical literature and comic books. The 1951 treason convictions of Julius and Ethel Rosenberg confirmed for many the extent of Communist subversion, although for many others, the Rosenberg executions represented the persecution of the innocents. Their trial, the Kefauver hearings, the college basketball and West Point cheating scandals, as well as the subsequent revelations of questionable gifts accepted by Truman's staff, gave further indication of the nation's weakened moral fiber. In 1952, the succession of five Democratic presidential victories came to an end.

Dwight Eisenhower swept into office on a campaign against Korea, Communism, and Corruption. He was a common-sense, down-to-earth man, a great military leader with a fatherly manner, who promised peace and prosperity. He vowed to take America down "the middle road," and with his victory, the quintessential fifties were set in gear. America returned to the business of business, and, as in the 1920s, businessmen were appointed to places of power in the government. Once again, material success assumed a place of reverence, and government's role as an agent of social reform was constrained.

In this climate of atomic anxiety, political paranoia, and moral self-doubt, most Americans looked to the time-honored virtues of home, church, and community. It was time to cultivate the gardens of ever-growing suburbia, to learn the new mambo steps, and to make every effort to find group acceptance as a sign of moral health and patriotism. There was a virtual revival of Victorian respectability and domesticity (marriage age and divorce rates fell) and of the pioneer sense of community (leagues of young baseball players and women voters proliferated). In a booming economy, corporate America offered many opportunities for those willing to conform—the organization men in their gray flannel suits and their wives who remained at home to bear children at the highest birthrate ever.

Female college attendance dropped well below twenties' levels. More than ever, the work world became the man's domain, as though the wish to enter it were abnormal. Women were offered the rewards of glittering new homes (stocked with new appliances), surrounded by other new homes, and the companionship of neighbors who might be potential ladies' club members, cobarbecuers, and cochauffeurs to and from the kids' piano and ballet classes. For those for whom this was not enough, there were the newly marketed tranquilizers whose sales were astonishing.

Uniform styles of dress and properly buttoned down attitudes concerning sexual mores helped assure acceptance. Stern undergarments like boned girdles and stiff, pointed, or padded bras helped confine the body, and styles like long, broad, crinolined skirts and Dior's A, H, and Y shapes helped conceal its natural shape. Buxomness, a display of femininity and maternal potential, was "in"—for perhaps the last time in this century.

Bible sales, like construction and babies, also boomed, and once again, not unlike the twenties, religion and success allied themselves. Best-sellers, such as the Reverend Norman Vincent Peale's *The*

Rock Hudson and Doris Day struggle over her chastity in *Pillow Talk.* Oscar Levant quips: "I knew Doris Day before she was a virgin." *Movie Star News.*

Power of Positive Thinking, confirmed that belief enhanced material well-being; the president made repeated references to the Almighty and reinforced the motto that the family that prays together stays together. Popular culture also provided reassurance and role models. Songs extolled "Love and Marriage" and were sung by wholesome stars like Pat Boone, Rosemary Clooney, Doris Day, and Perry Como. Hollywood began producing the big blockbusters like *Ben Hur* and *The Ten Commandments.* TV shows like "Father Knows Best" and "Leave It to Beaver" gave humorous demonstration that all was well in the well-run family. Lovable, dizzy Lucy, and lovable, capable Ricky even increased their tribe on the day of Ike's inauguration (both on and off the tube!). Popular fads like white bucks, crew cuts, hula hoops, and Davy Crockett paraphernalia were all manifestations of an endless wholesomeness.

The early fifties youth were unusual in the extent to which they assumed the mores of their elders; they also watched TV more hours than they attended school. As rock and Elvis became popular in the mid-fifties, the young people found their own music and language, and with money to spend, they became more highly defined than any other youth group in history. James Dean, the *Rebel without a Cause,*

became their alienated idol; the Beats also appeared. Interestingly, two fictional portrayals of teenagers, although decidedly different, became classics as well as best-sellers, Salinger's *The Catcher in the Rye* and Nabokov's *Lolita.*

Subtle dichotomies marked other areas of American culture. *The Seven-Year Itch, My Fair Lady, The Sound of Music,* and *Peter Pan* seem most representative of the fifties' stage, but *Waiting for Godot,* on Broadway, and the efflorescence of Off-Broadway theater of the absurd, indicated less cheerful sensibilities at work. Edward Albee's *Zoo Story,* which ends with the murder of an establishment man by an alienated youth, may well be seen as a coda of the decade. Films like the daring *From Here to Eternity,* and novels like *The Caine Mutiny, Bonjour Tristesse,* and *Marjorie Morningstar,* while cautioning the need to retain the accepted mores, bespoke a certain yearning among the middle class and youth for new rules. Two important nonfiction works expressed grave qualms. *The Lonely Crowd* described a society in which appearance and acceptance had replaced inner values as guidelines to life, and *The Affluent Society* decried the lack of public purpose in a society exalting accumulation. Self-doubt was more prominent in foreign films like *The Seventh Seal; Hiroshima, Mon Amour; Room at the Top;* and *La Dolce Vita;* all of which gained a devoted following.

In television, westerns were especially popular, but the fifties were also the Golden Age of serious and original drama, with shows like "Marty," "Patterns," and "Requiem for a Heavyweight" on regular programs such as "Playhouse 90" and "Philco Playhouse." An innovative kind of news reporting was represented by Edward R. Murrow, and television gained a new public role.

Many look back upon the fifties with distaste

Joseph Albers, *Homage to the Square: "With Rays"* 1959. Oil on masonite. 48⅛ × 48⅛". *The Metropolitan Museum of Art, Arthur H. Hearn Fund.*

J. Robert Oppenheimer, who questions the morality of the atomic weapons he helped to create. *Library of Congress*.

Elvis Presley's singing and body gyrations cause teenage hysteria and adult consternation. *Movie Star News*.

and call it an uncreative and unidealistic time. Among their evidence are the carbon-copy suburban housing developments and shopping areas of the period, as well as the boxlike apartment buildings and garishly decorated hotels in Miami and Las Vegas, 3-D movies, painting by number, grape and "sick" jokes, the invention of TV dinners, and gaudy fashion styles like pink ties and shirts with charcoal suits, felt skirts with sequined poodle appliques, and rhinestone-speckled, plastic shoes. Nixon's Checkers speech, endless speculations about flying saucers, and Christine Jorgensen's sex change, as well as the new phenomena of *Playboy* and Mickey Spillane fiction (which everyone pored over behind closed doors), are other emblems of the times.

Although there is still evidence of the "ticky-tacky" houses that dotted the nation, this was also the time when many of the magnificent glass and steel towers that characterize the American metropolis were built by architects like the Saarinens, Mies van der Rohe, Skidmore, Owings, and Merrill, and Philip Johnson. An aesthetic revolution continued with the abstract expressionists Jackson Pollock, Willem de Kooning, and Robert Motherwell. Great opera stars also came of age—Renata Tebaldi, Maria Callas, Richard Tucker—as well as the great choreographers George Balanchine and Jerome Robbins. Musical exchanges between the United States and the USSR introduced the American public to Richter,

Gilels, Oistrakh, and Rostropovich; attendance at symphony concerts reached record heights.

Among the personalities whose fascination has endured are Marilyn Monroe, the sensual, vulnerable child-woman in search of male protectors; Grace Kelly, the cool beauty who married a prince; and Elvis Presley, the talented musician whose uninhibited demeanor remains an influence today. The Salk and Sabin vaccines, which lifted forever the annual summer siege of polio, are perhaps the unequivocal stars of the period.

Throughout it all, imperative forces were at work. Those that forever changed American life include the 1954 ruling that segregated schools are not equal and Rosa Parks's 1955 refusal to go to the back of a Montgomery bus; images of black schoolchildren harangued by white parents in Little Rock remain indelible. In 1957, Russia fired a shot heard around the world when it launched its Sputnik. America's first efforts to match the USSR proved humiliating failures. As the decade ended and the economy slowed, TV quiz scandals gave rise to additional moral self-doubt, and America's continuing failures in space and the "missile gap" brought its scientific and military preeminence into question. As a chipper Khrushchev proclaimed "We will bury you" to a well-fed, well-clothed, and well-housed bourgeois nation, America wondered if it was on the right track.

1950

Facts and Figures

Economic Profile
Dow-Jones: ↑ High 235–
  Low 193
GNP: +13%
Inflation: +5.7%
Unemployment: 5.3%
Brick ranch home, Bayside
  Hills, N.Y., 2 bedrooms, 2
  baths: $12,900
Median price, nationally, for
  single-family home:
  $10,050 (at 4.09% interest)
Mink stole: $250
Stepladder: $3.44–$5.44
Mastercraft oil paint: $2.66
  (gal.)
12′ wide Congoleum: 69¢ (sq.
  yd.)
Sears 3-piece bedroom set:
  $49.98
Lionel trains, complete:
  $14.95
Toddling Twin dolls: $2.97
Slate blackboard, with drop
  lid, easel, rack: $4.98
Havana cruise, SS *Europe:*
  $135–$150 (8 days)
North American Airlines,
  New York–California: $88
  (round trip)

Invasion Beach at Inchon,
where MacArthur's surprise
landing leads to the recapture
of Seoul and the anticipation
of an early victory.
Department of the Navy.

Deaths

Walter Damrosch, Walter
  Huston, Emil Jannings, Al
  Jolson, Harold Laski,
  Vaslav Nijinsky, George
  Orwell, Eliel Saarinen,
  George Bernard Shaw,
  Kurt Weill

In the News

HOOVER AND TAFT CALL FOR PROTECTION OF FORMOSA . . . BRINKS EXPRESS IS HELD UP FOR RECORD $1.8 MILLION . . . BRITAIN RECOGNIZES COMMUNIST CHINA . . . TRUMAN BARS MILITARY AID TO FORMOSA . . . ALGER HISS IS FOUND GUILTY OF PERJURY . . . RACE RIOTS ERUPT IN JOHANNESBURG OVER NEW APARTHEID POLICY . . . CHINESE COMMUNISTS SEIZE U.S. CONSULATE, U.S. WITHDRAWS . . . TRUMAN TELLS AEC TO DEVELOP H-BOMB . . . RUSSIA AND CHINA SIGN 3-YEAR TREATY . . . BRITISH SCIENTIST KLAUS FUCHS IS FOUND GUILTY OF TREASON . . . RUSSIANS SHOOT DOWN UNARMED U.S. PLANE IN BALTIC FOR "SPYING" . . . NATO LEADERS AGREE ON 5-YEAR INTEGRATED DEFENSE PLAN . . . RUSSIA ANNOUNCES A-BOMB . . . POSTMASTER CUTS MAIL DELIVERY TO ONCE A DAY . . . KEFAUVER CRIME COMMISSION OPENS HEARINGS . . . GENERAL MOTORS–UNITED AUTOWORKERS PACT GRANTS PENSIONS . . . 15% OF FACULTY ARE DISCHARGED AT UNIVERSITY OF CALIFORNIA FOR FAILURE TO SIGN NONCOMMUNIST AFFIRMATION PLEDGE . . . NORTH KOREA INVADES SOUTH KOREA, U.S. GROUND FORCES ARE SENT, NAVY BLOCKADES COAST . . . SENATOR JOSEPH McCARTHY CHARGES COMMUNIST INFILTRATION OF STATE DEPARTMENT . . . UN SECURITY COUNCIL AUTHORIZES UNIFIED UN COMMAND UNDER DOUGLAS MacARTHUR . . . TRUMAN SEIZES RAILROADS TO AVERT STRIKE . . . U.S. FORCES LAND AT INCHON IN MAJOR VICTORY . . . CHINESE COMMUNISTS INVADE TIBET . . . McCARRAN'S INTERNAL SECURITY ACT PASSES OVER TRUMAN VETO . . . $500 THOUSAND IS VOTED FOR POINT FOUR ASSISTANCE . . . TRUMAN SAYS VICTORY IN KOREA STILL MEANS HANDS OFF ASIA . . . U.S. FORCES ADVANCE IN NORTH KOREA AND REACH YALU RIVER . . . COMMUNIST CHINESE ENTER WAR IN MASS NUMBERS, UN TROOPS ARE FORCED TO RETREAT.

Quotes

"The attack upon Korea makes it plain that Communism has passed beyond the use of subversion to conquer independent nations and will now use armed invasion and war. Accordingly, I have ordered the Seventh Fleet to prevent any attack on Formosa."

— Harry S Truman

"I have here in my hand a list of 205 names known to the Secretary of State as being members of the Communist party who nevertheless are still working and shaping the policy of the State Department.

— Sen. Joseph McCarthy (R-Wis.)

"I affirm my innocence."—Alger Hiss
"Disgusting."—Richard M. Nixon

Senator Estes Kefauver: You refuse to testify further?
Frank Costello: Mr. Senator, I want to think of my health first. When I testify, I want to testify truthfully, and my mind don't function.

— Kefauver committee hearings

"You goddamn bastards. I hope an atom bomb falls on every one of you."

— Bugsy Siegel's girlfriend, Virginia Hill Hauser, to Kefauver committee

"If the television craze continues with the present level of programs, we are destined to have a nation of morons."

— Boston University president Daniel Marsh

"We must accelerate obsolescence. . . . Basic utility cannot be the foundation of a prosperous apparel industry."

— B. E. Puckett, businessman

"I have just read your lousy review of Margaret's concert. . . . Some day I hope to meet you. When that happens, you'll need a new nose, a lot of beefsteak for black eyes, and perhaps a supporter below."

— Harry Truman to *Washington Post* critic Paul Hume

Margaret Truman, the president's daughter. The *Washington Daily News* ran her father's angry letter to *Washington Post* critic Paul Hume, who refused to print it. *Library of Congress.*

Ads

Know the Bomb's True Dangers. Know the Steps You Can Take to Escape Them!
—You Can Survive.
(Government pamphlet)

FOR SALE
Small Farms—Out Beyond Atom Bombs
(Ad for property outside of Washington, D.C.)

We're tobacco men . . . not medicine men.
Old Gold cures just one thing. The World's Best Tobacco.
(Old Gold Cigarettes)

If you're a "golf widow," then here's a gift for your man that will remind him of you.
—Gold-plated Golf Tees.
(Barton's of Ridgewood)

Many, many women are enveloped in self-consciousness . . . *needlessly* hampered by imagined shortcomings. . . . *No woman* has any right to keep on feeling insecure about herself. *(Ponds)*

Darling, you're right to be narrow-minded! Fashion puts the emphasis on that slim-as-an-exclamation-point figure.
(Warner's Three-way Corsets)

The thrill of Roses
Spiced with excitement
Speaking of love.
(Old Spice Toiletries)

Munsingwear gowns . . . turn you into a Princess Charming.
(Munsingwear Lingerie)

Which orange juice tastes better than just-squeezed?
—Birds Eye, guaranteed or money back.
(Birds Eye Foods)

TV

Premieres

"Robert Montgomery Presents" ("The Letter")
"The Garry Moore Show"
"Your Hit Parade," Dorothy Collins, Snooky Lanson
"The Kate Smith Hour"
"Pulitzer Prize Playhouse"
"The Steve Allen Show"
"The Colgate Comedy Hour," Eddie Cantor, Dean
    Martin, Jerry Lewis, Fred Allen
"Your Show of Shows," Sid Caesar, Imogene Coca
"This Is Show Business," Clifton Fadiman, George
    S. Kaufman, Abe Burrows
"What's My Line?" John Daly, Dorothy Kilgallen,
    Bennett Cerf, Arlene Francis
"You Bet Your Life," Groucho Marx
"Beat the Clock," Bud Collyer
"Arthur Murray's Dance Party"
"The Stork Club," Peter Lind Hayes, Mary Healy
"The George Burns and Gracie Allen Show"
"The Jack Benny Program"
"Truth or Consequences," Ralph Edwards

Top Ten (Nielsen)

"Texaco Star Theater," "Fireside Theatre," "Philco
TV Playhouse," "Your Show of Shows," "The
Colgate Comedy Hour," "Gillette Cavalcade of
Sports," "The Lone Ranger," "Arthur Godfrey's
Talent Scouts," "Hopalong Cassidy," "Mama"

Specials

"Departure of Marines for Korea," "Arrival of
Cruiser from Korea," "Vienna Philharmonic,"
"Marshall Plan," "What to Do during an A-Bomb
Attack," "The Journey Back" (Edward R. Murrow)

Emmy Awards

"Pulitzer Prize Playhouse" (drama); "The Alan
Young Show" (variety); "Time for Beany" (children);
"Truth or Consequences" (game); Alan Young (actor,
"The Alan Young Show"); Gertrude Berg (actress,
"The Goldbergs"); Groucho Marx (personality)

Of Note

Eleanor Roosevelt begins a weekly forum with
"What to Do with the Hydrogen Bomb?" • Bob Hope
makes his debut on "Star Spangled Revue," the first
major radio comedian on TV • "Broadway Open
House," with Morey Amsterdam, Jerry Lester, and
Dagmar, is the first late-night talk show • Paul Draper
is dismissed from Ed Sullivan's show because of
complaints concerning his leftist associations, the
first public indication of blacklisting • For the first
time, TV ratings match radio ratings • Radio
superstars leave for TV.

Movies

Openings

All about Eve (Joseph L. Mankiewicz), Bette Davis,
    Anne Baxter, Celeste Holm, George Sanders
Born Yesterday (George Cukor), Judy Holliday,
    William Holden, Broderick Crawford
Father of the Bride (Vincente Minnelli), Elizabeth
    Taylor, Spencer Tracy, Joan Bennett
Sunset Boulevard (Billy Wilder), Gloria Swanson,
    William Holden, Erich von Stroheim
The Asphalt Jungle (John Huston), Sterling Hayden
Cyrano de Bergerac (Michael Gordon), José Ferrer
Harvey (Henry Koster), James Stewart, Josephine
    Hull, Peggy Dow
Adam's Rib (George Cukor), Katharine Hepburn,
    Spencer Tracy
The Men (Fred Zinnemann), Marlon Brando
Samson and Delilah (Cecil B. De Mille), Hedy
    Lamarr, Victor Mature
Cheaper by the Dozen (Walter Lang), Clifton Webb,
    Myrna Loy, Jeanne Crain
La Ronde (Max Ophuls), Simone Signoret, Jean-
    Louis Barrault, Danielle Darrieux
Bitter Rice (Giuseppe de Santis), Silvano Mangano,
    Vittorio Gassman
Kind Hearts and Coronets (Robert Hamer), Alec
    Guinness, Joan Greenwood
Los Olvidados (Luis Buñuel), Alfonso Méfia

Academy Awards

Best Picture: *All about Eve*
Best Director: Joseph L. Mankiewicz *(All about Eve)*
Best Actress: Judy Holliday *(Born Yesterday)*
Best Actor: José Ferrer *(Cyrano de Bergerac)*

Top Box-Office Stars

John Wayne, Bob Hope, Bing Crosby, Betty Grable,
James Stewart, Abbott and Costello, Clifton Webb,
Esther Williams, Spencer Tracy, Randolph Scott

Stars of Tomorrow

Dean Martin and Jerry Lewis, William Holden,
Arlene Dahl, Ruth Roman, Vera-Ellen, John Lund,
William Lundigan, Dean Jagger, Joanne Dru

Popular Music

Hit Songs
"Autumn Leaves"
"A Bushel and a Peck"
"Music! Music! Music!"
"It's So Nice to Have a Man
    around the House"
"Rag Mop"
"Tzena, Tzena, Tzena"
"La Vie en Rose"
"My Heart Cries for You"
"There's No Tomorrow"

Top Records

Albums: *Cinderella* (Ilene
Woods); *Young Man with a Horn*
(Harry James, Doris Day); *Three
Little Words* (original cast); *Merry
Christmas* (Bing Crosby)

Singles: *Goodnight Irene* (The
Weavers); *It Isn't Fair* (Sammy
Kaye); *Third Man Theme* (Anton
Karas); *Mule Train* (Frankie
Laine); *Mona Lisa* (Nat "King"
Cole); *I Wanna Be Loved*
(Andrews Sisters); *Twilight Time*
(Three Suns); *Frosty, the Snow
Man* (Gene Autry); *If I Knew You
Were Coming I'd Have Baked a
Cake* (Eileen Barton); *Be My Love*
(Mario Lanza); *The Thing* (Phil
Harris); *Tennessee Waltz* (Patti
Page); *September in the Rain*
(Lionel Hampton); *You Go to My
Head* (Lee Konitz). Country:
Chattanooga Shoe Shine Boy
(Red Foley); *Long Gone
Lonesome Blues* (Hank Williams)

Jazz and Big Bands
Stan Kenton organizes a 40-piece
"Innovations in Modern Music
Orchestra." Count Basie breaks
up his big band and starts a septet;
Dizzy Gillespie dismantles his big
band. Horace Silver joins Stan
Getz. The Red Norvo Trio
includes Charles Mingus and Tal
Farlow. Mahalia Jackson holds her
first Carnegie Hall concert.

Top Performers (*Downbeat*): Stan
Kenton (band); George Shearing
(jazz group); Stan Getz, Serge
Chaloff, Maynard Ferguson, Bill
Harris, Terry Gibbs
(instrumentalists); Sarah Vaughan,
Billy Eckstine (vocalists); Mills
Brothers (vocal group)

Theater

Broadway Openings

Plays
The Member of the Wedding (Carson McCullers),
    Julie Harris, Ethel Waters, Brandon De Wilde
Come Back, Little Sheba (William Inge), Stanley
    Blackmer, Shirley Booth
The Cocktail Party (T. S. Eliot), Alec Guinness,
    Cathleen Nesbitt
The Country Girl (Clifford Odets), Paul Kelly, Uta
    Hagen
Bell, Book, and Candle (John Van Druten), Rex
    Harrison, Lilli Palmer
The Happy Time (Samuel Taylor), Claude Dauphin,
    Eva Gabor
The Wisteria Trees (Joshua Logan), Helen Hayes
The Lady's Not for Burning (Christopher Fry), John
    Gielgud, Pamela Brown
The Innocents (William Archibald), Beatrice Straight

Musicals
Guys and Dolls (Frank Loesser), Robert Alda,
    Vivian Blaine, Sam Levene
Call Me Madam (Irving Berlin), Ethel Merman,
    Russell Nype, Paul Lukas
Peter Pan (Leonard Bernstein), Jean Arthur, Boris
    Karloff

Classics and Revivals On and Off Broadway
The Devil's Disciple (George Bernard Shaw),
Maurice Evans; *As You Like It*, Katharine Hepburn;
The Tower beyond Tragedy (Robinson Jeffers), Judith
Anderson; *Twentieth Century* (Ben Hecht, Charles
MacArthur), Gloria Swanson, José Ferrer. *Founded:*
Arena Theater, Hotel Edison (first theater-in-the-
round): *The Show Off*, Lee Tracy; *Julius Ceasar*,
Basil Rathbone, Alfred Ryder; *Arms and the Man*
(Shaw), Francis Lederer, Sam Wanamaker

Regional

Founded: Arena State Theatre, Washington, D.C.,
by Zelda and Thomas Fichandler, Edward Mangum

Alley, Houston: *Season with Ginger* [*Time Out for
Ginger*] (Ronald Alexander)

Pulitzer Prize
South Pacific, Richard Rodgers, Oscar Hammerstein
II, Joshua Logan

Tony Awards
The Cocktail Party, T. S. Eliot (play); *South Pacific*,
Richard Rodgers, Oscar Hammerstein II, Joshua
Logan (musical)

Classical Music _____

Compositions

Aaron Copland, *Twelve Poems of Emily Dickinson*
Norman Dello Joio, *Psalm of David*
John Cage, *Cartridge Music*
William Schuman, String Quartet no. 4
Walter Piston, Symphony no. 4
Douglas Moore, *Giants in the Earth*
Ross Lee Finney, String Quartet no. 6

Important Events

The bicentennial of Johann Sebastian Bach's death is celebrated throughout the world.
The Royal Philharmonic Orchestra, with Sir Thomas Beecham, tours the United States.
The Israeli Symphony, with Serge Koussevitsky, Eleanor de Carvalho, and Leonard Bernstein, tours 40 cities.
Robert, Gaby, and Jean Casadesus play the *Bach Concerto in C* arranged for three pianos and orchestra at Carnegie Hall.
Charles Munch pays tribute to Boston Symphony Hall's 50th anniversary by performing its original program, which included Handel's Organ Concerto no. 4 (now performed by E. Power Biggs).
Georges Enesco is violinist, pianist, and composer at the 60th-anniversary concert of his first appearance in New York.

Debuts: Claude Frank, Gerard Souzay, William Warfield

Lauren Bacall and Humphrey Bogart dining out. They met as costars of *To Have and Have Not* (1944). *Movie Star News.*

Metropolitan Opera impresario Rudolph Bing is gaining a reputation for his often stormy relationships with the company's prima donnas. *Movie Star News.*

First Performances

Paul Hindemith, conducting, Sinfonietta in E (Louisville); Francis Poulenc, playing, Piano Concerto (Boston); Paul Creston, Concerto for Piano and Orchestra (Washington, D.C.); Aaron Copland, Concerto for Clarinet, String Quartet, Harp and Piano (New York); Howard Hanson, Short Symphony (New York); Virgil Thomson, Concerto for Cello (Philadelphia); Samuel Barber, Piano Sonata (New York, Vladimir Horowitz)

Opera

Numerous chamber opera premieres include Norman Dello Joio's *The Triumph of Joan* (New York); Bernard Rogers's *The Veil,* and Lucas Foss's *The Jumping Frog* (Indiana University).

Metropolitan: Controversial Rudolf Bing is appointed; Bing plans for fewer singers and a smaller repertory. Roberta Peters (debut), *Don Giovanni;* Cesare Siepi, Lucine Amara (debuts), Robert Merrill, *Don Carlo;* Paul Schoeffler, *Die Meistersinger;* Erna Berger, *The Magic Flute;* Fedora Barbieri, *Il trovatore.* Kirsten Flagstad and Helen Traubel share honors as top Wagner sopranos.

San Francisco: Set Svanholm, Kirsten Flagstad, *Tristan und Isolde;* Renata Tebaldi, Mario del Monaco (debuts), *Aïda;* Kirsten Flagstad, *Parsifal*

Music Notes

Because of a financial deficit, the Philharmonic Symphony Society of New York plays on the stage of the Roxy Theater between movie shows, four times a day, for two weeks.

Art

Painting

Willem de Kooning,
Excavation, Woman I
(1950–1952)
Hans Hofmann,
Magenta and Blue
Jackson Pollock,
Autumn Rhythm, One
(Number 31, 1950)
Franz Kline, *Chief*
Morris Graves, *Spring*
Mark Rothko, *Number
10, 1950*
George Tooker, *The
Subway*
Barnett Newman,
Tundra, The Wild
Bradley Walker Tomlin,
*In Praise of Gertrude
Stein*
Kurt Seligmann, *The
Balcony, I*

Sculpture

Herbert Ferber, *He Is
Not a Man*
Richard Lippold,
*Variation within a
Sphere, No. 10: The
Sun*

Louise Bourgeois,
Sleeping Figure
David Smith, *Blackburn:
Song of an Irish
Blacksmith, Twenty-
Four Greek Ys*

Architecture

Bavington House,
Norman, Okla. (Bruce
Goff)
Christ Lutheran Church,
Minneapolis (Saarinen
and Saarinen)
Harvard Graduate
Center, Cambridge,
Mass. The Architects
Collaborative [TAC].
Farnsworth House,
Plano, Ill. (Mies van
der Rohe)
UN Headquarters, New
York (Harrison, Le
Corbusier, Niemeyer,
Markelius)
Construction begins on
the Lever House, New
York (Skidmore,
Owings, and Merrill).

Important Exhibitions

Museums

New York: *Metropolitan:* Art treasures from the
Vienna collection; "American Painting Today" (with
works from a nationwide competition); "307
Paintings from 34 States"; Masterpieces of bronze;
The world of silk. *Museum of Modern Art:* Klee,
Demuth, Soutine retrospectives. *Whitney:* Hopper
retrospective

Washington: *National:* Makers of history in
Washington, 1800–1950; Art treasures from the
Vienna collection. *Corcoran:* "American
Processional 1492–1900"

Boston: American art (largest survey ever held,
government-supported with $100,000); Iranian art;
Hopper

Philadelphia: Diamond Jubilee—"Masterpieces in
America"; 250 works from private collections:
Angelico Crucifix to Picasso's *Three Musicians*

Cleveland: Hopper retrospective

Detroit: From David to Courbet

Richmond: Impressionism and postimpressionism

Venice Biennale: Marin, Gorky, Pollock, de
Kooning, and Bloom represent the United States.

Art Briefs

The Metropolitan Museum of Art announces that its
annual American show will include sculpture and
alternate living painters and sculptors • Edvard
Munch's work tours the United States • Major sales
include Rembrandt's *Portrait of a Young Man*
($130,000) and *Portrait of a Student* ($135,000),
Gilbert's full-length Washington portrait ($17,500),
and Matisse's "Woman in Green" ($5,500) • Twenty-
eight avant-garde artists issue a manifesto attacking
the Metropolitan Museum of Art's aesthetic
provincialism.

Dance

Ballet Theatre, New York City Ballet, Les Ballets
Americains, and Martha Graham companies tour in
Europe. Sadler's Wells, Ballets de Paris, and Marquis
de Cuevas visit the United States.
Ballet Theatre celebrates its tenth anniversary. The
company is renamed the American National Ballet
Theatre and becomes the official company of the
Metropolitan Opera. Dancers include Alicia Alonso,
Nora Kaye, John Kriza, John Taras, Mary Ellen
Moylan, and Igor Youskevitch. Jerome Robbins joins
the New York City Ballet; the New York City Dance
Theatre debuts with *The Moor's Pavanne* (José
Limón).
Martha Graham dances *Judith* (William Schuman) in
Louisville, Ky.; Sadler's Wells tour breaks box-office
records.

Premieres

New York City Ballet: *The Age of Anxiety,* (Jerome
Robbins, Leonard Bernstein), Tanaquil Le Clercq,
Todd Bolender; *Illuminations* (Frederick Ashton),
Nicholas Magallanes, Le Clercq, Melissa Hayden.

Books

Fiction

Critics' Choice

Collected Stories, William Faulkner
The Delicate Prey, Paul Bowles
Cast a Cold Eye, Mary McCarthy
The Family Moskat, Isaac Bashevis Singer
World Enough and Time, Robert Penn Warren
The Martian Chronicles, Ray Bradbury
The Town and the City, Jack Kerouac
The Trouble of One House, Brendan Gill
The Roman Spring of Mrs. Stone, Tennessee Williams

Best-Sellers

The Cardinal, Henry Morton Robinson
Joy Street, Frances Parkinson Keyes
Across the River and into the Trees, Ernest Hemingway
The Wall, John Hersey
Floodtide, Frank Yerby
The Adventurer, Mika Waltari
The Disenchanted, Budd Schulberg
Star Money, Kathleen Winsor
The Parasites, Daphne Du Maurier
Jubilee Trail, Gwen Bristow

Nonfiction

Critics' Choice

Decision in Germany, Lucius Clay
The Human Use of Human Beings, Norbert Wiener
Virgin Land, Henry Nash Smith
The American Mind, Henry Steele Commager
The Liberal Imagination, Lionel Trilling
A Rhetoric of Motives, Kenneth Burke
Classics and Commercials, Edmund Wilson
The Lonely Crowd, David Riesman, Jr., Reuel Denney, Nathan Glazer
Worlds in Collision, Immanuel Velikovsky
The Index of American Design, Edwin O. Christensen
Herman Melville, Newton Arvin

Best-Sellers

Betty Crocker's Picture Cook Book
The Baby
Look Younger, Live Longer, Gayelord Hauser
How I Raised Myself from Failure to Success in Selling, Frank Bettger
Kon-Tiki, Thor Heyerdahl
Your Dream Home, Hubbard Cobb
The Mature Mind, H. A. Overstreet

Bells on Their Toes, Frank Gilbreth, Jr., Ernestine Gilbreth Carey
Campus Zoo, Clare Barnes, Jr.
Mr. Jones, Meet the Master, Peter Marshall

Poetry

Wallace Stevens, *The Auroras of Autumn*
Robert Lowell, *Poems 1938–1949*
William Carlos Williams, *The Collected Later Poems*
Howard Nemerov, *Guide to the Ruins*
E. E. Cummings, *Xaïpe*
Delmore Schwartz, *Vaudeville for a Princess*
W. H. Auden, *Collected Shorter Poems 1930–1944*

Pulitzer Prizes

The Town, Conrad Richter (fiction)
The Old Northwest, Pioneer Period 1815–1840, vols. 1–2, R. Carlyle Buley (U.S. history)
John C. Calhoun: American Portrait, Margaret Louise Coit (biography)
Complete Poems, Carl Sandburg (poetry)

Science and Technology

Tritium, a hydrogen isotope and the basis for the new H-bomb, is discovered in ordinary water.
New elements Berkelium 97 and Californium 98 are created by the Berkeley cyclotron. The existence of subatomic "V" particles is confirmed.
On the basis of the La Jolla cave finds, George Carter, of Johns Hopkins, reports that man lived in North America 40,000 years ago.
Tromexan, an anticoagulant, is reported by Dr. Irving Wright to be a potential heart attack inhibitor.
Dr. Richard Lawler performs the first kidney transplant.
The first successful heart massage is performed at St. John's Hospital, Brooklyn, N.Y.

The first successful aorta transplant is performed on a fifty-seven-year-old man at Ford Hospital, Detroit.
B. J. Ludwig and E. C. Pich, of Wallace Labs, synthesize the tranquilizer meprobamate.

Nobel Prize

Philip S. Hench and Edward C. Kendall win the prize in physiology and medicine for their discoveries about the hormones of the adrenal cortex.

Sports

Baseball

Gil Hodges (Brooklyn, NL), hits four home runs in one game.

Connie Mack retires after fifty years as the Philadelphia A's manager.

The major leagues sign a $6 million TV contract for World Series rights, with benefits to go to the pension fund.

Champions

Batting	Pitching
Stan Musial (St. Louis, NL), .346	Sal Maglie (New York, NL), 18–4
William Goodman (Boston, AL), .354	Vic Raschi (New York, AL), 21–8
	Home runs
	Ralph Kiner (Pittsburgh, NL), 47

Football

The Cleveland Browns, of the old All-America Conference (AAC), win in the first year of the merged leagues.

NFL Season Leaders: Norm Van Brocklin (Los Angeles), passing; Marion Motley (Cleveland), rushing; Tom Fears (Los Angeles), passing

College All-Americans: Kyle Rote (B), Southern Methodist; Vic Janowicz (Q), Ohio State; Bill McColl (E), Stanford

Bowls (Jan. 1, 1951)

Rose: Michigan 14–California 6	Cotton: Tennessee 20–Texas 14
Orange: Clemson 15–Miami 14	Sugar: Kentucky 13–Oklahoma 6

Basketball

City College of New York wins the NCAA and the NIT, the first team to win both; Irwin Dambrot, Ed Roman, and Floyd Lane star.

NBA All-Pro First Team: George Mikan (Minneapolis), Jim Pollard (Minneapolis), Alex Groza (Indianapolis), Bob Davies (Rochester), Max Zaslofsky (Chicago)

Other Sports

Golf: In a comeback after his car accident, Ben Hogan wins the U.S. Open. Sam Snead is the PGA leader with $37,000 in winnings.

Boxing: Sugar Ray Robinson, middleweight champion, challenges Joey Maxim, light heavyweight champion, for his crown. Robinson is ahead on points but because of the heat can't come out for the 14th and loses by TKO.

Tennis: Gussie Moran's tennis outfit, including lace underwear, creates a stir on the pro circuit.

Winners

World Series	*College Basketball*
New York (AL) 4	C.C.N.Y. (NCAA, NIT)
Philadelphia (NL) 1	*Player of the Year*
MVP	Paul Arizin, Villanova
NL–Jim Konstanty, Philadelphia	*Stanley Cup*
AL–Phil Rizzuto, New York	Detroit
NFL	*US Tennis Open*
Cleveland 30–Los Angeles 28	Men: Arthur Larsen
College Football	Women: Margaret Osborne DuPont
Oklahoma	*USGA Open*
Heisman Trophy	Ben Hogan
Vic Janowicz, Ohio State	*Kentucky Derby*
NBA Championship	Middleground (W. Boland, jockey)
Minneapolis 4–Syracuse 2	

Fashion

For Women: The flapper revival at the beginning of the year is accompanied by more "wearable," "pretty," and "feminine" clothes: the belted chemise, sleeveless dresses, tailored suits, loose and fleecy topcoats. Velvet and velveteen are popular in ballgowns (with little jackets), suits, and dresses. Transparent fabrics, chiffons, and organdies in sherbet tones and white or gray tulle are worn at night with stoles in matching fabrics and patent leather shoes, bags, and belts. Most fashionable is the black/white combination, worn year round, with big, glittery rhinestone jewelry. Hair is longer, chignons are stylish, makeup is lighter, lips are pink and white, eyes are accented and elongated, eyebrows are natural.

High-fashion note: Balenciaga's belted jacket

Kaleidoscope _____

- Twelve live Russian sables are sent to the United States for breeding purposes in return for twelve U.S. minks; the sables arrive sterilized.
- Gen. Frank McConnell, at Fort Jackson, S.C., orders integration in the armed services following Truman's and the secretary of the army's directives.
- Bomb-shelter plans, like the government pamphlet *You Can Survive,* become widely available. Many leading scientists warn of Russia's race to achieve the H-bomb; Einstein and others argue that "general annihilation beckons."
- Blacklisting of performers with alleged Communist affiliations becomes widespread. CBS requires that a loyalty oath be signed; *Red Channels,* the "Report of Communist Influence in Radio and TV" lists Leonard Bernstein, Lee J. Cobb, Ben Grauer, Gypsy Rose Lee, Philip Loeb, Burgess Meredith, Arthur Miller, Zero Mostel, Pete Seeger, Howard K. Smith, and Orson Welles.
- Herblock coins the term *McCarthyism.*
- Thirty million people watch the Kefauver Commission crime hearings, which matches the World Series in TV ratings; one Chicago department store offers "10% off during Kefauver hours."
- Hallmark Greeting Cards buys reproduction rights for eighteen of Winston Churchill's canvases; he donates his stipend to Cambridge University.
- A Columbia University Press editor conducts a poll of librarians for the most boring books; the results are Bunyan's *Pilgrim's Progress,* Melville's *Moby Dick,* Milton's *Paradise Lost,* and Spenser's *Faerie Queene.*
- Americans consume 320 million pounds of potato chips annually and 750 million pounds of hotdogs; per capita consumption is 63.1 pounds of beef; 8.2 pounds of veal; 69.9 pounds of pork, and 3.9 pounds of lamb or mutton.
- At the 10,600 houses at Levittown, N.Y., rules mandate that grass be cut at least once a week and laundry washed on specific days.
- Polls indicate that President Truman's decisions to continue H-bomb research and to send the navy and air force to Korea have won him support from many who believe that America is finally taking a stand against Communism.
- The UN reports that half of the world's 800 million children are undernourished.
- A new low in illiteracy is recorded: 3.2 percent.
- A national survey reports that children spend 27 hours a week watching TV, three-fourths of an hour less than their weekly time in school.
- David Reisman's acclaimed *The Lonely Crowd* describes how rugged individualism has given way to the quest for peer group approval.
- After the Kefauver hearings, Young and Rubicam, one of the United States' largest advertising agencies, takes a full-page newspaper ad to express shock at "what's happened to public and private standards of morality."
- Congressman E. C. Johnson attacks the alleged immorality of film stars like Ingrid Bergman and Roberto Rossellini (who have conceived an out-of-wedlock child) and introduces a bill to license film producers and distributors.
- Jane Russell and Roy Rogers become born-again Christians. Miss Russell says of God: "He's a livin' doll."
- A *Downbeat* poll lists as the most popular male singers Billy Eckstine, Perry Como, Frankie Laine, Frank Sinatra, Louis Armstrong, and Mel Torme; female singers include Sarah Vaughan, Ella Fitzgerald, Doris Day, Kay Starr, Peggy Lee, Billie Holiday, Patti Page, Jo Stafford, and Fran Warren.
- A *Life* survey lists as the most popular teen idols Louisa May Alcott, Joe DiMaggio, Vera-Ellen, FDR, Lincoln, Roy Rogers, General MacArthur, Clara Barton, Doris Day, Sister Elizabeth Kenny, Babe Ruth, and Florence Nightingale.
- A Pan American flight from New York to London is recorded in 9 hours and 16 minutes.
- Flying saucers are sighted in Israel, Hong Kong, and Italy.
- UN diplomat Ralph J. Bunche receives the Nobel Peace Prize.
- Carol Fox, debutante daughter of a wealthy Chicago furniture manufacturer, founds the Chicago Lyric Theatre, goes to Europe, and lines up La Scala's Tito Gobbi, along with Guiseppe di Stefano, Giulietta Simionato, and Maria Callas.
- Without any evidence, Senator McCarthy names as the "top Russian espionage agent" Owen Lattimore of the State Department.
- "I do not intend to turn my back on Alger Hiss," says Dean Acheson, after his friend's conviction.
- Russian spy Klaus Fuchs says he had complete faith in Russian policy and no hesitation in giving away secrets.
- Russians, who have been boycotting the Security Council for five months, refuse Trygve Lie's invitation to return for the debate on Korea.

New Words and Usages: apartheid, captive audience, Cinerama, colorcast, dianetics, fusion bomb, H-bomb, integration, mambo, rat pack, spaceman, theater-in-the-round, triton bomb

Fads: Hopalong Cassidy outfits for children, along with toy guns, spurs, and boots; black molasses; the mambo; square dancing; antihistamine pill popping

First Appearances: Learn-When-Sleeping machine, phototransistor, Sugar Pops, orlon, Miss Clairol, Smokey the Bear, Otis elevator with self-opening doors, Minute Rice, Sony tape recorders, syndicated "Peanuts," Diners Club, Corning Ware, cyclamates, Air Call (beepers), A. C. Nielsen Co. (rating service, formerly of C. E. Hooper)

1951

In the News _____

CHINESE COMMUNISTS AND NORTH KOREANS RETAKE SEOUL AND INCHON . . . U.S. RESUMES ARMS SUPPLY TO CHINESE NATIONALISTS . . . TRUMAN SAYS RUSSIA SEEKS WORLD CONQUEST, ASKS CONGRESS FOR FULL MOBILIZATION AND WAGE-PRICE FREEZE . . . U.S. TESTS A-BOMB NEAR LAS VEGAS . . . UN RESOLUTION CONDEMNS CHINESE COMMUNIST AGGRESSION . . . PENN RAILROAD ACCIDENT IN N.J. KILLS 84 . . . RAIL STRIKE ENDS UNDER THREAT OF FIRINGS . . . U.S. WILL SEND 100,000 TROOPS TO EUROPE . . . LABOR BALKS AT 10% WAGE INCREASE LIMIT . . . 22D AMENDMENT TAKES EFFECT LIMITING THE PRESIDENT TO TWO TERMS . . . GENERAL OMAR BRADLEY ANNOUNCES THAT 250,000 GIs ARE NOW IN KOREA . . . J. EDGAR HOOVER WARNS THAT COMMUNISTS ARE GOING UNDERGROUND . . . ETHEL AND JULIUS ROSENBERG ARE FOUND GUILTY OF TREASON AND SENTENCED TO DEATH . . . GENERAL MACARTHUR URGES CROSSING THE YALU RIVER INTO CHINA . . . TRUMAN RELIEVES MACARTHUR, GIANT PARADE GREETS MACARTHUR IN NEW YORK . . . MOSSADEGH BECOMES PREMIER OF IRAN, PLANS TO NATIONALIZE OIL . . . THE DRAFT AGE IS LOWERED TO 18 . . . CHINESE COMMUNISTS ACCEPT U.S. PROPOSAL TO DISCUSS CEASE-FIRE . . . CEASE-FIRE TALKS BEGIN IN KAESONG . . . U.S. ASKS EGYPT TO OPEN SUEZ CANAL TO ISRAELIS . . . WASHINGTON ANNOUNCES SECOND SOVIET A-BOMB TEST . . . MUTUAL SECURITY ACT PROVIDES $7.5 BILLION FOR FOREIGN AID . . . CEASE-FIRE TALKS REOPEN IN PANMUNJOM . . . TRUMAN OFFERS "FOOLPROOF" DISARMAMENT PLAN . . . WEST GERMANY IS GRANTED SOVEREIGNTY . . . BRIEF CEASE-FIRE ENDS.

Gen. Douglas MacArthur's farewell address to a joint session of Congress. *Library of Congress.*

"We must . . . limit the war to Korea . . . to prevent a third World War. . . . General MacArthur did not agree with that policy. I have therefore considered it essential to relieve General MacArthur."
— Harry S Truman

"When you put on a uniform there are certain inhibitions which you accept."
— Gen. Dwight D. Eisenhower

"President Truman has given [the Communists] . . . just what they were after—MacArthur's scalp."
— Senator Richard M. Nixon

" 'Old soldiers never die; they just fade away.' And like the old soldier of that ballad, I now close my military career and just fade away—an old soldier who tried to do his duty as God gave him the light to see that duty. Good-bye.
— Gen. Douglas MacArthur

Ads

Quotes

"I saw a young kid of an outfielder I can't believe. He can run, hit to either field, and has a real good arm. Don't ask any questions. You've got to get this boy."
— New York Giants scout's report on Willie Mays

"One nice thing about television. You don't have to pick out where to look."
— *New Yorker* cartoon by Gardner Rea

"She has a favorite charity. . . . She belongs to the Arts and Literature Committee of the Women's Club, the DAR, and the Garden Club, . . . a charter member of the Wednesday Shakespeare Society."
— *Fortune* editorial, on the successful businessman's wife

"When you find an intellectual, you will probably find a Red."
— *Washington Confidential* (best-seller)

"I killed more people tonight than I have fingers on my hands. . . . I enjoyed every minute of it. . . . They were Commies. . . . They figure us all to be as soft as horse manure."
— Mike Hammer, *In a Lonely Night* by Mickey Spillane

Spencer Tracy. ("I've learned more about acting from watching Tracy than in any other way," says Laurence Olivier.) *Movie Star News.*

TV

Premieres

"The Cisco Kid," Duncan Renaldo
"Search for Tomorrow"
"Hallmark Hall of Fame," Sarah Churchill (host)
"Celanese Theater" ("Ah, Wilderness!")
"The Chevy Show Starring Dinah Shore"
"Treasury Men in Action," Walter Greaza
"See It Now," Edward R. Murrow
"Schlitz Playhouse of Stars" ("Not a Chance," Helen Hayes, David Niven)
"Wild Bill Hickok," Guy Madison, Andy Devine
"The Jack LaLanne Show"
"The Sam Levenson Show"
"Rocket Squad," Reed Hadley
"The Name's the Same," Robert Q. Lewis
"I Love Lucy," Lucille Ball, Desi Arnaz, Vivian Vance, William Frawley
"The Roy Rogers Show"
"The Red Skelton Show"
"Superman," George Reeves

Top Ten (Nielsen)

"Arthur Godfrey's Talent Scouts," "Texaco Star Theater," "I Love Lucy," "The Red Skelton Show," "The Colgate Comedy Hour," "Arthur Godfrey and His Friends," "Fireside Theatre," "Your Show of Shows," "The Jack Benny Show," "You Bet Your Life"

Emmy Awards

"Studio One" (drama); "The Red Skelton Show" (comedy); "Your Show of Shows" (variety); Sid Caesar (actor, "Your Show of Shows"); Imogene Coca (actress, "Your Show of Shows"); Senator Estes Kefauver (special achievement)

Of Note

The first commercial color broadcast takes place • The "eye" becomes CBS's logo • Many repeatedly "take the Fifth" on the Senate Crime Committee hearings chaired by Senator Estes Kefauver; underworld figures who appear include Joe Adonis, Frank Erickson, and Frank Costello (who allows only his hands to be televised) • "Amos 'n' Andy" is condemned by the NAACP for depicting "the Negro in a stereotyped and derogatory manner" • The Brooklyn and Golden Gate bridges appear simultaneously live on screen, as the coast-to-coast coaxial cable is completed ("See It Now").

Movies

Openings

An American in Paris (Vincente Minnelli), Gene Kelly, Leslie Caron, Oscar Levant
A Place in the Sun (George Stevens), Montgomery Clift, Elizabeth Taylor, Shelley Winters
Quo Vadis (Mervyn LeRoy), Robert Taylor, Deborah Kerr
A Streetcar Named Desire (Elia Kazan), Vivien Leigh, Marlon Brando, Kim Hunter
The African Queen (John Huston), Humphrey Bogart, Katharine Hepburn
Detective Story (William Wyler), Kirk Douglas, Eleanor Parker
David and Bathsheba (Henry King), Gregory Peck, Susan Hayward
Strangers on a Train (Alfred Hitchcock), Farley Granger, Robert Walker, Ruth Roman
Show Boat (George Sidney), Kathryn Grayson, Howard Keel, Ava Gardner
The Red Badge of Courage (John Huston), Audie Murphy, Bill Mauldin
The Great Caruso (Richard Thorpe), Mario Lanza, Ann Blyth, Dorothy Kirsten
Oliver Twist (David Lean), Alec Guinness, John Howard Davies
Cry, the Beloved Country (Zoltan Korda), Canada Lee, Sidney Poitier
The Lavender Hill Mob (Charles Crichton), Alec Guinness, Stanley Holloway
Rashomon (Akira Kurosawa), Toshiro Mifune

Academy Awards

Best Picture: *An American in Paris*
Best Director: George Stevens (*A Place in the Sun*)
Best Actress: Vivien Leigh (*A Streetcar Named Desire*)
Best Actor: Humphrey Bogart (*The African Queen*)

Top Box-Office Stars

John Wayne, Dean Martin and Jerry Lewis, Betty Grable, Abbott and Costello, Bing Crosby, Bob Hope, Randolph Scott, Gary Cooper, Doris Day, Spencer Tracy

Stars of Tomorrow

Howard Keel, Thelma Ritter, Shelley Winters, Frank Lovejoy, Debra Paget, David Brian, Piper Laurie, Gene Nelson, Dale Robertson, Corinne Calvet

Popular Music

Hit Songs
"Cold, Cold Heart"
"The Little White Cloud That
    Cried"
"Hello, Young Lovers"
"Mockin' Bird Hill"
"Jezebel"
"Shrimp Boats"
"Tell Me Why"
"In the Cool, Cool, Cool of the
    Evening"
"I Get Ideas"
"Unforgettable"

Top Records

Albums: *Guys and Dolls* (original cast); *Voice of the Xtabay* (Yma Sumac); *The Great Caruso* (Mario Lanza); *Showboat* (sound track); *Mario Lanza Sings Christmas Songs* (Mario Lanza)

Singles: *How High the Moon* (Les Paul, Mary Ford); *Loveliest Night of the Year* (Mario Lanza); *On Top of Old Smoky* (The Weavers); *I Apologize* (Billy Eckstine); *Because of You* (Tony Bennett); *Come On-a My House* (Rosemary Clooney); *Too Young* (Nat "King" Cole); *If* (Perry Como); *A Guy Is a Guy* (Doris Day); *The Syncopated Clock* (Leroy Anderson); *Aba Daba Honeymoon* (Debbie Reynolds); *Cry* (Johnnie Ray); *My Heart Cries for You* (Mitch Miller, Guy Mitchell). Country: *Shotgun Boogie* (Tennessee Ernie Ford); *I'm Movin' On* (Hank Snow)

Jazz and Big Bands
Dave Brubeck forms a quartet with Paul Desmond. Louis Bellson joins Duke Ellington.

First Recording: Sonny Rollins as leader

New Band: Count Basie reorganizes a big band.

Top Performers (*Downbeat*): Charlie Parker (soloist); Stan Kenton (band); George Shearing (jazz group); Stan Getz, Serge Chaloff, Buddy De Franco, Bill Harris, Maynard Ferguson (instrumentalists); Sarah Vaughan, Billy Eckstine (vocalists); Mills Brothers (vocal group)

Theater

Broadway Openings

Plays
The Rose Tattoo (Tennessee Williams), Maureen Stapleton, Eli Wallach
I Am a Camera (John Van Druten), Julie Harris, William Prince
Point of No Return (Paul Osborne), Henry Fonda, Leora Dana
The Moon Is Blue (F. Hugh Herbert), Barbara Bel Geddes, Donald Cook, Barry Nelson
Stalag 17 (Donald Bevin, Edmund Trzcinski), Robert Strauss, Harvey Lembeck
Gigi (Anita Loos), Audrey Hepburn
The Fourposter (Jan de Hartog), Jessica Tandy, Hume Cronyn
Darkness at Noon (Sidney Kingsley), Claude Rains, Kim Hunter
Billy Budd (Louis Coxe, Robert Chapman), Charles Nolte, Dennis King
The Autumn Garden (Lillian Hellman), Florence Eldridge, Fredric March
Barefoot in Athens (Maxwell Anderson), Barry Jones

Musicals
The King and I (Richard Rodgers, Oscar Hammerstein II), Gertrude Lawrence, Yul Brynner
Top Banana (Johnny Mercer), Phil Silvers
A Tree Grows in Brooklyn (Arthur Schwartz, Dorothy Fields), Shirley Booth, Johnny Johnston
Paint Your Wagon (Alan Jay Lerner, Frederick Loewe), James Barton, Olga San Juan

Classics and Revivals On and Off Broadway
Richard II, Maurice Evans; Reading of *Don Juan in Hell* (George Bernard Shaw), Charles Laughton, Charles Boyer, Cedric Hardwicke, Agnes Moorehead; *Caesar and Cleopatra, Antony and Cleopatra,* Laurence Olivier, Vivien Leigh; *Romeo and Juliet,* Olivia de Havilland, Jack Hawkins; *St. Joan* (Shaw), Uta Hagen, James Daly; *Peer Gynt* (Ibsen), John Garfield; *The Constant Wife* (W. Somerset Maugham), Katharine Cornell, Gladys George, Brian Aherne; *Diamond Lil* (Mae West), Mae West. *Founded:* Circle in the Square (three-sided theater): *Dark of the Moon; Summer and Smoke,* Geraldine Fitzgerald

Pulitzer Prize
No prize is awarded.

Tony Awards
The Rose Tattoo, Tennessee Williams (play); *Guys and Dolls,* Frank Loesser (musical)

Classical Music ———————

Compositions
Elliott Carter, String Quartet
Gail Kubik, Symphony Concertante
Morton Feldman, *Intersection I: Projections*
Walter Piston, String Quartet no. 4
Roger Sessions, Quartet no. 2
Roy Harris, Symphony no. 7
John Cage, *Imaginary Landscape* no. 4
Harold Shapero, Concerto for Orchestra
Aaron Copland, *Pied Piper*

Important Events
The 50th anniversary of Verdi's death is celebrated throughout the United States. Toscanini conducts the Requiem in New York.
Wanda Landowska records Bach's *Well-Tempered Clavier,* Book I.
Rudolf Serkin and Adolf and Hermann Busch perform at the first concert at the Marlboro Music School and Festival, Marlboro, Vermont.

Debut: Charles Rosen, Stephen Bishop-Kovacevich, Bruce Hungerford

First Performances
Charles Ives, Symphony no. 2 (New York), Symphony no. 4 (Minneapolis), Piano Concerto (Boston, with Lukas Foss, 29); Arthur Honegger, *Suite Archaique* (Louisville), Symphony no. 5

Imogene Coca and Sid Caesar in one of their satiric routines from "Your Show of Shows." Carl Reiner costars, and script writers include Mel Brooks, Neil Simon, Woody Allen, and Larry Gelbart. *Billy Rose Theatre Collection. The New York Public Library at Lincoln Center. Astor, Lenox and Tilden Foundations.*

Stuart Davis, *Owh! in San Pāo*, 1951. 52¼ × 41¾". *Whitney Museum of American Art, G. Clements.*

(Boston); Roy Harris, *Cumberland* Concerto (Cincinnati)

Opera

NBC-TV Opera Theater: *Amahl and the Night Visitors* (Gian Carlo Menotti, premiere)

Columbia University: *Giants in the Earth* (Douglas Moore, premiere)

Metropolitan: Cesare Siepi, *Fidelio;* Patrice Munsel, *Die Fledermaus;* Kurt Baum, *Wozzeck;* Victoria de los Angeles (debut), *Faust;* Mario del Monaco, *Otello;* Nell Rankin, George London, *Aïda;* Roberta Peters, Leonard Warren, *Rigoletto*

New York City: *The Dybbuk* (David Tamkin); *The Four Ruffians* (Wolf-Ferrari), premieres

San Francisco: Lily Pons, Jan Peerce, *La traviata;* Dorothy Kirsten, Jussi Bjoerling, *Tosca*

Music Notes
Seven hundred orchestras play in the United States.

Art ———————————————

Painting

Richard Pousette-Dart;
Chavade
Clyfford Still, *Painting,
1951 Yellow, 1951-N*
Stuart Davis, *Owh! In
San Pão*
Franz Kline, *Ninth
Street*
Jackson Pollock,
*Number 26, 27, Echo
(Number 25, 1951)*
Ellsworth Kelly, *Colors
for a Large Wall*
Barnett Newman, *Vir
Heroicus Sublimis*
Fritz Glarner, *Relational
Painting* (1949–51)
William Baziotes, *Sea
Forms*
Adolph Gottlieb, *The
Frozen Sounds, No. 1*
John Marin, *Sea Piece*

Sculpture

David Smith, *Australia,
Cloak, Family
Decision, Hudson
River Landscape*
Seymour Lipton, *Cloak*
Theodore Roszak, *Maja*
José de Rivera,
*Construction Blue and
Black*

Marcel Duchamp, *Wedge
of Chastity*

Architecture

Umbrella House,
Aurora, Ill. (Bruce
Goff)
860 Lake Shore Drive
Apartments, Chicago
(Mies van der Rohe)
General Motors
Technical Research
Center Auditorium,
Detroit (Eero
Saarinen)
First Unitarian Meeting
House, Madison,
Wisc. (Frank Lloyd
Wright)
Wayfarers' Chapel, Palos
Verdes, Calif. (Wright)
First Presbyterian
Church, Cottage
Grove, Ore. (Pietro
Belluschi)
Charles Eames House,
Santa Monica, Calif.
(Eames)
Indian Chapel,
University of
Oklahoma (Eero
Saarinen and Coe)

Important Exhibitions

Museums

New York: *Metropolitan:* 75th anniversary of the
Art Students League; Eakins, LaFarge, Bellows,
Chase; All-sculpture show. *Museum of Modern Art:*
"Abstract Painting and Sculpture in America"; 100
works from 85 artists, 1913 to the present; Matisse
retrospective. *Brooklyn:* "Italy at Work" (Crafts,
industrial art since World War II)

Boston: Edward Jackson Holmes memorial
exhibition of Persian art treasures of the Vienna
collection; German expressionism

Chicago: Art of Vienna; Artists of Chicago; Munch;
"Italy at Work"

Eugene O'Neill. *Billy
Rose Theatre
Collection. The New
York Public Library at
Lincoln Center. Astor,
Lenox and Tilden
Foundations.*

Washington: European paintings of the Gulbenkian
collection; Audubon

Cleveland, San Francisco, Chicago: Matisse

Pittsburgh: Eight centuries of French painting 1100–
1900

Baltimore, Yale: "Gertrude Stein as Collector and
Writer"

Detroit, Toledo: "Artists in Italy 1830–1875"

Indiana, Dayton, Davenport: Art in Colonial Mexico

Individual Shows

Gorky (Whitney, Minneapolis, San Francisco); Lovis
Corinth (Boston); Modigliani, Soutine, Lautrec
(Cleveland); Tobey (San Francisco, Seattle,
Whitney)

Art Briefs

The Metropolitan Museum of Art purchases a
Leonardo drawing *Head of the Virgin* and expands
and modernizes at a cost of $5,436,000 • At a
Whitney show, $100 provides entrance and the
purchase of one painting or sculpture • Top sales
include Lautrec's print *Partie de Compagne* ($1,600),
Delacroix's *Académie de Femme* ($10,500),
Boucher's *Pastorale* ($13,000), and Watteau's *Feast
of Pan* ($12,500) • The Houston Fine Arts Museum
acquires a Carl Milles fountain.

Dance ———————————————

Lew Christensen becomes director of the San
Francisco Ballet; Nora Kaye, Diana Adams, and
Hugh Laing move from Ballet Theatre to the New
York City Ballet.

Premieres

New York City Ballet: *Cakewalk* (Ruthanna Boris);
Tanaquil Le Clercq, Yvonne Mounsey; *The Cage*
(Jerome Robbins, Stravinsky), Nora Kaye, Mounsey;
The Miraculous Mandarin (Todd Bolender, Bartók),
Melissa Hayden, Hugh Laing; *La Valse* (Balanchine),
Le Clercq, Nicholas Magallanes, Francisco Moncion;
Swan Lake (Balanchine)

Books

Fiction
Critics' Choice
The Morning Watch, James Agee
The Grass Harp, Truman Capote
Requiem for a Nun, William Faulkner
Notes on a Horse Thief, William Faulkner
The Beetle Leg, John Hawkes
Lie Down in Darkness, William Styron
Barbary Shore, Norman Mailer
The Ballad of the Sad Café, Carson McCullers
The Catcher in the Rye, J. D. Salinger
The Strange Children, Caroline Gordon
In the Absence of Angels, Hortense Calisher
🙚 *The Masters*, C. P. Snow

Best-Sellers
From Here to Eternity, James Jones
The Caine Mutiny, Herman Wouk
Moses, Sholem Asch
The Cardinal, Henry Morton Robinson
A Woman Called Fancy, Frank Yerby
The Cruel Sea, Nicholas Monsarrat

Melville Goodwin, U.S.A., John P. Marquand
Return to Paradise, James A. Michener
The Foundling, Cardinal Francis B. Spellman
The Wanderer, Mika Waltari

Nonfiction
Critics' Choice
The Necessary Angel, Wallace Stevens
Life in America, Marshall B. Davidson
American Diplomacy, 1900–1950, George F. Kennan
The Far Side of Paradise, Arthur Mizener
Henry James, F. W. Dupee
White Collar, the American Middle Classes, C. Wright Mills
Jefferson and the Rights of Man, Dumas Malone
God and Man at Yale, William F. Buckley
The Origins of Totalitarianism, Hannah Arendt

Best-Sellers
Look Younger, Live Longer, Gayelord Hauser
Betty Crocker's Picture Cook Book

Washington Confidential, Jack Lait and Lee Mortimer
Better Homes and Gardens Handyman's Book
The Sea around Us, Rachel L. Carson
Pogo, Walt Kelly
The New Yorker Twenty-Fifth Anniversary Album
Kon-Tiki, Thor Heyerdahl

Poetry
Robert Lowell, *The Mills of the Kavanaughs*
Adrienne Rich, *A Change of World*
James Merrill, *First Poems*
William Carlos Williams, *Paterson, Book Four*
Randall Jarrell, *The Seven-League Crutches*
Theodore Roethke, *Praise to the End*

Pulitzer Prizes
The Caine Mutiny, Herman Wouk (fiction)
The Uprooted, Oscar Handlin (U.S. history)
Charles Evans Hughes, Merlo J. Pusey (biography)
Collected Poems (Marianne Moore)

Science and Technology

Scientists led by Edward Teller set off the first thermonuclear reaction.

Operation Greenhouse begins, a secret mission in the Pacific Islands believed to be related to hydrogen bomb testing.

The AEC completes its facility, called the "atomic apothecary," at Oak Ridge, Tenn., for processing radioisotopes for medical research.

Robert Leighton, at the California Institute of Technology, reports the discovery of the negative proton, a fundamental subatomic particle.

Remington Rand's UNIVAC is the first commercially produced, large-scale business computer; the first one is purchased by the U.S. Bureau of Census.

The U.S. Public Health Service reports that fluoridation of water greatly reduces tooth decay.

Antabuse, a drug that produces a powerful adverse reaction to alcohol, is marketed.

Carl Rogers, in *Client-Centered Therapy*, develops his nondirective approach.

Erik Erikson's *Childhood and Society* integrates psychoanalytical and anthropological studies.

🙚 The "electrical artificial pacemaker" is developed in Canada.

Nobel Prize
Glenn T. Seaborg wins the prize in chemistry for the discovery of plutonium.

Sports

Baseball

Bobby Thomson hits a three-run home run in the bottom of the ninth off Ralph Branca to win the NL playoff for the New York Giants over the Brooklyn Dodgers; the Giants, managed by Leo Durocher had overcome a 13½ game deficit in the last two months.

Willie Mays (New York, NL) is the league rookie of the year.

Mickey Mantle (New York, AL) debuts; Joe DiMaggio (New York, AL) retires with a lifetime BA of .325 and 361 home runs.

Champions

Batting	Pitching
Stan Musial (St. Louis, NL), .355	Preacher Roe (Brooklyn, NL), 22–3
Ferris Fain (Philadelphia, AL), .344	Bob Feller (Cleveland, AL), 22–8
	Home runs
	Ralph Kiner (Pittsburgh, NL), 42

Football

Norm Van Brocklin (Los Angeles) passes for a record 554 yards in one game.

NFL Season Leaders: Bob Waterfield (Los Angeles), passing; Eddie Price (New York), rushing; Elroy Hirsh (Los Angeles), passing

College All-Americans: Hugh McElhenny (B), Washington; Babe Parilli (Q), Kentucky; Dick Kazmaier (B), Princeton

Bowls (Jan. 1, 1952)

Rose: Illinois 40–Stanford 7	Cotton: Kentucky 20–Texas Christian 7
Orange: Georgia Tech 14–Baylor 14	Sugar: Maryland 28–Tennessee 13

Basketball

Allegations of point-shaving involving City College of New York, Long Island University, Kentucky, and Bradley, all major national powers, shake college basketball.

NBA All-Pro First Team: George Mikan (Minneapolis), Alex Groza (Indianapolis), Ed McCauley (Boston), Bob Davies (Rochester), Ralph Beard (Indianapolis)

Other Sports

Boxing: Sugar Ray Robinson, welterweight

Bobby Thomson's home run, "the shot heard round the world."

champion, becomes a double titleholder when he beats middleweight champion Jake LaMotta in 13.

Winners

World Series	College Basketball
New York (AL) 4	Kentucky
New York (NL) 2	*Player of the Year*
MVP	Richard Groat, Duke
NL–Roy Campanella, Brooklyn	*Stanley Cup*
AL–Yogi Berra, New York	Toronto
NFL	*US Tennis Open*
Los Angeles 24–Cleveland 17	Men: Frank Sedgman
	Women: Maureen Connolly
College Football	*USGA Open*
Tennessee	Ben Hogan
Heisman Trophy	*Kentucky Derby*
Dick Kazmaier, Princeton	Count Turf (C. McCreary, jockey)
NBA Championship	
Rochester 4–New York 3	

Fashion

For Women: The look is youthful and pretty in (1) the full skirt and small waist magnified through bulky crinolines, and (2) the "feminine" suit with molded jacket, rounded waist and bosom, high lapel, and small round collar. Separates appear in a mix of colors; coats, both fitted and loose, have large collars and pockets. The high-waisted, beltless empire gains much attention, and Dior launches his "princess line" with dresses fitted through the midriff and unmarked waistline. Balenciaga goes on to indicate the waist with a loose bow or indented curve; he even drops the waistline to the hip, re-creating a new middy line. Pointed shoes with spike heels have occasional straps at the ankles. Two new markets grow, for (1) at-home wear, for the growing time spent with TV, and (2) the teenager who also demands her own look (from the square dancer in a spinning skirt to the girl who wears a pony tail and a strapless dress). Hair is sometimes shorter, brushed up and back; the "poodle" first appears.

High-fashion notes: Balenciaga's shantung charcoal suit, collarless yoke, coolie hat

Kaleidoscope _____

- The 1939 dollar is now worth 59.3 cents; wartime inflation increases, and the sale of horsemeat triples in Portland; the New Jersey Telephone Company serves its employees whale pot roast; hoarding begins, and Macy's advertises: "Buy Nothing from Fear," although sales increase 25 percent.
- An estimated 3 million attend the MacArthur parade in New York City; six recordings of "Old Soldiers Never Die" appear, along with the MacArthur geranium, orchid, gladiola, and tea rose (which "needs no coddling or favor").
- Les Paul and Mary Ford perfect a method of superimposing their rendition of songs several times on a single record.
- Lyrics for "Come On-a My House" are written by William Saroyan on a bet by a relative.
- Margaret Sanger urges the development of an oral contraceptive.
- Monogram cancels a movie about Henry Wadsworth Longfellow, since Hiawatha, an Indian peacemaker, might be viewed as a Communist sympathizer.
- TV sponsors discover that dressing actors as doctors is good advertising.
- Ninety West Point cadets, including several football stars, are dismissed for cheating, although the Army coach remarks: "God help this country if we don't play football."
- It becomes public knowledge that Truman's assistant Harry Vaughn received a $520 deep freezer after World War II from a man who did business with the government.
- Korea becomes a battlefield of hills and valleys that gain designations such as Heartbreak Ridge, Sniper Ridge, Old Baldy, and The Punch Bowl.
- The North Koreans deliver a list of POWs that is 8,000 less than American figures.
- *Time* discontinues the "March of Time" newsreels after 16 years.
- The U.S. produces 350,000 pounds of streptomycin and 400,000 pounds of penicillin.
- Dorothy Stevens is discovered frozen stiff in a Chicago alley; she is thawed from a record low temperature of 64°.
- Hiroshima A-bomb survivor Shigeki Tanaha, 19, wins the Patriots Day Marathon in Boston.
- When Sioux City Memorial Park in Iowa refuses to bury John Rice, an American Indian who died in combat, Truman dispatches an air force plane to carry his family and his remains to Arlington National Cemetery.
- During National Music Week President Truman plays an impromptu concert on a piano made of materials from all the UN countries.
- Elizabeth Taylor and Conrad Hilton divorce; Janet Leigh and Tony Curtis marry.
- Milton Berle signs a 30-year contract in seven figures with NBC.
- Two-shows-a-day vaudeville is revived at the Palace; Judy Garland, booked for four weeks, plays 19.

Arthur Godfrey is the host of two of TV's top rated shows, as well as a popular radio program. *Billy Rose Theatre Collection. The New York Public Library at Lincoln Center. Astor, Lenox and Tilden Foundations.*

- Duke University researchers report that burned toast, strong tea, and milk of magnesia are universal antidotes for poisons of an unknown nature.
- The 5 cent phone call goes to 10 cents in New York and other large cities.
- "Don't tell my father we've been smoking," says a teenage Massachusetts girl who, with two babysitting friends, has stolen $18,000 and gone to New York on a shopping and sex spree.
- A Metropolitan Life Insurance Company report links fifteen pounds of overweight with early death.
- E. Merle Young, wife of a former RFC loan officer, receives a $9,540 mink coat from a company her husband did business with.
- Mrs. Blair Moody, wife of the Republican senator, wears a muskrat coat with its $381.25 price tag attached; mink farmers complain of an "unjust stigma."

First Appearances: Sugarless chewing gum, commercial electronic computer, dacron suits, pushbutton-controlled garage doors, hotels with all-foam rubber mattresses and pillows, telephone company answering service, college credit course in TV (Marquette), power steering (Chrysler), N.J. Turnpike, "Dennis, the Menace," Marimekko (textiles), Tropicana, Ore-Ida, Park's sausages, trading stamps (revival of S&H), orlon, infrared stoves, vibrating mattresses (300 times a minute), automatic gates for ranches and estates

1952

Economic Profile
- Dow-Jones:—High 252–Low 232
- GNP: +5%
- Inflation: +1.7%
- Unemployment: 3.0%

TV production: 6,096,000
AM radio stations: 2,355
Household telephones: 66%
Toll rate, New York–San Francisco: $2.50
Advertising expenditures: $7.7 billion
21″ Admiral console TV, radio, phonograph: $399.95
Folding TV table: $2.95
Pizza pie: 75¢ (large), 50¢ (small)
Complete Chinese dinner, House of Chan, New York: $1.50
Canaries: $9.95
Haig & Haig: $4.99 (⅘)
Fleischmann gin: $3.55 (qt.)
Body massager: $6.95
Vitatone: $9.95
Bulova watch: $27.50; Omega: $71.50

In the News

IKE ANNOUNCES HE WILL ACCEPT NOMINATION IF DRAFTED . . . BRITISH AND EGYPTIANS CLASH AT SUEZ, 25 DIE . . . FRENCH BATTLE TUNISIAN NATIONALISTS, 50 DIE . . . GEORGE VI DIES, ELIZABETH II SUCCEEDS TO THE THRONE . . . GREECE AND TURKEY JOIN NATO . . . WINSTON CHURCHILL ANNOUNCES THAT BRITAIN HAS ATOM BOMB . . . GENERAL FULGENCIO BATISTA OUSTS ELECTED LEADERS IN CUBA . . . TRUMAN SAYS HE WILL NOT RUN AGAIN . . . TRUMAN ORDERS SEIZURE OF STEEL MILLS TO AVERT STRIKE . . . RUSSIA CALLS FOR ALL-GERMAN ELECTIONS . . . U.S. ENDS OCCUPATION OF JAPAN . . . SUPREME COURT RULES THAT STEEL TAKEOVER IS UNCONSTITUTIONAL . . . IKE IS NOMINATED BY GOP, DEMOCRATS NOMINATE ADLAI STEVENSON . . . IKE PROMISES TO GO TO KOREA IF ELECTED . . . GENERAL MOHAMMED NAGUIB SEIZES POWER IN EGYPT, FAROUK ABDICATES . . . HUSSEIN BECOMES KING OF JORDAN . . . IRANIAN PARLIAMENT GIVES MOSSADEGH DICTORIAL POWERS . . . EVA PERON DIES . . . 14 CALIFORNIA COMMUNISTS ARE CONVICTED UNDER SMITH ACT . . . STALIN AND CHOU EN-LAI CONFER IN MOSCOW OVER KOREA . . . MOSCOW DEMANDS RECALL OF AMBASSADOR GEORGE KENNAN FOR "INSULTS" . . . IKE WINS LARGE VICTORY, 33 MILLION TO 27 MILLION . . . ATOMIC ENERGY COMMISSION ANNOUNCES SUCCESS OF H-BOMB TESTS AT ENIWETOK ATOLL . . . EISENHOWER COMPLETES 3-DAY BATTLEFRONT TOUR . . . CHOU EN-LAI REJECTS U.S. PEACE PLAN.

Deaths

John Dewey, John Garfield, Karen Horney, Sister Elizabeth Kenny, Hattie McDaniel, Maria Montessori, George Santayana, Chaim Weizmann.

The U.S. verifies "leaked" reports that it exploded a hydrogen bomb on Eniwetok Atoll, November 1st. *Library of Congress.*

Quotes

"I did get something, a gift, . . . a little cocker spaniel dog, . . . and our little girl, Trisha, the six-year-old, named it Checkers. . . . Pat and I have satisfaction that every dime that we've got is honestly ours. I should say this—that Pat doesn't have a mink coat, but she does have a respectable Republican cloth coat."
— Vice-presidential candidate Richard M. Nixon

"Our government makes no sense unless it is founded in a deeply felt religious faith and I don't care what it is."
— Dwight D. Eisenhower

"Some of us worship in churches, some in synagogues, some on golf courses.
— Adlai Stevenson

"Female card-holders are required to show their loyalty to the cause through indiscriminate intercourse where it will do the most good.
— *USA Confidential* by Lait and Mortimer, on the C.P.

"You can't fight Communism with perfume."
— Joseph McCarthy

"Adlai [is] the appeaser . . . who got his Ph.D. from Dean Acheson's College of Cowardly Communist Containment."
— Richard M. Nixon

"I cannot and will not cut my conscience to fit this year's fashions."
— Lillian Hellman, testifying before the House

"They'll wear toilet seats around their necks if you give 'em what they want to see."
— Bill Thomas, on 3-D glasses

"Late commuters, lost among identical rows of houses along identical street blocks, sometimes reported a sense of panic like bewildered children suddenly turned loose in a house of mirrors."
— P. Kimball, describing Levittown

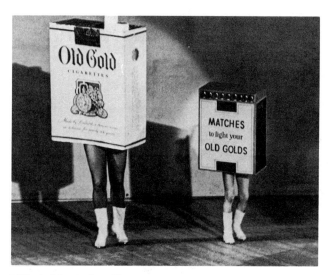

TV ad. *Movie Star News.*

Ads

America's Biggest Change
The Humble Diaper [is] . . . the greatest single fact in America's continued growth and prosperity. . . . The average American girl now marries at 20, has her first child at 22, . . . younger than ever before. . . . Victory goes to those who get there "fastest with the mostest," and MODERN ROMANCES gives you the answer with the "mostest of the firstest."
(Modern Romances)

Riddle: "What's college?"
"That's where girls who are above cooking and sewing go to meet a man they can spend their lives cooking and sewing for."
(Gimbel's ad for campus clothes)

STOP TRIPLE "O"
    Stop Breath Odor
    Stop Body Odor
    Stop Other Personal Odors
(Ennds Chlorophyll Tablets)

Don't be an e.s.s.*
    Wear smart *seamless* stockings by Hanes
        *eternal seam straightener!
(Hanes)

Dancing pleats that won't sit out.
(Orlon)

Second honeymoon. . . . Bruce and Peggy Walden spent a priceless two-weeks in Britain for only $209 each.
(Come to Britain)

Korea, Communism, and Corruption
    [K_1C_2]
(GOP slogan)

TV

Premieres
"Arthur Godfrey Time"
"I've Got a Secret," Garry Moore
"The Jackie Gleason Show," Jackie Gleason, Art
    Carney, Audrey Meadows
"Death Valley Days," Stanley Andrews
"The Ernie Kovacs Show"
"The Today Show," Dave Garroway
"Dragnet," Jack Webb
"Mr. Peepers," Wally Cox
"Our Miss Brooks," Eve Arden, Gale Gordon
"The Adventures of Ozzie and Harriet [Nelson]"
"The Liberace Show"
"My Friend Irma," Marie Wilson
"This Is Your Life," Ralph Edwards
"My Little Margie," Gale Storm, Charles Farrell
"I Married Joan," Jim Backus, Joan Davis
"Omnibus," Alistair Cooke

Top Ten (Nielsen)
"I Love Lucy," "Arthur Godfrey's Talent Scouts,"
"Arthur Godfrey and His Friends," "Dragnet,"

"Texaco Star Theater," "The Buick Circus Hour,"
"The Colgate Comedy Hour," "Gangbusters," "You
Bet Your Life," "Fireside Theatre."

Specials
"Victory at Sea" (music by Richard Rodgers);
"President Truman's Tour of the White House"

Emmy Awards
"Robert Montgomery Presents" (drama); "I Love
Lucy" (situation comedy); "Your Show of Shows"
(variety); "Dragnet" (action); "Time for Beany"
(children); "What's My Line?" (game); "See It
Now" (public service); Jimmy Durante (comedian);
Lucille Ball (comedienne); Bishop Fulton J. Sheen
(personality)

Of Note
Walter Cronkite is CBS anchor at the Republican
National Convention • Atomic bomb explosions are
televised April 2 and May 1.

Movies

Openings
The Greatest Show on Earth (Cecil B. De Mille),
    Betty Hutton, Cornel Wilde, Charlton Heston
High Noon (Fred Zinnemann), Gary Cooper, Grace
    Kelly
Ivanhoe (Richard Thorpe), Robert Taylor, Elizabeth
    Taylor, George Sanders
Moulin Rouge (John Huston), José Ferrer, Colette
    Marchand, Zsa Zsa Gabor
The Quiet Man (John Ford), John Wayne, Maureen
    O'Hara
Five Fingers (Joseph L. Mankiewicz), James Mason,
    Danielle Darrieux, Michael Rennie
Viva Zapata! (Elia Kazan), Marlon Brando, Jean
    Peters, Anthony Quinn
The Member of the Wedding (Fred Zinnemann),
    Ethel Waters, Julie Harris, Brandon De Wilde
Singin' in the Rain (Gene Kelly, Stanley Donen),
    Gene Kelly, Debbie Reynolds, Donald O'Connor
Limelight (Charles Chaplin), Charles Chaplin, Claire
    Bloom, Buster Keaton
The Snows of Kilimanjaro (Henry King), Gregory
    Peck, Susan Hayward, Ava Gardner
Come Back, Little Sheba (Daniel Mann), Shirley
    Booth, Burt Lancaster
The Importance of Being Earnest (Anthony Asquith),
    Michael Redgrave, Edith Evans

Bend of the River (Anthony Mann), James Stewart,
    Arthur Kennedy
Forbidden Games (René Clement), Brigitte Fossey,
    Georges Poujouly
Umberto D (Vittorio de Sica), Carlo Battista

Academy Awards
Best Picture: *The Greatest Show on Earth*
Best Director: John Ford *(The Quiet Man)*
Best Actress: Shirley Booth *(Come Back, Little
    Sheba)*
Best Actor: Gary Cooper *(High Noon)*

Top Box-Office Stars
Dean Martin and Jerry Lewis, Gary Cooper, John
Wayne, Bing Crosby, Bob Hope, James Stewart,
Doris Day, Gregory Peck, Susan Hayward, Randolph
Scott

Stars of Tomorrow
Marilyn Monroe, Debbie Reynolds, Marge and
Gower Champion, Mitzi Gaynor, Kim Hunter, Rock
Hudson, Audie Murphy, David Wayne, Forrest
Tucker, Danny Thomas

Popular Music ────────────

Hit Songs
"Anywhere I Wander"
"Botch-a-Me"
"Don't Let the Stars Get in Your Eyes"
"High Noon"
"How Do You Speak to an Angel"
"Pretend"
"Your Cheatin' Heart"
"Somewhere along the Way"
"I Saw Mommy Kissing Santa Claus"

Top Records

Albums: *An American in Paris* (sound track); *I'll See You in My Dreams* (Doris Day); *With a Song in My Heart* (Jane Froman); *The Merry Widow* (original cast); *Because You're Mine* (Mario Lanza)

Singles: *Blue Tango* (Leroy Anderson); *Wheel of Fortune* (Kay Starr); *You Belong to Me* (Jo Stafford); *Auf Widerseh'n* (Vera Lynn); *Tell Me Why* (Four Aces); *Till I Waltz Again with You* (Teresa Brewer); *Hold Me, Thrill Me, Kiss Me* (Karen Chandler); *Kiss of Fire* (Georgia Gibbs); *Why Don't You Believe Me?* (Joni James); *Lover* (Peggy Lee); *Glow Worm* (Mills Brothers); *Wish You Were Here* (Eddie Fisher). Country: *Wild Side of Life* (Hank Thompson); *Let Old Mother Nature Have Her Way* (Carl Smith)

Jazz and Big Bands
The Modern Jazz Quartet is organized; its *Vendôme* and *La Ronde* gain wide attention. Gerry Mulligan organizes a quartet without piano. Large jazz clubs, like Birdland, Box City, and the Royal Roost, present jazz without dancing; an interest in Latin American rhythms enters jazz, as in the music of Machito.

Top Performers (*Downbeat*): Louis Armstrong (soloist); Stan Kenton (band); George Shearing (jazz group); Les Paul, Gene Krupa, Harry Carney, Terry Gibbs, Art Van Damme (instrumentalists); Sarah Vaughan, Billy Eckstine (vocalists); Mills Brothers (vocal group)

Theater ────────────

Broadway Openings

Plays
The Shrike (Joseph Kramm), José Ferrer, Judith Evelyn
Mrs. McThing (Mary Chase), Helen Hayes, Brandon De Wilde
Dial "M" for Murder (Frederic Knott), Maurice Evans, Gusti Huber
The Seven-Year Itch (George Axelrod), Tom Ewell, Vanessa Brown
Venus Observed (Christopher Fry), Rex Harrison, Lilli Palmer
The Time of the Cuckoo (Arthur Laurents), Shirley Booth
The Deep Blue Sea (Terence Rattigan), Margaret Sullavan
Charles Dickens, readings and impersonations by Emlyn Williams

Musicals
Wish You Were Here (Harold Rome), Sheila Bond, Jack Cassidy
Two's Company (Vernon Duke, Ogden Nash), Bette Davis, David Burns
New Faces of 1952 (June Carroll, Arthur Siegal, et al.), Robert Clary, Carol Lawrence, Ronny Graham, Eartha Kitt, Alice Ghostley, Paul Lynde
An Evening with Beatrice Lillie

Classics and Revivals On and Off Broadway
Candida (George Bernard Shaw), Olivia de Havilland; *Anna Christie* (Eugene O'Neill), Celeste Holm, Kevin McCarthy; *Golden Boy* (Clifford Odets), John Garfield; *The Wild Duck* (Ibsen), Maurice Evans, Diana Lynn; *The Children's Hour* (Lillian Hellman), Patricia Neal, Kim Hunter; *The Millionairess* (George Bernard Shaw), Katharine Hepburn

Regional

Founded: Actor's Workshop, San Francisco, by Herbert Blau and Jules Irving

Pulitzer Prize
The Shrike, Joseph Kramm

Tony Awards
The Fourposter, Jan de Hartog (play): *The King and I,* Richard Rodgers, Oscar Hammerstein II (musical)

Classical Music ───────

Compositions
John Cage, *4'4*, Music for *Carillon, Imaginary Landscape,* no. 5
Elliott Carter, Sonata for Flute, Oboe, Cello, and Harp
Otto Luening, *Fantasy in Space, Low Speed, Invention*
Ned Rorem, *A Childhood Miracle*

Important Events
An unprecedented international exchange of performers includes the Boston Symphony's tour of Europe and participation in the Paris Festival of 20th-Century Music; *Porgy and Bess* goes to Berlin, Vienna, and London.
The most frequently performed composers by 31 leading orchestras are Beethoven, Mozart, Sibelius, and Prokofiev; Gershwin and Barber are the most frequently performed Americans.

First Performances
Roy Harris, Symphony no. 7 (Chicago); John Cage, *Water Music* (New York); Paul Creston, Symphony no. 4 (Washington); Gail Kubik, Symphony Concertante (New York); Igor Stravinsky, Cantata (Los Angeles, Stravinsky conducting); Boguslaw Schaeffer, *Symphony pour un homme seul, composed for tape recording machine* (Waltham, Mass.); Ralph Vaughan Williams, Romance in D flat for Harmonica, String Orchestra and Piano (New York); Morton Gould, Concerto for Tap Dancer and Orchestra (Rochester); Virgil Thomson, *Sea Piece with Birds* (Dallas)

Gary Cooper and Grace Kelly in *High Noon.* Kelly's first starring role is with this prototypical strong, silent hero. *Movie Star News.*

Opera

Metropolitan: Rudolph Bing raises prices to $8 (evening) and $30 (opening) and brings in stage directors Margaret Webster (*Aïda,* with Zinka Milanov), Tyrone Guthrie *(Carmen),* and Alfred Lunt *(Così fan tutte);* Kirsten Flagstad returns with *Alcestis.* Set Svanholm, Hans Hotter, Elizabeth Hoengen, Ljuba Welitsch, *Salomé;* Cesare Siepi, *Don Giovanni;* Jerome Hines, *La forza del destino*

NBC-TV: *Billy Budd* (Benjamin Britten, premiere from Covent Garden)

New York City: *Wozzeck, The Dybbuk, Bluebeard's Castle* (premieres)

San Francisco: Nicola Rossi-Lemeni, *Mefistofele*

Music Notes
Conductor Manuel Rosenthal is fired from the Seattle Symphony for living with a woman • Noah Greenberg organizes the New York Pro Musica Antiqua.

Louis "Satchmo" Armstrong tours Europe with his All Stars and becomes an international ambassador of American jazz. *Movie Star News.*

Art _____

Painting
Willem de Kooning,
  Woman I, Woman II
Peter Blume, *Castle of
  Euryalus*
Helen Frankenthaler,
  Mountains and Sea
Ad Reinhardt, *Red
  Painting, No. 15*
Mark Rothko, *Black,
  Pink and Yellow over
  Orange*
Jackson Pollock,
  *Number 12,
  Convergence*
Barnett Newman, *Day
  One*
Andrew Wyeth, *April
  Wind*
Adolph Gottlieb, *Unstill
  Life, Frozen Sounds II*
Bradley Walker Tomlin,
  Number 5

Sculpture
David Hare, *Juggler*
  (1950–52)
Alexander Calder,
  Sumac
Jacques Lipchitz,
  Sacrifice, II (1948–52)
Ibram Lassaw,
  Monoaros, Kwannon
David Smith, *The Hero*
Joseph Cornell,
  Dovecote

Architecture
Alcoa Building,
  Pittsburgh (Harrison
  and Abramovitz)
Lever House, New York
  (Skidmore, Owings,
  and Merrill)
Hinds House, Los
  Angeles (Richard
  Neutra)

Important Exhibitions
International exchanges continue.

Museums

New York: *Metropolitan:* Cézanne, Rembrandt, da
Vinci quincentenary anniversary. *Museum of Modern
Art:* Fifteen American abstract painters and
sculptors; "Rodin to the Present"; "Fauves and De
Stijl from 1917 to 1927." *Whitney:* John Sloan
Retrospective

Chicago: Cézanne, Rembrandt

Cleveland, Chicago, San Francisco: Matisse
retrospective

Philadelphia: Twentieth-century sculpture

Boston: Kandinsky; Gropius; Charles Bain Hoyt
memorial; Watercolors; Costume from the 18th to the
20th century; The Arts of England in the 18th
century; Kandinsky

Detroit: Venice and the 18th century

Hartford: "2,000 Years of Tapestry Weaving"

Ed Sullivan, host of "The Toast of the Town." *Billy Rose
Theatre Collection. The New York Public Library at
Lincoln Center. Astor, Lenox and Tilden Foundations.*

Venice Biennale: Hopper, Kuniyoshi, Davis, Calder
represent the United States.

Art Briefs
Rousseau's *Sleeping Gypsy,* Picasso's *Girl before a
Mirror* and *Three Musicians,* Léger's *Three Women,*
and Modigliani's *Stone Caryatid* are purchased for
the Museum of Modern Art by Mrs. Simon
Guggenheim • Private Paul Calle wins first prize for
Sad-Eyed Little Girl in a worldwide army
competition • Other major prizes include David
Smith's *Beach Scene* (Chicago Art Institute),
Lipchitz's *Prometheus Strangling the Vulture*
(Pennsylvania Academy of Arts), and Calder's
Giraffe (Venice International) • The International
Graphic Arts Society is formed • Major sales include
Corot's *l 'Odalisque sicilienne* ($17,500) and
Pollaiuolo's *Battle of the Nudes* ($6,000).

Dance _____

New York City Ballet makes history with the longest
continuous season on record, four months. The
American Ballet Center is founded by Robert Joffrey,
in New York City. Merce Cunningham forms his own
company.

Premieres

New York City Ballet: *Harlequin Pas de Deux*
(George Balanchine), Maria Tallchief, André
Eglevsky; *Metamorphoses* (Balanchine), Tanaquil Le
Clercq, Nicholas Magallanes, Todd Bolender; *Scotch
Symphony* (Balanchine), Tallchief

Books

Fiction

Critics' Choice
Invisible Man, Ralph Ellison
The Natural, Bernard Malamud
The Groves of Academe, Mary McCarthy
The Catherine Wheel, Jean Stafford
Player Piano, Kurt Vonnegut
The Long March, William Styron
Wise Blood, Flannery O'Connor
The Works of Love, Wright Morris
Winds of Morning, H. L. Davis

Best-Sellers
The Silver Chalice, Thomas B. Costain
The Caine Mutiny, Herman Wouk
East of Eden, John Steinbeck
My Cousin Rachel, Daphne Du Maurier
Steamboat Gothic, Frances Parkinson Keyes
Giant, Edna Ferber
The Old Man and the Sea, Ernest Hemingway
The Saracen Blade, Frank Yerby

Nonfiction

Critics' Choice
Struggle for Europe, Chester Wilmot
The Confident Years: 1885–1915, Van Wyck Brooks
Poetry in Our Time, Babette Deutsch
Midcentury Journey, William Shirer
The Traitors, Allan Morehead
The Hidden History of the Korean War, I. F. Stone
Democracy and the Economic Challenge, R. M. MacIver
Faces in the Crowd, David Riesman, Nathan Glazer
Social History of Art, Arnold Hauser
A History of Jazz in America, Barry Ulanov
Discovery of the Civil War, Thomas Harry Williams
Christ and Culture, Reinhold Niebuhr

Best-Sellers
The Holy Bible: Revised Standard Version
A Man Called Peter, Catherine Marshall
U.S.A. Confidential, Jack Lait and Lee Mortimer
The Sea around Us, Rachel L. Carson
Tallulah, Tallulah Bankhead
The Power of Positive Thinking, Norman Vincent Peale
This I Believe, ed. Edward P. Morgan
This Is Ike, ed. Wilson Hicks
Witness, Whittaker Chambers

Poetry
T. S. Eliot, *The Complete Poems and Plays*
W. S. Merwin, *A Mask for Janus*
Adrienne Rich, *(Poems)*
Wallace Stevens, *Selected Poems*
Kenneth Rexroth, *The Dragon and the Unicorn*
Robert Creeley, *Le Fou*

Pulitzer Prize
The Old Man and the Sea, Ernest Hemingway (fiction)
The Era of Good Feeling, George Dangerfield (U.S. history)
Edmund Pendleton, 1721–1803, David J. Mays (biography)
Collected Poems, 1917–1952, Archibald MacLeish (poetry)

Science and Technology

Jonas Salk, 38, at the University of Pittsburgh, tests his vaccine against polio.

Gamma globulin is administered to 25,000 children in Utah, Texas, and Iowa, in an attempt to prevent polio.

The first mitral valve heart operation is performed by Dr. Forest Dewey Dodrill in Detroit.

The first plastic artificial heart valve is used on a patient at the Georgetown Medical Center.

John Gibbons develops the heart-lung machine to allow the separation of the heart from the circulatory system during surgery.

Chlorpromazine (Thorazine), reserpine, isoniazid, and tri-iodothyronine are developed.

RCA announces the development of bean-size transistors that can replace vacuum tubes.

William G. Pfann develops two techniques to purify silicon and germanium crystals, facilitating electronics research.

W. F. Libby, of the University of Chicago, dates Stonehenge to about 1842 B.C.

Astronomer Milton Humason, at Mt. Palomar, describes runaway stars as further support for the "expanding theory of the universe."

Linus Pauling and Robert Corey, at MIT, reveal the molecular structure of certain proteins.

At Edwards Air Force Base, California, an experimental D-558-2 Douglas skyrocket goes a record 70,000 feet in altitude; later, William Bridgeman goes to 72,300 feet.

Nobel Prize
Edward Mills Purcell and Felix Bloch win the prize in physics for work in the measurement of magnetic fields in atomic nuclei. Selman A. Waksman wins in physiology and medicine for the codiscovery of streptomycin.

Sports

Baseball
Walt Dropo (Boston, AL) gets 12 consecutive hits.

Champions

Batting
Stan Musial (St. Louis, NL), .335
Ferris Fain (Philadelphia, AL), .327
Pitching
Hoyt Wilhelm (New York, NL), 15–3

Bob Shantz (Philadelphia, AL), 24–7
Home runs
Ralph Kiner (Pittsburgh, NL), 37
Hank Sauer (Chicago, NL), 37

Football
Sammy Baugh, Washington, retires.

NFL Season Leaders: Norm Van Brocklin (Los Angeles), passing, Dan Towler (Los Angeles), rushing; Mac Speedie (Cleveland), receiving

College All-Americans: Paul Giel (B), Minnesota; Don Heinrich (Q), Washington; Johnny Lattner (B), Notre Dame

Bowls (Jan. 1, 1953)
Rose: Southern California 7– Wisconsin 0
Orange: Alabama 61– Syracuse 6

Cotton: Texas 16– Tennessee 0
Sugar: Georgia Tech 24– Mississippi 7

Basketball

NBA All-Pro First Team: Paul Arizin (Philadelphia), George Mikan (Minneapolis), Bob Cousy (Boston), Ed McCauley (Boston), Bob Davies (Rochester).

Olympics
In the Summer Games at Helsinki, U.S. winners include Lindig Rimigino (100m, 10.4s), Andy Stanfield (200m, 20.7s), Mal Whitfield (800m, 1:49.2), Harrison Dillard (110mh, 13.7s), Bob Richards (pole vault, 14'14"), Bob Mathias (decathlon). In the Winter Games at Oslo, Richard Button wins figure skating and Mrs. Andrea Mead Lawrence, giant slalom.

Other Sports

Boxing: Jersey Joe Walcott, 37, knocks out Ezzard Charles to become the oldest heavyweight champion to date.

Tennis: Australians Frank Sedgman and Ken McGregor beat the U.S. in Davis Cup play for the third straight time; Jack Kramer then signs them up as pros for a record $100,000 guaranteed minimum.

Winners

World Series
New York (AL) 4
Brooklyn 3
MVP
NL–Hank Sauer, Chicago
AL–Bobby Shantz, Philadelphia
NFL
Detroit 17–Cleveland 7
College Football
Michigan State
Heisman Trophy
Billy Vessels, Oklahoma
NBA Championship
Minneapolis 4–New York 3

College Basketball
Kansas
Player of the Year
Clyde Lovellette, Kansas
Stanley Cup
Detroit
US Tennis Open
Men: Frank Sedgman
Women: Maureen Connolly
USGA Open
Julius Boros
Kentucky Derby
Hill Gail (E. Arcaro, jockey)

Fashion

For Women: Numerous styles appear. One is toward a slimmer and softer look. The "siren sheath" is introduced for both day and evening, along with a coat that replaces the tent with a new "column" shape. The "sweater girl" returns in form-fitting clothing in stripes and plaids. At the same time, new permanent pleating processes bring forth the "morning glory" blouse with pleats, and big crinoline skirts are narrowed; elasticized belts and cummerbunds are relaxed. The silhouette gets bulky on top as the fitted jacket is replaced with a front, concave style. The accession of Queen Elizabeth revives Elizabethan fashions: collars, tiaras, and jeweled velvet dresses; the mink stole is extremely popular. Italian and Spanish fashions are stylish: the Italian mule sandal with a narrow instep band, shawls, hoop earrings, multiple strands of pearls and pearl bibs. "Mamie bangs," the "poodle" cut, and ponytails are everywhere. Sixty percent of the women who used to go to beauty shops stay home with recent developments in hair dyes and drying methods.

High-fashion notes: Jacques Heim's wrapped jersey blouse, tapered blue and green velvet pants and lilac cummerbunds; Dior's shantung dustcoat

Kaleidoscope

- "Eggheads of the world unite. You have nothing to lose but your yolks," says the Democratic presidential candidate, the intellectual and balding Adlai Stevenson.
- "The great problem of America today," says Dwight D. Eisenhower, "is to take that straight road down the middle."
- "Dum-De-Dum Dum . . . the story you are about to hear is true; only the names have been changed to protect the innocent," begins the enormously popular "Dragnet" with Jack Webb.
- George Jorgensen, 26, is surgically transformed into a woman (Christine) in Denmark.
- A priest, minister, and rabbi sanction the appearance of Lucille Ball's pregnancy on her TV show.
- Fifty-six million watch Nixon's speech on TV when he describes his mortgage loan, 1950 auto, and $4,000 life insurance policy; Eisenhower later praises Nixon's brave defense against improper gifts, and in response to Nixon's request for public support, post offices are flooded, 350 to 1, in favor of Nixon.
- Subversives are barred from teaching in public schools.
- Salt Lake City Colleen Hutchens is the first blonde in 13 years to win the Miss America contest; she is also the tallest (5′10″), the oldest (25), and the heaviest (143 pounds).
- The penny postcard becomes 2 cents.
- Leo Durocher, New York Giants manager, is fined and suspended for two days for "beanball pitching."
- A potato shortage sets black-market prices at $5 to $8 for a 100-pound bag; the ceiling price is $3.55.
- A. S. Rosenbach sells his 73-volume collection of Shakespeare folios and quartos for $1 million.
- The complete Torah is published in English for the first time.
- Thirty-seven-year-old *Birth of a Nation* is barred in Maryland as "morally bad and crime inciting."
- A *New York Times* study reveals that 90 percent of all university funding is distributed to the physical and biological sciences; 10 percent goes to the humanities.
- A poliomyelitis epidemic strikes more than 50,000.
- Physicist Arthur Robert's *Overture to the Dedication of a Nuclear Reactor,* inspired by atomic energy, is performed at Oak Ridge, Tenn.
- Ruth Simmons gains wide interest in her claim to be a reincarnation of the nineteenth-century Bridey Murphy.
- ILGWU members demonstrate in New York against the efforts of crime syndicates to enter their industry.
- Bank robber Willie "the Actor" Sutton is captured five years after he escaped from jail by tricking guards with a dummy of himself.
- Arnold Schuster, an ordinary citizen whose tip led to Willie Sutton's arrest, is shot and killed.
- A Louis Seltzer editorial in the *Cleveland Press* alluding to the need for religious belief is reprinted in 41 publications; Mickey Spillane turns to Jehovah Witnesses.

- Although never implemented, the Fort Worth Plan is the first to propose banning cars from a business district in order to create a pedestrian shopping mall.

New Words and Usages: Miniaturization, globalist, Manchurian fever, cool jazz, cronyism, hot rod, Pentagonese, poodle cut, stretch-out, telethon, drag, hack, panty raid, ponytail, printed circuit, psycholinguistics, teleprompter, whirlybird.

Fads: Flying saucer watching (and "man from Mars" theories), panty raids; "beanies" with propeller tops; chlorophyll (even in deodorants and dog food); collecting stamps, autographs, seals, and labels; needlework, gardening

First Appearances: "Saralee" black doll, mechanical lawn mower, 16mm home movie projector, cigarette with built-in lighter, midget adding machine, two-way radio cars, adjustable shower head, bowling alley automatic pin boy, revolving grocery check-outs, circular bed, plastic vinylite swimming pool, automatic food vending machines on trains, marketing of frozen bread, transistorized hearing aids, plastic lens for cataract patients, nylon stretch yarn, parachutist to make 124 jumps in one day, Cinerama, "Mad" comics, Kellogg's Sugar Frosted Flakes, Gleem, Kent filter tips, Holiday Inn (Memphis), BMW, Sony pocket-size transistor radio, No-Cal ginger ale, fiberglass

Casey Stengel (left), famous both as New York Yankees manager and rambling rhetorician ("stengelese"). *Movie Star News.*

1953

Economic Profile
- Dow-Jones: ↑ High 293– Low 255
- GNP: +5%
- Inflation: +0.6%
- Unemployment: 2.9%

Korean Conflict
- Total deaths: 54,246
- Battle deaths: 33,629
- Other deaths: 20,617
- Wounded in action: 103,284

Daily newspapers: 2,009
Books published: 12,050
Airmail: 7¢ (oz.)
Postcard: 2¢
IRS total collections: $69.6 billion
Coronado Empire stove: $99.95
Coronado refrigerator: $199.95 (9 cubic ft.)
Revere pots (11-piece set): $39.95
Dormeyer deep-fry cooker: $19.50

Deaths

Hilaire Belloc, Raoul Dufy, John Marin, Queen Mary, Robert A. Millikan, Eugene O'Neill, Sergei Prokofiev, Robert Taft, Jacques Thiabaud, Fred M. Vinson, Jonathan Wainwright.

In the News

TRUMAN ANNOUNCES THE DAWN OF HYDROGEN POWER, WARNS OF THE HORROR OF WARFARE . . . RUSSIA CLAIMS JEWISH DOCTORS CONSPIRED TO KILL STALIN . . . IKE, INAUGURATED, PLEDGES TO SEEK PEACE . . . STALIN DIES AT 72, GEORGI MALENKOV BECOMES SOVIET PREMIER . . . WAGE AND PRICE CONTROLS ARE ENDED . . . SWEDE DAG HAMMARSKJÖLD IS ELECTED UN SECRETARY GENERAL . . . CONRAD ADENAUER VISITS U.S. . . . BOTH SIDES IN KOREA AGREE TO EXCHANGE WOUNDED . . . HEALTH, EDUCATION AND WELFARE DEPARTMENT IS CREATED, OVETA CULP HOBBY IS FIRST SECRETARY . . . SYNGMAN RHEE ORDERS RELEASE OF 27,000 ANTICOMMUNIST NORTH KOREAN PRISONERS . . . TRUCE NEGOTIATIONS BEGIN AT PANMUNJOM . . . OFFSHORE OIL BILL GIVES TITLE TO STATES . . . EDMUND HILLARY AND TENZING NORKAY REACH PEAK OF MOUNT EVEREST . . . ELIZABETH IS CROWNED BRITISH QUEEN . . . ANTICOMMUNIST RIOTS IN EAST BERLIN ARE SUPPRESSED . . . 129 DIE IN AIR FORCE GLOBEMASTER CRASH, WORST AIR ACCIDENT IN HISTORY . . . JULIUS AND ETHEL ROSENBERG ARE ELECTROCUTED AT SING SING PRISON, N.Y. . . . COMMUNISTS LAUNCH HEAVY OFFENSIVE, ALLIES COUNTERATTACK . . . 100,000 EAST GERMANS DEFY THREATS AND ENTER THE WEST FOR FOOD PACKAGES . . . POW EXCHANGE BEGINS . . . MALENKOV DECLARES THAT RUSSIA HAS H-BOMB . . . ROYALIST UPRISING OVERTHROWS MOSSADEGH, SHAH TAKES IRANIAN THRONE . . . EARL WARREN IS NOMINATED CHIEF JUSTICE, SUPREME COURT . . . ATTORNEY GENERAL HERBERT BROWNELL CHARGES THAT TRUMAN PROMOTED SPY HARRY DEXTER WHITE, TRUMAN RIDICULES CHARGE . . . LAVRENTI BERIA, STALIN'S KGB HEAD, IS EXECUTED.

Quotes _____

"[In San Antonio] the main question is: Should books on the public library shelves whose authors are either identified as Communists or suspected of Communist sympathies be branded with a red stamp?"

— Stanley Walker, "Book Branding"

"The Soviet government deems it necessary to report that the United States has no monopoly in the production of the hydrogen bomb."

— Premier Georgi Malenkov

"What was good for our country was good for General Motors and vice versa."

— Secretary of Defense Charles Wilson

"A climate favorable to business has been substituted for the socialism of recent years."

— Secretary of Commerce Sinclair Weeks

THE WORLD DEMANDS
CLEMENCY FOR THE ROSENBERGS
FRENCH DEPUTIES SAY CLEMENCY
300 BRITISH SCIENTISTS SAY CLEMENCY
POPE PIUS SAYS CLEMENCY
2500 MINISTERS SAY CLEMENCY
RABBIS OF ISRAEL SAY CLEMENCY
— Poster on behalf of Ethel and Julius Rosenberg

Not One to Turn Your Back On

Anti-McCarthy cartoon. Albert Einstein, Harry Truman, and Milton Eisenhower are among those who attack McCarthy, as he and his cohorts continue to investigate Communist influence in the State Department, Army, Harvard, the media, and the Methodist Church. *Library of Congress.*

"America is so terribly grim in spite of all that material prosperity. . . . Compassion and the old neighborliness are gone, people stand by and do nothing when friends and neighbors are attacked, libeled and ruined."

— Charles Chaplin

"The smart woman will keep herself desirable. It is her duty to be feminine and desirable at all times in the eyes of the opposite sex."

— Leland Kirdel, *Coronet*

Ads _____

Tasty uranium burger, 45¢
(Salt Lake City Fast Food Store)

Any melon worth its salt . . .
(Morton)

For you who love to flirt with fire, / who dare to skate on ice . . . / A lush and passionate scarlet / like flaming diamonds dancing on the moon.
(Revlon's Fire and Ice)

To bring the wolves out—Riding Hood Red.
(Max Factor)

Double Power—[to take] a husband away from his wife or a sweetheart away from the arms of his loved one.
(Diablo's Secret Cologne)

You're the girl who *can* do something wonderful with her looks. Do you know why? Because you're in a unique spot—as a WAF.
(Women's Air Force)

Smart Secretaries keep up with the times—the *New York Times,* of course.
(New York Times)

What does Atomic Energy really mean to YOU? —Dramatic new developments in medicine, agriculture, and industry promise long-time benefits for us all.
(Union Carbide and Carbon Corp.)

"Just what the doctor ordered."
—L & M with Alpha-cellulose filter.
(L & M Cigarettes)

TV

Premieres
"You Are There," Walter Cronkite
"I Led Three Lives," Richard Carlson
"Person to Person," Edward R. Murrow
"Topper," Leo G. Carroll
"The Jack Paar Show"
"Romper Room," Gloria Flood
"The Tonight Show," Steve Allen
"Soupy Sales"
"General Electric Theater," Ronald Reagan (host)
"Coke Time with Eddie Fisher"
"Make Room for Daddy," Danny Thomas
"U.S. Steel Hour" ("P.O.W.," Gary Merrill, Richard Kiley)

Top Ten (Nielsen)
"I Love Lucy," "Dragnet," "Arthur Godfrey's Talent Scouts," "You Bet Your Life," "The Milton Berle Show," "Arthur Godfrey and His Friends," "Ford Theatre," "The Jackie Gleason Show," "Fireside Theatre," "The Colgate Comedy Hour"

Specials
"Marty" (Paddy Chayefsky, with Rod Steiger); "King Lear" (Orson Welles, TV debut); Coronation of Queen Elizabeth II

Emmy Awards
"U.S. Steel Hour" (drama); "I Love Lucy" (situation comedy); "Omnibus" (variety); "Dragnet" (action); "Kukla, Fran, and Ollie" (children); "Victory at Sea" (public affairs); Donald O'Connor (actor, "Colgate Comedy Hour"); Eve Arden (actress, "Our Miss Brooks"); Edward R. Murrow (personality)

Of Note
Ed Murrow uses film clips on "See It Now" to accuse Joe McCarthy of character assassination in the case of Lt. Milo Radulovich. McCarthy appears in rebuttal • Bob Hope hosts the first Academy Awards show • Marilyn Monroe makes her TV debut on "The Jack Benny Show" • Mary Martin and Ethel Merman celebrate Ford's 50th anniversary on both NBC and CBS.

Movies

Openings
From Here to Eternity (Fred Zinnemann), Burt Lancaster, Deborah Kerr, Montgomery Clift, Frank Sinatra
Stalag 17 (Billy Wilder), William Holden, Don Taylor, Otto Preminger
Roman Holiday (William Wyler), Gregory Peck, Audrey Hepburn
Julius Caesar (Joseph L. Mankiewicz), Louis Calhern, James Mason, Marlon Brando
The Bad and the Beautiful (Vincente Minnelli), Lana Turner, Kirk Douglas
The Robe (Henry Koster), Richard Burton, Jean Simmons (first Cinemascope)
Shane (George Stevens), Alan Ladd, Jean Arthur, Van Heflin, Brandon De Wilde
Lili (Charles Walters), Leslie Caron, Mel Ferrer
Mogambo (John Ford), Clark Gable, Ava Gardner, Grace Kelly
The Moon Is Blue (Otto Preminger), William Holden, David Niven, Maggie McNamara
Pickup on South Street (Sam Fuller), Richard Widmark, Jean Peters
The Captain's Paradise (Anthony Kimmins), Alec Guinness, Yvonne de Carlo
The Big Heat (Fritz Lang), Glenn Ford, Lee Marvin, Gloria Grahame, Alexander Scourby
The Band Wagon (Vincente Minnelli), Fred Astaire, Cyd Charisse, Jack Buchanan
Gentlemen Prefer Blondes (Howard Hawks), Jane Russell, Marilyn Monroe, Charles Coburn
Bwana Devil (Arch Oboler) Robert Stack, Barbara Britton (first 3-D)
Wages of Fear (Georges Clouzot), Yves Montand

Academy Awards
Best Picture: *From Here to Eternity*
Best Director: Fred Zinnemann *(From Here to Eternity)*
Best Actress: Audrey Hepburn *(Roman Holiday)*
Best Actor: William Holden *(Stalag 17)*

Top Box-Office Stars
Gary Cooper, Dean Martin and Jerry Lewis, John Wayne, Alan Ladd, Bing Crosby, Marilyn Monroe, James Stewart, Bob Hope, Susan Hayward, Randolph Scott

Stars of Tomorrow
Janet Leigh, Gloria Grahame, Tony Curtis, Terry Moore, Rosemary Clooney, Julie Adams, Robert Wagner, Scott Brady, Pier Angeli, Jack Palance

Popular Music ⎯⎯⎯⎯⎯⎯⎯⎯⎯⎯⎯⎯⎯⎯⎯⎯⎯⎯⎯⎯

Hit Songs
"And This Is My Beloved"
"Baubles, Bangles and Beads"
"Hi-Lili, Hi-Lo"
"I Love Paris"
"My Love, My Love"
"Secret Love"
"Stranger in Paradise"
"That's Amore"
"You, You, You"
"Ebbtide"
"Ruby [Ruby Gentry]"

Top Records

Albums: *Hans Christian Andersen* (Danny Kaye); *Music for Lovers Only* (Jackie Gleason); *Music of Victor Herbert* (Mantovani); *Strauss Waltzes* (Mantovani); *Radio Bloopers* (Kermit Schafer)

Singles: *Crying in the Chapel* (June Valli); *Rags to Riches* (Tony Bennett); *Eh, Cumpari* (Julius La Rosa); *Song from Moulin Rouge* (Percy Faith); *Vaya con Dios* (Les Paul and Mary Ford); *Doggie in the Window* (Patti Page); *I'm Walking behind You* (Eddie Fisher); *Till I Waltz Again with You* (Teresa Brewer); *No Other Love, Don't Let the Stars Get in Your Eyes* (Perry Como). Country: *Kaw Liga* (Hank Williams); *It's Been So Long* (Webb Pierce)

Jazz and Big Bands
In the search for new sounds, Bud Shank, Frank Wess, and Herbie Mann introduce the flute; Count Basie, the Hammond organ; Oscar Pettiford, the cello.

New Band: The Dorsey Brothers are reunited.

Top Performers (*Downbeat*): Glenn Miller (soloist); Stan Kenton, Les Brown (bands); Dave Brubeck (jazz group); Les Paul, Ray Brown, Gerry Mulligan, Chet Baker, Don Elliott (instrumentalists); Ella Fitzgerald, Nat "King" Cole (vocalists); Four Freshmen (vocal group)

Theater ⎯⎯⎯⎯⎯⎯⎯⎯⎯⎯⎯⎯⎯⎯⎯⎯⎯⎯⎯⎯⎯⎯⎯⎯⎯⎯⎯⎯

Broadway Openings

Plays
The Teahouse of the August Moon (John Patrick), David Wayne, John Forsythe, Larry Gates
Picnic (William Inge), Ralph Meeker, Janice Rule, Paul Newman, Kim Stanley, Eileen Heckart, Arthur O'Connell
The Solid Gold Cadillac (Howard Teichmann, George S. Kaufman), Josephine Hull, Loring Smith
Tea and Sympathy (Robert Anderson), Deborah Kerr, John Kerr
The Crucible (Arthur Miller), Walter Hampden, Beatrice Straight, Arthur Kennedy, E. G. Marshall
Camino Real (Tennessee Williams), Eli Wallach, Frank Silvera, Jo Van Fleet, Martin Balsam
John Brown's Body (Stephen Vincent Benét), Raymond Massey, Tyrone Power, Judith Anderson
Sabrina Fair (Samuel Taylor), Margaret Sullavan, Joseph Cotten
The Love of Four Colonels (Peter Ustinov), Lilli Palmer, Rex Harrison

Musicals
Kismet (Alexander Borodin, Robert Wright, George Forest), Alfred Drake, Joan Diener, Richard Kiley
Wonderful Town (Leonard Bernstein, Betty Comden, Adolph Green), Rosalind Russell, Edith Adams
Can-Can (Cole Porter), Gwen Verdon, Lilo, Peter Cookson, Hans Conried
Hazel Flagg (Jule Styne, Bob Hilliard), Helen Gallagher
Me and Juliet (Richard Rodgers, Oscar Hammerstein II), Isabel Bigley, Joan McCracken
Comedy in Music with Victor Borge
John Murray Anderson's Almanac (Richard Adler, Jerry Ross), Harry Belafonte, Orson Bean, Polly Bergen
Porgy and Bess (George and Ira Gershwin, revival) Leontyne Price, Cab Calloway

Classics and Revivals On and Off Broadway
The Misalliance (George Bernard Shaw), Richard Kiley, Roddy McDowall. *Founded:* Phoenix Theatre by T. Edward Hambleton and Norris Houghton: *Richard III* (José Ferrer), *The Merchant of Venice* (Luther Adler)

Pulitzer Prize
Picnic, William Inge

Tony Awards
The Crucible, Arthur Miller (play); *Wonderful Town*, Leonard Bernstein, Betty Comden, Adolph Green (musical)

William "Count" Basie was first associated with Fats Waller, Walter Page, and Bennie Moten before his debut with his own group at the Reno Club in Kansas City. *Movie Star News.*

Ella Fitzgerald, *Downbeat's* most popular singer this year and from 1937 to 1939, when she took over the late Chick Webb's band. *Movie Star News.*

Compositions
Chou Wen-chung, *All in the Spring Wind*
Earle Brown, *Folio, 25 Pages—for 1 to 25 Pianos*
Quincy Porter, Concerto for Two Pianos and
    Orchestra
Alan Hovhaness, *Triptych*
Stefan Wolpe, *Enactment* for Three Pianos
Arthur Berger, *Ideas of Order*
John Cage, *Music for Piano—"4–84 to 1–84 Pianists"*
George Antheil, *Capital of the World*
Roger Sessions, Sonata for Solo Violin

Important Events
In addition to a $200,000 grant to the New York City Center, the Rockefeller Foundation gives $400,000 to the Louisville Philharmonic Society to encourage the performance, composition, and recording of contemporary music.
Of 4,000 performances of 900 works by 30 orchestras, European compositions dominate. Most frequently performed Americans are Aaron Copland, George Gershwin, Samuel Barber, Virgil Thomson, Paul Creston, and Gian Carlo Menotti.

Debut: Phillippe Entremont

Deborah Kerr and Burt Lancaster in *From Here to Eternity;* their passionate beach scene shocks audiences. *Movie Star News.*

Classical Music _____

First Performances
Roy Harris, Piano Concerto no. 2 (Louisville); Ernest Bloch, *Suite Hebraïque* (Chicago); Henry Cowell, Symphony no. 8 (Wilmington); Peter Mennin, Symphony no. 6 (Louisville); Darius Milhaud, *Christophe Columbe* (New York, in opera form)

Opera

Metropolitan: Hilde Gueden, *The Rake's Progress* (Stravinsky, premiere); Irmgard Seefried (debut), *Le nozze di Figaro;* Theodor Uppman, *Pelléas et Mélisande;* Cesare Siepi/George London, *Boris Godunov;* Victoria de los Angeles, Jussi Bjoerling, Robert Merrill, conductor Pierre Monteux (debut), *Faust*

New York City: *The Trial* (Von Einem, premiere)

Cincinnati: *Taming of the Shrew* (Vittorio Giannini)

Hartford: *The Mighty Casey* (William Schuman, premiere)

Dayton: *The Miracle of Saint Nicholas* (Benjamin Britten, premiere)

Central City, Colo.: *The Merry Wives of Windsor* (Giannini, premiere)

San Francisco: Giulietta Simionato, *Il barbiere di Siviglia;* Inge Borkh, *Elektra;* Cesare Valetti, *Werther* (Massenet)

Art

Painting

I. Rice Pereira, *Spirit of Air*

Jackson Pollock, *Portrait and a Dream, Ocean Grayness*

Richard Lindner, *The Meeting*

Jack Levine, *Gangster Funeral* (1952–53)

Willem de Kooning, *Woman and Bicycle, Woman VI*

Mark Tobey, *Edge of August*

Stuart Davis, *Something on the Eight Ball*

Barnett Newman, *Onement No. 6*

Josef Albers, *Homage to the Square*

Franz Kline, *New York*

Sam Francis, *Big Red*

Ad Reinhardt, *Blue Painting*

Moses Soyer, *Girl in Orange Sweater*

Jose Vela Zanetti completes a 20-yard mural for the UN Headquarters Building in New York.

Sculpture

Joseph Cornell, *Hôtel du Nord*

Louise Bourgeois, *Garden at Night*

David Smith, *Tanktotem II*

Seymour Lipton, *Sanctuary*

Architecture

General Motors Building, Warren, Mich. (Saarinen and Saarinen)

Private House, Madison, Wis. (James Dressler)

North Carolina State Fair Building, Raleigh (Nowicki and Dietrich)

Ford Rotunda, Dearborn, Mich. (Buckminster Fuller)

Mini-Earth Sphere Geoscope, Cornell University, Ithaca, N.Y. (Fuller)

Corning Glass Center, Corning, N.Y. (Harrison, Abramovitz, and Abbe)

David Smith, *Tanktotem II*, 1953. Steel and bronze 49½ × 80½". *The Metropolitan Museum of Art, Fletcher Fund, 1953.*

Important Exhibitions

Major visiting shows include De Stijl (from Amsterdam) and Japanese paintings and sculpture (sponsored by the Japanese government).

New York: *Metropolitan:* American painting from 1754–1954; "From the Land of the Bible"; Watercolors contest and show: Ivan Le Lorraine Albright, Claude Bentley, Charles Burchfield, John Marin; Japanese painting and sculpture. *Museum of Modern Art:* "The Juxtaposition of the Traditional and Modern" (in the newly opened sculpture garden). *Guggenheim:* Foundations of abstractionism; Living architecture

Washington: *Corcoran:* First prize to Abraham Rattner

Boston: Early American Jewish portraits and silver; Japanese paintings and sculpture

Chicago: International exhibition of contemporary drawings of 12 countries; Léger; Japanese paintings and sculpture; Jean Metzinger

San Francisco: Ward Lockwood retrospective; Léger

Cleveland: Rouault

Art Briefs

Forty-four painters and sculptors compose the *Reality* manifesto attacking the Museum of Modern Art and nonobjective art; the Museum defends "the moderns." Frank Lloyd Wright attacks the international style • Auction prices are lower than in recent years: Manet's *Mme. Jeanne Martin*, $28,000; Degas's *Laundress Carrying Linen*, $10,500

Dance

New York City Ballet: A record-breaking 12 new productions are mounted, including *Fanfare* (Jerome Robbins) and *Afternoon of a Faun* (Robbins), Kay Mazzo.

San Francisco: *Con Amore* (Lew Christensen); *Creatures of Beethoven* (Christensen)

Alwin Nikolais: *Masks, Props, and Mobiles*

Books

Fiction

Critics' Choice

The Adventures of Augie March,
  Saul Bellow
*The Enormous Radio and Other
  Stories*, John Cheever
The Deep Sleep, Wright Morris
Plexus, Henry Miller
Nine Stories, J. D. Salinger
Children Are Bored on Sunday,
  Jean Stafford
The Outsider, Richard Wright
Junkie, William Burroughs
The Stones of the House,
  Theodore Morrison
Go Tell It on the Mountain, James
  Baldwin
The Bridges at Toko Ri, James
  Michener
❧ *The Erasers*, Alain Robbe-
  Grillet

Best-Sellers

The Robe, Lloyd C. Douglas
The Silver Chalice, Thomas B.
  Costain
Désirée, Annemarie Selinko
Battle Cry, Leon M. Uris
From Here to Eternity, James
  Jones
The High and the Mighty, Ernest
  K. Gann
Beyond This Place, A. J. Cronin
Time and Time Again, James
  Hilton

Nonfiction

Critics' Choice

Science and Human Behavior, B.
  F. Skinner
*Shame and Glory of the
  Intellectuals*, Peter Viereck
The Conservative Mind, Russell
  Kirk
*The Challenge to American
  Foreign Policy*, John Jay
  McCloy
*The Natural Superiority of
  Women*, Ashley Montague
*The Interpersonal Theory of
  Psychiatry*, Harry Stack
  Sullivan
*Modern Science and Modern
  Man*, James Bryant Conant
In Search of Theater, Eric Bentley
Poetry and the Age, Randall
  Jarrell
The New England Mind, Roger
  Williams, Perry Miller
❧ *The Hedgehog and the Fox*,
  Isaiah Berlin

Best-Sellers

The Holy Bible: Revised Standard
  Version
The Power of Positive Thinking,
  Norman Vincent Peale
*Sexual Behavior in the Human
  Female*, Alfred C. Kinsey
Angel Unaware, Dale Evans
  Rogers

Life Is Worth Living, Fulton J.
  Sheen
A Man Called Peter, Catherine
  Marshall
The Greatest Faith Ever Known,
  Fulton Oursler, G. A. O.
  Armstrong
How to Play Your Best Golf,
  Tommy Armour
A House Is Not a Home, Polly
  Adler

Poetry

John Ashbery, *Turandot and Other
  Poems*
Richard Eberhart, *Undercliff:
  Poems 1946–1963*
Conrad Aiken, *Collected Poems*
Karl Shapiro, *Poems 1940–1953*
Wallace Stevens, *Selected Poems*
Robert Penn Warren, *Brother to
  Dragons*
Archibald MacLeish, *This Music
  Crept by Me upon the Waters*
May Sarton, *The Land of Silence*

Pulitzer Prizes

No prize is awarded in fiction.
A Stillness at Appomattox, Bruce
  Catton (U.S. history)
The Spirit of St. Louis, Charles A.
  Lindbergh (autobiography)
The Waking: Poems 1933–1953,
  Theodore Roethke (poetry)

Science and Technology

Francis Crick and James Watson solve the structure
  of DNA, the basic unit of heredity, with their
  double helix model.
The Salk vaccine is formally certified to prevent
  infantile paralysis; Salk says mass inoculations
  can begin.
The first successful open-heart surgery is performed
  at Jefferson Medical College, Philadelphia.
R. Bunge, at the University of Iowa, describes his
  work with artificial insemination using semen
  preserved by freezing.
Dr. Alfred Kinsey's *Sexual Behavior in the Human
  Female* concludes that women have less sex
  drive than men and engage in less forbidden
  sexual activity.

Oxytocin, the uterine contracting hormone, is
  synthesized.
Charles Yaeger goes a record 1,600 m.p.h. in a Bell
  X-1A at Edwards Air Force Base, California.
The atomic nucleus is shown to be twice as dense
  and smaller than previously believed.
University of Chicago archeologists unearth a 10,000-
  year-old Indian village at Prairie du Rocher, Ill.
The first atomic shell is fired at the Nevada Training
  Grounds.

Nobel Prize

Fritz A. Lipmann wins in physiology and medicine
for his studies of living cells.

Sports

Baseball

The Boston Braves are permitted by the NL to move to Milwaukee, the first franchise shift in the century.

The New York Yankees under Casey Stengel win a record fifth straight pennant and World Series.

Champions

Batting	Pitching
Mickey Vernon (Washington, AL), .337	Carl Erskine (Brooklyn, NL), 20–6
Carl Furillo (Brooklyn, NL), .344	Ed Lopat (New York, AL), 16–4
	Home runs
	Ed Matthews (Milwaukee, NL), 47

Football

Lou Groza (Cleveland) kicks a record 23 field goals; Burt Rechichar (San Francisco) kicks a record 56-yard field goal.

NFL Season Leaders: Otto Graham (Cleveland), passing; Joe Perry (San Francisco), rushing; Pete Pihos (Philadelphia), receiving.

College All-Americans: J. C. Caroline (B), Illinois; Paul Cameron (B), UCLA; Matt Hazeltine (G), California.

Bowls (Jan. 1, 1954)

Rose: Michigan State 28– UCLA 20	Cotton: Rice 28– Alabama 6
Orange: Oklahoma 7– Maryland 0	Sugar: Georgia Tech 42– West Virginia 19

Basketball

NBA All-Pro First Team: Neil Johnston (Philadelphia), George Mikan (Minneapolis), Bob Cousy (Boston), Ed McCauley (Boston), Adolph Schayes (Syracuse)

Other Sports

Boxing: Rocky Marciano knocks out Joe Walcott in the 13th for the heavyweight title.

Golf: Ben Hogan wins the Masters, U.S. Open, and British Open.

Racing: Bill Vukovich wins the Indianapolis 500.

Winners

World Series	*College Basketball*
New York (AL) 4	Indiana
Brooklyn (NL) 2	*Player of the Year*
MVP	Robert Houbregs,
NL–Roy Campanella, Brooklyn	Washington
AL–Al Rosen, Cleveland	*Stanley Cup*
NFL	Montreal
Detroit 16–Cleveland 10	*US Tennis Open*
College Football	Men: Tony Trabert
Maryland	Women: Maureen Connolly
Heisman Trophy	*USGA Open*
John Lattner, Notre Dame	Ben Hogan
NBA Championship	*Kentucky Derby*
Minneapolis 4–New York 1	Dark Star (H. Moreno, jockey)

Fashion

For Women: A mood of elegance and "femininity" is emphasized. Hair, waistlines, and hems become shorter. The semifitted suit with brief, narrow jacket is cinched at the waist and worn with a full, gathered skirt. The form-fitting sheath is also softened as widened or slashed necklines appear and are filled in with scarves or jewelry. Narrow skirts gain huge pockets. Dior moves the hemline to nearly 16 inches and reintroduces the low hip style. A new sophistication characterizes sportswear: sweaters are trimmed and even jeweled; slacks taper to the ankle or are molded to the leg in "toreador" pants.

Interesting accessories include hoop earrings, jeweled heels on plain shoes, and multipatterned scarves, which are worn with almost everything. The "poodle" hairdo gives way to the Italian "pixie," short and layered or casually pushed forward onto the face. Evening makeup includes new liquid rouges, foundations, heavy powder, dark brown eyeshadow, penciled eyebrows and eyelines, and pale, nearly white lipstick.

High-fashion note: Dior's skirt, 15½ inches off the ground

Kaleidoscope ————————

- Citizen groups in Central, New Mexico, halt the filming of the controversial *Salt of the Earth,* which has been produced with alleged Communist screenwriters and actors.
- The Screen Actors Guild adopts a by-law banning Communists from membership.
- Senator Joseph McCarthy announces that he has arranged for the Greeks to stop trading at Soviet ports.
- Charlie Chaplin says he finds it "virtually impossible" to continue work in the United States owing to "vicious propaganda" by powerful reactionary groups; once in Europe, he gives up his reentry permit.
- Vice President Richard Nixon attends a Boy Scout jamboree of 50,000 near his hometown in Newport Beach, California, and demonstrates how to scramble eggs.
- A member of the Indiana State Textbook Committee charges that "there is a Communist directive in education now to stress the story of Robin Hood . . . because he robbed the rich and gave to the poor."
- A jury acquits Yvonne Chevallier of shooting her husband, Pierre, mayor of New Orleans and newly appointed cabinet member, after he requested a divorce to marry his mistress.
- The gold in Fort Knox is counted and found to accord with records: $30,442,415,581.70.
- Rectifying an 1803 oversight, the House Interior Committee votes to admit Ohio to the Union.
- Senator Wayne Morse's 22-hour, 26-minute Senate speech, opposing a bill to return offshore oil reserves to their individual states, is unsuccessful.
- Air Force pilots report chasing clusters of red, white, and green lights over northern Japan, a report similar to recent UFO sightings in the United States and elsewhere.
- Easter egg rolling is revived at the White House.
- Thirty million attend performances of classical music, 15 million major league baseball; 7,250,000 children and young adults take music lessions.
- Arthur Godfrey fires Julius La Rosa on the air because La Rosa "lacks humility"; the public sympathizes with La Rosa.
- Actress June Havoc renounces her career to enter a Roman Catholic convent; six months later, she returns to Hollywood.
- Lucille Ball and Desi Arnaz sign TV's biggest contract ($8 million) to continue "I Love Lucy" for 30 months; the birth of their baby occurs on the show on the same day as in real life.
- Elvis Presley pays four dollars to cut "My Happiness" in Memphis for his mother's birthday.
- His career still at a low, Frank Sinatra takes the role of Maggio in *From Here to Eternity.*
- New sexual jargon includes baseball terms like "first base" and "home run."
- The comic book market expands to 650 titles; Scrabble also becomes a fad.

Christine Jorgensen elicits wide public interest after her sex change from George, achieved last year in Denmark by a combination of surgical and hormonal techniques. *Library of Congress.*

- The New York Fifth Avenue double-decker bus goes out of service.
- General Motors introduces the Chevrolet Corvette, the first plastic laminated fiberglass sports car, for $3,250.
- A correlation is indicated between coronary heart disease and diets high in animal fats.
- Oleo heir Minot (Mickey) Frazier is sentenced to three to six years on charges of running a ring of high-priced call girls.
- "Eight millionaires and a plumber" is a description given Ike's cabinet, the plumber a reference to Martin Durkin, head of a plumber's union and now secretary of labor.
- McCarthy staff members Roy Cohn and David Schine make an 18-day European trip to determine subversion in U.S. overseas programs; librarians are ordered to remove books by "Communists, fellow travelers, and the like."

New Words and Usages: Main Man, drag strip, name-dropper, bit, cookout, countdown, discount house, doublethink, egghead, girlie magazine, jet stream, metalinguistics, split-level, 3-D

First Appearances: DC-7 propeller plane, Japan Airlines, Sugar Smacks, bottled Schweppes quinine water, Irish Coffee, White Rose Redi-Tea, underground freezer storage (Kansas City, Mo.), *TV Guide, Playboy,* L & M cigarettes, Tareyton filter tips, 3-D Cinerama in stereo and wide screen, tufted plastic carpeting, 3-D newspaper ad (Waukesha, Wis.), aluminum-faced building (Alcoa, Pittsburgh), burglar alarm operated by ultrasonic or radio waves, element 100, 3-D cartoon and movies (*Melody, Bwana Devil, House of Wax*)

1954

Facts and Figures

Economic Profile
  Dow-Jones: ↑ High 404–
    Low 279
  GNP: +5%
  Inflation: +0.4%
  Unemployment: 5.5%
Expenditures
  Recreation: $13 billion
  Spectator sports: $224
    million
  European travel: $420
    million
Golf courses: 478
Bowlers: 2,500,000
Macy's Gregg Suisse skis:
  $17.98
Imported ski boots: $17.98
Best & Co. mink cape: $499
Saks 5th Ave. alligator bags:
  $115–$185
Russek's pastel cashmere
  coats: $135
Robert Hall all-nylon topper:
  $18.95
Rogers Peet broadcloth shirt:
  $3.95, oxford shirt: $4.95
Wallach's Bannister shoes,
  wing tip: $27.95
Arthur Godfrey ukelele:
  $4.98

Deaths

Wilhelm Furtwängler, Sidney
  Greenstreet, Cedric
  Hardwicke, Will Hays,
  Charles Ives, William
  Kapell, Henri Matisse,
  Grantland Rice.

In the News

FOUR SUPERPOWERS MEET AT BERLIN CONFERENCE . . . MOLOTOV PROPOSES A UNIFIED NEUTRAL GERMANY, DULLES REFUSES . . . MCCARTHY PROBE OF ARMY BEGINS . . . GAMAL ABDEL NASSER BECOMES PREMIER OF EGYPT . . . FIVE U.S. CONGRESSMEN ARE SHOT BY PUERTO RICAN NATIONALISTS . . . LARGEST THERMONUCLEAR BLAST OCCURS AT BIKINI ATOLL . . . ARMY CHARGES THAT MCCARTHY AND ROY COHN SOUGHT FAVORS FOR PRIVATE DAVID SCHINE . . . SOVIETS PROPOSE JOINING NATO AS PART OF GENERAL PEACE TREATY . . . ADMIRAL LEWIS STRAUSS SAYS H-BOMB CAN DESTROY CITY OF ANY SIZE . . . SUPREME COURT UPHOLDS INTERNAL SECURITY ACT . . . SENATE HEARINGS ON ARMY-MCCARTHY DISPUTE BEGIN . . . FRENCH FORTRESS AT DIEN BIEN PHU, VIETNAM, FALLS, THE ENTIRE GARRISON IS CAPTURED . . . SURGEON SAM SHEPPARD IS ACCUSED OF WIFE'S MURDER . . . SUPREME COURT RULES THAT RACIAL SEGREGATION IN PUBLIC SCHOOLS IS UNCONSTITUTIONAL . . . CHOU EN-LAI AND MENDES-FRANCE AGREE ON INDOCHINA SETTLEMENT . . . GENERAL MOTORS ANNOUNCES $1 BILLION EXPANSION . . . AEC VOTES 4–1 TO DENY SECURITY CLEARANCE TO J. ROBERT OPPENHEIMER . . . VIETNAM IS DIVIDED AT 17TH PARALLEL, PENDING THE 1956 ELECTION . . . HEAVY RIOTING OCCURS IN MOROCCO . . . HOLLAND ENDS UNION WITH INDONESIA . . . IKE SIGNS ESPIONAGE AND SABOTAGE ACT . . . BRITISH AGREE TO RETURN SUEZ CANAL TO EGYPT IN 1956 . . . DEMOCRATS GAIN IN HOUSE AND SENATE . . . U.S. SIGNS MUTUAL DEFENSE TREATY WITH NATIONALIST CHINA . . . SENATE VOTES TO CONDEMN MCCARTHY FOR CONTEMPT OF SENATE.

Quotes

WELCH: . . . You were asked for something different from the thing that hung on Schine's wall?

JULIANA: I never knew what hung on Schine's wall. . . .

WELCH: Did you think this [picture] came from a pixie? . . .

MCCARTHY (*interrupting*): Will counsel for my benefit define—I think he might be an expert on that—what a pixie is?

WELCH: Yes. I should say, Mr. Senator, that a pixie is a close relative of a fairy.
— Army-McCarthy hearings

"Have you left no sense of decency?"
— Joseph Welch to Senator Joseph McCarthy

"The doctrine of 'separate but equal' has no place [in public education]. . . . Separate facilities are inherently unequal."
— Supreme Court Decision, *Brown* v. *Board of Education of Topeka*

"[The U.S. needs a] deterrent of massive retaliatory power, . . . a great capacity to retaliate instantly by means and at times of our own choosing."
— Secretary of State John Foster Dulles

Ads

"The average American male stands five feet nine inches . . . 158 pounds, prefers brunettes, baseball, beefsteak, and French fried potatoes, and thinks the ability to run a home smoothly and efficiently is the most important quality in a wife. [The average American woman] . . . is five feet four, weighs 132, [and] can't stand an unshaven face."
— *Reader's Digest*

"College women in general have greater difficulty in marrying. . . . Men still want wives who will bolster their egos rather than detract from them."
— Paul H. Landis, *Your Marriage and Family Living*

(*Left*) Howdy Doody and "Buffalo Bob" Smith, who first aired in 1947, remain a popular afternoon babysitter. *Billy Rose Theatre Collection. The New York Public Library at Lincoln Center. Astor, Lenox and Tilden Foundations.*

(*Right*) Lucille Ball (and her husband Desi Arnaz) in "I Love Lucy" move CBS ratings ahead of NBC for the first time. *Billy Rose Theatre Collection. The New York Public Library at Lincoln Center. Astor, Lenox and Tilden Foundations.*

TV

Premieres
"Father Knows Best," Robert Young, Jane Wyatt
"Private Secretary," Ann Sothern
"The Jimmy Durante Show"
"People Are Funny," Art Linkletter
"Disneyland/Walt Disney"
"Lassie," George Cleveland
"The Secret Storm"
"The George Gobel Show"
"Producer's Showcase" ("State of the Union," Nina Foch, Joseph Cotten, Margaret Sullavan)
"The Loretta Young Show"
"Stop the Music," Bert Parks

Top Ten (Nielsen)
"I Love Lucy," "The Jackie Gleason Show," "Dragnet," "You Bet Your Life," "The Toast of the Town," "Disneyland," "The Jack Benny Show," "The Martha Raye Show," "The George Gobel Show," "Ford Theatre"

Specials
"Twelve Angry Men" (Robert Cummings); "Babes in Toyland" (Jack E. Leonard, Wally Cox); "Crime in the Streets" (Reginald Rose, with John Cassavetes); "Naughty Marietta" (Alfred Drake, Patrice Munsel); "Macbeth" (Judith Anderson); "Christmas Carol" (Fredric March); "Visit to a Small Planet" (Gore Vidal); "The Petrified Forest" (Humphrey Bogart, Henry Fonda, Lauren Bacall); "Scenes from South Pacific" (Mary Martin, Ezio Pinza); "McCarthy Hearings"; "Satins and Spurs" (Betty Hutton)

Emmy Awards
"U.S. Steel Hour" (drama); "Make Room for Daddy" (situation comedy); "Disneyland" (variety); "Stories of the Century" (action); "Lassie" (children); "This Is Your Life" (game); Danny Thomas (actor, "Make Room for Daddy"); Loretta Young (actress, "The Loretta Young Show"); John Daly (news); George Gobel (personality)

Movies

Openings
On the Waterfront (Elia Kazan), Marlon Brando, Karl Malden, Eva Marie Saint, Lee J. Cobb
The Country Girl (George Seaton), Bing Crosby, Grace Kelly, William Holden
The Caine Mutiny (Edward Dmytryk), Humphrey Bogart, Van Johnson, José Ferrer
Seven Brides for Seven Brothers (Stanley Donen), Howard Keel, Jane Powell
Three Coins in the Fountain (Jean Negulesco), Clifton Webb, Dorothy McGuire, Jean Peters, Louis Jourdan, Rossano Brazzi
Rear Window (Alfred Hitchcock), James Stewart, Grace Kelly
Sabrina (Billy Wilder), Humphrey Bogart, Audrey Hepburn, William Holden
A Star Is Born (George Cukor), Judy Garland, James Mason
The Barefoot Contessa (Joseph L. Mankiewicz), Ava Gardner, Humphrey Bogart
Bad Day at Black Rock (John Sturges), Spencer Tracy, Robert Ryan
Dial M for Murder (Alfred Hitchcock), Ray Milland, Grace Kelly
La Strada (Federico Fellini), Giulietta Masina, Anthony Quinn
Mr. Hulot's Holiday (Jacques Tati), Jacques Tati
The Wild One (Laslo Benedek), Marlon Brando
Beat the Devil (John Huston), Humphrey Bogart, Jennifer Jones, Gina Lollobrigida
Doctor in the House (Ralph Thomas), Dirk Bogarde, Kenneth More
Pather Panchali (Satyajit Ray), Subir Banerji
Diabolique (Henri-Georges Clouzot), Simone Signoret, Veral Clouzot
The Seven Samurai (Akira Kurosawa), Toshiro Mifune

Academy Awards
Best Picture: *On the Waterfront*
Best Director: Elia Kazan (*On the Waterfront*)
Best Actress: Grace Kelly (*The Country Girl*)
Best Actor: Marlon Brando (*On the Waterfront*)

Top Box-Office Stars
John Wayne, Dean Martin and Jerry Lewis, Gary Cooper, James Stewart, Marilyn Monroe, Alan Ladd, William Holden, Bing Crosby, Jane Wyman, Marlon Brando

Stars of Tomorrow
Audrey Hepburn, Maggie McNamara, Grace Kelly, Richard Burton, Pat Crowley, Guy Madison, Suzan Ball, Elaine Stewart, Aldo Ray, Cameron Mitchell

Popular Music

Hit Songs
"The Man That Got Away"
"Three Coins in the Fountain"
"Teach Me Tonight"
"Young and Foolish"
"Hernando's Hideaway"
"Cara Mia"
"If I Give My Heart to You"
"Mambo Italiano"
"Steam Heat"
"Papa Loves Mambo"
"Shake, Rattle, and Roll"
"Let Me Go, Lover"

Top Records

Albums: *Music for Lovers Only* (Jackie Gleason); *Selections from "The Glenn Miller Story"* (Glenn Miller); *The Student Prince* (Mario Lanza); *Songs for Young Lovers* (Frank Sinatra); *Music, Martinis, and Memories* (Jackie Gleason)

Singles: *Sh-boom* (Chords, Crew Cuts); *Rock around the Clock* (Bill Haley and the Comets, best-selling single to date); *Little Things Mean a Lot* (Kitty Kallen); *Hey, There* (Rosemary Clooney); *Wanted* (Perry Como); *Oh! My Pa-Pa* (Eddie Fisher); *Young at Heart* (Frank Sinatra). Country: *I Don't Hurt Anymore* (Hank Snow); *More and More* (Webb Pierce)

Jazz and Big Bands
J. J. Johnson and Kai Winding form a trombone-duo-lead quartet. Joe Williams joins Count Basie. The Miles Davis quintet includes John Coltrane; Art Blakey's Jazz Messengers include Horace Silver and Kenny Dorham. Hard bop, or "soul jazz," "gospel jazz," and "funky jazz," gain a following in reaction to the cool style. Sonny Rollins's *Oleo* gains wide interest. The Newport Jazz Festival begins.

Top Performers (*Downbeat*): Stan Kenton (soloist); Kenton, Les Brown (bands); Dave Brubeck (jazz group); Johnny Smith, Ray Brown, Shelly Manne, Charlie Parker, Chet Baker (instrumentalists); Ella Fitzgerald, Frank Sinatra (vocalists); Four Freshman (vocal group)

Theater

Broadway Openings

Plays
The Caine Mutiny Court Martial (Herman Wouk), Henry Fonda, John Hodiak, Lloyd Nolan
The Bad Seed (Maxwell Anderson), Nancy Kelly, Patty McCormack, Eileen Heckart
Witness for the Prosecution (Agatha Christie), Patricia Jessel, Frances L. Sullivan
Ondine (Jean Giraudoux), Audrey Hepburn, Mel Ferrer
Anastasia (Marcelle Maurette), Viveca Lindfors, Eugenie Leontovich
The Rainmaker (N. Richard Nash), Geraldine Page, Darren McGavin
The Immoralist (Ruth and Augustus Goetz), Geraldine Page, Louis Jourdan, James Dean
The Flowering Peach (Clifford Odets), Menasha Skulnik, Janice Rule
The Confidential Clerk (T. S. Eliot), Ina Claire, Douglas Watson, Claude Rains, Joan Greenwood

Musicals
The Pajama Game (Richard Adler, Jerry Ross), John Raitt, Janis Paige, Eddie Foy, Jr., Carol Haney
The Boy Friend, (Sandy Wilson), Julie Andrews
Fanny (Harold Rome), Ezio Pinza, Walter Slezak, Florence Henderson
Peter Pan (Mark Charlap, Carolyn Leigh), Mary Martin, Cyril Ritchard
The Golden Apple (Jerome Moross, John Latouche), Kay Ballard
The Threepenny Opera (Kurt Weill, Marc Blitzstein), Lotte Lenya, Scott Merrill

Classics and Revivals On and Off Broadway
A Midsummer Night's Dream, Stanley Hollaway, Robert Helpmann, Moira Shearer; *What Every Woman Knows* (James Barrie), Helen Hayes; *The Seagull* (Chekhov), Judith Evelyn, George Voskovic, Maureen Stapleton, Montgomery Clift

Regional

Founded: Milwaukee Repertory Theater Company by Mary John and Charles McCallum; the Front Street Theatre of Memphis; the Dallas Theater Center by Paul Baker

Pulitzer Prize
The Teahouse of the August Moon, John Patrick

Tony Awards
The Teahouse of the August Moon, John Patrick (play); *Kismet,* Alexander Borodin, Robert Wright, George Forest (musical)

Classical Music _____

Compositions
Edgard Varèse, *Déserts*
Ralph Shapey, Concerto for Clarinet with Six
    Instruments
Walter Piston, Symphony no. 5
Wallingford Riegger, Variations for Piano and
    Orchestra
Samuel Barber, *Souvenirs*

Important Events
Toscanini retires; Fritz Reiner spends his first year
with the Chicago Symphony; Enrique Jorda conducts
the San Francisco, Josef Krips, the Buffalo.
International exchanges continue: the
Concertgebouw travels through the United States.
Most frequently performed modern European
composers are Prokofiev, Stravinsky, and Bártok;
most frequently performed Americans include
Barber, Copland, Piston, and Gould.

Debuts: Mieczyslaw Horszowski, Andre Watts

First Performances
Stravinsky, Septet (Dumbarton Oaks); *Three Songs
for William Shakespeare, Four Russian Peasant
Songs, In Memoriam: Dylan Thomas* (Los Angeles);
Roy Harris, Symphonic Fantasy (Pittsburgh);
Charles Ives, *Washington's Birthday* (New York);
Alan Hovhaness, Piano Concerto no. 5 (New York);
Ernst Krenek, Cello Concerto (Los Angeles); Ernest
Bloch, *War no. 4* (Lenox, Mass.); David Diamond,
Ahavah (Washington, D.C., to celebrate the 300th

Watts Tower, Los Angeles. *Roger Whitehouse.*

Niccola Rosi-Lemeni and Maria Callas in *Norma*. Callas,
who became a public personality because of her
tempestuous personality and her love affair with Aristotle
Onassis, turns down an offer from the Metropolitan and
makes her American debut in Chicago. *Chicago Lyric
Opera.*

anniversary of the first Jew in America); Samuel
Barber, *Prayers of Kierkegaard* (Boston); Walter
Piston, Fantasy for English Horn, Strings, and Harp
(Boston); Ernest Bloch, Concerto Grosso no. 2
(Boston)

Opera

Metropolitan: Nicola Rossi-Lemeni, *Boris
Godunov;* Ettore Bastianini, *Aïda;* Richard Tucker,
Andrea Chenier

New York City: *The Tender Land* (Aaron Copland),
The Saint of Bleecker Street (Gian Carlo Menotti);
The Trial (Gottfried Von Einem), premieres

Chicago: Carol Fox founds the Lyric Opera, with
Lawrence V. Kelly and Nicola Rescigno. "Calling
Card" performance of *Don Giovanni;* Maria Callas
(debut), *Norma, Lucia di Lammermoor;* Leopold
Simoneau, Tito Gobbi, *Il barbiere di Siviglia*

San Francisco: *The Portuguese Inn* (Cherubini,
premiere); *Joan of Arc at the Stake* (Arthur
Honegger, first full production); *Carmina Burana*
(Carl Orff, premiere)

Music Notes
For their 100th anniversary Steinway & Sons sponsor
a charity concert at Carnegie Hall with dozens of
pianists performing together: one Chopin Polonaise is
played on ten pianos • Paul Hindemith receives the
distinguished Sibel Award ($35,000).

Art

Painting

Jackson Pollock, *White Light*
Mark Tobey, *Canals*
William Baziotes, *Congo, Flame*
Jasper Johns, *Flag*
Franz Kline, *Third Avenue*
Mark Rothko, *Earth and Green*
Edward Hopper, *Morning Sun*
Robert Motherwell, *Elegy to the Spanish Republic* (1953–54)
Robert Rauschenberg, *Charlene, Collection*
Stuart Davis, *Colonial Cubism*
Charles Sheeler, *Architectural Cadences*
Grace Hartigan, *Grand Street Brides*
Philip Guston, *Painting*

Sculpture

Sam Rodia, *Watts Towers* (1921–54)
Milton Hebald, *Convalescent Returns*
Reuben Nakian, *The Emperor's Bedroom*
The Iwo Jima Monument is dedicated at Washington, D. C.

Architecture

Oasis House, Ojai, Calif. (Richard Neutra)
First United Methodist Church, Midland, Mich. (Alden B. Dow)
Manufacturer's Hanover Bank, New York (Skidmore, Owings, and Merrill)
Bubble Prefab Houses, Hobe Sound, Fla. (Eliot Noyes)

Cincinnati: The Peale painters

San Francisco: Dufy

Minneapolis: Reality and fantasy

New Orleans: Sesquicentennial of Louisiana Purchase: 22 Louisiana Works

Chicago: Three expatriates: Sargent, Whistler, Cassatt; "Designer-Craftsmen, U.S.A"; Masterpieces of religious art

Venice Biennale: de Kooning, Shahn, Lachaise, Smith, Lassaw represent the United States

Art Briefs

The Metropolitan Museum of Art opens 44 renovated galleries with 700 masterpieces from the 13th to the 20th century • Major sales include Matisse's *Odalisque* ($75,000), which sold in 1930 for $25,000; Cézanne's *Baigneurs et Baigneuses* ($10,000); Grant Wood's charcoal study for *Daughters of the American Revolution* ($2,800).

Important Exhibitions

Museums

New York: *Metropolitan:* "Art 1754–1954" (to celebrate Columbia University's bicentennial); The Lehman collection; Masterpieces of Pre-Columbian gold; Ancient art of the Andes; Art of three expatriates—Sargent, Whistler, Cassatt; Dutch painting. *Museum of Modern Art:* Spencer retrospective; Vuillard; 25th-anniversary retrospective of modern art. *Whitney:* Grosz retrospective. *Guggenheim:* "Young European Painters," "Younger American Painters"

Toledo: Dutch painting

Boston: American arts of the 18th and early 19th centuries; Masterpieces from ancient civilizations; John Marin memorial

Philadelphia: The newly acquired Walter Arensberg collection; van Gogh

Indianapolis: Mannerism

Dance

Paul Taylor forms his own company.
The Robert Joffrey Ballet debuts with *Pas des déesses, Le Bal Masques*; the 25th anniversary of Diaghilev's death is commemorated throughout the ballet world.

Premieres

New York City Ballet: *Western Symphony* (George Balanchine), Diana Adams, Jacques d'Amboise; *Opus 34, Nutcracker, Ivesiana* (Balanchine), Adams, Francisco Moncion

Alvin Ailey: *House of Flowers*

Martha Graham: *Night Journey*

Ballet Theatre: *A Streetcar Named Desire* (Valerie Bettis)

Books

Fiction

Critics' Choice

The Goose on the Grave, John Hawkes

The Bird's Nest, Shirley Jackson

A Spy in the House of Love, Anaïs Nin

The Ponder Heart, Eudora Welty

The Dollmaker, Harriette Arnow

Cress Delahanty, Jessamyn West

The Tunnel of Love, Peter De Vries

ε *The Fellowship of the Ring*, J. R. R. Tolkien

ε *Lord of the Flies*, William Golding

Best-Sellers

Not as a Stranger, Morton Thompson

Mary Anne, Daphne Du Maurier

Love Is Eternal, Irving Stone

The Royal Box, Frances Parkinson Keyes

The Egyptian, Mika Waltari

No Time for Sergeants, Mac Hyman

Sweet Thursday, John Steinbeck

The View from Pompey's Head, Hamilton Basso

Never Victorious, Never Defeated, Taylor Caldwell

Benton's Row, Frank Yerby

Nonfiction

Critics' Choice

The Verbal Icon, Monroe C. Beardsley, W. K. Wimsatt

A Child of the Century, Ben Hecht

Realities of American Foreign Policy, George F. Kennan

The China Tangle, Herbert Feis

Call to Greatness, Adlai E. Stevenson

The American Presidency, Sidney Hyman

The Future of Architecture, Frank Lloyd Wright

Individualism Reconsidered, David Reisman

Freedom, Loyalty, Dissent, Henry Steele Commager

McCarthy and His Enemies, William F. Buckley, L. Brent Bozell

McCarthy and the Communists, James Rorty, Moshe Decter

Best-Sellers

The Holy Bible: Revised Standard Version

The Power of Positive Thinking, Norman Vincent Peale

Better Homes and Gardens New Cook Book

Betty Crocker's Good and Easy Cook Book

The Tumult and the Shouting, Grantland Rice

I'll Cry Tomorrow, Lillian Roth, Gerold Frank, Mike Connolly

The Prayers of Peter Marshall, ed. Catherine Marshall

This I Believe, 2d, ed., Raymond Swing

But We Were Born Free, Elmer Davis

Poetry

Louise Bogan, *Collected Poems 1923–1953*

E. E. Cummings, *Poems 1923–1954*

Robinson Jeffers, *Hungerfield and Other Poems*

W. S. Merwin, *The Dancing Bears*

William Carlos Williams, *The Desert Music and Other Poems*

Anthony Hecht, *A Summoning of Stones*

Weldon Kees, *Poems 1947–1954*

Leonie Adams, *Collected Poems*

Pulitzer Prizes

A Fable, William Faulkner (fiction)

Great River, the Rio Grande in North American History, Paul Horgan (U.S. history)

The Taft Story, William S. White (biography)

Collected Poems, Wallace Stevens

Nobel Prize

Ernest Hemingway

Science and Technology

Jonas Salk begins inoculation of schoolchildren in Pittsburgh; 900,000 children are eventually vaccinated nationwide.

A kidney transplant patient survives a record five months.

Vincent Du Vigneaud synthesizes two important pituitary hormones, oxytocin and vasopressin.

More resilient hybrid wheats are developed, based on wheat genetics work by Ernest Sears.

An electronic analog computer capable of mathematical logic is demonstrated at Princeton.

Bell Telephone Labs develop a solar battery.

The Boeing 707, the first jet-powered transport, is tested.

The first atomic-powered submarine, USS *Nautilis*, is commissioned at Groton, Conn.

An atomic-powered railway locomotive is developed at Utah University.

Nobel Prize

John F. Enders, Thomas H. Weller, and Frederick C. Robbins share the prize in physiology and medicine for their work in the cultivation of a polio virus.

Linus C. Pauling wins in chemistry for the study of forces holding together protein and other molecules.

Sports

Baseball

The Cleveland Indians win a record 111 games led by pitchers Bob Lemon, Early Wynn, Mike Garcia and Bob Feller.

Henry Aaron (Milwaukee-NL) debuts.

Stan Musial (St. Louis, NL) hits a record five home runs in a doubleheader.

Joe Adcock (Milwaukee, NL) hits four home runs and a double in one game.

Champions

Batting	Pitching
Willie Mays (New York, NL), .345	John Antonelli (New York, NL), 21–7
Bob Avila (Cleveland, AL), .341	Sandy Consuegra (Chicago, AL), 16–3
	Home runs
	Ted Kluszewski (Cincinnati, NL), 49

Football

Adrian Burk (Philadelphia) throws a record-tying seven touchdown passes in one game.

NFL Season Leaders: Norm Van Brocklin (Los Angeles), passing; Joe Perry (San Francisco), rushing; Pete Pihos (Philadelphia), receiving.

College All-Americans: Ralph Guglielmo (B), Notre Dame; Howard Cassady (B), Ohio State; Alan Ameche (B), Wisconsin.

Bowls (Jan. 1, 1955)

Rose: Ohio State 20–Southern California 7

Orange: Duke 34–Nebraska 7

Cotton: Georgia Tech 14–Arkansas 6

Sugar: Navy 21–Mississippi 0

Basketball

The NBA institutes the 24-second clock.

NBA All-Pro First Team: Neil Johnston (Philadelphia), Bob Cousy (Boston), Ed Macauley (Boston), George Mikan (Minneapolis), Ray Felix (Baltimore)

Other Sports

Running: Roger Bannister, of England, runs the mile in 3:59.4, the first under four minutes.

Racing: Bill Vukovich wins his second straight Indianapolis 500.

Tennis: Pancho Gonzales makes a comeback and defeats Pancho Segura and Frank Sedgman in round-robin matches.

Winners

World Series	*College Basketball*
New York (NL) 4	Kentucky
Cleveland (AL) 0	*Player of the Year*
MVP	Tom Gola, LaSalle
NL–Willie Mays, New York	*Stanley Cup*
AL–Yogi Berra, New York	Detroit
NFL	*US Tennis Open*
Cleveland 56–Detroit 10	Men: Tony Trabert
College Football	Women: Doris Hart
Ohio State	*USGA Open*
Heisman Trophy	Ed Furgol
Alan Ameche, Wisconsin	*Kentucky Derby*
NBA Championship	Determine (R. York,
Minneapolis 4–Syracuse 3	jockey)

Fashion

For Women: If Dior gave women curves in 1947, this year he rescinded them. The new look is the "H" with deemphasized bosom (necessitating a new lingerie line) and a straighter, longer silhouette, accented at the hips with low belts, sashes, and cuffs. The "costume ensemble" is also new: matched or blended dresses and coats, suits and overblouses. Jackets of various lengths include the long "skyscraper" worn with the hip-length pullover. Coats are flared from the shoulder, in ¾ or ⅞ lengths. The jumper is also popular, along with shorter slacks, again worn with sweaters that fall over the hip. A new interest appears in furs — sable, fox, leopard, and mink (for trim and full wear)—and the rope necklace of various beads and stones, as well as pearls. Of note, a silken shimmer covers most fabrics, even textured and flecked materials. Synthetics, like "miracle orlon," are enormously successful. The most popular casual clothes are the shirtwaist, worn with wide cinched belt, the off-the-shoulder top with ¾-length slacks, Bermuda shorts, and hooded shirts.

High-fashion notes: Dior's H-line; Balenciaga's "semi-fit" (close in front, straight in back)

1954

Kaleidoscope _____

- President Eisenhower modifies the Pledge of Allegiance from "one nation indivisible" to "one nation, under God, indivisible."
- The Supreme Court declares that membership in the Communist party is sufficient grounds for deportation of aliens.
- Televised Army-McCarthy hearings make Army counsel Joseph Welch a popular hero; McCarthy's repeated interruptions "point of order" and "Mr. chairman, Mr. chairman" cost him public support.
- "This is no time for men who oppose Senator McCarthy's methods to keep silent," says Edward R. Murrow on his prime-time "See It Now" show.
- Seventy-eight percent of Americans polled think it important to report to the FBI relatives or acquaintances suspected as Communists.
- Alan Freed, paid $75,000 a year, plays what he calls "rock 'n' roll" on radio station WINS, which becomes number one in only a few months.
- The first color TV sets are marketed for $1,000 (RCA).
- The Toledo Water Commission notes strange intervals of increased usage and discovers they coincide with TV commercials.
- Twenty million horror books are sold a month; there are more "deaths" portrayed on TV than occurred (of Americans) in the Korean War.
- A noticeable interest develops in group membership and mass culture; industrial workers, farmers, and businessmen join organizations in record numbers.
- One in ten households is headed by women, who number 21 million in the nation's 64 million workers.
- Although he is attacked by critics, Wladziu Valentino Liberace becomes a TV sensation with his candelabras, soft lights, and wide smiles.
- Jimmy Durante's famed nose is injured as it is accidentally caught under pianist Liberace's piano during a TV rehearsal.
- J. Robert Oppenheimer becomes controversial when the AEC calls him "loyal" but a "security risk" and guilty of "lack of enthusiasm."
- A record $3,135,000,000 is spent in new construction.
- Gas prices rise from 21 cents (1944) to 29 cents.
- The AEC thermonuclear tests at Bikini Atoll wound 31 Americans, 236 natives, and 23 Japanese fishermen. The United States offers an $800,000 indemnity.
- The AEC denies charges that its experiments were responsible for the death of 1,000 sheep in Utah.
- The Tobacco Industry Research Committee reports there is "no proof . . . that cigarette smoking is a cause of lung cancer."
- The public is alerted to the dangers of radioactive wastes.
- The Davy Crockett episodes on TV's "Disneyland" initiate a national mania for Davy Crockett products.
- Elvis Presley makes his first commercial recording and signs with RCA to promote "Elvis, the Pelvis."
- San Francisco's City Lights Bookshop becomes a gathering place for the beat generation and poets like Allen Ginsberg and Lawrence Ferlinghetti.
- The raccoon look describes the heavy eye makeup that "beat" girls wear; 10 million cakes of Max Factor pancake makeup are sold.
- There are 154 Americans with annual incomes of over $1 million (513 in 1929).
- Marilyn Monroe and Joe DiMaggio are married on January 14; they file for divorce October 5.
- A Gallup Poll reports that a family of four can live on $60 a week and that 94 percent of the population believes in God.
- Salvador Dali sues Mrs. William Woodward for $7,000, "the value of his services"; she walked away from her portrait "scared," as though she were "walking away from a monster."
- Miltown and Equanil, brands of the tranquilizer meprobamate, are marketed; sales are high.
- Mississippi voters approve a constitutional amendment to abolish public schools if there is no other way to avoid segregation.
- For the first time a senator is elected by write-in vote: Strom Thurmond, South Carolina.

New Words and Usages: Cat music, massive retaliation, desegregation, windfall profit, crazy pants, do-it-yourself, dragster, fall-out, goof, hard sell, hotline, hairy, greaser, hip, togetherness, cool (acceptable), bread (money)

Fads: Felt skirts with poodle appliques, "grape" jokes, the mambo, the "creep," raffles, bingo, "droodles," panty raids, roller skating marathons, flattops and crew cuts, the "ducktail" haircut.

First Appearances: Gas turbine car and bus, verified bridge hand, in which each player is dealt a perfect hand, automatic toll collector (Garden State Parkway, N.J.), newspaper vending machine, electric computers in business, Fontainebleau (Miami, Fla.); Ohrbach's (34th St., New York), Statler-Hilton Hotels, Inc., Studebaker-Packard Corp., Mercedes 300 SL with fuel injection, New York's Chemical Bank; cha-cha, U.S. Air Force Academy, Shakey's Pizza Parlors, Veterans' Day (replacing Armistice Day), F-100 Supersabre (supersonic fighter), Trix, Frozen TV brand dinners (turkey, sweet potatoes, peas), breath-inhaler alcoholism detector, check cashing with ID camera, vacation houseboy (light), wrist radio, language translating machine, Levi's faded blue denims, "Marmeduke"

1955

Economic Profile
Dow-Jones: ↑ High 488–
    Low 391
GNP: +9%
Inflation: −0.3%
Unemployment: 4.4%
Infant mortality/1,000: 26.0
Maternal mortality/10,000:
    4.1
Physicians in U.S.: 214,000
Dentists in U.S.: 95,000
Hospital beds: 1,604,000
Air France, New York–Nice:
    $520 (round trip)
National Airlines, New York–
    Havana: $176.50 (round
    trip)
Budapest String Quartet
    (Kaufman auditorium, New
    York City): $2–3
New York City Center: $3.60
LP records: $3.98
Annie Oakley cowgirl outfit:
    $4.90
"Morgan" stuffed animal:
    $2.95
English bike: $47.50
Croquet set: $12.98
Gimbel's professional ice
    skates: $17.95

Deaths

Theda Bara, Lionel
    Barrymore, Albert
    Einstein, Enrico Fermi,
    Alexander Fleming,
    Cordell Hull, Fernand
    Léger, Thomas Mann,
    Carmen Miranda, Charlie
    Parker

In the News

Congress Authorizes President to Use Force to Defend Formosa . . . U.S. Begins Aid to Indochina with $216 Million . . . Nikita Khrushchev Becomes Party Secretary, Malenkov Is Ousted for "Deviation" . . . West Germany Enters NATO . . . 8 Eastern European Countries Sign Warsaw Treaty of Mutual Defense . . . Ike Says A-Bomb Would Be Employed in War . . . Supreme Court Orders School Segregation to End "In Reasonable Time" . . . Afro-Asian Conference Meets at Bandung . . . Big Four Meet in Geneva, Ike Proposes Mutual Aerial Reconnaissance . . . Chinese Announce Release of 11 U.S. Airmen . . . Revolts Continue in Morocco and Algeria, 2,200 Die . . . General Motors Splits 3 for 1 . . . West Germany and Russia Agree to Diplomatic Relations . . . Military Ousts Juan Peron in Argentina . . . Ike Suffers Heart Attack in Colorado, Market Plunges $14 Billion . . . UN Votes to Take up Algeria, France Walks Out . . . Bao Dai Is Ousted, South Vietnam Proclaims Republic . . . James Dean, 24, Dies in Car Crash . . . Israel Attacks Syria in Retaliation for Shelling . . . Ford Foundation to Give $500 Million to Colleges . . . Interstate Commerce Commission Bans Segregation on Interstate Trains and Buses . . . AFL and CIO Merge, George Meany Becomes President . . . Khrushchev Criticizes Aerial Inspection Plan and Attacks Colonialism.

Quotes _____

"It's nice to be included in people's fantasies, but you also like to be accepted for your own sake."
— Marilyn Monroe

"Ah just act the way ah feel."
— Elvis Presley

"Sincerity is the quality that comes through on television."
— Richard M. Nixon

"Recognition of the Supreme Being is the first, the most basic, expression of Americanism. Without God, there could be no American form of government, nor American way of life."
— Dwight D. Eisenhower

"The south stands at Armageddon. . . . We cannot make the slightest concession to the enemy in this dark and lamentable hour of struggle. There is no more difference in compromising the integrity of race on the playing field than in doing so in the classroom."
— Governor Marvin Griffin, Georgia, on the Supreme Court *Brown* decision (1954)

Ads _____

He was a first-name kind of guy. He was everybody's kind of guy. . . . He was God's kind of guy.
(*film* A Man Called Peter)

Boys and Girls! Join the Davy Crockett Club at Bullock's Downtown—To qualify for the Davy Crockett Club, you need courage and common sense, an adventurous spirit and the will to succeed. Come to Bullock's . . . and get your . . . badge at no cost."
(*Bullock's Department Store, Los Angeles*)

Is there an angel in the house?—Give her a fabulous cherry colored nylon tricot gown.
(*Kayser*)

Our doubts are traitors,
And make us lose the good we oft might win,
By fearing to attempt.—Shakespeare, *Measure for Measure*
(*Container Corp. of America*)

How you gonna keep 'em away from the farm after they've seen this machine?
(*New Departure Ball Bearings*)

Jackie Gleason, Art Carney, Audrey Meadows, and Joyce Randolph in "The Honeymooners." "The Great One," Gleason, signs for 78 episodes but decides to stop after 39. *Movie Star News.*

Popular singer Eddie Fisher and popular actress Debbie Reynolds form what fan magazines call "a perfect union."

James Dean and Natalie Wood in *Rebel without a Cause.* Dean also stars in *East of Eden.* In both, he plays a sensitive young man not understood by parental figures. *Movie Star News.*

More Jobs Through Science
(*Union Carbide and Carbon*)

TV

Premieres

"The Lawrence Welk Show"
"The $64,000 Question," Hal March
"The Millionaire," Marvin Miller
"The Alcoa Hour"
"Gunsmoke," James Arness (first adult western)
"The Honeymooners," Jackie Gleason, Art Carney,
    Audrey Meadows, Joyce Randolph
"You'll Never Get Rich [Sergeant Bilko]," Phil
    Silvers
"The Life and Legend of Wyatt Earp," Hugh
    O'Brien
"Alfred Hitchcock Presents"
"Captain Kangaroo," Bob Keeshan
"The Mickey Mouse Club," The Mouseketeers,
    Annette Funicello

Top Ten (Nielsen)

"The $64,000 Question," "I Love Lucy," "The Ed
Sullivan Show," "Disneyland," "The Jack Benny
Show," "December Bride," "You Bet Your Life,"
"Dragnet," "The Millionaire," "I've Got a Secret"

Specials

"Patterns" (Rod Serling, with Ed Begley, Richard
Kiley); "A Catered Affair" (Paddy Chayefsky); "Our
Town" (musical, Frank Sinatra, Paul Newman, Eva
Marie Saint); "The Caine Mutiny Court Martial"
(Lloyd Nolan); "A-Bomb Test Coverage"; "Davy
Crockett and the River Pirates" on "Disneyland";
"Promenade" (Tyrone Power, Judy Holliday, Janet
Blair); "Tosca" (Leontyne Price); "She Stoops to
Conquer" (Michael Redgrave)

Emmy Awards

"Producer's Showcase" (drama); "Phil Silvers'
You'll Never Get Rich" (comedy); "Ed Sullivan
Show" (variety); "Disneyland" (action); "Lassie"
(children); "The $64,000 Question" (game); Phil
Silvers (actor, "You'll Never Get Rich"); Lucille Ball
(actress, "I Love Lucy"); Edward R. Murrow (news)

Of Note

CBS passes NBC to become number one for the first
time • "The Honeymooners" ends after 39 episodes.

Movies

Openings

Marty (Delbert Mann), Ernest Borgnine, Betsy Blair
The Rose Tattoo (Daniel Mann), Burt Lancaster,
    Anna Magnani
East of Eden (Elia Kazan), James Dean, Julie Harris
Rebel without a Cause (Nicholas Ray), James Dean,
    Sal Mineo, Natalie Wood
To Catch a Thief (Alfred Hitchcock), Cary Grant,
    Grace Kelly
The Blackboard Jungle (Richard Brooks), Glenn
    Ford, Sidney Poitier, Vic Morrow
Love Is a Many-Splendored Thing (Henry King),
    Jennifer Jones, William Holden
Mister Roberts (John Ford, Mervyn LeRoy), Henry
    Fonda, James Cagney, Jack Lemmon
Picnic (Joshua Logan), William Holden, Kim Novak
Love Me or Leave Me (Charles Vidor), James
    Cagney, Doris Day
The Man with the Golden Arm (Otto Preminger),
    Frank Sinatra, Eleanor Parker
I'll Cry Tomorrow (Daniel Mann), Susan Hayward
Guys and Dolls (Joseph L. Mankiewicz), Marlon
    Brando, Jean Simmons
The Bridges at Toko-Ri (Mark Robson), William
    Holden, Grace Kelly
Oklahoma! (Fred Zinnemann), Gordon McRae,
    Shirley Jones

The Night of the Hunter (Charles Laughton), Robert
    Mitchum, Lillian Gish
It's Always Fair Weather (Stanley Donen, Gene
    Kelly), Grace Kelly, Dan Dailey, Cyd Charisse
Smiles of a Summer Night (Ingmar Bergman), Ulla
    Jacobsson, Eva Dahlbeck

Academy Awards

Best Picture: *Marty*
Best Director: Delbert Mann *(Marty)*
Best Actress: Anna Magnani *(The Rose Tattoo)*
Best Actor: Ernest Borgnine *(Marty)*

Top Box-Office Stars

James Stewart, Grace Kelly, John Wayne, William
Holden, Gary Cooper, Marlon Brando, Dean Martin
and Jerry Lewis, Humphrey Bogart, June Allyson,
Clark Gable

Stars of Tomorrow

Jack Lemmon, Tab Hunter, Dorothy Malone, Kim
Novak, Ernest Borgnine, James Dean, Anne Francis,
Richard Egan, Eva Marie Saint Russ Tamblyn

Popular Music

Hit Songs

"The Ballad of Davy Crockett"
"Dance with Me, Henry"
"Cherry Pink and Apple Blossom
  White"
"Domani"
"Whatever Lola Wants"
"Cry Me a River"
"Love and Marriage"
"Love Is a Many-Splendored
  Thing"
"Moments to Remember"

Top Records

Albums: *Crazy Otto* (Crazy
Otto); *Starring Sammy Davis, Jr.*

(Sammy Davis, Jr.); *Lonesome
Echo* (Jackie Gleason); *Love Me
or Leave Me* (Doris Day)

Singles: *The Yellow Rose of
Texas* (Mitch Miller); *Sixteen Tons*
(Tennessee Ernie Ford); *Tweedle
Dee* (Georgia Gibbs); *Mr.
Sandman* (Chordettes); *Ain't It a
Shame* (Fats Domino); *Maybelline*
(Chuck Berry); *Earth Angel*
(Penguins); *I've Got a Woman*
(Ray Charles); *Unchained Melody*
(Roy Hamilton); *Everyday* (Count
Basie); *Only You* (The Platters).
Country: *Loose Talk* (Carl Smith);
Cattle Call (Eddy Arnold)

Jazz and Big Bands

First Recordings: Cannonball
Adderley

Top Performers (*Downbeat*):
Charlie Parker (soloist); Count
Basie, Les Brown (bands);
Modern Jazz Quartet (jazz group);
Erroll Garner, Max Roach, Paul
Desmond, Milt Jackson, Stan
Getz, Gerry Mulligan, J. J.
Johnson, Miles Davis
(instrumentalists); Ella Fitzgerald,
Frank Sinatra, Joe Williams
(vocalists); Four Freshmen (vocal
group).

Theater

Broadway Openings

Plays

Cat on a Hot Tin Roof (Tennessee Williams), Barbara
  Bel Geddes, Burl Ives, Pat Hingle, Mildred
  Dunnock
Inherit the Wind (Jerome Lawrence, Robert E. Lee),
  Ed Begley, Paul Muni, Tony Randall
The Lark (Jean Anouilh), Boris Karloff, Julie Harris,
  Christopher Plummer
Tiger at the Gates (Jean Giraudoux), Michael
  Redgrave, Leueen MacGrath, Leo Ciceri
The Matchmaker (Thornton Wilder), Robert Morse,
  Arthur Hill, Ruth Gordon, Eileen Herlie
Bus Stop (William Inge), Kim Stanley, Albert Salmi
The Diary of Anne Frank (Frances Goodrich, Albert
  Hackett), Joseph Schildkraut, Susan Strasberg
No Time for Sergeants (Ira Levin), Andy Griffith,
  Roddy McDowall
The Desperate Hours (Joseph Hayes), Paul Newman,
  George Grizzard, Karl Malden
A View from the Bridge (Arthur Miller), Van Heflin,
  Jack Warden, Eileen Heckart
The Chalk Garden (Enid Bagnold), Gladys Cooper,
  Siobhan McKenna
A Hatful of Rain (Michael V. Gasso), Ben Gazzara,
  Anthony Franciosa, Shelley Winters
The Dark Is Light Enough (Christopher Fry), Tyrone
  Power, Katharine Cornell, Christopher Plummer

Musicals

Damn Yankees (Richard Adler, Jerry Ross), Gwen
  Verdon, Stephen Douglass, Ray Walston

Plain and Fancy (Albert Hague, Arnold B. Horwitt),
  Shirl Conway, Richard Derr
Silk Stockings (Cole Porter), Hildegarde Neff, Don
  Ameche

Classics and Revivals On and Off Broadway

The Skin of Our Teeth (Thornton Wilder), Helen
Hayes, Mary Martin, George Abbott; *Six Characters
in Search of an Author* (Luigi Pirandello), Kurt
Kasznar

Regional

Founded: American Shakespeare Theatre,
Stratford, Conn., by Lawrence Langner: *Julius
Caesar, The Tempest,* Raymond Massey, Jack
Palance, Roddy McDowall, Christopher Plummer,
Fritz Weaver; Second City, Chicago

Dallas Theater Center: *Hamlet,* Burgess Meredith

Pulitzer Prize

Cat on a Hot Tin Roof, Tennessee Williams

Tony Awards

The Desperate Hours, Joseph Hayes (play); *The
Pajama Game,* Richard Adler, Jerry Ross (musical)

Classical Music

Compositions
Ross Lee Finney, Quartet
Ernest Toch, Symphony no. 3
Milton Babbitt, Two Sonnets
John Cage, Music for Piano
H. Owen Reed, *Michigan Dream*

Debuts: Glenn Gould, Emil Gilels, Lorin Hollander, David Oistrakh, Alicia de Larrocha, Geza Anda

First Performances
Walter Piston, Symphony no. 5 (Boston); Edgard Varèse, *Déserts* (Bennington, Vt.); Heitor Villa-Lobos, Symphony no. 18 (Philadelphia), Cello Concerto (New York); Howard Hanson, Symphony no. 5, *Sinfonia Sacra* (Philadelphia); Leonard Bernstein, Serenade (Boston); Arthur Honegger, *A Christmas Cantata* (Boston); Roy Harris, *Symphonic Epigram* (New York); Sergei Prokofiev, Suite of Waltzes (Cincinnati); Darius Milhaud, Symphony no. 8.

Opera
Porgy and Bess is the first American opera to be performed at La Scala. Lukas Foss's *Gruffelkin* is commissioned for TV.

Metropolitan: Marian Anderson (debut), *Un Ballo in Maschera;* Renata Tebaldi (debut), *Otello,* Risë

Stevens, *Orfeo ed Euridice;* Richard Tucker, Roberta Peters, Zinka Milanov, Marian Anderson, Leonard Warren, *Un ballo in Maschera; Arabella* (Richard Strauss, premiere)

New York City: *The Golden Slippers* (Tchaikovsky), *Troilus and Cressida* (William Walton)

Indiana University: *The Ruby* (Norman Dello Joio, premiere)

Florida State University: *Susannah* (Carlisle Floyd, premiere)

Chicago: Maria Callas, *I Puritani;* Renata Tebaldi, *Aïda;* triple bills: *Il tabarro, Il ballo delle ingrate, The Merry Widow,* and *Cavalleria rusticana, Lord Byron's Love Letter,* and *Revanche.*

San Francisco: Robert Weede, Inge Borkh, *Macbeth;* Elisabeth Schwarzkopf, Licia Albanese, Cesare Siepi, *Don Giovanni*

Music Notes
Eugene Ormandy and the Philadelphia Symphony Orchestra is officially sent abroad to exemplify the breadth of American culture • The Berlin Philharmonic gives its first concert in Washington, D.C., as the State Department rejects protests of musicians' unions that von Karajan is an ex-Nazi.

Glenn Gould, famous for his brilliant interpretations of Bach and his keyboard mannerisms, such as reduced use of pedal and a nearly horizontal piano posture. *Movie Star News.*

Nat "King" Cole. From Montgomery, Alabama, Cole is the first jazz-grounded male voice since Louis Armstrong to gain world wide fame. *Movie Star News.*

Art

Painting

Morris Graves, *Flight of Plover*
Robert Rauschenberg, *Satellite*
Larry Rivers, *Double Portrait of Birdie*
Hans Hofmann, *Exuberance*
Jasper Johns, *Flag, Target with Four Faces*
Robert Motherwell, *Je t'aime, IIA*
Philip Guston, *The Room* (1954–55)
William Baziotes, *The Beach, Pompeii*
Helen Frankenthaler, *Blue Territory*

Sculpture

Louise Nevelson, *Black Majesty*
Richard Stankiewicz, *Gross Bathers, Kabuki Dancer*
Sidney Gordin, *Construction, No. 10*

Louise Bourgeois, *One and Others*
Raoul Hague, *Sawkill Walnut*

Architecture

Socony-Mobil Building, New York (Harrison and Abramovitz)
H. C. Price Tower, Bartlesville, Okla. (Frank Lloyd Wright)
MIT Chapel, Kresge Auditorium (Eero Saarinen)
Under construction: $17 million Walt Disney Amusement Park, Anaheim, Calif.; $35 million New York Coliseum; $18 million Los Angeles County Courthouse.

Important Exhibitions

Loan shows include over 100 Goyas from Spain (at the National, Metropolitan, San Francisco, Los Angeles, Boston); 70 Dutch paintings of the 17th century and French drawings from the Louvre (at the Metropolitan and Toledo).

Museums

New York: *Metropolitan:* The Comédié Française and the theatre in France; Art of the Hebrew tradition; Persian and Assyrian art. *Museum of Modern Art:* 22 contemporary Europeans; Tanguy; de Chirico. *Whitney:* 35 contemporary Americans; Levine and Bloom. *Guggenheim:* Giacometti; Brancusi retrospective

Washington: Renaissance prints by Lucan van Leyden; Austrian drawings and prints; German drawings of five centuries

Chicago: French drawings from the 14th to the 19th century; Japanese prints

National, Cleveland, San Francisco, Fogg: German old masters

Los Angeles, San Francisco: Renoir

Cleveland: Chinese landscapes

Boston: Matisse bronzes and drawings; Sport in art

Pasadena: The blue four: Jawlensky, Kandinsky, Klee, Feininger

Art Briefs

Edward Steichen assembles "The Family of Man" show at the Museum of Modern Art • Major sales include Soutine's *The Old Mill near Cannes* ($20,500) and Cézanne's *The Water Can* ($19,000).

George Balanchine, distinguished for his modern productions and the famous statement: "Ballet is woman." Balanchine was married to Tamara Geva, Vera Zorina, Maria Tallchief, and Tanaquil LeClerq. *Library of Congress.*

Dance

Chicago Opera Ballet debuts, founded by Ruth Page; New York City Ballet tours Europe; Ballet Theatre visits South America; Sadler's Wells, Royal Danish, and several Spanish companies tour the United States.

Premieres

New York City Ballet: *Pas de Dix* (George Balanchine), Maria Tallchief, André Eglevsky

Books

Fiction

Critics' Choice

The Recognitions, William Gaddis
The Deer Park, Norman Mailer
A Charmed Life, Mary McCarthy
Lolita, Vladimir Nabokov
A Good Man Is Hard to Find,
 Flannery O'Connor
Satan in Goray, Isaac Bashevis
 Singer
Band of Angels, Robert Penn
 Warren
The Simple Truth, Elizabeth
 Hardwick
Sincerely, Willis Wayde, John P.
 Marquand
❧ *Cards of Identity*, Nigel Dennis

Best-Sellers

Marjorie Morningstar, Herman
 Wouk
Auntie Mame, Patrick Dennis
Andersonville, MacKinlay Kantor
Bonjour Tristesse, Françoise
 Sagan
The Man in the Gray Flannel Suit,
 Sloan Wilson
Something of Value, Robert Ruark
Not as a Stranger, Morton
 Thompson
No Time for Sergeants, Mac
 Hyman
The Tontine, Thomas B. Costain
Ten North Frederick, John O'Hara

Nonfiction

Critics' Choice

The Scrolls from the Dead Sea,
 Edmund Wilson
The Armed Vision, Stanley Edgar
 Hyman
A Democrat Looks at His Party,
 Dean Acheson
The African Giant, Stuart Cloete
Notes of a Native Son, James
 Baldwin
*The Life and Work of Sigmund
 Freud*, Ernest Jones
Dylan Thomas in America, John
 Malcolm Brinnin
An End to Innocence, Leslie
 Fiedler
The Strange Career of Jim Crow,
 C. Vann Woodward
Black Power, Richard Wright
American in Italy, Herbert Kubly

Best-Sellers

Gift from the Sea, Anne Morrow
 Lindbergh
The Power of Positive Thinking,
 Norman Vincent Peale
The Family of Man, Edward
 Steichen
A Man Called Peter, Catherine
 Marshall
How to Live 365 Days a Year,
 John A. Schindler
*Better Homes and Gardens Diet
 Book*

The Secret of Happiness, Billy
 Graham
Why Johnny Can't Read, Rudolf
 Flesch
Inside Africa, John Gunther
Year of Decisions, Harry S
 Truman

Poetry

W. H. Auden, *The Shield of
 Achilles*
Gregory Corso, *The Vestal Lady
 on Brattle*
Adrienne Rich, *The Diamond
 Cutters and Other Poems*
A. R. Ammons, *Ommateum*
Howard Nemerov, *The Salt
 Garden*
William Carlos Williams, *Journey
 to Love*
Lawrence Ferlinghetti, *Pictures of
 a Gone World*

Pulitzer Prizes

Andersonville, MacKinlay Kantor
 (fiction)
*The Age of Reform; From Bryan
 to FDR*, Richard Hofstadter
 (U.S. history)
Benjamin Henry Latrobe, Talbot
 F. Hamlin (biography)
*Poems: North and South—A Cold
 Spring*, Elizabeth Bishop
 (poetry)

Science and Technology

Retrolental fibroplasia, which causes childhood
 blindness, is associated with high doses of
 oxygen usually given premature babies.
An oral contraceptive ("the pill") made of a
 progesterone-type substance is discovered by
 Gregory Pincus.
The steroid prednisone is introduced.
Thorazine and reserpine are found effective for
 severe mental illness.
Albert Sabin, at the University of Cincinnati, says he
 believes a live virus anti-polio vaccine to be
 more effective than the dead one (Salk's).
RNA- and DNA-like molecules are synthesized by
 Severo Ochoa of New York University.
Experiments with "anti-protons" that annihilate

protons on contact are reported.
The AEC reports that fallout from last year's H-
 bomb tests at Bikini will affect human life in a
 7,000-square-mile area.
The U.S. Army announces that German rocket
 pioneer Herman Oberth will join 100 others in
 missile research at Redstone Arsenal, Alabama.

Nobel Prize

Polykarp Kusch and Willis E. Lamb, Jr., win the
prize in physics for atomic measurements. Vincent
Du Vigneaud wins in chemistry for work on pituitary
hormones.

Sports

Baseball

The Brooklyn Dodgers win the first ten games of the season and go on to win their first World Series, over the Yankees.

Champions

Batting	Pitching
Richie Ashburn (Philadelphia, NL), .338	Don Newcombe (Brooklyn, NL), 20–5
Al Kaline (Detroit, AL), .340	Tommy Byrne (New York, AL), 16–5
	Home runs
	Willie Mays (New York, NL), 51

Football

Otto Graham (QB), Cleveland, retires.
Johnny Unitas (QB), Baltimore, a free agent pickup, debuts.

NFL Season Leaders: Otto Graham (Cleveland), passing; Alan Ameche (Baltimore), rushing; Pete Pihos (Philadelphia), receiving

College All-Americans: Tommy McDonald (B), Oklahoma; Paul Hornung (B), Notre Dame

Bowls (Jan. 1, 1956)

Rose: Michigan State 17–UCLA 14
Orange: Oklahoma 20–Maryland 6
Cotton: Georgia Tech 7–Pittsburgh 0
Sugar: Mississippi 14–Texas Christian 13

Basketball

NBA All-Pro First Team: Neil Johnston (Philadelphia), Paul Arizin (Philadelphia), Bob Cousy (Boston), Bob Pettit (Milwaukee), Larry Foust (Fort Wayne)

Other Sports

Horse Racing: Nashua, ridden by Willie Hartack, wins the Preakness and Belmont.

Boxing: Sugar Ray Robinson comes out of retirement to knock out Bobo Olson and win the middleweight title for the third time.

Winners

World Series	*NBA Championship*
Brooklyn (NL) 4	Syracuse 4–Fort Wayne 3
New York (AL) 3	*College Basketball*
MVP	San Francisco
NL–Roy Campanella, Brooklyn	*Player of the Year*
AL–Yogi Berra, New York	Bill Russell, San Francisco
NFL	*Stanley Cup*
Cleveland 38–Los Angeles 14	Detroit
MVP	*US Tennis Open*
Harlon Hill, Chicago Bears	Men: Tony Trabert
College Football	Women: Doris Hart
Oklahoma	*USGA Open*
Heisman Trophy	Jack Fleck
Howard Cassady, Ohio State	*Kentucky Derby*
	Swaps (W. Shoemaker, jockey)

Fashion

For Women: Twenties' "siren simplicity" combines with the French empire style to create an unusual blend of willowy and youthful sexiness. The sheath is semifitted and beltless, and it emphasizes a long bodice and high bosom; hips remain rounded. Dior and Balenciaga introduce the Oriental tunic and semifitted coat and jacket worn with a straight tube dress or narrow skirt. Sari silks and Indian/Persian brocades and silks also appear in unusual color combinations: pink-orange, green-peacock blue, red-black. Jeweled jackets also gain popularity. For more formal wear, long evening gowns return with long, tight sleeves, high fronts, and low backs; the World War I wrap-around dance dress also returns. The market for at-home fashions grows: tapered satin, velvet, brocade pants with decorative sweaters or satin tops. Brilliant colors are everywhere, especially reds, emerald greens, and sapphire blues. College girls wear black leotards, tweed jumpers, camel-hair and gray coats; blazers appear in new, boldly contrasting stripes.

High-fashion notes: Balenciaga's black tunic with black fox collar and shoulder "flying panel"; Dior's A-line

For Men: The continental influence begins to be felt in sports clothes—cotton jersey pullovers, bateau necklines, lower cut, more flexible shoes, and moccasin slip-ons.

Kaleidoscope

An H-bomb
shelter in
Garden City,
Long Island.
*Library of
Congress.*

- Revlon buys "The $64,000 Question" and begins TV's big quiz era. Marine Corps Captain Richard S. McCutchen wins $64,000 by identifying the seven courses served King George and his guests in 1939; Joyce Brothers wins $64,000 but then misses on Sugar Ray Robinson's welterweight victory.
- Weekly church attendance is 49 million adults, half the total adult population.
- Wayne Morse, of Oregon, is the first senator to move from one party to another when he becomes a Democrat.
- Construction of suburban shopping centers and motels increases.
- Over 3.8 million people play golf on approximately 5,000 courses.
- Altman's department store, in New York, sells mink-handled can openers; a Beverly Hills shop offers 14k gold charge cards.
- Ira Hayes, Pima Indian and one of the six who raised the flag on Iwo Jima, dies of exposure and alcoholism.
- After an eight-month marriage, stripteaser Anita Manville wins a $400,000 settlement from Tommy Manville; she was his ninth wife.
- Richard J. Daley becomes mayor of Chicago.
- HEW Secretary Oveta Culp Hobby opposes free distribution of the Salk vaccine to poor children as "socialized medicine . . . by the back door."
- Twenty-five women scarred in the Hiroshima A-bomb blast arrive in New York for free plastic surgery.
- Walter Winchell tips audiences that Pentepec Oil is a good stock; those who follow his advice lose 21 percent.
- Eddie Fisher and Debbie Reynolds marry.
- Dior, Fath, Lanvin, and Patou sue U.S. manufacturers for "dress piracy."
- The U.S. Information Agency changes its address from 1778 to 1776 Pennsylvania Avenue.
- A campaign is launched to cultivate European interest in American culture and lessen the publicity of American scandals. The State Department sends to France Judith Anderson in *Medea, Oklahoma, The Skin of Our Teeth;* Balanchine and the New York City Ballet; Eugene Ormandy and the Philadelphia Orchestra; and an exhibit of 50 years in American art.
- "Pop art" gains attention with Robert Rauschenberg's *Bed,* which incorporates a real pillow and quilt on a stretcher, along with other objects and design materials.
- At its peak *Confidential* magazine has a circulation of 4.5 million readers.
- The population explosion creates a shortage of 120,000 teachers and 300,000 schoolrooms.
- "Smog," or "poisoned air," becomes a public concern.
- J. Edgar Hoover turns down mayor Wagner's $25,000-a-year offer to be New York City police commissioner.
- Textron American is incorporated as the first business conglomerate.

- The first TV presidential press conference occurs on January 19.
- The minimum wage goes up from 75 cents to $1.
- Richard Byrd is greeted by pickets in Dallas that read: "Little America [Antarctica] Needs the Little Woman" in response to his comment: "No woman has ever set foot on Little America, . . . the most silent and peaceful place in the world."
- Jackie Gleason applies to the U.S. Patent Office for "And away we go."

New Words and Usages: Automated, certified mail, junk mail, rock-and-roll, A-line, atomic rain, Thorazine, church key, cue card, one-take, bombed, stoned, isolation booth, blast off, har-dee-har, passion pit, Third World

Fads: Davy Crockett hats, books, and T-shirts; pink shirts; charcoal gray suits; mooning; raccoon coats; stuffing people into a car; pizza (replacing hamburger snacks); the new games of Chuggedy Chug, Annie-Oakley, Uncle Wiggley, Chutes and Ladders; Tutti-Frutti; Maybelline; driving around

First Appearances: Ten-story display ad on Times Square, plastic containers for shipping, polyglot typewriters, Disneyland (Anaheim, Calif.), army male nurse (E. L. T. Lyon), woman flying faster than the speed of sound (Jacqueline Cochran), sun-powered auto demonstration, auto seat belt safety law (Illinois), solar-heated and radiator-cooled house (Phoenix), element 101, electric stove for home use, commercial telephone using electricity generated by the sun's rays, Nieman-Marcus (Houston), Merengue (dance), Eden Roc (Miami Beach, Fla.), Crest, Gorton's Fish Sticks, Special K, Colonel Sanders' Kentucky Fried Chicken, New York alternate side of the street parking, Ford Thunderbird (two-seater), Karmann-Ghia, Long Island Expressway, Tappan Zee Bridge, "Ann Landers Says," "Dondi," Chase Manhattan Bank, First National City Bank, Sperry-Rand, H & R Block, Dreyfus Fund, *National Review, Village Voice,* Whirlpool, roll-on deodorant, Revlon "no-smear" Lanolite lipstick

1956

In the News

AUTHERINE LUCY, FIRST BLACK AT UNIVERSITY OF ALABAMA, IS SUSPENDED AFTER RIOTS . . . KHRUSHCHEV, AT 20TH PARTY CONGRESS, ASSAILS STALIN AS TERRORIST, EGOTIST, AND MURDERER . . . 11 BLACKS ARE ARRESTED DURING MONTGOMERY BUS BOYCOTT . . . SIX MARINE RECRUITS ARE DROWNED DURING A MARCH AT PARRIS ISLAND, S.C. . . . MOROCCO GAINS INDEPENDENCE . . . NGO DIEM IS ELECTED PRESIDENT OF SOUTH VIETNAM . . . TUNISIA GAINS INDEPENDENCE . . . GRACE KELLY MARRIES PRINCE RAINIER OF MONACO . . . KHRUSHCHEV SAYS RUSSIA WILL PRODUCE AN ICBM . . . COLUMNIST VICTOR RIESEL IS BLINDED BY ACID ATTACK . . . ADLAI STEVENSON IS RENOMINATED BY DEMOCRATS, IKE BY GOP . . . IKE UNDERGOES SURGERY FOR ILEITIS . . . BRITAIN LEAVES SUEZ AFTER 74 YEARS . . . UNITED DC-7 AND TWA SUPERCONSTELLATION CRASH OVER GRAND CANYON, 128 DIE . . . U.S. AND BRITAIN WITHDRAW ASWAN DAM AID FROM EGYPT . . . "ANDREA DORIA" SINKS AFTER COLLISION WITH "STOCKHOLM," 50 ARE DEAD, 1,652 ARE SAVED . . . SALK VACCINE GOES ON THE OPEN MARKET . . . 33-DAY STEEL STRIKE ENDS . . . NATIONAL GUARD IS CALLED OUT FOR ANTI-BLACK RIOTING AT CLINTON, TENNESSEE, HIGH SCHOOL . . . LABOR RIOTS ARE QUELLED IN POLAND, KHRUSHCHEV ATTACKS LIBERALIZATION . . . ANTI-SOVIET DEMONSTRATIONS IN HUNGARY ARE SUPPRESSED, HUNGARIANS REVOLT . . . EGYPT AND ISRAEL CLASH, GAZA STRIP FALLS TO ISRAEL . . . SOVIET FORCES CRUSH HUNGARIAN REVOLT . . . IKE WINS LANDSLIDE VICTORY, 36 MILLION TO 26 MILLION . . . FRENCH AND BRITISH LAND IN SUEZ, ISRAEL TAKES SINAI, IKE URGES THAT ALL WITHDRAW . . . U.S. EMERGENCY FORCE IS SENT TO SINAI . . . BUS SEGREGATION IN MONTGOMERY, ALABAMA, ENDS.

Senator Estes Kefauver, campaigning for the presidential nomination in a popular style of the day. *Copyright Washington Post. Reprinted courtesy D.C. Library.*

Quotes

"History is on our side. We will bury you!"
> — Nikita Khrushchev, to Western ambassadors at Kremlin reception

"Of all the accomplishments of the American woman, the one she brings off with the most spectacular success is having babies."
> — *Life* magazine

"[The U.S. and USSR] are like two scorpions in a bottle, each capable of killing the other but only at the risk of his own life. . . . The atomic clock ticks faster and faster."
> — J. Robert Oppenheimer

"Nonviolence is the most potent technique for oppressed people. Unearned suffering is redemptive."
> — Martin Luther King, Jr.

"I intend to continue not to be angry or bear ill will to anyone."
> — Autherine Lucy, expelled from the University of Alabama

"Many unconsciously wondered if they deserved better conditions. Their minds were so conditioned to segregation that they submissively adjusted to things as they were. This is the ultimate tragedy of segregation."
> — Martin Luther King, Jr.

"The ability to get to the verge without getting into war is the necessary art."
> — Secretary of State John Foster Dulles, on "brinkmanship"

Nobel Peace Prize winner and Harvard government professor Ralph Bunche and Democratic nominee for president Adlai Stevenson at a breakfast meeting. *Library of Congress.*

Ads

TV

Premieres
"As the World Turns"
"The Edge of Night"
"NBC News—Huntley-Brinkley"
"The Price Is Right," Bill Cullen
"The $64,000 Challenge," Sonny Fox
"Playhouse 90" ("Requiem for a Heavyweight," Jack Palance, Ed Wynn)
"Twenty-One," Jack Barry
"Tic Tac Dough," Jay Jackson
"The Steve Allen Show"

Top Ten (Nielsen)
"I Love Lucy," "The Ed Sullivan Show," "General Electric Theater," "The $64,000 Question," "December Bride," "Alfred Hitchcock Presents," "I've Got a Secret," "Gunsmoke," "The Perry Como Show," "The Jack Benny Show"

Specials
"The Plot to Kill Stalin" (Melvyn Douglas); "Charley's Aunt" (Art Carney); "Tragedy in a Temporary Town" (Reginald Rose); "A Night to Remember" (George Roy Hill); "Composing, Conducting" (Leonard Bernstein); "Born Yesterday" (Paul Douglas, Mary Martin); "High Tor" (Julie Andrews, Bing Crosby); Grace Kelly–Prince Rainier wedding

Emmy Awards
"Requiem for a Heavyweight" (program); "Phil Silvers Show," "Caesar's Hour" (series); "See It Now" (public service); Robert Young, (actor, "Father Knows Best"); Loretta Young (actress, "The Loretta Young Show"); Perry Como, Dinah Shore (personality)

Of Note
"Hillbilly singer" Elvis Presley debuts on "Stage Door," hosted by the Dorsey Brothers • The first of the pre-1948 film sales is made, and *The Wizard of Oz,* with Judy Garland, and *Richard III,* with Laurence Olivier, are aired.

Movies

Openings
Around the World in Eighty Days (Lindsay Anderson), David Niven, Shirley MacLaine, Cantinflas
The King and I (Walter Lang), Yul Brynner, Deborah Kerr
War and Peace (King Vidor), Audrey Hepburn, Mel Ferrer, Henry Fonda
Giant (George Stevens), Rock Hudson, James Dean, Elizabeth Taylor
Friendly Persuasion (William Wyler), Gary Cooper, Dorothy McGuire, Anthony Perkins
The Ten Commandments (Cecil B. De Mille), Charlton Heston, Yul Brynner, Anne Baxter
Lust for Life (Vincente Minnelli), Kirk Douglas, Anthony Quinn
Anastasia (Anatole Litvak), Ingrid Bergman, Yul Brynner
Baby Doll (Elia Kazan), Carroll Baker, Eli Wallach
Love Me Tender (Robert D. Webb), Elvis Presley
Bus Stop (Joshua Logan), Marilyn Monroe, Don Murray
The Searchers (John Ford), John Wayne, Natalie Wood, Jeffrey Hunter
High Society (Charles Walters), Frank Sinatra, Louis Armstrong, Bing Crosby, Grace Kelly
Invasion of the Body Snatchers (Donald Siegel), Dana Wynter, Kevin McCarthy
The Seventh Seal (Ingmar Bergman), Max von Sydow, Bibi Andersson
Rififi (Jules Dassin), Jean Servais, Carl Mohner

Academy Awards
Best Picture: *Around the World in Eighty Days*
Best Director: George Stevens *(Giant)*
Best Actress: Ingrid Bergman *(Anastasia)*
Best Actor: Yul Brynner *(The King and I)*

Top Box Office Stars
William Holden, John Wayne, James Stewart, Burt Lancaster, Glenn Ford, Martin and Lewis, Gary Cooper, Marilyn Monroe, Kim Novak, Frank Sinatra

Stars of Tomorrow
Rod Steiger, Jeffrey Hunter, Natalie Wood, Dana Wynter, Tim Hovey, Yul Brynner, George Nader, Joan Collins, Sheree North, Sal Mineo

Popular Music

Hit Songs

"Blue Suede Shoes"
"Friendly Persuasion"
"Hound Dog"
"Love Me Tender"
"Mack the Knife"
"Mr. Wonderful"
"My Prayer"
"The Party's Over"
"Too Close for Comfort"
"You're Sensational"

Top Records

Albums: *Oklahoma* (sound track); *Belafonte* (Harry Belafonte); *Elvis Presley* (Elvis Presley); *My Fair Lady* (original cast); *Calpyso* (Harry Belafonte); *Elvis* (Elvis Presley); *The Eddy Duchin Story* (sound track); *The King and I* (sound track)

Singles: *Que Sera, Sera* (Doris Day); *Moonglow* (Morris Stoloff); *Hot Diggity* (Perry Como); *Wonderful, Wonderful* (Johnny Mathis); *The Great Pretender* (The Platters); *Why Do Fools Fall in Love?* (Teenagers with Frankie Lyman); *On the Street Where You Live* (Vic Damone); *Heartbreak Hotel* (Elvis Presley); *Standing on the Corner* (Four Lads). Country: *Singing the Blues* (Marty Robbins); *Crazy Arms* (Ray Price)

Jazz and Big Bands

Horace Silver forms his own quartet. The first U.S. government–sponsored jazz tour travels to the Near and Middle East.

Top Performers (*Downbeat*): Duke Ellington (soloist); Count Basie, Les Brown (bands); Modern Jazz Quartet (jazz group); Stan Getz, J. J. Johnson, Dizzy Gillespie, Milt Jackson, Bud Shank (instrumentalists); Ella Fitzgerald, Frank Sinatra (vocalists); Four Freshmen (vocal group)

Theater

Broadway Openings

Plays

Middle of the Night (Paddy Chayefsky), Edward G. Robinson, Gena Rowlands
Waiting for Godot (Samuel Beckett), Bert Lahr, E. G. Marshall, Alvin Epstein, Kurt Kasznar
Long Day's Journey into Night (Eugene O'Neill), Fredric March, Florence Eldridge, Bradford Dillman, Katharine Ross, Jason Robards, Jr.
Separate Tables (Terence Rattigan), Margaret Leighton, Eric Portman
The Great Sebastians (Howard Lindsay, Russel Crouse), Alfred Lunt, Lynn Fontanne
Auntie Mame (Jerome Lawrence, Robert E. Lee), Rosalind Russell, Peggy Cass

Musicals

My Fair Lady (Alan Jay Lerner, Frederick Loewe), Julie Andrews, Rex Harrison
The Most Happy Fella (Frank Loesser), Robert Weede, Jo Sullivan, Art Lund
Mr. Wonderful (Jerry Bock), Sammy Davis, Jr. and Sr., Chita Rivera
Li'l Abner (Gene de Paul, Johnny Mercer), Peter Palmer, Edie Adams, Julie Newmar
Bells Are Ringing (Jule Styne, Betty Comden, Adolph Green), Judy Holliday, Sydney Chaplin
Candide (Leonard Bernstein, Richard Wilbur), Robert Rounseville, Barbara Cook

Classics and Revivals On and Off Broadway

King Lear, Orson Welles; *Major Barbara* (George Bernard Shaw), Eli Wallach, Burgess Meredith, Glynis Johns, Charles Laughton; *Saint Joan* (Shaw), Siobhan McKenna; *Troilus and Cressida,* Claire Bloom, Rosemary Harris, John Neville

Regional

American Shakespeare Festival: *King John,* Mildred Dunnock, Arnold Moss; *Measure for Measure,* Moss, Nina Foch; *The Taming of the Shrew,* Foch, Pernell Roberts

Actor's Workshop, San Francisco: *Mother Courage* (Bertolt Brecht), American premiere

Coconut Grove Playhouse, Miami: *Waiting for Godot* (Samuel Beckett, directed by Alan Schneider), Bert Lahr, Alvin Epstein, American premiere

Pulitzer Prize

The Diary of Anne Frank, Frances Goodrich, Albert Hackett

Tony Awards

The Diary of Anne Frank, Frances Goodrich, Albert Hackett (play); *Damn Yankees,* Richard Adler, Jerry Ross (musical)

Classical Music _____

Compositions

Hugo Weisgall, *Six Characters in Search of an Author, The Stranger*
Elliott Carter, *Narrations* for Orchestra
Norman Dello Joio, *Mediations on Ecclesiastes*
Vladimir Ussachevsky, A Piece for Tape Recorder
William Schuman, *New England Triptych*
George Rochberg, Sinfonia Fantasy
Igor Stravinsky, *Canticum sacrum*
Lejarin Hiller and L. M. Isaacson, *Illiac* Suite (computer composition)

Important Events

Musical celebrations include Sibelius's 90th birthday; the 50th anniversary of Artur Rubinstein's American debut, the 25th of Lily Pons's Metropolitan debut, and the much-celebrated Mozart bicentennial. Eduard Van Beinum becomes musical director of the Los Angeles Philharmonic.
International exchanges reach a peak: in the United States, the Berlin Philharmonic (Herbert von Karajan); Vienna Philharmonic; Salzburg Mozart Orchestra; Emil Gilels; David Oistrakh; and Mstislav Rostropovich. Americans abroad include Jan Peerce, Isaac Stern, the New Orleans Orchestra, Los Angeles Philharmonic, Juilliard String Quartet, and Robert Shaw Chorale; the Boston Symphony visits the USSR. To celebrate its 50th anniversary, Juilliard commissions work for six concerts from Roger Sessions (Piano Concerto); Peter Mennin (Cello Concerto); David Diamond (*Diaphony*); Roy Harris (*Festival Folk Fantasy*); Walter Piston (Symphony no. 5); and a William Bergsma opera. Artur Rubinstein plays the complete Beethoven and Brahms piano concerti at Carnegie Hall.

First Performances

Heitor Villa-Lobos, conducting, Symphony no. 11 (Boston); Miklós Rósza, Violin Concerto (Dallas); Paul Creston, Symphony no. 5 (Washington, D.C.); Gail Kubik, Symphony no. 2 (Louisville); Norman Dello Joio, *The Trial at Rouen* (NBC Opera); Carlos Chávez, Symphony no. 3 (New York); Darius Milhaud, Symphony no. 7 (Chicago); Ned Rorem, Symphony no. 2 (La Jolla, Calif.); Ernest Toch, Symphony no. 3 (Pittsburgh); Samuel Barber, *The School for Scandal* (New York); Charles Ives, *Robert Browning* (New York); Rolf Libermann, *The School for Wives* (Louisville)

Opera

Metropolitan: Maria Callas's debut in *Norma* grosses a record $75,510.50. Other performances include Mattiwilda Dobbs, *Rigoletto;* Carlo Bergonzi, *Aïda;* Richard Tucker, Renata Tebaldi, *Tosca;* Lisa Della Casa, *Der Rosenkavalier.*

New York City: *The Tempest* (Frank Martin, premiere); *The Moon* (Carl Orff, premiere)

Chicago: Eleanor Steber, *La fanciulla del West;* Inge Borkh, Martha Lipton, Ramon Vinay, *Salomé;* Borkh, Birgit Nilsson, *Die Walküre;* Renata Tebaldi, Jussi Bjoerling, *Tosca*

San Francisco: Debuts: Leonie Rysanek, *Die Walküre;* Boris Christoff, *Boris Godunov;* Eileen Farrell, *Il trovatore*

Central City, Colo.:   Beverly Sills (debut), "The Ballad of Baby Doe" (Douglas Moore)

Julie Andrews and Rex Harrison in *My Fair Lady.*

Below: *Waiting for Godot. Billy Rose Theatre Collection. The New York Public Library at Lincoln Center. Astor, Lenox and Tilden Foundations.*

Art

Painting
Georgia O'Keeffe, *Patio with Cloud*
George Tooker, *Government Bureau*
Helen Frankenthaler, *Eden*
Larry Rivers, *George Washington Crossing the Delaware*
Mark Rothko, *Orange and Yellow*
Adolph Gottlieb, *Unstill Life III*
Stuart Davis, *Colonial Cubism*
Franz Kline, *Mahoning*
Philip Guston, *Dial*

Sculpture
Ibram Lassaw, *Procession*
David Smith, *Tanktotem V, Five Spring, History of LeRoy Borton*
Joseph Cornell, *Homage to Blériot*
Louise Nevelson, *First Personage, Royal Voyage*
Leonard Baskin, *Man with a Dead Bird*
Theodore Roszak, *Sea Sentinel*

Herbert Ferber, *Sun Wheel*

Architecture
John Olin Library, Washington University, St. Louis (John Hejduk)
Navy Chapel, Miramar, Calif. (Richard Neutra)
Kneses Tifeth Israel Synagogue, Port Chester, N.Y. (Philip Johnson)
Brandeis University Chapel, Waltham, Mass. (Harrison and Abramovitz)
St. Louis Airport (Harrison and Abramovitz)
Crown Hall, Illinois Institute of Technology (Mies van der Rohe)
Graf House, Dallas (Edward Durell Stone)
Frank Lloyd Wright exhibits a design for a mile-high skyscraper, 528 stories.

Important Exhibitions

Museums

New York: *Metropolitan:* British painting 1800–1950; Costumes and decorative arts of Japan; Feininger, Kuhn, Kuniyoshi, Marin, Nordfeldt; Asian artists in crystal. *Museum of Modern Art:* Kirchner; Nolde. *Whitney:* Burchfield; Graves. *Guggenheim:* Brancusi

Kurt Kaznar, E.G. Marshall, Alvin Epstein, and Bert Lahr in *Waiting for Godot*, Samuel Beckett's existential query into friendship, loneliness, and the passage of time. *Billy Rose Theatre Collection. The New York Public Library at Lincoln Center. Astor, Lenox and Tilden Foundations.*

Chicago: "Louis Sullivan and the Architecture of Free Enterprise"; Toulouse-Lautrec; Design in Scandinavia

Washington: The Kress collection; contemporary German prints; "A Century and a Half of Painting in Argentina"

Boston: Sargent's Boston; German prints; Burchfield watercolors

Minneapolis: Kirchner; Nolde

Houston: "Caribbean International"

Venice Biennale: "[46] American Artists Paint the City," including Marin, Hopper, Davis, Pollock

Art Briefs
"Modern Art in the U.S.," which includes works by Pollock, de Kooning, Rothko, and Kline, is sent by the Museum of Modern Art to the Tate Gallery, London • The National Gallery celebrates its 15th birthday with a "World Masterpieces Show," which 2,250,000 people visit • A canvas purchased in Chicago for $450 is discovered to be a Leonardo valued at $1 million • Frank Lloyd Wright begins construction on the new Guggenheim Museum, New York.

Dance

Jerome Robbins starts his own company, Ballets U.S.A.; Sadler's Wells's *Sleeping Beauty,* on TV, is viewed by 30 million people.

Premieres

New York City Ballet: *Divertimento, No. 15* (George Balanchine, for the Mozart celebration), Diana Adams, Melissa Hayden, Yvonne Mounsey, Nicholas Magallanes; *Allegro Brillante* (Balanchine), Maria Tallchief, Magallanes; *The Still Point* (Bolender), Hayden, Jacques d'Amboise

Alwin Nikolais: *Kaleidoscope*

Paul Taylor: *Three Epitaphs*

Books

Fiction

Critics' Choice
The Floating Opera, John Barth
Seize the Day, Saul Bellow
The Long March, William Styron
The Field of Vision, Wright Morris
Further Fables for Our Time,
    James Thurber
Comfort Me with Apples, Peter De
    Vries
Bang the Drum Slowly, Mark
    Harris
A Walk on the Wild Side, Nelson
    Algren
The Presence of Grace, J. F.
    Powers
Giovanni's Room, James Baldwin

Best-Sellers
Don't Go Near the Water, William
    Brinkley
The Last Hurrah, Edwin
    O'Connor
Peyton Place, Grace Metalious
Auntie Mame, Patrick Dennis
Eloise, Kay Thompson
Andersonville, MacKinlay Kantor
A Certain Smile, Françoise Sagan
The Mandarins, Simone de
    Beauvoir
The Tribe That Lost Its Head,
    Nicholas Monsarrat
Boon Island, Kenneth Roberts

Nonfiction

Critics' Choice
Testament of a Liberal, Albert
    Guérard
The Meaning of Yalta, John F.
    Snell
*The Permanent Purge: Politics in
    Soviet Totalitarianism*, Zbigniew
    Brezinski
Conservatism in America, Clinton
    Rossiter
The Power Elite, C. Wright Mills
The Art of Loving, Erich Fromm
*Form and Idea in Modern
    Theatre*, John Gassner
The Case for Modern Man,
    Charles Frankel
*Freud and the Crisis of Our
    Culture*, Lionel Trilling
Eros and Civilization, Herbert
    Marcuse
*The Crucial Decade: America
    1945–1955*, Eric F. Goldman
*American Politics in a
    Revolutionary World*, Chester
    Bowles

Best-Sellers
Arthritis and Common Sense, Dan
    Dale Alexander
*Webster's New World Dictionary
    of the English Language*,
    Concise ed., ed. David B.
    Guralnik

Betty Crocker's Picture Cook Book
Etiquette, Frances Benton
*Better Homes and Gardens
    Barbecue Book*
The Search for Bridey Murphy,
    Morey Bernstein
Love or Perish, Smiley Blanton
The Nun's Story, Kathryn Hulme
How to Live 365 Days a Year,
    John A. Schindler
*Better Homes and Gardens
    Decorating Book*

Poetry

Donald Hall, *Exiles and Marriages*
John Ashbery, *Some Trees*
John Berryman, *Homage to
    Mistress Bradstreet*
Marianne Moore, *Like a Bulwark*
Elizabeth Bishop, *Poems*
Allen Ginsberg, *Howl*

Pulitzer Prizes

No prize is awarded in fiction.
Russia Leaves the War, George F.
    Kennan (U.S. history)
Profiles in Courage, John F.
    Kennedy (biography)
Things of This World, Richard
    Wilbur (poetry)

Science and Technology

Albert Sabin announces the development of three
    types of oral polio vaccine, which, together, will
    produce long-term immunity.
Techniques of hemodialysis, blood purification on an
    artificial kidney machine, are pioneered.
Wendell Stanley, at the University of California,
    reports the chemical creation of a virus capable
    of reproduction.
The DNA molecule is photographed.
The "neutrino," a particle of no electrical charge, is
    observed at Los Alamos.
The first photos of the birth of stars are taken.
The first American test rocket for sending a

manmade satellite into orbit ascends 125 miles at
    4,000 m.p.h.
James Pritchard, of the Chicago Divinity School,
    unearths biblical Gibeon, where the "sun stood
    still."

Nobel Prize

John Bardeen, Walter Brattain, and William Shockley
win the prize in physics for work in the development
of the electronic transistor. D. W. Richards, Jr., and
André Cournand win in physiology and medicine for
work in treating heart disease.

Sports

Baseball

Don Larsen (New York, AL) pitches the first perfect game in a World Series. The Cy Young Award, honoring the best major league pitcher, begins; Don Newcombe (Brooklyn, NL) is the first winner.

Champions

Batting	Pitching
Hank Aaron (Milwaukee, NL), .328	Don Newcombe (Brooklyn, NL), 27–7
Mickey Mantle (New York, AL), .340	Whitey Ford (New York, AL), 19–6
	Home runs
	Mickey Mantle (New York, AL), 52

Football

NFL Season Leaders: Ed Brown (Chicago), passing; Rick Casares (Chicago), rushing; Billy Wilson (San Francisco), receiving

College All-Americans: Jim Brown (B), Syracuse; Ron Kramer (E), Michigan; Alex Karras (G), Iowa

Bowls (Jan. 1, 1957)

Rose: Iowa 35–Oregon State 19

Orange: Colorado 27–Clemson 21

Cotton: Texas Christian 28–Syracuse 27

Sugar: Baylor 13–Tennessee 7

Basketball

Bill Russell, Boston, debuts.

NBA All-Pro First Team: Bob Pettit (St. Louis), Paul Arizin (Philadelphia), Neil Johnston (Philadelphia), Bill Cousy, Bill Sharman (Boston)

Olympics

At the Melbourne Summer Games, U.S. winners include Bobby Morrow (100m, 10.5s and 200m, 20.6s.), Glenn Davis (400mh, 50.1s.), Charley Dumas (high jump, 6'11¼"), Parry O'Brien (16 lb. shotput, 60'11"), Al Oerter (discus, 184'11"), Harold Connolly (16 lb. hammer, 207'3½"), Milton Campbell (decathlon), Patricia McCormick (diving, 2). In the Winter Games at Cortina D'Ampezzo, Italy, Tenley Albright wins figure skating.

Other Sports

Winners

World Series	*NBA Championship*
New York (AL) 4	Philadelphia 4–Fort
Brooklyn (NL) 3	Wayne 1
MVP	*MVP*
NL–Don Newcombe,	Bob Pettit, St. Louis
Brooklyn	*College Basketball*
AL–Mickey Mantle, New	San Francisco
York	*Player of the Year*
NFL	Bill Russell, San Francisco
New York 47–Chicago	*Stanley Cup*
Bears 7	Montreal
MVP	*US Tennis Open*
Frank Gifford, New York	Men: Ken Rosewall
College Football	Women: Shirley Fry
Oklahoma	*USGA Open*
Heisman Trophy	Cary Middlecoff
Paul Hornung, Notre Dame	*Kentucky Derby*
	Needles (D. Erb, jockey)

Fashion

For Women: *My Fair Lady* and late Edwardian decor influence fashion. Emphasis is on both flowing and clinging fabrics, ribbons, and feathers; the long-legged figure is created through long drapery, a high waistline, and sashes or belts under the bosom. Bloused backs and low-backed bodices give a "slouch" to the profile. Hair is swept up in a pompadour or chignon; capes and big hats become popular.

High-fashion notes: Dior's sac dress, the PVC (vinyl-coated raincoat); Chanel's quilted shoulder bag with intertwined gold metal, Rose Marie Reid's elasticized swimsuit with wide shorts and contrasting color trim at the top

For Men: Many boys wear crew cuts ("flattops") and "fabulous" dirty, white bucks, pants and bermudas with buckles on the back. Unlike these boys—"bananas," "weenies," and "yo-yos"—the "greasers," "skids," and "rocks" wear ducktail haircuts, black leather jackets, and T-shirts. The college boy chooses either the button-down "ivy" look or pegged pants, padded shoulders, and the newly popular and colorful Hawaiian shirts. Madison Avenue will soon be filled with young men in gray flannel suits, pink shirts, skinny bow or pink and black striped ties.

Kaleidoscope _____

- Ed Sullivan vows never to allow Elvis Presley's vulgar performance on his TV show; he later pays Presley $50,000 for three appearances; the last is televised only from the waist up.
- Boston religious leaders urge the banning of rock 'n' roll; a Connecticut psychiatrist calls rock a "communicable disease."
- William Whyte describes how corporations force their officers to toe the company line in his popular *The Organization Man.*
- Increasing numbers of lower-middle-class people move to the suburbs; colleges actively recruit from the middle classes.
- Eleanor Roosevelt receives the First Woman of Valor award.
- Clark Gable and Yul Brynner refuse to play Stalin in a projected movie.
- Mickey Hargitay, Mr. Universe, is KO'ed during a press conference in Mae West's dressing room.
- Artur Rubinstein calls Neil Sedaka the best high school pianist he has heard and gives him a Juilliard scholarship.
- Marilyn Monroe and Arthur Miller marry on June 29; she wears a sweater and skirt; he, a blue linen suit, white shirt, and no tie; on July 2, a rabbi performs a religious ceremony.
- European autos gain popularity, such as the Volkswagen, TR-2, Jaguar, Ferrari, Hillman Minx, Saab, Mercedes, Citroen, and Fiat.
- Golda Myerson, former Milwaukee schoolteacher, becomes the Israeli prime minister and accepts Premier Ben-Gurion's suggestion that she hebraize her name to Meir.
- Jean Seberg, daughter of an Iowa druggist, is selected from 18,000 applicants to play Joan of Arc in a movie.
- Disc jockey Jean Shepperd promotes as "turbulent" and "tempestuous" a nonexistent book, "I Libertine," which a month later he and Theodore Sturgeon write.
- The ex-Mrs. Adlai Stevenson, Ellen Borden, announces that she will vote for Eisenhower.
- Nat "King" Cole is knocked down by six white men on a Birmingham, Alabama, stage because they protest his appearance.
- Audiences find movies so expensive ($2 in New York, $1.50 in Los Angeles) that they stay home and watch TV.
- Seventeen recordings of "The Ballad of Davy Crockett" are made; Estes Kefauver campaigns in a coonskin cap.
- Harry Belafonte's "Jamaica Farewell" begins a widespread interest in calypso.
- The last Union veteran of the Civil War, Albert Woolson, dies; he was a drummer boy at seventeen.
- Oxford University confers the doctorate of civil law honorary degree on Harricum Truman.
- Eleven percent of all cars sold are station wagons; airlines carry as many passengers as railroads.
- Drive-in theaters multiply to 7,000 in number.
- "The sum and substance of it all is that God and I are

Arthur Miller and Marilyn Monroe, who met while she was studying acting in New York with Lee and Paula Strasberg. *Movie Star News.*

tired of men taking advantage of women," says Beatrice Adams, who runs her car over her 300-pound boyfriend several times until a passerby rips out the car's ignition wires.
- Procter & Gamble produces disposable Pampers after it discovers that women change babies' diapers 25 billion times a year.
- Ford Motor Company goes public and sells over 10 million shares ($650 million) to over 250,000 investors.
- Jackie Collins sells 500,000 copies of *James Dean Returns,* presumably dictated by the dead star; bits from his death car sell from $20; people can sit behind the wheel for 25 cents.
- For the first time since 1848, neither branch of Congress is won by the party of the elected president.
- Seventy-seven percent of college-educated women marry; 41 percent work part time, 17 percent full time.

New Words and Usages: Fuzz, the most, the greatest, cop-out, put-on, headshrinker, hero sandwich, lay-off pay

Fads: Wearing a "steady's" ring on a gold necklace, Captain Midnight decoders, Elvis Presley products

First Appearances: Bert and Harry Piel (Bob and Ray), Betty Furness and Westinghouse, Julia Mead and Lincoln-Mercury, gorilla born in captivity, Midas Muffler shop, Comet, Raid, Salem cigarettes, La Leche League, Imperial margarine, circular school building (Kankakee, Ill.), circular office building (Los Angeles), motto of the United States ("In God We Trust") authorized, motion picture actor on stamp (Gene Kelly), woman ordained as minister in Presbyterian church (M. E. Tower, Syracuse, N.Y.), all-steel convertible top (Ford), hair-splitting by .001 inch drill

1957

Economic Profile
 Dow-Jones:—High 520–
  Low 425
 GNP: +5%
 Inflation: +2.9%
 Unemployment: 4.3%
Average salary: $4,230
 Teacher: $4,085
 Physician: $22,100
 Factory Worker: $4,786
Cannon color sheets: $.49
Noritake china (53 pieces):
 $39.95
Martex giant towels: $1.49
Vanity bar set (32 pieces):
 $4.98
Plummer holiday glasses:
 $7.50 (for 8)
Sloane's 4-piece cherry
 bedroom: $524
Hutch cabinet (55"): $328
Twin foam mattress set:
 $124.50
Baker side chair: $139
Louis XIV dining table: $539

Deaths

Dennis Brain, Constantin
 Brancusi, Richard E. Byrd,
 Jimmy Dorsey, Joseph
 McCarthy, Ezio Pinza,
 Jean Sibelius, Arturo
 Toscanini, Erich von
 Stroheim.

In the News

ANTHONY EDEN RESIGNS OVER SUEZ DEBACLE, HAROLD MACMILLAN IS NEW BRITISH P.M. . . . NEW YORK "MAD BOMBER" IS ARRESTED . . . ISRAEL LEAVES EGYPTIAN TERRITORY, UN EMERGENCY FORCE TAKES OVER . . . EISENHOWER DOCTRINE IS STATED, TO HELP INDEPENDENT COUNTRIES IN THE MIDEAST . . . BRITAIN BECOMES H-BOMB POWER AT CHRISTMAS ISLAND . . . TEAMSTER DAVE BECK IS EXPELLED FROM AFL-CIO FOR MISUSE OF FUNDS . . . U.S. AGREES ON LOAN TO POLAND . . . USSR WILL AID SYRIA . . . GEORGI MALENKOV IS OUSTED FROM POLITBURO FOR "ANTIPARTY ACTIVITIES" . . . RUSSIA REJECTS AERIAL INSPECTION . . . IKE PROPOSES TWO-YEAR TEST BAN . . . USSR ANNOUNCES SUCCESSFUL INTERCONTINENTAL BALLISTIC MISSILE TEST . . . MCCLELLAN COMMITTEE DENOUNCES JIMMY HOFFA AND TEAMSTERS UNION . . . REVEREND BILLY GRAHAM DRAWS 92,000 AT YANKEE STADIUM . . . ARKANSAS NATIONAL GUARD BLOCKS BLACK HIGH SCHOOL STUDENTS IN LITTLE ROCK . . . IKE SENDS FEDERAL TROOPS TO STOP "MOB RULE" IN LITTLE ROCK . . . SPUTNIK I, FIRST SPACE SATELLITE, IS LAUNCHED BY RUSSIA . . . HOFFA BECOMES PRESIDENT OF TEAMSTERS . . . SPUTNIK II, WITH DOG LAIKA, GOES INTO ORBIT . . . EDWARD TELLER URGES STRONGER BOMBER BASE DEFENSE . . . POLICE RAID MAFIA MEETING AT APPALACHIN, N.Y. . . . U.S. SATELLITE EXPLODES AT CAPE CANAVERAL, FLORIDA . . . FIRST U.S. ATLAS ICBM IS TESTED.

Rock 'n' Roll, a teenage "fad" that is not passing. *Library of Congress.*

"The first artificial earth satellite in the world . . . was successfully launched in the USSR. . . . The new socialist society turns even the most daring of man's dreams into reality."
— Tass, the Soviet news agency

"[Sputnik is] a hunk of iron anybody could launch."
— Rear Adm. Lawson Bennett

"The balance of terror is more and more the foundation of peace."
— *Le Monde* editorial

"Everything I have is hers—and brother, that's plenty."
— Mike Todd, 54, newly married to Elizabeth Taylor, 24

Ads

New technique helps Los Alamos scientists take a sharp look at shock waves. . . . If you are a scientist or engineer of superior qualifications, interested in a creative atmosphere with a minimum of administrative detail, . . . write for an illustrated brochure.
(Los Alamos Scientific Lab, Los Alamos, N.M.)

College Dean Discovers Delicious New Casserole Made with Carnation Milk!
(Carnation Evaporated Milk)

Martini drinkers are divided into two glasses! says Ernie Kovacs. But the on the rocks faction is growing.
(Heublein Cocktails)

The road isn't built that can make it breathe hard!
(Chevrolet)

Quotes

"[This drive-in church] . . . with its loudspeakers set among the trees, provides an extra spiritual dimension, brought on by the sun, pines and the birds."
— Announcement of the Presbyterian Drive-in Church, Florida

"I like Charlie. He's the only man in the administration who doesn't talk about God."
— Reporter's comment on Secretary of Defense Charles Wilson

"The American satellite ought to be called Civil Servant. It won't work and you can't fire it."
— Popular joke

The Edsel, named after Henry Ford's son, one of the all-time manufacturing flops. *Library of Congress.*

Italian actress Sophia Loren is promoted as the new sex goddess. *Movie Star News.*

Keep the curves where they count.
(Sealtest Skim Milk)

Winstons taste good like a cigarette should.
(Winston Cigarettes)

TV

Premieres
"Mike Wallace Interviews"
"Tales of Wells Fargo," Dale Robertson
"Perry Mason," Raymond Burr
"Have Gun, Will Travel," Richard Boone
"Wagon Train," Robert Horton, Ward Bond
"To Tell the Truth," Bud Collyer
"Bat Masterson," Gene Barry
"The Pat Boone Show"
"Leave It to Beaver," Jerry Mathers, Hugh
    Beaumont
"Maverick," James Garner, Jack Kelly
"Bachelor Father," John Forsythe
"American Bandstand," Dick Clark

Top Ten (Nielsen)
"Gunsmoke," "The Danny Thomas Show," "Tales of Wells Fargo," "Have Gun, Will Travel," "I've Got a Secret," "The Life and Legend of Wyatt Earp," "General Electric Theater," "The Restless Gun," "December Bride," "You Bet Your Life"

Specials
"The Comedian" (Rod Serling); "The Miracle Worker" (William Gibson, with Teresa Wright); "The Helen Morgan Story" (Polly Bergen); "Oedipus the King" (Christopher Plummer, William Shatner); "Annie Get Your Gun" (John Raitt, Mary Martin); "Face the Nation" (interview with Khrushchev in Moscow); Senate Rackets Investigation (Senator John F. Kennedy, Counsel Robert Kennedy)

Emmy Awards
"Gunsmoke" (drama); "Phil Silvers Show" (comedy); Robert Young (actor), Jane Wyatt (actress), "Father Knows Best"; Jack Benny, Dinah Shore (personality)

Of Note
Important TV directors include John Frankenheimer, George Roy Hill, and Arthur Penn • Five of the top ten shows are Westerns • Jack Paar replaces Steve Allen on "The Tonight Show" • Video tape comes into general use, anticipating the end of live television.

Movies

Openings
The Bridge on the River Kwai (David Lean), William Holden, Alec Guinness
The Three Faces of Eve (Nunnally Johnson), Joanne Woodward, Lee J. Cobb, Vince Edwards
Peyton Place (Mark Robson), Lana Turner, Diane Varsi, Hope Lange
Sayonara (Joshua Logan), Marlon Brando, Red Buttons, Miyoshi Umeki
Twelve Angry Men (Sidney Lumet), Henry Fonda, Martin Balsam
Witness for the Prosecution (Billy Wilder), Marlene Dietrich, Charles Laughton, Tyrone Power
The Prince and the Showgirl (Laurence Olivier), Laurence Olivier, Marilyn Monroe
Silk Stockings (Rouben Mamoulian), Fred Astaire, Cyd Charisse
Love in the Afternoon (Billy Wilder), Gary Cooper, Audrey Hepburn
Les Girls (George Cukor), Gene Kelly, Kay Kendall
St. Joan (Otto Preminger), Jean Seberg
Paths of Glory (Stanley Kubrick), Kirk Douglas, Adolph Menjou
A Face in the Crowd (Elia Kazan), Andy Griffith, Patricia Neal, Anthony Franciosa
And God Created Woman (Roger Vadim), Brigitte Bardot
Wild Strawberries (Ingmar Bergman), Victor Sjöström, Ingrid Thulin

Academy Awards
Best Picture: *The Bridge on the River Kwai*
Best Director: David Lean (*The Bridge on the River Kwai*)
Best Actress: Joanne Woodward (*The Three Faces of Eve*)
Best Actor: Alec Guinness (*The Bridge on the River Kwai*)

Top Box-Office Stars
Rock Hudson, John Wayne, Pat Boone, Elvis Presley, Frank Sinatra, Gary Cooper, William Holden, James Stewart, Jerry Lewis, Yul Brynner

Stars of Tomorrow
Anthony Perkins, Sophia Loren, Jayne Mansfield, Don Murray, Carroll Baker, Martha Hyer, Elvis Presley, Anita Ekberg, Paul Newman, John Kerr

Popular Music _____

Hit Songs
"All Shook Up!"
"An Affair to Remember"
"All the Way"
"April Love"
"A White Sport Coat—and a Pink Carnation"
"Chances Are"
"Fascination"
"I'm Gonna Sit Right Down and Write Myself a Letter"
"Jailhouse Rock"
"Maria"

Top Records

Albums: *Love Is the Thing* (Nat "King" Cole); *Around the World in 80 Days* (sound track); *Loving You* (Elvis Presley); *Elvis' Christmas Album* (Elvis Presley); *Merry Christmas* (Bing Crosby)

Singles: *Diana* (Paul Anka); *Banana Boat Song* (Harry Belafonte); *Bye, Bye Love* (Everly Brothers); *Tammy* (Debbie Reynolds); *Blueberry Hill* (Fats Domino); *Love Letters in the Sand* (Pat Boone); *Lucille* (Little Richard). Country: *Gone* (Ferlin Husky); *Whole Lot of Shaking Going On* (Jerry Lee Lewis)

Jazz and Big Bands
Sonny Rollins forms his own combo. The School of Jazz is founded at Music Inn, Lenox, Massachusetts. Gunther Schuller coins "Third Stream," referring to the combination of jazz with European classical music forms, exemplified by the Modern Jazz Quartet; Charlie Mingus, in reaction to the style, moves to freer, open-ended, improvisational forms.

First Recordings: Miles Davis with Gil Evans; Shelly Manne with André Previn (jazz renditions of Broadway musicals); Ray Charles

Top Performers (*Downbeat*): Benny Goodman (soloist); Count Basie, Les Brown (bands); Modern Jazz Quartet (jazz group); Barney Kessel, Ray Brown, Errol Garner, Jimmy Giuffre, Miles Davis, Herbie Mann (instrumentalists); Ella Fitzgerald, Frank Sinatra (vocalists); Hi-Lo's (vocal group)

Theater _____

Broadway Openings

Plays
Look Homeward, Angel (Ketti Frings), Anthony Perkins, Jo Van Fleet, Hugh Griffith
The Dark at the Top of the Stairs (William Inge), Pat Hingle, Eileen Heckart, Teresa Wright
Romanoff and Juliet (Peter Ustinov), Peter Ustinov
Look Back in Anger (John Osborne), Alan Bates, Mary Ure, Kenneth Haigh
Time Remembered (Jean Anouilh), Susan Strasberg, Helen Hayes, Richard Burton
Visit to a Small Planet (Gore Vidal), Cyril Ritchard
A Clearing in the Woods (Arthur Laurents), Kim Stanley
The Waltz of the Toreadors (Jean Anouilh), Ralph Richardson, Mildred Natwick, Betty Field
Nude with Violin (Noel Coward), Noel Coward
Compulsion (Meyer Levin), Roddy McDowall, Dean Stockwell, Barbara Loden
A Moon for the Misbegotten (Eugene O'Neill), Wendy Hiller, Franchot Tone, Cyril Cusack
Orpheus Descending (Tennessee Williams), Maureen Stapleton, Cliff Robertson

Musicals
West Side Story (Leonard Bernstein, Stephen Sondheim), Carol Lawrence, Larry Kert, Chita Rivera
The Music Man (Meredith Willson), Robert Preston, Barbara Cook, David Burns
Ziegfeld Follies (Sammy Fain et al.), Beatrice Lillie, Billy De Wolfe (the last *Ziegfeld*)

Classics and Revivals On and Off Broadway
Mary Stuart (Friedrich Schiller), Irene Worth; *The Lady's Not for Burning* (Christopher Fry)

Regional

Founded: Charles Playhouse, Boston, by Murray Sugrue

American Shakespeare Festival: *Much Ado about Nothing*, Alfred Drake, Katharine Hepburn; *Othello*, Drake; *The Merchant of Venice*, Hepburn, Morris Carnovsky

Pulitzer Prize
Long Day's Journey into Night, Eugene O'Neill

Tony Awards
Long Day's Journey into Night, Eugene O'Neill (play); *My Fair Lady*, Alan Jay Lerner, Frederick Loewe (musical)

The Modern Jazz Quartet, with its "cerebral" style, manipulating classical forms within a jazz context, tours the British Isles with 88 performances in 4 months.

Classical Music

Compositions
Aaron Copland, Piano Fantasy
Gunther Schuller, *Transformation*
David Diamond, *The World of Paul Klee*
John Cage, Piano Concerto
Roger Sessions, Symphony no. 3
Walter Piston, Concerto for Viola

Important Events
A ten-day Festival of American Music takes place in Brussels.
Igor Stravinsky's 75th birthday is celebrated in Los Angeles with the premiere of *Agon* and *Canticum sacrum*.
The Philharmonic-Symphony Orchestra of New York changes its name to the New York Philharmonic; Leonard Bernstein becomes musical director.
A 44-story, vermillion-colored office building is proposed as the replacement for Carnegie Hall, scheduled to be razed August 7.
Most frequently performed symphonies are of Beethoven and Mozart; most performed American moderns are Samuel Barber, William Schuman, George Gershwin; most performed European moderns: Paul Hindemith, Ralph Vaughan Williams

Debuts: Daniel Barenboim, Lynn Harrell

First Performances
Charles Ives, Symphony no. 2 (New York); Roger Sessions, Symphony no. 3 (Boston); William Walton, Concerto for Cello and Orchestra (Boston, Gregor Piatigorsky, performing); Walter Piston, Symphony no. 4 (Minneapolis); Morton Gould, *Jekyll and Hyde Variations* (New York); Ernst Bacon, *Great River* (Dallas); Arthur Honegger, Symphony no. 5 and no. 6 (Boston); Gian Carlo Menotti, *Apocalypse* (Pittsburgh); Gian Francesco Malipiero, Sinfonia-Cantata (New York); Howard Hanson, *The Song of Democracy* (Philadelphia); Wallingford Riegger, Symphony no. 4 (University of Illinois); Lukas Foss, *Psalms* (New York); Morton Gould, *Declaration* (Washington, D.C.); Paul Creston, *Lydian Ode* (Wichita)

Opera

NBC Opera: *War and Peace* (Sergei Prokofiev)

Metropolitan: Renata Tebaldi, *La traviata;* Wolfgang Windgassen, Martha Mödl, *Das Rheingold;* George London, Lucine Amara, Martha Lipton, Richard Tucker, *Eugene Onègin;* Zinka Milanov, *Ernani;* premiere: *La périchole* (Jacques Offenbach). The complete *Ring* returns after six years.

Central City, Colo.: Cornell MacNeil, *Rigoletto*

Chicago: Giulietta Simionato, *Mignon;* Tito Gobbi, Renata Tebaldi, Mario del Monaco, *Andrea Chenier;* Maria Tallchief dances in *La Gioconda.*

San Francisco: *Dialogues of the Carmelites* (Francis Poulenc, premiere); Dorothy Kirsten, Eileen Farrell, Jussi Bjoerling, *Manon Lescaut*

Santa Fe: *The Rake's Progress* (Igor Stravinsky)

Art ────────

Painting

Mark Rothko, *Black over Reds, Red, White and Brown*

Adolph Gottlieb, *Blast I*

Mark Tobey, *New Life (Resurrection)*

Philip Guston, *The Clock, Painter's City*

William Baziotes, *Red Landscape*

Clyfford Still, *D No. 1*

Andrew Wyeth, *Brown Swiss*

Robert Rauschenberg, *Painting with Red Letter "S"*

Richard Diebenkorn, *Girl Looking at Landscape*

Ellsworth Kelly, *New York, New York*

Helen Frankenthaler, *Jacob's Ladder*

Sculpture

Seymour Lipton, *Pioneer*

Reuben Nakian, *The Burning Walls of Troy*

Important Exhibitions

Museums

New York: *Metropolitan:* Paintings from the New São Paulo, Brazil, Museum from the 18th to the 20th centuries; "Children in Style"; Greek vases; Rodin and French sculpture. *Museum of Modern Art:* Pollock; Smith; 20th-century German art; Chagall; Matta. *Guggenheim:* Duchamp, Duchamp-Villon, Jacques Villon; Mondrian

Museum of Modern Art, Chicago, Philadelphia: Picasso—75th anniversary, 328 works

Boston: Monet; Jan Cox; Feininger; New England miniatures; William Blake; Tessai; Venetian villas

Chicago: Monet; 60th annual show—Artists of Chicago and vicinity; Japanese stencils; African sculpture; Midwest designer-craftsmen

Cleveland: "The Venetian Tradition from the 16th Century to the Present"

Robert Motherwell, *Elegy to the Spanish Republic,* 1957. Oil on canvas, 70 × 7'6¼". *The Museum of Modern Art, given anonymously.*

Alexander Calder, *Black, White and 10 Red*

Calder's *.125,1957* is installed in the new International Arrivals Building, Idlewild Airport, N.Y.

Architecture

Old Orchard Shopping Center, Skokie, Ill. (Loebl, Schlossman, Bennett and Dart)

Connecticut General Life Insurance Company Building, Bloomfield, Conn. (Skidmore, Owings, and Merrill)

Skidmore, Owings, and Merrill present their design for the Air Force Academy, Colorado Springs.

Minneapolis: Rare Print Exhibition; Davis; Matta

Baltimore: 4,000 works of Modern art

National: Bellows; American primitives; 100 years of American architecture; Masterpieces of Korean art

Art Briefs

The New York Public Library sells 10 paintings for $169,000, including Gainsborough's *Woody Landscape* ($20,500) and Turner's *A Scene on the French Coast* ($56,000) • Record sales include Renoir's *La Serre* ($200,000) • Oil tanker magnate Stavros Niarchos buys 58 paintings for $3–4 million from Edward G. Robinson and his wife in their divorce settlement. Works include El Greco's *Deposition,* Cézanne's *Eternal Woman,* and Renoir's *Two Sisters.*

Dance ────────────

American Ballet Theatre (name changed from Ballet Theatre) encourages young choreographers and experimental performances: 15 new works, like *Sebastian* (Agnes de Mille), are performed without orchestral accompaniment or new scenery; dancers wear practice clothes.

Margot Fonteyn and Michael Somes dance *Cinderella* with the Royal Ballet for TV.

Premieres

New York City Ballet: *Square Dance* (George Balanchine), Patricia Wilde, Nicholas Magallanes; *Agon* (Balanchine, Stravinsky), Diana Adams, Melissa Hayden

Books

Fiction

Critics' Choice

The Short Reign of Pippin IV, John Steinbeck
The Wapshot Chronicle, John Cheever
The Town, William Faulkner
On the Road, Jack Kerouac
The Assistant, Bernard Malamud
Love among the Cannibals, Wright Morris
63: Dream Stories, James Purdy
Gimpel the Fool, Isaac Bashevis Singer
Stories, Jean Stafford
🕭 *Justine*, Lawrence Durrell

Best-Sellers

By Love Possessed, James Gould Cozzens
Peyton Place, Grace Metalious
Compulsion, Meyer Levin
Rally Round the Flag, Boys! Max Shulman
Blue Camellia, Frances Parkinson Keyes
Eloise in Paris, Kay Thompson
The Scapegoat, Daphne Du Maurier
On the Beach, Nevil Shute
Below the Salt, Thomas B. Costain
Atlas Shrugged, Ayn Rand

Nonfiction

Critics' Choice

The Function of Criticism, Yvor Winters
Anatomy of Criticism, Northrop Frye
The Crisis of the Old Order, 1919–1933, Arthur Schlesinger, Jr.
The Price of Power: America since 1945, Herbert Agar
America as a Civilization, Max Lerner
Theodore Roosevelt and the Rise of America to World Power, Howard K. Beale
The Hidden Persuaders, Vance Packard
The Roots of American Communism, Theodore Draper
Memoirs of a Revolution, Dwight MacDonald
Day of Infamy, Walter Lord
The Road to Miltown, or Under the Spreading Atrophe, S. J. Perelman
Syntactic Structures, Noam Chomsky

Best-Sellers

Kids Say the Darndest Things! Art Linkletter
The FBI Story, Don Whitehead
Stay Alive All Your Life, Norman Vincent Peale
To Live Again, Catherine Marshall

Better Homes and Gardens Flower Arranging
Where Did You Go? Out. What Did You Do? Nothing, Robert Paul Smith
Baruch: My Own Story, Bernard M. Baruch
Please Don't Eat the Daisies, Jean Kerr
The American Heritage Book of Great Historic Places
The Day Christ Died, Jim Bishop

Poetry

Denise Levertov, *Here and Now*
Theodore Roethke, *The Exorcism*
Richard Wilbur, *Poems 1943–1956*
Wallace Stevens, *Opus Posthumous*
Robert Hillyer, *The Relic*
James Wright, *The Green Wall*
🕭 Nellie Sachs, *And No One Knows How to Go On*

Pulitzer Prizes

A Death in the Family, James Agee (posthumous, fiction)
Banks and Politics in America—from the Revolution to the Civil War, Bray Hammond (U.S. history)
George Washington, Douglas Southall Freeman (biography)
Promises: Poems 1954–56, Robert Penn Warren (poetry)

Science and Technology

The U.S. Thor ICBM is successfully tested.

An intended U.S. earth satellite, the six-foot Viking blows up at the launching pad at Cape Canaveral, Florida.

Maj. John Glenn sets a new transcontinental record in a Navy BV-1P Voight Crusader—3 hours, 23 minutes, 8.4 seconds.

Despite record admissions, the number of long-term patients in mental hospitals decreases significantly as new medicines reduce lengths of stay.

Anticoagulants are shown to aid stroke victims by reducing permanent damage.

Darvon, a new pain killer, is marketed.

🕭 The USSR launches a 180-pound satellite, Sputnik I, into orbit around the earth; it also launches a second satellite, Sputnik II (carrying an Eskimo dog), to study conditions for a living organism in space.

🕭 Soviets successfully test an intercontinental ballistic missile.

Sports _____

Baseball

After the season, the Brooklyn Dodgers and New York Giants move to Los Angeles and San Francisco.

Warren Spahn (Milwaukee) wins the Cy Young Award.

Jackie Robinson retires.

Champions _____

Batting	*Pitching*
Stan Musial (St. Louis, NL), .351	Bob Buhl (Milwaukee, NL) 18–7
Ted Williams (Boston, AL), .388	Tom Sturdivant (New York, AL), 16–6
	Dick Donovan (Chicago, AL), 16–6
	Home runs
	Henry Aaron (Milwaukee, NL), 44

Football

Jim Brown (Cleveland), a rookie, gains a league-leading 942 yards rushing, including a record 237 in one game.

Other NFL Season Leaders: Tom O'Connell (Cleveland), passing; Ray Berry (Baltimore), receiving

College All-Americans: King Hill (B), Rice; John Crow (B), Texas A & M; Lou Michaels (T), Kentucky

Bowls (Jan. 1, 1958)

Rose: Ohio State 10–Oregon 7	Cotton: Navy 20–Rice 7
Orange: Oklahoma 48–Duke 21	Sugar: Mississippi 39–Texas 7

Jim Brown, former Syracuse star, debuts with the Cleveland Browns. *Pro Football Hall of Fame.*

Basketball

NBA All-Pro First Team: Paul Arizin (Philadelphia), Bob Pettit (St. Louis), Dolph Schayes (Syracuse), George Yardley (Fort Wayne), Bob Cousy (Boston), Bill Sharman (Boston)

Other Sports

Tennis: Australian Lew Hoad turns pro for a record offer of $125,000 guaranteed.

Boxing: Sugar Ray Robinson wins the middleweight title for the fourth time, beating Gene Fullmer.

Winners _____

World Series	*MVP*
Milwaukee (NL) 4	Bob Cousy, Boston
New York (AL) 3	*College Basketball*
MVP	North Carolina
NL–Henry Aaron, Milwaukee	*Player of the Year*
AL–Mickey Mantle, New York	Len Rosenbluth, North Carolina
NFL	*Stanley Cup*
Detroit 59–Cleveland 14	Montreal
MVP	*US Tennis Open*
John Unitas, Baltimore	Men: Mal Anderson
College Football	Women: Althea Gibson
Auburn	*USGA Open*
Heisman Trophy	Dick Mayer
John Crow, Texas A & M	*Kentucky Derby*
NBA Championship	Iron Liege (W. Hartack, jockey)
Boston 4–St. Louis 1	

Fashion _____

For Women: In the search for a new look, Balenciaga and Givenchy create the sack silhouette with sheath beneath, a combination of loose overdress of transparent fabric on top of a form-fitting dress. Generally, the look is slim, and necklines are revealing. Coat shapes expand, and large cape collars stand away from the face and neck. Rounded at the waist and swept wide at the hem, these bulky coats and suits appear in orange, yellow, red, brilliant blue, and emerald green. Fancy shoes with pointed toes and buckles are popular. The silk dress with bubble skirt, rounded neck, and ¾-length tight sleeves is high style for evening. Long dresses in royal blue and green silks and satins have deep V necklines and uneven trails.

For Men: Change in men's style since the depression has been slow and subtle. Dramatic this year, however, are the small glen plaids for suits and the huge plaids for sport jackets; four, not six, buttons; oriental raw silks; the Hapi coat; and fake furs. Synthetics in pastels also make news, as well as the increasingly fashionable ascot and paisley prints for handkerchiefs, scarves, and ties.

On "The $64,000 Question" contestants enter an "isolation booth" to avoid audience prompting. *Library of Congress.*

- Columbia College professor Charles Van Doren, 30, becomes a national hero, winning $129,000 on TV's quiz show "Twenty-One"; he loses on the question "Who is the king of Belgium?" Van Doren receives many letters praising him as a role model in contrast to Elvis Presley.
- Allen Ginsberg's *Howl,* seized by the police as obscene, brings a great deal of attention to the Beat movement; a judge later releases the book.
- Average wages for a factory production worker are $2.08 an hour, or $82.00 a week.
- The first civil rights legislation since 1872 passes, despite Strom Thurmond's (Dem., S.C.) record 24-hour, 18-minute filibuster.
- The 16-year search for the Mad Bomber of New York City, who planted 32 homemade bombs, ends with the arrest of an electric company ex-employee.
- Mobsters fill the headlines: Frank Costello is shot in a New York apartment; Frank Scalice is shot at a peach stand in the Bronx; Albert Anastasia, "Lord High Executioner" of Murder, Inc., is shot in the barber shop of New York's Park Sheraton Hotel.
- The Cadillac Eldorado Brougham has on its dashboard a lipstick, vanity case, and four gold cups.
- Montgomery Ward's catalog includes a Shetland pony for $300 and a Great Dane for $120.
- The Supreme Court rules that Congress can only investigate matters related to potential legislation, rather than for the purposes of exposé.
- Khrushchev muses that Soviet Sputniks are "lonely . . . waiting for American satellites to join them in space."
- Philip Morris, aware that its brown cigarette package will not sell on color TV, invests $250,000 to develop a colorful package.
- The recreational fishing industry grows, as 21 million people spend $2 billion on the sport.
- Briefly popular are whiskey-flavored toothpaste and radarlike fishing poles; one in three women goes regularly to a beauty shop, many for apricot- or silver-colored hair.

Kaleidoscope _____

- The United Nations Emergency Force is the first multinational peacekeeping force in history.
- Industry begins supporting education; in the fall, the first of the 556 National Merit Scholars go to 160 colleges.
- Volkswagen sells 200,000 Beetles.
- A replica of the Mayflower goes from England to Plymouth Rock in 54 days.
- The yearly per capita consumption of margarine overtakes that of butter, 8.6 pounds to 8.3 pounds.
- An intensive study of birth control with pills is begun in Puerto Rico.
- Edward Teller, Ernest O. Lawrence, and others report that radioactive fallout from H-bomb detonations has been reduced by 95 percent and is "negligible."
- Twelve leading scientists warn of fallout concentrated in the northern hemisphere beneath the high-altitude jet stream. Linus Pauling also states that 10,000 persons are dying or have died of leukemia because of nuclear weapons testing.
- The Massachusetts governor reverses the 1692 witchcraft convictions of six Salem women.
- *Fortune* names Paul Getty the richest American; his real estate is estimated at $1 billion.
- Humphrey Bogart, dies, after reportedly saying to his wife, Lauren Bacall, "Goodbye, kid."
- Animal lovers throughout the world protest Russia's use of an animal (Laika) in flight.
- The VD rate increases from 122,000 to 126,000, the first increase since 1948.
- Ford introduces a new model, the Edsel.
- The Everly Brothers' "Wake Up Little Susie" is banned in Boston; a Columbia University psychiatrist compares rock dancing to the medieval St. Vitus plague where victims were unable to stop dancing.

New Words and Usages: Asian flu, Common Market, Sputnik, meter maid, factsheet, subliminal projection, total theater, bird dog, shook up, funky

Fads: Crinolines, poodle haircuts, saddle shoes, girls wearing their boyfriends' varsity sweaters, silly putty, Slinky, raccoon coats (from the leftover Davy Crockett raccoon materials), Dick Clark's "American Bandstand" with the bunny hop, hula hoops, bowling, frisbees, Bloody Mary jokes, Daisy Mae, Dog Patch outfits, sack dresses

First Appearances: Commercial building heated by the sun (Albuquerque), charting of Northwest Passage, element 102, pocket-size transistor (Sony), installment sales law, car with retractable hardtop (Ford), Zysser vegetable steamer, animal insurance, marketing of electric typewriter, Union Carbide Corp., Gulf and Western, Newport, Americana (Florida), Gino's

1958

Economic Profile
  Dow-Jones: ↑ High 583–
    Low 451
  GNP: 0%
  Inflation: +1.9%
  Unemployment: 6.8%
Balance of international
  payments: +$5.8 billion
Military on duty: 2,600,000
Voter participation: 63%
  (1952), 61% (1956)
Population with religious
  affiliation: 109 million
Oldsmobile: $2,933
Renault: $1,345
Simca: $1,775
Wheel alignment: $7.50
Emerson 7½ amp, 115-volt
  air conditioner: $128
Air France, New York–Paris:
  $489.60 (round trip,
  economy class)
Delta, New York–Houston:
  $66.65
Harvard tuition: $1,250
Blue jeans: $3.75
Macy's rhinestone-decorated
  silk shoes: $19.94

Deaths

Claire L. Chennault, Ronald
  Colman, Christian Dior,
  Robert Donat, W. C.
  Handy, Ernest O.
  Lawrence, Louis B.
  Mayer, Tyrone Power,
  Mike Todd, Ralph Vaughan
  Williams.

In the News

TWO INTERMEDIATE-RANGE BALLISTIC MISSILE SQUADRONS ARE FORMED UNDER THE STRATEGIC AIR COMMAND . . . BULGANIN ASKS FOR SUMMIT, IKE AGREES . . . IKE WARNS AGAINST WAGE AND PRICE INCREASES . . . U.S. AND USSR AGREE TO CULTURAL EXCHANGES . . . EXPLORER I, FIRST U.S. SATELLITE, IS LAUNCHED FROM CAPE CANAVERAL . . . TRUMAN BLAMES RECESSION ON IKE . . . UNITED ARAB REPUBLIC IS FORMED BY EGYPT AND SYRIA . . . IRAQ AND JORDAN UNITE . . . RIOTS AGAINST PRESIDENT CHAMOUN TEAR BEIRUT . . . IKE ASKS FOR ON-SITE INSPECTION . . . RIGHTISTS SEIZE POWER IN ALGERIA, ASK DE GAULLE TO FORM NEW FRENCH GOVERNMENT . . . VICE PRESIDENT NIXON IS STONED IN CARACAS WHILE ON GOODWILL TOUR . . . ONE-AND-A-HALF-TON SPUTNIK III ORBITS . . . LAST TROOPS LEAVE ARKANSAS . . . DE GAULLE BECOMES FRENCH PREMIER . . . FREE HUNGARY LEADER, IMRE NAGY, IS EXECUTED . . . ALASKA IS ADMITTED TO THE UNION . . . IKE ORDERS THE MARINES TO LEBANON TO SAFEGUARD ITS INDEPENDENCE . . . MAO TSE-TUNG AND KHRUSHCHEV PARLEY IN PEKING . . . IKE ORDERS ONE-YEAR TEST BAN . . . CHINESE BOMBARD QUEMOY AND MATSU ISLANDS OFF CHINA COAST . . . SEVENTH FLEET SUPPLIES QUEMOY, CHINESE HOLD FIRE . . . PRESIDENT'S CHIEF AIDE SHERMAN ADAMS RESIGNS OVER ALLEGED BRIBE OF VICUNA COAT . . . PIONEER ROCKET GOES UP 7,300 MILES . . . POPE PIUS XII DIES, POPE JOHN XXIII IS ELECTED . . . BORIS PASTERNAK REFUSES NOBEL PRIZE . . . CASTRO–LED REBELS SEIZE PROVINCIAL CAPITAL IN CUBA.

Quotes

"The Strip" in Las Vegas. The gambling center is a rapid growth industry. *Roger Whitehouse.*

"In the field of marketing, . . . the trend toward selling [has] reached something of a nadir with the unveiling . . . of so-called subliminal projection. That is the technique designed to flash messages past our conscious guard."

— Vance Packard

"If the public wants to lower its standard of living by driving a cheap crowded car, we'll make it."

— Anonymous General Motors Executive

Ads

Do you arise irked with life? Are you prone to snap at loved ones? Our strong, hearty breakfast coffee will change all this! Breakfast becomes a spirited, even hilarious affair.

(General Foods Gourmet Foods)

"The way she talks, you'd think she was in *Who's Who*. Well! I found out what's what with her. . . . Why that palace of theirs has wall-to-wall mortgages! And that car? Darling . . . they won it in a fifty-cent raffle! . . . Of course, she *does* dress divinely. But really . . . I found out about that too."

(Ohrbach's)

C'est magnifique! Une maison Ranch très original, 2½ baths . . . 2-Cadillac garage . . . $21,000 . . . No cash for Veterans.

(Real Estate Ad)

"The schools are in terrible shape. . . . What has long been an ignored material problem, Sputnik has made a recognized crisis. [The] spartan Soviet system is producing many students better equipped to cope with the technicalities of the Space Age."

— *Life* editorial

"[The Russian sputnik is] an outer-space raspberry to a decade of American pretensions that the American way of life is a gilt-edge guarantee of our national security."

— Clare Boothe Luce

"In their mauve and cerise, air-conditioned, power-steered and power-braked automobiles, . . . [people] pass through cities that are badly paved, made hideous by blighted buildings, billboards, . . . decaying refuse. Is this, indeed, American genius?"

— John Kenneth Galbraith

"Is That All There Is?" remains Peggy Lee's theme song; she began her career with Benny Goodman. *Movie Star News.*

YOUR FUTURE IS GREAT IN A GROWING AMERICA
If ever there was a time for optimism—it's now! Here's what's coming: (1) More People . . . (2) More jobs . . . (3) More income . . . (4) More production . . . (5) More savings . . . (6) More research . . . (7) More need.

(Public Service Ad)

Where hearts are gay
There's Blond Dubonnet.

(Dubonnet)

TV

Premieres
"The Donna Reed Show"
"Naked City," John McIntire
"77 Sunset Strip," Efrem Zimbalist, Jr., Edd "Kookie" Byrnes
"Peter Gunn," Craig Stevens
"Dr. Joyce Brothers"
"The Rifleman," Chuck Connors
"Wanted: Dead or Alive," Steve McQueen
"The Lawman," John Russell
"Concentration," Hugh Downs
"Open End," David Susskind

Top Ten (Nielsen)
"Gunsmoke," "Wagon Train," "Have Gun, Will Travel," "The Danny Thomas Show," "Maverick," "Tales of Wells Fargo," "The Real McCoys," "I've Got a Secret," "The Life and Legend of Wyatt Earp"

Specials
"Days of Wine and Roses" (Piper Laurie, Cliff Robertson); "Little Moon of Alban" (James Costigan, with Christopher Plummer, Julie Harris); "The Old Man" (Horton Foote); Leonard Bernstein and the New York Philharmonic; "Face of Red China"; "Little Women" (Margaret O'Brien, Risë Stevens, Florence Henderson)

Emmy Awards
"An Evening with Fred Astaire" (program); "Playhouse 90," "Alcoa-Goodyear" (drama); "Jack Benny Show" (comedy); "Dinah Shore—Chevy Show" (variety); "Maverick" (western); "Omnibus" (public service); "What's My Line?" (game); Raymond Burr (actor, "Perry Mason"); Loretta Young (actress, "The Loretta Young Show")

Of Note
"A Turkey for the President" stars Ronald Reagan and Nancy Davis on the G.E. Theater, Thanksgiving Day • ABC tries out prime-time news with John Daly for 15 minutes at 10:30 P.M., but popular response is poor.

Movies

Openings
Gigi (Vincente Minnelli), Louis Jourdan, Leslie Caron, Maurice Chevalier
Separate Tables (Delbert Mann), Deborah Kerr, Burt Lancaster, David Niven, Rita Hayworth
Auntie Mame (Morton DaCosta), Rosalind Russell, Forrest Tucker
Cat on a Hot Tin Roof (Richard Brooks), Paul Newman, Elizabeth Taylor, Burl Ives
The Defiant Ones (Stanley Kramer), Sidney Poitier, Tony Curtis
The Inn of the Sixth Happiness (Mark Robson), Ingrid Bergman, Curt Jurgens
Some Came Running (Vincente Minnelli), Frank Sinatra, Shirley MacLaine, Dean Martin
Lonelyhearts (Vincent J. Donehue), Montgomery Clift, Myrna Loy, Robert Ryan
The Young Lions (Edward Dmytryk), Montgomery Clift, Marlon Brando, Dean Martin
The Goddess (John Cromwell), Kim Stanley, Lloyd Bridges
South Pacific (Joshua Logan), Mitzi Gaynor, Rossano Brazzi
Touch of Evil (Orson Welles), Charleton Heston, Orson Welles
Vertigo (Alfred Hitchcock), James Stewart, Kim Novak
The Magician (Ingmar Bergman), Max von Sydow, Ingrid Thulin

Academy Awards
Best Picture: *Gigi*
Best Director: Vincente Minnelli (*Gigi*)
Best Actress: Susan Hayward (*I Want to Live*)
Best Actor: David Niven (*Separate Tables*)

Top Box-Office Stars
Glenn Ford, Elizabeth Taylor, Jerry Lewis, Marlon Brando, Rock Hudson, William Holden, Brigitte Bardot, Yul Brynner, James Stewart, Frank Sinatra

Stars of Tomorrow
Red Buttons, Diane Varsi, Andy Griffith, Anthony Franciosa, Hope Lange, Brigitte Bardot, Burl Ives, Mickey Shaughnessy, Russ Tamblyn

Popular Music

Hit Songs
"All I Have to Do Is Dream"
"Bird Dog"
"A Certain Smile"
"Gigi"
"Pink Shoe Laces"
"Tears on My Pillow"
"Tom Dooley"
"Chanson d'amour"
"Nel blu dipinto di blu (Volare)"
"The Purple People Eater"

Top Records

Albums: *Ricky* (Ricky Nelson); *Come Fly with Me* (Frank Sinatra); *The Music Man* (original cast); *South Pacific* (sound track); *Johnny's Greatest Hits* (Johnny Mathis); *The Kingston Trio*

Singles: *Catch a Falling Star* (Perry Como); *He's Got the Whole World in His Hands* (Laurie London); *Twilight Time* (Platters); *Lollipop* (Chordettes); *Who's Sorry Now?* (Connie Francis); *Tea for Two Cha Cha* (Tommy Dorsey); *Fever* (Peggy Lee); *Hard-Headed Woman* (Elvis Presley). Country: *Ballad of a Teenage Queen* (Johnny Cash); *Blue Boy* (Jim Reeves)

Grammy Awards
Nel blu dipinto di blu (Volare), Domenico Modugno (record); *The Music from "Peter Gunn,"* Henry Mancini (album); "Nel blu dipinto di blu" (song)

Jazz and Big Bands
The Monterey, California, Jazz Festival takes place.
Lambert, Hendricks & Ross are organized; Ella Fitzgerald and Duke Ellington give a concert at Carnegie Hall.
Miles Davis's *Milestones* experiments with modal improvisation.

Top Performers (*Downbeat*): Count Basie (soloist, big band); Les Brown (dance band); Modern Jazz Quartet (jazz quartet); Oscar Peterson, Shelly Manne, Paul Desmond, Tony Scott, Milt Jackson, Herbie Mann, Art Van Damme (instrumentalists); Ella Fitzgerald, Frank Sinatra (vocalists); Four Freshmen (vocal group)

Theater

Broadway Openings

Plays
J. B. (Archibald MacLeish), Pat Hingle, Christopher Plummer, Raymond Massey
Two for the Seesaw (William Gibson), Henry Fonda, Anne Bancroft
Sunrise at Campobello (Dore Schary), Ralph Bellamy
A Touch of the Poet (Eugene O'Neill), Kim Stanley, Eric Portman, Helen Hayes, Betty Field
The Pleasure of His Company (Samuel Taylor), Cyril Ritchard, Cornelia Otis Skinner
The Marriage-Go-Round (Leslie Stephens), Charles Boyer, Claudette Colbert, Julie Newmar
The Visit (Friedrich Dürrenmatt), Alfred Lunt, Lynn Fontanne, Eric Porter
Ages of Man (Shakespeare scenes and sonnets), John Gielgud
The Disenchanted (Bud Schulberg, Harvey Breit), Rosemary Harris, George Grizzard, Jason Robards, Jr.
The Cold Wind and the Warm (S. N. Behrman), Eli Wallach, Maureen Stapleton
Epitaph for George Dillon (John Osborne, Anthony Creighton), Eileen Herlie, Robert Stephens
The Entertainer (John Osborne), Laurence Olivier, Joan Plowright

Musicals
Flower Drum Song (Richard Rodgers, Oscar Hammerstein II), Pat Suzuki, Juanita Hall, Larry Blyden
A Party with Betty Comden and Adolph Green
La Plume de Ma Tante (Gerard Calvi), Robert Dhéry, Colette Brosset

Classics and Revivals On and Off Broadway
Old Vic: *Hamlet, Twelfth Night, Garden District* (Tennessee Williams); *Blood Wedding* (Garcia Lorca); *Endgame* (Samuel Beckett); *Family Reunion* (T. S. Eliot), Lillian Gish, Florence Reed, Fritz Weaver; *Ivanov* (Chekhov); *The Quare Fellow* (Brendan Behan); *Ulysses in Nighttown* (Oliver Saylor), Zero Mostel; *The Chairs*, Eli Wallach, and *The Lesson* (Eugene Ionesco), Joan Plowright, Wallach; *The Infernal Machine* (Jean Cocteau), Claude Dauphin

Pulitzer Prize
Look Homeward, Angel, Ketti Frings

Tony Awards
Sunrise at Campobello, Dore Schary (play); *The Music Man,* Meredith Willson (musical)

Classical Music

Compositions
Edgard Varèse, *Poème electronique*
John Cage, *Fontana Mix*
Salvatore Martirano, *0,0,0,0, that Shakespeherian Rag*
Roger Sessions, Symphony no. 4
George Rochberg, Symphony no. 2
John La Montaine, Concerto for Piano and Orchestra

Important Events
Touring orchestras include the New York Philharmonic to South and Central America, and the Philadelphia to the USSR, Romania, and Poland. Four composers are invited to the USSR: Roger Sessions, Peter Mennin, Roy Harris, and Ulysses Kay.

Benno Moiseiwitsch plays the three Rachmaninoff concerti with the Symphony of the Air, at Carnegie Hall.

Harvey Lavan Cliburn, Jr. (Van Cliburn), 23, wins first prize in the International Tchaikovsky Piano Competition and gains instant fame, including a ticker tape parade in New York.

Debuts: Leonid Kogan, Vladimir Ashkenazy

First Performances
Roger Sessions, Symphony no. 3 (Boston); Deems Taylor, *The Dragon* (New York); Gian Carlo Menotti, Piano Concerto (Cleveland); Paul Creston, *Pre-Classic Suite* (New Orleans); Henry Humphreys, *The Waste Land of T. S. Eliot* (Cincinnati)

Opera

Metropolitan: During this 75th anniversary year, there are 240 performances; Inge Borkh (debut), *Salomé;* Borkh, Nicolai Gedda, *Cavalleria rusticana, I pagliacci;* Antonietta Stella, *Madama Butterfly;* Eleanor Steber, *Vanessa* (Samuel Barber, premiere); Rudolph Bing cancels Maria Callas in *Macbeth,* which is rescheduled with Leonie Rysanek (debut).

New York City: *The Silent Woman* (Richard Strauss), *Good Soldier Schweik* (Robert Kurka), premieres

Boston: Opera Group of Boston founded by Sarah Caldwell; *The Voyage to the Moon* (Offenbach)

Chicago: Birgit Nilsson, *Turandot;* William Wildermann, *Tristan und Isolde;* Tito Gobbi, *Falstaff*

San Francisco: *Medée* (Cherubini, premiere)

San Antonio: Lily Pons, *Lakmé*

Santa Fe: *Capriccio* (Richard Struass, premiere)

Music Notes
Pablo Casals's appearance at the UN General Assembly on UN Day, for the first time in over twenty years, is considered a symbol of the "exchange of peace through music" • Paul Robeson returns to New York after eleven years • President Truman and Jack Benny play in a benefit performance with the Kansas City Philharmonic.

Far left: Frank Lloyd Wright's innovative Solomon R. Guggenheim Museum. *Roger Whitehouse.*

Texan Van Cliburn is the first American to win the International Tchaikovsky Competition in Moscow. He studied with Rosina Lhévinne at Juilliard and made his debut with the Houston Symphony when he was 13. *Movie Star News.*

Art _____

Painting
Sam Francis, *Blue on a Point*
Philip Guston, *Passage*
Jan Müller, *Jacob's Ladder*
Abraham Rattner, *Song of Esther*
Morris Louis, *Russet*
Hans Hofmann, *Bird Cage—Variation II, Moloch*
Franz Kline, *King Oliver, Requiem, Siegfried*
Willem de Kooning, *Woman and Bicycle*
Jasper Johns, *Three Flags*
Mark Rothko, *Four Darks in Red, Red, Brown and Black*
Robert Motherwell, *Iberia No. 18*

Sculpture
Seymour Lipton, *Sorcerer*
Reuben Nakian, *The Rape of Lucrece*
Louise Nevelson, *Sky Cathedral*
George Rickey, *Omaggio a Bernini*

Naum Gabo, *Linear Construction in Space, Number 4*

Architecture
Solomon R. Guggenheim Museum, New York (Frank Lloyd Wright)
Main Library, Palo Alto, Calif. (Edward Durell Stone)
Seagram Building, New York (Mies van der Rohe, Philip Johnson)
Exterior, Museum of Fine Arts, Houston (Mies van der Rohe)
Four Seasons Restaurant, New York (Philip Johnson)
Inland Steel Building, Chicago (Skidmore, Owings and Merrill)
McGregor Memorial Center, Wayne State University, Detroit (Minoru Yamasaki)
Roofless Church, New Harmony, Ind. (Philip Johnson, Jacques Lipchitz)
Union Tank Car Co. Quarter Sphere Dome, Baton Rouge, La. (Buckminster Fuller)

Important Exhibitions
"Masterpieces of Korean Art" travels to Washington, Boston, and New York.

Museums

New York: *Metropolitan:* American art from Copley to O'Keeffe; Paintings by Sir Winston Churchill; "A Century of City Views"; Prints by Callot and Daumier; Paintings from colonial times to today; Korean art. *Museum of Modern Art:* 70th Anniversary of Chagall; Seurat; Modigliani; Arp. *Whitney:* "Nature in Abstraction"

Boston: Scenic painters and draughtsmen of 18th century Venice; Daumier; Primitive arts; Maillol's bronzes and drawings; Korean art

Washington: Photographs by Alfred Stieglitz; 150 Dutch drawings; Homer; Illuminated manuscripts; "The Fantastic, the Occult, and the Bizarre"; Blake's engravings; Korean art

Chicago: Seurat; Gris; Umberto Boccioni; Animals in Pre-Columbian art

Kansas City: Japanese art of the Edo period

Houston: The four Guardis; 18th century Venetian masters

Art Briefs
A workman is killed and 31 are injured in a fire at the Museum of Modern Art; works by Monet, Rivers, Tchelitchew, and others are damaged; the current exhibit, "U.S.A.: 1958—5,000 Works," is moved to the Madison Square Garden basement • Rothko begins his first commission, the monumental paintings for the Four Seasons Restaurant in New York • Major sales include Van Gogh's *Public Gardens at Arles* ($369,600), Manet's *La Rue de Berne* ($316,400), Renoir's *La Pensée* ($201,600), and Cézanne's *Garçon au Gilet Rouge* ($616,000, the highest price ever paid for a single painting at auction, by art dealer Georges Keller).

Dance _____

Alvin Ailey forms the American Dance Theater; the Moscow Moiseyev Dance Company tours with enormous success.

Premieres

New York City Ballet: *Stars and Stripes* (George Balanchine), Melissa Hayden, Jacques d'Amboise

Ballets U.S.A.: *New York Export: Op. Jazz* (Jerome Robbins)

San Francisco: *Beauty and the Beast* (Lew Christensen)

Merce Cunningham: *Antic Meet* (John Cage)

Martha Graham: *Clytemnestra*

Martha Graham and Bertram Ross: *Night Journey*

Books

Fiction

Critics' Choice
The End of the Road, John Barth
Breakfast at Tiffany's, Truman Capote
The Housebreaker of Shady Hill, John Cheever
The Violated, Vance Bourjaily
The Sundial, Shirley Jackson
The Subterraneans, Jack Kerouac
The Magic Barrel, Bernard Malamud
The Dharma Bums, Jack Kerouac
Home from the Hill, William Humphrey
Mrs. Bridge, Evan Connell

Best-Sellers
Doctor Zhivago, Boris Pasternak
Anatomy of a Murder, Robert Traver
Lolita, Vladimir Nabokov
Around the World with Auntie Mame, Patrick Dennis
From the Terrace, John O'Hara
Eloise at Christmastime, Kay Thompson
Ice Palace, Edna Ferber
The Enemy Camp, Jerome Weidman

Nonfiction

Critics' Choice
The Democratic Vista, Richard Chase
More in Anger, Marya Mannes
Irrational Man, William Barrett
Eisenhower, Captive Hero, Marquis Childs
The Shook-Up Generation, Harrison E. Salisbury
The Affluent Society, John Kenneth Galbraith
Russia, the Atom and the West, George F. Kennan
Our Nuclear Future, Edward Teller, Albert L. Latter
Mistress to an Age: A Life of Madame de Staël, J. Christopher Herold
🕭 *The Theatre and Its Double*, Antonin Artaud
🕭 *Structural Anthropology*, Claude Lévi-Strauss

Best-Sellers
Kids Say the Darndest Things! Art Linkletter
'Twixt Twelve and Twenty, Pat Boone
Only in America, Harry Golden
Masters of Deceit, J. Edgar Hoover
Please Don't Eat the Daisies, Jean Kerr

Better Homes and Gardens Salad Book
The New Testament in Modern English
Aku-Aku, Thor Heyerdahl
Dear Abby, Abigail Van Buren
Inside Russia Today, John Gunther

Poetry
William Meredith, *The Open Sea and Other Poems*
William Carlos Williams, *Paterson, Book V*
Karl Shapiro, *Poems of a Jew*
E. E. Cummings, *95 Poems*
Muriel Rukeyser, *Body of Waking*
William Jay Smith, *Poems 1947–1957*
Lawrence Ferlinghetti, *A Coney Island of the Mind*
Theodore Roethke, *Words for the Wind*
Gregory Corso, *Gasoline*

Pulitzer Prizes
The Travels of Jamie McPheeters, Robert Lewis Taylor (fiction)
The Republican Era: 1869–1901, Leonard D. White, with Jean Schneider (U.S. history)
Woodrow Wilson, Arthur Walworth (biography)
Selected Poems, 1928–1958, Stanley Kunitz (poetry)

Science and Technology

Integrated circuitry is invented; Jack Kilby describes the "monolithic idea," the basis of the microchip.

Stereo records are introduced by EMI and Decca.

John Enders develops a measles vaccine.

Joseph Wolpe in *Psychotherapy by Reciprocal Inhibition* develops a behavioral approach.

Explorer I, weighing 30.8 pounds, is launched by the army.

The navy fails for the sixth time to orbit Vanguard II.

The air force launches the heaviest U.S. missile to date, 8,750 pounds.

NASA is organized to unify and develop U.S. nonmilitary space efforts; it announces a space program, Project Mercury, with the goals of a man in space in two years, a man on the moon in six to ten years, and the exploration of Mars in ten to fifteen years.

James Van Allen describes two belts of cosmic radiation around the earth.

The first regular domestic jet service, from New York to Miami, begins.

Ultrasound for examination of the fetus during pregnancy is pioneered.

🕭 USSR orbits Sputnik III, weighing 2,925.53 pounds.

Nobel Prize
Sharing the prize in physiology and medicine are Joshua Lederberg, for work on genetic mechanisms, and George W. Beadle and Edward L. Tatum, for work on the genetic transmission of hereditary characteristics.

Jack Kerouac, spokesman of "the beat generation," whose San Francisco "subterraneans" are "hip without being slick, intelligent without being corny, . . . [and] very Christlike." *Courtesy Grove Press.*

Baseball

Stan Musial (St. Louis, NL) gets his 3,000th hit.
Bob Turley wins the Cy Young Award.

Champions

Batting
  Richie Ashburn
  (Philadelphia, NL), .350
  Ted Williams (Boston, AL), .328
Pitching
  Warren Spahn (Milwaukee, NL), 22–11

  Lew Burdette (Milwaukee, NL), 20–10
  Bob Turley (New York, NL), 21–7
Home runs
  Ernie Banks (Chicago, NL), 47

Football

Jim Brown (Cleveland) gains a record 1,527 yards rushing.
Johnny Unitas (Q) stars in Baltimore's sudden-death overtime victory over New York in the NFL playoff, the first title game televised coast to coast.

NFL Season Leaders: Eddie LeBaron (Washington), passing; Ray Berry (Baltimore), receiving

College All-Americans: Billy Cannon (B), LSU; Pete Dawkins (B), Army; Buddy Dial (E), Rice.

Bowls (Jan. 1, 1959)

Rose: Iowa 38–California 12
Orange: Oklahoma 21–Syracuse 6

Cotton: Air Force 0–Texas Christian 0
Sugar: Louisiana State 7–Clemson 0

Sports

Basketball

NBA All-Pro First Team: George Yardley (Detroit), Dolph Schayes (Syracuse), Bob Pettit (St. Louis), Bob Cousy (Boston), Bill Sharman (Boston)

Other Sports

Golf: Arnold Palmer is the PGA's top money-winner with $42,607.

Tennis: Pancho Gonzales beats Lew Hoad on the pro tour.

Winners

World Series
  New York (AL) 4
  Milwaukee (NL) 3
MVP
  NL–Ernie Banks, Chicago
  AL–Jackie Jensen, Boston
NFL
  Baltimore 23
  New York 17 (OT)
MVP
  Jim Brown, Cleveland
College Football
  Louisiana State University
Heisman Trophy
  Pete Dawkins, Army
NBA Championship
  St. Louis 4–Boston 2

MVP
  Bill Russell, Boston
College Basketball
  Kentucky
Player of the Year
  Elgin Baylor, Seattle
Stanley Cup
  Montreal
US Tennis Open
  Men: Ashley Cooper
  Women: Althea Gibson
USGA Open
  Tommy Bolt
Kentucky Derby
  Tim Tam (I. Valenzuela, jockey)

Fashion

For Women: The "chemise," "trapeze," and "empire" are ruby red, red-violet, lavender, orange, yellow, emerald, and fuchsia. The "shift," or sack dress, also strives for popularity. Nonfunctional dress decorations include big buttons, patch pockets, fringes, bows, sashes, and buckles. The trapeze, often called "a half-opened umbrella," is short-lived. Mohair is new, along with paisley and patterned wool knits; the new polished cottons are worn in the evening. Shoes are round or square, with thin heels; pumps have low straps and stitching (some have jeweled trim). In addition to beads in all colors and large pins, a rage grows for pearl drop earrings and gold hearts, and they are often worn together. The raccoon and loden coat are popular.

High-fashion notes: Yves St. Laurent's trapeze for Dior; Dior's 2d "demi-longeur"; Balenciaga's chemise; Cardin's blouse-backed jacket

Kaleidoscope _____

- Five months after Sputnik, *Life*'s series "Crisis in Education" focuses on major U.S. educational problems, including poor curricula, overcrowding of classrooms, poorly paid teachers, and lack of proper professional attention to substantive matters.
- For the 11th year, Eleanor Roosevelt is first on the "Most Admired Woman" list; Queen Elizabeth is second.
- John Kenneth Galbraith, in *The Affluent Society,* describes the materialism and conformity that characterize the United States and argues for a redistribution of income to end the poverty of public services.
- Paul Robeson, denied a passport for eight years because of his leftist affiliations, is allowed to tour abroad.
- Elvis Presley is inducted into the army on March 24 as no. 53310761.
- The Kingston Trio's "Tom Dooley" begins the folk music vogue.
- Colorado and Kansas are overrun by grasshoppers.
- Eisenhower tries but is unable to issue a "posthumous pardon" to O. Henry, who started writing fiction when jailed for an $854.08 embezzlement from an Austin, Texas, bank.
- Los Angeles Dodgers Roy Campanella fractures two back vertebrae and is paralyzed from the shoulders down.
- Lana Turner's 14-year-old daughter, Cheryl Crane, fatally stabs her mother's boyfriend, Johnny Stompanato, which the court rules "justifiable homocide."
- Approximately 250,000 attend the Jehovah's Witnessess's Convention at Yankee Stadium.
- Treason charges against Ezra Pound are dropped because he is "not competent" to stand trial.
- College tuition doubles since 1940 and is expected to double again by 1970; the average cost is $1,300 a year.
- A survey indicates that 40 percent of college students admit to cheating, many with no regrets.

In "Alfred Hitchcock Presents" stars like Barbara Bel Geddes, Gary Merrill, and Brian Keith make multiple appearances. *Billy Rose Theatre Collection. The New York Public Library at Lincoln Center. Astor, Lenox and Tilden Foundations.*

Harry Belafonte's renditions of "Scarlet Ribbons" and "Shenandoah" are becoming classics. *Movie Star News.*

- Brigitte Bardot becomes the new sex symbol.
- Jack Webb marries Miss America 1952, Jackie Loughery.
- The paperback edition of *Lolita* sells a million copies.
- A nationwide scandal involves a number of quiz shows giving answers beforehand; 12 of 20 contestants who won between $500 and $220,500 plead guilty but receive suspended sentences because of their "humiliation."
- City College of New York student Herbert Stempel, who won $49,500 on "Twenty One," claims that he was forced to lose to Charles Van Doren, "a guy that had a fancy name, Ivy League education, parents all his life."
- Nathan Leopold, jailed with Richard Loeb (who was killed in prison) for their 1924 kidnapping, is paroled.
- SANE is formed with 25,000 members.
- The food additive amendment prohibits the use of any substance that induces cancer in animals or people.
- The Elizabeth Taylor, Eddie Fisher, and Debbie Reynolds love triangle is widely publicized.
- The construction of a nuclear power plant at Bodega Head, California, is stopped by court action of environmental groups.

New Words and Usages: Beatniks, DNA, lunar probe, action-painting, carry-out, moon dust, news satellite, reentry, sex kitten, sick joke, trapeze dress

Fads: Waterskiing, British bobbies' capes

First Appearances: Privately owned atomic reactor, solid state electronic computer, bifocal contact lens, presidential pension, two-way moving sidewalk, John Birch Society, Grammy award, Chevrolet Impala, Green Giant canned beans, Sweet 'n Low, Cocoa Puffs, Cocoa Krispies, Pizza Hut (Kansas City), Synanon, acupuncture (in United States), Bankamericard, American Express, UPI, National Defense Education Act

1959

Facts and Figures

Economic Profile

Dow-Jones: ↑ High 679– Low 574

GNP: +8%

Inflation: +0.7%

Unemployment: 5.5%

Police expenditures, federal, state, local: $1.9 billion

Persons arrested: 2,613,000

Executions: 49

Prisoners, federal and state: 207,400

Juvenile court: 63,038

Castro convertible king-size sofa: $199.75

Caribbean cruise: $355 (15 days, 7 ports)

Greyhound, New York– Florida: $87.74 (9 days)

Willoughby's Bell & Howell 8mm moving picture camera: $19–$48

Hi-fi tape recorder: $49.95

Macy's "trapeze suit in transition": $59.95

Rogers Peet young men's tropical suit: $38.50

Summer sport coat: $14.95–$19.95

Deaths

George Antheil, Ethel Barrymore, Ernest Bloch, Raymond Chandler, Lou Costello, Cecil B. De Mille, Errol Flynn, George C. Marshall, Mel Ott, Tyrone Power, Frank Lloyd Wright.

In the News

FIDEL CASTRO TAKES HAVANA, BATISTA FLEES . . . POPE JOHN CALLS FOR ECUMENICAL COUNCIL . . . KHRUSHCHEV BOASTS OF SOVIET MILITARY SUPERIORITY . . . NORFOLK, VIRGINIA, SCHOOLS INTEGRATE . . . CYPRUS IS GIVEN INDEPENDENCE BY BRITAIN . . . CASTRO VISITS U.S. AND IS WARMLY RECEIVED . . . HAWAII BECOMES THE 50TH STATE . . . KAMBA TRIBES IN TIBET FIGHT CHINESE, DALAI LAMA SEEKS ASYLUM . . . IKE CALLS FOR ON-SITE MISSILE INSPECTION AND IS AGAIN REJECTED . . . UNITED ARAB REPUBLIC HALTS ISRAELI CARGO IN SUEZ CANAL . . . MONKEYS ABEL AND BAKER ARE RECOVERED AFTER ORBIT . . . RUSSIANS FIRE 4,400-POUND PAYLOAD INTO SPACE WITH TWO DOGS AND A RABBIT . . . 500,000 STEELWORKERS STRIKE . . . CUBAN PRESIDENT URRUTIA RESIGNS, ALLEGING COMMUNIST CONTROL . . . NIXON, ON RUSSIAN T.V., DEFENDS U.S. AND ASKS THAT RUSSIANS IMPROVE . . . INDIA CHARGES THAT CHINA SEIZED BORDER TERRITORY . . . LAOS ASKS FOR U.S. AID AGAINST NORTH VIETNAM AGGRESSION . . . EISENHOWER AND KHRUSHCHEV MEET AT CAMP DAVID . . . KHRUSHCHEV TOURS THE U.S. . . . CHARLES VAN DOREN ADMITS HIS T.V. QUIZ ROLE WAS FIXED . . . LUNIK II HITS THE MOON . . . HUNGARIAN LEADER JANOS KADAR SAYS RUSSIAN TROOPS WILL STAY AS LONG AS NECESSARY . . . IKE WILL TAKE 22,370-MILE GOODWILL TOUR.

Quotes ――――――――――

"It is necessary to provide every person in the U.S. with a shelter."
— Edward Teller, "father" of the H-bomb

"The immediate cause of World War III is the preparation of it."
— C. Wright Mills

"Let us never forget that there can be no second place in a contest with Russia and there can be no second chance if we lose."
— Adm. H. G. Rickover

"America when will we end the human war?
 Go F—— yourself with your atomic bomb"
— Allen Ginsberg, *Howl*, 2d ed.

"I am not willing to accept the idea that there are no Communists left in this country. I think if we lift enough rocks we'll find some."
— Sen. Barry Goldwater (R, Ariz.)

"We have beaten you to the moon, but you have beaten us in sausage making."
— Nikita S. Khrushchev in Des Moines

"Probably we will never be able to determine the psychic havoc of the concentration camp and the atomic bomb. One is Hip or one is Square, . . . one is a rebel or one conforms."
— Norman Mailer, "The White Negro"

The Mercury Seven, test pilots selected by NASA. *Courtesy NASA.*

"It got to the point where there were just too many quiz shows. Ratings began to drop. . . . Some producers turned to rigging. . . . They just couldn't afford to lose their sponsors."
— Hal March, host, "The $64,000 Question"

"[The producer] instructed me on how to answer the questions. . . . He gave me a script to memorize. . . . I would give almost anything I have to reverse the course of my life in the last three years."
— Charles Van Doren

Ads ――――――――――

TV

Premieres

"Rawhide," Eric Fleming, Clint Eastwood
"The G. E. College Bowl"
"The Bell Telephone Hour"
"The Many Loves of Dobie Gillis," Dwayne
    Hickman
"The Untouchables," Robert Stack
"Bonanza," Lorne Green, Dan Blocker, Pernell
    Roberts, Michael Landon
"The Late Show"
"The Twilight Zone," Rod Serling

Top Ten (Nielsen)

"Gunsmoke," "Wagon Train," "Have Gun, Will
Travel," "The Danny Thomas Show," "The Red
Skelton Show," "Father Knows Best," "77 Sunset
Strip," "The Price Is Right," "Wanted: Dead or
Alive," "Perry Mason"

Specials

"The Turn of the Screw" (Ingrid Bergman); "The
Moon and Sixpence" (Laurence Olivier); "Biography
of a Missile" (Ed Murrow, Fred Friendly); "Ethan
Frome" (Julie Harris); "Give My Regards to
Broadway" (Jimmy Durante, Ray Bolger); "The
Violent World of Sam Huff"; "Twentieth Century"
(Walter Cronkite, host)

Emmy Awards

"Playhouse 90" (drama); "Art Carney Special"
(comedy); "Fabulous Fifties" (variety);
"Huckleberry Hound" (children); Robert Stack
(actor, "The Untouchables"); Jane Wyatt (actress,
"Father Knows Best"); Rod Serling (writing
achievement)

Of Note

Ed Murrow interviews Fidel Castro, who is wearing
pajamas, on "Person to Person" • George Reeves,
star of "Superman," commits suicide.

Movies

Openings

Ben-Hur (William Wyler), Charlton Heston, Stephen
    Boyd
Anatomy of a Murder (Otto Preminger), James
    Stewart, Lee Remick, Ben Gazzara
The Nun's Story (Fred Zinnemann), Audrey
    Hepburn, Peter Finch
Room at the Top (Jack Clayton), Laurence Harvey,
    Simone Signoret
Some Like It Hot (Billy Wilder), Tony Curtis,
    Marilyn Monroe, Jack Lemmon
Pillow Talk (Michael Gordon), Doris Day, Rock
    Hudson, Tony Randall
Suddenly, Last Summer (Joseph L. Mankiewicz),
    Elizabeth Taylor, Katharine Hepburn,
    Montgomery Clift
Imitation of Life (Douglas Sirk), Lana Turner,
    Juanita Moore, John Gavin
North by Nothwest (Alfred Hitchcock), Cary Grant,
    Eva Marie Saint, James Mason
On the Beach (Stanley Kramer), Gregory Peck, Ava
    Gardner, Fred Astaire
The Best of Everything (Jean Negulesco), Hope
    Lange, Suzy Parker, Joan Crawford, Louis
    Jourdan
Gidget (Paul Wendkos), Sandra Dee, Cliff Robertson
Rio Bravo (Howard Hawks), John Wayne, Dean
    Martin, Ricky Nelson
Hiroshima, Mon Amour (Alain Resnais), Eiji Okada
The 400 Blows (François Truffaut), Jean-Pierre Leaud
La Dolce Vita (Federico Fellini), Marcello
    Mastroianni, Anita Ekberg, Anouk Aimée
Breathless (Jean-Luc Godard), Jean-Paul Belmondo,
    Jean Seberg
Black Orpheus (Marcel Camus), Breno Mello,
    Marpessa Dawn

Academy Awards

Best Picture: *Ben-Hur*
Best Director: William Wyler *(Ben-Hur)*
Best Actress: Simone Signoret *(Room at the Top)*
Best Actor: Charlton Heston *(Ben-Hur)*

Top Box-Office Stars

Rock Hudson, Cary Grant, James Stewart, Doris
Day, Debbie Reynolds, Glenn Ford, Frank Sinatra,
John Wayne, Jerry Lewis, Susan Hayward

Stars of Tomorrow

Sandra Dee, Ricky Nelson, James Garner, Curt
Jurgens, Lee Remick, John Saxon, Sidney Poitier,
Ernie Kovacs, Kathryn Grant, Carolyn Jones

Popular Music

Hit Songs
"Everything's Coming up Roses"
"Personality"
"Put Your Head on My Shoulder"
"The Sound of Music"
"I'm Just a Lonely Boy"
"Small World"
"Do-Re-Mi"
"Franky"
"Kookie, Kookie"

Top Records

Albums: *Flower Drum Song* (original cast); *Peter Gunn* (Henry Mancini); *The Kingston Trio at Large* (Kingston Trio); *Heavenly* (Johnny Mathis); *Film Encores* (Mantovani)

Singles: *Mack the Knife* (Bobby Darin); *I Loves You Porgy* (Nina Simone); *Misty* (Johnny Mathis); *Tiger* (Fabian); *What'd I Say?* (Ray Charles); *A Teenager in Love* (Dion and the Belmonts); *What a Difference a Day Makes* (Dinah Washington). Country: *Battle of New Orleans* (Johnny Horton); *Three Bells* (Browns)

Grammy Awards
Mack the Knife, Bobby Darin (record); *Come Dance with Me,* Frank Sinatra (album); "Battle of New Orleans," Jimmy Driftwood (song)

Jazz and Big Bands
Ornette Coleman's *The Shape of Jazz to Come* gains wide attention; Coleman's arrival in New York stirs the greatest controversy since Dizzy Gillespie's and Charlie Parker's in 1944. Miles Davis and John Coltrane, in *Kind of Blue,* create "free jazz."

Top Performers (*Downbeat*): Lester Young (soloist); Count Basie, Les Brown (bands); Dave Brubeck (jazz group); Stan Getz, Gerry Mulligan, Tony Scott, J. J. Johnson, Miles Davis (instrumentalists); Ella Fitzgerald, Frank Sinatra (vocalists); Lambert, Hendricks and Ross (vocal group)

Theater

Broadway Openings

Plays
A Raisin in the Sun (Lorraine Hansberry), Claudia McNeil, Sidney Poitier
The Miracle Worker (William Gibson), Anne Bancroft, Patty Duke
The Tenth Man (Paddy Chayefsky), George Voskovec, Lou Jacobi, Jack Gilford
Five Finger Exercise (Peter Shaffer), Jessica Tandy, Michael Bryant, Brian Bedford
A Majority of One (Leonard Spigelgass), Cedric Hardwicke, Gertrude Berg
Sweet Bird of Youth (Tennessee Williams), Geraldine Page, Paul Newman
The Andersonville Trial (Saul Levitt), George C. Scott, Herbert Berghof, Albert Dekker
Rashomon (Fay and Michael Kanin), Rod Steiger, Claire Bloom
Mark Twain Tonight, Hal Holbrook

Musicals
Fiorello! (Jerry Bock, Sheldon Harnick), Tom Bosley, Patricia Wilson, Howard da Silva
The Sound of Music (Richard Rodgers, Oscar Hammerstein II), Mary Martin, Theodore Bikel, Kurt Kazner

Once upon a Mattress (Mary Rodgers, Marshall Barer), Carol Burnett
Gypsy (Jule Styne, Stephen Sondheim), Ethel Merman, Jack Klugman, Sandra Church
Take Me Along (Robert Merrill), Jackie Gleason, Walter Pidgeon, Eileen Herlie, Robert Morse
At the Drop of a Hat, played and written by Michael Flanders, Donald Swann

Classics and Revivals On and Off Broadway
Much Ado about Nothing, Margaret Leighton, Maurice Evans; *Heartbreak House* (George Bernard Shaw), Maurice Evans, Pamela Brown; *The Connection* (Jack Gelber), Leonard Hicks, Ira Lewis; *The Zoo Story* (Edward Albee), George Maharis; *The Balcony* (Jean Genet), Nancy Marchand

Regional

Founded: Dallas Theater Center by Robert D. Stecker, Sr., and Beatrice Handel

Pulitzer Prize
J. B., Archibald MacLeish

Tony Awards
J. B., Archibald MacLeish (play); *Redhead,* Albert Hague, Dorothy Fields (musical)

Classical Music _____

Compositions

Walter Piston, Concerto for Piano and Orchestra
William Schuman, *Three Moods*
David Diamond, Symphony no. 7
Ralph Shapey, Violin Concerto
Virgil Thomson, *Collected Poems*
Wallingford Riegger, Variations for Violin and
    Orchestra
Elliott Carter, Second String Quartet
Gian Carlo Menotti / Samuel Barber, *A Hand of
    Bridge*
Gunther Schuller, Concertino, *Conversations*

Important Events

Celebrations include the tercentenary of Purcell's
birth, the bicentennial of Handel's death, the
sesquicentenary of Haydn's death, and the
sesquincentennial of Mendelssohn's birth.
Mischa Elman, celebrating his fifty years of
performance, presents a gala concert (New York).
The New York Philharmonic, under the auspices of
Eisenhower's International Program for Cultural
Presentations, gives 50 concerts in 17 countries,
including its first performance in Russia since the
revolution (*Rites of Spring* and *The Age of Anxiety*).
Closer international relations between the United
States and USSR are also marked by visits in the
United States of Dmitri Shostakovich, Tikhon
Khrennikov, Dmitri Kabelevsky, Konstantin
Dankevitch, and Fikret Amirov.
Pablo Casals leads the Third Festival in San Juan.
Maria Callas and Van Cliburn perform to capacity
audiences at the Philadelphia Academy of Music
($100 a ticket).
Jaime Laredo wins the Belgian International Prize
and debuts at Carnegie Hall.

First Performances

Paul Hindemith, *Pittsburgh Symphony*
(commissioned for the city's birthday); Bohuslav
Martinů, *Parables* (Boston); Walter Piston, *Three
New England Sketches* (Worcester, Mass.); George
Rochberg, Symphony no. 2 (Cleveland); Paul
Creston, *Janus* (Denver); Howard Hanson, *Summer
Seascape* (New Orleans); John Vincent, *Symphonic
Poem after Descartes* (Philadelphia); Ned Rorem,
Symphony no. 3 (New York)

Opera

Metropolitan: Eleanor Steber, Hermann Uhde,
Wozzeck (Alban Berg, premiere); Giulietta Simionato
(debut), *Il trovatore;* Cornell MacNeil (debut),
Rigoletto; Renata Tebaldi, Mario del Monaco,
George London, *Tosca;* Birgit Nilsson, *Tristan und
Isolde*

New York City: *Six Characters in Search of an
Author* (Hugo Weisgall, premiere)

Chicago: Leontyne Price, *Thaïs;* Sylvia Fisher, Gre
Brouwenstijn (debuts), *Jenůfa;* Christa Ludwig, *Così
fan tutte*

San Francisco: Sena Jurinac, *Madama Butterfly;
Die Frau ohne Schatten* (Richard Strauss, American
premiere)

Music Notes

Columbia and Princeton universities receive $175,000
from the Rockefeller Foundation to establish an
electronic music center.

Far left: Tennessee Williams,
author of *Sweet Bird of
Youth. Billy Rose Theatre
Collection. The New York
Public Library at Lincoln
Center. Astor, Lenox and
Tilden Foundations.*

Sidney Poitier in the
Broadway production of *A
Raisin in the Sun,* Lorraine
Hansberry's play about the
aspirations of a black family.
*Billy Rose Theatre
Collection. The New York
Public Library at Lincoln
Center. Astor, Lenox and
Tilden Foundations.*

Art

Painting

Adolph Gottlieb, *Brink*
Franz Kline, *Orange and Black Wall, Dahlia,*
Jasper Johns, *Numbers in Color* (1958–59)
Hans Hofmann, *Cathedral*
Larry Rivers, *The Last Civil War Veteran*
Frank Stella, *The Marriage of Reason and Squalor*
Willem de Kooning, *Merritt Parkway*
Morris Louis, *Blue Veil* (1958–59), *Saraband*
Stuart Davis, *The Paris Bit*
Ellsworth Kelly, *Gate, Running White*
Josef Albers, *Homage to the Square: With Rays*
Kenneth Noland, *Virginia Site*

Sculpture

Alexander Calder, *Big Red, Black Widow*
Isamu Noguchi, *Integral*
Richard Lippold, *Variation No. 7: Full Moon*

Louise Nevelson, *Dawn's Wedding Feast, Sky Columns— Presences*
John Chamberlain, *Wildroot*
Peter Voulkos, *Little Big Horn*

Architecture

Beth Sholom Synagogue, Elkins Park, Penn. (Frank Lloyd Wright)
Kalita Humphreys Theatre, Dallas (Frank Lloyd Wright)
Concordia Senior College, Fort Wayne, Ind. (Eero Saarinen)
Time-Life Building, New York (Harrison, Abramovitz, Harris)
Hockey Rink, Yale University, New Haven, Conn. (Eero Saarinen)
Stanford University Medical Center, Palo Alto, Calif. (Edward Durell Stone)
Asia House, New York (Philip Johnson)

Important Exhibitions

Museums

New York: *Metropolitan:* French drawings from American collections; Homer and Gauguin retrospectives; Ceramic international exhibition. *Museum of Modern Art:* 20th-century design; Miró retrospective; The new American painting; Recent U.S. sculpture; "New Talent": David Hayes, Ronni Solbert, among others. *Whitney:* American sculpture, including Hopper, Zorach, Weber, O'Keeffe, Calder, Smith, Lipton

Chicago: Lithographs by Max Kahn; Contemporary Swedish fabrics; Rare Dutch drawings; Claude Bentley drawings; Homer and Gauguin retrospectives

Washington, Cleveland, Chicago, San Francisco: 150 Dutch paintings from the 15th to the 20th century

Washington: Impressionist and postimpressionist painting (on loan from private collections)

Toledo, Minneapolis: Poussin

Cincinnati: Robert Lehmann's American art collection

Baltimore: "The Age of Elegance: The Rococo"

Art Briefs

The Solomon R. Guggenheim Museum, New York City, opens • A Gilbert Stuart portrait of Thomas Jefferson is discovered • Van Gogh's *Park of the Hospital at Saint Rémy* sells for $74,000.

Dance

Raissa Struchkova, and Vladimir Levashev. Jerome Robbins's Ballets U.S.A. creates a sensation in Europe.

Premieres

New York City Ballet: *Episodes* (Martha Graham, George Balanchine), Graham, Sallie Wilson

San Francisco: *Danses Concertantes* (Lew Christensen, Stravinsky)

Alwin Nikolais, *Totem*

Bolshoi Ballet. *Movie Star News.*

The Bolshoi Theatre Ballet of Moscow performs to record audiences with Galina Ulanova in *Romeo and Juliet;* other dancers include Maya Plisetskaya,

Books

Fiction

Critics' Choice
Malcolm, James Purdy
Goodbye Columbus and Five Short Stories, Philip Roth
The Poorhouse Fair, John Updike
The Sirens of Titan, Kurt Vonnegut
Henderson, the Rain King, Saul Bellow
The Mansion, William Faulkner
The Haunting of Hill House, Shirley Jackson
The Little Disturbances of Man, Grace Paley
The Empire City, Paul Goodman
The Naked Lunch, William Burroughs
🐦 *A Change of Heart*, Michel Butor

Best-Sellers
Exodus, Leon Uris
Doctor Zhivago, Boris Pasternak
Hawaii, James Michener
Advise and Consent, Allen Drury
Lady Chatterley's Lover, D. H. Lawrence
The Ugly American, William J. Lederer, Eugene L. Burdick
Lolita, Vladimir Nabokov
Poor No More, Robert Ruark
Mrs. 'Arris Goes to Paris, Paul Gallico
Dear and Glorious Physician, Taylor Caldwell

Nonfiction

Critics' Choice
Education and Freedom, Hyman Rickover
The American High School Today, James Bryant Conant
The Americans: The Colonial Experience, Daniel Boorstein
Advertisements for Myself, Norman Mailer
Life against Death. Norman O. Brown
The Question of Hamlet, Harry Levin
The Tragedy of American Diplomacy, William Appleman Williams
The Coming of the New Deal, Arthur Schlesinger, Jr.
The House of Intellect, Jacques Barzun
The Civil War: A Narrative, Shelby Foote
A History of Western Morals, Crane Brinton
James Joyce, Richard Ellmann
🐦 *The Two Cultures*, C. P. Snow
🐦 *The Phenomenon of Man*, Pierre Teilhard de Chardin

Best-Sellers
'Twixt Twelve and Twenty, Pat Boone
Folk Medicine, D. C. Jarvis
For 2¢ Plain, Harry Golden

The Status Seekers, Vance Packard
Act One, Moss Hart
Charley Weaver's Letters from Mamma, Cliff Arquette
The General Foods Kitchens Cookbook
Only in America, Harry Golden
Mine Enemy Grows Older, Alexander King
Elements of Style, William Strunk, Jr., E. B. White

Poetry
Robert Lowell, *Life Studies*
E. E. Cummings, *100 Selected Poems*
James Wright, *Saint Judas*
Robert Duncan, *Selected Poems, 1942–1950*
Jack Kerouac, *Mexico City Blues*
David Wagoner, *A Place to Stand*

Pulitzer Prizes
Advise and Consent, Allen Drury (fiction)
In the Days of McKinley, Margaret Leech (U.S. history)
John Paul Jones, Samuel Eliot Morison (biography)
Heart's Needle, William Snodgrass (poetry)

Science and Technology

Louis Leakey discovers the skull of Australopithecus (man-ape), 1.78 million years old, in the Olduvai Gorge, Tanganyika.
The Pioneer IV space probe passes the moon and heads into orbit around the sun.
The navy successfully orbits a Vanguard satellite, which will be the first weather station in space.
The navy develops a radar system to monitor Soviet nuclear tests and rocket launchings.
The red-eye, a heat-seeking missile, is developed.
Hypnosis, as a medical aid, is sanctioned by the AMA.

DNA isolated from a cancer-causing virus is found to cause cancer on its own.
🐦 Soviet Lunik II becomes the first man-made object to strike the moon; Lunik III takes the first photos of the moon's hidden side.

Nobel Prize
Emilio Segrè and Owen Chamberlain win the prize in physics for demonstrating the existence of the anti-proton. Severo Ochoa and Arthur Kornberg win in physiology and medicine for work on chromosomes.

Sports

Baseball

Harvey Haddix (Pittsburgh, NL) pitches 12 perfect innings against Milwaukee before giving up a hit in the 13th inning.

Rocky Colavito (Cleveland, AL) hits four home runs in one game.

Early Wynn (Chicago, AL) wins the Cy Young Award.

Champions

Batting	Pitching
Henry Aaron (Milwaukee, NL), .355	Elroy Face (Pittsburgh, NL), 18–1
Harvey Kuenn (Detroit, AL), .353	Robert Shaw (Chicago, AL), 18–6
	Home runs
	Ed Matthews (Milwaukee, NL), 46

Football

The American Football League is organized by Lamar Hunt with eight teams.

Vince Lombardi becomes Green Bay coach.

NFL Season Leaders: Charles Conerly (NY), passing; Jim Brown (Cleveland), rushing, 1,329 yards; Ray Berry (Baltimore), receiving.

College All-Americans: Bill Carpenter (E), Army; Charley Flowers (B), Mississippi; Billy Cannon (B), Louisiana State; Maxie Baughan (C), Georgia Tech

Bowls (Jan. 1, 1960)

Rose: Washington 44–Wisconsin 8

Orange: Georgia 14–Missouri 0

Cotton: Syracuse 23–Texas 14

Sugar: Mississippi 21–Louisiana State 0

Basketball

Wilt Chamberlain (Philadelphia) debuts.

NBA All-Pro First Team: Bob Pettit (St. Louis), Elgin Baylor (Minneapolis), Bill Russell (Boston), Bob Cousy (Boston), Bill Sharman (Boston)

Other Sports

Hockey: The Montreal Canadiens win their third straight Stanley Cup.

Winners

World Series	MVP
Los Angeles (NL) 4	Bob Pettit, St. Louis
Chicago (AL) 2	*College Basketball*
MVP	California
NL–Ernie Banks, Chicago	*Player of the Year*
AL–Nelson Fox, Chicago	Oscar Robertson,
NFL	Cincinnati
Baltimore 31–New York 16	*Stanley Cup*
MVP	Montreal
Charles Conerly, New York	*US Tennis Open*
College Football	Men: Neale Fraser
Louisiana State, Syracuse	Women: Maria Bueno
Heisman Trophy	*USGA Open*
Billy Cannon, Louisiana	Bill Casper, Jr.
State University	*Kentucky Derby*
NBA Championship	Tommy Lee (W.
Boston 4–Minneapolis 0	Shoemaker, jockey)

Fashion

For Women: College girls wear brass button blazers, chesterfields, reversible or belted fur-trimmed coats, straight skirts with a dirndl fullness at the hip, and pleated skirts. Leotards with sleeveless jumpers are especially popular with massive jewelry or multiple strands of necklaces, along with tartans, madras plaids, and leather ensembles. Soft boots of tight, hugging, light suede appear. Shirtwaists remain a favorite, but more stylish dresses redefine the waistline in fitted styles in muted taupes, blues, black-white, blue-orange, and blue, the color of the year. At night the black cocktail dress with plunging neckline appears. A medium heel with rounded toe replaces spike heels.

High-fashion notes: Givenchy's soft jacket and cuffed skirt; Balenciaga and Givenchy's loose sleeve, and high neck blouse over slim skirt

For Men: The Continental look challenges the Ivy look, and pattern becomes predominant with richer fabrics and offbeat colors. Cuffless pants are more form fitting, and although still three-buttoned, jackets are narrower and shorter, with square shoulders and side vents; lapels are semipeaked, and pockets slant backward. Vests appear in different fabrics and colors, along with spread-collar shirts and silk, figure-decorated ties. Shoes are slimmer, with pointed toes.

Kaleidoscope

- A *Look* magazine poll on moral attitudes reports a moral relativity based on group acceptance: one should do whatever he wants as long as it would be accepted by the neighbors.
- TV quiz shows remain under investigation; in House hearings, producers Jack Barry and Dan Enright and contestant Charles Van Doren admit to "controls." Disc jockeys also come under investigation for accepting "payola."
- Letters to NBC are 5 to 1 against the firing of Charles Van Doren, hired by the network as an announcer; Columbia College students also rally to protest Van Doren's dismissal.
- After rigorous testing, the "Mercury Seven" astronauts are chosen: John Glenn, Scott Carpenter, Virgil Grissom, Gordon Cooper, Walter Schirra, Donald Slayton, and Alan Shepard.
- Eighty-six percent of the population owns a TV; the average person watches it 42 hours a week.
- Perry Como signs a $25 million contract with Kraft Foods.
- To combat TV's popularity, Hollywood makes more racy films like *Pillow Talk, Some Like It Hot, North by Northwest,* and *Anatomy of a Murder.*
- The government experiments with programs for bright students; languages are introduced in grade school; early college admissions are encouraged.
- Japanese-Americans whose citizenship was surrendered during the war gain restitution.
- Nixon and Khrushchev debate in the kitchen of a model home at the U.S. National Exhibition in Moscow.
- On Khrushchev's visit to Washington, he comments to CIA director Allen Dulles: "I believe we get the same reports—and probably from the same people."
- Oklahoma finally repeals Prohibition, which came with statehood in 1907.
- The Lincoln penny is redesigned with the Lincoln Memorial on one side.
- At the American National Exhibition in Moscow, Rep. Frances E. Walters (D, Pa.) associates many of the 67 artists on display with "communist fronts and causes"; Eisenhower stands by the artists, who include Andrew Wyeth, Ben Shahn, Robert Motherwell, Willem de Kooning, and Jackson Pollock.
- Modern art is declared duty free by a bill signed into law.
- After a USSR nuclear testing period, reports are released of a 300 percent increase in atmospheric radioactivity in the eastern United States.
- A contaminated-cranberries scare around Thanksgiving frightens millions of Americans.
- General Motors redesigns its cars with larger portholes and more chrome; small cars, like the Falcon, become popular; the Lark is introduced. Cadillac is designed with a large expanse of rear glass, a "jeweled" rear grill, pointed fins, "cruise control" heating units, electric door locks, and air conditioning.

Jonas Salk, inventor of the first polio vaccine. *Copyright Washington Post. Reprinted by permission of D.C. Public Library.*

The Chrysler has swivel seats, electric mirrors, and automatic headlight dimmers.
- The total of deaths from auto accidents in the U.S. surpasses the total of American deaths in war.
- The average car costs $1,180 ($1,300 in 1939).
- Rock and roll stars Buddy Holly, Ritchie Valens, and the Big Bopper are killed in a plane crash.
- Dell pays a record $265,000 for the paperback rights to *Return to Peyton Place.*
- Khrushchev is denied entrance to Disneyland because security cannot be guaranteed.
- Eisenhower is welcomed by millions in India and hailed as the "Prince of Peace."
- In *Life against Death,* a psychoanalytic interpretation of history, Norman O. Brown argues for "polymorphous perversity," a return to intuition and rejection of rationality.

Fads: Go-karting; black leotards; do-it-yourself sports (boating, bowling); western paraphernalia, like toy guns; parachute jumping as a sport

New Words and Usages: A gas, cut out, get with it, gung ho, joint, head, make the scene, a groove, bugged, chick

First Appearances: Transparent plastic bags for clothing, weather station, movies with scent (*Behind the Great Wall),* nuclear merchant ship (*Savannah)*

THE *Sixties*

"Think of the time we're living through. Both of us young, with health, and two wonderful children—and to live through all this." Jacqueline Kennedy. *Library of Congress.*

Statistics

Vital
Population: 177,830,000
  Urban/rural: 125/54
  Farm: 8.7%
Life expectancy
  Male: 66.6
  Female: 73.1
Births/1,000: 23.7
Marriages/1,000: 8.5
Divorces/1,000: 2.2
Deaths/1,000: 9.5
  per 100,000
    Heart: 522
    Cancer: 149
    Tuberculosis: 6
    Car accidents: 21.3

Economic
Unemployed: 3,852,000
GNP: $503.7 billion
Federal budget: $92.3 billion
National debt: $286.3 billion
Union membership: 17.5
  million
Strikes: 3,333
Prime rate: 3.9%
Car sales: 6,674,200
Average salary: $4,743

Social
Homicides/100,000: 4.7
Suicides/100,000: 10.6
Lynchings: 0
Labor force male/female:
  49/23
Social welfare: $52.3 billion
Public education: $15.6 billion
College degrees
  Bachelors'
    Male: 253,000
    Female: 157,000
  Doctorates
    Male: 8,801
    Female: 1,028
Attendance
  Movies (weekly): 40 million
  Baseball (yearly): 20.3
    million

Consumer
Consumer Price Index
  (1967 = 100): 88.7
Eggs: 58¢ (doz.)
Milk: 26¢ (qt.)
Bread: 20¢ (loaf)
Butter: 75¢ (lb.)
Bacon: 66¢ (lb.)
Round steak: $1.06 (lb.)
Oranges: 75¢ (doz.)
Coffee: 75¢ (lb.)

The sixties were a time of momentous social movements and sweeping legislation, of remarkable space achievements and tragic assassinations, a time during which the longest war and most active antiwar protest in American history took place. Although the economy prospered, a social and political idealism challenged the materialistic values and conformity of the fifties with an energy that effected changes throughout the American scene. The youth movement, with its assault on authority ("the establishment"), gained an influence that was unprecedented in American history.

The decade began with a new type of leadership. John Kennedy—young, handsome, Harvard educated, wealthy, and Catholic—won broad public acclaim on the first televised presidential debate. By the barest popular majority, the dashing knight of Camelot defeated Richard Nixon to succeed the fatherly Dwight Eisenhower. Kennedy faltered at the Bay of Pigs but demonstrated his capability in the Cuban missile crisis. He built conventional forces, accelerated the production of atomic missiles, cut taxes to stimulate the economy, and embarked on a massive space program; he also established the Peace Corps and proposed civil rights legislation. Kennedy brought to the presidency a youthful, sophisticated, and widely admired style. His wife, Jacqueline, possessed a vibrant beauty and caché that also elicited voguish emulation. By 1963, the country was alive and hopeful, although, on the domestic scene, few changes had yet been made.

The day of Kennedy's assassination, much like December 7, 1941, is one of the few days of national import on which most Americans alive at the time can trace their whereabouts. The tragic, senseless death of a man in the prime of life who embodied so much of the American ideal of intelligence, power, and generosity of spirit was taken by the grieving nation as evidence of a violent, dark side to the national character, of a spiritual viciousness that underlay the country's material well being.

Indeed, there did remain an intolerable shame in American life—the persistent denial of rights and subjection to humiliating indignities of blacks. Starting in the late fifties, increasing numbers of civil rights advocates had begun to challenge racial bigotry in the laws and mores of the land. In the early sixties, a major assault was mounted: blacks and some white supporters sat in at segregated lunch counters, boycotted segregated buses, sought to integrate white colleges, and organized marches on southern towns for voting rights. Their efforts were often brutally opposed, and the struggle was bloody. Their unifying force, nevertheless, was one of those great leaders that just causes sometimes find. Espousing the Gandhian ideology of nonviolent civil disobedience, Martin Luther King led many of the marches, and his courage and brilliant power of expression gave an irresistible moral and spiritual impetus to the undeniable justice of his message. More than 250,000 at the 1963 Washington, D.C., civil rights march heard his "I have a dream" speech. In JFK's successor, Lyndon Johnson, Dr. King found an ally who would propose the legislation to codify the rights for which he fought. The civil rights bill of 1964 and the Voting Rights Act of 1965 made blacks at least equal before the law. That Congress passed these bills and other Johnson "Great Society" legislation, like Medicare and the poverty program, indicated, perhaps, that America yearned to fulfill its basic ideals and that material well-being alone was not sufficient; government had a responsibility for social change.

Much of the remaining decade involved youthful revolt against the establishment. Although Johnson had campaigned and won a giant victory as a champion of peace and social progress, he began sending combat troops to Vietnam in 1965. Many young people, already involved in the civil rights movement, saw the war as a further example of imperialistic might and materialist greed. As the "best and the brightest" of the administration pursued the war with increasing troop requirements and military power, a widening gap grew between a government that promised victory "around the corner" for a just cause and an increasing portion of the public that saw wanton destruction and defeat in a dubious or immoral war. America's lasting involvement in Vietnam undoubtedly gave energy and a broad base of adult support to the rebel youth and their cause.

The manifestations of antiestablishment sentiments were diverse, and they filtered through much of society. Dress and grooming changes were most visible. Hairstyles, especially for men, grew longer and wilder; beards and mustaches became popular. Women's skirts rose to mid-thigh, and bras were discarded. A casual unisex style favored faded jeans and decorated T-shirts. Large numbers of young people, many from middle-class backgrounds, "dropped out." Called "hippies," they advocated "alternate life-styles," "doing your own thing," and being "laid back." They proposed "turning on" and "making love, not war." Drug use increased, especially marijuana and LSD ("acid"), as a vehicle to more authentic experience ("trips"). Some went to live together in "communes"; others espoused meditation, Zen, astrology, and cult religions. Many sought to evade the draft by remaining in school or leaving the country. They adored the Beatles and later turned to "acid rock," practiced by such groups as the Rolling Stones, Big Brother with Janis Joplin, Jimi Hendrix, Grateful Dead, and Jefferson Airplane. Bob Dylan's and Joan Baez's folk lyrics vocalized

Martin Luther King with Lyndon Johnson, as the president signs the Voting Rights Act. Johnson, in proposing the bill, uses the civil rights motto "We Shall Overcome." *LBJ Library.*

their credo: "The Times They Are a-Changin'." They danced with uninhibited sensuality in discos with light shows and psychedelic posters. Late in the decade, they gathered, in astonishing numbers, at public concerts to celebrate their values and community.

College campuses became a major site of demonstration. Initially focused in forums such as teach-ins and marches, protest later took the form of militant sit-ins (for example, at Columbia University) or armed occupation (Cornell), and many colleges and universities were forced to close down temporarily. Students later demanded the right to assess faculty, determine curriculum, and monitor university policy. They gathered off-campus as well, their most electrifying demonstration the 1967 March on the Pentagon celebrated in Norman Mailer's *Armies of the Night.*

The black movement also changed from the passive resistance of Martin Luther King to the "black power" of Stokely Carmichael. The initial unity of the civil rights movement fragmented, as groups such as SNIC, CORE, and the Black Panthers espoused a more militant black posture, ranging from an emphasis on black identity ("Black is Beautiful") to black separatism. From Watts to Harlem, ghetto riots resulted in numerous deaths and widespread property destruction.

The Supreme Court, headed by Earl Warren, issued rulings that led to major social change. Those that prohibited school prayer, assured legal counsel for the poor, limited censorship of sexual material, and increased the rights of the accused were among the most far-reaching.

Changes were evident elsewhere in American life. Pop artists, like Robert Rauschenberg, Roy Lichtenstein, Andy Warhol, and Jasper Johns, blurred the distinction between popular and high culture. "Camp" did the same. "Happenings" expressed a wish for a more spontaneous, less conventionally structured art form, as in the sculptured forms of Edward Kienholz or the music of John Cage; the Moog synthesizer produced an entirely new sound. Writers such as Truman Capote *(In Cold Blood),* Norman Mailer, and Tom Wolfe, blurred the distinction between fact and fiction. Postmoderns like John Barth, Donald Barthelme, and Robert Coover challenged the sanctity of language as a viable expression of perception and communication.

More traditional in form, works like Joseph Heller's *Catch-22* and Ken Kesey's *One Flew over the Cuckoo's Nest* portrayed as heroes the victims of what they envisioned as a basically insane, inhuman, authoritarian system. A vigorous black literature condemned a racist white society, ranging from James Baldwin's warning *The Fire Next Time* to Eldridge Cleaver's savage denunciation *Soul on Ice.* Conventional attitudes about women came under attack as Betty Friedan condemned the "feminine mystique" of the woman as housewife and mother in a male-dominated culture that subjugates women to male needs. Masters and Johnson demonstrated the myth of vaginal orgasm. Rachel Carson in *The Silent Spring* indicted industry for poisoning the environment; in *Unsafe at Any Speed,* Ralph Nader attacked the automakers and government for callous disregard of highway safety. (Nader, like Friedan and Baldwin, gathered large, idealistic followings.) Enovid, the first marketed oral contraceptive, enhanced the ease of sexual liberation, and institutes like Esalen presented opportunities for freedom from social and sexual convention.

A number of films also expressed the unique sixties sensibility—*Dr. Strangelove, The Graduate, Bob and Carol and Ted and Alice,* and *Easy Rider. Who's Afraid of Virginia Woolf?* violated accepted movie standards in its language and subject matter and was responsible for a new film code. In the late sixties, the legitimate stage, as well as movies, began to routinely portray the previously taboo. *Hair, Oh! Calcutta!,* and *I Am Curious (Yellow)* contained nudity, simulated and real sex, and unrestricted language. Among other emblems of the times were the epic of onanism *Portnoy's Complaint,* topless bathing suits, the Truth in Packaging law, Valium, go-go girls, and the list of rare and endangered species.

Although protest may have been the leading edge of the sixties, it was not, as Nixon's election was to indicate, everyone's "bag." With a booming economy, many Americans were not involved in

The Beatles revolutionize American song and hairstyles. Their first hit is "I Want to Hold Your Hand."

Neil Armstrong and Buzz Aldrin plant the American flag on the moon, July 20, 1969. *Courtesy NASA.*

protest, and they pursued less rebellious life-styles. Rural sit-coms like "The Beverly Hillbillies" and "Green Acres" topped the TV ratings, along with detective fare like "Kojak" and spy spoofs like "The Man from U.N.C.L.E." Films like Sean Connery's James Bond series enjoyed great popularity, as did Julie Andrews flying about as *Mary Poppins.* Barbra Streisand became a superstar, and her frizzed look and eclectic dress style were much copied. Neil Simon began his Broadway career with *Barefoot in the Park,* and Charles Shultz's *Peanuts* books sold widely. *Valley of the Dolls* (about show biz pill popping) and *The Godfather* were the enormous sellers, and *The Games People Play,* the top self-help book of the decade. The art and music worlds of the sixties produced some of the most interesting works in American cultural history; in sculpture alone were the great works of David Smith, Reuben Nakian, Louise Nevelson, Eva Hesse, George Segal, and Richard Lippold. In sports a new pro-football league, the AFL, challenged the NFL, and eventually the two merged to create a sensational new championship game to rival the World Series, the Super Bowl. Sports superstars included Joe Namath, Willie Mays, Sandy Koufax, Bill Russell, Wilt Chamberlain, and Cassius Clay.

When the North Vietnamese mounted their Tet offensive in 1968, many believed that despite 500,000 combat troops in Vietnam, the United States was still far from victory. After antiwar candidate Eugene McCarthy showed strongly in the New Hampshire primary, LBJ announced that he would not seek reelection, and Robert Kennedy entered the race. With student rebellions sweeping the world from Mexico to France to Japan, 1968 may well be seen as

the apotheosis of the sixties; Martin Luther King, Jr. was assassinated, and widespread rioting followed; Robert Kennedy, like his brother John, was assassinated; protesters led by the Youth International Party (yippies), clashed with Chicago mayor Richard Daley's police and turned the Democratic Convention into a battlefield.

Although the presidential election was close, Richard Nixon, appealing to the "silent majority," won. Committed to "peace with honor," he nonetheless called for, and in 1969 began, troop withdrawal. He established a lottery system for the draft, hoping to undercut student rebellion. While 1969 was the year that 500,000 young people gathered at Woodstock for a free concert, the public tide that was already turning against youth was further strengthened by two highly publicized crimes, the Manson family murders and a killing at a Rolling Stones concert. Adult sympathy for protest had centered on the young people's ideals, but these two events appeared to lend credence to the Nixon-Agnew indictment of the "permissivists."

Indeed, 1969 was also the year of a great establishment triumph. Space accomplishments had multiplied during the decade, and while some condemned the space program as pyramid building, most of the public watched with intense interest as men with "the right stuff," like Neil Armstrong, Buzz Aldrin, and Michael Collins, made increasingly complex journeys into space. On July 20, 1969, 700 million throughout the world witnessed, via television, an American plant the first step on the moon—a happening to forever fire the imagination of human possibility.

1960

In the News

IKE SAYS ATLAS ICBM CAN GO 5,000 MILES . . . KHRUSHCHEV CLAIMS SOVIET ICBM GOES 7,762 MILES . . . BLACKS SIT IN AT GREENSBORO, NORTH CAROLINA, LUNCH COUNTER . . . FRENCH TEST FIRST A-BOMB IN SAHARA . . . CASTRO AND RUSSIANS SIGN ECONOMIC AGREEMENT . . . SOUTH AFRICAN POLICE KILL 92 BLACKS DURING DEMONSTRATION AT SHARPEVILLE . . . CIVIL RIGHTS ACT PROVIDES VOTING REFEREES . . . CHINESE COMMUNISTS ATTACK MODERN REVISIONISM IN FIRST RIFT WITH MOSCOW . . . U-2 RECONNAISSANCE JET, WITH PILOT GARY POWERS, IS SHOT DOWN OVER RUSSIA . . . MURDERER-WRITER CARYL CHESSMAN IS EXECUTED, INTERNATIONAL PROTESTS OCCUR . . . BRITISH PRINCESS MARGARET AND PHOTOGRAPHER TONY ARMSTRONG-JONES MARRY . . . KHRUSHCHEV, IN PARIS, DENOUNCES U.S. OVER POWERS INCIDENT, SUMMIT IS CALLED OFF . . . ATLAS ICBM GOES 9,000 MILES . . . ISRAELIS KIDNAP ADOLF EICHMANN FROM ARGENTINA TO JERUSALEM . . . IKE POSTPONES VISIT TO JAPAN BECAUSE OF ANTI-U.S. DEMONSTRATIONS . . . BELGIAN CONGO BECOMES INDEPENDENT . . . IKE CUTS CUBAN SUGAR QUOTA AND THREATENS COMMUNISTS IN WESTERN HEMISPHERE, KHRUSHCHEV THREATENS RETALIATION . . . JOHN F. KENNEDY WINS DEMOCRATIC NOMINATION, NIXON WINS GOP . . . UN FORCES ARE SENT TO CONGO TO RESTORE PEACE . . . CUBA EXPROPRIATES U.S. ASSETS . . . GARY POWERS IS SENTENCED TO 70 YEARS IN MOSCOW . . . CONGO PRESIDENT KASAVUBU EJECTS LEFTIST PREMIER LUMUMBA . . . KHRUSHCHEV AT U.N. POUNDS SHOE IN ANGER . . . DE GAULLE ANNOUNCES SELF-RULE AND REFERENDUM FOR INDEPENDENCE IN ALGERIA . . . KENNEDY WINS NARROW VICTORY BY 112,881, DEMOCRATS SWEEP CONGRESS . . . TWO WHITE PUBLIC SCHOOLS IN NEW ORLEANS ARE FIRST TO INTEGRATE . . . TWO AIRLINERS COLLIDE OVER STATEN ISLAND, 134 DIE.

Quotes

We've grown unbelievably prosperous, and we maunder along in a stupor of fat."

— Eric Goldman

"The politics of the Fifties were . . . the politics of fatigue . . . [and student] apathy probably unexampled in history. . . . [We chose] to invest not in people but in things."

— Arthur Schlesinger, Jr., "The Mood in Politics"

"We don't expect to live in [these houses] . . . very long. Some of the junior executives expect to become seniors . . . and a lot of us will be transferred all over the U.S. . . . We want to be sure there is a good re-sale value."

— Deerfield, Illinois, couple agitating against black occupancy

"Our society is an immense stamping ground for the careless production of underdeveloped and malformed human beings . . . [not] concerned with moral issues, with serious purposes, or with human dignity."

— Robert Heilbroner

"[Nixon] never told the truth in his life."

— Harry S Truman

"Our Secretary of Defense now frankly concedes that . . . the Soviet Union . . . will have a three-to-one superiority in the intercontinental ballistic missile."

— John F. Kennedy

"The Democrats were going to nominate a man who, no matter how serious his political dedication might be, was indisputably and willy-nilly going to be seen as a great box-office actor, and the consequences of that were staggering."

— Norman Mailer, "Superman Comes to the Supermarket"

"[We need] a new generation of leadership—new men to cope with new problems and new opportunities."

— John F. Kennedy

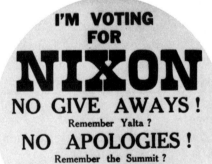

Pro-Nixon button. An October Gallup poll calls the race too close to call. *Smithsonian Institution.*

Ads

One thing leads to another. Babies just like mother used to make. But . . . young adults make them faster than ever. . . . These growing families buy by the gallon. . . . You see them throng shopping centers and [we] got them first.

(Redbook)

Stop right now and forget everything you ever knew about being a blonde. Up to now you could never be any of these delicate blondes.

(Clairol)

Here's the new white hexachlorophene paste with the cool clean refreshing minty taste. It's the one that kills decay germs best of all leading brands.

(Ipana)

No hits and misses. No dibs, dabs, and splatters.

(5-Day Deodorant Pads)

Around the world, the same standard of excellence you have learned to expect—250 branch offices, 14 manufacturing plants, 33,000 employees.

(IBM Machines)

Small wonder.

(Volkswagen)

Nothing else you use so often does so much yet costs so little. And the more you use it the more valuable it becomes.

(Bell Telephone)

Don't spread the cold. . . . Spread the word.

(Coldene Cold Tablets)

A homemade product, juvenile delinquency can be stopped at home.

(Public Service Ad)

TV

Premieres

"Route 66," George Maharis, Martin Milner
"Sing Along with Mitch"
"My Three Sons," Fred MacMurray
"The Flintstones" (first prime-time cartoon)
"The Andy Griffith Show"
"The Bob Newhart Show"
"Saturday Night at the Movies"
"Eyewitness to History," Charles Kuralt
"Face the Nation," Stuart Movins

Party," "Leonard Bernstein and the New York Philharmonic," "Harvest of Shame" (Fred Friendly, David Lowe, Edward R. Murrow), "Astaire Time," "Macbeth" (Maurice Evans, Judith Anderson), "Interview with Nikita Khrushchev" (David Susskind)

Top Ten (Nielsen)

"Gunsmoke," "Wagon Train," "Have Gun, Will Travel," "The Andy Griffith Show," "The Real McCoys," "Rawhide," "Candid Camera," "The Untouchables," "The Price Is Right," "The Jack Benny Show"

Emmy Awards

"Macbeth" (program and drama); "Jack Benny Show" (comedy); "Astaire Time" (variety); Raymond Burr (actor, "Perry Mason"); Barbara Stanwyck (actress, "The Barbara Stanwyck Show"); "Huntley-Brinkley Report" (news)

Specials

"The Nixon-Kennedy Debate," "Winston Churchill: The Valiant Years," "Aaron Copland's Birthday

Of Note

"Howdy Doody" ends after 13 years and 2,343 episodes, as Clarabell, the silent clown, finally speaks: "Goodnight, kids" • CBS's unsponsored coverage of the winter Olympic Games draws unexpectedly high ratings.

Movies

Openings

The Apartment (Billy Wilder), Jack Lemmon, Shirley MacLaine, Fred MacMurray
The Alamo (John Wayne), John Wayne, Richard Widmark, Laurence Harvey
Elmer Gantry (Richard Brooks), Burt Lancaster, Jean Simmons
Never on Sunday (Jules Dassin), Melina Mercouri, Jules Dassin
Psycho (Alfred Hitchcock), Anthony Perkins, Janet Leigh
Inherit the Wind (Stanley Kramer), Spencer Tracy, Fredric March, Gene Kelly
Spartacus (Stanley Kubrick), Kirk Douglas, Laurence Olivier, Jean Simmons
Exodus (Otto Preminger), Paul Newman, Eva Marie Saint, Sal Mineo
Butterfield 8 (Daniel Mann), Elizabeth Taylor, Laurence Harvey
The Fugitive Kind (Sidney Lumet), Marlon Brando, Anna Magnani, Joanne Woodward
The Magnificent Seven (John Sturges), Yul Brynner, Steve McQueen, Eli Wallach
Where the Boys Are (Henry Levin), George Hamilton, Yvette Mimieux

The Virgin Spring (Ingmar Bergman), Max von Sydow, Birgitta Valberg
L'Avventura (Michelangelo Antonioni), Monica Vitti, Gagride Ferzetti
Big Deal on Madonna Street (Mario Monicelli), Vittorio Gassman, Marcello Mastroianni

Academy Awards

Best Picture: *The Apartment*
Best Director: Billy Wilder (*The Apartment*)
Best Actress: Elizabeth Taylor (*Butterfield 8*)
Best Actor: Burt Lancaster (*Elmer Gantry*)

Top Box-Office Stars

Doris Day, Rock Hudson, Cary Grant, Elizabeth Taylor, Debbie Reynolds, Tony Curtis, Sandra Dee, Frank Sinatra, Jack Lemmon, John Wayne

Stars of Tomorrow

Jane Fonda, Stephen Boyd, John Gavin, Susan Kohner, Troy Donahue, Angie Dickinson, Tuesday Weld, Fabian, James Darren, George Hamilton

Popular Music

Art Blakey. *Movie Star News.*

Hit Songs
"Alley Oop"
"Are You Lonesome To-Night"
"Chain Gang"
"If Ever I Would Leave You"
"Never on Sunday"
"Theme from 'The Apartment' "
"Tracy's Theme"
"You Talk Too Much"
"Itsy Bitsy Teenie Weenie Yellow
    Polka Dot Bikini"

Top Records

Albums: *The Sound of Music* (original cast); *Persuasive Percussion* (Terry Snyder and the All Stars); *Nice 'n' Easy* (Frank Sinatra)

Singles: *The Twist* (Chubby Checker); *Georgia on My Mind* (Ray Charles); *It's Now or Never* (Elvis Presley); *Everybody's Somebody's Fool* (Connie Francis); *Where or When* (Dion and the Belmonts); *Puppy Love* (Paul Anka); *Let It Be Me* (Everly Brothers); *I Want to Be Wanted* (Brenda Lee); *Handy Man* (Jimmy Jones); *Ramona* (The Blue Diamonds). Country: *He'll Have to Go* (Jim Reeves)

Grammy Awards
Theme from "A Summer Place," Percy Faith (record); *The Button-Down Mind of Bob Newhart,* Bob Newhart (album); "Theme from *Exodus*" (song)

Jazz and Big Bands
Dave Brubeck continues his experiments with irregular meter in *Time Out;* Ornette Coleman makes "Free Jazz" with free group improvisation and the use of African instruments.
Joe Williams leaves Count Basie; John Coltrane leaves Miles Davis to form his own quartet and records *Meditations.*
A riot occurs at the Newport Jazz Festival.

Top Performers (*Downbeat*)**:** Dizzy Gillespie (soloist); Count Basie, Les Brown (bands); Modern Jazz Quartet (jazz group); Cannonball Adderley, John Coltrane, Buddy DeFranco, Milt Jackson, Herbie Mann (instrumentalists); Ella Fitzgerald, Frank Sinatra (vocalists); Lambert, Hendricks and Ross (vocal group)

Theater

Broadway Openings

Plays
All the Way Home (Tad Mosel), Lillian Gish, Colleen Dewhurst, Arthur Hill
Toys in the Attic (Lillian Hellman), Jason Robards, Jr., Maureen Stapleton, Irene Worth
A Taste of Honey (Shelagh Delaney), Joan Plowright, Angela Lansbury, Billy Dee Williams
Becket (Jean Anouilh), Laurence Olivier, Anthony Quinn
The Best Man (Gore Vidal), Melvyn Douglas, Frank Lovejoy, Lee Tracy
A Thurber Carnival (James Thurber), Tom Ewell, Peggy Cass, Paul Ford
Period of Adjustment (Tennessee Williams), James Daly, Barbara Baxley, Robert Webber
Advise and Consent (Loring Mandel), Richard Kiley, Ed Begley, Chester Morris
The Hostage (Brendan Behan), Alfred Lynch
An Evening with Mike Nichols and Elaine May
Duel of Angels (Jean Giraudoux), Vivien Leigh, Mary Ure

Little Moon of Alban (James Costigan), Robert Redford, Julie Harris, John Justin

Musicals
Irma La Douce (Marguerite Monnot, Julian More, et al.), Keith Mitchell, Elizabeth Seal, Clive Revill
Do Re Mi (Jule Styne, Betty Comden, Adolph Green), Nancy Walker, Phil Silvers
The Fantasticks (Harvey Schmidt, Tom Jones), Jerry Orbach (to be longest running musical in history)
Bye, Bye Birdie (Charles Strouse, Lee Adams), Dick Van Dyke, Chita Rivera, Dick Gautier
Camelot (Frederick Leowe, Alan Jay Lerner), Robert Goulet, Julie Andrews, Richard Burton
The Unsinkable Molly Brown (Meredith Willson), Tammy Grimes, Harve Presnell

Classics and Revivals On and Off Broadway
Krapp's Last Tape (Samuel Beckett), Donald Davis; *Women of Trachis* (Sophocles), Judith Malina; *The Prodigal* (Jack Richardson). *Founded:* Repertory Theatre of Lincoln Center with directors Robert Whitehead and Elia Kazan; APA by Ellis Raab

Theater (cont.)

Regional

Founded: Cincinnati Playhouse in the Park by Brook Jones

Actor's Workshop, San Francisco: *The Birthday Party* (Harold Pinter); *Saint's Day* (John Whiting), premieres

Pulitzer Prize

Fiorello: George Abbott, Jerry Bock, Sheldon Harnick, Jerome Weidman

Tony Awards

The Miracle Worker, William Gibson (play); *Fiorello!* George Abbott, Jerry Bock, Sheldon Harnick, Jerome Weidman, and *The Sound of Music,* Richard Rodgers, Oscar Hammerstein II (musical)

Classical Music

Compositions

Elliott Carter, String Quartet no. 2
Walter Piston, Symphony no. 7
George Perle, Three Movements for Orchestra
Irving Fine, *V-Alcestis*
Paul Creston, Violin Concerto
Milton Babbitt, Composition for Tenor and Six
    Instruments
Aaron Copland, Nonet for Strings
John Cage, *Theatre Piece*
Lukas Foss, *Time Cycle*

Important Events

Anniversaries celebrated throughout the world include the 250th birthday of Pergolesi, 150th of Chopin and Schumann, and 100th of Mahler. Pierre Monteux and Fritz Kreisler are 85; Aaron Copland is 60; Wallingford Riegger is 75. Musical exchanges are numerous: the Israeli Philharmonic and Moscow State symphonies visit the United States. Emil Gilels plays an all-Tchaikovsky concert, New York; Copland, Foss, and Byron Janis visit the USSR. A growing number of festivals present avant-garde "serialism" and electronic pieces. Malcolm Frager, 25, wins the Queen Elisabeth International Music Competition in Brussels after premiering Marcel Poot's Piano Concerto. Sviatoslav Richter tours the United States. At Eugene Ormandy's request, Leopold Stokowski returns, after 19 years, to conduct the Philadelphia Orchestra; he introduces Shirley Verrett, in de Falla's *El amor brujo.*

Conductors in New Locations: Stanislaw Skrowaczewski replaces Antal Dorati in Minneapolis; Georg Solti goes to Los Angeles; John Barbirolli goes to Houston.

First Performances: William Schuman, Symphony no. 7 (Boston); Roger Sessions, Symphony no. 4 (Minneapolis); Walter Piston, Concerto no. 2 for Violin (Pittsburgh); Paul Hindemith, Sinfonietta in E Major (Minneapolis); Samuel Barber, *Toccata Festiva* (Philadelphia), *A Hand of Bridge* (Boston).

Opera

Metropolitan: Anselmo Colzani (debut), *Simon Boccanegra;* Jon Vickers (debut), *I pagliacci;* Leonie Rysanek, Cesare Siepi, Rosalind Elias, Cornell MacNeil, *Nabucco;* Eileen Farrell (debut), *Alcestis;* Hermann Prey, *Tannhaüser.* During *La forza* Leonard Warren dies on stage.

New York City: *The Inspector General* (Werner Egk, premiere)

Dallas: Joan Sutherland (debut), *Alcina;* Sutherland, Giuseppi Taddei, Elisabeth Schwarzkopf, *Don Giovanni*

Chicago: Renata Scotto (debut), Richard Tucker, *La bohème;* Renata Tebaldi, *Fedora* (Giordano); Jon Vickers, Birgit Nilsson, *Die Walküre*

San Francisco: Marilyn Horne, Geraint Evans, *Wozzeck*

Music Notes

Isaac Stern leads a campaign to save Carnegie Hall from destruction; New York City takes title and gives the hall to a nonprofit organization to run • Harold Schonberg replaces Howard Taubman as *New York Times* music critic.

Art _____

Painting

Willem de Kooning, *Door to the River, A Tree in Naples*
Kenneth Noland, *Provence, Whirl*
Frank Stella, *Marquis de Portago*
Sam Francis, *Middle Blue, No. 5*
Edward Hopper, *Second-Story Sunlight*
Robert Indiana, *Moon*
Philip Evergood, *Virginia in the Grotto*
Adolph Gottlieb, *Circular*
Jasper Johns, *Light Bulb*
Morris Louis, *Beta Lambda*

Sculpture

Louise Nevelson, *Sky Cathedral*
Mark di Suvero, *Hankchampion*

Architecture

T.W.A. Terminal, John F. Kennedy Airport, New York (Eero Saarinen)
Union Carbide Building, New York City (Skidmore, Owings, and Merrill)
Climatron, St. Louis, Mo. (Murphy and Mackay)
Colonnades Apartments, Newark, N.J. (Mies van der Rohe)
IBM Watson Research, Yorktown Heights, N.Y. (Edward Durell Stone)
Gateway Center, Pittsburgh (Harrison and Abramovitz)
First Presbyterian Church, Stamford, Conn. (Harrison and Abramovitz)

Important Exhibitions

Museums

New York: *Metropolitan:* "Ancient Art: Sumerian, Mesopotamian, Phoenician, Egyptian, Etruscan, and Roman Works"; 18th-century design; The arts of Denmark. *Museum of Modern Art:* "Monet: Seasons and Moments"; "New Images of Man"; 16 Americans; Art nouveau

Washington: Haniwa—Japanese Burial Mound Figures (sent by the Japanese government to commemorate the centennial of U.S.-Japanese diplomatic relations); Daumier

Detroit: "Masterpieces of Flemish Art—Van Eyck to Bosch"

Chicago: Corot; Japan's modern prints; Primitive art; Prints by Lasansky, Harold Altman, Rembrandt, and Ensor; Corot

Boston: Buddhist sculpture from Gandhara: Courbet; Feininger and Prendergast memorials; Corot

Philadelphia: Cassatt; Courbet; Corot

Robert Rauschenberg, *Summer Rental, Number 2*, 1960. Oil on canvas, 70 × 54″. *Collection of Whitney Museum of American Art. Gift of the Friends of the Whitney Museum of American Art.*

Dallas: Magritte

Venice Biennale: Kline, Guston, and Hofmann represent the United States.

Art Briefs

An unprecedented number of galleries opens throughout the country, with numerous museums under construction • Levels of bidding at auctions soar • The first large-scale American sculpture exhibit is held in Paris; it includes Nevelson and Lassaw • Major sales include Cézanne's *Paysan en blouse bleue* ($406,000) and *Apples* ($200,000), and Braque's *The Violin* ($145,000).

Dance _____

The American Ballet Theatre is the first U.S. company to tour the USSR; Maria Tallchief and Toni Lander join the company.

Premieres

Alvin Ailey: *Revelations*

American Ballet Theatre: *Lady from the Sea* (Birgit Cullberg), Nora Kaye

New York City Ballet: *Monumentum pro Gesualdo* (Balanchine, Stravinsky), Diana Adams, Conrad Ludlow; *Liebeslieder Waltzer* (Balanchine), Adams

Martha Graham: *Acrobats of God*

San Francisco: *Con Amore* (Lew Christensen)

Books

Fiction

Critics' Choice
The Sot-Weed Factor, John Barth
The Waters of Kronos, Conrad Richter
The Magician of Lublin, Isaac Bashevis Singer
Set This House on Fire, William Styron
Rabbit, Run, John Updike
The Magic Christian, Terry Southern
The Violent Bear It Away, Flannery O'Connor
The Ferguson Affair, Ross MacDonald
ᐱ *The Affair,* C. P. Snow

Best-Sellers
Advise and Consent, Allen Drury
Hawaii, James A. Michener
The Leopard, Giuseppe di Lampedusa
The Chapman Report, Irving Wallace
Ourselves to Know, John O'Hara
The Constant Image, Marcia Davenport
Sermons and Soda-Water, John O'Hara

Nonfiction

Critics' Choice
Human Nature and the Human Condition, Joseph Wood Krutch
Love and Death in the American Novel, Leslie Fiedler
Grant Moves South, Bruce Catton
The Politics of Upheaval, Arthur M. Schlesinger, Jr.
Victory in the Pacific, 1945, Samuel Eliot Morison
The End of Ideology, Daniel Bell
The Liberal House, John Kenneth Galbraith
The Stages of Economic Growth, Eugene Rostow
Dictionary of American Slang, ed. Harold Wentworth, Stuart Berg Flexner
The Papers of Benjamin Franklin, ed. L. W. Larabee, W. J. Bell
Growing Up Absurd, Paul Goodman
Listen Yankee: The Revolution in Cuba, C. Wright Mills
Rococo to Cubism in Art and Literature, Wylie Sypher

Best-Sellers
Folk Medicine, D. C. Jarvis
The General Foods Kitchens Cookbook
May This House Be Safe from Tigers, Alexander King
Better Homes and Gardens Dessert Book

The Rise and Fall of the Third Reich, William L. Shirer
The Conscience of a Conservative, Barry Goldwater

Poetry
James Dickey, *Into the Stone and Other Poems*
Kenneth Koch, *Ko: or, A Season on Earth*
W. H. Auden, *Homage to Clio*
Randall Jarrell, *The Woman at the Washington Zoo*
W. S. Merwin, *The Drunk in the Furnace*
Anne Sexton, *To Bedlam and Part Way Back*
Denise Levertov, *With Eyes at the Back of Our Heads*
Charles Olson, *The Maximus Poems*
Gregory Corso, *The Happy Birthday of Death*

Pulitzer Prizes
To Kill a Mockingbird, Harper Lee (fiction)
Between War and Peace: The Potsdam Conference, Herbert Feis (U.S. history)
Charles Sumner and the Coming of the Civil War, David Donald (biography)
Times Three: Selected Verse from Three Decades, Phyllis McGinley (poetry)

Science and Technology

The laser (light amplification caused by stimulated emission of radiation) is created by Theodore Maiman.

Nick Holonyak invents the digital display for pocket calculators and electronic watches.

The first robot to imitate the grasping human hand is employed in a nuclear plant.

Echo I is launched, the world's first communications satellite.

The world's first weather satellite, Tiros I, is launched.

Robert Burns Woodward and German Martin Strell independently synthesize chlorophyll.

Drs. A. Jefferson and D. Gordon use ultrasound to diagnose brain damage.

Several new synthetic penicillins are developed, including cephalosporin, effective against penicillin-resistant organisms.

Nobel Prize
D. A. Glaser wins the prize in physics for the invention of the bubble chamber for the study of subatomic particles. Willard F. Libby wins in chemistry for the atomic time clock to estimate the age of objects by measuring their radioactivity.

Sports

Baseball

The Cy Young Award winner is Vernon Law
(Pittsburgh, NL).

Champions

Batting	Pitching
Pete Runnels (Boston, AL), .320	Ernie Broglio (St. Louis, NL), 21–9
Dick Groat (Pittsburgh, NL), .325	Jim Coates (New York, AL), 13–3
	Home runs
	Ernie Banks (Chicago, NL), 41

Football

Pete Rozelle becomes NFL commissioner.
Paul Hornung (Green Bay) scores a record 176
points. The AFL plays its first season; Houston beats
Los Angeles 24–16 before 32,183 spectators; the
winning player's share is $1,025.

NFL Season Leaders: Milt Plum (Cleveland),
passing; Jim Brown (Cleveland), rushing; Ray Berry
(Baltimore), receiving. **AFL Season Leaders:** Jack
Kemp (Los Angeles), passing; Abner Haynes
(Dallas), rushing; Lionel Taylor (Denver), receiving

College All-Americans: Mike Ditka (E) Pittsburgh,
Bob Lilly (T) Texas Christian, Bill Kilmer (UCLA)

Bowls (Jan. 1, 1961)

Rose: Washington 17–
  Minnesota 7
Orange: Missouri 21–
  Navy 14

Cotton: Duke 7–
  Arkansas 6
Sugar: Mississippi 14–
  Rice 6

Basketball

NBA All-Pro First Team: Bob Pettit (St. Louis),
Elgin Baylor (Minneapolis), Wilt Chamberlain
(Philadelphia), Bob Cousy (Boston), Oscar Robertson
(Cincinnati)

Olympics

At Rome, American gold medal winners include
Rafer Johnson (decathlon, 8,392 pts.), Cassius Clay
(light heavyweight boxing), Wilma Rudolph (100,
11.0s. and 200m, 24.0s.), Ralph Boston (broad jump,
26'7¾"), Don Bragg (pole vault, 15'5⅛"), Al Oerter
(discus, 184'1"). In the Winter Games at Squaw
Valley, California, Carol Heiss and David Jennings
win figure skating. The United States wins ice
hockey.

Other Sports

Boxing: Floyd Patterson knocks out Ingemar
Johansson in the fifth, becoming the first
heavyweight to regain his crown.

Golf: Jack Nicklaus, 20, is second to Arnold Palmer
in the U.S. Open.

Winners

World Series	*MVP*
Pittsburgh (NL) 4	Wilt Chamberlain,
New York (AL) 3	Philadelphia
MVP	*College Basketball*
NL–Richard Groat,	Ohio State
Pittsburgh	*Player of the Year*
AL–Roger Maris, New	Oscar Robertson,
York	Cincinnati
NFL	*Stanley Cup*
Philadelphia 17–Green Bay	Montreal
13	*US Tennis Open*
MVP	Men: Neal Fraser
Norm Van Brocklin, Los	Women: Darlene Hard
Angeles	*USGA Open*
College Football	Arnold Palmer
Minnesota	*Kentucky Derby*
Heisman Trophy	Venetian Way (W. Hartack,
Joe Bellino, Navy	jockey)
NBA Championship	
Boston 4–St. Louis 3	

Fashion

For Women: Mrs. Kennedy becomes the model of
good style in the empire-waist coat and dress, the
slim dirndl or elongated skirt that ends in a tapered
hem, the loose blouse worn with braided sash belt,
and the rich and patterned fabrics. Popular hair
styling involves the bouffant or "fluid bang." The
college set wears abstract expressionist designs in
colors of the harvest or stained glass. Coeds
especially favor culottes, skirts above the knee, and
knickers. Also "really in" are the bikini and chemise.

*High-fashion notes: Norrell's culottes; Thocolette's
topless Liberty Lawn nightdress; Chanel's rough
white tweed suit bound with navy braid; Gernreich's
cutaway diamond swimsuit*

For Men: Continental and British influences appear
in (1) bold prints, plaids, stripes, and checks for sport
jackets and topcoats, and (2) shirt colors in muted
olives, golds, heathers, blue, and grape.

Kaleidoscope ————————————

- Enovid 10, the first oral contraceptive, is marketed at 55 cents a pill.
- Eisenhower summarizes the progress of his presidency as including a 15 percent increase in average family income, 20 percent in real wages, 25 percent in output of goods, and more housing and school construction than ever before.
- Daniel Bell, describing the 1950s' sense of unity and moderation, publishes *The End of Ideology.* Herman Kahn's *On Thermonuclear War* discusses how, with careful planning, only 20 to 30 million Americans will be killed in a nuclear attack.
- Following the Greensboro, N.C., incident when four blacks sit down at a white lunch counter, 70,000 blacks and whites hold sit-ins in more than 100 cities.
- Brooklyn singer Barbra Streisand wins a Thursday night talent contest at a small Greenwich Village club with "A Sleepin' Bee."
- Berry Gordy borrows $800 and starts Motown Records.
- Ebbets Field, former home of the Brooklyn Dodgers, is demolished to become an apartment project site.
- The number of women over 14 in the work force increases from 25 percent in 1940 to 34 percent.
- The census shows large population gains in Nevada, Florida, Alaska, Arizona, and California.
- An estimated 850,000 "war baby" freshmen enter college, bringing total enrollment to 4 million; emergency living quarters are set up in dorm lounges, hotels, and trailer camps.
- Recognizing the new youth power, Pepsi-Cola begins a "For those who think young" campaign.
- John F. Kennedy, Jr., is born on November 25 by cesarean delivery.
- Aluminum cans for food and beverages are manufactured, although 95 percent of all soft drinks and 50 percent of all beer are sold in reusable bottles (reused 40 to 50 times).
- Lucille Ball and Desi Arnaz file for divorce.
- Ernest Evans, playing on Fats Domino's name, becomes Chubby Checker.
- Hollywood continues its permissive trend with films on so-called adult themes, such as *Butterfield 8.*
- The New York Circuit Court of Appeals moves that *Lady Chatterley's Lover* is not obscene.
- A new style that marks home furnishing includes the fusion of different period or national styles with unusual woods like African zebra wood.
- The year's most publicized joke results from NBC's censorship of Jack Paar's story of a WC mistaken for a wayside chapel. Paar is cut off the air for tasteless humor.
- Americans consume 73% fewer potatoes but 25% more fish, poultry, and meat, and 50% more citrus and tomato than in 1940.
- According to a *Downbeat* pool, the most popular male jazz singers are Frank Sinatra, Joe Williams, Mel Torme, Ray Charles, Jon Hendricks, Johnny Mathis, Jimmy Rushing, Bill Henderson, and Nat "King"

"The Flintstones," often compared to "The Honeymooners," is an animated sitcom intended for adult audiences. *Movie Star News.*

Cole; the most popular females are Ella Fitzgerald, Sarah Vaughan, Anita O'Day, Nina Simone, Annie Ross, Peggy Lee, June Christy, Chris Connor, and Dinah Shore.
- The largest TV audience to date, 75 million, watches the first Kennedy-Nixon debate.
- A record number of Broadway shows with distinguished stars fail; the stars include Bette Davis, Lucille Ball, Jack Lemmon, Henry Fonda, Charlton Heston, and John Wayne.
- The Museum of Modern Art, in New York, hosts Swiss Jean Tinguely's *Happening,* a self-destroying mechanical contraption 23 by 27 feet driven by 15 motors and consisting of 80 wheels, a bathtub, toy wagon, and junk objects; it makes musical sounds as it self-destroys.
- The year's most popular hobbies include science kits, rocket models, and plastic car sets; a survey reports that the most popular cartoons are "Peanuts," "Li'l Abner," and "Pogo."

Fads: Comedy records, talkathons, "Ken" (Barbie doll's friend), folk singing in coffee houses

New Words and Usages: Anchorman, bluegrass, compact car, sit-in, American Football League, area rug, balloon satellite, beehive hairdo, cosmonaut, laser, wild card rule, freedom rider

First Appearances: Bulova Accutron, Librium, Xerox 914 copier, felt-tip pen, underseas park (Reef Reserve, Fla.), artificial tanning creams, astroturf, Avron (rayon), soul music ("Spanish Harlem," Ben E. King), law to reduce auto fumes (California), OPEC meeting

1961

Facts and Figures

Economic Profile
  Dow-Jones: ↑ High 734–
    Low 610
  GNP: +3%
  Inflation: +1.9%
  Unemployment: 6.7%
Median age, first marriage:
  Male: 22.8 Female: 20.3
Average household size: 3.34
Population over 65: 9%
Population under 10: 21%
Kinney Rent-a-Car, compact:
  $119 a month
Sam Goody hi-fi package
  (Garrard, Harman,
  Kardon): $498
Abercrombie & Fitch:
  Fly rod outfit: $49.95
  Menabone plates: $25 (for
  4)
Schirmer's soprano (13″)
  recorder: $4.50
Black Angus Christmas
  dinner, 8-course: $3.75
Albert's all-the-sirloin-you-
  can-eat: $2.65
Carnegie Hall, Christmas eve
  concert: 50¢
Broadway musical, top: $8.60
Longchamps, New Year's
  Eve: $5–$6

Deaths

Sir Thomas Beecham, Ty
  Cobb, Gary Cooper,
  Marion Davies, Joan
  Davis, Lee De Forest, Carl
  Jung, George S. Kaufman,
  Chico Marx, Richard
  Wright.

In the News

U.S. SEVERS DIPLOMATIC RELATIONS WITH CUBA . . . FRENCH APPROVE DE GAULLE'S ALGERIA REFERENDUM . . . KENNEDY, AT INAUGURATION, CALLS FOR "GRAND, GLOBAL ALLIANCE FOR PROGRESS" . . . PATRICE LUMUMBA IS KILLED BY "HOSTILE TRIBESMEN," USSR BLAMES U.S. . . . 29 ELECTRIC EQUIPMENT MANUFACTURERS ARE CONVICTED OF PRICE FIXING . . . KENNEDY CREATES THE PEACE CORPS . . . DEAN RUSK URGES FREE NATIONS TO AID THREATENED SOUTHEAST ASIAN COUNTRIES . . . WARSAW PACT NATIONS CALL NATO "HOTBED OF DANGER" . . . ADOLF EICHMANN GOES ON TRIAL IN JERUSALEM . . . RUSSIANS SEND FIRST MAN INTO SPACE . . . ANTI-CASTRO CUBANS FAIL IN ASSAULT AT BAY OF PIGS . . . FIRST U.S. MANNED FLIGHT, WITH ALAN SHEPARD, STAYS IN SPACE FOR 15 MINUTES . . . JFK URGES ACCELERATED SPACE PROGRAM . . . KENNEDY AND KHRUSHCHEV MEET AT VIENNA SUMMIT . . . EAST GERMANS BUILD BERLIN WALL, TENSIONS RISE . . . FREEDOM RIDERS ARE ATTACKED BY MOBS IN BIRMINGHAM, ALABAMA . . . MARTIAL LAW IS DECLARED IN MONTGOMERY, ALABAMA, AFTER ANTIBLACK VIOLENCE . . . KENNEDY ORDERS REAPPRAISAL OF U.S. MILITARY POWER . . . RAFAEL TRUJILLO, DOMINICAN DICTATOR, IS ASSASSINATED . . . ERNEST HEMINGWAY DIES OF SELF-INFLICTED GUNSHOT . . . SECOND SOVIET MANNED FLIGHT LASTS 25 HOURS . . . RUSSIA WILL RESUME NUCLEAR TESTING . . . KENNEDY ORDERS U.S. RESUMPTION OF N-TESTS . . . JFK ADVISES THE "PRUDENT FAMILY" TO HAVE BOMB SHELTER . . . NONALIGNED NATIONS MEET IN YUGOSLAVIA . . . JFK ASKS TARIFF LIBERALIZATION.

Quotes —————————————

"I invite you to sit down in front of your television sets . . . and stay there. You will see a vast wasteland—a procession of game shows, violence, audience participation shows, formula comedies about totally unbelievable families . . . blood and thunder . . . mayhem, violence, sadism, murder . . . and, endlessly, commercials—many screaming, cajoling, and offending."
— FCC Chairman Newton N. Minow

"What our time needs is mystery. . . . There is a hex on us, the specters in books, the authority of the past; and to exorcise these ghosts is the great work of magical self-liberation. . . . What education does is to put a series of filters over your awareness so that year by year . . . you experience less and less."
— Norman O. Brown

"[We will] pay any price, bear any burden, meet any hardship, support any friend, oppose any foe, to assure the survival and the success of liberty."
— John F. Kennedy

"Orr was crazy and he could be grounded. All he had to do was ask: and as soon as he did he would no longer be crazy and would have to fly more missions. Or be crazy to fly more missions and sane if he didn't, but if he was sane he had to fly them. If he flew them he was crazy, didn't have to; but if he didn't want to he was sane and had to."
— Joseph Heller, *Catch-22*

President John F. Kennedy. At his inauguration he says: "We observe today not a victory of a party but a celebration of freedom. . . . Ask not what your country can do for you; ask what you can do for your country." *Library of Congress.*

"I believe this nation should commit itself to achieving the goal, before this decade is out, of landing a man on the moon and returning him safely to earth."
— John F. Kennedy

"Of a power leading from its strength and pride / Of young ambition eager to be tried, / Firm in our beliefs without dismay, / In any game the nations want to play, / A golden age of poetry and power / Of which this noonday's the beginning hour."
— Robert Frost, "For John F. Kennedy," on his inauguration

Ads —————————————

A, B, C, D, E, . . .
Your public library has arranged these in ways that make you cry, giggle, laugh, love, hate, wonder, ponder and understand.
(American Library Association)

The corset department is obsolete. The slimwear department is here.
(Warner's)

The unwashables. Take 'em for a ride.
(Evan-Picone)

No wonder the English have kept cool for 192 years.
(Gordon's Gin)

Pavlova danced, Caruso sang,
And Mercedes was winning races.
(Mercedes-Benz)

A little green gives you a lot of spring at Ohrbach's.
(Ohrbach's)

Ignore it.
(Western Union)

TV

Premieres
"The Mike Douglas Show"
"Dr. Kildare," Richard Chamberlain
"The Defenders," E. G. Marshall
"Ben Casey," Vince Edwards
"Hazel," Shirley Booth
"Password," Allen Ludden
"Wide World of Sports," Jim McKay
"The Dick Van Dyke Show"
"The Lucy Show," Lucille Ball, Vivian Vance

Top Ten (Nielsen)
"Wagon Train," "Bonanza," "Gunsmoke," "Hazel,"
"Perry Mason," "The Red Skelton Show," "The
Andy Griffith Show," "The Danny Thomas Show,"
"Dr. Kildare," "Candid Camera"

Movies

Openings
West Side Story (Jerome Robbins, Robert Wise),
     Natalie Wood, Rita Moreno, Richard Beymer
The Guns of Navarone (John Lee Thompson),
     Gregory Peck, David Niven, Anthony Quinn
The Hustler (Robert Rossen), Paul Newman, Piper
     Laurie, George C. Scott
Judgment at Nuremberg (Stanley Kramer), Spencer
     Tracy, Burt Lancaster, Judy Garland,
     Maximilian Schell
The Mark (Guy Green), Stuart Whitman, Rod
     Steiger, Maria Schell
Two Women (Vittorio De Sica), Sophia Loren, Raf
     Vallone, Jean-Paul Belmondo
Breakfast at Tiffany's (Blake Edwards), Audrey
     Hepburn, George Peppard
Splendor in the Grass (Elia Kazan), Natalie Wood,
     Warren Beatty
One-Eyed Jacks (Marlon Brando), Marlon Brando,
     Karl Malden
A Raisin in the Sun (Daniel Petrie), Sidney Poitier,
     Diana Sands
The Misfits (John Huston), Clark Gable, Marilyn
     Monroe, Montgomery Clift
Through a Glass Darkly (Ingmar Bergman), Harriet
     Andersson, Max von Sydow, Gunner
     Bjornstrand
Last Year at Marienbad (Alain Resnais), Delphine
     Seyrig
Saturday Night and Sunday Morning (Karel Reisz),
     Albert Finney, Rachel Roberts
Viridiana (Luis Buñuel), Fernando Rey, Sylvia Pinal
Divorce—Italian Style (Pietro Germi), Marcello
     Mastroianni, Daniela Rocca

Specials
"Victoria Regina" (Julie Harris); "Vincent van
Gogh—A Self-Portrait"; "Judy Garland Show";
"Biography of a Bookie Joint" (Jay McMullen)

Emmy Awards
"Victoria Regina" (program); "The Defenders"
(drama); "Bob Newhart Show" (comedy); "Garry
Moore Show" (variety); "New York Philharmonic—
Young People's Concert with Leonard Bernstein"
(children); E. G. Marshall (actor, "The Defenders");
Shirley Booth (actress, "Hazel"); "Huntley-Brinkley
Report" (news)

Paul Newman,
who studied at
Kenyon
College and
the Yale
School of
Drama, stars
in *The Hustler.*
*Movie Star
News.*

Academy Awards
Best Picture: *West Side Story*
Best Director: Robert Wise and Jerome Robbins
     (*West Side Story*)
Best Actress: Sophia Loren (*Two Women*)
Best Actor: Maximilian Schell (*Judgment at
     Nuremberg*)

Top Box-Office Stars
Elizabeth Taylor, Rock Hudson, Doris Day, John
Wayne, Cary Grant, Sandra Dee, Jerry Lewis,
William Holden, Tony Curtis, Elvis Presley

Stars of Tomorrow
Hayley Mills, Nancy Kwan, Horst Buchholtz, Carol
Lynley, Delores Hart, Paula Prentiss, Jim Hutton,
Juliet Prowse, Connie Stevens, Warren Beatty

Popular Music

Hit Songs
"Big Bad John"
"Dum Dum"
"Exodus"
"Michael—Row the Boat Ashore"
"Moon River"
"Pocketful of Miracles"
"Wimoweh"
"Tossin' and Turnin' "
"I Fall to Pieces"
"Runaway"

Top Records

Albums: *The Button-Down Mind Strikes Back* (Bob Newhart); *Wonderland by Night* (Bert Kaempfert); *Exodus* (sound track); *Calcutta* (Lawrence Welk), *Judy at Carnegie Hall* (Judy Garland)

Singles: *Don't Be Cruel / It's Now or Never* (Elvis Presley); *My Heart Has a Mind of Its Own / Where the Boys Are* (Connie Francis); *I Want to Be Wanted* (Brenda Lee); *Tonight, My Love, Tonight / Summer's Gone* (Paul Anka); *Cryin'* (Roy Orbison); *My True Story* (Jive Five); *Tossin' and Turnin'* (Bobby Lewis); *I Fall to Pieces* (Patsy Cline). Country: *Wings of a Dove* (Ferlin Husky); *Hello Wall Street* (Faron Young)

Grammy Awards
Moon River, Henry Mancini (record); *Judy at Carnegie Hall*, Judy Garland (album); "Moon River" (song)

Jazz and Big Bands
Stan Getz's quartet includes Scott LaFaro, Lem Winchester, and Booker Little.

Top Performers *(Downbeat):* Billie Holiday (soloist); Count Basie (band); Modern Jazz Quartet (jazz group); Wes Montgomery, Ray Brown, Max Roach, Cannonball Adderley, John Coltrane (instrumentalists); Ella Fitzgerald, Frank Sinatra (vocalists); Lambert, Hendricks, and Ross (vocal group)

Theater

Broadway Openings

Plays
A Man for All Seasons (Robert Bolt), Paul Scofield
The Night of the Iguana (Tennessee Williams), Margaret Leighton, Alan Webb, Patrick O'Neill
Mary, Mary (Jean Kerr), Barbara Bel Geddes, Barry Nelson
A Far Country (Henry Denker), Sam Wanamaker, Lili Darvas, Patrick O'Neil, Kim Stanley
The Caretaker (Harold Pinter), Alan Bates, Donald Pleasence, Robert Shaw
Gideon (Paddy Chayefsky), Fredric March, George Segal, Douglas Campbell
Rhinoceros (Eugene Ionesco), Zero Mostel, Eli Wallach, Anne Jackson
Come Blow Your Horn (Neil Simon), Hal March
Ross (Terence Rattigan), John Mills
A Shot in the Dark (Harry Kurnitz), Julie Harris, William Shatner, Walter Matthau
Purlie Victorious (Ossie Davis), Ruby Dee, Ossie Davis, Alan Alda, Godfrey Cambridge
The Complaisant Lover (Graham Greene), Michael Redgrave, Googie Withers

Musicals
How to Succeed in Business without Really Trying (Frank Loesser), Robert Morse, Rudy Vallee
Carnival (Bob Merrill), Jerry Orbach, Anna Maria Alberghetti

Milk and Honey (Jerry Herman), Mimi Benzell, Robert Weede, Molly Picon
From the Second City (William Mathieu, revue), Alan Arkin, Barbara Harris
An Evening with Yves Montand, Yves Montand

Classics and Revivals On and Off Broadway
The American Dream (Edward Albee); *The Death of Bessie Smith* (Albee); *Under Milk Wood* (Dylan Thomas); *The Hostage* (Brendan Behan); *Happy Days* (Beckett); *The Blacks* (Jean Genet), James Earl Jones; *The Automobile Graveyard* (Fernando Arrabal). *Founded:* Judson Poets' Theater by Al Carmines

Regional

Actor's Workshop, San Francisco: *Serjeant Musgrave's Dance* (John Arden), premiere

Arena Stage, Washington, D.C.: *The Caucasian Chalk Circle* (Bertolt Brecht, directed by Alan Schneider), American premiere

Pulitzer Prize
All the Way Home, Tad Mosel

Tony Awards
Becket, Jean Anouilh (play); *Bye, Bye Birdie*, Charles Strouse, Lee Adams (musical)

Classical Music _____

Compositions
Earle Brown, *Available Forms II*
Roy Harris, *Canticle of the Sun*
Milton Babbitt, *Composition for Synthesizer, Vision and Prayer*
Morton Feldman, *Durations*
Ralph Shapey, *Incantations*
Karl Korte, Symphony no. 2
Robert Ashley, *Public Opinion Descends upon the Demonstrators*
Robert Ward, *The Crucible*

Important Events
Celebrations include the 150th anniversary of the birth, and 75th anniversary of the death, of Liszt.
Pablo Casals, 84, Alexander Schneider, and Miezeslaw Horszowski play Mendelssohn, Schumann, and Couperin at a White House state dinner, November 13.
Sviatoslav Richter plays six concerts at Carnegie Hall; Artur Rubinstein, 75, gives a "Great Recitals" series—10 concerts in 40 days—and decides not to retire.
Van Cliburn performs and conducts the Prokofiev Piano Concerto no. 3 at Carnegie Hall's "Tribute to Dimitri Mitropoulos."
The lost recordings of Dinu Lipatti are recovered.
The Boston Symphony travels to the Far East.

First Performances
Walter Piston, Symphony no. 7 (Philadelphia), *Symphonic Prelude* (Cleveland); Francis Poulenc, *Gloria* (Boston); Elliott Carter, Double Concerto for Harpsichord, Piano, and Two Chamber Orchestras (New York); David Diamond, Symphony no. 8 (New York); Easley Blackwood, Symphony no. 2 (Cleveland); Henry Cowell, Symphony no. 14 (Washington, D.C.); Roy Harris, *Give Me the Splendid Silent Sun* (Washington, D.C.)

Opera
Grace Bumbry sings in *Tannhäuser* at the Wagner Festival, Bayreuth, under the direction of Wagner's grandson Wieland Wagner.

Metropolitan: A labor controversy between management and orchestra almost cancels the season; JFK asks Secretary of Labor Arthur Goldberg to intervene; Leopold Stokowski, on crutches because of a broken leg, leads *Turandot*. Joan Sutherland (debut), *Lucia di Lammermoor;*

Quote by President Kennedy: "We must regard artistic achievement and action as an integral part of our free society." *CBS Records.*

Leontyne Price, Franco Corelli (debuts), *Il trovatore;* Galina Vishnevskaya (debut), *Aïda;* Franco Corelli, Birgit Nilsson, *Turandot;* Price, Richard Tucker, Anselmo Colzani, *La fanciulla del West*

New York City: *The Wings of the Dove* (Douglas Moore, premiere)

Dallas: Denise Duval (debut), *Thaïs*

Chicago: Joan Sutherland, *Lucia di Lammermoor* (Teatro Massimo, Palermo production) Boris Christoff, *Mefistofele;* Jon Vickers, Birgit Nilsson, *Fidelio; The Harvest* (Vittorio Giannini, premiere)

San Francisco: *Blood Moon* (Norman Dello Joio, premiere)

Music Notes
Modern works most performed include Samuel Barber's Adagio for Strings; Benjamin Britten's *Young Person's Guide to the Orchestra;* Debussy's *La Mer;* Hindemith's *Symphonic Metamorphoses on Themes by Weber;* Prokofiev's *Classical Symphony,* Piano Concerto no. 1 and Violin Concerto no. 2; Ravel's *Second Suite from Daphnis and Chloe* and *La valse;* and Stravinsky's *Firebird Suite.*

Art

Painting

Larry Rivers, *Parts of the Face*
Andrew Wyeth, *Distant Thunder*
Robert Indiana, *Eat/Die, The American Dream I*
Robert Rauschenberg, *Black Market, First Landing Jump*
James Rosenquist, *Waves* (1960–61)
Jim Dine, *Hair*
Cy Twombley, *The Italians*
Robert Motherwell, *Elegy to the Spanish Republic*
Frank Stella, *New Madrid*
Tom Wesselmann, *Still-Life No. 14*
Jasper Johns, *Device, First Landing Jump*

Sculpture

John Chamberlain, *Mr. Press*
Leonard Baskin, *Seated Birdman*
George Segal, *The Man*

Sitting at the Table
David Smith, *Zig IV, Zig III*
Naum Gabo, *Linear Construction No. 4*

Architecture

Assembly Hall, University of Illinois (Harrison and Abramovitz)
Willow Creek Apartments, Palo Alto, Calif. (John C. Warnecke)
Alfred Newton Richards Medical Research Building, University of Pennsylvania (Louis I. Kahn)
Crown Zellerbach, San Francisco (Hertzka and Knowles, Skidmore, Owings, and Merrill)
New York Equitable Building, Chase Manhattan Bank, First National City Bank, New York (Skidmore, Owings, and Merrill)

Important Exhibitions

Shows include "Chinese Treasures" and "Italian Drawings: Masterpieces of Five Centuries" and "34 Objects from King Tutankhamen's Tomb," which begins in Washington, D.C.

Museums

New York: *Metropolitan:* The Arts of Thailand; "The Splendid Century: French 17th-Century Art"; "Italian Drawings"; "Chinese Treasures"; "Musical Instruments of Five Continents." *Museum of Modern Art:* Rothko; Max Ernst retrospective; Steichen; "The Art of Assemblage"; Norbert Kricke. *Guggenheim:* Arensberg and Gallatin collections (Duchamp's "Nude Descending a Staircase, No. 2"). *Brooklyn:* Egyptian sculpture of the Late Period, 700 B.C.–A.D. 100

Washington: The Civil War; Ingres; "34 Objects from King Tutankhamen's Tomb"; "Italian

Drawings"; "The Splendid Century: French 17th-Century Art"; Eakins retrospective

Worcester: Roman portrait sculpture

Boston: "Latin America—New Departures"; "Italian Drawings"; Modigliani; Art of Thailand; Art of Peru; "Chinese Treasures"

Chicago: The arts of Denmark; Contemporary Spanish Painting; Sculptures of Africa; "Dinner with the Presidents"; "Chinese Treasures"; "Max Ernst"; "Italian Drawings"

Chicago, Cleveland: Japanese decorative arts

Pittsburgh: Carnegie International Prize to Alberto Giacometti

Individual Shows

Ryder (Corcoran); Modigliani (Los Angeles); Hartley (Cincinnati, Minneapolis, St. Louis, Portland, New York); Magritte (Dallas); Ernst (New York, Chicago); Rothko (New York); Kuhn (Cincinnati)

Art Briefs

André Breton and Marcel Duchamp organize "Surrealist Intrusion in the Enchanters' Domain," a show that travels through the United States • Philip Johnson's Amon Carter Museum of Western Art opens in Fort Worth, Texas • An unprecedented wave of thefts occurs, including ten Picassos and numerous works by Léger, Miró, and Dufy • Rembrandt's *Artistotle Contemplating the Bust of Homer* is sold to the Metropolitan Museum of Art for a record $2.3 million.

Dance

Russian Rudolf Nureyev asks for political asylum in Paris.

Premieres

American Ballet Theatre: *Moon Reindeer* (Birgit Cullberg); *Etudes* (Harold Lander), Toni Lander, Bruce Marks, Royes Fernandez

New York City Ballet: *Donizetti Variations*

Books

Fiction

Critics' Choice

The Moviegoer, Walker Percy
Seduction of the Minotaur, Anaïs Nin
Catch-22, Joseph Heller
Children Is All, James Purdy
The Spinoza of Market Street, Isaac Bashevis Singer
Tell Me a Riddle, Tillie Olsen
A New Life, Bernard Malamud
Canary in a Cathouse, Kurt Vonnegut
Some People, Places and Things, John Cheever
🐝 *Riders in the Chariot,* Patrick White
🐝 *A House for Mr. Biswas,* V. S. Naipaul

Best-Sellers

The Agony and the Ecstasy, Irving Stone
Franny and Zooey, J. D. Salinger
To Kill a Mockingbird, Harper Lee
Mila 18, Leon Uris
The Carpetbaggers, Harold Robbins
Tropic of Cancer, Henry Miller
Winnie Ille Pu, trans. Alexander Lenard
Daughter of Silence, Morris West
The Winter of Our Discontent, John Steinbeck

Nonfiction

Critics' Choice

Russia and the West under Lenin and Stalin, George F. Kennan
Soviet Foreign Policy after Stalin, David J. Dallin
The Necessity for Choice, Henry A. Kissinger
The Death and Life of Great American Cities, Jane Jacobs
The Predicament of Democratic Man, Edmund Cahn
The Price of Liberty, Alan Barth
The City in History, Lewis Mumford
The Coming Fury, Bruce Catton
The Death of Tragedy, George Steiner
Nobody Knows My Name, James Baldwin
The Myth of Mental Illness, Thomas Szasz

Best-Sellers

The New English Bible: The New Testament
The Rise and Fall of the Third Reich, William L. Shirer
Better Homes and Gardens Sewing Book
Casserole Cook Book
A Nation of Sheep, William Lederer
Better Homes and Gardens Nutrition for Your Family
The Making of the President, 1960, Theodore H. White
Calories Don't Count, Dr. Herman Taller
Betty Crocker's New Picture Cook Book: New Edition
Ring of Bright Water, Gavin Maxwell

Poetry

Richard Wilbur, *Advice to a Prophet*
Charles Olson, *The Distances: Poems*
Allen Ginsberg, *Kaddish, and Other Poems, 1958–60*
Langston Hughes, *Mama*
Lawrence Ferlinghetti, *Starting from San Francisco*
Robert Frost, *Dedication: The Gift Outright*
Robert Lowell, *Imitations*
May Sarton, *Cloud, Stone, Sun, Vine*

Pulitzer Prizes

The Edge of Sadness, Edwin O'Connor (fiction)
The Triumphant Empire, Thunder-Clouds Gather in the West, Lawrence H. Gipson (U.S. history)
Poems, Alan Dugan
No prize is awarded in biography.

Science and Technology

Alan B. Shepard, on the Freedom 7, becomes the first American in space on a suborbital flight, which lasts 15 minutes.

The U.S. Air Force sends a chimpanzee, Enos, on two 17,500-mile revolutions around the earth in 3 hours, 21 minutes.

High-voltage electron beam welding becomes available so silicon chips can be better incorporated into integrated chips.

Jack Lippes produces an inert plastic contraceptive, the intrauterine device (IUD).

Antirhesus serum is administered to Rh-negative mothers to reduce the harmful antibodies produced during pregnancy.

🐝 Russian Yuri Gagarin becomes the first man to travel in space, orbiting in a 6-ton satellite for 1 hour, 48 minutes.

🐝 Russia's G. S. Titov orbits 17 times.

Nobel Prize

Robert Hofstadter wins the prize in physics for work on the shape and size of the atomic nucleus. Georg von Békésy wins in physiology and medicine for work on the cochlea. Melvin Calvin wins in chemistry for establishing the chemical steps during photosynthesis.

Sports

Baseball

Roger Maris (New York, AL) hits 61 home runs in the newly expanded 162-game season. Commissioner Ford Frick decides on an asterisk to distinguish Maris's record from Babe Ruth's; Maris hit 59 in the first 154 games.

Willie Mays (San Francisco, NL) hits 4 home runs in one game.

The American League expands to ten teams with Los Angeles and Washington.

The Cy Young Award is won by Whitey Ford.

Champions

Batting	Pitching
Roberto Clemente (Pittsburgh, NL), .351	John Podres (Los Angeles, NL), 18–5
Norm Cash (Detroit, AL), .361	Whitey Ford (New York, AL), 25–4
	Home runs
	Roger Maris (New York, AL), 61

Football

The NFL championship game at Green Bay draws its first million-dollar gate; the winner's share is a record $5,195.

Canton, Ohio is chosen as the site for the Pro Football Hall of Fame.

NFL Season Leaders: Milt Plum (Cleveland), passing; Jim Brown (Cleveland), rushing; James Phillips (Los Angeles), receiving

AFL Season Leaders: George Blanda (Houston), passing; Billy Cannon (Houston); Lionel Taylor (Denver), receiving

College All-Americans: Ernie Davis (B), Syracuse; Merlin Olsen (T), Utah State; Sandy Stephens (B), Minnesota

Bowls (Jan. 1, 1962)

Rose: Minnesota 21–UCLA 3

Orange: Louisiana State 25–Colorado 7

Cotton: Texas 12–Mississippi 7

Sugar: Alabama 10–Arkansas 3

Basketball

NBA All-Pro First Team: Wilt Chamberlain (Philadelphia), Elgin Baylor (Minneapolis), Oscar Robertson (Cincinnati), Bob Pettit (St. Louis), Jack Twyman (Cincinnati)

Winners

World Series
New York (AL) 4
Cincinnati (NL) 1
MVP
NL–Frank Robinson, Cincinnati
AL–Roger Maris, New York
NFL
Green Bay 37–New York 0
MVP
Y.A. Tittle, New York
College Football
Alabama
Heisman Trophy
Ernie Davis, Syracuse
NBA Championship
Boston 4–St. Louis 1

MVP
Bill Russell, Boston
College Basketball
Cincinnati
Player of the Year
Jerry Lucas, Ohio State
Stanley Cup
Chicago
US Tennis Open
Men: Roy Emerson
Women: Darlene Hard
USGA Open
Gene Littler
Kentucky Derby
Carry Back (J. Sellers, jockey)

Fashion

For Women: Gloves and hats gain a new importance, especially Mrs. Kennedy's pillbox, the cloche, and the high, rounded styles. Hair is teased into the "beehive," following Mrs. Kennedy, Princess Margaret, and Brigitte Bardot. The biggest news of the year is the "Little Nothing" dinner and evening dress—slender, low-bloused, and simple. Fashion appears to be moving away from the ornate and formal. Suits, coats, and dress fabrics are, in addition, textured and ridged in coral reds, oranges, greens, blues, and off-whites. The simple pump and low square shoe in the stacked and medium heel are also popular. Large costume jewelry includes bright

Audrey Hepburn and George Peppard in *Breakfast at Tiffany's*, the film version of Truman Capote's novella. *Movie Star News.*

beads and stones in irregular shapes, heavy, ornate earrings, and the year's fashionable jet.

High-fashion notes: Norell's "little black dress"; Madame Gres's draped jersey; revival of old furs, such as curly lamb, fox, and raccoon

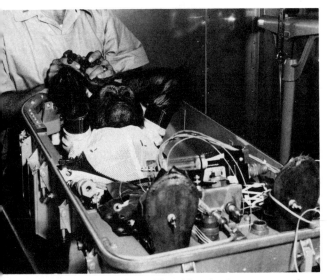

Enos preparing for flight. The chimp looks content as he prepares to circle the earth in space. *Courtesy NASA.*

- President Kennedy calls for "broad participation in exercise" by all Americans.
- Timothy Leary and Richard Alpert are fired from Harvard for using undergraduates in their research experiments; they create the International Foundation for International Freedom (IF-IF), publish *Psychedelic Review,* and prescribe that individuals can be free only through hallucinogenic drugs.
- CORE organizes Freedom Rides to integrate buses, trains, and terminals.
- The ICC bans segregation on all interstate facilities.
- Henry Miller's long-banned *Tropic of Cancer* is published in the United States; many cities censor it.
- The twist craze begins.
- Le Club, the first disco in the United States, opens in New York.
- Ray Kroc borrows $2.7 million, buys out the McDonald brothers, organizes 200 stands, and begins the McDonald's empire.
- Four thousand servicemen are sent to Vietnam as "advisers."
- JFK sign a law making airplane hijacking punishable by death.
- The Civil War Centennial celebration begins.
- The minimum wage rises from $1 to $1.25.
- Michael Rockefeller, the New York governor's son, is lost at sea off the coast of New Guinea.
- An updated version of the *Merriam-Webster Dictionary* takes a more permissive view of language and arouses the ire of purists.
- Reading specialists prefer the phonetic to the whole-word method of reading instruction, which is said to have caused reading retardation in 35 percent of the youth population.
- JFK signs a bill reducing the amount of duty-free goods that may be brought back to the United States from $500 to $100.
- Civil Defense officials distribute 22 million copies of the pamphlet *Family Fallout Shelter.*
- Eisenhower, in his farewell address, warns that the

Kaleidoscope

immense civilian arms industry and military establishment have "grave implications for the very structure of our society."
- A university poll reports that 72 percent of elementary and high school teachers approve of corporal punishment as a disciplinary measure.
- A Gallup Poll indicates that 74 percent of the teens interviewed believe in God; 58 percent plan to go to college. Of the 16-to-21 year-old girls interviewed, almost all expect to be married by age 22, and most want four children.
- The Supremes sign a four-year contract with Motown.
- Robert Zimmerman (Bobby Dylan), 20, begins singing in a Greenwich Village nightclub; he gets his first recording opportunity as a backup harmonica player.
- Clark Gable dies at the conclusion of filming *The Misfits.*
- JFK appoints a committee to study the status of women.

Fads: Guitars, yo-yos, rocking chairs

New Words and Usages: Microsurgery, new wave, Peace Corps, troika, third stream, high rise, New Frontier, go ape, soul, zonked

First Appearances: Woman appointed as personal physician to the president (J. G. Travell), vending machine with fresh flowers, First National Bank Certificates of Deposit (New York), IBM Selectric, self-wringing mops, freezers with front door, IBM golf ball, electric toothbrush, Coffee-mate, Total, Country corn flakes, Green Giant vegetables in pouch with butter sauce, Century City (Los Angeles), Haleakala National Park (Hawaii)

The Beat Poets: Peter Orlovsky, William Burroughs, Allen Ginsberg, Alan Ansen, Gregory Corso, Paul Bowles, and Ian Sommerville. *Courtesy Allen Ginsberg.*

1962

Facts and Figures

Economic Profile
  Dow Jones: ↑ High 767–
    Low 723
  GNP: +7%
  Inflation: +0.4%
  Unemployment: 5.5%
TV production: 6,047,000
AM radio stations: 5,710
Household telephones: 80%
Toll rate: New York–San
  Francisco: $2
Advertising expenditures:
  $12.3 billion
Van Cleef & Arpels 18k leaf
  pin: $115
Black Starr & Gorham
  diamond circle pin, on
  platinum: $660–$1975
Tiffany sapphire-centered
  cuff links, 14k: $35;
  matching tie bar: $19
Perfumes:
  Shalimar: $25 (1 oz.)
  Replique: $30 (2 oz.)
  Joy: $50 (1 oz.)
I. W. Harper bourbon:
  $6.70 (⅘)
Taster's Choice Scotch:
  $6.59 (⅘)
Four Roses: $6 (qt.)

Above: Lt. Col. John Glenn
and Atlas VI, the first
manned orbital launch on
the Freedom 7, makes 3
orbits and is picked up at
sea by a force of 24 ships,
126 aircraft, and 26,000
personnel. *Courtesy NASA.*

Deaths

Niels Bohr, Arthur Compton,
  William Faulkner, Kirsten
  Flagstad, Moss Hart, Ernie
  Kovacs, Charles Laughton,
  Eleanor Roosevelt, James
  Thurber, Bruno Walter.

In the News

KENNEDY EMBARGOES TRADE WITH CUBA, CASTRO DECRIES U.S. IMPERIALISM . . . U.S. REMOVES TANK FORCE FROM BERLIN WALL . . . U-2 PILOT GARY POWERS IS TRADED FOR SOVIET SPY RUDOLF ABEL . . . JOHN GLENN ORBITS EARTH THREE TIMES . . . SUPREME COURT RULES FEDERAL GOVERNMENT CAN OVERSEE STATE LEGISLATURE DISTRICTING . . . NEW ORLEANS ARCHBISHOP ORDERS ALL CATHOLIC SCHOOLS DESEGREGATED . . . U.S. RESUMES ATMOSPHERIC NUCLEAR TESTING AT CHRISTMAS ISLAND . . . BAY OF PIGS PRISONERS ARE RANSOMED FOR $2.5 MILLION . . . RANGER IV SPACECRAFT HITS THE MOON . . . STOCK MARKET PLUNGES, $20 BILLION IS LOST IN ONE DAY, LARGEST DROP SINCE 1929 . . . ADOLF EICHMANN IS HANGED IN JERUSALEM . . . SUPREME COURT RULES AGAINST OFFICIAL PRAYER IN PUBLIC SCHOOLS . . . BOEING 707 CRASHES IN PARIS, 130 DIE, THE WORST SINGLE PLANE DISASTER TO DATE . . . ALGERIA VOTES FOR INDEPENDENCE, 5.98 MILLION TO 16,000 . . . RUSSIA RESUMES ATMOSPHERIC TESTS IN ARCTIC . . . MARILYN MONROE DIES OF OVERDOSE . . . TWO RUSSIANS ORBIT SEPARATELY . . . DE GAULLE ESCAPES ASSASSINATION ATTEMPT IN PARIS . . . SOVIETS ANNOUNCE ARMS AND TECHNOLOGY FOR CUBA, KHRUSHCHEV WARNS U.S. NOT TO INTERFERE . . . ROSS BARNETT, MISSISSIPPI GOVERNOR, BARS BLACK, JAMES MEREDITH, FROM UNIVERSITY OF MISSISSIPPI, KENNEDY SENDS FEDERAL TROOPS . . . CHINA ATTACKS INDIA OVER DISPUTED BORDER . . . ADLAI STEVENSON IN UN ACCUSES USSR OF PLACING MISSILES IN CUBA . . . JFK ANNOUNCES AIR AND SEA QUARANTINE OF CUBA, U.S. INTERCEPTS CUBA-BOUND SOVIET TANKER . . . RUSSIA AGREES TO DISMANTLE CUBAN MISSILES . . . KENNEDY ORDERS END OF SEGREGATION IN FEDERAL HOUSING . . . INDIA ANNOUNCES CHINESE WITHDRAWAL.

Demonstrations against segregation occur throughout the south. *National Archives.*

"There are tens of millions of Americans who are beyond the welfare state. Taken as a whole there is a culture of poverty . . . bad health, poor housing, low levels of aspiration and high levels of mental distress. Twenty per cent of a nation, some 32,000,000."
— Michael Harrington, *The Culture of Poverty*

"We may be the last generation in the experiment with living."
— Tom Hayden, announcing the birth of SDS, Students for a Democratic Society

"Man does not live by ratings alone."
— Newton Minow, chairman, Federal Communications Commission

Quotes

"The medium *is* the message."
— Marshall McLuhan, *The Gutenberg Galaxy*

"As I leave you I want you to know—just think how much you're going to be losing: you won't have Nixon to kick around anymore, because, gentlemen, this is my last press conference."
— Richard M. Nixon, after losing to Pat Brown in the California gubernatorial race.

"I made two mistakes during my first year. One was Cuba. The other was letting it be known that I read as much as I do."
— John F. Kennedy

"Esteemed Mr. President . . .
    I understand very well your anxiety. . . . In order to liquidate with greater speed the dangerous conflict, . . . the Soviet government . . . has issued an order for the dismantling of weapons, which you describe as 'offensive,' their crating, and return to the Soviet Union. . . . The UN may verify the dismantling. . . .
    Respectfully yours,
    Nikita Khrushchev"

"Heeeeeere's Johnny."
— "The Tonight Show," as Johnny Carson begins, October 1

"It was quite a day. I don't know what you can say about a day when you see four beautiful sunsets. . . . This is a little unusual, I think."
— Col. John Glenn

Ads

Your client is a poor, rejected stepchild, whose best friends are dwarfs. Can you insure her against poisoned apples?
(Continental Insurance Co.)

My son, the pilot.
(El Al Airlines)

Has anyone given you a handful of emeralds? . . . Does traffic stop when you arrive in Paris? No? Then start wearing the fragrance that can take you places.
(Yardley)

Why be color-blind? . . . This fall more than ⅔ of nighttime programming will be in color.
(NBC)

Dr. Spock is worried. If you've been raising a family on Dr. Spock's books you know he doesn't worry easily.
(National Committee for SANE Nuclear Policy)

TV

Premieres

"The Virginian" (first 90-minute western), James Drury
"The Andy Williams Show"
"The Beverly Hillbillies," Buddy Ebsen
"Combat," Vic Morrow
"McHale's Navy," Ernest Borgnine
"The Merv Griffin Show"
"The Tonight Show Starring Johnny Carson"

Top Ten (Nielsen)

"The Beverly Hillbillies," "Candid Camera," "The Red Skelton Show," "Bonanza," "The Lucy Show," "The Andy Griffith Show," "Ben Casey," "The Danny Thomas Show," "The Dick Van Dyke Show"

Specials

Barbara Walters's report on Mrs. Kennedy's goodwill tour of India, "The Today Show" (her first major on-the-air assignment); "Julie [Andrews] and Carol [Burnett] at Carnegie Hall"; "The Tunnel" (Piers Anderson, Berlin news correspondent); "The Political Obituary of Richard Nixon" (Howard K. Smith)

Emmy Awards

"The Tunnel" (program); "The Defenders" (drama); "The Dick Van Dyke Show" (comedy); "The Andy Williams Show" (variety); "Walt Disney's Wonderful World of Color" (children); "G.E. College Bowl" (game); E. G. Marshall (actor, "The Defenders"); Shirley Booth (actress, "Hazel").

Of Note

Walter Cronkite replaces Douglas Edwards on the CBS "Evening News" • Benny "Kid" Paret dies in a boxing match with Emile Griffith on ABC's "Fight of the Week" • The bill requiring UHF capabilities on all TV sets greatly aids educational and other nonnetwork TV.

Movies

Openings

Lawrence of Arabia (David Lean), Peter O'Toole, Omar Sharif, Alec Guinness, Anthony Quinn, Jose Ferrer
The Longest Day (Andrew Marton, Ken Annakin, Bernhard Wicki), John Wayne, Henry Fonda, Robert Ryan
To Kill a Mockingbird (Robert Mulligan), Gregory Peck, Mary Badham, Brock Peters
The Miracle Worker (Arthur Penn), Anne Bancroft, Patty Duke
Birdman of Alcatraz (John Frankenheimer), Burt Lancaster, Karl Malden
Days of Wine and Roses (Blake Edwards), Lee Remick, Jack Lemmon
Whatever Happened to Baby Jane? (Robert Aldrich), Bette Davis, Joan Crawford
Long Day's Journey into Night (Sidney Lumet), Katharine Hepburn, Ralph Richardson, Jason Robards, Jr., Dean Stockwell
Sweet Bird of Youth (Richard Brooks), Paul Newman, Geraldine Page
The Manchurian Candidate (John Frankenheimer), Frank Sinatra, Janet Leigh, Laurence Harvey
Jules and Jim (François Truffaut), Oskar Werner, Jeanne Moreau
Lolita (Stanley Kubrick), James Mason, Shelley Winters, Sue Lyon, Peter Sellers
Freud (John Huston), Montgomery Clift, Susannah York
The Chapman Report (George Cukor), Shelley Winters, Efrem Zimbalist, Jr.
The Counterfeit Traitor (George Seaton), William Holden, Lilli Palmer
The Four Horsemen of the Apocalypse (Vincente Minnelli), Glenn Ford, Ingrid Thulin
Dr. No (Terence Young), Sean Connery, Ursula Andress (first James Bond film)
Advise and Consent (Otto Preminger), Henry Fonda, Charles Laughton

Academy Awards

Best Picture: *Lawrence of Arabia*
Best Director: David Lean (*Lawrence of Arabia*)
Best Actress: Anne Bancroft (*The Miracle Worker*)
Best Actor: Gregory Peck (*To Kill a Mockingbird*)

Top Box-Office Stars

Doris Day, Rock Hudson, Cary Grant, John Wayne, Elvis Presley, Elizabeth Taylor, Jerry Lewis, Frank Sinatra, Sandra Dee, Burt Lancaster

Stars of Tomorrow

Bobby Darin, Ann-Margret, Richard Beymer, Suzanne Pleshette, Capucine, George Peppard, James MacArthur, Peter Falk, Michael Callan, Yvette Mimieux

Popular Music _____

Hit Songs
"Shout! Shout! (Knock Yourself Out)"
"The Sweetest Sounds"
"Days of Wine and Roses"
"I Left My Heart in San Francisco"
"Walk on By"
"What Kind of Fool Am I?"
"Fly Me to the Moon"
"As Long as He Needs Me"
"Go Away Little Girl"

Top Records

Albums: *Holiday Sing along with Mitch* (Mitch Miller); *Breakfast at Tiffany's* (Henry Mancini); *West Side Story* (sound track); *Modern Sounds in Country and Western Music* (Ray Charles); *Peter, Paul and Mary* (Peter, Paul and Mary)

Singles: *Stranger on the Shore* (Acker Bilk); *I Can't Stop Loving You* (Ray Charles); *Mashed Potato Time* (Dee Dee Sharp); *Roses Are Red* (Bobby Vinton); *Johnny Angel* (Shelley Fabares); *Loco-Motion* (Little Eva); *Soldier Boy* (Shirelles); *Breaking Up Is Hard to Do* (Neil Sedaka); *Where Have All the Flowers Gone?* (Kingston Trio); *Hey! Baby* (Bruce Channel). Country: *Wolverton Mountain* (Claude King); *Mama Sang a Song* (Bill Anderson)

Grammy Awards
I Left My Heart in San Francisco, Tony Bennett (record, album); "What Kind of Fool Am I?" Anthony Newley (song)

Jazz and Big Bands
Archie Shepp leaves Cecil Taylor to form the Shepp-Dixon Quartet. The government sends Benny Goodman to the USSR on a cultural exchange program; his band includes Zoot Sims, Joe Newman, Teddy Wilson, and Victor Feldman.
Stan Getz, Charlie Byrd, Joao Gilberto, and Antonio Carlos Jobim continue to popularize the bossanova.

Top Performers *(Downbeat):* Miles Davis (soloist); Duke Ellington, Count Basie (band); Dave Brubeck (jazz group); Wes Montgomery, Max Roach, Cannonball Adderley, Stan Getz (instrumentalists); Ella Fitzgerald, Frank Sinatra (vocalists); Lambert, Hendricks and Ross (vocal group)

Theater _____

Broadway Openings

Plays
Who's Afraid of Virginia Woolf? (Edward Albee), Uta Hagen, Arthur Hill, George Grizzard
A Thousand Clowns (Herb Gardner), Jason Robards, Jr., Sandy Dennis
Never Too Late (Sumner Arthur Long), Paul Ford, Maureen O'Sullivan, Orson Bean
Tchin-Tchin (Sidney Michaels), Margaret Leighton, Anthony Quinn

Musicals
Stop the World—I Want to Get Off (Leslie Bricusse, Anthony Newley), Anthony Newley
I Can Get It for You Wholesale (Harold Rome), Elliott Gould, Barbra Streisand, Lillian Roth
A Funny Thing Happened on the Way to the Forum (Stephen Sondheim), Zero Mostel, Jack Gilford
Little Me (Neil Simon, Cy Coleman, Carolyn Leigh), Sid Caesar, Virginia Martin
No Strings (Richard Rodgers), Diahann Carroll, Richard Kiley
Beyond the Fringe, written and performed by Dudley Moore, Peter Cook, Jonathan Miller,

Classics and Revivals On and Off Broadway
Oh Dad, Poor Dad, Mamma's Hung You in the Closet and I'm Feelin' So Sad (Arthur Kopit), Barbara Harris, Jo Van Fleet; *The Collection* (Harold Pinter); *The Dumb Waiter* (Harold Pinter); *Brecht on Brecht,* Viveca Lindfors, George Voskovec; *Plays for Bleeker Street* (Thornton Wilder); *Romeo and Juliet,* John Stride, Joanna Dunham, directed by Franco Zeffirelli. *Founded:* La Mama E.T.C. (Experimental Theatre Club) by Ellen Stewart

Regional
Ford Foundation makes the largest grant to date: $2.1 million to the Alley Theatre (Houston), among others.

Pulitzer Prize
How to Succeed in Business without Really Trying, Frank Loesser

Tony Awards
A Man for All Seasons, Robert Bolt (play); *How to Succeed in Business without Really Trying,* Frank Loesser (musical)

Artur Rubinstein, who made his U.S. debut in 1906, continues to give concerts despite frequent considerations of retirement. *Move Star News.*

Compositions

Samuel Barber, Piano Concerto, no. 1, Cello Sonata
Charles Whittenberg, Fantasy
Earle Brown, *Available Forms II*
Walter Piston, *Lincoln Center,* String Quartet no. 5
David Diamond, Nonet
Ross Finney, *Still Are New Worlds*

Important Events

Birthday celebrations include the centennial for Claude Debussy and Frederick Delius; 80th for Zoltán Kodály and Gian Francesco Malipiero; 65th for Henry Cowell, Virgil Thomson, and Howard Hanson.

Igor Stravinsky celebrates his 80th birthday with numerous tours, including his first to the USSR in 48 years; he conducts *Oedipus Rex* (Washington, D.C.); CBS televises the premiere of *Noah and the Flood;* Kennedy honors him at a White House dinner.

Philharmonic Hall, the first completed building at Lincoln Center, New York, opens September 23, and dominates the musical year. Leonard Bernstein conducts the New York Philharmonic at the Inaugural Concert, broadcast on TV and radio: "Gloria," from Beethoven's *Missa Solemnis;* first movement, Mahler, Symphony no. 8; Ralph Vaughan Williams, *Serenade to Music;* Aaron Copland, *Connotations for Orchestra* (commissioned). Because of acoustical problems with the hall, Bernstein asks Daniel Pinkham to write *Catacoustical Measures* with every possible orchestral sonority; Bernstein later performs it at a Young People's Concert.

The American Symphony debuts with Leopold Stokowski, 80, at Carnegie Hall.

The Robert Shaw Chorale performs Bach's *B Minor Mass* in Moscow.

Classical Music _____

New Appointments: Jean Martinon at the Chicago Symphony; Erich Leinsdorf, the Boston Symphony; Josef Krips, the San Francisco Orchestra; Otto Klemperer returns after 20 years to New York to conduct the Philharmonic; William Schuman becomes president of Lincoln Center for the Performing Arts.

Visiting Orchestras: Concertgebouw, Leningrad, National French.

Debuts: Peter Serkin, Igor Oistrakh, Jean-Marie Darré, Stern-Rose-Istomin trio

First Performances

William Schuman, Symphony no. 8 (New York); Roy Harris, Symphony no. 8 (San Francisco); Darius Milhaud, Symphony no. 12 (San Francisco); Abraham Ellstein, *The Golem* (New York); George Antheil, *Cabeza de Vaca* (CBS-TV, New York); Henry Cowell, Symphony no. 15 (New York); Paul Creston, Piano Concerto (New York); Carlisle Floyd, *The Passion of Jonathan Wade* (New York); Pablo Casals, *El Pesebre* (San Francisco); David Diamond, Symphony no. 7 (Philadelphia), Symphony no. 8 (New York); Alexei Haieff, Symphony no. 3 (New York); Walter Piston, Violin Concerto no. 2 (New York)

Opera

Metropolitan: Longest season in history: Joan Sutherland, *La sonnambula;* Renata Tebaldi, *Adriana Lecouvreur;* Anneliese Rothenberger, Hertha Toepper, *Der Rosenkavalier* (directed by Lotte Lehmann); James McCracken, Renata Tebaldi, *Otello;* Judith Raskin (debut), *Le nozze di Figaro*

Boston: Beverly Sills, *Manon*

Chicago: Boris Christoff, dancers Sonia Arova and Rudolph Nureyev, *Prince Igor; Orfeo ed Euridice* (production of the Royal Opera House, Covent Garden)

San Francisco: *Le rossignol* (in Russian, Stravinsky); *Joan at the Stake* (Arthur Honegger)

Fort Worth: Placido Domingo (debut), Lily Pons (last time in role), *Lucia di Lammermoer*

Aspen: *The Pearl Fishers* (Georges Bizet)

Art

Paintings

Robert Indiana, *American Gas Works* (1961–62), *Star*

Andy Warhol, *Four Campbell's Soup Cans, 100 Cans, Green Coca-Cola Bottles, Gold Marilyn Monroe*

Josef Albers, *Homage to the Square*

Robert Rauschenberg, *Ace*

James Rosenquist, *Marilyn Monroe, I*

Jack Youngerman, *Anajo, Black, Red and White*

Edward Hopper, *New York Office*

Hans Hofmann, *Memoria in Aeternum*

Jules Olitski, *Cleopatra Flesh*

Roy Lichtenstein, *Flatten—Sand Fleas!*

Sculpture

Tony Smith, *Cigarette, Die*

Claes Oldenburg, *Two Cheeseburgers with Everything (Dual Hamburgers)*

Robert Morris, *I-Box*

Raoul Hague, *Sculpture in Walnut*

John Chamberlain, *Velvet White, Dolores James*

Marisol, *The Family*

George Segal, *The Bus Driver*

Lee Bontecou, *Untitled*

Isamu Noguchi, *Shrine of Aphrodite*

David Smith, *Voltri XVII, XIX*

Mark DiSuvero, *Blue Arch for Matisse*

Architecture

T.W.A. Terminal, Idlewild Airport (Mies van der Rohe)

Fine Arts Center, Howard University, Washington, D.C. (Le Corbusier)

"Century 21," Science Pavilion, Seattle World's Fair (Minoru Yamasaki)

Philharmonic Hall, Lincoln Center, New York (Harrison and Abramovitz)

Dulles International Airport Terminal Building, Chantilly, Va. (Eero Saarinen)

Air Force Academy, Colorado Springs, Colo. (Skidmore, Owings, and Merrill)

Marin County Civic Center, San Rafael, Calif. (Frank Lloyd Wright)

Greek Orthodox Church, Milwaukee (Frank Lloyd Wright, posthumous)

Important Exhibitions

Rare objects from King Tutankhamen's tomb tour the United States for a second year, sent by the Cairo Museum to raise funds to preserve the Nile temples threatened by flood. "Treasures of Versailles" tours Chicago, Toledo, San Francisco, and Los Angeles.

Museums

New York: *Metropolitan:* 141 drawings purchased in 1961 (Poussin, Delacroix, David, Rubens, Bruegel); Rowland's England; Drawings and watercolors from British collections. *Museum of Modern Art:* Dubuffet, Redon, Moreau, Rodolphe Bresdin; José Orozco drawings; "Recent Painting: U.S.A." *Whitney:* 30th-anniversary celebration: "American Art of Our Century"; "Geometric Abstraction in America." *Morgan:* Chinese paintings from the collection of John M. Crawford, Jr.

Chicago: Eakins; Redon-Moreau-Bresdin; Dubuffet retrospective; Chinese art treasures; Last works of Matisse

Washington: Samuel H. Kress and Andrew Myer collection; 16 German abstract artists; Eakins

Pittsburgh: Carnegie International Awards—Mark Tobey, Jules Olitski, Adolph Gottlieb, Ellsworth Kelly

Venice Biennale: Louise Nevelson, Loren MacIver, Jan Müller, Dimitri Hadzi, and Arshile Gorky represent the United States.

Art Briefs

Henry Moore has his first one-man show in eight years, at the Knoedler Gallery, New York • Leonardo da Vinci's *Mona Lisa* arrives in New York on December 19 for the Metropolitan Museum of Art's exhibit • The Dallas Museum of Fine Arts purchases Wyeth's *That Gentleman* for $58,000, the highest price ever paid by a museum to a living American artist • The National Museum of Sports Show in New York, "Fine Arts in Sports," is highly successful.

Dance

Rudolf Nureyev makes his American debut in the grand pas de deux from *Don Quixote* (Ruth Page's Chicago Opera Ballet), at the Brooklyn Academy. Rebecca Harkness makes a major financial contribution to the Joffrey.

Premieres

New York City Ballet: *A Midsummer Night's Dream* (George Balanchine), Melissa Hayden, Edward Villella, Arthur Mitchell

Paul Taylor: *Aureole.* **Alvin Ailey:** *Hermit Songs, Feast of Ashes.* **Martha Graham:** *Phaedra*

Books

Fiction

Critics' Choice

Pale Fire, Vladimir Nabokov
One Flew over the Cuckoo's Nest, Ken Kesey
Letting Go, Philip Roth
Another Country, James Baldwin
Stern, Bruce Jay Friedman
Big Sur, Jack Kerouac
Pigeon Feathers, John Updike
Eleven Kinds of Loneliness, Richard Yates
🔊 *Labyrinths, Ficciones*, Jorge Luis Borges
🔊 *The Tin Drum*, Günter Grass

Best-Sellers

Ship of Fools, Katherine Anne Porter
Dearly Beloved, Anne Morrow Lindbergh
A Shade of Difference, Allen Drury
Youngblood Hawke, Herman Wouk
Franny and Zooey, J. D. Salinger
Fail-Safe, Eugene Burdick, Harvey Wheeler
Seven Days in May, Fletcher Knebel, Charles W. Bailey II
The Prize, Irving Wallace
The Agony and the Ecstasy, Irving Stone

Nonfiction

Critics' Choice

Thinking about the Unthinkable, Herman Kahn
The Structure of Scientific Revolutions, T.S. Kuhn
The Paradoxes of Freedom, Sidney Hook
Silent Spring, Rachel Carson
Six Crises, Richard M. Nixon
Mark Twain's Letters from the Earth, ed. Bernard De Voto
Patriotic Gore, Edmund Wilson
The Legacy of Hiroshima, Edward Teller
A Sad Heart at the Supermarket, Randall Jarrell
Theatre of the Absurd, Martin Esslin
🔊 *The Gutenberg Galaxy*, Marshall McLuhan

Best-Sellers

Calories Don't Count, Dr. Herman Taller
The New English Bible: The New Testament
Happiness Is a Warm Puppy, Charles M. Schulz
The Joy of Cooking: New Edition, Irma S. Rombauer, Marion Rombauer Becker
My Life in Court, Louis Nizer
The Rothschilds, Frederic Morton
Sex and the Single Girl, Helen Gurley Brown

Travels with Charley, John Steinbeck

Poetry

Robert Frost, *In the Clearing*
Sylvia Plath, *The Colossus and Other Poems*
Anne Sexton, *All My Pretty Ones*
Brother Antoninus, *The Hazards of Holiness*
Kenneth Koch, *Thank You and Other Poems*
Howard Nemerov, *The Next Room of the Dream*
James Merrill, *Water Street*
William Stafford, *Traveling through the Dark*
Robert Bly, *Silence in the Snowy Fields*
🔊 Yevgeny Yevtushenko, *Selected Poems*

Pulitzer Prizes

The Reivers, William Faulkner (fiction)
Washington, Village and Capital, 1800–1878, Constance M. Green (U.S. history)
The Guns of August, Barbara Tuchman (nonfiction)
Henry James: The Middle Years, Henry James: The Conquest of London, Leon Edel (biography)
Pictures from Brueghel, William Carlos William (poetry)

Nobel Prize
John Steinbeck

Science and Technology

John Glenn, on the Friendship VII mission, becomes the first American to orbit the earth; later in the year, Scott Carpenter orbits three times, and Walter Schirra, six times.

Mariner II is the first successful interplanetary probe; it passes Venus in 109 days and confirms that with temperatures of 800° to 2000° F., Venus is inhospitable to life.

Ranger IV makes the first lunar impact, but picture taking fails.

Telstar is launched, initiating transatlantic TV broadcasts of 20 minutes' duration at one time.

Bell Labs directs a laser beam at the moon's surface and 2½ seconds later receives its reflection.

The MOS (metal odide semicondenser) integrated circuit is perfected by RCA scientists; it allows increased circuit information on a chip.

The first industrial robot is marketed by Unimation.

Digital markets a minicomputer for $15,000.

The Braille system of printing and writing is applied to the typewriter.

🔊 Pavel Popovich and Andrian Nikolayev make the first simultaneous space flights.

Nobel Prize

James D. Watson wins the prize in medicine and physiology for work on the molecular structure of DNA.

Sports

Baseball

Maury Wills (Los Angeles, NL) steals 104 bases, breaking Ty Cobb's 1915 record of 96.

Sandy Koufax (Los Angeles, NL) strikes out 18 men in a nine-inning game.

Jackie Robinson is the first black inducted into the Hall of Fame.

The National League expands to ten teams with the Houston Colts and New York Mets; the Mets under Casey Stengel lose a record 120 games.

Don Drysdale (Los Angeles, NL) wins the Cy Young Award.

Champions

Batting
Tommy Davis (Los Angeles, NL), .346
Pete Runnels (Washington, AL), .326
Pitching
Bob Purkey (Cincinnati, NL), 23–5

Ray Herbert (Chicago, AL), 20–9
Home runs
Willie Mays (San Francisco, NL), 49

Football

NFL Season Leaders: Bart Starr (Green Bay), passing; Jim Taylor (Green Bay), rushing; Bobby Mitchell (Washington), receiving; Taylor gains 1,474 yards. **AFL Season Leaders:** Len Dawson (Kansas City), passing; Cookie Gilchrist (Buffalo), rushing; Lionel Taylor (Denver) receiving.
College All-Americans: Jerry Stovall (B), Louisiana State; Lee Roy Jordan (C) Alabama

Bowls (Jan. 1, 1963)

Rose: Southern California 42–Wisconsin 37
Orange: Alabama 17–Oklahoma 0

Cotton: Louisiana State 13–Texas 0
Sugar: Mississippi 17–Arkansas 13

Basketball

Wilt Chamberlain (Philadelphia) scores 100 points in an NBA game, as Philadelphia beats New York 169–147.

NBA All-Pro Team: Bob Pettit (St. Louis), Elgin Baylor (Los Angeles), Wilt Chamberlain (Philadelphia), Jerry West (Los Angeles), Oscar Robertson (Cincinnati)

Other Sports

Tennis: Rod Laver wins the Grand Slam, all four major tournaments.

Golf: Jack Nicklaus wins his first major tournament, beating Arnold Palmer in overtime in the U.S. Open.

Horse Racing: Kelso is named Horse of the Year for the third straight year.

Winners

World Series
New York (AL) 4
San Francisco (NL) 3
MVP
NL–Maury Wills, Los Angeles
AL–Mickey Mantle, New York
NFL Championship
Green Bay 16–New York 7
MVP
Jim Taylor, Green Bay
College Football
Southern California
Heisman Trophy
Terry Baker, Oregon State
NBA Championship
Boston 4–Los Angeles 3

MVP
Bill Russell, Boston
College Basketball
Cincinnati
Player of the Year
Paul Hogue, Cincinnati
Stanley Cup
Toronto
US Tennis Open
Men: Rod Laver
Women: Margaret Smith
USGA Open
Jack Nicklaus
Kentucky Derby
Decidedly (W. Hartack, jockey)

Fashion

For Women: International styles and films contribute to an eclectic and casual vogue. One popular mix includes the Basque sheepherder coat, Wild West cowboy boots and bandanas, blue jeans, sheriff jackets, suspenders, and the combination of odd jackets, suede shirts, skirts, vests, pants, and Breton middies. "Breen" (brown/green) is fashionable in hooded jacketlike sweaters of thick mohair; the crocheted or flat turtleneck pullover is also popular. Generally, the silhouette is less abstract and more anatomical, the bosom the fashion focus. From *Last Year at Marienbad* comes short straight hair pushed behind the ear and swept across the forehead. From *Breakfast at Tiffany's,* and also the style set by Mrs. Kennedy, comes the high-bosomed look in coats, suits, and dresses, as well as the "princess" dress, which discards sleeves and belt, and the long, slim evening dress. Also fashionable are widespread color contrasts with black accents, influenced by the Picasso show.

High-fashion note: Gernreich's wool tank and topless swimsuit

Kaleidoscope _____

- "I'll say it again, I've said it before / Archie Moore will fall in four" and "He knocks them all out in the round he'll call / And that's why he's called the greatest of all" are examples of Cassius Marcellus Clay's poetry.
- After Decca and other recording companies turn him down, Brian Epstein convinces George Martin at EMI to sign the Beatles for 1 cent per side and 10 cents per song album.
- *My Fair Lady* closes after 2,717 performances, the longest running musical in Broadway history.
- Bobby Kennedy, on TV, asks: "Are we to say to the world that this is the land of the free except for the Negroes?"
- SNCC (Students' Nonviolent Coordinating Committee) organizes the "freedom ballot" and registers black voters in Georgia, Mississippi, and Alabama.
- President Kennedy awards Dr. Frances O. Kelsey of the Federal Drug Administration the Gold Medal of Distinguished Public Service for his "rigorous demands" to clear the market of birth-defects-producing thalidomide.
- Scientist Linus Pauling wins the Nobel Peace Prize.
- JFK instructs U.S. troops in Vietnam to protect themselves if fired upon but to understand that they are "not combat troops in the generally understood sense of the word."
- As they film *Cleopatra,* Richard Burton and Elizabeth Taylor pursue a romance that makes worldwide headlines.
- Richard Avedon's photograph of high-fashion model Christina Paolozzi, nude in a full-page color ad in *Harper's Bazaar,* causes a furor.
- The United States and USSR sign a two-year agreement to expand cultural, scientific, technical, and educational exchanges.
- JFK awards poet Robert Frost, on his 88th birthday, a special medal voted by Congress.
- Benny Goodman plays a jazz concert at Red Army Sports Palace in Moscow, which Khrushchev attends unexpectedly; the crowds and Khrushchev are highly responsive.
- Ralph Ginzberg's conviction for pornography is upheld by the Supreme Court; he has applied for bulk-mail privileges from cities with such names as Intercourse, Climax, and Blue Balls.
- Over $2.5 million is found in an abandoned 1947 Plymouth in Jersey City, N.J. The IRS files an immediate claim for $3.4 million from its owner, a 50-ish former newsboy and numbers runner.
- Horror movies like *Premature Burial* and *Tales of Terror* make a comeback; they offer audiences a violence TV cannot provide and are inexpensive to produce.
- Erle Stanley Gardner, author of the Perry Mason mysteries, announces a major archeological find of prehistoric cave paintings in California.
- With auto sales running high, the Big Three emphasis

Mary Tyler Moore and Dick Van Dyke, in "The Dick Van Dyke Show." Carl Reiner created this sitcom, which ranked 80th during its first season. *Movie Star News.*

is on longer, heavier, and more powerful cars.
- Eleanor Roosevelt wins a Gallup Poll for the "Most Admired Woman" for the thirteenth time.
- When the United States decides to resume nuclear testing, a major problem is "Where?"
- "We're eyeball to eyeball and I think the other fellow just blinked," comments Dean Rusk when Soviet vessels turn back from the U.S. quarantine.
- Paul Guilhard, 30, an Agence Presse reporter covering James Meredith's admission to the University of Mississippi, is fatally shot in the back; his last dispatch is: "The Civil War never came to an end."
- Tom Hayden's "Port Huron Statement" pledges SDS to the New Left and places particular emphasis on the university as an agency of social change.
- An advertising company promoting Brahms, Beethoven, and Bach faces on sweatshirts sues a competitor who brings out a similar item at a lower cost; it claims copyright infringement.
- Hulda Clark, 14 and the daughter of a black laborer, is given a $2,000 scholarship to a Moscow boarding school and air fare by Madame Khrushchev.
- Van Kemp bakes a 25,000-pound cake for the Seattle World's Fair.
- Rachel Carson, in *Silent Spring,* indicates that over 500 new chemicals are entering our bodies because of widespread insecticide usage.
- JFK contributes his presidential salary to charity.

Fads: JFK coloring books, worry beads

New Words and Usages: Splashdown, bank (as verb), status report, corner back, join-in, weather girl, mono, moononaut, unword

First Appearances: Diet Rite; Tab; powdered orange juice; child's molded car seat with seatbelt; "The Incredible Hulk"; Polaroid color film; national monuments: homes of (1) Abraham Lincoln (Lincoln City, Ind.), (2) Alexander Hamilton (New York City), and (3) Theodore Roosevelt (three in New York state); Esalen Institute encounter group (Big Sur, Calif.); merged Pennsylvania and New York Railroad; E. J. Korvette on 5th Avenue, New York City; K Mart; Petrified National Park (Arizona); Baxter State Park (Maine); Americana Hotel (New York City); "We Shall Overcome" copyright by Guy Carawan; Electronic Data Systems; Lear Jet Corp.; COMSAT (Communications Satellite Corp.)

1963

Facts and Figures

Economic Profile
Dow-Jones:—High 767–
Low 646
GNP: +5%
Inflation: +1.7%
Unemployment: 5.7%
Daily newspapers: 1,974
Books published: 25,784
Airmail postage: 8¢
Postcard: 4¢
IRS total collections: $105.9
billion
Shoes:
Hush Puppies: $8.75–$9.95
Baker leather pumps: $7.99
Chandler's golden mesh:
$12.99
Bloomingdale's sleeveless
silk dress: $59.95
Macy's suede coat, zip-out
pile lining: $84.97
A&S eight-button leather
gloves: $8.79
Balenciaga scarf: $20
Jack Winter stretch pants:
$13
Lord & Taylor leather bag:
$36–$60
Hammacher Schlemmer foot
scraper: $5.95

Above: after the
assassination of John F.
Kennedy, Lyndon Baines
Johnson takes the oath of
office aboard Air Force I.
Library of Congress.

Deaths

Richard Barthelmess, Jean
Cocteau, W. E. B.
Du Bois, Robert Frost,
Paul Hindemith, Rogers
Hornsby, Aldous Huxley,
Estes Kefauver, Clifford
Odets, Dick Powell, Monty
Woolley.

In the News

KENNEDY ASKS $13.5 BILLION TAX CUT TO STIMULATE ECONOMY
. . . DISARMAMENT CONFERENCE MEETS AT GENEVA . . .
KHRUSHCHEV SAYS DE-STALINIZATION ALLOWS NO INDIVIDUAL
LIBERTY . . . SUPREME COURT RULES THAT STATES MUST PROVIDE
FREE LEGAL COUNSEL FOR THE POOR . . . NEW YORK NEWSPAPER
STRIKE ENDS AFTER 114 DAYS . . . MOSCOW AND WASHINGTON
ESTABLISH HOT LINE . . . SUBMARINE "THRESHER" SINKS WITH 129
ABOARD . . . MASS BLACK ANTISEGREGATION DEMONSTRATION
OCCURS IN BIRMINGHAM, ALABAMA, 1,000 ARE ARRESTED . . .
BLACKS RIOT AFTER BIRMINGHAM HEADQUARTERS ARE BOMBED, JFK
SENDS TROOPS . . . ASTRONAUT GORDON COOPER CIRCLES THE EARTH
TWICE . . . POPE JOHN XXIII DIES, POPE PAUL VI IS ELECTED . . .
FEDERAL NATIONAL GUARD HELPS TWO BLACKS TO ENROLL AT
UNIVERSITY OF ALABAMA . . . RUSSIA REJECTS CHINESE POSITION AND
SAYS NUCLEAR WAR MUST BE AVERTED . . . USSR AND U.S.
AGREE TO NUCLEAR TEST BAN IN AIR, ATMOSPHERE, AND WATER
. . . U.S. EMBARGOES ARMS TO SOUTH AFRICA . . . 250,000 MARCH
FOR CIVIL RIGHTS IN WASHINGTON, D.C. . . . PUBLIC SCHOOLS IN
SOUTH CAROLINA AND LOUISIANA INTEGRATE . . . BOMB EXPLOSION
KILLS FOUR GIRLS AT BLACK CHURCH IN BIRMINGHAM . . . $250
MILLION OF WHEAT FOR RUSSIA IS AUTHORIZED . . . RUSSIA DELAYS
WEST BERLIN CONVOY . . . NGO DIEM IS ASSASSINATED IN SOUTH
VIETNAM . . . JFK IS ASSASSINATED IN DALLAS . . . LEE HARVEY
OSWALD IS ARRESTED . . . LYNDON BAINES JOHNSON TAKES OFFICE,
THE NATION MOURNS KENNEDY . . . OSWALD IS KILLED BY TEXAN
JACK RUBY DURING LIVE NEWS COVERAGE . . . ZANZIBAR AND
KENYA BECOME INDEPENDENT . . . 500,000 WEST BERLINERS VISIT
EAST BERLIN ON HOLIDAY SPECIAL.

Quotes _____

"Before the Pilgrims landed at Plymouth, we were here. Before the pen of Jefferson etched across the pages of history the majestic words of the Declaration of Independence, we were here. If the inexpressible cruelties of slavery cannot stop us, the oppression we now face will surely fail.
— Martin Luther King, Jr., from a Birmingham jail

"I have a dream that one day this nation will rise up and live out the true meaning of its creed . . . that all men are created equal. I have a dream that my four little children will one day live in a nation where they will not be judged by the color of their skin but by the content of their character. I have a dream today. And if America is to be a great nation, this must become true. So let freedom ring. From the prodigious hilltops of New Hampshire, let freedom ring. From the heightening Alleghenies of Pennsylvania, let freedom ring. But not only that; let freedom ring from Stone Mountain of Georgia. Let freedom ring from every hill and molehill of Mississippi. And when this happens, when we let it ring, we will speed that day when all of God's children, black men and white men, Jews and Gentiles, Protestants and Catholics, will be able to join hands and sing in the words of the old Negro spiritual:
    'Free at last, free at last,
    Thank God Almighty, we're free at last.' "
    — Martin Luther King, Jr., speech in
    Washington, D.C.

"She was very worried about a civilization which produced those five policemen standing on the Negro woman's neck in Birmingham."
— James Baldwin, citing Lorraine Hansberry

"I am called Baldwin because I was sold by my African tribe and kidnappd out of it into the hands of a white Christian named Baldwin, who forced me to

The "March on Washington for Jobs and Freedom," at which Martin Luther King, Jr., gives his "I have a dream" speech. *National Archives.*

kneel at the foot of the cross. . . . God gave Noah the rainbow sign, no more water, the fire next time!"
— James Baldwin, *The Fire Next Time*

"America wept tonight not alone for its dead young President, but for itself. . . . Somehow the worst prevailed over the best. . . . Some strain of madness and violence had destroyed the highest symbol of law and order."
— James Reston

"He died as a soldier under fire, doing his duty in the service of his country."
— Charles de Gaulle

"We are in this country . . . watchmen on the walls of freedom. . . . We ask, therefore, that we may be worthy of our power and responsibility, . . . that we may achieve the ancient vision of peace on earth, goodwill toward men."
— JFK's speech planned for November 22

Ads _____

Author James Baldwin, active in the civil rights movement, calls for "the unconditional freedom of the Negro." *Courtesy Sedat Pakay.*

Premieres

"The Fugitive," David Janssen
"Bob Hope Presents the Chrysler Theater"
"The Patty Duke Show"
"My Favorite Martian," Bill Bixby
"Petticoat Junction," Bea Benaderet
"Let's Make a Deal," Monty Hall
"General Hospital"
"The Saint," Roger Moore

TV

Top Ten (Nielsen)

"The Beverly Hillbillies," "Bonanza," "The Dick Van Dyke Show," "Petticoat Junction," "The Andy Griffith Show," "The Lucy Show," "Candid Camera," "The Ed Sullivan Show," "The Danny Thomas Show," "My Favorite Martian"

Specials

"The Making of the President, 1960"; "Abe Lincoln in Illinois" (Jason Robards, Jr.); "One Day in the Life of Ivan Denisovich"; "Cuba: The Bay of Pigs, The Missile Crisis"; "Elizabeth Taylor in London"

Emmy Awards

"The Defenders" (drama); "Dick Van Dyke Show" (comedy); "Danny Kaye Show" (variety); "Discovery '63–'64" (children); "Huntley-Brinkley Report" (news); Dick Van Dyke (actor, "The Dick Van Dyke Show"); Mary Tyler Moore (actress, "The Dick Van Dyke Show")

Of Note

Julia Child, on "The French Chef," becomes NET's first star.

Movies

Openings

Tom Jones (Tony Richardson), Albert Finney, Susannah York, Hugh Griffith
Cleopatra (Joseph L. Mankiewicz), Elizabeth Taylor, Rex Harrison, Richard Burton
How the West Was Won (John Ford, Henry Hathaway, George Marshall), Gregory Peck, Henry Fonda, James Stewart, Debbie Reynolds
Lilies of the Field (Ralph Nelson), Sidney Poitier, Lilia Skala
8 ½ (Federico Fellini), Marcello Mastroianni, Anouk Aimée
Hud (Martin Ritt), Paul Newman, Patricia Neal, Melvyn Douglas, Brandon De Wilde
It's a Mad, Mad, Mad, Mad World (Stanley Kramer), Sid Caesar, Buddy Hackett, Mickey Rooney
All the Way Home (Alex Segal), Robert Preston, Jean Simmons
The Birds (Alfred Hitchcock), Rod Taylor, Jessica Tandy, Tippi Hedren
Charade (Stanley Donen), Cary Grant, Audrey Hepburn, Walter Matthau
The Ugly American (George Englund), Marlon Brando, Eiji Okada
America, America (Elia Kazan), Stathis Giallelis
The Trial (Orson Welles), Anthony Perkins, Orson Welles
Irma La Douce (Billy Wilder), Shirley MacLaine, Jack Lemmon

Academy Awards

Best Picture: *Tom Jones*
Best Director: Tony Richardson *(Tom Jones)*
Best Actress: Patricia Neal *(Hud)*
Best Actor: Sidney Poitier *(Lilies of the Field)*

Top Box-Office Stars

Doris Day, John Wayne, Rock Hudson, Jack Lemmon, Cary Grant, Elizabeth Taylor, Elvis Presley, Sandra Dee, Paul Newman, Jerry Lewis

Stars of Tomorrow

George Chakiris, Peter Fonda, Stella Stevens, Diane McBain, Pamela Tiffin, Pat Wayne, Dorothy Provine, Barbara Eden, Ursula Andress, Tony Bill

Popular Music ⎯⎯⎯⎯⎯⎯⎯⎯⎯⎯⎯⎯⎯⎯

Hit Songs
"Wipeout"
"Call Me Irresponsible"
"If I Had a Hammer"
"More"
"Puff (the Magic Dragon)"
"Da Doo Ron Ron"
"The Times They Are A-
    Changin' "
"Dominique"

Top Records

Albums: *My Son, the Celebrity*
(Allan Sherman); *Jazz Samba*
(Stan Getz, Charlie Byrd); *Days of
Wine and Roses* (Andy Williams);
*Little Stevie Wonder, the 12-Year-
Old Genius* (Stevie Wonder);
Blowin' in the Wind (Peter, Paul
and Mary).

Singles: *Sugar Shack* (Jimmy
Gilmer and the Fireballs); *Surfin'
U.S.A.* (Beach Boys); *The End of
the World* (Skeeter Davis);
Rhythm of the Rain (Cascades);
He's So Fine (Chiffons); *Blowin'
in the Wind* (Peter, Paul and
Mary); *Heatwave* (Martha and the
Vandellas); *Fingertips* (Little
Stevie Wonder). Country: *Don't
Let Me Cross Over* (Carl Butler);
Love's Gonna Live Here (Buck
Owens)

Grammy Awards
The Days of Wine and Roses,
    Henry Mancini (record, song);
    The Barbra Streisand Album
    (album)

Jazz and Big Bands
Jazz, both traditional and more
progressive, is widely written
about as an art form.
Don Ellis tours with his jazz
"happenings."
New York City's jazz clubs begin
closing, and the Lower East Side
replaces Greenwich Village for
avant-garde jazz.

Top Performers *(Downbeat):*
Thelonius Monk (soloist); Duke
Ellington, Count Basie (bands);
Dave Brubeck (jazz group);
Charlie Byrd, Ray Brown, Joe
Morello, Roland Kirk, Jimmy
Smith (instrumentalists); Ella
Fitzgerald, Ray Charles
(vocalists); Lambert, Hendricks,
and Ross (vocal group)

Theater ⎯⎯⎯⎯⎯⎯⎯⎯⎯⎯⎯⎯⎯⎯⎯

Broadway Openings

Plays
Barefoot in the Park (Neil Simon), Robert Redford,
    Elizabeth Ashley, Kurt Kasznar, Mildred
    Natwick
Enter Laughing (Joseph Stein), Vivian Blaine, Alan
    Arkin, Sylvia Sidney
A Case of Libel (Henry Denker), Sidney Blackmer,
    Van Heflin
Nobody Loves an Albatross (Ronald Alexander),
    Robert Preston
Luther (John Osborne), Albert Finney
Ballad of the Sad Café (Edward Albee), Colleen
    Dewhurst, Michael Dunn
Mother Courage and Her Children (Bertolt Brecht),
    Anne Bancroft
The Milk Train Doesn't Stop Here Anymore
    (Tennessee Williams), Mildred Dunnock
The Private Eye (Peter Shaffer), Barry Foster
One Flew over the Cuckoo's Nest (Dale Wasserman),
    Gene Wilder, Kirk Douglas
The Rehearsal (Jean Anouilh), Keith Michell, Alan
    Badel

Musicals
Oliver! (Lionel Bart), Clive Revill, Bruce Pochnik,
    Georgia Brown
She Loves Me (Jerry Bock, Sheldon Harnick), Jack
    Cassidy, Barbara Baxley, Barbara Cook, Daniel
    Massey
110 in the Shade (Harvey Schmidt, Tom Jones),
    Robert Horton, Inga Swenson
Tovarich (Lee Pockriss, Anne Crosswell), Vivien
    Leigh, Jean Pierre Aumont

Classics and Revivals On and Off Broadway
School for Scandal (Sheridan), Ralph Richardson,
John Gielgud, Geraldine McEvan; *Desire under the
Elms* (Eugene O'Neill), George C. Scott, Colleen
Dewhurst; *Strange Interlude* (O'Neill), Geraldine
Page, Ben Gazzara, Pat Hingle, Franchot Tone, Jane
Fonda; *A Month in the Country* (Turgenev), Celeste
Holm; *Too True to Be Good* (George Bernard Shaw),
David Wayne, Cyril Ritchard, Glynis Johns, Ray
Middleton, Eileen Heckart, Robert Preston, Lillian
Gish; *The Trojan Women* (Euripides), Mildred
Dunnock, Carrie Nye; *The Bald Soprano, The
Lesson* (Eugene Ionesco); *In White America* (Martin
B. Duberman); *The Maids* (Jean Genet), Lee Grant

Regional

Founded: Minnesota Theatre Company (Guthrie
Theater), Minneapolis, by Sir Tyrone Guthrie, Peter

Theater (cont.)

Ziesler, Oliver Rea: *Hamlet, The Miser, The Three Sisters, Death of a Salesman,* Hume Cronyn, Jessica Tandy, George Grizzard, Rita Gam, Zoë Caldwell; Seattle Repertory Theatre by Stuart Vaughan; Center Stage, Baltimore

Boston Theatre Company: *The Knack* (Ann Jellicoe)

Arena Stage, Washington, D.C.: *The Devils* (John Whiting), Joan Van Ark, Ned Beatty, Hurd Hatfield, René Auberjonois, Anthony Zerbe, premiere

Pulitzer Prize
No prize is awarded.

Le Guichet (The box office), by Alexander Calder, at Lincoln Center for the Performing Arts. *Marjorie Cox.*

Tony Awards
Who's Afraid of Virginia Woolf, Edward Albee (play), *A Funny Thing Happened on the Way to the Forum,* Stephen Sondheim (musical)

Classical Music

Compositions
Roy Harris, *Epilogue to Profiles in Courage: JFK, Salute to Death*
Roger Reynolds, *The Emperor of Ice Cream*
Lukas Foss, *Echoi*
Leonard Bernstein, Symphony no. 3 *(Kaddish)*
Roger Shapey, Brass Quintet, String Quartet no. 6
Lejaren Hiller, *Computer Cantata*

Important Events
Celebrations include the sesquicentennial birthdays of Wagner and Verdi.
The International Festival of Visiting Orchestras opens at Carnegie Hall with the Royal Philharmonic of London (Sir Malcolm Sargent); participating are the Hamburg, Hague, Leningrad, and National French Orchestras.
The most celebrated composition of the year is Benjamin Britten's *War Requiem.*
Of the works played by 262 orchestras, 812 were composed before 1899, 357 between 1900 and 1955, and 574 between 1955 and 1963. The Prelude to Wagner's *Die Meistersinger* is most performed, as well as an excerpt from *Lohengrin,* Beethoven's Symphony no. 5 and his Overtures; also, the symphonies of Mozart, Brahms, and Tchaikovsky.

Conductors in New Locations: Lukas Foss takes over the Denver; Jean Martinon goes to Chicago; Eleazar de Carvalho, to St. Louis.

Debut: Itzhak Perlman

First Performances
Roy Harris, Symphony no. 9 (Philadelphia); Benjamin Lees, Violin Concerto; (Boston); Samuel Barber, *Andromache's Farewell* (New York); Francis Poulenc, *Sept répons des ténébres* (New York); Paul Hindemith, Concerto for Organ and Orchestra (New York); Alan Hovhanness, Symphony no. 17 (Cleveland); Howard Hanson, *Song of Human Rights* (text includes excerpts from JFK's Inaugural Address, Washington, D.C.).

Opera

Premieres
Labyrinth (Gian Carlo Menotti, NBC-TV); *Death of the Bishop of Brindisi* (Menotti, Cincinnati); *Highway No. 1, U.S.A.* (William Grant Still, Miami); *Gentlemen, Be Seated!* (Jerome Moross, New York); *The Sojourner and Mollie Sinclair* (Carlisle Floyd, Raleigh, N.C.); *The Long Christmas Dinner* (Paul Hindemith, New York)

Metropolitan: George Shirley, *Madama Butterfly;* Joan Sutherland, *La sonnambula;* Régine Crespin, Herta Topper, *Der Rosenkavalier;* James McCracken, *Otello;* Raina Kabaivanska, *Don Carlo;* Eileen Farrell, Franco Corelli, *Andrea Chénier;* Leonard Bernstein debuts, conducting *Eugene Onègin;* Lorin Maazel, *Don Giovanni*

Chicago: Jon Vickers, Régine Crespin, *Un ballo in maschera;* Vickers, Sena Jurinac, *Otello*

Dallas: *L'incoronazione di Poppea* (Monteverdi, American premiere)

San Francisco: *Lulu* (Alban Berg, American premiere); Regina Resnik, *The Queen of Spades*

Art _____

Painting
Andy Warhol, *Mona Lisa*

Roy Lichtenstein, *Okay Hot Shot, Okay, Wham!, Drowning Girl*

Larry Rivers, *Dutch Masters and Cigars II*

Helen Frankenthaler, *Blue Atmosphere*

Richard Lindner, *The Actor*

Jack Levine, *Witches' Sabbath*

Ellsworth Kelly, *Red, Blue, Green*

Jasper Johns, *Map, Periscope (Hart Crane)*

Jim Dine, *Walking Dream with a Four-Foot Clamp*

Tom Wesselmann, *Great American Nude No. 44, Still-Life No. 34*

Sculpture
David Smith, *Zig VII, Cubi XVII, Cubi I, Voltron XVIII*

Reuben Nakian, *Leda and the Swan*

Richard Lippold, *Orpheus and Apollo* (Philharmonic Hall, New York)

Herbert Ferber, *Homage to Piranesi II*

Edward Kienholz, *Back Seat Dodge*

George Segal, *Cinema*

Claes Oldenburg, *Bedroom Ensemble*

Lippold's sculptures are placed in the Pan American Building, New York.

Architecture
Sheldon Memorial Art Gallery, University of Nebraska, Lincoln (Philip Johnson)

Yale School of Art and Architecture (Paul Rudolph)

Carpenter Center for Visual Arts, Harvard University, Cambridge, Mass. (Le Corbusier)

Science Library, Lake Forest College, Illinois (Perkins and Will)

University of California, Music Building, Santa Barbara, and Macgowan Hall, Los Angeles (Charles Luckman)

College of Education, Wayne State University, Detroit (Minoru Yamasaki)

Teneco Building, Houston (Skidmore, Owings, and Merrill)

O'Hare Centralized Terminal Building, Chicago (C. F. Murphy)

Important Exhibitions

Museums

New York: *Metropolitan: Mona Lisa* (on loan); "Treasure from the Mannean Land"; American art. *Museum of Modern Art:* Nolde memorial; Hofmann retrospective; "Americans 1963"; Sculpture of Rodin and Medardo Rosso. *Guggenheim:* Francis Bacon; Kandinsky retrospect

Whitney: "The Decade of the Armory Show"

Philadelphia: "A World of Flowers: Masterpieces of Flower Paintings and Fruit"; Breughel, von Huysum, Manet, Degas, Matisse; Clyfford Still

Guggenheim, Los Angeles, Ann Arbor, Minneapolis: "6 Artists and the Object" (first pop art show)

Washington: Turner; *Mona Lisa* (on loan)

Virginia Museum of Fine Arts: Mellon collection from 1700 to 1950

Boston: "She Walks in Splendor: Great Costumes 1550–1950"

Minneapolis: "The Nabis and Their Circle"

Boston, Toledo, Cleveland, San Francisco: "Barbizon Revisited—Millet, Dupré, Rousseau, Corot

Utica, N.Y.: 320 works from the 1913 Armory show

Art Briefs
Major sales include Rembrandt's *The Merry Lute Player* ($600,000) and *Portrait of a Young Girl* ($260,000), and Wyeth's *Her Room* ($65,000) • The highest purchase price at a Sears & Roebuck show hosted by Vincent Price is $750 for a Chagall lithograph • University of Mississippi professor G. Ray Kerciu is arrested for desecrating a Confederate flag in his painting *America the Beautiful,* inspired by desegregation riots on campus.

Dance _____

Willam Christensen goes from San Francisco to Salt Lake City and founds Ballet West.
The Pennsylvania Ballet develops from Barbara Weisberger's Philadelphia school.

Premieres

New York City Ballet: *Movements for Piano and Orchestra* (George Balanchine), Susan Farrell, Jacques D'Amboise; *Bugaku* (Balanchine)

Paul Taylor: *Scudorama*

Alwin Nikolais: *Imago*

Books

Fiction

Critics' Choice

V, Thomas Pynchon
The Centaur, John Updike
The Bell Jar, Sylvia Plath
Idiot's First, Bernard Malamud
Textures of Life, Hortense Calisher
Names and Faces of Heroes, Reynolds Price
Cat's Cradle, Kurt Vonnegut
The Island, Robert Creeley
❦ *One Day in the Life of Ivan Denisovich*, Alexander Solzhenitsyn

Best-Sellers

The Shoes of the Fisherman, Morris L. West
The Group, Mary McCarthy
Raise High the Roof Beam, Carpenters, and Seymour—An Introduction, J. D. Salinger
Caravans, James A. Michener
Elizabeth Appleton, John O'Hara
Grandmother and the Priests, Taylor Caldwell
City of Night, John Rechy
The Glass-Blowers, Daphne Du Maurier
The Sand Pebbles, Richard McKenna

Nonfiction

Critics' Choice

Eichmann in Jerusalem: A Report on the Banality of Evil, Hannah Arendt
The Rise of the West: A History of Human Community, William H. McNeill
The Great Ascent, Robert Heilbroner
The Feminine Mystique, Betty Friedan
Prospect for the West, J. William Fulbright
The American Way of Death, Jessica Mitford
The Fire Next Time, James Baldwin
John F. Kennedy, President, Hugh Sidey
The Deadlock of Democracy, James McGregor Burns
The American Economic Republic, Adolf A. Berle
Beyond the Melting Pot, Nathan Glazer, Daniel P. Moynihan
John Keats: The Making of a Poet, Aileen Ward
Man-Made America, Christopher Tunnard, Boris Pushkarev

Best-Sellers

Happiness Is a Warm Puppy, Charles M. Schulz
Security Is a Thumb and a Blanket, Charles M. Schulz
J.F.K.: The Man and the Myth, Victor Lasky
Profiles in Courage: Inaugural Edition, John F. Kennedy
O Ye Jigs & Juleps!, Virginia Cary Hudson
Better Homes and Gardens Bread Cook Book
The Pillsbury Family Cookbook
I Owe Russia $1200, Bob Hope
Heloise's Housekeeping Hints

Poetry

James Wright, *The Bough Will Not Break*
E. E. Cummings, *73 Poems*
Conrad Aiken, *The Morning Song of Lord Zero*
W. S. Merwin, *The Moving Target*
James Merrill, *The Thousand and Second Night*
Adrienne Rich, *Snapshots of a Daughter-in-Law*

Pulitzer Prizes

No prize is awarded in fiction.
Puritan Village: The Formation of a New England Town, Sumner Chilton Powell (U.S. history)
Anti-Intellectualism in American Life, Richard Hofstadter (nonfiction)
John Keats, Walter Jackson Bate (biography)
At the End of the Open Road, Louis Simpson (poetry)

Science and Technology

The laser is developed for retinal operations.
F. D. Moore and T. E. Starzl perform the first liver transplant.
J. D. Hardy performs the first human lung transplant.
The FDA declares cancer "cures" Krebiozen and laetrile to be worthless.
Roche Labs introduces the tranquilizer Valium.
The electrical hospital "watchdog" is developed to record up to twelve postoperative patients' body functions.
Gordon Cooper, on the Faith 7 mission, makes 22 orbits and orients manually for reentry.
The Minuteman ICBM is declared combat-ready; its weight is 70,000 pounds, speed capability 15,000 m.p.h., and range, 6,300 miles.
A Polaris missile is launched from a submarine.
The first commercial nuclear reactor, at the Jersey Central Power Company, becomes operational.
❦ Phillips introduces the compact cassette.
❦ Russian Valentina Tereshkova becomes the first woman in space.

Nobel Prize

E. P. Wigner wins the prize in physics for work in nuclear and theoretical physics. Maris Goppert-Mayer and J. H. D. Henson win for discoveries in the shell structure of atomic nuclei.

Sports _____

Baseball

Sandy Koufax (Los Angeles, NL) pitches his second no-hitter, strikes out 306 in the season, and strikes out 15 in a World Series game.

Stan Musial retires; his lifetime totals include an NL record 3,630 hits, 475 homers, and a .330 BA.

Sandy Koufax (Los Angeles, NL) wins the Cy Young Award.

Champions _____

Batting
  Tommy Davis (Los Angeles, NL), .326
  Carl Yastrzemski (Boston, AL), .321
Pitching
  Ron Perranoski (Los Angeles, NL), 16–3
  Whitey Ford (New York, AL), 24–5
Home runs
  Henry Aaron (Milwaukee, NL), 44
  Willie McCovey (San Francisco, NL), 44

Football

Don Shula becomes Baltimore Colt coach and Weeb Ewbank becomes New York Jet coach.

The Supreme Court turns down the AFL antitrust suit.

The Pro Football Hall of Fame begins; original selections include Sammy Baugh, Earl Clarke, Red Grange, George Halas, Wilbur Henry, Cal Hubbard, Don Hutson, Curly Lambeau, Bronko Nagurski, Ernie Nevers, and Jim Thorpe.

Paul Hornung (Green Bay) and Alex Karras (Detroit) are suspended one year for betting on games.

Jim Brown (Cleveland) gains a record 1,863 yards; Y. A. Tittle (New York) throws a record 36 TD passes.

NFL Season Leaders: Y.A. Tittle (New York), passing; Bobby Joe Conrad (St. Louis), receiving.
AFL Season Leaders: Tobin Rote (San Diego), passing; Clem Daniels (Oakland), rushing; Lionel Taylor (Denver), receiving

Cassius Clay (Muhammad Ali) and Howard Cosell. Cosell's "Tell-It-Like-It-Is" interviews alter the style of sports reporting. *Movie Star News.*

College All-Americans: Roger Staubach (QB), Navy; Dick Butkus (C), Illinois; Gale Sayers (B), Kansas; Carl Eller (T), Minnesota

Bowls (Jan. 1, 1964)

Rose: Illinois 17–Washington 7
Orange: Nebraska 13–Auburn 7
Cotton: Texas 28–Navy 6
Sugar: Alabama 12–Mississippi 7

Basketball

NBA All-Pro First Team: Bill Russell (Boston), Elgin Baylor (Los Angeles), Oscar Robertson (Cincinnati), Bob Pettit (St. Louis), Jerry West (Los Angeles)

Other Sports

Winners _____

World Series
  Los Angeles (NL) 4
  New York (AL) 0
MVP
  NL–Sandy Koufax, Los Angeles
  AL–Elston Howard, New York
NFL
  Chicago Bears 14–New York 10
MVP
  Y. A. Tittle, New York
  Jim Brown, Cleveland
College Football
  Texas
Heisman Trophy
  Roger Staubach, Navy

NBA Championship
  Boston 4–Los Angeles 2
MVP
  Bill Russell, Boston
College Basketball
  Loyola, Chicago
Player of the Year
  Art Heyman, Duke
Stanley Cup
  Toronto
US Tennis Open
  Men: Rafael Osuna
  Women: Maria Bueno
USGA Open
  Julius Boros
Kentucky Derby
  Chateaugay (B. Baeza, jockey)

Fashion _____

For Women: The sleeveless dress virtually disappears, and the "offbeat look" sweeps through fashion in layered outfits of various textures and styles. Boots reach over woolen tights and the thigh. Saint Laurent taps the Robin Hood and Joan of Arc look. Desired bulk is, in part, accomplished through turtlenecks and decorative scarves worn with collared shirts, all of which go beneath V-neck cardigans. Chunky tweed jackets and trench coats borrow men's styling. The offbeat look includes blouses modeled after the peasant smock shirt with double stitching, low-slung pants, fishnet stockings, sporty oxfords, white kid boots, thirties' open-back T-strap sandals, and sport watches. The woman who affects the hearty outdoor look moves easily from bulky textures to willowy silks and skinny coats. For the more mature woman, travel coordinates, by Norell, include woolen slacks, jerkins, skirts, capes, and coats. Evening wear is more beautiful than ever with brocade theater suits and full-length tailored coats.

High-fashion note: Dior's evening chemise with flounces and low back

Kaleidoscope

- Joseph M. Valachi publicly identifies the chiefs of organized crime on a televised Senate hearing.
- Eighty-one Teamster officials are indicted, and 58 convicted, by Attorney General Robert Kennedy.
- JFK, visiting the Berlin wall, says, "Ich bin ein Berliner."
- Bayard Rustin and A. Philip Randolph, black president of the Union of Sleeping Car Porters, organize the March on Washington for Jobs and Freedom, at which Martin Luther King delivers his "I have a dream" speech.
- Police chief Bull Connor of Birmingham uses police dogs, fire hoses, and cattle prods on Martin Luther King and the marching schoolchildren and adults in Birmingham.
- A Gallup Poll shows Nelson Rockefeller's fall in popularity after his divorce and remarriage to a divorcée.
- Betty Friedan, in *The Feminine Mystique,* attacks the myth of the happy homemaker.
- The Zapruder film, an amateur movie of the JFK assassination, shows Texas governor John Connally being shot 1.8 seconds after the president and leads to controversy over whether the same bullet hit both men; this lends support to the possibility of a conspiracy.
- California passes New York as the most populous state.
- The Beatles have their first big success, "I Want to Hold Your Hand"; the group includes John Lennon, 23, Paul McCartney, 22, George Harrison, 20, and Ringo Starr, 24.
- "Hootenanies"—group folk concerts with audience participation—gain in popularity, especially with Joan Baez and Bobby Dylan.
- Although unemployment is at 6.1 percent, U.S. factory workers earn more than $100 a week, their highest earnings in history.
- On June 10, congressional legislation guarantees equal pay for equal work.

Birmingham, Alabama's police force confronting civil rights marchers. *Courtesy Dr. Archie Allen.*

Eleanor Roosevelt and Helen Keller meet during the Year of the Woman. *Copyright* Washington Post. *Reprinted by permission of D.C. Public Library.*

- Illegitimate births among teenage mothers are up 150 percent since 1940.
- Frank Sinatra, Jr., is kidnapped at Lake Tahoe and released unhurt in Los Angeles after his father pays a $240,000 ransom. The FBI arrests three suspects two days later and recovers most of the money.
- Two fatal botulism cases are tied to canned tuna fish.
- Julia Child prepares Boeuf Bourguignon on TV, beginning the popularization of French food through cooking demonstrations.
- New Hampshire passes a sweepstakes bill authorizing government-operated lotteries for educational programs.
- Fourteen thousand are arrested in 75 southern cities during civil rights demonstrations.
- "South Vietnam is on its way to victory," United States ambassador Fred Nolting writes, as Diem's campaign against the Buddhists continues.
- Sarah Lawrence graduate Hope Cooke marries Crown Prince Palden Thondup Namgyal of Sikkim; he becomes maharajah when his father dies at the end of the year.
- Fifty girls each week apply to *Playboy* to be "Playmate of the Month."

New Words and Usages: Beatlemania, rat fink, fake out

First Appearances: Kodak Instamatic camera with film cartridge, New York Hilton, Weight Watchers, Trimline phone, commercial service of push-button telephones (Carnegie and Greensburg, Pa.), illuminated nine-hole regulation golf course (Sewell, N.J.), international postcard, John F. Kennedy Airport (Idlewild), gerenuk born in U.S. (Bronx Zoo), the "Amazing Spider Man"

1964

In the News

LBJ CALLS FOR AN END TO POVERTY AND RACIAL DISCRIMINATION . . . RIOTS OCCUR IN PANAMA CANAL ZONE OVER DISPLAY OF AMERICAN FLAG . . . SUPREME COURT RULES THAT CONGRESSIONAL DISTRICTS MUST BE EQUAL . . . JAMES HOFFA IS SENTENCED TO EIGHT YEARS FOR JURY RIGGING . . . JACK RUBY IS SENTENCED TO DEATH FOR LEE HARVEY OSWALD'S MURDER . . . IAN SMITH, WHITE SUPREMACIST, WILL HEAD RHODESIA . . . KHRUSHCHEV AND NASSER HAIL FIRST STAGE OF ASWAN DAM . . . 24TH AMENDMENT, PROHIBITING POLL TAX, PASSES . . . CIVIL RIGHTS ACT OF 1964 PASSES, FORBIDDING PUBLIC, EMPLOYMENT, AND UNION DISCRIMINATION . . . GOP NOMINATES BARRY GOLDWATER FOR PRESIDENT, DEMOCRATS NOMINATE LBJ . . . HARLEM AND BROOKLYN BLACKS RIOT, 141 ARE INJURED . . . RANGER VII TRANSMITS PHOTOS OF MOON . . . FBI FINDS BODIES OF THREE SLAIN CIVIL RIGHTS WORKERS IN PHILADELPHIA, MISSISSIPPI . . . U.S. PLANES BOMB NORTH VIETNAM AFTER ATTACK ON U.S. DESTROYER IN THE GULF OF TONKIN, THE SENATE VOTES RESOLUTION OF U.S. SUPPORT . . . $947 MILLION IS VOTED FOR ANTIPOVERTY PROGRAM, JOB TRAINING, DOMESTIC PEACE CORPS . . . BLACKS IN PHILADELPHIA, PA., RIOT OVER POLICE BRUTALITY, 248 ARE INJURED . . . WARREN COMMISSION REPORT CONCLUDES THAT OSWALD ACTED ALONE IN KENNEDY ASSASSINATION . . . AT CAIRO, 47 NONALIGNED NATIONS DENOUNCE THE U.S. . . . MARTIN LUTHER KING WINS NOBEL PEACE PRIZE . . . KHRUSHCHEV IS REMOVED, LEONID BREZHNEV AND ALEKSEI KOSYGIN TAKE OVER . . . CHINA EXPLODES ITS FIRST A-BOMB . . . LBJ WINS LANDSLIDE VICTORY, 43 MILLION TO 27 MILLION . . . ECUMENICAL COUNCIL EXONERATES JEWS OF CHRIST'S DEATH . . . SUPREME COURT UPHOLDS THE CIVIL RIGHTS ACT.

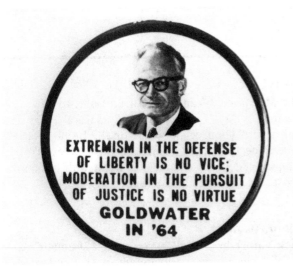

Campaign button for Barry Goldwater with the presidential candidate's famous dictum. *Smithsonian Institution.*

"I'm the only President you've got."
— Lyndon B. Johnson

"I don't see an American dream; . . . I see an American nightmare. . . . Three hundred and ten years we worked in this country without a dime in return."
— Malcolm X

"Why does integration have to begin with *our* children?"
— Anonymous (quoted in *New York Times*)

Quotes

"Camp is the answer to the problem: how to be a dandy in an age of mass culture. Camp asserts . . . there is a good taste of bad taste . . . [for example] The *Enquirer* . . . 'Swan Lake' . . . Shoedsack's 'King Kong' . . . Jayne Mansfield . . . Victor Mature . . . Bette Davis . . . Art Nouveau."
— Susan Sontag, "Notes on Camp"

"[Pop art is] the use of commercial art as a subject matter in painting. . . . It was hard to get a painting that was despicable enough so that no one would hang it. . . . The one thing everyone hated was commercial art; apparently they didn't hate that enough either."
— Roy Lichtenstein

"In the electronic age, we wear all mankind as our skin."
— Marshall McLuhan, *Understanding Media*

"By continuously embracing technologies we relate ourselves to them. . . . That is why we must, to use them at all, serve these objects as gods or minor religions."
— Marshall McLuhan

Ads

Trichinosis, encephalitis, scarlet fever, amoebiasis, jungle rot.
We think you'll find them more challenging than the sniffles.
(Peace Corps)

I quit school when I were sixteen.
(Public Service Ad)

Act your age—today is Election Day. If you're over 21, make sure you vote.
(Public Service Ad)

Does it make sense to jump out of a warm bed into a cold cereal?
(Quaker Oats)

Only 1 out of 25 men is color blind. The other 24 just dress that way.
(Mohara Suits)

167 days of foggy, foggy dew can't claim all the credit for beautiful English complexions.
(Elizabeth Arden)

Peter Sellers as a former Nazi missile expert in Stanley Kubrick's *Dr. Strangelove, or How I Learned to Stop Worrying and Love the Bomb. Movie Star News.*

TV

Premieres
"The Man from U.N.C.L.E.," Robert Vaughn, David McCallum
"Flipper," Brian Kelly
"Gomer Pyle, U.S.M.C.," Jim Nabors
"Daniel Boone," Fess Parker
"Jeopardy"
"Peyton Place," Mia Farrow, Ed Nelson
"Bewitched," Elizabeth Montgomery
"Mr. Magoo"
"Gilligan's Island," Jim Backus, Alan Hale, Jr.
"The Munsters," Yvonne De Carlo, Al Lewis
"The Addams Family," John Astin, Carolyn Jones

Top Ten (Nielsen)
"Bonanza," "Bewitched," "Gomer Pyle, U.S.M.C.," "The Andy Griffith Show," "The Fugitive," "The Red Skelton Show," "The Dick Van Dyke Show," "The Lucy Show," "Peyton Place II," "Combat"

Specials
"The Magnificent Yankee" (Alfred Lunt, Lynn Fontanne); "My Name Is Barbra" (Barbra Streisand); "The Decision to Drop the Bomb" (NBC White Paper); "What Is Sonata Form?" (New York Philharmonic Young People's Concert with Leonard Bernstein); "Profiles in Courage"

Emmy Awards
"Dick Van Dyke Show" (program); "I, Leonardo da Vinci," "The Louvre" (documentaries); Leonard Bernstein, Dick Van Dyke (performers)

Of Note
An American version of the British "That Was the Week That Was," with Elliot Read, Henry Morgan, and David Frost, initiates a biting form of topical political satire on prime-time TV • Owing to its great success, "Peyton Place" is aired twice weekly in prime time.

Movies

Openings
My Fair Lady (George Cukor), Audrey Hepburn, Rex Harrison
Becket (Peter Glenville), Richard Burton, Peter O'Toole, John Gielgud
Dr. Strangelove (Stanley Kubrick), Peter Sellers, George C. Scott
Mary Poppins (Robert Stevenson), Julie Andrews, Dick Van Dyke
Zorba the Greek (Michael Cacoyannis), Anthony Quinn, Alan Bates, Lila Kedrova
The Pumpkin Eater (Jack Clayton), Anne Bancroft, Peter Finch, James Mason
Seven Days in May (John Frankenheimer), Burt Lancaster, Kirk Douglas, Fredric March
Hush, Hush, Sweet Charlotte (Robert B. Aldrich), Bette Davis, Olivia de Havilland
A Hard Day's Night (Richard Lester), Beatles
The Pink Panther (Blake Edwards), Peter Sellers, David Niven, Capucine
The Americanization of Emily (Arthur Hiller), James Garner, Julie Andrews
Cheyenne Autumn (John Ford), Richard Widmark, Carroll Baker
The Umbrellas of Cherbourg (Jacques Demy), Catherine Deneuve
Woman in the Dunes (Hiroshi Teshigahara), Eiji Okada, Kyoko Kishida
The Servant (Joseph Losey), Dirk Bogarde, James Fox, Sarah Miles
From Russia with Love (Terence Young), Sean Connery, Daniela Bianchi, Lotte Lenya
Goldfinger (Guy Hamilton), Sean Connery, Honor Blackman
The Gospel According to St. Matthew (Pier Paolo Pasolini), Enrique Irazoqui

Academy Awards
Best Picture: *My Fair Lady*
Best Director: George Cukor (*My Fair Lady*)
Best Actress: Julie Andrews (*Mary Poppins*)
Best Actor: Rex Harrison (*My Fair Lady*)

Top Box-Office Stars
Doris Day, Jack Lemmon, Rock Hudson, John Wayne, Cary Grant, Elvis Presley, Shirley MacLaine, Ann-Margret, Paul Newman, Richard Burton

Stars of Tomorrow
Elke Sommer, Annette Funicello, Susannah York, Elizabeth Ashley, Stefanie Powers, Harve Presnell, Dean Jones, Keir Dullea, Nancy Sinatra, Joey Heatherton

Popular Music

Hit Songs
"Chim Chim Cher-ee"
"I Want to Hold Your Hand"
"Downtown"
"People"
"Pink Panther Theme"
"Walk on By"
"We'll Sing in the Sunshine"
"King of the Road"

Top Records

Albums: *Hello Dolly!* (original cast); *Honey in the Horn* (Al Hirt); *The Barbra Streisand Album, West Side Story* (sound track); *The Second Barbra Streisand Album; Meet the Beatles*

Singles: *She Loves You* (Beatles); *Baby, I Need Your Loving* (Four Tops); *Oh, Pretty Woman* (Roy Orbison); *Hello Dolly!* (Louis Armstrong); *I Get Around* (Beach Boys); *Everybody Loves Somebody* (Dean Martin); *Baby Love* (Supremes); *A Hard Day's Night* (Beatles); *Leader of the Pack* (Shangri-La). Country: *Understand Your Man* (Johnny Cash); *Dang Me* (Roger Miller)

Grammy Awards
The Girl from Ipanema, Stan Getz, Astrud Gilberto (record); *Getz / Gilberto* (album); "Hello Dolly!" (song)

Jazz and Big Bands
Successful concerts include those of Charlie Mingus, Earl Hines, Cecil Taylor, Jimmy Giuffre, Paul Bley, and Rod Levill; Andrew Hill and Charles Lloyd attract much attention.
Frank Zappa introduces jazz into rock with The Mothers of Invention.

Top Performers *(Downbeat)*: Eric Dolphy (soloist); Duke Ellington, Count Basie (bands); Dave Brubeck (jazz group); Jim Hall, Charlie Mingus, Bill Evans (instrumentalists); Ella Fitzgerald, Ray Charles (vocalists); Double Six (vocal group)

Theater

Broadway Openings
Plays
The Subject Was Roses (Frank D. Gilroy), Martin Sheen, Jack Albertson, Irene Dailey
Dylan (Sidney Michaels), Alec Guinness, Kate Reid
Any Wednesday (Muriel Resnik), Sandy Dennis, Gene Hackman, Rosemary Murphy
Luv (Murray Schisgal), Eli Wallach, Anne Jackson, Alan Arkin
The Owl and the Pussycat (Bill Manhoff), Diana Sands, Alan Alda
The Deputy (Rolf Hochhuth), Emlyn Williams, Jeremy Brett
Tiny Alice (Edward Albee), John Gielgud, Irene Worth
The Sign in Sidney Brustein's Window (Lorraine Hansberry), Rita Moreno, Gabriel Dell
The Physicists (Friedrich Dürrenmatt), Jessica Tandy, George Voskovec, Hume Cronyn
Blues for Mr. Charlie (James Baldwin), Al Freeman, Jr., Rip Torn, Diana Sands
After the Fall (Arthur Miller), Barbara Loden, Jason Robards, Jr.
Incident at Vichy (Arthur Miller), David Wayne, Hal Holbrook

Musicals
Hello Dolly! (Jerry Herman), Carol Channing, David Burns, Charles Nelson Reilly
Fiddler on the Roof (Jerry Bock, Sheldon Harnick), Zero Mostel, Maria Karnilova
Funny Girl (Jule Styne), Barbra Streisand, Sydney Chaplin

Golden Boy (Charles Strouse, Lee Adams), Sammy Davis, Jr.

Classics and Revivals On and Off Broadway
Hamlet, Richard Burton; *The Slave, The Toilet* (LeRoi Jones), Jaime Sanchez; *Othello*, James Earl Jones; *A Slight Ache, The Room, The Lover* (Harold Pinter); *The Old Glory* (Robert Lowell); *Three Sisters* (Chekhov), Geraldine Page, Kim Stanley, Shirley Knight; *The Blood Knot* (Athol Fugard), James Earl Jones; *The New Tenant, Victims of Duty* (Eugene Ionesco); Royal Shakespeare: *King Lear* (Paul Scofield), *Comedy of Errors. Founded:* The American Place Theatre by Wynn Handman and Sidney Lanier

Regional
Founded: Eugene O'Neill Memorial Theater, Waterford, Conn., by George C. White; Hartford Stage Company by Jacques Cartier; Actors Theatre of Louisville, by Richard Block, Ewel Cornett; Trinity Square Repertory, Providence, R.I., by Adrian Hall

Minnesota Theatre Company: *Henry V, St. Joan, Volpone*, George Grizzard, Ed Flanders

Pulitzer Prize
No prize is awarded.

Tony Awards
Luther, John Osborne (play), *Hello Dolly!* Jerry Herman (musical)

Classical Music _____

Compositions
Milton Babbitt, *Philomel*
Ferde Grofé, *World's Fair Suite*
Roy Harris, *Horn of Plenty*
William Schuman, Symphony no. 7
Leo Sowerby, Symphony no. 5
John Cage, *Atlas Elipticales*
Henry Brant, *Voyage Four*
Charles Wuorinen, Piano Variations

Important Events
Interest grows in electronic music: the Ojai Festival, California, includes *Ensembles for Synthesizer* (Milton Babbitt); Duo for Clarinet and Recorded Clarinet (William O. Smith); and *Rhythm Studies Performed on Perforated Piano* (John Powell).
The Festival of Chamber Music, Library of Congress, includes *In Time of Daffodil* (Riccardo Malipiero); *Amaryllis* (William Schuman); String Septet (Darius Milhaud); *Four Psalms* (Howard Hanson); String Sextet (Walter Piston); and *The Feast of Love* (Virgil Thomson).
Jascha Heifetz and Gregor Piatigorsky give three chamber music and concerto concerts, New York; Artur Rubinstein gives three major concerts, New York.
The Los Angeles Music Center for the Performing Arts opens: the Los Angeles Philharmonic with Zubin Mehta, 28, conductor, gives a week of concerts, including *American Festival Overture* (William Schuman); Beethoven Violin Concerto and Symphony no. 9, and *Le sacre du printemps* (Igor Stravinsky).

Debut: John Ogdon

Newcomer Régine Crespin, with Richard Tucker, one of the Metropolitan's leading tenors since 1945, in *Tosca*. *Chicago Lyric Opera: David H. Fishman.*

First Performances
Leonard Bernstein, Third Symphony *(Kaddish)*, Boston; Carlos Chávez, Symphony no. 6 (New York); Peter Mennin, Symphony no. 7 (Cleveland); Roger Sessions, Symphony no. 5 (Philadelphia); Quincy Porter, Symphony no. 2 (Louisville); Lukas Foss, *Elytres* (Los Angeles); Henry Cowell, Concerto for Koto and Orchestra (Philadelphia); Igor Stravinsky, *Elegy for JFK* (Los Angeles)

Opera

Metropolitan: Roberta Peters, George London, *The Last Savage* (Gian Carlo Menotti, premiere); Joan Sutherland, *Lucia di Lammermoor;* Rita Gorr, Jess Thomas, *Samson et Delila;* Gabriella Tucci, Regina Resnik, Anselmo Colzani, *Falstaff;* Elisabeth Schwarzkopf (debut), *Der Rosenkavalier;* Donald Gramm (debut), *Ariadne auf Naxos*

New York City: *Natalia Petrovna* (Lee Hoiby, premiere)

Boston: Joan Sutherland, *I Puritani; Lulu*

Philadelphia: Renata Tebaldi returns to the stage in *La bohème;* Joan Sutherland, *La traviata*

Chicago: Fiorenza Cossotto, *La favorita;* Irmgard Seefried, Regine Crespin, *Ariadne auf Naxos*

Santa Fe: *Daphne* (Richard Strauss)

San Francisco: *Der Freischütz, Susanna*

Fiddler on the Roof, the highly successful musical based on Sholem Aleichem's stories of Jewish life in Russia. *Billy Rose Theatre Collection. The New York Public Library at Lincoln Center. Astor, Lenox and Tilden Foundations.*

Art

Painting

Jasper Johns, *Field Painting, Studio*
Agnes Martin, *The Tree*
Ad Reinhardt, *Abstract Painting*
Kenneth Noland, *Tropical Zone, Prime Course*
Frank Stella, *Ifafa II, Fez*
Jack Youngerman, *Black, Yellow, Red*
Jim Dine, *Double Self-Portrait (The Green Line)*
Robert Rauschenberg, *Retroactive*
Andy Warhol, *Brillo Boxes*

Sculpture

David Smith, *Cubi XVIII, Cubi XIX*
Louise Nevelson, *Black Cord, Silent Music I*
George Segal, *Woman in a Doorway I*
Edward Kienholz, *The Birthday*
Jasper Johns, *Painted Bronze II (Ale Cans)*
Alexander Calder designs sculpture for the Federal Center, Chicago.

Important Exhibitions

Museums

New York: *Metropolitan:* "The World's Fairs—Architectures of Fantasy." *Gallery of Modern Art:* Tchelitchew; The Pre-Raphaelites. *Museum of Modern Art:* Sculpture retrospective; Hofmann; Bonnard. *Whitney:* Joseph Stella and Hopper retrospectives. *Guggenheim:* Francis Bacon Retrospective

Chicago: Albright; Chinese art of the Ming and Ch'ing dynasties

Architecture

Verrazano-Narrows Bridge, New York (Ammann, Hermann)
New York World's Fair, New York Pavilion (Philip Johnson)
Kline Science Tower, Yale University, New Haven, Conn. (Philip Johnson)
Chicago Federal Center, United States Courthouse, Federal Office Building, Post Office, Chicago (Mies van der Rohe)
Venturi House, Philadelphia (Venturi and Rausch)
Gallery of Modern Art, New York (Edward Durell Stone)
New York State Theater, Lincoln Center, New York (Harrison and Johnson)
Green Center for the Earth Sciences, M.I.T., Cambridge (I.M. Pei)

Richmond: Elizabethan art (to celebrate Shakespeare's 400th birthday); Dutch 17th-century paintings

Baltimore: 250 works from 1914

Washington: *Corcoran:* John Singer Sargent; Contemporary Japanese painting. *National:* Turner; 7,000 years of Persian art

Cleveland, Brooklyn, Kansas City, Houston, San Francisco: Turner—80 watercolors

Art Briefs

Michelangelo's *Pièta* is displayed at the New York World's Fair (Vatican Pavilion) • The Museum of Modern Art in New York opens two new wings and expands the sculpture garden; the first permanent photo gallery is installed • Chagall completes a stained-glass memorial panel to Dag Hammarskjöld for the UN Building, New York • Mark Rothko completes murals for a Houston interdenominational chapel later named the Rothko Chapel • Major prizes of the year are awarded to painters Rauschenberg, Motherwell, and Kelly, and architects David, Georges, Conway, and McCullough.

Dance

The Boston Ballet is founded by E. Virginia Williams. Rebecca Harkness and Robert Joffrey separate because of conflicting artistic policies; she forms the Harkness Ballet. The New York City Ballet opens in the new New York State Theater, Lincoln Center. The Ford Foundation gives $7.7 million to the company.

Premieres

New York City Ballet: *Tarantella* (George Balanchine), Patricia McBride, Edward Villella; *Irish Fantasy* (Jacques D'Amboise)

Merce Cunningham: *Event Number One*

Books

Fiction

Critics' Choice
Because I Was Flesh, Edward Dahlberg
Second Skin, John Hawkes
Julian, Gore Vidal
Come Back, Dr. Caligari, Donald Barthelme
Cabot Wright Begins, James Purdy
Little Big Man, Thomas Berger
The Wapshot Scandal, John Cheever
Teeth, Dying and Other Matters, Richard G. Stern
Last Exit to Brooklyn, Hubert Selby
ᔒ *The Interrogation*, J. G. Le Clézio

Best-Sellers
The Spy Who Came in from the Cold, John Le Carré
Candy, Terry Southern, Mason Hoffenberg
Herzog, Saul Bellow
Armageddon, Leon Uris
The Man, Irving Wallace
The Rector of Justin, Louis Auchincloss
The Martyred, Richard E. Kim
You Only Live Twice, Ian Fleming

Nonfiction

Critics' Choice
Waiting for the End, Leslie Fiedler
Crowell's Handbook of Classical Literature, Lillian Feder
Understanding Media, Marshall McLuhan
Science: The Glorious Entertainment, Jacques Barzun
The Games People Play, Eric Berne
Experiment, Willie Lee Rose
The End of Alliance, Ronald Steel
The Theatre of Revolt, Robert Brustein
Of Poetry and Power: A Tribute to John F. Kennedy, ed. Pierre Salinger, Sander Vanocur
The Warren Commission Report
God and Golem, Inc., Norbert Wiener
The Life of Lenin, Louis Fischer
The Oysters of Locmariaquer, Eleanor Clark
ᔒ *The Wretched of the Earth*, Franz Fanon

Best-Sellers
Four Days, American Heritage, United Press International
I Need All the Friends I Can Get, Charles M. Schulz
Profiles in Courage: Memorial Edition, John F. Kennedy
In His Own Write, John Lennon
Christmas Is Together-Time, Charles M. Schulz
A Day in the Life of President Kennedy, Jim Bishop
The Kennedy Wit, Bill Adler
A Moveable Feast, Ernest Hemingway

Poetry
Robert Lowell, *For the Union Dead*
Theodore Roethke, *The Far Field* (posthumous)
Karl Shapiro, *The Bourgeois Poet*
Charles Olson, *Signature to Petition on Ten Pound Island*
James Dickey, *Helmets, Two Poems of the Air*
Richard Eberhart, *The Quarry*
Ted Berrigan, *The Sonnets*
J. V. Cunningham, *To What Strangers, What Welcome*

Pulitzer Prizes
Collected Stories of Katherine Anne Porter, Katherine Anne Porter (fiction)
The Greenback Era, Irwin Unger (U.S. history)
O Strange New World, Howard Mumford (nonfiction)
Henry Adams, 3 vols., Ernest Samuels (biography)
77 Dream Songs, John Berryman (poetry)

Science and Technology

A total of 4,316 high-resolution photos of the moon's surface are taken by Ranger VII.

IBM introduces chips into its 360 system; it also demonstrates a word processor that stores, corrects, and retypes.

Motions of an orbiting satellite are visualized by an IBM 7090 digital computer.

The fundamental subatomic particle, omega-minis, is discovered.

Home dialysis for kidney patients is introduced in the United States and England.

Dr. Michael DeBakey replaces a section of the aorta with Dacron.

The U.S. Surgeon General links cigarette smoking and cancer.

The "battered-child syndrome" is described.

Methadone is developed as a means of rehabilitating heroin users by Vincent Dole and Marie Nyswander.

The Verrazano-Narrows Bridge, in New York, opens, the world's largest single-span suspension bridge.

ᔒ A new strain of "miracle" rice, suitable for tropical cultivation, is developed.

Nobel Prize
Dr. Konrad Bloch wins the prize in physiology and medicine for work on the relationship between heart disease and cholesterol. C. H. Townes wins in physics for work on high-intensity radiation.

Sports

Baseball

Dean Chance (Los Angeles, AL) pitches a record 11 shutouts. He also wins the Cy Young Award.

Champions

Batting
Roberto Clemente (Pittsburgh, NL), .339
Tony Oliva (Minnesota, AL), .323
Pitching
Sandy Koufax (Los Angeles, NL), 19–5
Wally Bunker (Baltimore, AL), 19–5
Home runs
Harmon Killebrew (Minneapolis, AL), 49

Football

Jim Brown (Cleveland) ties Don Hutson's career record of 105 touchdowns.

NFL Season Leaders: Bart Starr (Green Bay), passing; Jim Brown (Cleveland), rushing; John Morris (Chicago), receiving. **AFL Season Leaders:** Len Dawson (Kansas City), passing; Cookie Gilchrist (Buffalo), rushing; Charlie Hennigan (Houston) receiving

College All-Americans: Gale Sayers (B), Kansas; Jerry Rhome (QB), Tulsa; Dick Butkus (LB), Illinois

Bowls (Jan. 1, 1965)

Rose: Michigan 34–Oregon State 7
Orange: Texas 21–Alabama 17
Cotton: Arkansas 10–Nebraska 7
Sugar: Louisiana State 13–Syracuse 10

Basketball

NBA All-Pro First Team: Wilt Chamberlain (Philadelphia), Oscar Robertson (Cincinnati), Bob Pettit (St. Louis), Walt Bellamy (Baltimore), Jerry West (Los Angeles)

Olympics

In the Summer Games at Tokyo, Don Schollander wins four gold medals in swimming (100m, 400m, two relays). Other U.S. winners include Robert Hayes (100m, 10.0s.); Henry Carr (200m, 20.35s.); Michael Larrabee (400m, 45.1s.); Robert Schul (5000m, 13:48.8); Walter Mills (10,000m, 28.24.4); Fred Hansen (pole vault, 16'8¾"); Dallas Long (shot put, 66'8¼"); Al Oerter (discus, 200'1½"); Wyomia Tyus (100m, 11.4s.); Edith McGuire (200m, 23.0s.); Virginia Duenkel (swimming, 400m, 4:43.3); Joseph Frazier (HW boxing). In the Winter Games at Innsbruck, Austria, R. Terrance McDermott wins the 500m.

Other Sports

Boxing: Cassius Clay, an 8–1 underdog, beats Sonny Liston in seven rounds for the heavyweight title before 8,200 in Miami.

Running: Seventeen-year old Jim Ryun runs the mile in 3:50.0.

Winners

World Series
St. Louis (NL) 4
New York (AL) 3
MVP
NL–Ken Boyer, St. Louis
AL–Brooks Robinson, Baltimore
NFL
Cleveland 27–Baltimore 0
MVP
Len Moore, Baltimore
College Football
Alabama
Heisman Trophy
John Huarte, Notre Dame
NBA Championship
Boston 4–San Francisco 1

MVP
Oscar Robertson, Cincinnati
College Basketball
UCLA
Player of the Year
Walt Hazzard, UCLA
Stanley Cup
Toronto
US Tennis Open
Men: Roy Emerson
Women: Maria Bueno
USGA Open
Ken Venturi
Kentucky Derby
Northern Dancer (W. Hartack, jockey)

Fashion

For Women: Colored or textured tights give the body a sculpted look. Bold blocks of strongly contrasting color and pattern, in sharp outlines and with colored borders, echo pop art. Barbra Streisand's "eclectic look" shares fashion honors with that of the more traditionally elegant Mrs. Kennedy and the Duchess of Windsor. Mary Quant and Sally Triffin's "mod" emphasizes "the nude look" (Gernreich's topless tank has already appeared). The body stocking is a great success, along with transparent sports blouses and décolletages that reach both the navel and the base of the spine. Courrèges pursues the opposite fashion extreme with tops that cover all except the face and hands and are worn with narrow pipe-stem pants. Generally, the "superfeminine look" replaces the sporty one, with accents from North Africa, and the Middle and Far East. Long hair is pulled back into designer scarves; the raincoat becomes ubiquitous.

High-fashion notes: Picciu's draped and folded pants from Bali, India, and Africa; Cashin's evening sportswear; Ferraud's see-throughs

Kaleidoscope _____

- A controversial LBJ TV ad portrays a little girl picking daisies, an atomic explosion, and the statement: "These are the stakes."
- "Go-go" girls on raised platforms in "discos" set the dance pace to the frug, swim, watusi, dog, children, and monkey. A San Francisco bar introduces topless go-go girls on June 19; on September 3, they go bottomless.
- Marshall McLuhan popularizes his belief that "the medium is the message," that the experience of seeing and hearing, rather than content, matters.
- The Hell's Angels receive a great deal of publicity with their huge Harley-Davidson motorcycles, colored and unwashed clothing (like sleeveless vests), helmets, huge sunglasses, and tattoos.
- The largest mass arrest of student demonstrators includes 732 sit-ins at Sproul Hall at the University of California (Berkeley), led by Mario Savio, Bettina Aptheker, and Jack Weinberg.
- The Warren Commission, finding no conspiracy in JFK's assassination, issues a paperback report 80 hours after its conclusions are made.
- Some 464,000 black students boycott the New York public schools to end, through busing, de facto segregation.
- Lester Maddox closes his Atlanta restaurant, Pickwick, rather than serve blacks; he had previously distributed pickax handles to anyone willing to cudgel entering blacks.
- Martin Luther King donates most of his $54,600 Nobel Peace Prize to the civil rights movement.
- James Chaney, Andrew Goodman, and Michael Schwerner are murdered, along with 12 others, after SNCC's Freedom Summer; the FBI arrests 21, including Sheriff Lawrence Rainey of Neshoba County, Mississippi.
- Ten thousand await the Beatles at JFK Airport: the group gets $2,400 for its Ed Sullivan appearance, and, later, a record $150,000 in Kansas City; "Can't Buy Me Love" has the biggest advance sale to date.
- Rudy Gernreich's topless bathing suit begins the no-bra fad.
- Over 250 million paperback books are sold.
- Movies have their most successful year since TV began.
- Elizabeth Taylor divorces Eddie Fisher and marries Richard Burton 10 days later.
- As evidence of his thriftiness, LBJ goes around the White House turning off lights.
- LBJ promises not "to send American boys 9 or 10,000 miles away from home to do what Asian boys should do for themselves."
- LBJ appoints Sargent Shriver head of the Office of Economic Opportunity in the "national war on poverty"; he is to coordinate the Job Corps, Neighborhood Youth Corps, VISTA, Head Start, and other organizations.
- The surgeon general's reports linking cigarettes and

The New York World's Fair. *Museum of the City of New York.*

cancer lead the Federal Trade Commission to require that cigarette packages carry health warnings.
- A record 276 million gallons of alcohol is consumed, averaging 1.45 gallons per capita; bourbon is the largest-selling whiskey.
- Thieves, led by Murph the Surf, are caught after stealing rare stones from the Museum of Natural History in New York, including the world's largest sapphire, the 565-carat Star of India.
- The motto of the New York World's Fair is "Peace through Understanding"; 27 million attend, less than anticipated.
- Cigarette advertising is halted in magazines, sports programs, and college papers, and on radio stations.
- Michelangelo's *Pièta*, on loan from St. Peters for the New York World's Fair, arrives in a special waterproof, floatable crate designed to free itself from a sinking ship.
- An outraged public reads about an indifferent public on the occasion of Kitty Genovese's assault: many neighbors watched but no one phoned the police until after she was beaten to death.
- Police capture the suspected "Boston Strangler," Albert Henry De Salvo.
- "In your heart you know he might [push the button]" is one takeoff on Barry Goldwater's campaign slogan "In your heart you know he's right."

Fads: Beatles items, the Prince Valiant hairdo, GI Joe dolls

First Appearances: Films shown on airplanes, Ford Mustang, Awake, Pop-Tarts, Lucky Charms, Dole fresh pineapple, Dynel, rivets removed from Levi Straus blue jean pockets, Carlton, Reverend Ike (Frederick J. Eikeronkoetter), Klear, zip codes, Canyonlands National Park (Utah), Campobello International Park, Brunswick Island, freeze-dried coffee (Maxim), artificial leather (Corfam), electronic voting machines, elliptical-shaped office building, geodesic dome, Washington's Capital Beltway, self-service post office (Wheaton, Md.), bridge player to earn a lifetime total of 8,000 points (Oswald Jacoby), picture-phone service (New York, Chicago), presidential election in which votes are tallied electronically, Allan and Midge dolls (to go with Barbie and Ken), Kennedy half dollar, *Crawdaddy* (first rock magazine), Robert Moog synthesizer

1965

Facts and Figures

Economic Profile
  Dow-Jones: ↑ High 969–
    Low 867
  GNP: +8%
  Inflation: +1.6%
  Unemployment: 4.5%
Infant mortality/1,000: 24.7
Maternal mortality/10,000:
  3.2
Physicians in U.S.: 297,000
Dentists in U.S.: 109,000
Hospital beds: 1,703,000
New York City apartments:
  5th Ave. (60s), 6-room
    duplex: $575
  Broadway, 72nd St., 2
    bedrooms: $200
  Park West Village, 2
    bedrooms, with view of
    Central park: $239
Help wanted (*New York
  Times*):
  Receptionist: $65–$80
  Clerk-typist: $70–$90
  TV programmer: $125
  IBM key punch: $65–$90
  Dental assistant: $150

Deaths

Bernard Baruch, Clara Bow,
  Winston Churchill, Nat
  "King" Cole, T. S. Eliot,
  Felix Frankfurter, Judy
  Holliday, Stan Laurel,
  Georgi Rimsky-Korsakov,
  Edward R. Murrow,
  Helena Rubinstein, Albert
  Schweitzer, Adlai E.
  Stevenson

In the News

LBJ PLEDGES TO SUPPORT SOUTH VIETNAM AND TO BUILD "THE GREAT SOCIETY" . . . FIRST U.S. COMBAT TROOPS LAND IN VIETNAM . . . MALCOLM X IS ASSASSINATED IN HARLEM . . . $1.4 BILLION IS APPROPRIATED FOR APPALACHIA . . . SOVIET COSMONAUT LEONOV IS THE FIRST MAN TO FLOAT IN SPACE . . . 3,200 MAKE A 54-MILE "FREEDOM MARCH" FROM SELMA TO MONTGOMERY, ALABAMA, MARCHER VIOLA LIUZZO IS MURDERED . . . GEMINI MAKES THE FIRST TWO-MAN U.S. ORBIT . . . TERRORIST BOMB DEVASTATES U.S. SAIGON EMBASSY . . . LBJ OFFERS NORTH VIETNAM UNCONDITIONAL PEACE AND $1 BILLION FOR RECONSTRUCTION . . . CIVIL WAR BREAKS OUT IN DOMINICAN REPUBLIC, JOHNSON SENDS TROOPS . . . 100,000 ON 100 CAMPUSES ATTEND NATIONAL TEACH-IN ON VIETNAM . . . BOMBING OF NORTH VIETNAM RESUMES AS HO CHI MINH REJECTS LBJ OFFER . . . ED WHITE TAKES A RECORD 20-MINUTE WALK FROM GEMINI IV . . . SUPREME COURT STRIKES DOWN COMPULSORY ANTI–BIRTH CONTROL LAWS . . . MARINER FLIES PAST MARS AND TRANSMITS PHOTOS . . . MEDICARE BILL PASSES . . . VOTING RIGHTS ACT OF 1965 PASSES . . . 34 DIE IN WATTS GHETTO RIOTS . . . MAO CALLS FOR REVOLUTIONARY WARS IN DEVELOPING NATIONS . . . OAS PEACE PLAN FOR DOMINICAN REPUBLIC IS ACCEPTED . . . FRANCE LEAVES NATO . . . HUD IS CREATED . . . INDONESIAN ARMY CRUSHES COMMUNIST COUP AND BEGINS ERADICATION . . . $2.3 BILLION HIGHER EDUCATION ACT IS PASSED . . . RHODESIA DECLARES INDEPENDENCE OF BRITAIN, BRITISH P.M. WILSON ORDERS SANCTIONS . . . 25,000 IN WASHINGTON, D.C., MARCH TO PROTEST WAR . . . LBJ STOPS BOMBING AND OFFERS PEACE . . . VIETNAM: U.S. TROOP STRENGTH, 190,000; U.S. DEAD, 1,350; WOUNDED, 5,300; ENEMY DEAD, 34,585.

Antiwar march. Protest accelerates at home, alongside military buildup in Vietnam. *Photographer: Richard Hofmeister.*

"The Vietcong are going to collapse within weeks."
— National Security Adviser Walt Rostow

"This is a theatre of assault. The play that will split the heavens will be called THE DESTRUCTION OF AMERICA. The heroes will be Crazy Horse, Denmark Vesey, Patrice Lumumba."
— Leroi Jones, "The Revolutionary Theatre"

"Once it was power that created style. But now high styles come from low places, from people who have no power, . . . who are marginal, who carve out worlds for themselves in the nether depths, in tainted 'undergrounds.' "
— Tom Wolfe, "Girl of the Year"

"We like books that have a lot of *dreck* in them, matter which presents itself as not wholly relevant . . . but which, carefully attended to, can supply a 'sense' of what is going on."
— Donald Barthelme, *Snow White*

Quotes

"Let us march on segregated schools. Let us march on poverty. Let us march on ballot boxes, until the Wallaces of our nation tremble away in silence. My people, my people, listen! The battle is in our hands."
— Martin Luther King, Jr., en route from Selma to Montgomery

"At times, history and fate meet at a single time in a single place to shape a turning point in man's unending search for freedom. So it was at Lexington and Concord. So it was a century ago at Appomattox. So it was last week at Selma."
— President Lyndon Johnson

Vietnam: Orange Beach, South of Danang. In the first year ground troops are sent to Vietnam, LBJ declares "the people of South Vietnam have chosen to resist aggression from the north. The U.S. has taken its place beside them." *U.S. Navy Department.*

Ads

TV

Premieres
"Days of Our Lives"
"Green Acres," Eva Gabor, Eddie Albert
"Run for Your Life," Ben Gazzara
"The Dean Martin Show"
"The Wild, Wild West," Robert Conrad, Ross Martin
"Get Smart," Don Adams, Barbara Feldon
"The Big Valley," Barbara Stanwyck
"I Dream of Jeannie," Barbara Eden
"The FBI," Efrem Zimbalist, Jr.
"F Troop," Forrest Tucker, Larry Storch
"Hogan's Heroes," Werner Klemperer, Bob Crane
"The Avengers," Patrick Macnee, Diana Rigg
"I Spy," Robert Culp, Bill Cosby

Top Ten (Nielsen)
"Bonanza," "Gomer Pyle, U.S.M.C.," "The Lucy Show," "The Red Skelton Hour," "Batman," "The Andy Griffith Show," "Bewitched," "The Beverly Hillbillies," "Hogan's Heroes," "Green Acres"

Specials
"Ages of Man"; "Frank Sinatra: A Man and His Music"; "A Charlie Brown Christmas"; "Inherit the Wind" (Melvyn Douglas, Ed Begley); "Eagle in a Cage" (Trevor Howard, James Daly); "Senate Hearings on Viet Nam" (NBC)

Emmy Awards
"The Fugitive" (drama); "The Dick Van Dyke Show" (comedy); "Andy Williams Show" (variety); Bill Cosby (actor, "I Spy"); Dick Van Dyke (comedic actor, "The Dick Van Dyke Show"); Barbara Stanwyck (actress, "The Big Valley"); Mary Tyler Moore (comedic actress, "The Dick Van Dyke Show")

Of Note
NBC is the first network to present early evening, 30-minute news • Forty new shows, the highest number in TV history, appear in the fall • For the first time, all the top shows are in color.

Movies

Openings
The Sound of Music (Robert Wise), Julie Andrews, Christopher Plummer, Eleanor Parker
The Collector (William Wyler), Terence Stamp, Samantha Eggar
Cat Ballou (Elliot Silverstein), Jane Fonda, Lee Marvin
The Spy Who Came in from the Cold (Martin Ritt), Richard Burton, Claire Bloom
Othello (Stuart Burge), Laurence Olivier, Frank Finlay, Maggie Smith
The Pawnbroker (Sidney Lumet), Rod Steiger, Geraldine Fitzgerald
Juliet of the Spirits (Federico Fellini), Giulietta Masina, Sandra Milo, Sylva Koscina
Darling (John Schlesinger), Julie Christie, Dirk Bogarde, Laurence Harvey
Dr. Zhivago (David Lean), Julie Christie, Omar Sharif, Tom Courtenay, Alex Guinness
A Thousand Clowns (Fred Coe), Jason Robards, Barbara Harris
Ship of Fools (Stanley Kramer), Simone Signoret, Oskar Werner, Vivien Leigh, Lee Marvin
To Die in Madrid (documentary), narrated by John Gielgud
Help! (Richard Lester), The Beatles
Alphaville (Jean-Luc Godard), Eddie Constantine, Anna Karina
The Agony and the Ecstasy (Carol Reed), Charlton Heston, Rex Harrison
The Ipcress File (Stanley T. Furie), Michael Caine, Nigel Green
The Shop on Main Street (Jan Kadar, Elmar Klos), Ida Kaminska, Josef Kroner

Academy Awards
Best Picture: *The Sound of Music*
Best Director: Robert Wise (*The Sound of Music*)
Best Actress: Julie Christie (*Darling*)
Best Actor: Lee Marvin (*Cat Ballou*)

Top Box-Office Stars
Sean Connery, John Wayne, Doris Day, Julie Andrews, Jack Lemmon, Elvis Presley, Cary Grant, James Stewart, Elizabeth Taylor, Richard Burton

Stars of Tomorrow
Rosemary Forsythe, Michael Anderson, Jr., Michael Parks, Michael Caine, Mary Ann Mobley, Jocelyn Lane, Mia Farrow, Julie Christie, Richard Johnson, Senta Berger

Popular Music

Hit Songs
"Crying in the Chapel"
"Goldfinger"
"It's Not Unusual"
"Help!"
"Like a Rolling Stone"
"Look of Love"
"Mr. Tambourine Man"
"Mrs. Brown, You've Got a
   Lovely Daughter"
"Red Roses for a Blue Lady"
"The Shadow of Your Smile"
"What the World Needs Now Is
   Love"
"Stop! In the Name of Love"

Top Records
Albums: *Roustabout* (Elvis Presley); *Beatles '65* (Beatles); *Mary Poppins* (sound track); *Goldfinger* (sound track); *Out of Our Heads* (Rolling Stones)

Singles: *Wooly Bully* (Sam the Sham and the Pharaohs); *I Can't Help Myself* (Four Tops); *(I Can't Get No) Satisfaction* (Rolling Stones); *King of the Road* (Roger Miller); *What's New Pussycat?* (Tom Jones); *Ferry Cross the Mersey* (Gerry and the Pacemakers); *I Got You Babe* (Sonny and Cher); *Downtown* (Petula Clark). Country: *Is It Really Over?* (Jim Reeves); *Make the World Go Away* (Eddy Arnold)

Grammy Awards
A Taste of Honey, Herb Alpert and the Tijuana Brass (record); *September of My Years,* Frank Sinatra (album); "The Shadow of Your Smile" (song)

Jazz and Big Bands
Maynard Ferguson and Lionel Hampton break up their big bands and form small combos.

New Bands: Stan Kenton and the Los Angeles Neophonic Orchestra; Don Ellis, the Hindustani Jazz Sestet

Top Performers *(Downbeat):* John Coltrane (soloist); Duke Ellington, Count Basie (bands); Dave Brubeck (jazz group); Jim Hall, Charles Mingus, Bill Evans, J. J. Johnson (instrumentalists); Ella Fitzgerald, Frank Sinatra (vocalists); Double Six (vocal group)

Theater

Broadway Openings

Plays
The Persecution and Assassination of Marat as Performed by the Inmates of the Asylum at Charenton under the Direction of the Marquis de Sade (Peter Weiss), Patrick Magee, Glenda Jackson, Ian Richardson
The Odd Couple (Neil Simon), Art Carney, Walter Matthau
Cactus Flower (Abe Burrows), Lauren Bacall, Barry Nelson
Generation (William Good Hart), Henry Fonda
The Royal Hunt of the Sun (Peter Shaffer), Christopher Plummer, George Rose
Inadmissible Evidence (John Osborne), Nicol Williamson
The Right Honourable Gentleman (Michael Dyne), Charles D. Gray
The Amen Corner (James Baldwin), Bea Richards
Entertaining Mr. Sloane (Joe Orton), Dudley Sutton
The Devils (John Whiting), Anne Bancroft, Jason Robards

Musicals
Man of La Mancha (Mitch Leigh, Joe Darion), Richard Kiley, Joan Diener
Do I Hear a Waltz? (Richard Rodgers, Stephen Sondheim), Elizabeth Allen, Sergio Franchi
The Roar of the Grease Paint—the Smell of the Crowd (Leslie Bricusse, Anthony Newley), Cyril Ritchard, Anthony Newley
On a Clear Day You Can See Forever (Burton Lane, Alan Jay Lerner), John Cullum, Barbara Harris
Flora, the Red Menace (John Kander, Fred Ebb), Liza Minnelli, Bob Dishy

Classics and Revivals On and Off Broadway
Hogan's Goat (William Alfred), Faye Dunaway, Cliff Gorman; *A View from the Bridge* (Arthur Miller), Robert Duvall, Jon Voight; *Happy Days* (Samuel Beckett), Ruth White; *The Zoo Story* (Edward Albee); *Baal* (Bertolt Brecht); *An Evening's Frost* (Donald Hall), Will Geer; *Danton's Death* (Buechner); *The Condemned of Altona* (Jean-Paul Sartre); *The Caucasian Chalk Circle* (Brecht); *Happy Ending, Day of Absence* (Douglas Turner Ward), Robert Hooks. *Founded:* Roundabout Theatre by Gene Feist

Regional

Founded: Philadelphia Theatre of the Living Arts by André Gregory; Long Wharf, New Haven, by Jon Jory and Harlan Kleiman; American Conservatory Theatre (A.C.T.), Pittsburgh, by William Ball; Studio Arena, Buffalo, by Neal Du Broch

Theater (cont.)

Alley, Houston: *The Effect of Gamma Rays on Man-in-the-Moon Marigolds* (Paul Zindel), premiere

Theatre Company of Boston: *Live Like Pigs* (John Arden), premiere

Goodman, Chicago: *The Ballad of the Sad Café* (Edward Albee); *Anna Karenina* (adapted by Eugenie Leontovich, James Goodwin), premieres

Minneapolis Theatre Company: *Richard III*, Jessica Tandy, Hume Cronyn; *The Way of the World*, Zoë Caldwell, Tandy, Ed Flanders; *The Caucasian Chalk Circle*, Flanders, Caldwell

Pulitzer Prize
The Subject Was Roses, Frank D. Gilroy

Tony Awards
The Subject Was Roses, Frank D. Gilroy (play), *Fiddler on the Roof*, Jerry Bock, Sheldon Harnick

Classical Music

Compositions
Gunther Schuller, Symphony no. 1
Roy Harris, Symphony no. 10
Roger Sessions, Piano Sonata no. 3
Walter Piston, Symphony no. 8
George Rochberg, *Music for the Magic Theater*
Charles Wuorinen, *Orchestral and Electronic Exchanges*
Karl Korte, String Quartet no. 2

Important Events
Vladimir Horowitz returns to the concert stage (Carnegie) after 12 years and plays the Bach-Busoni Chromatic Fantasy and Fugue and Schumann *Kinderscenen.*
The Rockefeller Foundation, Ford Foundation, and National Council on the Arts make unprecedented contributions to the musical arts.
Leonard Bernstein, after his sabbatical, begins a two-year survey of 20th-century music with the New York Philharmonic.
The Chicago Symphony Orchestra, for its 75th birthday, commissions works from Gunther Schuller, Jean Martinon, and performs world premieres of Stravinsky's *Variations* and *T. S. Eliot in Memoriam.* Numerous avant-garde concerts, as in Buffalo and Washington, D.C., premiere Luis Escobar, Robert Evett, Carlos Chávez, Ezra Laderman, Walter Piston, Armando Krieger, and Bernal Flores.

Acclaimed Concerts: The Berlin Philharmonic, with Herbert von Karajan, plays a Beethoven cycle in five concerts (New York). Wilhelm Kempff's U.S. debut includes Beethoven's last four sonatas; the New York Philharmonic performs a Bruckner cycle. The touring Munich Bach Choir and Orchestra present, in one week, the St. Matthew Passion, St. John Passion, B-minor Mass, and Christmas Oratorio.

Debuts: Jacqueline Du Pré, James Oliver Buswell, Rolf Smedvig

First Performances
Benjamin Britten, *Voices for Today* (for UN anniversary, New York); Walter Piston, Symphony no. 8 (Boston); Charles Ives, Symphony no. 4 (Washington, D.C.); Easley Blackwood, Symphony no. 3 (Chicago); Roy Harris, *Abraham Lincoln Symphony* (Long Beach, Calif.); Gustav Mahler, Symphony no. 10 (Philadelphia).

Opera

Metropolitan: Montserrat Caballé (debut), *Faust;* Renata Tebaldi, Anna Moffo, Regina Resnik, *Carmen;* Mirella Freni, *La bohème;* Grace Bumbry (debut), *Don Carlo;* Martina Arroyo, *Madama Butterfly;* Nicolai Ghiaurov (debut), *Faust, Don Carlo*

New York City: *Lizzie Borden* (Jack Beeson), *The Flaming Angel* (Sergei Prokofiev), *Miss Julie* (Ned Rorem), premieres

Kansas City: Evelyn Lear, *Julius Caesar*

Boston: *Intolleranza* (Luigi Nono, American premiere); *Boris Godunov* (original version)

Santa Fe: *The King Stag* (Hans Werner Henze); *The Nose* (Shostakovich)

Dallas: Montserrat Caballé, *La traviata*

Chicago: Nicolai Ghiaurov, *Mefistofele;* Grace Bumbry, Jon Vickers, *Samson et Dalila;* Leontyne Price, *Aïda;* double bill: Teresa Berganza, Alfredo Kraus, *L'heure espagnole* and *Carmina Burana;* Geraint Evans, *Wozzeck*

San Francisco: *La forza del destino, Don Giovanni, Un ballo in maschera,* each with Leontyne Price

Art

Painting

Frank Stella, *Empress of India*

Jim Dine, *Double Isometric Self-Portrait*

Jules Olitski, *Prince Patutsky Command*

Andy Warhol, *Campbell's Tomato Soup*

Roy Lichtenstein, *Little Big Painting*

Marc Chagall designs murals for the Metropolitan Opera House, New York.

Sculpture

Robert Arneson, *Typewriter*

Donald Judd, *Untitled*

Richard Tuttle, *The Fountain*

Tony Smith, *Generation*

Edward Kienholz, *The Friendly Grey Computer—Star Gauge Model #54, The Beanery*

Carl Andre, *Crib, Coin, and Compound*

Henry Moore's *Reclining Figure* as well as Alexander Calder's *Stabile,* are placed at Lincoln Center, New York.

Eero Saarinen's 630-foot concrete and steel Gateway Arch is installed in St. Louis.

Architecture

Salk Institute for Biological Studies, La Jolla, Ill. (Louis I. Kahn)

CBS Building, New York (Eero Saarinen)

Smith House, Darien, Conn. (Richard Meier)

At Lincoln Center, New York: Vivian Beaumont Theater (Harrison and Saarinen); Library, Museum of the Performing Arts (Harrison and Skidmore, Owings and Merrill)

Woodrow Wilson School, Princeton University, Princeton, N.J. (Minoru Yamasaki)

Medical Center, New Haven, Conn. (Perkins and Will)

Henry Miller, whose sexually explicit 1930s novels were banned in the U.S. but have since become popular sellers. *Photographer: Cedric Wright. Courtesy Grove Press.*

Important Exhibitions

Museums

New York: *Metropolitan:* Indian sculpture; American painting from Copley to Johns. *Museum of Modern Art:* Giacometti and Magritte retrospectives; Beckmann. *Guggenheim:* Baziotes memorial

Washington: Copley, Terbrugghen; Watercolorists

Pittsburgh: *Carnegie International:* 400 works from 30 nations; Awards to Kelly (United States); Pasmore (Great Britain), Soulages, Arp (France), Chilida, Saura (Spain)

Detroit: Art of Italy, 1600–1700

Art Briefs

The National Council for the Arts is founded • Shows expand and travel: The Museum of Modern Art's "The Responsive Eye" (op art) travels across the United States and includes Smith, Poons, Davis, Dorazio, Riley, Neal, Kelly, Goodyear, Anuszkiewicz, Reinhardt, and Noland • Sculpture has an unprecedented renaissance; works invite more active spectator participation • Exhibitions of color and music and the special uses of lighting have wide success • Rembrandt's portrait of his son Titus sells for $2,234,000 to Norton Simon.

Richard Kiley in *Man of La Mancha,* a musical based on Cervantes's *Don Quixote. Billy Rose Theatre Collection. The New York Public Library at Lincoln Center. Astor, Lenox and Tilden Foundations.*

Dance

Premieres

American Ballet Theatre: *Les Noces* (Jerome Robbins); *The Four Marys; The Wind and the Mountains* (Agnes de Mille); *Tank Dive* (Twyla Tharp)

New York City Ballet: *Don Quixote* (George Balanchine), Richard Rapp, Suzanne Farrell; *Harlequinade* (Balanchine), Patricia McBride; Edward Villella

Books

Fiction

Critics' Choice

Going to Meet the Man, James Baldwin
The Painted Bird, Jerzy Kosinski
Everything that Rises Must Converge, Flannery O'Connor
God Bless You, Mr. Rosewater, Kurt Vonnegut
Thirteen Stories, Eudora Welty
Dune, Frank Herbert
An American Dream, Norman Mailer
Miss MacIntosh, My Darling, Marguerite Young
At Play in the Fields of the Lord, Peter Matthiessen
❧ *The Clown*, Heinrich Böll

Best-Sellers

The Source, James A. Michener
Up the Down Staircase, Bel Kaufman
Herzog, Saul Bellow
The Looking Glass War, John Le Carré
The Green Berets, Robin Moore
Those Who Love, Irving Stone
The Man with the Golden Gun, Ian Fleming
Hotel, Arthur Hailey

Nonfiction

Critics' Choice

The Troubled Partnership, Henry A. Kissinger
The Making of a Quagmire, David Halberstam
Letters to Anaïs Nin, Henry Miller
Manchild in the Promised Land, Claude Brown
The Autobiography of Malcolm X
The Kandy-Colored, Tangerine-flake Stream-line Baby, Tom Wolfe
The Psychedelic Reader, Timothy Leary
The Americans: The National Experience, Daniel Boorstein
Starting Out in the Thirties, Alfred Kazin
Paris Journal (1944–1965), Janet Flanner

Best-Sellers

How to Be a Jewish Mother, Dan Greenburg
A Gift of Prophecy, Ruth Montgomery
Games People Play, Eric Berne, M.D.
World Aflame, Billy Graham
Happiness Is a Dry Martini, Johnny Carson

Markings, Dag Hammarskjöld
My Shadow Ran Fast, Bill Sands
Kennedy, Theodore C. Sorensen
The Making of the President, 1964, Theodore H. White

Poetry

Randall Jarrell, *The Lost World*
James Dickey, *Buckdancer's Choice*
Elizabeth Bishop, *Questions of Travel*
Robert Lowell, *Selected Poems*
Sylvia Plath, *Ariel, Uncollected Poems*
Amiri Baraka (Leroi Jones), *The Dead Lecturer*
❧ Salvatore Quasimodo, *Selected Poems*

Pulitzer Prizes

Collected Stories, Katharine Anne Porter (fiction)
The Life of the Mind in America, Perry Miller (U.S. history)
A Thousand Days: John F. Kennedy in the White House, Arthur M. Schlesinger, Jr. (biography)
Selected Poems, Richard Eberhart (poems)

Science and Technology

Mariner IV transmits 21 photos of Mars.
The world's first commercial satellite, Early Bird, is put into orbit by COMSAT; it relays transatlantic telephone and TV.
Virgil Grissom and John Young, the first U.S. two-man crew, use the orbital maneuvering system on the Gemini III mission.
Edward White walks in space and uses a personal propulsion system on his mission with James McDivitt (on Gemini IV).
Gordon Cooper and Charles Conrad, on Gemini V, make 120 orbits in eight days, demonstrating the human physiologic feasibility of a lunar mission.
Frank Borman and James Lovell make 206 orbits on Gemini VII.

Walter Shirra and Thomas Stafford, on Gemini VIA, accomplish the first docking in space and come within six feet of Gemini VII.
Minuscule integrated circuits on a semiconductor material, silicon, are marketed.
The discovery of "blue galaxies" lends support to the big-bang theory of creation.

Nobel Prize

Richard P. Feynman and Julian S. Schwinger win the prize in physics for work in quantum electrodynamics. Robert B. Woodward wins in chemistry for research on the synthesizing of complicated organic compounds.

Sports

Baseball

Sandy Koufax (Los Angeles, NL) strikes out a record 382, pitches a perfect game (1–0 over Chicago), and wins his second Cy Young Award.

Willie Mays (San Francisco, NL) hits 52 home runs, a record-tying 17 in one month.

Casey Stengel retires.

Warren Spahn retires with 363 wins, a record for a lefthander.

Champions

Batting
  Roberto Clemente (Pittsburgh, NL), .329
  Tony Oliva (Minnesota, AL), .321
Pitching
  Sandy Koufax (Los Angeles, NL), 26–5
  Wally Bunker (Baltimore, AL), 19–5
Home runs
  Willie Mays (San Francisco, NL), 52

Football

Joe Namath, Alabama quarterback, is drafted by the AFL's New York Jets and signed for a record $400,000 bonus.

Gayle Sayers (Chicago) scores a record 22 TD's, including 6 in one game to tie Ernie Nevers's record.

NFL attendance is a record 4.6 million, AFL's, 1.7 million.

NFL Season Leaders: Rudy Bukich (Chicago), passing; Jim Brown (Cleveland), rushing; Dave Parks (San Francisco), receiving. **AFL Season Leaders:** Len Dawson (Kansas City), passing; Paul Lowe (San Diego), rushing; Lionel Taylor (Denver), receiving

College All-Americans: Tom Nobis (G), Texas; Howard Twilley (E), Tulsa; George Webster (DB), Michigan State; Bob Griese (QB), Purdue

Bowls (Jan. 1, 1966)

Rose: UCLA 14–Michigan State 12
Orange: Alabama 39–Nebraska 28
Cotton: Louisiana State 14–Arkansas 7
Sugar: Missouri 20–Florida 18

Basketball

NBA All-Pro First Team: Bill Russell (Boston), Elgin Baylor (Los Angeles), Oscar Robertson (Cincinnati), Jerry Lucas (Cincinnati), Jerry West (Los Angeles)

Other Sports

Boxing: Underdog heavyweight champion Cassius Clay knocks out Sonny Liston in one round at Lewiston, Maine.

Winners

World Series
  Los Angeles (NL) 4
  Minnesota (AL) 3
MVP
  NL–Willie Mays, San Francisco
  AL–Zoilo Versalles, Minnesota
NFL
  Green Bay 23–Cleveland 12
MVP
  Jim Brown, Cleveland
College Football
  Michigan State (UPI)
  Alabama (AP)
Heisman Trophy
  Mike Garrett, Southern California

NBA Championship
  Boston 4–Los Angeles 1
MVP
  Bill Russell, Boston
College Basketball
  UCLA
Player of the Year
  Bill Bradley, Princeton
Stanley Cup
  Montreal
US Tennis Open
  Men: Manuel Santana
  Women: Margaret Smith
USGA Open
  Gary Player
Kentucky Derby
  Lucky Debonair (W. Shoemaker, jockey)

Fashion

For Women: Popular are op art fabrics in swirling, eye-teasing designs, along with black and white contrasting patterns, like checkerboard prints. Saint Laurent's "Mondrian" chemise is enormously successful. Lengths extend from above the knee to the ankle. Leotards attenuate "the leggy look." The "nothing-under" effect for see-through blouses and cut-out fabrics is accomplished with "invisible lingerie" by Gertrude Seperak and Warner. Ankle-to-shoulder underwear is available for slacks and tights. Peekaboo fashions extend from midriff tops to cut-out shoes and hats. Popular day fabrics include suede, suede cloth, and crocheted yarn. In the evening, firmer silks, satins, and gabardines replace more traditional chiffons and crepes. Summer innovations include huge, round goggles, canoe-shaped, white, mid-calf, kid boots, and Cole's one-piece Lycra swimsuit, which plunges to the navel with a mesh V.

High-fashion note: The ultra short skirt by John Bates, Courrèges

Kaleidoscope

- Unemployment is the lowest in 8 years, 4.2 percent.
- The first teach-in is held March 2 at the University of Michigan; the largest is held at Berkeley, where 12,000 hear Dr. Benjamin Spock, Norman Mailer, I. F. Stone, and Senator Ernest Gruening, among others.
- "Flower Power" is coined by Allen Ginsberg at a Berkeley antiwar rally.
- The Medicaid rider to the Medicare bill provides funds to states for care of the poor.
- Studies show that American cities are becoming progressively more dangerous with public services increasingly less adequate; New York City has a water shortage and blackout during the year.
- In *The Psychedelic Reader* Harvard professor Timothy Leary advises: "Drop out, turn on, tune in."
- Students carry Viet Cong and North Vietnam flags in demonstrations and chant: "Hey, hey, LBJ, how many kids did you kill today?"
- The Voting Rights Act, eliminating literacy tests and authorizing federal supervision of voting procedures, stimulates an increase in black voting registration from 29 percent to 52 percent.
- "Clad" coins eliminate 90 percent of the silver in dollars, half dollars, quarters, and dimes.
- Since the Vietnam conflict is a guerrilla war, battle reports emphasize casualties ("body counts") and political progress, rather than decisive battles or territorial gains.
- Vietnam news reportage familiarizes the nation with places like Danang, Cam Ranh Bay, and Bien Hoa, sites of major U.S. installations, as well as combat zones like the Mekong Delta, Dakto, and Pleiku.
- Over $60 million is spent for prescription drugs to lose weight, twice the amount spent in 1960.
- More than 70 percent of the world's orchestras reside in the United States, 1,401 (600 in 1939).
- Pope Paul visits New York to address the UN; he speaks for peace: "No more war, war never again."
- Ralph Nader, who has left his job with the Department of Labor, intensifies his crusade for consumer protection; *Unsafe at Any Speed,* concerning auto safety, is published.
- The Clean Air Act allows for federal regulation of auto emissions; the Water Quality Act requires that states set antipollution standards for interstate waters.
- A group planning to destroy the Washington Monument, Statue of Liberty, and Liberty Bell is arrested.
- Quaker Norman Morrison immolates himself on the steps of the Pentagon.
- Congress passes a bill making it an offense to mutilate or destroy a draft card; the penalty is set at $10,000 or five years in jail.
- Robert Lowell's refusal to attend the White House Festival of the Arts because he is "dismayed" at foreign policy is widely publicized; the president later comments: "Some of them insulted me by staying away and some of them insulted me by coming."
- Of 2,560 cadets at the Air Force Academy, 105 resign for cheating on exams.
- The first singles community is built in Los Angeles.
- The birth rate falls to 19 per 1,000 people, the lowest since 1940.
- Sheriff Jim Clark of Selma, Alabama, leads an attack with tear gas and clubs against civil rights marchers led by Martin Luther King.
- Fourteen thousand National Guardsmen are called out at Watts, a black ghetto in South Los Angeles; 34 die, 4,000 are arrested, and the area is in ashes after five days.
- The truth in packaging bill is written to standardize weights in packaged goods.
- César Chavez's 25-day fast convinces the Brown Power militants to align themselves with his nonviolent strike against the grape growers; shoppers boycott table grapes in sympathy.
- The word *soul* replaces *rhythm and blues* on hit charts.
- Ads for men's colognes and face lotions increase eightfold since 1960, and body-building ads virtually disappear.
- The Beatles and Elvis Presley meet in Bel Air, California.
- The Supreme Court eliminates state and local film censorship.
- The Grateful Dead begin in San Francisco, their name taken from an Oxford English Dictionary notation on the burial of Egyptian pharaohs.
- The Fillmore, in San Francisco, begins rock concerts; the first stars Jefferson Airplane and Grateful Dead.
- At Lady Bird's urging, Congress appropriates funds to beautify U.S. highways and remove their large number of billboards.

Fads: I Ching, macrobiotic foods, body painting, trivia contests, computer dating, disposable paper dresses, James Bond toys

New Words and Usages: Camp, campy, computerize, degradable, discotheque, electronic music, hardware, kook, op art, printout, program, quark, skateboard, crash, dude, do your own thing, groupie, no way, old lady, old man, rap, vibes, straight

First Appearances: Miniskirt (Mary Quant), International Society for Krishna Consciousness (Hare Krishna, by A. C. Bhaktivedanta), domed stadium (Astrodome), Bravo, Diet Pepsi, Apple Jacks, Cranapple, Avis Rent-a-Car acquired by ITT, all-news radio station (New York), master skyscraper antenna (Empire State Building, New York), American Stock Exchange women members (J. M. Walsh, P. K. S. Peterson, New York), Sony home video tape recorder

1966

In the News

ROBERT WEAVER IS APPOINTED SECRETARY OF HUD, THE FIRST BLACK IN CABINET . . . B-52 AND JET TANKER COLLIDE, 7 CREW DIE, 4 H-BOMBS ARE LOST, 3 ARE RECOVERED . . . JOHNSON ASKS $4 BILLION MORE FOR DEFENSE, $3 BILLION FOR THE GREAT SOCIETY . . . JOHNSON AND SOUTH VIETNAM LEADER KY MEET AND ISSUE DECLARATION OF HONOLULU . . . BOMBING OF NORTH VIETNAM IS RESUMED . . . OPERATION WHITE WING SUCCEEDS IN QUANG NGAT . . . RUSSIA MAKES FIRST SOFT MOON LANDING . . . SUHARTO TAKES OVER IN INDONESIA . . . LBJ ASKS $1 BILLION FAMINE AID FOR INDIA . . . STOKELY CARMICHAEL IS ELECTED HEAD OF STUDENT NONVIOLENT COORDINATING COMMITTEE . . . LOST H-BOMB IS FOUND OFF SPANISH COAST . . . STUDENTS DEMONSTRATE NATIONWIDE AGAINST THE WAR . . . SURVEYER MAKES FIRST U.S. SOFT LANDING ON THE MOON . . . SUPREME COURT RULES ON RIGHTS OF ACCUSED IN MIRANDA CASE . . . MICHAEL COLLINS AND JOHN W. YOUNG DOCK AND WALK IN SPACE AT A RECORD 474 MILES . . . SNIPER ON TOWER IN TEXAS SHOOTS 45, KILLS 12 AND SELF . . . 8 NURSES ARE SLAIN IN CHICAGO DORMITORY . . . AIRLINE STRIKE ENDS AFTER 43 DAYS . . . GEMINI GOES TO RECORD 850-MILE ALTITUDE . . . LBJ MAKES 26,000-MILE FAR EAST TOUR . . . UN AMBASSADOR ARTHUR GOLDBERG PLEDGES U.S. FORCE REDUCTION IF NORTH VIETNAM ASSENTS . . . COMMUNIST CHINA TESTS INTERCONTINENTAL BALLISTIC MISSILE . . . REPUBLICANS GAIN IN CONGRESSIONAL ELECTIONS . . . VIETNAM: U.S. TROOP STRENGTH, 400,000; U.S. DEAD, 6,358; ENEMY DEAD, 77,115.

Quotes

"Their symbol is the black panther, a bold, beautiful animal, representing the strength and dignity of black demands today."
— Stokely Carmichael, describing a new party in Loundes County, Alabama

"We have stopped losing the war."
— General William Westmoreland

"[We seek]" to confront with concrete action the conditions which now prevent women from enjoying equality of opportunity and freedom of choice which is their right as individual Americans and as human beings."
— NOW manifesto

"If you want to join the New York intellectual establishment, . . . all you've got to do is make the right friends and then attack them, claim that the establishment doesn't exist and that everyone in it is brilliant, and denounce the mass media while they are lionizing you."
— Victor S. Navasky

"I noticed that mannequins in windows were smiling and Elizabeth Taylor from an enormous poster advertising the film *Cleopatra* several times gestured for me to come to her."
— Report of psychedelic drug experience in R. Masters and J. Houston, *The Varieties of Psychedelic Experience*

"Just when you think you're getting famous, somebody comes along and makes you look like a warm-up act for amateur night. . . . Pope Paul VI [for example, just arrived]. Talk about advance PR—I mean for centuries."
— Andy Warhol, *Popism*

"We came, therefore (and with many Western thinkers before us), to suspect civilization may be overvalued."
— Gary Snyder

"The mad truth: the boundary between sanity and insanity is a false one. . . . The proper posture is to listen and learn from lunatics as in former times."
— Norman O. Brown, *Love's Body*

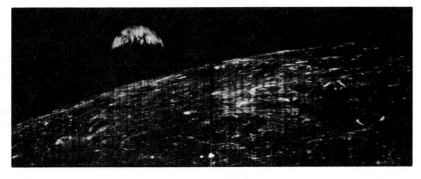

The first view of the earth from the vicinity of the moon is taken by Lunar Orbiter 1. *Courtesy NASA.*

Ads

TV

Premieres

"The Newlywed Game," Bob Eubanks
"Mission: Impossible," Martin Landau, Barbara Bain, Peter Graves
"The Hollywood Squares," Peter Marshall
"Batman," Adam West
"Family Affair," Brian Keith
"Star Trek," William Shatner, Leonard Nimoy
"The Monkees," David Jones
"That Girl," Marlo Thomas
"Felony Squad," Howard Duff
"The Dating Game," Jim Lange
"The Smothers Brothers Comedy Hour"

Top Ten (Nielsen)

"Bonanza," "The Red Skelton Hour," "The Andy Griffith Show," "The Lucy Show," "The Jackie Gleason Show," "Green Acres," "Daktari," "Bewitched," "The Beverly Hillbillies," "Gomer Pyle, U.S.M.C."

Specials

"Death of a Salesman" (Lee J. Cobb); "Barefoot in Athens" (Peter Ustinov); "Anastasia" (Lynn Fontanne, Julie Harris); "The Glass Menagerie" (Shirley Booth); "China: The Roots of Madness" (Theodore White); "Organized Crime in America" (NBC); "The Homosexuals" (CBS); "A Christmas Memory" (Geraldine Page); "Bob Hope's Christmas Tour of the GI Bases"; "Ages of Man" (John Gielgud)

Emmy Awards

"Mission: Impossible" (drama); "The Monkees" (comedy); "Andy Williams Show" (variety); "Jack and the Beanstalk" (children); Bill Cosby (actor, "I Spy"); Don Adams (comedic actor, "Get Smart"); Barbara Bain (actress, "Mission: Impossible"); Lucille Ball (comedic actress, "The Lucy Show")

Of Note

Movies in prime time increase to five evenings a week • ABC's "Scope" joins "Vietnam Weekly Review" (NBC) and "Vietnam Perspective" (CBS), as coverage of the war intensifies • "The Bridge on the River Kwai" receives a 60 percent rating, the most popular movie shown on TV to date; network interest in high-cost, quality, made-for-TV movies also increases.

Movies

Openings

A Man for All Seasons (Fred Zinnemann), Paul Scofield, Robert Shaw
Who's Afraid of Virginia Woolf? (Mike Nichols), Richard Burton, Elizabeth Taylor, George Segal, Sandy Dennis
The Professionals (Richard Brooks), Burt Lancaster, Lee Marvin, Claudia Cardinale
Georgy Girl (Silvio Narizzano), Lynn Redgrave, Alan Bates, James Mason
Morgan! (Karel Reisz), Vanessa Redgrave, David Warner
Closely Watched Trains (Jiri Menzel), Vaclay Neckar, Jitka Bendova
Khartoum (Basil Dearden), Charlton Heston, Laurence Olivier
Blow-up (Michelangelo Antonioni), Vanessa Redgrave, David Hemmings
Fahrenheit 451 (François Truffaut), Oskar Werner, Julie Christie
Harper (Jack Smight), Paul Newman, Lauren Bacall, Arthur Hill
Madame X (David Lowell Rich), Lana Turner, John Forsythe, Ricardo Montalban
La guerre est fini (Alain Resnais), Yves Montand, Ingrid Thulin, Genevieve Bujold
Alfie (Lewis Gilbert), Michael Caine, Shelley Winters

Academy Awards

Best Picture: *A Man for All Seasons*
Best Director: Fred Zinnemann (*A Man for All Seasons*)
Best Actress: Elizabeth Taylor (*Who's Afraid of Virginia Woolf?*)
Best Actor: Paul Scofield (*A Man for All Seasons*)

Top Box-Office Stars

Julie Andrews, Sean Connery, Elizabeth Taylor, Jack Lemmon, Richard Burton, Cary Grant, John Wayne, Doris Day, Paul Newman, Elvis Presley

Stars of Tomorrow

Elizabeth Hartman, George Segal, Alan Arkin, Raquel Welch, Geraldine Chaplin, Guy Stockwell, Robert Redford, Beverly Adams, Sandy Dennis, Chad Everett

Popular Music

Hit Songs
"The Ballad of the Green Berets"
"Born Free"
"Good Vibrations"
"The Impossible Dream"
"Sunny"
"What Now, My Love"
"Winchester Cathedral"
"Alfie"
"The Sounds of Silence"
"Georgy Girl"

Top Records

Albums: *Rubber Soul* (Beatles); *Going Places* (Herb Alpert and the Tijuana Brass); *If You Can Believe Your Eyes and Ears* (Mamas and the Papas); *Doctor Zhivago* (sound track); *The Monkees* (Monkees)

Singles: *Strangers in the Night* (Frank Sinatra); *These Boots Are Made for Walking* (Nancy Sinatra); *Last Train to Clarksville* (Monkees); *Yellow Submarine, Eleanor Rigby* (Beatles); *Scarborough Fair* (Simon and Garfunkel); *Rainy Day Women #12 and 35* (Bob Dylan); *Cherish* (Association); *You're My Soul and Inspiration* (Righteous Brothers); *Reach Out and I'll Be There* (Four Tops); *Monday, Monday* (Mamas and the Papas). Country: *Almost Persuaded* (David Houston); *Giddy Up Go* (Red Sovino)

Grammy Awards
Strangers in the Night, Frank Sinatra (record); *Sinatra: A Man and His Music* (album); "Michelle" (song)

Jazz and Big Bands
Don Ellis's *Synthesis* attempts to fuse jazz and raga.

Top Performers *(Downbeat):* Ornette Coleman (soloist); Duke Ellington (band); Miles Davis (jazz group); Wes Montgomery, Ray Brown, Oscar Peterson, Elvin Jones, Paul Desmond (instrumentalists); Ella Fitzgerald, Frank Sinatra (vocalists); Double Six (vocal group); Ornette Coleman, *At the Golden Circle, Vol. I* (album)

Theater

Broadway Openings

Plays
Wait until Dark (Frederick Knott), Lee Remick
The Investigation (Peter Weiss), Richard Castellano
Don't Drink the Water (Woody Allen), Lou Jacobi
The Star-Spangled Girl (Neil Simon), Anthony Perkins, Richard Benjamin, Connie Stevens
A Delicate Balance (Edward Albee), Jessica Tandy, Hume Cronyn, Rosemary Murphy
America Hurrah (Jean-Claude Van Itallie), Ruth White, Bill Macy
Malcolm (Edward Albee, James Purdy), Estelle Parsons, Ruth White, John Heffernan
The Lion in Winter (James Goldman), Robert Preston, Rosemary Harris
Philadelphia, Here I Come! (Brian Friel), Patrick Bedford, Donal Donnelly
The Killing of Sister George (Frank Marcus), Beryl Reid, Eileen Atkins
Slapstick Tragedy (Tennessee Williams), Kate Reid, Margaret Leighton, Zoë Caldwell

Musicals
Cabaret (John Kander, Fred Ebb), Jill Haworth, Joel Grey, Lotte Lenya, Bert Convy
Viet-Rock (Megan Terry), Seth Allen
Sweet Charity (Cy Coleman, Dorothy Fields), Gwen Verdon, Helen Gallagher, John McMartin
Mame (Jerry Herman), Angela Lansbury, Beatrice Arthur
The Apple Tree (Jerry Bock, Sheldon Harnick), Barbara Harris, Alan Alda, Larry Blyden
I Do! I Do! (Harvey Schmidt, Tom Jones), Mary Martin, Robert Preston

Classics and Revivals On and Off Broadway
Galileo (Bertolt Brecht), Anthony Quayle; *School for Scandal* (Sheridan), Helen Hayes, Ellis Rabb, Rosemary Harris; *Serjeant Musgrave's Dance* (John Arden), Dustin Hoffman; *Ivanov* (Chekhov), John Gielgud, Vivien Leigh, Claire Bloom; *The Kitchen* (Arnold Wesker), Sylvia Miles

Regional

Founded: Repertory Theatre, New Orleans, by the National Endowment for the Humanities; Theatre Atlanta; Ypsilanti Greek Festival: *Oresteia,* Judith Anderson; *The Birds,* Bert Lahr

Pulitzer Prize No prize is awarded.

Tony Awards
Marat/Sade, Peter Weiss (play), *Man of La Mancha,* Mitch Leigh, Joe Darion (musical)

Classical Music _____

Compositions
Salvatore Martirano, Ballad
Roger Reynolds, *Blind Men*
David Saturen, Sonata for Clarinet and Piano
Walter Piston, Variations for Cello and Orchestra
Roger Sessions, Symphony no. 6, Six Pieces for
  Cello
Leon Kirchner, Quartet no. 3
Earl Brown, *Modules 1 and 2*

Important Events
New York hosts the Igor Stravinsky Festival, Lincoln
Center; the David Diamond Concert at the New York
Philharmonic, with the first performance of the
Symphony no. 5 for Piano and Orchestra; Arturo
Benedetti Michelangeli's return to the stage after
fifteen years; Jascha Heifetz's first solo recital in ten
years, and the Heifetz and Gregor Piatigorsky series
of four chamber concerts.
Leonard Bernstein announces his plan to retire from
the New York Philharmonic; his two-year survey of
symphonic music includes all of Sibelius's and
Nielsen's symphonies, both celebrated for their 100th
birthday.

Debuts: Martha Argerich, Radu Lupu

First Performances
Roger Sessions, "Psalm 140" (Boston), Symphony
no. 6 (Newark); Virgil Thomson, Fantasy (Kansas
City); Ulysses Kay, *Markings* (Rochester); Paul
Creston, *Variations* (La Jolla, Calif.); Henry Cowell,
Hymn and Fuguing Tune no. 16 (New York); Igor
Stravinsky, *Requiem Canticles* (Princeton, N.J.);
Douglas Moore, *Carry Nation* (University of Kansas,
commissioned for university centennial); Busoni,
Piano Concerto (New York)

Elizabeth Taylor and Richard Burton in the uncensored
movie adaptation of Edward Albee's *Who's Afraid of
Virginia Woolf? Movie Star News.*

CBS Records.

Opera

Metropolitan: After a gala performance at the old
Met, with excerpts from 23 operas, the new Met, at
Lincoln Center for the Performing Arts, opens with
the world premiere of *Antony and Cleopatra* (Samuel
Barber) with an all-American cast: Leontyne Price,
Justino Diaz; the top price is $250; other productions
for the season include Walter Berry (debut), Christa
Ludwig, Leonie Rysanek, *Die Frau ohne Schatten;*
Birgit Nilsson, Rysanek, *Elektra;* Zinka Milanov,
Andrea Chenier

New York City Opera: Opening at the New York
State Theatre—Beverly Sills, Norman Treigle, *Don
Rodrigo* (Alberto Ginastera, premiere)

Fort Worth: Beverly Sills: *I pagliacci; Die schöne
Galatea* (Suppé)

Boston: *Moses und Aron* (Schoenberg, American
premiere); Placido Domingo, Beverly Sills, *Hippolyte
et Aricie* (Rameau, American premiere)

Chicago: Alfredo Kraus, *The Pearl Fishers; Angel
of Fire;* Nicolai Ghiaurov, *Boris Godunov*

San Francisco: Evelyn Lear, *Lulu*

Music Notes
The touring company of the Met disbands because of
rising costs • The Jesse H. Jones Hall for the
Performing Arts, Houston, opens with the world
premiere of Alan Hovhaness's *Ode to the Temple of
Sound.*

Art

Paintings
Ad Reinhardt, *Black Painting* (1960–66)

Barnett Newman, *Who's Afraid of Red, Yellow, Blue I* (1966–67)

Allan D'Arcangelo, *Proposition No. 9*

Richard Lindner, *Checkmate*

Kenneth Noland, *Par Transit*

Philip Pearlstein, *Woman Reclining on Couch*

Roy Lichtenstein, *Yellow and Red Brushstrokes*

Willem de Kooning, *Woman Acabonic*

Sculpture
Eva Hesse, *Hang Up*

Louise Nevelson, *Atmosphere and Environment*

Reuben Nakian, *Hiroshima*

Chryssa, *Variations on the Ampersand*

Robert Indiana, *Love*

Mark di Suvero, *Elohim Adonai*

Edward Kienholz, *The State Hospital*

Sol LeWitt, *B-258, Open Modular Cube*

Lucas Samaras, *Mirror Room*

Carl Andre, *Lever, Sanbornville III*

Robert Smithson, *Alogon*

Alexander Calder, *Totems*

Architecture
School of Social Service Administration, University of Chicago (Mies van der Rohe)

Whitney Museum of American Art, 945 Madison Avenue, New York City (Marcel Breuer)

University Plaza, New York City (I. M. Pei)

Metropolitan Opera House, New York City (Wallace K. Harrison)

Johnson Museum, New Canaan, Conn. (Philip Johnson)

Charles Gwathmey Residence and Studio, Amagansett, N.Y. (Charles Gwathmey)

Richard J. Daley Center, Chicago (C. F. Murphy; Skidmore, Owings, and Merrill)

Construction begins on the World Trade Center, New York City (Yamasaki, Roth).

Important Exhibitions

Museums

New York: *Metropolitan:* 3,000 years of Chinese metalwork; "200 Years of Watercolors." *Museum of Modern Art:* Motherwell, Turner retrospectives; Magritte. *Whitney:* Davis; "7 Decades—Cross Currents in Modern Art: 277 Major Modern Artists." *Guggenheim:* Munch; Gauguin

Chicago: Manet; Great works from the Polish collection

Philadelphia: Manet; Mondrian retrospective; "The Older Tradition"

Washington: Art treasures of Turkey; Chinese art objects

San Francisco, Toledo, Boston: Rembrandt

Art Briefs
Popular interest grows in the avant-garde—"Nine Evenings, Theatre and Engineerings," in New York, combines several forms of "happenings": John Cage, Robert Whitman, Robert Rauschenberg, Andy Warhol, Roy Lichtenstein; the ideal is an environment of sensory saturation. Minimalist shows gain interest, along with "object" art, "primary structures," and "kinetic sculpture." The Guggenheim's "systemic painting" show displays shaped and multiple canvases and modular paintings. Edward Kienholz's *The Beanery*, with its taped sound effects and cooking smells, gains much attention • The National Gallery in Washington, D.C., purchases a 4⅛-by-5⅝-inch painting, *St. George and the Dragon*, by Rogier van der Weyden for $616,000. Brancusi's "Bird in Space" sells for $140,000 • Chagall's *Le Triomphe de la Musique* is installed at the Metropolitan Opera House, New York.

Dance

The Joffrey Ballet moves to New York's City Center; Bruce Marks joins Willam Christensen at Ballet West, Salt Lake City.

Premieres

New York City Ballet: *Variations* (George Balanchine), Suzanne Farrell; *Brahms-Schoenberg Quartet* (Balanchine), Edward Villella, Suzanne Farrell, Jacques D'Amboise, Melissa Hayden

American Ballet Theatre: *Ricarcare, Sargasso* (Glen Tetley), Sallie Wilson

Books

Fiction

Critics' Choice

The Crying of Lot 49, Thomas Pynchon

Giles Goat-Boy, John Barth

Up above the World, Paul Bowles

Nothing Ever Breaks Except the Heart, Kay Boyle

A Christmas Memory, Truman Capote

The Last Gentleman, Walker Percy

Been Down So Long It Looks like Up to Me, Richard Fariña

The Origin of the Brunists, Robert Coover

Criers and Kibitzers, Kibitzers and Criers, Stanley Elkin

The Diary of a Rapist, Evan S. Connell, Jr.

Omensetter's Luck, William Gass

🍃 *Hopscotch*, Julio Cortázar

Best-Sellers

Valley of the Dolls, Jacqueline Susann

The Adventurers, Harold Robbins

The Secret of Santa Vittoria, Robert Crichton

Capable of Honor, Allen Drury

The Double Image, Helen MacInnes

The Fixer, Bernard Malamud

Tell No Man, Adela Rogers St. Johns

Tai-Pan, James Clavell

The Embezzler, Louis Auchincloss

All in the Family, Edwin O'Connor

Nonfiction

Critics' Choice

Against Interpretation, Susan Sontag

Freedom in the Modern World, Herbert J. Miller

The Report on the Warren Report

The Social Novel at the End of an Era, Warren French

Cannibals and Christians, Norman Mailer

La Vida, Oscar Lewis

Inquest: The Warren Commission, Edward Jay Epstein

The Enlightenment, Peter Gay

Papa Hemingway, A. E. Hotchner

The Proud Tower, Barbara Tuchman

🍃 *Quotations of Chairman Mao*

🍃 *On Aggression*, Konrad Lorenz

Best-Sellers

How to Avoid Probate, Norman F. Dacey

Human Sexual Response, William Howard Masters, Virginia E. Johnson

In Cold Blood, Truman Capote

Games People Play, Eric Berne, M.D.

A Thousand Days, Arthur M. Schlesinger, Jr.

Everything But Money, Sam Levenson

The Random House Dictionary of the English Language

Rush to Judgment, Mark Lane

The Last Battle, Cornelius Ryan

Phyllis Diller's Housekeeping Hints, Phyllis Diller

Poetry

John Ashbery, *Rivers and Mountains*

Robert Creeley, *Poems 1950–1965*

Adrienne Rich, *Necessities of Life*

May Sarton, *A Private Mythology*

James Merrill, *Nights and Days*

🍃 Andrei Voznesensky, *Anti-World*

Pulitzer Prizes

The Fixer, Bernard Malamud (fiction)

Exploration and Empire, William H. Goetzmann (U.S. history)

The Problem of Slavery in Western Culture, David Brion Davis (nonfiction)

Mr. Clemens and Mark Twain, Justin Kaplan (biography)

Live or Die, Anne Sexton (poetry)

Science and Technology

Har Gobind Khorana completes the deciphering of the DNA code.

The FDA concludes that there are no adequate scientific reasons to declare "the pill" unsafe, in reply to concern over blood clots.

Biodegradable liquid detergents are produced to reduce pollution.

Astronauts who walk in space include Eugene Cernan (Gemini IX), Michael Collins (Gemini X), Richard Gordon (Gemini XI), and Buzz Aldrin (Gemini XII).

Gemini XIII, manned by Neil Armstrong and David Scott, is the first dual launch in space to dock with a target rocket, Agena.

Surveyor I achieves a soft lunar landing in the Ocean of Storms.

Sealab II, with a crew led by astronaut Scott Carpenter, spends 45 days under the sea to test survival problems.

Nobel Prize

The prize in physiology and medicine is shared by Charles Brenton Huggins, for work on the hormone treatment of cancer of the prostate, and Francis P. Rous, for work on tumor-producing viruses. Robert S. Mulliken wins in chemistry for his work on the bond that holds atoms together in molecules.

Sports

Coach Vince Lombardi: "Winning isn't everything. It's the only thing." *Football Hall of Fame.*

Baseball

The Major League Players Association is formed.
Frank Robinson (Baltimore, AL) becomes the first player to win an MVP award in each league.
Sandy Koufax (Los Angeles, NL) wins a record third Cy Young Award and retires.

Champions

Batting
Matty Alou (Pittsburgh, NL), .342
Frank Robinson (Baltimore, AL), .326
Pitching
Juan Marichal (San Francisco, NL), 25–6
Mudcat Grant (Minnesota, AL), 21–5
Home runs
Frank Robinson (Baltimore, AL), 49

Football

The Green Bay Packers, under Vince Lombardi, win a record third straight NFL title.
The NFL and AFL announce their plan to merge in 1970 and to begin a championship series.
Jim Brown (Cleveland) retires with a career rushing record of 12,312 yards.

NFL Season Leaders: Bart Starr (Green Bay), passing; Gale Sayers (Chicago), rushing; Charles Taylor (Washington), receiving
AFL Season Leaders: Len Dawson (Kansas City), passing; Jim Nance (Boston), rushing; Lance Alworth (San Diego), receiving

College All-Americans: Ray Perkins (E), Alabama; Mel Farr (B), UCLA; Nick Eddy (B), Notre Dame

Bowls (Jan. 1, 1967)
Rose: Purdue 14– Southern California 13
Orange: Florida 27– Georgia Tech 12
Cotton: Georgia 24– Southern Methodist 9
Sugar: Alabama 34– Nebraska 7

Winners

World Series
  Baltimore (AL) 4
  Los Angeles (NL) 0
MVP
  NL–Roberto Clemente, Pittsburgh
  AL–Frank Robinson, Baltimore
Sugar Bowl I (Jan. 1967)
  Green Bay 35–Kansas City 10
MVP
  Bart Starr, Green Bay
College Football
  Notre Dame
Heisman Trophy
  Steve Spurrier, Auburn

NBA Championship
  Boston 4–Los Angeles 3
MVP
  Wilt Chamberlain, Philadelphia
College Basketball
  Texas Western
Player of the Year
  Cazzie Russell, Michigan
Stanley Cup
  Montreal
US Tennis Open
  Men: Fred Stolle
  Women: Maria Bueno
USGA Open
  Billy Casper
Kentucky Derby
  Kauai King (D. Brumfield, jockey)

Basketball

NBA All-Pro First Team: Rick Barry (San Francisco), Jerry Lucas (Cincinnati), Wilt Chamberlain (Philadelphia), Jerry West (Los Angeles), Oscar Robertson (Cincinnati)

Other Sports

Boxing: Cassius Clay becomes a Muslim and changes his name to Muhammed Ali; he makes five successful title defenses.

Running: Jim Ryun runs the half-mile in a record 1:44.9; he also runs 3:51.3 and 3:51.1 miles.

Fashion

For Women: Emphasis is on "femininity," despite the Carnaby or English mod look: short shirts, T-shirt dresses with chin-high necklines and turtlenecks, scarves, and headbands. Coats include the tent, the straight, slim style, and the military coat with epaulettes and brass buttons. Long, straight hair and op art glasses complete the look, which also includes low-slung bell bottoms, wide belt or hip-riding miniskirts five to six inches above the knee, and daytime pantsuits of twill and bright tartans. With the growing interest in surfing, the two-piece bathing suit replaces the bikini. Harem pants, wide trousers with matching tops, and elaborate jumpsuits are worn all year around. Mia Farrow's hair, cut to the scalp, sets a style, along with tiny pearl stud earrings.

High-fashion note: Mary Quant's midi

For Men: Men begin to devote as much money and time to their hair as women, with permanent waves, hair coloring, transplants, and replacements. It is no longer fashionable for a man to look as if he has just had a haircut.

Kaleidoscope

- "Black Power" is introduced into the civil rights movement, clarifying the rift between the pacifist followers of Martin Luther King, SCLC, and the militants following Stokely Carmichael, SNCC, and Floyd McKissick, CORE.
- March 25–27 are International Days of Protest against the war in Vietnam in seven American and seven foreign cities.
- Senator William Fulbright, at Johns Hopkins University, attacks the administration for its foreign policy, condemning those who "feel qualified to play God."
- Much attention is paid to the controversial elite combat unit in Vietnam, the Green Berets.
- Blanket student deferments are abolished; draft calls reach 50,000 a month.
- "Can you pass the acid test?" is author Ken Kesey's motto at the San Francisco Trips Festival, an acid-rock, multimedia happening of rock, light shows, and acid dropping, which begins the "San Francisco Sound."
- A new style of dance hall, like the Fillmore in San Francisco, replaces discos with strobe lights, liquid color blobs, glow paint, and psychedelic posters.
- The publication of the Catholic edition of the Bible in the Revised Standard Version is considered a milestone in the mid-century ecumenical movement.
- Roman Catholic bishops rule that except during Lent, American Catholics may eat meat on Friday.
- The Clean Waters Restoration Act allocates funds for preventing river and air pollution.
- The Traffic Safety Act, long urged by Ralph Nader, provides for auto safety standards and recalls.
- James Roche, General Motors president, apologizes for spying into Ralph Nader's private life after he cited the GM Corvair as dangerous; Nader sues Roche and two private detectives and settles out of court for $500,000.
- César Chavez's National Farm Workers Union, in its strike against grape growers, is recognized as the bargaining agent for farm workers.
- James Meredith is shot walking from Memphis to Jackson; the walk is then joined by Dick Gregory, Martin Luther King, Floyd B. McKissick (CORE), and Stokely Carmichael (SNCC).
- The social event of the year is Truman Capote's New York Plaza Hotel party to celebrate *In Cold Blood*'s success.
- John Lindsay faces his first crisis the day he becomes New York City mayor—the city's first "official" transit strike; an estimated 850,000 cars enter Manhattan in a single day.
- Virginia Masters and William Johnson's *Human Sexual Response* asserts, among other things, that women possess at least as much sexual energy as men and enjoy a variety of sexual responses, including multiple orgasms.
- The National Association of Broadcasters instructs all disc jockeys to screen all records for hidden (drug) or obscene meanings.
- *Time* magazine's "Man of the Year" is actually a group: the "Twenty-Five and Under . . . Generation."
- At what is presumably the last performance at the old Metropolitan Opera House, a five-hour gala evening ends with the audience and performers joining hands and singing "Auld Lang Syne"; the gold curtain is cut into small patches and packaged with a souvenir recording.
- *Who's Afraid of Virginia Woolf?* is a landmark film whose shocking language receives the new seal "suggested for mature audiences"; the new production code is voluntarily accepted by the studios.
- Beginning the conglomerate takeover of the big film studios, Gulf and Western absorbs Paramount; Kinney National Service takes over Warner and Seven Arts. The big studios make TV films as well.
- Per capita consumption of processed potato chips rises from 6.3 pounds a year (1958) to 14.2 pounds a year.
- A nationwide sports poll tallies 59 million bikers, 40 million boaters and volleyball players, 36 million fishers and campers, and 2 million tennis players.
- Because of the smog, California imposes standards on car exhausts, to take effect in 1969.
- A study reports that food prices are higher in the poorer rather than the more affluent neighborhoods.
- The President's Commission on Food Marketing reports that consumers pay 29 percent more for nationally advertised brands than high-quality local brands.
- Jimi Hendrix helps popularize the electric guitar.
- "Batman" airs twice weekly and becomes a national fad. Batman's adversaries include the Archer (Art Carney), the Penguin (Burgess Meredith), and the Joker (Cesar Romero).

Fads: Monkee items, underground newspapers, Batman accessories, Ouija boards, astrology, Tarot cards

New Words and Usages: Abort, big-bang theory, bowser bag, cable TV, chip, flashcube, glitch, commune, flower children, psychedelic, acid rock, mind blowing, zap, go-go, gypsy cab, hawk, hippy, interface, intrauterine device, loop, LSD, miniskirt, mod, pop, Third World

First Appearances: Medicare ID card (presented to Harry Truman, Jan. 20), sandwich grill toaster, tape cartridges, stereo cassette decks, NOW, Bank Americard, Interbank Card, Laker Airways, Product 19, Taster's Choice, BacOs, Maxwell's Plum (New York), Guadelupe National Park (Texas), Fifth Avenue (New York) as one-way south-bound street, Madison Avenue (New York) as one-way northbound street, Chicago Civic Center, UN Plaza, Random House acquired by RCA, lyrics on record albums, Rare and Endangered Species List (Department of the Interior)

1967

Facts and Figures

Economic Profile
- Dow-Jones: ↑ High 943–Low 786
- GNP: +5%
- Inflation: +2.8%
- Unemployment: 3.8%

Average salary: $6,230
- Teacher: $6,605
- Physician: $34,600
- Factory worker: $6,880

Bonwit Teller Bengal lizard bags: $75–$90
Altman's trench coat: $26–$110
A&S African cotton tent dress: $30
"Teddy-Bra" slip: $7
Alexander's cashmere sweater: $12.99
Sloane's Afskar rug: $268 (12′ by 8′)
- Tabriz rug, used: $548 (12′ by 9′)
- Cambridge upholstered chair: $159

Altman's upholstered sofa: $439–$569
Ironstone, 93-piece set: $39.99

Deaths

Dan Duryea, Mischa Elman, Geraldine Farrar, Dorothy Gish, Fannie Hurst, Vivien Leigh, Thomas Merton, Ramon Novarro, Basil Rathbone, Upton Sinclair, Robert Taylor, Spencer Tracy.

In the News

Roger Chaffee, Virgil Grissom, and Edward White Are Killed in Apollo Test Launch Fire . . . Kosygin Meets Pope Paul . . . U.S. Bombers Raid Hanoi . . . Ho Chi Minh Letters Reject LBJ Peace Proposal . . . Army Junta Seizes Power in Greece . . . Svetlana Alliluyeva, Stalin's Daughter, Defects to West . . . Soviet Cosmonaut Komarov Dies in Reentry . . . Nasser Demands Withdrawal of UN Forces in Sinai, Secretary-General U Thant Complies . . . UN Appoints Commission on Southwest Africa, Now Claimed by South Africa . . . Nasser Closes Aqaba Gulf to Israeli Ships . . . East Nigeria Claims Independence as Biafra . . . Israel Smashes Arabs, Takes Sinai, Gaza, Old Jerusalem, Golan Heights, and West Bank in Six Days . . . Thurgood Marshall Is First Black Appointed to Supreme Court . . . Communist China Announces It Has H-Bomb . . . Johnson and Kosygin Talk at Glassboro, N.J. . . . Newark Black Riots End after Six Days with 26 Dead . . . Detroit Black Riots End after 8 Days, 43 Are Dead . . . De Gaulle, on Canada Visit, Calls for "Québec Libre" . . . Cambridge Riots Follow Stokely Carmichael Speech . . . U.S. Troop Level in Vietnam Reaches 525,000 . . . Red Guards Sack British Compound in Peking . . . U.S. and USSR Present Anti–Nuclear Proliferation Treaty to General Disarmament Conference . . . U.S. Announces Anti–Ballistic Missile Defense Plan against Chinese Attack . . . Bolivia Confirms Capture and Death of Che Guevara . . . Antiwar Protesters Make Night March on Pentagon . . . Expo '67 Opens in Montreal . . . Christiaan Barnard Performs First Heart Transplant . . . Vietnam: U.S. Dead, 15,997.

Vietnam: near the Bassac River. National Security Advisor Walt Rostow states that "Victory is just around the corner." *Department of the Navy.*

"I don't have no personal quarrel with those Viet Congs."

— Muhammad Ali

"We believe that all men somehow possess a divine potentiality. . . . We reject the tired dualism that seeks God and human potentialities in denying the joys of the senses."

— George B. Leonard, Esalen

"There [in Haight-Ashbury], in a daily street-fair atmosphere, upwards of 15,000 unbonded girls and boys interact in a tribal love-seeking, free-winging, acid-based society, where if you are a hippie and you have a dime, you can put it in a parking meter and lie down in the street for an hour's sunshine."

— Warren Hinckle, *Social History of the Hippies*

Ads

Quotes

"I have tried to show that contemporary society is a repressive society in all its aspects, that even the comfort and the prosperity, the alleged political and moral freedom, are utilized for repressive ends."

— Herbert Marcuse

"If I could turn you on, if I could drive you out of your wretched mind, if I could tell you, I would let you know."

— R. D. Laing, *Politics of Experience*

" 'An investigation into Sex' is now offered at Dartmouth. 'Analogues to the LSD Experience' can now be studied at Penn. 'Guerilla Warfare' is being examined by DePauw students. Stanford undergraduates are studying 'American Youth in Revolt,' and 'The Origins and Meaning of Black Power' is a course at Brooklyn College. Has higher education finally caught up with the times?"

— Ralph Keyes, "The Free Universities"

"Batman." *Movie Star News.*

TV

Premieres
"Mannix," Mike Connors
"Judd for the Defense," Carl Betz
"The David Susskind Show"
"N.Y.P.D.," Jack Warden, Robert Hooks
"The Flying Nun," Sally Field
"The Carol Burnett Show," Carol Burnett, Vicki
    Lawrence, Tim Conway, Harvey Korman
"Ironside," Raymond Burr
"The Phil Donahue Show"

Top Ten (Nielsen)
"The Andy Griffith Show," "The Lucy Show,"
"Gomer Pyle, U.S.M.C.," "Gunsmoke," "Family
Affair," "Bonanza," "The Red Skelton Show," "The
Dean Martin Show," "The Jackie Gleason Show,"
"Saturday Night at the Movies"

Specials
"Elizabeth the Queen" (Dame Judith Anderson); "St.
Joan" (Genevieve Bujold); "The Crucible" (Colleen
Dewhurst); "Do Not Go Gentle into That Good
Night" (Melvyn Douglas); "Crisis in the Cities"
(NET); "Eric Hoffer: The Passionate State of Mind"

Emmy Awards
"Mission: Impossible" (drama); "Get Smart"
(comedy); "He's Your Dog, Charlie Brown"
(children); Bill Cosby (Actor, "I Spy"); Don Adams
(comedic actor, "Get Smart"); Barbara Bain (actress,
"Mission: Impossible"); Lucille Ball (comedic
actress, "The Lucy Show")

Of Note
Both CBS and NBC televise the Super Bowl • The
Public Broadcasting Act, which funds public TV, is a
great aid for educational TV.

Movies

Openings
In the Heat of the Night (Norman Jewison), Sidney
    Poitier, Rod Steiger
Bonnie and Clyde (Arthur Penn), Warren Beatty,
    Faye Dunaway
The Graduate (Mike Nichols), Dustin Hoffman,
    Anne Bancroft, Katharine Ross
Guess Who's Coming to Dinner (Stanley Kramer),
    Spencer Tracy, Sidney Poitier, Katharine
    Hepburn
In Cold Blood (Richard Brooks), Robert Blake, Scott
    Wilson, John Forsythe, Paul Stewart
Cool Hand Luke (Stuart Rosenberg), Paul Newman,
    George Kennedy
The Dirty Dozen (Robert Aldrich), Lee Marvin,
    Ernest Borgnine, Charles Bronson
Barefoot in the Park (Gene Saks), Robert Redford,
    Jane Fonda
Two for the Road (Stanley Donen), Audrey Hepburn,
    Albert Finney
Elvira Madigan (Bo Widerberg), Pia Degermark,
    Thommy Berggren
Accident (Joseph Losey), Dirk Bogarde, Stanley
    Baker
The Battle of Algiers (Gillo Pontecorvo), Yacef
    Saadi, Jean Martin
The Night of the Generals (Anatole Litvak), Peter
    O'Toole, Omar Sharif, Tom Courtenay
Persona (Ingmar Bergman), Bibi Andersson, Liv
    Ullmann

Reflections in a Golden Eye (John Huston), Elizabeth
    Taylor, Marlon Brando
Belle de Jour (Luis Buñuel), Catherine Deneuve,
    Jean Sorel

Academy Awards
Best Picture: *In the Heat of the Night*
Best Director: Mike Nichols (*The Graduate*)
Best Actress: Katharine Hepburn (*Guess Who's
    Coming to Dinner*)
Best Actor: Rod Steiger (*In the Heat of the Night*)

Top Box-Office Stars
Julie Andrews, Lee Marvin, Paul Newman, Sean
Connery, Elizabeth Taylor, Sidney Poitier, John
Wayne, Richard Burton, Steve McQueen

Stars of Tomorrow
Lynn Redgrave, Faye Dunaway, James Caan, John
Phillip Law, Michele Lee, Michael Sarrazin, Sharon
Tate, Michael York, Hywell Bennett, David
Hemmings

Popular Music

Hit Songs
"A Natural Woman"
"Soul Man"
"I Never Loved a Man"
"Make Me Yours"
"I Was Made to Love Her"
"Penny Lane"
"By the Time I Get to Phoenix"
"Cabaret"
"Can't Take My Eyes off You"
"It Must Be Him"

Top Records

Albums: *More of the Monkees; Diana Ross and the Supremes' Greatest Hits; Sounds Like* (Herb Alpert and the Tijuana Brass)

Singles: *To Sir with Love* (Lulu); *The Letter* (Box Tops); *San Francisco (Wear Some Flowers in Your Hair)* (Scott McKenzie); *The Beat Goes On* (Sonny and Cher); *Light My Fire* (Doors); *I'm a Believer* (Monkees); *Lucy in the Sky with Diamonds* (Beatles); *Windy* (Association); *Jimmy Mack* (Martha and the Vandellas). Country: *There Goes My Everything* (Jack Greene)

Grammy Awards
Up, Up and Away, 5th Dimension (record); *Sgt. Pepper's Lonely Hearts Club Band,* Beatles (album); "Up, Up and Away" (song)

Jazz and Big Bands
Charles Lloyd records *Forest Flower* with a basso ostinato.

Top Performers (*Downbeat*): Charles Lloyd (soloist); Duke Ellington (band); Miles Davis (jazz group); Wes Montgomery, Ray Brown, Buddy Rich, Stan Getz (instrumentalists); Ella Fitzgerald, Lou Rawls (vocalists); Beatles (vocal group); *Miles [Davis] Smiles* (album)

Theater

Broadway Openings

Plays
The Homecoming (Harold Pinter), Vivien Merchant, Ian Holm, Paul Rogers
The Birthday Party (Harold Pinter), Ruth White, Ed Flanders, James Patterson
Rosencrantz and Guildenstern Are Dead (Tom Stoppard), Brian Murray, John Wood
Black Comedy (Peter Shaffer), Geraldine Page, Michael Crawford, Lynn Redgrave
There's a Girl in My Soup (Terence Frisby), Gig Young, Barbara Ferris
You Know I Can't Hear You When the Water's Running (Robert Anderson), Martin Balsam, Eileen Heckart, George Grizzard
More Stately Mansions (Eugene O'Neill), Ingrid Bergman, Colleen Dewhurst, Arthur Hill
Little Murders (Jules Feiffer), Elliott Gould, Barbara Cook

Musicals
How Now, Dow Jones (Elmer Bernstein, Carolyn Leigh) Anthony Roberts, Brenda Vaccaro
Hallelujah, Baby! (Jules Styne, Betty Comden, Adolph Green), Leslie Uggams, Robert Hooks
You're a Good Man, Charlie Brown (Clark Gesner), Gary Burghoff, Reva Rose
Judy Garland at the Palace

Classics and Revivals On and Off Broadway
The Little Foxes (Lillian Hellman), Margaret Leighton, E. G. Marshall, Anne Bancroft, George C. Scott; *Scuba Duba* (Bruce Jay Friedman), Jerry Orbach; *Macbird* (Barbara Garson), Cleavon Little, Stacy Keach, William Devane; *Fortune and Men's Eyes* (John Herbert); *Iphigenia in Aulis* (Euripides), Irene Papas; *The Ceremony of Innocence* (Ronald Ribman), Sandy Duncan, Donald Madden. Founded: CSC (Classic Stage Company) by Christopher Martin, Harris Laskawy, and Kathryn Wyman.

Regional

Founded: Mark Taper Forum, Los Angeles, by Gordon Davidson: *The Sorrows of Frederick* (Romulus Linney), premiere; Center Theatre Group (Dal Manson), Los Angeles: *More Stately Mansions* (Eugene O'Neill), Ingrid Bergman, Arthur Hill, Colleen Dewhurst, premiere; *The Happy Time* (John Kander and Fred Ebb), Robert Goulet, premiere
Arena Stage, Washington, D.C.: *The Great White Hope* (Howard Sackler), James Earl Jones, Jane Alexander, premiere
Minneapolis: *The House of Atreus* (John Lewin's adaptation of *The Oresteia*)
A.C.T., San Francisco: Three versions of *Hamlet*

Pulitzer Prize
A Delicate Balance, Edward Albee

Tony Awards
The Homecoming, Harold Pinter (play), *Cabaret,* John Kander, Fred Ebb (musical)

Classical Music

Compositions
Walter Piston, Clarinet Concerto
David Diamond, Violin Concerto no. 3
Roger Sessions, Symphony no. 7
Lukas Foss, Cello Concerto
William Albright, *Tic*
George Crumb, "Echoes of Time and the River"

Important Events
For the New York Philharmonic's 125th anniversary, Leonard Bernstein repeats its inaugural program (1842), which includes Beethoven, Weber, Rossini, Mozart, Hummel, and Kalliwoda. For the remainder of the season, each concert presents at least one work that the orchestra premiered or commissioned.
Zubin Mehta and the Los Angeles Philharmonic begin a world tour.
Celebrating their 40th year on the stage are Vladimir Horowitz, Robert Goldsand, and Yehudi Menuhin.
In its first U.S. appearance, La Scala performs Verdi's Requiem at Carnegie Hall.
Mstislav Rostropovich and the London Symphony play eight concerts in 18 days.
Dietrich Fischer-Dieskau sings three lieder concerts of Shumann, Schubert, and Beethoven (New York). Other highly acclaimed New York recitals are by Jacqueline du Pré, Lily Kraus (Mozart's 25 solo piano concerti), and Rostropovich with Galina Vishnevskaya.

The House of Atreus, the first regional theater production to tour the country. *Minneapolis Theatre Company.*

Contemporary music festivals proliferate from New York and Cleveland to Dallas and Seattle; the Third International Webern Festival is held in Buffalo, N.Y.
Robert Shaw becomes director of the Atlanta Symphony.

Debuts: Kyung-Wha Chung, Alexis Weissenberg

First Performances
Webern, Three Pieces for Orchestra (Philadelphia); Krzysztof Penderecki, *St. Luke Passion* (Chicago); Elliott Carter, Piano Concerto (Boston); Morton Subotnick, *An Electronic Christmas* (New York); Walter Piston, Variations for Cello and Orchestra (New York); Paul Creston, *Chthonic Ode* (Detroit); Alan Hovhannes, *The Holy City* (Portland, Me.), *To Vishnu* (New York); Lalo Schifrin, *The Rise and Fall of the Third Reich* (Hollywood); Aaron Copland, *Inscape* (Ann Arbor, Mich.)

Opera

Metropolitan: Evelyn Lear, Marie Collier, *Mourning Becomes Elektra* (Marvin Levy, premiere); Grace Bumbry, *Carmen;* Jon Vickers, *Peter Grimes;* Pilar Lorengar, Teresa Berganza (debut), *Le nozze di Figaro;* Marc Chagall sets are used for *Die Zauberflöte.*

City Center: *The Servant of Two Masters* (Vittorio Giannini, premiere)

Washington, D.C.: *Bomarzo* (Alberto Ginastera)

Chicago: Season canceled because of labor disputes

San Francisco: Luciano Pavarotti, *La bohème;* Irene Dalis, *Tristan und Isolde*

Boston: *Voyage to the Moon* (in modern style at the White House for LBJ and Turkish president); double bill: *Bluebeard's Castle* and *The Miraculous Mandarin* (Béla Bartók)

Santa Fe: House burns down after *Cardillac.*

Music Notes
Owing to deficits, the Met raises its ticket prices to a maximum $15.50.

Art

Painting

Kenneth Noland, *Wild Indigo, Via Blues*

Alfred Leslie, *Notan Study for the Killing of Frank O'Hara, Alfred Leslie*

Tom Wesselmann, *Great American Nude, No. 98*

James Rosenquist, *U-Haul It*

Ellsworth Kelly, *Spectrum III*

Jules Olitski, *High a Yellow*

Andrew Wyeth, *The Apron*

Helen Frankenthaler, *Guiding Red*

Sculpture

George Segal, *Portrait of Sidney Janis with Mondrian*

Claes Oldenburg, *Giant Soft Fan* (1966–67)

Richard Tuttle, *Gray Extended Seven*

Carl Andre, *Cuts*

Donald Judd, *Untitled*

Barnett Newman, *Broken Obelisk*

Lucas Samaras, *Corridor*

Bruce Nauman, *From Hand to Mouth*

Picasso's abstract steel sculpture is placed at the Richard J. Daley Center, Chicago.

Architecture

Hanselmann House, Ft. Wayne, Ind. (Michael Graves)

Stuhr Museum, Grand Island, Neb. (Edward Durell Stone)

Bell Tower, St. John's Abbey Church, Collegeville, Minn. (Marcel Breuer)

Ford Foundation, New York (Roche and Dinkeloo)

National Center for Atmospheric Research, Boulder, Colo. (I. M. Pei)

Gulf Life Tower, Jacksonville, Fla. (Welton Becket)

Sante Fe Opera House, Sante Fe, N.M. (McHugh and Kidder)

Marina City, Chicago (Bertrand Goldberg)

Hyatt Regency Hotel, Atlanta, Ga. (John Portman)

First Unitarian Church, Rochester (Louis I. Kahn)

Important Exhibitions

"The Art of India and Nepal" tours the United States.

The year is dominated by retrospectives, theme shows, and sculpture. Retrospectives include Ingres, Gilbert, Smart (Washington); Hogarth (Richmond); Degas (Philadelphia); Manet (Chicago, Philadelphia); The Peale family (Detroit, Utica); Wyeth (Whitney); Pollock (Museum of Modern Art); Klee (Guggenheim); and Léger (Chicago).

Protest shows include "Angry Artists against the War in Vietnam," a week-long demonstration with D'Arcangelo, di Suvero, Rosenquist, Golub, and Greene; "Protest and Hope": New School works by Indiana, Levine, Segal, and Shahn.

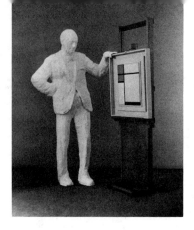

George Segal, *Portrait of Sidney Janis with Mondrian Painting* 1967. Plaster figure with Mondrian's *Composition,* 1933, on an easel; figure, 66″ high; easel 67″ high. *The Sidney and Harriet Janis Collection. Gift to the Museum of Modern Art, New York.*

As the "sculpture renaissance" continues, numerous avant-garde shows are held (Guggenheim, Washington, Los Angeles, Minneapolis). Various exhibits travel through the United States: environmental projects, serial ideas, mass production techniques, and minimalism.

Shows on experimental work include polyurethane pieces, colored plastics, electromagnetics, plexiglass reliefs, rearranged modules: Piero Gilardi, John Chamberlain, Dan Flavin, David Weinrib, Craig Kauffman, Robert Morris, Isamu Noguchi, along with the enormous projects of Sol LeWitt, and Claes Oldenburg.

Art Briefs

Five and a half tons of Picasso sculpture arrive at the Museum of Modern Art for the exhibition October 11–January 1 • Sidney Janis donates his $2 million collection to the Museum of Modern Art • Thomas P. F. Hoving becomes director of the Metropolitan Museum of Art • The United States joins the world in efforts to save the art treasures damaged by the flood in Florence, Italy • Support for technical experiments extend from organizations such as AT&T, IBM, and AFL-CIO to EAT (Experiments in Art and Technology) • The National Gallery purchases Leonardo da Vinci's *Ginevra dei Benci* from the prince of Liechtenstein for $5–6 million, the highest price ever paid for a painting; it also receives $20 million from the Andrew Mellon family • Monet's *La Terasse à Saint-Adresse,* purchased in 1926 for $11,000, sells for $1.4 million.

Dance

Premieres

American Ballet Theatre: *Las Hermanas, Concerto* (Kenneth Macmillan)

New York City Ballet: *Jewels* (George Balanchine), Violette Verdy, Patricia McBride, Suzanne Farrell

Eliot Feld: *At Midnight, Harbinger*

Alwin Nikolais: *Triptych*

Books

Fiction
Critics' Choice
The Manor, Isaac Bashevis Singer
When She Was Good, Philip Roth
Stop Time, Frank Conroy
Snow White, Donald Barthelme
Why Are We in Vietnam?, Norman Mailer
Fathers, Herbert Gold
A Garden of Earthly Delights, Joyce Carol Oates
A Bad Man, Stanley Elkin
Trout Fishing in America, Richard Brautigan
Hall of Mirrors, Robert Stone

Best-Sellers
The Arrangement, Elia Kazan
The Confessions of Nat Turner, William Styron
The Chosen, Chaim Potok
Topaz, Leon Uris
Christy, Catherine Marshall
The Eighth Day, Thornton Wilder
Rosemary's Baby, Ira Levin
The Plot, Irving Wallace
The Gabriel Hounds, Mary Stewart
The Exhibitionist, Henry Sutton

Nonfiction
Critics' Choice
The Fabulators, Robert Scholes
Hell's Angels, Hunter S. Thompson
Selected Essays, William Troy
The New Industrial State, John Kenneth Galbraith
Death at an Early Age, Jonathan Kozol
Like a Conquered Province: The Moral Ambiguity of America, Paul Goodman
The Temper of Our Time, Eric Hoffer
F. Scott Fitzgerald: The Last Laocoön, Robert Sklar
The Naked Ape, Desmond Morris
ᴥ *Twenty Letters to a Friend*, Svetlana Alliluyeva
ᴥ *Writing Degree Zero*, Roland Barthes
ᴥ *The Medium Is the Massage*, Marshall McLuhan, Quentin Fiore

Best-Sellers
Death of a President, William Manchester
Misery Is a Blind Date, Johnny Carson
Games People Play, Eric Berne, M.D.
A Modern Priest Looks at His Out-Dated Church, Father James Kavanaugh
Everything But Money, Sam Levenson
Our Crowd, Stephen Birmingham
Phyllis Diller's Marriage Manual
Stanyan Street (poetry), Rod McKuen
Edgar Cayce—The Sleeping Prophet, Jess Stearn
Better Homes and Gardens Favorite Ways in Chicken

Poetry
Howard Nemerov, *The Blue Swallows*
W. S. Merwin, *The Lice*
Robert Bly, *The Light around the Body*
Elizabeth Bishop, *Selected Poems*
Denise Levertov, *The Sorrow Dance*
Marianne Moore, *Complete Poems*

Pulitzer Prizes
The Confessions of Nat Turner, William Styron (fiction)
The Ideological Origins of the American Revolution, Bernard Bailyn (U.S. history)
Rousseau and Revolution, William and Ariel Durant (nonfiction)
Memoirs 1925–1950, George F. Kennan (biography)
The Hard Hours, Anthony Hecht (poetry)

Science and Technology

Rene Favaloro, at the Cleveland Clinic, develops the coronary bypass operation.

A connection between a cholesterol-lowering diet and reduced incidence of heart disease is shown in the report of a five-year study on 412 men.

The structure of the enzyme ribonuclease (RNA) is discovered.

R. M. Dolby develops a system for eliminating background hiss in audio recordings.

Multiple Independent Reentry Vehicles (MIRV) are developed, permitting many separate missiles from one launch.

The laser range finder is developed.

Pioneer VIII is launched to investigate and monitor interplanetary phenomena at diverse points in space throughout the solar system.

Lunar Orbiter V is launched to obtain a complete photo mapping of the lunar surface.

Biosatellite II is the first successful United States satellite for bioscientific research.

E. Hay and Y. Yellott build a solar house with ponds of water on the roof to act as insulation.

ᴥ Dr. Christiaan Barnard performs the first heart transplant in Capetown, South Africa; the patient, Lewis Washansky, lives 18 days.

Nobel Prize
Hans A. Bethe wins the prize in physics for work on the energy production of stars. H. K. Hartline, George Wald, and Ragnar Granit win in physiology and medicine for work on the human eye.

Sports

Baseball

The Boston Red Sox go from ninth place, last season, to the pennant; Carl Yastrzemski leads the league with .326, 121 RBIs, and 44 home runs (triple crown).

Cy Young Awards go to Mike McCormick (San Francisco, NL) and Jim Lonborg (Boston, AL).

Champions

Batting	
Roberto Clemente (Pittsburgh, NL), .357	Sonny Siebert (Cleveland, AL), 16–8
Carl Yastrzemski (Boston, AL), .326	*Home runs*
Pitching	Harmon Killebrew (Minnesota, AL), 49
Richard Hughes (St. Louis, NL), 16–6	Carl Yastrzemski (Boston, AL), 49

Football

The first interleague championship, called the Super Bowl, is played January 15 at Los Angeles; the score is Green Bay 35–Kansas City 10.

Lou Groza retires with a record 1,349 points.

Raymond Berry retires with a record 631 receptions.

NFL Season Leaders: Sonny Jurgensen (Washington), passing; Leroy Kelley (Cleveland), rushing; Charles Taylor (Washington), receiving

AFL Season Leaders: Darryl Lamonica (Oakland), passing; Jim Nance (Boston), rushing; George Sauer (New York Jets), receiving

Bowls (Jan. 1, 1968)

Rose: Southern California 14–Indiana 3	Cotton: Texas A & M 20–Alabama 16
Orange: Oklahoma 26–Tennessee 24	Sugar: Louisiana State 20–Wyoming 13

College All-Americans: O. J. Simpson (B), Southern California; Larry Csonka (B), Syracuse; Ted Hendricks (DE), Miami

Basketball

The Philadelphia 76'ers post a record 68–13 season led by Wilt Chamberlain, 24.1 p.p.g., 24 r.p.g. The ABA begins; stars include Connie Hawkins, Roger Brown, and Mel Daniels.

NBA All-Pro First Team: Rick Barry (San Francisco), Elgin Baylor (Los Angeles), Wilt Chamberlain (Philadelphia), Jerry West (Los Angeles), Oscar Robertson (Cincinnati)

Other Sports

Winners

World Series	*MVP*
St. Louis (NL) 4	Wilt Chamberlain,
Boston (AL) 3	Philadelphia
MVP	*College Basketball*
NL–Orlando Cepeda, San Francisco	UCLA
AL–Carl Yastrzemski, Boston	*Player of the Year*
Super Bowl II (Jan. 1968)	Lew Alcindor, UCLA
Green Bay 33–Oakland 14	*Stanley Cup*
MVP	Toronto
John Unitas, Baltimore	*US Tennis Open*
College Football	Men: John Newcombe
Southern California	Women: Billie Jean King
Heisman Trophy	*USGA Open*
Gary Beban, UCLA	Jack Nicklaus
NBA Championship	*Kentucky Derby*
Philadelphia 4–San Francisco 2	Proud Clarion (R. Ussery, jockey)

Fashion

For Men: A revolution occurs in men's wear: color is at its most unrestrained; coordinates are carefully matched. Jackets are double-breasted in plaids, tattersall, cavalry twill, and whipcord; citified tweeds are used for all styles. Turtlenecks join both formal and casual wear, along with colored or boldly striped shirts with spread collars and French cuffs. Soft, square-toed leather shoes, hand-sewn slip-ons, and saddle stitching are popular.

For Women: Fashion model Twiggy arrives in New York in March with short skirts, boots, pin-striped jumpsuits, and the boldest contrasting colors yet. The maxi is worn over the mini; white wool tents, velvet knickers and jeweled, embroidered, sequined, and lace fabrics appear. Underwear no longer hides body shape. Made of laces, net, and marquisette, it reveals and controls the natural shape. Bras, almost invisible in wear, are wire and padding free. Gernreich coordinates mini slips and mini bras; stockings are virtually replaced by tights.

High-fashion note: Deliss's linen and lace peasant dress, pleated and embroidered

Kaleidoscope _____

- Colorado leads in the liberalization of abortion laws.
- Estimates report 50,000–100,000 hippies in the San Francisco area: "Haight is Love" is a popular slogan; 1,000 psychedelic bands play in the area.
- The Esalen Institute in northern California ("Third Force Psychiatry") practices a gestalt therapy that encourages people to act out their dreams, role play, and take nude hot baths together; it grosses $1 million and is followed by T-groups throughout the United States.
- Secretary of Defense Robert McNamara becomes World Bank president after resigning his office.
- Army physician Captain Harold Levy refuses to train Green Berets in the treatment of skin disease on the grounds that they commit war crimes and are "killers of women and children"; he is court-martialed and sent to Fort Leavenworth Prison.
- U.S. troop levels in Vietnam pass 475,000, exceeding the total troop strength in Korea; U.S. total bombing tonnage, 1,630,000, exceeds that of World War II.
- "Pacification," "strategic revolutionary development," and "strategic hamlets" are key concepts in American efforts to control the countryside.
- Muhammad Ali, heavyweight champion, is denied conscientious objector status; after refusing induction into the army, he is arrested, given a five-year sentence, and fined $10,000; ring authorities have already removed his title.
- A black, Carl Stokes, is elected mayor of Cleveland.
- Over 700,000 people march in a Fifth Avenue parade against the war.
- Norman Mailer mythologizes the October 21 March on the Pentagon in *Armies of the Night;* Dr. Benjamin Spock, Paul Goodman, Philip Hirschkop, Robert Lowell, Noam Chomsky, and Dwight McDonald are prominent figures in both.
- Black leader Rap Brown says of the ghetto riots: "Violence is as American as cherry pie," and adds, they are "a dress rehearsal for revolution."
- The Supreme Court rules unconstitutional state laws against interracial marriage.
- The National Student Association reveals that it has secretly been receiving CIA funds.
- Coed dorms open at numerous colleges across the country.
- Violence in movies escalates in such films as *Bonnie and Clyde, The Dirty Dozen,* and *In Cold Blood;* a landmark interracial film is *Guess Who's Coming to Dinner.*
- The final TV episode of "The Fugitive," when the killer is caught and the innocent David Janssen hero is vindicated, is advertised as "the day the running stopped"; it draws over a 50 percent rating.
- Record albums begin to outsell singles; *Sgt. Pepper* introduces electronic rock.
- The first rock festival is held at Monterey, Calif., with Grateful Dead and Big Brother and the Holding Company (Janis Joplin).

Dustin Hoffman and Anne Bancroft (as Mrs. Robinson) in *The Graduate,* a story of the alienation of educated youth in a materialistic society. *Movie Star News.*

- The world's largest outdoor Monopoly game, 550 by 470 feet, is played at Juniata College, Huntington, Pa.
- Lynda Bird Johnson marries Marine Captain Charles Robb in the White House.
- George Lincoln Rockwell, president of the U.S. Nazi party, is shot to death.
- Annual beef consumption, per capita, is 105.6 pounds, up from 99 pounds in 1960.
- Pillsbury buys Burger King.
- The U.S. population has doubled since 1917; college enrollment has almost doubled since 1960 (6,963,687, from 3,570,000).
- Operation Match, a two-year-old computer dating corporation, reports that 130,000 of its 5 million clients have married.
- James Garrison, New Orleans district attorney, claims he has solved the JFK assassination and arrests Clay Shaw, a retired businessman for conspiracy; Shaw is acquitted.
- Journalist Bernard Fall is killed in Vietnam by a land mine.
- The *New York Times* Sunday magazine publishes an article by General Maxwell Taylor entitled "The Cause in Vietnam Is Being Won."

Fads: Jogging, Mickey Mouse watches, protest buttons, Finnish saunas, psychedelic art

New Words and Usages: Guru, hangup, blow your cool, narc, kicky, beautiful, head shop, shades, ballsy, peacenik, boondocks, Spirit of Glassboro

First Appearances: "Be-In" (Golden Gate Park, San Francisco), combination knife–can opener, UHF-VHF combination, laser surgery operating theater (Cincinnati), general who rose from draftee (K. L. Ware), Zen Buddist monastery (Tassajara Springs, Calif.), horse motel (Marshfield, Mo.), wine museum (Hammondsport, N.Y.) large-type weekly *(New York Times),* electric fishing reel, Hertz acquired by RCA, Hilton Hotels International acquired by TWA, compact microwave (Amana), Holt, Rinehart & Winston acquired by CBS, Phoenix House, airmail postcard commemorative (Charlotte Amalie, Virgin Islands)

1968

Facts and Figures

Economic Profile
  Dow-Jones: ↑ High 985–
    Low 825
  GNP: +8%
  Inflation: +4.2%
  Unemployment: 3.6%
Balance of international
  payments: +$1.5 billion
Military on duty: 3,548,000
Voter participation: 64%
  (1960), 61% (1968)
Population with religious
  affiliation: 128 million
Zenith 20″ color TV: $399.95
Sunbeam cannister vacuum:
  $49.95
Allen carpet: $5.88–$9.88 (sq.
  yd.)
Chrysler: $2,249
Plymouth: $2,049
Toyota: $1,666
Chock Full O'Nuts:
  Coffee, milk, orange juice:
    15¢
  Sandwich (chicken salad,
    nutted cheese): 35¢
  Frankfurter: 25¢
  Beefburger: 45¢
  Whole wheat doughnut:
    10¢
  Coconut layer cake,
    huckleberry pie: 25¢

Deaths

John Coltrane, Nelson Eddy,
  Woody Guthrie, Langston
  Hughes, Jayne Mansfield,
  Ann Sheridan, Alice B.
  Toklas, Paul Whiteman.

In the News

ALEXANDER DUBCEK IS ELECTED CZECH LEADER . . . NORTH KOREA SEIZES USS "PUEBLO" AND CREW . . . VIET CONG BEGIN TET OFFENSIVE ON SAIGON, HUE, AND OTHER MAJOR CITIES, SAIGON EMBASSY IS INVADED . . . HUE IS RECAPTURED . . . EUGENE MCCARTHY GIVES LBJ CLOSE RACE IN NEW HAMPSHIRE DEMOCRATIC PRIMARY . . . ROBERT KENNEDY DECLARES PRESIDENTIAL CANDIDACY . . . JOHNSON ANNOUNCES PARTIAL HALT IN BOMBING AND DECLARES HE WILL NOT RUN AGAIN . . . MARTIN LUTHER KING, JR. IS ASSASSINATED IN MEMPHIS, MASSIVE RIOTING ERUPTS IN 125 CITIES, 46 ARE KILLED . . . "OPERATION COMPLETE VICTORY" IS LAUNCHED WITH 100,000 TROOPS . . . THE 1968 CIVIL RIGHTS ACT PASSES . . . COLUMBIA UNIVERSITY IS OCCUPIED BY STUDENT REBELS . . . U.S. AND NORTH VIETNAM SCHEDULE PARIS PEACE TALKS . . . FRENCH STUDENTS CLASH WITH POLICE . . . ROBERT KENNEDY IS ASSASSINATED IN CALIFORNIA, ALLEGED KILLER SIRHAN SIRHAN IS ARRESTED ON THE SPOT . . . JAMES EARL RAY, ALLEGED MARTIN LUTHER KING ASSASSIN, IS ARRESTED . . . CREIGHTON ABRAMS REPLACES WESTMORELAND AS VIETNAM COMMANDER . . . INCOME TAX SURCHARGE IS PASSED . . . JOHNSON AND SOUTH VIETNAMESE THIEU MEET IN HONOLULU . . . GOP NOMINATES RICHARD NIXON . . . USSR INVADES CZECHOSLOVAKIA . . . 200,000 MEXICAN STUDENTS DEMONSTRATE . . . YIPPIES LEAD MAJOR RIOTS AT DEMOCRATIC CONVENTION IN CHICAGO, HUBERT HUMPHREY IS NOMINATED . . . JACKIE KENNEDY WEDS ARISTOTLE ONASSIS . . . JOHNSON CALLS FOR BOMBING HALT . . . NIXON IS ELECTED BY MARGIN OF 500,000 . . . U.S. "ADMITS GUILT" AND NORTH KOREA RELEASES "PUEBLO" CREW . . . ASTRONAUTS CIRCLE MOON TEN TIMES . . . VIETNAM: U.S. TROOP STRENGTH, 540,000; U.S. DEAD, 30,857; ENEMY DEAD, 422,979.

Martin Luther King is assassinated April 4th. *Copyright* Washington Post. *Reprinted by permission of D.C. Public Library.*

Students take over the president's office at Columbia University. *L. Strong.*

"We've got some difficult days ahead. But it really doesn't matter with me now. Because I've been to the mountain top. Like anybody, I would like to live a long life, [but] I've seen the Promised Land. I may not get there with you, [but] we as a people will get [there]. . . . So I'm happy tonight. I'm not fearing any man. Mine eyes have seen the glory of the coming of the Lord."
— Martin Luther King, Jr., in Memphis, shortly before his assassination

"I shall not seek, and I will not accept, the nomination of my party for another term as your President" (Lyndon Baines Johnson). "I don't know quite what to say" (Bobby Kennedy). "I went and had another drink" (Everett Dirksen). "THANKS, LBJ" (Youths outside the White House). "Congratulations. It was the best thing you could possibly have given up for Lent" (Unidentified photographer).
(all cited in *Time*)

Quotes

"I know some of you have been through defeats, as I have, and had your hearts broken. It has been said that great philosophy is not won without defeat. But a great philosophy is always won without fear."
— Richard M. Nixon

"[Those] phony intellectuals . . . don't understand what we mean by hard work and patriotism. . . . If you've seen one ghetto area, you've seen them all."
— Spiro T. Agnew

"We are at a crisis point in the history of American education and probably in that of the Western world."
— Richard Hofstadter, Columbia University professor

"The youth rebellion is a worldwide phenomenon that has not been seen before in history. I do not believe they will calm down and be ad execs at thirty as the Establishment would like us to believe."
— William Burroughs

"Shoot to kill."
— Chicago mayor Richard Daley

"Slave catchers, slave owners, murderers, butchers, oppressors—the white heroes have acquired new names."
— Eldridge Cleaver, *Soul on Ice*

"No girl child born today should responsibly be brought up to be a housewife. Too much has been made of defining human personality and destiny in terms of the sex organs. After all, we share the human brain."

— Betty Friedan

Ads

The new color portable that won't give you a hernia
(*Sony Trinitron*)

Farewell to the ugly cigarette.
(*Eve*)

The Temptation of Brother Domenico
(*Sara Lee Devil's Food Cake*)

Honor thy self
(*Johnny Walker Black*)

The sexual revolution is spreading a lot more than love.
(RN *magazine*)

Will the cost of living going up stop your hemline from coming down?
(*Ohrbach's*)

Don't go home with strangers.
(*Swissair*)

If you depend on the LIRR to get home in time for dinner . . .
(*Salton Hottray*)

TV

Premieres

"It Takes a Thief," Robert Wagner
"The Dick Cavett Show"
"The Mod Squad," Peggy Lipton, Michael Cole,
    Clarence Williams III
"Rowan and Martin's Laugh-In"
"The Ghost and Mrs. Muir," Hope Lange, Edward
    Mulhare
"Hawaii Five-O," Jack Lord
"The Prisoner," Patrick McGoohan
"60 Minutes," Harry Reasoner, Mike Wallace
"Adam-12," Martin Milner
"Mayberry R.F.D.," Ken Berry
"Here's Lucy," Lucille Ball
"Julia," Diahann Carroll

Top Ten (Nielsen)

"Rowan and Martin's Laugh-In," "Gomer Pyle,
U.S.M.C.," "Bonanza," "Mayberry R.F.D.,"
"Family Affair," "Gunsmoke," "Julia," "The Dean
Martin Show," "Here's Lucy," "The Beverly
Hillbillies"

Specials

"Hunger in the United States" (Martin Carr); "Police
after Chicago" (John Laurence); "Martin Luther
King;" "Man Who Dances: Edward Villella";
"Teacher, Teacher" (Billy Schulman); "Vladimir
Horowitz: A Television Concert at Carnegie Hall"

Emmy Awards

"NET Playhouse" (drama); "Get Smart" (comedy);
"Rowan and Martin's Laugh-In" (variety); "Mister
Rogers' Neighborhood" (children); Carl Betz (actor,
"Judd for the Defense"); Don Adams (comedic actor,
"Get Smart"); Barbara Bain (actress, "Mission:
Impossible")

Of Note

"Rowan and Martin" regulars include Goldie Hawn,
Lily Tomlin, Eileen Brennan, Richard Dawson, and
Judy Carne • Fifteen-minute soap operas ("Search for
Tomorrow," "The Guiding Light") expand to half an
hour • CBS cuts the successful Smothers Brothers
after they publicly attack the network for censorship
of Joan Baez.

Movies

Openings

Oliver! (Carol Reed), Ron Moody, Oliver Reed, Shani
    Wallis, Mark Lester
Funny Girl (William Wyler), Barbra Streisand, Omar
    Sharif
The Lion in Winter (Anthony Harvey), Peter
    O'Toole, Katharine Hepburn
Rachel, Rachel (Paul Newman), Joanne Woodward,
    Estelle Parsons, Kate Harrington
Romeo and Juliet (Franco Zeffirelli), Olivia Hussey,
    Leonard Whiting
2001: A Space Odyssey (Stanley Kubrick), Keir
    Dullea, Gary Lockwood
Charly (Ralph Nelson), Cliff Robertson, Claire
    Bloom
Faces (John Cassavetes), John Marley, Gena
    Rowlands
The Producers (Mel Brooks), Zero Mostel, Gene
    Wilder
Rosemary's Baby (Roman Polanski), Mia Farrow,
    John Cassavetes, Ruth Gordon
The Thomas Crown Affair (Norman Jewison), Steve
    McQueen, Faye Dunaway
Barbarella (Roger Vadim), Jane Fonda
Pretty Poison (Noel Black), Anthony Perkins,
    Tuesday Weld
Yellow Submarine (George Duning), animation with
    music by the Beatles

Planet of the Apes (Franklin Schaffner), Charlton
    Heston, Roddy McDowall
Charlie Bubbles (Albert Finney), Albert Finney, Liza
    Minnelli
Petulia (Richard Lester), Julie Christie, George C.
    Scott, Richard Chamberlain

Academy Awards

Best Picture: *Oliver!*
Best Director: Carol Reed (*Oliver!*)
Best Actress: Katharine Hepburn (*The Lion in
    Winter*) and Barbra Streisand (*Funny Girl*)
Best Actor: Cliff Robertson (*Charly*)

Top Box-Office Stars

Sidney Poitier, Paul Newman, Julie Andrews, John
Wayne, Clint Eastwood, Dean Martin, Steve
McQueen, Jack Lemmon, Lee Marvin, Elizabeth
Taylor

Stars of Tomorrow

Dustin Hoffman, Katharine Ross, Katharine
Houghton, Estelle Parsons, Judy Geeson, Robert
Drivas, Robert Blake, Jim Brown, Gayle Hunnicut,
Carol White

Popular Music

Hit Songs
"Folsom Prison Blues"
"Sunshine of Your Love"
"The Windmills of Your Mind"
"Galveston"
"Spinning Wheel"
"Blond on Blond"
"Lady Madonna"
"Do Your Own Thing"

Top Records

Albums: *Magical Mystery Tour* (Beatles); *Bookends* (Simon and Garfunkel); *Cheap Thrills* (Big Brother and the Holding Company); *The Beatles* (Beatles); *The Graduate* (sound track)

Singles: *(Sittin' on) The Dock of the Bay* (Otis Redding); *Little Green Apples* (O. C. Smith); *Stoned Soul Picnic* (5th Dimension); *Does Your Mama Know about Me?* (B. Taylor/Vancouvers); *This Guy's in Love with You* (Herb Alpert); *Slip Away* (Clarence Carter); *Love Is Blue* (Paul Mauriat); *Midnight Confessions* (Grass Roots); *Love Child* (Diana Ross and the Supremes). Country: *Honey* (Bobby Goldsboro); *Fist City* (Loretta Lynn)

Grammy Awards
Mrs. Robinson, Simon and Garfunkel (record); *By the Time I Get to Phoenix,* Glen Campbell (album); "Little Green Apples" (song)

Jazz and Big Bands
Walter Carlos uses the Moog synthesizer in *Switched-on Bach.*

Top Performers (*Downbeat*): Gary Burton (soloist); Duke Ellington (band): Miles Davis (jazz group); Kenny Burrell, Richard Davis, Herbie Hancock, Elvin Jones, Cannonball Adderley, Pee Wee Russell (instrumentalists); Ella Fitzgerald, Ray Charles (vocalists); Beatles (vocal group); Don Ellis, *Electric Bath* (album)

Theater

Broadway Openings

Plays
The Great White Hope (Howard Sackler), James Earl Jones, Jane Alexander
The Prime of Miss Jean Brodie (Jay Allen), Zoë Caldwell
Loot (Joe Orton), George Rose
The Seven Descents of Myrtle (Tennessee Williams), Harry Guardino, Estelle Parsons
The Man in the Glass Booth (Robert Shaw), Donald Pleasence
Plaza Suite (Neil Simon), Maureen Stapleton, George C. Scott
The Price (Arthur Miller), Arthur Kennedy, Pat Hingle, Kate Reid
A Day in the Death of Joe Egg (Peter Nichols), Elizabeth Hubbard, Albert Finney
We Bombed in New Haven (Joseph Heller), Jason Robards, Diana Sands
Forty Carats (Jay Allen), Julie Harris
I Never Sang for My Father (Robert Anderson), Hal Holbrook, Lillian Gish, Teresa Wright
Lovers (Brian Friel), Art Carney

Musicals
Promises, Promises (Burt Bacharach, Hal David), Jerry Orbach, Jill O'Hara
George M! (George M. Cohan), Joel Grey
Hair (Galt MacDermot, James Rado, revised version), James Rado, Gerome Ragni
Zorba (John Kander, Fred Ebb), Herschel Bernardi, Maria Karnilova
Jacques Brel Is Alive and Well and Living in Paris (Jacques Brel), Ellie Stone, Mort Shuman
Dames at Sea (Jim Wise, Robin Miller), Bernadette Peters
Marlene Dietrich, program of songs

Classics and Revivals On and Off Broadway
The Boys in the Band (Mart Crowley), Cliff Gorman, Laurence Luckinbill; *The Basement* (Harold Pinter); *King Lear,* Lee J. Cobb; *In the Matter of J. Robert Oppenheimer* (Heinar Kipphardt), Joseph Wiseman; *Futz* (Rochelle Owens), Sally Kirkland; *No Place to Be Somebody* (Charles Gordone), Ron O'Neal; Living Theater: *Frankenstein, Paradise Now* (Julian Beck, Judith Malina). *Founded:* Negro Ensemble, with *The Song of the Lusitanian Bogey* (Peter Weiss), American premiere

Regional

Founded: Atlanta Repertory Theatre opens with John Dryden's masque *King Arthur*

Theater (cont.)

Mark Taper, Los Angeles: *In the Matter of J. Robert Oppenheimer* (Heinar Kipphardt); *The Golden Fleece* (A. R. Gurney), premieres

Long Wharf, New Haven: *A Whistle in the Dark* (Thomas Murphy), premiere

Studio Arena, Buffalo: *Box, Quotations from Chairman Mao Tse-Tung* (Edward Albee), premieres

Trinity Square Repertory, Providence: *Years of the Locust* (Norman Holland), premiere

Theater Atlanta: *Red, White and Maddox* (Jay Broad and Don Tucker), premiere

Dallas Theater Center: *The Latent Heterosexual*

Hair, a musical about a draftee's experiences with the flower children. *Billy Rose Theatre Collection. The New York Public Library. Astor, Lenox and Tilden Foundations.*

(Paddy Chayefsky, directed by Burgess Meredith), Zero Mostel, premiere

Goodman, Chicago: *Othello,* James Earl Jones

Pulitzer Prize
No prize is awarded.

Tony Awards
Rosencrantz and Guildenstern Are Dead, Tom Stoppard (play), *Hallelujah, Baby!,* Jule Styne, Betty Comden, Adolph Green (musical)

Classical Music

Compositions
Howard Hanson, Symphony no. 6
Roger Sessions, Symphony no. 8
Roy Harris, Concerto for Amplified Piano, Brass, and Percussion
Karl Korte, Symphony no. 3
Michael Colgrass, *The Earth's a Baked Apple*
Charles Whittenberg, *Games of Fire*
Karel Huse, String Quartet no. 3

Important Events
Numerous electronic music festivals include the Buffalo with Lukas Foss, John Cage, and Iannis Xenakis.
The New York Philharmonic premieres thirteen symphonies, including the composers Richard Rodney Bennett, Roberto Gerhard, Howard Hanson, Nicolas Nabokov, and Roger Sessions.

New Appointments: Seiji Ozawa, San Francisco; William Steinberg, Boston; George Szell, New York Philharmonic

Debut: Maurizio Pollini

First Performances
Roy Harris, Symphony no. 11 (New York); Benjamin Lees, Piano Concerto no. 2 (Boston); Ulysses Kay, Symphony (Macomb, Ill.); Dave Brubeck, *Oratorio* (Cincinnati); Paul Creston, Concerto for Two Pianos (New Orleans); Philip Glass, *Piece in the Shape of a Square* (New York)

Opera

Metropolitan: *Das Rheingold* (Herbert von Karajan, Salzburg production); Luciano Pavarotti (debut), *La bohème;* Teresa Zylis-Gara, *Don Giovanni;* Shirley Verrett (debut), *Carmen;* Birgit Nilsson, *Elektra;* Montserrat Caballé, Richard Tucker, Sherrill Milnes, *Luisa Miller;* Martti Talvela (debut), *Don Carlo*

New York City: Beverly Sills, *Manon; Nine Rivers from Jordan* (Hugo Weisgall)

Santa Fe: *Die Jakobsleiter*

Chicago: Elena Suliotis, *Norma;* Tito Gobbi, *Falstaff;* Renata Tebaldi, *Manon Lescaut*

San Francisco: Anja Silja (debut), *Salome;* Régine Crespin, *Les Troyens;* premieres: *Fra Diavolo* (Daniel Auber); *Royal Palace* (Kurt Weill)

Music Notes
The $13 million Atlanta Memorial Arts Center opens with the premiere of *King Arthur* (Purcell). Also opening are the Blossom Music Center, between Cleveland and Akron, Ohio; the Santa Fe Opera; San Antonio Theater for the Performing Arts; Powell House, St. Louis; Jackson, Mississippi, Music Hall; and Garden State Arts Center (New Jersey).

Art _____

Painting

Frank Stella, *Hatra II, Sinjerli-Variation IV*
Romare Bearden, *Eastern Barn*
Ellsworth Kelly, *Yellow Black, Green Blue*
Marisol, *Portrait of Sidney Janis Selling Portrait of Sidney Janis by Marisol*
Chuck Close, *Self-Portrait*
Robert Mangold, *¹/₂ W Series*

Sculpture

Robert Smithson, *Non-site (Palisades—Edgewater, N.J.)*
Walter De Maria, *Dirt Room, Mile Long Drawing*
Carl Andre, *Joint*
Robert Morris, *Earthworks*
Claes Oldenburg, *Toilet—Hard Model, Soft Toilet*
Richard Serra, *Splashing*
Eva Hesse, *Repetition 19, III*

Christo, *The Museum of Modern Art Packed*
Michael Heizer, *Isolated Man/Circumflex*
Dan Flavin, *Untitled (to the "innovator" of Wheeling Peachblow)*

Architecture

General Motors Building, New York (Edward Durell Stone)
Lake Point Tower, Chicago (Shipporeit and Heinrich)
Xerox Square Building, Rochester, N.Y. (Welton Becket)
One Main Place, Dallas (Skidmore, Owings, and Merrill)
Department of Housing and Urban Development, Washington, D.C. (Marcel Breuer)
Juilliard School of Music, Lincoln Center, New York (Harrison & Belluschi)

Mark Rothko, standing before one of his paintings shortly before his death. *Courtesy Sedat Pakay.*

Brooklyn, Richmond, San Francisco: "The Triumph of Realism"

Buffalo: "Plus by Minus": The constructivist tradition from Malevich to Minimalism

Venice Biennale: Dickinson, Nakian, Gallo, Grooms represent the U.S.

Other Avant-Garde Shows: "Foundings"—Rauschenberg; "Machine Art" (Museum of Modern Art); "Options" (Metropolitan, Chicago); "Object and Image," with the use of light and kinetic materials (Whitney)

Art Briefs

The Egyptian Temple of Dendur, rescued from the rising Nile, arrives at the Metropolitan Museum of Art in 661 crates • Renoir's *Le Pont des Arts* sells for $1,550,000.

Important Exhibitions

"Negro Art" originates in Minnesota and travels throughout the United States; also touring are "New Primitive Paintings" (from Los Angeles) and "Painting in France 1900–1967" (organized by the French government), which travels to New York, Washington, Boston, Chicago, and Detroit. Important retrospectives include Noguchi, Ray, Arp, Smith, Lipchitz, Kollwitz, and Feeley.

Museums

New York: *Metropolitan:* The Great Age of the Fresco—from Giotto to Pontormo. *Museum of Modern Art:* "The Art of the Real: O'Keeffe, Kelly, Smith"; "Dada, Surrealism and their Heritage"; Word and Image (posters)

Dance _____

George Balanchine revives *Slaughter on Tenth Avenue* from *On Your Toes* with Suzanne Farrell and Arthur Mitchell

Premieres

American Ballet Theater: *Giselle* (David Blair); *Coppélia* (Enrique Martinez)

Merce Cunningham: *Rainforest* (for which Andy Warhol fills the stage with rectangular silver balloons)

New York City Ballet: *Metastaseis and Pithoprakta* (George Balanchine)

Books ━━━━━━━━━━━━━━━━━━━━━━━━━━━

Fiction
Critics' Choice
The Universal Baseball Association, Robert Coover
Up, Ronald Sukenick
Expensive People, Joyce Carol Oates
Mosby's Memoirs, Saul Bellow
Lost in the Funhouse, John Barth
Stranger in a Strange Land, Robert A. Heinlein
In the Heart of the Heart of the Country, William H. Gass
Steps, Jerzy Kosinski
The Seance and Other Stories, Isaac Bashevis Singer

Best-Sellers
Airport, Arthur Hailey
Couples, John Updike
The Salzburg Connection, Helen MacInness
A Small Town in Germany, John Le Carré
Testimony of Two Men, Taylor Caldwell
Preserve and Protect, Allen Drury
Myra Breckenridge, Gore Vidal

Nonfiction
Critics' Choice
Soul on Ice, Eldridge Cleaver
The Electric Kool-Aid Acid Test, Tom Wolfe
The Double Helix, James D. Watson
While Six Million Died, Arthur J. Morse
Death in Life: Survivors of Hiroshima, Robert Jay Lifton
Slouching towards Bethlehem, Joan Didion
The Whole Earth Catalog, Stewart Brand
Making It, Norman Podhoretz
The Algiers Motel Incident, John Hersey
36 Children, Herbert R. Kohl
🖎 *The Visible and the Invisible*, Maurice Merleau-Ponty
🖎 *The Teachings of Don Juan: A Yaqui Way of Knowledge*, Carlos Castaneda

Best-Sellers
Random House Dictionary of the English Language, ed. Laurence Urdang
Listen to the Warm (poetry), Rod McKuen
Between Parent and Child, Haim G. Ginott
Lonesome Cities (poetry), Rod McKuen
The Doctor's Quick Weight Loss Diet, Erwin M. Stillman, Samm Sinclair Baker
The Money Game, Adam Smith
Stanyon Street (poetry), Rod McKuen
The Weight Watcher's Cook Book, Jean Nidetch

Poetry
Gwendolyn Brooks, *In the Mecca*
W. D. Snodgrass, *After Experience: Poems and Translations*
Allan Ginsberg, *T.V. Baby Poems, Planet News*
John Berryman, *His Toy, His Dream, His Rest: 308 Dream Songs*
Diane Wakoski, *Inside the Blood Factory*
Richard Brautigan, *The Pill Versus the Springhill Mine Disaster*
Nikki Giovanni, *Black Judgment*
Philip Levine, *Not This Pig*

Pulitzer Prizes
House Made of Dawn, N. Scott Momaday (fiction)
Origins of the Fifth Amendment, Leonard W. Levy (U.S. history)
Armies of the Night, Norman Mailer (nonfiction)
So Human an Animal, Dr. René Jules Dubos (nonfiction)
Of Being Numerous, George Oppen (poetry)

Science and Technology ━━━━━━━━━━━━━━

ILLIAC is developed; it performs 39 million computations per second.

New, fast-growing crops bring about a worldwide "green revolution."

The largest reservoir of petroleum in North America is discovered on Alaska's North Slope.

Pulsars, radio waves emitted by neutron stars, are discovered.

An asteroid, Icarus, comes within 395,000 miles of the earth.

Amniocentesis, a technique for investigating amniotic fluid early in pregnancy for genetic disorders, is developed.

Dr. Denton Cooley performs the first U.S. heart transplant and gives a 47-year-old a 15-year-old's heart.

The first Poseidon, a submarine-launched strategic missile, is fired from Cape Kennedy.

Apollo VII, manned by Walter Shirra, Donald Eisale, and Walter Cunningham, performs eight successful propulsion firings and transmits seven live TV sessions with its crew.

🖎 Dr. Christiaan Barnard performs a heart transplant on Philip Blaiberg, who survives 18 months.

Nobel Prize
Luis W. Alvarez wins the prize in physics for work on subatomic particles. R. W. Holley, H. G. Khorana, and M. W. Nirenberg win in physiology and medicine for work on the genetic code. Lars Onsager wins in chemistry for work in thermodynamics.

Sports

Baseball

Denny McLain (Detroit, AL) is the first since Dizzy Dean in 1934 to win 30 games.

Don Drysdale (Los Angeles, NL) pitches a record 58⅔ consecutive scoreless innings.

Bob Gibson has a record low ERA of 1.12.

Frank Howard (Washington) hits a record 10 home runs in six games; Luis Tiant (Cleveland) strikes out 19 in a 10-inning game and Don Wilson (Houston, NL) 18 in 9.

The Cy Young Award is won by Bob Gibson (St. Louis, NL) and Denny McLain (Detroit, AL).

Champions

Batting
Pete Rose (Cincinnati, NL), .335
Carl Yastrzemski (Boston, AL), .301

Pitching
Bill Blass (Pittsburgh, NL), 18–6
Denny McLain (Detroit, AL) 31–6

Home runs
Frank Howard (Washington, AL), 44

Football

The first combined NFL–AFL draft is held. Johnny Unitas (Baltimore) becomes the all-time passing leader with 2,261 completions for 33,340 yards and 252 touchdowns.

George Halas retires as Chicago Bears coach.

NFL Season Leaders: Earl Morrall (Baltimore), passing; Leroy Kelley (Cleveland), rushing; Clifton McNeil (San Francisco), receiving

AFL Season Leaders: Len Dawson (Kansas City), passing; Paul Robinson (Cincinnati), rushing; Lance Alworth (San Diego), receiving

College All-Americans: Terry Hanratty (Q), Notre Dame; Roger Wehrli (DB), Missouri; Ted Kwalick (E), Pennsylvania State

Olympics

The Summer Games are held in Mexico City. American gold medal winners include James Hines (100m, 9.9s.), Tommy Smith (20m, 19.8s.), Lee Evans (400m, 43.8s.), Willie Davenport (110mh, 13.3s.), Dick Fosbury (high jump, 7'4¼"), Bob Beamon (broad jump, 29'2½"), Randy Matson (shot put, 67'4¾"), Al Oerter (200'1¼"), William Toomey (decathlon, 8,193 points), Wyomia Tyus (100m, 11.0s.), George Foreman (heavyweight boxing), Debby Meyer (3 in swimming), Michael Burton (2 in swimming). Two athletes give the black power salute on the winners' stand.

Peggy Fleming wins women's figure skating at the Winter Games at Grenoble, France.

Winners

World Series
Detroit (AL) 4
St. Louis (NL) 3

MVP
NL–Bob Gibson, St. Louis
AL–Dennis McLain, Detroit

Super Bowl III (Jan. 1969)
New York (Jets) 16–
Baltimore 7

MVP
Earl Morrall, Baltimore

College Football
Ohio State

Heisman Trophy
O. J. Simpson, Southern California

NBA Championship
Boston 4–Los Angeles 2

MVP
Wilt Chamberlain, Philadelphia

College Basketball
UCLA

Player of the Year
Lew Alcindor, UCLA

Stanley Cup
Montreal

US Tennis Open
Men: Arthur Ashe
Women: Margaret Smith Court

USGA Open
Lee Trevino

Kentucky Derby
Dancer's Image (R. Ussery, jockey)

Fashion

For Women: A "do-your-own-thing" attitude prevails in a year of contrasts and contradictions, but styles are generally more feminine while flamboyant. Pants of all fabrics are worn for every occasion by women of all ages, with shirt jackets, long white sweaters, hip-length vests, and multiple chains. Jumpers and sweater-tunics are also worn over pants with large and unusual buckled belts. Scarves, sashes, pendants, and chains accompany everything. Leather appears in dresses and vests. The stylish look begins with a belted leather skirt and turtleneck with matching tights, novelty rings on all five fingers, long scarves, and the safari pouch bag.

High-fashion notes: Valentino's stockings; Anne Klein's navy blazer, white skirt, and gray flannel pants; the Afro and corn-row hairdos

For Men: Bolder plaids and bigger tattersalls appear, along with new colors—cobalt blue, shocking pink, emerald green, and fire-engine red. Blazers are white with blue trim and are worn with shirts in blazing colors, decorative scarves, belts, chains, and pendants. Ties, infrequently worn, become increasingly wider.

Kaleidoscope _____

- Following the assassinations of Martin Luther King and Robert Kennedy, Sears & Roebuck removes toy guns from its Christmas catalog and orders its 815 stores to cease advertising them; this is followed by stores throughout the country.
- Riots occur in over 100 cities following Martin Luther King's assassination; 46 die (41 blacks) and 21,000 federal and 34,000 state troops are called out, the largest military civil emergency force in modern times.
- The Poor People's Campaign, led by the Reverend Ralph Abernathy, arrives in Resurrection City, Washington, a 15-acre meadow between the Lincoln and Washington monuments that houses the poor blacks, Indians, Mexican, and Appalachian whites.
- On the nightly TV news the nation watches the Saigon chief of police calmly shoot a prisoner in the head.
- Polls in February indicate that only 35 percent support LBJ's policies.
- Yale College admits women.
- Film courses become popular at universities.
- Black Studies programs are developed at many universities.
- Black militancy increases on campuses; the president of San Francisco State resigns as black instructors urge black students to bring guns on campus.
- Protesting the war, Daniel Berrigan, Jesuit priest-writer, his brother, Phil, and seven other priests enter the Maryland Selective Service offices and burn hundreds of 1-A classification records.
- Protesting an off-campus gym and the university's ties to the Institute for Defense Analysis, Columbia University students seize President Grayson Kirk's office and hold three hostages.
- Student protest leaders at the Democratic Convention in Chicago include Abbie Hoffman and Jerry Rubin of the Youth International Party, Tom Hayden of SDS, and Bobby Seale and David Dillinger.
- Four permanent three-day weekends—Washington's Birthday, Memorial Day, Columbus Day, and Veterans' Day—are created by shifting the holidays to Monday.
- Vietnam casualties exceed Korean War totals.
- Occupational and graduate school deferments are cut back.
- Nixon's 43.4 percent victory is the lowest presidential margin since 1912.
- Violent crimes are up 57 percent since 1960.
- "Come tiptoe through the tulips," sings new cult hero Tiny Tim, in orange socks and plaid shirt.
- John Lennon and Yoko Ono's nude record album cover is banned.
- There is a marked increase in college courses in Oriental theology, religion, sorcery, witchcraft, Zen, and Oriental magic; *I Ching* sales (Princeton University Press) go from 1,000 a year to 50,000.
- Rock ballrooms include the Fillmore (San Francisco), Fillmore East (New York), Boston Tea Party (Boston), and Kinetic Playground (Chicago).
- Valerie Solanos, a bit player in Andy Warhol's movies, shoots Warhol; he dictates a novel while recuperating; she is also founder of SCUM (Society for Cutting Up Men).
- Off-off-Broadway's *Hair,* billed as "the first tribal-love-rock musical," sets a fad and is followed by numerous productions with nudity, sexuality and antiestablishment values, such as *Futz* (New York) and *Big-Time Buck White* (Los Angeles).
- Judith Malina and Julian Beck tour *Paradise Now* (the new improvisational "living theater"), which protests drug laws and clothing; they are arrested fifteen times.
- The AMA formulates a new standard of death, "brain death."
- Celibacy of the priesthood becomes an issue in the Catholic church; Pope Paul VI's ban on contraception is also challenged by 800 U.S. theologians.
- The New York Hilton rents rooms on a travelers' one-day hour plan; $12 for the first three hours and $3, each hour after.
- Jackie Onassis's wedding gift from Aristotle Onassis is a large ruby ring surrounded by large diamonds and matching earrings, valued at $1.2 million.
- A nine-day sanitation strike hits New York City.
- Twenty thousand are added monthly to New York's welfare rolls; one-fourth of the city's budget goes to welfare.
- IBM stocks split, up from $320, 20 months ago, to $667.50. One hundred shares purchased in 1914 ($2,750) are now 59,320 shares valued at more than $20 million.
- A Florida heiress leaves $450,000 to 150 stray dogs.
- Feminists picket the Miss America Contest and drop girdles and bras in trash cans.
- Joe Namath buys a mink coat.
- In April, following the Vietnamese Tet offensive, General Westmoreland states, "We have never been in a better relative position."
- The Vietnam war becomes the longest war in U.S. history.

First Appearances: Mobile coronary-care ambulance (St. Vincent's Hospital, New York), woman on the "Ten Most Wanted" list (Ruth Eisemann-Schier), professional school exclusively for training circus clowns (Venice, Fla.), North Cascades National Park (Washington State), Redwood National Park, investigations into "Chinese Restaurant Syndrome," Zero Population Growth Inc., "Zap" (underground comic book), Little, Brown acquired by Time, Inc., enzyme detergents, Sheraton Hotels acquired by ITT, *Queen Elizabeth II,* direct service, New York–USSR (Pan American, Aeroflot), *New York* magazine, book set into type completely by electronic composition, Bureau of Customs receipts totaling over $3 billion, legislation permitting postage stamps to be illustrated in color, water bed filtration system (East Chicago, Ind.), Clinique fragrance-free makeup

1969

Facts and Figures

Economic Profile
  Dow-Jones: ↓ High 952–
    Low 769
  GNP: +7%
  Inflation: +5.7%
  Unemployment: 3.5%
Police expenditures, federal,
    state, local: $4.4 billion
Persons arrested: 5,577,000
Executions: 0
Prisoners, federal and state:
    196,000
Juvenile court: 69,669
SS France, Caribbean: $240
    (2 wks.)
Willoughby Yashica zoom
    moving picture camera: $79
Henri Bendel bikini,
    matching robe, nylon and
    Lycra: $90
Saks 5th Ave. leotard, brass
    buttons: $40
Halston terry wrap, Indian
    print muffler: $130
Bill Blass "silco" brown knit:
    $100
Calvin Klein gray wool skirt,
    tube, with slit: $165
Diane von Furstenberg
    cotton midi dress, elastic
    waist, Bloomingdale's and
    Neiman Marcus: $100

Deaths

Maureen Connolly, Dwight
    D. Eisenhower, Walter
    Gropius, Walter Hagen,
    Sonja Henie, Boris
    Karloff, Joseph P.
    Kennedy, Jack Kerouac,
    John L. Lewis, Drew
    Pearson, Thelma Ritter.

In the News

HENRY CABOT LODGE IS APPOINTED CHIEF NEGOTIATOR IN PARIS . . . GIANT OIL SLICK CONTAMINATES SANTA BARBARA COAST . . . VIETNAMIZATION POLICY OF WAR IS INITIATED . . . RUSSIA AND CHINA CLASH ON BORDER, 31 SOVIETS ARE KILLED . . . JAMES EARL RAY PLEADS GUILTY TO MARTIN LUTHER KING, JR.'S MURDER AND IS SENTENCED TO 99 YEARS . . . SENATE RATIFIES ANTI–NUCLEAR PROLIFERATION TREATY . . . NIXON ASKS FUNDS FOR ABM AROUND MISSILE BASES . . . POLICE REMOVE 400 HARVARD UNIVERSITY SIT-INS . . . SOVIETS REPLACE ALEXANDER DUBCEK WITH GUSTAV HUSAK . . . SIRHAN SIRHAN IS CONVICTED OF ROBERT KENNEDY'S MURDER . . . NIGERIA CAPTURES BIAFRA HEADQUARTERS . . . DE GAULLE RESIGNS AFTER ELECTION DEFEAT . . . NIXON APPOINTS WARREN BURGER CHIEF JUSTICE, SUPREME COURT . . . TED KENNEDY ADMITS TO PART IN CHAPPAQUIDDICK DEATH OF MARY JO KOPECHNE . . . ASTRONAUT NEIL ARMSTRONG IS THE FIRST MAN TO WALK ON THE MOON . . . BRITAIN BEGINS AIRLIFTING TROOPS TO IRELAND AS VIOLENCE INCREASES . . . JUNTA OVERTHROWS LIBYAN KING IDRIS . . . NIXON ANNOUNCES REMOVAL OF 25,000 MORE TROOPS . . . HIPPIE CULT LEADER CHARLES MANSON AND "FAMILY" ARE CHARGED WITH MURDERS OF PREGNANT SHARON TATE POLANSKI AND THREE OTHERS . . . MANY PARTICIPATE IN VIETNAM MORATORIUM DAY . . . STUDENTS HOLD MASS RALLIES IN JAPAN . . . SENATE VETOES CLEMENT HAYNESWORTH SUPREME COURT NOMINATION . . . FRED HAMPTON, BLACK PANTHER LEADER, IS KILLED IN CHICAGO POLICE RAID . . . LIEUTENANT WILLIAM CALLEY TO BE TRIED FOR MY LAI MASSACRE . . . FIRST DRAFT LOTTERY IS HELD . . . VIETNAM: U.S. TROOP STRENGTH, 484,000; U.S. DEAD, 39,893; WOUNDED, 250,000; MISSING, 1,400; ENEMY DEAD, 568,989.

1969

Quotes _____

"Houston, Tranquility Base here. The Eagle has landed. . . . I'm at the foot of the ladder. I'm going to step off the LM now. That's one small step for man, one giant step for mankind. The surface is fine and powdery. I can kick it up with my toe. . . . It's different but it's very pretty out here."

— Neil Armstrong, landing on the moon

"READ THIS BOOK STONED

The Youth International Revolution will begin with a mass breakdown of authority. . . . Tribes of long hairs, blacks, armed women, workers, peasants and students will take over. . . . The White House will become one big commune. . . . The Pentagon will be replaced with an LSD experimental farm. . . . To steal from the rich is a sacred and religious act."

— Jerry Rubin, *Do It*

"[The protesters are] a vocal minority. The great silent majority support us."

— Richard M. Nixon

"Drugs, crime, campus revolution, racial discord, draft resistance . . . on every hand we find old standards violated, old values discarded, old principles ignored. [This threatens] the fundamental values, the process by which a civilization maintains its continuity."

— Richard M. Nixon

Left: Janis Joplin, famed for her hoarse voice, stamping feet, and "hooker clothes" (her description), drinks Southern Comfort while she performs. *Movie Star News.*

"A spirit of national masochism prevails encouraged by an effete core of impudent snobs who characterize themselves as intellectuals, . . . instant analysis and querulous criticism . . . [by] a tiny enclosed fraternity of privileged men [the media]. . . . [Americans want] a cry of alarm to penetrate the cacophony of seditious drivel."

— Spiro Agnew

"[The counterculture stands against] the final consolidation of a technocratic totalitarianism in which we shall find ourself ingeniously adapted to an existence wholly estranged from anything that has ever made the life of man an interesting adventure."

— Theodore Roszak, *The Making of a Counterculture*

Ads _____

TV

Premieres
"The David Frost Show"
"The Brady Bunch," Florence Henderson, Robert Reed
"The Johnny Cash Show"
"Hee Haw," Buck Owens, Roy Clark
"This Is Tom Jones"
"Marcus Welby, M.D.," Robert Young, James Brolin
"Medical Center," Chad Everett
"The Bold Ones," John Saxon, David Hartman, E. G. Marshall, Burl Ives, Joseph Campanella
"The Bill Cosby Show"

Top Ten (Nielsen)
"Rowan and Martin's Laugh-In," "Gunsmoke," "Bonanza," "Mayberry R.F.D.," "Family Affair," "Here's Lucy," "The Red Skelton Hour," "Marcus Welby, M.D.," "Walt Disney's Wonderful World of Color," "The Doris Day Show"

Specials
"The Forsyte Saga"; "The Sound of Burt Bacharach"; "Model Hippie" (Huntley-Brinkley); "The Desert Whales" ("The Undersea World of Jacques Cousteau"); "An Investigation of Drug Addiction—Odyssey House" (Huntley-Brinkley); "Apollo: A Journey to the Moon"; "Silent Night, Lonely Night" (Robert Anderson); "Solar Eclipse: A Darkness at Noon"; "Man on the Moon: The Epic Journey of Apollo XI" (Walter Cronkite); "Artur Rubinstein"

Emmy Awards
"Marcus Welby, M.D." (drama); "My World and Welcome to It" (comedy); "The David Frost Show" (variety); "Sesame Street" (children); Robert Young (actor, "Marcus Welby, M.D."); William Windom (comedic actor, "My World and Welcome to It"); Susan Hampshire (actress, "The Forsyte Saga"); Hope Lange, (comedic actress, "The Ghost and Mrs. Muir")

Of Note
CBS's "Morning News" is the first hour-long daily news show • Doctor shows increase • Ninety-five percent of all homes have TV sets; 40 percent are color TVs • The first-year lineup for PBS includes "The Forsyte Saga" and "Sesame Street."

Movies

Openings
Midnight Cowboy (John Schlesinger), Dustin Hoffman, Jon Voight
Butch Cassidy and the Sundance Kid (George Roy Hill), Paul Newman, Robert Redford
Hello, Dolly! (Gene Kelly), Barbra Streisand, Walter Matthau
Z (Costa-Gavras), Yves Montand, Irene Pappas, Jean-Louis Trintignant
Alice's Restaurant (Arthur Penn), Arlo Guthrie, Pat Quinn, James Broderick
They Shoot Horses, Don't They (Sydney Pollack), Jane Fonda, Michael Sarrazin, Gig Young
The Sterile Cuckoo (Alan Pakula), Liza Minnelli, Wendell Burton
Bob and Carol and Ted and Alice (Paul Mazursky), Natalie Wood, Robert Culp, Dyan Cannon, Elliott Gould
Easy Rider (Dennis Hopper), Peter Fonda, Jack Nicholson, Dennis Hopper
Goodbye Columbus (Larry Peerce), Richard Benjamin, Ali MacGraw
The Damned (Luchino Visconti), Dirk Bogarde, Ingrid Thulin
The Wild Bunch (Sam Peckinpah), William Holden, Ernest Borgnine, Robert Ryan
Medium Cool (Haskell Wexler), Robert Foster, Verna Bloom
True Grit (Henry Hathaway), John Wayne, Glen Campbell, Kim Darby
I am Curious (Yellow) (Vilgot Sjoman), Lena Nyman, Peter Lindgren
My Night at Maud's (Eric Rohmer), Jean-Louis Trintignant, Françoise Fabian

Academy Awards
Best Picture: *Midnight Cowboy*
Best Director: John Schlesinger (*Midnight Cowboy*)
Best Actress: Maggie Smith (*The Prime of Miss Jean Brodie*)
Best Actor: John Wayne (*True Grit*)

Top Box-Office Stars
Paul Newman, John Wayne, Steve McQueen, Dustin Hoffman, Clint Eastwood, Sidney Poitier, Lee Marvin, Jack Lemmon, Katharine Hepburn, Barbra Streisand

Stars of Tomorrow
Jon Voight, Kim Darby, Glen Campbell, Richard Benjamin, Mark Lester, Olivia Hussey, Leonard Whiting, Ali MacGraw, Barbara Hershey, Alan Alda

Popular Music

Hit Songs
"Good Morning Starshine"
"Hair"
"I've Got to Be Me"
"Lay Lady Lay"
"Get Back"
"It's Your Thing"
"Oh Happy Day"
"Honky Tonk Women"
"Sugar Baby"
"Crimson and Clover"
"Love (Can Make You Happy)"

Top Records

Albums: *Hair* (original cast); *Abbey Road* (Beatles); *Blood, Sweat and Tears* (Blood, Sweat and Tears); *Led Zeppelin II* (Led Zeppelin); *Green River* (Creedence Clearwater Revival)

Singles: *Sugar, Sugar* (Archies); *Everyday People* (Sly and the Family Stone); *Aquarius / Let the Sun Shine In* (5th Dimension); *Give Peace a Chance* (John Lennon and the Plastic Ono Band); *I'll Never Fall in Love Again* (Tom Jones); *Spinning Wheel* (Blood, Sweat and Tears); *Yester-Me, Yester-You, Yesterday* (Stevie Wonder); *Raindrops Keep Falling on My Head* (B. J. Thomas); *Leaving on a Jet Plane* (Peter, Paul and Mary); *I Can't Get Next to You* (Temptations). Country: *All I Have to Offer You* (Charley Pride); *Wichita Lineman* (Glen Campbell)

Grammy Awards
Aquarius / Let the Sun Shine In, 5th Dimension (record); *Blood, Sweat and Tears* (album); "Games People Play" (song)

Jazz and Big Bands
Miles Davis's *In a Silent Way* integrates rock and jazz. Archie Shepp plays with African musicians in *Jazz Meets Arabia.*

Top Performers *(Downbeat):* Miles Davis, Ornette Coleman (soloists); Duke Ellington (band); Miles Davis (jazz group); Stan Getz, Gerry Mulligan, Jimmy Hamilton, J. J. Johnson, Gary Burton, Herbie Mann (instrumentalists); Ella Fitzgerald, Ray Charles (vocalists); Blood, Sweat and Tears (vocal group); Miles Davis, *Filles de Kilimanjaro* (album)

Theater

Broadway Openings

Plays
Hadrian VII (Peter Luke), Alec McCowen
Play It Again, Sam (Woody Allen), Woody Allen, Diane Keaton, Anthony Roberts
Butterflies Are Free (Leonard Gershe), Blythe Danner, Keir Dullea, Eileen Heckart
Indians (Arthur Kopit), Stacy Keach, Sam Waterston
A Patriot for Me (John Osborne), Maximilian Schell
Last of the Red Hot Lovers (Neil Simon), James Coco, Linda Lavin
Ceremonies in Dark Old Men (Lonnie Elder), Billy Dee Williams
No Place to Be Somebody, (Charles Gordone), Ron O'Neal

Musicals
1776 (Sherman Edwards), William Daniels, Ken Howard, Howard da Silva
Oh! Calcutta (devised by Kenneth Tynan and various contributors, first nude musical)
Coco (André Previn, Alan Jay Lerner), Katharine Hepburn (musical debut), René Auberjonois
Dear World (Jerry Herman), Angela Lansbury, Milo O'Shea

Classics and Revivals, On and Off Broadway
Ché (Lennox Raphael); *Hamlet,* one version, Nichol Williamson; another, Ellis Rabb; *To Be Young, Gifted, and Black* (Lorraine Hansberry); *The Front Page* (Ben Hecht, Charles MacArthur), Bert Convy; *Our Town* (Thornton Wilder), Henry Fonda; *Private Lives* (Noel Coward), Tammy Grimes, Brian Bedford. *Founded:* Circle Repertory Company by Lanford Wilson, Marshall W. Mason, Rob Thirkield, and Tanya Berezin

Regional

Arena Stage, Washington, D.C.: *Indians* (Arthur Kopit), Stacy Keach, premiere

Charles Playhouse, Boston: *The Indian Wants the Bronx* (Israel Horovitz), premiere

A.C.T., San Francisco: *Glory! Hallelujah!* (Anna Marie Barlow), premiere; *The Architect and the Emperor of Assyria* (Fernando Arrabal), American premiere

Pulitzer Prize
The Great White Hope, Howard Sackler

Tony Awards
The Great White Hope, Howard Sackler (play), *1776,* Sherman Edwards (musical)

Classical Music

Compositions
Roy Harris, Symphony no. 12
Samuel Barber, *Despite and Still*
William Schuman, *In Praise of Shahn*
Earl Brown, *Modules 3*
John Cage, *Cheap Imitation, HPSCHD*
Charles Wuorinen, *Time's Encomium*

Important Events
Byron Janis performs two Chopin waltzes that he discovered in 1967 in Yvelines.
Rising costs threaten the musical world. The Met closes for three months over a strike; the Atlanta Opera closes; the Cincinnati and Indiana orchestras merge; a proposal is considered for merging the Buffalo and Rochester orchestras; Washington's National Symphony strikes. Five major orchestras (Boston, Chicago, Cleveland, New York, and Philadelphia) and 77 others meet to apply for assistance from the National Endowment for the Arts.
To stimulate concertgoers, a variety of programs is devised: Leonard Bernstein and Leopold Stokowski present a concert of Bach, rock, and the Moog synthesizer; Rosalyn Tureck plays Bach on the Moog; Seattle Opera: *Fidelio* with junk-sculpture sets; Kansas City: "Love-In" (ballet with baroque orchestra, rock, and amplified instruments); Fresno Philharmonic: "The Electric Eye": concert and light show; Lorin Hollander: the Baldwin electronic amplified concert grand.

Debut: Garrick Ohlsson, Ursula Oppens

First Performances
Luciano Berio, *Sinfonia,* with Swingle Singers and electronic harpsichord and organ (New York); William Schuman, "To Thee Old Cause [Martin Luther King]" (New York); Alberto Ginastera, Piano Concerto no. 2 (Indianapolis); Carlos Chávez, conducting, *Fuego Olimpico* (New York); Gian Carlo Menotti, Triple Concerto (New York); Peter Mennin, *Pied Piper of Hamlin* (Cincinnati, Mayor John Lindsay of New York narrating); Dmitri Shostakovich, Symphony no. 12 (Oregon); Leo Smit, Piano Concerto (Kansas City)

Opera

Metropolitan: Leonie Rysanek, Régine Crespin, Christa Ludwig, *Der Rosenkavalier;* Ludwig, Walter Berry, *Die Frau ohne Schatten;* Geraint Evans, *Wozzeck;* Jon Vickers, *Peter Grimes;* Renato Bruson, *Lucia di Lammermoor;* Marilyn Horne (debut), *Norma*

New York City: *Mefistofele* (Boito), first staging in New York in 40 years

Washington, D.C.:   *Comte Ory, The Turn of the Screw*

Santa Fe: *Help! Help! The Globolinks* (Gian Carlo Menotti, premiere)

Chicago: Nicolai Ghiaurov, *Khovanshchina; El amor brujo* (Falla); The *Ring* cycle begins.

San Francisco: *Götterdämerung; Christopher Columbus* (Darius Milhaud, premiere)

Music Notes
Leonard Bernstein ends his tenure as conductor of the New York Philharmonic with Mahler's Symphony no. 3 • Other shifts in conductors include Pierre Boulez, New York; Georg Solti, Chicago; Thomas Schippers, Cincinnati; Antonio de Almeida, Houston; and Antal Dorati, National • The Juilliard School opens at Lincoln Center for the Performing Arts.

Vladimir Horowitz, legendary for his dazzling technique and unique interpretations, continues to perform and record.

Art

Paintings

James Rosenquist, *Horse Blinders* (1968–69)
Brice Marden, *Point*
Philip Pearlstein, *Nude Seated on Green Drape*
Helen Frankenthaler, *Commune*
Malcolm Bailey, *Hold, Separate but Equal*
Chuck Close, *Phil*
Cy Twombley, *Untitled*
Frank Stella, *Abra Variation I*

Michael Heizer, *Double Negative*
Robert Smithson, *First Mirror Displacement*
Nancy Graves, *Camel VI, Camel VII, Camel VIII*
Sol LeWitt, *Serial Project No. I (ABCD)*
Robert Morris, *37 Pieces of Work*

Sculpture

Carl Andre, *144 Pieces of Lead*
Dan Flavin, *An Artificial Barrier of Green Fluorescent Light (to Trudie and Enno Develing)*
Richard Serra, *House of Cards*

Architecture

Oakland Museum, Oakland, Calif. (Roche and Dinkeloo)
City Hall, Boston (Kallmann, McKinnell and Knowles)
Rotating House, Wilton, Conn. (Richard T. Foster)
John Hancock Center, Boston (I. M. Pei)

Important Exhibitions

Winslow Homer Show travels to 14 cities.

Museums

New York: *Metropolitan:* Primitive art; New York painting and sculpture, 1940 to the present; "Harlem on My Mind"; Florentine Baroque art; Stained glass and illuminated manuscripts of the Middle Ages (Cloisters); Jules Olitski. *Museum of Modern Art:* de Kooning, Kandinsky, Oldenburg. *Guggenheim:* Peggy Guggenheim's Picassos, Giacomettis, Légers, among others; David Smith retrospective

Washington: 19th-century American painting; William Sidney Mount; Turner

Chicago, Boston: The old masters; Rembrandt

Philadelphia: Mexican art from the 16th century to the present; Comic strips and American art

Chicago: Moholy-Nagy

Illinois Institute of Technology: German Bauhaus (over 2,500 objects)

Leonard Bernstein, the first native-born director of the New York Philharmonic, sometimes conducts so strenuously that he must be carried off the podium. *Movie Star News.*

Milwaukee: "New Realism": Jack Beal, Gabriel Laderman, Robert Bechtle, Philip Pearlstein, Sidney Tillim, Alfred Leslie, Wayne Thiebaud

Art Briefs

Robert Lehman bequeaths 3,000 works valued at over $100 million to the Metropolitan Museum of Art • Nelson Rockefeller donates his primitive collection to the Metropolitan, for which a new wing is to be built • James Michener gives his American collection to the University of Texas • New museums include the Everson Museum of Art (Syracuse) and Des Moines Art Center • The Museum of Modern Art purchases the Gertrude Stein collection for $6 million • Other major sales include Bierstadt's *Emigrants Crossing the Plains, Sunset* ($115,000), and Rembrandt's *Self-Portrait* ($1,159,200).

Dance

Eliot Feld forms his own company to stage his own works; Jerome Robbins rejoins the New York City Ballet.

Premieres

New York City Ballet: *Dances at a Gathering* (Jerome Robbins), Allegra Kent, Patricia McBride, Violette Verdy, John Clifford

Alvin Ailey: *Masakela Language*

Books ───────────────────────

Fiction

Critics' Choice
Them, Joyce Carol Oates
Pictures of Fidelman: An Exhibition, Bernard Malamud
Slaughterhouse-Five, Kurt Vonnegut
Bullet Park, John Cheever
Going Down Fast, Marge Piercy
Tell Me That You Love Me, Junie Moon, Marjorie Kellogg
Pricksongs and Descants, Robert Coover
Going Places, Leonard Michaels

Best-Sellers
Portnoy's Complaint, Philip Roth
The Godfather, Mario Puzo
The Love Machine, Jacqueline Susann
The Inheritors, Jerome Robbins
The Andromeda Strain, Michael Crichton
The Seven Minutes, Irving Wallace
Naked Came the Stranger, Penelope Ashe
Ada, or Ardor, Vladimir Nabokov

Nonfiction

Critics' Choice
Ernest Hemingway, Carlos Baker
Living Room War, Michael Arlen
I Know Why the Caged Bird Sings, Maya Angelou
The Establishment Is Alive and Well in Washington, Art Buchwald
The Making of the President, 1968, Theodore H. White
The Burden of Southern History, C. Vann Woodward
The Children of the Dream, Bruno Bettelheim
The Valachi Papers, Peter Maas
The Kingdom and the Power, Gay Talese
On Death and Dying, Elizabeth Kubler-Ross
The 900 Days: The Siege of Leningrad, Harrison Salisbury
The Trial of Dr. Spock, Jessica Mitford

Best-Sellers
American Heritage Dictionary of the English Language, ed. William Morris
The Peter Principle, Laurence J. Peter, Raymond Hull
The Graham Kerr Cookbook
In Someone's Shadow (poetry), Rod McKuen
Between Parent and Teenager, Dr. Haim Ginott
The Selling of the President, 1968, Joe McGinniss
My Life and Prophecies, Jeanne Dixon with Rene Noorbergen

Poetry
Robert Lowell, *Notebooks 1967–68*
Kenneth Koch, *The Pleasures of Peace*
Amiri Baraka, *Black Magic: Poetry 1961–1967*
Donald Hall, *The Alligator Bride*
Richard Wilbur, *Waking to Sleep*
Elizabeth Bishop, *The Complete Poems*
W. H. Auden, *City without Walls*

Pulitzer Prizes
Collected Stories, Jean Stafford (fiction)
Present at the Creation, Dean Acheson (U.S. history)
Gandhi's Truth, Erik H. Erikson (nonfiction)
Huey Long, T. Harry Williams (biography)
Untitled Subjects, Richard Howard (poetry)

Science and Technology ───────────

Apollo X, manned by Eugene Cernan, James Young, and Thomas Stafford, evaluates lunar module performance in the lunar environment.

Apollo XI, manned by Neil Armstrong, Buzz Aldrin, and Michael Collins, is the first lunar landing mission. Armstrong walks on the moon on July 20; he and Aldrin collect 9 pounds, 12 ounces of rock and soil. They remain on the moon 21 hours, 31 minutes.

Apollo XII, manned by Charles Conrad, Richard Gordon, and Alan Bean, lands on the moon; EVA time is 15 hours, 30 minutes; it returns with samples of the lunar surface.

A magnetic device that stores information on tiny "bubbles" that can be retrieved within 100 microseconds is developed; hundreds of thousands of bubbles can be placed on a single microchip.

A scanning electron microscope is developed that permits stereoscopic images of thicker specimens.

Rubella (German measles) vaccine is made available

The chemical structure of antibodies is discovered.

The FDA removes cyclamates from the market.

DDT usage in residential areas is banned.

The first commercial 747 goes into service.

The Concorde makes its first trans-U.S. flight, from Seattle to New York.

🐚 A human egg is fertilized out of the mother's body in Cambridge, England.

Nobel Prize
M. Gell-Mann wins the prize in physics for his theory of elementary particles. Max Delbruck, Alfred Hershey, and Salvador Luria win in physiology and medicine for work on the genetic structure of viruses.

Sports

Baseball
Bowie Kuhn becomes commissioner.
Each major leagues is split into two divisions, with pennant playoffs.
Denny McLain (Detroit, AL) wins his second straight Cy Young Award. Tom Seaver (New York, NL) also wins the award.
The New York Mets (NL) are the first expansion team to win the pennant.

Champions

Batting	Jim Palmer (Baltimore,
Pete Rose (Cincinnati, NL),	AL), 16–4
.348	*Home runs*
Rod Carew (Minnesota,	Harmon Killebrew
AL), .332	(Minnesota, AL), 49
Pitching	
Tom Seaver (New York,	
NL), 25–7	

Football
The 17-point underdog New York Jets, led by Joe Namath (QB), who promises a victory, upset the Baltimore Colts, 16–7, to become the first AFL Super Bowl winner.
Johnny Unitas is named Player of the Decade.
Vince Lombardi leaves Green Bay for Washington.

NFL Season Leaders: Sonny Jurgensen (Washington), passing; Gale Sayers (Chicago), rushing; Danny Abramowicz (New Orleans), receiving. **AFL Season Leaders:** Greg Cook (Cincinnati), passing; Dickie Post (San Diego), rushing; Lance Alworth (San Diego), receiving

College All-Americans: Mike Phipps (Q), Purdue; Mike McCoy (T), Notre Dame

Bowls (Jan. 1, 1970)
Rose: Southern California 10–Michigan 3
Orange: Pennsylvania State 10–Missouri 3
Cotton: Texas 21–Notre Dame 7
Sugar: Mississippi 27–Arkansas 22

Basketball
UCLA, with Lew Alcindor at center, wins its third straight NCAA tournament.
Bill Russell, in his last season, leads Boston to a 4–3 play-off win over Wilt Chamberlain and Los Angeles; it is the Celtics' 11th title in 12 years.

NBA All-Pro First Team: Billy Cunningham (Philadelphia), Elgin Baylor (Los Angeles), Wes Unseld (Baltimore), Earl Monroe (Baltimore), Oscar Robertson (Cincinnati)

Winners

World Series	*NBA Championship*
New York (NL) 4	Boston 4–Los Angeles 3
Baltimore (AL) 1	*MVP*
MVP	Wes Unseld, Baltimore
NL–Willie McCovey, San	*College Basketball*
Francisco	UCLA
AL–Harmon Killebrew,	*Player of the Year*
Minnesota	Lew Alcindor, UCLA
Super Bowl IV (Jan. 1970)	*Stanley Cup*
Kansas City 23–	Montreal
Minnesota 7	*US Tennis Open*
MVP	Men: Rod Laver
Roman Gabriel, Los	Women: Margaret Smith
Angeles	Court
College Football	*USGA Open*
Texas	Orville Moody
Heisman Trophy	*Kentucky Derby*
Steve Owens, Oklahoma	Majestic Prince (W.
	Hartack, jockey)

Fashion

For Women: Contributing to the eclectic look are (1) the unisex revolution in jackets, vests, and other apparel, (2) the thirties' "Bonnie and Clyde" look, (3) "gypsy" fashions, (4) the Gibson Girl hairdo, and (5) art deco touches in belts, bags, jewelry, and fabrics. Basic are body-hugging and layered clothes: shirts, trousers, and dresses in clinging crepes, knit jersey, silk chiffons, velvets, and the hip-length sweaters or long blazers that fit over both ripple-pleated skirts and straight cuffed pants. The summer brings forth midriff blouses with Dietrich pants or Gable shorts, clogs, and wide-strapped, clunky platforms. Everything appears in faded, murky colors and thirties' "wallpaper prints." The Gibson girl haircut frames the face in a soufflelike puff with the hair pulled to the crown in a tiny knot, tendrils framing the face in a soft, sexy way. Hair is colored only for highlights.

High-fashion note: Cerutti's unisex look

For Men: The indented waist, longer jacket vest, cuffed trousers, and wider lapels and shoulders recall the thirties. Shirts, in huge stripes, prints, and weaves, hug the body; collars are higher, with longer points. Ties, 3½ to 5 inches wide, are patterned and worn with striped shirts and suits. Long hair is styled with conditioners, hair dyes, and sprays at salons.

Joe Namath. Three days before the Super Bowl, he says: "I think we'll win it; in fact, I'll guarantee it." *Movie Star News.*

Kaleidoscope _____

- The FBI is exposed for tapping Martin Luther King's phones, following an LBJ order for "national security."
- Nixon proposes a federally maintained income minimum.
- After weeks of debate, the United States and Vietnam delegates agree on the shape of the table to be used when South Vietnam and the National Liberation Front join the peace talks.
- A total of 448 universities have strikes or are forced to close; student demands broaden to include revision of admissions policies and reorganization of entire academic programs.
- Billboards appear with signs such as "Keep America Clean. Take a Bath" and "Get a Haircut."
- John Lennon and Yoko Ono marry.
- Jackie and Aristotle Onassis reportedly spend $20 million their first year together, a rate of $384,000 a week.
- Police raid a Greenwich Village, New York, gay bar after which a march takes place; the Gay Liberation Front later participates in the Hiroshima Day March, the first homosexual participation in a peace march as a separate constituency.
- Dr. Benjamin Spock's conviction for encouraging draft evasion is reversed by a U.S. court of appeal.
- Writers Norman Mailer and Jimmy Breslin run for mayor on a platform to make New York City the 51st state; their intention is to stop the state government from taking all of the city's tax money.
- *I am Curious (Yellow)* begins a series of "cultural" skin-flicks; it is exhibited after several court battles and depicts frontal nudity and simulated intercourse.
- The "Smothers Brothers Comedy Hour" is canceled because the show has not been submitted to prescreening, for "mindless" censorship, as one spokesman describes it.
- Harold Robbins receives a $2.5 million advance for *The Inheritors.*
- Rock concerts proliferate as the Rolling Stones, the Who, Joan Baez, Ravi Shankar, Jimi Hendrix, and the Jefferson Airplane draw record audiences: 100,000 at Atlanta, 150,000 at Dallas, and an estimated 400,000 to 500,000 at Woodstock.
- An estimated 300,000 attend a free Rolling Stones concert at the Altamont Music Festival in San Francisco. The Stones hire the Hell's Angels as their own security guards and the Angels stab to death a

boy who tries to reach the stage; the Stones are singing "Sympathy for the Devil."
- Richard Schechner's *Dionysus 69* introduces group participation into the theater: each night a girl from the audience is selected to be made love to on stage; many plays of "communal celebration" follow, such as *Sweet Eros* and *Ché.*
- Richard Burton buys Elizabeth Taylor a 69.42-carat diamond from Cartier; its price is not revealed, although Cartier says it paid $1,050,000 for it the day before and has now "made a profit."
- Bobby Seale is ordered bound and gagged by Judge Julius Hoffmann when Seale repeatedly disrupts the Chicago Eight trial.
- Ted Kennedy's long delay in reporting Mary Jo Kopechne's drowning elicits widespread questioning of his character.
- Many universities make ROTC voluntary or abolish it; Defense Department contracts with universities drop from 400 to 200.
- A group of black students armed with machine guns take over a building at Cornell University; they leave after negotiations with the administration.
- "Hip, Hip, Hippocrates. . . . Up with the service, down with the fees," shout demonstrators at an AMA meeting.
- The addition of MSG to commercially prepared infant food is halted as studies indicate damage to the hypothalamus.
- A copy of the first printing of the Declaration of Independence sells for $404,000.
- On his 70th birthday, Duke Ellington is presented the Medal of Freedom by President Nixon.

Fads: Underground newspapers *(Berkeley Barb, L. A. Free Press, East Village Other),* dune buggies

New Words and Usages: Downs, uppers, command module, lunar module, mini beard, "-wise" (fashionwise, careerwise), crunch, hair weaving, headhunter, noise pollution, hunk, total

First Appearances: Army war college women graduates; medals of army, navy, air force presented to one person at the same time (L. L. Lemnitrev), city commissioner who is a former Miss America (Bess Meyerson, New York City), transatlantic solo rowboat (January 20–July 19, Canary Islands to Florida), senator to become movie actor (Everett Dirksen, *The Monitors), Penthouse,* Frosted Mini-Wheats, bank to install automatic teller (Chemical, New York), vasectomy outpatient service (Margaret Sanger Research Bureau, New York), postage stamp to depict living American (moon issue, Neil Armstrong), harness race track to handle more than $300 million in bets (Yonkers), ship to pass both ways through the Northwest Passage

THE *Seventies*

Nixon's farewell. *Congressional Library.*

Statistics

Vital

Population: 204,879,000
  Urban/rural: 149/54
  Farm: 4.8%
Life expectancy
  Male: 67.1
  Female: 74.8
Births/1,000: 18.4
Marriages/1,000: 10.6
Divorces/1,000: 3.5
Deaths/1,000: 9.5
  per 100,000
    Heart: 521
    Cancer: 163
    Tuberculosis: 3
    Car accidents: 26.9

Economic

Unemployed: 4,088,000
GNP: $977.1 billion
Federal budget: $197.2 billion
National debt: $382 billion
Union membership: 20.7
  million
Strikes: 5,716
Prime rate: 7.7%
Car sales: 6,546,800
Average salary: $7,564

Social

Homicides/100,000: 8.3
Suicides/100,000: 11.6
Percent below poverty level:
  12.6
Labor force, male/female: 27/
  16
Social welfare: $145.9 billion
Public education: $40.7 billion
College degrees
  Bachelors'
    Male: 484,000
    Female: 343,000
  Doctorates
    Male: 22,890
    Female: 3,976
Attendance
  Movies (weekly): 18 million
  Baseball (yearly): 28.9
    million

Consumer

Consumer Price Index
  (1967 = 100): 116.3
Eggs: 61¢ (doz.)
Milk: 33¢ (qt.)
Bread: 24¢ (loaf)
Butter: 87¢ (lb.)
Bacon: 95¢ (lb.)
Round steak: $1.30 (lb.)
Oranges: 86¢ (doz.)
Coffee: 91¢ (lb.)

The seventies witnessed many unprecedented events in American life—the first peacetime gas shortage, the first lost war, and the first president to resign. It is perhaps no wonder that self-doubt clouded the nation's bicentennial, and many questioned whether the era of American preeminence was passing. Close inspection of the social fabric, however, provides a more auspicious view.

The decade began with a tragic event when, during an antiwar rally at Kent State University, Ohio National Guardsmen opened fire and killed four students. Nationwide protest followed, and it appeared that the unrest of the late sixties was to continue. A more hopeful period ensued, however, as Nixon wound down the war and prepared to swallow the bitter pill of peace without victory. The president also took far-reaching initiatives in foreign affairs. Long a vaunted anticommunist, he and his shuttling minister, Henry Kissinger, made friendly overtures to Red China. Nixon, in addition, developed a policy of détente with Russia and eventually exchanged visits with Russian premier Leonid Brezhnev; in 1972, the first major postwar arms agreement, the Strategic Arms Limitation Treaty (SALT), was signed.

Elected in 1972 by a landslide that rivaled FDR's in 1936, and at the pinnacle of his roller-coaster public life, Nixon soon plummeted to scandal and ignominy. The Senate Watergate committee, chaired by Sam Ervin, pursued an investigation of the preelection break-in at Democratic Committee headquarters, and an extraordinary tale of suspense and intrigue unfolded. White House and other party underlings confessed and implicated their superiors, and the cover-up question arose. As Howard Baker succinctly put it: what did the president know, and when did he know it? All varieties of the shabby abuse of power came to light, from an "enemies list" of administration opponents targeted for IRS hassling and the employment of clandestine teams of "plumbers" for illicit break-ins to the president's predilection for secretly taping White House conversations and his typically obscene language. In due course, the president's counsel, John Dean, implicated Nixon, who then fired his chief aides, H. R. Haldeman and John Erlichman; Nixon later fired Archibald Cox, his own appointee as Watergate prosecutor. Finally, after battling the Supreme Court, Nixon agreed to release his secret tapes, and their publication sealed his fate. With the president's criminal complicity widely accepted, a House committee in 1974 voted articles of impeachment. During this time, Vice President Spiro Agnew resigned over corruption charges, and Gerald Ford was appointed vice president. Nixon, then facing an impeachment trial, elected to resign, and Ford became America's first appointed president; Ford's first official act was to pardon his disgraced predecessor. Continuing Senate investigations subsequently revealed dubious practices of both the FBI and CIA.

The country was shocked at the extent of its leaders' moral turpitude, and the immediate post-Vietnam War period, concurrent with Watergate, contributed to the national disillusionment. When, in 1975, North Vietnam occupied Saigon, a final American tally recorded over fifty thousand soldiers dead and more than 6 million veterans of the lost war. An unclarified sense of defeat and moral disaffection troubled many. Returning soldiers experienced great difficulties reintegrating into society. Most were greeted with ambivalence, in contrast to the glory and honor bestowed on veterans of previous wars. Perhaps in recognition of the widespread popular skepticism about the war's validity, Ford, in a limited way, and later Jimmy Carter, unconditionally, offered amnesty to those who had exiled themselves to avoid the draft. Throughout the decade, popular books and movies continued to question the nature and meaning of America's involvement in the war, including *The Best and the Brightest, Fire in the Lake, Coming Home, The Deer Hunter,* and *Apocalypse Now.*

Between Vietnam and Watergate, the most cynical of Americans lost faith in the integrity and judgment of the national leadership. In the meantime, the economy suffered, as inflation and recession ("stagflation") combined in an unprecedented manner. Then, in 1973, the nation's lifeline, its oil supply, became imperiled when OPEC, an organization of Third World oil producers, embargoed oil exports in response to America's posture toward the Arab-Israeli war. The erosion of America's might, as well as its moral prestige, seemed evident.

In 1976, America elected a little-known, born-again Christian from the Deep South, Jimmy Carter, who advocated human rights and promised executive candor. During his administration, however, the country's economic problems grew worse, and double-digit inflation and soaring interest rates (the "great inflation") devalued the dollar both at home and abroad. Gold prices jumped, and banks began to advertise borrowing as a means of hedging against inflation. Pan Am advised: "Live Today. Tomorrow Will Cost More."

Central to the crisis was the ever-increasing cost of oil, as OPEC relentlessly manipulated supply and increased prices of crude. The economy, in general, fared poorly, and basic industries like automaking and steel suffered enormous losses; Chrysler required a government loan to prevent bankruptcy. Other problems mounted. Crime, especially among the young, reached record heights; college enrollments fell; an accident at the Three Mile Island nuclear plant increased fears of a poisoned environment.

Carter's foreign policy, in the beginning, showed great promise. He negotiated the Panama Canal treaties and was instrumental in helping Egypt and Israel reach accord at Camp David. It was, however, in foreign affairs that America suffered its most severe humiliation as a world power. America's staunch ally, the shah of Iran, was overthrown by a theocratic revolution that installed a religious fanatic, the Ayatollah Khomeini, as ruler. In late 1979, the new Iranian government imprisoned forty-six Americans in the U.S. embassy, leaving America and its president to wring their hands and tie yellow ribbons.

There is another story to be told of this decade, but it is a more subtle one. It tells of the gradual integration of many of the ideals of the sixties into the mainstream of American consciousness. To the extent that these supported equality, diversity, and the individual's right to a private determination of social, moral, sexual, and spiritual beliefs, the history of the seventies takes on a brighter aspect.

Despite controversies over busing and affirmative action, and the persistence of racial bigotry and economic disadvantage, the ideals and legislation of the civil rights movement gained significant acceptance during the seventies. Segregation was officially eliminated, and blacks were free to vote everywhere. In southern towns, as well as northern cities, more blacks than ever entered political life and gained office, from Carl Stokes of Cleveland to Thomas Bradley of Los Angeles. Even sports reflected a responsible change in attitude, as blacks who had played in the early Negro baseball leagues were elected to the Major League Hall of Fame. Movies and television shows, like "The Jeffersons" and "Sanford and Son," began to portray blacks as role models and ordinary people, rather than as stereotypes and victims. *Roots*, Alex Haley's epic of black American history, became a blockbuster best-seller and, when dramatized on TV for seven nights later in the decade, drew all-time record audiences. Perhaps the black struggle for freedom had become an American, not just a black, story. Needless to say, ingrained prejudice still remained in many areas of society, but the principle of equality was taking hold. Children raised during this decade probably lacked the color line distinctions that surrounded their parents as recently as twenty years before.

The ideal of female equality also became further amalgamated into the national consciousness. Despite the failure of sufficient states to ratify the ERA—a great setback to many—numerous positive changes took place. A federal law forbidding discrimination based on gender was passed. More women went to medical, law, and business schools, and more women worked and demanded and received dignified treatment. The growth of child care helped women to work and parent at the same time. Early in the decade, Gloria Steinem's *Ms.* magazine got underway, and a number of important feminist books reached a wide audience, telling of *Sexual Politics, The Female Eunuch, Our Bodies, Ourselves,* and *Against Our Will.* Women gained a sense of community with one another, and new role models were visible. Barbara Jordan became the first woman and first black to give the keynote address at a presidential convention; Barbara Walters became the first female major network anchor. As women's roles expanded, male roles also became more flexible. Men were encouraged to be more sensitive; the emergence of the witty but insecure Woody Allen as a romantic hero in *Annie Hall,* the sophisticated romance of the decade, further defined changing role models. Other films like *Kramer vs. Kramer* addressed the dilemma of parents fulfilling their identities and still sharing in the raising of children. Probably the most controversial and far-reaching event concerning individual rights was the 1973 Supreme Court ruling on first-trimester abortion.

During the seventies, ethnic uniqueness also became a source of enrichment, rather than embarrassment, as Hispanics, Chicanos, American Indians, and Italians celebrated their heritage. *Bury My Heart at Wounded Knee,* Dee Brown's work on Indian history, was a best-seller, and "Chico and the Man," a popular TV show. Although not without problems, laws were passed supporting bilingual education.

Other issues, like the future of the environment—the danger of its exhaustion as well as the reality of its pollution—entered the mainstream of national awareness. The oil crisis jolted the public into a recognition of the limits of the earth's natural resources, and public attention focused on smaller, gas-efficient cars. Environmental concerns also prompted numerous industrial regulations geared toward reducing toxic waste in the air and water. An expanding health food industry promised uncontaminated ("natural") foods.

There was also a trend toward self-awareness, self-improvement, and self-fulfillment. Part of this was expressed in the explosive interest in exercise (especially running), health foods and gourmet cuisine, and psychologically oriented self-help books like *I'm O.K., You're O.K., Be Your Own Best Friend,* and *Your Erroneous Zones,* along with the many assertiveness-training manuals like *Looking Out for #1*. Later age at marriage and lower birth and higher divorce rates were perhaps also evidence of greater freedom of individual choice and self-awareness, as were books like *Fear of Flying* and

Passages. The growth of singles' communities and activities, as well as the marketing of singles' products, also indicated new life-styles.

It was during this time that the nation grew better able to own up to its Archie Bunkers. Norman Lear virtually elevated the sit-com into an art form by exaggerating realistic human foibles whereby his audience could laugh at itself and confront genuine social issues. A new candor was also evident in television movies, which portrayed subjects like interracial love affairs and homosexuality. Movies portrayed a more realistic and open attitude toward sex as a natural and mutual expression of romantic and/or erotic feelings, rather than as the reward women give scheming men as the prize for marriage in the way the earlier, coy, and tortured Doris Day–Rock Hudson films had portrayed it.

The new openness toward sexuality became widespread. *Last Tango in Paris,* an X-rated movie, starred a major box-office actor, Marlon Brando. *Deep Throat,* a hard-core porno film, played at posh neighborhood theaters. Two graphic self-help books, *Everything You Always Wanted to Know about Sex* and *The Joy of Sex,* became best-sellers, along with *The Sensuous Man* and *The Sensuous Woman. Open Marriage,* which advocated shelving sexual fidelity, had a vogue, and *Carnal Knowledge,* a film about this very subject, was well received. Jane Fonda, in many ways the female star of the decade, won an Oscar for her realistic portrayal of a prostitute. In an allied vein, streaking (running nude in public) became a fad.

Of course, as with all social change, there was resistance. Marabel Morgan's best-selling *Total Woman* advocated a more submissive female role. Clint Eastwood's emergence as the number one box-office star indicated the persistence of more or less traditional macho role models. The return among youth to the materialistic concerns of "getting on" and "getting ahead" indicated the sway of tradition. Adam Smith's *The Money Game* and Sylvia Porter's *The Money Book* also reflected this trend, as did the return to preppie clothes late in the decade.

Also in the seventies, Saul Bellow won the Nobel prize in literature, and E. L. Doctorow's critically acclaimed *Ragtime* received a record paperback advance. Three film directors were so successful as to virtually displace actors as Hollywood stars: George Lucas *(Star Wars),* Francis Ford Coppola *(The Godfather),* and Steven Spielberg *(Jaws).* In the world of opera, Beverly Sills became a leading personality; in ballet, many new companies flourished, and dancers such as Rudolf Nureyev and Mikhail Baryshnikov gained enormous popularity. Major popular music personalities and groups included Diana Ross, Elton John, Chicago, Earth, Wind and Fire, and Peter Frampton; there was a

Beverly Sills, who was "Bubbles" on radio at age 3, becomes general director of the New York City Opera in 1979. *Ian Howarth.*

renewed interest in country and jazz. Regional theater expanded, initiating shows like *Crimes of the Heart* and *Children of a Lesser God.* On Broadway, innovative musicals included *Jesus Christ Superstar* and *A Chorus Line.* Dominant sports figures were Henry Aaron, Kareem Abdul-Jabbar, O. J. Simpson, and Muhammad Ali. Interestingly, the sports world reflected the new role changes in its own good-natured way. New York Jets quarterback Joe Namath, for example, advertised mink coats and pantyhose. A huge television audience watched the battles between aging, self-proclaimed male chauvinist tennis star Bobby Riggs and the two current women champions, Margaret Smith Court and Billie Jean King. The sex symbols of the decade were Charlie's Angel detective Farrah Fawcett-Majors and the laconic he-man Burt Reynolds. In the trial of the decade, heiress Patty Hearst, kidnapped by a small terrorist group, was later found guilty of joining her captors in bank robbery. In another sequela of the sixties, nine hundred religious cult members committed suicide at their pastor's direction.

Finally, alongside America's political and economic trials and its social and cultural transfigurations, the seventies witnessed another phenomenon—the dawning of the Microchip Age. From calculators and digital electronics to personal computers, Atari, and video arcade games, computer technology became part of everyone's awareness. Genetic engineering, test-tube babies, and the experimental space shuttle seemed to give further reality to sci-fi fantasies. The children who flocked three and four times to see the movie *Star Wars,* making it the greatest box-office hit of all time, themselves demonstrated an addictive interest in the new computer gadgetry. In fact, a technological revolution, and with it perhaps yet another industrial revolution, was in the making, promising vast, exciting, but uncertain changes whose tale those Star Wars children, and their children, will tell.

1970

Facts and Figures

Economic Profile
Dow-Jones: ↓ High 842–
Low 669
GNP: +5%
Inflation: +6.5%
Unemployment: 4.9%
Stanley Blacker Borg
Alaskan men's coats:
$89.99
Lloyd and Haig calf shoes,
wing tip: $20.90
Dior giana tie: $8.50
Brooks Brothers shirts: from
$8; ties, from $5
Altman cotton, lace
nightgown: $16; matching
robe: $25
Gimbel's "Flower Bride"
ensemble (gown,
headpiece): $260
Ma Griffe perfume: $25 (oz.)
Lady Schick mist curler set:
$19.88
Norelco electric comb:
$10.88
Macy's shoe polisher: $24.99
Cartier miniature octagonal
silver salt shakers: $25
(for 4)

Deaths

Sir John Barbirolli, Erle
Stanley Gardner, Jimi
Hendrix, Richard
Hofstadter, Janis Joplin,
Gypsy Rose Lee, Sonny
Liston, Charles Ruggles,
John Scopes, George Szell.

In the News

U.S. AND CHINA RESUME TALKS IN WARSAW . . . SENATE CURBS DE FACTO SCHOOL SEGREGATION . . . CHICAGO 7 ARE ACQUITTED OF CONSPIRACY TO RIOT, 5 ARE FOUND GUILTY OF LESSER CHARGES . . . SOUTH CAROLINA WHITES STORM BUSES TO PREVENT INTEGRATION . . . NUCLEAR NONPROLIFERATION TREATY GOES INTO EFFECT . . . ARMY ACCUSES GEN. SAMUEL KOSTER OF SUPPRESSING INFORMATION ABOUT MY LAI CIVILIAN MASSACRE . . . . SENATE REJECTS SUPREME COURT NOMINEE CARSWELL OVER RACIST BACKGROUND . . . 2D ROUND OF STRATEGIC ARMS LIMITATION TREATY TALKS BEGINS . . . NIXON PLEDGES TO BRING 150,000 TROOPS BACK IN THE NEXT YEAR . . . NATION CELEBRATES EARTH DAY . . . NIXON ADMITS SENDING TROOPS INTO CAMBODIAN SANCTUARIES, STUDENTS PROTEST ACROSS THE COUNTRY . . . FOUR STUDENTS ARE KILLED AT KENT STATE UNIVERSITY WHEN NATIONAL GUARD OPENS FIRE . . . TWO STUDENTS ARE KILLED IN JACKSON STATE DEMONSTRATION . . . MAO CALLS FOR WORLD REVOLUTION . . . STOCKS RISE 32.04 ON RECORD DAY . . . PENN CENTRAL ASKS FOR BANKRUPTCY REORGANIZATION . . . NIXON ASKS VOTE FOR 18-YEAR-OLDS . . . NEW YORK ABORTION LAW TAKES EFFECT, THE MOST LIBERAL IN U.S. . . . 747 JUMBO JET WITH 379 ABOARD IS HIJACKED TO CUBA . . . FOUR NEW YORK–BOUND AIRLINERS ARE HIJACKED IN EUROPE, 300 HOSTAGES ARE HELD IN JORDANIAN DESERT . . . KING HUSSEIN CRUSHES PALESTINIAN REVOLT IN JORDAN . . . EGYPTIAN RULER NASSER DIES OF HEART ATTACK, VICE PRESIDENT ANWAR SADAT TAKES OVER . . . 200,000 ARE KILLED IN EAST PAKISTAN CYCLONE TIDAL WAVE . . . U.S. FAILS IN ATTEMPT TO FREE NORTH VIETNAM POW'S . . . VIETNAM: U.S. TROOP STRENGTH, 343,700; U.S. DEAD 44,241; WOUNDED, 293,529; ENEMY DEAD, 687,648.

Woodstock, the film of the 1969 rock festival dubbed by Abbie Hoffman "Woodstock Nation." *Movie Star News.*

"The senate must not remain silent now while the President uses the armed forces of the United States to fight an undeclared and undisclosed war in Laos."
— Senator William Fulbright (D-Ark.)

"We are not a weak people. We are a strong people. America has never been defeated in the proud, 199-year history of this country and we shall not be defeated in Vietnam. . . . We will not be humiliated. The world's most powerful nation [will not act] like a pitiful, helpless giant."
— Richard M. Nixon, on the bombing of Cambodia

"Unnecessary, unwarranted, and inexcusable."
— Scranton Report, on the Kent State shootings

"Pablum for the permissivists."
— Spiro Agnew, on the Scranton Report

Quotes

"Youth in its protest must be heard."
— Secretary of the Interior Walter Hickel

"I know that probably most of you think I'm an S.O.B., but I want you to know I understand just how you feel."
— Nixon, to student demonstrators

"The issue of race has been too much talked about. . . . We may need a period in which Negro progress continues and racial rhetoric fades, . . . [a policy of] benign neglect."
— Daniel Moynihan

"This is not a bedroom war. This is a political movement."
— Betty Friedan, on women's rights

Feminist Betty Friedan leads a nationwide women's demonstration on the occasion of the 50th anniversary of women's suffrage. *Philippe Halsman.*

Ads

TV

Premieres

"The Flip Wilson Show"
"Monday Night Football," Howard Cosell, Don
    Meredith
"The Odd Couple," Jack Klugman, Tony Randall
"The Mary Tyler Moore Show," Ed Asner, Valerie
    Harper
"The Partridge Family," Shirley Jones
"The Don Knotts Show"
"All My Children"
"Flipper"

Top Ten (Nielsen)

"Marcus Welby, M.D.," "The Flip Wilson Show,"
"Here's Lucy," "Ironside," "Gunsmoke," "ABC
Movie of the Week," "Hawaii Five-O," "Medical
Center," "Bonanza," "The F.B.I."

Specials

"The Andersonville Trial" (Jack Cassidy); "My
Sweet Charlie" (Al Freeman, Patty Duke); "The
Price" (George C. Scott, Colleen Dewhurst); "The
Neon Ceiling" (Gig Young, Lee Grant); "David
Copperfield" (Sir Laurence Olivier); "Civilisation"
(Sir Kenneth Clark); "The World of Charlie
Company" (CBS); "LBJ: The Decision to Halt the
Bombing"; "VD: A Plague on Our Houses" (Frank
Field); "Hamlet" (Richard Chamberlain)

Emmy Awards

"The Senator—The Bold Ones" (drama); "All in the
Family" (comedy, premiered 1/71); "The Flip Wilson
Show" (variety); "Sesame Street" (children); Hal
Holbrook (actor, "The Senator"); Jack Klugman
(comedic actor, "The Odd Couple"); Susan
Hampshire (actress, "The First Churchills"); Jean
Stapleton (comedic actress, "All in the Family")

Of Note

PBS takes over NET • Despite network complaints,
Nixon refuses to distribute advance copies of his
speeches in order to forestall "instant analysis" •
Thirty-three percent of the TV audience watches
ABC's "Monday Night Football," the first prime-
time football event.

Movies

Openings

Patton (Franklin J. Schaffner), George C. Scott, Karl
    Malden
Airport (George Seaton), Burt Lancaster, Dean
    Martin, Helen Hayes
Five Easy Pieces (Bob Rafelson), Jack Nicholson,
    Karen Black
Love Story (Arthur Hiller), Ali MacGraw, Ryan
    O'Neal
M*A*S*H (Robert Altman), Elliott Gould, Donald
    Sutherland, Sally Kellerman
Women in Love (Ken Russell), Alan Bates, Glenda
    Jackson
Diary of a Mad Housewife (Frank Perry), Richard
    Benjamin, Carrie Snodgress
Lovers and Other Strangers (Cy Howard), Gig Young,
    Richard Castellano, Beatrice Arthur
Satyricon (Federico Fellini), Martin Potter, Hiram
    Keller
Tora! Tora! Tora! (Richard Fleischer, Toshio Masuda,
    Kinji Fukasada), Jason Robards, Martin Balsam
Husbands (John Cassavetes), John Cassavetes, Ben
    Gazzara, Peter Falk
Gimme Shelter (David Maysles, Albert Maysles,
    Charlotte Zwerin), Mick Jagger, Charlie Watts,
    Melvin Belli
The Wild Child (François Truffaut), François
    Truffaut, Jean-Pierre Cargol, Jean Daste
Woodstock (Michael Wadleigh), Jimi Hendrix, Joan
    Baez, Joe Cocker, Arlo Guthrie
The Boys in the Band (William Friedkin), Cliff
    Gorman, Laurence Luckinbill
Little Big Man (Arthur Penn), Dustin Hoffman, Faye
    Dunaway, Martin Balsam
Ryan's Daughter (David Lean), Robert Mitchum,
    Sarah Miles, John Mills

Academy Awards

Best Picture: *Patton*
Best Director: Franklin Schaffner *(Patton)*
Best Actress: Glenda Jackson *(Women in Love)*
Best Actor: George C. Scott *(Patton)* (declined)

Top Box-Office Stars

Paul Newman, Clint Eastwood, Steve McQueen,
John Wayne, Elliott Gould, Dustin Hoffman, Lee
Marvin, Jack Lemmon, Barbra Streisand, Walter
Matthau

Stars of Tomorrow

Donald Sutherland, Liza Minnelli, Goldie Hawn,
Jack Nicholson, Genevieve Bujold, Dyan Cannon,
Marlo Thomas, Beau Bridges, Sharon Farrell, Peter
Boyle

Popular Music

Hit Songs
"We've Only Just Begun"
"Do the Funky Chicken"
"I'll Be There"
"I Like Your Lovin' "
"Psychedelic Shack"
"Signed, Sealed, Delivered I'm Yours"
"Love on a Two Way Street"
"The Love You Save"

Top Records

Albums: *Bridge over Troubled Water* (Simon and Garfunkel); *Cosmo's Factory* (Creedence Clearwater Revival); *Abraxas* (Santana); *McCartney* (Paul McCartney); *Woodstock* (Sound track)

Singles: "*(They Long to Be) Close to You*" (Carpenters); *American Woman / No Sugar Tonight* (Guess Who); *War* (Edwin Starr); *Ain't No Mountain High Enough* (Diana Ross); *Let It Be* (Beatles); *Get Ready* (Rare Earth); *Everything Is Beautiful* (Ray Stevens); *Rainy Night in Georgia* (Brook Benton). Country: *Wonder Could I Live There Anymore* (Charlie Pride); *Baby, Baby* (David Houston)

Grammy Awards
Bridge over Troubled Water, Simon and Garfunkel (record, album, song)

Jazz and Big Bands
Top Performers (*Downbeat*): Miles Davis, Jimi Hendrix (soloists); Duke Ellington (band); Miles Davis (jazz group); Rahsaan Roland Kirk, Wayne Shorter (instrumentalists); Ella Fitzgerald, Leon Thomas (vocalists); Frank Zappa (rock/blues musician); Blood, Sweat, and Tears (vocal group); Miles Davis, *Bitches Brew;* Blood, Sweat, and Tears, *B.S. & T3* (albums)

Theater

Broadway Openings

Plays
Child's Play (Robert Marasco), Pat Hingle, Fritz Weaver
Conduct Unbecoming (Barrie England), Paul Jones, Jeremy Clyde
Sleuth (Anthony Shaffer), Anthony Quayle, Keith Baxter
Borstal Boy (Brendan Behan), Niall Tolbin, Frank Grimes
Home (David Storey), Ralph Richardson, John Gielgud
The Gingerbread Lady (Neil Simon), Maureen Stapleton

Musicals
Purlie (Gary Geld, Peter Udell), Melba Moore, Cleavon Little, John Heffernan
Applause (Charles Strouse, Lee Adams), Lauren Bacall, Len Cariou, Penny Fuller
Company (Stephen Sondheim), Elaine Stritch, Dean Jones
Two by Two (Richard Rodgers, Martin Charnin), Danny Kaye
The Rothschilds (Jerry Boch, Sheldon Harnick), Hal Linden
The Me Nobody Knows (Gary Friedman, Will Holt), Melanie Henderson, Laura Michaels, Irene Cara
Bob and Ray, The Two and Only, written and performed by Bob Elliott, Ray Goulding

Classics, Revivals, and Off-Broadway Premieres
The Effect of Gamma Rays on Man-in-the-Moon Marigolds (Paul Zindel), Sada Thompson; *Steambath* (Bruce Jay Friedman), Anthony Perkins; *Happy Birthday, Wanda June* (Kurt Vonnegut, Jr.), Marsha Mason, Kevin McCarthy; *Colette* (Elinor Jones), Zoë Caldwell; Emlyn Williams as Charles Dickens; *Landscape, Silence* (Harold Pinter); *The Good Woman of Setzuan* (Bertolt Brecht), Colleen Dewhurst; *Jack McGowan in the Works of Beckett; The Basic Training of Pavlo Hummel* (David Rabe), William Atherton; *Harvey* (Mary Chase), Helen Hayes, James Stewart; *The White House Murder Case* (Jules Feiffer); *What the Butler Saw* (Joe Orton), Laurence Luckinbill; *Boesman and Lena* (Athol Fugard), James Earl Jones, Ruby Dee. *Founded:* Manhattan Theatre Club

Regional
Long Wharf, New Haven: *Country People* (Gorky); *A Place without Doors* (Marguerite Duras); *Yegor Bulichov* (Gorky), Martha Schlamme, Morris Carnovsky, American premieres

Seattle Repertory Theatre: *Richard III,* Richard Chamberlain

Mark Taper Forum, Los Angeles: *A Dream on Monkey Mountain* (Derek Wolcott), *Crystal and Fox* (Brian Friel); *Murderous Angels* (Conor Cruise O'Brien), premieres

Theater (cont.)

Dallas Theater Center: *The Night Thoreau Spent in Jail* (Jerome Lawrence, Robert E. Lee), premiere

Studio Arena, Buffalo: *Scenes from American Life* (A. R. Gurney), premiere

Pulitzer Prize
No Place to Be Somebody, Charles Gordone

Tony Awards
Borstal Boy, Brendan Behan (play); *Applause,* Charles Strouse, Lee Adams (musical)

Ralph Richardson and John Gielgud in *Home. Billy Rose Theatre Collection. The New York Public Library at Lincoln Center Astor, Lenox and Tilden Foundations.*

Classical Music

Compositions
Roger Sessions, Rhapsody, *When Lilacs Last in the Dooryard Bloom'd*
Walter Piston, Fantasia for Violin
Philip Glass, *Music with Changing Parts*
David Saturen, *Ternaria* for Organ and Orchestra
Steve Reich, Four Organs
George Crumb, *Ancient Voices of Children*
Ulysses Kay, *The Capitoline Venus*
Charles Wuorinen, *Time's Encomium*

Important Events
Beethoven's 200th birthday is celebrated throughout the country. Rudolf Serkin, Daniel Barenboim, and Claude Frank perform in the two-week Casals Festival. In New York, Barenboim plays the complete piano sonatas; Stern-Istomin-Rose play the complete piano trios; the Juilliard and Guarneri perform the quartets.
For Copland's 70th birthday, the composer leads the New York Philharmonic in his most famous works. At the MacDowell Colony, Isaac Stern and Leonard Bernstein perform *Aaron's Canon;* William Warfield sings "Old American Songs."
Garrick Ohlsson, 22, wins the Eighth International Chopin Festival in Warsaw.

Debut: Israela Margalit

First Performances
William Walton, Improvisations on an Impromptu of Benjamin Britten (San Francisco); Dmitri Shostakovich, Symphony no. 13 (Philadelphia); Elliott Carter, Concerto for Orchestra (New York); Charles Ives, *The Yale-Princeton Football Game* (New York); Hans Werner Henze, Symphony no. 6 (New York); Norman Dello Joio, *Mass* (Chicago); Karlheinz Stockhausen, *Carré* (Minneapolis); William Schuman, *In Praise of Shahn* (New York)

Opera

Metropolitan: Joan Sutherland, Marilyn Horne (debut), *Norma;* Franco Corelli, Grace Bumbry in Zeffirelli production of *Cavalleria rusticana;* Richard Tucker, Lucine Amara, Sherrill Milnes in Zeffirelli's *I pagliacci;* Martina Arroyo, Milnes, *Ernani;* Grace Bumbry, *Orfeo ed Euridice;* Placido Domingo, Cornell MacNeil, *La traviata;* Gabriel Bacquier, *Les contes d'Hoffmann*

Boston: *Good Soldier Schweik* (Robert Kurka); Beverly Sills, *Daughter of the Regiment*

Minneapolis: *17 Days and 4 Minutes* (Werner Egk)

Chicago: Theodor Uppman, *Billy Budd* (Benjamin Britten, premiere); Birgit Nilsson, *Turandot;* Marilyn Horne, *L'Italiana in Algieri* (Rossini)

San Francisco: Completes four-year *Ring* cycle; Geraint Evans, *Falstaff*

Music Notes
Unconventional efforts to enlarge audiences continue throughout the United States • The Los Angeles Philharmonic tries to enlarge its audience with "Contemporary '70–20th Century Music: How It Was, How It Is," a fusion of the classics and rock • On national TV: *Switched-On Symphony* (classical/rock).

Buckminster
Fuller. *Movie
Star News.*

Art

Painting

Philip Pearlstein, *Two Female Nudes with Red Drape*

Philip Guston, *Courtroom, Cellar*

Jim Dine, *Twenty Hearts*

Vija Celmins, *Ocean Image*

Richard Hamilton, *Kent State*

Red Grooms, *The Discount Store*

Alice Neel, *Andy Warhol*

Alfred Leslie, *Act and Portrait* (1968–70)

Dorothea Rockburne, *A, C and D from Group/And*

Romare Bearden, *Patchwork Quilt*

Wayne Thiebaud, *Still Life with Bowl*

Sculpture

Robert Smithson, *Spiral Jetty*

Jackie Ferrara, *Untitled*

Eva Hesse, *Untitled (Seven Poles)*

Architecture

John Hancock Center, Chicago (Skidmore, Owings and Merrill)

Central Library, University of California, San Diego (William L. Pereira)

Knights of Columbus Building, New Haven, Conn. (Roche and Dinkeloo)

Mailman Clinic, Miami (Ferendino, Grafton, Spillis and Candela)

John F. Kennedy Memorial, Dallas (Philip Johnson)

Hyatt House, Chicago (Portman, Grafton, Spillis)

Outdoor Theatre, Santa Fe, N.M. (Paolo Soleri)

Sculpture Museum, New Canaan, Conn. (Philip Johnson)

Important Exhibitions

Museums

New York: *Metropolitan:* Before Cortès; Sculpture of Middle America; "The Year 1200"; New York Painting and Sculpture (Pollock, Calder, Rauschenberg); 19th-Century America; Masterpieces of Painting from the Boston Museum of Fine Arts. *Museum of Modern Art:* Stella, Archipenko, Oldenburg retrospectives; Hector Guimard. *Whitney:* Nineteenth-century trompe l'oeil; "The Reality of Appearance"; "New Realism": William Bailey, Jack Beal, John Clarke, Alfred Leslie, Wayne Thiebaud

Boston: Afro-American artists—Alvin Loving, Bill Rivers, Jack White, Norman Lewis, "New York and Boston"

Chicago: Brancusi retrospective

San Francisco, Washington, Detroit, Whitney: "The Reality of Appearance": William Harnett, J. F. Peto, John Haberle

Washington: Robert Morris retrospective; Selections from the Nathan Cummings collection

Detroit: Robert Morris retrospective

Art Briefs

The U.S. Pavilion at the Japan World's Fair ignores traditionalism; prominent is Andy Warhol's *Rain Curtain* • Artists join in political and social protest such as "The New York Artists' Strike against Racism, Sexism, Repression, War"; numerous shows collect funds for antiwar political candidates • Jacques Lipchitz begins large-scale commissions for the Municipal Plaza in Philadelphia and Columbia University • The University of Wisconsin opens a $3.5 million Elvehjem Art Center; other museums open at the University of California (Berkeley) and SUNY (Purchase) • Major sales include Cézanne's *Study of His Father* ($1.5 million) and Andy Warhol's *Campbell Soup Can with Peeling Label* ($60,000).

Dance

Natalia Makarova joins the American Ballet Theatre and debuts in *Giselle.*

Alvin Ailey tours North Africa prior to visiting the USSR on a cultural exchange program.

Premieres

American Ballet Theatre: Thirtieth anniversary, *The River* (Alvin Ailey, Duke Ellington)

New York City Ballet: *Who Cares?* (George Balanchine), Patricia McBride, Jacques d'Amboise; *In the Night* (Jerome Robbins)

Joffrey: *Trinity* (Gerald Arpino)

National Ballet of Washington: *Cinderella* (Ben Stevenson)

Books

Fiction

Critics' Choice
Mr. Sammler's Planet, Saul Bellow
Islands in the Stream, Ernest Hemingway (posthumous)
Jeremy's Version, James Purdy
The Estate, A Friend of Kafka, Isaac Bashevis Singer
Bech: A Book, John Updike
The Perfectionist, Gail Godwin
Standing Fast, Harvey Swados
Going All the Way, Dan Wakefield
The Stunt Man, Paul Brodeur
❒ *One Hundred Years of Solitude*, Gabriel García Márquez

Best-Sellers
Love Story, Erich Segal
The French Lieutenant's Woman, John Fowles
Deliverance, James Dickey
Great Lion of God, Taylor Caldwell
The Crystal Cave, Mary Stewart
The Gang That Couldn't Shoot Straight, Jimmy Breslin
Travels with My Aunt, Graham Greene
God Is an Englishman, R. F. Delderfield
The Secret Woman, Victoria Holt
Calico Palace, Gwen Bristow

Nonfiction

Critics' Choice
Jefferson and the Presidency: First Term, 1801–1805, Dumas Malone
Sexual Politics, Kate Millett
On Violence, Hannah Arendt
Future Shock, Alvin Toffler
George Washington and the New Nation, James T. Flexner
Science in the British Colonies of America, Raymond Phineas Stearns
Hard Times: An Oral History of the Great Depression, Studs Terkel
Nixon Agonistes, Garry Wills
My Lai 4, Seymour M. Hersh
The Game of Nations, Miles Copeland
Cocteau, Francis Steegmuller
The End of the American Era, Andrew Hacker
The Limits of Intervention, Townsend Hoopes
The Greening of America, Charles Reich

Best-Sellers
Everything You Always Wanted to Know about Sex but Were Afraid to Ask, David Reuben
The New English Bible
The Sensuous Woman, "J"
American Heritage Dictionary of the English Language, ed. William Morris

Up the Organization, Robert Townsend
Ball Four, Jim Bouton
Zelda, Nancy Milford
Inside the Third Reich, Albert Speer
Body Language, Julius Fast
Human Sexual Inadequacy, William Masters, Virginia E. Johnson

Poetry

Robert Creeley, *The Finger: Poems 1966–1969*
Nikki Giovanni, *Black Talk / Black Judgement*
John Berryman, *Love and Fame*
Robert Lowell, *Notebook 1967–1968*
Don Lee, *Walk the Way of the New World*
James Dickey: *The Eye-Beaters, Blood, Victory, Madness, Buckhead, and Mercy*
Philip Levine, *5 Detroits*

Pulitzer Prizes
No prize is awarded in fiction.
Roosevelt: The Soldier of Freedom, James McGregor Burns (U.S. history)
The Rising Sun, John Toland (nonfiction)
Robert Frost: The Years of Triumph, 1915–1938, Lawrance Thompson (biography)
The Carrier of Ladders, W. S. Merwin (poetry)

Science and Technology

University of Wisconsin scientists, led by Har Gobind Khorana, perform the first complete synthesis of a gene.
The IBM Model 145 is the first mainframe computer to use monolithic semiconductor circuits for the entire main memory.
The floppy disc, a computer storage record, is introduced by the IBM 3740.
The FDA approves Lithium for the treatment of manic-depression and L-DOPA for the treatment of Parkinson's disease.

The FDA warns that "the pill" can cause blood clots.
The first known survivor from rabies is a six-year-old who is treated with vigorous supportive measures.
Lasers are used to improve bombing accuracy.

Nobel Prize
Julius Axelrod wins the prize in physiology and medicine for work on human nerve impulse transmission.

Sports _____

Baseball

Curt Flood (St. Louis, NL) sues the major leagues for contractual freedom and loses.

Hank Aaron (Atlanta, NL) and Willie Mays (San Francisco, NL) both get their 3,000th hit.

Jim Bunning (Philadelphia, NL) becomes the first pitcher to win 100 games in each league.

Tom Seaver (New York, NL) strikes out 19 men in a nine-inning game, the last 10 in a row.

The Cy Young awards go to Bob Gibson (St. Louis, NL) and Jim Perry (Minnesota, AL).

Champions _____

Batting	Bob Gibson (St. Louis,
Rico Carty (Atlanta, NL),	NL), 23–7
.366	Miguel Cuellar (Baltimore,
Alex Johnson (California,	AL), 23–8
AL), .329	*Home runs*
Pitching	Johnny Bench (Cincinnati,
	NL), 45

Football

The NFL and AFL merge into the NFL with an NFC and AFC.

NFC Season Leaders: John Brodie (San Francisco), passing; Larry Brown (Washington), rushing; Dick Gordon (Chicago), passing

AFC Season Leaders: Darryl Lamonica (Oakland), passing; Floyd Little (Denver), rushing; Fred Biletnikof (Oakland), receiving

College All-Americans: Joe Theisman (Q), Notre Dame; Jim Stillwagon (MG), Ohio State; Jack Ham (LB), Penn State

Bowls (Jan. 1, 1971)

Rose: Stanford 27–Ohio State 17	Cotton: Notre Dame 24–Texas 11
Orange: Nebraska 17–Louisiana State 12	Sugar: Tennessee 24–Air Force 13

Basketball

NBA All-Pro Team: Billy Cunningham (Philadelphia), Connie Hawkins (Phoenix), Willis Reed (New York), Jerry West (Los Angeles), Walt Frazier (New York)

Other Sports

Hockey: Bobby Orr, 23, Boston Bruins, scores 120 points, a record for a defenseman.

Boxing: Muhammad Ali returns to boxing with a third round TKO over Jerry Quarry.

Winners _____

World Series	*MVP*
Baltimore (AL) 4	Willis Reed, New York
Cincinnati (NL) 1	*College Basketball*
MVP	UCLA
NL–Johnny Bench,	*Player of the Year*
Cincinnati	Pete Maravich, Louisiana
AL–Boog Powell, Baltimore	State
Super Bowl V (Jan. 1971)	*Stanley Cup*
Baltimore 16–	Boston
Dallas 13	*US Tennis Open*
MVP	Men: Ken Rosewall
John Brodie, San Francisco	Women: Margaret Smith
College Football	Court
Texas (UPI)	*USGA Open*
Nebraska (AP)	Tony Jacklin
Heisman Trophy	*Kentucky Derby*
Jim Plunkett, Stanford	Dust Commander (M.
NBA Championship	Manganello, jockey)
New York 4–Los Angeles 3	

Fashion _____

For Women: Freedom in fashion is unprecedented: skirts are all lengths; pants are worn for any occasion; young people shop in army-navy surplus stores and thrift shops for the eclectic look; the thirties' influence is still felt. The slow demise of the mini appears as the polo dress and slithering look take over. The "midi" shows up in early spring at mid-calf lengths in denims, ginghams, and cinch-waist skirts. Heavy wool skirts are slit or buttoned, and dark stockings and boots are worn with everything. Long trench coats of canvas, leather, vinyl, and poplin are also worn over everything; men dislike the midi (64 percent), and during the controversy, pants and pant-sets prevail for all occasions and jobs; they appear in every shape, fabric, and design: straight-legged, to midcalf (gaucho), knickers, jumpsuits, blue jeans, in velvets with tunics. Anything ethnic or folksy is also fashionable, especially the Indian/Eastern Indian peasant look: cross stitching, feathers, fringes, deerskin, and beaded headbands. Cosmetics become "pure"; hair teasing is out; the Afro is chic for both blacks and whites; makeup is natural and subtle, with blush used to give a healthy, shining look; more makeup is used to give a less made-up look.

High-fashion notes: Blass's Persian embroidery, gaucho hat and Zhivago boots; de la Renta's "steppe" look.

Kaleidoscope _____

Mr. and Mrs. David Bowie, who favor futuristic costumes. *Movie Star News.*

- A bomb is planted in the math building at the University of Wisconsin as a protest against war research; a student working late is killed.
- A Greenwich Village townhouse in New York is destroyed by an explosion in what is believed to be a "bomb factory" of a radical group known as the Weathermen; three bodies are found.
- Nearly 100,000 students demonstrate in Washington; Nixon, unable to sleep, goes to the Lincoln Memorial before dawn to address them.
- Six construction workers are arrested after they attack 70 students carrying antiwar posters at Pace College in New York. Union leader Peter Brennan presents Nixon with an honorary hard hat.
- Nixon orders the Scranton committee to gather information about campus unrest; the committee reports a counterculture dedicated to "humanity, equality, and the sacredness of life."
- Agricultural scientist Norman Borlaug wins the Nobel Peace Prize.
- At demonstrations celebrating the 50th anniversary of the Nineteenth Amendment, sample placards read: "REPENT MALE CHAUVINISTS, YOUR WORLD IS COMING TO AN END," "DON'T COOK DINNER TONIGHT—STARVE A RAT TODAY,"and "DON'T IRON WHILE THE STRIKE IS HOT."
- Environmentalists and ecologists sponsor Earth Day (April 22), a national teach-in to publicize the problems of the environment.
- The amount of collected urban garbage, per capita, has risen from 2.75 pounds per day (1920) to 5 pounds per day.
- As boots become a fad, Golo Footwear sells 100,000 $30 patent leather boots in two months.
- An estimated 69,000 abortions are performed in the first six months after the New York state abortion law takes effect.
- The smallest ratio of men to women in history is recorded: 94.8 to 100.
- The National Research Council tells expectant mothers not to restrict weight gain; 20 to 25 pounds is desirable.
- Construction at "Acrosanti," Cords Junction, Arizona, begins for a ten-acre, ecologically sound environment for 3,000 people in 25-story buildings.
- Alexander Calder designs 74 feet of sidewalk on Madison Avenue, New York, in front of the Karl Perls Gallery.
- Slogans for the three major TV stations reflect current usage: "It's Happening on NBC!" "Let's Get it Together on ABC," and "We're Putting It All Together on CBS."
- "Let It Be," "Jesus Christ Superstar," and "Spirit in the Sky" mark the religious trend in rock music.
- Allstate Insurance Company offers to cut rates as much as 20 percent if manufacturers will improve the resistance of their bumpers to low-speed crash damage.
- The FDA orders a massive recall of canned tuna for possible mercury poisoning.

- An independent postal service replaces the U.S. Post Office.
- The Supreme Court rules that if necessary, trial judges may bind, gag, jail, or expel from court unruly defendants.
- Jane Alpert, convicted of bombing "military and war-related corporate buildings" in New York, breaks bail and goes underground.
- Financier Robert Vesco arranges a loan to save Bernie Cornfeld's International Overseas Services.
- With Howard Hughes in seclusion in the Bahamas, legal maneuverings over the control of his vast financial empire begin.
- Pop rock folk documentaries such as "Gimme Shelter" and "Woodstock" become a new genre.
- Health food sales rise to $3 billion.
- Vassar College becomes coed.
- The Bureau of Census reports that 143,000 unmarried couples live together (17,000 in 1960); a *New York Times* survey estimates that there are 2,000 communes in the United States.

Fads: Wigs, Mickey Mouse watches, sweatshirts

New Words and Usages: Fortran, ergonomics, psycho-technology, blahs, fast-food, head shop, hype, megafamily, Oreo, plastic (credit), ripoff, sexploitation, T-group, marathon group, sensitivity training, encounter group, Jesus people, hassle, putdown, trash, preppie, radical chic

First Appearances: Quadraphonic sound and records, commercial videophone, Gray Panthers, safety tops on drugs and dangerous products like turpentine, electronic editing terminal for newspapers, 30 cents New York City subway fare (20 cents since 1966), commissioned women generals, nun in the air force, cabinet member to serve in four different capacities (Elliot Richardson), no-fault divorce law (California), no-fault auto insurance (Massachusetts), lottery with $1 million top prize (New York City), European king buried in United States (Peter Karageorgevich), Boeing 747 transatlantic service (Pan American), ambulatory surgical facility independently operated (Surgicenter, Phoenix), woman jockey to ride in the Kentucky Derby (Diane Crump), strike of postal employees

1971

Facts and Figures

Economic Profile
  Dow-Jones: ↑ High 950–
    Low 790
  GNP: +8%
  Inflation: +5.7%
  Unemployment: 5.9%
Median age, first marriage:
  male: 23.2
  female: 20.8
Average household size: 3.14
Population over 65: 10%
Population under 10: 18%
Apollo 11 JFK medal,
  bronze: $6.50
Apollo 11 dollar: $2.50;
  silver: $39.95
Skis, Fisher Imperator: $175
Fisher 707 glass skis: $95
Dacron ski jacket: $35
Wines:
  1966 Chassagne
    Montrachet, Etienne
    Laurel: $3.79
  1957 Chambertin, Marion
    Perri Gelin: $11.90
  1966 Chambertin, J.
    Verchere: $8.98
  1967 Lafite Rothschild:
    $16.50
  1967 Graves, Entr'
    Boutant: $1.98

Deaths

Bennett Cerf, Jeff Chandler,
  Van Heflin, Rockwell
  Kent, Harold Lloyd, Paul
  Lukas, Audie Murphy,
  Allan Nevins, J. C.
  Penney, Igor Stravinsky.

In the News

PRIEST DANIEL BERRIGAN IS CHARGED WITH CONSPIRACY TO KIDNAP HENRY KISSINGER . . . ROBERT BYRD OUSTS TED KENNEDY AS SENATE MAJORITY WHIP . . . IDI AMIN BECOMES UGANDA RULER . . . APOLLO XIV LANDS ON MOON . . . TREATY IS SIGNED TO KEEP NUKES OFF OCEAN FLOOR . . . BOMB DAMAGES SENATE FLOOR . . . CHARLES MANSON AND HIS "FAMILY" ARE SENTENCED TO DEATH . . . LIEUTENANT WILLIAM CALLEY IS FOUND GUILTY IN MY LAI MASSACRE . . . SOCIALIST SALVADOR ALLENDE WINS CHILE ELECTION . . . FIRST LEGALIZED OFF-TRACK BETTING BEGINS IN N.Y. . . . CHOU EN-LAI WELCOMES U.S. PING PONG TEAM . . . "NEW YORK TIMES" PUBLISHES PENTAGON PAPERS, DANIEL ELLSBERG IS ARRESTED FOR THEIR DISCLOSURE . . . SUPREME COURT UPHOLDS BUSING FOR DESEGREGATION . . . 200,000 RALLY AGAINST VIETNAM WAR IN WASHINGTON, D.C. . . . SUPREME COURT SAYS THAT JURIES CAN PASS DEATH SENTENCE . . . NIXON INSTITUTES WAGE AND PRICE CONTROLS . . . BRITAIN WILL ENTER COMMON MARKET . . . NIXON ENDS 21-YEAR TRADE EMBARGO ON CHINA . . . PRISONERS RIOT AT ATTICA, 10 HOSTAGES AND 39 CONVICTS DIE AS TALKS FAIL . . . HUNGARIAN CARDINAL MINDSZENTY IS EXILED TO ROME . . . SHAH CELEBRATES PERSIA'S 2500TH ANNIVERSARY . . . UN VOTES TO SEAT PEKING . . . U.S. WILL SELL $136 MILLION IN LIVESTOCK TO USSR . . . 45,000 MORE TROOPS ARE RECALLED FROM VIETNAM . . . INDIA AND PAKISTAN FIGHT IN EAST PAKISTAN, U.S. BRANDS INDIA AGGRESSOR . . . AIR ATTACKS ON NORTH VIETNAM INCREASE . . . 26TH AMENDMENT IS PASSED, LOWERING THE VOTING AGE TO 18 . . . NIXON ANNOUNCES HE WILL VISIT CHINA . . . NIXON SEVERS GOLD-DOLLAR TIE AND ASKS TAX CUT, STOCK MARKET LEAPS RECORD 32.93 . . . VIETNAM: U.S. TROOP STRENGTH, 152,000; U.S. DEAD, 45,543.

Feminist and editor of *Ms.* magazine, Gloria Steinem. *Courtesy of* Ms.

Quotes

"We are men. We are not beasts. We only want to live."

— Attica inmates

"There was the whole rule of law to consider . . . the whole fabric of society."

— Governor Nelson Rockefeller, on Attica

"It is indisputably clear . . . that the Justice Department was simply wrong as a matter of law in advising that [Muhammad] Ali's beliefs were not religiously based and were not sincerely held."

— Supreme Court ruling

"The Constitution is larger than the executive branch."

— Daniel Ellsberg

"Every senator in this chamber is partly responsible for sending 50,000 young Americans to an early grave."

— Senator George McGovern (D-S. Dak.)

"I've suffered more as a woman than as a black."

— Shirley Chisholm

"Eliminating the patriarchal and racist base of the existing social system requires a revolution, not a reform."

— *Ms.* magazine, first issue

"A woman's liberty and right to privacy may include the right to remove an unwanted child."

— Gerhard Gesell, federal judge

"Let me make one thing perfectly clear. I wouldn't want to wake up next to a lady pipefitter."

— Richard M. Nixon (quoted in *Ms.*)

"Send me your poor, your deadbeats, your filthy . . . all of them free to live together in peace and harmony in their little, separate sections where they feel safe, and break your head if you go in there."

— Archie Bunker, "All in the Family"

Jack Klugman and Tony Randall in "The Odd Couple": "Can two divorced men share an apartment without driving each other crazy?" *Movie Star News.*

Ads

TV

Premieres
"All in the Family," Carroll O'Connor, Jean Stapleton
"The Sonny and Cher Comedy Hour"
"Owen Marshall, Counselor at Law," Arthur Hill, Lee Majors
"Columbo," Peter Falk
"Cannon," William Conrad
"McMillan and Wife," Susan St. James, Rock Hudson

Top Ten (Nielsen)
"All in the Family," "The Flip Wilson Show," "Marcus Welby, M.D.," "Gunsmoke," "ABC Movie of the Week," "Sanford and Son," "Mannix," "Funny Face," "Adam 12," "The Mary Tyler Moore Show"

Specials
"Brian's Song" (James Caan, Lou Gossett); "The Selling of the Pentagon" (Peter Davis); "Elizabeth R"; "Beethoven's Birthday: A Celebration in Vienna with Leonard Bernstein"; "Look Homeward, Angel" (Ben Edwards); "The Pentagon Papers" (PBS); "The China Trip" (ABC); "The Homecoming"; "The Six Wives of Henry VIII"

Emmy Awards
"Elizabeth R" (drama); "All in the Family" (comedy); "The Carol Burnett Show" (variety); "Sesame Street" (children); Peter Falk (actor, "Columbo"); Carroll O'Connor (comedic actor, "All in the Family"); Glenda Jackson (actress, "Elizabeth R"); Jean Stapleton (comedic actress, "All in the Family")

Of Note
After much debate, the three major networks agree to limit prime time to 8:00–11:00 P.M. • John Chancellor becomes solo anchor on NBC nightly news.

Movies

Openings
The French Connection (William Friedkin), Gene Hackman, Fernando Rey, Roy Scheider
A Clockwork Orange (Stanley Kubrick), Malcolm McDowell, Patrick Magee
The Last Picture Show (Peter Bogdanovich), Timothy Bottoms, Jeff Bridges, Ben Johnson, Cloris Leachman, Ellen Burstyn, Eileen Brennan
Sunday, Bloody Sunday (John Schlesinger), Peter Finch, Glenda Jackson
The Hospital (Arthur Hiller), George C. Scott, Diana Rigg
McCabe and Mrs. Miller (Robert Altman), Julie Christie, Warren Beatty
The Go-Between (Joseph Losey), Julie Christie, Alan Bates
Carnal Knowledge (Mike Nichols), Jack Nicholson, Candice Bergen, Arthur Garfunkel, Ann-Margret
The Garden of the Finzi-Continis (Vittorio De Sica), Dominique Sanda
Summer of '42 (Robert Mulligan), Jennifer O'Neill, Gary Grimes
Diamonds Are Forever (Guy Hamilton), Sean Connery, Jill St. John
Klute (Alan J. Pakula), Jane Fonda, Donald Sutherland
Shaft (Gordon Parks), Richard Roundtree, Moses Gunn
Bananas (Woody Allen), Woody Allen, Louise Lasser
Dirty Harry (Don Siegel), Clint Eastwood, Harry Guardino
Harold and Maude (Hal Ashby), Ruth Gordon, Bud Cort

Academy Awards
Best Picture: *The French Connection*
Best Director: William Friedkin (*The French Connection*)
Best Actress: Jane Fonda (*Klute*)
Best Actor: Gene Hackman (*The French Connection*)

Top Box-Office Stars
John Wayne, Clint Eastwood, Paul Newman, Steve McQueen, George C. Scott, Dustin Hoffman, Walter Matthau, Ali MacGraw, Sean Connery, Lee Marvin

Stars of Tomorrow
Jennifer O'Neill, Karen Black, Gary Grimes, Sally Kellerman, Arthur Garfunkel, Bruce Davison, Richard Roundtree, Deborah Winters, Jane Alexander, Rosalind Cash

Popular Music

Hit Songs
"How Can You Mend a Broken Heart?"
"Rainy Days and Mondays"
"Joy to the World"
"Maggie May"
"One Bad Apple"
"Got to Be There"
"Theme from *Shaft*"
"Ain't No Sunshine"

Top Records

Albums: *All Things Must Pass* (George Harrison); *Jesus Christ Superstar* (various artists); *Pearl* (Janis Joplin); *Tapestry* (Carole King); *Santana* (Santana)

Singles: *Family Affair* (Sly and the Family Stone); *Got to Be There* (Michael Jackson); *All I Ever Need Is You* (Sonny and Cher); *It's Too Late* (Carole King); *She's a Lady* (Tom Jones); *That's the Way I've Always Heard It Should Be* (Carly Simon); *Every Picture Tells a Story* (Rod Stewart); *Take Me Home, Country Roads* (John Denver with Fat City); *Go Away Little Girl* (Donny Osmond). Country: *Rose Garden* (Lynn Anderson); *Help Me Make It through the Night* (Sammi Smith)

Grammy Awards
It's Too Late, Carole King (record); *Tapestry,* Carole King (album); "You've Got a Friend," Carole King (song)

Jazz and Big Bands
T.T.T. (Twelve Tone Tune) is recorded by Bill Evans.

Top Performers (*Downbeat*): Miles Davis, Charles Mingus (soloists); Duke Ellington (band); Miles Davis (jazz group); Kenny Burrell, Richard Davis, Herbie Hancock, Buddy Rich, Cannonball Adderley (instrumentalists); Roberta Flack, Leon Thomas (vocalists); Frank Zappa (rock/blues musician); Blood Sweat, and Tears (vocal group); Weather Report, (album)

Theater

Broadway Openings

Plays
The Prisoner of Second Avenue (Neil Simon), Lee Grant, Peter Falk
Twigs (George Furth), Sada Thompson
Lenny (Julian Barry), Cliff Gorman, Joe Silver
And Miss Reardon Drinks a Little (Paul Zindel), Estelle Parsons, Julie Harris, Nancy Marchand
Abelard and Heloise (Ronald Millar), Keith Mitchell, Diana Rigg
How the Other Half Loves (Alan Ayckbourn), Phil Silvers, Sandy Dennis
Old Times (Harold Pinter), Robert Shaw, Mary Ure, Rosemary Harris
All Over (Edward Albee), Jessica Tandy, Colleen Dewhurst, George Voskovec, Betty Field
The Philanthropist (Christopher Hampton), Alec McCowen

Musicals
Follies (Stephen Sondheim), Alexis Smith, Dorothy Collins, Gene Nelson, Yvonne DeCarlo
No, No, Nanette (Vincent Youmans, revival), Ruby Keeler, Helen Gallagher, Patsy Kelly, Jack Gilford
Jesus Christ Superstar (Andrew Lloyd Webber, Tim Rice), Jeff Fenholt, Ben Vereen
Ain't Supposed to Die a Natural Death (Melvin Van Peebles), Carl Gordon, Barbara Alston
Two Gentlemen of Verona (Galt MacDermot, John Guare), Raul Julia, Clifton Davis, Jonelle Allen
Godspell (Stephen Schwartz), David Haskell

Classics, Revivals, and Off-Broadway Premieres
The Trial of the Catonsville Nine (Daniel Berrigan), Sam Waterston, Michael Moriarty; A *Doll's House* (Ibsen), Claire Bloom; *Hamlet,* Judith Anderson (as Hamlet); *Hedda Gabler* (Ibsen), Claire Bloom, Donald Madden; *Othello,* James Earl Jones; *Waiting for Godot* (Samuel Beckett), Tom Ewell; *Long Day's Journey into Night* (Eugene O'Neill), Robert Ryan, Stacy Keach, Geraldine Fitzgerald; *School for Wives* (Molière, Richard Wilbur), Brian Bedford; *Sticks and Bones* (David Rabe), Tom Aldredge; *The House of Blue Leaves* (John Guare), William Atherton, Anne Meara

Regional

Long Wharf, New Haven: *Solitaire, Double Solitaire* (Robert Anderson), Martha Schlamme

Ivanhoe, Chicago: *Out Cry* (Tennessee Williams)

Arena Stage, Washington, D.C.: *The Ruling Class*

Theater (cont.)

(Peter Barnes); *Moonchildren* (Michael Weller), premieres

Washington Theatre Club, D.C.: *The Web and the Rock* (Dolores Sutton), premiere

Mark Taper Forum, Los Angeles: *The National Health* (Peter Nichols); *The Trial of the Catonsville Nine* (Daniel Berrigan), Beau Bridges, James Daly, Peter Strauss, Anthony Zerbe, premieres

Yale Repertory Theatre: *Where Has Tommy Flowers Gone* (Terrence McNally) Henry Winkler, premiere

Classical Music

Compositions
Roger Sessions, Concerto for Viola and Cello
Aaron Copland, Duo for Flute and Piano
Peter Mennin, Sinfonia for Orchestra
Karl Korte, *Remembrances* (for Flute and Tape)
Lawrence Moss, *Auditions*
George Crumb, *Songs, Drones and Refrains of Death*
Mario Davidovsky, *Synchronisms,* no. 6
Jacob Druckman, *Windows*

Important Events
The John F. Kennedy Center for the Performing Arts, Washington, D.C., opens with a variety of concerts: Leonard Bernstein's *Mass,* with 200 participants, jazz and taped material, and the Alvin Ailey Dance Company; the National Symphony (Antal Dorati) and the premiere of Alberto Ginastera's *Beatrix Cenci.* During the year the varied programs include Beverly Sills, *Ariodante, Candide,* Eugene Istomin–Isaac Stern–Leonard Rose, and the Fifth Dimension.
Pierre Boulez becomes director of the New York Philharmonic and performs the avant-garde; he conducts the Juilliard Ensemble in "New and Newer Music." Boulez plans "preconcerts," recitals for subscription holders.
Alexander Schneider celebrates the New School's (New York) 40th anniversary with Pinchas Zukerman and Peter Serkin.
For Roger Sessions's 75th birthday, Virgil Thomson and the New York Philharmonic premiere *Nativity* and perform *The Mother of Us All.*

Other New Facilities: Heinz Hall for the Performing Arts (Pittsburgh); University of Michigan Power Center for the Performing Arts; Wolf Trap Farm Park, Vienna, Va.

Leading opera stars Joan Sutherland and Marilyn Horne in *Semiramide. Chicago Lyric Opera.*

Debut: Pinchas Zukerman, Yo-Yo Ma

First Performances
Ingolf Dahl, Saxophone Concerto (New York); Dmitri Shostakovich, Symphony no. 4; Lalo Schifrin, *Pulsations* (Los Angeles); Pablo Casals, 94, conducting, *Hymn to the United Nations* (UN); Samuel Barber, *The Lovers* (Philadelphia)

Opera

Metropolitan: Rudolph Bing retires after 22 years of managing the company and is knighted by Queen Elizabeth. Goeran Gentele replaces him and dies in December; Schuyler G. Chapin takes over. James Levine debuts, conducting *Tosca.* Birgit Nilsson, Jess Thomas, *Tristan und Isolde;* Luigi Alva, *L'elisir d'amore;* Adriana Maliponte (debut), *La bohème;* Stuart Burrows (debut), *Don Giovanni;* William Dooley, *Fidelio*

Boston: Beverly Sills, *Norma*

Minneapolis: *The Mother of Us All; Faust Counter Faust* (H. Wesley Balk)

St. Paul: *Summer and Smoke* (Lee Hoiby)

Santa Fe: *Yerma* (Heitor Villa-Lobos, premiere)

Chicago: Joan Sutherland, Marilyn Horne, *Semiramide*

San Francisco: Christa Ludwig, *Der Rosenkavalier*

Art

Painting
Helen Frankenthaler, *Chairman of the Board*
Audrey Flack, *Macarena of Miracles*
Al Held, *Black Nile III*
Jack Tworkov, *Partitions*
Richard Estes, *Helena's Florist*
Richard Artschwager, *Doors*
Red Grooms, *Mr. and Mrs. Rembrandt*
Jasper Johns, *Decoy*
Ellsworth Kelly, *Chatham XI, Blue, Yellow*
Richard Diebenkorn, *Ocean Park, N. 36*

Sculpture
Mark di Suvero, *Il Ook*
Robert Morris, *Observatory*
Claes Oldenburg, *Three Way Plug, Scale A (Soft), Prototype in Blue*
Alexander Calder, *Animobiles*
Lynda Benglis, *For Darkness: Situation and Circumstance*
Michael Heizer, *Adze Dispersal*
Hammarskjöld Plaza, United Nations, New York (Alexander Liberman)
Welded steel construction, Seagram Building, New York (Louise Nevelson)

Architecture
Cleo Rodgers Memorial Library, Columbia, Ind. (I. M. Pei)
Bank of America, San Francisco (Wurster and Associates)
Hyatt-Regency Hotel, San Francisco (John C. Portman)
New Haven Pre-Fab Housing (Paul Rudolph)
John F. Kennedy Center for the Performing Arts, Washington, D.C. (Edward Durell Stone)
Lyndon Baines Johnson Library, Austin, Texas (Skidmore, Owings and Merrill)
Mummer's Theater, Oklahoma City, Okla. (John Johnson)
National Airlines Terminal, J. F. Kennedy Airport, New York (I. M. Pei)

Important Exhibitions
Albrecht Dürer's 500th birthday and Picasso's 90th birthday prompt shows throughout the United States. The Marin and Sloan centennial shows travel widely.

Museums
New York: *Metropolitan:* "The Cubist Epoch"; Joseph Cornell; "Arts from the Rooftops of Asia"; Dürer; "Greek and Roman Art: Triumphs and Tribulations." *Museum of Modern Art:* "The Collections of Gertrude Stein and Her Family"; Marin Centennial; Retrospectives: Philip Johnson, Kevin Roche, Paul Rudolph. *Whitney:* O'Keeffe, Eakins

Philadelphia: "The Multiple": Duchamp, Warhol, Oldenburg, Vasarely

Washington: Cézanne; Ingres; Sloan centennial

Boston: Zen painting and calligraphy; "Earth, Air, Water, Fire: Elements of Art" (live show)

Baltimore, San Francisco: Matisse

Minneapolis: Dutch masters

Chicago, San Francisco: Vuillard

Art Briefs
Avant-garde exhibitions include various "confrontation shows," the new "street" and "wall" artists, the "new realists," the minimalists, and pop. The Guggenheim Museum in New York sponsors a show of kinetic sculpture as a metaphor for the creative process • The Salvador Dali Museum in Cleveland opens • The Whitney's "Contemporary Black Artists in America" becomes controversial because of the museum's lack of a black curator; eight well-known artists reply to the article "Why Have There Been No Great Women Artists?" and a long public controversy follows. The Whitney and Brooklyn museums hold shows of women artists. The Museum of Modern Art sponsors "The Artist as Adversary" • The Metropolitan Museum of Art pays a record $5,544,000 for a Velasquez portrait.

Dance

The American Ballet Theatre is named the official company of the John F. Kennedy Center for the Performing Arts.
Dance Company of Harlem is founded by Arthur Mitchell and Karel Shook.
The Joffrey dances at Filene Center, Wolf Trap Farm Park, the first national park for the performing arts.

Premieres
New York City Ballet: *The Goldberg Variations* (Jerome Robbins), Gelsey Kirkland, Peter Martins

Joffrey: *Feast of Ashes* (Alvin Ailey)

National Ballet of Washington: *The Sleeping Beauty* (Marius Petipa, full-length version), Margot Fonteyn

Alvin Ailey: *Cry* (Alvin Ailey, Alice Coltrane, Laura Nyro), Judith Jamison; *Flowers* (Ailey, Big Brother and the Holding Company, Janis Joplin), Lynn Seymour

Books

Fiction
Critics' Choice

Blood Oranges, John Hawkes
City Life, Donald Barthelme
Being There, Jerzy Kosinski
The Tenants, Bernard Malamud
Birds of America, Mary McCarthy
Love in the Ruins, Walker Percy
The Pagan Rabbi and Other Stories, Cynthia Ozick
Fire Sermon, Wright Morris
Grendel, John Gardner
The Death and Life of Harry Goth, D. Keith Mano
The Complete Stories, Flannery O'Connor
&. *Maurice*, E. M. Forster (posthumous)

Best-Sellers

Wheels, Arthur Hailey
The Exorcist, William Peter Blatty
The Passions of the Mind, Irving Stone
The Day of the Jackal, Frederick Forsyth
The Betsy, Harold Robbins
The Winds of War, Herman Wouk
The Drifters, James Michener
The Other, Thomas Tryon
Rabbit Redux, John Updike

Nonfiction
Critics' Choice

Steal This Book, Abbie Hoffman
Ordeal of the Union, vols. 7, 8, Allan Nevins
Living on the Earth, Alicia Bay Laurel
The Female Eunuch, Germaine Greer
The Memoirs of Chief Ned Fox, Ned Fox
Fiction and the Figures of Life, William H. Gass
The Classic Style: Haydn, Mozart, Beethoven, Charles Rosen
The European Discovery of America, Samuel Eliot Morison
The Prisoner of Sex, Norman Mailer
Beyond Freedom and Dignity, B. F. Skinner
Roots of Involvement: The U.S. in Asia 1784–1971, Marvin Kalb, Elie Abel
A Theory of Justice, John Rawls

Best-Sellers

The Sensuous Man, "M"
Bury My Heart at Wounded Knee, Dee Brown
Better Homes and Gardens Blender Cook Book
I'm O.K., You're O.K., Thomas Harris
Any Woman Can! David Reuben
Inside the Third Reich, Albert Speer
Honor Thy Father, Gay Talese

Fields of Wonder (poetry), Rod McKuen

Poetry

Anne Sexton, *Transformations*
Erica Jong, *Fruits and Vegetables*
Adrienne Rich, *The Will to Change: Poems 1968–1970*
A. R. Ammons, *Briefings: Poems Small and Easy*
David Shapiro, *A Man Holding an Acoustic Panel*
Diane Wakoski, *The Motorcycle Betrayal Poems*
Frank O'Hara, *The Collected Poems*
&. Ted Hughes, *Crow*

Pulitzer Prizes

Angle of Repose, Wallace Stegner (fiction)
Neither Black nor White: Slavery and Race Relations in Brazil and the United States, Carl N. Degler (U.S. history)
Stilwell and the American Experience in China, 1911–1945, Barbara W. Tuchman (nonfiction)
Eleanor and Franklin, Joseph P. Lash (biography)
Collected Poems, James Wright (poetry)

Science and Technology

Intel of California introduces the microprocessor, the "computer on a chip."
Illiac IV can handle 200 million instructions per second.
Direct dialing begins between New York and London.
Choh Hao Li, at the University of California, synthesizes the growth hormone, somatrotropin, for the treatment of pituitary dwarfism in children.
The USPHS no longer advises smallpox vaccination.
Diethylstilbesterol (DES), used since the 1930s to prevent miscarriage, is found to be carcinogenic for children of those pregnancies.
Interest in acupuncture revives.

The world's largest proton accelerator is built at Batavia, Illinois.
Apollo XIV, manned by Alan Shepard, Allen Roosa, and Edgar Mitchell, explores the moon's surface.
Apollo XV, manned by David Scott, Alfred Worden, and James Irwin, utilizes the lunar roving vehicle, spends 18 hours EVA time, and gathers 180 pounds of samples.
Mariner IX orbits Mars.
&. The diamond-bladed scalpel is developed for eye microsurgery.

Nobel Prize

Earl Sutherland wins in chemistry for work on the enzyme cyclic AMP.

Sports

Baseball

A special commission is formed to select Negro League players for the Baseball Hall of Fame.

The Supreme Court upholds baseball's "unique exemption" from antitrust laws.

Willie Mays scores his 1,950th run.

Rookie Vida Blue (Oakland, AL) wins the MVP and Cy Young Awards.

Ferguson Jenkins (Chicago, NL) also wins the Cy Young award.

Champions

Batting
Joe Torre (St. Louis, NL), .363
Tony Oliva (Minnesota, AL), .337
Pitching
Don Gullet (Cincinnati, NL), 16–6
Steve McNally (Baltimore, AL), 21–5
Home runs
Willie Stargell (Pittsburgh, NL), 48

Football

Joe Kapp begins an antitrust suit against the NFL.

NFC Season Leaders: Roger Staubach (Dallas), passing; John Brockington (Green Bay), rushing; Bob Tucker (New York Giants), receiving

AFC Season Leaders: Bob Griese (Miami), passing; Floyd Little (Denver), rushing; Fred Biletnikof (Oakland), receiving

College All-Americans: Gregg Pruitt (B), Oklahoma; Ed Marinaro (B), Cornell; Lydell Mitchell (B), Penn State

Bowls (Jan. 1, 1972)

Rose: Stanford 13– Michigan 12

Orange: Nebraska 38– Alabama 6

Cotton: Penn State 30– Texas 6

Sugar: Oklahoma 40– Auburn 22

Basketball

NBA All-Pro First Team: John Havlicek (Boston), Billy Cunningham (Philadelphia), Lew Alcindor (Milwaukee), Jerry West (Los Angeles), Dave Bing (Detroit)

ABA All-Pro First Team: Roger Brown (Indiana), Rick Barry (NY), Mel Daniels (Indiana), Mack Calvin (Floridians), Charlie Scott (Virginia)

Other Sports

Boxing: The Muhammad Ali–Joe Frazier fight draws the largest gate ever, with closed-circuit TV; Frazier wins in 15. and each earns $3.5 million.

Golf: Jack Nicklaus wins a record $244,000 on the pro tour. Ken Rosewall is the World Championship Tennis (WCT) champion.

Winners

World Series
Pittsburgh (NL) 4
Baltimore (AL) 3
MVP
NL–Joe Torre, St. Louis
AL–Vida Blue, Oakland
Super Bowl VI (Jan. 1972)
Dallas 24–Miami 3
MVP
Bob Griese, Miami
College Football
Nebraska
Heisman Trophy
Pat Sullivan, Auburn
NBA Championship
Milwaukee 4–Baltimore 0

MVP
Lew Alcindor, Milwaukee
College Basketball
UCLA
Player of the Year
Sidney Wicks, UCLA
Stanley Cup
Montreal
US Tennis Open
Men: Stan Smith
Women: Billie Jean King
USGA Open
Lee Trevino
Kentucky Derby
Canonero II (G. Avila, jockey)

Fashion

For Women: Hot pants save the day for the controversial midi, now used as a cover-up. No longer "drab and dowdy," it is slashed thigh high in front or on the side, revealing a sleek, booted, bare, or stockinged leg. Pants are suspendered and cuffed, worn below a bare midriff with a knit, velvet, or brocade vest and a number of varied accessories. Tie-dye shirts, slinky sweaters, halters, open-laced sandals, high and low boots, all in many colors, add to the wardrobe, Denim dungarees turn fashionable with do-it-yourself patches, butterflies, stars, and macramé belts. T-shirts are hand-painted with Disneyland pictures, but anything goes in front and back. The "military look" also becomes popular, with shoulder patches on coats, and insignias on everything from hot pants to bikinis. A nostalgia for the forties is apparent in wedgies and platform shoes, chubby jackets, and fake furs, the ¾-length pinstripe coat, herringbone tweeds, and striped skirts. Pants are pleated at the waist, worn with blouses flowing to the elbow or waist in soft, clinging fabrics with deep V necklines. Hems fall to about the knee. Hair is both long and short, cut to the shoulder but layered above in the shag or gypsy cut; teasing and spraying are out.

High-fashion notes: Syndica's layers of bubble-knit sweaters; Ungaro's hot pants

Kaleidoscope

- The *New York Times* publishes the first installment of "The Pentagon Papers" June 13, a secret (classified) history of American involvement in Vietnam since World War II.
- Seventy-five percent of those polled oppose the publication of "The Pentagon Papers"; 15 percent want to know more about "government secrecy."
- Attorney General John Mitchell denounces the federal courts for restricting his wiretapping privileges.
- The Supreme Court mandates busing as a means of school desegregation where no acceptable alternative is offered.
- President Nixon revives the Subversive Activities Control Board.
- Returning Vietnam veterans have an increasingly difficult time adjusting to a public that, according to a Harris Poll, considers them "suckers" for risking their lives "in the wrong place, at the wrong time."
- The Supreme Court rules that qualification for conscientious-objector status necessitates opposing all wars, not just Vietnam.
- Two thousand Vietnam veterans protest the war by throwing away their medals on the steps of the Capitol.
- The National Cancer Act is passed to provide $1.5 billion a year for research; the president has urged an all-out attempt to find a cure.
- The Senate votes down funding for an American supersonic transport, which leaves the field to the British-French Concorde.
- Nixon vetoes Congress's approval of the Child Development Act, which would authorize federal funding of child-care centers.
- A Yankelovich poll indicates that 34 percent of the general population believes marriage is obsolete, up from 24 percent in 1969.
- *Gourmet* magazine circulation doubles since 1967 to 550,000, and the fancy food industry rapidly expands.
- The Boston Women's Health Collective attacks the myth of the female vaginal orgasm and of lesbianism as a perversion.
- Mick and Bianca Jagger marry, and also become parents; Margaret Sinclair, 22, and Canadian prime minister Pierre Trudeau marry.
- A survey of upper-class women at a major eastern college indicates that 18 percent would stop working if they became mothers, compared with 59 percent in 1943.
- George Harrison appears in the Benefit for Bangladesh concert at Madison Square Garden.
- Diana Ross begins a solo career; the Beatles break up.
- Many traditional barbers go out of business or become hair stylists.
- Three-fourths of all moviegoers are under 30.
- Sears reprints its 1903, 1908, and 1927 catalogs after its 1902 edition sells 400,000 copies.
- William Reinquist becomes the fourth Nixon appointee to the Supreme Court.
- Ralph Nader contends that $1 billion is spent yearly

English model Twiggy, in *The Boyfriend;* her slender frame inspires a vogue. *Movie Star News.*

on worthless drugs and fraudulent home repairs.
- *Scientific American* devotes its September issue to "Energy and Power" and warns that the United States will face critical shortages by the year 2000.
- The FDA warns against mercury-tainted swordfish.
- Cigarette advertising is banned from TV.
- Beef consumption per capita rises from 113 pounds to 128.5 pounds.
- The nickel candy bar goes to 6 cents and 7 cents; Wrigley's gum is 10 cents for seven sticks (5 cents since 1893).
- Alleged Mafia leader Joseph Colombo organizes the Italo-American Unity Day in New York; at the parade, he is shot and left brain dead.
- *Look* magazine ceases publication.
- Billie Jean King becomes the first woman athlete to earn $100,000 in one year.

Fads: Gourmet foods, jogging, tote bags, directors' chairs

New Words and Usages: Think tank, demo, lib, body language, gross out, hot line, hot pants, right on, sexism, up front, workaholic

First Appearances: College with tuition based on family income (Beloit, Wisc.), the Jesus Movement, OTB, RMG (New York City), snowmobiles, EST, dunebuggies, *Family Circle* acquired by *New York Times,* Park Lane Hotel (New York City), ice skater to cover 100 miles in less than 6 hours, state litter legislation (Ore.), auto-train to transport passengers and their autos on the same train, road paved with glasphalt (Omaha, Neb.), public school built in conjunction with apartment house (Bronx, N.Y.), technical school for American Indians (Albuquerque, N.M.), state law banning sex discrimination (Wash.).

1972

Facts and Figures

Economic Profile
  Dow-Jones: ↑ High 1036–
    Low 921
  GNP: 0%
  Inflation: +4.3%
  Unemployment: 5.6%
TV production: 59,550,000
AM radio stations: 7,120
Household telephones: 92%
Toll rate: New York–San
  Francisco: $1.25
Advertising expenditures: $20
  billion
Altman's dynel wig: $20
Houbigant musk perfume oil:
  $3.50 (4 oz.)
Hoffritz mustache comb:
  $5.50
Saks Fifth Ave. suede jacket,
  plaid wool lining: $150
All-weather Apollo jacket:
  $29.50
Stowe, skiing (Stowehof Inn);
  $252 (5 days)
Concord Hotel, New York:
  $130 (6 days)
Mercedes 250: $7,800
Hornet: $2,995
Duster: $1,993

Deaths

John Berryman, William
  Boyd, Maurice Chevalier,
  Brian Donlevy, Rudolph
  Friml, Gil Hodges, George
  Sanders, Helen Traubel,
  Harry S Truman, Walter
  Winchell.

In the News

U.S. AND USSR TO POOL MEDICAL RESEARCH . . . ALABAMA GOVERNOR GEORGE WALLACE ENTERS DEMOCRATIC PRIMARIES . . . ATTORNEY GENERAL JOHN MITCHELL RESIGNS, WILL HEAD COMMITTEE TO REELECT THE PRESIDENT . . . NIXON CONFERS WITH MAO IN CHINA . . . U.S. SUSPENDS PARIS TALKS . . . NORTH VIETNAM LAUNCHES MAJOR EASTER OFFENSIVE . . . CHARLIE CHAPLIN RETURNS TO U.S. AFTER 20 YEARS ABROAD . . . U.S. BOMBS HAIPHONG FOR THE FIRST TIME SINCE 1968 . . . J. EDGAR HOOVER DIES . . . U.S. MINES HAIPHONG HARBOR . . . WALLACE IS SHOT IN LAUREL, MD., AND PARALYZED . . . NIXON AND BREZHNEV SIGN TWO SALT AGREEMENTS . . . ANGELA DAVIS IS ACQUITTED OF MURDER IN CALIFORNIA . . . SOCIAL SECURITY IS INCREASED 20% . . . U.S. WILL SELL USSR $750 MILLION IN GRAIN . . . DEMOCRATS NOMINATE GEORGE McGOVERN FOR PRESIDENT AND THOMAS EAGLETON FOR VICE PRESIDENT . . . SADAT EXPELS SOVIETS . . . EAGLETON REVEALS HOSPITALIZATION FOR DEPRESSION, IS REPLACED BY SARGENT SHRIVER . . . SENATE APPROVES SALT . . . LAST U.S. GROUND TROOPS LEAVE VIETNAM . . . 11 ISRAELIS ARE KILLED BY PALESTINIAN TERRORISTS AT MUNICH OLYMPICS . . . AGRICULTURE SECRETARY EARL BUTZ DENIES THAT GRAIN SALE LEAK LED TO WINDFALL PROFITS . . . BREAK-IN OCCURS AT DEMOCRATIC HEADQUARTERS IN WATERGATE BUILDING, FIVE ARE CAUGHT . . . KISSINGER AND LE DUC THO TALK IN PARIS . . . NORTH VIETNAM ACCEPTS CEASE-FIRE, THIEU REJECTS PLAN . . . "WASHINGTON POST" CONNECTS WATERGATE WITH COMMITTEE TO REELECT THE PRESIDENT . . . NIXON WINS LANDSLIDE VICTORY, 47 MILLION TO 29 MILLION, DEMOCRATS KEEP CONGRESS . . . DOW JONES TOPS 1,000 . . . U.S. RESUMES BOMBING OF HANOI AND HAIPHONG.

Quotes

"What really hurts is if you try to cover it up. . . . I can categorically say that no one on the present White House staff, no one in this administration, presently employed, was involved in this very bizarre incident."
— Richard M. Nixon, on the Watergate break-in

"I'm not going to comment on a third-rate burglary attempt."
— Ron Ziegler, press secretary

"All that crap, you're putting it in the paper? It's all been denied. [*Washington Post* publisher] Katie Graham's gonna get her tit caught in a big fat wringer if that's published."
— John Mitchell

"I love my husband very much, but I'm not going to stand for all those dirty things that go on. . . . They threw me down on the bed—five men did it—and stuck a needle in my behind. . . . They're afraid of my honesty. . . . Yes, Martha's honesty."
— Martha Mitchell

"Once the toothpaste is out of the tube, it's hard to get it back in."
— H. R. Haldeman, presidential aide

"I'm 1000% for Tom Eagleton, and I have no intention of dropping him from the ticket."
— Senator George McGovern

Chou En Lai: "What do you think of the wall?"
Richard Nixon: "I think you would have to conclude that this is a great wall."
— Exchange during President Nixon's trip to China

"Everywhere new hopes are rising for a world no longer overshadowed by fear, and want and war."
— Richard M. Nixon, on the SALT signing

"You are only as good as the people you dress."
— Halston

Ads

Have you ever had a bad time in Levi's?
(Levi's)

What this commercial is trying to sell you won't make your breath any sweeter, your clothes any whiter or your acid indigestion any better. It'll just make you more human.
Support the Arts for your [own] sake.
(Business Committee for the Arts)

Women: Stand up for your right to sit down at dinner time.
(Salton Hottray)

Most women hear better than men, so when she screams turn down the sound what she really means is turn down the damn distortion because the distortion is driving her bananas.
(Marantz Stereo)

Play it again, Sam.
(New York State Lottery)

With a Timme fake you can have a beautiful tiger, and he can have his.
(Timme Fake Furs)

Consumer advocate, lawyer, and author Ralph Nader. *Movie Star News.*

Vacation is a world where there are no locks on the doors or the mind or the body.
(Club Med)

The rich need Volvos too.
(Volvo)

I'd like to teach the world to sing in perfect harmony, / I'd like to buy the world a Coke and keep it company. It's the Real Thing.
(Coca-Cola)

TV

Premieres

"Sanford and Son," Redd Fox, Demond Wilson
"The Streets of San Francisco," Karl Malden,
    Michael Douglas
"Maude," Beatrice Arthur
"M*A*S*H," Alan Alda, Wayne Rogers, Loretta
    Swit, McLean Stevenson
"The Joker's Wild," Jack Barry
"Kung Fu," David Carradine
"The Bob Newhart Show"
"The Waltons," Michael Learned, Ralph Waite,
    Richard Thomas

Top Ten (Nielsen)

"All in the Family," "Sanford and Son," "Hawaii
Five-O," "Maude," "Bridget Loves Bernie," "The
NBC Sunday Mystery Movie," "The Mary Tyler
Moore Show," "Gunsmoke," "The Wonderful World
of Disney," "Ironside"

Specials

"Long Day's Journey into Night" (Laurence Olivier);
" 'Sleeping Beauty': Bernstein in London"; "The
Marcus-Nelson Murders" (Telly Savalas); "A War of
Children" (James Costigan); "Singer Presents Liza";
"The U.S./Soviet Wheat Deal: Is There a Scandal?"
(Walter Cronkite); "The Watergate Affair" (CBS);
"The Great American Dream Machine"

Emmy Awards

"The Waltons" (drama); "All in the Family"
(comedy); "The Julie Andrews Hour" (variety);
Richard Thomas (actor, "The Waltons"); Jack
Klugman (comedic actor, "The Odd Couple");
Michael Learned (actress, "The Waltons"); Mary
Tyler Moore (comedic actress, "The Mary Tyler
Moore Show")

Of Note

Time/Life HBO, subscription cable TV, begins with a
National Hockey League contest and the film
"Sometimes a Great Notion" • Controversy builds
when mid-life "Maude" becomes pregnant and
decides, after much soul-searching, to have an
abortion • "That Certain Summer," with Hal
Holbrook and Martin Sheen, is an early TV drama on
male homosexuality.

Movies

Openings

The Godfather (Francis Ford Coppola), Marlon
    Brando, Al Pacino, James Caan, Robert Duvall
Cabaret (Bob Fosse), Liza Minnelli, Michael York,
    Joel Grey
Deliverance (John Boorman), Jon Voight, Burt
    Reynolds
Sounder (Martin Ritt), Cicely Tyson, Paul Winfield,
    Kevin Hooks
Sleuth (Joseph L. Mankiewicz), Laurence Olivier,
    Michael Caine
The Ruling Class (Peter Medak), Peter O'Toole,
    Harry Andrews
Lady Sings the Blues (Sidney J. Furie), Diana Ross,
    Billy Dee Williams, Richard Pryor
The Heartbreak Kid (Elaine May), Charles Grodin,
    Cybill Shepherd
The Candidate (Michael Ritchie), Robert Redford,
    Melvyn Douglas, Peter Boyle
The Discreet Charm of the Bourgeoisie (Luis
    Buñuel), Fernando Rey, Delphine Seyrig
The Poseidon Adventure (Ronald Neame), Gene
    Hackman, Ernest Borgnine, Shelley Winters
Cries and Whispers (Ingmar Bergman), Harriet
    Andersson, Ingrid Thulin, Liv Ullmann
Play It Again, Sam (Herbert Ross), Woody Allen,
    Diane Keaton, Tony Roberts
Last Tango in Paris (Bernardo Bertolucci), Marlon
    Brando, Maria Schneider
Deep Throat, Linda Lovelace, Harry Reems

Academy Awards

Best Picture: *The Godfather*
Best Director: Bob Fosse (*Cabaret*)
Best Actress: Liza Minnelli (*Cabaret*)
Best Actor: Marlon Brando (*The Godfather*)

Top Box-Office Stars

Clint Eastwood, Ryan O'Neal, Steve McQueen, Burt
Reynolds, Robert Redford, Barbra Streisand, Paul
Newman, Charles Bronson, John Wayne, Marlon
Brando

Stars of Tomorrow

Al Pacino, Edward Albert, Jeff Bridges, Joel Grey,
Sandy Duncan, Timothy Bottoms, Madeline Kahn,
Cybill Shepherd, Malcolm McDowell, Ron O'Neal

Popular Music

Hit Songs
"Let's Stay Together"
"I'd Like to Teach the World to
    Sing"
"Oh Girl"
"Lean on Me"
"Where Is the Love?"
"Alone Again (Naturally)"
"Anticipation"
"Last Night I Didn't Get to Sleep
    at All"
"I'll Take You There"

Top Records
Albums: *Music* (Carole King);
American Pie (Don McLean);
Chicago V (Chicago); *First Take*
(Roberta Flack); *America*
(America); *Honky Chateau* (Elton
John)

Singles: *The First Time Ever I
Saw Your Face* (Roberta Flack);
Candy Man (Sammy Davis, Jr.); *If
Loving You Is Wrong* (Luther
Ingram); *Rocket Man* (Elton
John); *Morning Has Broken* (Cat
Stevens); *Without You* (Nilsson); *I
Gotcha* (Joe Tex); *Baby Don't Get
Hooked on Me* (Mac Davis).
Country: *The Happiest Girl in the
Whole U.S.A.* (Donna Fargo); *All
His Children* (Charlie Pride)

Grammy Awards
*The First Time Ever I Saw Your
    Face,* Roberta Flack (record);
    The Concert for Bangla Desh,
    George Harrison et al. (album);
    "The First Time Ever I Saw
    Your Face" (song)

Jazz and Big Bands
The main part of the Newport
Jazz Festival moves to New York
City.

Top Performers *(Downbeat):*
Ornette Coleman (soloist); Thad
Jones and Mel Lewis (band);
Weather Report (jazz group);
Kenny Burrell, Richard Davis,
Herbie Hancock, Hubert Laws,
Wayne Shorter (instrumentalists):
Roberta Flack, Leon Thomas
(vocalists); Frank Zappa (rock/
blues musician); Blood, Sweat,
and Tears (vocal group);
Mahavishnu Orchestra, *Inner
Mounting Flame* (album)

Theater

Broadway Openings
Plays
The Sunshine Boys (Neil Simon), Jack Albertson,
    Sam Levene
The Last of Mrs. Lincoln (James Prideaux), Julie
    Harris
Butley (Simon Gray), Alan Bates
Vivat! Vivat Regina! (Robert Bolt), Claire Bloom,
    Eileen Atkins
Moon Children (Michael Weller), James Woods,
    Kevin Conway, Edward Herrmann
6 Rms Riv Vu (Bob Randall), Jerry Orbach, Jane
    Alexander
Night Watch (Lucille Fletcher), Joan Hackett, Len
    Cariou
The Creation of the World and Other Business
    (Arthur Miller), Zoë Caldwell, George Grizzard

Musicals
Grease (Jim Jacobs, Warren Casey), Barry Bostwick,
    Carole Demas
Pippin (Stephen Schwartz), Ben Vereen, John
    Rubinstein, Jill Clayburgh
Sugar (Jule Styne, Bob Merrill), Tony Roberts,
    Elaine Joyce, Robert Morse, Cyril Ritchard

Classics, Revivals, and Off-Broadway
    Premieres
The Country Girl (Clifford Odets), Jason Robards,
Maureen Stapleton, George Grizzard; *Captain
Brassbound's Conversion* (George Bernard Shaw),

Ingrid Bergman; *Mourning Becomes Electra* (Eugene
O'Neill), Colleen Dewhurst; *That Championship
Season* (Jason Miller), Michael McGuire, Walter
McGinn; *Don't Bother Me I Can't Cope* (Micki
Grant); *Small Craft Warnings* (Tennessee Williams),
The Great God Brown (Eugene O'Neill), Patrick
Macnee, Jordan Christopher; *Much Ado about
Nothing,* Sam Waterston, Kathleen Widdoes; *The
Real Inspector Hound, After Magritte* (Tom
Stoppard), Carrie Nye. Founded: The Acting
Company by John Houseman and Margot Harley;
Negro Ensemble Company: *The River Niger* (Joseph
A. Walker), Douglas Turner Ward, premiere

Regional

Long Wharf, New Haven: *The Changing Room*
(David Storey), premiere

Cleveland: *A Yard of Sun* (Christopher Fry),
directed by José Ferrer, premiere

A.C.T., San Francisco: *The Mystery Cycles* (Nagle
Jackson)

Pulitzer Prize
No prize is awarded.

Tony Awards
Sticks and Bones, David Rabe (play), *Two Gentlemen
of Verona,* Galt MacDermot, John Guare (musical)

Classical Music

Compositions

Elliott Carter, String Quartet, no. 3
Aaron Copland, Three Latin-American Sketches
George Rochberg, String Quartet no. 3,
    Electrikaleidoscope
Lukas Foss, *Cave of the Winds*
Earle Brown, *Time Spans, Sign Sounds*

Important Events

New facilities include Philharmonic Hall, Miami;
Eastman Theater (renovated), Rochester, N.Y.;
Indiana University $11.3 million Musical Arts
Theater; and the University of Cincinnati Patricia
Corbett Pavillion.
Centennials of Ralph Vaughan Williams and
Alexander Scriabin are celebrated.
Interesting concerts include a musical marathon of
sixteen pianists at Carnegie Hall, at which Czerny's
Overture to Rossini's *Semiramide* is performed on
eight pianos, and John Philip Sousa's *Stars and
Stripes,* on ten; the Bach Aria Group celebrates its
25th anniversary with a cantata aria series; the J. F.
Kennedy Center performs 31 concerts in a 12-day
series with "The Old and the New" (a survey of
Italian Baroque to modern music).
Murray Perahia is the first American to win the
Leeds International Pianoforte Competition.

Debuts: Eugene Fodor, Radu Lupu, Vladimir
Pleshakov

First Performances

Jacob Druckman, *Windows* (Chicago); Olivier
Messiaen, *La transfiguration de notre seigneur,*
Jésus-Christ (Washington, D.C.); John La Montaine,
Wilderness Journal (Washington, D.C.); Oscar
Morawetz, *From the Diary of Anne Frank* (New
York)

Opera

Metropolitan: Final new Bing productions: Teresa
Zylis-Gara, James McCracken, *Otello;* Marilyn
Horne, James McCracken, *Carmen* (Leonard
Bernstein, conducting); Montserrat Caballé, *Don
Carlo;* Joan Sutherland, *Norma;* Sherrill Milnes,
Sutherland, Luciano Pavarotti, *Rigoletto;* Anja Silja
(debut), *Fidelio*

New York City: Beverly Sills, *Maria Stuarda;* Sills,
Norman Treigle, *Les contes d'Hoffmann*

Atlanta: *Treemonisha* (Scott Joplin, premiere)

Seattle: *Black Widow* (Thomas Pasatieri)

Chicago: *I due Foscari* (Verdi)

San Francisco: Regina Resnik, *The Visit*

Boston: Régine Crespin, *Les Troyens* (first U.S.
complete staging)

Music Notes

On January 26, bombs explode in Sol Hurok's offices
in protest against the importation of Russian artists; a
receptionist is killed.

Cicely Tyson wins an Academy Award nomination for her
role in *Sounder,* about black sharecroppers during the
depression. *Movie Star News.*

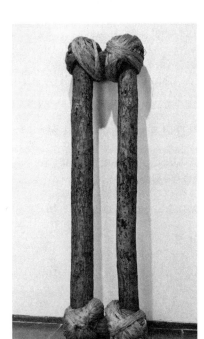

Jackie Winsor,
Bound Logs, 1972–
1973. Wood and
hemp, 114 × 29 ×
18". *Collection of
Whitney Museum of
American Art. Gift
of the Howard and
Jean Lipman
Foundation, Inc.*

Art

Painting
Robert Mangold,
*Incomplete Circle
No. 2*
Andrew Wyeth, *Bale*
Richard Serra, *Untitled*
Thomas Hart Benton,
*Turn of the Century
Joplin*
Jules Olitski, *Willemite's
Vision*
Brice Marden, *Star (for
Patti Smith)*
Adja Yunkers, *The
Pinned-Up Woman*

Sculpture
Tony Smith, *Gracehoper*
H. C. Westermann,
*American Death Ship
on the Equator*
Sylvia Stone, *Another
Place*
Jackie Winsor, *Bound
Logs, Bound Square*

Architecture
Kimball Art Museum,
Fort Worth, Texas
(Louis I. Kahn)

One Shell Plaza,
Houston (Skidmore,
Owings & Merrill)
Graduate School of
Design, Harvard
University,
Cambridge, Mass.
(Andrews, Anderson,
Baldwin)
College Life Insurance
Company, Indianapolis
(Roche and Dinkeloo)
One Liberty Plaza, New
York (Skidmore,
Owings and Merrill)
Pennsylvania Mutual
Life Insurance
Company building,
Philadelphia (Romaldo
Giurgola)
Federal Reserve Bank,
Minneapolis (Gunnar
Birkerts)
Crown Center, Kansas
City, Mo. (Edward
Larrabee Barnes)
Omni Coliseum, Atlanta,
(Thompson, Ventulett
and Stainbeck)

Important Exhibitions
Exhibits of Soviet arts and crafts, as well as Mexican
decorative arts, tour the United States. Numerous
American Indian and Eskimo art shows also tour.

Museums

New York: *Metropolitan:* Chinese calligraphy;
Lipchitz. *Museum of Modern Art:* Modern European
sculpture; Matisse; The 90th birthday of Picasso is
celebrated with a show of 84 paintings, 69 works of
sculpture. *Guggenheim:* Mondrian centennial; Rodin.
Cultural Center: Giorgio de Chirico retrospective.

Boston: Ancient art of the Americas

Washington: National parks and the American
landscape

Minneapolis, Toledo: Dutch masterpieces of the 18th
century; Matisse

Los Angeles: Gericault; The American West

Buffalo: Nostalgia for the fifties: Pollock, de
Kooning, Gorky, Guston, Still, Kline, Motherwell,
Rothko, Frankenthaler

Cleveland: Caravaggio and his followers

Art Briefs
Accused of discrimination against women and blacks,
the Whitney devotes its 40th Annual to both groups •
Women artists become active in (1) workshops with
Kate Millet and Yoko Ono, (2) the New York Interart
Center, and (3) "Dream-Space" in Los Angeles •
James Rosenquist gains a great deal of attention with
F-111, 86 feet long • A 1914 living room of Frank
Lloyd Wright, from Wayzata, Minnesota, is installed
in the Metropolitan Museum of Art • Moore's
Reclining Figure is auctioned for $260,000 • The
Norton Simon Foundation pays a record $3 million
for Zubarán's *Still Life* • Headline news reports that
Michelangelo's *Pièta* in St. Peter's basilica has been
badly damaged by a deranged man with a 12-pound
hammer • Christo's $700,000 *Orange Valley Curtain,*
made of parachute cloth, is torn to ribbons by a wind
storm at Rifle Gap, Colo.

Dance

Ballet attendance increases 500 percent since 1905,
with dance performances increasing 600 percent.
At the New York State Theatre celebration of
Stravinsky's birthday (he would have been 90),
Balanchine stages nine ballets to Stravinsky's music,
including *Duo Concertante, Pulcinella,* and the
Violin Concerto.
Benjamin Harkarvy becomes co-artistic director of
the Pennsylvania Ballet.

Premieres

New York City Ballet: *Watermill* (Jerome Robbins),
Edward Villella

Boston Ballet: *Les Sylphides,* Liliana Cosi

Ballet of the 20th Century: *Nijinsky Clown of God*
(Maurice Béjart), Jorge Donn

Twyla Tharp: *Raggedy Dances* (Scott Joplin,
Mozart), *The Bix Pieces*

Alvin Ailey: *The Lark Ascending*

Books —————————————————————

Fiction
Critics' Choice
Chimera, John Barth
The Breast, Philip Roth
The Western Coast, Paula Fox
I Am Elijah Thrush, James Purdy
Mumbo-Jumbo, Ishmael Reed
Fredi and Shirl and the Kid,
    Richard Elman
Augustus, John Williams
The Sunlight Dialogues, John
    Gardner

Best-Sellers
Jonathan Livingston Seagull,
    Richard Bach
August 1914, Alexander
    Solzhenitsyn
The Odessa File, Frederick
    Forsyth
The Day of the Jackal, Frederick
    Forsyth
The Word, Irving Wallace
The Winds of War, Herman Wouk
Captains and the Kings, Taylor
    Caldwell
Two from Galilee, Marjorie
    Holmes
My Name Is Asher Lev, Chaim
    Potok
Semi-Tough, Dan Jenkins

Nonfiction
Critics' Choice
Who Pushed Humpty Dumpty?
    Donald Barr

The New 100 Years War, Georgie
    Geyer
The Closing Circle, Barry
    Commoner
The Children of Pride, Robert
    Manson Myers
The New Chastity, Midge Dechter
Papers on the War, Daniel
    Ellsberg
The Boys of Summer, Roger Kahn
*The United States and the Origins
    of the Cold War 1941–1947*,
    John Lewis Gaddis
Eleanor: The Years Alone, Joseph
    P. Lash
A Study in Suicide, A. Alvarez
Intuition, R. Buckminster Fuller
*George Washington: Anguish and
    Farewell (1793–1799)*, James
    Thomas Flexner

Best-Sellers
The Living Bible, Kenneth Taylor
I'm O.K., You're O.K., Thomas
    Harris
Open Marriage, Nena O'Neill,
    George O'Neill
Harry S Truman, Margaret
    Truman
Dr. Atkins' Diet Revolution,
    Robert A. Atkins
*Better Homes and Gardens Menu
    Cook Book*
The Peter Prescription, Laurence
    J. Peter
A World Beyond, Ruth
    Montgomery

Journey to Ixtlan, Carlos
    Castaneda
*Better Homes and Gardens Low-
    Calorie Desserts*

Poetry
John Berryman, *Delusions, Etc.*
James Merrill, *Braving the
    Elements*
Howard Nemerov, *Gnomes and
    Occasions*
A. R. Ammons, *Collected Poems,
    1951–1971*
Sylvia Plath, *Winter Trees*
James Tate, *Absences*
Nikki Giovanni, *My House*
John Ashbery, *Three Poems*

Pulitzer Prizes
The Optimist's Daughter, Eudora
    Welty (fiction)
*People of Paradox: An Inquiry
    Concerning the Origin of
    American Civilization*, Michael
    Kammen (U.S. history)
*Fire in the Lake: The Vietnamese
    and the Americans in Vietnam*,
    Frances FitzGerald (nonfiction)
Children of Crisis, vols. 1 and 2,
    Robert Coles (nonfiction)
Luce and His Empire, W. A.
    Swanberg (biography)
Up Country, Maxine Kumin
    (poetry)

Science and Technology —————————

Genetic engineering, biochemical methods of joining
    genes, is developed.
The sites of DNA production on genes are
    discovered.
Hexachlorophene is ordered off the market by the
    FDA; it causes brain lesions in monkeys and is
    suspect in several newborn deaths.
Storage software is marketed by IBM.
Einstein's prediction of a time difference in a moving
    clock is validated.
Pioneer X is launched to explore the nature of the
    asteroid belt and Jupiter.
Apollo XVII is the sixth and last currently planned
    lunar landing; manned by Eugene Cernan,

Ronald Evans, and Harrison Schmitt, it returns
    with 250 pounds of samples.
≈ A brainscanner is introduced (in England), which
    provides cross sectional X rays; the technique is
    called Computerized Axial Tomography, CAT.

Nobel Prize
John Bardeen, Leon N. Cooper, and John R.
Schrieffer win in physics for work on the theory of
superconductivity. G. M. Edelman wins in
physiology and medicine for work on antibodies. C.
B. Anfinsen, Stanford Moore, and William H. Stein
win in chemistry, for research on enzymes.

Sports

Baseball

The Players Association strike delays the season's opening 13 days, the first major sports strike.

Roberto Clemente (Pittsburgh, NL) gets his 3,000th hit in his last at-bat of the season. In December, he dies in a plane crash while taking part in the Nicaragua earthquake relief effort.

The Cy Young awards go to Steve Carlton (Philadelphia, NL) and Gaylord Perry (Cleveland, AL).

Champions

Batting	NL), 15–5
Billy Williams (Chicago,	Catfish Hunter (Oakland,
NL), .333	AL), 21–7
Rod Carew (Minnesota,	*Home runs*
AL), .318	Johnny Bench (Cincinnati,
Pitching	NL), 40
Gary Nolan (Cincinnati,	

Football

The undefeated Miami Dolphins win a record 17 straight games; Larry Czonka and Mercury Morris both rush over 1,000 yards.

NFC Season Leaders: Fran Tarkenton (Minnesota), passing; Larry Brown (Washington), rushing; Harold Jackson (Philadelphia) receiving

College All-Americans: Randy Gradishar (LB), Penn State; John Hannah (G), Alabama; Otis Armstrong (B), Purdue

Bowls (Jan. 1, 1973)

Rose: Southern	Cotton: Texas 17–
California 42–Ohio	Alabama 13
State 19	Sugar: Oklahoma 14–
Orange: Nebraska 40–	Penn State 0
Notre Dame 6	

Basketball

NBA All-Pro First Team: John Havlicek (Boston), Spencer Haywood (Seattle), Kareem Abdul-Jabbar (Milwaukee), Walt Frazier (New York), Gail Goodrich (Los Angeles)

ABA Stars: Don Issel (Kentucky), Rick Barry (New York), Artis Gilmore (Kentucky), Dan Freeman (Dallas)

Olympics

At Munich, Arab terrorists seize Israeli Olympians as hostages, and eleven die in an attempt to free them. Swimmer Mark Spitz wins a record seven gold medals. Other American winners include Vincent Matthews (400m, 44.6s). Frank Shorter (marathon, 2:12:19.7), and Melissa Belote (2 in swimming). The USSR beats the United States in basketball for the first time on a disputed continuation of the game, after the United States had originally won. In the Winter Games at Sapporo, Japan, Anne Henning (500m, 42.3s.), Diane Holum (1500m, 2:20.8), and Barbara Cochran (slalom) win.

Winners

World Series	*MVP*
Oakland (AL) 4	Kareem Abdul-Jabbar,
Cincinnati (NL) 3	Milwaukee
MVP	*College Basketball*
NL–Johnny Bench,	UCLA
Cincinnati	*Player of the Year*
AL–Dick Allen, Chicago	Bill Walton
Super Bowl VII (Jan. 1973)	*Stanley Cup*
Miami 14–Washington 7	Boston
MVP	*US Tennis Open*
Larry Brown, Washington	Men: Ille Nastase
College Football	Women: Billie Jean King
Southern California	*USGA Open*
Heisman Trophy	Jack Nicklaus
Johnny Rodgers, Nebraska	*Kentucky Derby*
NBA Championship	Riva Ridge (R. Turcotte,
Los Angeles 4–New York 1	jockey)

Fashion

For Women: Despite hot pants in mini lengths, it is width, rather than length, that makes the news: tent coats, beltless chemises, bat-wing sleeves, and evening caftans. Influencing style is the president's visit to China, after which lacquer-red colors, silk evening pajamas, and lotus and patterned gowns appear. The London King Tutankhamen exhibit prompts colorful Nile prints. Pants are replaced by beltless chemises and two-piece sweater dresses; "natural" and "organic" makeups gain a following.

High-fashion notes: Peretti's ivory egg pendant; Dior's cuffed trousers; Ruffin's T-shirt dress of polyester jersey; wooden combs for the Afro/natural hairdo; Cartier's tank watch

For Men: The male "peacock revolution" *(Esquire)* is at a peak with straight hip huggers or flared and cuffed bell bottoms. Men of all ages wear large herringbones and suits in colorful prints, heavy wools in lumber jacket plaids, the Hudson Bay blanket coat, and in spring, the twenties off-white suit. There is also an interesting display of chest hair. The British "bobby" coat in navy blue melton with silver buttons and whistle becomes popular for both men and women, an example of the unisex clothing revolution.

Kaleidoscope —————

- The budget of the Law Enforcement Assistance Administration goes from $63 million to $700 million.
- In a 5-to-4 decision, the Supreme Court rules that capital punishment is "cruel and unusual punishment," pending further legislation from the states.
- A black political convention is organized in Gary, Ind., at which New York representative Shirley Chisholm announces her candidacy for president.
- The number of fast-food establishments increases to 6,784 (3,418, in 1967; 1,120, in 1958).
- High-rated TV "Bridget Loves Bernie" is canceled because religious groups object to its intermarriage (Catholic-Jewish) situation. The stars marry in real life.
- David Bowie introduces "glitter rock."
- The Rolling Stones earn $4 million in a 30-city tour and appear before 750,000 people.
- The first graphically erotic movie with a major star opens— *Last Tango in Paris,* with Marlon Brando.
- Porno films find a wide audience and include *Deep Throat* and an X-rated cartoon, *Fritz the Cat;* sex-oriented radio programs also become popular (Bill Ballance, KGBS, Los Angeles).
- After 3,242 performances, *Fiddler on the Roof* closes, the longest running show in Broadway history.
- China sends a pair of giant pandas to Washington.
- Bobby Fisher beats Boris Spassky and becomes the first American world chess champion.
- McGraw-Hill proudly announces the publication of a long-awaited Howard Hughes autobiography; the book turns out to be a fraud perpetrated by Clifford Irving, who has received a $750,000 advance.
- Frank Sinatra is subpoened by a House committee on crime and indignantly denies all Mafia connections: "I'm not a second-class citizen," he states; "Let's get that straight."
- Mafia boss Joey Gallo is shot during a birthday party at Umberto's Clam House in New York; 26 flower-decked limosines serve in his funeral cortege.

Henry Kissinger, U.S. representative to the Paris peace talks, at the Playboy Club, Chicago. *Courtesy Morton Tanner.*

"M*A*S*H" begins with low TV ratings, but CBS gives it time to build an audience. *Movie Star News.*

- The Massachusetts Supreme Court rules unconstitutional the law prohibiting the sale of contraceptives to single persons.
- Jack Anderson accuses Acting Attorney General R. Kleindienst of settling an ITT antitrust case for a $400,000 contribution to the GOP convention.
- Congress passes Title IX, which entitles women to participate equally in all areas of sports.
- Published annual salaries include the following: Julia Child ("French Chef," $13,000), Walter Cronkite (CBS, $250,000), Hugh Hefner (*Playboy,* $303,847), Tom Seaver (New York Mets, $120,000), Harold S. Geneen (ITT, $382,494), Thomas Watson, Jr. (IBM, $413,735); Gaspare Greco (subway pretzel vendor, $2,600), Sue Long (second-grade private-school teacher, $7,500).
- Items in the Watergate burglars' possession include: one AWOL bag, 39 rolls of film, two spotlight bulbs and clamps, one extension cord, one small battery, one screwdriver, one roll of black tape, one piece of white plastic, four sponges, and one pair of needle-nose pliers.

Fads: Health food, acupuncture, pinball, Jesus freaks, TM (transcendental meditation)

First Appearances: Walter Pollution Control Act, Washington, D.C., Metro, bank to provide motion pictures for its customers waiting in line (Chemical, New York), corporation to have more than 3 million stockholders (AT&T), electric power using municipal refuse as a boiler fuel (Union Electric, St. Louis, Mo.), acupuncture treatment center (New York), statewide noise-control legislation (New Jersey), block of four postage stamps combined in 1 design in which each stamp is an entity (Cape Hatteras National Seashore stamps), pictorial postal card, Polaroid SC-70, pocket calculators, electronic lock and key system with plastic card

1973

The great red spot on Jupiter,
the photo taken by Pioneer
10, launched in 1972.
Courtesy NASA.

In the News

U.S. SUSPENDS ALL ACTIVITIES OVER NORTH VIETNAM . . . MARCOS
DECLARES INDEFINITE MARTIAL LAW IN PHILIPPINES . . . SUPREME
COURT RULES ALL FIRST-TRIMESTER ANTIABORTION LAWS
UNCONSTITUTIONAL . . . KISSINGER AND LE DUC THO AGREE TO
CEASE-FIRE . . . DEFENSE SECRETARY LAIRD SAYS DRAFT WILL END
. . . U.S. AND CUBA SIGN ANTIHIJACK PACT . . . MCCORD LETTER
TO JUDGE JOHN SIRICA IMPLICATES COMMITTEE TO REELECT THE
PRESIDENT . . . MILITANT INDIANS SEIZE HOSTAGES AT WOUNDED
KNEE, S.D. . . . LAST U.S. COMBAT TROOPS LEAVE VIETNAM . . .
ERVIN SENATE COMMITTEE BEGINS WATERGATE HEARINGS . . . JOHN
DEAN, PRESIDENTIAL COUNSEL, IMPLICATES THE PRESIDENT . . .
NIXON ADMITS MAJOR WATERGATE RESPONSIBILITY AND ANNOUNCES
RESIGNATION OF HALDEMAN AND EHRLICHMAN . . . MITCHELL AND
STANS ARE INDICTED . . . ALL CHARGES AGAINST DANIEL ELLSBERG
ARE DROPPED . . . ARCHIBALD COX IS APPOINTED SPECIAL
WATERGATE PROSECUTOR . . . BRANDT AND BREZHNEV SIGN 10-YEAR
PACT . . . MONARCHY IS ABOLISHED IN GREECE, DEMOCRACY IS
ESTABLISHED . . . NIXON'S SECRET TAPING SYSTEM IS REVEALED . . .
LAST PRICE CONTROLS ARE LIFTED . . . SIRICA ORDERS TAPE
RELEASE, NIXON REFUSES . . . JUAN PERON IS ELECTED PRESIDENT OF
ARGENTINA . . . SALVADOR ALLENDE TAKES HIS LIFE AS CHILEAN
MILITARY OVERTHROWS HIM . . . SYRIA AND EGYPT ATTACK ISRAEL
ON YOM KIPPUR . . . AGNEW RESIGNS, PLEADING "NOLO
CONTENDERE" TO CORRUPTION CHARGES . . . GERALD FORD IS
APPOINTED V.P. . . . OPEC IMPOSES OIL EMBARGO . . . NIXON
DISMISSES COX OVER WEEKEND . . . ISRAEL RETAKES SINAI, GOLAN,
NEGEV . . . CEASE-FIRE IS AGREED TO IN MIDEAST . . . ALASKAN
PIPELINE IS AUTHORIZED . . . MILITARY RETAKES POWER IN GREECE.

Senate Watergate Committee: standing (left to right)—
Lowell Weicker (R-Conn.), Daniel Inouye (D-Hawaii),
Herman Talmadge (D-Ga.), Edward Gurney (R-Fla.);
seated (left to right)—Howard Baker (R-Tenn.), Sam Ervin
(D-So. Car.). *U.S. Senate.*

Quotes

"Lee took the blame. 'It was all my fault,' he said to
Pickett's troops. That's quite different from some
people I know."

— Senator Sam Ervin

". . . a beauty contest."

— Spiro Agnew, on the Ervin committee

"We have a cancer within, close to the presidency,
that is growing."

— John Dean to Richard M. Nixon

"People have got to know whether or not their
President is a crook. Well, I'm not a crook."

— Richard M. Nixon

"I have had to speak against the President of the
United States."

— John W. Dean

"I was hoping you fellows wouldn't ask me about
that."

— Alexander Butterfield, about the White House
taping system

"Under the doctrine of separation of powers, . . . the
President is not subject to questioning by another
branch of government."

— Richard M. Nixon

"Executive poppycock."

— Senator Sam Ervin

"It's beginning to be like the Teapot Dome. There's a
smell to it; let's get rid of the smell."

— Senator Barry Goldwater (R-Ariz.)

"Every tree in the forest will fall."

— James McCord, accused Watergate burglar

"I'll probably do better in the next four years, having
gone through a few crises in the White House. I
confront tough problems without flapping. Actually, I
have a reputation for being the coolest person in the
room. I've trained myself to be that."

— Richard M. Nixon

"The burglers who broke into the Democratic
National Committee were in effect breaking into the
home of every American."

— Senator Sam Ervin (D-N. Car.)

"There can be no whitewash at the White House."

— Richard M. Nixon

Ads

TV

Premieres
"Barnaby Jones," Buddy Ebsen
"Kojak," Telly Savalas
"Police Story," Ed Asner
"The Young and the Restless"
"The Six-Million-Dollar Man," Lee Majors

Top Ten (Nielsen)
"All in the Family," "The Waltons," "Sanford and Son," "M*A*S*H," "Hawaii Five-O," "Maude," "Kojak," "The Sonny and Cher Comedy Hour," "The Mary Tyler Moore Show," "Cannon"

Specials
"Marlo Thomas and Friends in Free to Be . . . You and Me"; "The Autobiography of Miss Jane Pittman" (Cicely Tyson); "Pueblo" (Hal Holbrook): "The Merchant of Venice" (Laurence Olivier); "The Execution of Private Slovik" (Martin Sheen); "A Case of Rape" (Elizabeth Montgomery); "Watergate: The White House Transcripts" (CBS); "Watergate Coverage" (PBS); "America's Nerve Gas Arsenal" (NBC); "Solzhenitsyn" (CBS); "Steambath" (Bruce Jay Friedman); "QB VII" (Anthony Hopkins)

Emmy Awards
"Upstairs, Downstairs" (drama); "M*A*S*H" (comedy); "The Carol Burnett Show" (variety); "A Charlie Brown Thanksgiving" (children); Telly Savalas (actor, "Kojak"); Alan Alda (comedic actor, "M*A*S*H"); Michael Learned (actress, "The Waltons"); Mary Tyler Moore (comedic actress, "The Mary Tyler Moore Show")

Of Note
Particularly popular are shows about families like "The Waltons" • 50 percent of the new programs are on law and order.

Movies

Openings
The Sting (George Roy Hill), Paul Newman, Robert Redford, Robert Shaw
American Graffiti (George Lucas), Richard Dreyfuss, Ronny Howard
The Exorcist (William Friedkin), Ellen Burstyn, Max Von Sydow, Linda Blair
Mean Streets (Martin Scorsese), Robert De Niro, Harvey Keitel
Sleeper (Woody Allen), Woody Allen, Diane Keaton
Save the Tiger (John G. Avildsen), Jack Lemmon, Jack Gilford
The Last Detail (Hal Ashby), Jack Nicholson, Otis Young, Randy Quaid
Serpico (Sidney Lumet), Al Pacino, John Randolph
A Touch of Class (Melvin Frank), George Segal, Glenda Jackson
The Way We Were (Sydney Pollack), Barbra Streisand, Robert Redford
The Paper Chase (James Bridges), Timothy Bottoms, John Houseman, Lindsay Wagner
Bang the Drum Slowly (John Hancock), Michael Moriarty, Robert De Niro, Vincent Gardenia
Scenes from a Marriage (Ingmar Bergman), Liv Ullmann, Erland Josephson
Day for Night (François Truffaut), François Truffaut, Jacqueline Bisset, Valentina Cortese
Blume in Love (Paul Mazursky), George Segal, Susan Anspach, Kris Kristofferson

Produced on a "Head Start" grant and aimed at teaching letters and numbers to ghetto preschoolers, Jim Henson's "Sesame Street" continues its great success. *Billy Rose Theatre Collection. The New York Public Library at Lincoln Center. Astor, Lenox and Tilden Foundations.*

Academy Awards
Best Picture: *The Sting*
Best Director: George Roy Hill (*The Sting*)
Best Actress: Glenda Jackson (*A Touch of Class*)
Best Actor: Jack Lemmon (*Save the Tiger*)

Top Box-Office Stars
Clint Eastwood, Ryan O'Neal, Steve McQueen, Burt Reynolds, Robert Redford, Barbra Streisand, Paul Newman, Charles Bronson, John Wayne, Marlon Brando

Stars of Tomorrow
Diana Ross, Michael Moriarty, Marsha Mason, Joe Don Baker, Jeannie Berlin, Candy Clark, Robert De Niro, Jan-Michael Vincent, Tatum O'Neal

Popular Music ━━━━━━━━━━━━━━━━━━━━━━━━━━━━

Hit Songs
"Tie a Yellow Ribbon"
"Delta Dawn"
"Let's Get It On"
"Me and Mrs. Jones"
"Bad, Bad Leroy Brown"
"Why Me?"
"Rocky Mountain High"
"Natural High"
"Could It Be I'm Falling in
   Love?"

Top Records

Albums: *Goodbye Yellow Brick Road* (Elton John); *No Secrets* (Carly Simon); *Living in the Material World* (George Harrison); *Chicago VI* (Chicago); *Brothers and Sisters* (Allman Brothers Band); *Goat's Head Soup* (Rolling Stones)

Singles: *Killing Me Softly with His Song* (Roberta Flack); *You Are the Sunshine of My Life* (Stevie Wonder); *Touch Me in the Morning* (Diana Ross); *You're So Vain* (Carly Simon); *Crocodile Rock* (Elton John); *Will It Go Round in Circles?* (Billy Preston); *My Love* (Paul McCartney and Wings); *We're an American Band* (Grand Funk Railroad); *The Night the Lights Went Out in Georgia* (Vicki Lawrence). Country: *Behind Closed Doors* (Kenny O'Dell/Charlie Rich); *Till I Get It Right* (Tammy Wynette)

Grammy Awards
Killing Me Softly with His Song, Roberta Flack (record); *Innervisions,* Stevie Wonder (album); "Killing Me Softly with His Song," Roberta Flack (song)

Jazz and Big Bands
The New York Jazz Festival features swing musicians Benny Goodman, Gene Krupa, Lionel Hampton, and Slam Stewart.

Top Performers (*Downbeat*): Chick Corea (soloist); Thad Jones and Mel Lewis (band); Weather Report (jazz group); John McLaughlin, Ron Carter, Gary Burton, Billy Cobham, Freddie Hubbard (instrumentalists); Roberta Flack, Leon Thomas (vocalists); Stevie Wonder (rock/blues musician); Mahavishnu Orchestra (vocal group); Mahavishnu Orchestra, *Birds of Fire* (album)

Theater ━━━━━━━━━━━━━━━━━━━━━━━━━━━━━━━━━━

Broadway Openings

Plays
The Changing Room (David Storey), John Lithgow
The Jockey Club Stakes (William Douglas Home), Wilfred Hyde-White
Finishing Touches (Jean Kerr), Barbara Bel Geddes
Crown Matrimonial (Royce Ryton), Eileen Herlie, George Grizzard
Veronica's Room (Ira Levin), Arthur Kennedy, Eileen Heckart
The Good Doctor (Neil Simon), Christopher Plummer, Marsha Mason
Out Cry (Tennessee Williams), Michael York, Cara Duff-MacCormick
Hot L Baltimore (Lanford Wilson), Trish Hawkins, Judd Hirsch
The River Niger (Joseph A. Walker), Douglas Turner Ward, Les Roberts

Musicals
A Little Night Music (Stephen Sondheim), Glynis Johns, Len Cariou, Hermione Gingold
Seesaw (Cy Coleman, Dorothy Fields), Michele Lee, Ken Howard, Tommy Tune
Raisin (Judd Woldin, Robert Brittan), Virginia Capers, Joe Morton

Good Evening, revue written and performed by Peter Cook, Dudley Moore
The Tooth of Crime (Performance Group, Sam Shepard), Stephen Borst

Classics, Revivals, and Off-Broadway Premieres
A Moon for the Misbegotten (Eugene O'Neill), Colleen Dewhurst, Jason Robards; *Uncle Vanya* (Chekhov), George C. Scott, Nicol Williamson, Julie Christie, Lillian Gish; *A Streetcar Named Desire* (Tennessee Williams), Rosemary Harris; *Henry IV* (Pirandello), Rex Harrison; *The Iceman Cometh* (O'Neill), James Earl Jones; *The Contractor* (David Storey), Kevin O'Connor, George Taylor; *The Women* (Clare Boothe Luce), Dorothy Loudon, Myrna Loy, Kim Hunter, Rhonda Fleming; *Medea* (Euripides), Irene Papas; *When You Comin' Back, Red Ryder?* (Mark Medoff), Brad Dourif

Regional
Arena Stage, Washington, D.C.: Takes *Inherit the Wind* and *Our Town* to the Soviet Union, sponsored by the U.S. Department of State; *Raisin* (Robert Brittan, Judd Woldin); *A Public Prosecuter Is Sick of It All* (Max Frisch), premieres; *Bartholomew Fair* (Ben Jonson), American premiere

Theater (cont.)

Goodman, Chicago: *The Freedom of the City* (Brian Friel), premiere

Long Wharf, New Haven: *Forget-Me-Not Lane* (Peter Nichols); *The Widowing of Mrs. Holroyd* (D. H. Lawrence); *The Contractor* (David Storey), premieres

Minneapolis Theatre Company: *Cyrano* (musical by Anthony Burgess, Michael J. Lewis), Christopher Plummer

Pulitzer Prize
That Championship Season, Jason Miller

Tony Awards
That Championship Season, Jason Miller (play), *A Little Night Music,* Stephen Sondheim (musical)

Classical Music

Compositions
Donald Martino, *Notturno*
Virgil Thomson, *Cantata based on Nonsense Rhymes*
Peter Mennin, Symphony no. 8
Walter Piston, *Fantasy*
William Schuman, *A Story of Orpheus,* Concerto on Old English Rounds for Viola, Female Chorus, and Orchestra

Important Events
Gregor Piatigorsky is honored on his 70th birthday at Lincoln Center; Sol Hurok on his 85th (with vignettes by his star performers at the Met); John Cage, on his 60th birthday, is the subject of several retrospectives (New York, Boston).
Symphony of the New World presents "Black Week"; the New York Philharmonic gives Haydn and Stravinsky retrospectives.
The Philadelphia Orchestra is the first to tour the People's Republic of China.

Debut: Elmar Oliveira, Ida Levin

First Performances
Leonardo Balada, *Steel Symphony* (Pittsburgh); Arne Norheim, *Greeting* for Orchestra (Los Angeles); Louis Ballard, *Devil's Promenade* (Tulsa); Marvin David Levy, *Masada* (Washington, D.C.); Luciano Berio, Concerto for Two Pianos and Orchestra (New York)

Opera

Metropolitan: Nicolai Gedda, Raina Kabaivanska, *Pique Dame* (Tchaikovsky, in Russian); Montserrat Caballé, *Norma;* Shirley Verrett, Christa Ludwig, Jon Vickers, *Les Troyens;* Marilyn Horne, *L'Italiana in Algeri;* Clamma Dale, Hilda Harris, *Four Saints in Three Acts;* Carlo Cossutta (debut), *Norma;* Teresa Kubiak (debut), *Pique Dame;* "Opera at the Forum" begins (three short operas)

New York City: Beverly Sills, *Anna Bolena; The Young Lord* (Sarah Caldwell, conducting), with Rudolf Bing as Sir Edgar

Houston: William Dooley, Donald Gramm, John Alexander, *Don Carlos* (1867, 4½-hour version)

New Orleans: Carol Neblett, *Thaïs*

Boston: *Don Carlos* (in original Paris version of 1867); Emmett Kelly, Sr., Mary Costa, James Atherton, *The Bartered Bride; Mahagonny*

Santa Fe: *Melusine* (Reimann, premiere); Alan Titus, Regina Resnik, *Owen Wingrave* (Benjamin Britten)

Chicago: Montserrat Caballé, *Maria Stuarda;* Luciano Pavarotti, Ileana Cotrubas, *La bohème*

San Francisco: Jess Thomas, *Peter Grimes*

Music Notes
At the Norton Lectures, at Harvard, Leonard Bernstein draws a parallel between the structure of music and language • The New York Philharmonic institutes "Rug Concerts," where seats are removed and the audience sits on the floor and stage pillows • The Santa Fe Chamber Music Festival begins • Music and politics clash before Nixon's inauguration as (1) members of the New York Philharmonic Orchestra refuse to perform for a president whose politics they "deplore," (2) Charlton Heston reads portions of the Declaration of Independence against a musical background, and (3) Leonard Bernstein conducts *Mass in Time of War* at a "Counterconcert."

Art _____

Paintings

Jim Dine, *Untitled Tool Series*
Richard Artschwager, *Interior*
Jasper Johns, *Two Flags*
James Bishop, *Untitled, No. 2*
Andy Warhol, *Mao*
Al Held, *South Southwest*
Frank Stella, *Targowica*
Sam Francis, *Untitled #7*
David Hockney, *The Weather Series: Sun*

Sculpture

Robert Rauschenberg, *Untitled*
Donald Judd, *Untitled*
Christopher Wilmarth, *My Divider*
Brice Marden, *Grove Group, I*

Robert Smithson, *Amarillo Ramp*

Architecture

Frank House study, Cornwall, Conn. (Peter Eisenman)
Boston Public Library Wing (Philip Johnson, John Burgee)
Murray Lincoln Center, University of Massachusetts, Amherst (Marcel Breuer)
American Institute of Architects, Washington, D.C. (The Architects Collaborative)
IDS Center, Minneapolis (Johnson, Burgee)
88 Pine Street Building, New York (I. M. Pei)

Important Exhibitions

The United States hosts shows from the Soviet Union, China, India, and Japan, including "Impressionists and Post-Impressionists from the USSR," 41 paintings from the Hermitage and Pushkin museums.

Museums

New York: *Metropolitan:* American realism: Sargent, Robinson, Hassam, Chase; 125 photograhic works of Man Ray; Frank Lloyd Wright; Japanese work, 2700 B.C.–19th century. *Museum of Modern Art:* Ellsworth Kelly; Miró; Duchamp; Matisse's sculpture: "Collage and the Photo Image." *Guggenheim:* Miró, Dubuffet. *Whitney:* Nineteenth-century America. *Asia House:* Works, 1520–1900.

Chicago: Renoir; "Multitudinous uses of Gold"; The arts and crafts movement in America; Nineteenth-century America

Indianapolis: Religion in American art

Avant-garde Shows: Abstract art: Jules Olitski (Boston, Whitney); Morris Louis, Larry Poons (New York); Ellsworth Kelly, Philip Woffard (Washington)

Group Shows: "Women Choose Women: Unmanly Art" (New York Cultural Center); "The Art Heritage of Puerto Rico" (Museo del Barrio and Metropolitan Museum of Art); "United Graffiti Artists" (Razor Alley, New York); "The Art of Maximum Security Prisoners" (National Gallery); "Fakes and Forgeries" (Minneapolis)

Art Briefs

Several museums open in California, including the Desert Museum in Palm Springs. In Texas, museums open at Fort Worth, Corpus Christi, and Amarillo • Artrain begins, organized by the Michigan Council on the Arts and the NEA; it is a six-railroad-car traveling museum show that visits remote communities in the Rocky Mountain states • The Salvador Dali Holographic Room opens at M. Knoedler, in New York • The Metropolitan's "de-accessioning" controversy continues • The Italian government questions the Metropolitan's 1972, $1,000 purchase of the calyx krater by Euphronios, valued at $1 million • Japanese collectors and dealers buy a great many Western works, including Kuniyoshi's *Little Joe with Cow* ($220,000) and Stuart Davis's *Hot Still-Scape for Six Colors* ($175,000) • Major sales include Georgia O'Keeffe's *Poppies* ($120,000) and Jasper Johns's *Double White Map* ($240,000). Jackson Pollock's *Blue Poles* sells to the National Museum of Australia for $2 million, the highest price ever paid for an American painting.

Dance _____

A Los Angeles company is formed by John Clifford of the New York City Ballet; Michael Smuin leaves the American Ballet Theatre to join the San Francisco Ballet.

Premieres/Important Productions

New York City Ballet: *Cortège Hongrois* (George Balanchine), for retiring Melissa Hayden, Jacques d'Amboise; *An Evening's Waltzes* (Jerome Robbins), Patricia McBride, Jean-Pierre Bonnefous, John Clifford; Sara Leland, Bart Cook

American Ballet Theatre: *Tales of Hoffmann* (Peter Darrell, full length), for Cynthia Gregory

Joffrey: *The Dream* (Sir Frederick Ashton); *Deuce Coupe* (Twyla Tharp, Beach Boys)

Alvin Ailey: *Hidden Rites*

Books

Fiction

Critics' Choice

Gravity's Rainbow, Thomas Pynchon

Ninety-two in the Shade, Thomas McGuane

People Will Always Be Kind, Wilfred Sheed

Do with Me What You Will, Joyce Carol Oates

Rembrandt's Hat, Bernard Malamud

Theophilus North, Thornton Wilder

Nickel Mountain, John Gardner

Best-Sellers

Jonathan Livingston Seagull, Richard Bach

Once Is Not Enough, Jacqueline Susann

Breakfast of Champions, Kurt Vonnegut, Jr.

The Odessa File, Frederick Forsyth

Burr, Gore Vidal

Evening in Byzantium, Irwin Shaw

The Matlock Paper, Robert Ludlum

The Billion Dollar Sure Thing, Paul E. Erdman

The Honorary Consul, Graham Greene

Nonfiction

Critics' Choice

The Best and the Brightest, David Halberstam

Franklin D. Roosevelt: Launching the New Deal, Frank Freidel

Pentimento, Lillian Hellman

A Second Flowering, Malcolm Cowley

Sincerity and Authenticity, Lionel Trilling

The Anxiety of Influence, Harold Bloom

The New Left and the Origins of the Cold War, Robert James Maddox

Deeper into Movies, Pauline Kael

The World of Nations, Christopher Lasch

Economics and the Public Purpose, John Kenneth Galbraith

The Living Presidency, Emmet John Hughes

Marilyn, Norman Mailer

Bright Book of Life, Alfred Kazin

The Briar Patch, Murray Kempton

Life: The Unfinished Experiment, S. E. Luria

Best-Sellers

The Living Bible, Kenneth Taylor

Dr. Atkins' Diet Revolution, Robert C. Atkins

I'm O.K., You're O.K., Thomas Harris

The Joy of Sex, Alex Comfort

Weight Watchers Program Cookbook, Jean Nidetch

How to Be Your Own Best Friend, Mildred Newman et al.

The Art of Walt Disney, Christopher Finch

Alistair Cooke's America, Alistair Cooke

Sybil, Flora R. Schreiber

Poetry

Robert Bly, *Sleepers Joining Hands*

Allen Ginsberg, *The Fall of America*

Muriel Rukeyser, *Breaking Open*

W. S. Merwin, *Writings to an Unfinished Accompaniment*

Alice Walker, *Revolutionary Petunias and Other Poems*

Adrienne Rich, *Diving into the Wreck*

🙠 Czselaw Milosz, *Selected Poems*

Pulitzer Prizes

No prize is awarded in fiction.

The Americans: The Democratic Experience, vol. 3, Daniel Boorstin (U.S. history)

The Denial of Death, Ernest Becker (nonfiction)

O'Neill, Son and Artist, Louis Sheaffer (biography)

The Dolphin, Robert Lowell (poetry)

Science and Technology

Pioneer X approaches closer to Jupiter and shows the planet and its great red spot in significant detail.

The first manned Skylab launch is accomplished with Charles Conrad, Joseph Kerwin, and Paul Weitz as crew. They spend 28 days in space and conduct medical experiments related to manned space flight.

The second manned Skylab launch, with Alan Bean, Owen K. Garriott, and Jack Lousma, continues medical experiments; the mission spends 59½ days in space.

A computerized brain scanner (CAT) is marketed.

Heinz Kohut's *Analysis of the Self* challenges psychoanalytic theory by emphasizing self-worth rather than instinctual drives.

The multiple accurate reentry vehicle is developed (MARV), which permits accurate multiple missile guidance.

A cigarette-pack-size electronic brain-wave reader is developed that can detect and signal lapses in concentration.

Nuclear Magnetic Resonance (NMR) is developed; it measures the absorption of radio waves in a magnetic field to distinguish healthy from diseased tissue.

Nobel Prize

Ivar Giaever wins the prize in physics for work in miniature electronics.

Sports

Baseball

Arbitrator Peter Seitz rules, in the Andy Messersmith case, that after one season without a contract, a player is a free agent.

The AL begins allowing the designated hitter.

Nolan Ryan (California, AL) pitches two no-hitters and strikes out a record 393.

Tom Seaver (New York, NL) and Jim Palmer (Baltimore, AL) receive the Cy Young awards.

Champions

Batting
Pete Rose (Cincinnati, NL), .338
Rod Carew (Minnesota, AL), .350
Pitching
Tommy John (Los Angeles, NL), 16–7

Catfish Hunter (Oakland, AL), 21–5
Home runs
Willie Stargell (Pittsburgh, NL), 44

Football

O. J. Simpson (Buffalo, AFC) rushes for a record 2,003 yards.

Congress prohibits TV blackouts for sold-out games.

NFC Season Leaders: Roman Gabriel (Philadelphia), passing; John Brockington (Green Bay), rushing; Harold Carmichael (Philadelphia), receiving
AFC Season Leaders: Ken Anderson (Cincinnati), passing; Fred Willis (Houston), receiving

College All-Americans: Lynn Swann (E), Southern California; Roosevelt Leaks (B), Texas; Lucius Selmon (L), Oklahoma

Bowls (Jan. 1, 1974)

Rose: Ohio State 42–Southern California 21
Orange: Penn State 16–Louisiana State 9
Cotton: Nebraska 19–Texas 3
Sugar: Notre Dame 24–Alabama 23

Basketball

NBA All-Pro First Team: John Havlicek (Boston), Spencer Haywood (Seattle), Kareem Abdul-Jabbar (Milwaukee), Nate Archibald (Kansas City, Omaha), Jerry West (Los Angeles)
ABA All-Pro First Team: Billy Cunningham (Carolina), Julius Erving (Virginia), Artis Gilmore (Kentucky), James Jones (Utah), Warren Jabali (Denver)

Other Sports

Tennis: Long-retired tennis star Bobby Riggs beats current star Margaret Smith Court on Mother's Day in a $10,000 winner-take-all match. Later, Billie Jean King beats Bobby Riggs in the Astrodome in a $100,000 match; 30,000 attend and 40 million watch on TV. She arrives by elephant; he, by rickshaw.

Golf: Jack Nicklaus wins his 14th major tournament, one more than Bobby Jones.

Winners

World Series
Oakland (AL) 4
New York (NL) 3
MVP
NL–Pete Rose, Cincinnati
AL–Reggie Jackson, Oakland
Super Bowl VIII (Jan. 1974)
Miami 24–Minnesota 7
MVP
O. J. Simpson, Buffalo
College Football
Alabama (UPI)
Notre Dame (AP)
Heisman Trophy
John Cappelletti, Penn State
NBA Championship
New York 4–Los Angeles 3

MVP
Dave Cowens, Boston
College Basketball
UCLA
Player of the Year
Bill Walton, UCLA
Stanley Cup
Montreal
US Tennis Open
Men: John Newcombe
Women: Margaret Smith Court
USGA Open
Johnny Miller
Kentucky Derby
Secretariat (R. Turcotte, jockey)

Fashion

For Men: "The look" is easy, bright, and youthful, the Mark Spitz look: loosely brushed black hair, dark mustache, slim figure—elegant but casual—the decorative sport shirt over jeans or hiphuggers, the knit turtleneck with flared slacks, the textured sports shirt with collar outside the jacket. The shift to "casual" even extends to business: not only do sleeveless sweaters replace the vest but print shirts and patterned jackets and ties are also prominent. Shirts appear in every print, including polka dots; white shirts are a rarity. Any variety of dot, plaid, and solid color is used for bow and wide ties. The "Great Gatsby" look, with white hat, shoes, open shirt, wide pants, and slim jacket, is stylish. Shoes get bolder, in cream with bright red bands, or they copy the twenties' golfing style with flopping tongue; the "chunky" shoe is also very popular. T-shirts are decorated with names or cartoon characters.

For Children: With the casual look and jeans and underwear-type T-shirts decorated with names of children or odd animals, for the first time, rich and poor kids look alike.

High-fashion note: Biba's sequined dress and matching skull cap

Kaleidoscope

- Questionable government activities alluded to during the Watergate hearings include an administration "enemies list" of journalists, businessmen, politicians, and others (like Barbra Streisand and Joe Namath), who might be subjected to IRS harassment.
- After Archibald Cox is fired during the "Saturday Night Massacre," more than 250,000 telegrams arrive at the White House denouncing the president; crowds march there day and night.
- Nine hundred delegates to the AFL-CIO convention in Florida adopt a resolution asking for Nixon's impeachment.
- Eighty-four congressmen in the House sponsor 22 bills calling for impeachment.
- Long gas lines are seen throughout the nation during the OPEC embargo.
- Fuel prices since 1964 have risen at an annual rate of 3.7 percent; OPEC raises the price for crude oil 300 percent during the last four months of the year.
- The Nobel Peace Prize is awarded to Henry Kissinger and North Vietnamese Le Duc Tho, who refuses it.
- Screening of airline passengers to prevent hijacking begins.
- Oregon is the first state to decriminalize marijuana.
- There is a rise of interest in pentecostal and charismatic religions, as well as in Eastern movements such as Hare Krishna, yoga, Zen, Tibetan Buddhism, and I Ching.
- Michael Novak, in *The Rise of the Unmeltable Ethnics* defines the revival of ethnicity ("Kiss me, I'm Italian") as a rejection of American white, Anglo-Saxon, Protestant domination and a return to old values like loyalty.
- It is estimated that one out of three meals is consumed out of the house (one in eight in 1965).
- Vodka outsells whiskey for the first time.
- The median sale price of a single-family house is $28,900, up from $20,000 in 1968.
- A *Playboy* survey indicates that sexual liberalism is now the dominant ideal but that highly organized standards of love, marriage, and family remain.
- The popular PBS show "An American Family" focuses on the disintegration of a family ("Oh, we're mad at each other all the time," says the father, Bill Loud) and reflects the increasing divorce rate, nearly double since 1966.
- Elvis gives Priscilla $750,000 in their divorce settlement.
- The Supreme Court rules that employment ads cannot specify gender.
- The American Psychiatric Association revises its categorization of homosexuality; it is no longer considered a mental disorder.
- The Supreme Court establishes a narrower definition of pornography and allows the use of local, not national, standards to define what is obscene.
- New young Hollywood directors include George Lucas, Peter Bogdanovich, and Martin Scorsese; new male screen heroes include Robert De Niro, Martin Sheen, and Al Pacino.

Singer Barbra Streisand, whose look set a vogue, and top male box office star Robert Redford in *The Way We Were*. *Movie Star News.*

- Fifty rock stars earn $2–6 million a year.
- Most single records are country and western.
- The *Washington Post* wins a Pulitzer for its Watergate investigative reporting by Bob Woodward and Carl Bernstein.
- The FDA standardizes nutritive information on food labels, which lists such items as calories and grams of protein, fat, and carbohydrates.
- According to a Gallup Poll, 25 percent of all consumers (50 million people) participate in boycotts against food inflation; groups, like Operation Pocketbook, form and set up pickets ("NUTS TO BUTZ," "NIX-ON BEEF").
- Charles Revson signs Lauren Hutton, 28, for a record-breaking $200,000 as exclusive model for his Ultima II eye makeup and skin creams.
- "Pet rocks," which become a fad, are said to be an ironic testimony to the individual's power over his environment.
- An estimated 600,000 attend the Watkins Glen Rock Music Festival to hear the Grateful Dead and Allman Brothers.
- Because there are so many art thefts, Interpol publishes the first "Most Wanted Paintings" list.
- "I'm a Ford, not a Lincoln," says the new vice president, Gerald Ford.

Fads: CB radios, martial arts, backgammon

New Words and Usages: Skylab, spacelab, space shuttle, juggernaut, biofeedback, interface, consensus of opinion, doomster, ego trip, let it all hang out, time frame, nouvelle cuisine

First Appearances: Balloon flight powered by solar energy (Statesville, N.C.), college belly dancing course (University of Texas, Arlington), college to offer athletic scholarship to women (University of Miami, Coral Gables), woman prison guard in maximum security prison for men (Iowa State Penitentiary), state highway metric-distance-marker system (Ohio), vote recorded by electronic means in the House of Representatives, twilight zoo (Highland Park, Pittsburgh), floating international currencies

1974

In the News

55-MILE-PER-HOUR SPEED LIMIT IS ENACTED . . . NIXON REJECTS ERVIN SUBPOENA . . . 18½-MINUTE NIXON TAPE GAP IS EXPOSED . . . ISRAEL AND EGYPT SIGN TROOP DISENGAGEMENT ACCORD . . . MAO LAUNCHES CULTURAL REVOLUTION . . . HEIRESS PATTY HEARST IS KIDNAPPED BY SYMBIONESE LIBERATION ARMY . . . HOUSE VOTES 410–4 TO INVESTIGATE THE PRESIDENT . . . SOLZHENITSYN IS DEPORTED FROM RUSSIA . . . GRAND JURY INDICTS PRESIDENT'S AIDES HALDEMAN, EHRLICHMAN, COLSON . . . TURKISH DC-10 JET CRASHES, 346 DIE . . . OPEC OIL EMBARGO ENDS . . . KISSINGER AND BREZHNEV MEET IN MOSCOW . . . NIXON AGREES TO PAY $432,000 IN BACK TAXES . . . PORTUGUESE ARMY SEIZES POWER TO END DICTATORIAL RULE . . . NIXON WILL MAKE PUBLIC 2,100 PAGES OF TAPES . . . BRANDT RESIGNS IN SPY SCANDAL, HELMUT SCHMIDT IS NEW GERMAN P.M. . . . PALESTINIAN TERRORISTS SEIZE SCHOOL IN MAALOT, 21 CHILDREN DIE . . . INDIA ANNOUNCES IT HAS A-BOMB . . . NIXON AND BREZHNEV HOLD SUMMIT, 10-YEAR ECONOMIC PACT IS SIGNED . . . JUAN PERON DIES, HIS WIFE ISABEL TAKES OVER . . . TURKEY INVADES CYPRUS . . . CIVILIAN GOVERNMENT RETURNS IN GREECE . . . HOUSE JUDICIARY APPROVES BILL OF IMPEACHMENT . . . EHRLICHMAN IS SENTENCED 1½–5 YEARS FOR ELLSBERG CIVIL RIGHTS VIOLATION . . . JOHN DEAN PLEADS GUILTY, IS SENTENCED 1–4 YEARS . . . NIXON ADMITS "SERIOUS ACT OF OMISSION" . . . PRESIDENT RESIGNS . . . FORD IS SWORN IN AS PRESIDENT . . . NELSON ROCKEFELLER IS APPOINTED VICE PRESIDENT . . . FORD GIVES NIXON ABSOLUTE PARDON . . . ETHIOPIAN EMPEROR HAILE SELASSIE IS DEPOSED BY ARMY COUP . . . PRESIDENT OFFERS "EARNED CLEMENCY" TO DRAFT EVADERS . . . DEMOCRATS INCREASE MAJORITY IN MID-TERM ELECTIONS . . . PLO IS GIVEN OBSERVER STATUS AT UN . . . OIL IS FOUND IN MEXICO.

Quotes

"Don't lie to them to the extent to say 'No involvement,' but just say this is a comedy of errors, without getting into it; the President believes that it is going to open the whole Bay of Pigs thing up again. . . . I know these people. . . . When they detect weakness somewhere, they would not hesitate to harden their position. If they want to put me behind bars, let them."

— Richard M. Nixon on tape

"The question is: What did the President know, and when did he know it?"

— Senator Howard Baker (R-Tenn.)

"There are only so many lies you can take, and now there has been one too many. Nixon should get his ass out of the White House today."

— Senator Barry Goldwater (R-Ariz.)

"Whatever we learn or conclude, let us now proceed with such care and decency and thoroughness and honor that the vast majority of the American people, and their children after them, will say: 'This was the right course. There was no other way.'"

— Peter Rodino, chairman, House Judiciary Committee on Impeachment

"Richard M. Nixon has acted in a manner contrary to his trust as President and subversive of constitutional government. . . . Wherefore Richard M. Nixon by such conduct warrants impeachment and trial and removal from office."

— House Judiciary Committee

"[I am, in the words of Teddy Roosevelt,] the man in the arena whose face is marred by dust and sweat and blood, who at the best knows in the end the triumphs of high achievement and with the worst fails, at least fails while daring greatly."

— Richard M. Nixon, on leaving the presidency

"I, Gerald Ford, President of the United States, . . . do grant a full, free, and absolute pardon unto Richard Nixon for all offenses against the United States."

— Gerald Ford

"[This nation is becoming] a nation of hamburger stands, a country stripped of industrial capacity and meaningful work, . . . a service economy, . . . a nation of citizens busily buying and selling cheeseburgers and rootbeer floats."

— AFL-CIO Public Statement

"[Two million dollars worth of food to] all people with welfare cards, social security pension cards, food stamps, medical cards, parole or probation papers, and jail or bail release slips."

— Symbionese Liberation Army ransom demand for Patty Hearst

White House counsel John Dean gives testimony incriminating the president. *U.S. Senate.*

Ads

Live today. Tomorrow will cost more.

(Pan Am)

If you can't decide between a Shepherd, a Setter, or a Poodle, get them all. . . . Adopt a mutt.

(ASPCA)

Have a child. It's as beautiful as having a baby.

(New York State Board of Adoption)

Einstein's Theory of Relativity: give strangers the same price you give relatives.

(Einstein-Moomjy Carpets)

Our readers knew Henry [Kissinger] was getting married before Henry did.

(National Enquirer)

Equal Pay / Equal Time

(Bulova Accutron, for Men and Women)

If gas pains persist, try Volkswagen.

(Volkswagen)

We sell more cars than Ford, Chrysler, Chevrolet, and Buick combined.

(Matchbox Toy Cars)

TV

Premieres

"The Rockford Files," James Garner
"Tony Orlando and Dawn"
"Happy Days," Henry Winkler, Ron Howard
"Good Times," Esther Rolle, Jimmy Walker
"$25,000 Pyramid," Bill Cullen
"Monty Python's Flying Circus"
"Rhoda," Valerie Harper
"Little House on the Prairie," Michael Landon
"Chico and the Man," Freddie Prinze, Jack
　　Albertson
"Police Woman," Angie Dickinson

Top Ten (Nielsen)

"All in the Family," "Sanford and Son," "Chico and
the Man," "The Jeffersons" (premiered 1/75),
"M*A*S*H," "Rhoda," "Good Times," "The
Waltons," "Maude," "Hawaii Five-O"

Specials

"Love among the Ruins" (Laurence Olivier,
Katharine Hepburn); "Queen of the Stardust
Ballroom" (Jean Stapleton, Charles Durning); "The
Missiles of October" (William Devane); "The
American Film Institute Salute to James Cagney";
"Profile in Music: Beverly Sills"; "An Evening with
John Denver"

Emmy Awards

"Upstairs, Downstairs" (drama); "The Mary Tyler
Moore Show" (comedy); "The Carol Burnett Show"
(variety); "Yes, Virginia, There Is a Santa Claus"
(children); Jim McKay (sportscaster); Robert Blake
(actor, "Baretta," premiered 1/75); Tony Randall
(comedic actor, "The Odd Couple"), Jean Marsh
(actress, "Upstairs, Downstairs"); Valerie Harper
(comedic actress, "Rhoda")

Of Note

NBC pays a record $10 million for the movie *The
Godfather* and will charge $225,000 per minute for
commercials during its airing • "J.J." (Jimmy
Walker), on "Good Times," coins a new catchphrase:
"Dyn-o-mite."

Movies

Openings

The Godfather, Part II (Francis Ford Coppola), Al
　　Pacino, Robert De Niro, Diane Keaton, Robert
　　Duvall
Alice Doesn't Live Here Anymore (Martin Scorsese),
　　Ellen Burstyn, Kris Kristofferson
Chinatown (Roman Polanski), Jack Nicholson, Faye
　　Dunaway
The Conversation (Francis Ford Coppola), Gene
　　Hackman, Allen Garfield
Lenny (Bob Fosse), Dustin Hoffman, Valerie Perrine
The Towering Inferno (John Guillermin), Steve
　　McQueen, Paul Newman
Harry and Tonto (Paul Mazursky), Art Carney, Ellen
　　Burstyn
Murder on the Orient Express (Sidney Lumet),
　　Albert Finney, Ingrid Bergman, Lauren Bacall
Blazing Saddles (Mel Brooks), Cleavon Little, Gene
　　Wilder, Madeline Kahn, Mel Brooks
Young Frankenstein (Mel Brooks), Gene Wilder,
　　Peter Boyle, Madeline Kahn
Badlands (Terrence Malick), Martin Sheen, Sissy
　　Spacek
That's Entertainment (Jack Haley, Jr.), Fred Astaire,
　　Judy Garland, Gene Kelly
Andy Warhol's Frankenstein (Paul Morrissey), Joe
　　Dallesandro, Monique Van Vooren
The Pedestrian (Maximilian Schell), Maximilian
　　Schell, Mary Tamar

Amarcord (Federico Fellini), Puppela Maggio, Magali
　　Noel
The Great Gatsby (Jack Clayton), Robert Redford,
　　Mia Farrow, Sam Waterston
Death Wish (Michael Winner), Charles Bronson,
　　Vincent Gardenia, Hope Lange

Academy Awards

Best Picture: *The Godfather, Part II*
Best Director: Francis Ford Coppola (*The Godfather,
　　Part II*)
Best Actress: Ellen Burstyn (*Alice Doesn't Live Here
　　Anymore*)
Best Actor: Art Carney (*Harry and Tonto*)

Top Box-Office Stars

Robert Redford, Clint Eastwood, Paul Newman,
Barbra Streisand, Steve McQueen, Burt Reynolds,
Charles Bronson, Jack Nicholson, Al Pacino, John
Wayne

Stars of Tomorrow

Valerie Perrine, Richard Dreyfuss, Randy Quaid,
Deborah Raffin, Joseph Bottoms, Ron Howard, Sam
Waterston, Linda Blair, Keith Carradine, Steven
Warner

Popular Music

Hit Songs
"Seasons in the Sun"
"The Most Beautiful Girl"
"The Streak"
"The Entertainer"
"Please, Mister Postman"
"Mandy"
"Top of the World"
"Just You and Me"

Top Records

Albums: *Elton John—Greatest Hits* (Elton John); *You Don't Mess around with Him* (Jim Croce); *The Sting* (Sound track); *Planet Waves* (Bob Dylan); *Band on the Run* (Paul McCartney and Wings); *461 Ocean Boulevard* (Eric Clapton)

Singles: *The Way We Were* (Barbra Streisand); *Cats in the Cradle* (Harry Chapin); *Love's Theme* (Love Unlimited Orchestra); *(You're) Having My Baby* (Paul Anka); *If You Love Me* (Olivia Newton-John); *Feel Like Makin' Love* (Roberta Flack); *Come and Get Your Love* (Redbone); *Dancing Machine* (Jackson Five); *The Loco-Motion* (Grand Funk Railroad); *Bennie and the Jets* (Elton John). Country: *I Will Always Love You* (Dolly Parton); *A Very Special Love Song* (Charlie Rich)

Grammy Awards
I Honestly Love You, Olivia Newton-John (record); *Fulfillingness' First Finale*, Stevie Wonder (album); "The Way We Were" (song)

Jazz and Big Bands
Rick Ulman records *Hillbilly Jazz*. Jazz hits the big charts again with John McLaughlin, Freddy Hubbard, Donald Byrd, Herbie Hancock, Keith Jarrett, and Mahavishnu.

Top Performers (*Downbeat*): Herbie Hancock (soloist), Thad Jones and Mel Lewis (band); Weather Report (jazz group); John McLaughlin, Ron Carter, Stanley Clarke, McCoy Tyner, Garnett Brown, Airto Moreira, Jean-Luc Ponty (instrumentalists); Flora Purim, Stevie Wonder (vocalists); Pointer Sisters (vocal group); Weather Report, *Mysterious Traveller*, Stevie Wonder, *Fulfillingness' First Finale* (albums)

Theater

Broadway Openings

Plays
Equus (Peter Shaffer), Anthony Hopkins, Peter Firth
Noel Coward in Two Keys (Noel Coward), Anne Baxter, Hume Cronyn, Jessica Tandy
My Fat Friend (Charles Laurence), Lynn Redgrave, George Rose
Jumpers (Tom Stoppard), Brian Bedford, Jill Clayburgh
Absurd Person Singular (Alan Ayckbourn), Richard Kiley, Geraldine Page, Sandy Dennis
The National Health (Peter Nichols), Rita Moreno, Leonard Frey
In Praise of Love (Terence Rattigan), Rex Harrison, Julie Harris, Martin Gabel
Sizwe Banzi Is Dead / The Island (Athol Fugard), John Kani, Winston Ntshona

Musicals
Lorelei (Jule Styne, Leo Robin), Carol Channing, Dody Goodman
The Magic Show (Stephen Schwartz), Doug Henning
Mack and Mabel (Jerry Herman), Robert Preston, Bernadette Peters
Over Here! (Richard and Robert Sherman), Janie Sell, Andrews Sisters

Classics, Revivals, and Off-Broadway Premieres
Ulysses in Nighttown (Majorie Barkentin), Zero Mostel, Fionnuala Flanagan; *Cat on a Hot Tin Roof* (Tennessee Williams), Elizabeth Ashley, Keir Dullea; *Scapino* (Molière), Jim Dale; *As You Like It* (all-male cast); Henry Fonda as Clarence Darrow; *The Wager* (Mark Medoff), Kristoffer Tabori; *The Dance of Death* (Strindberg), Robert Shaw, Zoë Caldwell; *A Doll's House* (Ibsen), Liv Ullmann; *The Sea Horse* (Edward Moore); *Sherlock Holmes* (Arthur Conan Doyle, William Gillette), John Wood

Regional

Founded: St. Nicholas Theater, Chicago, by William H. Macy, David Mamet, Patricia Cox, and Stephen Schachter

Mark Taper Forum, Los Angeles: *Savages* (Christopher Hampton), premiere

Stage Arena, Washington, D.C.: *Zalmen, or the Madness of God* (Elie Wiesel), premiere

Theater (cont.)

Dallas Theater Center: *A Texas Trilogy: The Last Meeting of the Knights of the White Magnolia, Lu Ann Hampton Laverty Oberlander, The Oldest Living Graduate* (Preston Jones)

Yale Repertory: *The Tubs (The Ritz)* (Terrence McNally), premiere

Goodman, Chicago: *The Sea* (Edward Bond), premiere

Long Wharf, New Haven: *Sizwe Banzi Is Dead* (Athol Fugard), premiere

Classical Music ⸻

Compositions
Dominick Argento, *From the Diary of Virginia Woolf*
Milton Babbitt, *Reflections*
George Rochberg, *Imago Mundi*
Elliott Carter, Violin and Piano Duo, Brass Quintet
Walter Piston, Concerto for String Quartet and
    Orchestra
Milton Feldman, Instruments I, Voice and
    Instruments II

Important Events
Numerous festivals celebrate the Arnold Schoenberg and Charles Ives centennials.
The New York Philharmonic continues its unusual programming with such works as Robert Schumann's Scenes from Goethe's *Faust,* Aaron Copland's *Connotations,* and the premieres of Aribert Reimann's *Cycle* for Baritone, Alberto Ginastera's *Serenata,* and Marvin Levy's *In Memoriam, W. H. Auden.*
The Chicago and Los Angeles symphonies visit twelve European cities; the Cleveland tours Japan. Virgil Fox performs on the new $200,000 Rodgers electric organ (Carnegie Hall) with a concert of Bach, Dupré, Louis Vierne, and César Frank.
Vladimir Horowitz, at the Met, in his first concert in six years, plays Clementi, Schumann, Chopin, and Scriabin; proceeds go to the opera company. Maria Callas and Giuseppe di Stefano participate in other Met benefits.

Debut: Myung-Whun Chung

First Performances
Alberto Ginastera, String Quartet no. 3 (Dallas); Richard Rodney Bennett, Concerto for Orchestra (Denver); Sir Michael Tippett, Symphony no. 3 (Boston); Philip Glass, Music in 12 Parts (New York)

Pulitzer Prize
No prize is awarded.

Tony Awards
The River Niger, Joseph A. Walker (play), *Raisin,* Judd Woldin, Robert Brittan (musical)

Sarah Caldwell often produces, as well as directs and conducts, operas at the Opera Company of Boston. *Copyright* Washington Post. *Reprinted courtesy of D.C. Public Library.*

Opera

Metropolitan: Peter Pears (debut), *Death in Venice* (Benjamin Britten); Maureen Forrester, *Das Rheingold;* Kiri Te Kanawa (debut), *Otello;* double bill: *Bluebeard's Castle* and *Gianni Schicchi;* Montserrat Caballé, Nicolai Gedda / Placido Domingo, *I vespri siciliani*

New York State: Beverly Sills in all three Donizetti "English Queen" operas: *Maria Stuarda, Roberto Devereaux, Anna Bolena;* Sills, *I Puritani*

Boston: Donald Gramm, John Moulson, Arlene Saunders, *War and Peace* (Prokofiev, American premiere, performed at Wolf Trap, Washington, D.C.)

Chicago: Jon Vickers, *Peter Grimes*

Houston: Richard Stilwell, Frederica von Stade, John Reardon, *The Seagull* (Thomas Pasatieri)

Santa Fe: *Lulu*

Washington, D.C.: Frederica von Stade, Richard Stilwell, *Il ritorno d'Ulisse in patria* (Monteverdi)

San Francisco: Leontyne Price, *Manon Lescaut;* John Sutherland, *Esclarmonde*

Art

Paintings

Fairfield Porter, *The Cliffs of Isle au Haut*

Chuck Close, *Robert/ 104,072*

Richard Estes, *Woolworth's America*

Frank Stella, *Pratfall, York Factory*

Richard Artschwager, *Rockefeller Center*

Ralph Goings, *McDonald Pickup*

Helen Frankenthaler, *Savage Breeze*

Sculpture

Lynda Benglis, *Victor*

Carl Andre, *Decks*

Joel Shapiro, *Untitled (house on shelf)*

Richard Serra, *Ollantoyambo*

Robert Morris, *Labyrinth*

Michael Heizer, *The City, Complex One*

Calder's *Universe* is installed in the Sears Tower, Chicago.

Architecture

J. Paul Getty Museum, Malibu, Calif. (Langdon and Wilson)

Air and Space Museum, Washington, D.C. (Hellmuth, Obata, Kassabaum)

Sears Tower, Chicago (Skidmore, Owings and Merrill), world's tallest building (1,450 feet)

Roche and Dinkeloo design a downtown plan for Denver; the revitalization of Burlington Square, Vermont, is designed by Mies van der Rohe and Freeman-French-Freeman.

Important Exhibitions

Museums

New York: *Metropolitan:* Medieval tapestries; "A Centenary of Impressionism"; American Indian art. *Museum of Modern Art:* Miró, Duchamp. *Whitney:* Pop art, organized by Lawrence Alloway: Johns's flag paintings, Warhol's soup cans, Ramos's Batmen, Lichtenstein's comic strip frames. *Guggenheim:* Retrospective of 200 works of Giacometti

Philadelphia: Achievement of women in the arts; Duchamp

Washington: "American Self-Portraits": West, Copley, Whistler, Sargent, Eakins, Shahn, Warhol

Minneapolis: Willem de Kooning drawings and sculptures

Richmond, Whitney, San Francisco: The flowering of American folk art, 1776–1876.

Art Briefs

Numerous museums open, including the J. Paul Getty Museum in Malibu, Calif.; the Hirschhorn Museum and Sculpture Garden, Washington, D.C.; the Newberger Modern Museum (State University of New York, Purchase); the Walters, in Baltimore, builds a $4 million wing • Major sales include Willem de Kooning's *Woman V* ($850,000, the highest price ever paid a living artist; the painting brought $30,000 in 1955), Brancusi's *La Negresse* ($750,000), and Dali's *Resurrection of the Flesh* ($240,000).

Andy Warhol, in front of one of his paintings. *Courtesy Sedat Pakay.*

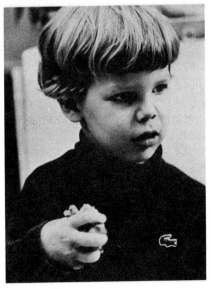

Designer clothing becomes fashionable for children.

Books

Fiction

Critics' Choice
Look at the Harlequins, Vladimir Nabokov
The War between the Tates, Alison Lurie
The Shadow Knows, Diane Johnson
Enormous Changes at the Last Minute, Grace Paley
The Hair of Harold Roux, Thomas Williams
The Last Days of Louisiana Red, Ishmael Reed
The Odd Woman, Gail Godwin
The House of the Solitary Maggot, James Purdy
Fear of Flying, Erica Jong
The King and India, John Gardner
Guilty Pleasures, Donald Barthelme
Dog Soldiers, Robert Stone
Sula, Toni Morrison

Best-Sellers
Centennial, James A. Michener
Watership Down, Richard Adams
Jaws, Peter Benchley
Tinker, Tailor, Soldier, Spy, John le Carré
Something Happened, Joseph Heller
The Dogs of War, Frederick Forsyth
The Pirate, Harold J. Robbins

The Seven-Per-Cent Solution, John H. Watson, M.D.
The Fan Club, Irving Wallace

Nonfiction

Critics' Choice
Time on the Cross, Robert Fogel, Stanley L. Engerman
Seduction and Betrayal, Elizabeth Hardwick
From Reverence to Rape, Molly Haskell
Flying, Kate Millet
Kissinger, Marvin and Bernard Kalb
The Diary of Anaïs Nin
The Real America, Ben Wattenberg
A Bridge Too Far, Cornelius Ryan
The Lives of a Cell, Lewis Thomas
Zen and the Art of Motorcycle Maintenance, Robert M. Pirsig
Choosing Our Language, Michael Novak
Marcel Proust, Roger Shattuck
The Life of Emily Dickinson, Richard Sewall

Best-Sellers
The Total Woman, Marabel Morgan
All the President's Men, Carl Bernstein and Bob Woodward
Plain Speaking: An Oral Biography of Harry S Truman, Merle Miller
More Joy: A Lovemaking

Companion to the Joy of Sex, ed. Alex Comfort
Alistair Cooke's America, Alistair Cooke
Tales of Power, Carlos A. Castaneda
You Can Profit from a Monetary Crisis, Harry Browne
All Things Bright and Beautiful, James Herriot
The Bermuda Triangle, Charles Berlitz, with J. Manson Valentine
The Memory Book, Harry Lorayne, Jerry Lucas

Poetry
Anne Sexton, *The Death Notebooks*
Robert Creeley, *Sitting Here*
W. H. Auden, *Thank You, Fog: Last Poems* (posthumous)
Marilyn Hacker, *Presentation Piece*
James Merrill, *The Yellow Pages: 59 Poems*

Pulitzer Prizes
The Killer Angels, Michael Shaara (fiction)
Jefferson and His Time, Dumas Malone (U.S. history)
Pilgrim at Tinker Creek, Annie Dillard (nonfiction)
The Power Broker: Robert Moses and the Fall of New York, Robert A. Caro (biography)
Turtle Island, Gary Synder (poetry)

Science and Technology

Mariner X's fly-by pictures show Venus surrounded by a shell of haze.
Pioneer II transmits pictures of Jupiter that include its large moon, Callisto.
Ultrasound diagnostic techniques are developed.
A new particle "J" or "psi" is discovered.
An air force SR-71 jet flies from New York to London in 1 hour, 55 minutes.
The National Academy of Science calls a halt to research in genetic engineering, pending safer techniques.

A USSR space probe lands on Mars and detects more water vapor than previously observed.
Great Britain, France, China, and India conduct nuclear tests.

Nobel Prize
Paul Jon Flory wins the prize in chemistry for his experiments with polymers. George E. Palade and Christian de Duve win in physiology and medicine for studies on the inner workings of living cells.

Sports

Baseball

Henry Aaron (Atlanta, NL) hits his 715th home run, off Al Downing, breaking Babe Ruth's lifetime record.

Lou Brock (St. Louis, NL) steals a record 118 bases.

Nolan Ryan (California, AL) strikes out a record-tying 19 in one game and also pitches his third no-hitter and wins the Cy Young Award.

Mike Marshall (Los Angeles, NL) appears in a record 106 games and also wins the Cy Young Award.

Champions

Batting
Ralph Garr (Atlanta, NL), .353
Rod Carew (Minnesota, AL), .364

Pitching
Andy Messersmith (Los Angeles, NL), 20–6
Miguel Cuellar (Baltimore, AL), 22–10

Home runs
Mike Schmidt (Philadelphia, NL), 36

Football

Kickoffs are moved to the 35-yard line in the NFL.

NFL Season Leaders: Sonny Jurgensen (Washington), passing; Larry McCutcheon (Los Angeles), rushing; Charlie Young (Philadelphia), receiving

AFC Season Leaders: Ken Anderson (Cincinnati), passing; Otis Armstrong (Denver), rushing; Lydell Mitchell (Baltimore), receiving

College All-Americans: Steve Bartkowski (Q), California; Randy White (L), Maryland; Joe Washington (RB), Oklahoma

Bowls (Jan. 1, 1975)

Rose: Southern California 18–Ohio State 17

Orange: Notre Dame 13–Alabama 11

Cotton: Penn State 41–Baylor 20

Sugar: Nebraska 13–Florida 10

Basketball

NBA All-Pro First Team: John Havlicek (Boston), Rick Barry (Golden State), Kareem Abdul-Jabbar (Milwaukee), Walt Frazier (New York), Gail Goodrich (Los Angeles)

ABA All-Pro First Team: Julius Erving (New York), George McGinnis (Indiana), Artis Gilmore (Kentucky), Jimmy Jones (Utah), Mack Calvin (Carolina)

Other Sports

Boxing: Muhammad Ali, using "rope-a-dope" tactics, knocks out George Foreman, in the eighth round, in Zaire.

Tennis: John Newcombe is the World Championship Tennis (WCT) champion.

Winners

World Series
Oakland (AL) 4
Los Angeles (NL) 1

MVP
NL–Steve Garvey, Los Angeles
AL–Jeff Burroughs, Texas

Super Bowl IX (Jan. 1975)
Pittsburgh 16–Minnesota 6

MVP
Ken Stabler, Oakland

College Football
Southern California (UPI)
Oklahoma (AP)

Heisman Trophy
Archie Griffin, Ohio State

NBA Championship
Boston 4–Milwaukee 3

MVP
Kareem Abdul-Jabbar, Milwaukee

College Basketball
North Carolina State

Player of the Year
David Thompson, North Carolina State

Stanley Cup
Philadelphia

US Tennis Open
Men: Jimmy Connors
Women: Billie Jean King

USGA Open
Hale Irwin

Kentucky Derby
Cannonade (A. Cordero, jockey)

Fashion

For Women: Fashion is marked by both the "covered" and "uncovered" look: (1) the string bikini, two soft, clinging, fabric postage stamps held together by string ties at the hip, and (2) the blanketed look with wide capes, along with coats and skirts that fall below the knee to mid and low calf and loose blouses. A nostalgia for the twenties and thirties also characterizes the year, with art deco revived in silver accessories and geometric prints. T-shirt graphics include comic characters and historical, musical, and contemporary personalities; screen-print dresses have color reproductions of Rolls-Royces and heroes of the twenties and thirties. Victorian camisoles are worn on top of skirts; garter belts, twenties' teddy lingerie (loose pants with one-piece camisole tops) are also worn. Ethnic clothing includes Russian-style tunics that are side-buttoned and belted, and pants that tuck into ankle boots, Chinese worker shirts, pants, and quilted vests. Capes become fashionable again.

High-fashion notes: St. Laurent's "Steppes look"; Missone's knit stripes and zigzags; Lagerfeld's smocks atop midis; Valentino's long, pleated knits; Biba's naughty thirties' look; Hermès's envelop bag

Kaleidoscope _____

- The nation witnesses the House Judiciary Committee roll-call vote, 27–11, on the first article of impeachment (obstruction of justice) against the president; 28–10 on the second (abuse of power); and 21–17 on the third (violation of congressional subpoena).
- Director William Colby admits that the CIA has thousands of illegally obtained secret files on various Americans.
- White House associates who leave the administration because of Watergate include Robert Haldeman, John Ehrlichman, John Dean, Charles Colson, John Mitchell, Jeb Stuart Magruder, Gordon Strachen, Herbert Porter, John Caulfield, Anthony Ulasewicz, Howard Hunt, Maurice Stans, Robert Mardian, Donald Segretti, Herbert Kalmbach, L. Patrick Gray, and Dwight Chapin.
- After Gerald Ford gives Richard Nixon his "full" and "absolute" pardon, his popularity drops from 72 percent to 49 percent.
- The Equal Opportunity Act forbids discrimination based on sex or marital status.
- The number of Vietnam veterans totals 6,558,000.
- Forty-two nuclear plants are operable, 56 are under construction, 101 have been ordered, 14 are in the planning stage.
- An antitrust suit is brought against AT&T, Western Electric, and Bell Labs.
- Because of gasoline shortages, daylight savings time is observed year around to save fuel.
- Car sales are down 35 percent from 1973; home construction is down 40 percent.
- Thousands bare their buttocks in the year's streaking fad: 1,543 at the University of Georgia boast the largest number; hundreds at Texas Tech stay naked for hours; streaking also marks major academic, cultural, and sports gatherings, including the Academy Awards.
- Philippe Petit dances along a one-inch wire strung between the twin towers of the World Trade Center, New York, 1,350 feet high; Petit gets a job as high-wire man with Barnum and Bailey.
- Frank Sinatra makes news as he calls the press "bums" and women "broads" and "hookers."
- Newlyweds of the year include Henry and Nancy Kissinger and singer Sly of the Family Stone and Kathy; the latter marry at Madison Square Garden before a record audience.
- AT&T, the world's largest private employer, bans discrimination against homosexuals.
- Four Episcopal bishops defy church law and ordain 11 women as priests.
- During court-ordered busing in Boston, Louise Day Hicks leads a group called Restore Our Alienated Rights (ROAR) to halt integration; rioting follows.
- The public is warned of the environmental carcinogen polyvinyl chloride used in plastic containers.
- Lt. William Calley, convicted for his role in the My Lai massacre, is paroled.

"All in the Family," the Norman Lear-Bud Yorkin production with Jean Stapleton and Carroll O'Connor, continues as Number 1 for the third year. *Movie Star News.*

- Soul music moves into discos; in addition to the renewed interest in jazz, ragtime is revived.
- CBGB, New York, introduces Blondie, the Ramones, and Talking Heads, among other glitter-backlash groups.
- Evel Knievel fails to launch across the Idaho Snake River in his Sky-Cycle X-2, and riots and stampedes follow.
- The "singles" industry is estimated at $40 billion.
- Gay Gaer Luce helps found SAGE, Senior Actualization and Growth Exploitation, bringing greater attention to "gray power," senior citizens who comprise 10 percent of the population.
- The biggest money-making films are all-star disaster movies like *Towering Inferno* and *Earthquake* and films of supernatural violence like *The Exorcist.*
- Although a disgruntled artist sprays "KILL YES ALL" on Picasso's *Guernica,* in the Museum of Modern Art, the painting is undamaged.

New Words and Usages: Nuke, yen, stonewalling, striking, scientism

First Appearances: An avowed homosexual elected to state office (Elaine Noble, Boston), girls allowed into the Little League, bachelor's degree awarded by a recognized institution without requiring a single college credit (N. E. France, SUNY, Albany), woman mayor of a major city (J. G. Hayes, San Jose, Calif.), woman police officer killed in the line of duty (G. A. Cobb), pressure-sensitized adhesive postage stamp

1975

Facts and Figures

Economic Profile
  Dow-Jones: − High 860–
    Low 610
  GNP: +10%
  Inflation: +14.1%
  Unemployment: 9.1%
Vietnam War wounded:
  300,000
Vietnam War deaths:
  U.S., in combat: 45,884
  U.S., noncombat: 10,281
  South Vietnam in Combat:
    184,494
  South Vietnam civilians:
    205,000
  North Vietnam, Vietcong:
    904,000
Total: 1,300,000
Cartier tank watch, gold
  plated: $180
Louis Vuitton attaché case:
  $1,200
Pulsar electronic watch:
  $295–$395
Halston perfume: $18.50 (¼
  oz.)
Elsa Peretti bean-shaped
  compact: $6.50
Mood rings: $2.99
Texas Instruments SR-52
  hand calculator: $3.95
Hewlett-Packard hand
  calculator: $125–$795
Tappan microwave oven:
  $449
Braun coffeemaker: $49.95

Deaths

Cannonball Adderly, Thomas
  Hart Benton, Chiang Kai-
  shek, Fredric March,
  Aristotle Onassis, Haile
  Selassie, Rod Serling,
  Casey Stengel, Richard
  Tucker, William Wellman.

In the News

H. R. HALDEMAN, JOHN EHRLICHMAN, AND JOHN MITCHELL ARE CONVICTED OF CONSPIRACY . . . PRESIDENT FORD ANNOUNCES RECESSION POLICY . . . HOUSE DEMOCRATS REMOVE THREE CHAIRMEN IN SUCCESSFUL CHALLENGE TO SENIORITY SYSTEM . . . FORD SIGNS $22.8 BILLION TAX CUT . . . U.S. AIR FORCE PLANE WITH VIETNAMESE ORPHANS CRASHES, 200 ARE KILLED . . . FORD OFFICIALLY ENDS AMERICAN ROLE IN VIETNAM . . . SAIGON FALLS TO NORTH VIETNAM, THOUSANDS FLEE BY BOAT . . . UNEMPLOYMENT REACHES 8.9%, HIGHEST SINCE 1941 . . . MARINES RESCUE 39 FROM USS "MAYAGUEZ," SEIZED BY CAMBODIA . . . CAMBODIAN KHMER ROUGE EVACUATE POPULACE FROM CITIES, MASSIVE DEATH TOLL IS FEARED . . . INDIRA GANDHI DECLARES STATE OF EMERGENCY AND ARRESTS OPPONENTS . . . APOLLO-SOYEZ LINK-UP MISSION IS LAUNCHED . . . 35 EAST AND WEST NATIONS MEET IN HELSINKI, ACCORDS ON HUMAN RIGHTS ARE DECLARED . . . TEAMSTER LEADER JIMMY HOFFA DISAPPEARS, FOUL PLAY IS SUSPECTED . . . VOTING RIGHTS ACT IS EXTENDED SEVEN YEARS . . . ISRAEL AND EGYPT SIGN SINAI INTERIM AGREEMENT . . . LYNETTE FROMME, MANSON FAMILY MEMBER, IS ARRESTED FOR POINTING GUN AT PRESIDENT . . . PATTY HEARST IS ARRESTED BY FBI . . . FORD ESCAPES SHOT FIRED BY SARA JANE MOORE . . . U.S. AND RUSSIA AGREE ON FIVE-YEAR GRAIN EXPORT PLAN . . . OPEC INCREASES OIL PRICES 10% . . . PORTUGUESE LEAVE ANGOLA . . . SPANISH DICTATOR FRANCISCO FRANCO DIES . . . FORD REJECTS FEDERAL BAILOUT OF N.Y.C. . . . ARAB TERRORISTS SEIZE HOSTAGES AT OPEC MEETINGS IN VIENNA . . . CIA ACKNOWLEDGES PLOTS TO KILL UNDESIRABLE HEADS OF STATE . . . BOMB AT LA GUARDIA AIRPORT, N.Y.C., KILLS 11.

Quotes

"Today, accountants look like Shakespearean actors, space salesmen look like art directors, hair stylists wear short hair, clothes designers dress conservatively, . . . an orthodontist comes on like a cowboy. . . . Everybody's into reverse role-playing."
— John Weitz, fashion designer

"A total woman caters to her man's special quirks, whether it be in salads, sex, or sports."
— Marabel Morgan, *The Total Woman*

"FORD TO CITY: DROP DEAD"
— *New York Daily News* headline

"I don't know of any foreign leader that was ever assassinated by the CIA. . . . There were always discussions of everything . . . things that may not be acceptable to the American people."
— Richard Helms, former CIA director

"In addition to the inflation, we have stagnating productivity. People don't work the way they used to."
— Arthur Burns, chairman, Federal Reserve

"[The lesson of Vietnam is] we must throw off the cumbersome mantle of world policeman and limit our readiness to areas where our interests are truly in danger."
— Senator Edward Kennedy (D-Mass.)

President Gerald Ford, the first appointed president. *Library of Congress.*

"The United States is no longer in a position to take on warmongering adventures. . . . Only fifteen years ago, the United States was very powerful—but no more."
— Fidel Castro

"Though we are no longer predominant, we are inescapably a leader."
— Henry Kissinger

Ads

The Arabs have the oil.
America has the corn.
(CPC International Corn Products)

"Some of my favorite performers are horses."
(Frank Sinatra for Off-Track Betting)

When it comes to buying an engagement ring, don't let love get in the way.
(Fortunoff)

Send yourself across the country in four minutes or less.
(Xerox Telecopier)

If you forget to have your children vaccinated, you could be reminded of it the rest of your life.
(Metropolitan Life Insurance Company)

Warren Beatty, in *Shampoo*, portrays a womanizing hairdresser. *Movie Star News.*

Perform a death-defying act. Have your blood pressure checked.
(American Heart Association)

Due to a lack of funds, there will be a shortage of justice this year.
(Give to the Legal Aid Society)

TV _____

Premieres
"A.M. America"
"Robert MacNeil Report"
"Baretta," Robert Blake
"S.W.A.T.," Steve Forrest
"The Jeffersons," Isabel Sanford, Sherman Hemsley
"Barney Miller," Hal Linden
"Starsky and Hutch," David Soul, Paul Michael Glaser
"One Day at a Time," Bonnie Franklin
"Phyllis," Cloris Leachman
"NBC's Saturday Night Live," Chevy Chase, John Belushi, Gilda Radner, Dan Akroyd
"Welcome Back, Kotter," Gabriel Kaplan, John Travolta

Top Ten (Nielsen)
"All in the Family," "Rich Man, Poor Man," "Laverne and Shirley," "Maude," "The Bionic Woman," "Phyllis," "Sanford and Son," "Rhoda," "The Six-Million-Dollar Man," "ABC Monday Night Movie"

Specials
"Eleanor and Franklin" (Edward Herrmann, Jane Alexander); "A Moon for the Misbegotten" (Jason Robards); "Rich Man, Poor Man" (Nick Nolte, Peter Strauss); "The Adams Chronicles" (George Grizzard); "Vietnam: A War That Is Finished"; "7,382 Days in Vietnam"; "Vietnam: Lessons Learned, Prices Paid"

Emmy Awards
"Policy Story" (drama); "The Mary Tyler Moore Show" (comedy); "NBC's Saturday Night Live" (variety); "You're a Good Sport, Charlie Brown" (children); Jim McKay (sports personality); Peter Falk (actor, "Columbo"); Jack Albertson (comedic actor, "Chico and the Man"); Michael Learned, (actress, "The Waltons"); Mary Tyler Moore (comedic actress, "The Mary Tyler Moore Show")

Of Note
Situation comedy peaks with shows such as "All in the Family," "M*A*S*H," "The Mary Tyler Moore Show," "The Odd Couple," "Barney Miller," "Rhoda," and "Chico and the Man" • As a result of protests over TV violence and sex, as well as subsequent FCC pressure, the networks agree to establish 8:00–9:00 P.M. as the "family hour."

Movies _____

Openings
One Flew over the Cuckoo's Nest (Milos Forman), Jack Nicholson, Louise Fletcher
Barry Lyndon (Stanley Kubrick), Ryan O'Neal, Marisa Berenson
Dog Day Afternoon (Sidney Lumet), Al Pacino, John Cazale, James Broderick, Charles Durning
Jaws (Steven Spielberg), Roy Scheider, Robert Shaw, Richard Dreyfuss
Nashville (Robert Altman), Karen Black, Ronee Blakley, Keith Carradine
Shampoo (Hal Ashby), Warren Beatty, Julie Christie, Goldie Hawn, Lee Grant, Jack Warden
The Story of Adele H. (François Truffaut), Isabelle Adjani, Bruce Robinson
Hester Street (Joan Micklin Silver), Steve Keats, Carol Kane
The Man Who Would Be King (John Huston), Michael Caine, Sean Connery
Monty Python and the Holy Grail (Terry Gilliam, Terry Jones), Graham Chapman, John Cleese, Terry Gilliam, Eric Idle, Terry Jones
Swept Away (Lina Wertmuller), Mariangela Melato, Giancarlo Giannini
Three Days of the Condor (Sydney Pollack), Robert Redford, Faye Dunaway
Tommy (Ken Russell), Roger Daltrey, Ann-Margret, Oliver Reed, Elton John
Seven Beauties (Lina Wertmuller), Giancarlo Giannini, Shirley Stoler

Academy Awards
Best Picture: *One Flew over the Cuckoo's Nest*
Best Director: Milos Forman (*One Flew over the Cuckoo's Nest*)
Best Actress: Louise Fletcher (*One Flew over the Cuckoo's Nest*)
Best Actor: Jack Nicholson (*One Flew over the Cuckoo's Nest*)

Top Box-Office Stars
Robert Redford, Barbra Streisand, Al Pacino, Charles Bronson, Paul Newman, Clint Eastwood, Burt Reynolds, Woody Allen, Steve McQueen, Gene Hackman

Stars of Tomorrow
Stockard Channing, Bo Svenson, Susan Blakely, William Atherton, Brad Dourif, Bo Hopkins, Conny Van Dyke, Ronee Blakley, Paul Le Mat

Popular Music

Hit Songs
"Rhinestone Cowboy"
"Fame"
"Best of My Love"
"Laughter in the Rain"
"The Hustle"
"Have You Never Been Mellow?"
"One of These Nights"
"Jive Talkin' "
"Black Water"

Top Records

Albums: *Captain Fantastic & the Brown Dirt Cowboy* (Elton John); *Physical Graffiti* (Led Zeppelin); *Chicago X—Chicago's Greatest Hits* (Chicago); *Red Octopus* (Jefferson Starship); *Rock of the Westies* (Elton John)

Singles: *Philadelphia Freedom* (Elton John); *Before the Next Teardrop Falls* (Freddy Fender); *My Eyes Adored You* (Frankie Valli): *Shining Star* (Earth, Wind and Fire); *Thank God I'm a Country Boy* (John Denver); *You're No Good* (Linda Ronstadt). Country: *San Antonio Stroll* (Tanya Tucker); *A Legend in My Time* (Ronnie Milsap)

Grammy Awards
Love Will Keep Us Together, Captain and Tennille (record); *Still Crazy after All These Years,* Paul Simon (album); "Send in the Clowns" (song)

Jazz and Big Bands
Electronic keyboard instruments gain in popularity with one-man bands: Herbie Hancock, Chick Corea.

Popular mainstream performers include Cecil Taylor, Bill Evans, Dizzy Gillespie, Miles Davis, Gerry Mulligan, Oscar Peterson, and Jim Hall.

Top Performers *(Downbeat):* McCoy Tyner (soloist); Thad Jones and Mel Lewis (band); Weather Report (jazz group); Joe Pass, Phil Woods, Bill Watrous (instrumentalists); Flora Purim, Stevie Wonder (vocalists); Pointer Sisters (vocal group); Earth, Wind and Fire (rock/blues group); Weather Report, *Tale Spinnin',* Jeff Beck, *Blow by Blow* (albums)

Theater

Broadway Openings
Plays
Seascape (Edward Albee), Deborah Kerr, Frank Langella
Travesties (Tom Stoppard), John Wood
Same Time, Next Year (Bernard Slade), Ellen Burstyn, Charles Grodin
The Ritz (Terrence McNally), Rita Moreno, Jack Weston, F. Murray Abraham
The Norman Conquests (Alan Ayckbourn), Barry Nelson, Ken Howard, Estelle Parsons, Richard Benjamin, Paula Prentiss
Habeas Corpus (Alan Bennett), Alan Bennett, Donald Sinden

Musicals
The Wiz (Charlie Smalls), Stephanie Mills
Shenandoah (Peter Udell, Gary Geld), John Cullum
Chicago (John Kander, Fred Ebb), Gwen Verdon, Jerry Orbach, Chita Rivera
A Chorus Line (Edward Kleban, Marvin Hamlisch), Donna McKechnie, Ann Reinking, choreographed by Michael Bennett

Classics, Revivals, and Off-Broadway Premieres
A Doll's House (Ibsen), Liv Ullmann; *Private Lives* (Noel Coward), Maggie Smith, Brian Bedford; *The Misanthrope* (Molière), Diana Rigg, Alec McCowen; *Hamlet,* Sam Waterston; *All God's Chillun Got Wings* (Eugene O'Neill), Trish Van Devere; *Death of a Salesman* (Arthur Miller), George C. Scott, Teresa Wright; *Sweet Bird of Youth* (Tennessee Williams), Christopher Walken, Irene Worth; *The Constant Wife* (W. Somerset Maugham), Ingrid Bergman; *The Skin of Our Teeth* (Thornton Wilder), Elizabeth Ashley, Alfred Drake; *Trelawny of the Wells* (Pinero), John Lithgow, Meryl Streep; *The Devils* (John Whiting), Anne Bancroft, Jason Robards

Regional
Goodman, Chicago: *American Buffalo* (David Mamet), premiere

Long Wharf, New Haven: *Ah, Wilderness!* (Eugene O'Neill), Teresa Wright, Geraldine Fitzgerald, Paul Rudd, revival

Mark Taper Forum, Los Angeles: *The Shadow Box* (Michael Cristofer), premiere

Pulitzer Prize
Seascape, Edward Albee

Tony Awards
Equus, Peter Shaffer (play), *The Wiz,* Charlie Smalls (musical)

Classical Music

Compositions
Ned Rorem, *Air Music*
John Cage, *Etudes Australes*
George Rochberg, Piano Quintet, Violin Concerto
Roy Harris, Symphony no. 14
Roger Sessions, Three Choruses on Biblical Texts
Leonard Bernstein, Seven Dances and Suite no. 1
    from *Dybbuck*
Morton Feldman, *Piano and Orchestra*
Floyd Carlisle, *Flower and Hawk*
Garrett List, Process #1, #2

Rudolf
Nureyev.
*Movie Star
News.*

Important Events
Birthday celebrations include Strauss's 150th,
Britten's and Ravel's 100th, and Copland's 75th.

New Appointments: Mstislav Rostropovitch
(National) and André Previn (Pittsburgh)

Debut: Emanuel Ax

First Performances
Dominick Argento, *From the Diary of Virginia Woolf*
(Minneapolis); Elliott Carter, Duo for Violin and
Piano (New York); Michael Colgrass,
Concertmasters (Detroit); Henry Brant, *Homage to
Ives* (Denver); Eric Stokes, *Continental Harp and
Band Report* (Minneapolis); Alberto Ginastera
Turbae ad Passionem Gregioranam (Philadelphia);
Lewis Weingarden, Piano Concerto (Denver); George
Rochberg, Piano Concerto (Pittsburgh)

A Chorus Line, Michael Bennett's musical psychodrama
concerning the hardships of show business. *Movie Star
News.*

Opera

Metropolitan: James Levine is appointed musical
director; Anthony Bliss becomes executive director.
Beverly Sills (debut), *Siege of Corinth; Ring* cycle is
completed after seven years (in the von Karajan,
Salzburg productions), with Birgit Nilsson, Mignon
Dunn, Berit Lindholm (debut), Maureen Forrester,
Thomas Stewart, Jess Thomas, Ragnar Ulfung;
Teresa Kubiak, *Un ballo in maschera;* Régine
Crespin, *Carmen; Boris Godunov* (based on two
original versions)

New York City: Beverly Sills, *Daughter of the
Regiment*

Dallas: Beverly Sills, *Lucrezia Borgia;* Marilyn
Horne, *Rinaldo*

Houston: *Treemonisha*

Chicago: Ileana Cotrubas, Richard Stilwell, *Orfeo
ed Euridice;* Nicholai Ghiaurov, *Don Quichotte;*
Carlo Cossutta, Gilda Cruz-Romo, *Otello*

Boston: Jon Vickers, Donald Gramm, John
Reardon, Patricia Wells, *Benvenuto Cellini* (Berlioz,
American premiere)

Seattle: Complete *Ring* (once in German, once in
English)

Music Notes
On its first visit to the United States, the Moscow
Bolshoi Opera performs six operas • James Dixon
conducts the University of Iowa Symphony in
Aleksandr Scriabin's *Prometheus,* which features a
laser apparatus that renders the visualization of color
that Scriabin envisioned.

Art

Paintings
Richard Estes, *Central Savings*
Jasper Johns, *Scent*
Bill Beckley, *Hot and Cold Faucets with Drain*
Frank Stella, *Grodno (1–7)*
Willem de Kooning, *Whose Name Was Writ in Water*

Sculpture
Carl Andre, *Twenty-Ninth Copper Cardinal*
Lynda Benglis, *Bravo 2*
Louise Nevelson, *Transparent Horizon*
Jackie Winsor, *Fifty-five*
Larry Le Va, *Center Points and Lengths (through Tangents)*
Richard Serra, *Sight Point*
Claes Oldenburg, *Geometric Mouse—Scale A*
Scott Burtain, *Bronze Chair*
Sheila Hicks, *Communications Labyrinth*

Important Exhibitions
Museums
Visiting the Metropolitan, Philadelphia, and Detroit museums: "French Painting 1774–1830: From David to Delacroix"; also touring: "Archeological Finds of the People's Republic of China"; "Master Paintings from the Hermitage and State Russian Museums"; "King Tutankhamen's Treasures"

New York: *Metropolitan:* Scythian Ancient Treasures; "The Impressionist Epoch." *Whitney:* "The Flowering of American Folk Art"; Sheldon Peck; Mark di Suvero retrospective. *Whitney, Hirshhorn:* Elie Nadelman retrospective. *Guggenheim:* Max Ernst retrospective

Boston: *Institute of Fine Arts:* "Boston Celebrations: Jubilee Projects for the Bicentennial"

Washington, D.C.: *John F. Kennedy Center:* "Art

Alexander Calder's *Flying Colors of the United States* is installed at Braniff International.

Architecture
Herbert F. Johnson Museum, Cornell University (I. M. Pei)
Best Products Showroom, Houston (Site, Inc.)
Pennzoil Plaza, Houston (Philip Johnson, John Burgee)
"Decade 80" Solar House, Tucson (Cooper Development Association)
INA Tower, Philadelphia (Mitchell, Guirgola)
Franklin Court, Philadelphia (Venturi and Rauch)
Crystal Court, IDS Center, Minneapolis (Philip Johnson)
Design competition for 1,000 housing units, Roosevelt Island, New York City, Philip Johnson in charge

Now, '75 Cartoon Festival" (first U.S. comprehensive comic art show)

Cleveland, Los Angeles, Metropolitan: Chinese paintings from the Arthur M. Sackler collection

San Francisco: *Palace of Legion of Honor:* De Young; "Rainbow Show." *Museum of Modern Art:* Benefit on theme of artists' soapbox derby with five nudes, pumpernickel sports car

Chicago: Monet

Art Briefs
The Metropolitan sponsors a rare one-man show of Francis Bacon • Bicentennial celebrations begin and include an exhibition of Calder's red, white, and blue flagship sculpture • The Metropolitan sends an exhibition of 19th- and 20th-century realistic art to the Hermitage and Pushkin museums • Paul Gauguin's *Hina Maruru* sells for $950,000.

Dance

The Bolshoi Ballet visits the United States after almost ten years. Rudolf Nureyev dances with the Martha Graham and Murray Louis modern dance companies. Bicentennial celebrations begin, such as Alvin Ailey's *The Mooche* and *Night Creature*.

Premieres/Important Productions
American Ballet Theatre: For its 35th anniversary gala—*The Sleeping Beauty* (Anton Dolin); *Pillar of Fire, Fancy Free, Three Virgins and a Devil, Raymonda*, and the premiere of *The Leaves Are Falling* (Anthony Tudor, Dvorak)

New York City Ballet: *Homage à Ravel—six new works, including Gaspard de la Nuit, Daphnis and Chloe, Tzigane* (Balanchine, Taras, Robbins)

San Francisco: *Shinju* (Michael Smuin); *Romeo and Juliet* (Smuin, full length)

Joffrey: *Deuce Coupe* (Twyla Tharp)

Martha Graham: *The Scarlet Letter*

Of Interest
Valery Panov and Galina Panova dance in *Lady and Hooligan* and *The Corsair* • Nureyev and Dame Margot Fonteyn dance with Martha Graham in *Lucifer* for her 50th anniversary gala.

Books

Fiction
Critics' Choice

A Month of Sundays, John Updike
The Dead Father, Donald Barthelme
Cockpit, Jerzy Kosinski
The Underground Woman, Kay Boyle
J R, William Gaddis
Tyrants Destroyed and Other Stories, Vladimir Nabokov
I Would Have Saved Them If I Could, Leonard Michaels
Beyond the Bedroom Wall, Larry Woiwode
A Dove of the East and Other Stories, Mark Helprin

Best-Sellers

Ragtime, E. L. Doctorow
The Moneylenders, Arthur Hailey
Curtain, Agatha Christie
Looking for Mister Goodbar, Judith Rossner
The Choirboys, Joseph Wambaugh
The Eagle Has Landed, Jack Higgins
The Great Train Robbery, Michael Crichton
Shōgun, James Clavell

Nonfiction
Critics' Choice

Anarchy, State, and Utopia, Robert Nozick
Sociobiology, Edward O. Wilson
The War against the Jews, 1933–1945, Lucy Davidowicz
Synergetics, Buckminster Fuller
Against Our Will: Men, Women and Rape, Susan Brownmiller
A Time to Die, Tom Wicker
The Courage to Create, Rollo May
Before the Fall, William Safire
Thinking about Crime, James Q. Wilson
The Great Railway Bazaar, Paul Theroux
Fathers and Children, Michael Rogin
A Century of Struggle, Eleanor Flexner
American Slavery, American Freedom, Edmund S. Morgan
The Great War and Modern Memory, Paul Fussell
Passage to Ararat, Michael J. Arlen
The Problem of Slavery in the Age of Revolution, David Brion Davis

Best-Sellers

Angels: God's Secret Agents, Billy Graham
Winning through Intimidation, Robert Ringer
TM, Harold H. Bloomfield
The Ascent of Man, Jacob Bronowski
Sylvia Porter's Money Book, Sylvia Porter
Total Fitness in 30 Minutes a Week, Laurence E. Morehouse, Leonard Gross

Poetry

Anne Sexton, *The Awful Rowing toward God*
Nikki Giovanni, *The Women and the Men*
A. R. Ammons, *Diversifications*
Galway Kinnell, *The Avenue Bearing the Initial of Christ into the New World*
Denise Levertov, *The Freeing of the Dust*
William Meredith, *Hazard, the Painter*

Pulitzer Prizes

Humboldt's Gift, Saul Bellow (fiction)
Lamy of Santa Fe, Paul Horgan (U.S. history)
Why Survive? Being Old in America, Robert N. Butler (nonfiction)
Edith Wharton: A Biography R. W. B. Lewis (biography)
Self-Portrait in a Convex Mirror, John Ashbery (poetry)

Science and Technology

Apollo 18 and the USSR's Soyuz 19 dock in space, perform experiments together, and indicate the possibility of space rescue.

A telephone transmission device is developed to analyze a distant patient's heartbeat.

EMI develops a scanner that takes cross-sectional X-rays through any part of the body.

The highly controversial DES is approved for limited use, such as "morning-after" contraception.

The Heimlich Maneuver, for people who choke on food, is approved.

Leading scientists try to formulate safety precautions for genetic engineering at the Asilomar (California) Conference.

Discovered in Texas, a pterosaur fossil with a 51-foot wing span offers evidence of the largest known flying animal.

☙ Encephalin, "the brain's own opiate," is isolated, leading to further research in the production of a natural analgesic without addictive properties.

☙ Atari/Sears of Japan produces the first low-priced integrated circuits for TV games.

Nobel Prize

James Brainwater wins in physics for demonstrating that the atomic nucleus is asymmetrical. David Baltimore, Howard M. Temin, and Renato Dulbecco win in physiology and medicine for work on the interaction between tumor viruses and the genetic material of the cell.

Sports

Baseball

Newly declared free agent Catfish Hunter signs a record $2.85 million contract with New York Yankee owner George Steinbrenner.

Cincinnati's "Big Red Machine" wins 108 games, the most won by any team in the National League since 1906, when Chicago won 116.

Fred Lynn (Boston, AL) is the first player to win Rookie of the Year and MVP in the same season.

A record TV audience of 75.9 million watches the seventh game of the World Series.

The Cy Young awards are won by Tom Seaver (New York, NL) and Jim Palmer (Baltimore, NL).

Champions

Batting
Bill Madlock (Chicago, NL), .354
Rod Carew (Minnesota, AL), .359
Pitching
Don Gullett (Cincinnati, NL), 15–4
Mike Torrez (Baltimore, AL), 20–9
Home runs
Mike Schmidt (Philadelphia, NL), 38

Football

Archie Griffin (Ohio State) is the first player to win a second Heisman Trophy.

Oklahoma's 37-game unbeaten streak is ended.

NFL Season Leaders: Fran Tarkenton (Minnesota), passing; Jim Otis (St. Louis), rushing; Chuck Foreman (Minnesota), receiving

AFC Season Leaders: Ken Anderson (Cincinnati), passing; O. J. Simpson (Buffalo), rushing, 1,827 yards; Reggie Rucker (Cleveland), receiving

College All-Americans: Tony Dorsett (B), Pittsburgh; Ricky Bell (B), Southern California.

Bowls (Jan. 1, 1976)

Rose: UCLA 23–Ohio State 10
Orange: Oklahoma 14–Michigan 6
Cotton: Arkansas 31–Georgia 10
Sugar: Alabama 13–Penn State 6

Basketball

NBA All-Pro First Team: John Havlicek (Boston), Rick Barry (Golden State), Kareem Abdul-Jabbar (Milwaukee), Walt Frazier (New York), Gail Goodrich (Los Angeles)

Other Sports

Boxing: In the "Thrilla in Manila," Muhammad Ali beats Joe Frazier by a TKO in the 15th round to regain the title.

Golf: Jack Nicklaus wins the Masters and PGA, misses the U.S. Open by two and the British Masters by one; he has won 16 majors.

Soccer: The New York Cosmos soccer team signs Brazilian star Pelé to a $1 million contract.

Tennis: Arthur Ashe wins Wimbledon and is the leading money winner with $325,000.

Horse racing: Unbeaten three-year-old Ruffian breaks an ankle and must be destroyed.

Winners

World Series
  Cincinnati (NL) 4
  Boston (AL) 3
MVP
  NL–Joe Morgan, Cincinnati
  AL–Fred Lynn, Boston
Super Bowl X (Jan. 1976)
  Pittsburgh 21–Dallas 17
MVP
  Fran Tarkenton, Minnesota
College Football
  Oklahoma
Heisman Trophy
  Archie Griffin, Ohio State
NBA Championship
  Golden State 4–Washington 0

MVP
  Bob McAdoo, Buffalo
College Basketball
  UCLA
Player of the Year
  David Thompson, North Carolina State
Stanley Cup
  Philadelphia
US Tennis Open
  Men: Manuel Orantes
  Women: Chris Evert
USGA Open
  Lou Graham
Kentucky Derby
  Foolish Pleasure (J. Vasquez, jockey)

Fashion

For Women: East and West meet in the ethnic and layered look: from Britain come the Sherlock Holmes cape, Norfolk jacket, and tartan kilt; from China, the velvet gown, cossack coat, pants tucked in boots-style, and hats with ear flaps; from France, skin-tight jeans rolled at the knee with boots. Also popular are khaki and blue fatigues and jumpsuits, along with wide-shouldered pinafore dresses and other early American dress styles (for the bicentennial) with prim, high necks, fitted bodices, and gathered skirts. The T-shirt fad continues.

For Men: The casual look dominates: leisure suits with large patch pockets, worn with open shirts (collars extended over the lapels), or sweaters, scarves, ascots, and string ties. Women's designers, like Halston, turn to men's wear.

High-fashion notes: For Women—the Louis Vuitton duffle bag; Dorothy Bis's sweater coat. For Men—the St. Laurent fitted, double-breasted, "banker-gangster" suit

Kaleidoscope

- When Apollo 18 and USSR Soyez dock in space, the astronauts celebrate with a dinner of borscht, turkey, and lamb.
- A national opinion survey indicates that 69 percent of the population believes that "over the last 10 years, this country's leaders have consistently lied to the people"; public confidence in physicians drops from 73 percent (1966) to 42 percent; in big business, 55 percent to 16 percent.
- Attorney General Edward Levi confirms that J. Edgar Hoover kept files on the private lives of prominent people, including presidents and congressmen.
- Former CIA director Richard Helmes divulges CIA sponsorship of the assassination of foreign leaders—the attempt, for example, to enlist the Mafia's aid in killing Castro. One plot involved poisoned pens; another, poisoned cigars.
- The so-called typical nuclear family, with working father, housewife, and two children, represents only 7 percent of the population; average family size is 3.43 (in 1970, 3.58; in 1920, 4.3).
- Harvard changes its 5 to 2 male-female admissions policy to equal admissions.
- Vandalism and violence increase in public schools; homicides increase nearly 20 percent, rapes and robberies, 40 percent; since 1965, crimes against students escalate 3,000 percent and against teachers 7,000 percent.
- Despite the International Women's Year, efforts to pass statewide ERAs in New York and New Jersey suffer defeat.
- The Atomic Energy Commission is dissolved.
- A Massachusetts physician is convicted of manslaughter by a Boston jury for aborting a fetus and is sentenced to a year on probation.
- California and New York doctors publicize their enormous malpractice insurance increases by withholding all but emergency services; premiums have increased 93.5 percent in New York since last year.
- The Supreme Court rules that the mentally ill cannot be hospitalized against their will unless they are dangerous to themselves or others.
- A New Jersey superior court denies the petition of Karen Ann Quinlan's parents, which asks to remove her life support systems; she has suffered irreversible brain damage after an overdose of alcohol and tranquilizers.
- New York City, under threat of default, is bailed out by union pension funds, which buy Municipal Assistance Corporation bonds; MAC is headed by Felix Rohatyn.
- Governor James Rhodes and the Ohio National Guard are acquitted of all claims against them in the Kent State deaths of 1970.
- Joanne Little is declared "not guilty" of stabbing a white prison guard who tried to rape her.
- Rape laws are changed in nine states, narrowing the amount of corroborative evidence necessary for

conviction and also restricting the trial questions permitted regarding the victim's past sex life.
- Sixty-nine cents shops replace 5 and 10 cents stores.
- The Rolling Stones tour grosses $13 million; Elton John signs a record contract for $8 million; Stevie Wonder later signs for $13 million; Bruce Springsteen appears on both *Time* and *Newsweek* covers.
- New dances include the hustle, bump, and robot.
- *Penthouse* sales surpass *Playboy*'s.
- Bantam pays a record $1,850,000 for the paperback rights to E. L. Doctorow's *Ragtime*.
- The Brewers' Society reports that Americans consume an average of 151 pints of beer per year, 11.5 pints of wine, and 9.1 pints of spirits.
- Studies indicate a decrease in heart attack deaths because of better diet, exercise, and decreased smoking.
- Many big cities are hit by strikes, including San Francisco (police), Charleston, West Virginia, and Chicago (teachers), and New York (sanitation workers).
- Chrysler, followed by other auto companies, offers rebates to counter record low sales.
- The first bulletproof fashion collection for men and women is manufactured.
- Vice President Nelson Rockefeller buys a bed designed by Max Ernst for $35,000.
- Charleston, S.C., passes a law requiring horse owners to diaper their animals.

Fads: Pie throwing, dance marathons, skateboards, mood rings, Spiderman

New Words and Usages: Fireperson, chairperson

First Appearances: Whooping crane born in captivity (Laurel, Md.), commencement exercises within a prison (Jackson, Mich.), black chief justice of a federal court (J. B. Parsons, Illinois), hotel for dogs, (Kennilworth, New York City); state finding unconstitutional the ban against girls competing with boys in athletics on a state basis (Pa.), ski carousel, individuals permitted to buy gold (since 1933), word processing equipment, digital records, women's bank (New York City), Swingline multiple-shot-fastening staple gun, disposable razor, Altair home computer kit, electronic watch (Commodore), doll that "grows," American canonized by the Catholic church (Elizabeth Seton), nonstick chewing gum for denture wearers (Wrigley), satellite TV cable, videocassette recorders (VCR, Betamax), computerized supermarket checkout, Pulitzer prize for cartoon ("Doonesbury"), legislation enabling women to attend Annapolis, West Point, and the Air Force Academy, advertisement for tampons on TV

1976

Facts and Figures

Economic Profile
  Dow-Jones: ↑ High 1004–
    Low 858
  GNP: +10%
  Inflation: +8.7%
  Unemployment: 8.3%
Entering college students:
  31%
Four-year colleges: 1,913
Public/private schools: 7.5/1
VW Rabbit: $3,499
Plymouth Cordoba: $4,899
Cadillac Seville: $13,442
Puma "Clydes": $21.95
Rossignol ski sets: $99–$229
Vacation packages:
  Hawaii from Chicago (8
  days, American Airlines):
  $329
  Mexico from Denver (8
  days, Mexicana): $119–
  $139
  Disneyland from New York
  (8 days, Eastern): $206
House, Pine Hill, N.J.
  (former home of Al
  Capone): $180,000
Veterans' mortgage rates,
  Milwaukee: 7.¾%

Deaths

Busby Berkeley, Benjamin
  Britten, Alexander Calder,
  Agatha Christie, André
  Malraux, Sal Mineo,
  Walter Piston, Lily Pons,
  Paul Robeson, Rosalind
  Russell.

In the News

CHINESE PREMIER CHOU EN-LAI DIES . . . SPAIN ANNOUNCES PLAN FOR DEMOCRACY . . . FORD ANNOUNCES REORGANIZATION OF U.S. INTELLIGENCE SERVICES . . . PORTUGAL ESTABLISHES DEMOCRACY . . . LOCKHEED BRIBE OF JAPANESE IS EXPOSED . . . PATTY HEARST IS FOUND GUILTY OF BANK ROBBERY . . . LEBANESE CIVIL WAR ERUPTS, SYRIAN TROOPS MOVE IN . . . SUPREME COURT ALLOWS REMOVAL OF KAREN QUINLAN'S LIFE SUPPORT SYSTEMS . . . NIXON SAYS KISSINGER AIDES' PHONES WERE TAPPED . . . FRENCH PRESIDENT GISCARD D'ESTAING ADDRESSES CONGRESS, ASKS FOR "CONFIDENCE IN US" . . . CONCORDE BEGINS REGULAR TRANSATLANTIC SERVICE . . . U.S. AND USSR SIGN UNDERGROUND NUCLEAR LIMITATIONS TREATY . . . SUPREME COURT RULES THAT CAPITAL PUNISHMENT IS CONSTITUTIONAL . . . VIETNAM IS REUNIFIED, HANOI IS NAMED CAPITAL, SAIGON IS RENAMED HO CHI MINH CITY . . . ISRAELI COMMANDOS RAID ENTEBBE AIRPORT, UGANDA, AND FREE 103 HOSTAGES . . . DEMOCRATS NOMINATE JIMMY CARTER FOR PRESIDENT, FORD IS NOMINATED BY GOP . . . RHODESIAN P.M. IAN SMITH ACCEPTS PLAN TO TRANSFER POWER TO BLACKS . . . 26 CHILDREN ON SCHOOL BUS ARE KIDNAPPED AND LATER FREED IN CHOWCHILLA, CALIF. . . . VIKING I LANDS ON MARS, SENDS BACK PHOTOS . . . FORD, ON TV DEBATE, DENIES RUSSIA'S POWER OVER POLES . . . U.S. AND IRAN SIGN $10 BILLION ARMS SALE . . . CHILEAN EXILE ORLANDO ATELIER IS ASSASSINATED IN WASHINGTON, D.C. . . . MAO TSE-TUNG DIES . . . SECRETARY OF AGRICULTURE EARL BUTZ RESIGNS OVER ALLEGED RACIST REMARK . . . CARTER WINS PRESIDENCY, 40.8 MILLION TO 39.1 MILLION, DEMOCRATS RETAIN CONGRESS . . . SEPARATISTS GAIN LARGE VICTORY IN QUEBEC . . . OPEC ANNOUNCES 5%–10% OIL PRICE HIKE.

President Jimmy Carter and his family. "I'll never tell a lie," Mr. Carter promises. *Library of Congress.*

Quotes

"I speak to you as a direct descendant from George III. . . . It seems to me that Independence Day, the Fouth of July, should be celebrated in both our countries. . . . Let Freedom Ring."
— Queen Elizabeth II, presenting a new liberty bell

"It's the Me-Decade."
— Tom Wolfe, *New York* magazine

"[This is a time of] hedonism, . . . narcissism, . . . cult of the self."
— Christopher Lasch, *New York Review of Books*

"What we succeeded in doing in the Sixties was in dealing with the constitutional issue of rights. We've won that battle. . . . [Now] we're dealing with real equality."
— James Farmer, former head, CORE

"I have looked upon a lot of women with lust. I've committed adultery in my heart many times."
— Jimmy Carter, *Playboy* interview

"In his heart, he knows your wife."
— Bumper sticker, following Jimmy Carter's *Playboy* interview

"I can't type, I can't file, I can't even answer the phone."
— Elizabeth Ray, secretary to Congressman Wayne Hayes

"For some reason, self-doubt appears to thrive in our Bicentennial year."
— Arthur Schlesinger, Jr.

"I've got a momma who joined the Peace Corps and went to India when she was sixty-eight. I've got one sister [Ruth], who's a Holy Roller preacher, another sister [Gloria], who . . . rides a motorcycle. So that makes me the only sane person in the family."
— Jimmy Carter

"Governor Reagan and I have one thing in common. We both played football. . . . I played for Michigan. He played for Warner Brothers."
— Gerald Ford

"That word would be 'faith.' "
— Jimmy Carter's one-word summary of his campaign

Ads

How strong is the Chiquita name?
How many banana commercials can you sing?
(*Chiquita Banana Company*)

Now your kids don't have to miss Monday Night Football because they're studying for a Tuesday morning exam.
(*Betamax, Sony*)

How kinky is Barbra?
Only her hairdresser knows for sure.
(People *magazine*)

In 1944 you won the war together. Isn't it worth $1.50 to spend five minutes with him again?
(*Northwestern Bell*)

Look your best while you wear your least.
(*Jockey Shorts*)

Fly now. Shovel later.
(*Eastern Airlines*)

Maybe your squeaky hair is really crying out for help.
(*Pantene*)

At last. A pickle that bites back.
(*Marcus Valley Pickles*)

TV

Premieres
"The Muppet Show," Jim Henson
"Quincy, M.E.," Jack Klugman
"The Gong Show," Chuck Barris
"Mary Hartman, Mary Hartman," Louise Lasser
"The Bionic Woman," Lindsay Wagner
"Laverne and Shirley," Cindy Williams, Penny Marshall
"Donny and Marie [Osmond]"
"Charlie's Angels," Jaclyn Smith, Farrah Fawcett-Majors, Kate Jackson
"Alice," Linda Lavin
"Wonder Woman," Lynda Carter

Top Ten (Nielsen)
"Happy Days," "Laverne and Shirley," "ABC Monday Night Movie," "M*A*S*H," "Charlie's Angels," "The Big Event," "The Six-Million-Dollar Man," "ABC Sunday Night Movie," "Baretta," "One Day at a Time"

Specials
"Sybil"; "Rich Man, Poor Man, Book II"; "American Ballet Theatre: 'Swan Lake' " ("Live from Lincoln Center"); "Eleanor and Franklin: The White House Years" (Edward Herrmann, Jane Alexander); "Arthur Rubinstein at 90"; "Jesus of Nazareth" (Franco Zeffirelli)

Emmy Awards
"Upstairs, Downstairs" (drama); "The Mary Tyler Moore Show" (comedy); "Van Dyke and Company" (variety); "Ballet Shoes, Parts I and II, Piccadilly Circus" (children); James Garner (actor, "The Rockford Files"); Carroll O'Connor (comedic actor, "All in the Family"); Lindsay Wagner (actress, "The Bionic Woman"); Beatrice Arthur (comedic actress, "Maude")

Of Note
There are 20 police–private eye shows • Showtime becomes the second major pay-cable TV network • The film *Gone with the Wind* draws the highest ratings to date • The Gerald Ford–Jimmy Carter debate is the first presidential campaign debate since Nixon and Kennedy's in 1960 • Barbara Walters signs a 5-year, $1 million-a-year contract with ABC as co-anchor with Harry Reasoner • ABC, under Fred Silverman's guidance, becomes number one in ratings, after many years of CBS dominance.

Movies

Openings
Rocky (John G. Avildsen), Sylvester Stallone, Talia Shire, Burgess Meredith
All the President's Men (Alan J. Pakula), Dustin Hoffman, Robert Redford, Jason Robards
Bound for Glory (Hal Ashby), David Carradine, Melinda Dillon, Ronny Cox, Gail Strickland
Network (Sidney Lumet), Faye Dunaway, William Holden, Peter Finch
Taxi Driver (Martin Scorsese), Robert De Niro, Harvey Keitel, Cybill Shepherd
Carrie (Brian De Palma), Sissy Spacek, Piper Laurie
Marathon Man (John Schlesinger), Dustin Hoffman, Laurence Olivier, Roy Scheider
The Sailor Who Fell from Grace with the Sea (Lewis John Carlino), Sara Miles, Kris Kristofferson
The Front (Martin Ritt), Woody Allen, Zero Mostel
King Kong (John Guillermin), Jeff Bridges, Jessica Lange, Charles Grodin
A Star Is Born (Frank Pierson), Barbra Streisand, Kris Kristofferson
The Omen (Richard Donner), Gregory Peck, Lee Remick
Harlan County, U.S.A. (Barbara Kipple), documentary
The Bad News Bears (Michael Ritchie), Walter Matthau, Tatum O'Neal
The Man Who Fell to Earth (Nicolas Roeg), David Bowie, Rip Torn
The Memory of Justice (Marcel Ophuls), documentary
Cousin, Cousine (Jean-Charles Tacchelia), Marie-Christine Barrault, Victor Lanoux

Academy Awards
Best Picture: *Rocky*
Best Director: John G. Avildsen *(Rocky)*
Best Actress: Faye Dunaway *(Network)*
Best Actor: Peter Finch *(Network)*

Top Box-Office Stars
Robert Redford, Jack Nicholson, Dustin Hoffman, Clint Eastwood, Mel Brooks, Burt Reynolds, Al Pacino, Tatum O'Neal, Woody Allen, Charles Bronson

Stars of Tomorrow
Sylvester Stallone, Talia Shire, Jessica Lange, Sissy Spacek, Robby Benson, Sam Elliott, Margaux Hemingway, Susan Sarandon, Ellen Greene

Popular Music

Hit Songs
"Silly Love Songs"
"Don't Go Breaking My Heart"
"Play that Funky Music"
"A Fifth of Beethoven"
"(Shake, Shake, Shake) Shake
Your Booty"
"Breaking Up Is Hard to Do"
"Love Is Alive"
"Sara Smile"
"Get Closer"

Top Records

Albums: *Songs in the Key of Life*
(Stevie Wonder); *Peter Frampton
Comes Alive!* (Peter Frampton);
Desire (Bob Dylan); *Their
Greatest Hits 1971–1975* (Eagles);
Black and Blue (Rolling Stones);
Gratitude (Earth, Wind and Fire)

Singles: *Disco Lady* (Johnnie
Taylor); *December 1963* (Four

Seasons); *Kiss and Say Goodbye*
(Manhattans); *50 Ways to Leave
Your Lover* (Paul Simon); *I Write
the Songs* (Barry Manilow); *Love
Hangover* (Diana Ross); *Lonely
Night* (Captain and Tennille).
Country: *Stranger* (Johnny
Duncan); *If I Had to Do It All
Over Again* (Roy Clark)

Grammy Awards
The Masquerade, George Benson
(record); *Songs in the Key of
Life,* Stevie Wonder (album); "I
Write the Songs" (song)

Jazz and Big Bands
Bob Marley and the Wailers
popularize reggae ("Rastaman
Vibration").

Popular Performers: Carlos
Santana, Cal Tjader, Eddie
Palmieri, Ray Barretto, Johnny
Pachecho, Tito Puente, Willie
Colon

**Popular Jazz-Rock-Blues
Groups:** Weather Report,
Mahavishnu Orchestra, Blood,
Sweat, and Tears, Chicago; the
avant-garde: Keith Jarrett,
Roswell Rud and Jazz Composers
Orchestra, Gato Barbieri; space
jazz: Lonnie Liston Smith,
"Astral Traveling"; African jazz:
Dollar Brand "Sangoma"; the
revival of old sounds: National
Jazz Ensemble (Chuck Israel).

Top Performers *(Downbeat):*
McCoy Tyner (soloist); Thad
Jones and Mel Lewis (band);
Weather Report (jazz group);
Chick Corea, George Benson,
Wayne Shorter, Phil Woods,
Sonny Rollins, Gerry Mulligan,
Bill Watrous, Freddie Hubbard,
Airto Moreira (instrumentalists);
Flora Purim, Mel Torme
(vocalists); Pointer Sisters (vocal
group); Weather Report, *Black
Market,* McCoy Tyner, *Trident*
(albums)

Theater

Broadway Openings

Plays
A Matter of Gravity (Enid Bagnold), Katharine
Hepburn
The Belle of Amherst (William Luce), Julie Harris
California Suite (Neil Simon), Barbara Barrie,
George Grizzard, Tammy Grimes, Jack Weston
Texas Trilogy (Preston Jones), Diane Ladd
The Comedians (Trevor Griffins), John Lithgow,
Jonathan Pryce, Milo O'Shea
Days in the Trees (Marguerite Duras), Madeleine
Renard, in French; Mildred Dunnock, in English
No Man's Land (Harold Pinter), Ralph Richardson,
John Gielgud
Poor Murderers (Pavel Kahout), Maria Schell,
Laurence Luckinbill
The Innocents (William Archibald), Claire Bloom,
Pauline Flanagan
Sly Fox (Larry Gelbart), George C. Scott, Robert
Preston, Jack Gilford
The Heiress (Ruth Augustus Goetz), Richard Kiley,
Jane Alexander
Knock Knock (Jules Feiffer), Lynn Redgrave, John
Heffernan, Charles Durning

Musicals
Pacific Overtures (Stephen Sondheim), Mako, Yuki
Shimodo, Sab Shimono
Bubbling Brown Sugar (various authors), Avon Long,
Josephine Premice
Your Arms Too Short to Box with God (Alex
Bradford), Delores Hall, William Hardy, Jr.

Classics, Revivals, and Off-Broadway
Premieres
The Old Glory (Robert Lowell), Roscoe Lee Browne;
The Lady from the Sea (Ibsen), Vanessa Redgrave,
Pat Hingle; *Who's Afraid of Virginia Woolf?* (Edward
Albee), Ben Gazzara, Colleen Dewhurst; *Mrs.
Warren's Profession* (George Bernard Shaw), Ruth
Gordon; *For Colored Girls Who Have Considered
Suicide When the Rainbow Is Enuf* (Ntozake
Shange), Trazana Beverley; *American Buffalo* (David
Mamet), Michael Egen; *Long Day's Journey into
Night* (Eugene O'Neill), Zoë Caldwell, Jason
Robards, Michael Moriarty, Kevin Conway

Regional
Arena Stage, Washington, D.C., is the first company
outside New York to win a Tony Award.

Theater (cont.)

Long Wharf, New Haven: *Streamers* (David Rabe), premiere

Pulitzer Prize
A Chorus Line, Edward Kleban, Marvin Hamlisch

Tony Awards
Travesties, Tom Stoppard (play); *A Chorus Line,* Edward Kleban, Marvin Hamlisch (musical)

Classical Music

Compositions
Richard Wernick, *Visions of Terror and Wonder*
Karl Korte, Concerto for Piano and Winds
Gian Carlo Menotti, *Landscapes and Remembrances, First Symphony*
Don Gillis, *The Secret History of the Birth of the Nation*
Vivian Fine, Romantic Ode; *Meeting for Equal Rights 1866*
William Schuman, *Concerto on Old English Rounds; The Young Dead Soldiers*
Morton Feldman, *Voices and Instruments*

Important Events
Avery Fisher Hall at Lincoln Center reopens, after acoustical adjustments, with a month of Mahler and a nine-day festival of 20th-century music performed by Juilliard and the New York Philharmonic.
The Kennedy Center in Washington, D.C., presents a year-long Bicentennial Parade of American Music, sponsored by a $200,000 grant from Exxon.
Lorin Maazel conducts the Cleveland in programs devoted to individual modern composers Boris Blacher, Luciano Berio, and Raymond Premru.
On the event of its 85th birthday, Carnegie Hall raises over a million dollars at a concert at which Isaac Stern, Yehudi Menuhin, Mstislav Rostropovitch, Dietrich Fischer-Dieskau, Leonard Bernstein, and Vladimir Horowitz perform and together sing the Hallelujah chorus from Handel's *Messiah.*
Artur Rubinstein, 89, gives a 70th-anniversary concert at Carnegie Hall.

New Appointments: Seiji Ozawa, Boston (full time); Eduardo Mata, Dallas; Edo de Waart, San Francisco

Debuts: Ken Noda, Lazar Berman, James Galway

First Performances
Mario Davidorsky, Synchronism 7 (New York); John Cage, *Renga, Apartment House 1776* (Boston); Lukas Foss, Folk Song (Baltimore); Roy Harris, Symphony no. 14 (Washington); Ned Rorem, *Air Music* (Cincinnati); Ross Lee Finney, Violin Concerto, (Dallas); William Bolcom, Piano Concerto (Seattle); Michael Colgrass, *New People* (Minneapolis)

Opera

Metropolitan: Sarah Caldwell (debut), Beverly Sills, Stuart Burrows, Ingvar Wixell, *La traviata;* Renata Scotto, Shirley Verrett, Luciano Pavarotti, *Il trovatore;* Joan Sutherland, *Esclarmonde;* Giuseppe Giacomini, Ezio Flagello, *La forza del destino*

New York State: Beverly Sills, Donald Gramm, Samuel Ramey, *Il barbiere di Siviglia* (Sarah Caldwell, conducting)

Chicago: Nicolai Ghiaurov, *Khovanshchina* (Mussorgsky); Richard Gill, William Dooley, Alan Titus, Klara Barlow, *The Love for Three Oranges*

Boston: Donald Gramm, Brent Ellis, Phyllis Bryn-Julson, *Montezuma* (Roger Sessions, American premiere)

Santa Fe: *The Mother of Us All* (Virgil Thomson)

Dallas: Alfredo Kraus, *Les contes d'Hoffmann*

Houston: *Bilby's Doll* (Carlisle Floyd, premiere)

Minnesota: *The Voyage of Edgar Allan Poe* (Dominick Argento, premiere)

Baltimore: Richard Stilwell, *Ines de Castro* (Thomas Pasatieri, premiere). Visiting for the Bicentennial: Paris Opera (*Le nozze di Figaro*), La Scala (Strehler's *Macbeth; La Cenerentola*)

Music Notes
Philip Glass's *Einstein on the Beach* is performed in numerous European cities and in New York • Particular attention to women musicians includes a "Meet the Woman Composer" series of 11 concerts in New York and premieres of works by Jean Eichelberger-Ivey (Baltimore) and Marga Richter (Tucson) • The Festival Institute at Round Top, Texas, begins • Artur Rubinstein receives the Medal of Freedom from Gerald Ford.

Art

Paintings

Jasper Johns, *Corpse and Mirror, End Paper*

Jim Dine, *Four Robes Existing in This Vale of Tears*

Chuck Close, *Linda no. 6646*

Red Grooms, *Ruckus Manhattan*

Philip Guston, *Wharf: Source*

Frank Stella, *Wake Island Rail*

Lee Krasner, *Present Perfect*

Isabel Bishop, *Recess #3*

William Jensen, *Heaven, Earth*

Willem de Kooning, *Untitled VI*

Duane Hanson, *Couple with Shopping Bags*

Jackie Winsor, *Cement Piece, #1 Rope*

Claes Oldenburg, *Inverted Q*

Sol LeWitt, *Lines to Points on a Grid*

Sculpture

Christo, *Running Fence*

Architecture

Occupational Health Center, Columbia, Ind. (Holzman, Pfeiffer)

Richardson-Merrell Headquarters, Wilton, Conn. (Roche and Dinkeloo)

Liberty Bell Pavilion, Living History Center, Philadelphia (Mitchell, Giurgola)

Columbus East High School, Indiana (Mitchell, Giurgola)

Important Exhibitions

For the bicentennial, the Prado sends a collection of Spanish paintings that tours the United States. The King Tutankhamen Treasures exhibition begins its tour to New York, Chicago, Los Angeles, New Orleans, Oakland, and Seattle.

Museums

New York: *Metropolitan:* "The Two Worlds of Andrew Wyeth: Kuerners and Olsons." *Museum of Modern Art:* "Fauvism and Its Affinities" (travels to San Francisco, Fort Worth); Retrospective: André Masson. *Whitney:* 200 Years of American Sculpture

Yale: "American Art 1750–1800 toward Independence"

Philadelphia: "Three Centuries of American Art" (the largest bicentennial show)

National: "The Age of Jefferson"; "The European Vision of America" (also at Cleveland)

Worcester: "The Early Republic: Consolidation of Revolutionary Goals"

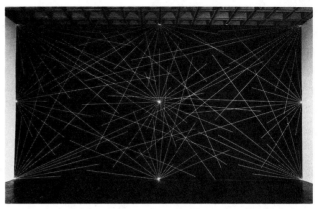

Sol LeWitt, *Lines to Points on a Grid,* 1976. Six-inch pencil grid and white chalk on four black walls. *Collection of Whitney Museum of American Art. Gift of the Gilman Foundation, Inc.*

Chicago: Ecclesiastical vestments from the 11th–20th centuries

Art Briefs

Much attention is given to the disposition of Mark Rothko's multimillion-dollar estate • A Rembrandt portrait at the Boston Museum, valued at $1–2 million, is stolen, adding to an estimated $1 billion of stolen or smuggled art in the United States • Major sales include Gauguin's *Nature Morte à l'estampe Japonaise* ($1.4 million) and a marble bust of Ben Franklin by Jean-Antoine Houdon ($310,000).

Dance

Bruce Marks becomes artistic director of Ballet West, Salt Lake City.

Premieres/Important Productions

American Ballet Theatre: *Push Comes to Shove* (Twyla Tharp); *Le sacre du printemps* (Glen Tetley); *The Nutcracker* (Mikhail Baryshnikov), *La Bayadère* (Natalia Makarova); *Other Dances* (Jerome Robbins); dancing in the company are Baryshnikov, Makarova, Erik Bruhn, Fernando Bujones, Gelsey Kirkland, Ivan Nagy, Carla Fracci, Alicia Alonso, Marcia Haydee, Lynn Seymour.

New York City Ballet: *Union Jack* (Balanchine); *Chaconne* (Balanchine); *Calcium Light Night* (Peter Martins)

Alvin Ailey: *Pas de Duke* (Ailey, Duke Ellington), Baryshnikov, Judith Jamison

Paul Taylor: *Cloven Kingdom*

Saul Bellow. *Thomas Victor.*

Books

Fiction

Critics' Choice
The Public Burning, Robert Coover
Kinflicks, Lisa Alther
Meridian, Alice Walker
Lovers and Tyrants, Francine du Plessix Gray
Will You Please Be Quiet, Please?, Raymond Carver
Searching for Caleb, Anne Tyler
Ordinary People, Judith Guest
Chilly Scenes of Winter, Ann Beattie
The Spectator Bird, Wallace E. Stegner
* *Autumn of the Patriarch,* Gabriel García Márquez

Best-Sellers
Trinity, Leon Uris
Sleeping Murder, Agatha Christie
Dolores, Jacqueline Susann
The Deep, Peter Benchley
1876, Gore Vidal
Slapstick or Lonesome No More! Kurt Vonnegut, Jr.

Nonfiction

Critics' Choice
Born on the Fourth of July, Ron Kovic
The Uses of Enchantment, Bruno Bettelheim
World of Our Fathers, Irving Howe
The Black Family in Slavery and Freedom 1750–1925, Herbert Gutman
Friendly Fire, C. D. B. Bryan
Lyndon Johnson and the American Dream, Doris Kearns
The Survivor, Terrence Des Pres
The Woman Warrior, Maxine Hong Kingston
The Russians, Hedrick Smith
Plagues and People, William McNeill
The Time of Illusion, Jonathan Schell
Norman Thomas: The Last Idealist, W. A. Swanberg

Best-Sellers
The Final Days, Bob Woodward, Carl Bernstein
Roots, Alex Haley
Your Erroneous Zones, Dr. Wayne W. Dyer
Passages, Gail Sheehy
Born Again, Charles W. Colson
The Grass Is Always Greener over the Septic Tank, Erma Bombeck
Blind Ambition: The White House Years, John Dean
The Hite Report: A Nationwide Study of Female Sexuality, Shere Hite

Poetry
Robert Lowell, *Selected Poems*
James Dickey, *The Zodiac*
Muriel Rukeyser, *The Gates*
Richard Eberhart, *Collected Poems, 1930–76*
Philip Levine, *The Names of the Lost*

Pulitzer Prizes
No prize is awarded in fiction.
The Impending Crisis: 1841–1861, David M. Potter (U.S. history) (posthumous)
Beautiful Swimmers, William W. Warner (nonfiction)
A Prince of Our Disorder, John E. Mack (biography)
Divine Comedies, James Merrill (poetry)

Nobel Prize
Saul Bellow

Science and Technology

Viking I makes a successful soft landing on Mars and returns photos of a rusty brown landscape with rocky desert and pink sky; its findings indicate the presence of nitrogen in Mars's atmosphere.

The Pershing IA ground-to-ground guided missile system permits firing from an unsurveyed site.

The Navy tests Tomahawk, a sea-launched cruise missile (SLCM) with a high-explosive warhead.

The Air-Launched Cruise Missile (ALCM) system is developed to intentionally confuse the distinctions between tactical or strategic and conventional or nuclear weapons.

Cimetidine (Tagamet) is marketed for peptic ulcers; it prevents the secretion of excessive acid.

A swine flu virus is cultured for mass inoculation to avoid a recurrence of the 1918–19 epidemic.

U.S. and Soviet surgeons implant artificial hearts in calves, the first joint project to develop an artificial heart for human beings.

Richard Leakey discovers the most complete homo erectus skull (like Peking man) to date, in Kenya; its estimated age is 1.5 million years.

* British scientists develop PGE, a prostaglandin, which prevents blood clotting.

Nobel Prize
Burton Richter and Samuel C. C. Ting win in physics for the discovery of the J and psi subatomic particles. Baruch S. Blumberg and D. Carleton Gajdusek win in physiology and medicine for their work on infectious disease. William N. Lipscom wins in chemistry for work on the structure and bonding mechanism of boranes.

Sports

Baseball

Players and owners negotiate a contract allowing for free agency for players with more than six years of service; after the season Reggie Jackson signs for a record $2.9 million for five years.

Pitcher Mark "The Bird" Fydrich (Detroit, AL) wins Rookie of the Year and excites fans with antics such as talking to the baseball.

Henry Aaron retires with a career total of 755 home runs.

The Cy Young awards are won by Randy Jones (San Diego, NL) and Jim Palmer (Baltimore, AL).

Champions

Batting
Bill Madlock (Chicago, NL), .339
George Brett (Kansas City, AL), .333
Pitching
Steve Carlton (Philadelphia, NL), 20–7
Bill Campbell (Minnesota, AL), 17–5
Home runs
Mike Schmidt (Philadelphia, NL), 38

Football

O. J. Simpson (Buffalo) signs a record $2.9 million, three-year pact; he also rushes for a single-game record of 273 yards. Rocky Bleier and Franco Harris each gain over 1,000 yards rushing for Pittsburgh.

NFC Season Leaders: Fran Tarkenton (Minnesota), passing; Walter Payton (Chicago), rushing; Drew Pearson (Dallas), receiving

AFC Season Leaders: Ken Stabler (Oakland), passing; O. J. Simpson (Buffalo), rushing, 1,503 yards; MacArthur Lane (Kansas City), receiving

College All-Americans: Rob Lyttle (B), Michigan; Tommy Kramer (Q), Rice; Ricky Bell (B), Southern California

Bowls (Jan. 1, 1977)

Rose: Southern California 14–Michigan 6
Orange: Ohio State 27–Colorado 10
Cotton: Houston 30–Maryland 21
Sugar: Pittsburgh 27–Georgia 3

Basketball

Four ABA teams—Denver, Indiana, New York, San Antonio—merge with the NBA after the season. An NBA playoff game goes to triple overtime: Boston 128–Phoenix 126.

NBA All-Pro First Team: Rick Barry (Golden State), George McGinnis (Philadelphia), Kareem Abdul-Jabbar (Los Angeles), Nate Archibald (Kansas City), Pete Maravich (New Orleans)

ABA All-Pro First Team: Julius Erving (New York), Billy Knight (Indiana), Artis Gilmore (Kentucky), James Silas (San Antonio), Ralph Simpson (Denver)

Olympics

At the Summer Games in Montreal, security, of foremost concern, costs over $100 million. U.S. winners include John Nabor (4 in swimming), Edwin Moses (400 mh, 47.64s.). Arnie Robinson (broad jump, 27'4.7"), Bruce Jenner (decathlon, 8,618 pts.), Mac Wilkins (discus, 221'5.4"), Ray Leonard (LW boxing), Michael Spinks (MW boxing), and Leon Spinks (HW boxing). In the Winter Games at Innsbruck, Austria, winners are Dorothy Hamill (figure skating), Peter Mueller (1,000m, 1:19.32), and Sheila Young (500m, 42.7s.).

Other Sports

Boxing: Muhammad Ali fights a Japanese wrestler to a draw in a highly publicized match.

Tennis: Transexual René Richards is barred from the U.S. Open, as players demand chromosomal sex determination.

Winners

World Series
Cincinnati (NL) 4
New York (AL) 0
MVP
NL–Joe Morgan, Cincinnati
AL–Thurman Munson, New York
Super Bowl XI (Jan. 1977)
Oakland 32–Minnesota 14
MVP
Bert Jones, Baltimore
College Football
Pittsburgh
Heisman Trophy
Tony Dorsett, Pittsburgh
NBA Championship
Boston 4–Phoenix 2
MVP
Kareem Abdul-Jabbar, Los Angeles
College Basketball
Indiana
Player of the Year
Adrian Dantley, Notre Dame
Stanley Cup
Montreal
US Tennis Open:
Men: Bjorn Borg
Women: Chris Evert
USGA Open
Jerry Pate
Kentucky Derby
Bold Forbes (A. Cordero, jockey)

Fashion

For Women: Split-pea-colored loden coats regain popularity and are worn with knit mufflers and wide-brim hats, along with a variety of pants (particularly harem or culotte), tube skirts and tunics, caftans, and long blouses. The layered and bulky look remains, but fabrics are lighter (in silk and cashmere); checked pants are often matched with striped tunics, shirts, and scarves. Large smocks, big capes, and large, loose blazers fit over a variety of skirts—dirndls and culottes, or pleated, gypsy, flared, tube, or wraparound styles. The tailored look is also popular in gabardines and Harris tweeds. Bags are either businesslike or rugged, in canvas, pigskin, or buckskin. Lapel pins, link bracelets, hoop earrings, and tiny, widely separated diamonds on gold chains are stylish accessories. Dorothy Hamill popularizes a short brush-and-bang haircut.

For Men: Men begin to show an interest in traditional, conservative styles. Vests, windbreakers, peacoats, and classical pullovers regain attention.

High-fashion notes: Halston's strapless dress; Mollie Parnis's peasant cotton

Kaleidoscope

- Bicentennial festivities include a reenactment of a Revolutionary War battle in Western Springs, Illinois; a reenactment of the Minutemen battling the British on Lexington Green; "Operation Sail" in New York City, with 16 of the world's tallest old windjammers and thousands of other ships; and the Freedom Train, traveling over 17,000 miles to 80 cities, with 12 cars of Americana exhibitions.
- In the preelection presidential debate with Gerald Ford, Jimmy Carter defines a new economic barometer, the "misery index," the sum of the unemployment and inflation rates, which he views as an excessive 12.4.
- The Supreme Court rules that employers are not required to give paid maternity leave.
- FBI chief Clarence Kelly apologizes publicly for bureau excesses, such as the Martin Luther King and Black Panther surveillances.
- Amy Carter, nine, attends a predominantly black Washington public school.
- Renowned lawyer F. Lee Bailey defends Patty Hearst, daughter of publisher William Randolph Hearst, with expert witnesses such as psychiatrist Robert J. Lifton who claim she was "brainwashed."
- The *Encyclopaedia Britannica* reports that roughly 15 percent of American adults are functional illiterates, unable to read an average newspaper or write a simple letter.
- Numerous will forgeries appear claiming the estate of Howard Hughes, who apparently left no will.
- President Ford orders a major inoculation campaign against a projected swine flu epidemic (which does not occur).
- With the repeal of the Fair Trade law, manufacturers can no longer fix retail prices; this is anticipated to save consumers $2 billion through discount shopping.
- The arrest rate for women since 1964 has risen three times faster than the rate for men.
- Sales of bran cereals increase 20 percent and of high-fiber bread 30 percent, as consumers respond to widely published medical studies reporting health benefits from high-fiber diets.
- Daniel Schorr is suspended from CBS after he gives the *Village Voice* newspaper a House Intelligence Committee report on alleged illegal CIA activities.
- California is the first state to legalize "living wills," the right of the terminally ill to decree their own deaths.
- Legionnaire's disease, from a bacterium of unknown origin, fatally strikes 34 at an American Legion convention in Philadelphia.
- Two amateur electronics enthusiasts develop the Apple computer in a California garage.
- In his revised *Baby and Child Care,* Dr. Benjamin Spock redefines the sex roles: "The father's responsibility is as great as the mother's," he writes.
- Richard Nixon is disbarred in New York State.
- Former president and Mrs. Nixon visit China, where they are warmly welcomed.
- Cars, like the Cadillac Seville, are reduced in weight and size; production of the Eldorado, the last U.S. convertible model, ceases.
- Average SAT scores drop to 472 in math and 435 in English (501 and 480 in 1968).
- Shirley Temple Black becomes the U.S. State Department chief of protocol.
- Barbara Jordan becomes the first woman and first black to deliver a convention keynote speech at the Democratic convention.
- One out of five children now lives in a one-parent home; three out of five marriages end in divorce.

Fads: Mattress stacking, Farrah Fawcett-Majors posters

First Appearances: Rhodes scholarship to a woman, six-star general (George Washington, posthumously), woman president of *Harvard Law Review,* women in NASA training program for astronauts, electronic sewing machine (Singer), commercial supersonic airline service (Concorde), protoplasts (animal and plant cells combined), underground school (Artesia, N.M.)

1977

Facts and Figures

Economic Profile
  Dow-Jones: ↓ High 999–
    Low 800
  GNP: +11%
  Inflation: +11.0%
  Unemployment: 7.6%
Infant mortality/1,000: 16.1
Maternal mortality/10,000:
  12.8
Physicians: 393,700
Dentists: 107,000
Hospital beds: 1,466,000
Herman's sporting
  equipment:
  Adidas finalist tennis
    shoes: $12.99
  Butchart Nicholls golf
    shoes: $19.99
  Whitely trim ride exercise
    bike: $54.99
Billard 115-lb. barbell set:
  $24.99
Hudson vitamin C, 250 mg.:
  $4.09 (250)
Megavitamin B complex:
  $5.75–$13.20 (250)
Radio Shack CB: $59.99–
  $159.95
Cuisinart: $224.99
Tiffany 15-inch chain, 14
  diamonds: $395

Deaths

Maria Callas, Charles
  Chaplin, Joan Crawford,
  Bing Crosby, Anthony
  Eden, Guy Lombardo,
  Groucho Marx, Vladimir
  Nabokov, Anaïs Nin, Elvis
  Presley, Leopold
  Stokowski.

Anti-Shah Demonstration.
Copyright Washington Post.
*Reprinted courtesy of D.C.
Public Library.*

In the News

GARY GILMORE IS KILLED BY FIRING SQUAD, THE FIRST U.S. EXECUTION IN 10 YEARS . . . CARTER GRANTS UNCONDITIONAL AMNESTY TO VIETNAM DRAFT EVADERS . . . CARTER LIFTS ALL TRAVEL BANS TO CUBA, VIETNAM, NORTH KOREA, AND CAMBODIA . . . INDIRA GANDHI IS DEFEATED AND RESIGNS . . . SENATE APPROVES RIGOROUS CODE OF SENATE ETHICS, LIMITS SENATORS' OUTSIDE INCOME . . . 570 DIE AS TWO 747'S COLLIDE IN CANARY ISLANDS . . . MARTIN LUTHER KING'S ASSASSIN, JAMES EARL RAY, IS RECAPTURED AFTER PRISON ESCAPE . . . EGYPTIAN LEADER ANWAR SADAT VISITS CARTER . . . CARTER SAYS B-1 BOMBER IS UNNECESSARY . . . MENACHEM BEGIN IS ELECTED ISRAELI PREMIER . . . LEON JAWORSKI IS NAMED "KOREAGATE" PROSECUTOR TO INVESTIGATE BRIBES BY U.S. CORPORATIONS . . . DEPT. OF ENERGY IS CREATED . . . "SON OF SAM" KILLER IS ARRESTED IN N.Y.C. . . . BERT LANCE, BUDGET DIRECTOR, RESIGNS OVER ISSUE OF BANKING PRACTICES . . . UNEMPLOYMENT FALLS TO 7% . . . ALI BHUTTO, FORMER PAKISTANI P.M., IS ARRESTED FOR MURDER . . . U.S. AND PANAMA SIGN CANAL ZONE TREATIES . . . SHAH OF IRAN VISITS WHITE HOUSE DESPITE PROTEST DEMONSTRATIONS . . . EGYPTIAN PRESIDENT ANWAR SADAT VISITS JERUSALEM . . . ISRAELI PREMIER MENACHEM BEGIN VISITS EGYPT.

Quotes

"Ring the bells for your sons. Tell them that those wars were the last of wars and the end of sorrows."
— Anwar Sadat

"The time of the flight between Cairo and Jerusalem is short . . . [but] the distance between them . . . until yesterday, quite large. . . . Sadat passed this distance with heartfelt courage. . . . We, the Jews, know how to appreciate this courage."
— Menachem Begin

"We need a better family life to make us better servants of the people. So those of you living in sin, I hope you get married. And those of you who have left your spouses, go back home."
— Jimmy Carter

"Which of you is going to step up and put me out to pasture?"
— John Wayne, to Congressional Committee on Aging

"For the first time in our history, a small group of nations controlling a scarce resource [oil] could, over time, be tempted to pressure us into foreign policy decisions not dictated by our national interests."
— Henry Kissinger

"Society cannot continue to live on oil and gas. Those fossil fuels represent nature's savings accounts which took billions of years to form."
— Buckminster Fuller

"The massive failure in basic skills—particularly reading and writing—is nothing short of scandalous."
— Fred M. Hechinger, editor, *New York Times*

"We don't so much want to see a female Einstein become an assistant professor. We want a woman schlemiel to get promoted as quickly as a male schlemiel."
— Bella Abzug

"I think Gerald Ford will be remembered as a man who bumped his head, had a wonderful wife, and left Americans more at peace with themselves and the rest of the world than at any time since it became a world power."
— Senator Daniel Moynihan (D-N.Y.)

"You can always find something on the evening news to take your mind off life."
— "Mary Hartman, Mary Hartman"

Ads

Woody Allen and Diane Keaton in *Annie Hall,* a romantic comedy about the difficulties of relating to oneself and others in a modern, urban environment. *Movie Star News.*

TV

Premieres

"Family Feud," Richard Dawson
"The Dick Cavett Show"
"Three's Company," Suzanne Somers, John Ritter
"Eight Is Enough," Dick Van Patten
"Chips," Erik Estrada
"Soap," Robert Mandan
"Lou Grant," Edward Asner
"The Love Boat," Gavin MacLeod

Top Ten (Nielsen)

"Laverne and Shirley," "Happy Days," "Three's Company," "60 Minutes," "Charlie's Angels," "All in the Family," "Little House on the Prairie," "Alice," "M*A*S*H," "One Day at a Time"

Specials

"Roots" (Ben Vereen, Cicely Tyson, Lloyd Bridges, LeVar Burton, Maya Angelou); "Holocaust"; "The Body Human"; "I, Claudius"; "American Ballet Theatre's 'Giselle' "; Bette Midler: Ol' Red Hair Is Back"; "The Great Whales: National Geographic"; "The Gathering"; Interview with Anwar Sadat and Menachem Begin (Walter Cronkite); Interviews with Richard Nixon (David Frost)

Emmy Awards

"The Rockford Files" (drama); "All in the Family" (comedy); "The Muppet Show" (variety); "Hollywood Is Grinch Night" (children); Ed Asner (actor, "Lou Grant"); Carroll O'Connor (comedic actor, "All in the Family"); Sada Thompson (actress, "Family"); Jean Stapleton (comedic actress, "All in the Family")

Of Note

"Roots" draws the largest audience in TV history, 130 million people; "Holocaust" draws 120 million.

Movies

Openings

Annie Hall (Woody Allen), Woody Allen, Diane Keaton
The Goodbye Girl (Herbert Ross) Richard Dreyfuss, Marsha Mason
Julia (Fred Zinnemann), Jane Fonda, Vanessa Redgrave, Jason Robards
Star Wars (George Lucas), Mark Hamill, Harrison Ford, Carrie Fisher
The Turning Point (Herbert Ross), Anne Bancroft, Shirley MacLaine, Mikhail Baryshnikov
Close Encounters of the Third Kind (Steven Spielberg), Richard Dreyfuss, François Truffaut, Teri Garr
The Late Show (Robert Benton), Art Carney, Lily Tomlin
Looking for Mr. Goodbar (Richard Brooks), Diane Keaton, Richard Kiley, Tuesday Weld
Saturday Night Fever (John Badham), John Travolta, Karen Lynn Gorney, Donna Pescow
Providence (Alain Resnais), Ellen Burstyn, Dirk Bogarde, John Gielgud
Oh, God! (Carl Reiner), George Burns, John Denver, Teri Garr
Pumping Iron (George Butler, Robert Fiore), Arnold Schwarzenegger
That Obscure Object of Desire (Luis Buñuel), Fernando Rey, Carole Bouquet
Madame Rosa (Moshe Mizrahi), Simone Signoret, Claude Dauphin
Handle with Care (Jonathan Demme), Ann Wedgeworth, Paul Le Mat
Stroszek (Werner Herzog), Bruno S., Eva Mattes, Clemens Scheitz

Academy Awards

Best Picture; *Annie Hall*
Best Director: Woody Allen (*Annie Hall*)
Best Actress: Diane Keaton (*Annie Hall*)
Best Actor: Richard Dreyfuss (*The Goodbye Girl*)

Top Box-Office Stars

Sylvester Stallone, Barbra Streisand, Clint Eastwood, Burt Reynolds, Robert Redford, Woody Allen, Mel Brooks, Al Pacino, Diane Keaton, Robert De Niro

Stars of Tomorrow

John Travolta, Karen Lynn Gorney, Michael Ontkean, Mark Hamill, Harrison Ford, Carrie Fisher, Kathleen Quinlan, Peter Firth, Richard Gere, Melinda Dillon

Popular Music

Hit Songs
"Tonight's the Night"
"Nobody Does It Better"
"Theme from 'Rocky' (Gonna Fly Now)"
"I Like Dreamin' "
"Don't Leave Me This Way"
"Feels Like the First Time"
"Star Wars (Main Title)"
"Couldn't Get It Right"
"Torn between Two Lovers"

Top Records
Albums: *Rumours* (Fleetwood Mac); *A Star Is Born* (Barbra Streisand, Kris Kristofferson); *Simple Dreams* (Linda Ronstadt); *Wings over America* (Wings); *Barry Manilow/Live* (Barry Manilow)

Singles: *I Just Want To be Your Everything* (Andy Gibb); *Best of My Love* (Emotions); *Angel in Your Arms* (Hot); *Handy Man* (James Taylor); *I Wish* (Stevie Wonder); *You're My World* (Helen Reddy); *(Your Love Has Lifted Me) Higher and Higher* (Rita Coolidge); *I'm Your Boogie Man* (K. C. and the Sunshine Band). Country: *Heaven's Just a Sin Away* (Kendalls); *Lucille* (Kenny Rogers)

Grammy Awards
Hotel California, Eagles (record); *Rumours,* Fleetwood Mac (album); "You Light Up My Life" (song)

Jazz and Big Bands
Scott Hamilton, on tenor sax, gains attention with his revival of swing.
"Second Generation of Fusion Jazz" includes Spyro Gyra, Seawind, Auracle, Caldera.

Top Performers *(Downbeat):* McCoy Tyner (soloist); Thad Jones/Mel Lewis (band); Weather Report (jazz group); Dexter Gordon, Jean-Luc Ponty, Rahsaan Roland Kirk, Hubert Laws, Joe Pass, Anthony Braxton, Phil Woods (instrumentalists); Flora Purim, Al Jarreau (vocalists); Earth, Wind and Fire (vocal group); Weather Report, *Heavy Weather* (album)

Theater

Broadway Openings
Plays
Chapter Two (Neil Simon), Judd Hirsch, Anita Gillette
The Gin Game (D. L. Coburn), Hume Cronyn, Jessica Tandy
Dirty Linen/New-Found-Land (Tom Stoppard), Stephen D. Newman, Remak Ramsay
Gemini (Albert Innaurato), Danny Aiello
Golda (William Gibson), Anne Bancroft
Vieux Carré (Tennessee Williams), Sylvia Sidney
Miss Margarida's Way (Roberto Athayde), Estelle Parsons
Otherwise Engaged (Simon Gray), Tom Courtenay
American Buffalo (David Mamet), Robert Duvall, John Savage
The Shadow Box (Michael Christofer), Laurence Luckinbill
Dracula (Hamilton Deane, John L. Balderston), Frank Langella

Musicals
Annie (Charles Strouse, Martin Charnin), Andrea McArdle, Dorothy Loudon, Reid Shelton
The Act (John Kander, Fred Ebb), Liza Minnelli, Barry Nelson
Side by Side by Sondheim (Stephen Sondheim et al.) Millicent Martin, Julie N. McKenzie, David Kernan
Beatlemania (John Lennon, Paul McCartney, George Harrison, Ron Rabinowitz et al.), Mitch Weissman
The King and I (Richard Rodgers, Oscar Hammerstein II, revival), Yul Brynner

Classics, Revivals, and Off-Broadway Premieres
A Life in the Theatre (David Mamet), Ellis Rabb, Peter Evans; *A Touch of the Poet* (Eugene O'Neill), Geraldine Fitzgerald, Jason Robards, Milo O'Shea; *Agamemnon* (Aeschylus), Gloria Foster, Earle Hyman; *The Cherry Orchard* (Chekhov), Irene Worth, George Voskovec; *St. Joan* (George Bernard Shaw), Lynn Redgrave; *Tartuffe* (Molière), John Wood, Tammy Grimes; *Caesar and Cleopatra* (Shaw), Rex Harrison, Elizabeth Ashley; *The Basic Training of Pavlo Hummel* (David Rabe), Al Pacino; *Anna Christie,* (O'Neill), Liv Ullmann; *The Three Sisters* (Chekhov), Rosemary Harris, Tovah Feldshuh, Ellen Burstyn

Regional
Goodman, Chicago: *The Sport of My Mad Mother* (Ann Jellicoe); *A Life in The Theatre* (David Mamet), premieres

Actors Theater of Louisville: *Getting Out* (Marsha Norman); *The Gin Game* (D. L. Coburn); *Whose Life Is It Anyway?* (Brian Clark, joint production with Folger Theatre Group); premieres

Theater (cont.)

Pulitzer Prize
The Shadow Box, Michael Cristofer

Tony Awards
The Shadow Box, Michael Cristofer (play); *Annie,* Charles Strouse, Martin Charnin (musical)

Classical Music

Compositions
Michael Colgrass, *Déjà Vu* for Percussion Quartet and Orchestra
George Crumb, *Star Child*
Harold Faberman, *War Cry*
Ralph Shapey, *The Covenant*
Lou Harrison, *Serenade*
Garrett List, *Slugging Rocks*
Ned Rorem, Six Songs, *Romeo and Juliet*
Elliott Schwartz, Chamber Concerto III

Important Events
Numerous festivals include the 150th anniversary of Beethoven's death and the New York Philharmonic's Celebration of Black Composers series. Charleston, S.C., hosts the new Spoleto Festival U.S.A., which opens with *Pique Dame* (Magda Olivero).
For the first time, Congress appropriates the full budget request of the National Endowment of the Arts, $123.5 million (in 1969, $8 million).

New Appointments: Antal Dorati, Detroit; Mstislav Rostropovich, National; John Nelson, Indianapolis; Leonard Slatkin, New Orleans Philharmonic

Debut: Thomas Lorango

First Performances
David Del Tredici, *Final Alice* (performed by six orchestras); Elliott Carter, A Symphony of Three Orchestras (New York); Jacob Druckman, *Chiaroscuro* (Cleveland); Toru Takemitsu, *Quatrain* (Boston); Sir Michael Tippett, Symphony no. 4 (Chicago); Dominick Argento, *In Praise of Music* (Minnesota)

Opera
PBS broadcasts four operas live from the Met, one from the New York City Opera, and five from the Vienna and La Scala companies.

Metropolitan: Marilyn Horne, *Le prophète;* Régine Crespin, Shirley Verrett, *Dialogues des Carmelites;* Leontyne Price, Placido Domingo, Cornell MacNeil, Martti Talvela, *La forza del destino;* Elena Obraztsova, Guy Chauvet, *Samson et Dalila;* Marius Rintzler, Yvonne Minton, *Der Rosenkavalier*

New York City: *Henderson, the Rain King* (Leon Kirchner, premiere); *The Voice of Ariadne* (Thea Musgrave, premiere)

San Francisco: Eric Tappy, *Idomeneo;* Leontyne Price, *Ariadne auf Naxos;* Montserrat Caballé, Luciano Pavarotti, *Turandot*

Houston: *Tancredi* (Rossini, revised and cut edition); *Of Mice and Men*

Boston: *Russlan and Ludmilla* (Glinka, American premiere)

Santa Fe: *The Italian Straw Hat* (Nino Rota, premiere)

Chicago: *Idomeneo;* "Maria Callas Tribute"

San Antonio: *Rienzi*

Roots, taken from Alex Haley's current best-seller, "remakes the TV world" (*Variety*) with its saga of black history beginning with Kunte Kinte, an African hunter brought to the colonies as a slave. *Movie Star News.*

Star Wars. This sci-fi epic rapidly earns the highest box office receipts in history. Many children see it more than once—or twice. *Movie Star News.*

Art

Painting

Agnes Martin, *Untitled No. 11, No. 12*
Audrey Flack, *Marilyn*
Richard Estes, *Ansonia*
Ellsworth Kelly, *Blue Panel I*
Philip Guston, *Cabal*
Nicholas Africano, *The Cruel Discussion*
Red Grooms, *Quick Elysées*
Frank Stella, *Sinjerli Variations, Steller's Albatross*

Sculpture

Dan Flavin, *Untitled (for Robert with Fond Regards)*
Louise Nevelson, *Mrs. N's Place*
Luccio Pozzi, *Four Windows*
Alice Aycock, *Studies*

Architecture

World Trade Center, New York City (Minoru Yamasaki, Emery Roth)
Faneuil Hall Marketplace, Boston (restoration design, Benjamin Thompson)
Yale University Center for British Art, New Haven (Louis I. Kahn)
Citicorp Center, New York (Hugh Stubbins)
Thanksgiving Square, Dallas (Johnson, Burgee)
Renaissance Center, Detroit (John Portman)
Lehman Wing, Metropolitan Museum (Roche and Dinkeloo)
Cesar Pelli is commissioned, with Gruen Associates, for the addition to the Museum of Modern Art.

Important Exhibitions

Museums

New York: *Metropolitan:* Celtic art; Islamic, Egyptian art; Thracian art treasures; Russian costumes. *Whitney:* "Turn of the Century America"; Retrospective: Richard Diebenkorn

Washington, D.C.: Henri Matisse's paper cut-outs. *Smithsonian:* "A Nation of Nations" (on exhibit until 1981)

Boston: Winslow Homer

Houston, Boston: Nineteenth-century French art

Yale: Paul Mellon collection of British paintings: Constable, Reynolds, Gainsborough

St. Petersburg, Fla.: "Art of European Glass 1600–1800"

Cleveland: Japanese screens

Richard Estes, *Ansonia* 1977. Oil on canvas. 48 × 60″. *Collection of Whitney Museum of American Art. Gift of Frances and Sydney Lewis.*

Los Angeles: Sixty-two Chinese jade carvings

Los Angeles, Carnegie Institute, University of Texas (Austin), Brooklyn: Women artists 1550–1950

Art Briefs

Thomas Hoving leaves the Metropolitan after ten years; the building facade is redesigned; the sidewalk and fountains are modernized • Sales: Van Gogh: *La fin de la journée* ($880,000); Renoir, *Baigneuse Couchée* ($600,000).

Dance

Rudolf Nureyev dances *Pierrot Lunaire* (Glen Tetley) and other ballets on Broadway.

Premieres/Important Productions

American Ballet Theatre: *The Firebird* (Michel Fokine), Natalia Makarova

New York City Ballet: *Vienna Waltzes* (George Balanchine); *Bournonville Divertissements* (Bournonville, Stanley Williams)

Joffrey: *Les Patineurs* (Ashton), Christian Holder

Merce Cunningham: *Images*

Books

Fiction
Critics' Choice
Falconer, John Cheever
The Professor of Desire, Philip Roth
True Confessions, John Gregory Dunne
Song of Solomon, Toni Morrison
Torch Song, Anne Roiphe
A Book of Common Prayer, Joan Didion
Lancelot, Walker Percy
In the Future Perfect, Walter Abish
The Women's Room, Marilyn French

Best-Sellers
The Silmarillion, J. R. R. Tolkien
The Thorn Birds, Colleen McCullough
Illusions, Richard Bach
The Honourable Schoolboy, John le Carré
Oliver's Story, Erich Segal
Dreams Die First, Harold Robbins
Beggarman, Thief, Irwin Shaw
How to Save Your Own Life, Erica Jong
Delta of Venus: Erotica, Anaïs Nin
Daniel Martin, John Fowles

Nonfiction
Critics' Choice
Gates of Eden, Morris Dickstein
Origins, Richard E. Leakey, Roger Lewin
A Rumor of War, Philip Caputo
Dispatches, Michael Herr
Coming into the Country, John A. McPhee
The Age of Uncertainty, John Kenneth Galbraith
The Path between the Seas: The Creation of the Panama Canal, 1870–1914, David McCullough
Ontogeny and Phylogeny, Stephen Jay Gould
The Origin of Consciousness in the Breakdown of the Bicameral Mind, Julian Jaynes
Convention, Richard Reeves
The Economic Transformation of America, Robert Heilbroner, Aaron Singer
On Photography, Susan Sontag
Winners and Losers: Battles, Retreats, Gains, Losses and Ruin from a Long War, Gloria Emerson

Best-Sellers
Roots, Alex Haley
Looking Out for #1, Robert Ringer
All Things Wise and Wonderful, James Herriot
Your Erroneous Zones, Dr. Wayne W. Dyer
The Book of Lists, David Wallechinsky
The Possible Dream: A Candid Look at Amway, Charles Paul Conn
The Dragons of Eden: Speculations on the Evolution of Human Intelligence, Carl Sagan
The Second Ring of Power, Carlos Castaneda
The Grass Is Always Greener over the Septic Tank, Erma Bombeck
The Amityville Horror, Jay Anson

Poetry
Kenneth Koch, *The Duplications*
John Berryman, *Henry's Fate and Other Poems, 1967–1972* (posthumous)
Robert Lowell, *Day by Day* (posthumous)
John Ashbery, *Houseboat Days*
A. R. Ammons, *The Snow Poems*
Hayden Carruth, *Brothers, I Loved You All*
W. S. Merwin, *The Compass Flower*

Pulitzer Prizes
Elbow Room, James Alan McPherson (fiction)
The Invisible Hand: The Managerial Revolution in American Business, Alfred D. Chandler, Jr. (U.S. history)
The Dragons of Eden, Carl Sagan (nonfiction)
Samuel Johnson, W. Jackson Bate (biography)
The Collected Poems, Howard Nemerov (poetry)

Science and Technology

The first fusion reactions by laser are achieved.

The neutron bomb is developed, which, through neutron radiation, destroys population but leaves property intact.

A U.S. space shuttle, Enterprise, makes its first gliding test flight after being carried on the back of a Boeing 747.

Voyagers I and II are launched to explore Jupiter, Saturn, and Uranus.

A study reports that alcohol consumed during pregnancy may injure the fetus.

Charles I. Reford and Richard J. Whitley, at the University of Alabama, develop a drug (ara-A) to treat the viral disease herpes encephalitis.

Solomon Snyder, at Johns Hopkins, traces brain pathways where endorphins (natural tranquilizers) act.

🦋 The Japanese car industry employs 7,000 robots for painting, welding, and assembly.

Nobel Prize
Rosalyn S. Yalow, Roger C. L. Guillemin, and Andrew V. Schally win in physiology and medicine for work on the role of hormones in body chemistry.

Sports

Baseball

Many stars sign free-agent contracts, including Rollie Fingers, Gary Matthews, Dave Cash, and Don Gullett.

Reggie Jackson (New York, AL) hits three home runs in successive at-bats in the final game of the World Series.

Nolan Ryan strikes out 341, a record fifth time over 300.

"Billy Martin should win the Nobel Peace Prize for winning this season," says Reggie Jackson.

The Cy Young awards are won by Steve Carlton (Philadelphia, NL) and Sparky Lyle (New York, AL).

Champions

Batting	Pitching
Dave Parker (Pittsburgh, NL), .338	John Candeleria (Pittsburgh, NL), 20–5
Rod Carew (Minnesota, AL), .388	Paul Splitorff (Kansas City, AL), 16–6
	Home runs
	George Foster (Cincinnati, NL), 52

Football

Walter Payton, Chicago, sets a single-game rushing record of 275.

NFC Season Leaders: Roger Staubach (Dallas), passing; Walter Payton (Chicago), rushing; Ahmad Rashad (Minnesota), receiving

AFL Season Leaders: Bob Griese (Miami), passing; Mark Van Eeghen (Oakland), rushing; Lydell Mitchell (Baltimore), receiving

College All-Americans: Joe Montana (Q), Notre Dame; Earl Campbell (B), Texas; Terry Miller (B), Oklahoma

Bowls (Jan. 1, 1978)

Rose: Washington 27–Michigan 20	Cotton: Notre Dame 38–Texas 7
Orange: Arkansas 31–Oklahoma 6	Sugar: Alabama 35–Ohio State 6

Basketball

Al McGuire, Marquette, wins the NCAA in his last season of coaching.

NBA All-Pro First Team: Elvin Hayes (Washington), David Thompson (Denver), Kareem Abdul-Jabbar (Los Angeles), Pete Maravich (New Orleans), Paul Westphal (Phoenix)

Other Sports

Car Racing: A. J. Foyt wins the Indianapolis 500 a record fourth time.

Horse Racing: Seventeen-year-old jockey Steve Cauthen earns a record $6.1 million in purses with 487 wins.

Tennis: Jimmy Connors is the leading pro tennis money winner with $822,656.

Winners

World Series	*MVP*
New York (AL) 4	Bill Walton, Portland
Los Angeles (NL) 2	*College Basketball*
MVP	Marquette
NL–George Foster, Cincinnati	*Player of the Year*
AL–Rod Carew, Minnesota	Marques Johnson, UCLA
Super Bowl XII (played Jan. 1978)	*Stanley Cup*
Dallas 27–Denver 10	Montreal
MVP	*US Tennis Open*
Walter Payton, Chicago	Men: Guillermo Vilas
College Football	Women: Chris Evert
Notre Dame	*USGA Open*
Heisman Trophy	Hubert Greene
Earl Campbell, Texas	*Kentucky Derby*
NBA Championship	Seattle Slew (J. Cruguet, jockey)
Portland 4–Philadelphia 2	

Fashion

For Men: The return to conservatism is marked by narrow, silk challis ties with small patterns and oxford and broadcloth shirts (no longer tapered) in tattersall and solids with small button-down collars. Also popular are pin-stripe and herringbone double-breasted suits with narrow lapels, soft shoulders, and straight, uncuffed trousers. The layered look characterizes casual dress in tweeds and textured fabrics, suede and leather elbow patches, vests, and classic V-neck pullovers. Specific fabrics create the traditional and country look: Harris, Donegal, and Shetland tweeds, corduroy, twill, flannel, camel hair, and cashmere. Soft leather, high-polished shoes with tassels or stitching are popular, along with wing tips and a variety of loafers, moccasins, and low boots. Limited accessories are in keeping with the new understated look: little jewelry (a small collar pin, watch, and ID bracelet) and narrow belts, in soft leathers with decorative buckles.

High-fashion notes: John Weitz's pin stripe and glen plaid suits, blue blazer, and tan cavalry twill pants

Kaleidoscope _____

- The Supreme Court rules that the spanking of schoolchildren by teachers is constitutional.
- Three first ladies—Rosalynn Carter, Betty Ford, and Lady Bird Johnson—attend the National Women's Conference in Houston.
- Twenty-six-year-old George Willig scales the side of New York's World Trade Center tower, 1,350 feet high, and is fined $1.10 for each story.
- The *New York Times* reports on the CIA's program to develop mind control techniques.
- Larry Flint resigns as publisher of *Hustler* when he becomes a born-again Christian, under the guidance of Ruth Carter Stapleton, the president's sister.
- A parking ticket leads to the arrest of David Berkowitz, "Son of Sam" killer, so named after a dog that, he says, instructed him to kill.
- Two million Elvis Presley records sell within a day of his death; Presley's funeral costs $47,000.
- The Supreme Court rules that states do not have to use Medicaid funds for elective abortion.
- Freddie Prinze, 22 and star of the hit TV show "Chico and the Man," commits suicide.
- Forty-five million people watch the highest rated TV interview in history—Richard Nixon's appearance on David Frost's program—for which Nixon receives $600,000 and 10 percent of the show's profits.
- CBS anchor Walter Cronkite acts as an intermediary between Anwar Sadat and Menachem Begin in arranging their meeting in Israel.
- A study at Princeton University reveals that 6.8 million married couples have elected surgical contraception (3.8 million women, 3 million men).
- Sales of smoke detecters surpass 8 million.
- Singer Connie Francis is awarded $1,475,000 from the Howard Johnson motel chain after she is raped; she charged that she was not provided a safe and secure room.
- Widespread looting occurs during a blackout in New York and Westchester that affects 9 million people.
- The FDA bans Red No. 2 additive in foods, drugs, and cosmetics, and Red No. 4 in maraschino cherries; Yellow No. 5 is indicated to be a potential allergen.
- International tourism breaks records, despite the rise in hotel rates abroad; especially popular are Venice, London, and Paris.
- The Supreme Court reverses a New York law that prohibits the distribution of contraceptives to minors.
- Spencer Sacco receives a proclamation in Boston from Massachusetts governor Michael Dukakis that states that his grandfather, Nicola Sacco, and Bartolomeo Vanzetti were improperly tried for murder in 1927; both were executed.
- A California judge grants temporary custody to the parents of several young adults ("Moonies") said to be under the brainwashing influence of the Rev. Sun Myung Moon's Unification church.
- "Go back to oranges and leave the other fruits alone" reads one placard outside a Kansas City auditorium the day of Anita Bryant's concert appearance. Bryant

Farah Fawcett, whose posters are best-sellers, plays one of three braless female detectives on "Charlie's Angels"; "jiggling" (an ABC executive's term) leads to high ratings. *Movie Star News.*

campaigns to repeal a Dade County ordinance outlawing discrimination against homosexuals in housing and employment.
- The number of imported cars breaks all records with sales of 1.5 million.
- Because of soaring prices, consumers boycott coffee.
- CB radios achieve record sales as 25 million anonymous callers create a new language and make new friends.
- Over 400,000 teenage abortions are performed, a third of the total in the United States; 21 percent of the pregnant unmarried teens give birth and 87 percent of these keep their children.
- Cheryl Tiegs, the world's highest paid model, earns $1,000 a day.
- Billy Carter, the president's brother, endorses Billy Beer.
- Jimmy Carter, in a cardigan sweater, begins his fireside chats.
- "Li'l Abner" ceases publication.
- J. R. R. Tolkien's *Silmarillion* sells a record 1,056,696 copies in the first three months after its publication.

Fads: Roller disco; mopeds, food processors (20 brands), TV recorders, T-shirts, cheese, health foods, bottled water, poster saloons

First Appearances: Presidential call-in, lethal-drug capital punishment authorized (Oklahoma), killer whale born in captivity, no-brand generic products (Chicago), "Supercall" (electronic line judge for tennis play decisions), public automatic blood pressure machines, pocket TV ($300), Life Achievement Academy Award (Bette Davis), parade with music from transistor radios (Steamwood, Ill.), woman referee for heavyweight championship fight (Eva Shain, Ali vs. Shavers, New York City); American male saint (J. N. Neumann)

1978

Facts and Figures

Economic Profile
  Dow-Jones: − High 893–
    Low 807
  GNP: +11%
  Inflation: +12.4%
  Unemployment: 6.3%
Balance of international
  payments: −$14.8 billion
Military on duty: 2,062,000
Voter participation: 55.2%
  (1972), 53.5% (1976)
Population with religious
  affiliation: 132,500,000
Wines:
  1978 Pinot Chardonnay:
    $3.99
  1976 Saint Veran: $4.49
  1966 Chateau Lafite:
    $45.00
United Supersaver, New
  York–California: $233
  (round trip)
Cuba (7 nights): $573
Queen Elizabeth II, New
  York–London, fly back:
  $695–$2,165
Rosemary Reid leather-look
  bathing suit: $25

In the News

37 ISRAELIS ARE SLAIN IN PLO RAID ON HAIFA BUS . . . CARTER DEFERS NEUTRON BOMB . . . SECOND CANAL TREATY IS RATIFIED, CANAL WILL GO TO PANAMA IN 1999 . . . SOUTH KOREAN AIRLINER IS FORCED DOWN IN RUSSIA, 2 ARE KILLED, 110 SURVIVE . . . BODY OF ALDO MORO, ITALIAN LEADER KIDNAPPED BY TERRORISTS, IS FOUND IN ROME . . . "BUGS" ARE DISCOVERED IN U.S. EMBASSY IN MOSCOW . . . U.S. RECALLS AMBASSADOR TO CHILE OVER LETELIER MURDER . . . SUPREME COURT RULES AGAINST REVERSE DISCRIMINATION IN ALLAN BAKKE CASE . . . 100,000 MARCH IN WASHINGTON, D.C., FOR THE ERA . . . ANTISHAH RIOTS SPREAD IN IRAN . . . POPE PAUL VI DIES, JOHN PAUL I IS ELECTED . . . CAMP DAVID TALKS END IN ACCORD BETWEEN SADAT AND BEGIN . . . JOHN PAUL I DIES, POLISH CARDINAL IS NAMED POPE JOHN PAUL II . . . WALL POSTERS CRITICIZING MAO APPEAR IN PEKING . . . ETHIOPIA AND RUSSIA SIGN FRIENDSHIP TREATY . . . GOP GAINS IN CONGRESS, DEMOCRATS KEEP CONTROL . . . 900 AMERICAN CULT MEMBERS COMMIT SUICIDE IN GUYANA, REPRESENTATIVE RYAN AND 4 OTHERS ARE SLAIN . . . PIONEER VENUS II ENTERS VENUS ATMOSPHERE . . . OPEC RAISES PRICES 14% . . . CITY OF CLEVELAND DEFAULTS . . . STRIKES PARALYZE IRAN . . . INFLATION RATE: 12.4%; PRIME RATE: 12%.

Deaths

Edgar Bergen, Charles
  Boyer, Dan Dailey, Hubert
  Humphrey, Aram
  Khachaturian, Margaret
  Mead, Golda Meir,
  Norman Rockwell, William
  Steinberg, Gene Tunney.

Quotes _____

"Hurry, my children, hurry. They will start parachuting out of the air. They'll torture our children. Lay down your life with dignity. Let's get gone. Let's get gone."
— Reverend Jim Jones, People's Temple, Guyana

"We trust the Shah to maintain stability in Iran, to continue with the democratic process, and also to continue the progressive change in the Iranian social-economic structure."
— Jimmy Carter

"With credit, you can buy everything you can't afford."
— Edith Bunker, "All in the Family"

The president's intensive conversations with both Begin and Sadat at Camp David help them to reach accord. *Jimmy Carter Library.*

Billie Jean King, many-time U.S. Open and Wimbleton champion, has helped popularize women's tennis. *Copyright* Washington Post. *Reprinted courtesy of D.C. Public Library.*

"ERA would nullify any laws that make any distinction between men and women. When the good Lord created the earth, he didn't have the advice of Gloria Steinem or Bella Abzug."
— Sam Ervin

"The country is fed up with radical causes . . . the unisex movement . . . the departure from basics, decency, from the philosophy of the monogamous home."
— Jerry Falwell

"My esteem in this country has gone up substantially. It is very nice now [that] when people wave at me, they use all their fingers."
— Jimmy Carter

Ads _____

TV

Premieres
"The Incredible Hulk," Bill Bixby, Lou Ferrigno
"Fantasy Island," Ricardo Montalban, Herve Villechaize
"Dallas," Larry Hagman, Barbara Bel Geddes
"WKRP in Cincinnati," Loni Anderson
"Diff'rent Strokes," Gary Coleman, Conrad Bain
"Mork and Mindy," Robin Williams, Pam Dawber
"20/20," Hugh Downs
"Vegas," Robert Urich
"Taxi," Judd Hirsch

Top Ten (Nielsen)
"Laverne and Shirley," "Three's Company," "Mork and Mindy," "Happy Days," "Angie," "60 Minutes," "M*A*S*H," "The Ropers," "All in the Family," "Taxi"

Specials
"Balanchine IV, Dance in America"; "Friendly Fire"; "The Jericho Mile"; "Who Are the De Bolts—and Where Did They Get Nineteen Kids?" "Live from Lincoln Center with Luciano Pavarotti and Joan Sutherland"; "Strangers: The Story of a Mother and Daughter" (Bette Davis)

Diana Ross, Motown recording star, who began in the sixties with the Supremes. *Movie Star News*.

Emmy Awards
"Lou Grant" (drama); "Taxi" (comedy); "Christmas Eve on Sesame Street" (children); "The Tonight Show Starring Johnny Carson" (special class); Ron Leibman (actor, "Kaz"); Carroll O'Connor (comedic actor, "All in the Family"); Mariette Hartley (actress, "The Incredible Hulk"); Ruth Gordon (comedic actress, "Taxi")

Of Note
Fred Silverman, former CBS executive who brought ABC to a number one rating, moves to NBC as president.

Movies

Openings
The Deer Hunter (Michael Cimino), Robert De Niro, Meryl Streep, Christopher Walken
Coming Home (Hal Ashby), Jane Fonda, Jon Voight, Bruce Dern
Midnight Express (Alan Parker), Brad Davis, John Hurt, Randy Quaid
An Unmarried Woman (Paul Mazursky), Jill Clayburgh, Alan Bates, Michael Murphy
Interiors (Woody Allen), E. G. Marshall, Geraldine Page, Maureen Stapleton, Diane Keaton
Autumn Sonata (Ingmar Bergman), Ingrid Bergman, Liv Ullmann
Get Out Your Handkerchiefs (Bertrand Blier), Gerard Depardieu, Patrick Dewaere
Foul Play (Colin Higgins), Goldie Hawn, Chevy Chase
Grease (Randal Kleiser), John Travolta, Olivia Newton-John
Superman (Richard Donner), Christopher Reeve, Marlon Brando, Gene Hackman
Pretty Baby (Louis Malle), Keith Carradine, Brooke Shields, Susan Sarandon
National Lampoon's Animal House (John Landis), Tim Matheson, John Belushi, Donald Sutherland, Tom Hulce
Days of Heaven (Terence Malick), Sam Shepard, Linda Manz, Richard Gere
La Cage aux Folles (Edouard Molinaro), Ugo Tognazzi, Michel Serrault, Michel Galabru

Academy Awards
Best Picture: *The Deer Hunter*
Best Director: Michael Cimino (*The Deer Hunter*)
Best Actress: Jane Fonda (*Coming Home*)
Best Actor: Jon Voight (*Coming Home*)

Top Box-Office Stars
Burt Reynolds, John Travolta, Richard Dreyfuss, Warren Beatty, Clint Eastwood, Woody Allen, Diane Keaton, Jane Fonda, Peter Sellers, Barbra Streisand

Stars of Tomorrow
Christopher Reeve, John Belushi, Brad Davis, Amy Irving, John Savage, Brooke Adams, Gary Busey, Brooke Shields, Harry Hamlin, Tim Matheson

Popular Music

Hit Songs
"Night Fever"
"Stayin' Alive"
"I Go Crazy"
"Love Is Thicker than Water"
"Boogie Oogie Oogie"
"Three Times a Lady"
"Miss You"
"With a Little Luck"

Top Records

Albums: *Saturday Night Fever* (Sound track); *Grease* (Sound track); *52nd Street* (Billy Joel); *Some Girls* (Rolling Stones); *Don't Look Back* (Boston); *Live and More* (Donna Summer)

Singles: *Shadow Dancing* (Andy Gibb); *Kiss You All Over* (Exile); *How Deep Is Your Love* (Bee Gees); *Baby Come Back* (Player); *If I Can't Have You* (Yvonne Elliman); *Feels So Good* (Chuck Mangione); *Last Dance* (Donna Summer); *Our Love* (Natalie Cole). Country: *Mammas Don't Let Your Babies Grow Up to Be Cowboys / I Can Get Off on You* (Waylon Jennings and Willie Nelson); *Sleeping Single in a Double Bed* (Barbara Mandrell)

Grammy Awards
Just the Way You Are, Billy Joel

(record); *Saturday Night Fever*, Bee Gees (album); "Just the Way You Are" (song)

Jazz and Big Bands

Top Performers (*Downbeat*): Dexter Gordon (soloist); Toshiko Akiyoshi and Lew Tabackin (band); Weather Report (jazz group); Elvin Jones, Ron Carter, Jaco Pastorius, Woody Shaw, Wayne Shorter, Jimmy Smith, Airto Moreira (instrumentalists); Al Jarreau, Flora Purim (vocalists); Woody Shaw, *Rosewood* (album)

Theater

Broadway Openings

Plays
Tribute (Bernard Slade), Jack Lemmon
First Monday in October (Jerome Lawrence, Robert E. Lee), Henry Fonda, Jane Alexander
The Kingfisher (William Douglas Home), Claudette Colbert, Rex Harrison
Deathtrap (Ira Levin), John Wood, Marian Seldes
The Crucifer of Blood (Paul Giovanni), Glenn Close, Paxton Whitehead

Musicals
Ballroom (Billy Goldenberg, Alan and Marilyn Bergman), Dorothy Loudon, Vincent Gardenia
The Best Little Whorehouse in Texas (Carol Hall), Carlin Glynn, Henderson Forsythe
Ain't Misbehavin' (Fats Waller, revue), Nell Carter, Andre De Shields
On the 20th Century (Betty Comden, Adolph Green, Cy Coleman), John Collum, Kevin Kline, Madeline Kahn
Dancin' (numerous authors), Ann Reinking, choreographed by Bob Fosse
Eubie! (Eubie Blake, Nobel Sissle, et al.), Gregory Hines

Classics, Revivals, and Off-Broadway Premieres
Da (Hugh Leonard), Barnard Hughes; *13 Rue de l'Amour* (Feydeau), Louis Jourdan, Patricia Elliott;

Buried Child (Sam Shepard), Jacqueline Brookes; *Once in a Lifetime* (Moss Hart, George S. Kaufman), John Lithgow; *Man and Superman* (Shaw), George Grizzard; *The Inspector General* (Gogol), Theodore Bikel; *5th of July* (Lanford Wilson), William Hurt; *Getting Out* (Marsha Norman); *Molly* (Simon Gray), Tammy Grimes; *St. Mark's Gospel*, Alec McCowen; *Taming of the Shrew*, Meryl Streep, Raul Julia; *The Show-off* (George Kelly), Paul Rudd

Regional

Mark Taper Forum, Los Angeles: *Zoot Suit* (Luis Valdez), premiere

Alley, Houston: *Echelon* (Mikhail Raschin), directed by Soviet Galina Volchek, with American actors, American premiere

Actors Theater, Louisville: *Crimes of the Heart* (Beth Henley), premiere

Pulitzer Prize
The Gin Game, D. L. Coburn

Tony Awards
Da, Hugh Leonard (play), *Ain't Misbehavin'*, Fats Waller (musical)

Classical Music _____

Compositions
Joseph Schwantner, *Aftertones of Infinity*
John Cage, *Etudes Borealis, Freeman Etudes*
Morton Feldman, *Neither: Spring of Chosroes*
Charles Wuorinen, *Fast Fantasy*
Morton Subotnik, *Game Room, Wild Beasts*
Milton Babbitt, *A Solo Requiem*
Ezra Laderman, Piano Concerto
William Kraft, *Andirivieni*

Important Events
The year's celebrations include the 150th anniversary
of the death of Schubert (with national tours by
Andre Watts, Charles Treger, and others), and the
50th of Janáček. Horowitz, for the 50th anniversary
of his U.S. debut, performs the Rachmaninoff Piano
Concerto, no. 3 in New York and the White House.
Andrés Segovia, on the 50th anniversary of his New
York debut, gives his first performance with an
orchestra in 25 years (Avery Fisher Hall, New York).
Leonard Bernstein's 60th birthday is commemorated
by the National Symphony at Wolf Trap Farm Park;
Roy Harris, on his 80th birthday, is honored at his
hometown, Chandler, Okla.

New Appointments: Zubin Mehta, New York
Philharmonic; Carlo Maria Giulini, Los Angeles;
Eduardo Mata, Dallas

Debuts: Youri Egorov, Dylan Jenson, Mark Kaplan

Pulitzer Prize winner Carl Sagan. *Copyright* Washington
Post. *Reprinted courtesy of D.C. Library.*

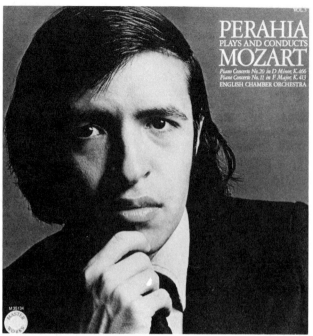
CBS records.

First Performances
Gene Gutche, *Helios Kenetic* (Miami); Krzysztof
Penderecki, Violin Concerto (Minneapolis); Percy
Grainger, *Free Music, no. 1* (Oakland); Pierre
Boulez, *Notations* (New York); Karlheinz
Stockhausen, *Sirius* (Houston); William Kraft, Tuba
Concerto (Los Angeles); Ralph Shapey, *O Jerusalem*
(Pittsburgh)

Opera
Metropolitan: *Don Pasquale;* Maria Ewing, Jerome
Hines, *Dialogues of the Carmelites;* Richard Stilwell,
Peter Pears, *Billy Budd;* Jon Vickers, *Peter Grimes;*
Beverly Sills, Sherrill Milnes, *Thaïs*

Houston: Marilyn Horne, Joan Carden (debut),
Tancredi (with long-lost, 80-bar "tragic finale");
Donald Gramm, *Falstaff* (in English)

Chicago: Arnold Moss, William Stone, *Paradise
Lost* (premiere, Krzysztof Penderecki)

Washington, D.C.: *Poro* (Handel, premiere)

Virginia: *Mary, Queen of Scots* (Thea Musgrave,
premiere)

Temple University, Philadelphia: *Every Good Boy
Deserves Favor* (André Previn, Tom Stoppard,
premiere)

San Francisco: Placido Domingo, *Elegy for Young
Lovers* (Hans Werner Henze)

Art

Painting
Willem de Kooning, *Untitled III*
Jennifer Bartlett, *Summer Lost at Night (for Tom Hess)*
Philip Guston, *Tomb, The Ladder*
Roy Lichtenstein, *Razzmatazz*
Susan Rothenberg, *For the Light*
Alice Neel, *Geoffrey Hendricks and Brian*
Ralph Goings, *Still Life with Sugars*
Audrey Flack, *Bounty*
Elizabeth Murray, *Children Meeting*

Sculpture
Louise Bourgeois, *Confrontation, Structure III—Three Floors*
Duane Hanson, *Woman Reading a Paperback*

William Tucker, *Arc*
Richard Long, *Cornish Stone Circle*
Alexander Calder's 980-pound aluminum mobile is placed in the National Gallery.
Isamu Noguchi's 36-foot portal is placed in the Justice Center, Cleveland.

Architecture
East Building, National Gallery of Art, Washington, D.C. (I. M. Pei)
Dallas City Hall, Dallas (Pei)
Moorehead Cultural Bridge, Fargo (Michael Graves)
Purchase Campus, State University of New York (Edward Larrabee Barnes)

Roy Lichtenstein, *Stepping Out*, 1978. Oil and magna on canvas. 86 × 70″. *The Metropolitan Museum of Art. Purchase, Lila Acheson Fund, Inc. Gift, Arthur Hoppock Hearn Fund, Stephen C. Swid, The Bernhill Fund, Walter Bareiss, and Louise Smith Gifts, 1980.*

Clint Eastwood, who gained movie fame as a star of "spaghetti westerns" in the sixties, remains a top box office attraction and often directs his own films. *Movie Star News.*

Important Exhibitions
"Pompeii 79 A.D." opens in Boston, Chicago, Dallas, and New York. The Pei Wing of the National Gallery opens with "The Splendor of Dresden," which goes to the Metropolitan and San Francisco.

Museums

New York: *Metropolitan:* "Monet's Years at Giverny"; "The Arts under Napoleon"

Guggenheim, Houston, Minneapolis, Los Angeles: Mark Rothko retrospective

Minneapolis, Washington, D.C. (National): "Noguchi's Imaginary Landscapes"

Washington, D.C.: *Hirschhorn:* "The 'Noble Buyer': John Quinn, Patron of the Avant-Garde." *National:* "Aspects of 20th Century Art"; American art at mid-century

Fort Worth: "Stella since 1970"

Art Briefs
The two-year King Tutankhamen show collects $5 million for the Cairo Museum • Nelson Rockefeller invests $4 million in a mail-order business of high quality reproductions of works from his collection • The J. Paul Getty Museum, Malibu, will receive $50 million a year under Getty's will to purchase works • Three Gutenberg Bibles are sold within three months, one for $2.2 million.

Books

Fiction

Critics' Choice

Shosha, Isaac Bashevis Singer
Picture Palace, Paul Theroux
The World According to Garp, John Irving
Final Payments, Mary Gordon
Going after Cacciato, Tim O'Brien
The Coup, John Updike
Natural Shocks, Richard G. Stern
Whistle, James Jones
Airships, Barry Hannah
Detour, Michael Brodsky

Best-Sellers

Chesapeake, James A. Michener
War and Remembrance, Herman Wouk
Fools Die, Mario Puzo
Bloodlines, Sidney Sheldon
Scruples, Judith Krantz
Evergreen, Belva Plain
Illusions, Richard Bach
The Holcroft Covenant, Robert Ludlum
Second Generation, Howard Fast
Eye of the Needle, Ken Follett

Nonfiction

Critics' Choice

The World within the Word, William Gass
American Caesar, William Manchester
On Moral Fiction, John Gardner
Inventing America, Garry Wills
The Snow Leopard, Peter Matthiessen
Lying: Moral Choice in Public and Private Life, Sissela Bok
Perjury: The Hiss-Chambers Case, Allen Weinstein
My Mother / Myself, Nancy Friday
Robert Kennedy and His Times, Arthur Schlesinger, Jr.
Intellectual Life in the Colonial South 1585–1763, Robert Beale Davis
The Rise of American Philosophy, Bruce Kuklick
Modern Art, Meyer Schapiro

Best-Sellers

If Life Is a Bowl of Cherries— What Am I Doing in the Pits? Erma Bombeck
Gnomes, Wil Huygen, with illustrations by Rien Poortvliet
The Complete Book of Running, James Fixx
Mommie Dearest, Christina Crawford
The Memoirs of Richard Nixon, Richard Nixon
A Distant Mirror, Barbara W. Tuchman
Faeries, Brian Froud, Alan Lee
In Search of History, Theodore H. White

Poetry

Maya Angelou, *And Still I Rise*
Anthony Hecht, *Millions of Strange Shadows*
Adrienne Rich, *The Dream of a Common Language*
John Hollander, *Spectral Emanations*
James Merrill, *Mirabell: Books of Numbers*
Peter Davidson, ed., *Hello, Darkness: The Collected Poems of L. E. Sissman*

Pulitzer Prizes

The Stories of John Cheever, John Cheever (fiction)
The Dred Scott Case, Don E. Fehrenbacher (U.S. history)
On Human Nature, Edward O. Wilson (nonfiction)
Days of Sorrow and Pain: Leo Baeck and the Berlin Jews, Leonard Baker (biography)
Now and Then, Robert Penn Warren (poetry)

Nobel Prize

Isaac Bashevis Singer

Science and Technology

The drug Anturane is discovered to reduce, by 50 percent, sudden death following heart attack.

A study of longshoremen shows that the risk of fatal heart attack is cut in half by physical labor.

A balloon compression method of opening arteries is developed.

Elective induced labor in pregnancy is banned because of the side effects of oxytocin.

Recombinant, self-replicating DNA is used to program E. choli bacteria to make insulin.

Stanford physicist William Fairbank questions whether "free" quarks exist only in combinations as subatomic particles or in isolation.

NASA's Seasat I satellite collects information on 95 percent of the world's oceans (70 percent of the total surface) every 36 hours.

Plate techtonics research shows a "Siberian connection"—a piece of North America joined to Asia 1.5 million years ago.

ᐬ Louise Brown, the first test-tube baby, is born in Oldham, England, after a fertilized egg is implanted in her mother's womb.

ᐬ Ultrasound techniques are developed in London to view the fetus through the mother's abdomen.

ᐬ Canadian researchers propose that aspirin reduces the chance of stroke.

Nobel Prize

Arno Penzias and Robert W. Wilson win in physics for work in cosmic microwave radiation. Daniel Nathans and Hamilton Smith win in physiology and medicine for their work in restriction enzymes and molecular genetics.

Sports

Baseball

Pete Rose sets an NL consecutive-game hitting streak record of 44.

New York (AL) beats Boston (AL), 5–4, on Bucky Dent's home run in the AL-East playoff.

The Cy Young awards are won by Gaylord Perry (San Diego, NL) and Ron Guidry (New York, AL).

Champions

Batting	Pitching
Dave Parker (Pittsburgh, NL), .334	Gaylord Perry (San Diego, NL), 21–6
Rod Carew (Minnesota, AL), .333	Ron Guidry (New York, AL), 25–3
	Home runs
	Jim Rice (Boston, NL), 46

Football

NFC Season Leaders: Roger Staubach (Dallas), passing; Walter Payton (Chicago), rushing; Ricky Young (Minnesota), receiving

AFC Season Leaders: Terry Bradshaw (Pittsburgh), passing; Earl Campbell (Houston), rushing; Steve Largent (Seattle), receiving

College All-Americans: Chuck Fusina (Q), Penn State; Joe Montana (Q), Notre Dame; Rick Leach (Q), Michigan

Bowls (Jan. 1, 1979)

Rose: Washington 27–Michigan 20	Cotton: Notre Dame 35–Houston 34
Orange: Oklahoma 31–Nebraska 24	Sugar: Alabama 14–Penn State 7

Basketball

NBA All-Pro First Team: Leonard Robinson (New Orleans), Julius Erving (Philadelphia), Bill Walton (Portland), George Gervin (San Antonio), David Thompson (Denver)

Other Sports

Soccer: North American Soccer League attendance rises 50 percent to 5.3 million.

Boxing: Leon Spinks, 24, former Olympic champion, decisions Muhammad Ali for the heavyweight title; Ali later regains the crown before 70,000 who pay $7 million.

Horse Racing: Affirmed, ridden by Steve Cauthen, wins the triple crown; Alydar is second in all three races. In the Marlboro Cup, Seattle Slew beats Affirmed in the first match between triple crown winners.

Tennis: Top money winners are Bjorn Borg ($691,886) and Martina Navratilova ($500,757).

Winners

World Series		MVP
New York (AL) 4		Bill Walton, Portland
Los Angeles (NL) 3		*College Basketball*
MVP		North Carolina
NL–Dave Parker, Pittsburgh		*Player of the Year*
AL–Jim Rice, Boston		Phil Ford, North Carolina
Super Bowl XIII (Jan. 1979)		*Stanley Cup*
Pittsburgh 35–Dallas 31		Philadelphia
MVP		*US Tennis Open*
Earl Campbell, Houston		Men: Jimmy Connors
College Football		Women: Chris Evert
Alabama		*USGA Open*
Heisman Trophy		Andy North
Billy Sims, Oklahoma		*Kentucky Derby*
NBA Championship		Affirmed (S. Cauthen, jockey)
Washington 4–Seattle 2		

Fashion

For Women: The exercise rage provides a new market for sportswear: T-shirts (with Mickey Mouses, for Mickey's 50th birthday), jogging outfits, bright terry-cloth fabrics, bloomers, and a variety of matching sports shoes. Jeans, even when ripped to the calf or mid-thigh, are coordinated with fancy tops, such as silk blouses and beaded cardigans, and are worn with a diversity of belt styles. Shorter boots reach only to the ankle or mid-calf and have a low heel. Denim gains even more popularity, now in blousons and jackets. For the evening, the forties style is revived in the broad-shouldered and slim-hipped silhouette (the "Joan Crawford" look, now called the "Joe Namath look"), black satins, high heels, large jeweled accessories, and vivid makeup (bright pinks, reds, purples on lips, fingers, and toes).

High-fashion notes: Perry Ellis's slouch coat; Bill Blass's red silk and satin draped skirt and jacket

Kaleidoscope

- Forty-seven percent of the adult population exercises daily or "almost daily" (up from 24 percent in 1961); 30 million play tennis (20 million in 1973); 3 million, racquetball (50,000 in 1970); one person in nine runs.
- Betty Ford announces that she has entered a treatment program for alcohol and pill addiction.
- The Karen Silkwood estate is awarded $10 million damages by a jury that finds she was poisoned by plutonium.
- Nelson Rockefeller dies of a heart attack in the apartment of one of his female assistants.
- The Mormons ordain their first black priest.
- The legal retirement age is raised to 70.
- NASA selects 35 new astronauts, including 6 women and 3 blacks.
- The Bee Gees' *Saturday Night Fever* album sells a record 12 million copies.
- A Soviet satellite, Cosmo 954, crashes in the Canadian wilderness by accident; the United States is forewarned by the Russians.
- Fifty percent of all shoe sales are sneakers; sales soar to 200 million.
- Unmarried couples living together number 1,137,000 (523,000 in 1970).
- The baseball commissioner's ban of female reporters in locker rooms is set aside by a federal judge.
- A Salem, Oregon, jury acquits John Rideout of raping his wife.
- A "Singles Expo" in California provides seminars on "Finding that Perfect Mate"; it also provides exhibits of singles products, like soup for one; there is a 60 percent increase in people living alone, 23 percent of the population.
- Alex Haley's *Roots* is followed by a growing interest in genealogy.
- Competing in the New York City marathon are 9,875 runners; 8,748 complete the 26 miles.
- Howard Jarvis, 75, becomes a national hero by organizing the petition to put Proposition 13 (reducing state property tax 57 percent) on the California June ballot; it passes.
- The Harvard University faculty votes 182–65 to return to a more structured undergraduate curriculum, thereby moving away from the more "relevant" one with greater options established during the 1960s.
- The USDA and FDA warn of the danger of nitrites in processed and cured meat products, saying that sodium nitrite may cause cancer.
- Attracted by seemingly unlimited employment and housing possibilities, more than 1,000 families move to Dallas each month.
- By mid-June, passengers have 18 different fares to choose from when flying from New York to London.
- Following a study of recidivism, the New York City police begin to arrest wife beaters.

Kareem Abdul-Jabbar continues as the dominant pro basketball player of the decade. *Copyright* Washington Post. *Reprinted courtesy of D.C. Public Library.*

- Nine Lives' (cat food) Morris dies in Chicago at the age of 17.
- U.S. and Egyptian researchers analyze the hair of a mummy in King Tutankhamen's tomb and identify King Tut's grandmother.
- The first American-made Volkswagen comes off the assembly line at New Stanton, Pa.
- Statewide limitations on indoor smoking are passed in Iowa and New Jersey.
- James Fixx earns $930,000 as *The Complete Book of Running* sells 620,000 copies.
- Some of TV's top salaries are paid to Johnny Carson ($4 million), James Garner ($1,700,000), Henry Winkler ($990,000), and Valerie Harper ($660,000).
- Bjorn Borg earns $50,000 for advertising headbands and Tuborg beer; $200,000 for endorsing Fila clothing; $100,000, Bancroft rackets; $2,000, VS gut; $50,000, Tretorn shoes; and $25,000, Scandinavian Airlines (on a shoulder patch).

Fads: Biorhythm, college toga parties

First Appearances: 45 RPM picture disc records, woman commemorated on a circulating coin (Susan B. Anthony dollar), pen with erasable ink (Eraser Mate), postage stamp to honor a black woman (Harriet Tubman), legalized gambling in N.J. (Atlantic City), slot machine payoff of $275,000 (Las Vegas), Garfield cartoon, "Battlestar Galactica," 2XL, Merlin, Master Mind, pocket math game calculator, microchip technology in washing machines, federal deregulation of airlines

1979

Facts and Figures

Economic Profile
  Dow-Jones: ↓ High 907–
    Low 742
  GNP: +12%
  Inflation: +13.3%
  Unemployment: 6.5%
Police expenditures, federal,
  state, local: $25.8 billion
Persons arrested: 10,500,000
Executions: 2
Prisoners, federal and state:
  301,470
Metropolitan Opera
  subscription, 8
  performances: $56–$320
Radio City Music Hall:
  $7.50–$10.50
Broadway musical, Saturday
  night (top): $25
Rental near Lincoln Center,
  New York City, studio to 3
  bedrooms: $535–$1,695
Calvin Klein linen suits:
  $175–$230
Ralph Lauren (Chaps) suits:
  $190–$245
Bill Blass vested suits: $205–
  $235
Franchises
  Philly Mignon: $25,000–
    $30,000
  Dunkin Donuts: $45,000
  Slimique: $30,000

Deaths

Mamie Eisenhower, Arthur
Fiedler, Roy Harris,
Emmett Kelly, Leonide
Massine, Thurman
Munson, Merle Oberon,
Mary Pickford, Richard
Rodgers, Jean Seberg,
Bishop Fulton Sheen, John
Wayne.

In the News

U.S. AND CHINA ESTABLISH DIPLOMATIC RELATIONS, FORMAL TIES WITH TAIWAN ARE SEVERED . . . VIETNAM TAKES OVER CAMBODIA . . . SHAH LEAVES IRAN FOR "VACATION" . . . AYATOLLAH KHOMEINI RETURNS TO IRAN FROM FRANCE . . . CHINA INVADES VIETNAM . . . VOYAGER I SENDS PHOTOS OF JUPITER . . . ACCIDENT AT THREE MILE ISLAND, PA., NUCLEAR PLANT THREATENS AREA . . . MARGARET THATCHER IS ELECTED, FIRST WOMAN BRITISH P.M. . . . CARTER DECONTROLS DOMESTIC OIL . . . U.S. AND RUSSIA ANNOUNCE COMPLETION OF SALT II AGREEMENT . . . DC-10 CRASHES IN CHICAGO, 274 ARE DEAD, ALL DC-10 FLIGHTS ARE HALTED . . . FIRST BLACK GOVERNMENT IS ELECTED IN RHODESIA . . . SOMOZA FLEES NICARAGUA, SANDINISTAS TAKE POWER . . . OPEC ANNOUNCES FURTHER OIL PRICE RAISE, 50% IN ONE YEAR . . . CARTER PROCLAIMS "MORAL EQUIVALENT OF WAR" ON OIL USAGE . . . CARTER DOUBLES INDOCHINA REFUGEE QUOTA TO 14,000 PER MONTH . . . PRESIDENT RESHUFFLES CABINET, JOSEPH CALIFANO AND JAMES SCHLESINGER LEAVE . . . U.N. AMBASSADOR ANDREW YOUNG RESIGNS AFTER HIS MEETING WITH PLO IS REVEALED . . . LORD MOUNTBATTEN IS ASSASSINATED BY IRA IN IRELAND . . . PIONEER XI RETURNS PHOTOS OF SATURN . . . CARTER PROPOSES MX MISSILES ON RACETRACK PLAN . . . SHAH COMES TO N.Y. FOR GALL BLADDER SURGERY . . . STUDENTS SEIZE U.S. EMBASSY IN IRAN, 62 AMERICANS ARE HELD HOSTAGE . . . $1.5 BILLION FEDERAL BAILOUT LOAN TO CHRYSLER IS APPROVED . . . RUSSIA INVADES AFGHANISTAN . . . GOLD REACHES A RECORD $524 PER OUNCE, UP FROM $223 IN 1978 . . . INFLATION: 13.3%; PRIME RATE: 15.75%.

Ronald Reagan, the former movie star and governor of California, and his wife Nancy. Reagan seeks the Republican nomination for president. *Courtesy Sedat Pakay.*

"[This] is the first day of the government of God."
— Ayatollah Khomeini

"My initial reaction was to do something. [But] none of us would want to do anything that would worsen the danger in which our fellow citizens have been placed."
— Jimmy Carter, following seizure of the hostages

"If one works for years at becoming a pitiful, helpless giant, one might just succeed."
— Former Secretary of Energy James Schlesinger

Quotes

"The poor . . . are your brothers and sisters in Christ. You must never be content to leave them just crumbs from the feast."
— Pope John Paul II, at Yankee Stadium

"Are we going to guarantee businessmen against their own incompetence?"
— Senator William Proxmire (D-Wis.), on the Chrysler bail-out

"The defeat of the Equal Rights Amendment is the greatest victory for women's rights since the woman's suffrage movement of 1920."
— Phyllis Schlafly

"No More Iranian Students Will be Permitted on These Premises Until the Hostages Are Released."
— Bordello sign near Reno

"Shouldn't we stop worrying whether someone likes us and decide once again we're going to be respected in the world?"
— Ronald Reagan

"For the average American, the message is clear. Liberalism is no longer the answer. It is the problem."
— Ronald Reagan

"The craze for genealogy . . . is connected with the epidemic for divorce. . . . If we can't figure out who our living relatives are, then maybe we'll have more luck with the dead ones."
— Jane Howard, *Families*

Ads

TV

Premieres

"Benson," Robert Guillaume
"Archie Bunker's Place," Carroll O'Connor, Martin Balsam
"Real People," Fred Willard
"The Dukes of Hazzard," Tom Wopat, John Schneider
"The Facts of Life," Charlotte Rae
"Trapper John, M. D.," Pernell Roberts, Gregory Harrison
"Knots Landing," Joan Van Ark, Michele Lee
"Hart to Hart," Robert Wagner, Stefanie Powers

Top Ten (Nielsen)

"60 Minutes," "Three's Company," "That's Incredible," "Alice," "M*A*S*H," "Dallas," "Flo," "The Jeffersons," "The Dukes of Hazzard," "One Day at a Time"

Specials

"The Miracle Worker" (Patty Duke Astin, Melissa Gilbert); "Every Little Movement" (Shirley MacLaine); "IBM Presents Baryshnikov on Broadway"; "Live from Studio 8H: A Tribute to Toscanini"; "The Body Human: The Magic Sense"; "Fred Astaire: Change Partners and Dance"; "Edward and Mrs. Simpson"; "Roots: The Next Generation" (Marlon Brando, James Earl Jones); "Blind Ambition" (Martin Sheen, Rip Torn); "Attica" (Marvin J. Chomsky); "Guyana Tragedy" (Powers Boothe)

Emmy Awards

"Lou Grant" (drama); "Taxi" (comedy); "IBM Presents Baryshnikov on Broadway" (variety or music); "The Body Human" (informational); "A Tribute to Toscanini" (classical); Ed Asner (actor, "Lou Grant"); Richard Mulligan (comedic actor, "Soap"); Barbara Bel Geddes (actress, "Dallas"); Cathryn Damon (comedic actress, "Soap")

Of Note

ABC begins a nightly report, "The Iran Crisis: America Held Hostage," with Frank Reynolds and Ted Koppel.

Movies

Openings

Kramer vs. Kramer (Robert Benton), Dustin Hoffman, Meryl Streep
All that Jazz (Bob Fosse), Roy Scheider
Apocalypse Now (Francis Ford Coppola), Marlon Brando, Robert Duvall, Martin Sheen
Breaking Away (Peter Yates), Dennis Christopher, Paul Dooley, Barbara Barrie
Norma Rae (Martin Ritt), Sally Field, Ron Leibman, Beau Bridges
Manhattan (Woody Allen), Woody Allen, Diane Keaton, Mariel Hemingway
The China Syndrome (James Bridges), Jane Fonda, Jack Lemmon, Michael Douglas
10 (Blake Edwards), Dudley Moore, Julie Andrews, Bo Derek
Being There (Hal Ashby), Peter Sellers, Shirley MacLaine, Melvyn Douglas
The Rose (Mark Rydell), Bette Midler, Alan Bates
The Black Stallion (D. Carroll Ballard), Kelly Reno, Mickey Rooney, Teri Garr
Fedora (Billy Wilder), William Holden, Marthe Keller, José Ferrer
Hair (Milos Forman), John Savage, Treat Williams
The Marriage of Maria Braun (Rainer Werner Fassbinder), Hanna Schygulla
Star Trek—The Motion Picture (Robert Wise), Leonard Nimoy, William Shatner

Kramer vs. Kramer, with Meryl Streep and Dustin Hoffman, wins five Academy Awards. *Movie Star News.*

Monty Python's Life of Brian (Terry Jones), John Cleese, Terry Gilliam
The Muppet Movie (James Frawley), Jim Henson and the Muppets

Academy Awards

Best Picture: *Kramer vs. Kramer*
Best Director: Robert Benton *(Kramer vs. Kramer)*
Best Actress: Sally Field *(Norma Rae)*
Best Actor: Dustin Hoffman *(Kramer vs. Kramer)*

Top Box-Office Stars

Burt Reynolds, Clint Eastwood, Jane Fonda, Woody Allen, Barbra Streisand, Sylvester Stallone, John Travolta, Jill Clayburgh, Roger Moore, Mel Brooks

Stars of Tomorrow

Bo Derek, Dennis Christopher, Treat Williams, Michael O'Keefe, Lisa Eichhorn, Sigourney Weaver, Chris Makepeace, Ricky Schroder, Karen Allen, Mary Steenburgen

Popular Music _____

Hit Songs
"Le Freak"
"I Will Survive"
"Reunited"
"Hot Stuff"
"Sad Eyes"
"Too Much Heaven"
"My Life"
"Mama Can't Buy You Love"

Top Records

Albums: *Bad Girls* (Donna Summer); *Barbra Streisand's Greatest Hits, vol. 2* (Barbra Streisand); *The Long Run* (Eagles); *Breakfast in America* (Supertramp); *Spirits Having Flown* (Bee Gees); *Minute by Minute* (Doobie Brothers)

Singles: *My Sharona* (Knack); *Bad Girls* (Donna Summer); *Da Ya Think I'm Sexy* (Rod Stewart); *Y.M.C.A.* (Village People); *Ring My Bell* (Anita Ward); *Makin' It* (David Naughton); *Fire* (Pointer Sisters); *A Little More Love* (Olivia Newton-John). Country: *Amanda* (Waylon Jennings); *Every Which Way but Loose* (Eddie Rabbitt)

Grammy Awards
What a Fool Believes, Doobie Brothers (record); *52nd Street,* Billy Joel (album); "What a Fool Believes" (song)

Jazz and Big Bands

Top Performers *(Downbeat):* Charles Mingus (soloist); Toshiko Akiyoshi/Lew Tabackin (band); Weather Report (jazz group); Phil Woods, Hubert Laws, McCoy Tyner, Jaco Pastorius, Gary Burton, Chick Corea, Tony Williams (instrumentalists), Al Jarreau, Sarah Vaughan (vocalists); Steely Dan (vocal group); Joni Mitchell, *Mingus* (album)

Theater _____

Broadway Openings
Plays
The Elephant Man (Bernard Pomerance), Philip Anglim, Carole Shelley, Kevin Conway
Wings (Arthur Kopit), Constance Cummings
Bedroom Farce (Alan Ayckbourn), Michael Gough
Whose Life Is It Anyway? (Brian Clark), Tom Conti, Jean Marsh
On Golden Pond (Ernest Thompson), Frances Sternhagen, Tom Aldredge
Loose Ends (Michael Weller), Kevin Kline, Roxanne Hart
Spokesong (Stewart Parker), John Lithgow, Virginia Vestoff
Romantic Comedy (Bernard Slade), Mia Farrow, Anthony Perkins
Night and Day (Tom Stoppard), Maggie Smith
Bent (Martin Sherman), Richard Gere
Strider: The Story of a Horse (Mark Rozorsky), Gerald Hiken
Knockout (Louis La Russa), Danny Aiello

Musicals
Sweeney Todd (Stephen Sondheim), Angela Lansbury, Len Cariou
I Remember Mama (Richard Rodgers, Martin Charnin), Liv Ullmann
Sugar Babies (Ralph C. Allen, Harry Rigby), Mickey Rooney, Ann Miller
Whoopee! (Gus Kahn, Walter Donaldson), Bob Allen, Charles Repole
Evita (Andrew Lloyd Weber, Tim Rice), Patti LuPone, Bob Gunton
They're Playing Our Song (Marvin Hamlisch, Carole Bayer Sager), Robert Klein, Lucie Arnaz
Every Good Boy Deserves Favour (André Previn, Tom Stoppard), René Auberjonois, Eli Wallach

Classics, Revivals, and Off-Broadway Premieres
Happy Days (Samuel Beckett), George Voskovec, Irene Worth; *Talley's Folly* (Lanford Wilson), Judd Hirsch, Trish Hawkins: *Hamlet,* William Hurt; *A Month in the Country* (Turgenev), Tammy Grimes, Farley Granger; *Gertrude Stein* (Marty Martin), Pat Carroll; *A Lovely Sunday for Creve Coeur* (Tennessee Williams), Shirley Knight; *Richard III,* Al Pacino; *Drinks before Dinner* (E. L. Doctorow), Christopher Plummer; *The Art of Dining* (Tina Horne), Dianne Wiest, George Guidall; *The Human Voice* (Cocteau), Liv Ullmann; *Taken in Marriage* (Thomas Babe), Colleen Dewhurst, Meryl Streep; *The Inspector General* (Gogol), Theodore Bikel

Regional
Goodman, Chicago: *Death and the King's Horseman* (Wole Soyinka), premiere

Mark Taper Forum, Los Angeles: *Children of a Lesser God* (Mark Medoff), premiere

Theater (cont.)

Arena, Washington, D.C.: *Loose Ends* (Michael Weller), premiere

Pulitzer Prize
Buried Child, Sam Shepard

Tony Awards
The Elephant Man, Bernard Pomerance (play), *Sweeney Todd,* Stephen Sondheim (musical)

Classical Music _____

Compositions
David Del Tredici, *In Memory of a Summer Day*
George Rochberg, Three String Quartets
Gunther Schuller, Sonata Serenata
Marvin Feinsmith, *Isaiah* Symphony
William Bolcomb, Second Sonata for Violin and
    Piano
Samuel Barber, Oboe Concerto
James Tenney, Harmonium #4; Saxony #2

Important Events
A total of 1,470 symphony orchestras perform before 25 million people.
Elliott Carter's 70th birthday is celebrated with numerous performances of *Syringa;* California honors Carter with a day named after him. Ernst Krenek is honored in an eight-day festival in Santa Barbara.
Beverly Sills, 50, retires from the stage: Gian Carlo Menotti writes a farewell opera in her honor, *La Loca,* premiered in San Diego.
A great deal of concertizing occurs abroad. After the first cultural pact, the Boston Symphony becomes the first U.S. orchestra to tour China. Eugene Istomin is the first American to concertize in Egypt. Numerous Russian émigrés give highly acclaimed recitals: Youri Egorov, Bella Davidovich, Gidon Kremer.

Retirements: Eugene Ormandy, Philadelphia Orchestra (after 44 years); Maurice Abravanel, Utah (32 years); Lorin Maazel, Cleveland (10 years)

New Appointments: Neville Marriner, Minnesota; Michael Gielen, Cincinnati; Leonard Slatkin, St. Louis; Julius Rudel, Buffalo; Pinchas Zukerman, St. Paul Chamber Orchestra

Debuts: Carmit Zori, Gennadi Rozhdestvensky

First Performances
William Schuman, Symphony no. 10 (Minneapolis); Jacob Druckman, *Aureole* (New York); Earl Kim, Violin Concerto (New York): Morton Subotnik, *Place* (Portland); Henry Brant, Antiphonal Responses (Oakland): Barbara Kolb, *Grisaille* (Portland); Alan Hovhaness, Symphony no. 36 for Solo Flute and Orchestra (Washington, D.C.); Easley Blackwood, Symphony no. 4 (Chicago)

Opera
Metropolitan: Birgit Nilsson returns with a gala concert; Placido Domingo, Gilda Cruz-Romo, *Otello* (PBS, televised); Teresa Zylis-Gara, Tatiana Troyanos, Kurt Moll (debut), *Tannhaüser;* Teresa Stratas, Nicolai Gedda, Martti Talvela, Jon Vickers, *The Bartered Bride;* Vasile Moldoveanu, *Don Carlo;* Astrid Varnay, *The Rise and Fall of the City of Mahagonny; Der Rosenkavalier*

New York City: Rita Shane, *Miss Havisham's Fire* (Dominick Argento, premiere). Sills becomes director on July 1.

Chicago: Richard Gill, Bill Dooley, *The Love for Three Oranges;* Jon Vickers, *Tristan und Isolde*

Boston: *The Ice Break* (Sir Michael Tippett, premiere); *Madama Butterfly* (original version, Puccini)

Santa Fe: *Lulu* (Alban Berg, premiere in English)

San Francisco: *A Winter's Tale* (John Harbison, premiere); *Mary, Queen of Scots* (Thea Musgrave)

Virginia: *A Christmas Carol* (Musgrave, premiere)

Aspen: *Houdini* (Peter Schat)

Spoleto: *The Desperate Husband* (Domenico Cimarosa)

Music Notes
The tour of the Moscow Philharmonic in the United States is canceled after the defections of the Bolshoi Ballet stars • AT&T begins the Bell System American Orchestras on Tour program with $10 million; major orchestras tour the United States; NEA increases aid to orchestras by $1.6 million ($10.8 million for 120 grants) • The Pierpont Morgan Library purchases the holograph manuscript of Mozart's Symphony in D major for an undisclosed price • 100,000 attend a memorial concert in Boston for Arthur Fiedler.

Art _____

Paintings

Robert Rauschenberg;
  Barge
Richard Diebenkorn,
  Ocean Park 105
Ellsworth Kelly,
  Diagonal with Curve 9
Susan Rothenberg,
  Pontiac
Frank Stella, *Guadalupe
  Island, Kastüra*
Jim Dine, *Jerusalem
  Nights, In the Harem*
Ida Applebroog, *Sure,
  I'm Sure*
Jack Beal, *The Harvest*
Hans Haacke, *Thank
  You, Paine Webber*
Julian Schnabel,
  *Procession for Jean
  Vigo*

Alice Adams, *Three
  Arches*
Christopher Wilmarth,
  *The Whole Soul
  Summed Up, Insert
  Myself within Your
  Story*
Vito Acconci, *The
  People Machine*

Architecture

Boettcher Concert Hall,
  Denver (Holzman,
  Pfeiffer)
Deere West Building,
  Moline, Ill. (Roche
  and Dinkeloo)
John F. Kennedy
  Library, Boston (I. M.
  Pei)

Sculpture

Richard Serra, *Left
  Corner Rectangles*

Important Exhibitions

"From Leonardo to Titian" (from the USSR) tours
Washington, New York, Detroit, and Los Angeles;
also touring is "5,000 years of Korean Art."

Museums

New York: *Metropolitan:* Greek Art of the Aegean
Islands; Costumes and designs of ballets. *Museum of
Modern Art:* Klee. *Guggenheim:* Matisse
retrospective; "The Planar Dimension: Europe 1912–
1932. *Whitney:* "William Carlos Williams and the
American Scene 1920–1930"; George Segal
retrospective; "Traditionalism and Modernism in
American Art, 1900–1930"

Brooklyn, Philadelphia, Detroit: "Victorian High
Renaissance"; "The Second High Empire: Art in
France under Napoleon III"

Washington: *National:* Munch; "Berenson and the
Connoisseurship of Italian Painting"

Chicago: Toulouse-Lautrec (100th anniversary), 109
paintings; 16th-century Roman drawings from the
Louvre

Isamu
Noguchi,
*Unidentified
Object,* 1979.
Black basalt.
11½ × 7'.
*Noguchi
Foundation
Inc.
Permission
granted by the
artist.*

Los Angeles: "Daumier in Retrospect, 1808–1879"

Madison, Seattle, Minneapolis: Art of Norway

Art Briefs

The Museum of Modern Art plans for a gigantic
Picasso retrospective • Controversy develops over the
removal of Gilbert Stuart's portraits of Martha and
George Washington from the Boston Atheneum and
their placement in the National Gallery.

Dance _____

Bolshoi principals Alexander Godunov and Leonid
and Valentina Kozlov defect to the United States;
Mikhail Baryshnikov returns to ABT as director.

Premieres/Important Productions

American Ballet Theatre: *The Tiller in the Fields*
(Anthony Tudor); a labor dispute continues for two
months.

New York City Ballet: *The Four Seasons* (Jerome
Robbins); abridged *Apollo* for Baryshnikov; *Opus 19*
(Jerome Robbins); *Sonate di Scarlatti* (Peter
Martins); George Balanchine's illness halts
productions.

Joffrey: Financial difficulties limit premieres,
although Rudolf Nureyev is guest artist; the company
does *Homage to Diaghilev, L'apres-midi d'un faune*
(Nureyev).

Books

Fiction
Critics' Choice
Letters, John Barth
Mulligan Stew, Gilbert Sorrentino
Dubin's Lives, Bernard Malamud
Great Days, Donald Barthelme
Good as Gold, Joseph Heller
The Ghost Writer, Philip Roth
Black Tickets, Jayne Anne Phillips

Best-Sellers
The Matarese Circle, Robert
 Ludlum
Sophie's Choice, William Styron
Overload, Arthur Hailey
Memories of Another Day, Harold
 Robbins
Jailbird, Kurt Vonnegut
The Dead Zone, Stephen King
The Last Enchantment, Mary
 Stewart
The Establishment, Howard Fast
*The Third World War: August
 1985*, Gen. Sir John Hackett et
 al.
Smiley's People, John le Carré

Nonfiction
Critics' Choice
The Powers That Be, David
 Halberstam
Truth in History, Oscar Handlin

The Medusa and the Snail, Lewis
 Thomas
The Right Stuff, Tom Wolfe
African Calliope, Edward
 Hoagland
The Culture of Narcissism,
 Christopher Lasch
*Sideshow: Nixon and the
 Destruction of Cambodia*,
 William Shawcross
Anatomy of an Illness, Norman
 Cousins
The Nature of Mass Poverty, John
 Kenneth Galbraith
The White Album, Joan Didion
Close to Home, Ellen Goodman
*Franklin D. Roosevelt and
 American Foreign Policy, 1932–
 1945*, Robert Dallek
The Gnostic Gospels, Elaine
 Pagels

Best-Sellers
Aunt Erma's Cope Book, Erma
 Bombeck
*The Complete Scarsdale Medical
 Diet*, Herman Tarnower, M.D.,
 Samm Sinclair Baker
*How to Prosper during the
 Coming Bad Years*, Howard J.
 Ruff
Cruel Shoes, Steve Martin
*The Pritikin Program for Diet and
 Exercise*, Nathan Pritikin,
 Patrick McGrady, Jr.

White House Years, Henry
 Kissinger
Lauren Bacall by Myself, Lauren
 Bacall
*The Brethren: Inside the Supreme
 Court*, Bob Woodward, Scott
 Armstrong
Restoring the American Dream,
 Robert J. Ringer

Poetry
Denise Levertov, *Life in the
 Forest*
John Hollander, *Blue Wine*
Louis Zukofsky, *A*
David Wagoner, *In Broken
 Country*
John Ashbery, *As We Know*
Irving Feldman, *New and Selected
 Poems*

Pulitzer Prizes
The Executioner's Song, Norman
 Mailer (fiction)
*Been in the Storm So Long: The
 Aftermath of Slavery*, Leon F.
 Litwack (U.S. history)
*Gödel, Esher, Bach: An Eternal
 Golden Braid*, Douglas R.
 Hofstadter (nonfiction)
The Rise of Theodore Roosevelt,
 Edmund Morris (biography)
Selected Poems, Donald Justice
 (poetry)

Science and Technology

Viking I discovers a thin, flat ring of particles around
 Jupiter.
Pioneer 11 reaches Saturn and reports that its rings
 are made up of ice-covered rocks; it is blue with
 bright bands near its North Pole.
Voyager I and II explore Jupiter's moons; they reveal
 that Io, the innermost moon, is the most
 volcanically active body discovered thus far in
 the solar system.
A fusion reactor at Princeton achieves a temperature
 of 60 million degrees F.
A microelectronic "syringe driver" is developed.
A new artificial kidney machine for dialysis is
 developed that can be carried in an attaché case.
Controlling mild hypertension is found to greatly
 reduce the incidence of heart attack.

Replantation surgery increases, incorporating many
 techniques learned from the Chinese.
A more effective, less painful six-shot rabies vaccine
 is developed.
Research into the use of interferon (a body protein)
 in the treatment of cancer is pioneered.
Work begins on robots able to "see"; they are
 programmed with "visual" coded memory.

Nobel Prize
Steven Weinberg and Sheldon L. Glashow win in
physics for work on radioactive decay in atomic
nuclei. Allan McLeod Cormack wins in physiology
and medicine for developing the CAT scan. Herbert
C. Brown wins in chemistry for work in developing
substances that facilitate difficult chemical reactions.

Sports _____

Baseball

Lou Brock (St. Louis, NL) and Carl Yastrzemski (Boston, AL) get their 3,000th hit, making a total of 15 players to accomplish this.

Willie Stargell wins the MVP awards of the season's playoffs and World Series.

Thurman Munson (New York, AL), catcher, dies when his private plane crashes.

The Cy Young awards go to Bruce Sutter (Chicago, NL) and Mike Flanagan (Baltimore, AL).

Champions _____

Batting	Pitching
Keith Hernandez (St. Louis, NL), .344	Tom Seaver (Cincinnati, NL), 16–6
Fred Lynn (Boston, AL), .333	Mike Caldwell (Milwaukee, AL), 16–6
	Home runs
	Dave Kingman (Chicago, NL), 48

Football

O. J. Simpson, Buffalo, retires with 11,236 yards rushing, second only to Jim Brown's 12,312.
Dan Fouts, San Diego, passes for a record 4,082 yards.

NFC Season Leaders: Roger Staubach (Dallas), passing; Walter Payton (Chicago), rushing; Ahmad Rashad (Minnesota), receiving

AFC Season Leaders: Dan Fouts (San Diego), passing; Earl Campbell (Houston), rushing; Joe Washington (Baltimore), receiving

College All-Americans: Billy Sims (B), Oklahoma; Jim Richter (C), North Carolina State

Bowls (Jan. 1, 1980)

Rose: Southern California 17–Ohio State 16	Cotton: Houston 17–Nebraska 14
Orange: Oklahoma 24–Florida State 7	Sugar: Alabama 24–Arkansas 0

Basketball

Ann Meyers becomes the first woman to sign an NBA contract ($50,000), with Indiana; she does not play during the season.

NBA All-Pro First Team: Marques Johnson (Milwaukee), Elvin Hayes (Washington), Moses Malone (Houston), George Gervin (San Antonio), Paul Westphal (Phoenix)

Other Sports

Boxing: Muhammad Ali "officially" retires; his record is 56 (37 KOs)–3–0; he has earned an estimated $50 million. Undefeated Sugar Ray Leonard defeats Wilfredo Benitez for the welterweight title.

Hockey: Montreal wins its fourth consecutive Stanley Cup; the WHA merges with the NHL.

Golf: Tom Watson wins a record $462,636; Nancy Lopez wins a women's record $197,489.

Tennis: Both Bjorn Borg and John McEnroe exceed $1 million in earnings; Borg wins a modern record fourth straight Wimbleton.

Winners _____

World Series	NBA Championship
Pittsburgh (NL) 4	Seattle 4–Washington 1
Baltimore (AL) 3	*MVP*
MVP	Moses Malone, Houston
AL–Don Baylor, California	*College Basketball*
NL–Keith Hernandez, St. Louis, Willie Stargell, Pittsburgh	Michigan State
	Player of the Year
Super Bowl XIV (Jan. 1980)	Larry Bird, Indiana State
Pittsburgh 31–Los Angeles 19	*Stanley Cup*
	Montreal
MVP	*US Tennis Open*
Earl Campbell, Houston	Men: John McEnroe
College Football	Women: Tracy Austin
Alabama	*USGA Open*
Heisman Trophy	Hale Irwin
Charles White, Southern California	*Kentucky Derby*
	Spectacular Bid (R. Franklin, jockey)

Fashion _____

For Women: High inflation and the energy crisis precipitate more traditional styles and less radical silhouette changes. Emphasis is on accessories, like blouses, camisoles, and jackets, that can expand the wardrobe. Interest in ethnic styles diminishes, and more popular, for day, are slim slit skirts worn with belted sweaters, and broad-shouldered suits worn with spike-heeled shoes. Soft silk blouses grow in popularity, along with black velvet jackets and plaid skirts and tartans. Pants take on a roomy pajama look. New to the fashion scene are disco clothes, like body suits and wraparound skirts, but tight jeans remain ubiquitous. Popular accessories (and investments) are gold chains, earrings, and bangles, as well as tiny diamond earrings.

High-fashion notes: Halston's sequined and "skin" lace chemise; Trigère's black chiffon gown with Chinese motif

Kaleidoscope _____

- Over 315,000 microcomputers are sold (172,000 in 1978).
- Health food sales reach $1.6 billion ($140 million in 1970).
- John Mitchell is freed from prison, the last Watergate convict; 25 people served 25 days to 53 months.
- The Supreme Court rules that "husbands-only" alimony laws are unconstitutional.
- The *Reader's Digest* plans to condense the revised standard version of the Bible by omitting repetitions and genealogies.
- Jane Fonda and Tom Hayden tour 50 cities to speak out against nuclear power.
- Patty Hearst's sentence is commuted to 22 months, and she leaves prison.
- California is the first state to initiate gas rationing via alternate-day purchasing; many states follow.
- With 3,243 performances, *Grease* passes *Fiddler on the Roof* as the longest playing Broadway show.
- Record sales drop from 4.3 billion in 1978 to 3.5 billion, the first major decline in many years.
- Chrysler Corporation's annual losses are $1.1 billion, the largest in U.S. corporate history.
- Massachusetts joins six other states to raise the legal drinking age from 18 to 20.
- A *New York Times* poll reports that 55 percent of the population sees nothing wrong with premarital sex, over double the statistic in 1969.
- Marlon Brando, Steve McQueen, Clint Eastwood, Burt Reynolds, and Robert Redford command $3 million per film.
- Eleven people are trampled to death rushing for seats at a Cincinnati concert by the Who.
- An amendment to the 1964 Civil Rights law says that employers with disability plans must provide disability for pregnancy.
- A California court awards Michelle Triola $104,000 in her "palimony" suit against Lee Marvin; she had asked for half of Marvin's $3.6 million earnings during the time they lived together.
- Jane Margaret Byrne becomes Chicago's first female mayor when she defeats Mayor Michael A. Bilandic,

Punk rock star Deborah Harry ("Blondie"), former beautician and *Playboy* bunny, sings "Heart of Glass." *Movie Star News*.

who had previously fired her as consumer affairs commissioner.
- The Supreme Court reverses a Massachusetts law requiring unmarried minors to obtain their parents' or a judge's permission for an abortion.
- Following the Three Mile Island accident, antinuclear rallies are held throughout the country.
- Numerous brands of hair dryers are recalled because of suspected harmful amounts of asbestos.
- Risks International, Inc., computes an up-to-the-minute data log of terrorist acts throughout the world and sells it to firms whose executives might be threatened by terrorists.
- Fifty-year-old Treasury bills worth $80,000 float through the air in Cleveland when a building is demolished; the bills are gathered by passersby.
- *U.S. Trust* reports that 520,000 Americans are millionaires, 1 in every 424.
- The divorce rate increases 69 percent since 1968, with the median duration of marriage 6.6 years; 40 percent of the children born during the decade will spend some time in a single-parent household, 90 percent headed by the mother.
- Judith Krantz receives a record $3.2 million advance for the paperback rights to *Princess Daisy*.
- A sociological study reports that clothing with designer labels, T-shirts with slogans, and bumper stickers with such mottoes as "I'd rather be fishing" express a wish for connection with other people.

Fads: Electronic games like Chess Challenger, backgammon, bridge, Microvision, Speak and Spell, Little Professor

First Appearances: Video digital sound disc, electronic blackboard, "tera" pocket calculator (connecting to company computer by three-way radio), throwaway toothbrushes, U.S. ambassador to the People's Republic of China (Leonard Woodcock), "Drabble" cartoon (in *Seventeen* magazine), nitrite-free hot dogs, railroad train operated exclusively by women (Port Washington, N.Y., to Penn Station), highest purchase price for a comic book (Marvel Comic, no. 1, $43,000), Cracker Jack ice cream bars, rocket vehicle to break the sound barrier on land (Stan Barrett, Edwards Air Force Base), woman commander of naval ship on regular patrol (Beverly Kelley)

Alfalfa sandwiches, one of the stock products in the expanding health food industry. *Copyright* Washington Post. *Reprinted courtesy of D.C. Library.*

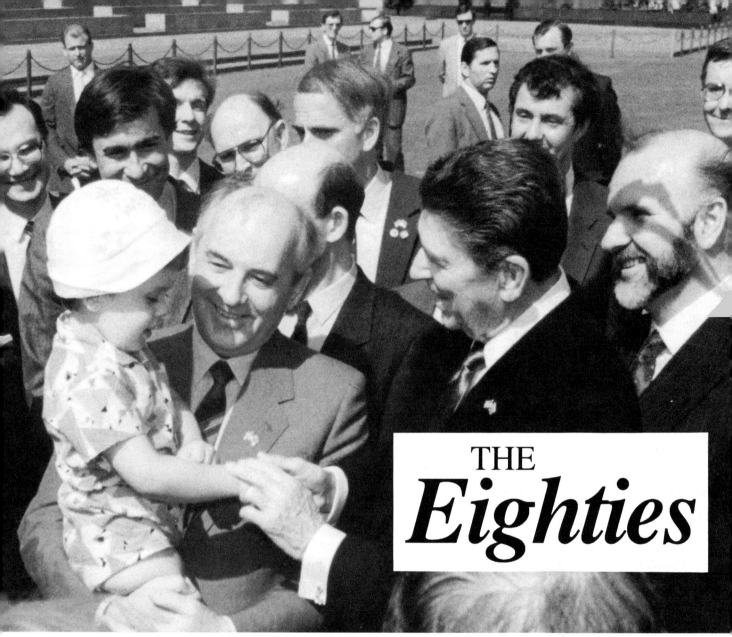

Ronald Reagan and Mikhail Gorbachev in 1988. *Pete Souza, The White House.*

Statistics ———————————————————

Vital

Population: 226,546,000
  Urban/Rural: 167/59
  Farm: 2.7%
Life Expectancy
  Male: 69.9
  Female: 77.6
Births/1,000: 15.8
Marriages/1,000: 10.6
Divorces/1,000: 5.2
Deaths/1,000: 8.7
  per 100,000
    Heart: 435
    Cancer: 183
    Tuberculosis: 1
    Car accidents: 24.3

Economic

Unemployed: 7,636,000
GNP: $2,633 billion
Federal budget: $579.6
  billion
National debt: $914 billion
Union membership: 21.7
  million
Strikes: 3,885
Prime rate: 21.5%
Car sales: 6,400,000
Average salary: $15,757

Social

Homicides/100,000: 12.4
Suicides/100,000: 10.2
Lynchings: 0
Labor force, male/female: 56/38
Public education: $164.7 billion
College degrees
  Bachelors'
    Male: 526,000
    Female: 473,000
  Doctorates
    Male: 22,900
    Female: 9,700
Attendance
  Movies (weekly): 20 million
  Baseball (yearly): 43.7 million

Consumer

Consumer Price Index
  (1967 = 100): 246.8
Eggs: 84¢ (doz.)
Milk: $1.04 (qt.)
Bread: 51¢ (loaf)
Butter: $1.87 (lb.)
Bacon: $1.44 (lb.)
Round steak: $2.37 (lb.)
Oranges: $1.37 (doz.)
Coffee: $2.98 (lb.)

Even if, as Hegel says, history is inevitable, then only God anticipated the events that concluded the eighties. With a stunning and unforeseen success, popular democratic movements overturned totalitarian communist governments in Poland, Hungary, East Germany, Czechoslovakia, and Rumania. In the words of America's new president, George Bush, the world seemed to be "witnessing the death of an idea—the final chapter of the communist experiment."

The decade, however, began ominously. Double-digit inflation accompanied declining productivity. Soviet troops exceeded even the Brezhnev doctrine by invading Afghanistan. Helpless outrage accompanied the government's failure to rescue the hostages in Iran. In 1980, the most unpopular incumbent since Herbert Hoover, Jimmy Carter, was challenged by Ronald Reagan, the elderly ex–movie star and former California governor, who for years was considered too far right by his own party. Reagan's message was straightforward: restore American respect abroad and reduce government at home. His tone, like that of his early hero, FDR, was one of genial, confident optimism. Reagan expounded a faith in America's "special destiny." He appealed to the nation's revulsion at its own sense of impotence and moral self-doubt and its disenchantment with utopian activism. Reagan won a dazzling victory and carried on his coattails the first Republican senate since 1948.

While many of Mr. Reagan's opponents feared that ideological rigidity, intellectual failure, or, finally, fatigue would undo both the man and the nation, Reagan's clear sense of direction and warmth of personality were remarkable assets in enlisting the public trust. The nation was buoyed by the hostages' release on the day of his inauguration. Only months later, it was moved to admiration by his courage and stamina after a nearly successful assassination attempt. America was willing to give the Reagan Agenda a chance.

Relying on "supply-side" economic theory and aided by a cooperative Congress, Reagan navigated a major tax reduction plan aimed at increasing incentives to productivity. Nonmandated social spending was limited, but with rising defense allocations, deficit spending went into high gear. After a serious recession in 1981–82, the economy recovered (1983) and continued to grow, with modest inflation, during the next seven years. The stock market rose to nearly triple pre-eighties levels and survived the 1987 crash.

In foreign affairs, the Reagan "revolution" was slower, and in this arena, Reagan himself underwent an extraordinary transformation. Taking his popularity as a mandate for a militarily mightier America, he gained Congressional approval for larger defense spending. Faced with the Soviets' medium-range missiles in Eastern Europe, he ordered comparable missiles deployed in the NATO nations. Public protests at home and abroad did not deter him, nor did the plethora of books, films, and editorials depicting the potential nuclear holocaust feared because of his actions (*The Day After, The Fate of the Earth*). When he denounced the Soviet Union as "the focus of evil in the modern world," made jokes about its imminent obliteration, and proposed a vast antimissile shield to protect the United States, he caused profound alarm in those who feared that his ideological fervor and inflammatory rhetoric were tempting Armageddon. At the same time, he satisfied others who looked upon these as demonstrations of "America . . . back—standing tall." On the whole, public approval also greeted his invasion of Grenada and bombing of Libya. His Contra support elicited a more divided response.

Neither the president's supporters nor his detractors—like Garry Wills (*Reagan's America*) and Arthur Schlesinger, Jr. (*The Cycles of American History*)—foresaw the startling turnabout in 1987, when Reagan and the bold reformist Mikhail Gorbachev both agreed to a treaty eliminating intermediate nuclear weapons from Europe and set unprecedented disarmament and verification agendas. Nor did anyone anticipate Gorbachev's domestic initiatives for market-oriented economic change (*perestroika*) and "democratic-style" reforms (*glasnost*), or, above all, his government's stunning decision to withdraw from Afghanistan. By 1988, with "peace breaking out all over," from the Persian Gulf to West Africa, with democratic governments in place in Argentina, Brazil, and the Philippines, and with free elections in South Korea and even Chile, the 77-year-old departing incumbent had reason to be pleased with his "watch." Bush's later victory was, in great likelihood, based on his promise to continue the *Pax Reaganica*.

In everyday life, the conservative turn found its incarnation in the "Yuppie." As the hippie had succeeded the bohemian and beatnik as the manifestation of anti-establishment sentiment, so the impeccably groomed (and toned) Wall Street financier reclaimed the "man in the gray flannel suit" as standard bearer of the entrepreneurial ethos. America, as in the twenties and fifties, would return to the "business of business."

Exalting such heroes as Chrysler's savior Lee Iacocca ("The pride is back, / Born in America") and superdealer Donald Trump, Yuppiedom witnessed with awe (and scurried to profit from) the incessant multibillion dollar takeovers stimulated by the Carl Icahns and Michael Milkens.

Business schools, investment banks, and "Wall Street" law firms overflowed with the eager and hopeful baby-boomers who, in their personal lives, placed gourmet cuisine, health clubs, high-performance autos, designer-decorated condos, supersneakers, suspenders, wine spritzers, and sushi high on their agendas. Low fat and fiber cereals, animals bred for low cholesterol, and Jane Fonda workout books and videos promised to preserve their insides, as well as add luster to their exteriors.

The Yuppie work and play ethic was everywhere—from

Norwest Center, Minneapolis. "We are now free to create a new generation of skyscrapers—optimistic, celebratory, joyful . . . accepting their role as icons," says architect Cesar Pelli. *Balthazar & Christian Korab.*

TV's Cosby family to the best-selling *In Search of Excellence.* With economic success paramount, the traditional middle-class values that had revived in the late seventies now gained ascendancy. The work ethic replaced "being yourself." Movies like *Chariots of Fire* and even, in their campy way, TV's "Dynasty" and "Dallas" manifested the new ethos, as well as, on a more analytical level, works like the Friedmans' neoconservative *Free to Choose* and Thomas Sowell's *Ethnic America*: the entrepreneur had replaced the social reformer, and the market, the state, as the operative means of salvation. Indeed, within the same week, one could find such political opposites as William F. Buckley and John Kenneth Galbraith publicly quoting Dr. Johnson on the relatively benign nature of wealth as a human motivation.

The conservatism of the decade, also like that of the twenties and fifties, was accompanied by revivalist cheerleading and a restrictive, moralistic social agenda. Led by veteran right-wing stalwarts like Jerry Falwell and his Moral Majority, conservatism boasted the membership of anti-feminist Phyllis Schlafly and North Carolina Senator Jesse Helms. It was also invigorated by Reagan's support for such items as school prayer, the undoing of Roe v. Wade, and the teaching of creation science. The fundamentalists gained a great deal of publicity early in the decade; however, neither the courts, Congress, nor public (judging from opinion polls) rallied to their causes. The defeat of their darling, Supreme Court nominee Robert Bork, epitomized their frustration. The country had turned conservative in the marketplace, but not in the bedroom.

Many of the social trends of the sixties and seventies actually continued into the eighties. The two-earner family became even more common, as more women worked, received college and advanced degrees, and then married and bore fewer children at later ages. Concern with more flexible gender roles persisted, as the popularity of movies such as *Tootsie* and *Three Men and a Baby* attested. The first female Supreme Court justice, vice presidential candidate, space rider, and space walker appeared. Minority membership in politics also increased during the decade, culminating in the New York mayoral and Virginia gubernatorial elections. Jesse Jackson electrified the nation when he came in second in the 1988 Democratic primaries.

The sexual revolution, although undaunted by the conservative prescription of chastity, nevertheless encountered a powerful adversary in 1982, with the formidable spread of an apparently fatal and sexually (and/or blood-product) transmitted illness, AIDS. Rock Hudson's death in 1985 imprinted the terror of the disease on the public imagination.

As information about AIDS came to light, safe sex replaced casual sex, and condom ads succeeded Brooke Shields and her Calvins. The popular movie *Fatal Attraction*, a tale of casual infidelity (an activity more benignly regarded in preceding decades), disguised in a saga of menace an allegory of the AIDS danger. Since changes in sexual manners reflected health, rather than morality, it is not surprising that earlier social trends, like unmarried couples living together and abortions, continued to increase. The divorce rate, however, stabilized.

Another trend on the conservative agenda was stricter law enforcement. Crime rates (1980) had tripled since 1960, and prisons were filled to capacity. Hope for safer streets was damaged, however, when crack appeared in 1985, and violent crime rates soared again. While indications of drug use among *Bright Lights, Big City* aspirants were legion, the dangers of recreational drug use (a sixties invention) became increasingly evident, and the romance of drugs was clearly on the wane. The death of young athlete Len Bias, as well as the career havoc of superstars like Dwight Gooden and Lawrence Taylor, also influenced public attitudes, even if they failed to reach hard-core addicts. Nancy Reagan's "Just Say No" may have sounded naive, but to many, abstinence became a workable notion. As with sexual habits, health, rather than morality, was the issue.

Finally, and recalling the fifties, American education came under fire. Liberals decried cuts in government support for both student costs and faculty salaries. Conservatives like William Bennett, Allan Bloom, and E. D. Hirsch, Jr., assaulted the "relativist" and "relevance" orientations begun in the sixties. They advocated a return to the classics of Western culture at the college level and to basic skills in earlier education.

The eighties were a quieter time in the arts. No new style or heroes emerged to assail the commercial burghers and the glorification of Yuppiedom. There were no F. Scott Fitzgeralds or James Deans. Writers like Saul Bellow and John Updike continued to produce excellent work in their (by now) own traditions. Raymond Carver, William Kennedy, Anne Tyler, and Toni Morrison gained a wider recognition. Don DeLillo, Joseph McElroy, and Robert Coover pursued their explorations of human cognition and mythmaking for a small but loyal following, but this was also a continuation of seventies interests.

The musical stage was dominated by vast British entertainments like *Cats* and *The Phantom of the Opera*. Although rock superstars such as Michael Jackson and Bruce Springsteen sold millions of records and had cable and VCR exposure, they created no cultural vogues. Film superstars—among them Eddie Murphy, Bill Murray, and Tom Hanks—also failed to elicit emulation. Perhaps the narrowing of the generation gap—with young people sharing their parents' material ambitions—accounts for the lack of a more innovative creative energy.

The major artistic achievements of the decade were in postmodern architecture. There was an enormous renewal of construction—in offices, apartments, concert halls, and museums. The exponents of these new styles, blending strict, geometric Corbusier-like forms with traditional decoration, included Michael Graves, Cesar Pelli, Robert Venturi, Robert A. M. Stern, Stanley Tigerman, and the ageless Philip Johnson.

For all the new buildings that rose in concert with the market, not everyone believed that as the Dow goes, so goes the nation. Indeed, as the decade progressed, the social benefits of private greed came into question. Issues arose concerning the moral turpitude of the rich and powerful. The Boesky and Drexel insider trading scandals made headlines, along with dubious Pentagon practices, administration sleaze, and spying for dollars. The president's lack of interest in environmental issues (nuclear waste, acid rain, the greenhouse effect), the growing homeless population, and the mounting drug problem undermined the "trickle down" theory of prosperity. The persistence of ghettos plagued by crime, teenage pregnancy and unemployment, and renewed racial tensions led to accusations of the Administration's indifference to the disenfranchised. The enormous trade and budget deficits fostered concern about the very foundations of the Reagan Revolution. Could the United States really compete against the rising capabilities of the Japanese and Europeans?

When the Iran-Contra affair surfaced, questions arose about Reagan's "loose managerial style." With the stock market crash, memories rekindled of an earlier panic, during another prosperous Republican decade. Gloomy predictions had, of course, been made throughout the decade. *Crisis Investing* warned of "the coming depression," and Lester Thurow foretold a "zero-sum society" (1980); Paul Kennedy and Benjamin Friedman later warned of "a day of reckoning," as did Tom Wolfe's *The Bonfire of the Vanities* and Ravi Batra's *The Great Depression of 1990.*

Science and technology gave some credence to Reagan's faith that "there are no limits to the human mind." The information-processing revolution continued to enhance industrial efficiency. Genetic engineering also came of age, with early successes at transplantation and gene mapping, which provided hope for medical and agricultural advances. Research in superconductivity

Vietnam Veterans Memorial, Washington, D.C. *National Park Service.*

promised a technology of less costly, safe energy. Before the 1986 Challenger tragedy, unmanned spaceships returned dazzling evidence regarding the nature and extent of the physical universe. And blending humanistic and scientific concerns, Stephen Hawking's *A Brief History of Time* attempted a cosmological explanation of the new physics—an attempt, as he put it, "to know the mind of God."

While scientists measured and contemplated infinity, considerable public attention remained on recent history. The tragedy of Vietnam continued in the American awareness. "Rambo" appealed to those for whom the war remained a noble cause doomed by a failure of American will; *Platoon* and *A Bright Shining Lie* demanded respect for the soldiers who followed their misguided leaders. At last, a stunning Washington memorial expressed to Vietnam veterans the same measure of their country's gratitude as had been shown the heroes of other American wars. The exuberant anniversary of the Statue of Liberty also said much about the mood of the period. It provided a marked contrast to the constrained celebrations that greeted the 1976 bicentennial.

Perhaps the extremes of hardship and material well-being provide the foundations of generosity. For those who feared the "Vanities" of the affluent eighties, the turning of many Yuppies and megacorporations to voluntarism at the end of the decade may have indicated the renewal of the altruism that recurs in American life (witness the Depression thirties and prosperous sixties). George Bush's call for a "kinder, gentler nation" found an already mobilized audience.

As one surveys the nineties, the mandates are clear: to enable the underclass to enter the economic mainstream; to maintain economic competitiveness at an international level; to continue rapprochement with the communist world during its own "revolutionary" changes, with, above all, a view to completely defusing the nuclear threat. Finally, there is the challenge to rally the world's resources against the growing ecological menaces. This is an awesome agenda, but given the unexpected successes of the eighties, a more hopeful one than we might have envisioned a decade ago.

1980

How do I deal with the Mafia?

01-24-80   23:10:46

In the News

CARTER ASKS SENATE TO DELAY SALT II CONSIDERATION . . . PRESIDENT HALTS GRAIN TO RUSSIA FOLLOWING AFGHANISTAN INVASION . . . ANDREI SAKHAROV IS EXILED TO GORKY . . . CARTER DECLARES U.S. WILL DEFEND PERSIAN GULF . . . "OPERATION ABSCAM" INDICTS 30 OFFICIALS . . . EGYPT AND ISRAEL EXCHANGE FIRST AMBASSADORS . . . GUERRILLA LEADER ROBERT MUGABE WINS LANDSLIDE IN ZIMBABWE . . . ARCHBISHOP ARNULFO ROMERO IS ASSASSINATED IN EL SALVADOR . . . CARTER SEVERS DIPLOMATIC TIES TO IRAN, KHOMEINI MILITANTS HOLD HOSTAGES . . . U.S. OLYMPIC COMMITTEE VOTES TO BOYCOTT MOSCOW SUMMER GAMES . . . 125,000 CUBAN REFUGEES, RELEASED BY CASTRO, ARRIVE IN MIAMI . . . REP. JOHN ANDERSON (R-IL) ANNOUNCES 3RD PARTY CANDIDACY . . . U.S. RESCUE MISSION TO IRAN FAILS, 8 DIE AS TWO AIRCRAFT COLLIDE, IRAN DISPERSES HOSTAGES . . . YUGOSLAV LEADER MARSHALL TITO, 87, DIES . . . WASHINGTON VOLCANO MOUNT ST. HELENS ERUPTS, 22 DIE . . . GOP NOMINATES RONALD REAGAN AND GEORGE BUSH, DEMOCRATS RENOMINATE CARTER AND MONDALE . . . DRAFT REGISTRATION BEGINS . . . SHAH OF IRAN, 60, DIES OF CANCER IN CAIRO . . . EXILED NICARAGUAN DICTATOR SOMOZA IS ASSASSINATED IN PARAGUAY . . . IRAQ INVADES IRAN . . . WORKERS SEIZE SHIPYARDS IN GDANSK, POLISH COURT RECOGNIZES SOLIDARITY AS UMBRELLA UNION . . . FORD LOSES $595 MILLION IN 3RD QUARTER, LARGEST CORPORATE LOSS TO DATE . . . REAGAN DEFEATS CARTER, 43 TO 35 MILLION, ANDERSON GAINS 5.6 MILLION, GOP ALSO TAKES SENATE . . . GANG OF FOUR, INCLUDING MAO'S WIFE, GOES ON TRIAL IN BEIJING . . . JOHN LENNON IS SHOT TO DEATH IN NYC . . . MODERATE NAPOLEÓN DUARTE IS ELECTED IN EL SALVADOR . . . PRIME RATE: 21%, GOLD: $880 PER OUNCE.

Quotes

"This is the most serious threat to world peace during my administration. It's even more serious than Hungary or Czechoslovakia."
—Jimmy Carter, on Afghanistan invasion

"Death to Carter, Death to the Shah."
—Iranian militants, at U.S. Embassy in Teheran

"And that's the way it is on this, the [100th, 300th] day of captivity for those 52 American hostages in Iran."
—Walter Cronkite, signing off the CBS evening news

"For me, a few hours ago, this campaign came to an end. For all those whose cares have been our concern, the work goes on, the cause endures, the hope still lives, and the dream shall never die."
—Ted Kennedy, to the Democratic Convention

"I had a discussion with my daughter, Amy, the other day, before I came here, to ask her what she thought the most important issue was. She said she thought nuclear weaponry and the control of nuclear arms."
—Jimmy Carter

"Sometimes when I look at all my children, I say to myself: 'Lillian, you should have stayed a virgin.'"
—Lillian Carter

"There you go again."
". . . Are you better off than you were four years ago? . . . Is America as respected throughout the world as it was?"
—Ronald Reagan to Jimmy Carter, during TV debate

"Marvelous."
—Jane Wyman, on Ronald Reagan's victory

The author of Medicare and youngest of four brothers, Edward Kennedy pursues a presidential campaign that falters under the weight of his personal past. *U.S. Senate.*

"It was not so clear to many of us as we talked of American imperialism how few options many of these countries had except for Soviet imperialism, which was maybe worse. . . . But history has been very cruel."
—Susan Sontag

"We are passing from one generation to another a group of people who are hopelessly locked into a permanent underclass."
—Congressman Louis Stokes (D-Ohio)

"The repeated failure of well-intentioned programs is not accidental. . . . The failure is deeply rooted in the use of bad means."
—Milton and Rose Friedman, *Free to Choose*

"Our optimism [must be] turned loose again. . . . People who talk about an age of limits are really talking about their own limitations, not America's."
—Ronald Reagan

Ads

You know what comes between me and my Calvins? Nothing!
(Brooke Shields, for Calvin Klein)

Everything a vegetable should be, except green . . .
(Potato Growers of America)

The Rise or Fall of our Empire depends upon our legs.
(Empire Chicken)

How to tell your mother
You're appearing in *Playboy* . . .
(Playboy Magazine)

Reach out and touch someone.
(Northwestern Bell)

Nine years without taking a leak.
(Herman Survivors Boot Company)

Contrary to the economic theories of your grandparents, there are actually times when it is smart to borrow.
(Central National Bank and Trust)

Getting oil from a stone?
Texaco's trying.
(Texaco)

TV

Premieres

"Magnum, P.I.," Tom Selleck, John Hillerman
"Barbara Mandrell and the Mandrell Sisters"
"Nightline," Ted Koppel
"Too Close for Comfort," Ted Knight, Nancy Dussault

Top Ten (Nielsen)

"Dallas," "M*A*S*H," "The Dukes of Hazzard," "60 Minutes," "Three's Company," "Private Benjamin," Diff'rent Strokes," "House Calls," "The Jeffersons," "Too Close for Comfort"

Specials

"Shōgun" (Richard Chamberlain); "Playing for Time" (Vanessa Redgrave, Jane Alexander); "Gideon's Trumpet" (Henry Fonda); "Arthur Miller on Home Ground"; "Happy Days" (Samuel Beckett); "Cosmos" (Carl Sagan); "Edward and Mrs. Simpson"; "The Body in Question"

Emmy Awards

"Hill Street Blues" (drama); "Taxi" (comedy); "Jerome Robbins Ballets" (classical); "Playing for Time" (limited series); Daniel J. Travanti (actor, "Hill Street Blues"); Judd Hirsch (comedic actor, "Taxi"); Barbara Bosson (actress, "Hill Street Blues"); Isabel Sanford (comedic actress, "The Jeffersons")

Of Note

"Shōgun is second to "Roots" in all-time series ratings • "Donahue" becomes the most widely watched syndicated TV talk show in America • ABC president Fred Silverman signs a three-year contract with NBC for an estimated $5 million a year • The Moral Majority responds to the new raciness in ads (as in jeans) and programming (as in "Bosom Buddies") • "Good Morning America" passes "Today" in ratings for the first time.

Movies

Openings

Ordinary People (Robert Redford), Donald Sutherland, Mary Tyler Moore, Timothy Hutton
Coal Miner's Daughter (Michael Apted), Sissy Spacek, Tommy Lee Jones
The Elephant Man (David Lynch), Anthony Hopkins, John Hurt
Raging Bull (Martin Scorsese), Robert De Niro
The Empire Strikes Back (Irvin Kershner), Mark Hamill, Carrie Fisher, Harrison Ford, Billy Dee Williams
Urban Cowboy (James Bridges), John Travolta, Debra Winger
The Great Santini (Lewis John Carlino), Robert Duvall, Blythe Danner
Stardust Memories (Woody Allen), Woody Allen, Charlotte Rampling

In *Hopscotch,* Walter Matthau plays a CIA agent exposing "the company's" ineptitude and amorality. *Movie Star News.*

Private Benjamin (Howard Zieff), Goldie Hawn, Eileen Brennan
Gloria (John Cassavetes), Gena Rowlands, John Adames, Buck Henry
Breaker Morant (Bruce Beresford), Edward Woodward, Jack Thompson
Airplane (Jim Abrahams), Lloyd Bridges, Peter Graves
Dressed to Kill (Brian De Palma), Michael Caine, Angie Dickinson
The Shining (Stanley Kubrick), Jack Nicholson, Shelley Duvall
The Last Metro (François Truffaut), Catherine Deneuve
Kagemusha (Akira Kurosawa), Tatsuya Nakadai
Return of the Secaucus 7 (John Sayles), Mark Arnott

Academy Awards

Best Picture: *Ordinary People*
Best Director: Robert Redford (*Ordinary People*)
Best Actress: Sissy Spacek (*Coal Miner's Daughter*)
Best Actor: Robert De Niro (*Raging Bull*)

Top Box-Office Stars

Burt Reynolds, Robert Redford, Clint Eastwood, Jane Fonda, Dustin Hoffman, John Travolta, Sally Field, Sissy Spacek, Barbra Streisand, Steve Martin

Stars of Tomorrow

Timothy Hutton, Debra Winger, Cathy Moriarty, Dennis Quaid, Diana Scarwid, William Hurt, Michael Biehn, Miles O'Keefe, Peter Gallagher, Martin Hewitt

Popular Music

Hit Songs
"Rock with You"
"Crazy Little Thing Called Love"
"Coming Up"
"Funkytown"
"It's Still Rock & Roll to Me"
"Lost in Love"
"Do That to Me One More Time"

Top Records
Albums: *The Wall* (Pink Floyd); *Eat to the Beat* (Blondie); *Off the Wall* (Michael Jackson); *Glass Houses* (Billy Joel); *Damn the Torpedoes* (Tom Petty and the Heartbreakers); *Against the Wind* (Bob Seger and the Silver Bullet Band); *In the Heat of the Night* (Pat Benatar)

Singles: *Magic* (Olivia Newton-John); *The Rose* (Bette Midler); *Shining Stars* (The Manhattans); *Cruisin'* (Smokey Robinson); *Let's Get Serious* (Jermaine Jackson); *Coward of the County* (Kenny Rogers). Country: *One Day at a Time* (Cristy Lane); *He Stopped Loving Her Today* (George Jones)

Grammy Awards
Sailing, Christopher Cross (record); *Christopher Cross,* Christopher Cross (album); "Sailing" (song)

Jazz and Big Bands
More big bands perform than in any time since the 1940s. New bands include Mel Lewis (NY), Baron Von Olen (Indianapolis), Rodger Pemberton (Chicago); Bill Berry (Los Angeles), Dallas Jazz Orchestra (Dallas), and the Blue Wisp (Cincinnati).

Top Performers *(Downbeat):* Dexter Gordon (soloist); Toshiko Akiyoshi/Lew Tabackin (band); Weather Report (jazz group); Woody Shaw, Wayne Shorter, Anthony Braxton, McCoy Tyner, Stephane Grappelli (instrumentalists); Al Jarreau, Sarah Vaughan (vocalists); Manhattan Transfer (vocal group); Jack De Johnette, *Special Edition* (album)

Gospel music has a renaissance.

Theater

Broadway Openings

Plays
Amadeus (Peter Shaffer), Ian McKellen, Tim Curry, Jane Seymour
Betrayal (Harold Pinter), Blythe Danner, Roy Scheider, Raul Julia
Fifth of July (Lanford Wilson), Christopher Reeve, Swoosie Kurtz
Talley's Folly (Lanford Wilson), Judd Hirsch, Trish Hawkins
The American Clock (Arthur Miller), William Atherton, Joan Copeland, John Randolph
A Lesson from Aloes (Athol Fugard), James Earl Jones, Harris Yulin, Maria Tucci (from Yale Repertory Theatre)
A Life (Hugh Leonard), Roy Dotrice, Pat Hingle
Children of a Lesser God (Mark Medoff), Phyllis Frelich, John Rubinstein
Whose Life Is It Anyway? (Brian Clark), Mary Tyler Moore, James Naughton
Nuts (Tom Topor), Anne Twomey

Musicals
Barnum (Michael Stewart, Cy Coleman), Jim Dale, Glenn Close
A Day in Hollywood/A Night in the Ukraine (Dick Vosburgh, Frank Lazarus), Priscilla Lopez, Stephen James, David Garrison
42nd Street (Harry Warren, Al Dubin), Jerry Orbach, Tammy Grimes
Your Arms Too Short to Box with God (Alex Bradford), Jennifer Yvette-Holliday

Classics, Revivals, and Off-Broadway Premieres
Morning's at Seven (Paul Osborne), Teresa Wright, Maureen O'Sullivan, Nancy Marchand; *The Philadelphia*

Old-time singing and dancing flourish on Broadway in this stage version of the 1933 film *42nd Street,* where the classic backstage ingenue steps in for the indisposed leading lady. *Billy Rose Theatre Collection. The New York Public Library at Lincoln Center. Astor, Lenox and Tilden Foundations.*

Theater (cont.)

Story (Philip Barry), Blythe Danner; *The Bacchae* (Euripides), Irene Papas; *John Gabriel Borkman* (Ibsen), E. G. Marshall, Irene Worth; *Camelot,* Richard Burton; *The Ik; The Blood Knot* (Athol Fugard); *The Sea Gull,* Rosemary Harris, Christopher Walken; *True West* (Sam Shepard), Tommy Lee Jones.

Regional
Actors Theater of Louisville: *Agnes of God* (John Pielmeier)

Pulitzer Prize
Talley's Folly, Lanford Wilson

Tony Awards
Children of a Lesser God, Mark Medoff (play); *Evita,* Andrew Lloyd Webber, Tim Rice (musical)

Classical Music

Compositions
Steve Reich, *Variations for Winds, Strings and Keyboards*
Elliott Carter, *Night Fantasies*
George Perle, *A Short Symphony*
Jacob Druckman, *Prism*
John Watts, *Ach*
Henry Brant, *The Glass Pyramid*

Important Events
Several milestone birthday celebrations include Aaron Copland's 80th, Samuel Barber's 70th, and William Schuman's 70th. At the 14-hour Symphony Space celebration in his honor, Copland conducts from *Appalachian Spring.*
The St. Louis and Boston symphonies begin their centennial celebrations; the Boston commissions 12 works that will be premiered over the next five years.
Interest mounts in contemporary works: the Los Angeles Philharmonic invites Morton Subotnick, John Cage, Thea Musgrave, and Dorrance Stalvey to introduce small-scale works in special series.

Appointments: Lukas Foss, Milwaukee; John Williams, Boston Pops; Sara Caldwell, Wolf Trap Farm Park of the Performing Arts.

Debuts: Anne-Sophie Mutter, Cecile Licad

Luciano Pavarotti and Renata Scotto in *Un Ballo in maschera,* at the Chicago Lyric Opera. *Tony Romano.*

First Performances
Krzysztof Penderecki, Symphony no. 2 (New York); David Del Tredici, *In Memory of a Summer Day* (St. Louis); John Harbison, Piano Concerto (Washington, D.C.); Leonard Bernstein, *Fanfare* (Boston); William Schuman, *Three Colloquies* (New York); Morton Subotnik, *After the Butterfly* (Los Angeles); Ned Rorem, *Santa Fe Songs* (Santa Fe); Mark Neikrug, *Eternity's Sunrise* (New York)

Opera
Metropolitan: Teresa Stratas, Franz Mazura, *Lulu* (complete version); Luciano Pavarotti, Katia Ricciarelli, *Masked Ball;* Hildegard Behrens, Jon Vickers, *Fidelio;* Birgit Nilsson, Leonie Rysanek, *Elektra;* Placido Domingo, Renata Scotto, *Manon Lescaut* (viewed in 20 countries via satellite)

Chicago (25th anniversary): Alfredo Kraus, Mirella Freni, Nicolai Ghiaurov, Richard Stilwell, *Faust* (PBS); Ghiaurov, *Boris Godunov, Attila* (Verdi); Domingo, *Andrea Chénier*

San Francisco: Shirley Verrett, Domingo, *Samson et Dalila;* Nilsson, Rysanek, *Die Frau ohne Schatten;* Margaret Price, Cesare Siepi, *Simon Boccanegra*

Washington, D.C.: *Radimisto* (Handel)

Dallas: Marilyn Horne, *Orlando Furioso* (Vivaldi)

Philadelphia: *Fierabras* (Schubert)

Santa Fe: Schoenberg's *Erwartung, Die Jakobsleiter; Von Heute auf Morgan* (American premiere)

Music Notes
With the San Francisco Symphony's new residence at the $27.5 million Louise M. Davies Symphony Hall, the San Francisco Opera gains full use of the Opera House • Continuing corporate support for the arts includes a $5-million grant from Texaco to the Metropolitan Opera Company • The secret autobiography of Shostakovich is smuggled out of the USSR and published.

Art

Painting
Willem de Kooning, *Untitled I*
Jasper Johns, *Dancers on a Plate*
Jim Dine, *A Tree that Shatters the Dancing*
Roy Lichtenstein, *American Indian Theme II*
Ellsworth Kelly, *Dark Blue Gray; Violet; Red-Orange*
Roger Brown, *First Continental Eruption*
Jules Kirschenbaum, *Dream of a Golem*
Randall Deihl, *Sweets*

Sculpture
Michael Heizer, *This Equals That*
Nancy Holt, *14 Concrete*

Discs and Fragments
Robert Irwin, *Running Fence*
Jeff Koons, New Hoover Deluxe Shampoo Polisher
Scott Burton, *Two Chairs*
Edward Kienholz, *Sollie 17*

Architecture
Atheneum Center, New Harmony, Indiana (Richard Meier)
Harborplace, Baltimore (Benjamin Thompson)
Corning Museum of Glass, Corning, N.Y. (Gunnar Birkerts)
Helen Bonfils Theater, Denver (Roche and Dinkeloo)

The glass-enclosed sculpture garden in the new $18-million American Wing of the Metropolitan Museum of Art (Roche and Dinkeloo). *The Metropolitan Museum of Art.*

Important Exhibitions
Touring the U.S. from abroad are "The Avant-Garde in Russia, 1910–1930" (450 works by 40 artists), "Post-Impressionism—Cross Currents in European Painting," and "Treasures from the Bronze Age of China."

Museums
New York: *Metropolitan:* "The Vikings" (550 exhibits); Clyfford Still (largest one-man show for a living artist in the Met's history); Barnett Newman; 19th-Century French Drawings. *Museum of Modern Art:* "Pablo Picasso: A Retrospective" (100th anniversary of Picasso's birth); Chagall; Pollock; Cornell; Postmodern Architecture: Six "windowless box" showrooms (by SITE), and plans by Michael Graves, Anthony Lunsden, Charles Moore, Allan Greenberg, Robert A. M. Stern, and Stanley Tigerman. *Whitney:* Hopper (more than 285 works); Reinhardt; Louise Nevelson (80th birthday); Noguchi. *Guggenheim:* "Expressionism: A German Intuition"

Washington: "American Light: The Luminist Movement"; "In Praise of America: 1650–1830"

Buffalo: Miró (87th birthday exposition)

Los Angeles, Minneapolis: "The Romantics to Rodin: French Nineteenth-Century Sculpture from North American Collections"

Art Briefs
One and a half million people visit the Picasso retrospective; 1,000 works cover an area of 3.5 miles • Auctions bring record highs: Turner's *Juliet and Her Nurse* ($6.4 million); Van Gogh's *Le Jardin du poète, Arles* ($5.2 million); a Tiffany spidernet lamp ($360,000) • The Whitney pays $1 million for Jasper Johns' *Three Flags,* the highest price ever paid a living artist ($600, 1959) • Rev. Robert Schuller's $18-million star-shaped *Crystal Cathedral,* by Philip Johnson (Garden Grove, Calif.), has 10,000 one-way mirrors to reflect the sky • Carter cancels the Hermitage show in Washington to indicate U.S. disapproval of the invasion of Afghanistan • Senator Daniel Moynihan proposes a "supervising architect" to improve the quality of federal architecture.

Dance

Newcomers include Ib Andersen, Darci Kistler (City Ballet), and Susan Jaffe (Ballet Theatre). Peter Schaufuss dances in the U.S. with the newly formed Makarova Company and with Ballet National de Marseilles (Petit's *Coppélia*). Brooklyn Academy of Music hosts "Ballet America."

Premieres/Important Productions
American Ballet Theatre: Mikhail Baryshnikov becomes director. Natalia Makarova, *La Bayadère* (Makarova, $500,000 production); Fernando Bujones, Marianna Tcherkassky, *Spectre de la Rose* (Fokine)

New York City Ballet: George Balanchine returns after 1979 heart surgery. Andersen, Patricia McBride, *Afternoon of a Faun;* Peter Martins, Heather Watts, *Davidsbündlertänze*

Joffrey: First gala at Metropolitan Opera House; *Night* (Laura Arpino, debut); *Postcards* (Joffrey, Satie)

Eliot Feld: *Anatomic Balm, Scenes for the Theater, Circa*

Books

Fiction
Critics' Choice
The Second Coming, Walker Percy
Loon Lake, E. L. Doctorow
Falling in Place, Ann Beattie
Bellefleur, Joyce Carol Oates
The Transit of Venus, Shirley Hazzard
The Collected Stories of Eudora Welty, Eudora Welty
How German Is It, Walter Abish
Ridley Walker, Russell Hoban
House-Keeping, Marilynne Robinson
🍃 *Man in the Holocene*, Max Frisch

Best-Sellers
The Covenant, James A. Michener
The Bourne Identity, Robert Ludlum
Rage of Angels, Sidney Sheldon
Princess Daisy, Judith Krantz
Firestarter, Stephen King
The Key to Rebecca, Ken Follett
Random Winds, Belva Plain
The Devil's Alternative, Frederick Forsyth
The Fifth Horseman, Larry Collins, Dominique Lapierre

Nonfiction
Critic's Choice
Walter Lippmann and the American Century, Ronald Steel
China Men, Maxine Hong Kingston
Lyndon: An Oral Biography, Merle Miller
The Panda's Thumb, Stephen Jay Gould
Walt Whitman, Justin Kaplan
Part of Nature, Part of Us, Helen Vendler
The Zero-Sum Society, Lester Thurow
At Odds, Carl Degler
White Supremacy, George M. Frederickson
The Cost of Good Intentions, Charles R. Morris

Best-Sellers
Crisis Investing, Douglas R. Casey
Cosmos, Carl Sagan
Free to Choose, Milton and Rose Friedman
Anatomy of an Illness as Perceived by the Patient, Norman Cousins
Thy Neighbor's Wife, Gay Talese
The Sky's the Limit, Dr. Wayne W. Dyer
The Third Wave, Alvin Toffler

Poetry
James Merrill, *Scripts for the Pageant*
Robert Penn Warren, *Being Here: Poetry 1977–1980*
Galway Kinnell, *Mortal Arts, Mortal Words*
Howard Nemerov, *Sentences*
Lisel Mueller, *The Need to Hold Still*
Frederick Seidel, *Sunrise*
Louis Glück, *Descending Figure*

Pulitzer Prizes
A Confederacy of Dunces, John Kennedy Toole (fiction)
American Education: The National Experience, 1783–1876, Lawrence A. Cremin (U.S. history)
Fin-de-Siècle Vienna, Carl E. Schorske (nonfiction)
Peter the Great, Robert K. Massie (biography)
The Morning of the Poem, James Schuyler (poetry)

Nobel Prize
Czeslaw Milosz

Science and Technology

Four hundred cases of toxic shock syndrome, caused by certain kinds of tampons, are reported.

A 10-year study shows negligible risk from oral contraceptives.

The genetic engineering of "miracle drug" Interferon and human insulin begins.

University of California, San Diego, researchers assert that "passive smoking" can lead to lung cancer.

The FDA adds caffeine to the list of warnings recently given pregnant women, including smoking and drinking.

Based on geological findings (an iridium layer), Walter and Luis Alvarez theorize that a giant meteor caused the dinosaur extinctions.

Mars Viking Lander 2 finds no evidence of earthlike life on Mars, and Pioneer Venus finds none on Venus.

Voyager I discovers that Saturn has at least 15, not 12, moons and a complex system of major and minor rings.

🍃 Two Soviet astronauts go a record 185 days on Salyut 6.

Nobel Prize
Paul Berg and Walter Gilbert win in chemistry for their work on recombinant DNA. James Cronin and Val Fitch win in physics for studying the asymmetry of subatomic particles. George Snell and Baruj Benacerraf win in physiology or medicine for their experiments with heredity, transplants, and disease susceptibility.

Unmanned spaceships return closeups of the distant solar system; here Voyager I discovers that Saturn has at least 15, not 12, moons and a complex system of major and minor rings. *Courtesy: NASA.*

Sports

Baseball

Rickey Henderson (Oakland, AL) becomes the third player to steal 100 bases.

George Brett (Kansas City, AL) hits .390, the highest since Ted Williams's .406, in 1941.

Houston-Philadelphia NLCS has four extra-inning games.

The Cy Young awards go to Steve Carlton (Philadelphia, NL) and Steve Stone (Baltimore, AL).

Champions

Batting	
Bill Buckner (Chicago, NL), .324	Steve Stone (Baltimore, AL), 25–7
George Brett (Kansas City, AL), .390	*Home runs*
Pitching	Mike Schmidt (Philadelphia, NL), 48
Steve Carlton (Philadelphia, NL), 24–9	

Football

Allegations of bogus courses and grades jolt many universities.

NFL Season Leaders: Ron Jaworski (Philadelphia), passing; Walter Payton (Chicago), rushing; Earl Cooper (San Francisco), receiving

AFL Season Leaders: Brian Sipe (Cleveland), passing; Earl Campbell (1,934 yards) (Houston), rushing; Kellen Winslow (San Diego) receiving

College All-Americans: Herschel Walker (B), Georgia; Hugh Green (LB), Pittsburgh; Anthony Carter (E), Michigan

Bowls (Jan. 1, 1981)

Rose: Michigan 23–Washington 6
Orange: Oklahoma 18–Florida State 17
Cotton: Alabama 30–Baylor 2
Sugar: Georgia 17–Notre Dame 10

Basketball

Larry Bird (Boston) and Magic Johnson (Los Angeles Lakers) debut; Johnson plays center for the injured Abdul-Jabbar in the sixth playoff game and scores 42 points in the Lakers' victory.

The NBA experiments with a 3-point shot.

NBA All-Pro First Team: Julius Erving (Philadelphia), Larry Bird (Boston), Kareem Abdul-Jabbar (Los Angeles Lakers), George Gervin (San Antonio), Paul Westphal (Phoenix)

Olympics

Thirty-six nations join the U.S. in boycotting the Moscow Summer Olympics to protest the Russian invasion of Afghanistan. At Lake Placid, New York, Eric Heiden wins five gold medals (500m–10,000m) and the U.S. hockey team upsets heavily favored Russia for the gold medal.

Other Sports

Boxing: Larry Holmes defeats Ali in Las Vegas; the gate is a record $6.2 million. Roberto Duran decisions Sugar Ray Leonard for the welterweight title; Leonard wins a rematch when Duran quits saying; "No más, no más."

Hockey: Wayne Gretzky (Edmonton) debuts, scoring 137 points and winning the MVP.

Running: Bill Rogers wins a third Boston Marathon.

Horse Racing: Spectacular Bid wins all nine starts and becomes the all-time money winner, with $2.7 million.

Winners

World Series	*MVP*
Philadelphia (NL) 4	Kareem Abdul-Jabbar, Los Angeles
Kansas City (AL) 2	*College Basketball*
MVP	Louisville
NL–Mike Schmidt, Philadelphia	*Player of the Year*
AL–George Brett, Kansas City	Darrell Griffith, Louisville
Super Bowl XV (Jan. 1981)	*Stanley Cup*
Oakland 27–Philadelphia 10	New York Islanders
MVP	*US Tennis Open*
Earl Campbell, Houston	Men: John McEnroe
College Football	Women: Chris Evert Lloyd
Georgia	*USGA Open*
Heisman Trophy	Jack Nicklaus
George Rogers, South Carolina	*Kentucky Derby*
NBA Championship	Genuine Risk (J. Vazquez, jockey)
Los Angeles 4–Philadelphia 2	

Fashion

The return to basics includes the "preppy look": navy blazer, challis skirt or kilt, and cardigan sweater or button-down shirt. The "Hapsburg" look is epitomized in the braid-trimmed jacket, velvet skirt (with shorter hem), and low-heeled pump. With disco challenged by country and western, cowboy and Indian dress also gain popularity, and fringe trims everything. Bo Derek's corn-row hairstyle (from the movie *10*) sets another style. Ubiquitous in winter is the bright nylon down coat.

High-fashion note for women: Yves Saint Laurent's bicolor, Pierrot suits, half black, half white. For men: Perry Ellis's gray flannel suit with rolled-up sleeves; Lacoste (alligator) shirts with the collar worn up

Kaleidoscope ────────────────────

- In an unprecedented third year of double-digit inflation, CDs typically offer 18 percent and mortgage rates exceed 20 percent.
- Yellow ribbons become a symbol of American concern for the hostages in Iran.
- When Ronald Reagan is heckled with cries of "Bonzo," referring to a movie he made about a monkey (*Bedtime for Bonzo*), he replies: "Well, they better watch out. Bonzo grew up to be King Kong."
- On hearing that Ted Kennedy plans to oppose him for the Democratic nomination, Jimmy Carter retorts: "I'll whip his ass."
- Headmistress of a Virginia girls' school Jean Harris shoots to death her longtime lover, famous Scarsdale diet doctor Herman Tarnower; he had become romantically involved with his office manager.
- Abbie Hoffman, who jumped bail in 1974 on cocaine possession and has lived in upstate New York as "Barry Freed," emerges from hiding; "Welcome, Wall Street, here I come! Let's make millions of dollars," says another ex-Yippie, Jerry Rubin.
- The trial of Elvis Presley's physician reveals that Elvis took 10,000 pills in the 20 months prior to his death.
- A UCLA and American Council on Education survey indicates that college freshmen are more interested in power, money, and status than at any time during the past 15 years (62.5 percent vs. 50 percent); business and management is the most popular major.
- Office gossip becomes media news when Mary Cunningham leaves Bendix: her high executive position was linked to her romance with chairman William Agee.
- New Equal Opportunity Commission regulations forbid sexual harassment of women by their superiors.
- On "Dallas," the largest audience on record for a regular series learns that it was J. R.'s girlfriend Kristin who shot "the man you love to hate."
- The divorce rate has grown from 1 in 3 marriages (1970) to 1 in 2; one-parent families have increased 50 percent; unmarried couples are up 300 percent; one million teenagers, two-thirds of them unmarried, become pregnant.
- The Senate investigates the White House after learning that the president's brother, Billy, has received money from Libya and is registered as a Libyan agent; remarks Jimmy Carter: "I love Billy. I can't control him."
- The November *Journal of the AMA* answers an airline stewardess's query: silicone breast implants may expand to twice normal size at 18,000 feet, and three times normal size at 30,000 feet.
- The Reagans' lucky monkey, Bob, dressed in a three-piece suit, is kidnapped and later recovered by the FBI.
- Bioengineering ventures are boosted when the Supreme Court rules that new biological forms produced by gene splicing are patentable.

- The World Health Organization announces that smallpox has finally been eradicated; viral samples remain in only six laboratories worldwide for future research.
- Widespread attention is given the health hazards of radiation exposure and toxic chemicals in dump sites (Love Canal, Niagara Falls) and nuclear plants (Three Mile Island); the Senate appropriates $1.6 billion for cleanup, and five nuclear plants are ordered to close.
- In August, six planes are hijacked to Cuba.
- Lillian Hellman files a $2.5 million libel suit against Mary McCarthy, who, on TV, called Hellman "a dishonest writer."
- Thousands mourn the death of John Lennon, shot by former mental patient Mark David Chapman, by praying and singing in front of his apartment in New York City.
- When Yale students filch a moosehead and write their college president: "Dear Bart—We have your moose. Cancel midterms or we'll eat him. The Moose Liberation Army," Giamatti responds: "Let them eat mousse."
- Fundamentalist ministers organize politically; the Rev. Jerry Falwell speaks to 18 million weekly on TV and radio; his Moral Majority opposes abortion, homosexual rights, and ERA, and endorses Ronald Reagan.
- The ten most endangered North American species include the dusky seaside sparrow, red wolf, and snail darter.
- An estimated 43 million people have tried drugs once.
- An ethical debate begins in the medical profession when four states mandate that doctors inject lethal drugs into criminals sentenced to death.
- Publisher Nelson Doubleday, Jr., buys a controlling interest in the New York Mets; his great-granduncle Abner is said to have invented baseball.

Fads: Rubik's Cube, Sony Walkman, mechanical bulls (as in the movie *Urban Cowboy*), Yoda, designer jeans

New Words and Usages: copresidency, voodoo economics, nerd; revival of 1950s jargon: bombed, loaded, smashed, wrecked, out to lunch, gut course, gross, cake course, easy ace, pig out

First Appearances: female Annapolis graduates, female motion-picture studio head (Sherry Lansing, 20th Century-Fox), *Science 80, Discover, Black Scholar,* the Pump (punk rock) and Jog (dances), electronic products with computerized speech (talking calculator, digital clock, microwave, doll, language translator), cordless telephones, Pulsetach (for runners), front-wheel-drive subcompact (Escort), 24-hour-a-day news coverage (Ted Turner's CNN), New York Futures Exchange (Wall Street), Synthetic Fuel Agency, situp sleeping bag, plastic sled, 3-D calculator

1981

Facts and Figures

Economic Profile

Dow-Jones: ↑ High 1,024–
   Low 824

GNP: +11.7%

Inflation: +10.2%

Unemployment: 7.6%

Median age, first marriage:
   male: 23.9
   female: 20.8

Average household size: 2.76

Population over 65: 11.3%

Population under 10: 14.7%

Dime Savings: 13.57% 30 mo.
   11.759% 6 mo.

Gimbels diamond, pierced
   earrings:
   5 pt: $49; 10 pt: $69; 15
   pt: $99

Brooks Brothers woman's
   cable wool cardigan:
   $94

Nippon stripe shirtdress,
   polyester: $105

Kniepp bath botanics, 3.4
   oz.: $9

Pan Am, N.Y.–California
   (free car): $219

Bell System, lowest rates (3
   minutes)
   U.S.–Belgium, Denmark,
   Finland: $3.15
   U.S.–Japan, Malaysia,
   Korea: $3.75

Parrots: $29.99

Tricolor sharks: $5.90

Silver Angels: 3/$1.00

Deaths

Samuel Barber, Omar
   Bradley, Moshe Dayan,
   Melvin Douglas, Will
   Durant, Ella T. Grasso,
   William Holden, Joe
   Louis, William Saroyan,
   Roy Wilkins

In the News

RONALD REAGAN IS INAUGURATED AS 40TH PRESIDENT, IRAN RELEASES 52 HOSTAGES . . . GM REPORTS $763 MILLION LOSS FOR '80, FIRST LOSS SINCE '21 . . . REAGAN PROPOSES TAX AND FEDERAL BUDGET CUTS TO COMBAT "ECONOMIC CALAMITY" . . . SPANISH KING JUAN CARLOS HELPS QUELL MILITARY COUP . . . U.S. SENDS MILITARY ADVISERS TO EL SALVADOR, CLAIMING CUBAN AND SOVIET PRESENCE . . . PRESIDENT IS SHOT IN CHEST IN ASSASSINATION ATTEMPT, PRESS SECRETARY JAMES BRADY SUFFERS HEAD WOUND, JOHN HINCKLEY IS CAPTURED . . . ROBERT CRIPPEN AND JOHN YOUNG ORBIT 36 TIMES ON COLUMBIA, THE FIRST SPACE SHUTTLE . . . REAGAN LIFTS USSR GRAIN EMBARGO . . . SEN. HARRISON A. WILLIAMS (D-NJ) IS CONVICTED ON ABSCAM CHARGES . . . IRA LEADER ROBERT SANDS DIES ON HUNGER STRIKE IN PRISON . . . SOCIALIST FRANÇOIS MITTERAND IS ELECTED FRENCH PRESIDENT . . . POPE JOHN PAUL II IS WOUNDED AT VATICAN IN ASSASSINATION ATTEMPT, MEHMET ALI AGCA IS ARRESTED . . . ISRAEL BOMBS IRAQI NUCLEAR REACTOR . . . WAYNE WILLIAMS IS ARRESTED IN ATLANTA MURDERS OF 23 BLACK CHILDREN . . . SANDRA DAY O'CONNOR BECOMES FIRST WOMAN SUPREME COURT JUSTICE . . . WALKWAY AT KANSAS CITY'S HYATT REGENCY COLLAPSES, 111 DIE . . . PRINCE CHARLES AND LADY DIANA SPENCER MARRY . . . KEMP-ROTH TAX CUT PASSES, 25% IN 3 YEARS . . . REAGAN FIRES STRIKING AIR CONTROLLERS . . . NAVY JETS SHOOT DOWN 2 LIBYAN PLANES IN GULF OF SIDRA . . . ANWAR SADAT IS ASSASSINATED IN CAIRO BY ISLAMIC FUNDAMENTALISTS . . . REAGAN PROPOSES ZERO OPTION ON INTERMEDIATE MISSILES IN EUROPE, SOVIETS REJECT OFFER . . . 500,000 IN AMSTERDAM AND WEST GERMANY MARCH AGAINST NUCLEAR WEAPONS . . . POLISH LEADER JARUZELSKI DECLARES MARTIAL LAW, SOLIDARITY GOES ON STRIKE.

1981

Quotes _____

"The idea has been established over the past ten years that almost every service that someone might need in life ought to be provided by the government. . . . We reject that notion."

—Ronald Reagan

"Dammit, the law is the law, and the law says they cannot strike. If they strike, they quit their jobs."
   —Ronald Reagan, on the strike of 13,000 air controllers

"For myself, [abortion] is simply offensive, but I'm over the hill. I'm not going to be pregnant again. It's easy for me to say now."
   —Sandra Day O'Connor, at her confirmation hearings

"Honey, I forgot to duck."
   —Ronald Reagan to Nancy, after being shot

"My visit to the Oval Office for lunch with the President was more in the nature of a visit to the woodshed after supper."
   —Budget Director David Stockman, on being reprimanded for his *Atlantic Monthly* interview

"If they haven't figured out how to get rid of the stuff after 30 years, they ought to shut the plants down. It's like building an eating place without a garbage disposal."
   —Environmentalist Alfred Coleman, Jr., on nuclear waste disposal

"I have indeed grown poor loving you, while a self-serving ignorant slut has grown very rich."
   —Jean Harris's "Scarsdale letter," used in the trial that convicted her of murdering diet doctor Herman Tarnower

"Sexual harassment on the job is not a problem for virtuous women. . . . Men hardly ever ask sexual favors of women from whom the certain answer is no."
   —Phyllis Schlafly

Ronald Reagan nominates Sandra Day O'Connor of the Arizona State Court of Appeals to the Supreme Court; O'Connor completed her undergraduate and graduate degrees at Stanford University in five years. *U.S. Supreme Court.*

"This isn't meant to take anything away from the hostages. We just want to remind people that there are guys without arms and legs lying in that hospital right now who never got a parade. . . . Where are the yellow ribbons for them?"
   —Gregory Steele, Vietnam veteran

"When it comes to giving tax breaks to the wealthy of this country, the president has a heart of gold."
   —Tip O'Neill

Financial wiz and federal budget director David Stockman, 35, makes problems for himself as he questions the wisdom of his own budget: "None of us really knows what's going on with all these numbers." *Library of Congress.*

Ads _____

Remove those unwanted lines in seconds.
   (IBM)

We have liftoff.
   (Nike Sneakers)

Last year handguns killed 48 people in Japan, 8 in Great Britain, 34 in Switzerland, 52 in Canada, 58 in Israel, 21 in Sweden, 42 in West Germany, 10,720 in the U.S. God Bless America.
   (Stop Handguns Before They Stop You Committee)

Only 29 shopping days 'til the Hamptons.
   (Barney's, New York)

There's a difference between being baptized and brainwashed.
   (The Episcopal Church)

In 1982, if you have a miscarriage you could be prosecuted for murder.
   (Planned Parenthood)

TV

Premieres
"Dynasty," Linda Evans, John Forsythe, Joan Collins
"Falcon Crest," Jane Wyman, Abby Dalton
"Hill Street Blues," Daniel J. Travanti, Michael Conrad
"Private Benjamin," Eileen Brennan
"The Fall Guy," Lee Majors
"Gimme a Break," Nell Carter
"Simon & Simon," Jameson Parker, Gerald McRaney

Top Ten (Nielsen)
"Dallas," "60 Minutes," "M*A*S*H," "The Dukes of Hazzard," "Three's Company," "Private Benjamin," "Diff'rent Strokes," "House Calls," "Archie Bunker's Place," "Too Close for Comfort"

Specials
"Masada" (Peter O'Toole, Peter Strauss); "Skokie"

(Danny Kaye); "Lily [Tomlin]: Sold Out"; "Shock of the New" (Robert Hughes); "Boston Symphony Celebration"

Emmy Awards
"Hill Street Blues" (drama); "Barney Miller" (comedy); "Night of 100 Stars" (variety); "The Wave" (children); Daniel J. Travanti (actor, "Hill Street Blues"); Alan Alda (comedic actor, "M*A*S*H"); Michael Learned (actress, "Nurse"); Carol Kane (comedic actress, "Taxi")

Of Note
Walter Cronkite retires as CBS anchor and is replaced by Dan Rather • News programs vie for audiences • Tom Brokaw and Roger Mudd are hired to replace John Chancellor (NBC); David Brinkley goes from NBC to ABC • MacNeil/Lehrer and Ted Koppel sharply increase in ratings • Despite initial poor ratings, "Hill Street Blues" wins a record eight Emmys.

Movies

Openings
Chariots of Fire (Hugh Hudson), Ben Cross, Ian Charleson
Atlantic City (Louis Malle), Burt Lancaster, Susan Sarandon
Reds (Warren Beatty), Diane Keaton, Warren Beatty, Jack Nicholson
On Golden Pond (Mark Rydell), Henry Fonda, Katharine Hepburn, Jane Fonda
Raiders of the Lost Ark (Steven Spielberg), Harrison Ford, Karen Allen
The French Lieutenant's Woman (Karel Reisz), Meryl Streep, Jeremy Irons
Gallipoli (Peter Weir), Mel Gibson, Mark Lee
Ragtime (Milos Forman), James Cagney, Mary Steenburgen, Howard E. Rollins, Jr.
Absence of Malice (Sydney Pollack), Paul Newman, Sally Field
Arthur (Steve Gordon), Dudley Moore, Liza Minnelli, John Gielgud
Body Heat (Lawrence Kasdan), William Hurt, Kathleen Turner
Superman II (Richard Lester), Christopher Reeve, Gene Hackman, Margot Kidder
My Dinner with André (Louis Malle), André Gregory, Wallace Shawn
Prince of the City (Sidney Lumet), Treat Williams
Napoleon (Abel Gance, 1927 unabridged), Albert Dieudonne

Academy Awards
Best Picture: *Chariots of Fire*
Best Director: Warren Beatty (*Reds*)
Best Actress: Katharine Hepburn (*On Golden Pond*)
Best Actor: Henry Fonda (*On Golden Pond*)

Top Box-Office Stars
Burt Reynolds, Clint Eastwood, Dudley Moore, Dolly Parton, Jane Fonda, Harrison Ford, Alan Alda, Bo Derek, Goldie Hawn, Bill Murray

Stars of Tomorrow
Matt Dillon, Rachel Ward, Griffin O'Neal, Henry Thomas, Kathleen Turner, Eric Roberts, Mel Gibson, Molly Ringwald, Sean Young, Elizabeth McGovern

Kathleen Turner debuts in *Body Heat* as a sexy and sophisticated socialite who plots the death of her husband. *Movie Star News.*

Popular Music

Hit Songs
"Lady"
"Starting Over"
"Kiss on My List"
"9 to 5"
"Take It On the Run"
"Morning Train"
"Slow Hand"

Top Records
Albums: *Hi Infidelity* (REO Speedwagon); *Greatest Hits* (Kenny Rogers); *Crimes of Passion* (Pat Benatar); *Paradise Theater* (Styx); *Voices* (Daryl Hall, John Oates); *Zenyatta Mondatta* (The Police); *Back in Black* (AC/DC)

Singles: *Endless Love* (Diana Ross, Lionel Richie); *Jessie's Girl* (Rick Springfield); *Celebration* (Kool & the Gang); *The Tide Is High* (Blondie); *Master Blaster* (Stevie Wonder); *Woman in Love* (Barbra Streisand). Country: *Fire and Smoke* (Earl Thomas Conley); *No Gettin' Over Me* (Ronnie Milsap)

Grammy Awards
Bette Davis Eyes, Kim Carnes

Bruce ("the Boss") Springsteen captures huge audiences with an earthy style and populist lyrics. *Movie Star News.*

(record); *Double Fantasy,* John Lennon, Yoko Ono (album); "Bette Davis Eyes" (song)

Jazz and Big Bands
Dizzy Gillespie heads the Newport Jazz Festival, in Rhode Island for the first time since 1971. Art Blakey is honored with numerous tributes at the New York City Kool Jazz Festival. Indiana University offers an M.A. in jazz.

Top Performers *(Downbeat):* Miles Davis (soloist); Toshiko Akiyoshi/Lew Tabackin (band); Weather Report (jazz group); Freddie Hubbard, Jimmy Knepper, Oscar Peterson, Phil Woods, Gerry Mulligan (instrumentalists); Sarah Vaughan, Al Jarreau (vocalists); Manhattan Transfer (vocal group); Miles Davis, *Man with the Horn* (album)

Theater

Broadway Openings

Plays
The Life and Adventures of Nicholas Nickleby (David Edgar), Roger Rees ($100 a ticket)
Crimes of the Heart (Beth Henley), Mary Beth Hurt, Mia Dillon
The Dresser (Ronald Harwood), Tom Courtenay, Paul Rogers
Mass Appeal (Bill C. Davis), Milo O'Shea, Michael O'Keefe
The Floating Light Bulb (Woody Allen), Beatrice Arthur
The West Side Waltz (Ernest Thompson), Katharine Hepburn, Dorothy Loudon

Musicals
Dreamgirls (Tom Eyen, Henry Krieger), Jennifer Holliday (choreographed and directed by Michael Bennett)

The Pirates of Penzance (W. S. Gilbert, Arthur Sullivan), Linda Ronstadt, Kevin Kline, Estelle Parsons
Woman of the Year (Fred Ebb, John Kander), Lauren Bacall
Sophisticated Ladies (Duke Ellington), Gregory Hines

Classics, Revivals, and Off-Broadway Premieres
A Soldier's Play (Charles Fuller), Adolph Caesar; *Candida,* Joanne Woodward, Jane Curtin; *The Little Foxes,* Elizabeth Taylor, Maureen Stapleton, Tom Aldredge; *American Buffalo* (David Mamet), Al Pacino; *Rockaby* (Samuel Beckett); *The Winslow Boy; Grown Ups* (Jules Feiffer); *Translations* (Brian Friel), Barnard Hughes; *The Dance and the Railroad* (David Henry Hwang), John Lone; *My Fair Lady,* Rex Harrison; *A Taste of Honey,* Amanda Plummer

Theater (cont.)

Regional
Arena Stage, Washington, D.C.: *Plenty* (David Hare)

Pulitzer Prize
Crimes of the Heart, Beth Henley

Tony Awards
Amadeus, Peter Shaffer (play); *42nd Street*, Harry Warren, Al Dubin (musical)

Al Pacino, "the Godfather," turns petty criminal in *American Buffalo*, David Mamet's staccato enunciation of human ignobility. *Billy Rose Theatre Collection. The New York Public Library at Lincoln Center. Astor, Lenox and Tilden Foundations.*

Classical Music

Compositions
Roger Sessions, Concerto for Orchestra
Philip Glass, *Glassworks*
Elliott Carter, *In Sleep, In Thunder*
Ned Rorem, *Winter Pages*
John Adams, *Harmonium*
Patrick Hardish, *Tremotrill*

Important Events
Numerous celebrations of Bartók's 100th birthday include a nine-day festival of the Detroit Symphony led by conductor laureate Antal Dorati.
On the occasion of Virgil Thomson's 85th birthday, *Four Saints in Three Acts* is revived at Carnegie Hall, the first full-length production in over a decade.

Debut: Ivo Pogorelich

First Performances
Mozart, *Symphony in F* (composed at age 9) (Washington, D.C.); in Boston: Peter Maxwell Davies, Symphony no. 2, Roger Sessions, Concerto for Orchestra, John Harbison, Violin Concerto, Robert Starer, Violin Concerto; Ned Rorem, *Double Concerto in 10 Movements for Cello and Orchestra* (Cincinnati); Erza Laderman, Symphony no. 4 (Los Angeles); David Del Tredici, *All in the Golden Afternoon* (Philadelphia); Charles Wuorinen, *Four Fragments of 1/f Music* (New York); John Cage, *Empty Words* (12-hour work) (Hartford); Karlheinz Stockhausen *Jubilee* (New York)

Opera
Metropolitan: triple bill—*Parade* (Satie), *Les Mamelles de Tirésias* (Poulenc), *L'Enfant et les sortilèges* (Ravel), designs by David Hockney; Régine Crespin, Maria Ewing, *Dialogues des Carmélites*; Teresa Stratas, José Carreras, *La bohème* (sets by Franco Zeffirelli); Eva Marton, Birgit Nilsson, *Die Frau ohne Schatten*; James Levine: "We're trying [for a] total theatrical experience, not . . . concerts in costume."

Boston: Shirley Verrett, James McCracken, *Otello*; Tatiana Troyanos, *Der Rosenkavalier*

San Francisco: Retiring Kurt Adler mounts 70 performances of 11 operas; Terry McEwen will assume his position. Thomas Stewart, *King Lear* (Aribert Reimann), U.S. premiere; *Lady Macbeth of Mtsensk* (original version); Kiri Te Kanawa, *Arabella;* Teresa Berganza, Franco Bonisolli/Domingo, *Carmen; Jenůfa* (in Czech); Pavarotti, Margaret Price, *Aïda*.

Chicago: Evelyn Lear, *The Merry Widow*; Ardis Krainik takes over Carol Fox's post as general manager.

Minnesota: *A Water Bird Talk* (Dominick Argento); Conrad Susa, *Black River*

Houston: *Willie Stark* (Carlisle Floyd)

Lewiston, N.Y.: *Satyagraha* (Philip Glass)

Music Notes
Shostakovich's conductor-son, Maksim, and his pianist grandson, Dmitri, defect from the USSR; on the composer's 75th birthday, they perform with Rostropovich and the National Symphony • On May 5, Carnegie Hall re-creates its 1881 opening program: *Marche solennelle* (Tchaikovsky), *Te Deum* (Berlioz), and the *Leonore Overture*.

Art ———————————

Painting
James Rosenquist, *House of Fire*

Robert Motherwell, *Dance, Dance*

Richard Estes, *Macdonald's*

David Salle and Julian Schnabel, *Jump*

Willem de Kooning, *Pirate*

Bill Jensen, *Memory of Closeness*

Craig Kauffman, *Cocque and Bell Jar*

Jim Dine, *Painting a Fortress for the Heart*

Eric Fischl, *Bad Boy*

Mark Tansey, *The Innocent Eye Test*

Sculpture
Louise Nevelson, *Moon-Star III; Moon-Star Zag XIII*

Alice Aycock, *The Savage Sparkler*

George Segal, *Cézanne Still Life, No. 4*

Deborah Butterfield, *Chestnut*

Architecture
Asia Society Building, New York (Edward Larrabee Barnes)

West Wing, Museum of Fine Arts, Boston (I. M. Pei)

Wing, Walters Art Gallery, Baltimore (Shepley, Bulfinch, Richardson & Abbott)

Loyola Law School, Los Angeles (Frank Gehry)

Pensacola Place II Apartments, Chicago (Stanley Tigerman)

Coatesville home, Coatesville, Pa. (Norman Gaffney)

Important Exhibitions
"5,000 Years of Korean Art," "The Search for Alexander," and "El Greco of Toledo" travel to numerous cities.

Museums
New York: *Metropolitan:* 19th-century German painting; "Renaissance of Islam: Art of the Mamluks"; Leonardo da Vinci: Nature Studies"; "18th-century Woman"; numerous new viewing areas include the print galleries (opening with "The Painterly Print," monotypes); the 12th-century Chinese (Astor) Garden design that complements the Douglas Dillon Galleries of Chinese Paintings; Sackler Gallery of Assyrian Art. *Museum of Modern Art:* Modigliani retrospective; "American Child"; Breuer; "American Landscapes." *Whitney:* Calder, O'Keeffe. *Pierpont Morgan:* "Masterpieces of Medieval Painting"

Kansas City, Cleveland: "Eight Dynasties of Chinese Painting"

Washington, Detroit: "Dutch Painting in the Age of Rembrandt"

Washington: Rodin—"The Age of Bronze"

Los Angeles: "Japanese Genre Paintings"; Art of Los Angeles (to celebrate city's bicentennial)

Controversy begins over Michael Graves' pastel-colored Portland Building, one of the decade's most influential structures. *Paschall/Taylor*

Art Briefs
Picasso's self-portrait "Yo" (1901) sells for $5.3 million, the highest price ever paid for a 20th-century work • His "Guernica" is returned to the Prado after 42 years at the Museum of Modern Art; Picasso ordered that it not be returned until Spain had a democratic government • The Whitney opens its first branch, in Stamford, Conn. • The $7.2 million San Antonio Museum opens • Joseph Hirshhorn leaves his entire collection of 6,000 works, with a multimillion-dollar gift, to the Hirshhorn Museum and Sculpture Garden • Andy Warhol, who began his career with shoe ads, designs ads for Halston.

Dance ———————————

Premieres/Important Productions
New York City Ballet: Tchaikovsky Festival—20 ballets (*Ice Palace*, designed by Philip Johnson and John Burgee); Mel Tomlinson, *Agon* (Balanchine); 900th *Nutcracker*

American Ballet Theatre: Natalia Makarova, Mikhail Baryshnikov, *The Wild Boy* (Kenneth MacMillan); Baryshnikov, Cynthia Gregory, *Prodigal Son* (Balanchine); Ib Andersen, Suzanne Farrell, *Mozartiana* (Balanchine)

Joffrey: 25th anniversary; Marcie Haydee, Richard Cragun, *The Taming of the Shrew* (John Cranko); *Return to the Strange Land* (Jiri Kylian); *Light Rain* (John Arpino)

Martha Graham (age 87): *Acts of Light* (Carl Nielsen); Elie Chaib, Susan McGuire, *Arden Court* (Paul Taylor)

Twyla Tharp: *The Catherine Wheel*

Books

Fiction
Critics' Choice
What We Talk About When We Talk About Love, Raymond Carver
Tar Baby, Toni Morrison
Ellis Island and Other Stories, Mark Helprin
Dad, William Wharton
The Men's Club, Leonard Michaels
Zuckerman Unbound, Philip Roth
The Chaneysville Incident, David Bradley

Best-Sellers
Nobel House, James Clavell
The Hotel New Hampshire, John Irving
Cujo, Stephen King
An Indecent Obsession, Colleen McCullough
Gorky Park, Martin Cruz Smith
Masquerade, Kit Williams
Goodbye, Janette, Harold Robbins
The Third Deadly Sin, Lawrence Sanders
The Glitter Dome, Joseph Wambaugh
No Time for Tears, Cynthia Freeman

Nonfiction
Critics' Choice
Philosophical Explanations, Robert Nozick
Ethnic America, Thomas Sowell
Waldo Emerson, Gay Wilson Allen
Mornings on Horseback, David McCullough
Lucy, Donald Johanson, Maitland Edey
Richard Nixon, Fawn Brodie
The Philosophy of Moral Development, Lawrence Kohlberg
The Mismeasure of Man, Stephen Jay Gould
Wealth and Poverty, George Gilder
The Gate of Heavenly Peace, Jonathan Spence
National Defense, James Fallows
Explaining America, Garry Wills
Psychoanalysis: The Impossible Profession, Janet Malcolm
❧ *The Drama of the Gifted Child*, Alice Miller

Best-Sellers
The Beverly Hills Diet, Judy Mazel
The Lord God Made Them All, James Herriot
Richard Simmons' Never-Say-Diet Book, Richard Simmons
A Light in the Attic, Shel Silverstein
Cosmos, Carl Sagan
Better Homes and Gardens New Cookbook
Miss Piggy's Guide to Life, Miss Piggy (as told to Henry Beard)
Weight Watchers* 365-Day Menu Cookbook
You Can Negotiate Anything, Herb Cohen
A Few Minutes with Andy Rooney, Andrew A. Rooney

Poetry
A. R. Ammons, *A Coast of Trees*
Anne Sexton, *The Complete Poems* (posthumous)
Philip Levine, *One for the Rose*
John Ashbery, *Shadow Train*
Jared Carter, *Work, For the Night Is Coming*
Carolyn Forché, *The Country Between Us*

Pulitzer Prizes
Rabbit Is Rich, John Updike (fiction)
Mary Chesnut's Civil War, ed. C. Vann Woodward (U.S. history)
The Soul of a New Machine, Tracy Kidder (nonfiction)
Grant, William S. McFeely (biography)
The Collected Poems, Sylvia Plath (poetry)

Science and Technology

Surgeons relieve coronary artery obstruction with a stretchable balloon-tipped catheter.

A 10-year, 7-country study correlates fatal heart disease to the saturated-unsaturated fat ratio in the diet.

The first successful surgery on a fetus is performed, to relieve urinary blockage.

The National Cancer Institute finds laetrile ineffective.

Voyager 2 takes more than 1,800 photos of Saturn, which has a temperature of −300°F and 1,000 mph winds.

Photographs from galaxies 10 billion light years away indicate the minimum age of the universe as 16 billion years.

Cave paintings of sacred Mayan ball games, circa A.D. 800, are found in Guatemala.

Tools found in Ethiopia, two-and-a-half million years old, are the oldest discovered to date.

Donald Johanson and Maitland Edey propose a new human ancestor, *Australopithecus afarensis*, or "Lucy," a four-foot fossil found in 1974, named after "Lucy in the Sky with Diamonds."

Nobel Prizes

Roald Hoffmann wins in chemistry for his theory of the quantum mechanics of chemical reactions. Nicolaas Bioembergen and Arthur Schawlow win in physics for their research in laser spectroscopy. In physiology or medicine, David H. Hubel and Torsten N. Wiesel win for their brain and vision studies; Roger Sperry, for brain hemisphere functions.

Sports

Baseball

A seven-week strike, the longest in U.S. sports history, causes a "split season"; the issue is free agency.

Pete Rose (Philadelphia, NL) passes Stan Musial's NL lifetime record of 3,630 hits.

Nolan Ryan (Houston, NL) pitches a record fifth no-hitter.

Mexican Fernando Valenzuela (Los Angeles, NL), who does not speak English, debuts with eight shutouts.

The Cy Young awards go to Fernando Valenzuela (Los Angeles, NL) and Rollie Fingers (Milwaukee, AL).

Champions

Batting
   Bill Madlock (Pittsburgh, NL), .341
   Carney Lansford (Boston, AL), .336
Pitching
   Fernando Valenzuela (Los Angeles, NL), 13–7
   Pete Vuckovich (Milwaukee, AL), 14–4
Home runs
   Mike Schmidt (Philadelphia, NL), 31

Football

Bear Bryant, Alabama, sets a major college coaching record with his 315th victory.

NFL Season Leaders: Joe Montana (San Francisco), passing; George Rogers (New Orleans), rushing; Dwight Clark (San Francisco), receiving

AFL Season Leaders: Ken Anderson (Cincinnati), passing; Earl Campbell (Houston), rushing; Kellen Winslow (San Diego), receiving

College All-Americans: Herschel Walker (B), Georgia; Dan Marino (Q), Pittsburgh; Homer Jordan (Q), Clemson

Bowls (Jan.1, 1982)
Rose: Washington 28–Iowa 0
Orange: Clemson 22–Nebraska 15

Cotton: Texas 14–Alabama 12
Sugar: Pittsburgh 24–Georgia 20

Basketball

NBA All-Pro First Team: Julius Erving (Philadelphia), Larry Bird (Boston), Kareem Abdul-Jabbar (Los Angeles Lakers), George Gervin (San Antonio), Dennis Johnson (Phoenix)

Other Sports

Boxing: Sugar Ray Leonard TKO's "Hitman" Thomas Hearns in 14, for a record $37 million.

Tennis: John McEnroe, "the Ugly American," wins his third straight Wimbledon.

Running: Alberto Salazar (2:08:13) and Alison Roe (2:25:13) set world records in the New York City Marathon.

Winners

World Series
   Los Angeles (NL) 4
   New York (AL) 2
MVP
   NL–Mike Schmidt, Philadelphia
   AL–Rollie Fingers, Milwaukee
Super Bowl XVI (Jan. 1982)
   San Francisco 26–Cincinnati 21
MVP
   Ken Anderson, Cincinnati
College Football
   Clemson
Heisman Trophy
   Marcus Allen, USC
NBA Championship
   Boston 4–Houston 2

MVP
   Julius Erving, Philadelphia
College Basketball
   Indiana
Player of the Year
   Ralph Sampson, Virginia
Stanley Cup
   New York Islanders
U.S. Tennis Open
   Men: John McEnroe
   Women: Tracy Austin
USGA Open
   David Graham
Kentucky Derby
   Pleasant Colony (J. Velazquez, jockey)

Fashion

The combination of Nancy Reagan's elegance and White House formality, along with Lady Di and Prince Charles's wedding, stimulates a return to opulent styles. Billowing skirts, capes, tentlike dresses and coats appear in bold patterns, paisleys, florals, and rich tapestries; even ruffles return. Sportswear is influenced by the Reagans' western dress, and designers show leather pants, blouses, and tunics. Gold in makeup, as well as fabrics, is fashionable: "golden khaki" and "bronze glow" eyeshadows, rouges, and lipsticks. Dramatic makeup and last year's red, red lipsticks remain popular.

High-fashion note: Rudy Gernreich's double-knit wool culotte dress; Anne Klein's pleated dress in gold and other metallic fabrics

Miss Piggy. *La grande dame* follows her television success with advice on manners and art appreciation; she has a best-seller this year. *Movie Star News.*

Kaleidoscope

- Minutes after Ronald Reagan's inauguration, the 52 hostages are released from their 444 days of captivity in Iran.
- The 69-year-old president recovers with remarkable speed after a bullet punctures his left lung; he leaves the hospital in 12 days.
- After reports of Libyan assassination teams headed for America, all U.S. citizens are advised to leave Libya.
- Reaganomics, or supply-side economics, proposes that government increase incentives to production, primarily through tax reform; "We must grow our way out of inflation," explains Rep. Jack Kemp (R-N.Y.).
- National unemployment rises to 8 percent, including 16.8 percent for blacks and 40 percent for black teenagers; "I did not come here today bearing the promise of government handouts," announces the president at the NAACP convention in June.
- The largest merger in U.S. history occurs when Dupont acquires Conoco for $7.9 billion.
- Says the president, after aide Edwin Meese waits five-and-a-half hours to wake him when U.S. fighter planes shoot down two Libyan jets: "If our planes were shot down, yes, they'd wake me up right away. If the other fellow's were shot down, why wake me up?"
- The *Washington Post*'s Janet Cook wins a Pulitzer for reporting on an eight-year-old heroin addict; she later confesses to having fabricated the story.
- Both Paula Parkinson, who alleges she "lobbied" various congressmen with sex, and Rita Jenrette, wife of the alleged Abscam congressman, appear in *Playboy*.
- Jack Henry Abbott, convicted murderer and best-selling jailhouse author (*In the Belly of the Beast*), is released from prison through the intervention of Norman Mailer; Abbott soon commits another murder.
- Kathy Boudin, wanted since 1970 for a bomb explosion in New York, is among several Weather Underground and BLA members captured during a Brink's robbery in Nyack, New York; three police were killed.
- The 1980 census reports the smallest rate of population growth in the United States, with the exception of the Depression; women from 15 to 44 average 1.9 children (2.5 in 1970), less than the 2.1 necessary for population replacement.
- The Rev. Jerry Falwell and Phyllis Schlafly, picket such "racy and X-rated" TV shows as "Flamingo Road" and "Knots Landing"; Procter and Gamble later removes sponsorship from specific shows.
- Congress votes 96–0 and 405–13 against changes in social security.
- An eight-year VA study reveals that Vietnam veterans suffer "more emotional, social, educational, and job-related problems" than veterans of other recent wars: 20 percent (vs. 70 percent) complete college, 24 percent (vs. 10 percent) are arrested.
- The president supports the Senate bill sponsored by Jesse Helms and Henry Hyde that human life "shall be deemed to exist from conception"; it is later defeated.
- VCR sales increase 72 percent from last year, with an estimated 34 million units in use; MTV cassette sales soar, with MTV on over 250 cable stations.
- The Rolling Stones achieve a record $25 million earnings from their U.S. tour of 40 cities; Art Garfunkel and Paul Simon perform before 400,000 in a reunion concert in Central Park. (They separated in 1970.)
- Elizabeth Taylor separates from Sen. John Warner, her seventh husband.
- On July 29, an estimated 750 million people watch the marriage of Prince Charles to kindergarten teacher Lady Diana Spencer; in November, the royal couple announces that a child is expected in June.
- Natalie Wood, 43, remarried to Robert Wagner for nine years, slips while sailing and drowns.
- The University of Pennsylvania Press publishes the complete *Sister Carrie* (Theodore Dreiser), with 36,000 expurgated words originally considered too sexually explicit.
- The Supreme Court rules that radio and TV coverage of criminal trials is constitutional.
- A furor arises when it is revealed that the administration wanted to count ketchup as a vegetable in subsidized school lunches.
- California Governor Jerry Brown stirs massive protest when he orders spraying of the pesticide malathion to counter Medfly crop infestation.

Fads: jelly beans (Reagan's favorite), diet fad books, potato skins, pasta al pesto, collectible comic books, cat books (*Garfield, 101 Uses for a Dead Cat, Fat Cats*), *The Solution to Rubik's Cube* (4 million copies), "how-to" video game books (*Mastering Pac Man*), Laffer curve

First Appearances: U.S. test-tube baby, NutraSweet (in U.S.), Hepatitis B vaccine (Merck), black-footed ferret (thought extinct), R 136 (most massive star), energy-saving jet (35 percent, Boeing 767), second honorary U.S. citizen (Raoul Wallenberg; the first: Winston Churchill), deregulation of financial systems, trillion-dollar national debt, Guardian Angels (New York City), "Dr. Ruth" (radio sex-talk show), Donkey Kong, Ms. Pac Man, Astroids, record video game (Defender: 16 hours, 34 minutes; score of 15,963,100), De Lorean sports coupe ($25,000), Isuzu, Le Baron, Chrysler K, invisible dental braces, Strawberry Shortcake doll, optical laser videodisc system (Magnavox), 288k memory chip (IBM), IBM PC, Kaypro II, Commodore Vic 20, Dolby C, satellite TV reception, hispanic mayor of large city (Henry Cisneros, San Antonio), female mayor of Houston (Kathryn Whitmire), designer chocolate (Bill Blass), Chipwich, electric wet-dry shaver, 20-cent first-class stamp, artificial skin (MIT, Harvard)

1982

Facts and Figures

Economic Profile
  Dow-Jones: ↑ High 1,070–
    Low 776
  GNP: +3.7%
  Inflation: +6%
  Unemployment: 9.7%
Household telephones: 93%
Advertising expenditures:
    $66.6 billion
Ski equipment:
  Rossignol EM: $185
  Elen: $250
  Lacroix Europa: $200
  Hanson Citation boots:
    $235
Ford Fairmont, Mercury
    Zephyr: $5,585
  Mustang, Capri: $5,880
  Lynx: $4,687
Cadillac El Dorado: $14,595
Zenith video recorder: $695
Radio Shack TRS-80 color
    computer: $399
Cordless "Walk-Talk" push-
    button phone: $99.95
Brother L-10+3 typewriter:
    $239.99
Fidelity Chess Challenger:
    $149.99

Deaths

Ingrid Bergman, John
    Cheever, Henry Fonda,
    Abe Fortas, Glenn
    Gould, Archibald
    MacLeish, Thelonious
    Monk, "Satchel" Paige,
    Arthur Rubinstein, Jack
    Webb, Vladimir
    Zworykin

In the News

KIDNAPPED U.S. GENERAL JAMES DOZIER IS RESCUED FROM ITALIAN RED BRIGADE TERRORISTS . . . REAGAN WARNS OAS OF "NEW CUBAS" . . . ARGENTINA INVADES FALKLAND ISLANDS, BRITAIN SENDS FLEET AND TROOPS . . . ISRAEL RETURNS SINAI TO EGYPT . . . BRITISH SUBMARINE SINKS ARGENTINE GENERAL BELGRANI, 321 DIE, EXOCET MISSILE SINKS HMS "SHEFFIELD," 30 DIE . . . IRAN CAPTURES 30,000 IRAQIS . . . SPAIN JOINS NATO . . . ISRAEL INVADES LEBANON TO HALT PLO ATTACKS, REACHES BEIRUT IN ONE WEEK . . . 600,000 MARCH IN NEW YORK PEACE RALLY . . . BRITISH TROOPS RECAPTURE FALKLANDS, 255 BRITISH, 1,000 ARGENTINES DIE . . . 1965 VOTING RIGHTS ACT IS EXTENDED 25 YEARS . . . JOHN HINCKLEY, FOUND NOT GUILTY ON INSANITY PLEA, IS SENT TO MENTAL HOSPITAL . . . HAIG RESIGNS AS SECRETARY OF STATE, GEORGE SHULTZ IS APPOINTED . . . SALVADOR GETS MILITARY AID AS HUMAN RIGHTS PROGRESS IS CERTIFIED . . . MULTINATIONAL PEACEKEEPING FORCES, INCLUDING U.S. MARINES, ARRIVE IN BEIRUT . . . NEW CHINESE CONSTITUTION ATTACKS MAOISM, ASSERTS END OF CLASS STRUGGLE . . . CHRISTIAN LEBANESE PREMIER BASHIR GEMAYEL IS ASSASSINATED . . . CHRISTIAN MILITIAMEN KILL 600 PALESTINIANS IN SABRA AND SHATILA REFUGEE CAMPS IN BEIRUT . . . PRINCESS GRACE OF MONACO DIES IN AUTO CRASH . . . POLAND OUTLAWS SOLIDARITY . . . 7 DIE FROM POISONED TYLENOL IN CHICAGO . . . LEONID BREZHNEV, 75, DIES, KGB HEAD YURI ANDROPOV, 69, TAKES OVER . . . REAGAN LIFTS HIS BAN ON EURO-SOVIET OIL PIPELINE TECHNOLOGY . . . FIRST ARTIFICIAL HEART IS IMPLANTED IN BARNEY CLARK, 61 . . . CONGRESS APPROVES MX FOR HARDENED SILOS, REJECTS "DENSEPACK."

Quotes

"Grace and I were old friends. We saw each other at Prince Charles's wedding, and we said, would anyone back then have believed she would marry a prince and I'd end up here?"

    —Nancy Reagan, recalling the late Princess of Monaco

"My program hasn't hurt anybody. No one has been thrown out in the snow to die."

    —Ronald Reagan

"Someone told me it was a round thing that gobbles up money. I thought it was Tip O'Neill.

    —Ronald Reagan, on Pac Man

"Waiting for supply-side economics to work is like leaving landing lights on for Amelia Earhart."

    —Walter Heller, economist

"Twenty Americans died at Yorktown. In the Napoleonic wars the British Navy lost scarcely 6,000 men. How are we to think of civilization disappearing in an hour's time?

    —Sen. Daniel Moynihan (D-N.Y.)

"Thank you, America . . . for finally remembering us."

    —Jan Scruggs, at dedication of Vietnam memorial

Alexander Haig (who in 1981 said, "I'm in control here") resigns, and George Shultz replaces him; Haig is said to be angry over Vice President Bush's appointment to the White House crisis team. *Library of Congress.*

"Our children should not grow up frightened. They should not fear the future."

    —Ronald Reagan, on Peacemaker MX

"I have always believed that this anointed land was set apart, . . . that a divine plan placed this great continent here between the oceans, to be found by people from every corner of the earth who had a special love of faith and freedom."

    —Ronald Reagan

Ads

TV

Premieres
"Cagney & Lacey," Tyne Daly, Meg Foster
"T. J. Hooker," William Shatner
"St. Elsewhere," William Daniels
"Matt Houston," Lee Horsley, Pamela Henderson
"Cheers," Ted Danson, Shelley Long

"Remington Steele," Stephanie Zimbalist, Pierce Brosnan
"Newhart," Bob Newhart

Top Ten (Nielsen)
"Dallas," "60 Minutes," "Three's Company," "The

TV (cont.)

Jeffersons," "One Day at a Time," "The Dukes of Hazzard," "Too Close for Comfort," "Alice," "The ABC Monday Night Movie," "M*A*S*H"

Specials

"Brideshead Revisited" (Jeremy Irons); "The Blue and the Gray" (Stacy Keach, John Hammond); "Marco Polo" (Ken Marshall, John Gielgud, Anne Bancroft); "A Woman Called Golda" (Ingrid Bergman); "Pleasure Drugs: The Great American High"; "Bernstein/Beethoven" (the nine symphonies)

Emmy Awards

"Hill Street Blues" (drama); "Cheers" (comedy); "Motown 25: Yesterday, Today, Forever" (variety); "Big Bird in China" (children); Ed Flanders (actor, "St. Elsewhere"); Judd Hirsch (comedic actor, "Taxi"); Tyne Daly (actress, "Cagney & Lacey"); Shelley Long (comedic actress, "Cheers")

Of Note

Top evening shows include the soaps "Dallas," "Knot's Landing," "Dynasty," "Flamingo Road," and "Falcon Crest" • General William Westmoreland sues CBS for $120 million for accusing him of conspiring to falsify information about enemy forces in Vietnam (on "60 Minutes") • Cable TV, including HBO, shows a decline in popularity, particularly shows on high culture.

Movies _____

Openings

Gandhi (Richard Attenborough), Ben Kingsley, John Gielgud

Missing (Costa-Gavras), Jack Lemmon, Sissy Spacek

Tootsie (Sydney Pollack), Dustin Hoffman, Jessica Lange

The Verdict (Sidney Lumet), Paul Newman

E.T. The Extra-Terrestrial (Steven Spielberg), Henry Thomas

Victor/Victoria (Blake Edwards), Julie Andrews, James Garner, Robert Preston

An Officer and a Gentleman (Taylor Hackford), Richard Gere, Debra Winger

Dudley Moore in *Arthur,* as a tipsy multimillionaire reformed by love (with Liza Minnelli), is one of the year's great box-office successes. *Movie Star News.*

Diner (Barry Levinson), Steve Guttenberg, Mickey Rourke

My Favorite Year (Richard Benjamin), Peter O'Toole, Mark Linn-Baker

Poltergeist (Tobe Hooper), JoBeth Williams, Heather O'Rourke

Sophie's Choice (Alan J. Pakula), Meryl Streep, Kevin Kline

Star Trek II: The Wrath of Khan (Nicholas Meyer), William Shatner, Leonard Nimoy

48 Hours (Walter Hill), Eddie Murphy, Nick Nolte

Eating Raoul (Paul Bartel), Mary Waronov, Robert Beltran

Conan the Barbarian (John Milius), Arnold Schwarzenegger

Rocky III (Sylvester Stallone), Sylvester Stallone, Mr. T

Quest for Fire (Jean-Jacques Annaud), Rae Dawn Chong

Academy Awards

Best Picture: *Gandhi*

Best Director: Richard Attenborough (*Gandhi*)

Best Actress: Meryl Streep (*Sophie's Choice*)

Best Actor: Ben Kingsley (*Gandhi*)

Top Box-Office Stars

Burt Reynolds, Clint Eastwood, Sylvester Stallone, Dudley Moore, Richard Pryor, Dolly Parton, Jane Fonda, Richard Gere, Paul Newman, Harrison Ford

Stars of Tomorrow

Tom Cruise, Sean Penn, Matthew Broderick, Jennifer Beals, Ally Sheedy, Cynthia Rhodes, Kevin Kline, Rosanna Arquette, Andrew McCarthy, Deborah Foreman

Popular Music

Hit Songs
"Any Day Now"
"Jack and Diane"
"Abracadabra"
"Hard to Say I'm Sorry"
"Gloria"
"I Can't Go for That"
"Hurts So Good"

Top Records
Albums: *Asia* (Asia); *Beauty and the Beat* (The Go-Go's); *4* (Foreigner); *American Fool* (John Cougar); *Freeze-Frame* (J. Geils Band); *Tattoo You* (Rolling Stones); *Get Lucky* (Loverboy)

Singles: *Physical* (Olivia Newton-John); *Eye of the Tiger* (Survivor); *Chariots of Fire* (Vangelis); *Ebony & Ivory* (Paul McCartney and Stevie Wonder); *Our Lips Are Sealed* (The Go-Go's); *Don't You Want Me* (Human League); *You Should Hear How She Talks About You* (Melissa Manchester). Country: *Nobody* (Sylvia); *What's Forever For* (Michael Murphey)

Grammy Awards
Rosanna, Toto (record); *Toto IV,* Toto (album); "Always on My Mind" (song)

Jazz and Big Bands
Numerous new jazz clubs open throughout the United States, as many rock clubs change to jazz formats. Ornette Coleman records *Of Human Feeling,* exploring electric instrumentation.

Top Performers (*Downbeat*):
Wynton Marsalis (soloist); Toshiko Akiyoshi/Lew Tabackin (band); Weather Report (jazz group); Jaco Pastorius, Airto Moreira, Sonny Rollins, Pepper Adams, Ron Carter (instrumentalists); Sarah Vaughan, Al Jarreau (vocalists); Manhattan Transfer (vocal group); Wynton Marsalis, *Mr. Marsalis* (album)

Theater

Broadway Openings

Plays
Torch Song Trilogy (Harvey Fierstein), Harvey Fierstein
The Curse of an Aching Heart (William Alfred), Faye Dunaway
Agnes of God (John Pielmeier), Elizabeth Ashley, Geraldine Page, Amanda Plummer
Come Back to the 5 & Dime, Jimmy Dean, Jimmy Dean (Ed Graczyk), Cher, Sandy Dennis
Foxfire (Susan Cooper, Hume Cronyn, Jonathan Holtzman), Jessica Tandy, Hume Cronyn
Good (C. P. Taylor), Alan Howard
Steaming (Nell Dunn), Judith Ivey
"Master Harold" . . . and the boys (Athol Fugard), Zakes Mokae, Danny Glover, Lonny Price (from Yale Repertory Theatre)
84 Charing Cross Road (Helene Hanff), Ellen Burstyn
Extremities (William Mastrosimone), Susan Sarandon

Musicals
Cats (T. S. Eliot, Andrew Lloyd Webber), Betty Buckley
Joseph and the Amazing Technicolor Dreamcoat (Andrew Lloyd Webber, Tim Rice), Bill Hutton, Gordon Stanley
Pump Boys and Dinettes (Jim Wann), Jim Wann
Nine (Maury Yeston), Raul Julia, Anita Morris

Classics, Revivals, and Off-Broadway Premieres
Othello, James Earl Jones, Christopher Plummer, Dianne Wiest; *Medea,* Zoe Caldwell, Dame Judith Anderson; *Present Laughter,* George C. Scott; *Angels Fall* (Lanford Wilson), Fritz Weaver, Barnard Hughes; *Plenty* (David Hare), Kate Nelligan; *The Dining Room* (A. R. Gurney); *True West* (Sam Shepard), John Malkovich; *Little Shop of Horrors,* Jennifer Leigh Warren, Leilani Jones

Regional
Goodman, Chicago: *A House Not Meant to Stand* (Tennessee Williams)

Long Wharf, New Haven: *Elegy for a Lady, Some Kind of Love Story* (Arthur Miller)

Arena Stage, Washington, D.C.: *On the Razzle* (Tom Stoppard), American premiere

Trinity Square Repertory, Providence: *The Hothouse* (Harold Pinter), George Martin

Pulitzer Prize
A Soldier's Play, Charles Fuller

Tony Awards
The Life and Adventures of Nicholas Nickleby, David Edgar (play); *Nine,* Maury Yeston (musical)

Classical Music ————————————

Compositions
Ellen Zwilich, *Three Movements for Orchestra*
Steve Reich, *Vermont Counterpoint*
Henry Brant, *Meteor Farm*
Joseph Schwantner, *Daybreak of Freedom*
Gian Carlo Menotti, *Notturno*
John Cage, *Postcard from Heaven*
Frederic Rzewski, *Antigone-legend*

Important Events
Major birthday celebrations include John Cage's 70th and
Stravinsky's 100th. Stravinsky festivities include a
worldwide, televised National Symphony concert
conducted by Leonard Bernstein and Michael Tilson
Thomas; at the Whitney, in New York, the complete
L'Histoire is performed with Aaron Copland, Roger
Sessions, and Virgil Thomson performing the spoken
parts.
"Minimalists," experimenting with confrontational
performing styles, play Reich, Glass, Rzewski, Monk, La
Barbara.
His hand crippled in 1965, Leon Fleischer plays Franck's
Symphonic Variations with the Baltimore Orchestra at the
new $22 million Meyerhoff Hall.
Zubin Mehta's 20th-century focus includes six Schoenberg
pieces and an all-Lutoslawski program.

Debuts: Barry Douglas, Dimitris Sgouros, Midori

First Performances
At the New World Festival of the Arts, Miami: Morton
Gould, Suite for Cello, Lukas Foss, *Solo Observed*;
Thomas Ludwig, Symphony no. 1 (Washington); Alvin
Curran, *Maritime Rites* (Chicago); Alvin Lucier, *Crossings*
(Chicago); Steve Reich, *Tehillim* (orchestral version) (New
York)

E.T. earns a record $235 million within three months; "I wanted
a creature only a mother could love," says director Steven
Spielberg. *Movie Star News.*

Opera
Metropolitan: Placido Domingo, Tatiana Troyanos, Ruth
Welting, *Tales of Hoffmann*; Kiri Te Kanawa, Donald
Gramm, *Così fan Tutte*; Marilyn Horne, Pablo Elvira, *Il
barbiere di Siviglia*; Joan Sutherland, Alfredo Kraus,
Lucia di Lammermoor; Luciano Pavarotti, Hildegard
Behrens, Eleana Cotrubas, *Idomeneo*; Simon Estes,
Leonie Rysanek, *Tannhaüser*, Sherrill Milnes, Renata
Scotto, *Macbeth* (Peter Hall production, booed by
audience)

New York City: *Candide; Die Feen* (Wagner); Gianna
Rolandi, *The Cunning Little Vixen* (Janáček, designs by
Maurice Sendak)

Santa Fe: *The Confidence Man* (George Rochberg)

San Francisco: Anja Silja, *Lady Macbeth*; Luciano
Pavarotti, *Aïda; The Triumph of Honor* (Scarlatti)

Boston: *Die Soldaten* (Bernd Alois Zimmerman),
American premiere

Houston: Elisabeth Söderström, *Kátya Kabanova*;
Horne, *La Donna del lago* (Rossini)

Music Notes
The Berlin Philharmonic visits the U.S. with a six-
program series in New York and Pasadena; the Kansas
City Philharmonic disbands and becomes the smaller
Kansas City Symphony • Filene Center at Wolf Trap Park
burns down • Grace Bumbry and Shirley Verrett perform in
a joint recital at Carnegie Hall to honor the 80th birthday
of Marian Anderson • Eugene Ormandy leaves the
Philadelphia with a parting *Zarathustra.*

Nam June Paik, *V-yramid.* 1982. 40 televisions. 180¾ × 85 × 74
inches. *Collection of Whitney Museum of American Art, New
York. Purchase, with funds from the Lemberg Foundation in
honor of Samuel Lemberg.*

Art

Painting
Frank Stella, *Thruxton*
Jasper Johns, *Perilous Night*
Alex Katz, *Yellow House*
Jim Dine, *The Apocalypse*
Robert Rauschenberg, *Kabal American Zephyr Series*
Mark Tansey, *Robbe-Grillet Cleansing Every Object in Sight*
Barbara Kruger, *Untitled (You Invest in the Divinity of the Masterpiece)*
Elizabeth Murray, *Fire Cup*
Robert Motherwell, *The Dedalus Sketchbooks*

Sculpture
Louise Bourgeois, *Femme Couteau*
James Croak, *Pegasus: Some Loves Hurt More than Others*
Jackie Winsor, *Burnt Paper Piece*

William Tucker, *The Promise*

Architecture
IBM headquarters, New York City (Edward Larrabee Barnes)
Trump Tower, New York City (Der Scutt & Swanke, Hayden, Connell)
Schulman House addition, Princeton, N.J. (Michael Graves)
Hartford Seminary, Hartford, Connecticut (Richard Meier)
Peoria Civic Center, Peoria, Illinois (Philip Johnson, John Burgee)
Humana Building, Louisville (Michael Graves)
Bank of South West Tower, Houston (Helmut Jahn)
Cohn Pool House, Llewelyn Park, N.J. (Robert A.M. Stern)

Important Exhibitions
Works from the Vatican Collection, "France in the Golden Age—17th-Century Painting," and "Dutch Painting from the Mauritshuis" travel across the country. Loan exhibits become less frequent because of the increasing costs of shipping and insurance. Replacing them are shows of a single artist or a family's collection, such as "The Collection of Lessing J. Rosenwald," which begins at the National, or "The Russian Avant-garde," the collection of George Costakis, which appears at the Guggenheim and in Boston and Houston.

Museums
New York: *Metropolitan:* The $18-million Michael C. Rockefeller Wing of 2,000 primitive works from Africa, the Pacific Islands, and the Americas opens; "Art of Chivalry"; Art of Central Asia—6th–10th Centuries; Rodin's "Gates of Hell" portal. *Museum of Modern Art:* de Chirico retrospective; Jonathan Borofsky; Louise Bourgeois. *Guggenheim:* Kandinsky in Munich

Los Angeles, Washington: U.S. Portraits, 1720–1920

Washington: Claude Lorrain retrospective; David Smith

Julian Schnabel, *Hope*. 1982. Oil on velvet. 110 × 158 inches. *Collection of Whitney Museum of American Art, New York. Purchase.*

Philadelphia, Boston: Eakins

Seattle: Asian Art from the Idemitsu Collection

Minneapolis, Washington: "De Stijl: Visions of Utopia"

Art Briefs
Daniel Terra, of the Terra Museum of American Art in Evanston, Illinois, buys from Syracuse University, for $3.25 million, "The Gallery of the Louvre" by Samuel F.B. Morse, the telegraph inventor; commissioned by James Fenimore Cooper, it is a series of masterworks in miniature • The Salvador Dali Museum opens in St. Petersburg, Florida • The J. Paul Getty Museum becomes the richest in the world with $1 billion from its founder • Postmodernist Robert Venturi lectures on "Relevance in Historicism" at Harvard • Henry Moore's elmwood "Reclining Figure" brings a record price for a living sculptor: $1,265,000 • Richard Haas covers bare walls throughout the U.S. with trompe l'oeil murals.

Dance

Premieres/Important Productions
New York City Ballet: Nine-day Stravinsky Celebration, including Nina Fedorova, Adam Lüders, *Noah and the Flood* (Balanchine-Jacques d'Amboise); Mel Tomlinson, Maria Calegari, *Création du Monde* (Joseph Duell, Milhaud); *The Magic Flute* (on PBS)

Joffrey: *Fire* (Laura Dean, designs and decor by Michael Graves); the company acquires a second home, in Los Angeles

Chicago City: Suzanne Farrell, Lüders, *Cinderella* (Paul Mejia)

Merce Cunningham: *Trails; Gallopade*

Paul Taylor: *Mercuric Tidings; Lost, Found and Lost*

Books

Fiction
Critics' Choice

The Dean's December, Saul Bellow

A Mother and Two Daughters, Gail Godwin

Dinner at the Homesick Restaurant, Anne Tyler

Oh What a Paradise It Seems, John Cheever (posthumous)

Bech Is Back, John Updike

The Names, Don DeLillo

Shiloh and Other Stories, Bobbie Ann Mason

A Midnight Clear, William Wharton

The Mosquito Coast, Paul Theroux

❧ *Chronicle of a Death Foretold*, Gabriel García Márquez

Best-Sellers

E.T. The Extra-Terrestrial Storybook, William Kotzwinkle

Space, James A. Michener

The Parsifal Mosaic, Robert Ludlum

Master of the Game, Sidney Sheldon

Mistral's Daughter, Judith Krantz

The Valley of Horses, Jean M. Auel

Different Seasons, Stephen King

North and South, John Jakes

2010: Odyssey Two, Arthur C. Clarke

The Man from St. Petersburg, Ken Follett

Nonfiction
Critics' Choice

The Journals of Sylvia Plath, ed. Ted Hughes and Frances McCullough

Years of Upheaval, Henry Kissinger

Edie: An American Biography, ed. Jean Stein, George Plimpton

The Fate of the Earth, Jonathan Schell

China: Alive in the Bitter Sea, Fox Butterfield

Voices of Protest: Huey Long, Father Coughlin and the Great Depression, Alan Brinkley

The Vineyard of Liberty, James MacGregor Burns

"Subtle Is the Lord . . ."—The Science and Life of Albert Einstein, Abraham Pais

The Path to Power: The Years of Lyndon Johnson, Robert Caro

Slavery and Freedom, Willie Lee Rose

On Deconstruction: Theory and Criticism after Structuralism, Jonathan Culler

Best-Sellers

Jane Fonda's Workout Book, Jane Fonda

Living, Loving and Learning, Leo Buscaglia

And More by Andy Rooney, Andrew A. Rooney

Better Homes and Gardens New Cookbook

Life Extension: Adding Years to Your Life and Life to Your Years, Durk Pearson, Sandy Shaw

When Bad Things Happen to Good People, Harold S. Kushner

A Few Minutes with Andy Rooney, Andrew A. Rooney

The Weight Watchers Food Plan Diet Cookbook, Jean Nidetch

Richard Simmons' Never-Say-Diet Cookbook, Richard Simmons

No Bad Dogs: The Woodhouse Way, Barbara Woodhouse

Poetry

Robert Creeley, *The Collected Poems of Robert Creeley*

Charles Wright, *Country Music*

Maxine Kumin, *Our Ground Time Here Will Be Brief*

Brad Leithauser, *Hundreds of Fireflies*

Pulitzer Prizes

The Color Purple, Alice Walker (fiction)

The Transformation of Virginia 1740–1790, Rhys L. Isaac (U.S. history)

Is There No Place on Earth for Me? Susan Sheehan (nonfiction)

Growing Up, Russell Baker (biography)

Selected Poems, Galway Kinnell (poetry)

Science and Technology

Homosexuals, blood product users (such as hemophiliacs), and Haitian immigrants are identified as major AIDS sufferers.

Research indicates that giving aspirin to children with common viruses can lead to Reyes' syndrome, a serious neurological disorder.

A theory that cancer may be caused by a single gene mutation is developed.

The FDA approves streptokinase, a clot-dissolving enzyme that can stop heart attacks in progress.

Fluorescent light is used to treat recurrent winter depression known as seasonal affective disorder (SAD).

Genital herpes reaches epidemic proportions: 400,000 new cases and 20 million total victims.

Decreased neurotransmitter binding sites and serotonin in the brain are found in suicides.

Space shuttle Columbia successfully launches two communications satellites.

Astronomers propose a new inflationary universe model: the universe is 10^{60} times larger in volume than assumed.

Nobel Prize

Kenneth G. Wilson wins in physics for work in second-order phase transitions.

Sports

Baseball

Rickey Henderson (Oakland, AL) steals 130 bases, breaking Lou Brock's record of 118.

Pete Rose (Philadelphia, NL) passes Henry Aaron and becomes second only to Ty Cobb in hits.

The Cy Young awards go to Steve Carlton (Philadelphia, NL) and Pete Vuckovich (Milwaukee, AL).

Champions

Batting
  Al Oliver (Montreal, NL), .331
  Willie Wilson (Kansas City, AL), .332
Pitching
  Phil Niekro (Atlanta, NL), 17–4

Jim Palmer (Baltimore, AL), 15–5
Home runs
  Reggie Jackson (California, AL), 39
  Gorman Thomas (Milwaukee, AL), 39

Football

A strike cuts the regular season to nine games; "a matter of dignity," says union leader Gene Upshaw.

NFL Season Leaders: Joe Theismann (Washington), passing; Tony Dorsett (Dallas), rushing; Dwight Clark (San Francisco), receiving

AFL Season Leaders: Ken Anderson (Cincinnati), passing; Freeman McNeil (New York Jets), rushing; Kellen Winslow (San Diego), receiving

College All-Americans: John Elway (Q), Stanford; Eric Dickerson (B), Southern Methodist; Todd Blackledge (Q), Penn State; Curt Warner (B), Penn State; Jim Kelly (Q), Miami

Bowls (Jan. 1, 1983)

Rose: UCLA 24–Michigan 14
Orange: Nebraska 21–LSU 20
Cotton: SMU 7–Pittsburgh 3
Sugar: Penn State 27–Georgia 23

Basketball

Pat Riley replaces Paul Westhead as Laker coach after Magic Johnson complains about Westhead's slow style.

NBA All-Pro First Team: Julius Erving (Philadelphia), Larry Bird (Boston), Moses Malone (Houston), Gus Williams (Seattle), George Gervin (San Antonio)

Other Sports

Boxing: Larry Holmes TKO's "great white hope" Gerry Cooney in 13; the overall gate is a record $40 million.

Brooke Shields's face and physique are famous from her jeans ads and numerous magazine covers; she now attends her home state's Princeton University. *Movie Star News.*

Golf: Tom Watson wins the U.S. Open with an "impossible" chip shot on the 17th hole; he is PGA Player of the Year for the fifth time in six years.

Hockey: Wayne Gretzky (Edmonton) scores 92 goals, breaking Phil Esposito's record of 76, and a record 212 points.

Winners

World Series
  St. Louis (NL) 4
  Milwaukee (AL) 3
MVP
  NL–Dale Murphy, Atlanta
  AL–Robin Yount, Milwaukee
Super Bowl XVII (Jan. 1983)
  Washington 27–Miami 17
MVP
  Dan Fouts, San Diego
College Football
  Penn State
Heisman Trophy
  Herschel Walker, Georgia
NBA Championship
  Los Angeles 4–Philadelphia 2

MVP
  Moses Malone, Houston
College Basketball
  North Carolina
Player of the Year
  Ralph Sampson, Virginia
Stanley Cup
  New York Islanders
US Tennis Open
  Men: Jimmy Connors
  Women: Martina Navratilova
USGA Open
  Tom Watson
Kentucky Derby
  Gato del Sol (E. De la Houssaye, jockey)

Fashion

For men: A sense of nostalgia, stimulated by the film *Chariots of Fire* and TV's *Brideshead Revisited,* influences style: the "Duke of Windsor look," with pin and wing collar shirts of plain oxford cloth or finely striped broadcloths, ties (in the Windsor knot) in foulard prints, thin stripes, Challis, or dark silk, and argyle or cable sweaters, worn with navy blue or gray pants. The business suit becomes less formal; most popular are the pinstripes and glen plaids; double-breasted jackets and double-pleated pants are especially stylish.

For women: The new, slim, unadorned and aristocratic look—"Minimalism"–characterizes the coats, pants, and dresses by the new designers Norma Kamali, Ronaldus Shamask, and Zoran.

Additional high-fashion note: Ralph Lauren's elongated, Norfolk jacket and long and lean button-front shirt

Kaleidoscope ————————

Dustin Hoffman, in *Tootsie*, plays a failing actor who succeeds as a feminist and female soap-opera heroine. *Movie Star News*.

- Two jokes of the year: "If your company is still paying taxes, you haven't read the new tax law"; "The good news is that they've found a cure for herpes. The bad news: it's Tylenol."
- A mysterious disease is reported that kills 40 percent of its victims—AIDS, acquired immune deficiency syndrome.
- The Vietnam Veterans Memorial, in Washington, D.C., designed by Yale student Maya Lin, is dedicated in November; it is inscribed with 57,939 names of American soldiers killed or missing in Vietnam.
- Some of the blockbuster mergers of the year include Gulf-Cities Service, U.S. Steel-Marathon ($6 billion), Allied-Bendix, Coca-Cola–Columbia; 58 were valued at more than $100 billion.
- Dun and Bradstreet reports 20,365 bankruptcies by October, the highest figure (along with unemployment) since the Depression; included were Braniff, F.W. Woolworth, and Revere.
- After an investigation begun by his stepchildren, Claus von Bülow is found guilty of twice attempting to murder his wealthy wife, Sunny, with insulin injections.
- John De Lorean, former GM executive, is arrested for alleged possession of 60 pounds of cocaine, supposedly to save his sports car business.
- Comic film and TV actor John Belushi, 33, dies suddenly in a posh Hollywood hotel; a female companion reveals that he died of drugs.
- Peter Pulitzer, of Palm Beach, wins custody and low alimony after allegations against his wife, Roxanne, include infidelity and sleeping with a trumpet.
- Prince Andrew's adventures with U.S. soft-porn star Koo Stark in the West Indies are closely followed by the press.
- Efforts at library censorship triple in the early 1980s; banned books in New York State include *The Adventures of Huckleberry Finn, The Grapes of Wrath,* and *The Catcher in the Rye.*
- The last all-male college in the Ivy League, Columbia College will accept women, beginning in autumn 1983.
- *Roget's Thesaurus* bans sexist categories: mankind becomes humankind; countryman, country dweller.
- The administration requires clinics on federal funds to notify parents when children under 18 receive oral birth control devices ("squeal rule").
- Congress passes legislation to facilitate the emigration of Amerasian children to the United States.
- A federal court in Arkansas invalidates a new state law mandating equal time in public schools for creation science.
- President Reagan proclaims May 6 "National Day of Prayer" and endorses a constitutional amendment to permit school prayer; it is defeated.
- With black support, reformed segregationist George Wallace is reelected Alabama governor.
- High-tech industries in the Silicon Valley begin layoffs for the first time.
- Photos taken from the space shuttle Columbia reveal that the Sahara was once criss-crossed with major waterways.
- Interior decorating rejects the Bauhaus style and returns to old-world comfort and romanticism, with belle epoque designs.
- Prices for computers plummet; Timex sells a personal computer for $99.95; Commodore VIC 20, $199; computers reach 1.5 million homes, five times the number in 1980.
- The proposed equal rights amendment (ERA) runs out of time; it received 35 of the required 38 state ratifications.
- The longest lunar eclipse since 1736 occurs on July 6; the first sighting of Halley's comet since 1911 also takes place.
- Rev. Sun Myung Moon marries 4,000 "Moonies" at Madison Square Garden; most of the couples were paired by him.
- A 49-room mansion in Glen Cove, New York, called Killenworth, is discovered to be a Soviet spy center; the Russians are forbidden to use local beaches.

Fads: Smurf and E.T. paraphernalia, designer underwear for men, discount air fares, community gardens in urban centers, starch blockers, Valspeak and Valley Girls ("grody to the max"), "lite" foods

First Appearances: IRA, largest one-day Dow drop (39 points), oncogene (isolated and reproduced), *USA Today,* unexpurgated *Red Badge of Courage,* Bradley Fighting Vehicle, Epcot, Accutane (acne drug), commercial product of genetic engineering (insulin), juice in paper bottles (Ocean Spray), compact disc (CD), Eastman Kodak disk camera, Mojave Desert solar plant (10,000 kilowatts), electronic Monopoly, polyurethane car bumpers, diamond branding, Porsche 944, Honda Accord (produced in U.S.), Boeing 757, laser stopwatch with smallest unit of time (femto, $1/10^{60}$ sec., Bell Labs), cabinet-level official held in contempt of Congress (Anne Gorsuch, EPA), CMA, largest cash robbery ($9.8 million, Brink's, New York), convicted murderer executed by lethal injection (Charlie Brooks, Texas), "Love" stamp, Paul Newman products, Jane Fonda aerobics video, stuffed croissants, NCAA major college basketball championship for women

1983

Facts and Figures

Economic Profile
- Dow-Jones: ↑ High 1,287–Low 1,027
- GNP: +7.6%
- Inflation: +3.2%
- Unemployment: 9.6%

Daily newspapers: 1,701
Books published: 53,380
First-class postage: 20¢
Postcard: 13¢
IRS total collections: $627.2 billion
PeoplExpress
- Washington, D.C.–Dallas, Baltimore, New York: $23
- Washington, D.C.–London: $172 (coach)

Calvin Klein men's hip briefs (teal, butter): $7.50
Ralph Lauren tank swim suit, nylon, lycra: $36
John Henry jeans: $30
Puma Guillermo Vilas tennis shoes: $41.99
Radio Shack CB with priority switch: $119.95
portable pocket computer: $119.95
Panasonic answering machine: $239.99
Sony Walkman D-6 (with Dolby): $229.99
WM-10: $78.88
RCA VCR-VHS: $399.99–$888.88
Sony Betamax: $439.99

Deaths

George Balanchine, Eubie Blake, Buster Crabbe, Jack Dempsey, Buckminister Fuller, Arthur Godfrey, Arthur Koestler, David Niven, Gloria Swanson, Tennessee Williams

In the News

RECORD $189 BILLION DEFICIT IS PROJECTED . . . KLAUS BARBIE, GESTAPO "BUTCHER OF LYONS," IS EXTRADITED FROM BOLIVIA TO FRANCE . . . ISRAELI MINISTER ARIEL SHARON RESIGNS, ACCUSED OF "INDIRECT RESPONSIBILITY" IN REFUGEE CAMP MASSACRE . . . PRESIDENT ASKS INCREASED MILITARY AID TO EL SALVADOR . . . REAGAN URGES HIGH-TECH ANTIBALLISTIC MISSILE RESEARCH . . . SCOWCROFT COMMISSION RECOMMENDS SINGLE WARHEAD MOBILE ICBM AND MX IN EXISTING SILOS . . . TERRORISTS BOMB U.S. EMBASSY IN BEIRUT, OVER 100 DIE . . . DOW EXCEEDS 1,200 FOR THE FIRST TIME . . . INDUSTRIAL PRODUCTION RISES 2.1% IN ONE MONTH, HIGHEST IN 8 YEARS . . . NATO MINISTERS AFFIRM DECISION TO DEPLOY INF . . . MARGARET THATCHER WINS LARGE VICTORY, LABOR PARTY FALLS TO POSTWAR LOW . . . POPE'S ASSAILANT, AGCA, CLAIMS KGB AND BULGARIAN SUPPORT . . . CONGRESS APPROVES MX FUNDING . . . HOUSE VOTES 228–195 TO BAR COVERT CONTRA AID . . . OPPOSITION LEADER BENIGNO AQUINO IS ASSASSINATED AT MANILA AIRPORT ON RETURN FROM EXILE IN U.S. . . . KOREAN AIR LINES 007 IS SHOT DOWN BY SOVIET MISSILE IN RUSSIAN AIRSPACE, 279 ARE KILLED . . . TERRORIST TRUCK BOMB HITS MARINE HEADQUARTERS AT BEIRUT AIRPORT, 239 MARINES ARE KILLED . . . 2 MILLION IN WESTERN EUROPE DEMONSTRATE AGAINST U.S. MISSILE DEPLOYMENT . . . U.S. AND CARIBBEAN TROOPS INVADE GRENADA "TO FORESTALL CUBAN TAKEOVER" . . . CIVILIAN RAUL ALFONSIN WINS ARGENTINE ELECTION . . . SOVIETS LEAVE GENEVA TO PROTEST INF DEPLOYMENT . . . SYRIA SHOOTS DOWN U.S. PLANE, PILOT IS CAPTURED . . . ARAFAT AND 4,000 PLO ARE EVACUATED TO TUNISIA.

Quotes _____

"The United States can overkill every Russian person 40 times. The Soviet Union can overkill every American person 20 times. To talk about negotiating from a position of strength . . . is obscene."
— Dr. Helen Caldicott, anti-nuclear activist

"Living with nuclear weapons is our only hope. It requires that we can persevere in reducing the likelihood of war, even though we cannot remove the possibility altogether."
— Harvard Nuclear Study Group

"The educational foundations of our society are presently being eroded by a rising tide of mediocrity that threatens our very future as a nation and a people."
— *A Nation at Risk*

"[The USSR] is a focus of evil in the modern world."
— Ronald Reagan

"We do not want a Central American country to go communist on our watch."
— James Baker, White House Chief of Staff, on Nicaragua

"The American people know that we have been down this road before and that it only leads to a dark tunnel of endless intervention."
— Sen. Christopher Dodd (D-Conn.)

"If they've been put there to fight, then there are far too few. If they've been put there to be killed, there are far too many."
— Sen. Ernest Hollings (D-S.C.),
after the Marine bombing in Beirut

"We tried to provide more for the poor and produced more poor instead."
— Charles Murray

All-American entrepreneur Lee Iacocca, who led the resurgence of the U.S. auto industry; his Chrysler Corporation went from "bailout" indignity to high profitability. *Courtesy: Chrysler Corporation.*

"It didn't upset my breakfast at all."
— Ronald Reagan, on UN disapproval of Grenada invasion

"We've had considerable information that people go to soup kitchens because the food is free. . . . That's easier than paying for it."
— Ed Meese, on the matter of hungry children

"We all felt the majesty of the body . . . [and] were reverent. . . . As we saw the artificial heart beat in Dr. Clark, the feeling was not, aren't we great, but aren't we small."
— Dr. William C. DeVries, surgeon

"I heard from my cat's lawyer today. My cat wants $12,000 a week for Tender Vittles."
— Johnny Carson

Ads _____

Handel with care.
(KSJN/91.1 FM)

Announcing life insurance for people who regularly walk a mile. But not for a camel.
(ITT)

Your heart doesn't know what a big shot you are.
(Cardio-Fitness Center, New York City)

Mint Summer Night's Dream.
(Godiva Chocolatier)

Four out of five convicts were abused children.
(San Francisco Child Abuse Inc.)

The joy of six.
(Guinness)

Stands head and antlers above the rest.
(Moosehead Beer)

How to avoid the draft . . .
(Apple Computers)

TV

Premieres

"The A-Team," George Peppard, Mr. T
"Wheel of Fortune," Pat Sajak, Vanna White
"Hardcastle and McCormick," Brian Keith, Daniel Hugh Kelly
"Scarecrow and Mrs. King," Kate Jackson, Bruce Boxleitner
"Hotel," James Brolin, Connie Selleca, Bette Davis
"Night Court," Harry Anderson, John Larroquette
"Webster," Alex Karras, Susan Clark, Emmanuel Lewis

Top Ten (Nielsen)

"60 Minutes," "Dallas," M*A*S*H"/"Magnum, P.I.,"
"Dynasty," "Three's Company," "Simon & Simon,"
"Archie Bunker's Place," "Newhart," "Falcon Crest"

Specials

"The Life and Adventures of Nicholas Nickleby";
"Vietnam: A Televised History"; "The Thorn Birds"
(Richard Chamberlain, Rachel Ward); "The Day After"
(Jason Robards, JoBeth Williams); "The Winds of War"
(Robert Mitchum); "Adam" (Daniel J. Travanti); "The
Ring" (videotaped at Bayreuth, Patrice Chereau-Pierre
Boulez Production)

Emmy Awards

"Hill Street Blues" (drama); "Cheers" (comedy);
Laurence Olivier (actor, limited series, "King Lear"); "A

"Dynasty," one of several fictionalized "Lifestyles of the Rich and Famous," becomes a prime-time Nielsen triumph. *Movie Star News.*

Walk Through the 20th Century with Bill Moyers"
(informational); Tom Selleck (actor, "Magnum, P.I.");
John Ritter (comedic actor, "Three's Company"); Tyne
Daly (actress, "Cagney & Lacey"); Jane Curtin (comedic
actress, "Kate and Allie")

Of Note

Over 100 million watch "The Day After," a made-for-TV
film about an all-out nuclear attack in Lawrence, Kansas •
The largest TV audience of the year watches the last
episode (251st) of "M*A*S*H," begun during the
Vietnam War (1972), and the first black-comedy sitcom •
Newly appointed solo news anchors are Tom Brokaw and
Peter Jennings • Joan Rivers signs as permanent guest host
for "The Tonight Show" • Controversy increases over
cable programming with obscenity and graphic sexuality.

Movies

Openings

Terms of Endearment (James L. Brooks), Shirley
MacLaine, Debra Winger, Jack Nicholson
Tender Mercies (Bruce Beresford), Robert Duvall
The Right Stuff (Philip Kaufman), Sam Shepard, Dennis
Quaid
The Big Chill (Lawrence Kasdan), Tom Berenger, Glenn
Close, William Hurt, Kevin Kline, JoBeth Williams,
Jeff Goldblum
Silkwood (Mike Nichols), Meryl Streep, Kurt Russell,
Cher
Zelig (Woody Allen), Woody Allen, Mia Farrow
Return of the Jedi (Richard Marquand), Mark Hamill,
Harrison Ford, Carrie Fisher
Fanny and Alexander (Ingmar Bergman), Bertil Guve,
Pernilla Allwin
Berlin Alexanderplatz (Rainer Werner Fassbinder), Gunter
Lamprecht, Hanna Schygulla
Flashdance (Adrian Lyne), Jennifer Beals

Mr. Mom (Stan Dragoti), Michael Keaton
The Return of Martin Guerre (Daniel Vigne), Gérard
Depardieu
The Year of Living Dangerously (Peter Weir), Mel Gibson,
Sigourney Weaver
Yentl (Barbra Streisand), Barbra Streisand, Mandy
Patinkin
Sudden Impact (Clint Eastwood), Clint Eastwood
Educating Rita (Lewis Gilbert), Michael Caine, Julie
Walters
War Games (John Badham), Matthew Broderick
The Dresser (Peter Yates), Albert Finney, Tom Courtenay

Academy Awards

Best Picture: *Terms of Endearment*
Best Director: James L. Brooks (*Terms of Endearment*)
Best Actress: Shirley MacLaine (*Terms of Endearment*)
Best Actor: Robert Duvall (*Tender Mercies*)

Both Jack Nicholson and Shirley MacLaine win Oscars for *Terms of Endearment*. *Movie Star News.*

The Hollywood newcomers in *The Big Chill* portray the reunion of prospering college friends who nostalgically rethink their 1960's idealism. *Movie Star News.*

Movies (cont.)

Top Box-Office Stars

Clint Eastwood, Eddie Murphy, Sylvester Stallone, Burt Reynolds, John Travolta, Dustin Hoffman, Harrison Ford, Richard Gere, Chevy Chase, Tom Cruise

Stars of the Future

Tom Berenger, Kurt Russell, Matthew Modine, Jeff Goldblum, Patrick Swayze, Rob Lowe, Esai Morales, Ralph Macchio, Emilio Estevez, Meg Tilly

Popular Music ─────────────

Hit Songs

"Down Under"
"Billie Jean"
"Every Breath You Take"
"Maniac"
"Total Eclipse of the Heart"
"Say, Say, Say"
"Islands in the Stream"

Top Records

Albums: *Business as Usual* (Men at Work); *Synchronicity* (The Police); *Metal Health* (Quiet Riot); *Flashdance* (soundtrack); *1999* (Prince); *Can't Slow Down* (Lionel Richie); *Pyromania* (Def Leppard)

Singles: *Africa* (Toto); *All Night Long* (Lionel Richie); *Come On Eileen* (Dexys Midnight Runners); *Let's Dance* (David Bowie); *Sweet Dreams* (Eurythmics); *Tell Her About It* (Billy Joel). Country: *Can't Even Get the Blues* (Reba McEntire); *Going Where the Lonely Go* (Merle Haggard)

Grammy Awards

Beat It, Michael Jackson (record); *Thriller,* Michael Jackson (album); "Every Breath You Take" (song)

Jazz and Big Bands

Electronic and eclectic sounds dominate. Young stars include Kevin Eubanks, James Newton, Chico Freeman, Hamiet Bluiett, Paquito D'Rivera, Anthony Davis, and the enormously popular Wynton and Branford Marsalis (trumpet, saxophone).

Top Performers (*Downbeat*):

Wynton Marsalis (soloist); Count Basie (band); Art Blakey's Jazz Messengers (acoustic jazz group); Weather Report (electric jazz group); James Newton, Ron Carter, Pat Metheny, Gerry Mulligan, Jimmy Smith (instrumentalists); Sarah Vaughan, Al Jarreau (vocalists); Manhattan Transfer (vocal group); Miles Davis, *Star* (album)

Theater ─────────────

Broadway Openings

Plays

Brighton Beach Memoirs (Neil Simon), Matthew Broderick

'night, Mother (Marsha Norman), Anne Pitoniak, Kathy Bates
Plenty (David Hare), Kate Nelligan, Edward Herrmann
Angels Fall (Lanford Wilson), Fritz Weaver, Barnard Hughes

Theater (cont.)

Passion (Peter Nichols), Frank Langella
Noises Off (Michael Frayn), Dorothy Loudon

Musicals
My One and Only (George and Ira Gershwin), Tommy
    Tune, Twiggy
La Cage aux Folles (Jerry Herman), George Hearn, Gene
    Barry
The Tap Dance Kid (Robert Lorick, Henry Krieger),
    Hinton Battle, Alfonso Ribeiro
La Tragédie de Carmen (adapted by Peter Brook),
    alternating cast

Classics, Revivals, and Off-Broadway Premieres
A View from the Bridge, Tony Lo Bianco; *On Your Toes*,
Natalia Makarova; *You Can't Take It With You*, Colleen
Dewhurst, Jason Robards; *The Caine Mutiny Court-
Martial*, Michael Moriarty, Philip Bosco; *Private Lives*,
Elizabeth Taylor, Richard Burton (each earning $70,000 a
week); *Quartermaine's Terms* (Simon Gray), Remak
Ramsey; *Zorba*, Anthony Quinn

Pulitzer Prize
'night, Mother, Marsha Norman

Tony Awards
Torch Song Trilogy, Harvey Fierstein (play); *Cats*, T. S.
Eliot, Andrew Lloyd Webber (musical)

Classical Music

Compositions
Bernard Rands, *Canti del Sole*
Ezra Laderman, Symphony no. 6
George Rochberg, Oboe Concerto
Pauline Oliveros, *The Wheel of Time*
Jacob Druckman, *Vox Humana*
Donald Erb, *Prismatic Variations*
Nicolas Roussakis, *Fire and Earth and Water and Air*
Lukas Foss, *Percussion Quartet*

Important Events
Mozart's first symphony, in A minor, composed 1764–
1765, is discovered in manuscript form in Denmark.
New York Philharmonic composer-in-residence Jacob
Druckman organizes "Horizons '83: Since 1968, a New
Romanticism," and focuses on Del Tredici, Crumb, and
Harbison.
Acclaimed recitals include those of Alfred Brendel,
Ronald Smith, Maurizio Pollini, Charles Rosen, Emil
Gilels, Salvatore Accardo, and Ivan Moravec.

New Appointments: James Levine (Metropolitan Opera,
1986–87); Sarah Caldwell (Israel); Charles Dutoit
(Minnesota)

Debut: Dmitry Sitkovetsky

First Performances
Joseph Schwantner, *New Morning for the World*
(Washington, D.C.), *Four Poems of Aguenda Pizarro* (St.

Louis); Vivian Fine, *Drama for Orchestra* (San
Francisco); Elliott Carter, *Triple Duo* (New York); Ezra
Pound, *Cavalcanti* (Berkeley); George Antheil, Violin
Sonata no. 1 (Buffalo)

Opera
Metropolitan: gala 100th birthday celebration of 100
artists, October 22. Placido Domingo, Tatiana Troyanos,
Jessye Norman (debut), *Les Troyens*; Kiri Te Kanawa,
Donald Gramm, *Arabella*; Luciano Pavarotti, *Ernani*;
Domingo, Mirella Freni, Nicolai Ghiaurov, *Don Carlo*;
Hildegard Behrens, *Tristan und Isolde*

New York City: *Cendrillon* (sung in French,
accompanied with English subtitles on the proscenium
arch)

Los Angeles: *Anna Karenina* (Iain Hamilton), U.S.
premiere

Minnesota: *A Death in the Family*, U.S. premiere

Waterloo Festival, New Jersey: *Das Liebesverbot*
(Wagner), U.S. premiere, concert performance

San Diego: Sherrill Milnes, *Henry VIII* (Saint-Saëns)

Houston: Theodor Uppman, *Billy Budd*; *A Quiet Place*
(Leonard Bernstein)

Boston: *The Legend of the Invisible City of Kitezh and
the Maiden Fevronia* (Rimsky-Korsakov)

Art

Painting

Jasper Johns, *Ventriloquist; Between the Clock and the Bed*
Willem de Kooning, *Morning; The Springs*
Jennifer Bartlett, *Shadow*
Philip Pearlstein, *Two Models with a Library Ladder*
Jean Michel Basquiat, *Flash in Naples*
Chuck Close, *Self-Portrait*
Frank Stella, *Valle Lunga; Mellieha Boy*
Louisa Chase, *Pink Cave*
James Valerio, *Still Life with Decoy*

Sculpture

Lucas Samaras, *Box #110*
Jim Dine, *The Crommelynck Gate with Tools*
Juan Hamilton, *Curve and Shadow No. 2*
Jon Borofsky, *Molecule Men*
Keith Haring and Kermit Oswald, *Untitled (TOTEM)*

Jenny Holzer, *Unex Sign #1* (performance)
Christo's *Surrounded Islands,* Biscayne Bay, Florida ($3.1 million)

Architecture

AT&T Building, New York City (Philip Johnson, John Burgee)
Portland Museum, Portland, Maine (Harry Cobb)
Point West Place, Framingham, Massachusetts (Robert A. M. Stern)
Dallas Museum, Dallas (Edward Larrabee Barnes)
Museum of Modern Art apartment tower, New York (Cesar Pelli)
Indiana University Art Museum, Bloomington (I. M. Pei)
Best Products headquarters, Richmond, Virginia (Hardy/Hardy/Holzman, Pfeiffer)

Important Exhibitions

New York: *Metropolitan:* Manet; "Impressionism-Postimpressionism"; "Constable's England"; Henry Moore retrospective; Holbein; Design in America: 1925–1950; Stieglitz; Sir Winston Churchill. *Museum of Modern Art:* "The Modern Drawing"; Three New Skyscrapers. *Guggenheim:* Peggy Guggenheim collection; Julio Gonzalez. *Whitney:* De Kooning; Biennial: Louise Bourgeois, Jasper Johns, Joan Mitchell, Frank Stella, and film and video work

Boston, Washington: American Art

Washington: "Manet and Modern Paris"; Raphael, Lorrain; "Leonardo da Vinci: Studies for *The Last Supper*"

Washington, Fort Worth, New Haven: Gainsborough

Minneapolis, Whitney: Grant Wood

Cleveland: Dürer

Art Briefs

Major sales include: Degas, "Waiting" ($3.7 million, record price for an impressionist painting); Goya, "The Marquesa de Santiago" ($4 million); and Mary Cassatt, "Reading *Le Figaro*" ($1.1 million) • As real estate entrepreneurs try to replace the 1953 Lever House, New York, with a 40-floor glass tower, the building gains landmark status.

In his postmodern AT&T building, Philip Johnson combines the decorative Chippendale motif with the stark Corbusier facade. *Courtesy: AT&T.*

Dance

Dance Black America Festival, in Boston, celebrates 300 years of black dance.

Premieres/Important Productions

American Ballet Theatre: Cynthia Gregory, Martine van Hamel, Patrick Bissell, *Symphonie Concertante* (Balanchine); *La Sylphide*; Mikhail Baryshnikov, *Once Upon A Time* (Twyla Tharp); Gelsey Kirkland, *Great Galloping Gottschalk* (Lynne Taylor-Corbett)

New York City Ballet: *Glass Pieces* (Jerome Robbins, Philip Glass); Bolshoi dancers Leonid and Valentina Kozlova join as soloists. Balanchine dies on April 29. Peter Martins and Robbins become artistic directors.

Joffrey: *Love Songs* (William Forsythe)

San Francisco (50th anniversary): History of the Company since *Ballet Mécanique*

Paul Taylor: Suzanne Farrell, Peter Martins, *Musette*

Books

Fiction
Critics' Choice
Cathedral, Raymond Carver
Moon Deluxe, Frederick Barthelme
Disturbances in the Field, Lynne Sharon Schwartz
The Cannibal Galaxy, Cynthia Ozick
Winter's Tale, Mark Helprin
The Anatomy Lesson, Philip Roth
Overnight to Many Distant Cities, Donald Barthelme
The Queen's Gambit, Walter Tevis

Best-Sellers
The Return of the Jedi Storybook, adapted by Joan D. Vinge
Poland, James A. Michener
Pet Sematary, Stephen King
The Little Drummer Girl, John le Carré
Christine, Stephen King
Changes, Danielle Steel
The Name of the Rose, Umberto Eco
White Gold Wielder: Book Three of the Second Chronicles of Thomas Covenant, Stephen R. Donaldson
Hollywood Wives, Jackie Collins
The Lonesome Gods, Louis L'Amour

Nonfiction
Critics' Choice
The Price of Power: Kissinger in the Nixon White House, Seymour M. Hersh
Promethean Fire, Charles J. Lumsden, Edward O. Wilson
Living with Nuclear Weapons, The Harvard Study Group
Revolution in Time, David S. Landes
The Rosenberg File, Ronald Radosh, Joyce Milton
Vietnam: A History, Stanley Karnow
Blue Highways, William Least Heat Moon
Hugging the Shore, John Updike
The Discoverers, Daniel Boorstin
The Spheres of Justice, Michael Walzer
❧ *Modern Times*, Paul Johnson

Best-Sellers
In Search of Excellence, Thomas J. Peters, Robert H. Waterman, Jr.
Megatrends, John Naisbitt
Motherhood, Erma Bombeck
The One Minute Manager, Kenneth Blanchard, Spencer Johnson
Jane Fonda's Workout Book, Jane Fonda
The Best of James Herriot, James Herriot
The Mary Kay Guide to Beauty, Beauty Experts at Mary Kay Cosmetics
On Wings of Eagles, Ken Follett
Creating Wealth, Robert G. Allen

William Kennedy. The author's Pulitzer Prize–winning Depression novel, *Ironweed*, focuses on the noble survival of Albany's indigents. *Bill DeMichele*.

Poetry
Gary Snyder, *Axe Handles*
W. S. Merwin, *Opening the Hand*
Amy Clampitt, *The Kingfisher*
James Merrill, *The Changing Light at Sandover*
Elizabeth Bishop, *The Complete Poems, 1927–1979* (posthumous)

Pulitzer Prizes
Ironweed, William Kennedy (fiction)
The Social Transformation of American Medicine, Paul Starr (nonfiction)
Booker T. Washington, Louis R. Harlan (biography)
American Primitive, Mary Oliver (poetry)

Science and Technology

The shuttle Challenger completes four missions, including the first spacewalk since 1972; Pioneer 10 becomes the first man-made object to leave the solar planetary system.

The Pershing II missile is tested, a single intermediate-range nuclear warhead.

Evidence of the bottom quark is found at Cornell.

Studies of Alzheimer's disease, which affects 2.5 million, focus on neurotransmitter acetylcholine deficiency.

Nonsurgical destruction of kidney stones with sound waves is pioneered.

The use of cyclosporin to deactivate T-lymphocytes is shown to improve transplant success by 30 percent.

Eric Kandel demonstrates structural change as a product of learning in a one-celled animal (alypsia).

A primitive tribe is discovered in Borneo that practices no agriculture and maintains its population by incest.

❧ The predicted intermediate vector bosons (W and Z), subatomic particles, are observed at CERN (European Center for Nuclear Research).

Nobel Prize

Henry Taube wins in chemistry for his work on electron transfer reactions. Subrahmanyan Chandrasekhar and William Fowler win in physics for studying how stars age and collapse. Barbara McClintock wins in physiology or medicine for researching genetic changes in plants.

Sports

Baseball

Nolan Ryan (Houston, NL) breaks Walter Johnson's strikeout record of 3,508, but Steve Carlton overtakes Ryan with 3,709.

Carl Yastrzemski (Boston, AL) retires with over 3,000 hits and 400 home runs.

In Toronto, Dave Winfield is arrested when his throw kills a sea gull.

The Cy Young awards go to John Denny (Philadelphia, NL) and LaMarr Hoyt (Chicago, AL).

Champions

Batting
  Bill Madlock (Pittsburgh, NL), .323
  Wade Boggs (Boston, AL), .361
Pitching
  John Denny (Philadelphia, NL), 19–6
  Rich Dotson (Chicago, AL), 22–7
Home runs
  Mike Schmidt (Philadelphia, NL), 40

Football

The USFL begins with 12 teams in a spring-summer format; Herschel Walker (B) and Jim Kelly (Q) sign multimillion-dollar contracts.

NFL draftees include Dan Marino and John Elway, who signs for a record $5 million for five years.

NFL Season Leaders: Steve Bartkowski (Atlanta), passing; Eric Dickerson (Los Angeles Rams), rushing, 1,808 yards; Roy Green (St. Louis), receiving

AFL Season Leaders: Dan Marino (Miami), passing; Curt Warner (Seattle), rushing; Todd Christensen (Los Angeles Raiders), receiving

College All-Americans: Irv Fryar (B), Nebraska; Bernie Kosar (Q), Miami; Dean Steinkuhler (L), Nebraska

Bowls (Jan. 1, 1984)

Rose: UCLA 45–Illinois 9
Orange: Miami 31–Nebraska 30
Cotton: Georgia 10–Texas 9
Sugar: Auburn 9–Michigan 7

Jennifer Beals, in *Flashdance,* sets a fashion trend—clothing with holes and tears. *Movie Star News.*

Basketball

NCAA champ North Carolina State had 10 regular-season losses.

The NBA contract is the first in sports to include revenue sharing (53 percent) with players.

NBA All-Pro First Team: Julius Erving, Moses Malone (Philadelphia), Larry Bird (Boston), Magic Johnson (Los Angeles Lakers), Sidney Moncrief (Milwaukee)

Other Sports

Boat Racing: Australia II defeats Liberty at Newport, R.I., in the America's Cup and becomes the first non-American boat to win in 132 years.

Hockey: The New York Islanders win their fourth straight Stanley Cup; Wayne Gretzky (Edmonton) wins his fourth straight MVP.

Winners

World Series
  Baltimore (AL) 4
  Philadelphia (NL) 1
MVP
  NL–Dale Murphy, Atlanta
  AL–Cal Ripken, Baltimore
Super Bowl XVIII (Jan. 1984)
  Los Angeles Raiders 38–
  Washington 9
MVP
  Joe Theismann, Washington
College Football
  Miami
Heisman Trophy
  Mike Rozier, Nebraska
NBA Championship
  Philadelphia 4–Los Angeles 0

MVP
  Moses Malone, Philadelphia
College Basketball
  North Carolina State
Player of the Year
  Ralph Sampson, Virginia
Stanley Cup
  New York Islanders
US Tennis Open
  Men: Jimmy Connors
  Women: Martina Navratilova
USGA Open
  Larry Nelson
Kentucky Derby
  Sunny's Halo (E. De la Houssaye, jockey)

Fashion

Sweaters of all lengths and styles return to high fashion and are decorated in every pattern or with beads and glitter; pants are well tailored. Japanese designs influence U.S. fashion in a less traditional direction, especially the designs of Issey Miyake, Rei Kawakubo, and Yohji Yamamoto: layered, oversized dresses that are knotted or tied at the waist or hip and that have uneven hems and even tears or holes in the fabric (an accompaniment to the popular *Flashdance*). The chemise also returns—with dolman sleeves or low V-back necklines.

High-fashion notes: Mariuccia Mandelli's pullovers with bird or polar bear designs; Perry Ellis's high-waisted pants with tapered ankles.

Kaleidoscope _____

- Several negative reports on U.S. public education appear: all observe the absence of bright students in the pursuit of teaching.
- In the Baby Jane Doe case at Stony Brook Hospital (New York), the Reagan Administration applies civil-rights laws to force active medical treatment of a severely, congenitally ill child.
- AIDS cases total 2,678, with 1,102 deaths since the disease's first appearance in 1978; it has been diagnosed in 33 countries.
- After four years, the auto industry reverses its losses: the Big Four earn $4.1 billion through September, the same amount lost in 1980.
- In New York City, there are 84,043 reported robberies and 7,351 convictions, 26,808 felonious assaults and 771 convictions; over 90 percent of the convictions are plea bargains.
- Per capita personal income in New York is $12,314; in Washington, D.C., $14,550; Alaska, $16,257; Alabama, $8,649; and Mississippi, $7,778.
- Martin Luther King, Jr., is the first person since George Washington whose birthday is declared a national holiday.
- Secretary of Interior James Watt resigns under criticism for depicting one of his commissions as "a black, a woman, two Jews, and a cripple."
- The Supreme Court reaffirms its 1973 (Roe v. Wade) decision for a woman's constitutional right to abortion.
- Several lawsuits raise the question of a "lover's right" to be told of herpes; three wives have sued their husbands.
- Auto accident fatalities drop to 43,028, the lowest figure in 20 years; seat-belt and anti–drunk driver campaigns are credited.
- Worldwide attention is paid to the publication of Hitler's diaries by *Time* magazine and the West German *Der Stern*; the material is later discovered to be a forgery.
- Reports indicate that Klaus Barbie was employed as a U.S. Army spy after World War II.
- A California court grants a divorcing couple joint custody of a dog, ruling that the dog is a child substitute to be shared on a monthly basis.
- Advertisers cater to "the thin look": the White Rock girl in 1874 was estimated at 5'4", 140 pounds; she is now 5'8" and 118 pounds; Campbell's soup kids and Aunt Jemima are also reduced.
- Top fashion designers such as Calvin Klein, Anne Klein, and John Anthony plan to market their "look" at lower prices; Halston signs with J.C. Penney to design clothes for $22 to $200.
- Magazines with the highest circulation are *Reader's Digest, TV Guide, National Geographic, Modern Maturity, Better Homes and Gardens,* and *AARP News Bulletin.*
- Average tuition in four-year private colleges is $7,475;

Mikhail Baryshnikov. A former Kirov star, the luminous dancer, administrator, and personality stimulates public interest in dance. *Move Star News.*

ranges include Yale, $9,050; Harvard, $8,195; University of Montana, $755; University of Alabama, $600.
- On September 29, *A Chorus Line* becomes the longest-running show in Broadway history, 3,389 performances.
- Two major antitrust actions begun in the 1970s are concluded: IBM is exonerated, whereas AT&T is forced to divest its Bell Systems.
- Psychologists report increased marital stress due to computer preoccupation, creating "computer widows" or "widowers."
- In the national spelling bee, the spelldown consists of ratatouille and Purim.
- The Supreme Court rules against tax deductions for racially biased private schools and colleges (Bob Jones University); the Court also upholds a Florida law denying high school diplomas to students who fail a literacy test.
- MTV, received in 17.5 million homes, revives the record industry; top videos include "Beat It" (Michael Jackson), "Be Good Johnny" (Men at Work), "She Works Hard for It" (Donna Summer), and "Sexy 17" (Stray Cats).
- Barney Clark, the first artificial heart recipient, dies after 112 days.

Fads: CD players, no-frills flying (PeoplExpress, Newark–London: $149), Menudo jeans and T-shirts, no-caffeine sodas (Coca-Cola, Pepsi), data banks, "networking," suspenders, men's color shirts with white collars, wine coolers, expensive cooking items (olive oil, goat cheese, designer ice creams, shiitake mushrooms), flavored popcorn (grape), Ray-Ban and Vuarnet sunglasses, break dancing, electroboogie, Cabbage Patch dolls (with birth certificate and adoption papers)

New Words and Usages: evil empire, Star Wars (SDI), yuppie, nuclear winter

First Appearances: vaginal contraceptive sponge, dial-a-porn, TV watch (Seiko, 1.2"), large ceiling TV screen (Kloss Video, 5'), Disneyland outside U.S. (Tokyo), fingerprinting infants (for kidnap solving), *Vanity Fair* (revived after 47 years), California condor hatched in captivity (San Diego Zoo), woman governor of Kentucky (Martha Layne Collins), black mayor of Chicago (Harold Washington) and Philadelphia (Wilson Goode), woman in space (Sally Ride), black in space (Guion Bluford, Jr.), worst AAA muni-bond default (WPPSS, nuclear power, $2.5 billion), female Secretary of Transportation (Elizabeth Dole)

1984

Facts and Figures

Economic Profile
- Dow-Jones:—High 1,287–Low 1,286
- GNP: +10.8%
- Inflation: +4.3%
- Unemployment: 7.5%

Expenditures
- Recreation: $168.3 billion
- Spectator sports: $2.9 billion
- European travel: $5.1 billion
- Golf courses: 12,278
- Chivas Regal Royal Paisley scotch, 750 ml: $11
- Carlyle Hotel, N.Y., Sunday brunch: $22.75
- Paddington bear, musical, 12″: $24; 48″: $150
- Merona long-sleeve knit shirt: $45–$48
  - cotton, short sleeve: $32.50–$50
  - suede pants: $265
  - suede rugby shirts: $295
- ilias LALAoUNIS: 18k, 22k, gold neolithic beads: $6,850–$9,700
- Rolex 14k gold octagon watch: $1,950
- Orrefors, classic 1934 bowl: $390

Deaths

Ansel Adams, Count Basie, Richard Burton, Truman Capote, Michel Foucault, George Gallup, Lillian Hellman, Ethel Merman, Jan Peerce, William Powell, Karen Ann Quinlan

In the News

JESSE JACKSON GAINS RELEASE OF NAVY PILOT FROM SYRIA . . . CHINESE PREMIER ZHAO ZIYANG SIGNS ECONOMIC ACCORDS AT WHITE HOUSE . . . $180 BILLION DEFICIT IS PROJECTED . . . REAGAN ORDERS MARINES OFFSHORE IN LEBANON . . . ANDROPOV, 69, DIES, KONSTANTIN CHERNENKO, 72, BECOMES GENERAL SECRETARY . . . CHALLENGER ASTRONAUTS MAKE TWO FREE-FLYING SPACE WALKS . . . U.S. DIPLOMAT WILLIAM BUCKLEY IS KIDNAPPPED IN BEIRUT . . . SENATE RESOLUTION OPPOSES CIA MINING OF NICARAGUAN HARBORS . . . RUSSIA ANNOUNCES BOYCOTT OF LOS ANGELES SUMMER OLYMPICS . . . INDIAN TROOPS STORM SIKH GOLDEN TEMPLE SEEKING TERRORISTS, 300 DIE . . . JACKSON MEETS CASTRO, 22 AMERICAN PRISONERS ARE FREED . . . GUNMAN KILLS 22 AT MCDONALD'S IN SAN YSIDRO, CA . . . DEMOCRATS NOMINATE WALTER MONDALE AND GERALDINE FERRARO, GOP NOMINATES REAGAN, BUSH . . . U.S. PLEDGES $4.5 BILLION TO RESCUE CONTINENTAL ILLINOIS BANK . . . BRITISH AGREE TO LEAVE HONG KONG IN 1997, CAPITALISM TO REMAIN . . . LABOR AND LIKUD AGREE TO SHARE POWER IN ISRAEL . . . FBI AGENT RICHARD MILLER IS ARRESTED FOR SPYING . . . KATHRYN SULLIVAN BECOMES FIRST U.S. WOMAN TO WALK IN SPACE . . . THATCHER ESCAPES IRA BOMB AT BRIGHTON HOTEL . . . CHINA PLANS FREER MARKET . . . INDIRA GANDHI, INDIAN PM, IS ASSASSINATED BY SIKH BODYGUARDS . . . REAGAN DEFEATS MONDALE BY LANDSLIDE, 54 TO 37 MILLION . . . U.S. CLAIMS USSR SHIPS MIGS TO NICARAGUA . . . GAS LEAK KILLS 2,000 AT UNION CARBIDE PLANT IN BHOPAL, INDIA, THE WORST INDUSTRIAL ACCIDENT IN HISTORY . . . U.S. CONFIRMS WITHDRAWAL FROM UNESCO . . . NYC SUBWAY "VIGILANTE" BERNHARD GOETZ SURRENDERS IN SHOOTING OF 4 YOUTHS.

Quotes

Before the election: "The truth is, politics and morality are inseparable. . . . Morality's foundation is religion" (Ronald Reagan). "I believe in an America that honors what Thomas Jefferson first called the 'wall of separation between church and state' " (Walter Mondale). "Mondale cannot, whatever he does, kiss her" (Pollster Patrick Cadell, on Geraldine Ferraro). "We tried to kick a little ass last night" (George Bush, on the Ferraro TV debate). "Look past the glitter, beyond the showmanship [to] the desperate, the disinherited, and the despised" (Jesse Jackson). "It's morning in America, and besides, there's a bear in the woods" (Republican campaign ad). "Where's the beef?" (Mondale, on Hart).

"My fellow Americans, I am pleased to tell you today that I've signed legislation that will outlaw Russia forever. We begin bombing in five minutes."
> —President Reagan, testing a microphone for radio broadcast

"Calling the MX a peacekeeper is like calling the guillotine a headache remedy."
> —Eugene Carroll, retired admiral

"One woman was furious when I turned down her request to sing at a benefit. She said she heard that I wasn't a homosexual but that I had sung for an AIDS benefit. I told her I belonged to the Audubon Society but I'm not a bird."
> —George Hearn, star of *La Cage aux Folles*

"If he didn't know, it scares me. If he did know, it scares me."
> —Robert Byrd (D-W. Va.), on whether President Reagan knew about the mining of the Nicaraguan harbors

"America is a land where dreams can come true for all of us," proclaims Geraldine Ferraro, Democratic vice-presidential candidate and daughter of a seamstress. *Library of Congress.*

"America is back—standing tall, looking to the Eighties with courage, confidence, and hope."
> —Ronald Reagan, State of the Union speech

"In my head I keep a picture of a pretty little miss, Someday, mister, I'm gonna lead a better life than this."
> —Bruce Springsteen, *Born in the U.S.A.*

"Over a thousand officials to choose from, and I get a moron like you."
> —John McEnroe, to a British tennis umpire

Democratic presidential candidate Jesse Jackson gains national recognition when he achieves the release of both political prisoners in Cuba and Navy pilot Robert Goodman in Syria. *Library of Congress.*

Ads

TV

Premieres

"Kate and Allie," Susan Saint James, Jane Curtin
"Miami Vice," Don Johnson, Philip Michael Thomas
"Hunter," Fred Dryer, Stepfanie Kramer
"The Bill Cosby Show," Bill Cosby, Phylicia Ayers-Allen
"Murder, She Wrote," Angela Lansbury
"Highway to Heaven," Michael Landon, Victor French

Top Ten (Nielsen)

"Dallas," "60 Minutes," "The A-Team," "Simon & Simon," "Falcon Crest," "Magnum, P.I.," "Dynasty," "Hotel," "Knot's Landing," "Newhart"

Specials

"The Jewel in the Crown" (Dame Peggy Ashcroft); "The Brain"; "The Gin Game"; "D-Day and Eisenhower"; "You Can't Take It with You"(Broadway production); "George Washington" (Barry Bostwick, Patty Duke Astin); "*Pagliacci* and *Cavalleria Rusticana*" (Placido Domingo, live from Metropolitan Opera)

Emmy Awards

"Cagney & Lacey" (drama); "The Cosby Show" (comedy); "The Jewel in the Crown" (limited series); William Daniels (actor, "St. Elsewhere"); Robert Guillaume (comedic actor, "Benson"); Tyne Daly (actress, "Cagney & Lacey"); Jane Curtin (comedic actress, "Kate and Allie")

Of Note

"The Cosby Show" is the first sitcom about a professional upper middle-class black family • A Utah referendum proposes banning stations like the Playboy Channel from cable • The National Coalition on TV Violence reports a 75 percent increase in TV violence since 1980, citing "Blue Thunder," "V," and "The A-Team." • Radio talk shows, following Don Imus, offend certain audiences with their ethnic slurs and general vulgarity.

Movies

Openings

Amadeus (Milos Forman), F. Murray Abraham, Tom Hulce
A Passage to India (David Lean), Dame Peggy Ashcroft, Alec Guinness
The Killing Fields (Roland Joffe), Sam Waterston, Haing S. Ngor
Places in the Heart (Robert Benton), Sally Field, John Malkovich
A Soldier's Story (Norman Jewison), Howard E. Rollins, Jr.
Beverly Hills Cop (Martin Brest), Eddie Murphy
Ghostbusters (Ivan Reitman), Bill Murray, Dan Aykroyd
The Bostonians (James Ivory), Christopher Reeve, Vanessa Redgrave
Broadway Danny Rose (Woody Allen), Woody Allen, Mia Farrow
The Brother from Another Planet (John Sayles), Joe Morton
The Gods Must Be Crazy (Jamie Uys), Marius Weyers
Indiana Jones and the Temple of Doom (Steven Spielberg), Harrison Ford
The Little Drummer Girl (George Roy Hill), Diane Keaton
The Natural (Barry Levinson), Robert Redford
Romancing the Stone (Robert Zemeckis), Michael Douglas, Kathleen Turner

The Terminator (James Cameron), Arnold Schwarzenegger
A Sunday in the Country (Bertrand Tavernier), Louis Ducreux, Sabine Azema
The Karate Kid (John G. Avildsen), Ralph Macchio, Noriyuki (Pat) Morita

Academy Awards

Best Picture: *Amadeus*
Best Director: Milos Forman (*Amadeus*)
Best Actor: F. Murray Abraham (*Amadeus*)
Best Actress: Sally Field (*Places in the Heart*)

Top Box-Office Stars

Clint Eastwood, Bill Murray, Harrison Ford, Eddie Murphy, Sally Field, Burt Reynolds, Robert Redford, Prince, Dan Akroyd, Meryl Streep

Stars of the Future

Willem Dafoe, Aidan Quinn, John Cusak, Melanie Griffith, Daryl Hannah, Robert Downey, Jr., Corey Haim, Rick Rossovich, Larry Fishborne

TV cops "Cagney & Lacey" gain critical acclaim for their tough and touching portrayal of female professionalism and camaraderie. *Movie Star News.*

Top box-office star Eddie Murphy continues to publicize his abstinence from smoking, drinking, and drugs; his only vices are jewelry and cars. *Movie Star News.*

Popular Music

Hit Songs
"Footloose"
"Jump"
"Time After Time"
"Owner of a Lonely Heart"
"Ghostbusters"
"Uptown Girl"
"Self Control"

Top Records
Albums: *Sports* (Huey Lewis and the News); *An Innocent Man* (Billy Joel); *Colour by Numbers* (Culture Club); *1984* (Van Halen); *Seven and the Ragged Tiger* (Duran Duran); *She's So Unusual* (Cindy Lauper); *Purple Rain* (Prince and the Revolution)

Singles: *I Just Called to Say I Love You* (Stevie Wonder); *Against All Odds* (Phil Collins); *Stuck on You* (Lionel Richie); *Dancing in the Dark* (Bruce Springsteen); *Let's Hear It for the Boy* (Deniece Williams); *Borderline* (Madonna); *Say It Isn't So* (Hall & Oates). Country: *To All the Girls I've Loved Before* (Julio Iglesias, Willie Nelson); *I Don't Wanna Be a Memory* (Exile)

Grammy Awards
What's Love Got to Do with It, Tina Turner (record); *Can't Slow Down,* Lionel Richie (album); "What's Love Got to Do with It" (song)

Jazz and Big Bands
Reissued: the works of Thelonious Monk, Dinah Washington, Gerry Mulligan-Chet Baker, Earl Hines, Duke Ellington, Count Basie, Miles Davis. At the N.Y.C. Jazz Festival: "The Future of Jazz"—in record reissues, video, symphonic collaboration, the new technology.

Top Performers *(Downbeat)*: Wynton Marsalis (soloist); Count Basie (band); Wynton Marsalis Quintet (acoustic jazz group); Weather Report (electric jazz group); Buddy De Franco, Sonny Rollins, Phil Woods, Oscar Peterson, Charlie Haden (instrumentalists); Sarah Vaughan, Bobby McFerrin (vocalists); Manhattan Transfer (vocal group); Miles Davis, *Decoy* (album)

Theater

Broadway Openings

Plays
Glengarry Glen Ross (David Mamet), Robert Prosky, Joe Mantegna (from Goodman Theater, Chicago)
The Real Thing (Tom Stoppard), Jeremy Irons, Glenn Close
Hurlyburly (David Rabe), William Hurt, Harvey Keitel, Ron Silver, Judith Ivey, Sigourney Weaver
Ma Rainey's Black Bottom (August Wilson), Theresa Merritt (from Yale Repertory Theatre)

Musicals
Sunday in the Park with George (Stephen Sondheim), Mandy Patinkin, Bernadette Peters
The Rink (Fred Ebb, John Kander), Liza Minnelli, Chita Rivera

Classics, Revivals, and Off-Broadway Premieres
Death of a Salesman, Dustin Hoffman, Kate Reid, John Malkovich; *Much Ado About Nothing, Cyrano de*

Samuel Beckett and Alan Schneider. The exploration of existential questions that began with *Waiting for Godot* (1953) continues off-Broadway. *Billy Rose Theatre Collection. The New York Public Library at Lincoln Center. Astor, Lenox and Tilden Foundations.*

Theater (cont.)

Bergerac, Derek Jacobi, Sinead Cusack (Royal Shakespeare Company); *Heartbreak House,* Rex Harrison, Amy Irving; *Endgame,* Alvin Epstein; *Rockaby, Footfalls,* and *Enough* (Samuel Beckett), all with Billie Whitelaw; *Balm in Gilead* (Lanford Wilson)

Regional
Yale Repertory, New Haven: *The Road to Mecca* (Athol Fugard)

American Repertory Theater, Cambridge, Mass.: *Big River: The Adventures of Huckleberry Finn* (Roger Miller)

Pulitzer Prize
Glengarry Glen Ross, David Mamet

Tony Awards
The Real Thing, Tom Stoppard (play), *La Cage aux Folles,* Harvey Fierstein, Jerry Herman (musical)

Classical Music

Compositions
Stephen Albert, *RiverRun*
Terry Riley, *The Harp of New Albion*
Ellen Zwilich, *Celebration for Orchestra*
Mario Davidovsky, String Quartet no. 4
Roger Reynolds, *Transfigured Wind II*

Important Events
Major festivals take place in San Antonio, at Juilliard, the Universities of Miami and Hartford, and Los Angeles. The New York Philharmonic's "Horizons '84: The New Romanticism" offers computer, synthesizer, and performance art.
The Northeast Orchestral Consortium of 15 orchestras commissions Charles Wuorinen's Piano Concerto no. 3, John Harbison's *Ulysses' Raft,* Earl Kim's *Cornet,* Tobias Picker's *The Encantadas,* Robert Starer's *Hudson Valley Suite,* and Ned Rorem's Violin Concerto; each will be performed at least twice over a five-season period.

Appointments: Lorin Maazel, Pittsburgh; Christoph von Dohnányi, Cleveland; Günther Herbig, Detroit; André Previn, Los Angeles (1986–87); Zubin Mehta's renewed contract gives him the longest tenure of any musical director of the New York Philharmonic.

Debut: Frank Peter Zimmerman

First Performances
George Crumb, *A Haunted Landscape* (New York); Michael Tippett, *The Mask of Time* (Boston); Donald Erb, *Prismatic Variations* (St. Louis)

Opera
Metropolitan: Carol Vaness, Samuel Ramey (debut), *Rinaldo* (Handel, first Baroque opera performed at Met); Placido Domingo, *Lohengrin*; Anna Tomowa-Sintow, Sherrill Milnes, *Simon Boccanegra*; Hildegard Behrens, *Wozzeck*; Jessye Norman, Edita Gruberova, *Ariadne auf Naxos*; Mirella Freni, *Manon Lescaut*; Leontyne Price, Giuseppe Giacomini, *La Forza del Destino*; Christa Ludwig, Ute Vinzing, *Elektra*; Domingo conducts *La bohème.*

Houston: *Akhnaten* (Philip Glass), U.S. premiere

Santa Fe: *We Come to the River* (Hans Werner Henze), U.S. premiere; *Violanta, A Florentine Tragedy* (Erich Korngold)

San Francisco: *Khovanshchina* (Shostakovich), U.S. premiere

Los Angeles (Olympic Arts Festival): Royal Opera of Covent Garden, *Peter Grimes, Turandot, Die Zauberflöte*

Music Notes
An $18 million Filene Center at Wolf Trap Farm Park replaces the auditorium that burned down in 1982.

Art

Painting

Jasper Johns, *Racing Thoughts*
Roy Lichtenstein, *Landscape with Figures*
Julian Schnabel, *King of the Wood*
Donald Sultan, *Black Lemons*
Robert Bechtle, *Sunset Intersection*
David Salle, *His Brain*
Robert Longo, *Still*
Richard Diebenkorn, *Ocean Park #137; #140*
Brice Marden, *Masking Drawing 4 (Red Drawing 4)*
Kenny Scharf, *When Worlds Collide*
Red Grooms, *Chance Encounter at 3 a.m.*

Sculpture

Frank Stella, *St. Michael's Counterguard*
Christopher Wilmarth, *Baptiste Longing Number 3*
Marisol, *Self Portrait*

Looking at the Last Supper
Isamu Noguchi, *Lightning Bolt: Memorial to Ben Franklin*
Mel Kendrick, *Five Piece Mahogany*

Architecture

General Foods Corporation headquarters, Rye, New York (Kevin Roche, John Dinkeloo)
High Museum of Art, Atlanta, Ga. (Richard Meier)
R.J. Reynolds Tobacco Company Building, Winston-Salem, N.C. (Croxton Collaborative)
Taft House, Cincinnati (Gwathmey Siegel & Associates)
Gordon Wu Hall, Princeton University, Princeton, N.J. (Venturi, Rauch & Scott Brown)
Center for the Fine Arts, Miami (Philip Johnson)

Important Exhibitions

Numerous Chinese exhibits travel throughout the United States; several shows celebrate Whistler's and Degas' 150th birthdays.

Museums

New York: *Metropolitan:* "Van Gogh in Arles"; Klee; Balthas; William Merritt Chase; African Ivories. *Museum of Modern Art:* Primitivism in 20th-Century Art; Aalto; International Survey of Recent Painting and Sculpture. *Whitney:* American Sculpture since 1970; "The Explosion of Pop, Minimalism, and Performance 1958–1969"; New York Painters: Davis, Murray, Stephan, Torreano. *Museum of American Folk Art:* "Expressions of a New Spirit: New Zealand Art"

Guggenheim, Atlanta: Kandinsky; Russian and Bauhaus Years 1915–1933

Washington: Bonnard; Watteau; "Orientalists: Delacroix to Matisse"; Leonardo: Drawings of Horses and Other Animals

Scott Burton, *Pair of Two-Part Chairs, Obtuse Angle.* 1984. Polished granite, 2 parts: 33 × 24 × 33 inches. *Collection of Whitney Museum of American Art, New York. Purchase, with funds from the Lemberg Foundation.*

Los Angeles, Chicago: "A Day in the Country"; Impressionism and Postimpressionism

Chicago: Degas; "Impressionism and the French Landscape"; "Chicago and New York"

Art Briefs

After four years and a cost of $55 million, the Museum of Modern Art reopens, more than twice its original size • The Getty Museum acquires the Luding collection of medieval manuscripts and numerous photograph collections to become one of the finest photo museums in the world • The Equitable Life Assurance Society buys the ten Thomas Hart Benton murals of life in America • Record auctions include J. M. W. Turner's "Seascape: Folkestone" (over $10 million, the highest price ever paid at auction) • Forty-five Renaissance "masterworks" at the Metropolitan are discovered to be forgeries.

Dance

The Los Angeles Olympic Arts Festival opens with Pina Bausch Wuppertaler Tanztheater, followed by companies from all over the world.

Premieres/Important Productions

American Ballet Theatre: Numerous debuts in the Peter Anastos-Mikhail Baryshnikov *Cinderella* include Megali Messac, Cheryl Yeager, Danilo Radoje, and Marianna Tcherkassy; Cynthia Gregory and Patrick Bissell dance in a $925,000 production; Baryshnikov, Elaine Kudo, *Sinatra Suite* (Twyla Tharp)

Pennsylvania Ballet: *Mozart Violin Concerto* (Peter Martins)

Merce Cunningham: *Pictures and Inlets*

Joffrey (in Los Angeles): *Jamboree* (Gerald Arpino)

Books

Fiction

Critics' Choice

Machine Dreams, Jayne Anne Phillips

Him with His Foot in His Mouth and Other Stories, Saul Bellow

Stolen Stories, Steve Katz

Lives of the Poets, E. L. Doctorow

God Knows, Joseph Heller

Edisto, Padgett Powell

Bright Lights, Big City, Jay McInerney

Victory Over Japan, Ellen Gilchrist

Love Medicine, Louise Erdrich

❧ *The War of the End of the World*, Mario Vargas Llosa

❧ *The Unbearable Lightness of Being*, Milan Kundera

Best-Sellers

The Talisman, Stephen King, Peter Straub

The Aquitaine Progression, Robert Ludlum

The Sicilian, Mario Puzo

Love and War, John Jakes

The Butter Battle Book, Dr. Seuss

". . . And Ladies of the Club," Helen Hooven Santmyer

The Fourth Protocol, Frederick Forsyth

Full Circle, Danielle Steel

The Life and Hard Times of Heidi Abramowitz, Joan Rivers

Lincoln: A Novel, Gore Vidal

Nonfiction

Critics' Choice

The March of Folly, Barbara Tuchman

Losing Ground, Charles Murray

An American Procession, Alfred Kazin

One Writer's Beginnings, Eudora Welty

Religion in the Secular City, Harvey Cox

The Bourgeois Experience: Victoria to Freud, vol. 1, Peter Gay

The Nature of the Child, Jerome Kagan

The Heyday of American Communism: The Depression Decade, Harvey Klehr

The Evolution of Cooperation, Robert Axelrod

Cities and the Wealth of Nations, Jane Jacobs

Inquiries into Truth and Interpretation, Donald Davidson

The Abandonment of the Jews: America and the Holocaust, 1941–1945, David S. Wyman

Of Mind and Other Matters, Nelson Goodman

Andrew Jackson and the Course of American Democracy, 1833–1845, vol. 3, Robert V. Remini

Best-Sellers

Iacocca: An Autobiography, Lee Iacocca with William Novak

Loving Each Other, Leo Buscaglia

Eat to Win, Robert Haas, M.D.

Pieces of My Mind, Andrew A. Rooney

Weight Watchers Fast and Fabulous Cookbook, Weight Watchers International

What They Don't Teach You at Harvard Business School, Mark H. McCormack

Women Coming of Age, Jane Fonda with Mignon McCarthy

The One Minute Salesperson, Spencer Johnson, M.D., Larry Wilson

Weight Watchers Quick Start Program Cookbook, Jean Nidetch

Poetry

Tess Gallagher, *Willingly*

Sharon Olds, *The Dead and the Living*

John Ashbery, *A Wave*

Philip Kenny, *The Evolution of the Flightless Bird*

❧ Ted Hughes, *River*

Pulitzer Prizes

Foreign Affairs, Alison Lurie (fiction)

The Prophets of Regulation, Thomas K. McCraw (U.S. history)

The Good War: An Oral History of World War II, Studs Terkel (nonfiction)

The Life and Times of Cotton Mather, Kenneth Silverman (biography)

Yin, Carolyn Kizer (poetry)

Science and Technology

American and French investigators both claim isolation of a virus (HTLV-3) that causes AIDS.

Twenty oncogenes in cancer-organizing viruses have been identified.

For the first time the American Cancer Society makes specific food recommendations: whole grains, and fruits and vegetables high in vitamins A and C.

Reports from Harvard and Stanford indicate that inactivity increases heart and lung disease.

Diet and exercise become the recommended treatment for mild hypertension.

The discovery that RNA can act as a catalyst to trim another RNA may indicate that RNA is the origin of life, the very first "information" molecule.

Challenger space shuttle performs in-orbit repair of a satellite; on another mission, Bruce McCandless and Robert McNair make untethered space walks using nitrogen backpacks.

Discovery becomes the third space shuttle.

❧ At CERN, the top quark is observed.

Nobel Prize

R. Bruce Merrifield wins in chemistry for developing an automated method to make proteins.

Sports ────────────────

Baseball

Olympics organizer Peter Ueberroth replaces Bowie Kuhn.

Pete Rose (Philadelphia, NL) becomes the second player to get over 4,000 hits.

Rookie Dwight Gooden (New York, NL) strikes out a record 45 in three games.

Reggie Jackson (California, AL) hits his 500th home run.

The Cy Young awards go to Rick Sutcliffe (Chicago, NL) and Willie Hernandez (Detroit, AL).

Champions ────────────

Batting	16–1
Tony Gwynn (San Diego, NL), .351	Doyle Alexander (Toronto, AL), 17–6
Don Mattingly (New York, AL), .343	*Home runs*
Pitching	Tony Armas (Oakland, AL), 43
Rick Sutcliffe (Chicago, NL),	

Football

Doug Flutie, BC, throws "The Pass," a 49-yarder with 6 seconds left to beat Miami 47–45.

Led by Donald Trump, the USFL files a $1.3 billion antitrust suit against the NFL.

Dan Marino sets season records of 48 TD passes and 5,084 yards passing.

Walter Payton breaks Jim Brown's rushing record of 12,213; Eric Dickerson rushes for 2,105 yards to break O. J. Simpson's record.

NFL Season Leaders: Joe Montana (San Francisco), passing; Eric Dickerson (Los Angeles Rams), rushing; Art Monk (Washington), receiving, record 106.

AFL Season Leaders: Dan Marino (Miami), passing; Earnest Jackson (San Diego), rushing; John Stallworth (Pittsburgh), receiving

College All-Americans: Robbie Bosco (Q), Brigham Young; Bernie Kosar (Q), Miami

Bowls (Jan 1, 1985)
Rose: USC 20–Ohio State 17
Orange: Washington 28–Oklahoma 17
Cotton: Boston College 45–Houston 18
Sugar: Nebraska 28–LSU 10

Basketball

NBA All-Pro First Team: Larry Bird (Boston), Bernard King (New York Knicks), Kareem Abdul-Jabbar (Los Angeles Lakers), Magic Johnson (Los Angeles Lakers), Isiah Thomas (Detroit)

Olympics

The first time run as a private enterprise, the Olympics record a $150 million surplus. The Russians and other Eastern bloc countries boycott. Carl Lewis wins 4 gold, matching Jessie Owens (100m, 200m, long jump, relay); Mary Lou Retton wins 5 gold in gymnastics. Other winners include Edwin Moses (400m) and Greg Louganis, diving (2). In the Winter Games at Sarajevo, American gold winners include Bill Johnson, downhill (first American), and Phil Mahre, slalom.

Winners ────────────

World Series	*MVP*
Detroit (AL) 4	Larry Bird, Boston
San Diego (NL) 1	*College Basketball*
MVP	Georgetown
NL–Ryne Sandberg, Chicago	*Player of the Year*
AL–Willie Hernandez, Detroit	Michael Jordan, North Carolina
Super Bowl XIX (Jan. 1985)	*Stanley Cup*
San Francisco 38–Miami 16	Edmonton
MVP	*US Tennis Open*
Dan Marino, Miami	Men: John McEnroe
College Football	Women: Martina Navratilova
Brigham Young	*USGA Open*
Heisman Trophy	Fuzzy Zoeller
Doug Flutie, Boston College	*Kentucky Derby*
NBA Championship	Swale (L. Pincay, jockey)
Boston 4–Los Angeles 3	

Fashion ────────────────

"Androgynous" fashions gain popularity: pin-striped, double-breasted suits with skirts at ankle length, oversized coats over tailored and cuffed pants (with wide waistbands), and jackets with square shoulders. Flat- or low-heeled shoes accompany the tailored look, along with bags or totes in new fabrics—real or imitation crocodile, elephant, and buffalo. Accessories soften the look: pearl necklaces, gold chains, silk and challis shawls. Singer Michael Jackson's black leather penny loafers also create a vogue.

High-fashion note: Ralph Lauren's wrap, styled like a man's dressing gown, in silk velvet with a mink shawl collar

Androgynous rock singers become popular: Michael Jackson, Boy George, Prince, Annie Lennox (Eurythmics), Nick Rhodes (Duran Duran), and, here, Grace Jones. *Movie Star News.*

Kaleidoscope _____

Frederick Hart's sculpture facing the Vietnam Memorial Wall (Washington, D.C.). Critics wanted a "patriotic" work to balance the wall, which they viewed as a "political statement of shame and dishonor." *National Park Service.*

- According to *Life,* as she walks to work, the female yuppie reads *The Wall Street Journal,* wears Nikes, Brooks Brothers clothing, a Coach bag and Cartier tank watch, and listens to her Sony Walkman; she likes sushi, pasta salad, and wine spritzers.
- Metropolitan-area housing skyrockets: a typical San Francisco Haight house costs $385,000 ($87,000, 1977); an eight-room co-op, Fifth Avenue, New York, $800,000 ($150,000, 1975).
- Jesse Jackson creates a furor when he refers to New York City as "Hymietown"; Louis Farrakhan, Jackson's supporter, calls Judaism "a gutter religion"; Jackson refuses to repudiate Farrakhan.
- Donald Trump and Harrah's open a 614-room, 39-story hotel and casino in Atlantic City; the $125 million Trump Plaza and $200 million 68-story Trump Tower, in New York City, make Trump a media star.
- The Rhode Island Supreme Court overturns Claus von Bülow's conviction for attempting to murder his wife, Sunny; he stands to inherit $14 million of her $75-million estate.
- Broker Marina Verola claims she lost her E. F. Hutton job for posing in *Playboy*: "I went bare in a bull market."
- Vanessa Williams, the first black Miss America, resigns after her sexually explicit photos are scheduled for *Penthouse* magazine.
- The American Council on Education describes an eroding "generation gap" in college students, who now espouse the more traditional career, marriage, and financial goals of their parents.
- Ann Landers receives a huge mail response that says female readers prefer more affection and less of "the act."
- In New York and San Francisco, gays protest closing the bathhouses that health authorities claim spread AIDS.
- In the largest mergers to date, Texaco outbids Pennzoil for Getty ($10 billion), and SOCAL takes over Gulf ($13 billion).
- The Reagan administration threatens to withdraw aid from nations that advocate abortion as birth control.
- Dow and six other chemical companies settle with Agent Orange victims for $180 million.
- Incidents of child abuse at day-care centers increase; one Los Angeles preschool is charged with 208 counts of child molestation over the past 10 years.
- For the first time in 22 years, a woman suffers the death penalty; Margie Velma Barfield, 51, was convicted in 1978 of poisoning her fiancé.
- Prisons are filled beyond capacity; the United States incarcerates more people than any other Western country: 1 out of every 529; in some states, 1 out of 10 black males between 18 and 34.
- Modifying Miranda, the Supreme Court rules that illegally obtained evidence is admissible if otherwise obtainable.
- For the first time since 1968, the judiciary is a major issue in the national election: 5 out of the 9 Supreme Court justices are over 75.
- The California Wilderness Act is passed, designating 23 new areas in 20 states; efforts are made to save the dwindling black duck and wood stork from extinction.
- *Variety* reports on "Radio Breaking [the] Racial Barrier": black musicians like Michael Jackson are now featured on white-dominated Top Ten radio programs.
- Michael Jackson earns $1.5 million for a Pepsi commercial; during its filming, his hair catches fire.
- A photograph of the star Beta Pictoris, 293 trillion miles from earth, reveals another solar system in the first stages of formation.
- A three-volume *Ulysses* by James Joyce, with 5,000 corrections, is published by Garland.
- A pizza parlor customer keeps a promise when he splits his $6 million lottery winnings with a waitress.
- George Orwell's *1984* (1949) becomes a best-seller as schools across the country evaluate its predictions.

Fads: Trivial Pursuit, lottery sweepstakes, diet and religious books, Guess clothes, expensive matchmakers (Great Expectations, $525; People Resources, $700); gentrification, taco salads, mesquite grilling, tofutti, rosemary (the herb of the year, replacing basil, 1983)

First Appearances: U.S. as debtor nation (first time since 1913), full diplomatic relations between U.S. and Vatican, FBI agent arrested as spy, baboon heart transplant (Baby Fae), artificial Factor VIII (for hemophiliacs), chicken pox vaccine, second artificial heart surgery (William Schroeder), child born from frozen embryo (Australia), surrogate conception (conceived in one woman, carried in another), genetic fingerprinting, extinct species cloning (zebra fish), sheep cloning, woman to walk in space, Apple Macintosh, megabit memory chip (1 million bits, Bell Labs), state requiring seat belts (New York), plastic plane (Avtek 400), airborne public telephone, women jaycees, male bunnies at Playboy Club, Poet's Corner (Cathedral of St. John the Divine, New York City), movie rating PG-13

1985

In the News

WHITE HOUSE CHIEF OF STAFF JAMES BAKER AND DONALD REGAN, OF TREASURY, EXCHANGE POSTS . . . PHILIPPINE MILITARY IS CHARGED IN AQUINO MURDER . . . REAGAN ASKS RENEWED AID TO CONTRA "FREEDOM FIGHTERS" . . . ISRAELIS BEGIN PULLOUT FROM LEBANON . . . SOVIET LEADER CHERNENKO, 73, DIES, MIKHAIL GORBACHEV, 54, TAKES OVER . . . REAGAN VISITS SS CEMETERY AT BITBURG AND BERGEN-BELSEN CONCENTRATION CAMP . . . DOW TOPS 1,300 FOR THE FIRST TIME, PRIME RATE DROPS TO 10% . . . POLICE BOMB MILITANT ANARCHISTS IN PHILADELPHIA, KILL 11 . . . EX-NAVYMAN JOHN WALKER, SON, AND BROTHER ARE ARRESTED FOR ESPIONAGE . . . REAGAN SAYS U.S. WILL ABIDE BY UNRATIFIED SALT II . . . SHIITE TERRORISTS HIJACK TWA 847, DISPERSE AMERICANS IN BEIRUT . . . ISRAELIS FREE ARAB PRISONERS, TERRORISTS RELEASE TWA HOSTAGES, LINK IS DENIED . . . CONGRESS VOTES SANCTIONS AGAINST SOUTH AFRICA . . . NAZI WAR CRIMINAL DR. JOSEPH MENGELE'S REMAINS FROM 1979 ARE IDENTIFIED IN BRAZIL . . . GORBACHEV ASKS FOR ECONOMIC REFORMS, BETTER CONSUMER PRODUCTS . . . EARTHQUAKE HITS MEXICO CITY, 10,000 DIE . . . PALESTINIAN TERRORISTS SEIZE "ACHILLE LAURO" CRUISE SHIP, KILL LEON KLINGHOFFER IN WHEELCHAIR . . . U.S. AIR FORCE INTERCEPTS "LAURO" HIJACKERS OVER MEDITERRANEAN . . . REAGAN AND GORBACHEV HOLD SUMMIT IN GENEVA, AGREE TO "FRESH START" . . . TREATY WITH GREAT BRITAIN GIVES IRELAND ROLE IN NORTH IRELAND . . . COLOMBIAN VOLCANO ERUPTS, 25,000 ARE KILLED . . . PRESIDENT VETOES SHOE AND TEXTILE IMPORT QUOTAS . . . REAGAN SIGNS GRAMM-RUDMAN BILL MANDATING BUDGET CONTROL . . . 20 ARE KILLED IN ARAB TERRORIST ATTACKS AT VIENNA AND ROME AIRPORTS.

Quotes _____

"We are living in a material world
And I am a material girl."
    —Madonna, "Material Girl"

"[This is] a Second American Revolution of hope and opportunity. . . . There are no constraints on the human mind, . . . no barriers to progress, except those we ourselves erect."

    —Ronald Reagan

"That place, Mr. President, is not your place. Your place is with the victims of the SS."
    —Elie Wiesel, to Ronald Reagan, before his visit to Bitburg cemetery

"[We need] a return to the original intent of the Founding Fathers."

    —Attorney General Ed Meese

". . . arrogance cloaked in humility."
    —Supreme Court Justice William Brennan, in response to Meese

"After seeing the movie *Rambo,* I'll know what to do the next time something like this happens."
    —President Reagan, on the TWA hostage crisis

"To put it bluntly, female flies don't want to mate with a wimp. Larger flies have a more energetic serenade when they mate."
    —Entomologist John Sivinski, Department of Agriculture

"Do we get to win this time?" asks Sylvester Stallone, when in *Rambo* he returns to Vietnam to rescue POWs; the enormously popular movie creates widespread debate over the "macho-jingo" Rambo phenomenon. *Movie Star News.*

"If you corner a rat and you are about to butcher it— O.K.? The way I responded was viciously and savagely, just like a rat."
    —Alleged "subway vigilante" Bernhard Goetz

"The biggest problem this country faces is mismanagement, . . . the survival of the unfittest. The guy who gets to the top in 80 to 85 percent . . . is a political guy . . . good to have a drink with."
    —Carl Icahn, "corporate raider"

"The ultimate GM coat of arms will feature a robot dressed in a kimono seated in front of a word processor."
    —Ben Bidwell, Chrysler executive on GM's enterprises with Japan

"Shall I die? Shall I fly/Lovers' baits and deceits,/ sorrow breeding?"
    —Opening of newly discovered Shakespeare poem

Ads _____

TV

Premieres
"The Golden Girls," Beatrice Arthur, Betty White, Rue McClanahan

"Dynasty II: The Colbys," Charlton Heston, Barbara Stanwyck

"The Equalizer," Edward Woodward

"Spenser for Hire," Robert Urich

"The Oprah Winfrey Show," Oprah Winfrey

Top Ten (Nielsen)
"Dynasty," "Dallas," "The Cosby Show," "60 Minutes," "Family Ties," "The A-Team," "Simon & Simon," "Knots Landing," "Murder, She Wrote," "Falcon Crest"/"Crazy Like a Fox"

Specials
"45/85" (40 years following World War II); "Death of a Salesman" (Dustin Hoffman); "The Statue of Liberty"; "Television's Vietnam: The Real Story"; "Fresno" (Carol Burnett, Dabney Coleman); Leontyne Price, "Aïda" (farewell performance from the Metropolitan); "Live Aid: Concert to End World Hunger"

Emmy Awards
"Cagney & Lacey" (drama); "The Golden Girls" (comedy); William Daniels (actor, "St. Elsewhere"); Michael J. Fox (comedic actor, "Family Ties"); Sharon Gless (actress, "Cagney & Lacey"); Betty White (comedic actress, "The Golden Girls")

Of Note
ABC is acquired by Capital Cities Communications for $3.43 billion • CBS, which tops the ratings for the sixth consecutive year, foils a takeover attempt by Ted Turner Broadcasting System • Rupert Murdock buys seven TV stations and 20th Century-Fox Film Corporation; he plans to form the Fox television network.

Movies

Openings
Out of Africa (Sydney Pollack), Robert Redford, Meryl Streep

The Color Purple (Steven Spielberg), Whoopi Goldberg, Oprah Winfrey

Kiss of the Spider Woman (Hector Babenco), William Hurt, Raul Julia

Prizzi's Honor (John Huston), Jack Nicholson, Kathleen Turner

Witness (Peter Weir), Harrison Ford, Kelly McGillis

Back to the Future (Robert Zemeckis), Michael J. Fox

The Trip to Bountiful (Peter Masterson), Geraldine Page

Cocoon (Ron Howard), Don Ameche, Jessica Tandy, Hume Cronyn

The Jagged Edge (Richard Marquand), Glenn Close, Jeff Bridges

The Purple Rose of Cairo (Woody Allen), Mia Farrow, Jeff Daniels, Danny Aiello

Rambo: First Blood Part II (George P. Cosmatos), Sylvester Stallone

The Breakfast Club (John Hughes), Molly Ringwald, Anthony Michael Hall

Code of Silence (Andy Davis), Chuck Norris

Desperately Seeking Susan (Susan Seidelman), Rosanna Arquette, Madonna

Mad Max Beyond Thunderdome (George Miller, George Ogilvie), Mel Gibson, Tina Turner

Ran (Akira Kurosawa), Tatsuya Nakadai

Shoah (Claude Lanzmann), documentary on the Holocaust

Academy Awards
Best Picture: *Out of Africa*
Best Director: Sydney Pollack *(Out of Africa)*
Best Actress: Geraldine Page *(The Trip to Bountiful)*
Best Actor: William Hurt *(Kiss of the Spider Woman)*

Above: William Hurt *(right)*, in *Kiss of the Spider Woman*, with Raul Julia, wins an Oscar for his portrayal of a gay prisoner consoled by fantasies of old movies. *Movie Star News.*
Below: Steven Spielberg's film version of Alice Walker's *The Color Purple* with Whoopi Goldberg and Margaret Avery receives numerous Academy Award nominations but no Oscars. *Movie Star News.*

Movies (cont.)

Top Box-Office Stars
Sylvester Stallone, Eddie Murphy, Clint Eastwood, Michael J. Fox, Chevy Chase, Arnold Schwarzenegger, Chuck Norris, Harrison Ford, Michael Douglas, Meryl Streep

Stars of the Future
Whoopi Goldberg, Oprah Winfrey, Anjelica Huston, Kelly McGillis, Patrick Dempsey, Martha Plimpton, Laura Dern, Mary Stuart Masterson, Anthony Michael Hall

Popular Music

Hit Songs
"Wake Me Up Before You Go-Go"
"I Feel for You"
"Glory Days"
"Crazy for You"
"Careless Whisper"
"One Night in Bangkok"

Top Records
Albums: *Born in the U.S.A.* (Bruce Springsteen); *Reckless* (Bryan Adams); *Like a Virgin* (Madonna); *Make It Big* (Wham!); *Private Dancer* (Tina Turner); *Beverly Hills Cop* (sound track); *Suddenly* (Billy Ocean)

Singles: *We Are the World,* (U.S.A. for Africa); *Everybody Wants to Rule the World* (Tears for Fears); *I Want to Know What Love Is* (Foreigner); *Cherish* (Kool & the Gang); *Saving All My Love for You* (Whitney Houston); *Night Shift* (The Commodores). Country: *The Best Year of My Life* (Eddie Rabbitt); *Does Fort Worth Ever Cross Your Mind . . .* (George Strait)

Grammy Awards
We Are the World, U.S.A. for Africa (record); *No Jacket Required,* Phil Collins (album); "We Are the World" (song)

Jazz and Big Bands
The growing eclecticism in jazz includes jazz-pop collaborations, like Sting's *The Dream of the Blue Turtles,* with Wynton Marsalis, Kenneth Kirkland, and Darryl Jones. Big bands mix rhythm and blues, bebop, and gospel with jazz.

Top Performers (*Downbeat*):
Wynton Marsalis (soloist); Count Basie (band); Phil Woods (acoustic jazz group); Miles Davis (electronic jazz group); Steve Swallow, Stanley Jordan, Wayne Shorter (instrumentalists); Sarah Vaughan, Bobby McFerrin (vocalists); Jack De Johnette, *Album Album* (album)

Theater

Broadway Openings

Plays
Biloxi Blues (Neil Simon), Matthew Broderick
Pack of Lies (Hugh Whitemore), Rosemary Harris, Patrick McGoohan
The Boys of Winter (John Pielmeier), Matt Dillon, Andrew McCarthy
I'm Not Rappaport (Herb Gardner), Judd Hirsch, Cleavon Little (from Seattle Repertory Theater)
As Is (William M. Hoffman), Jonathan Hogan, Jonathan Hadary
Benefactors (Michael Frayn), Glenn Close, Sam Waterston, Mary Beth Hurt
The Search for Signs of Intelligent Life in the Universe (Jane Wagner), Lily Tomlin

Musicals
Big River: The Adventures of Huckleberry Finn (Roger Miller), Daniel Jenkins, Ron Richardson
Song and Dance (Andrew Lloyd Webber), Bernadette Peters
Leader of the Pack (Ellie Greenwich), Patrick Cassidy, Dinah Manoff

Classics, Revivals, and Off-Broadway Premieres
The Iceman Cometh, Jason Robards, Barnard Hughes; *The King and I,* Yul Brynner; *The Mystery of Edwin Drood,* George Rose; *Strange Interlude,* Glenda Jackson; *The Marriage of Figaro,* Christopher Reeve; *Arms and the Man,* Kevin Kline, Raul Julia; *The Odd Couple,* Rita Moreno, Sally Struthers; *Aren't We All?,* Rex Harrison, Claudette Colbert, Lynne Redgrave, Jeremy Brett; *Aunt Dan and Lemmon* (Wallace Shawn), Linda Hunt; *The Normal Heart* (Larry Kramer); *Talley and Son* (Lanford Wilson); *Penn and Teller; Vivat! Vivat Regina!,* Geraldine Page; *Joe Egg,* Jim Dale, Stockard Channing; *Curse of the Starving Class* (Sam Shepard); *The Marriage of Bette and Boo* (Christopher Durang, author and actor)

Regional
Yale Repertory Theatre, New Haven: *The Blood Knot* (Athol Fugard), Zakes Mokae: *Fences* (August Wilson), James Earl Jones

Goodman, Chicago: Gregory Mosher leaves to become director of the Vivian Beaumont Theater, Lincoln Center.

Big River, the Tony-winning musical version of *Huckleberry Finn. Billy Rose Theatre Collection. The New York Public Library at Lincoln Center, Astor, Lenox and Tilden Foundations.*

Noted, among other things, for her sartorial splendor, Tina Turner makes *Mad Max Beyond Thunderdome* and also wins three grammys. *Movie Star News.*

Theater (cont.)

Pulitzer Prize
Sunday in the Park with George, Stephen Sondheim, James Lapine

Tony Awards
Biloxi Blues, Neil Simon (play); *Big River*, William Hauptman, Roger Miller (musical)

Classical Music

Compositions
George Perle, Wind Quintet IV
Ralph Shapey, Symphonic Variations
William Schuman, *On Freedom's Ground*
John Harbison, Variations
Otto Luening, *Symphonic Fantasies VI*

Important Events
The Bach, Handel, and Scarlatti tercentenaries are celebrated throughout the world. Many rarely or never-performed Handel operas are staged, such as *Alessandro* (Washington and New York). At Yale, 33 recently discovered Bach chorale preludes are performed; in Birmingham, 120 artists and ensembles participate in a grass-roots Bach birthday celebration. Harpsichordist Scott Ross begins recording all 555 Scarlatti keyboard sonatas. In New York, Zubin Mehta celebrates the centenaries of Varèse and Webern.

New Appointments: Philippe Entremont, Denver; Maksim Shostakovich, New Orleans; Herbert Blomstedt, San Francisco; Edo de Waart, Minnesota

Debuts: Anne-Marie McDermott, Nigel Kennedy

First Performances
Ellen Zwilich, Symphony no. 2 (San Francisco); Henry Brant, *Desert Forests* (Atlanta); David Del Tredici, *March to Tonality* (Chicago); Toru Takemitsu, Piano Concerto (Los Angeles); Donald Erb, Contrabassoon Concerto (Houston)

Opera
Metropolitan: James Levine is named artistic director, with Bruce Crawford (general manager) and Jonathan Friend (casting). Martti Talvela, *Khovanshchina;* Grace Bumbry, Simon Estes, *Porgy and Bess;* Kathleen Battle, Carol Vaness, Frederica von Stade, *Marriage of Figaro* (Jean-Pierre Ponelle production); Jon Vickers, Leonie Rysanek, *Parsifal;* Vaness, Tatiana Troyanos, *La Clemenza di Tito;* Julia Migenes-Johnson, Evelyn Lear, Franz Mazura, *Lulu;* Giuseppe Taddei, *Falstaff;* Leontyne Price sings her farewell performance in *Aïda.*

New York City: Samuel Ramey, Linda Roark-Strummer, *Attila* (Verdi)

Seattle, San Francisco: Eva Marton, James A. Morris, Thomas Stewart, *Ring* cycle

San Francisco: Mirella Freni, *Adriana Lecouvreur;* Renata Scotto, Alfredo Kraus, *Werther;* Eva Marton, Franco Bonisolli, *Turandot;* Marilyn Horne, Ruth Ann Swenson, *Orlando*

Chicago: Cecilia Gasdia (debut), Tatiana Troyanos, *I Capuleti e i Montecchi* (Bellini); Placido Domingo, Margaret Price, Sherrill Milnes, *Otello;* Joan Sutherland, *Anna Bolena*

Minnesota: *Casanova's Homecoming* (Dominick Argento)

Music Notes
The Ordway Music Theatre, home of the Minnesota Opera and St. Paul Chamber Orchestra, opens in St. Paul • The first "American Music Week" is held Nov. 4–10, with 300 performances of both young and established composers, including Cage, Thomson, Copland, Schuman, Lou Harrison, and Robert Erikson.

Art

Painting
Sam Francis, *Fast and Dark II*
Philip Taafe, *Brest; Homo Fortissimus Excelsius*
Ross Bleckner, *Crocodile Tears*
Terry Winters, *Good Government*
Sherrie Levine, *Golden Knots* series
David Salle, *Very Few Cars*
Peter Schuyff, *The Well*

Sculpture
Richard Serra, *Clara-Clara: Pasolini*
Mark DiSuvero, *Huru*
Richard Artschwager, *Flayed Tables*
Ronald Bladen, *Aura*

Haim Steinbach, *Related and Different*
Martin Puryear, *Sanctum*

Architecture
Humana Building, Louisville, Kentucky (Michael Graves)
Procter & Gamble Building, Cincinnati (Kohn Pederson Fox)
PA Technology Building, Hightstown, N.J. (Richard Rogers)
Charles Shipman Payson Building, Portland Museum of Art (I. M. Pei)
American Academy of Pediatrics, Elk Grove Village, Ill. (Hammond, Beeby & Babka)

Important Exhibitions
Numerous exhibitions of the painting and sculpture of India travel across the United States, as well as "Maya: Treasures of an Ancient Civilization."

Museums
New York: *Metropolitan:* "The Art of Pre-Columbian Gold"; "Liechtenstein: The Princely Collection"; "The Age of Caravaggio"; Treasures of San Marco, Venice; India: 1300–1900; Clemente. *Museum of Modern Art:* "Contrasts of Form: Geometric Abstract Art"; Matisse; Toulouse-Lautrec; Rousseau; Schwitters. *Whitney:* Bicentennial–from Rodney Alan Greenblat to David Wojnarowic Johns and Cindy Sherman; Borofsky retrospective; Crawford. *Guggenheim:* Motherwell retrospective: "Kandinsky in Paris: 1933–44"

Philadelphia: Chagall retrospective

Elizabeth Murray, *Open Book*. 1985. Oil on canvas. 2 panels: (a) 90½ × 121 × 11 inches; (b) 88¼ × 111¼ × 9¾ inches. *Collection of Whitney Museum of American Art, New York. Gift of the Mnuchin Foundation.*

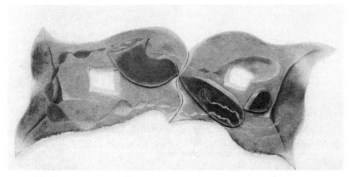

Minneapolis: "Jennifer Bartlett in midcareer"

Washington: Degas: "Treasure Houses of Britain: 500 Years of Private Patronage and Art Collecting"; "Old Master Drawings from the Albertina"; "The Sculpture of India 3000 B.C.–1300 A.D."

Boston: Renoir

Washington, Chicago, Los Angeles: "Leonardo to van Gogh" (from Museum of Fine Arts, Budapest)

Art Briefs
New York bars new high-rise buildings on residential side streets of the Upper East Side to protect their architectural character • More than 600 people sign a petition to reject Michael Graves' colorful addition to the Whitney Museum, saying it will "destroy" Marcel Breuer's "world-renowned" building • *Artnews* pressures the Austrian government to return 3,900 works seized by the Nazis to their appropriate owners; unclaimed works will be auctioned for Jewish charities • Controversy continues over Richard Serra's 1981 massive "Tilted Arc," in downtown Manhattan, which critics call "ugly and intrusive" • The Getty Museum pays $10.4 million for Andrea Mantegna's "Adoration of the Magi," the highest ever paid for a painting.

Dance

Premieres/Important Productions
New York City Ballet: Patricia McBride, Ib Andersen, *Valse Triste* (Peter Martins); Andersen, Kyra Nichols, Sean Lavery, Maria Calegari, *Eight Lines*

American Ballet Theatre: Clark Tippet, Martine van Hamel, *Field, Chair and Mountain* (David Gordon); Fernando Bujones resigns when Baryshnikov refuses to allow Maurice Béjart to create a work for him.

Joffrey (first repertory season at New York State Theater, Lincoln Center): *Forgotten Land* (Jiri Kylian); *Untitled* (Pilobolus); *Arden Court* (Paul Taylor)

Ballet West: *Abdallah* (August Bournonville), first performance in 125 years.

Dance Theatre of Harlem (funded by the new National Choreography Project): *Movers* (Gordon, Thelonious Monk)

Books

Fiction
Critics' Choice
Gerald's Party, Robert Coover
Carpenter's Gothic, William Gaddis
World's Fair, E. L. Doctorow
Glitz, Elmore Leonard
The Beans of Egypt, Maine, Carolyn Chute
Continental Drift, Russell Banks
The Accidental Tourist, Anne Tyler
Later the Same Day, Grace Paley
In Country, Bobbie Ann Mason
🐚 *Mr. Palomar*, Italo Calvino
🐚 *The Old Gringo*, Carlos Fuentes

Best-Sellers
The Mammoth Hunters, Jean M. Auel
Texas, James A. Michener
Lake Wobegon Days, Garrison Keillor
If Tomorrow Comes, Sidney Sheldon
Skeleton Crew, Stephen King
Secrets, Danielle Steel
Contact, Carl Sagan

Nonfiction
Critics' Choice
The Mind's New Science, Howard Gardner
Habitations of the Word, William Gass
Illiterate America, Jonathan Kozol
Popol Vuh, ed. Dennis Tedlock

The Broken Brain, Nancy Andreasen
The Workshop of Democracy, James MacGregor Burns
Crime and Human Nature, James Q. Wilson, Richard J. Hernstein
All Fall Down, Gary Sick
The Man Who Mistook His Wife for a Hat, Oliver Sacks
Crabgrass Frontier, Kenneth T. Jackson
The Flamingo's Smile, Stephen Jay Gould
Habits of the Heart, Robert Bellah et al.

Best-Sellers
Iacocca: An Autobiography, Lee Iacocca with William Novak
Yeager: An Autobiography, General Chuck Yeager and Leo Janos
Elvis and Me, Priscilla Beaulieu Presley with Sandra Harmon
Fit for Life, Harvey and Marilyn Diamond
The Be-Happy Attitudes, Robert Schuller
Dancing in the Light, Shirley MacLaine
A Passion for Excellence, Thomas J. Peters, Nancy K. Austin
The Frugal Gourmet, Jeff Smith

Poetry
Raymond Carver, *Where Water Comes Together with Other Water*

The reigning prince of the postmodern novel, Robert Coover continues to explore the nature of human mythmaking. *Grove Press.*

Louise Glück, *The Triumph of Achilles*
Galway Kinnell, *The Past*
June Jordan, *Living Room*
🐚 Seamus Heaney, *Station Island*

Pulitzer Prizes
Lonesome Dove, Larry McMurtry (fiction)
. . . The Heavens and the Earth, Walter McDougall (U.S. history)
Common Ground, J. Anthony Lukas (nonfiction)
Move Your Shadow, Joseph Lelyveld (nonfiction)
Louise Bogan: A Portrait, Elizabeth Frank (biography)
The Flying Change, Henry Taylor (poetry)

Science and Technology

The superstrings theory proposes that the most elementary particles are one-dimensional and that the universe is ten-, rather than four-, dimensional.

A 4.4-million-year-old anthropoid jawbone discovered in Burma indicates that human ancestors may have originated in Asia and then migrated to Africa.

Radioactive monoclonal antibodies are used to treat liver cancer.

An anxiety-producing peptide that binds to the same brain receptor sites as Valium is discovered.

A National Cancer Institute study indicates that half of new breast cancer patients might benefit from lumpectomy, a more limited form of surgery.

Harvard researchers discover angiogenin, a blood-vessel promoting protein, and the gene of its origin.

Reports indicate the potential health hazards of food additives, such as artificial sweeteners, dyes, sulfites, and caffeine.

Studies indicate that ECT may be effective and at times life-saving for certain kinds of depression.

On a Discovery shuttle flight, a satellite is recovered by a spacewalker, repaired, and relaunched.

Nobel Prizes
Michael S. Brown and Joseph L. Goldstein win in physiology or medicine for their studies of cholesterol metabolism. Herbert A. Hauptman and Jerome Karle win in chemistry for their work with crystal structures.

Sports

Baseball

Pete Rose breaks Ty Cobb's record with his 4,192nd hit.

Nolan Ryan (Houston, NL) is the first to record 4,000 strikeouts.

Keith Hernandez (New York, NL) and Dave Parker (Cincinnati, NL) testify, under immunity, to past drug use.

The Cy Young awards go to Dwight Gooden (New York, NL) and Bret Saberhagen (Kansas City, AL).

Champions

Batting	
Willie McGee (St. Louis, NL), .353	NL), 19–3
	Ron Guidry (New York, AL), 22–6
Wade Boggs (Boston, AL), .368	*Home runs*
Pitching	Darrell Evans (Detroit, AL), 40
Orel Hershiser (Los Angeles,	

Football

NFL salaries average $163,145 ($90,102 in 1982).

Mammoth Bears lineman William (Refrigerator) Perry becomes a media star when he scores as a fullback.

NFL Season Leaders: Joe Montana (San Francisco), passing; Gerald Riggs (Atlanta), rushing; Roger Craig (San Francisco), receiving

AFL Season Leaders: Ken O'Brien (New York Jets), passing; Marcus Allen (Los Angeles Raiders), rushing; Lionel James (San Diego), receiving

College All-Americans: Chuck Long (Q), Iowa; Tony Casillas (L), Oklahoma

Bowls (Jan. 1, 1986)

Rose: UCLA 45–Iowa 28
Orange: Oklahoma 25–Penn State 10
Cotton: Texas A&M 36–Auburn 16
Sugar: Tennessee 35–Miami 7

Basketball

The Knicks win the first NBA draft lottery and choose Patrick Ewing.

Dwight Gooden, 20, becomes the youngest pitcher to win 20 games with his incredible season: 24–4, 1.53 ERA, and 276 strikeouts. *New York Mets.*

Villanova upsets Georgetown in the NCAA final with 79 percent shooting.

NBA All-Pro First Team: Bernard King (New York), Larry Bird (Boston), Moses Malone (Philadelphia), Isiah Thomas (Detroit), Magic Johnson (Los Angeles Lakers)

Other Sports

Boxing: Light HW champ Michael Spinks decisions HW champ Larry Holmes (48–1), who fails to overtake Rocky Marciano (48–0).

Horse Racing: John Henry retires, having won a record $6.6 million. Spend-a-Buck cost $12,500.

Winners

World Series	*MVP*
Kansas City (AL) 4	Larry Bird, Boston
St. Louis (NL) 3	*College Basketball*
MVP	Villanova
NL–Willie McGee, St. Louis	*Player of the Year*
AL–Don Mattingly, New York	Chris Mullin, St. Johns
Super Bowl XX (Jan. 1986)	*Stanley Cup*
Chicago 46–New England 10	Edmonton
MVP	*US Tennis Open*
Walter Payton, Chicago	Men: Ivan Lendl
College Football	Women: Hana Mandlikova
Oklahoma	*USGA Open*
Heisman Trophy	Andy North
Bo Jackson, Auburn	*Kentucky Derby*
NBA Championship	Spend-a-Buck (A. Cordero, Jr.,
Los Angeles Lakers 4–	jockey)
Boston 2	

Fashion

The body silhouette takes one of two forms: a slim, sexy shape that emphasizes the curvaceous and sensuous, in the new popular jersey or crepe fabrics, or the flowing, broad-shouldered look that matches large shirts, sweaters, and jackets with either equally full skirts and trousers or contrasting tight, fitted, and tapered styles. Stirrup pants are shown with large sweaters with padded shoulders; skirts are decorated with silver or gold sequins or bright patterns in bold colors. For more formal dress, rich fabrics create an elegant, moneyed look: velvets, cashmeres, and ornate brocades. Coin jewelry, with reproductions of current or ancient coinage, is popular.

High-fashion note: Ralph Lauren's, Calvin Klein's, and Givenchy's short jacket (to the waist) with shaping tucks or a button tucking at the waist

Kaleidoscope

- Rock Hudson, 59, one of the first public figures to acknowledge his battle with AIDS, is instrumental in raising public awareness of the disease.
- A highly addictive, inexpensive cocaine derivative ($5–$10 a vial) appears; called "crack," it is, according to drug officials, "our worst nightmare."
- More than 2,000 people die in plane crashes, making this the worst year in civilian air travel; largest accidents include JAL (520), Air India (329), and Arrow (248).
- As Shiite extremists hold TWA 847 hostages, ABC's "Good Morning America" holds a live interview with the Lebanese justice minister regarding their release; controversy follows on the role of media in crisis situations.
- The "Live Aid" concert in Philadelphia and London is viewed by 1.6 billion on TV and grosses $70 million for famine-stricken Africa; the "We Are the World" record and video raises $50 million.
- Takeovers reach a record high, over $120 billion; largest acquisitions, in billions of dollars, include GM of Hughes Aircraft (5.2), R.J. Reynolds of Nabisco (4.9), GM of RCA (6.2), and Kohlberg Kravis of Beatrice (6).
- A Texas court awards $11 billion in damages to Pennzoil in its suit against Texaco for interfering with a Getty-Pennzoil deal sealed only with a handshake and an oral agreement.
- The Nobel Peace Prize goes to the International Physicians for the Prevention of Nuclear War, founded by two cardiologists, one at Harvard, the other in Moscow.
- Weddings of the year include Billy Joel and Christie Brinkley; Bruce Springsteen and Julianne Phillips; Springsteen's *Born in the U.S.A.* sells 15 million copies.
- Parents and local school boards fight over keeping AIDS-afflicted children in school.
- According to the AMA, medical malpractice suits have tripled since 1975; the average award has increased from $95,000 to $333,000; the average doctor pays $8,400 yearly for insurance; a neurosurgeon pays as much as $101,000.
- Claus von Bülow, convicted in 1982, is acquitted of the attempted murder of his wealthy wife, Sunny, despite the damaging testimony of his mistress.
- "Mayflower Madam" Sidney Biddle Barrows, descendant of Plymouth and social-register forebears, is arrested as the alleged proprietress of a New York townhouse brothel; she maintains the privacy of her clients.
- The 1979 sentence of Gary Dotson, of 25–50 years for the rape of Cathleen Crowell Webb, is commuted after his supposed victim admits she lied at the trial.
- Reputed Gambino mob boss Paul Castellano is shot to death on his way to Sparks steakhouse in New York.
- After 99 years, Coca-Cola markets a new formula, "New Coke"; three months later, after consumer objection, it reinstates "Coca-Cola Classic."
- Wendy's Hamburgers fires Clara Peller, 84 ("Where's the beef?"), after her Prego spaghetti sauce ad ("I finally found it").
- A jury finds that *Time* magazine defamed but did not libel Ariel Sharon, in associating him with the 1982 massacre of Palestinians in Lebanon.
- General Westmoreland drops his $120 million 1982 libel suit against CBS for its documentary alleging that he deceived the public concerning Vietcong strength.
- A high-ranking KGB defector, Yurchencko returns to the USSR embassy and claims the CIA kidnapped him.
- Spy John Walker is turned in by his wife and daughter.
- Videocassette movie-rental income equals movie theater receipts; *Billboard* begins a "Top 40 VC" listing.
- Barbie dolls surpass in number the American population.
- A Nielsen survey reports that young children watch a record 27 hours and 21 minutes of TV a week and will have spent more time in front of the TV than in the classroom when they graduate from high school.
- An estimated 27 million adults are functional illiterates.
- The U.S. Army rules that male officers are forbidden to carry umbrellas.
- Sen. William Cohen (D-Me.) derides the Pentagon for paying $640 for a toilet seat, giving "a new meaning to the word throne."
- An Indianapolis company manufactures "Arfi," a $10 video for dogs; they bark at "Recipes to Lick your Chops Over," with Julia Chow, and "Fitness with Figi," who says "Roll over, get those tails in shape."
- New Secretary of Education William J. Bennett defends the president's cuts and calls for students' "divestiture" of "stereos, cars, and vacations."

Fads: hot food and salad bars, ethnic restaurants, wafer-thin pizza with toppings like duck and lamb sausage, pastas with ingredients like goat cheese and broccoli, whole-grain pita bread, ice-cream substitutes (tofu, yogurt), calcium to prevent osteoporosis (Tums)

New Words: (takeover jargon) white knight, golden parachute, leveraged buyout, junk bond, poison pill

First Appearances: photos of missing children on milk cartons, Acyclovir (for herpes), Strawberry Fields (in memory of John Lennon), Taurus, Sable, Yugo ($3,990), septuplets (to Patti and Sam Frustaci), female Harlem Globetrotter (Lynette Woodard, 5'11"), Cuban-American Miami mayor (Xavier Suarez), congressman in space (Jake Garn), Japanese PM on TV pleading "Buy American," Wrestlemania, She-Ra, computer-designed stamp (F.A. Bartholi), Rock and Roll Hall of Fame

1986

Facts and Figures

Economic Profile

Dow-Jones: ↑ High 1,955–Low 1,502

GNP: +5.6%

Inflation: +1.9%

Unemployment: 7.0%

Urban/rural population: 184/56

Male/female ratio: 119/125

High school graduates entering college: 35%

Four-year colleges: 2,029

Public/private schools: 7/1

American Chardonnays: '83 Tualatin; '84 Deloach: $9.99; '83 Stonegate: $8.19

U.S. Air, PeoplExpress, Eastern, Braniff; Washington, D.C.–New York: $29–35; Pittsburgh, Kansas City: $99; Los Angeles: $179

Hyundai: $4,995

Yugo: $3,990

Mitsubishi: $4,999

Nissan Maxima: $13,295, Sentra: $4,959

Cadillac Brougham: $20,159, Coupe de Ville: $16,999

Fisher VHS-VCR: $299

Deaths

Desi Arnaz, Jorge Luis Borges, James Cagney, Roy Cohn, Benny Goodman, Cary Grant, Georgia O'Keeffe, Alan Jay Lerner, Kate Smith, Theodore White, Rudy Vallee, Minoru Yamasaki

In the News

CHALLENGER SHUTTLE EXPLODES 73 SECONDS AFTER LIFT-OFF, CREW OF SEVEN DIES INSTANTLY . . . REAGAN HALTS TRADE TO LIBYA, CALLS QADDAFI "BARBARIAN," "FLAKY" . . . HAITIAN DICTATOR BABY DOC DUVALIER IS OVERTHROWN . . . GORBACHEV ASKS "RADICAL REFORM," CONDEMNS FORMER LEADERSHIP . . . MARCOS CLAIMS VICTORY OVER CORAZON AQUINO, U.S. SENATE CALLS ELECTION A FRAUD . . . AQUINO TAKES OVER, MARCOS LEAVES FOR EXILE . . . DOW TOPS 1,800 . . . OIL FALLS TO $11 A BARREL . . . "THE NEW YORK TIMES" ACCUSES AUSTRIAN PRESIDENTIAL CANDIDATE KURT WALDHEIM OF NAZI PAST . . . ACCIDENT AT CHERNOBYL NUCLEAR PLANT ENDANGERS USSR AND EUROPE . . . LIBYA FIRES ON U.S. PLANES OVER "LINE OF DEATH," WARNS OF WORLDWIDE TERROR . . . U.S. BOMBS TRIPOLI AND BENGHAZI IN RETALIATION FOR LIBYAN ATTACK ON GI DISCO IN WEST GERMANY, 2 PILOTS ARE LOST . . . CHIEF JUSTICE WARREN BURGER RESIGNS, WILLIAM REHNQUIST IS NOMINATED . . . CONGRESS VOTES $70 MILLION MILITARY AID TO CONTRAS . . . PANAMANIAN ARMY CHIEF MANUEL NORIEGA IS ACCUSED OF DRUG DEALING . . . 1,000% INCREASE IN AIDS DEATHS IS PREDICTED BY 1991 . . . BASKETBALL STAR LEN BIAS DIES OF COCAINE USE . . . MAJOR TAX REFORM BILL CUTS DEDUCTIONS, INDIVIDUAL AND CORPORATE RATES . . . IMMIGRATION LAW OFFERS AMNESTY TO ALIENS . . . REAGAN AND GORBACHEV MEET IN ICELAND, DISAGREE ON SDI . . . DEMOCRATS GAIN SENATE MAJORITY, 55–45 . . . WALL STREET ARBITRAGEUR IVAN BOESKY PAYS $100 MILLION FINE FOR INSIDER TRADING . . . $30 MILLION SECRET WEAPONS SALE TO IRAN IS REVEALED, PROFITS WERE DIVERTED TO CONTRAS, NSC CHIEF JOHN POINDEXTER AND AIDE COL. OLIVER NORTH ARE IMPLICATED.

Quotes

"[They] slipped the surly bonds of earth to touch the face of God."
—Ronald Reagan, on the death of the Challenger crew

"We did not—repeat, did not—trade weapons or anything else for hostages—nor will we."
—President Reagan

"There is no evidence that AIDS is spread through casual contact occurring in the workplace."
—Dr. Robert Windom, U.S. Public Health Service

"We made the proposal, not the Soviets. We said . . . we will do away with all nuclear weapons. . . . We'll give it away if you let us continue our search for this defense [SDI]."
—White House Press Secretary Larry Speakes, on Iceland summit

"The long agony is over. We are finally freed."
—Philippine President Corazón Aquino

"I have no weaknesses for shoes."
—Imelda Marcos

"Hello, Johnny? . . . [click]."
—Joan Rivers, on telling Johnny Carson about her own late night talk show

"It's not the most intellectual job in the world, but I do have to know the letters."
—Vanna White, "Wheel of Fortune"

"I don't expect you'll hear me writing any poems to the greater glory of Ronald and Nancy Reagan."
—First U.S. Poet Laureate Robert Penn Warren

"I am very happy and proud to be the donor. Her mother carried her for nine months, and I am honored to give her a part of me."
—Sen. Jake Garn (R-Utah), on donating a kidney to his daughter

The Challenger crew: Elison S. Onizuka, Christa McAuliffe, Gregory B. Jarvis, Judith A. Resnik (standing), Michael J. Smith, Francis R. Scobee, Robert E. McNair. *Courtesy: NASA.*

Ads

—Dedicated to the proposition that news does not improve with age.
(The Wall Street Journal)

We sell appetite suppressants over the counter.
(Ted's Great Grinders, Michigan)

We employ more bozos, buffoons, jokesters, and weirdos than most other newspapers.
(The Oregonian)

We've been in this business since it started getting ugly.
(Volkswagen Beetle)

You can never be too powerful. Or too well connected.
(Macintosh, by Apple)

Improve your husband's sex life.
(Nike Sneakers)

For long wear and rugged good looks, just add water.
(Timberland Boat Shoes)

The best tasting bran flake has done more than just change its name. Now it's high in fiber and natural too.
(Post Natural Bran Flakes)

TV

Premieres

"L.A. Law," Harry Hamlin, Jill Eikenberry
"Our World," Linda Ellerbee
"Matlock," Andy Griffith
"Alf," Paul Fusco
"Crime Story," Dennis Farina, Darlanna Fluegel
"Perfect Strangers," Bronson Pinchot, Mark Linn-Baker

Top Ten (Nielsen)

"The Cosby Show," "Family Ties," "Murder, She Wrote," "60 Minutes," "Cheers," "The Golden Girls," "Dallas," "Dynasty," "Miami Vice," "Who's the Boss?"

Specials

"Peter the Great" (Lilli Palmer, Vanessa Redgrave, Maximillian Schell); "Goya" (Gian Carlo Menotti, with Placido Domingo); "Nobody's Child" (Marlo Thomas); "Planet Earth"; "The Story of English" (Robert MacNeil); "The Africans"; "The Vanishing Family—Crisis in America" (Bill Moyers)

Emmy Awards

"L.A. Law" (drama); "The Golden Girls" (comedy); "A Year in the Life" (miniseries); Bruce Willis (actor, "Moonlighting"); Michael J. Fox (comedic actor, "Family Ties"); Sharon Gless (actress, "Cagney & Lacey"); Rue McClanahan (comedic actress, "The Golden Girls")

Of Note

On July 29, 350 million watch Prince Andrew wed Sarah Ferguson at Westminster Abbey • General Electric takes over RCA and replaces Grant Tinker with Richard C. Wright • William S. Paley, 84, returns to CBS as active chairman, replacing Thomas H. Wyman • Bobby Ewing (Patrick Duffy) returns to "Dallas" in a well-publicized shower scene; his death, along with the entire last season, was just a dream.

Movies

Openings

Platoon (Oliver Stone), Tom Berenger, Willem Dafoe
A Room with a View (James Ivory), Maggie Smith, Denholm Elliott
Hannah and Her Sisters (Woody Allen), Mia Farrow, Woody Allen, Dianne Wiest, Michael Caine
Children of a Lesser God (Randa Haines), Marlee Matlin, William Hurt
Round Midnight (Bertrand Tavernier), Dexter Gordon
Mona Lisa (Neil Jordan), Bob Hoskins, Cathy Tyson
The Color of Money (Martin Scorsese), Paul Newman, Tom Cruise
Peggy Sue Got Married (Francis Ford Coppola), Kathleen Turner
Aliens (James Cameron), Sigourney Weaver
Crimes of the Heart (Bruce Beresford), Jessica Lange, Sissy Spacek, Diane Keaton

Star Trek IV: The Voyage Home (Leonard Nimoy), William Shatner, Leonard Nimoy
Ruthless People (Jim Abrahams), Bette Midler, Danny DeVito
Down and Out in Beverly Hills (Paul Mazursky), Nick Nolte, Bette Midler
My Beautiful Laundrette (Stephen Frears), Saeed Jaffrey
Crocodile Dundee (Peter Faiman), Paul Hogan
Top Gun (Tony Scott), Tom Cruise, Kelly McGillis
Stand by Me (Rob Reiner), Wil Wheaton, River Phoenix
Blue Velvet (David Lynch), Kyle MacLachlan, Isabella Rosellini

Academy Awards

Best Picture: *Platoon*
Best Director: Oliver Stone *(Platoon)*
Best Actress: Marlee Matlin *(Children of a Lesser God)*
Best Actor: Paul Newman *(The Color of Money)*

Top Box-Office Stars

Tom Cruise, Eddie Murphy, Paul Hogan, Rodney Dangerfield, Bette Midler, Sylvester Stallone, Clint Eastwood, Whoopi Goldberg, Kathleen Turner, Paul Newman

Stars of the Future

River Phoenix, Kiefer Sutherland, Rodney Harney, Keanu Reaves, Johnny Depp, Corey Feldman, Christian Slater, Alfre Woodard

Teenage hero and #1 box-office star Tom Cruise co-stars with Paul Newman in *The Color of Money,* for which Newman wins an Oscar. *Movie Star News.*

Popular Music

Hit Songs
"How Will I Know"
"Kyrrie"
"Greatest Love of All"
"Live to Tell"
"On My Own"
"There'll Be Sad Songs"
"Sledgehammer"

Top Records
Albums: *The Broadway Album* (Barbra Streisand); *Promise* (Sade); *Welcome to the Real World* (Mr. Mister); *Whitney Houston* (Whitney Houston); *5150* (Van Halen); *Winner in You* (Patti LaBelle)

Singles: *Sarah* (Starship); *These Dreams* (Heart); *Rock Me Amadeus* (Falco); *Kiss* (Prince and the Revolution); *Addicted to Love* (Robert Palmer); *West End Girls* (Pet Shop Boys); *Invisible Touch* (Genesis). Country: *In Love* (Ronny Milsap); *Always Have Always Will* (Janie Fricke)

Grammy Awards
Higher Love, Steve Winwood

Since his 1959 debut at the legendary Five Spot cafe in New York (where Leonard Bernstein proclaimed him "a genius"), saxophonist Ornette Coleman has remained on the leading edge of jazz innovation. *Movie Star News.*

(record); *Graceland,* Paul Simon (album); "That's What Friends Are For" (song)

Jazz and Big Bands
Run-DMC popularizes "rap music," with "Walk This Way" (Aerosmith), a rhythmic talk-over style originating in New York ghetto neighborhoods. New groups include Elektric Band, Red Alert, O.T.B., and Azymuth.

Top Performers (*Downbeat*): Wynton Marsalis (soloist); Count Basie (band); Art Blakey & the Jazz Messengers (acoustic jazz group); Miles Davis (electric jazz group); Eddie Daniels, Ron Carter, Gerry Mulligan, Stephane Grappelli, Steve Swallow (instrumentalists); Sarah Vaughan, Bobby McFerrin (vocalists); Manhattan Transfer (vocal group); Pat Metheny/Ornette Coleman, *Song X* (album)

Theater

Broadway Openings

Plays
Broadway Bound (Neil Simon), Linda Lavin
The World According to Me, written and acted by Jackie Mason
Wild Honey (Michael Frayn), Ian McKellen

Musicals
The Mystery of Edwin Drood (Rupert Holmes), George Rose, Betty Buckley
Me and My Girl (L. Arthur Rose, Douglas Furber, Noel Gay), Robert Lindsay

Classics, Revivals, and Off-Broadway Premieres
The Boys in Autumn, George C. Scott, John Cullum; *You Never Can Tell* (G. B. Shaw), Amanda Plummer, Uta Hagen; *The House of Blue Leaves,* Swoosie Kurtz, Stockard Channing; *Long Day's Journey into Night,* Jack Lemmon; *Hay Fever,* Rosemary Harris; *Arsenic and Old Lace,* Jean Stapleton; *The Front Page,* Richard Thomas; *Cuba and His Teddy Bear* (Reinaldo Povod), Robert DeNiro, Ralph Macchio

Pulitzer Prize
No prize is awarded.

Tony Awards
I'm Not Rappaport, Herb Gardner (play); *The Mystery of Edwin Drood,* Rupert Holmes (musical)

Classical Music

Compositions

John Harbison, *The Flight into Egypt*
William Bolcom, Symphony no. 4
Ralph Shapey, Symphonie Concertante
Elliott Carter, *A Celebration of Some 100 × 150 Notes*
Charles Wuorinen, *The W. of Babylon*
Ursula Mamlok, *Der Andreus Garten*
Wendy Chambers, *Liberty Overture*
Richard Wernick, Violin Concerto

Important Events

The centenary of Liszt's death is widely commemorated; in Washington, D.C., and New York, Jorge Bolet, Charles Rosen, and Earl Wild perform Liszt's piano works; an unpublished composition is scheduled for U.S. and world premiere at the end of the year.

As part of the cultural exchange program, Vladimir Horowitz, 81, returns to the USSR (after 61 years) and gives two recitals; performed on his nine-foot Steinway, flown from New York City, the concerts are televised to the United States and Western Europe.

The Tanglewood Festival of Contemporary Music includes minimalist works of electronic and computer music.

New Appointments: André Previn, Los Angeles

Debut: Gustavo Romero

First Performances

Jacob Druckman, *Athanor* (New York); Ellen Zwilich, Piano Concerto (Detroit); Leonard Bernstein, *Jubilee Games* (New York); Morton Feldman, *Coptic Light* (New York); Oliver Messiaen, *St. Francis of Assisi,* 3 scenes (Boston); Elliott Carter, String Quartet no. 4 (Miami)

Bette Midler earns a record number of awards this year for her stage and screen comedy; she is also expecting a child. *Movie Star News.*

Opera

Metropolitan: Simon Estes, Hildegard Behrens, Peter Hofmann, *Die Walküre* (designs by Gunther Schneider-Siemssen); Joan Sutherland (25th debut anniversary), *I Puritani;* Jon Vickers, Leona Mitchell, *Samson* (Handel); Alfredo Kraus, Cecilia Gasdia (debut), *Roméo et Juliette;* Anna Tomowa-Sintow, Brigitte Fassbaender (debut), Elisabeth Söderström, *Der Rosenkavalier;* Tatiana Troyanos, Kiri Te Kanawa, Vinson Cole (debut), *Die Fledermaus;* Söderström, José van Dam, Kathleen Battle, *La Nozze di Figaro;* Sherrill Milnes, Te Kanawa, *Simon Boccanegra*

New York City: Ben Holt, *The Life and Times of Malcolm X* (Anthony Davis)

Chicago: Jon Vickers, Tatiana Troyanos, *Parsifal;* Marilyn Horne, Jeffrey Gall, Gianna Rolandi, *Orlando*

San Francisco: Ghena Dimitrova, Franco Bonisolli, Piero Cappuccilli, *Il Trovatore;* Régine Crespin, *The Medium;* Cappuccilli, *I Pagliacci;* Firenza Cossotto, Cappuccilli, *Cavalleria rusticana*

Washington, D.C.:   *The Tzar's Bride* (directed by Galina Vishnevskaya, Mstislav Rostropovich); Placido Domingo, *Goya* (Gian Carlo Menotti), world premiere

Los Angeles Music Center Opera (opening):
Domingo, *Otello* (designs by Schneider-Siemmsen)

Boston: *Taverner* (Peter Maxwell Davies)

Lionel Richie, 36, attended Tuskegee Institute before singing with the Commodores and Diana Ross, and before writing and producing an album for Kenny Rogers; he went out on his own in 1980. *Movie Star News.*

Art

Painting

Jasper Johns, *The Seasons*
Robert Motherwell, *Work in Progress (The Golden Bough)*
Jim Waid, *Gazelle*
Gregory Gillespie, *Studio Corner*
Andy Warhol, *Last Self-Portrait, Mercedes Benz W125 (1937)*
Cy Twombley, *Gaeta Set III 6*
Meyer Vaisman, *Process Inks*
Julian Schnabel, *Stella and the Wooden Bird*
Frederick Brown, *Just Love*

Portrait of a Memory *(with a Blue Edge)*
Richard Artschwager, *Organ of Cause and Effect III*
Judy Pfaff, *Supermercado*

Sculpture

Isamu Noguchi, *Slide Mantra; Ojizousama*
Terry Allen, *Trees*
Group Material, *MASS*
Christopher Wilmarth,

Architecture

Battell Chapel, Yale University, New Haven (Herbert S. Newman)
Los Angeles Museum of Contemporary Art (Arata Isozaki)
Herring Hall, Rice University, Houston (Cesar Pelli)
Cleveland Clinic Foundation Building (Cesar Pelli)
IBM Corporate Office Building, Purchase, New York (I.M. Pei)

Important Exhibitions

Many nonwestern, traveling exhibitions include "Impressionist to Early Modern Paintings from the USSR."

Museums

New York: *Metropolitan:* "Treasures of the Holy Land"; Gothic and Renaissance Art in Nuremberg 1300–1550; Van Gogh in Saint-Rémy and Auvers; Boucher; Rodin. *Museum of Modern Art:* "Vienna: 1900—Art, Architecture and Design"; Mies van der Rohe (100th birthday); Jasper Johns; Richard Serra; Bill Jensen. *Whitney:* Eric Fischl; Alex Katz; Sargent; Storrs. *Guggenheim:* Four Decades of American, European Sculpture. *Pace:* Picasso's sketchbooks.

Detroit, Fort Worth: Donatello

Washington: Matisse; Goya; Winslow Homer

San Francisco: "The New Painting: Impressionism 1874–1886"

Detroit: Diego Rivera retrospective

Chicago: Louis Sullivan; The Great Eastern Temple: Treasures of Japanese Buddhist Art from Tōdaiji

Jasper Johns,
The Seasons.
Courtesy: Leo Castelli.

Phoenix, Santa Barbara, Met: "The Elegant Brush: Chinese Painting under the Quianlong Emperor, 1735–95"

Art Briefs

Television City, in New York, is proposed by postmodernist Helmut Jahn • *Art and Antiques* reports on a series of unknown Andrew Wyeth paintings, most of an unidentified blond nude known as Helga (Testorf), eventually identified as a Pennsylvania housekeeper • The Willard Hotel, Washington, D.C., reopens, restored to the grandeur it had during Ulysses S. Grant's day; here Grant coined the term "lobbyists" to describe his favor seekers • Equitable opens its $200-million building (New York City, by Edward Larrabee Barnes), also housing a branch of the Whitney Museum; at the entrance is the newly commissioned 68-foot "Mural with Blue Brushstroke" by Roy Lichtenstein • Topping the auction record for an American work, Rembrandt Peale's "Rubens Peale with a Geranium" brings $4.07 million; Jasper Johns' "Out the Window" sells for $3.6 million.

Dance

Premieres/Important Productions

New York City Ballet: Robert La Fosse, *Quiet City, Piccolo Balletto;* Heather Watts, Jock Soto, *Songs of the Auvergne* (Peter Martins)

American Ballet Theatre: Mikhail Baryshnikov, Clark Tippet, *Murder* (David Gordon); Cynthia Gregory, Patrick Bissell, *Francesca da Rimini* (John Taras)

Joffrey (30th anniversary): Glenn Edgerton, Dawn Caccamo, *Birthday Variations (Arpino);* Beatriz Rodriguez, David Palmer, *Passage* (James Kudelka, Thomas Tallis); Carl Corry, Charlene Gehm/Yoko Ichino, Fernando Bujones, *La fille mal gardée* (Frederick Ashton); *Force Field* (Laura Dean); *Esteemed Guests* (Mark Morris)

Martha Graham (60th anniversary): *Heretic, Every Soul Is a Circus*

Books

Fiction

Critics' Choice

The Garden of Eden, Ernest Hemingway (posthumous)
Kate Vaiden, Reynolds Price
Roger's Version, John Updike
Reckless Eyeballing, Ishmael Reed
Slaves of New York, Tama Janowitz
The Good Mother, Sue Miller
Paco's Story, Larry Heinemann
The Sportswriter, Richard Ford
The Endless Short Story, Ronald Sukenick
☙ *The Handmaid's Tale*, Margaret Atwood

Best-Sellers

It, Stephen King
Red Storm Rising, Tom Clancy
Whirlwind, James Clavell
The Bourne Supremacy, Robert Ludlum
Hollywood Husbands, Jackie Collins
Wanderlust, Danielle Steel
I'll Take Manhattan, Judith Krantz
Last of the Breed, Louis L'Amour
The Prince of Tides, Pat Conroy
A Perfect Spy, John le Carré

Nonfiction

Critics' Choice

Cities on a Hill: A Journey through Contemporary American Cultures, Frances FitzGerald
Murrow, His Life and Times, A. M. Sperber
Tombee: Portrait of a Cotton Planter, Theodore Rosengarten
The Nazi Doctors, Robert Jay Lifton
The Anthropic Cosmological Principle, John Barrow, Frank Tipler
Less Than One: Selected Essays, Joseph Brodsky
The Cycles of American History, Arthur M. Schlesinger, Jr.
The Reckoning, David Halberstam
A Machine That Would Go of Itself: The Constitution in American Culture, Michael G. Kammen
The Society of Mind, Marvin Minsky

Best-Sellers

Fatherhood, Bill Cosby
Fit for Life, Harvey and Marilyn Diamond
His Way: The Unauthorized Biography of Frank Sinatra, Kitty Kelley
The Rotation Diet, Martin Katahn
You're Only Old Once, Dr. Seuss
Callanetics: Ten Years Younger in Ten Hours, Callan Pinckney

The Frugal Gourmet Cooks with Wine, Jeff Smith
Be Happy—You Are Loved!, Robert H. Schuller, Thomas Nelson
Word for Word, Andrew A. Rooney
James Herriot's Dog Stories, James Herriot

Poetry

Derek Walcott, *Collected Poems, 1948–1984*
Edwin Denby, *The Complete Poems*
Adrienne Rich, *Your Native Land, Your Life*
Donald Hall, *The Happy Man*
Charles Simic, *Unending Blues*
Jane Kenyon, *The Boat of Quiet Hours*

Pulitzer Prizes

A Summons to Memphis, Peter Taylor (fiction)
Voyagers to the West, Bernard Bailyn (U.S. history)
Arab and Jew, David K. Shipler (nonfiction)
Bearing the Cross: Martin Luther King Jr. and the Southern Christian Leadership Conference, David Garrow (biography)
Thomas and Beulah, Rita Dove (poetry)

Science and Technology

Azidothymidine (AZT) shows promise for the lethal AIDS pneumonia.
A study of Harvard alumni reports that 2,000 calories of exercise per week reduces the death rate by 28 percent.
Adoptee research indicates that heredity is more important to obesity than environment.
Studies show that long-term oral contraceptive use does not increase the rate of breast cancer.
Training in inductive reasoning and spatial skills is found to prevent mental decline in the elderly.
Genetically engineered alpha-interferon is used to make a hepatitis B vaccine and to treat hairy cell leukemia.
The first successful intrauterine surgery on twins, for hydrocephalis, is performed at Baltimore's Sinai Hospital.

The deciphering of the Mayan language reveals bloodletting and self-mutilation rituals.
☙ The European Scientific Association's spaceship Giotto comes within 375 miles of Halley's comet; its findings support the "dirty snowball" (dust and ice) theory; photos also indicate a black nucleus.

Nobel Prizes

Dudley R. Herschback and Yuan T. Lee win in chemistry for their studies of "reaction dynamics." Rita Levi-Montalcini and Stanley Cohen win in physiology or medicine for their work on substances that influence cell growth.

Sports ———————————————————————

Baseball
Eleven players who admitted drug use under immunity are fined 10 percent of their salary.

Roger Clemens (Boston, AL) strikes out a record 20 in a single game.

In the All-Star game, Fernando Valenzuela (Los Angeles, NL) strikes out five in a row, matching Hubbell (1934).

The Cy Young awards go to Mike Scott (Houston, NL) and Roger Clemens (Boston, AL).

Champions ————————————

Batting	18–5
Tim Raines (Montreal, NL), .334	Roger Clemens (Boston, AL), 24–4
Wade Boggs (Boston, AL), .357	*Home runs*
Pitching	Jesse Barfield (Toronto, AL), 40
Bob Ojeda (New York, NL),	

Football
In the USFL's $1.69 billion suit, a jury rules that the NFL violated antitrust laws but awards only $1; the USFL disbands.

The NFL's top draft choice, Bo Jackson, chooses baseball and signs with Kansas City.

NFL Season Leaders: Tommy Kramer (Minnesota), passing; Eric Dickerson (Los Angeles Rams), rushing; Jerry Rice (San Francisco), receiving

AFL Season Leaders: Dan Marino (Miami), passing; Curt Warner (Seattle), rushing; Todd Christensen (Los Angeles Raiders), receiving

College All-Americans: Brian Bosworth (LB), Oklahoma; Cornelius Bennett (LB), Alabama; Paul Palmer (B), Temple

Bowls (Jan. 1, 1987)
Rose: Arizona State 22–Michigan 15
Orange: Oklahoma 42–Arkansas 8
Cotton: Ohio State 28–Texas A&M 12
Sugar: Nebraska 30–LSU 15
Fiesta: Penn State 20–Miami 14 (for #1)

Basketball
Len Bias had just been made Boston's first draft pick when he died of cocaine use.

Four-time all-star Micheal Ray Richardson is banned for two years for cocaine use.

NBA All-Pro First Team: Larry Bird (Boston), Dominique Wilkins (Atlanta), Kareem Abdul-Jabbar (Los Angeles Lakers), Magic Johnson (Los Angeles Lakers), Isiah Thomas (Detroit)

Other Sports
Golf: Jack Nicklaus, 46, becomes the oldest to win the Masters; Raymond Floyd wins his first Open at 43.

Boxing: Michael Tyson, 20, KO's Trevor Berbick, to become the youngest heavyweight champion.

Tennis: Martina Navratilova wins her fifth straight Wimbledon.

Winners ————————————

World Series	*MVP*
New York (NL) 4	Larry Bird, Boston
Boston (AL) 3	*College Basketball*
MVP	Louisville
NL–Mike Schmidt, Philadelphia	*Player of the Year*
AL–Roger Clemens, Boston	Walter Berry, St. John's
Super Bowl XXI (Jan. 1987)	*Stanley Cup*
New York Giants 39–Denver 20	Montreal
MVP	*US Tennis Open*
Lawrence Taylor, New York Giants	Men: Ivan Lendl
	Women: Martina Navratilova
College Football	*USGA Open*
Penn State	Ray Floyd
Heisman Trophy	*Kentucky Derby*
Vinnie Testaverde, Miami	Ferdinand (W. Shoemaker, jockey)
NBA Championship	
Boston 4–Houston 2	

Fashion ——————————————————

For young women, the soft, feminine, and casual look remains popular, with even skinnier body-hugging pants and jersey miniskirts and dresses. Denim skirts reach the knee or midthigh, and the shorter styles have side, or back, hem zippers; denim also remains popular in shirts, jackets, and coats. Accessories range from silk scarves to pearl necklaces and earrings. Tops, in the summer, of cotton or jersey, are still loose but now cut to the waist or above; skin is visible. Men's shirts are also fashionable, with the shirttails casually knotted in the front. *Out of Africa* safari bush-country styles in twill, khaki, or chino gain in vogue.

High-fashion note: Karl Lagerfeld's and Fendi's denim suits with stitching or embroidery

Kaleidoscope _____

Born in Brooklyn and a distinguished pediatric surgeon, Surgeon General C. Everett Koop crusades against the dangers of smoking, "the leading cause of preventable death." *National Health Service.*

- The July Fourth $30 million birthday party for the Statue of Liberty includes Chief Justice Burger's administering of citizenship oaths, and a 40,000-piece fireworks display.
- The oldest college in the United States, Harvard celebrates its 350th birthday.
- A presidential investigation reveals that leakage from an O-ring seal on the solid fuel booster rocket caused the Challenger explosion.
- Following the Challenger disaster, a Titan missile with a "spy" satellite blows up after lift-off.
- The prime rate drops to 7 percent, and the national debt passes $2 trillion, twice the amount of 1981.
- In the "preppie murder" case, Robert Chambers is accused of strangling Jennifer Levin in Central Park; he claims her death was accidental during rough sex.
- Drexel, Burnham, Lambert executive Dennis Levine, 33, pleads guilty to insider trading, by which he earned $12.6 million.
- After President Reagan addresses the nation on the secret Iran weapons deal, his popularity falls dramatically.
- Extensive coverage is given Austrian President Kurt Waldheim's insistence that he joined Nazi groups to advance his diplomatic career and knew nothing of the Final Solution.
- From Long Beach, California, to New York City, the Hands Across America chain raises $100 million for the poor and homeless.
- Estimates of the homeless in major cities include: 40,000, NYC; 38,000, Los Angeles; 25,000, Chicago; 20,000, St. Louis; 10,000, Boston and Washington.
- The Chainina is one of the new crossbreeds intended to provide less fatty, lower-calorie beef.
- Fitness foods—high in fiber and low in sodium, fat, cholesterol, calories, and caffeine—account for 10 percent of the $300 billion retail food market.
- Increased numbers of consumers seek professional assistance with home decorating and spend an average of $15,584 on the living room.
- After a presidential commission estimates that, per month, 20 million use marijuana, 5 million cocaine, and 500,000 heroin, federal workers in "sensitive" tasks are randomly drug tested; half of the Fortune 500 are said to be considering similar actions.
- Controversy intensifies over the death penalty for youths and their confinement in adult jails: 500,000 are held in adult jails each year; 30 states allow for the execution of children (in Indiana, at age 10).
- The FBI arrests Gennadi F. Zakharov, a Soviet physician at the UN, on charges of spying; he is exchanged for *U.S. News* reporter Nicholas Daniloff, arrested by the KGB for allegedly carrying secret maps.
- Many officials are implicated in a New York City Parking Violations Bureau scandal; a borough president, Donald Manes, under suspicion, commits suicide.
- The Supreme Court holds that the military may enforce a uniform dress code; the case involves three men who were prohibited from wearing yarmulkes indoors.
- In Bowers *v.* Hardwick, the Supreme Court reaffirms a Georgia statute making consensual sodomy a criminal offense.
- Because of the declining U.S. dollar and Chernobyl— and fear of reprisal after the U.S. raid at Libya—travel to Western European countries drops 45 percent.
- The Southeast has a month-long drought, during which crops and cattle die and over 430 forest fires occur.
- Joseph P. Kennedy II, son of Robert and nephew of President John Kennedy, enters Congress.
- *Dirty Harry* actor Clint Eastwood is elected mayor of Carmel-by-the-Sea, a California village of 4,700 homes.
- Much-discussed marriages of the year include: Caroline Bouvier Kennedy, 28, to Edwin A. Schlossberg, 41; John McEnroe, 27, to Tatum O'Neal, 22; Debra Winger, 30, to Timothy Hutton, 25.
- An estimated $1.5 billion is spent for religious radio and TV; Pentecostal preacher Jimmy Swaggart, 50, runs a 7,000-seat Family Worship Center near Baton Rouge.
- Two women vie for governor of Nebraska: Kay Orr defeats Helen Boosalis.
- Eli Wiesel wins the Nobel Peace Prize.

Fads: aerobics, grilled tuna, carpaccio (raw beef), Saurian Godzilla, foam diadem of Statue of Liberty, My Pet Monster, Clubman shades, telescopes (for Halley's comet)

First Appearances: ceramic that superconducts at −406°, official observance of Martin Luther King, Jr., Day, U.S. poet laureate (Robert Penn Warren), Cadillac Allante ($50,000), Honda Acura (in U.S.), Dodge Shadow, Hyundai Excel, Texas Air takeover of PeoplExpress, record auto auction price ($6.5 million, 1931 Bugatti Royale, Reno), $1.1 million TV ad minute (Super Bowl), microchip circuited talking toy (Smarty Bear), Candyland, Clue, Chutes and Ladders for VCR, Rubik's Magic, The Heart Family New Arrival Set (father, pregnant mother, newborn), one-stick Popsicle, microwave pizza (Pillsbury), tourist visa required for France, Carter Presidential Center (Atlanta), Spectra (Polaroid), outdoor testing of genetically engineered plants (Wisconsin)

1987

In the News

EVANGELIST JIM BAKKER ADMITS TO MAKING PAYMENTS TO COVER SEXUAL INFIDELITY . . . GARY HART WITHDRAWS WHEN SEXUAL INDISCRETION IS EXPOSED . . . IRAQI MISSILE HITS SS "STARK" IN PERSIAN GULF AND KILLS 37, IRAQ APOLOGIZES . . . WEST GERMAN MATHIAS RUST, 19, FLIES SMALL PLANE FROM FINLAND INTO MOSCOW, SOVIET DEFENSE MINISTER IS FIRED . . . ALAN GREENSPAN REPLACES PAUL VOLCKER AS FEDERAL RESERVE CHAIRMAN . . . THATCHER IS REELECTED BRITISH PM FOR THIRD TIME . . . NYC SUBWAY "VIGILANTE" GOETZ IS ACQUITTED OF ASSAULT, FOUND GUILTY OF ILLEGAL GUN POSSESSION . . . STRICT CONSTRUCTIONIST ROBERT BORK IS NOMINATED FOR JUSTICE LEWIS POWELL'S SEAT . . . OLIVER NORTH TAKES FIFTH AMENDMENT IN IRAN-CONTRA CONNECTION . . . EX-NSC CHIEF JOHN POINDEXTER TESTIFIES TO TRANSFERRING IRAN ARMS SALES PROFITS TO CONTRAS WITHOUT INFORMING REAGAN . . . U.S. SHIPS IN PERSIAN GULF ESCORT KUWAITI TANKER UNDER U.S. FLAG . . . IRANIANS RIOT IN MECCA, 400 ARE KILLED BY SAUDIS . . . COSTA RICAN PRESIDENT OSCAR ARIAS'S CENTRAL AMERICAN PEACE PLAN IS SIGNED . . . MARINE SERGEANT FROM MOSCOW EMBASSY IS CONVICTED OF SPYING . . . DOW TOPS 2,700 . . . DOW DROPS 508 POINTS IN ONE DAY, THE WORST FALL IN HISTORY . . . BORK NOMINATION IS REJECTED BY SENATE, 58–42 . . . CONGRESSIONAL REPORT CRITICIZES "DECEPTION, DISDAIN FOR THE LAW" IN IRAN-CONTRA AFFAIR . . . REAGAN AND GORBACHEV SIGN TREATY TO ELIMINATE INF IN EUROPE . . . PALESTINIANS RIOT ON WEST BANK AND GAZA STRIP . . . SOUTH KOREA HOLDS FIRST DIRECT PRESIDENTIAL ELECTION, RULING PARTY IS REELECTED . . . 338 OF 452 ARE CONVICTED IN MAFIA TRIAL IN PALERMO.

Quotes _____

"A few months ago, I told the American people I did not trade arms for hostages. My heart and best intentions still tell me this is true, but the facts and the evidence tell me it is not."

—Ronald Reagan

"I made a very deliberate decision not to ask the president so I could insulate him . . . and provide future deniability."

—National Security Adviser John Poindexter

"The problem at the heart was one of people, not process, . . . not that the structure was faulty. . . . The structure was not used."

—Brent Scowcroft, of the Tower Commission

"I came here to tell the truth—the good, the bad, and the ugly."

—Oliver North

"And yes, I can type."

—Fawn Hall, North's secretary

"We're all going to have to seriously question the system for selecting our national leaders. . . . It reduces the press of this nation to hunters."

—Gary Hart, after the *Miami Herald* reports his weekend adventure with Donna Rice

"Holy Wars: Money, Sex and Power"

—cover, *Newsweek* magazine, referring to Jim and Tammy Bakker

"When you have a man of this caliber, I think it's just terrible to try to make an ideological battle of it."

—Sen. Orrin Hatch (R-Utah), on Robert Bork's nomination to the Supreme Court

Michael Jackson maintains that he has never taken hormones to retain his high voice and never altered his cheekbones or eyes. *Movie Star News.*

"Robert Bork's America is a land in which women would be forced into back-alley abortions."

—Sen. Ted Kennedy (D-Mass.)

"Openness . . . now means accepting everything and denying reason's power. . . . Cultural relativism destroys . . . the good."

—Allan Bloom, *The Closing of the American Mind*

On the INF Treaty: "We make history. Changing its direction is within our power . . . when leaders of both sides have no illusions, talk with candor, and meet differences head-on" (Ronald Reagan). "It is our duty . . . to move together toward a nuclear-free world . . . for our children and grandchildren. . . . We can be proud of planting this sapling which may one day grow into a mighty tree of peace" (Mikhail Gorbachev).

Ads _____

TV

Premieres
"Tour of Duty," Stephen Caffrey, Miguel Nuñez
"Jake and the Fatman," William Conrad, Joe Penny
"A Different World," Lisa Bonet
"Beauty and the Beast," Ron Perlman, Linda Hamilton

Top Ten (Nielsen)
"The Cosby Show," "Family Ties," "Cheers," "Murder, She Wrote," "The Golden Girls," "60 Minutes"/"Night Court," "Growing Pains," "Moonlighting," "Who's the Boss?"

Specials
"Long Day's Journey into Night" (Jack Lemmon); "Silas Marner" (Ben Kingsley); "Mandela" (Danny Glover); "America by Design"; "We the People" (Peter Jennings); "The Constitution in Crisis" (Bill Moyers)

Emmy Awards
"L.A. Law" (drama); "The Golden Girls" (comedy); Gena Rowlands (actress in miniseries, "The Betty Ford Story"); Bruce Willis (actor, "Moonlighting"); Sharon Gless (actress, "Cagney & Lacey"); Michael J. Fox (comedic actor, "Family Ties")

Of Note
When overtime sports coverage of the U.S. Tennis Open intrudes on news time, Dan Rather storms off the set, and TV screens go black for six minutes • ABC airs the controversial "Amerika," a drama set in the United States ten years after a Soviet takeover • Joan Rivers is removed from her late-night talk show because of low ratings • The last "Hill Street Blues" show is broadcast • The Iran-Contra hearings gain a large audience.

Movies

Openings
The Last Emperor (Bernardo Bertolucci), John Lone
Broadcast News (James Brooks), William Hurt, Holly Hunter
Fatal Attraction (Adrian Lyne), Glenn Close, Michael Douglas
Hope and Glory (John Boorman), Sarah Miles
Moonstruck (Norman Jewison), Cher, Nicolas Cage
Wall Street (Oliver Stone), Michael Douglas, Charlie Sheen
Ironweed (Hector Babenco), Jack Nicholson, Meryl Streep
Good Morning, Vietnam (Barry Levinson), Robin Williams
The Untouchables (Brian De Palma), Kevin Costner, Sean Connery
Baby Boom (Charles Shyer), Diane Keaton
Three Men and a Baby (Leonard Nimoy), Tom Selleck, Steve Guttenberg, Ted Danson
Full Metal Jacket (Stanley Kubrick), Matthew Modine
Radio Days (Woody Allen), Woody Allen, Mia Farrow
Matewan (John Sayles), Chris Cooper, James Earl Jones
The Dead (John Huston), Anjelica Huston, Donal McCann
Empire of the Sun (Steven Spielberg), Christian Bale
House of Games (David Mamet), Lindsay Crouse, Joe Mantegna
Babette's Feast (Gabriel Axel), Stephane Audran

Left: Glenn Close, in *Fatal Attraction,* embodies the dangers of casual sex for the happily married man living in the AIDS era. *Movie Star News. Right:* Newly arrived on Oliver Stone's *Wall Street,* Charlie Sheen aspires to be like Gordon Gekko, the grandiose insider whose greed knows neither limits nor morality. *Movie Star News.*

Best Actress: Cher (*Moonstruck*)
Best Actor: Michael Douglas (*Wall Street*)

Top Box-Office Stars
Eddie Murphy, Michael Douglas, Michael J. Fox, Arnold Schwarzenegger, Paul Hogan, Tom Cruise, Glenn Close, Sylvester Stallone, Cher, Mel Gibson

Stars of the Future
Charlie Sheen, Adam Baldwin, Jennifer Rubin, Kyle MacLachlan, D. B. Sweeney, Kennan Ivory Wayans

Academy Awards
Best Picture: *The Last Emperor*
Best Director: Bernardo Bertolucci (*The Last Emperor*)

Popular Music

Hit Songs
"Nothing's Gonna Stop Us Now"
"Alone"
"Here I Go Again"
"The Way It Is"
"Shakedown"
"Livin' on a Prayer"
"Everybody Have Fun Tonight"

Top Records
Albums: *Slippery When Wet* (Bon Jovi); *Licensed to Ill* (Beastie Boys); *The Way It Is* (Bruce Hornsby and the Range); *Control* (Janet Jackson); *The Joshua Tree* (U2); *Fore!* (Huey Lewis and the News); *Invisible Touch* (Genesis)

Singles: *Walk like an Egyptian* (Bangles); *Shake You Down* (Gregory Abbott); *I Wanna Dance with Somebody* (Whitney Houston); *Always* (Atlantic Star); *I Think We're Alone Now* (Tiffany); *La Bamba* (Los Lobos). Country: *Give Me Wings* (Michael Johnson); *Half Past Forever* (T. G. Sheppard)

Grammy Awards
Graceland, Paul Simon (record); *The Joshua Tree,* U2 (album); "Somewhere Out There" (song)

Jazz and Big Bands
Major record companies continue to revitalize their jazz offerings: Columbia issues unreleased Duke Ellington on CD. Best-selling are George Howard, Dexter Gordon, Kenny G., Najee, Stanley Jordan.

Top Performers (*Downbeat*)
Ornette Coleman (soloist); Gil Evans (band); Art Blakey (acoustic jazz group); Pat Metheny Group (electric jazz group); Wynton Marsalis, Chic Corea, James Newton (instrumentalists); Sarah Vaughan, Bobby McFerrin (vocalists); Manhattan Transfer (vocal group); Michael Brecker, *Michael Brecker* (album)

Theater

Broadway Openings

Plays
Burn This (Lanford Wilson), John Malkovich, Joan Allen (from Mark Taper Forum, Los Angeles)
Fences (August Wilson), James Earl Jones
Les Liaisons Dangereuses (Christopher Hampton), Alan Rickman, Lindsay Duncan
Breaking the Code (Hugh Whitemore), Derek Jacobi, Michael Gough
Sweet Sue (A. R. Gurney), Mary Tyler Moore, Lynne Redgrave
The Nerd (Larry Shue), Robert Joy, Mark Hamill
Death and the King's Horseman (Wole Soyinka), Earle Hyman
Coastal Disturbances (Tina Howe), Annette Bening

Musicals
Starlight Express (Andrew Lloyd Webber, Richard Stilgoe), Greg Mowry, Robert Torti
Les Misérables, (Herbert Kretzmer, Claude-Michel Schönberg), Colm Wilkinson, Randy Graff, Terrence Mann
Into the Woods (Stephen Sondheim), Tom Aldredge, Bernadette Peters, Joanna Gleason

Classics, Revivals, and Off-Broadway Premieres
Driving Miss Daisy (Alfred Uhry), Dana Ivey, Morgan Freeman; *All My Sons,* Richard Kiley; *Steel Magnolias* (Robert Harling); *Serious Money* (Caryl Churchill); *Pygmalion,* Peter O'Toole, Amanda Plummer, Sir John Mills; *Anything Goes,* Patti LuPone; *Cabaret,* Joel Grey; *Frankie and Johnny in the Claire de Lune* (Terrence McNally); *The Mahabarata* (directed by Peter Brook); *The Widow Claire* (Horton Foote), Matthew Broderick; *Lily Dale,* Molly Ringwald; *Dreamgirls,* Lillias White

Regional
La Jolla and Los Angeles Theater Center: *Sarcophagus* (Vladimir Gubaryev)

Globe Theatre, San Diego: *Into the Woods; Another Antigone* (A. R. Gurney), George Grizzard

Alley, Houston: *Henceforward . . .* (Alan Ayckbourn)

Long Wharf, New Haven: *Dalliance* (Tom Stoppard)

American Repertory Theatre, Harvard University: *Sweet Table at the Richelieu* (Ronald Ribman)

Pulitzer Prize
Fences, August Wilson

Tony Awards
Fences, August Wilson (play), *Les Misérables,* Herbert Kretzmer, Claude-Michel Schönberg (musical)

Classical Music

Compositions
Milton Babbitt, *Transfigured Notes*
Nicholas Thorne, *Revelations*
Stephen Stucky, *Concerto for Orchestra*
William Schimmel, *Symphony no. 3 (Roy Harris)*
Max Schubel, *Divertimento*

Important Events
Birthday celebrations include Wilhelm Kempff's 92nd, Mstislav Rostropovich's 60th, and Sir George Solti's 75th. The complete Beethoven symphonies and concerti are performed at Carnegie Hall by the Vienna Philharmonic. The Louisville Orchestra celebrates its 50th anniversary with a 10-day series of concert-discussions.
Yo-Yo Ma and Luciano Pavarotti, among others, participate in a "Music for Life" concert at Carnegie Hall for AIDS victims.

Debut (U.S.):   Vladimir Feltsman

First Performances
William Bolcom, Symphony no. 4 (St. Louis); Ralph Shapey, Symphonie Concertante (Philadelphia); John Harbison, Symphony no. 2 (San Francisco); Donald Martino, *The White Island* (Boston); Steve Paulus, *Construction Symphony* (Los Angeles); George Perle, *New Fanfares, Songs for Praise and Lamentation, Concertino for Piano* (Tanglewood)

Opera
Numerous productions of *Otello* (100 years old) and *Don Giovanni* (200) are mounted.

Metropolitan: James Morris, Franz Mazura, Waltraud Meier (debut), *Das Rheingold* (designs by Gunther Schneider-Siemssen); Martti Talvela, Paul Plishka, Vladimir Popov, *Boris Godunov;* Eva Marton, Placido Domingo, *Turandot* (Franco Zeffirelli production); Jessye Norman, Leonie Rysanek, *Tannhäuser;* Catherine Malfitano, Neil Shicoff, *Manon* (Massenet, Jean-Pierre Ponnelle production); Tatiana Troyanos, Timothy Jenkins, Hans Sotin, *Parsifal;* Jon Vickers, Marilyn Horne, *Samson et Dalila*

Houston: *Nixon in China* (John Adams); Mirella Freni, Stefania Toczyska, *Aïda*

St. Louis: *Beauty and the Beast* (Stephen Oliver)

Chicago: *Satyagraha* (Philip Glass)

San Francisco: Leslie Richards, Paul Plishka, *Nabucco*

Los Angeles: *Fiery Angel* (Prokofiev); Domingo, Angelique Burzynsky, *La bohème* (Jean-Pierre Ponnelle production); Frederica von Stade, *La Cenerentola*

Music Notes
Sarah Caldwell organizes a three-week Boston-Moscow exchange • Numerous changes in performance policy occur: American works are regularly included in subscribed series; orchestras divide into smaller performing groups to offer nonsymphonic compositions; composers-in-residence take on greater professional capacities: Jacob Druckman (New York Philharmonic); John Harbison (L.A. Philharmonic); Charles Wuorinen (San Francisco) • Leonard Bernstein wins both the MacDowell Medal and Albert Schweitzer Music Award.

Pianist Vladimir Feltsman arrives in New York after an eight-year struggle to leave the USSR; he gains wide public acclaim. *Courtesy: CAMI.*

On both TV and movie screens, Michael J. Fox represents the '80s coming of age in a gentler fashion than his '60s or '70s predecessors. *Movie Star News.*

Art ───────────────

Painting

Peter Haley, *Cell with Smokestack*

Robert Mangold, *Brown Frame/Gold Ellipse*

Melissa Meyer, *My Father's Sketch Pad*

Gregory Amenoff, *Gnarl*

Tim Rollins & K.O.S., *Amerika VIII*

Christopher Brown, *Eighteen Blossoms*

Jim Dine, *For Margit van Leight-Frank*

Sculpture

Richard Serra, *My Curves Are Not Mad*

Richard Long, *Vermont Georgia South Carolina Wyoming Circle*

Tony Berland, *Zygote*

Architecture

Battery Park City, New York City (Cesar Pelli)

Menil Collection, Houston (Renzo Piano)

Robert O. Anderson Building, Los Angeles County Museum of Art (Hardy Holzman Pfeiffer)

Dartmouth College Gymnasium, Hanover, New Hampshire (Gwathmey Siegel), Hood Museum of Art (Charles W. Moore, Chad Floyd)

Lewis Thomas Laboratory, Princeton University, Princeton, New Jersey (Venturi, Rauch and Scott)

Computer Science and Engineering buildings, University of California, Irvine (Frank O. Gehry)

190 South La Salle Street, Chicago (Philip Johnson, John Burgee)

Important Exhibitions

Impressionist and postimpressionist paintings from London's Courtauld Collection travel to several cities; Anselm Kiefer's work tours; the controversial Andrew Wyeth "Helga Pictures" are refused by some museums, such as the Metropolitan.

Museums

New York: *Metropolitan:* "American Paradise: The World of the Hudson River School"; Ancient Chinese Art; "The Age of Correggio and Carracci"; Zurbarán. *Museum of Modern Art:* Frank Stella; Klee; American Prints; "Harlem Renaissance: Art of Black America." *Whitney:* Red Grooms; Demuth; Sheeler; Schnabel. *Guggenheim:* Kokoschka; Miró; Peggy Guggenheim Collection

Washington, Chicago, Metropolitan: Achievement of the Ottoman Empire of the 1550s

Boston, San Francisco, Washington: Georgia O'Keeffe; Wyeth's Helga Paintings

Houston: Contemporary Hispanic Art

Philadelphia, Houston, Los Angeles: "The Quest for Eternity: Chinese Ceramic Sculpture from the People's Republic of China"

Sherrie Levine, *Untitled (Gold Knots: I)*. (1987). Oil on polywood under plexiglass. 62⅛ × 50⁹/₁₆. *Collection of Whitney Museum of American Art, New York. Purchase.*

Art Briefs

The Met opens its $26 million Lila Acheson Wallace Wing (Kevin Roche, John Dinkeloo) for 20th-century art • The Arthur M. Sackler Gallery of Asian and Near Eastern Art opens at the Smithsonian • Richard Meier plans a $100 million J. Paul Getty Center in western Los Angeles • Major sales include Van Gogh's "Sunflowers" ($39.9 million) and "Irises" ($53.9 million) • Andres Duany and Elizabeth Plater-Zyberk plan a seaside pastel village in northwest Florida modeled on historic seafront towns.

Dance ───────────────

Moscow's Bolshoi visits the U.S. and performs, among others, *The Golden Age* (Yuri Grigorovich) with Irek Mukhamedov. Newly merged are the Pennsylvania and Milwaukee, under Robert Weiss, and the Minnesota Dance Theatre and Pacific Northwest. Thirteen New York companies perform "Dancing for Life" for AIDS research.

Premieres/Important Productions

American Ballet Theatre: Julio Bocca, Cheryl Yeager, *Sleeping Beauty* (Kenneth MacMillan); Bocca, Yeager, *La Sylphide* (Erik Bruhn)

New York City: *Les Petits Riens; Les Gentilhommes* (all male, Peter Martins); Darci Kistler, Robert La Fosse, *La Sonnambula* (Balanchine)

Joffrey: Beatriz Rodriguez, *The Rite of Spring* (Nijinsky)

Martha Graham: Rudolf Nureyev, Mikhail Baryshnikov, *Appalachian Spring;* Maya Plisetskaya, *Incense*

Books

Fiction
Critics' Choice
The Counterlife, Philip Roth
More Die of Heartbreak, Saul Bellow
The Thanatos Syndrome, Walker Percy
The Messiah of Stockholm, Cynthia Ozick
The Bonfire of the Vanities, Tom Wolfe
Women and Men, James McElroy
World's End, T. Coraghessan Boyle
Gone to Soldiers, Marge Piercy
🕮 *Anthills of the Savannah*, Chinua Achebe

Best-Sellers
The Tommyknockers, Stephen King
Patriot Games, Tom Clancy
Kaleidoscope, Danielle Steel
Misery, Stephen King
Leaving Home, Garrison Keillor
Windmills of the Gods, Sidney Sheldon
Presumed Innocent, Scott Turow
Fine Things, Danielle Steel
Heaven and Hell, John Jakes

Nonfiction
Critics' Choice
Cultural Literacy, E. D. Hirsch
And the Band Played On, Randy Shilts
Democracy Is in the Streets, James E. Miller
A Conflict of Visions, Thomas Sowell
The Fitzgeralds and the Kennedys, Doris Kearns Goodwin
Timebends: A Life, Arthur Miller
Chaos, James Gleick
The Renewal of Literature: Emersonian Reflections, Richard Poirier
Mortal Splendor: The American Empire in Transition, Walter R. Mead
Pagans and Christians, Robin Lane Fox
Neural Darwinism, Gerald Edelman
🕮 *Perestroika: New Thinking for Our Country and the World*, Mikhail Gorbachev

Best-Sellers
Time Flies, Bill Cosby
Spycatcher, Peter Wright with Paul Greengrass
Family: The Ties that Bind . . . and Gag! Erma Bombeck
Veil, Bob Woodward
A Day in the Life of America, Rick Smolan, David Cohen
The Great Depression of 1990, Ravi Batra
It's All in the Playing, Shirley MacLaine

Many believe that Tom Wolfe's first novel, *The Bonfire of the Vanities*, presents with Balzacian verisimilitude the panorama of urban life circa the 1980s. *Bill Blanchard.*

Man of the House, Thomas P. O'Neill, Jr., with William Novak
The Closing of the American Mind, Allan Bloom

Poetry
Denise Levertov, *Breathing the Water*
Christopher Logue, *War Music*
William Snodgrass, *Selected Poems 1957–1987*
Amy Clampitt, *Archaic Figure*

Pulitzer Prizes
Beloved, Toni Morrison (fiction)
The Launching of Modern American Science 1846–1876, Robert V. Bruce (U.S. history)
The Making of the Atomic Bomb, Richard Rhodes (nonfiction)
Look Homeward: A Life of Thomas Wolfe, David Herbert Donald (biography)
Partial Accounts, William Meredith (poetry)

Science and Technology

Paul Chu discovers a ceramic compound that superconducts at −238°, a much more feasible temperature than previously achieved.

The FDA approves pTA, a genetically engineered blood clot dissolver ($2,000 per dose).

Ursacholic acid is observed to dissolve gallstones, averting the need for surgery.

A 70-man team at Johns Hopkins separates 27-month-old Siamese twins joined at the head.

Dystrophin, a normal protein, is discovered to be missing in muscular dystrophy.

A three-hour-old infant becomes the youngest heart transplant recipient, at Loma Linda University, California.

The first open-air use of a genetically engineered bacteria, a frost retardant, is tried on strawberry plants.

Remains of 1.8-million-year-old *homo habilus* indicate that it was the first toolmaker but lived, like apes, partly in trees.

Supernova 1987A, a giant exploding star in the Large Magellanic Cloud galaxy, is observed, the brightest star since 1604.

The House authorizes the Superconducting Super Collider, which will use 40 trillion volts to accelerate particles in a 53-mile tunnel (to seek the Higg's boson).

Nobel Prize
Donald J. Cram and Charles J. Pedersen win in chemistry for creating artificial molecules that can mimic living chemical reactions.

Sports

Baseball

On TV, Dodger executive Al Campanis creates a furor when he says that blacks lack "some of the necessities" to become managers; he resigns under pressure.

Dwight Gooden (New York, NL), 22, tests positive for drugs and enters a rehab program.

Mark McGwire (Oakland, AL) sets a rookie record of 49 HRs; Don Mattingly (New York, AL) ties the record for grand slams (6) and HRs in consecutive games (8).

The Cy Young awards go to Steve Bedrosian (Philadelphia, NL) and Roger Clemens (Boston, AL).

Champions

Batting	
Tony Gwynn (San Diego, NL), .370	John Cerutti (Toronto, AL), 11–4
Wade Boggs (Boston, AL), .363	*Home runs*
Pitching	Mark McGwire (Oakland, AL), 49
Dennis Martinez (Montreal, NL), 11–4	Andre Dawson (Chicago, NL), 49

Football

The season is interrupted by a 24-day strike during which replacements ("scabs") play three games ("scabball"); the strike is broken when many regulars return.

NFL Season Leaders: Joe Montana (San Francisco), passing; Charles White (Los Angeles), rushing; J. T. Smith (St. Louis), receiving

AFL Season Leaders: Bernie Kosar (Cleveland), passing; Eric Dickerson (Indiana), rushing; Al Toon (New York Jets), receiving

College All-Americans: Don McPherson (Q), Syracuse; Chris Spielman (LB), Ohio State; Keith Jackson (TE), Oklahoma

Bowls (Jan. 1, 1988)

Rose: Michigan State 20–USC 17
Orange: Miami 20–Oklahoma 14
Cotton: Texas A&M 35–Notre Dame 10
Sugar: Auburn 16–Syracuse 16

Basketball

Magic Johnson is named playoff MVP as the Lakers win their fourth title in eight years.

Michael Jordan (Chicago) averages 37.1 ppg, the first since Wilt Chamberlain to score 3,000 points.

Julius Erving, the third player to top 30,000 career points, retires.

NBA All-Pro First Team: Larry Bird, Kevin McHale (Boston), Akeem Olajuwon (Houston), Magic Johnson (Los Angeles Lakers), Michael Jordan (Chicago).

Other Sports

Boat Racing: Stars and Stripes, helmed by Dennis Conner, defeats Kookaburra II in Australia to regain the America's Cup.

Auto Racing: Al Unser, 47, becomes the oldest man to win the Indy 500.

Tennis: Martina Navratilova ties Helen Wills with her eighth Wimbledon.

Winners

World Series	*MVP*
Minnesota (AL) 4	Magic Johnson, Los Angeles
St. Louis (NL) 3	Lakers
MVP	*College Basketball*
NL–Andre Dawson, Chicago	Indiana
AL–George Bell, Toronto	*Player of the Year*
Super Bowl XXII (Jan. 1988)	Dave Robinson, Navy
Washington 42–Denver 10	*Stanley Cup*
MVP	Edmonton
Jerry Rice, San Francisco	*US Tennis Open*
College Football	Men: Ivan Lendl
Miami	Women: Martina Navratilova
Heisman Trophy	*USGA Open*
Tim Brown, Notre Dame	Scott Simpson
NBA Championship	*Kentucky Derby*
Los Angeles Lakers 4–Boston 3	Alysheba (C. McCarron, jockey)

Fashion

The mini enjoys a major revival: some have slits in the back; most are in stretch materials of rubberized or jersey fabrics that shape a tight, sexy fit. The long skirt is also stylish, narrower and more feminine, like the blouses and jackets that accompany it. In either length, a more rounded, hourglass silhouette emerges. At night, the mini bubble dress with strapless top is fashionable. Red is the color of the year—in skirts, sweaters, hats, belts, bracelets, handbags, eyeglasses, earrings, and even shoes (particularly the fashionable high pump or ballerina style), worn with plain or textured black, pastel (lemon, vanilla), or white hose. Hair is shorter at the sides than at the top.

High-fashion note: New Paris designer Christian Lacroix's short gathered bubble skirt dress (the "pouf") with a shawled bodice

Kaleidoscope _____

- The Dow peaks at 2,722 on August 25; on Black Monday, October 19, it drops 508 points, representing $500 billion in lost equity.
- Lt. Col. Oliver North becomes a media hero, along with Senate counsel Arthur Liman and Fawn Hall; Hall, North's secretary, who smuggled shredded documents in her clothing, tells Congress: "Sometimes you have to go above the written law."
- Oral Roberts says God has told him that He will take Roberts' life if he can't raise $8 million; a millionaire dog-track owner donates the required sum.
- Jim Bakker leaves his PTL ministry when it is learned that he paid $250,000 for the silence of Jessica Hahn, 27, with whom he committed adultery in 1980.
- Sen. Joe Biden (D-Del.) withdraws as a presidential candidate after claims that he plagiarized a speech and exaggerated his law school grades.
- The *Miami Herald* stakes out presidential hopeful Gary Hart on his date with ex-model Donna Rice; later photos show Rice on Hart's lap aboard his friend's yacht, the Monkey Business.
- Ansell America is the first condom manufacturer to advertise on TV.
- Playtex, in TV ads for the "Cross Your Heart" bra, is the first to use live lingerie models.
- With the AIDS panic, monogamy and abstinence gain a vogue; "safe sex" becomes a social password, including the use of condoms and spermicides and the avoidance of specific sexual practices.
- Forty states and hundreds of cities restrict smoking in public buildings, restaurants, and schools, following the surgeon general's directives on passive smoking.
- The Supreme Court rules that states may require all-male private clubs to admit women.
- A California court rules that a frozen embryo (1981) from two subsequently deceased parents can be implanted without future claim to the donors' estate.
- In the "Baby M" case, Mary Beth Whitehead, who contracted to be artificially inseminated by William Stern and to then give the child to Stern, changes her mind; the New Jersey court gives full custody to Stern.
- Television reports the rescue of 18-month-old Jessica McClure 58 hours after she fell into a well 22 feet deep.
- John Gotti, alleged "boss of bosses," is acquitted of racketeering charges; he was prosecuted by Diane Giacalone ("the lady in red"), originally from his own Queens neighborhood.
- The Pennsylvania state treasurer, convicted of bribery, commits suicide during a televised press conference.
- Convictions in the "Pizza Connection" drug-rackets trial include that of major boss Gaetano Badalamenti.
- New Agers celebrate "harmonic convergence," the rare alignment of all nine planets, at "power points" including Mt. Olympus and Machu Picchu.

Cesar Pelli's Battery Park City. *Timothy Hursley.*

- Three white teens are charged with manslaughter after attacking three black men in Howard Beach, New York; one was killed by a car as he tried to flee his assailants.
- NASA confirms a 4 percent decrease in the ozone layer (1978) due to chlorohydrocarbons in the atmosphere.
- A garbage boat, the Mobro, leaves New York City and sails 6,000 miles in futile search of a disposal site; it returns to New York to burn the waste.
- Two best-sellers criticize U.S. education: E. D. Hirsch Jr.'s *Cultural Literacy* attacks progressive-skills orientation in favor of fact orientation; Allan Bloom's *The Closing of the American Mind* calls for a return to "great books" and attacks cultural relativism.
- Sixty percent of kitchens have microwave ovens; 40 percent of the food dollar is spent eating out.
- Congress overrides the president's veto of the $20 billion Clean Water Bill.
- Douglas Ginsburg withdraws his Supreme Court nomination, admitting that he tried marijuana in the past.
- Andy Warhol, 58, dies on February 22, of a heart attack after routine gall bladder surgery.
- Fifty thousand people gather at Graceland, in Memphis, Tennessee, on the 10th anniversary of Elvis's death.
- Ornithologists watch the last of the dusky seaside sparrows die of old age, as the species becomes extinct.

New Words and Usages: couch potato, glasnost, perestroika

First Appearances: U.S. budget exceeding $1 trillion, genetic marker for colon cancer, PC-2, Macintosh II and SE, Kodak Fling, Fuji Quick Snap (preloaded, disposable camera), Spuds MacKenzie, Max Headroom, computer performing 1.72 billion computations/second (NASA), 4-dram chip, Acuvue (disposable contact lenses), test-tube kittens (to save endangered species), female mayor of Dallas (Annette G. Strauss), Captain Power toys that interact with TV show (Mattel)

1988

Facts and Figures

Economic Profile
Dow-Jones: ↑ High 2,183–
Low 1,879
GNP: +6.8%
Inflation: +4.7%
Unemployment: 5.4%
Balance of international
payments: −$118
billion
Military on duty: 2,168,000
Voter Participation:
53.1% (1984), 50.0%
(1988)
Population with religious
affiliation: 142,800,000
Compaq SLT/286, laptop
computer: $5,399
Camcorders (8 millimeter):
Sony, CCD-V9: $1,800
VF3000 portable VHS,
Casio, headphones:
$1,399
Mitsubishi home theater, 35″
screen, stereo speakers,
CD, $5,000–$10,000
Crime-stopper alarm,
remote: $349
Bikeomatic (auto-
transmission for
multispeed bikes): $49
Brewmaster electronic beer
maker (11¢/bottle): $89
CIC talking heartbeat
monitor, attachable to
Walkman or chest: $299
Faxphone: $1,295
Diaper alarm: $10

Deaths

Charles Addams, Louis
L'Amour, Mary Astor,
Raymond Carver, Carl
Hubbell, Joshua Logan,
Frederick Loewe, Louise
Nevelson, Isamu
Noguchi, Roy Orbison

In the News

USSR PLANS TO WITHDRAW FROM AFGHANISTAN . . . MIAMI INDICTS NORIEGA ON DRUG DEALING CHARGES . . . HOUSE VOTES DOWN ARMS AID TO CONTRAS . . . TV PREACHER JIMMY SWAGGART RESIGNS AFTER PROSTITUTE REVEALS LIAISON . . . JESSE JACKSON WINS 5 PRIMARIES ON SUPER TUESDAY . . . STORMY DEBATES AT KREMLIN CP MEETING ARE TELEVISED . . . SENATE RATIFIES INF TREATY . . . WIDESPREAD DROUGHTS CAUSE MAJOR DAMAGE ACROSS U.S. . . . IRAN AIR 655 IS SHOT DOWN BY USS "VINCENNES" IN PERSIAN GULF, 290 ARE KILLED, HUMAN ERROR IS BLAMED, NOT COMPUTER SYSTEM . . . SPECIAL PROSECUTOR FINDS ATTORNEY GENERAL ED MEESE "UNINDICTABLE" . . . DEMOCRATS NOMINATE MICHAEL DUKAKIS AND LLOYD BENTSEN . . . IRAN ACCEPTS UN RESOLUTION FOR TRUCE WITH IRAQ . . . SOUTH AFRICA AND CUBA AGREE ON PLAN TO WITHDRAW FROM ANGOLA . . . VIETNAM PLANS TO WITHDRAW FROM CAMBODIA . . . RECORD HEAT WAVE HITS U.S., POLLUTION CLOSES BEACHES . . . GOP NOMINATES GEORGE BUSH AND DAN QUAYLE . . . SEC CHARGES DREXEL BURNHAM LAMBERT AND JUNK BOND KING MICHAEL MILKEN WITH INSIDER VIOLATIONS . . . U.S. ACCUSES IRAQ OF MUSTARD GAS ATTACKS ON KURDS . . . DISCOVERY SHUTTLE ORBITS, FIRST SINCE CHALLENGER CRASH . . . CHILE VOTES "NO" TO DICTATOR PINOCHET . . . BUSH WINS PRESIDENCY 47 TO 40 MILLION . . . PAKISTAN ELECTS BENAZIR BHUTTO, FIRST FEMALE LEADER OF MOSLEM COUNTRY . . . GORBACHEV, AT UN, ANNOUNCES UNILATERAL TROOP AND TANK CUTS IN EUROPE . . . EARTHQUAKE STRIKES ARMENIA, 25,000 DIE . . . U.S. AGREES TO TALKS WITH PLO AFTER ARAFAT "ACCEPTS" ISRAEL AND "REJECTS" TERRORISM . . . PAN AM 103 EXPLODES OVER SCOTLAND, 280 DIE, EVIDENCE INDICATES BOMB.

Quotes _____

"There will be a lot more hot summers than normal, and
the hottest ones will be hotter than normal."
> —Dr. James Hansen, on the presence
> of the greenhouse effect

"It's atavistic."
> —Former Secretary of Education William Bennett, on
> Stanford's decision to make the Western
> Civilization course noncompulsory

"The growth of democracy has become one of the most
powerful political movements of our age."
> —President Reagan to Moscow students

"You must lift people's options. . . . I was born to a
teenage mother. . . . I know the plight" (Jesse Jackson).
"[I am] a card-carrying member of the ACLU" (Michael
Dukakis). "I don't know what his problem is with the
Pledge of Allegiance. . . ." (George Bush). "He is out of
the mainstream. . . . Do we want this country to go that
far left?" (George Bush). "Senator, you're no Jack
Kennedy" (Lloyd Bentsen to Dan Quayle). "He's tan.
He's rested. He's ready. Nixon '88" (bumper sticker).

"The success of the West is . . . profound. . . . The
triumph of democratic capitalism as a model for the world
is nearly complete."
> —Charles Krauthammer, in *Time* magazine

"The sense of well-being . . . today is an illusion, . . .
based on borrowed time and borrowed money."
> —Benjamin Friedman, *The Day of Reckoning*

President-elect George Bush. *David Valdez, The White House.*

"It is obvious . . . that the use or threat of force no longer
can or must be an instrument of foreign policy. This
applies above all to nuclear arms."
> —Mikhail Gorbachev, at UN

"We have redefined the whole question of dependency.
This is no longer to be a permanent or even extended
circumstance."
> —Sen. Daniel Moynihan (D-N.Y.),
> on Welfare Reform Bill

"What do you expect from a bunch of pablum-puking
pinkos?"
> —Morton Downey, Jr.

"It's lonely at the top."
"Yeah, but it's not crowded."
> —David Mamet, *Speed-the-Plow*

Ads _____

Don't take the romance out of life.
> *(Modern Maturity Magazine)*

It's a jungle out there.
It's a matter of common sense.
> *(Ansell American LifeStyles Condoms)*

"Who gave weekend passes to murderers not even eligible
for parole? . . . And now he says he wants to do for
America what he's done for Massachusetts."
> *(Republican National Committee,*
> *with photo of Willie Horton)*

"Even a President is mortal."
> *(Democratic National Committee)*

IBM with Seoul.
> *(Hyundai Electronics)*

Just What the Doctor Ordered.
And the Lawyer. And the Architect.
> *(Quantus Microsystems)*

The TV of the ear.
> *(Toshiba)*

This is not your father's Oldsmobile.
> *(General Motors)*

How fast is the new Impulse Isuzu turbo? How does 950
miles an hour sound? Trust me.
> *(Joe Isuzu)*

Kinder-care. Proof that innovative thinking is not just
good for business but for everything.
> *(Drexel Burnham Lambert)*

TV _____

Premieres
"Roseanne," Roseanne Barr, John Goodman
"thirtysomething," Mel Harris, Ken Olin
"The Wonder Years," Fred Savage, Josh Saviano
"Dear John," Judd Hirsch
"Night Caller," Gary Cole
"Wiseguy," Ken Wahl
"Murphy Brown," Candice Bergen
"In the Heat of the Night," Carroll O'Connor, Howard
    Rollins, Jr.

Top Ten (Nielsen)
"The Cosby Show," "A Different World," "Cheers,"
"Roseanne," "Who's the Boss?" "The Golden Girls,"
"L.A. Law," "Murder, She Wrote," "Dear John," "60
Minutes"

Specials
"Voices and Visions" (13-part American poets series);
"War and Remembrance" (38 hours, $110 million, Robert
Mitchum, Jane Seymour); "The Mind"; "Joseph
Campbell and the Power of Myth" (Bill Moyers); "The
Bourne Identity" (Richard Chamberlain); "Favorite Son"

After eight years, Tom Selleck's "Magnum, P.I." retires from prime-time TV programming. *Movie Star News.*

(Harry Hamlin); "A Perfect Spy"; "Dear America: Letters
Home from Vietnam"; "The American Experience"

Emmy Awards
"thirtysomething" (drama); "The Wonder Years"
(comedy); "The Murder of Mary Phagan" (miniseries or
special); Richard Kiley (actor, "A Year in the Life");
Michael J. Fox (comedic actor, "Family Ties"); Beatrice
Arthur (comedic actress, "The Golden Girls")

Of Note
On "20/20," Jane Fonda describes her 1972 Hanoi
interview as "thoughtless and cruel" toward the POWs •
Numerous remembrances air on the 25th anniversary of
JFK's assassination • George Bush and Dan Rather
exchange harsh words when Rather asks the candidate
about the Iran-Contra affair • "Trash TV" peaks.

Movies _____

Openings
Dangerous Liaisons (Stephen Frears), Glenn Close, John
    Malkovich
Gorillas in the Mist (Michael Apted), Sigourney Weaver
Mississippi Burning (Alan Parker), Gene Hackman,
    Willem Dafoe
Big (Penny Marshall), Tom Hanks
Who Framed Roger Rabbit? (Robert Zemeckis), Bob
    Hoskins
Rain Man (Barry Levinson), Dustin Hoffman, Tom Cruise
The Last Temptation of Christ (Martin Scorsese), Willem
    Dafoe, Harvey Keitel
Bull Durham (Ron Shelton), Susan Sarandon, Kevin
    Costner
The Accidental Tourist (Lawrence Kasdan), William Hurt,
    Kathleen Turner
Working Girl (Mike Nichols), Melanie Griffith, Harrison
    Ford, Sigourney Weaver
Hotel Terminus (Marcel Ophuls), documentary
Another Woman (Woody Allen), Gena Rowlands
Die Hard (John McTiernan), Bruce Willis
Tequila Sunrise (Robert Towne), Mel Gibson, Kurt
    Russell, Michelle Pfeiffer
Running on Empty (Sidney Lumet), Judd Hirsch, Christine
    Lahti

Women on the Verge of a Nervous Breakdown (Pedro
    Almodóvar), Carmen Maura
Wings of Desire (Wim Wenders), Bruno Ganz, Solveig
    Dommartin, Otto Sander

Academy Awards
Best Picture: *Rain Man*
Best Director: Barry Levinson *(Rain Man)*
Best Actress: Jody Foster *(The Accused)*
Best Actor: Dustin Hoffman *(Rain Man)*

Top Box-Office Stars
Tom Cruise, Eddie Murphy, Tom Hanks, Arnold
Schwarzenegger, Paul Hogan, Danny DeVito, Bette
Midler, Robin Williams, Tom Selleck, Dustin Hoffman

Stars of the Future
Ricki Lake, Donovan Leitch, Jr., Glenne Headly, Eric
Bogosian, Kelly Lynch, Jonathan Silverman, Karen
Young, Uma Thurman

Popular Music

Hit Songs
"Faith"
"Need You Tonight"
"Sweet Child O' Mine"
"Hands to Heaven"
"One More Try"
"Wild, Wild West"
"Groovy Kind of Love"

Top Records
Albums: *Faith* (George Michael);
Dirty Dancing (soundtrack);
Hysteria (Def Leppard); *Kick*
(INXS); *Bad* (Michael Jackson);
Appetite for Destruction (Guns N'
Roses); *Tracy Chapman* (Tracy
Chapman). Country: *When You Say
Nothing At All* (Keith Whitley);
Hold Me (K. T. Oslin)

Singles: *Got My Mind Set On You*
(George Harrison); *Never Gonna
Give You Up* (Rick Astley); *So
Emotional* (Whitney Houston);
Heaven Is a Place on Earth (Belinda
Carlyle); *Could've Been* (Tiffany);
Wishing Well (Terence Trent
D'Arby); *Shake Your Love* (Debbie
Gibson)

Grammy Awards
"Don't Worry, Be Happy," Bobby
McFerrin (record); *Faith*, George
Michael (album); "Don't Worry, Be
Happy," Bobby McFerrin (song)

Jazz and Big Bands
Downtown school gains
popularity: Elliott Sharp, John
Zorn, Wayne Horvitz, Hank
Roberts, and George Cartwright.
Clint Eastwood's film *Bird* draws
attention to Charlie Parker, and
numerous records are reissued,
including "Bird at the Roost" and
"The Complete Savoy Sessions."

Top Performers *(Downbeat)*:
Wynton Marsalis (soloist); Count
Basie (band); Phil Woods (acoustic
jazz group); Chick Corea Elektric
Band (electric jazz group); Eddie
Daniels, Steve Lacy, Charlie Haden,
Joe Zawinul, Steve Swallow
(instrumentalists); Sarah Vaughan,
Bobby McFerrin (vocalists);
Manhattan Transfer (vocal group);
Wynton Marsalis, *Standard Time*
(album)

Theater

Broadway Openings

Plays
Joe Turner's Come and Gone (August Wilson), Ed Hall,
    Delroy Lindo
M. Butterfly (David Henry Hwang), John Lithgow, B. D.
    Wong
A Walk in the Woods (Lee Blessing), Robert Prosky, Sam
    Waterston
Speed-the-Plow (David Mamet), Joe Mantegna, Ron
    Silver, Madonna
The Road to Mecca (Athol Fugard), Amy Irving, Yvonne
    Bryceland
Spoils of War (Michael Weller), Kate Nelligan
Rumors (Neil Simon), Ron Leibman

Musicals
The Gospel at Colonnus (Bob Telson), Morgan Freeman
The Phantom of the Opera (Andrew Lloyd Webber, Richard
    Stilgoe, Charles Hart), Michael Crawford, Sarah Bright-
    man
Chess (Tim Rice, Benny Andersson, Bjorn Ulvaeus), Philip
    Casnoff, Judy Kuhn, David Carroll
Sarafina! (Mbongeni Ngema), Leleti Rhumalo

Classics, Revivals, and Off-Broadway Premieres
Macbeth, Christopher Plummer, Glenda Jackson; *The
Cherry Orchard*, Erland Josephson, Brian Dennehy; *A

Madonna began her career with a dance scholarship at the
University of Michigan and worked with the Alvin Ailey and
Pearl Lange dance companies; the singer now stars in David
Mamet's *Speed-the-Plow*. *Movie Star News*.

Midsummer Night's Dream, F. Murray Abraham; *Juno and
the Paycock*, Donald McCann, John Kavanagh (Gate
Theatre); *Ain't Misbehavin'*, Nell Carter; *Long Day's
Journey into Night*, Jason Robards, Colleen Dewhurst;
Cafe Crown (Hy Kraft), Eli Wallach, Anne Jackson; *The
Cocktail Hour* (A. R. Gurney), Nancy Marchand;
Coriolanus, Christopher Walken, Irene Worth; *The Heidi
Chronicles* (Wendy Wasserstein), Joan Allen; *Forbidden
Broadway* (Gerard Alessandrini); *Reckless* (Craig Lucas);
Eastern Standard (Richard Greenberg)

Colleen Dewhurst and Jason Robards, in the successful revival of *Long Day's Journey into Night. Movie Star News.*

Theater (cont.)

Regional
Long Wharf, New Haven: *National Anthems* (Dennis McIntyre), Tom Berenger, Kevin Spacey

Pulitzer Prize
Driving Miss Daisy, Alfred Uhry

Tony Awards
M. Butterfly, David Henry Hwang (play); *The Phantom of the Opera,* Charles Hart, Richard Stilgoe, Andrew Lloyd Webber (musical)

Classical Music

Compositions
Roger Reynolds, *Whispers Out of Time*
Wendy Chambers, *Symphony of the Universe*
Elliott Carter, *Remembrance*
Gunther Schuller, *Chimeric Images*
Ralph Shapey, *Variations on a Cantus*
George Rochberg, Symphony no. 6
Christopher Rouse, Symphony no. 1
Stephen Paulus, Violin Concerto

First Performances
Elliott Carter, Oboe Concerto (New York); Gunther Schuller, Concerto for Flute (Chicago); Paul Felter, *Three Excursions* (Buffalo); David Del Tredici, *Tattoo* (New York); Steve Stucky, Concerto for Orchestra (Philadelphia); George Lloyd, Symphony no. 7 (Chicago)

Important Events
Celebrations for Leonard Bernstein's 70th birthday and 45th anniversary of his New York Philharmonic conducting debut include programs with the Vienna Philharmonic, New York Philharmonic, and Boston Symphony (Tanglewood).
The Elliott Carter 80th birthday celebration includes *Variations for Orchestra: A Celebration of Some 100 × 150 Notes* (Houston, New York Philharmonic) and the Piano Concerto (Ursula Oppens, Houston, New York).
Bruce Crawford retires from the Metropolitan Opera; Zubin Mehta from the New York Philharmonic.
John Adams conducts excerpts of *Nixon in China* in concert form at Avery Fisher Hall.

Debut: Lily New

Opera
Metropolitan: Kathleen Battle, Martine Dupuy, *Giulio Cesare* (Handel); Ghena Dimitrova (debut), *Turandot*; Frederica von Stade, José van Dam, *Pélleas et Melisande*; von Stade, Alfredo Kraus, *Werther*; Kiri Te Kanawa, Susan Quittmeyer, *Così Fan Tutte*; Hildegard Behrens, Wolfgang Neumann, *Siegfried*; Behrens, Jeannine Altmeyer, Christa Ludwig, Frank Mazura, *Götterdämmerung*; Edita Gruberova, *Lucia di Lammermoor*; Judith Blegen, von Stade, *Hansel and Gretel*

San Francisco: Lofti Mansouri becomes new general director; Leona Mitchell, Domingo, *Aïda*; Eva Marton, Vyacheslav Polozov, *La Gioconda*

Chicago: Catherine Malfitano, Tatiana Troyanos, Mazura, *Lulu*; Marilyn Horne, Barbara Daniels, *Falstaff*; Samuel Ramey, Carol Vaness, *Don Giovanni*; Anna Tomowa-Sintow, Peter Dvorsky, *Madama Butterfly*

Dallas: Neil Rosenshein, *The Aspern Papers* (Argento), world premiere

Houston: *The Making of the Representative for Planet 8* (Philip Glass), world premiere

Music Notes
Fifteen internationally respected composers are invited to Telluride, California, to meet in panels and performances; their aesthetic is "to engage the listener rather than provide him with a soothing goal" • Material from Beethoven's sketchbooks for a 10th symphony, in E flat, is presented by the American Symphony Orchestra at Carnegie Hall to generally lukewarm reviews • After several years of negotiations, the Van Cliburn International Piano Competition announces that both the USSR and People's Republic of China will participate in the 1989 contest.

Art _____

Painting
Ellsworth Kelly, *Red Black*
Chuck Close, *Susan*
Julian Schnabel, *Flaubert's Letter to His Mother*
Philip Taafe, *Then and Now*
Jeff Koons, *Popples, Serpents*
Ashley Bickerton, *Tormented Self-Portrait*
Kenny Sharf, *Obglob*
Larry Rivers, *Seventy-Five Years Later: Sienna*

Sculpture
Ted Wesselmann, *Blonde Vivienne*
Rebecca Horn, *The Hot Circus*
Gilda Snowden, *Monument*
John Newman, *Inside the Cylindrical Mirror*

Architecture
Sunshine Skyway Bridge, St. Petersburg-Bradenton, Florida (Figg & Muller)
Queens Citicorp Building, Long Island City, New York (Skidmore, Owings & Merrill)
Chicago Art Institute Wing, Chicago (Thomas Beeby)
Tent City, Boston (Goody, Clancy)
Help I, Brooklyn, New York (Cooper, Robertson)
Union Station, Washington, D.C. (Benjamin Thompson)
135 East 57th Street, New York City; 1201 Third Avenue, Seattle (Kohn Pederson Fox)

Important Exhibitions
"Dutch and Flemish Paintings from the Hermitage" travels through the United States.

Museums
New York: *Metropolitan:* Degas; David Hockney; Georgia O'Keeffe; Umberto Boccioni; Painting in Renaissance Siena: 1420–1500; "The 1980s: A New Generation"; Fragonard. *Museum of Modern Art:* Cézanne; Deconstructivist Architecture; "Berlin Art: 1965–1987"; Anselm Kiefer; "Diebenkorn: Works on Paper." *Whitney:* Donald Judd retrospective; Artschwager; Guy Pène du Bois. *Guggenheim:* "Viewpoints: Postwar Poetry and Sculpture"; "Andy Warhol, Cars." *Brooklyn:* "Cleopatra's Egypt."

Philadelphia: "Jasper Johns: Work Since 1974"

Chicago: "Chicago Architecture, 1872–1922"

Washington, Chicago: Paul Gauguin

Washington: "The Human Figure in Early Greek Art—Athens"; "Cézanne: The Early Years, 1859–1872"; "Michelangelo: Draftsman, Architect"; Japan: The Shaping of Daimyo Culture, 1185–1868

Boston: "The BiNational": exchange between Boston and West Germany of 1980s art

Red Grooms. *Trump Tower. Marlborough Gallery.*

Fort Worth: "Poussin: The Early Years in Rome"

Cleveland: Greek bronzes

Art Briefs
P.S. 1, in Long Island City, New York, a renovated school, gains increased attention as an alternative space that assumes the function of a gallery or museum; its first show, covering its entire 35,000 feet, is devoted to Michelangelo Pistoletto • Important sales include Picasso's "Acrobat and Young Harlequin" ($38.4 million), the highest price paid for a 20th-century artist, and Jasper Johns' "False Start" ($17 million), a record price for a living artist.

Dance _____

The Paris Opera Ballet School makes its U.S. debut.

American Ballet Theatre: Mikhail Baryshnikov, Julio Bocca, *Drink to Me Only with Thine Eyes* (Mark Morris, Virgil Thomson)

Martha Graham (age 94): Baryshnikov, *El Penitente*; Maya Plisetskaya, *The Dying Swan*

New York City Ballet (40th anniversary): 21 world premieres, including Valentina Kozlova, *The Unanswered Question* (Eliot Feld)

Joffrey: "Robert Joffrey Memorial Season"; Edward Stierle, *Cotillion* (George Balanchine); *"La Vivandière"* (Arthur Saint-Leon); Gerald Arpino succeeds Joffrey.

Alvin Ailey (30th anniversary): Dudley Williams, *Opus McShann*

Books

Fiction
Critics' Choice
The Tenants of Time, Thomas Flanagan

Where I'm Calling From, Raymond Carver

Wheat That Springeth Green, J. F. Powers

Libra, Don DeLillo

Paris Trout, Pete Dexter

Prisoner's Dilemma, Richard Powers

Stories in an Almost Classical Mode, Harold Brodkey

Quinn's Book, William Kennedy

Krazy Kat, Jay Cantor

The Mysteries of Pittsburgh, Michael Chabon

Best-Sellers
The Bonfire of the Vanities, Tom Wolfe

Love in the Time of Cholera, Gabriel García Márquez

The Shell Seekers, Rosamunde Pilcher

The Icarus Agenda, Robert Ludlum

Alaska, James Michener

Zoya, Danielle Steel

The Cardinal of the Kremlin, Tom Clancy

Till We Meet Again, Judith Krantz

Donald Trump purchases a 282-foot yacht with solid-gold sinks and a bullet-proof sauna, as well as the Eastern Shuttle ($365 million) and New York's Plaza Hotel. *Trump Corporation.*

Nonfiction
Critics' Choice
Reconstruction, Eric Foner

Freud: A Life for Our Time, Peter Gay

Day of Reckoning, Benjamin Friedman

Coming of Age in the Milky Way, Timothy Ferris

The New Historicism, ed. Stephen Greenblatt

The Power Game, Hedrick Smith

The Power of Myth, Joseph Campbell with Bill Moyers

Inventing the People, Edmund S. Morgan

The Trial of Socrates, I. F. Stone

Whose Justice? Which Rationality? Alasdair MacIntyre

Best-Sellers
The 8-Week Cholesterol Cure, Robert W. Kowalski

Trump: The Art of the Deal, Donald J. Trump with Tony Schwartz

Swim with the Sharks Without Being Eaten Alive, Harvey Mackay

Thriving on Chaos, Tom Peters

A Brief History of Time, Stephen W. Hawking

The Rise and Fall of the Great Powers, Paul Kennedy

Talking Straight, Lee Iacocca with Sonny Kleinfield

Love, Medicine and Miracles, Bernie S. Siegel

Poetry
Donald Hall, *The One Day*

James Schuyler, *Selected Poems*

Joseph Brodsky, *To Urania*

Czeslaw Milosz, *The Collected Poems*

🙛 Octavio Paz, *The Collected Poems, 1957–1987*

Pulitzer Prizes
Breathing Lessons, Anne Tyler (fiction)

Parting the Waters: America in the King Years 1954–1963, Taylor Branch; *Battle Cry of Freedom: The Civil War Era*, James M. McPherson (U.S. history)

A Bright Shining Lie, Neil Sheehan (nonfiction)

Oscar Wilde, Richard Ellmann (biography)

New and Collected Poems, Richard Wilbur (poetry)

Science and Technology

Harvard scientists obtain the first animal patent, for a genetically engineered mouse with special immune properties (patent: 4,736,866).

The specific genetic defect in schizophrenia, once thought environmental, is located.

A Harvard study indicates that taking aspirin every other day reduces, by half, risk of heart attack.

Paul Chu reports a new superconducting compound, at $-204°$, up 30 degrees.

The first image of benzene, ringlike as expected, is obtained by IBM scientists with the scanning tunneling microscope.

New scientific tests indicate that the Shroud of Turin dates from the Middle Ages, not Christ's death.

Allan Wilson discovers a 200,000-year-old black-skinned common ancestor, "Eve," in sub-Saharan Africa; her genes have been passed to all humans.

Grave robbers lead to fabulous gold and ceramic artifacts of the Moche culture in Peru.

NASA plans to commence, in 1992, a 10-year SETA project (Search for Signals of Extraterrestrial Intelligence); it will cost $95 million.

Nobel Prizes
Leon Lederman, Melvin Schwartz, and Jack Steinberger win in physics for their studies of subatomic neutrino particles. George H. Hitchings and Gertrude B. Elion win in physiology or medicine for their work on drug treatment for heart disease, ulcers, and leukemia.

Sports ⸺

Baseball

Orel Hershiser (Los Angeles, NL) breaks Don Drysdale's record by pitching 59 consecutive scoreless innings.

Jose Canseco (Oakland, AL) is the first to hit 40 HRs and steal 40 bases in a season.

Wade Boggs (Boston, AL), despite a palimony suit, makes 200 hits for a record fifth time.

The Cy Young awards go to Orel Hershiser and Frank Viola (Minnesota, AL).

Champions ⸺

Batting	20–3
Tony Gwynn (San Diego, NL), .313	Frank Viola (Minnesota, AL), 24–7
Wade Boggs (Boston, AL), .366	*Home runs*
Pitching	Jose Canseco (Oakland, AL), 42
David Cone (New York, NL),	

Football

Among those suspended for drug use are Lawrence Taylor, Dexter Manley, Mark Duper, and Bruce Smith.

NFL Season Leaders: Wade Wilson (Minnesota), passing; Herschel Walker (Dallas), rushing; Henry Ellard (Los Angeles Rams), receiving

AFC Season Leaders: Boomer Esiason (Cincinnati), passing; Eric Dickerson (Indianapolis), rushing; Al Toon (New York Jets), receiving

College All-Americans: Troy Aikman (Q), UCLA; Rodney Peete (Q), USC; Major Harris (Q), West Virginia

Bowls (Jan. 1, 1989)

Rose: Michigan 22–USC 14
Orange: Miami 23–Nebraska 3
Cotton: UCLA 17–Arkansas 3
Sugar: Florida State 13–Auburn 7
Fiesta (for #1): Notre Dame 34–West Virginia 21

Basketball

Michael Jordan is the first to lead in both scoring and steals and is named Defensive Player of the Year.

NBA All-Pro First Team: Larry Bird (Boston), Charles Barkley (Philadelphia), Akeem Olajuwon (Houston), Magic Johnson (L.A. Lakers), Michael Jordan (Chicago)

Olympics

A record 161 nations compete in Seoul. Ben Johnson, of Canada, is stripped of his gold medal in the 100m dash when he tests positive for steroids. Gold medal winners include Carl Lewis (100m, long jump), Florence Griffith-Joyner (100m, 200m, 400m relay), Jackie Joyner-Kersee (long jump, heptathalon), Matt Biondi (5 in swimming), and Greg Louganis (2 in diving). The Soviets upset the United States in basketball.

Other Sports

Boxing: Mike Tyson KO's Michael Spinks in 1; the gate is $40 million. Tyson's feuds with his wife, Robin Givens, and mother-in-law, Ruth Roper, dominate boxing news.

Hockey: Wayne Gretzky is traded from Edmonton to Los Angeles to be near his wife's career.

Winners ⸺

World Series	*MVP*
Los Angeles (NL) 4	Michael Jordan, Chicago
Oakland (AL) 1	*College Basketball*
MVP	Kansas
NL–Kirk Gibson, Los Angeles	*Player of the Year*
AL–Jose Canseco, Oakland	Danny Manning, Kansas
Super Bowl XXIII (Jan. 1989)	*Stanley Cup*
San Francisco 20–Cincinnati 16	Edmonton
MVP	*US Tennis Open*
Boomer Esiason, Cincinnati	Men: Mats Wilander
College Football	Women: Steffi Graf
Notre Dame	*USGA Open*
Heisman Trophy	Curtis Strange
Barry Sanders, Oklahoma State	*Kentucky Derby*
NBA Championship	Winning Colors (G. Stevens, jockey)
Los Angeles Lakers 4–Detroit 3	

Fashion ⸺

Along with the demise of both the pouf and minimal look come longer skirts, the return of pants, and generally, for day and evening, more comfortable designs with a softening of the hard-edged look. This is the year for simple designs with pragmatic details (pockets, buttons, snaps) and dramatic ornamentation—a style Chanel set 60 years ago that is now reinstituted by Karl Lagerfeld and numerous Chanel imitators. Yves Saint Laurent also returns to center stage, along with new designers Isaac Mizrahi and Marc Jacobs. The key to high fashion is variety—long and/or short skirts, sexy and/or bulky blouses and sweaters—whatever is comfortable.

High-fashion note: Donna Karan's bamboo wool crepe gabardine pants suit; sleek hair; custom-blended powders; Retin-A for wrinkles caused by the sun

Kaleidoscope _____

- Russia curtails political use of psychiatric hospitals, allows the teaching of Hebrew, stops jamming Radio Liberty, and proposes elected leadership; it also allows dissident Andrei Sakharov to visit the United States, and begins selling the *New York Times, Time,* and *Newsweek* magazines.
- Voluntarism increases: Xerox and IBM allow social-service leave; Bush advocates "a thousand points of light" and a "kinder, gentler nation."
- A 30-year leakage of radioactive materials from the Savannah River (Georgia) and Rocky Flats (Colorado) defense plants is exposed.
- Soaps are preempted by the live testimony of Hedda Nussbaum against lawyer Joel Steinberg, accused in the beating death of their daughter, Lisa, six.
- Two-parent families tally 27 percent of the population (49 percent in 1970); since 1980, singles are up 20 percent; unmarried couples, 63 percent.
- Women account for nearly half of all graduating accountants; one-third of MBAs; one-fourth of lawyers and physicians (up 300 percent in 10 years).
- The average pre-tax family income is $46,848 ($29,627 in 1980), an (adjusted) increase of $3,700.
- With ACLU assistance, homeless Joyce Brown, "Billy Boggs," is released from Bellevue; she gets a job, lectures at Harvard, and returns to street begging.
- "If you feel guilty, see a priest," says New York's Mayor Ed Koch, who advises saying "no" to panhandlers; public debate follows.
- Ninety percent of major corporations report sexual-harassment complaints.
- "George Bush reminds every woman of her first husband," remarks Democratic candidate Bruce Babbitt.
- The Supreme Court gives school administrators broad powers of newspaper censorship.
- Spending for cultural events ($3.4 billion) exceeds spectator sports spending for the first time. (It was half in 1960.)
- After Paul de Man's death, documents indicate that in 1942, the respected Yale deconstructionist wrote pro-Nazi, anti-Semitic articles.
- CBS fires sports announcer Jimmy "the Greek" Snyder after he says: "The black is a better athlete to begin with, because he's been bred to be that way."
- Former chief aide Donald Regan claims that Nancy Reagan uses astrology to plan her husband's activities.
- Nancy Reagan says she "broke her own little rule" when she continued to borrow dresses and jewelry, but she denies any ethical wrongdoing.
- Pat Robertson claims that revelations concerning Jimmy Swaggart's sex life were timed to hurt his election bid; *Penthouse* immediately sells out its Debra Mumphree issue, in which she describes her tryst with Swaggart.
- Tracy Chapman, 25 ("Fast Car"), gains enormous

The "homeless," estimated at several hundred thousand to several million, become a common urban problem during the eighties. *Library of Congress.*

popularity; she sings angry songs about poor people, race riots, and neurotic love.
- Fundamentalists picket *The Last Temptation of Christ;* the film is an unexpected financial success.
- TV talk show hosts gain attention: Geraldo's nose is broken during a debate with white supremacists; Donahue wears a dress on a show about transvestites; and Oprah Winfrey loses 67 pounds on a liquid diet.
- Three whites are found guilty in the death of a black in the Howard Beach, New York, racial attack.
- Black teenager Tawana Brawley claims she was raped by a group of white men, but a grand jury finds no evidence for her charges and calls her advisers, including the Rev. Al Sharpton, "unethical."
- Former Miss America (1945) Bess Myerson is found innocent of attempting to influence a judge to reduce the alimony payments of her boyfriend, Andy Capasso.
- Larry Davis is acquitted of shooting six uniformed Bronx officers on grounds of self-defense.
- Robert Chambers pleads guilty to murdering Jennifer Levin; the tape of a mock doll-strangling, which he made with friends, is later aired.
- "A Gatsby for the Reagan era [Dominick Dunne]," art collector–socialite Robert Polo is charged in a $100-million embezzlement of investor funds.
- Soviets and Americans work together to save two whales trapped off the Alaska coast.

Fads: "Elvis Lives," *E.T.* videocassettes, faxing, oat bran, heartland food, the sixties, suction Garfield cats (on car windows)

First Appearances: B-2 Stealth bomber ($500 million), Catastrophic Medicare Bill, Rogaine (for hair loss), oral abortion pill (RU486, France), felony conviction for computer-virus insertion, largest leveraged buyout ($25 billion, R.J.R. Nabisco by Kohlberg Kravis Roberts), largest corporate fine ($650 million, Drexel Burnham), FDIC loss, $20 million gift to black college (Bill Cosby to Spelman, Atlanta), Video Walkman (Sony), Ford Probe, smoking ban on U.S. flights of two hours and under, $165,000 shoes (Judy Garland's ruby slippers in *The Wizard of Oz*), proposed SEC offering of brothel (Mustang Ranch, Nevada), truffle water, Honey Teddy Grahams (Nabisco), Crunchy Bran (Quaker)

1989

Facts and Figures

Economic Profile
Dow-Jones: ↑ High 2,791–
Low 2,168
GNP: +7.0%
Inflation: +4.6%
Unemployment: 5.3%
Household VCR: 66%
Household cable TV: 57%
On sale, Bloomingdale's:
Berlin Wall: $12.50

Democratic revolutions:
China: 1.103 million
(suppressed)
Poland: 38 million
Hungary: 10.6 million
East Germany: 16.6
million
Czechoslovakia: 15.6
million
Bulgaria: 9 million
Rumania: 23 million

Barbara Bush admits, ''I
married the first man I ever
kissed. When I tell this to my
children, they just about throw
up.'' *The White House.*

Deaths

Lucille Ball, Donald
Barthelme, Samuel
Beckett, Irving Berlin,
Salvador Dali, Bette
Davis, Emperor
Hirohito, Abbie
Hoffman, Vladimir
Horowitz, Dolores
Ibarruri (''La
Pasionaria''), Herbert
von Karajan, Mary
McCarthy, Billy Martin,
Laurence Olivier, Sugar
Ray Robinson, Andre
Sakharov, Virgil
Thomson, Barbara
Tuchman, Robert Penn
Warren

In the News

SOVIETS COMPLETE TROOP WITHDRAWAL FROM AFGHANISTAN . . .
KHOMEINI OFFERS $5 MILLION FOR MURDER OF ''BLASPHEMOUS''
AUTHOR SALMAN RUSHDIE . . . SOVIETS HOLD OPEN ELECTIONS FOR
PARLIAMENT . . . TANKER ''EXXON VALDEZ'' SPILLS 11 MILLION
BARRELS OF OIL OFF ALASKAN COAST . . . JOGGING INVESTMENT
BANKER, 28, IS RAPED IN CENTRAL PARK, ''WILDING'' TEENAGERS
ARE CHARGED . . . ONE MILLION, LED BY STUDENTS, DEMONSTRATE
FOR DEMOCRACY IN BEIJING . . . OLIVER NORTH IS CONVICTED IN
IRAN-CONTRA AFFAIR . . . HOUSE SPEAKER JIM WRIGHT RESIGNS
OVER ALLEGATIONS OF FINANCIAL IMPROPRIETY . . . ARMY FIRES ON
DEMONSTRATORS IN TIANANMEN SQUARE, BEIJING, AND KILLS
HUNDREDS . . . KHOMEINI, 89, DIES, MOURNERS TOPPLE HIS BODY
SEEKING RELICS . . . SOLIDARITY WINS FIRST FREE POLISH
ELECTIONS IN 40 YEARS . . . SUPREME COURT RULES 5-4 THAT
STATES MAY RESTRICT ABORTION FUNDING . . . SUPREME COURT
RULES 5-4 THAT FLAG BURNING IS PROTECTED FREE SPEECH . . .
HUNGARY PERMITS EAST GERMANS TO EXIT TO WEST, THOUSANDS
FLEE . . . EARTHQUAKE HITS SAN FRANCISCO BAY AREA . . . EAST
GERMAN PRESIDENT RESIGNS, 250,000 EAST BERLINERS CHANT
''FREEDOM'' AND ''DEMOCRACY'' . . . EAST GERMANY OPENS BERLIN
WALL . . . BLACKS WIN ELECTIONS FOR VIRGINIA GOVERNOR AND
NYC MAYOR . . . 800,000 IN PRAGUE CHANT ''FREEDOM'' AND
''DEMOCRACY,'' CP LEADERS RESIGN . . . 50,000 DEMONSTRATE
AGAINST BULGARIAN GOVERNMENT . . . RUMANIANS OVERTHROW
NICOLAI CEAUSESCU AFTER POLICE MASSACRE THOUSANDS,
DICTATOR AND WIFE ARE EXECUTED . . . U.S. INVADES PANAMA,
DEPOSED DICTATOR NORIEGA IS LATER FOUND IN VATICAN EMBASSY
. . . PLAYWRIGHT VACLAV HAVEL BECOMES CZECH PRESIDENT.

Quotes

"And how stands the city on the winter night? More prosperous, more secure and happier than it was eight years ago. She's still a beacon . . . for all who must have freedom."

—Ronald Reagan, farewell address

"If all racial discrimination were abolished today, the life prospects facing many poor blacks would still constitute a major challenge for public policy."

—*A Common Destiny: Blacks and American Society* (National Research Council report)

"[This is] the clearest opportunity to reduce the risk of war since the dawn of the nuclear age."

—James Baker, on Gorbachev's reforms

"What we may be witnessing is not just the passing of a particular period in modern history but the end of history, . . . the end point of mankind's ideological evolution and the universalization of Western liberal democracy as the final form of human government."

—Francis Fukuyama, in *The National Interest*

On changes in the communist world: Q: "What is 150 yards long and eats potatoes?" A: "A Moscow queue waiting to buy meat" (Moscow joke). "Socialism is the system where the past is unpredictable" (*New York Times*). "The people remain silent for a long time, but they do not forget" (Budapest paper, on reburial of Imre Nagy, executed in 1956). "My beloved, what am I supposed to tell you today?" (Polish PM Mazowiecki). "We do not know how this experiment will end; we only know that . . . communism had reached the end of its usefulness" (Hungarian leader Imre Pozsgay). "They came. They saw.

At the Malta summit: "The world is leaving an era of cold war," says U.S.S.R.'s Mikhail Gorbachev. "We stand on the threshold of a brand-new era," states President George Bush. *David Valdez, The White House.*

They did a little shopping" (Berlin Wall graffiti). "Long ago I wanted freedom and democracy. . . . I never thought I would live to see it" (1968 hero Alexander Dubcek, in Prague). "It is like a dream" (Prague engineer Tom D.). "This is the moment of truth. We got rid of the monsters who mutilated our history. Let these tyrants be cursed" (Rumanian TV anchorman, on executions of the Ceausescus).

"We don't pay taxes. The little people pay taxes."

—Leona Helmsley

"You all look like happy campers to me. Happy campers you are. . . . Happy campers you will always be."

—Dan Quayle, during Samoan visit

"If Barney Frank [Rep. D-Mass.] can come out of the closet, why can't I come out of a suitcase?"

—Former Speaker Tip O'Neill, on his TV hotel ads

"The new sexual realism goes with the rediscovery of the joys of tonal music, . . . a career in investment banking and church windows."

—Susan Sontag

Ads

TV

Premieres
"Life Goes On," Christopher Burke, Patti LuPone
"Anything But Love," Jamie Lee Curtis, Richard Lewis
"The Amazing Teddy Z," Jon Cryer

Top Ten (Nielsen)
"Roseanne," "The Cosby Show," "Cheers," "A Different World," "Dear John," "The Golden Girls," "60 Minutes," "The Wonder Years," "L.A. Law," "Empty Nest"

Specials
"Lonesome Dove" (Robert Duvall, Tommy Lee Jones); "Billy Crystal: Midnight Train to Moscow" (from Moscow); "The Women of Brewster Place" (Oprah Winfrey); "Art of the Western World" (Michael Wood); "The Simon Wiesenthal Story" (Ben Kingsley)

Emmy Awards
"L.A. Law" (drama); "Cheers" (comedy); "War and Remembrance" (miniseries); "One Day"/"Roe vs. Wade" (drama special); Carroll O'Connor (actor, "In the Heat of the Night"); Richard Mulligan (comedic actor, "Empty

"Roseanne" stars Roseanne Barr and John Goodman: earthy people soar to the top of the Nielsen's. *Movie Star News.*

Nest"); Dana Delany (actress, "China Beach"); Candice Bergen (comedic actress, "Murphy Brown")

Of Note
Live news coverage of the Chinese and Eastern European revolutions, as well as of the San Francisco earthquake, exceeds $35 million • The alleged videotaped hanging of Colonel William Higgins by Shiite Lebanese terrorists stirs an intense reaction across the nation • Jane Pauley is replaced by Deborah Norville on NBC's "Today" show • Arsenio Hall and Pat Sajak vie with 27-year veteran Johnny Carson for late night attention • Because of low ratings, Morton Downey's show is canceled • "Beauty and the Beast" returns without "Beauty"; the actress is now a full-time mother; the show has spawned 20 fan clubs and 50 publications.

Movies

Openings
Born on the Fourth of July (Oliver Stone), Tom Cruise
Field of Dreams (Phil Alden Robinson), Kevin Costner, James Earl Jones, Burt Lancaster
When Harry Met Sally (Rob Reiner), Billy Crystal, Meg Ryan, Carrie Fisher
Crimes and Misdemeanors (Woody Allen), Martin Landau, Woody Allen, Alan Alda, Mia Farrow
Glory (Edward Zwick), Matthew Broderick, Denzel Washington, Cary Elwes, Morgan Freeman
My Left Foot (Jim Sheridan), Daniel Day-Lewis, Brenda Fricker
Driving Miss Daisy (Bruce Beresford), Morgan Freeman, Jessica Tandy, Dan Ackroyd
Dead Poet's Society (Peter Weir), Robin Williams
Do the Right Thing (Spike Lee), Danny Aiello, Spike Lee, Ruby Dee, Ossie Davis
Enemies, A Love Story (Paul Mazursky), Ron Silver, Lena Olin, Anjelica Huston
Batman (Tim Burton), Michael Keaton, Jack Nicholson
sex, lies and videotape (Steven Soderbergh), James Spader, Andie McDowell, Laura San Giacomo
The Little Mermaid (Ron Clements, John Musker), animation
Sea of Love (Harold Becker), Al Pacino, Ellen Barkin

Indiana Jones and the Last Crusade (Steven Spielberg), Harrison Ford, Sean Connery
Roger and Me (Michael Moore), documentary
The War of the Roses (Danny DeVito), Kathleen Turner, Michael Douglas, Danny DeVito
Drugstore Cowboy (Gus Van Sant, Jr.), Matt Dillon

Academy Awards
Best Picture: *Driving Miss Daisy*
Best Director: Oliver Stone (*Born on the Fourth of July*)
Best Actress: Jessica Tandy (*Driving Miss Daisy*)
Best Actor: Daniel Day-Lewis (*My Left Foot*)

Top Box-Office Stars
Jack Nicholson, Tom Cruise, Robin Williams, Michael Douglas, Tom Hanks, Michael J. Fox, Eddie Murphy, Mel Gibson, Sean Connery, Kathleen Turner

Stars of the Future
Ellen Barkin, Kenneth Branagh, Lolita Davidovich, Hugh O'Conor, Ron Eldard, Andie McDowell, Cinque Lee, Laura San Giacomo, Annabella Sciorra, Ron Silver

Popular Music ─────────────

Hit Songs
"My Prerogative"
"Straight Up"
"Giving You the Best that I Got"
"This Time I Know It's for Real"
"Fight the Power"
"Cold Hearted"
"Cherish"

Top Records
Albums: *Don't Be Cruel* (Bobby Brown); *Hangin' Tough* (New Kids on the Block); *Forever Your Girl* (Paula Abdul); *New Jersey* (Bon Jovi); *Appetite for Destruction* (Guns N' Roses); *The Raw and the Cooked* (Fine Young Cannibals)

Singles: *Look Away* (Chicago); *Every Rose Has Its Thorn* (Poison); *Miss You Much* (Janet Jackson); *Girl You Know It's True* (Milli Vanilli); *End of the Line* (Traveling Wilburys); *Wild Thing* (Tone Lōc); *Love Shack* (The B-52's). Country: *Better Man* (Clint Black); *Living Proof* (Ricky Van Shelton)

Grammy Awards
Wind Beneath My Wings, Bette Midler (record); *Nick of Time*, Bonnie Raitt (album); "Wind Beneath My Wings" (song)

Jazz and Big Bands
Duke Ellington's 90th birthday is celebrated throughout the U.S.

Interest mounts in Latin or Afro-Cuban jazz, with Mario Bauzo and reissues of Machito, and in improvisational computer-programmed jazz (Steve Coleman). The newly established Thelonius Monk Institute of Jazz, at Duke University, plans to admit students in 1991–92.

Top Performers (*Downbeat*): Wynton Marsalis (soloist); Sun Ra (big band); Phil Woods (acoustic jazz group); Miles Davis (electronic jazz group); Branford Marsalis, James Newton, J. J. Johnson, Phil Woods, Tito Puente, Milt Jackson (instrumentalists); Bobby McFerrin, Betty Carter (vocalists); Pat Metheny, *Letter from Home* (album)

Theater ─────────────

Broadway Openings

Plays
The Heidi Chronicles (Wendy Wasserstein), Joan Allen
Lend Me a Tenor (Ken Ludwig), Philip Bosco, Victor Garber, Tovah Feldshuh
Shirley Valentine (Willy Russell), Pauline Collins
Metamorphosis (Steven Berkoff adaptation), Mikhail Baryshnikov
Love Letters (A. R. Gurney), alternating casts
Largely New York (Bill Irwin), Bill Irwin
Mastergate (Larry Gelbart), Daniel von Bargen
A Few Good Men (Aaron Sorkin), Tom Hulce

Artist Descending a Staircase (Tom Stoppard), Stephanie Roth
Tru (Jay Presson Allen), Robert Morse

Musicals
Black and Blue (revue, Claudio Segovia, Héctor Orezzoli), Ruth Brown, Linda Hopkins, Carrie Smith
Jerome Robbins' Broadway (revue, directed by Robbins), Jason Alexander, Charlotte d'Amboise
City of Angels (Cy Coleman, David Zippel, Larry Gelbart), James Naughton, Randy Graff, Gregg Edelman
Sweeney Todd (Stephen Sondheim, revival), Bob Gunton, Beth Fowler
Meet Me in St. Louis (Hugh Martin, Ralph Blane), George Hearn, Betty Garrett, Donna Kane
Grand Hotel (Robert Wright, George Forrest, Maury Yeston), directed and choreographed by Tommy Tune
Gypsy (Jule Styne, Stephen Sondheim, revival), Tyne Daly

Classics, Revivals, and Off-Broadway Premieres
The Lisbon Traviata (Terrence McNally), Anthony Heald, Nathan Lane; *Other People's Money* (Jerry Sterner), Kevin Conway, Mercedes Ruehl; *Orpheus Descending*, Vanessa Redgrave; *Measure for Measure*, Len Cariou, Kate Burton; *What the Butler Saw* (Joe Orton), Joseph Maher; *Aristocrats* (Brian Friel), Niall Buggy; *The Talented Tenth* (Richard Wesley); *Big Hotel* (Charles Ludlam); *Mountain*

Kevin Costner, star of *Field of Dreams,* which produces a state motto: "Is this Heaven?" "No, it's Iowa." *Movie Star News.*

Theater (cont.)

Language, The Birthday Party (Harold Pinter), Jean Stapleton; *The Circle,* Rex Harrison, Stewart Granger, Glynis Johns; *The Lady in Question* (Charles Busch); *The Merchant of Venice* (Peter Hall, director), Dustin Hoffman

Regional
Doolittle Theatre, L.A.: *Who's Afraid of Virginia Woolf?* (Edward Albee), Glenda Jackson, John Lithgow

Goodspeed Opera House, East Haddam, Conn.: *Oh, Kay!* (George and Ira Gershwin)

Pulitzer Prize
The Heidi Chronicles, Wendy Wasserstein

Tony Awards
The Heidi Chronicles, Wendy Wasserstein (play); *Jerome Robbins' Broadway* (musical)

Classical Music

Compositions
Mel Powell, *Duplicates*
Eleanor Cory, *Hemispheres*
William Albright, *Chasm*
Martin Bresnick, *Pontoosuc*
Tod Machover, *Toward the Center*

Important Events
Van Cliburn makes a successful comeback after 11 years and plays the Liszt and Tchaikovsky piano concertos, in Philadelphia and Dallas. Memorable performances include those of Edward Aldwell, Shura Cherkassky, and Nigel Kennedy and Ken Noda, as well as Leonard Bernstein's Mahler's "Resurrection" Symphony in New York. Barbara Nissman is the first pianist to program Prokofiev's nine sonatas as a cycle. Peter Serkin commissions works from 11 composers which he plans to perform in 17 cities; works include John Adams's *The Wound-Dresser,* Lukas Foss's *American Landscape,* and Leon Kirchner's *Interlude.*

Appointments: Dennis Russell Davies for Lukas Foss, at the Brooklyn Philharmonic; Esa-Pekka Salonen for Philippe Entremont, at Denver; Daniel Barenboim for Solti, at Chicago (in 1991); André Previn resigns from the Los Angeles.

Debuts: Olivier Charlier, Gil Shaham

First Performances
John Adams, *Fearful Symmetry* (New York); John Cage, *101* (Boston); Jacob Druckman, *Brangle* (Chicago); Stephen Paulus, *Night Speech* (Spokane); George Perle, String Quartet no. 8 (New York); Marc Neikrug, Flute Concerto (Pittsburgh)

Opera
The trend continues to update opera in what become controversial settings: Peter Sellars's *Figaro* (set in Trump Tower), *Don Giovanni* (Spanish Harlem), *Così fan tutti* (a roadside disco), *Tannhaüser* (a tawdry motel with a Jimmy Swaggart look-alike).

Metropolitan: Hugh Southern succeeds Bruce Crawford as general manager. Three *Rings* (Hildegard Behrens, James Morris, Jessye Norman) are presented, each within a week (Otto Schenk, Gunther Schneider-Siemssen production, James Levine conducting). Norman, Samuel Ramey, *Bluebeard;* José van Dam, *Tales of Hoffmann;* June Anderson (debut), Luciano Pavarotti, *Rigoletto;* Teresa Strata, *Il Trittico;* Paolo Coni (debut), *La bohème.*

New York City: Beverly Sills retires; Christopher Keene plans to emphasize twentieth-century works.

Los Angeles: Maria Ewing, Eva Marton, *Salomé* (Peter Hall production); Anna Steiger, Gary Bachlund, *The Rise and Fall of the City of Mahagonny*

Chicago: Cecilia Gasdia, Frank Lopardo, *La Sonnambula;* Lella Cuberli, Marilyn Horne, Chris Merritt, Jan Galla (debut), *Tancredi*

San Francisco: van Dam, *The Flying Dutchman;* Gwyneth Jones, Janis Martin, Behrens, Franz Mazur, 4 *Ring* cycles; Ann Panagulias, *Lulu*

Santa Fe: *A Night at the Chinese Opera* (Judith Weir)

Music Notes
Roger Norrington's original instrument performances and workshops of Beethoven's Sixth and Ninth elicit great interest • The Chicago plans to perform a Liszt piano concerto newly discovered by a University of Chicago graduate student • Leonard Bernstein leads Beethoven's Ninth in an East Berlin Christmas concert and substitutes "Freiheit" ("Freedom") for "Freude" ("Joy").

Art _____

Paintings

Joan Mitchell, *Mountain*

Leon Golub, *The Prisoner; Night Scenes*

Sherrie Levine, *Untitled (Mr. Austridge: 3; 5)*

Ellsworth Kelly, *Dallas Panels* (Dallas Symphony Hall)

Kenneth Noland, *Curtains 1988–1989*

Sculpture

Matt Mullican, *Untitled [Idealized World City]*

Nam June Paik, *Fin de Siècle II*

Frank Stella, *Moby-Dick* series

Claes Oldenburg, Coosje Van Bruggen, *Knife Slicing Wall*

Richard Serra, *Blackmun and Brennan*

Scott Burton, *Battery Park Esplanade*

Architecture

Morton H. Meyerson Symphony Center, Dallas; C.A.A. Building, Beverly Hills (I. M. Pei)

Wexner Center for the Arts, Ohio State University, Columbus (Peter Eisenman, Richard Trott)

Morgan Building, New York City (Kevin Roche)

Kimball Museum extension, Fort Worth, Texas (Romaldo Giurgola)

Norwest Center, Minneapolis (Cesar Pelli)

Bridgeport Center, Bridgeport, Connecticut (Richard Meier)

Chrysler Museum, Norfolk, Virginia (Hartman-Cox)

Civil Rights Memorial, Montgomery, Alabama (Maya Lin)

Important Exhibitions

Traveling shows include "Goya and the Spirit of Enlightenment" and "Masterworks of Ming and Qing Painting from the Forbidden City, Beijing."

Museums

New York: *Metropolitan:* Velázquez; Canaletto; Bonnard; Flemish Drawings and Prints (Majolica); Remington. *Museum of Modern Art:* "Picasso and Braque: Pioneering Cubism"; "Andy Warhol: A Retrospective"; Helen Frankenthaler; Matt Mullican. *Whitney:* "Image World: Art and Media Culture"; Kiesler. *Guggenheim:* Mario Merz; Jenny Holzer; American Minimalism; "The German Image, 1960–88."

Washington, D.C.: *Hirshhorn:* Bacon; Giacometti; Sonnier. *National:* Hals; Veronese; Manship; Rare Dutch, Flemish, German Still Lifes, 1600–1750.

Forth Worth, San Francisco, Buffalo: "10 + 10: Contemporary Soviet and American Painting.

Chicago: "On the Art of Fixing a Shadow: 150 Years of Photography"; "The Human Figure in Early Greek Art"; Chuck Close.

Civil Rights Memorial, Montgomery, Alabama. *Southern Poverty Law Center.*

Los Angeles, Fort Worth: Guido Reni.

Los Angeles: Robert Longo; "Romance of the Taj Mahal"; German Expressionism 1915–1925; Masters of Jugendstil; East German Art. *L.A. Museum of Contemporary Art:* "A Forest of Signs."

Art Briefs

Large numbers protest the cancelation of Mapplethorpe's Corcoran show and later attend the Wadsworth Atheneum show • Chicago veterans protest an Art Institute exhibit where the American flag is draped on the floor • Richard Serra's controversial "Tilted Arc" (inscribed with "This government is savage. It is eating its culture") is finally removed from NYC's Federal Plaza and placed in storage • Record sales include Picasso's *Pierrette's Wedding* ($51.3 million) and Pontormo's *The Halberdier* ($35.2 million); sales mount in Fauvism and de Stijl • Willem de Kooning and I. M. Pei are American winners of the new $100,000 Japanese Imperial Prize for lifetime achievement in the arts.

Dance _____

Twyla Tharp disbands her troupe, joins ABT (with 15 of her company) as artistic associate, and retires from dancing. Alvin Ailey dies.

Premieres/Important Productions

American Ballet Theatre: Mikhail Baryshnikov resigns. Clark Tippett, *Some Assembly Required* (Bolcom); *Rigaudon* (Britten); *In the Upper Room* (Glass/Tharp)

New York City Ballet: Lincoln Kirstein resigns. Nichol Hlinka, *Raymonda Variations;* Darci Kistler, *A Midsummer Night's Dream* (Balanchine)

Ballet West: Peter Anastos, *The Gilded Bat* (Edward Gorey design)

Books

Fiction
Critics' Choice
Billy Bathgate, E. L. Doctorow
Spartina, John Casey
If the River Was Whiskey, T. Coraghessan Boyle
Affliction, Russell Banks
The Shawl, Cynthia Ozick
Oldest Living Confederate Widow Tells All, Allan Gurganus
The Other Side, Mary Gordon
Hence, Brad Leithauser
🍂 *Foucault's Pendulum*, Umberto Eco

Best-Sellers
The Joy Luck Club, Amy Tan
The Satanic Verses, Salman Rushdie
While My Pretty One Sleeps, Mary Higgins Clark
Star, Danielle Steel
The Temple of My Familiar, Alice Walker
The Russia House, John le Carré
The Cardinal of the Kremlin, Tom Clancy
The Negotiator, Frederick Forsyth
Red Phoenix, Larry Bond
The Sands of Time, Sidney Sheldon

Nonfiction
Critics' Choice
Citizens, Simon Shama
From Beirut to Jerusalem, Thomas L. Friedman
A Peace to End All Peace, David Fromkin
Among Schoolchildren, Tracy Kidder
Barbarian Sentiments, William Pfaff
Second Chances, Judith Wallerstein
Great Plains, Ian Frazier
Paul Robeson, Martin B. Duberman
The Tempting of America, Robert Bork
Danger and Survival, McGeorge Bundy
The Crosswinds of Freedom, James MacGregor Burns
The Encyclopedia of Southern Culture, ed. Charles R. Wilson, William Ferris
Albion's Seed, David H. Fischer
More Like Us, James Fallows
🍂 *A Critical Dictionary of the French Revolution*, ed. François Furet and Mona Ozouf

Best-Sellers
All I Really Need to Know I Learned in Kindergarten, Robert Fulgham
A Brief History of Time, Stephen Hawking
Wealth Without Risk, Charles Givens
The 8-Week Cholesterol Cure, Revised Edition, Robert Kowalski
The T-Factor Diet, Martin Katahn
It's Always Something, Gilda Radner
The Way Things Work, David Macauley
A Woman Named Jackie, C. David Heymann
Leadership Secrets of Attila the Hun, Wess Roberts
The Good Times, Russell Baker

Poetry
Robert Haas, *Human Wishes*
Adrienne Rich, *Time's Power*
🍂 Philip Larkin, *Collected Poems*

Pulitzer Prizes
The Mambo Kings Play Songs of Love, Oscar Hijuelos (fiction)
In Our Image: America's Empire in the Philippines, Stanley Karnow (U.S. history)
And Their Children After Them, Dale Maharidge, Michael Williamson (nonfiction)
Machiavelli In Hell, Sebastian de Grazia (biography)
The World Doesn't End, Charles Simic (poetry)

Science and Technology

Harvard studies indicate that 30–45 minutes of brisk walking five times a week reduces heart attack mortality by more than 50 percent.

AZT is shown to delay the onset of AIDS, indicating the value of treating HIV-positive individuals.

New treatments are discovered for hepatitis C (Alpha interferon), Parkinson's disease (depressyl), transplant rejection (FK506), osteoporosis (fluoride and calcium), depression (Prozac), and bed-wetting (DDAVP).

A Duke study indicates that only hostility (not "workaholism") related to the Type A personality is dangerous; the study links cynicism and mistrust to early death.

Through chromosome jumping, the genetic defect in cystic fibrosis is located.

Before leaving the solar system, Voyager II (launched in 1977) returns data from Neptune showing icy volcanos, six moons, and 1500 mph winds.

Physicists agree on three basic types of matter: up and down, charmed and strange, top and bottom quarks.

Astronomers discover a new galaxy in formation, which contradicts the belief that all have already been formed.

Nobel Prize

J. Michael Bishop and Harold Varmus win in medicine for their work on cancer-causing genes. Norman Ramsey wins in physics for atomic clock work, and Hans Dehmelt for subatomic particle study. Thomas Cech and Sidney Altman win in chemistry for their work on the active cellular role of RNA.

Sports ─────────────────────────

Baseball

Commissioner Bart Giamatti bans Pete Rose for life, for his alleged betting on baseball. A week later, Giamatti, 53, dies of a heart attack; Fay Vincent succeeds him.

The San Francisco earthquake strikes minutes before game three of the first Bay Area World Series; the game is delayed ten days.

Nolan Ryan, 42, records his 5,000th strikeout.

One-handed Jim Abbott goes 12–12 for California, AL.

Bill White is the first black to become NL president.

The Cy Young awards go to Mark Davis (San Diego, NL) and Bret Saberhagen (Kansas City, AL).

Champions ─────────────────

Batting
Tony Gwynn (San Diego, NL), .336
Kirby Puckett (Minnesota, AL), .339
Pitching
Sid Fernandez (New York, NL), 14–5

Scott Garrelts (San Francisco, NL), 14–5
Bret Saberhagen (Kansas City, AL), 23–6
Home runs
Kevin Mitchell (San Francisco, NL), 47

Football

NFL attorney Paul Tagliabue succeeds Pete Rozelle.

Bo Jackson (L.A. Raiders) gains 950 yards rushing after a 32 HR, 105 RBI season for Kansas City, AL.

Art Shell, L.A. Raiders, becomes the first (modern era) black NFL head coach.

NFC Season Leaders: Joe Montana (San Francisco), passing; Barry Sanders (Detroit), rushing; Sterling Sharpe (Green Bay), receiving

AFC Season Leaders: Boomer Esiason (Cincinnati), passing; Christian Okoye (Kansas City), rushing; Andre Reed (Buffalo), receiving

College All-Americans: Tony Rice (Q), Notre Dame; Anthony Thompson (B), Indiana

Bowls (Jan. 1, 1990)
Rose: USC 17–Michigan 10
Orange: Notre Dame 21–Colorado 6
Cotton: Tennessee 31–Arkansas 27
Sugar: Miami 33–Alabama 25

Basketball

Kareem Abdul-Jabbar retires after a record 20 years and 38,787 points.

NBA All-Pro First Team: Karl Malone (Utah), Charles Barkley (Philadelphia), Akeem Olajuwon (Houston), Magic Johnson (L.A. Lakers), Michael Jordan (Chicago)

Other Sports

Hockey: Wayne Gretzky breaks Gordy Howe's career scoring record of 1,850 points in half Howe's time.

Horse Racing: Secretariat, 19, dies.

Winners ─────────────────

World Series
Oakland (AL) 4
San Francisco (NL) 0
MVP
AL–Robin Yount, Milwaukee
NL–Kevin Mitchell, San Francisco
Super Bowl XXIV (Jan. 1990)
San Francisco 55–Denver 10
MVP
Joe Montana, San Francisco
College Football
Miami
Heisman Trophy
Andre Ware, Houston
NBA Championship
Detroit 4–Lakers 0

MVP
Magic Johnson, L.A. Lakers
College Basketball
Michigan
Player of the Year
Sean Elliott, Arizona
Stanley Cup
Calgary
US Tennis Open
Men: Boris Becker
Women: Steffi Graf
USGA Open
Curtis Strange
Kentucky Derby
Sunday Silence (Pat Valenzuela, jockey)

Fashion ─────────────────────

For Women: Diverse styles continue. Calvin Klein's lean and refined "new look" includes soft fabrics with little or no jewelry (like the short, strapless, silk crepe dress for evening). At the other extreme, Charlotte Neuville retains the boxy suit and jacket and introduces spicy colors, mixed textures, and metallics and laces. Giorgio di Sant'Angelo emphasizes the spare and bare look: the body sensually enshrined in gauze and sexy, exotic stretch fabrics. Décolleté and exposed midriffs—flashes of flesh everywhere—are in the fashion forecast.

For Men: Despite the above, tailored clothing remains the vogue, with even higher-buttoned (three button) jackets. Deep-notched, peaked lapels return in jackets and coats with both padded and softer shoulders (Jhane Barnes, Alexander Julian).

Additional high-fashion note: Gordon Henderson's minimalist and casual, low-priced women's styles ($80– 200 an item): linen skirts with hemlines no more than two inches from long jackets that have the "slouchy" look (no shoulder pads).

Kaleidoscope _____

- The longest peacetime period of economic expansion continues in its 85th month (December); per capita (adjusted) income is up 19 percent since 1982.
- On Friday, October 13, the Dow drops 190.58, the second worst drop in history; on the 16th, it revives.
- Demonstrations follow the Supreme Court abortion and flag-burning decisions; polls indicate that 60 percent oppose the former; 65 percent oppose the latter.
- NEA funding comes under attack (led by Jesse Helms) for Robert Mapplethorpe's "homoerotic" and Andres Serrano's "obscene" photography (*Piss Christ*).
- The *New York Times* reports that social service voluntarism is on the rise among yuppies.
- Pollsters record "a desire for . . . real values" (F. Popcorn); Daniel Yankelovich reports that "top-of-the-line in every category is no longer desirable."
- Demonstrators in Tiananmen Square carry a styrofoam Statue of Liberty; fax machines and CNN transmit the news worldwide.
- "Japan Invades Hollywood" appears on *Newsweek*'s cover after Sony buys Columbia Pictures; the Japanese purchase of Rockefeller Center adds to the controversy over the extensive U.S. holdings by the Japanese.
- It is disclosed that junk bond "king" Michael Milken earned $550 million from Drexel Burnham in 1987.
- A HUD scandal reveals $2 billion in losses in 1988, including "Robin HUD," who "gave" $5 million to the poor.
- Congress passes $166 billion legislation to bail out the Savings and Loan industry.
- Publisher Malcolm Forbes flies hundreds of celebrities to his $3 million 70th birthday party in Morocco.
- Zsa Zsa Gabor, convicted of slapping a Beverly Hills policeman who stopped her in her Rolls Corniche, is sentenced to three days in jail and to reveal her age.
- Billionaire hotel "queen" Leona Helmsley is convicted of income tax evasion, including deductions for girdles, and sentenced to four years in jail.
- Televangelist Jim Bakker is sentenced to 45 years for selling bogus lifetime vacations.
- More than a million people are serving prison sentences.
- Pepsi fires Madonna after her video "Like a Prayer," in which she receives stigmata and is dressed in underwear.
- Cocaine (including crack) addiction is up 35 percent since 1985, although the number of users has declined; one percent of sixth graders are regular users.
- An Illinois woman is charged with child abuse for cocaine use during pregnancy; pediatric AIDS has doubled since 1986.
- The president outlines a "war on drugs" and names William Bennett "drug czar."
- CCNY sociologists report that "dating" for teens has been replaced by "going out in groups."
- In a contested divorce, a Tennessee judge awards

College students embrace stars of the decade Michael Jordan and Oat Bran.

David Dinkins (right), seen here with Rabbi Gunter Hirschberg, runs a conciliatory New York mayoral campaign. *Congregation Rodeph Sholom.*

custody of seven frozen embryos to the wife.
- First births are up more than 400 percent for women between 30 and 39.
- Movies gross a record $5 billion; *Batman* earns $250 million, the fifth highest movie income in history.
- The Rolling Stones' tour grosses $70 million.
- Utah scientists claim an energy breakthrough with "cold fusion"; later efforts to replicate their findings fail.
- Fear arises over the pesticide Alar on apples.
- An explosion on the battleship Iowa kills 47; a controversial Navy probe implicates a suicidal sailor.
- Evidence indicates that monumental "new world" Peruvian architecture is as old as the Egyptian pyramids.
- Ornithologists fear the extinction of the American black duck, due, they speculate, to timid males who cannot woo the females away from more assertive, flashier mallards.

New Words and Usages: endism, Sinatra doctrine ("You do it your way"), common house of Europe, African American, extraditables, narcoterrorist

Fads: nonfat frozen yogurt, upscale takeout food, American bistros, talk radio, Tetris, Teenage Mutant Ninja Turtles (Nintendo), codependency groups, *Bat*pins.

First Appearances: black Chair for Joint Chiefs (Gen. Colin Wilson), liver transplant using live donor (Teresa Smith), 200th anniversary of French Revolution, private U.S. satellite, B-2 test flight, Trump shuttle, "Trump" (game), comedy cable TV, Golden Trim (low-fat meat), Michelob Dry, UFOs and ETs sighted in USSR, witches' coven granted tax-exempt status (Rhode Island), Pregaphone (to talk to fetus), pocket translator, Lynx (Atari), DAT, N-10 (Intel), X terminal, IDTV, law permitting live-in lovers to register (San Francisco, $35), Time-Warner, *Street News* (newspaper by the homeless, NYC), Penn State in Big Ten, Miata, Lexus, Infiniti, trading cards of famous rabbis, female soldier leading troops in combat (Linda L. Bray, Panama City), girl in Little League World Series, 90-year-old to finish NYC marathon

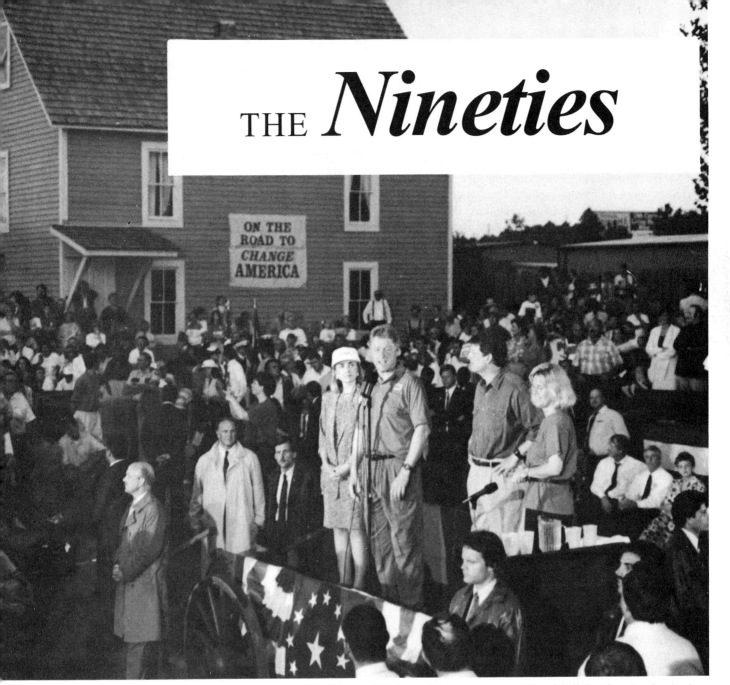

THE *Nineties*

ON THE
ROAD TO
CHANGE
AMERICA

Bill Clinton: "Without vision the people will perish." *Smithsonian Institution.*

Statistics

Vital

Population: 248,700,000
  Urban/Rural: 179/67
  Farm: 1.8%
Life expectancy:
  Male: 72.0
  Female: 78.8
Births/1,000: 16.4
Marriages/1,000: 9.7
Divorces/1,000: 4.7
Deaths/1,000: 8.7
  Heart: 289
  Cancer: 202
  Tuberculosis: 0.7
  Car accidents: 19.1

Economic

Unemployed: 6,874,000
GNP: $5,465.1 billion
Federal budget: $1.251.8 billion
National debt: $3,233.3 billion
Union membership: 16.7
  million
Strikes: 44
Prime rate: 10.0%
Car sales: 9,301,304
Average salary: $23,602

Social

Homicides/100,000: 10.2
Suicides/100,000: 12.3
Lynchings: 0
Labor force, male/female: 1.2/1
Public education: $371.9 billion
College degrees
  Bachelors'
    Male: 485,000
    Female: 558,000
  Doctorates
    Male: 24,000
    Female: 14,000
Attendance
  Movies (weekly): 20 million
  Baseball (yearly): 55.5
  million

Consumer

Consumer Price Index
  (1982–84 = 100): 130.7
Eggs: $1.00 (doz.)
Milk: 71¢ (qt.)
Bread: 76¢ (loaf)
Butter: $2.05 (lb.)
Bacon: $2.28 (lb.)
Round steak: $3.42 (lb.)
Oranges: $3.05 (doz.)
Coffee: $2.94

For all the tumult of American political life during the Nineties, when the popular President Bill Clinton spent much of his presidency under investigation for allegations of wrongdoing culminating in his impeachment, that same president could claim, with agreement by most of America and the world, that the U.S. had done well by its people and internationally. It demonstrated the efficiency of its flexible market system and willingness to use its high-tech military to combat ethnic atrocities, terrorism, and dangerous despots abroad; it also reconciled longstanding religious and ethnic enemies.

In its efforts to spread global freedom and tolerance and to engender cultural artifacts and heroes of worldwide admiration, America indeed fulfilled many of the hopes of its founders and leaders regarding its rendezvous with destiny. But in the "Nightmare Before Christmas" 1998, when House Republicans passed two articles of impeachment against overwhelming public sentiment, many feared for the Founders' dreams.

The exhilaration of the West's Cold War triumph in 1989 was surprisingly short-lived. First, in 1990, came economic recession, a ballooning national debt, and the full measure of the savings and loan debacle, requiring tens of billions of federal dollars to make good insured bank deposits. Record losses in the auto industry and stunning bankruptcy filings, involving household names like Bloomingdale's and Pan Am, made all too threatening the rumblings of disaster and "downsizing" from many of America's most stalwart companies. Eighties icons fell from grace with disturbing swiftness: junk bond maven Michael Milken, the $500-million-a-year wizard, was indicted for insider trading, Drexel Burnham, former king of investment banks, declared bankruptcy, and super-entrepreneur Donald Trump's financial empire trembled with debt. President George Bush broke his "Read My Lips" pledge and signed a record $500 billion deficit-reduction tax increase. Also in 1990, and taking the world completely by surprise, Iraq seized the tiny oil sheikhdom of Kuwait and made menacing gestures toward the globe's leading oil supplier, Saudi Arabia. With one of the world's largest standing armies, Saddam Hussein, known to be developing chemical and nuclear weapons, seemed poised to alter the world's balance of power.

America faced its first global challenge well. Bush moved with brilliant efficiency. Drawing "a line in the sand" and vowing, "This will not be another Vietnam," he organized an international fighting force under UN auspices, including the hitherto reclusive Saudis. Confronting Hussein's swaggering defiance of UN deadlines for withdrawal, the U.S. and other UN forces led by Generals Colin Powell and Norman Schwarzkopf made good Bush's promise. For six weeks, a missile and air assault, unprecedented in history, struck Iraqi military targets. Then, in what Hussein termed "the Mother of all battles," ground forces engaged. In 100 hours and with remarkably low casualties, Kuwait was liberated, the Iraqis were routed, and UN forces stood at the gates of Baghdad. Here, however, they halted, and Hussein remained—surrounded by his conquerors but still his country's undisputed ruler. The courage of America's valorous young men and women and the cold efficiency of its military weaponry had triumphed. At home and abroad Bush was acclaimed as an American Churchill—whose postwar fate he would also soon encounter.

The afterglow of victory was brief, as the economy still sputtered and company after company reported lower profits and larger layoffs. Bush seemed Hooveresque in his passive optimism. Rising drug use and crime in the cities—especially violent and random assaults—dominated headlines, and racial tensions rose. With the president's seeming inattentiveness to education, health care, homelessness, and AIDS, the Republican agenda came under attack. Its staunchest opposition came from academe, where it crystallized under the epithet of "political correctness."

Lacking an official definition, the meaning and purpose of "PC" were nonetheless clear—to reverse the alleged abuses of the Eighties—the "greed is good" mentality: the unaddressed hardships facing both the poor and middle class, as well as perceived racial, ethnic, and gender inequalities. Events like the televised Anita Hill–Clarence Thomas sexual harassment hearings and videotaped Rodney King police beating brought the credentials of the administration into question. Many believed that racial and ethnic tensions, heightened during twelve years of Republican neglect, were now blowing apart the American social fabric.

Polls indicated a widespread desire for change. Appealing to this powerful sentiment, multibillionaire Ross Perot announced his independent candidacy and quickly gained a dazzling (30 percent) poll rating. The Democrats united around Bill Clinton, a former Rhodes scholar and five-term Arkansas governor. Clinton seemed to combine intellectual brilliance in policy matters with an extraordinary empathy for everyday struggles. Suddenly the party had a chance to return to power, an unthinkable possibility the year before. The excitement of the 1992 election was due in part to Perot, the most formidable third-party candidate since Teddy Roosevelt in 1912. It was also due to the unprecedented role of round-the-clock cable TV, a new and powerful feature of the American scene. Live TV journalism had made an unusual appearance during the Gulf War, broadcast "live from Baghdad" by CNN. The public eagerly followed the war instant by instant, aided by voluminous "expert" commentary. Television had expanded its 1980s tabloid subject matter to cover history and political protagonists in the manner of daytime serial melodrama. Not only did Perot return to "Larry King Live" to accept the presidential nomination, but the Clintons discussed their marital problems on "60 Minutes."

Americans wanted change, and they elected a "new kind of Democrat" who, after an initial failure with a

Microsoft's Bill Gates, inventive genius of the computer age, becomes the world's wealthiest man. *Michael Moore.*

national health care plan overseen by his Yale lawyer wife, endorsed an essentially "conservative" agenda: balancing the budget, supporting global free markets, getting tough on crime, and promising to "end to welfare as we know it." During the 1994 congressional elections, however, the Republicans, led by Newt Gingrich's "Contract with America," which called for balanced budget and term limits constitutional amendments, orphanages in place of welfare, and an end to government funding for the arts, gained dominance in the House and Senate. By 1995, the president seemed doomed. But perhaps in the climate of a growing economy, the GOP's threat to shut down government by withholding funds frightened (or affronted) the public, for Clinton began, unexpectedly, to rise in the polls to become the first Democrat since FDR to gain reelection (alongside continuing GOP congressional dominance).

Guided by Federal Reserve chair Alan Greenspan and Treasury Secretary Robert Rubin and propelled by a mergermania reminiscent of the 1900s, Clinton's early efforts at budget balancing took hold, and the U.S. surpassed Japan's economic success with the best economic indicators in nearly three decades. By late 1998, the stock market had tripled, and job creation equaled Eighties heights, with an ever-falling—rather than rising—budget deficit. Crime rates, especially in urban areas, plummeted to levels unseen in three decades; welfare and illegitimacy rates declined as well. One might say that the decade's economic and social successes were fueled by Republican policies supported by a "new kind" of Democratic leadership.

The most revolutionary events of the decade were undoubtedly its scientific advances, which transformed former science fiction imaginings into mundane realities. Advances in computer hardware and software gave $500 personal computers a power once the preserve of multimillion-dollar apparatuses; the possibilities of armchair access to instantaneous global information seemed limitless. The repaired Hubble telescope provided incredible views of the universe and its origins, while small unmanned rovers on the Moon and Mars compelled intense interest. Creation of the first mammalian

clone and gene mapping were the stuff of dreams and nightmares. Cancer mortality declined with early detection tests and new treatments; drugs offered longer life for AIDS patients. Viagra offered yet another fantasy come true in relieving male impotence. Not only had the average lifespan increased over 30 years during the century, but so had the hope of a more vigorous twilight.

In every area of high and popular culture, America's global influence grew. Movies like *Titanic* and athletes like Michael Jordan were as popular in China as at home. Ben Heppner and the young Hilary Hahn joined the likes of Yo-Yo Ma, Itzhak Perlman, and Wynton Marsalis as world-class musicians. Architects and sculptors like Frank Gehry and Mark di Suvero built magnificent works abroad; Toni Morrison's drama of daily minority experience generated global regard. Steven Spielberg's films on prehistoric creatures, the Holocaust, slavery, and D-Day set an example of prodigious genius.

Throughout the decade, the cultural and social scene embraced many reversals and inconsistencies, typical of the nation's history in its tension between unfettered individualism and social conservatism. In the early 1990s, the venality of yuppiedom was the subject of best-sellers like *Barbarians at the Gate* and *The Firm.* "Politically correct" movies *Dances with Wolves* and *Unforgiven* won Oscars. Madonna wore underwear as outerwear, and underclass dress, "grungewear," became faddish. "The Simpsons," a TV satire of the two-parent family, and "Seinfeld," the "show about nothing," won extraordinary acclaim. The bestseller *Vox* described telephone sex between two characters who never meet, and problems of female self-assertion were the subject of *Backlash* and the "buddy" film *Thelma and Louise.*

But family values and the conservative agenda remained alive and well, their intensity perhaps a reaction to political correctness. Despite the Pulitzer Prize–winning show about gay life, *Angels in America,* homophobia gained support from the likes of Senate leader Trent Lott. Interest in "family values" may also account for the extraordinary attention paid to such scandals as the Joey Buttafuoco–Amy Fisher and Woody Allen–Soon-Yi liaisons, the Dan Quayle–"Murphy Brown" contretemps, Lorena Bobbitt's unkind cut, and the Lt. Kelly Flinn and Marv Albert affairs. A tide rose to limit abortion, strengthen punishment for criminals, replace welfare with work, end affirmative action, dissolve bilingual education, elevate educational standards, curtail rights of legal immigrants, and impose warnings on "unsuitable" material for children on the Internet, records, and TV. These were all in keeping with an old-fashioned morality of self-responsibility ("opportunity and responsibility") rather than "the abuse excuse." As the decade progressed, even rap music, with its themes of female submission and "gangsta" worship, became tamer; country music thrived, and retro-swing and a new kind of pop emerged. Emblematic of this mood was the transformation of Manhattan's sleazy 42nd Street into an

Nobel Prize–winner Toni Morrison. © *Bryan Lanker.*

urban Disney center. Perhaps the most extreme and controversial opposition to PC was *The Bell Curve,* which predicated a genetic racial, intellectual inferiority.

Scandalmania pervaded the decade. Two great athletes were sent to prison: Pete Rose for tax evasion, Mike Tyson for rape. The Teflon Don, John Gotti, was finally ensnared for life. The O. J. Simpson trial for Simpson's murder of his wife, Nicole, and her friend Ron Goldman enraptured the nation for over a year. The life and tragic death of Princess Diana attracted enormous attention. Other emblems of the decade included *Men Are from Mars, Women Are from Venus,* Anonymous's *Primary Colors, The Book of Virtues,* dinosaurs, Beanie Babies, Michael Jordan, and Mark McGwire's and Sammy Sosa's assaults on Roger Maris' homerun record.

Throughout the Nineties, the problems of being the world's leader became apparent. The attack on the World Trade Center by Muslim fanatics, the Oklahoma City bombing by a homegrown paramilitary paranoic, and the U.S. Capitol murders by a lone disturbed man showed American vulnerability at home. Abroad, our "infinite reach" was challenged by Hussein's repeated rejection of UN inspectors, India's and Pakistan's nuclear testing, Iranian and Korean missiles, the bombings of U.S. embassies in Kenya and Tanzania, and U.S. retaliation in Afghanistan and the Sudan. The sudden weakness in the thriving Asian economies and the Russian debacle appeared to threaten American prosperity. Political reconciliations sponsored by the U.S. remained precarious as well: in the Balkans, Ireland, and the Middle East.

The climactic drama of the decade involved what one newsmagazine called "The Two Bill Clintons," the brilliant political leader and the morally dubious individual. Pursued by Independent Prosecutor Kenneth Starr, whom most Americans saw as a partisan adversary, the president denied, for seven months, allegations of "sexual relations" with a White House intern, Monica Lewinsky. Given immunity, Lewinsky testified to their sexual intimacy before a grand jury—with no details spared. Private matters reached new levels of public rev-

elation as the press and TV routinely referred to previously unmentionable aspects of human sexuality. The drama continued when Clinton admitted on TV his "improper" relationship with Lewinsky following his day-long grand jury testimony; the House Judiciary's public release of Starr's sexually explicit, graphic report and tapes of Clinton's testimony; and, finally, the House hearings, which from the start many called a "witch-hunt" and "kangaroo court." Throughout, two-thirds of the public approved of the president's job performance while abhorring his private behavior, believing it did not rise to the level of "high crimes and misdemeanors."

Nothing of the decade overshadowed the Clinton-Starr war, with its intensifying dramatic scenario—Whitewater, Travelgate, Filegate, and finally Monicagate—and its cast, including taper Linda Tripp, devoted secretary Betty Currie, and the loyal Secret Service. At its climax, at the same moment American forces were attacking Iraq for rejecting UN efforts to thwart its development of instruments of mass destruction, the full House voted—along strictly partisan lines—to impeach the president. For only the second time in American history, a president faced Senate trial for removal from office.

The last year of the decade began with the "Trial of the Century," the Senate's judgment of the president as prescribed by the Constitution. With the GOP holding a 55–45 margin, and with sentiment running along virtually strict partisan lines, removal—requiring 67 votes—seemed unlikely. In early January 1999, the Senate, lacking clear precedent or constitutional guidelines, sought to establish itself as an impartial body, a reputation that had escaped the House. The 13 "House managers" presented their case for perjury and obstruction and the president's lawyers his defense—both on the specific charges and the issue of whether his wrongdoing met constitutional criteria. All involved repeatedly avowed the burden and gravity of their historic task. Overseen by Chief Justice William Rehnquist, the Senate took a bipartisan approach to avoid sexual material and unseemly tactics; the proceedings heard no live witnesses and took videotaped depositions, of little impact, from only three. On February 12, the Senate voted to acquit: 55–45 on perjury; 50–50 on obstruction. Efforts to obtain official Senate censure of the president's actions failed, although members of both parties repeatedly denounced Clinton's behavior.

With a sigh of relief, the nation generally accepted that "the Constitution [was] the clear winner" in protecting the will of the people. Although many felt that Clinton's reputation was irreparably damaged, the economy continued to grow, with low inflation and unemployment, in what was now the nation's longest peacetime expansion. As the millennium approached, the challenge to America's democracy to "provide the stage for liberty" and lead a world caught between relentless technological advances and recalcitrant human nature—as in Kosovo—remained as profound as ever.

1990

In the News

U.S. ARRESTS NORIEGA IN PANAMA FOR DRUG DEALING . . .
FEDERATED AND ALLIED STORES FILE FOR BANKRUPTCY . . .
DREXEL BURNHAM LAMBERT FILES FOR BANKRUPTCY . . .
VIOLETTA CHAMORRO DEFEATS SANDINISTA DANIEL ORTEGA
IN NICARAGUAN ELECTION . . . USSR BEGINS TROOP
WITHDRAWAL FROM CZECHOSLOVAKIA . . . LITHUANIA,
LATVIA DECLARE INDEPENDENCE FROM USSR . . . SOVIET
CONGRESS LIMITS CP POWER, ELECTS GORBACHEV PRESIDENT
FOR FIVE YEARS . . . 87 DIE IN SOCIAL CLUB FIRE IN BRONX,
N.Y. . . . MICHAEL MILKEN PLEADS GUILTY TO FELONY
SECURITIES FRAUD . . . BORIS YELTSIN IS ELECTED PRESIDENT
OF RUSSIAN FEDERATION . . . SUPREME COURT DECLARES
FLAG DESECRATION LAW UNCONSTITUTIONAL . . . OLIVER
NORTH'S CONVICTIONS IN IRAN-CONTRA ARE OVERTURNED . . .
BUSH NOMINATES DAVID SOUTER TO SUPREME COURT . . .
FEDERAL LAW FORBIDS DISCRIMINATION AGAINST THE
DISABLED . . . IRAQ SEIZES OIL SHEIKDOM OF KUWAIT . . .
SECURITY COUNCIL VOTES EMBARGO ON IRAQ, U.S. SENDS
TROOPS TO SAUDI ARABIA . . . BUSH AND GORBACHEV CALL
FOR IRAQI WITHDRAWAL FROM KUWAIT . . . CAMBODIAN
FACTIONS ACCEPT UN PLAN TO END CIVIL WAR . . . EAST AND
WEST GERMANY ARE REUNITED . . . BUSH VETO OF CIVIL
RIGHTS BILL IS UPHELD . . . NEW BUDGET PROVIDES FOR TAX
INCREASES AND $496 BILLION DEFICIT REDUCTION IN FIVE
YEARS . . . SECURITY COUNCIL APPROVES FORCE IF IRAQ
REMAINS IN KUWAIT AFTER JAN. 15 . . . CONTINENTAL
AIRLINES FILES FOR BANKRUPTCY . . . HUSSEIN FREES
FOREIGNERS IN IRAQ . . . POLAND ELECTS LECH WALESA
PRESIDENT . . . BUSH APPROVES $1 BILLION AND FOOD FOR
USSR . . . FORMER PRIEST JEAN-BERTRAND ARISTIDE WINS
FIRST FREE HAITIAN ELECTION.

Quotes ———————

"I've got to do what I think is right."
— George Bush, on breaking his
"Read My Lips" pledge

"Do you want nuns washing your underwear the rest
for your life?"
— Vatican emissary to Noriega, hiding in the
Vatican embassy

On Iraq's invasion of Kuwait:
"This will not stand. This will not stand, this
aggression against Kuwait" (Bush). "We are dealing
with Hitler revisited" (Bush). "Soviet support for our
position totally disoriented the Arab world" (U.S.
diplomat). "[U.S. planes] will fall down like dead
sparrows, and if any pilots try to parachute, . . . their
bodies will be torn into pieces . . . so that their souls
will go to hell" (Baghdad radio). "If we had had the
technology then, you'd have seen Eva Braun on the
'Donahue' show and Hitler on 'Meet the Press' " (Ed
Turner, CNN executive).

On political correctness:
"The goal is to eliminate prejudice, . . . the grand
prejudice that the intellectual tradition of Western
Europe occupies the central place in the history of
civilization" (*Newsweek*). "Either you support
multiculturalism . . . or you support white
supremacy" (Molefi Assate, Chair, African American
Studies, Temple University).

Gen. Colin Powell, the first African-American chief of
staff: "If you finally decide you have to commit military
force, you've got to be as massive and decisive as possible." *Department of the Army.*

"A lot of what we consider normal parenting is
abusive."
— John Bradshaw

"If we believe in decency—surely the least we can do
is protest the use of taxpayers' money to . . .
subsidize utterly filthy, so-called art."
— Sen. Jesse Helms (R-N.C.), on NEA grants
to artists

Marla Maples: "Are you in love with your husband?
 Because I am."
Ivana Trump: "Stay away from my husband."
Donald: "You're overreacting."
— Reported conversation in the
New York Daily News

"Best sex I've ever had."
— Marla Maples

"To have her walkin' funny we try to abuse it / A big
stinking p——y can't do it all / So we try real hard to
bust the walls."
— 2 Live Crew

Ads ———————————————

Thanks to the Miracle of Laser Technology
She's a Virgin All Over Again.
 (Madonna, Blond Ambition World Tour 90)

Please remember: ugly animals like being looked at,
too.
 (San Diego Zoo)

Thanks to video stores, kids have a whole new reason
to call television the boob tube.
 (WKYC-TV, Channel 3 news)

ingle ells
ingle ells
The holidays aren't the same without J&B
 (J&B Scotch whisky)

Drive Drunk and We'll See You Real Soon.
 *(Goodwine Funeral Homes, Flatrock, Palestine,
Robinson, Texas)*

Expect light, moderate and heavy winds through the
weekend.
 (Minnesota Symphony Orchestra)

Maybe if you gave your money a nicer home, it
would stay around longer.
 (Rolf's leather goods)

Unfortunately, the way to a man's heart really is
through his stomach.
 (1-800-EAT-LEAN)

Drop out of school and you can still get a job on Wall
Street.
 (Burger King, "Nourish Your Mind")

TV

Premieres

"The Simpsons"
"Law and Order," Chris Noth, Michael Moriarty
"Twin Peaks," Kyle MacLachlan, Michael Ontkean
"Evening Shade," Burt Reynolds, Marilu Henner
"In Living Color," Damon Wayans
"Fresh Prince of Bel Air," Will Smith, James Avery
"America's Funniest Home Videos," Bob Saget
"Seinfeld," Jerry Seinfeld

Top Ten (Nielsen)

"Roseanne," "The Cosby Show," "Cheers," "A Different World," "America's Funniest Home Videos," "The Golden Girls," "60 Minutes," "The Wonder Years," "Empty Nest," "Murder, She Wrote"

Specials

"The Civil War" (Ken Burns, 11 hours long, 5 years in production); "Eyes on the Prize II"; *The Ring* (from the Metropolitan Opera: Hildegard Behrens, Jessye Norman); "Caroline" (Stephanie Zimbalist); "Kennedys of Massachusetts"; "The Incident" (Walter Matthau)

Emmy Awards

"L.A. Law" (drama); "Murphy Brown" (comedy); Peter Falk (actor, drama, "Columbo"); Patricia Wettig (actress, drama, "thirtysomething"); Ted Danson (actor, comedy, "Cheers"); Candice Bergen (actress, comedy, "Murphy Brown"); "Drug Wars: The Camarena Story" (miniseries)

Of Note

Satellite broadcasting covers the Persian Gulf crisis; Dan Rather is the first to interview Hussein • Jim Henson, creator of the Muppets, dies of pneumonia • David Lynch's nighttime serial "Twin Peaks" popularizes the program's "Who Killed Laura Palmer?" • Sineád O'Connor and Nora Dunne refuse to appear on "Saturday Night Live" when Andrew Dice Clay is booked as guest host • "Cartoon All-Stars to the Rescue" airs on several Saturday morning networks simultaneously: an antidrug special, it targets 20 million 5- to 11-year olds • NBC is first in the Nielsen ratings for the fifth consecutive year • Efforts by San Francisco's KQED and other stations to televise executions fail.

Movies

Openings

Dances With Wolves (Kevin Costner), Costner
Ghost (Jerry Zucker), Patrick Swayze, Demi Moore, Whoopi Goldberg
Awakenings (Penny Marshall), Robert De Niro, Robin Williams
Goodfellas (Martin Scorcese), Robert De Niro, Ray Liotta, Joe Pesci
The Godfather Part III (Francis Ford Coppola), Al Pacino, Diane Keaton, Andy Garcia
Total Recall (Paul Verhoeven), Arnold Schwarzenegger
Pretty Woman (Garry Marshall), Richard Gere, Julia Roberts
Postcards from the Edge (Mike Nichols), Meryl Streep, Shirley MacLaine
Reversal of Fortune (Barbet Schroeder), Jeremy Irons, Glenn Close
Presumed Innocent (Alan Pakula), Harrison Ford, Raul Julia, Bonnie Bedelia
Dick Tracy (Warren Beatty), Beatty, Madonna, Al Pacino
The Grifters (Stephen Frears), Anjelica Huston, John Cusack, Annette Bening
Hamlet (Franco Zeffirelli), Mel Gibson, Glenn Close
Home Alone (Chris Columbus), Macauley Culkin
Metropolitan (Whit Stillman), Edward Clements, Christopher Eigman
Teenage Mutant Ninja Turtles (Steve Barron), Elias Koteas, Judith Hoag (voices)
Tie Me Up! Tie Me Down! (Pedro Almodóvar), Victoria Abril, Antonio Banderas
Cinema Paradiso (Guiseppe Tornatore), Philippe Noiret, Jacques Perrin

Academy Awards

Best picture: *Dances with Wolves*
Best director: Kevin Costner (*Dances with Wolves*)
Best actress: Kathy Bates (*Misery*)
Best actor: Jeremy Irons (*Reversal of Fortune*)

Top Box-Office Stars

Arnold Schwarzenegger, Julia Roberts, Bruce Willis, Tom Cruise, Mel Gibson, Kevin Costner, Patrick Swayze, Sean Connery, Harrison Ford, Richard Gere

Stars of the Future

Kenneth Branagh, Lolita Davidovich, Kelly Lynch, Andre Braugher, Laura San Giacomo, Madeleine Stowe, Ethan Hawke, Joanne Whalley-Kilmer

Popular Music

Hit Songs
"Black Velvet"
"Come Back to Me"
"Have You Seen Her"
"Do You Remember"
"It Must Have Been Love"
"Oh Pretty Woman"

Top Records
Albums: *Where've You Been* (Kathy Mattea); *Nick of Time* (Bonnie Raitt); *Janet Jackson's Rhythm Nation 1814* (Janet Jackson); *Soul Provider* (Michael Bolton); *Please Hammer, Don't Hurt 'Em* (M. C. Hammer); *Storm Front* (Billy Joel); *Johnny Gill* (Johnny Gill)

Singles: *Vision of Love* (Mariah Carey); *Escapade* (Janet Jackson);

How Am I Supposed to Live without You (Michael Bolton); *Hold On* (Wilson Phillips); *Vogue* (Madonna); *Talk to Me* (Anita Baker); *Step by Step* (New Kids on the Block). Country: *I've Come to Expect it from You* (George Strait); *Unanswered Prayers* (Garth Brooks)

Grammy Awards
Another Day in Paradise, Phil Collins (record); *Back on the Block*, Quincy Jones (album); "From a Distance" (song)

Jazz and Big Bands
Blind pianist Marcus Roberts gains an enormous following with *Deep in the Shed*. Joining Wynton Marsalis in the revival of classical jazz (1950s hard bop) and jazz-

rock fusion are his brother Branford Marsalis, Terence Blanchard, Brian Lynch, Donald Harrison, and Wallace Roney. Pianist Harry Connick, Jr., 23, revives swing-era styles. Bass player Milt Hinton is honored at the JVC Jazz Festival in New York; trumpeter-bandleader Kid Sheik Colar, at the New Orleans Jazz and Heritage festivals.

Top Performers (*Downbeat*): Wynton Marsalis (soloist); Count Basie (big band); Red Rodney (acoustic jazz group); Rolling Stones (rock group); Phil Woods, Steve Lacy, Eddie Daniels, Sonny Rollins, Steve Swallow (instrumentalists); Betty Carter, Joe Williams (vocalists); Miles Davis, *Aura* (album)

Theater

Broadway Openings

Plays
The Piano Lesson (August Wilson), Charles S. Dutton, S. Epatha Merkerson
Lettice and Lovage (Peter Shaffer), Maggie Smith, Margaret Tyzack
The Grapes of Wrath (Steinbeck, adapted by Frank Galati), Gary Sinise, Lois Smith, Terry Kinney
Six Degrees of Separation (John Guare), Stockard Channing, John Cunningham
Shadowlands (William Nicholson), Nigel Hawthorne, Jane Alexander
Prelude to a Kiss (Craig Lucas), Timothy Hutton, Mary-Louise Parker, Barnard Hughes
Jackie Mason—Brand New, Jackie Mason

Musicals
Aspects of Love (Andrew Lloyd Webber, Don Black, Charles Hart), Michael Ball, Ann Crumb, Kevin Colson
Once on This Island (Stephen Flaherty, Lynn Ahrens), La Chanze, Jerry Dixon
Buddy: The Buddy Holly Story (Buddy Holly), Paul Hipp
Falsettoland (William Finn), Stephen Bogardus, Michael Rupert

Classics, Revivals, and Off-Broadway Premieres
Cat on a Hot Tin Roof, Kathleen Turner, Daniel Hugh Kelly, Charles Durning; *By and For Havel: Audience* (Havel), *Catastrophe* (Beckett); *Hamlet,* Kevin Kline; *King Lear,* Hal Holbrook; *Fiddler on the Roof,* Topol; *Sex, Drugs, Rock & Roll* (Eric Bogosian); *Oh! Kay* (George and Ira Gershwin), Brien Mitchell; *Monster in a Box* (Spalding Gray); *Machinal* (Sophie Treadwell), Jodie Markell; *The Taming of the Shrew,* Morgan Freeman, Tracey Ullman

Regional

Yale Repertory Theater, New Haven: *Two Trains Running* (August Wilson)

Mark Taper Forum, Los Angeles: *Jelly's Last Jam* (Jelly Roll Morton, George C. Wolfe)

Seattle Repertory Theater: *Conversations with My Father* (Herb Gardner), Judd Hirsch

Pulitzer Prize
The Piano Lesson, August Wilson

Tony Awards
The Grapes of Wrath, Steinbeck, adapted by Frank Galati (play), *City of Angels,* Cy Coleman, David Zippel, Larry Gelbart (musical)

Classical Music _____

Compositions
Shulamit Ram, Symphony
Joan Tower, *Silver Ladders, Flute Concerto*
Jacob Druckman, *Brangle*
David Del Tredici, *Steps*
Ezra Laderman, Cello Concerto
George Perle, *Windows of Order*

Important Events
The Chicago Symphony and Carnegie Hall begin their 100th anniversary celebrations; Tanglewood, its fiftieth anniversary.

Notable Performances: Celebrating his reinstated Soviet citizenship, Mstislav Rostropovich returns to Russia after sixteen years and tours with the National Symphony Orchestra; he plays and conducts the Dvorak Cello Concerto. Highly acclaimed performances in the U.S. include Margaret Argerich's Prokofiev's Third Piano Concerto with the Boston Symphony; Christa Ludwig's Schubert's *Wintereise* (ordinarily sung by men), accompanied by James Levine; and Yevgeny Kissin's interpretations of Chopin, Schumann, and Prokofiev

Debut: Yevgeny Kissin

First Performances
Mario Davidovsky, Concertante for String Quartet and Orchestra (Philadelphia); Liszt, Piano Concerto (Chicago); Ned Rorem, *Goodbye My Fancy* (Chicago); Shulamit Ram, First Symphony (Philadelphia); Elliott Carter, Violin Concerto (Philadelphia); Toru Takemitsu, *Visions* (Chicago); John Corigliano, Symphony, no. 1 (Chicago)

Opera

Metropolitan: Productions of the complete *Ring* continue; Thomas Hampson, Cheryl Studer, *Don Giovanni;* Gwyneth Jones, Vladimir Popov, Aprile Milo, *Turandot* (Zeffirelli production); June Anderson (debut), Luciano Pavarotti, *Rigoletto;* Barbara Bonney, Anne Sofie von Otter, *Der Rosenkavalier* (Carlos Kleiber, conducting); Placido Domingo, *Otello* (Kleiber, conducting); Marilyn Horne, Lella Cuberli, *Semiramide*

New York City: Christopher Keene becomes director. Schoenberg, *Moses und Aron; House of the Dead* (Jánaĉek, premiere)

Seattle: *War and Peace* (for Prokofiev centenary, $2 million production)

Spoleto Festival, Charleston, S.C.: *Hydrogen Jukebox* (Philip Glass, Allen Ginsberg); William Pell, *Parsifal*

Minnesota: *Frankenstein: The Modern Prometheus* (Libby Larsen), premiere

Chicago: Jessye Norman, *Alceste* (Gluck); *Voyage of Edgar Allen Poe* (Argento)

Music Notes
Intense interest in authentic instrumentation raises controversy over the proper selection of instruments • The Sante Fe, Ravinia, and Saratoga festivals join in a rare collaborative commission of works from Ned Rorem, Jacob Druckman, and John Harrison • The joint benefit concert in Rome of José Carreras, Placido Domingo, and Luciano Pavarotti creates enormous interest and record sales.

The Simpson family. Bart's filial irreverence and Homer's "Father knows little" attitude contrast with previous family visions. *"The Simpsons"*° and ™ *Twentieth Century Fox Film Corporation—All Rights Reserved.*

Mac Adams's Korean War memorial, Battery Park, New York City.

Art

Painting
Robert Rauschenberg, *Lock-Out*
Tom Wesselman, *Monica Lying Down on Robe*
Brice Marden, *Cold Mountain 3* (1989–91)
Jim Nutt, *Daft*
Elizabeth Murray, *Terrifying Terrain*
Philip Taaffe, *Necromancer*
Joan Mitchell, *Champs*
Mark Tansey, *Bridge over the Cartesian Gap*

Sculpture
Christo, *Lower Manhattan Wrapped Buildings* (1964–90)
John Miller, *Echo and Narcissus*
Jeff Koons, *Jeff and Ilona*

Kiki Smith, *Projects Room*
Michael Todd, *Jazz*

Architecture
333 West Wacker Drive building, Chicago (Kohn Pederson Fox)
Broward Center for the Performing Arts, Fort Lauderdale (Benjamin Thompson)
John Madden Co. building, Denver (Urban Design Group)
NBC Tower, Chicago (SOM)
Armand Hammer Museum, Los Angeles (Edward Larrabee Barnes)
The largest restoration in history takes place at Ellis Island (Beyer Blinder Belle, Notter Finegold & Alexander)

Important Exhibitions

Museums
The most comprehensive exhibit of Monet's works including all 16 of the series paintings, begins traveling through the U.S.

New York: *Metropolitan:* "From Poussin to Matisse"; "Gericault's Heroic Landscapes"; Art of Central Africa; "Mexico: Splendors of 30 Centuries"; Caravaggio; Joseph Wright. *Museum of Modern Art:* "Matisse in Morocco"; "High and Low: Modern Art and Popular Culture." *Brooklyn:* Albert Pinkham Ryder; Vuillard. *Guggenheim:* the museum closes for a $40 million renovation and expansion.

Washington (Corcoran), Brooklyn: "Facing History: The Black Image in American Art, 1710–1940"

Washington (National): Titian (quincentenary of his birth); Church; Hals; "The Art of Glass"; "Eva/Ava: Woman in Renaissance and Baroque Prints"

Baltimore: Grace Hartigan; "Lalique: A Century of Glass"

Metropolitan, San Antonio, Los Angeles: Mexican art from the pre-Columbian to modern period

Minneapolis, Houston, San Francisco, St. Louis: Jasper Johns

Seattle, Minneapolis: Russian Constructivism

Art Briefs
Dennis Barrie, director of the Contemporary Arts Center in Cincinnati, is acquitted of obscenity charges, following the museum's Robert Mapplethorpe exhibit, "The Perfect Moment" • The world's largest art theft since 1911 (of the *Mona Lisa*) occurs at the Gardner Museum in Boston ($200 million), for which the museum is uninsured • After selling works by Kandinsky, Modigliani, and Chagall, the Guggenheim purchases a group of minimalist works ($30 million) • Record sales include Brancusi's 1919 *Golden Bird,* $12 million; van Gogh's *Portrait du Gachet,* $83 million; Renoir's *Au Moulin de la Galette,* $78.1 million (both paintings purchased by Japanese businessman Ryoei Saito); and the American Willem de Kooning's *July,* $8.8 million.

Dance

American Ballet Theatre: Jane Hermann and Oliver Smith are appointed directors. Julio Bocca, Cheryl Yeager, *Brief Fling* (Twyla Tharp)

New York City Ballet: Jerome Robbins retires. Darci Kistler, Robert LaFosse, *Danses Concertantes* (Balanchine); Lauren Hausen, Ben Huys, *Dances at a Gathering; Fearful Symmetries* (Martins)

San Francisco: *The Sleeping Beauty* (Helgi Tomasson), for the 150th anniversary of Tchaikovsky's birth

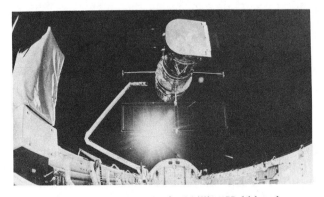

Despite its flawed mirrors, the $1.5 billion Hubble telescope delivers unprecedented views of outer space. *NASA, IMAX, Smithsonian.*

Books

Fiction

Critics' Choice
Vineland, Thomas Pynchon
East is East, T. Coraghessan Boyle
Seventh Heaven, Alice Hoffman
Natural Selection, Frederick Barthelme
Because It Is Bitter, and Because It Is My Heart, Joyce Carol Oates
Shuffle, Leonard Michaels

Best-Sellers
Oh, The Places You'll Go, Dr. Seuss
Clear and Present Danger, Tom Clancy
The Stand: The Complete and Uncut Version, Stephen King
The Burden of Proof, Scott Turow
The Bourne Ultimatum, Robert Ludlum
September, Rosamund Pilcher
Message From Nam, Danielle Steele
An Inconvenient Woman, Dominick Dunne
Devices and Desires, P. D. James

Nonfiction

Critics' Choice
The House of Morgan, Ron Chernow
What I Saw at the Revolution, Peggy Noonan

From their New Hampshire farm, married poets Donald Hall and Jane Kenyon command devoted followings and critical acclaim. Kenyon's photo: *Donald Hall.* Hall's photo: *Gary Samson.*

Middle Passage, Charles Johnson
Tenured Radicals, Roger Kimball
The Worst Years of Our Lives, Barbara Ehrenreich
A Natural History of the Senses, Diane Ackerman
Darkness Visible, William Styron
The Years of Lyndon Johnson: Means of Ascent, Robert Caro
The Book of J, Harold Bloom, David Rosenberg
Sexual Personae: Art and Decadence from Nefertiti to Emily Dickinson, Camille Paglia

Best-Sellers
Wealth Without Risk, Charles Givens
Barbarians at the Gate: The Fall of R. J. Nabisco, Bryan Burrough and John Helyar
Megatrends 2000, John Naisbitt and Patricia Aburdene
It Was on Fire When I Lay Down On It, Robert Fulghum
Liar's Poker: Rising Through the Wreckage on Wall Street, Michael M. Lewis
Men at Work, George Will
Dave Barry Turns Forty, Dave Barry

You Just Don't Understand: Men and Women in Conversation, Deborah Tannen
Homecoming: Reclaiming and Championing Your Inner Child, John Bradshaw
Secrets About Men Every Woman Should Know, Barbara DeAngelis

Poetry
Laurie Sheck, *Io at Night*
Charles Simic, *The Book of Gods and Devils*
Dave Smith, *Cuba Night*
Maya Angelou, *I Shall Not Be Moved*

Pulitzer Prizes
Rabbit at Rest, John Updike (fiction)
A Midwife's Tale: The Life of Martha Ballard, Laura Thatcher Ulrich (U.S. history)
The Ants, Bert Holldobler, Edward O. Wilson (nonfiction)
Jackson Pollack: An American Saga, Steven Naifeh, Gregory White Smith (biography)
Near Changes, Mona Van Duyn (poetry)

Science and Technology

Test-tube work on human gene therapy for cystic fibrosis begins.

A 4-year-old girl, with ADA deficiency, is the first to receive human gene therapy.

Accutane is discovered to block regrowth of mouth and throat cancer.

Dietary calcium (800 mg) is demonstrated to be of benefit to postmenopausal women in slowing osteoporosis.

The first successful fetal surgery for diaphragmatic hernias is performed.

Two studies that indicate brain volume differences support the biological origin of schizophrenia.

Cortical human brain cells are grown in a laboratory.

Studies indicate that a growth hormone given men between 61 and 81 have made their bodies 20 years younger.

Measurements of the Cosmic Background Explorer satellite support the big bang theory.

Nobel Prizes
Elias James Corey wins in chemistry for new ways of synthesizing complex natural molecules. Jerome I. Friedman and Henry Kendall win in physics for their "breakthrough in understanding matter." In medicine, Joseph E. Murray wins for the first kidney transplant; E. Donnall Thomas, for bone marrow transplants.

Sports _____

Baseball

Pete Rose is sentenced to five months for income tax evasion.

A record 9 no-hitters are pitched, 7 in the AL, 2 in the NL.

Nolan Ryan, 43, pitches a record 6th no-hitter.

Bobby Thigpen makes a record 57 saves.

The Cy Young Awards go to Bob Welch (Oakland, AL) and Doug Drabek (Pittsburgh, NL).

Champions _____

Batting
  Willie McGee (St. Louis, NL), .335
  George Brett (Kansas City, AL), .329
Pitching
  Doug Drabek (Pittsburgh, NL), 22–6

Bob Welch (Oakland, AL), 27–6
Home runs
  Cecil Fielder (Detroit, AL), 51

Football

Matt Bahr's last second field goal wins the NFC championship for the N.Y. Giants over San Francisco, 15–13.

NFC Season Leaders: Phil Simms (New York Giants), passing; Barry Sanders (Detroit), rushing, 1,502 yards; Jerry Rice (San Francisco), receiving, 100 catches, 1,502 yards

College All-Americans: Raghib "Rocket" Ismail (E), Notre Dame; Russell Maryland (G), Miami; Eric Bienemy (B), Colorado

Bowls (Jan. 1, 1991):

Rose: Washington 46–Iowa 34
Orange: Colorado 10–Notre Dame 9
Cotton: Miami 46–Texas 3
Sugar: Tennessee 23–Virginia 22

Basketball

Super college star Hank Gathers, Loyola Marymount, dies suddenly of cardiac arhythmia.
Michael Jordan wins a 4th straight scoring title.

NBA All-Pro First Team: Magic Johnson (Los Angeles Lakers), Michael Jordan (Chicago), Patrick Ewing (New York Knicks), Charles Barkley (Philadelphia), Karl Malone (Utah)

Other Sports

Boxing: 35–1 underdog James "Buster" Douglas KOs undefeated Mike Tyson (37–0) in the 10th in Tokyo. Evander Holyfield takes the title from Douglas in a 3rd round KO at Las Vegas.

Golf: Hale Irwin, 45, becomes the oldest to win the US Open.

Hockey: Edmonton wins its 5th Stanley Cup in 7 years and first without Wayne Gretzky.

Tennis: Martina Navratilova wins a record 9th Wimbledon. Pete Sampras is the youngest male to win the Open.

Winners _____

World Series
  Cincinnati (NL) 4
  Oakland (AL) 0
MVP
  NL—Barry Bonds, Pittsburgh
  AL—Rickey Henderson, Oakland
Super Bowl XXV (Jan. 1991)
  New York Giants 20–Buffalo 19
MVP
  Randall Cunningham, Philadelphia
College Football
  Colorado
  Georgia Tech
Heisman Trophy
  Ty Detmer, Brigham Young

NBA Championship
  Detroit 4–Portland 1
MVP
  Magic Johnson, L.A. Lakers
College Basketball
  UNLV
Player of the Year
  Lionel Simmons, La Salle
Stanley Cup
  Edmonton
US Tennis Open
  Men: Pete Sampras
  Women: Gabriela Sabatini
USGA Open
  Hale Irwin
Kentucky Derby
  Unbridled (Craig Perret, jockey)

Fashion _____

A revival of 1960s styling brings back hot pants, mini-skirts, psychedelic and op art prints, the tent dress, pants-suits, and the A-line. Mini-skirts, in a slim line or with flared or pleated shirts, are worn with tunic-length sweaters or overblouses. Bright-colored tights or leggings, often in textured or lace patterns, contrast with the patterning of the blouses or skirts. Black becomes a color worn at any time of day—for every style and for females of all ages, even children. Natural colors are also popular: earth browns, copper tones, and stone grays, as well as shades of curry, cinnamon, olive, paprika, and plum. Younger people wear bicycle shorts, baseball caps (often backward), new age symbols (the word *Nirvana* on shirts, sweaters, and jackets), and astrology signs. At the end of the year, Madonna's flair for underwear becomes contagious, and black bras, with metallic studs, rhinestones, and other embellishments, gain popularity as outerwear.

High-fashion notes: Sonia Rykiel's pink velour slip dress; Gigli's narrow pants with stirrup leggings.

Kaleidoscope _____

- The GNP falls after a record eight years of growth; consumer confidence falls to a low, 61.3 (113, 1989).
- Housing values plummet; bad loans of the 1980s undermine new construction; factory orders fall 10.5 percent; personal bankruptcies rise 60 percent.
- The savings and loan debacle of the eighties is expected to cost $250–$500 billion; Congress appropriates $68 billion for this year.
- Females constitute a record 11% of U.S. troops (3 percent, 1973).
- Satellite broadcasting covers Saddam Hussein's parading of hostages before the camera as he also pats the heads of children.
- After claiming that a black mugger had murdered his pregnant wife and wounded him, Boston businessman Charles Stuart commits suicide; evidence had already mounted that he murdered her.
- Washington, D.C. mayor Marion Barry is videotaped smoking a crack pipe; convicted of misdemeanor charges, he is sentenced to six months in jail.
- Donald Trump's financial empire is threatened by his $3.2 billion debt; his creditors put him on a $450,000 a month allowance (down from $583,000).
- Drexel Lambert Burnham distributes $200 million in bonuses two months before declaring bankruptcy.
- Violence reaches young children; a 6-month-old in Chicago and a 9-month-old in New York are randomly shot to death.
- "Gangsta rap" groups, including Ice Cube, Geto Boys, and N.W.A., sing of violent life in the inner city; M. C. Hammer's *Please Don't Hurt 'Em Hammer* sells over 4 million copies, the best-selling rap album in history.
- Fab Morvan and Rob Piatus (Milli Vanilli) admit not singing "Girl You Know It's Not True" on their Grammy-winning album; the award is rescinded.
- One in nine college women experiences date rape; 16 women are raped hourly in the U.S., twenty times the rate in Britain; thirty that of Japan.
- 375,000 children are born to crack-addicted mothers.
- The EPA estimates that 3,800 die yearly from secondhand smoke.
- An estimated 15 million, including smokers, crossdressers, alcoholics, sexual compulsives, and gamblers, attend weekly self-help support groups.
- A controversy on euthanasia begins after Dr. Jack Kevorkian provides Alzheimer sufferer Janet Adkin, 53, with a suicide device.
- The U.S. Census estimates that 25 percent of the population is a member of a minority group; the fastest growing groups are the Asians and Pacific Islanders.
- Fifty-one percent of mothers with children under one work; 56 percent, with children under six; 73 percent, with children between 6 and 17.
- In keeping with multicultural and "PC" ideals, the University of Texas adopts the freshman course "Racism and Sexism: An Integrated Study."
- "You have a brain in your head / You have feet in your shoes / You can steer yourself wherever you choose," writes Dr. Seuss in his final book, *Oh, The Places You'll Go.*

- Imelda Marcos holds a birthday party for her husband, in attendance in a refrigerated casket; she changes his shirt twice a week.
- Record book auction prices include Audubon's *Birds of America,* $3,960,000; *The Federalist* (bound for George Washington), $1,430,000; and a first folio edition of Shakespeare (4 volumes), $1,320,000.
- New NEA requirements stipulate that funded artists subject their final work to review, and, if judged obscene, return their grants.
- Leonard Bernstein dies in October, five days after announcing his retirement; he conducted his last concert at Tanglewood in August.
- In *The Book of J,* an unexpected bestseller, critic Harold Bloom attributes the "Yahweh" portion of the Bible to a female Israelite poet.
- Dieting becomes a $33 billion industry; Oprah Winfrey tells viewers she has lost 67 pounds on a liquid diet.
- Roseanne Barr's screeching version of "The Star-Spangled Banner," accompanied by an unseemly physical gesture at a San Diego Padres game, causes national irritation; Barr apologizes publicly.
- Hemophiliac Ryan White dies at 14; he had gained national sympathy in 1985, when he was not permitted to enter school due to his AIDS infection.
- The northwest spotted owl is declared an endangered species, due to the timber industry in the Pacific Northwest.
- An eleven-year study of Trinidadian guppies indicates that changes in reproductive behavior are due to environment, supporting the theory of natural selection.
- Colorado fossil fragments of a dinosaur 30 million years before Tyrannosaurus rex are named Epanterias amplexus; it could have consumed a 1,400-pound cow in one gulp.

First Appearances: Moscow McDonald's, Kobe beef from Japan ($100 a serving), Infiniti, Saturn, Lexus, Sensor shaving cream, Reebok pump, dolphin-free tuna, 2-liter Coke and Pepsi in recycled plastic, gender-specific disposable diapers, Caller ID system (Bell), Norplant (in U.S.), Simplesse (fat substitute), "Decade of the Brain" (NIMH), genes for retinitis pigmentosa and elephant man's disease, genetically engineered calves and enzymes for cheese making, Revised Clean Air Act, White House drug testing

Fads: condom boutiques, pre-ripped jeans, wide headbands, Lambada, roller blading, Batman logos, "The Simpsons" and Ninja Turtles paraphernalia, potatoes, canola oil, Hong Kong food, bistros, Waldo books, high-priced sneakers ($125–$175)

New Words and Usages: sandwich generation, glass ceiling, mom's war, white collar recession, new world order, differently abled (challenged), people of color, sexual orientation, heterosexism, outing

1991

In the News

GENEVA TALKS BETWEEN BAKER AND IRAQI TARIQ AZIZ FAIL . . . CONGRESS AUTHORIZES FORCE IN GULF . . . JAN. 15 DEADLINE FOR IRAQI COMPLIANCE EXPIRES, UN FORCES LED BY U.S. LAUNCH MASSIVE AIR AND MISSILE ASSAULT . . . UN LAUNCHES GROUND ASSAULT ON IRAQI TROOPS IN KUWAIT AND IRAQ . . . KUWAIT IS LIBERATED AND IRAQIS SURRENDER AFTER 100 HOURS . . . FOUR WHITE L.A. POLICE OFFICERS ARE INDICTED FOR BEATING MOTORIST RODNEY KING, INCIDENT WAS VIDEOTAPED BY AMATEUR . . . FEDERAL RESERVE LOWERS INTEREST RATE TO 5.5% . . . BUSH IS BRIEFLY HOSPITALIZED FOR HEART IRREGULARITY . . . INDIAN PM RAJIV GANDHI IS ASSASSINATED . . . ANGOLAN FACTIONS AGREE TO END 16-YEAR CIVIL WAR . . . BORIS YELTSIN IS ELECTED RUSSIAN PRESIDENT BY POPULAR VOTE . . . BUSH AND GORBACHEV SIGN STRATEGIC ARMS REDUCTION TREATY . . . JEFFREY DAHMER IS ARRESTED FOR MULTIPLE MURDERS AND CANNIBALISM . . . HARDLINER COUP IN MOSCOW FAILS TO OUST GORBACHEV, YELTSIN LEADS RESISTANCE . . . SOVIET COUNCIL RECOGNIZES BALTICS . . . CROATIA AND SLOVENIA DECLARE INDEPENDENCE FROM YUGOSLAVIA . . . ELECTED HAITIAN PRESIDENT ARISTIDE IS OVERTHROWN BY MILITARY COUP . . . SENATE CONFIRMS CLARENCE THOMAS TO SUPREME COURT AFTER LAW PROFESSOR ANITA HILL CHARGES SEXUAL HARRASSMENT . . . MAGIC JOHNSON ANNOUNCES HE IS HIV-POSITIVE . . . U.S. INDICTS TWO LIBYAN AGENTS IN 1988 PAN AM BOMBING . . . PAN AM CEASES OPERATIONS . . . LAST U.S. HOSTAGE IN LEBANON, TERRY ANDERSON, IS RELEASED . . . RUSSIA, UKRAINE, AND BYELORUSSIA FORM COMMONWEALTH TO REPLACE USSR . . . GM TO CLOSE 21 PLANTS, LAY OFF 70,000.

Quotes _____

On the Gulf War:
"Should the Americans become embroiled, we will make them swim in their own blood, Allah willing" (Saddam Hussein). "No blood for oil" (peace protesters). "We have before us the opportunity to forge for ourselves and future generations, a new world order" (Bush to Gulf coalition). "Something is happening outside. . . . The skies over Baghdad have been illuminated. We're seeing flashes going off all over the sky" (CNN correspondent Bernard Shaw, Jan. 16, 6:35 p.m. EST). "[Prepare for] the mother of all battles" (Hussein, anticipating land war). "He is neither a strategist, nor is he schooled in the operational arts, nor is he a tactician, nor is he a general, nor is he a soldier. Other than that, he's a great military man" (Gen. Schwarzkopf, on Hussein).

"Vice President Gennady Yanayev has taken over, . . . due to Gorbachev's inability to perform . . . for health reasons."
— Tass bulletin

"On a lighter note, shall we now sign a decree suspending the activities of the Russian Communist Party?"
— Yeltsin to Gorbachev

On Christopher Columbus:
"He was interested in discovery. He wasn't interested in genocide" (Prof. Davril Alden, U. of Washington). "He represents the worst of his era" (Prof. Jack Weatherford, Macalester College).

General Norman Schwarzkopf. In 100 hours, 800,000 troops from 30 nations conquer 545,000 entrenched Iraqi veterans. *Department of the Army.*

From the Clarence Thomas-Anita Hill hearings:
"I felt I had to tell the truth" (Hill). "He . . . went over to his desk to get the Coke and asked: 'Who has put a pubic hair on my Coke?' " (Hill). "Enough is enough. This is a circus, . . . a national disgrace, . . . a high-tech lynching for uppity blacks" (Thomas). "Are you a scorned woman? . . . Are you interested in writing a book?" (Sen. Howell Heflin, D-Ala., questioning Hill).

"I confess that after I arrived in L.A. in 1979, I did my best to accommodate as many women as I could—most of them through unprotected sex."
— Magic Johnson, on how he contracted AIDS

Ads _____

TV

Premieres
"Northern Exposure," Rob Morrow, Barry Corbin, Janine Turner

"I'll Fly Away," Sam Waterston, Regina Taylor

"Brooklyn Bridge," Marion Ross, Danny Gerard

"Civil Wars," Mariel Hemingway, Peter Onorati

"Homefront," ensemble cast

Top Ten (Nielsen)
"Cheers," "60 Minutes," "Roseanne," "A Different World," "The Cosby Show," "America's Funniest Home Videos," "Murphy Brown," "Murder, She Wrote," "Home Improvement," "Designing Women"

Specials
The Mahabarata; "Columbus and the Age of Discovery"; "Separate but Equal" (Sidney Poitier, Burt Lancaster); *Uncle Vanya* (David Warner, Ian Bannen); "Pearl Harbor: Two Hours that Changed the World"; *The Grapes of Wrath* (Steppenwolf production); "Sarah: Plain and Tall" (Glenn Close); "Prisoners of Honor" (Richard Dreyfus); "Stop at Nothing," Veronica Hamel

Emmy Awards
"L.A. Law" (drama); Patricia Wettig (actress, drama, "thirtysomething"); James Earl Jones (actor, drama, "Gabriel's Fire"); "Cheers" (comedy); Burt Reynolds (actor, comedy, "Evening Shade"); Kirstie Alley (comedy, actress, "Cheers"); "Separate but Equal" (drama)

Of Note
Vast numbers watch history as it occurs: during the Persian War, Soviet coup to depose Gorbachev, Clarence Thomas-Anita Hill hearings • William Kennedy Smith's rape trial gains a large audience • The 24-hour-a-day Courtroom TV Network begins • NBC chooses Jay Leno to succeed Johnny Carson; David Letterman "has a snit" • "Dallas" ends after 13 years • "Studs" raises a controversy about tastelessness: single women rate their dates sexually.

Movies

Openings
The Silence of the Lambs (Jonathan Demme), Anthony Hopkins, Jodie Foster

Bugsy (Barry Levinson), Warren Beatty, Annette Bening

JFK (Oliver Stone), Kevin Costner, Gary Oldman

The Prince of Tides (Barbra Streisand), Streisand, Nick Nolte

Beauty and the Beast (Gary Trousdale, Krik Wise), animated film

Thelma and Louise (Ridley Scott), Susan Sarandon, Geena Davis

Terminator 2: Judgment Day (James Cameron), Arnold Schwarzenegger

Robin Hood: Prince of Thieves (Kevin Reynolds), Kevin Costner, Morgan Freeman

Jungle Fever (Spike Lee), Wesley Snipes, Annabella Sciorra

Boyz 'N the Hood (John Singleton), Ice Cube, Larry Fishburne

The Fisher King (Terry Gilliam), Robin Williams, Jeff Bridges

Homicide (David Mamet), Joe Mantegna

City Slickers (Ron Underwood), Billy Crystal, Jack Palance

My Own Private Idaho (Gus Van Sant, Jr.), River Phoenix, Keanu Reeves

Barton Fink (Joel Coen), John Turturro, John Goodman

Grand Canyon (Lawrence Kasdan), Danny Glover, Kevin Kline

Fried Green Tomatoes (John Avnet), Jessica Tandy, Kathy Bates

Mediterraneo (Gabriele Salvatores), Diego Abatantuono

Academy Awards
Best picture: *The Silence of the Lambs*

Best director: Jonathan Demme (*The Silence of the Lambs*)

Best actress: Jodie Foster (*The Silence of the Lambs*)

Best actor: Anthony Hopkins (*The Silence of the Lambs*)

Top Box-Office Stars
Kevin Costner, Arnold Schwarzenegger, Robin Williams, Julia Roberts, Macaulay Culkin, Jodie Foster, Billy Crystal, Dustin Hoffman, Robert De Niro, Mel Gibson

Stars of the Future
Annette Bening, Edward Clements, Harry Connick, Jr., Marcia Gay Harden, Tony Goldwyn, Harley Jane Kozak, Mary McDonnell, Stephen Mailer, Mary-Louise Parker, Wesley Snipes

Popular Music ━━━━━━━━━━━━━━━━━━━━━━

Hit Songs

"(Everything I Do) I Do for You"
"I Wanna Sex You Up"
"One More Try"
"Someday"
"How Can I Ease the Pain"
"The First Time"

Top Records

Albums: *The Immaculate Collection* (Madonna); *Luck of the Draw* (Bonnie Raitt); *Use Your Illusion I* and *II* (Guns N'Roses); *Rhythm of the Saints* (Paul Simon); *Mariah Carey* (Mariah Carey); *Gonna Make You Sweat* (C&C Music Factory); *Wilson Phillips* (Wilson Phillips)

Singles: *From a Distance* (Bette Midler); *Written All Over Your Face* (Rude Boys); *All the Man that I Need* (Whitney Houston); *Rush Rush* (Paula Abdul); *Love Me Down* (Freddie Jackson). Country: *Don't Rock the Jukebox* (Alan Jackson); *She's in Love with the Boy* (Trisha Yearwood)

Grammy Awards

Unforgettable, Natalie Cole (record); *Unforgettable,* Natalie Cole (album); "Unforgettable" (song)

Jazz and Big Bands

As jazz gains increased scholarly interest as an art form, Gunther Schuller and David Baker begin a series of historical jazz concerts at the Smithsonian. Receiving special attention are the young saxophonist Amani A. W. Murray, 15, pianist Stephen Scott Henry, Marcus Roberts, as well as the veteran Ornette Coleman, who returns to the JVC Jazz Festival; George Gruntz leads *Chicago Cantata* at the Chicago Jazz Festival.

Top Performers *(Downbeat):* Wynton Marsalis (soloist); Count Basie (big band); Phil Woods (acoustic jazz combo); Living Colour (pop/rock group); Lee Morgan (Hall of Fame); Tito Puente, John McLaughlin, Joe Zawinul, J. J. Johnson; Betty Carter, Joe Williams (vocalists); Charlie Haden's Liberation Music Orchestra, *Dream Keeper* (album)

Theater ━━━━━━━━━━━━━━━━━━━━━━━━━

Broadway Openings

Plays

Lost in Yonkers (Neil Simon), Mark Blum, Mercedes Ruehl, Irene Worth
Dancing at Lughnasa (Brian Friel), Brid Brennan, Donal Donnelly
Mule Bone (Langston Hughes, Zora Neale Hurston), Arthur French, Eric Ware, Vanessa Williams
Penn and Teller: The Refrigerator Tour, Penn Jillette, Teller

Musicals

Miss Saigon (Claude-Michel Schönberg, Richard Maltby, Jr., Alain Boubil), Jonathan Pryce, Lea Salonga
The Secret Garden (Lucy Simon, Marsha Norman) Mandy Patinkin, Daisy Egan
The Will Rogers Follies (Betty Comden, Adolph Green, Cy Coleman), Keith Caradine, Dee Hoty

Classics, Revivals, and Off-Broadway Premieres

Lips Together, Teeth Apart (Terrence McNally), Swoosie Kurtz, Nathan Lane; *Assassins* (Stephen Sondheim), Victor Garber; *A Room of One's Own,* Eileen Atkins; *Getting Married* (Shaw), Victoria Tennant, Simon Jones; *The Homecoming,* Roy Dotrice, Lindsay Crouse; *On Borrowed Time* (Paul Osborn), George C. Scott, Teresa Wright; *Gypsy,*

Whoopi Goldberg's *Sister Act,* following her success in *Ghost* (1990), establishes her as a leading box office star. *Movie Star News.*

Tyne Daly; *Lyndon* (James Prideaux), Laurence Luckinbill; *Forbidden Broadway 1991 1/2* (Gerard Alessandrini)

Regional

American Repertory Theatre, Cambridge: *Oleanna* (David Mamet), William H. Macy, Rebecca Pidgeon

Intiman Theatre, Seattle: *The Kentucky Cycle* (Robert Schenkkan)

Pulitzer Prize

Lost in Yonkers, Neil Simon

Tony Awards

Lost in Yonkers, Neil Simon (play), *The Will Rogers Follies,* Betty Comden, Adolph Green, Cy Coleman (musical)

Classical Music _____

The bicentennial of Mozart's death dominates performance, recording, lectures, and publications.

Compositions
Wayne Peterson, *The Face of the Night, the Heart of the Dark*
Gunther Schuller, Impromptus and Cadenzas
Peter Lieberson, *World Turning*
Ellen Zwillich, Concerto for Flute and Orchestra
Elliot Carter, Violin Concerto

Important Events
Lincoln Center begins a 19-month Mozart celebration during which all 835 surviving works are performed. For the centenary of Prokofiev's birth, pianists Barbara Nissman, Boris Berman, John Lill, and Murray McLachlan begin surveys. Works of the important Soviet composer Alfred Schnittke are premiered in Boston (Cello Concerto, Mstislav Rostropovich) and Cleveland (Concerto Grosso, no. 5). The Santa Fe Chamber Music Festival performs Shostakovich's complete chamber music. Jerome Lowenthal plays the newly discovered Liszt Piano Concerto in E Flat with the New York Philharmonic. At his conductorial farewell with the Chicago, Georg Solti's performs Verdi's *Otello,* with Kiri Te Kanawa and Luciano Pavarotti; Zubin Mehta, nearing the end of his tenure at the New York Philharmonic, conducts Schoenberg's *Guerre-Lieder.*

New Appointment: Daniel Barenboim, Chicago

First Performances
Mozart, Rondo for Horn (original version), New York; Michael Tippett, *Byzantium* (Chicago); John Harbison, Symphony no. 3 (Baltimore); York Höller, Piano Concerto (Chicago); David del Tredici, *Alice Symphony* (Boston); Aaron Jay Kernis, *Symphony in Waves* (New York); Ned Rorem, *Swords and Ploughshares* (Boston)

Opera
The Bolshoi performs *Eugene Onegin, Mlada,* and *The Maid of Orleans* in Washington, D.C. and New York.

Metropolitan: Gabriela Benackova, Aage Haugland, Susan Quittmeyer, *Katya Kabanova* (Jánaček, premiere); Kathleen Battle, Kurt Moll, *The Magic Flute;* Placido Domingo, Jessye Norman, Ekkehard Wiaschiha, Robert Lloyd, *Parsifal;* Edita Gruberova, *I Puritani;* Carole Vaness, Delores Ziegler, *Cosi Fan Tutte;* Teresa Stratas, Hakian Hagegard, *The Ghosts of Versailles* (John Corigliano, premiere)

Jo Davidson's "Gertrude Stein."

New York City: *Die Soldaten* (Zimmerman); *The Mother of Three Sons* (Bill T. Jones, Leroy Jenkins, premiere, jazz-dance opera)

Brooklyn Academy of Music: *Death of Klinghoffer* (John Adams, premiere)

Chicago: *The Gambler* (Prokofiev); *Antony and Cleopatra* (Barber); June Anderson, Alfredo Kraus, *Lucia di Lammermoor*

Boston: Deborah Voigt (debut), *Ariadne auf Naxos*

Houston: *The Magic Flute* (Maurice Sendak sets)

St. Louis: *Mithridates: King of Pontus* (Mozart, Ken Cazan's production)

Music Notes
Interest in authentic instruments extends to performances of Brahms • Lincoln Center opens a jazz department, with Rob Gibson director • Jazz artists Danny Barker, Clark Terry, Buck Clayton, and Andy Kirk receive awards from the NEA • An early example of J. S. Bach's handwriting is discovered on a prelude and fugue by Buxtehude • The 18-year Teldec project to record Bach's 200 church cantatas is completed • Shostakovich's Preludes and Fugues, op. 87, are recorded by Tatiana Nikolayeva, for whom they were written 40 years ago • Pianist David Owen Norris receives the first Irving S. Gilmore Award of $250,000 • Due to financial difficulties, the New Orleans Symphony Orchestra disbands.

Art ━━━━━━━━━━━━━━━━━━━━━━━━━━━━━━━━

Painting
Al Held, *Victoria XIV*

Lucas Samaras, *Mosaic Painting #10*

Jeff Koons, *Wolfman*

Dorothea Rockburn, *Roman Wall Painting*

Ed Moses, *Khotan, Turfan*

David Salle, *Ugolino's Room, E.A.J.A.*

Sculpture
George Segal, *Depression Bread Line*

Donald Judd, *Untitled [Anodized Aluminum in 12 works]*

Charles Ray, *Mannequin Fall '91*

Barnett Newman, *Zum Zum II*

Architecture
Seattle Museum, Seattle (Venturi, Rauch, Scott)

Disney Corporation building, Burbank, Calif. (Michael Graves)

First Interstate World Center, Los Angeles (Pei Cobb Freed)

Art Institute of Chicago, Rice building (Hammond Beeby and Babka)

Myerson Symphony Center, Dallas (Pei Cobb Freed)

Carnegie Hall tower, New York (Cesar Pelli)

1585 Broadway building, New York (Gwathmey & Siegel)

Important Exhibitions
Traveling shows of African-American artists include the Romare Bearden (Harlem, Chicago) and Henry Ossawa Tanner (Detroit, Atlanta, San Francisco).

Museums

New York: *Metropolitan:* Seurat retrospective; "The Fauve Landscape: Matisse, Derain, Braque and their Circle, 1904–1908"; "Caspar David Friederick: Paintings from the USSR"; Indonesian sculpture; Delacroix; Malevich; Sargent; Stuart Davis. *Museum of Modern Art:* Popova retrospective; "Art of the Forties"; "Dislocations"; Tadao Ando; Reinhardt. *Whitney:* Calder; Rauschenberg.

Washington, D.C.: *National* (50th anniversary): 320 Old Masters to Moderns acquired from donors; "The Drawings of Anthony Van Dyck"

Cleveland (75th anniversary): 70 major works purchased by curators; "The Triumph of Japanese Art"

Los Angeles, Chicago: "Degenerate Art: The Fate of the Avant-Garde in Nazi Germany"

Brooklyn, San Francisco, Washington: Albert Bierstadt

Buffalo: "Jenny Holzer: The Venice Installation"

Atlanta: Lynda Benglis

Art Briefs
Walter Annenberg donates over 50 Impressionist and Post-Impressionist works to the Metropolitan, valued at $1 billion • The controversial exhibition in Washington—"The West as America: Reinterpreting Images of the Frontier"—raises questions over public support of shows that display white violence and racism • With U.S. construction near a standstill, architects continue working abroad: Robert Venturi completes the Sainsbury wing of London's National Gallery of Art; Cesar Pelli continues his ongoing renewal of the London Docklands • Auction prices continue to fall; among the highest sales are Degas' *Racehorses,* $9.98 million; Leger's *Les Maisons Sous les Arbres,* $9.9 million, and *Petit Déjeuner,* $7.7 million; also Matisse's *The Persian Robe,* $4.5 million and Warhol's *Red Jackie* silk screen, $352,000 ($825,000 in 1989).

Dance ━━━━━━━━━━━━━━━━━━━━━━━━━━━━━━━━

The Guangdong Modern Dance Company from China appears in the U.S. for the first time, performing Western works.

American Ballet Theatre: Cynthia Gregory retires. Carla Fracci, *Fall River Legend*

New York City Ballet: Ben Huys, Darci Kistler, *Sleeping Beauty* (Martins, $2.8 million); *Ash* (Torke); *Waltz Trilogy* (La Fosse)

Joffrey (anniversary): *Panoramagram* (Charles Moulton); *Empyrean Dances, Lacrymosa* (Edward Stierle), *Runaway Train* (d'Amboise), all premieres

Martha Graham (memorial): *The Eyes of the Goddess* (Graham, unfinished, Marisol set)

Paul Taylor, Houston: *Company B* (Taylor, Andrews Sisters)

Dance Theatre of Harlem: *Dialogues* (Glen Tetley, Ginastera)

Books

Fiction

Critics' Choice

Harlot's Ghost, Norman Mailer
The Runaway Soul, Harold Brodkey
A Dangerous Woman, Mary McGarry Morris
Maus: A Survivor's Tale II, Art Spiegelman
A Soldier of the Great War, Mark Helprin
Lila: An Inquiry into Morals, Robert Pirsig
The Gold Bug Variations, Richard Powers
Pinocchio in Venice, Robert Coover
Mating, Norman Rush

Best-Sellers

The Firm, John Grisham
Loves Music, Loves to Dance, Mary Higgins Clark
Possession: A Romance, A. S. Byatt
As the Crow Flies, Jeffrey Archer
Star Wars: Heir to the Empire, Timothy Zahn
The Kitchen God's Wife, Amy Tan
The Sum of All Fears, Tom Clancy
Damage, Josephine Hart
Heartbeat, Danielle Steele

Nonfiction

Critics' Choice

Den of Thieves, James B. Stewart
Backlash: The Undeclared War Against American Women, Susan Faludi
Patrimony, Philip Roth
Savage Inequalities: Children in Americas's Schools, Jonathan Kozol
Lone Star Rising: Lyndon Johnson and His Times 1908–1960, Robert Dallek
Anne Sexton, Diane Wood Middlebrook
Make No Law: The Sullivan Case and the First Amendment, Anthony Lewis
Freedom, Orlando Patterson
The Promised Land, Nicholas Lemann
There are No Children Here, Alex Kotlowitz
Holocaust Testmonies, Lawrence Langer

Best-Sellers

Iron John: A Book About Men, Robert Bly
Wealth Without Risk, Charles J. Givens
Financial Self Defense, Charles J. Givens

Homecoming, John Bradshaw
Parliament of Whores, P. J. Rourke
Chutzpah, Alan Dershowitz
Toujours Provence, Peter Mayle
Fire in the Belly: On Being a Man, Sam Keene
Final Exit, Derek Humphry
DO IT! Get Off Our Buts, John-Roger and Peter McWilliams
The Civil War: An Illustrated History, Geoffrey C. Ward and Ken Burns
A Life on the Road, Charles Kuralt

Poetry

Flow Chart, John Ashbery
Selected Poems, Robert Creeley
What Work Is, Philip Levine

Pulitzer Prizes

A Thousand Acres, Jane Smiley (fiction)
The Fate of Liberty: Abraham Lincoln and Civil Liberties, Mark E. Neely, Jr. (U.S. history)
The Prize: The Epic Quest for Oil, Daniel Yergin (nonfiction)
Fortunate Son: The Healing of a Vietnam Vet, Lewis Puller, Jr. (biography)
Selected Poems, James Tate (poetry)

Science and Technology

Streptokinase, an inexpensive blood clot preventer, is shown to be as effective as the costly TPA.

A ten-year study of 48,000 nurses indicates that estrogen administration after menopause cuts the risk of heart disease by almost half.

Green tea is reported to contain a powerful anticancer agent.

PSA (prostate-specific antigen) tests, combined with rectal examination, are demonstrated to greatly aid in the early detection of prostate cancer.

NCI researchers make the first attempt to treat cancer patients with genetically altered cells.

Taxol, from the rare yew tree, is found to be effective in ovarian, breast, and lung cancer; efforts proceed to manufacture the drug synthetically.

Successful transplant of the small intestine occurs at the University of Pittsburgh.

Successful heart surgery is performed on a fetus in the womb.

Questions arise over the safety of the widely used tranquilizer Halcion.

Fortifications and the tomb of an 8th-century Mayan king lend support to the theory that wars brought about that society's collapse in the 900s.

Sports

Baseball

The Atlanta Braves and Minnesota Twins are the first
teams to go from last to first place in one year.
Nolan Ryan, 44, pitches a record 7th no-hitter.
Rickey Henderson (Oakland, AL) breaks Lou
Brock's record when he steals his 939th base.
Cy Young Awards go to Tom Glavine (Atlanta, NL)
and Roger Clemens (Boston, AL).

Champions

Batting	Jose Rijo (Cincinnati, NL),
Terry Pendleton (Atlanta,	15–6
NL), .319	Scott Erickson (Minnesota,
Julio Franco (Texas, AL)	AL), 20–9
.341	*Home runs*
Pitching	Cecil Fielder (Detroit, AL) 44
John Smiley (Pittsburgh,	Jose Canseco (Oakland, AL)
NL), 20–8	44

Football

NFC Season Leaders: Steve Young (San Francisco),
passing; Emmitt Smith (Dallas), rushing; Michael
Irvin (Dallas), receiving

AFC Season Leaders: Jim Kelly (Buffalo), passing;
Thurman Thomas (Buffalo), rushing; Haywood
Jeffires (Houston), receiving

College All-Americans: Steve Emtman (DT),
Washington; Casey Weldon (QB), FSU; David
Klingler (QB), Houston

Bowls (Jan 1, 1992)
Rose: Washington 34–Michigan 14
Orange: Miami 22–Nebraska 0
Cotton: FSU 10–Texas A&M 2
Sugar: Notre Dame 39–Florida 28

Basketball

Magic Johnson retires after announcing he is HIV
positive; he was league MVP 3 times. Larry Bird
becomes the 5th to collect 20,000 points, 5,000
rebounds, and 5,000 assists.

NBA All-Pro First Team: Michael Jordan (Chicago),
Magic Johnson (L.A. Lakers), David Robinson (San
Antonio), Charles Barkley (Philadelphia), Karl
Malone (Utah)

Other Sports

Hockey: Pittsburgh wins the first Stanley Cup in its
24 years in the NHL.

Tennis: Jimmy Connors, now 39, stirs great
excitement by reaching the quarterfinals in the U.S.
Open.

Boxing: Cheeseburger-eater, George Foreman, 42,
257 lbs., earns $12.5 million, as he loses to Evander
Holyfield. Mike Tyson is accused of raping a beauty
contestant in Indianapolis. Sugar Ray Leonard fails in
an attempted comeback.

Winners

World Series	*MVP*
Minnesota (AL) 4	Michael Jordan, Chicago
Atlanta (NL) 3	*College Basketball*
MVP	Duke
NL—Terry Pendleton,	*Player of the Year*
Atlanta	Larry Johnson, UNLV
AL—Cal Ripken, Jr.,	*Stanley Cup*
Baltimore	Pittsburgh
Super Bowl XXVI (Jan. 1992)	*US Tennis Open*
Washington 37–Buffalo 24	Men: Stefan Edberg
MVP	Women: Monica Seles
Thurman Thomas, Buffalo	*USGA Open*
College Football	Payne Stewart
Washington	*Kentucky Derby*
Miami	Strike The Gold (C. Antley,
Heisman Trophy	jockey)
Desmond Howard, Michigan	
NBA Championship	
Chicago 4–L.A. Lakers 1	

Fashion

With the recession, designers try a number of ways to
attract buyers: Ralph Lauren reduces prices; Anne
Klein and Giorgio Armani create a less expensive
line. The revival of 1960s styles continues, but the
Gulf War and rap music also affect fashion.
Accessories are decorated with red, white, and blue,
and flags and other patriotic decals are everywhere.
Bomber jackets and multi-zippered black leather
motorcycle jackets are also popular and worn with
everything—from pleated skirts to evening dresses.
Hemlines vary, from just above the knee to mid or
below the calf (with lengthy slits) or uneven lengths in
front and back. The demand grows for evening wear
that looks like lingerie—black lace over spandex,
satin slips or corselette tops with cancan skirts,
transparent chiffons and laces. Plaids—both
traditional tartans and new designer patterns—are
introduced for both outerwear and underwear.

*High-fashion notes: Karl Lagerfeld's garter purse;
Jean-Paul Gaultier's body suit in houndstooth with
matching accessories; Bob Mackie's black lace over
nude spandex teddy.*

Kaleidoscope

- As Allied forces attack Iraq, all regular television programming is canceled for full coverage of the Gulf War; CNN's Bernard Shaw, Peter Arnett, and John Holliman report directly from Baghdad.
- 1,000 sorties are flown during the first 14 hours of the Gulf War (the maximum in Vietnam, 3,000 a week); 2,232 tons of explosives are dropped the first day, the largest strike in history; only 8 Allied planes are downed during the first 2,000 sorties.
- "Smart" bombs with laser-guidance systems lead to 90% target accuracy (25%, for "dumb" bombs).
- $60 billion is pledged toward war costs from other nations, including Saudi Arabia and Kuwait ($16 billion); Japan (10); and Germany (6.5).
- A record 23,300 U.S. homicides are tallied; 52 occurred in Dallas on the same day 24 soldiers died in the Gulf War land assault.
- In the worse mass shooting in U.S. history, George Hennard drives his truck through the window of a Texas cafeteria and randomly kills 22 and wounds 23 others.
- Arlette Schweitzer, 42, acts as surrogate mother for her daughter, born without a uterus, hence giving birth to her own grandchildren (twins).
- The FDA questions the safety of silicone breast implants, which are now in over 2 million women.
- Recent computer technology includes hand-held scanners that read copy aloud; auto navigators (map interpreters); and "virtual [or artificial] reality."
- The number of single parents is up 41% from 1980; of unmarried couples living together, 80%; 26% of all newborns are born to single women.
- Psychologists determine that within one day a child recognizes its mother by smell.
- After Demi Moore appears nude on the cover of *Vanity Fair, Spy* magazine simulates a cover image of her husband, Bruce Willis, also nude and pregnant.
- Kitty Kelley's negative portrayal of Nancy Reagan is the fastest-selling book in American history.
- Michael Jackson signs a $1.1 billion multi-year contract with Sony.
- Elizabeth Taylor marries her eighth husband, Larry Fortensky, 39.
- Donald and Ivana Trump settle their divorce case out of court; she will receive $10 million, the Connecticut mansion, and Manhattan apartment.
- Cartoon character (60-year-old) Blondie, wife of Dagwood Bumstead, announces her need for a career.
- The economy officially goes into recession for the first time since 1982; disposable income falls, and unemployment claims rise dramatically.
- Eastern and Pan Am go into bankruptcy; Delta takes over most Pan Am routes and becomes the leading carrier.
- Kimberly Bergalis, who contracts AIDS from her dentist, tells Congress her "life has been taken away"; she campaigns for testing of all health care employees.
- Derek Humphry's *Final Exit: The Practicalities of Self-Deliverance and Assisted Suicide in the Dying* becomes number one on the *New York Times* "How to" bestseller list.
- Simon LeVay's study shows anatomical hypothalmic differences in gay and heterosexual men, lending credibility to the biological origin of sexual orientation.
- Alleged "Fatal Attraction" killer Carol Warmus is tried for the murder of her lover's wife; several books and two TV movies are planned.
- In Crown Heights, Brooklyn, a 3-day riot follows the accidental killing of a 7-year-old black child by a Hasidic Jewish driver; a Jewish student is murdered in the ensuing riot.
- A single sheet of the first printing of the Declaration of Independence sells for $2,420,000; it was found at a flea market (for $4) in the backing of a painting.
- Three unpublished witty and scatological canon texts by Mozart are discovered at Harvard; they had been replaced by less racy lyrics in the first edition of his work.
- *Scarlett,* Alexandra Ripley's sequel to *Gone with the Wind,* sells a record 250,000 copies in one day.
- In his autobiography, Wilt Chamberlain claims to have had sex with 20,000 women.
- Ostriches are raised for healthy meat consumption.
- School violence escalates, and 25% of whites and 20% of blacks say they fear attack in school; many principals install metal detectors.
- Polls reveal that 21% of all women have been harassed at work.
- Roseanne Barr says that she is an incest survivor, as daytime talk shows focus on family abuse.
- Former Klansman David Duke, who loses the Louisiana gubernatorial primary, has had plastic surgery to make his face appear more Aryan.
- The House banking scandal reveals that 134 Congress members overdrew 581 checks for more than $1,000.
- Generals Colin Powell and Norman Schwarzkopf lead in the most extensive parade since the end of World War II: 4.7 million attend "Operation Welcome Home" in New York and throw 87 tons of confetti.

First Appearances: McDonald's McLean, female director of NIH (B. Healy), Happy-To-Be-Me Doll (36–27–38), Oregon Health Care Plan, Motorola 7.7 oz. cellular telephone, R. W. Frookies natural, fat-free cookies, Wal-Mart food line

New words: "The mother of all . . . ," date rape, dis, boy toy, homeboy, living will, new world order

"My confidence in you is total, our cause is just. Now you must be the thunder and lightning of Desert Storm," says Gen. Norman Schwarzkopf to his troops. *Department of the Army.*

1992

President-elect Bill Clinton
The White House.

Hillary Clinton. The Yale-educated lawyer's potential power as First Lady creates controversy. *The White House.*

In the News

U.S. Reports First Decline in Economy Since 1982, Unemployment is Highest in Five Years, 7.1% . . . Gennifer Flowers Alleges Long Affair with Candidate Bill Clinton, Clinton Denies Accusation . . . "Big 3" Car Makers Report Record Losses . . . Paul Tsongas Wins N.H. Primary, Clinton is Second . . . Mike Tyson is Sentenced to Six Years for Rape . . . Clinton and Bush Win Super Tuesday Primaries . . . House Reports that Members Overdrew 20,000 Checks . . . Billionaire Ross Perot Rises to over 30% in Polls . . . UN Troops Arrive in Croatia, U.S. and EC Recognize Bosnia Herzegovina . . . L.A. Riots Follow Acquittal of Officers Accused of Rodney King Beating, 52 Die, Damages Reach over $1 Billion . . . John Gotti is Convicted of Racketeering, Testimony of Right-Hand Man Salvatore "Bull" Gravano Is Key . . . Arthur Ashe Announces He Has AIDS, Contracted by Blood Transfusion . . . Bush and Yeltsin Hold First U.S.-Russia Summit, Agree to Major Nuclear Reductions . . . UN Troops Take Over Sarajevo Airport, Report Mass Atrocities by Serbs Including "Ethnic Cleansing" and Rape . . . Democrats Nominate Clinton and Gore, Ross Perot Drops Out, Citing "Revitalized" Democrats . . . Czechs and Slovaks Agree to Split . . . GOP Renominates Bush and Quayle . . . Hurricane Andrew Devastates Florida and Louisiana . . . Perot Reenters Presidential Race . . . Clinton Wins with 42%, Bush Gains 38%, Perot, 19% . . . U.S. Bombs Iraq for Failure to Comply with UN Inspection . . . U.S. Sends Troops to Supply Famine Relief to Somalia.

Deaths

John Cage, "Red" Barber, Marlene Dietrich, José Ferrer, Alex Haley, Bert Parks, Anthony Perkins, Lee Salk, Eric Severeid, Lawrence Welk

Quotes

During the Presidential election:
"I'm certainly going into this as a dog-eat-dog fight, and I will do whatever it takes to be reelected" (Bush). "If you the people are that serious, you register me in fifty states" (Ross Perot, on "Larry King Live"). "All I've been asked about by the press are a woman I didn't sleep with and a draft I didn't dodge" (Clinton). "I'm not some little woman . . . standing by my man like Tammy Wynette" (Hillary Clinton). "I mean, if black people kill black people every day, why not have a week and kill white people?" (Rap singer Sister Souljah). "Sister Souljah's comments before and after Los Angeles were filled with a kind of hatred that you do not honor today and tonight" (Clinton, to the Rainbow Coalition). "I didn't inhale" (Clinton). "It doesn't help matters when prime time had Murphy Brown . . . mocking the importance of fathers by bearing a child alone and calling it just another 'lifestyle choice' " (Vice President Dan Quayle). "I suppose I could have stayed home and baked cookies and had teas. But what I decided to do was to fulfill my profession" (Hillary Clinton). "That's fine phonetically, but you're missing just a little bit" (Quayle, adding an "e" to a 6th grader's spelling of potato). "The total national debt was only $1 trillion in 1980. . . . It is now $4 trillion. Maybe it was voodoo economics. . . . Whatever it was, we are in deep voodoo" (Perot). "Don't Stop Thinking about Tomorrow" (Unofficial Clinton campaign song). "Those two bozos know less about foreign policy than my dog Millie" (Bush).

George Stephanopolous and James Carville, in the Clinton campaign's "War Room" in Little Rock; their swift and incisive responses are considered essential to the Democratic victory.

"American workers don't work hard enough. They don't work but demand high pay."
— Yoshio Sakurauchi, Japanese House speaker

"The heart wants what it wants."
— Woody Allen, on his love for Mia Farrow's teenage daughter

"'M 'bout to dust some cops off. . . . Die, pig, die."
— "Cop Killer," Ice-T

"I bid you all a very heartfelt good night."
— Johnny Carson's last words on "The Tonight Show"

Ads

TV

Premieres
"Picket Fences," Tom Skerritt, Kathy Baker
"Love and War," Susan Dey, Jay Thomas
"Hearts Afire," John Ritter, Markie Post
"You Bet Your Life," Bill Cosby
"The Tonight Show," Jay Leno

Top Ten (Nielsen)
"60 Minutes," "Roseanne," "Murphy Brown,"
"Cheers," "Home Improvement," "Designing
Women," "Coach," "Full House," "Murder, She
Wrote," "Unsolved Mysteries"

Specials
"Memento Mori" (Maggie Smith); "The Best of
Friends" (Sir John Gielgud, Patrick McGoohan,
Wendy Hiller); "A Woman Scorned: The Betty
Broderick Story" (Meredith Baxter); "Without
Warning: The James Brady Story" (Beau Bridges)

Emmy Awards
"Northern Exposure" (drama); Dana Delany (actress,
drama "China Beach"); Christopher Lloyd (actor,
drama, "Avonlea"); "Murphy Brown" (comedy);
Craig T. Nelson (actor, comedy, "Coach"); Candice
Bergen (actress, comedy, "Murphy Brown"); "A
Woman Named Jackie" (drama or miniseries)

Of Note
Presidential candidates hold three 90-minute debates
in different formats over 8 days and draw record
audiences • "Murphy Brown" gains high ratings when
"she" responds to Vice President Quayle's attack on
the program's lack of family values • David
Letterman is offered a $16 million contract to move to
CBS opposite Jay Leno • Clinton plays the saxophone
for Arsenio Hall • New cable channels include the
Sci-Fi and Cartoon stations • 23 million watch Ross
Perot's 30-minute prime time "infomercials" • Johnny
Carson's last show draws a record 55 million viewers.

Movies

Openings
Unforgiven (Clint Eastwood), Eastwood, Gene
  Hackman, Morgan Freeman
The Crying Game (Neil Jordan), Stephen Rea, Jaye
  Davidson
Howards End (James Ivory), Emma Thompson,
  Vanessa Redgrave, Anthony Hopkins
A Few Good Men (Rob Reiner), Tom Cruise, Jack
  Nicholson, Demi Moore
Scent of a Woman (Martin Brest), Al Pacino
The Player (Robert Altman), Tim Robbins
Glengarry Glen Ross (David Mamet), Al Pacino, Jack
  Lemmon, Alec Baldwin
Malcolm X (Spike Lee), Denzel Washington, Lee, Al
  Freeman
The Last of the Mohicans (Michael Mann), Daniel
  Day-Lewis
Wayne's World (Penelope Spheeris), Mike Myers,
  Dana Carver, Rob Lowe
A River Runs Through It (Robert Redford), Tom
  Skerritt, Craig Sheffer, Brad Pitt
White Men Can't Jump (Ron Shelton), Wesley
  Snipes, Woody Harrelson
Basic Instinct (Paul Verhoeven), Michael Douglas,
  Sharon Stone
Aladdin (John Musker, Ron Clements), Scott
  Wringer, Brad Kane, animated
Sister Act (Emile Ardolino), Whoopi Goldberg
Passion Fish (John Sayles), Mary McDonnell, Angela
  Bassett
Indochine (Régis Wargnier), Catherine Deneuve,
  Vincent Perez

Under Siege (Andrew Davis), Steven Seagal, Tommy
  Lee Jones

Academy Awards
Best Picture: *Unforgiven*
Best Director: Clint Eastwood (*Unforgiven*)
Best Actress: Emma Thompson (*Howards End*)
Best Actor: Clint Eastwood (*Unforgiven*)

Top Box-Office Stars
Tom Cruise, Mel Gibson, Kevin Costner, Jack
Nicholson, Macaulay Culkin, Whoopi Goldberg,
Michael Douglas, Clint Eastwood, Steven Seagal,
Robin Williams

Stars of the Future
Tyra Ferrell, Cuba Gooding, Jr., Anthony La Paglia,
Robin Givens, Juliette Lewis, John Leguizamo, John
Cameron Mitchell, Adrienne Shelly, Brad Pitt, Juliet
Stevenson

Spike Lee's film
Malcolm X rekindles
public interest in its
title figure. *Movie
Star News.*

Popular Music

Hit Songs
"Save the Best for Last"
"Baby Got Back"
"Jump"
"When a Man Loves a Woman"
"Under the Bridge"
"All 4 Love"

Top Records

Singles: *Losing My Religion* (R.E.M.); *Something to Talk About* (Bonnie Raitt); *I Will Always Love You* (Whitney Houston); *How Can I Ease the Pain* (Lisa Fischer); *Just Another Day* (Jon Secada); *Diamonds and Pearls* ((Prince and the N.P.G.). Country: *Don't Let Our Love Start Slippin' Away* (Vince Gill); *Lonesome Standard Time* (Kathy Mattea)

Albums: *Dangerous* (Michael Jackson); *The Comfort Zone* (Vanessa Williams); *Ropin' the Wind* (Garth Brooks); *Some Gave All* (Billy Ray Cyrus); *Achtung Baby* (U2); *Cooleyhighharmony* (Boyz II Men)

Grammy Awards
Tears in Heaven, Eric Clapton (record); *Unplugged,* Eric Clapton (album); "Tears in Heaven," (song)

Jazz and Big Bands
Steve Lacy wins the MacArthur Award; Billy Taylor, the National Medal of Arts. The Lila Wallace-Reader's Digest Foundation distributes $1 million in grants for jazz concerts and jazz education programs. The JVC Festival focuses on tributes to the swing and bop era, and recordings of jazz's "Golden Age" continue to be reissued. Improvisation also marks the year, from portions of Anthony Davis's opera *X* to performances of Anthony Braxton, Peter Brötzmann, and the Tony Bevan-Paul Rogers-Steve Noble trio. Dizzy Gillespie's birthday is widely celebrated.

Top Performers (Downbeat):
Joe Henderson (soloist); Count Basie (big band); John Scofield (jazz electronic combo); Wynton Marsalis (jazz acoustic combo); Neville Brothers (blues/soul/R&B group); Maynard Ferguson (Hall of Fame); Betty Carter, Joe Williams (vocalists); Joe Henderson, *Lush Life* (album)

Theater

Broadway Openings

Plays
Conversations with My Father (Herb Gardner), Judd Hirsch, David Margulies
Someone Who'll Watch Over Me (Frank McGuinness), Alec McCowen, Stephen Rea
Death and the Maiden (Ariel Dorfman), Glenn Close, Richard Dreyfuss, Gene Hackman
Two Trains Running (August Wilson), Larry Fishburne, Cynthia Martell
Jake's Women (Neil Simon), Alan Alda, Helen Shaver, Kate Burton

Musicals
Five Guys Named Moe (Louis Jordan), Doug Eskew
Jelly's Last Jam (Jelly Roll Morton, Susan Birkenhead, Luther Henderson), Gregory Hines
Crazy For You (George Gershwin, Ira Gershwin), Harry Groener, Jodi Benson, Jane Connell

Classics, Revivals, and Off-Broadway Premieres
Guys and Dolls, Nathan Lane, Faith Prince, Josie de Guzman; *The Most Happy Fella,* Spiro Malas, Sophie Hayden; *Oleanna* (David Mamet), William H. Macy; *Texts for Nothing* (Beckett), Bill Irwin; *A Streetcar Named Desire,* Alec Baldwin, Jessica Lange; *The Sisters Rosensweig* (Wendy Wasserstein), Jane

"I'm all ears," says the on-again, off-again, folksy Ross Perot, scoring heavily in the first presidential debate after rejecting both parties' advances. *United We Stand America.*

Alexander, Madeleine Kahn, Frances McDormand; *The Price,* Eli Wallach, Hector Elizondo; *The Real Inspector Hound* and *The Fifteen Minute Hamlet* (Stoppard); *The Destiny of Me* (Larry Kramer); *Spic-o-Rama* (John Leguizamo); *Les Atrides* (Mnouchkine, Théâtre du Soleil)

Regional

Mark Taper Forum, Los Angeles: *Angels in America* (Tony Kushner)

Pulitzer Prize
The Kentucky Cycle, Robert Schenkkan

Tony Awards
Dancing at Lughnasa, Brian Friel (play), *Crazy for You,* George and Ira Gershwin (musical)

Classical Music ──────────────

Compositions
Christopher Rouse, Trombone Concerto
Ralph Shapey, *Concerto Fantastique*
Michael Torke, *Music on the Floor, Chalk, Ash*
Steve Reich, *The Four Sections*
Joan Tower, Concerto for Orchestra

Important Events
Celebrations of the Mozart bicentennial are completed. Lincoln Center ends its 19-month Mozart festival with nine unknown operas in concert form, including *Lucio Silla* and *La Finta Semplice*. The 200th birth of Rossini and 500th anniversary of Columbus's voyage are also celebrated. The New York Philharmonic, commemorating its 150th anniversary, commissions 36 new works. Leonard Slatkin conducts Bolcom's *Songs of Innocence and of Experience* with the St. Louis; Pierre Boulez conducts contemporary works with the Chicago. The Steinway Foundation commissions three piano concertos that premiere with Rostropovich and the National in Washington, D.C.: Lalo Schifrin's second; Lowell Liebermann's second; and Rodion Shchedrin's fourth.

New Appointments: Wolfgang Sawallisch, Philadelphia; Esa-Pekka Salonen, Los Angeles

First Performances
John Harbison, Oboe Concerto (San Francisco); Olivier Messiaen, *Éclairs sur l'Au-delà* (New York); Lowell Liebermann, Flute Concerto (St. Louis); Charles Wuorinen, *Genesis* (Minneapolis); Liszt, *Cantata for the Unveiling of the Beethoven Monument in Bonn* (Indianapolis); Joan Tower, Violin Concerto (Salt Lake City); Thomas Lee, Concerto for French Horn and Orchestra (Pittsburgh); William Bolcom, Concerto for Clarinet (New York); Andrzej Panufnik, Piano Concerto (Denver).

Opera
Olga Borodina debuts with the Kirov in *The Queen of Spades*.

Metropolitan: *The [Columbus] Voyage* (Glass, $2 million premiere); Gabriela Benackova, Leonie Rysanek, *Jenůfa;* Thomas Hampson, *Billy Budd;* Stanford Olsen, Ruth Ann Swenson, *L'Elisir d'Amore;* Olsen, Barbara Bonney, *Falstaff;* Thomas Hampson, Frederica von Stade, Samuel Ramey, *The Barber of Seville;* Mirella Freni, Jerry Hadley, Sergei Leiferkus, Nicolai Ghiaurov, *Eugène Onègin*

New York City Opera: *Doktor Faust* (Busoni)

Chicago: Eva Marton, Lando Bartolini, *Turandot* (sets, David Hockney); Catherine Malfitano, Ben Heppner, *McTeague* (Bolcom, premiere)

Oklahoma: *Armida* (Rossini, premiere)

Austin, Texas: *La Pietra del Paragone* (Rossini, premiere)

Houston: *Desert of Roses* (Moran, premiere); *Beauty and the Beast*

Philadelphia: *Tania* (Anthony Davis, premiere)

San Francisco: Jean-Philippe Lafont, *Christophe Colomb* (Milhaud)

Music Notes
U.S. orchestras and dance companies report record financial loses • Sony releases videos of Glenn Gould in performance • Jazz pianist Keith Jarrett records Shostakovich's Preludes and Fugues • Young conductors Ion Marin and Carol Crawford receive unusual attention • *Symphony* magazine reports that John Adams is the most frequently performed living composer • The long-awaited 4-volume *New Grove Dictionary of Opera* is published; *Musical America* ceases publication.

The father of sociobiology and student of ants, Harvard professor Edward O. Wilson has won Pulitzer prizes for *The Ants* and *On Human Nature*. *Courtesy: Edward O. Wilson.*

Art _____

Painting
Jennifer Bartlett, *Five A.M., One A.M.*
Roy Lichtenstein, *Interior with Mirrored Closet*
Dorothea Rockburne, *Parameters and Perimeters*
Susan Rothenberg, *Galisteo Creek*
Sue Williams, *Victim Ranting*

Sculpture
Chris Burden, *The Other Vietnam Memorial* (1991–92)
Bill Barrett, *Lago di Garda*
William Morris, *Suspected Artifact*
Nancy Graves, *Unending Revolution of Venus*

Architecture
Solomon R. Guggenheim Museum, New York, ten-story annex (Gwathmey Siegel)
Chiat/Day/Mojo building, Venice, Calif. (Frank Gehry, in collaboration with Claes Oldenburg and Coosejevan Bruggen)
Oriole Park at Camden yards, Baltimore (Hellmuth, Obata & Kassabaum)
Mall of America, Bloomington, Minn. (Jerde), $625 million
Disney Corporation Convention Center, Orlando, Fla. (Gwathmey Siegel)
Robert Venturi and Denise Scott Brown design the Staten Island Ferry terminal, N.Y.C.
Robert A. M. Stern is commissioned to revitalize New York's Times Square.

Important Exhibitions
"Czech Cubism: Architecture and Design" travels through the U.S.

Museums

New York: *Metropolitan:* Magritte; Andrea Mantegna; Brass and ivory sculptures from Africa; "Barbizon: French Landscapes of the 19th Century"; Poussin. *Museum of Modern Art:* Henri Matisse retrospective (largest showing of his work, 400 pieces); "Allegories of Modernism"; William S. Paley collection; Louis Kahn. *Whitney:* Agnes Martin. *Guggenheim* (reopens): "The Guggenheim Museum

Ann Sperry, *Personal Interiors XIII*. Welded and painted steel. 5'2" × 5'8" × 19". *Courtesy: Ann Sperry.*

and the Art of this Century"; The Russian Avant-Garde.

Chicago, Boston, San Francisco, New York: "Master European Paintings from the National Gallery of Ireland"

Philadelphia: "The Loves of the Gods"; Martin Puryear retrospective

Atlanta: "Landscape Painting in France: Corot to Monet"

Dallas: "Art Treasures Stolen from Germany during World War II"

Los Angeles: "Parallel Visions: Modern Artists and Outsider Art"; "Helter Skelter: Los Angeles Art in the 1990s"

Art Briefs
Important gallery debuts include Janine Artoni, Dennis Balk, Jack Pierson, and Thomas Trosch • The Solomon R. Guggenheim Museum opens a gallery in Manhattan's Soho area with Chagall and Rauschenberg exhibits • UCLA's Fowler Museum of Cultural History, the new Seattle Art Museum, and the west wing of the National open • After Patrick Buchanan accuses the Bush administration of supporting "pornographic and blasphemous art" through the NEA, John E. Frohmayer resigns • Sales, highest since the beginning of the 1990 recession, include Matisse's *Harmony in Yellow,* $14.5 million, and *Waterlily Basin,* $12.1 million.

Dance _____

For its 100th anniversary, *The Nutcracker* is staged throughout the country. Mark Morris's version, *The Hard Nut,* is inspired by cartoons and set in the 1960s. The Kirov returns with the much-lauded 1940 staging of Prokofiev's *Romeo and Juliet* (Lavrovsky).

American Ballet Theatre: Jane Hermann resigns over the company's increasing financial problems.

Kevin McKenzie and Gary Dunning become the new directors. *Symphonic Variations* (Tudor); *The Other* (de Mille); *Undertow* (Tudor)

New York City Ballet: *Diamond Project* (Stiefel and premieres by 11 other choreographers)

Paul Taylor: Elie Chaib, Karla Wolfangle, *Epic; Oz*

Books

Fiction

Critics' Choice

All the Pretty Horses, Cormac McCarthy
Jazz, Toni Morrison
Vox, Nicholson Baker
Clockers, Richard Price
The Volcano Lover: A Romance, Susan Sontag
Natural History, Maureen Howard
The Secret History, Donna Tartt
Outerbridge Reach, Robert Stone
Regeneration, Pat Barker
A Case of Curiosities, Allen Kurzweil

Best-Sellers

Dolores Claiborne, Stephen King
The Pelican Brief, John Grisham
Gerald's Game, Stephen King
Mixed Blessings, Danielle Steel
Jewels, Danielle Steel
The Stars Shine Down, Sidney Sheldon
The Tale of the Body Thief, Anne Rice
Mexico, James A. Michener
Waiting to Exhale, Terry McMillan
All Around the Town, Mary Higgins Clark

Nonfiction

Critics' Choice

Young Men and Fire, Norman Maclean
Genius: The Life and Science of Richard Feynman, James Gleick
Head to Head: The Coming Economic Battle Among Japan, Europe and America, Lester Thurow
The Overworked American: The Unexpected Decline of Leisure, Juliet Schor
Can Poetry Matter? Dana Gioia
Their Ancient Glittering Eyes, Donald Hall
Reinventing Government: How the Entrepreneurial Spirit Is Transforming the Public Sector, David Osborne
Debating P.C.: The Controversy Over Political Correctness on College Campuses, ed. Paul Berman
The End of History and the Last Man, Francis Fukuyama
The Disuniting of America, Arthur Schlesinger
We Were Soldiers Once . . . And Young, Harold Moore, Joseph Galloway
Two Nations: Black and White, Separate and Unequal, Andrew Hacker
The Diversity of Life, Edward O. Wilson
Earth in the Balance, Albert Gore
❧ *Summer Meditations*, Vaclav Havel

Best-Sellers

The Way Things Ought to Be, Rush Limbaugh
It Doesn't Take a Hero, H. Norman Schwarzkopf
How to Satisfy a Woman Every Time, Naura Hayden
Every Living Thing, James Herriot
A Return to Love, Marianne Williamson
Sam Walton, Sam Walton
Diana, Andrew Morton
Silent Passage, Gail Sheehy
Sex, Madonna

Poetry

Gjertrud Schnackenberg, *A Gilded Lapse of Time*
Lucille Clifton, *Quilting: Poems 1987–1990*
John Ashbery, *Hotel Lautréamont*
David Ferry, *Gilgamesh*
Alexander Theroux, *The Lollipop Trollop*

Pulitzer Prizes

A Good Scent from a Strange Mountain, Robert Olen Butler (fiction)
The Radicalism of the American Revolution, Gordon S. Wood (U.S. history)
Lincoln at Gettysburg: The Words that Remade America, Garry Wills (nonfiction)
Truman, David McCullough (biography)
The Wild Iris, Louise Glück (poetry)

Science and Technology

In his cosmic radiation studies, George Smoot announces: "We have observed the largest and oldest structures in the universe."
The genes for muscular dystrophy and Marfan's syndrome are located.
A Harvard study shows that Caprotil markedly reduces mortality in patients with heart failure.
Research indicates that levels of HDL, the "good" cholesterol, may be more important than overall blood cholesterol.
MRI studies demonstrate left temporal lobe abnormalities in schizophrenia.
New findings support the hypothesis that primates originated in Africa.
In Kenya, Mave Leakey discovers the oldest hominoid fossil to date, about 25 million years old, from about the period of the ape-human divergence.

Nobel Prizes

Rudolph Marcus wins in chemistry for his theory of electron-transfer reactions; Edmond Fischer and Edwin S. Krebs, for discoveries of reverse phosphorylation in the metabolism of proteins.

Sports _____

Baseball

Fay Vincent resigns under pressure when he tries to realign the leagues; Milwaukee owner Bud Selig becomes interim commissioner.

Robin Yount and George Brett become the 17th and 18th players to get 3,000 hits.

The Cy Young Awards go to Greg Maddux (Chicago, NL) and Dennis Eckersley (Oakland, AL).

Champions _____

Batting
  Gary Sheffield (San Diego, NL), .330
  Edgar Martinez (Seattle AL), .343
Pitching
  Bob Tewksbury (St. Louis, NL), 16–5

  Mike Mussina (Baltimore, AL), 18–5
Home runs
  Juan Gonzalez (Texas, AL), 43

Football

Facing an antitrust suit loss in the Freeman McNeill case, the NFL finally agrees to a tentative free-agency labor settlement.

NFC Season Leaders: Steve Young (San Francisco), passing; Emmitt Smith (Dallas), rushing; Sterling Sharpe (Green Bay), receiving

AFC Season Leaders: Dan Marino (Miami), passing; Barry Foster (Pittsburgh), rushing; Haywood Jeffires (Houston), receiving

College All-Americans: Garrison Hearst (RB), Georgia; Marvin Jones (LB), Florida State; Will Shields (G), Nebraska

Bowls (Jan. 1, 1993)
Rose: Michigan 38–Washington 31
Orange: Florida State 27–Nebraska 14
Sugar: Alabama 34–Miami 13
Cotton: Notre Dame 28–Texas A&M 3

Basketball

Larry Bird retires.

NBA All-Pro First Team: Karl Malone (Utah), Chris Mullin (Golden State), David Robinson (San Antonio), Michael Jordan (Chicago), Clyde Drexler (Portland)

Olympics

In the Summer Games at Barcelona, Spain, the U.S. basketball "Dream Team," with 11 pros and one collegian headed by Bird, Magic, and Michael Jordan, devastates its opposition. The former USSR competes as the Unified Team. Other U.S. gold winners include Gail Devers (100m), Jackie Joyner-Kersee (heptathlon), Carl Lewis (long jump), Mike Barroman (200m, world record), Kevin Young (400m, world record), Pablo Morales, and Jennifer Capriati (tennis). In the Winter Games at Albertville, France, Kristi Yamaguchi wins the gold medal in figure skating, the first American since Dorothy Hamill in 1976.

Other Sports

Boxing: Riddick Bowe decisions Evander Holyfield for the heavyweight title.

Tennis: Andre Agassi wins at Wimbledon; Jim Courier, the Australian Open.

Winners _____

World Series
  Toronto (AL) 4
  Atlanta (NL) 3
MVP
  NL—Barry Bonds, Pittsburgh
  AL—Dennis Eckersley, Oakland
Super Bowl XXVII (Jan. 1993)
  Dallas 52–Buffalo 17
MVP
  Steve Young, San Francisco
College Football
  Alabama
Heisman Trophy
  Gino Torretta, Miami
NBA Championship
  Chicago 4–Portland 2

MVP
  Michael Jordan, Chicago
College Basketball
  Duke
Player of the Year
  Christian Laettner, Duke
Stanley Cup
  Pittsburgh
US Tennis Open
  Men: Stefan Edberg
  Women: Monica Seles
USGA Open
  Tom Kite
Kentucky Derby
  Lil E. Tee (P. Day, jockey)

Fashion _____

For women: Although animal prints are popular in everything from T-shirts to evening dress, the revival of 40s, 50s, and 70s styles is the industry's most dramatic effort to revive sales. The result is an entirely eclectic look—with skirts of every length, width, fabric, and design. For the very popular elasticized long tube skirt, the cinch belt and bulky platform shoe returns. Pants are as narrow as leggings. Juxtapositions of the most casual materials (like denim) with sheer and delicate fabrics represent the epitome of democratization in fashion—the merging of high and low culture.

High-fashion note: Ralph Lauren's tailored suit worn with a man's tie; Isaac Mizrahi's transparent black bodysuit worn over black bra; Christian Dior's body-hugging leather corselet with fake fur trim.

For Men: With the recession, designers focus on multicolored shirts and on ties with floral and geometric patterns. Men wear lycra stretch bodysuits for casual wear, as well as for running and exercise. The "grunge" look moves into the mainstream: college students sport (often temporary) tattoos, slashed and tattered clothing (particularly shirts and trousers), and exposed seams and torn linings.

Kaleidoscope ─────────────────────────

- Poverty rises to 14.2 percent, the highest level since 1983.
- Macy's and TWA file for bankruptcy; IBM has its first annual loss, $564 million.
- "The economy, stupid," reads a sign in the Little Rock Clinton campaign "War Room"; Clinton emphasizes "change"; Bush, "character" and "trust."
- Clinton and Gore's *Putting People First* and Perot's *United We Stand* become bestsellers.
- Presidential candidates appear on "Larry King Live" thirteen times.
- Assistant Secretary of State Elizabeth Tamposi is forced to resign after having the passport records of Clinton (and his mother) improperly searched.
- Over 20,500 Californians buy guns after the Los Angeles riots, following the acquittals in the Rodney King case.
- Woody Allen files charges against Mia Farrow for custody of three children; Farrow claims that Allen has sexually molested their adopted daughter Dylan; Allen denies the charge but admits to an affair with 19-year-old Soon-Yi Farrow Previn.
- Amy Fisher, 17, the "Long Island Lolita," pleads guilty to shooting the wife of Joey Buttafuoco, 42, whom she alleges was her lover; two TV movies air during the year.
- Madonna's book, *Sex,* which includes graphic pictures ranging from bisexuality to bestiality, sells for $49.95 and grosses $25 million in its first week of sales.
- Prince negotiates $100 million with Warner; Michael Jackson receives $20 million from HBO for rights to his "Dangerous" concert; Time-Warner gives Madonna an estimated $50 million.
- Singer Sinéad O'Connor stirs wide controversy after tearing a photograph of the Pope on "Saturday Night Live."
- The U.S. has the highest incarceration rate in the world: 455 per 100,000 citizens (double, 1980).
- Jeffrey Dahmer is sentenced to 15 consecutive life terms; he says he only ate the ones he liked because he wanted them to become a part of him, adding: "You don't forget your first one."
- With his execution imminent, Roger Coleman claims his innocence on "Donahue" and other TV shows; when he fails a lie detector test, Virginia governor Wilder refuses to stay his execution.
- After decades of decline, tuberculosis resurges in major cities.
- The Supreme Court rules that cross burning is protected speech under the First Amendment, that prayer at public school graduations is unconstitutional, and that states may enforce a 24-hour waiting period on abortion.
- The FDA restricts the use of silicone-gel breast implants to reconstructive purposes.
- A copy of the first *Superman* comic (1938) sells for $82,500.
- The first half of *Huckleberry Finn* is discovered in an attic and placed with its other half in the Buffalo Public Library.
- Royalties for the Bush dog's "autobiography" (*Millie's Book,* ghostwritten by Barbara Bush) earn $890,000.
- Physicists announce the discovery of "cosmic seeds," which began the stars and galaxies after the Big Bang.

- A record 46 women run for congress; four are elected to the Senate.
- A baboon liver is transplanted into a 35-year-old man; he dies after 71 days due to a brain hemorrhage.
- After 26 women allege sexual assault and harrassment at the 1991 Tailhook Convention in Las Vegas, the Pentagon begins an investigation.
- Fewer Americans marry than in any year since 1965; the median age is 26.3 for men; 24.1, for women (first marriages).
- Warren Beatty, 54, marries Annette Bening, 33, and they become parents; "the highest level of sexual excitement is in a monogamous relationship," says Beatty.
- Over 500,000 march in Washington, D.C. for abortion rights.
- Marvel comic book hero Northstar reveals he is gay, adding: "Silence equals death."
- Bobby Fischer returns to chess; in violation of U.S. sanctions on Serbia, he goes to Yugoslavia and defeats Boris Spassky, 10–5.

First appearances: child divorcing parents (Gregory Kingsley, Florida), black woman in space (Mae C. Jemison), black female senator (Carol Moseley Braun), female poet laureate (Mona Van Duyn), the mommy-to-be and rollerblade dolls, serial commercial (Taster's Choice), EuroDisneyland (Paris), poisonous bird (pitohui, New Guinea), marriage in space, 27th Amendment, nicotine patches, Intel 486 chip, juice- and tea-based drinks, Colgate standup toothpaste, McDonald's fettucini Alfredo and lasagna (in Tennessee), Kiwi Airlines, "New age" clear beverages (Coke, Pepsi), AT&T's Video Phone 2500, Apple portable computers, Mega CD video game, Mall of America (largest in U.S., Minnesota), vaginal pouch ("female condom")

Fads: Barney the purple dinosaur, olive oil, red wine, Snapple

Over 1.1 million voters choose the young Elvis Presley portrait over the older one for the new commemorative stamp.

1993

Israeli PM Rabin urges "enough of blood and tears," as he shakes hands with Palestinian leader Arafat at a meeting arranged by President Clinton. *The White House.*

Shoemaker-Levy, a comet shaped like a chain of pearls, is discovered at Mount Palomar; it will presumably crash into Jupiter in 1994. *NASA.*

Deaths

Marian Anderson, Arthur Ashe, Raymond Burr, Dizzy Gillespie, Helen Hayes, Audrey Hepburn, Erich Leinsdorf, Myrna Loy, Thurgood Marshall, Rudolf Nureyev, Albert Sabin

In the News

BUSH AND YELTSIN SIGN *START II* MISSILE REDUCTION TREATY . . . CLINTON IS INAUGURATED AS 42ND PRESIDENT . . . HILLARY RODHAM CLINTON IS NAMED CHAIR OF HEALTH REFORM TASK FORCE . . . FAMILY MEDICAL LEAVE BILL IS PASSED . . . PRESIDENT PROPOSES $495 BILLION DEFICIT REDUCTION THROUGH REDUCED SPENDING AND INCREASED TAXES ON UPPER INCOMES . . . NATIONAL SERVICE PROGRAM IS PASSED . . . HUGE CAR BOMB EXPLODES IN WORLD TRADE CENTER GARAGE, 6 DIE, 1,000 ARE INJURED, 50,000 ARE EVACUATED . . . U.S. AIR FORCE SENDS RELIEF TO BESIEGED MUSLIMS IN BOSNIA . . . FEDERAL JURY IN L.A. CONVICTS 2 POLICE OFFICERS OF VIOLATING RODNEY KING'S CIVIL RIGHTS . . . BRANCH DAVIDIAN COMPOUND AT WACO, TEX., IS BURNED TO GROUND BY CULT LEADER DAVID KORESH, 80 DIE . . . 23 UN PEACE-KEEPERS ARE KILLED BY SOMALIAN WARLORD . . . FBI ARRESTS 8 MUSLIM EXTREMISTS FOR PLOTTING TERRORIST ATTACKS ON N.Y.C. . . . U.S. ATTACKS IRAQ IN RESPONSE TO BUSH ASSASSINATION PLOT IN KUWAIT . . . CLINTON DECREES "DON'T ASK, DON'T TELL" POLICY ON GAYS IN MILITARY . . . DEPUTY PRESIDENTIAL COUNSEL VINCENT FOSTER IS FOUND DEAD IN VA. PARK, AN APPARENT SUICIDE . . . BRITAIN RATIFIES EUROPEAN UNION TREATY . . . RECORD FLOODS ENGULF MIDWEST, CONGRESS VOTES $6.2 BILLION IN RELIEF . . . PLO LEADER YASIR ARAFAT AND ISRAELI PM YITZHAK RABIN AGREE ON PEACE ACCORD . . . CLINTON ORDERS 15,000 TROOPS TO SOMALIA . . . CONGRESS APPROVES NORTH AMERICAN FREE TRADE AGREEMENT WITH MEXICO . . . BRADY BILL IS PASSED, MANDATES WAITING PERIOD ON HANDGUN PURCHASES.

Quotes

"Here, on the pulse of this new day / You may have the grace to look up and out / And into your sister's eyes, and into / Your brother's face, your country / And say simply / Very simply / With hope— / Good morning."
—Maya Angelou, at the Presidential Inauguration

"Radical feminism, male lesbians, transsexuals, musical condoms with suspenders, and lotsa drummers drumming are all manifestations of a political agenda with roots in the 1960s. This is all fruit we are reaping from the sexual revolution."
—Rush Limbaugh, *See, I Told You So*

"The health system is badly broken, and it's time to fix it."
—Bill Clinton

"I have courted some of these congressmen longer than I courted my wife."
—Treasury Secretary Lloyd Bentsen, on his advocacy of NAFTA

"I let him live on a farm. I guess he learned naturally from the animals that were around."
—Pat Robertson, opposed to sex education in school, explaining his son's understanding of the facts of life

Ads

I know bourbon gets better with age, because the older I get the more I like it.
(Jim Beam)

Next month you'll be blowing your nose with this ad.
(Ad Council, Earth Share Recycling)

While you don't necessarily dress for men, it doesn't hurt, on occasion, to see one drool like the pathetic dog that he is.
(Body Slimmers)

We remove crows' feet.
Forgive us, ASPCA.
(Center for Cosmetic Surgery or Bosom Buddy)

No one will ever accuse you of being dressed by your mother.
(Harley-Davison)

Re-live the days when being a Washington Senator was nothing to be ashamed of.
(Beverly Hills Baseball Card Shop)

"For a plate of spaghetti, he'd leave home. For another woman? Never!"
—Luciano Pavarotti's wife, responding to the remark that her husband was unfaithful

"She should . . . have a serious talk with Denis Thatcher. He knew how to behave."
—Sir Bernard Ingram, press secretary to ex-P.M. Thatcher, on Mrs. Clinton

"I guess I can see how, if you were a salamander, 'Amphibian-American' would be a step up. But it seems to me you should call a toad a toad."
—Kermit the Frog, on "political correctness"

"I always say I don't know whether it's the finest public housing in America or the crown jewel of the prison system."
—Bill Clinton, on the White House

"Unlike the president, I inhaled. And then I threw up."
—New Jersey Governor–elect Christine Todd Whitman

Left: Robin Williams as *Mrs. Doubtfire,* a divorced father who becomes an English nanny to be near his children. Right: The versatile Anthony Hopkins savors *The Remains of the Day* as a repressed butler, two years after his "Hannibal, the cannibal" Oscar. *Movie Star News.*

In the U.S., this would be a crime. In Romania, it's day care.
(Free Romania Fund)

Americans are the best fed people on earth. The ones who eat, that is.
(United Way of St. Louis)

For 11,000 women, every day the moon will be a safer place to be.
(National Coalition against Domestic Violence)

For a night on the town, we recommend the following bars.
(The Richmond Symphony)

TV

Premieres
"NYPD Blue," David Caruso, Dennis Franz
"Ellen," Ellen DeGeneres
"Frasier," Kelsey Grammer
"Grace under Fire," Brett Butler
"Walker, Texas Ranger," Chuck Norris
"Homicide," Ned Beatty, Richard Belzer
"The X-Files," David Duchovny, Gillian Anderson

Top Ten (Nielsen)
"Home Improvement," "60 Minutes," "Seinfeld,"
"Roseanne," "Frasier," "Coach," "Murphy Brown,"
"Grace under Fire," "Murder, She Wrote," "NFL
Monday Night Football"

Specials
"Parsifal" (from Metropolitan, Siegfried Jerusalem);
"Apollo Theatre Hall of Fame"; "Tosca" (Plácido
Domingo, Catherine Malfitano); "Healing of the Mind
with Bill Moyers"; "The Prize" (documentary); "Fame
in the Twentieth Century"; "Innocence Lost"; "The
Positively True Adventures of the Alleged Texas
Cheerleading-Murdering Mom"

Tom Hanks, in *Philadelphia*, first
mainstream movie to deal with AIDS.
Movie Star News.

Emmy Awards
"Picket Fences" (drama); Kathy Baker (actress, drama,
"Picket Fences"); Tom Skerritt (actor, drama, "Picket
Fences"); "Seinfeld" (comedy); Roseanne Arnold
(actress comedy, "Roseanne"); Ted Danson (actor,
comedy, "Cheers"); "Barbarians at the Gate" / "Stalin"
(tie, made-for TV movie)

Of Note
Drawing particularly large audiences are Oprah Winfrey's
interview with Michael Jackson and Ross Perot's debate
with Al Gore on NAFTA • Over 98 million watch the last
"Cheers"; ads are $650,000 for 30 seconds; for each
episode, Danson has earned a reported $450,000 • CBS
hires David Letterman from NBC for $42 million over
three years • Fox outbids CBS to broadcast the NFC •
HBO earns more Emmys than any other network • The
Amy Fisher–Joey Buttafuoco scandal has three dramati-
zations on commercial networks • "NYPD Blue," TV's
graphic prime-time show, is immediately controversial.

Movies

Openings
Schindler's List (Steven Spielberg), Liam Neeson, Ben
   Kingsley
The Remains of the Day (James Ivory), Anthony
   Hopkins, Emma Thompson
The Piano (Jane Campion), Holly Hunter, Harvey Keitel
In the Name of the Father (James Sheridan), Daniel
   Day-Lewis, Emma Thompson
The Fugitive (Andrew Davis), Harrison Ford, Tommy
   Lee Jones
In the Line of Fire (Wolfgang Petersen), Clint Eastwood,
   John Malkovich
The Firm (Sydney Pollack), Tom Cruise, Jean
   Tripplehorn, Gene Hackman
Jurassic Park (Steven Spielberg), Sam Neill, Laura Dern
Sleepless in Seattle (Nora Ephron), Tom Hanks, Meg
   Ryan
Falling Down (Joel Schumacher), Michael Douglas,
   Robert Duvall
Mrs. Doubtfire (Chris Columbus), Robin Williams,
   Sally Field
Indecent Proposal (Adrian Lyne), Demi Moore, Robert
   Redford
The Age of Innocence (Martin Scorsese), Daniel Day-
   Lewis, Michelle Pfeiffer

Philadelphia (Jonathan Demme), Tom Hanks, Denzel
   Washington
Shadowlands (Richard Attenborough), Anthony
   Hopkins, Debra Winger
The Pelican Brief (Alan Pakula), Julia Roberts, Denzel
   Washington
Farewell My Concubine (Chen Kaige), Leslie Cheung
Like Water for Chocolate (Alfonso Arau), Lumi Cavazos

Academy Awards
Best Picture: *Schindler's List*
Best Director: Steven Spielberg, *Schindler's List*
Best Actress: Holly Hunter, *The Piano*
Best Actor: Tom Hanks, *Philadelphia*

Top Box-Office Stars
Clint Eastwood, Tom Cruise, Robin Williams, Kevin
Costner, Harrison Ford, Julia Roberts, Tom Hanks, Mel
Gibson, Whoopi Goldberg, Sylvester Stallone

Stars of the Future
Juliette Lewis, Brad Pitt, Leonardo DiCaprio, Sandra
Bullock, Ralph Fiennes, Jason Scott Lee, Jeanne
Tripplehorn, Will Smith, Janine Turner, Wendy Crewson

Popular Music

Hit Songs
"That's the Way Love Goes"
"All That She Wants"
"No Ordinary Love"
"Again"
"I'd Do Anything for Love"
"Rebirth of Slick"
"Hey Jealousy"

Top Records

Albums: *Get a Grip* (Aerosmith); *Music Box* (Mariah Carey); *janet* (Janet Jackson); *Ten* (Pearl Jam); *Plush* (Stone Temple Pilots); *Are You Gonna Go My Way* (Lenny Kravitz)

Singles: *Freak Me* (Silk); *Weak* (SWV); *Dream Lover* (Mariah Carey); *Bed of Roses* (Bon Jovi); *Nuthin' but a 'G' Thang* (Dr. Dre);

Two Princes (Spin Doctors). Country: *Passionate Kisses* (Mary Chapin Carpenter); *Ain't That Lonely Yet* (Dwight Yoakam)

Grammy Awards
I Will Always Love You, Whitney Houston (record); *The Bodyguard,* Whitney Houston (album); "A Whole New World (Aladdin's Theme)" (Alan Menken, Tim Rice) (song)

Jazz and Big Bands
The merging of outside influences continues—e.g., Digital Planets blend rap and cool jazz; Greg Osby, "street jazz" with rap. Wynton Marsalis and Rosemary Clooney join in a jazz celebration at the White House. Marsalis also leads

"Jazz for Young People" concerts at Lincoln Center. Jazz pianists on the rise include Cyrus Chestnut, Jacky Terrasson, Eric Reed, and Peter Martin; tenor saxophonists, James Carter and Eric Alexander. The Smithsonian begins a three-and-a-half-year project on Duke Ellington.

Top Performers (*Downbeat*): Joe Henderson (soloist); McCoy Tyner (big band); Red Rodney (jazz acoustic group); B. B. King (blues/soul musician); Joe Zawinul, Milt Jackson, Steve Lacy, James Newton, Gerry Mulligan, Max Roach (instrumentalists); Gerry Mulligan (Hall of Fame); Betty Carter, Joe Williams (vocalists); Joe Henderson, *So Near, So Far* (album)

Theater

Broadway Openings

Plays
The Sisters Rosensweig (Wendy Wasserstein), Jane Alexander, Madeline Kahn, Robert Klein
Laughter on the 23rd Floor (Neil Simon), Nathan Lane
Angels in America, Part I: Millennium Approaches (Tony Kushner), Ron Leibman, Jeffrey Wright
Angels in America, Part II: Perestroika (Tony Kushner), Ron Leibman, Jeffrey Wright
Shakespeare for My Father (Lynn Redgrave), Redgrave
Fool Moon (Bill Irwin, David Shiner), Irwin, Shiner

Musicals
Kiss of the Spider Woman (John Kander, Fred Ebb), Brent Carver, Chita Rivera
The Who's Tommy (Peter Townshend, rock opera), Michael Cerveris, Marcia Mitzman
Blood Brothers (Willy Russell), Con O'Neill, Mark Michael Hutchison, Stephanie Lawrence
She Loves Me (Jerry Bock, Sheldon Harnick), Boyd Gaines, Judy Kuhn

Classics, Revivals, and Off-Broadway Premieres
The Kentucky Cycle (Robert Schenkkan), Stacy Keach; *A Perfect Ganesh* (Terrence McNally), Frances Sternhagen, Zoë Caldwell; *The Last Yankee* (Arthur Miller); *Timon of Athens; Jeffrey* (Paul Rudnick); *Anna Christie,* Natasha Richardson, Liam Neeson; *Joseph and*

the Amazing Technicolor Dreamcoat (Andrew Lloyd Webber); *Marisol* (Joe Rivera); *Measure for Measure,* Kevin Kline; *My Fair Lady,* Richard Chamberlain; *Medea,* Diana Rigg

Regional

Mark Taper Forum, Los Angeles: *Twilight, Los Angeles, 1992* (Anna Deavere Smith); *Sunset Boulevard* (Andrew Lloyd Webber), Glenn Close

Steppenwolf, Chicago: *Einstein and Picasso at the Lapin Agile* (Steve Martin)

American Conservatory Theatre, Pittsburgh: *The Pope and the Witch* (Dario Fo)

Pulitzer Prize
Angels in America, Tony Kushner

Tony Awards
Angels in America, Tony Kushner (play), *Kiss of the Spider Woman,* Fred Ebb, John Kander (musical)

Tony Kushner, author of *Angels in America,* the two-part, seven-hour epic of gay life. *FDU.*

Classical Music

Compositions

Gunther Schuller, *Of Reminiscences and Reflections*
Karel Husa, Cello Concerto
Ned Rorem, *Concerto for Left Hand*
Leon Kirchner, Music for Cello and Orchestra
Mikel Kuehn, *Five Parables* (based on Kafka)

Important Events

Serious financial problems face most U.S. orchestras; the Buffalo and Houston seasons are canceled. The 100th anniversary of *The New World Symphony* stimulates a Dvorak revival, but modest celebrations mark the deaths of Monteverdi (350th), Tchaikovsky (100th), and Rachmaninoff (50th), as well as Grieg's 150th birthday; two gala concerts at Carnegie Hall celebrate Ella Fitzgerald's 75th birthday. The New York Philharmonic's 150th anniversary commemoration includes Zubin Mehta's return to conduct the world premiere of Messiaen's *Eclairs sur l'au-délà;* repetition of the orchestra's first complete Overture to *Der Freischütz* (1843) and its premiere of Berlioz's *Symphonie fantastique* (1866), as well as "A Philharmonic Celebration: Remembering Lenny [Bernstein]" (for their 47-year-association). Unusual events include the Cracow Philharmonic's first appearance since the fall of communism; Kurt Mazur's leading Shostakovich's 13th Symphony, its first performance in 30 years (containing an indictment of Soviet anti-Semitism in the "Babi Yar" movement during which Yevgeny Yevtushenko reads his poems); Andras Schiff's six concerts (Schubert's Piano Sonatas); and Evgeny Kissin's all-Chopin recital.

First Performances

Witold Lutoslawski, Symphony no. 4 (Los Angeles); William Bolcom, Flute Concerto (St. Louis); Lucio Berio, *Continuo* (Chicago); Ellen Taaffe Zwilich, Symphony no. 3 (New York); John Adams, Chamber Symphony (San Francisco); Alfred Schnittke, Sixth Symphony (Washington, D.C.); George Walker, Sinfonia no. 2 (Detroit); Aaron Jay Kernis, *Still Movement with Hymn* (Princeton, N.J.); Charles Wuorinen, *Microsymphony* (Philadelphia)

Opera

Metropolitan: James Morris, Robert Hall, Gwyneth Jones, *The Ring* cycle (three times in a row); Plácido Domingo and Luciano Pavarotti in celebration of their Met debut 25 years ago includes Domingo in a new production of *Stiffelio* and Pavarotti's in *I Lombardi;* each also does his own *Tosca;* Jessye Norman, *Ariadne auf Naxos;* Donald McIntyre, Hermann Prey, *Die Meistersinger;* Domingo, Carol Vaness, Richard Croft,

Left: Since his 1991 debut, Arcadi Volodos has been compared to the century's greatest pianists. *Peter Zander. Sony.* Right: Cecilia Bartoli. *J. Henry Fair, Sony.*

Otello; Gabriela Benackova, Neil Rosenshein, *Rusalka* (Dvorak, premiere); Angela Gheorghiu, Manuel Lanza (debuts), *La Bohème*

New York City (50th anniversary): World premieres: *Marilyn* (Ezra Laderman); *Griffelkin* (Lukas Foss); *Esther* (Hugo Weisgall); *Midsummer Marriage* (Michael Tippett); *Madama Butterfly* (original version)

Brooklyn Academy of Music: *The Cave* (Steve Reich, Beryl Korot, multimedia)

Chicago: *McTeague* (Bolcom), *The Ring;* Renée Fleming, Samuel Ramey, *Susannah* (Carlisle Floyd)

Houston: Cecilia Bartoli (debut), *Barber of Seville; Aïda*

Washington, D.C., Dallas: *The Dream of Valentino* (premiere, Argento, costumes by Valentino)

Cleveland: *Mrs. Dalloway* (Libby Larsen)

Music Notes

U.S. News and World Report writes that 16 percent of the population has attended an opera or classical music concert in the past year; opera attendance has grown 35 percent in ten years • San Francisco hosts a "Wet Ink Festival," primarily with music of the Pacific Rim • Carnegie Hall begins a two-year survey of Mahler, with performances by the Berlin, Vienna, Israeli, Boston, St. Louis, and Pittsburgh orchestras • Sony releases the first of 12 video cassettes and six laser discs of *The Glenn Gould Collection* • Mstislav Rostropovitch returns to Russia after 20 years' exile to lead the Washington National Symphony before 100,000 at Moscow's Red Square • Concerned with predominantly "graying audiences," musical directors try to attract a broader group with more American and less traditional programming.

Art ─────────────

Painting

Ellsworth Kelly, *Blue Relief with Black*

James Rosenquist, *Gift Wrapped Doll #23*

Dorothea Rockburne, *Quasar*

Lucian Freud, *Working in the Studio*

Chuck Close, *Kiki*

David Salle, *Lifesaver, Picture Builder*

Robert Longo, *Bodyhammer 30 Special*

Sculpture

Jennifer Pastor, *Bridal Cave*

Louise Bourgeois, *The Locus of Memory*

Ann Hamilton, *Tropos*

Architecture

U.S. Holocaust Memorial Museum, Washington, D.C. (James Ingo Freed)

Recycling Center, Phoenix (Linnea Glatt, Michael Singer)

Wexner Center for the Arts, Ohio State University, Columbus (Peter Eisenman)

Seaman's Church Institute, N.Y.C. (James Stewart Polshek)

Performing Arts Center, Charlotte, N.C. (Cesar Pelli)

Davis Museum, Wellesley College, Mass. (Rafael Moneo)

The University of Minnesota Art Museum, designed by Frank Gehry. *Don Wong.*

Important Exhibitions

Traveling across the U.S. are "Great French Paintings from the Barnes Foundation"; "Gates of Mystery: The Art of Russia"; "The Greek Miracle: Classical Sculpture from the Dawn of Democracy"; and "Rolywholyover: A Circus" (multimedia, John Cage and others). The year's large number of retrospectives include Miró, Lichtenstein, de Kooning, and Ryman.

Museums

New York: *Metropolitan:* Abstract Expressionism; Master drawings of the Hudson River School; "Daumier Drawings"; "The Greek Flowering of Democracy, the 5th Century B.C."; Verrocchio's *Christ and St. Thomas;* "Painters of the Great Ming: The Imperial Court and Zhe School"; Arthur B. Davies landscapes; Frederick E. Church; Lucian Freud. *Museum of Modern Art:* "Max Ernst: Dada and the Dawn of Surrealism" (200 works); Ryman; Joseph Beuys. *Guggenheim:* "Picasso and the Age of Iron"; Lichtenstein; Klee. *Whitney:* "Controversial Political Art [including video art of the Rodney King beating]"; "Abject Art: Repulsion and Desire in American Art." *Museum for African Art:* Old and New African and African-American Altars

Boston: "The Art of Rubens"; "Awash in Color [Homer and Sargent]"; "In and Out of Place: Contemporary Art and the American Social Landscape"; "Sculptures from Greece, the Islands, and Asia Minor"

Dallas, Philadelphia: Late French Impressionism

Art Briefs

The Robert Mapplethorpe Foundation gives the Guggenheim a $5 million gift for a gallery named in his honor • Numerous painters and sculptors hold photo shows: Cy Twombly, Frank Stella, George Segal, Bryan Hunt, Philip Smith • The Norman Rockwell Museum in Stockbridge, Mass., opens on Rockwell's 100th birthday • "42nd Street Now," by Robert A. M. Stern and others, is designed to replace the sleazy theaters and shops between Times Square and 8th Avenue • Record sales include a 15th-century pottery candlestick, $975,000; 12th-century bronze lion, $3.6 million; and Cézanne's *Still Life with Apples,* $28.6 million • Walter Annenberg buys Van Gogh's *Wheat Field with Cypresses* ($57 million) for MoMA • The Getty acquires Michelangelo's *Holy Family on the Flight into Egypt* for $6.3 million, the highest price ever paid for a drawing; a Steiglitz photo of Georgia O'Keeffe sells for $398,500, the highest ever paid for a photograph.

Dance ─────────────

American Ballet Theatre: Julie Kent (debut), *Swan Lake; Symphonic Variations; Drink to Me Only with Thine Eyes* (Mark Morris); *Manon* (Kenneth MacMillan)

New York City Ballet: For the Balanchine festival Peter Martins invites dancers from other U.S. and European companies to participate in 73 ballets, including revivals of works not seen since the 1940s and 1950s. Damian Woetzel, *Harlequinade; Pas de Deux* (Glinka); premiere: *Jazz* (Wynton Marsalis)

Joffrey: *Billboards* (Prince)

San Francisco: Elizabeth Loscavio, Eric Hoisington, *Swan Lake*

Martha Graham: *Demeter and Persephone* (Twyla Tharpe, premiere)

Books

Fiction

Critics' Choice
The Road to Wellville, T. C. Boyle
Operation Shylock: A Confession, Philip Roth
Pigs in Heaven, Barbara Kingsolver
Operation Wandering Soul, Richard Powers
Feather Crowns, Bobbie Ann Mason
Body and Soul, Frank Conroy
Einstein's Dream, Alan Lightman
Van Gogh's Room at Arles: Three Novellas, Stanley Elkin
❧ *Dream of Fair to Middling Women*, Samuel Beckett (posthumous)

Best-Sellers
The Bridges of Madison County, Robert James Waller
The Client, John Grisham
Slow Waltz at Cedar Bend, Robert James Waller
Without Remorse, Tom Clancy
Nightmares and Dreamscapes, Stephen King
Vanished, Danielle Steel
Lasher, Anne Rice
Pleading Guilty, Scott Turow
Like Water for Chocolate, Laura Esquivel
The Scorpio Illusion, Robert Ludlum

Nonfiction

Critic's Choice
Balkan Ghosts, Robert D. Kaplan
Culture of Complaint: The Fraying of America, Robert Hughes
Race Matters, Cornel West
Remembering Denny, Calvin Trillin
The Moral Sense, James Q. Wilson
Listening to Prozac, Peter D. Kramer
The Culture of Disbelief, Stephen L. Carter
Case Closed: Lee Harvey Oswald and the Assassination of JFK, Gerald Posner
Protecting Soldiers and Mothers, Theda Skocpol
The Fifties, David Halberstam
The Real Anita Hill, David Brock
Crime and Punishment in American History, Lawrence Friedman
The Cultivation of Hatred, Peter Gay

Best-Sellers
See, I Told You So, Rush Limbaugh
Private Parts, Howard Stern
Seinlanguage, Jerry Seinfeld
Embraced by the Light, Betty J. Eadie, with Curtis Taylor
Ageless Body, Timeless Mind: The Quantum Alternative to Growing Old, Deepak Chopra
Stop the Insanity! Susan Powter
Women Who Run with the Wolves, Clarissa Pinkola Estés
Men Are from Mars, Women Are from Venus, John Gray

Supreme Court Justice Ruth Bader Ginsberg has been called the "legal architect of the modern women's movement." *Supreme Court Historical Society.*

The Hidden Life of Dogs, Elizabeth Marshall Thomas
And If You Play Golf, You're My Friend, Harvey Penick, with Bud Shrake

Poetry
Mona Van Duyn, *Firefall: Poems*
Mark Doty, *My Alexandria*
Brenda Hillman, *Bright Existence*
W. S. Merwin, *Travels*

Pulitzer Prizes
The Shipping News, E. Annie Proulx (fiction)
No prize is awarded in U.S. history
Lenin's Tomb: The Last Days of the Soviet Empire, David Remnick (nonfiction)
W. E. B. Du Bois: Biography of a Race, 1868–1919, David Levering Lewis (biography)
Neon Vernacular, Yusef Komunyakaa (poetry)

Nobel Prize
Toni Morrison

Science and Technology

Higher levels of high density lipoprotein (HDL), "the good cholesterol," are found to correlate with lower levels of coronary disease.

EPA labels secondhand smoke a carcinogen, causing 3,000 deaths yearly.

Studies indicate that vasectomy increases a man's chances of prostate cancer.

Genes are identified with Lou Gehrig's disease, hyperactivity disorder, Alzheimer's, colon cancer, and diabetes.

An Aramaic stone monument mentions King David, the first ancient reference outside the Bible.

The remains of *Pseudoryx*, a 220-pound horned ancestor of the ox, is discovered in Southeast Asia, the first new mammal species found in 50 years.

A three-foot-long carnivore, Eoraptor, is discovered in Argentina, the most primitive dinosaur yet (228 million years old).

Scientists argue over whether Neanderthals are human ancestors.

Nobel Prizes
Joseph H. Taylor, Jr., and Russell A. Hulse win in physics for their discovery of the binary pulsar; Kary B. Mullis in chemistry for the polymerase chain reaction permitting DNA individual identification; Phillip A. Sharp in physiology or medicine for locating split genes, which help diagnose cancer.

Sports

Baseball

This is the last year of two-division play.

Bobby Bonds wins his third MVP in four years.

Paul Molitor becomes the 19th player to get 3,000 hits.

Greg Maddux wins 20 games for the 3rd straight year, the first in 20 years.

Joe Carter's HR is the second to end a WS.

The Cy Young awards go to Greg Maddux (Atlanta, NL) and Jack McDowell (Chicago, AL).

Champions

Batting
Andres Galarraga (Colorado, NL), .370
John Olerud (Toronto, AL), .363

Pitching
Mark Portugal (Houston, NL), 18–4

Jimmy Key (New York, AL), 18–8

Home runs
Barry Bonds (San Francisco, NL)
Juan Gonzales (Texas, AL), 46

Football

Liberalized free agency rules lead to many big contracts. Don Shula wins his 325th game to pass George Halas.

NFC Season Leaders: Steve Young (San Francisco), passing; Emmitt Smith (Dallas), rushing; Sterling Sharpe (Green Bay), receiving, record 112 receptions

AFC Season Leaders: Dan Marino (Miami), passing; Thurman Thomas (Buffalo), rushing; Reggie Langhorne (Indianapolis), receiving

College All-Americans: Dan Wilkinson (OL), Ohio State; J. J. Stokes (WR), UCLA

Bowls (Jan. 1, 1994)
Rose: Wisconsin 21–UCLA 16
Orange: Florida State 18–Nebraska 16
Cotton: Notre Dame 24–Texas A&M 21
Sugar: Florida 41–Washington 7

Basketball

Chicago Bulls "threepeat," the first team to win 3 straight titles since the 57–66 Boston Celtics. Michael Jordan wins his 7th-straight scoring title, tying Wilt Chamberlain, and retires shortly after his father's murder, saying: "I have nothing more to prove."

NBA All-Pro First Team: Karl Malone (Utah), Charles Barkley (Phoenix), Hakeem Olajuwon (Houston), Michael Jordan (Chicago), Mark Price (Cleveland)

Other Sports

Tennis: Arthur Ashe dies of AIDS; he had been infected by a blood transfusion. Pete Sampras wins at Wimbledon.

Boxing: Evander Holyfield, 6–1 underdog, beats Riddick Bowe for the HW title.

Racing: Arcangues, at 133–1, wins the $3 million Breeders' Cup.

Winners

World Series
Toronto (AL) 4
Philadelphia (NL) 2

MVP
NL–Barry Bonds, San Francisco
AL–Frank Thomas, Chicago

Super Bowl XXVIII (Jan. 1994)
Dallas 30–Buffalo 13

MVP
Emmitt Smith (Dallas)

College Football
Florida State

Heisman Trophy
Charles Ward, Florida State

NBA Championship
Chicago 4–Phoenix 2

MVP
Charles Barkley, Phoenix

College Basketball
North Carolina

Player of the Year
Calbert Cheaney, Indiana

Stanley Cup
Montreal

U.S. Tennis Open
Men: Pete Sampras
Women: Steffi Graff

USGA Open
Lee Janzen

Kentucky Derby
Sea Hero (Jerry Bailey, jockey)

Fashion

Designers attempt to revive sales by again rejecting the hard-edged look of the 1980s. With the revival of 1970s styles come shorter and thinner models than in the 1980s, combining the flower-power look with the recent grunge style. Continuing the 1970s revival are sheer fabrics, bell bottoms, elongated vests, crocheted tops, and shaggy, short, or layered hair styles. The punk look includes bare midruffs, tattoos, brightly colored hair, and body-piercing jewelry. African-American women choose short Afro braids and dreadlocks. The casual look extends to men's wear, with sweaters replacing shirts with suits; hiking boots are worn to the office.

High-fashion notes: Ralph Lauren's czarist Cossack outfits; Karl Lagerfeld and Yves St. Laurent's thigh-high skirt.

Kaleidoscope

- Implementing his promise that government leadership "look more like America," Clinton names an unprecedented number of blacks, women, and Hispanics to high posts.
- The president promises "universal [health] coverage" comparable to that of Fortune 500 companies; 64 million people lack adequate coverage.
- Mohammed A. Salameh is arrested for the WTC bombing when he reclaims his $400 car rental deposit.
- Claiming sexual abuse, Lorena Bobbitt cuts off the penis of her sleeping husband, John, and reports the event to the police; the penis, found on the lawn, is reattached.
- Howard Stern's *Private Parts,* with its graphic cover, posts large sales.
- An Oregon law permits physician assisted suicide; Michigan's Jack Kevorkian, M.D., is jailed twice for assisting patients' suicide.
- Clinton ends the ban on fetal tissue research and lifts the "gag rule" against abortion counseling in federally funded clinics.
- *Official and Confidential: The Secret Life of J. Edgar Hoover* asserts that Hoover was blackmailed by organized crime as a cross-dresser and homosexual.
- Vince Foster, White House counsel and Clinton's boyhood friend, remarks of a *Wall Street Journal* attack: "Here ruining reputations is considered sport."
- *Jurassic Park* is the highest-grossing movie of all time.
- Movie star River Phoenix, 23, dies of a drug overdose.
- The Department of Education reports that 25 percent of 12th graders cannot read properly.
- Compared with other developed countries, U.S. teachers earn lower salaries ($38,000–$70,000 in Switzerland) and teach larger classes.
- The brown uniform of the Brownies changes after 66 years to include pastel tops, culotte jumpers, and floral print vests.
- Food poisoning afflicts 300 after they consume meat at Jack In The Box restaurants.
- After living with the De Boerses for seven years, Baby "Jessica," now "Anna Lee," is legally reclaimed by her birth parents, Cara and Dan Schmidt; the man who signed the adoption consent was not her biological father.
- The Menendez brothers' trial for the murder of their parents begins; they mount a sexual abuse defense.
- The U.S. begins testing the French abortion pill RU-486.
- The U.S. Supreme Court rules against North Carolina's congressional redistricting plan as racial gerrymandering.
- Princeton's Andrew Wiles offers proof of Fermat's last theorem, 350 years old.
- Cosmologists find that stars and other observable matter occupy less than 10 percent of the universe, reinforcing theories of the universe's mammoth undetected "dark matter."
- Scientists discover the largest known bacterium; it is visible to the naked eye (.0015″).
- As country music sales soar, Billy Ray Cyrus's *Some Gave All* is the fastest-selling debut album in history.
- Sears ends its mail-order catalog business.
- A Pentagon report prompted by the "Tailhook Scandal" (1991) indicates widespread sexual misconduct in the military.
- The UN establishes a tribunal to try war criminals of the former Yugoslavia.
- The Ford Taurus tops the Honda Accord in total car sales.

The Holocaust via *Schindler's List. Movie Star News.*

- "Waif" models, like Kate Moss and Amber Valletta, are criticized for encouraging eating disorders among women.
- Random House signs a $6 million contract with Gen. Colin Powell for his memoirs.
- The most populated cities in the world, in millions, are São Paulo (11.1), Mexico City (10.2), Seoul (9.6), Moscow (8.8), Bombay and Shanghai (8.2), Tokyo (8.1), Beijing (7.3), New York City (7.3), and Jakarta (6.7).
- Largest populations in the U.S., in millions, are N.Y.C. (7.3), L.A. (3.4), Chicago (2.7), Houston (1.6), Philadelphia (1.5), San Diego (1.1), and Detroit and Dallas (1).
- A Florida court rules that a 14-year-old girl, switched at birth with another child, cannot be forced to have contact with her biological parents.
- Six foreign tourists are murdered in Florida during robberies.
- The First Lady wears clothes of moderately priced designers like Randy Kemper; her violet bouffant Inaugural gown is designed by little-known Sarah Phillips.
- Clinton's withdrawal of Lani Guinier's Justice Department nomination for her alleged "antidemocratic" writings stirs controversy.
- IBM loses $6 billion worldwide and plans for 35,000 layoffs, as widespread business "downsizing" continues.
- 30-year mortgages drop to 6.7%, the lowest in 25 years.
- Dr. Dre, whose *The Chronic* sells 3 million copies, says: "People in the suburbs, they can't go to the ghetto, so they like to hear what's goin' on."
- Bill Clinton suffers wide criticism when his $200 haircut by Christophe at LAX delays air traffic.
- Mia Farrow wins her custody battle with Woody Allen, although he retains supervised visitation; he stays with his stepdaughter-girlfriend Soon-Yi Previn.

Fads: unfinished hems, torn-apart clothing, the "cold shoulder" dress, Rollerblading, Snapple in exotic flavors, TV home shopping, Elvis Presley 29¢ stamp, Mortal Kombat (video game), Joey Buttafuoco jokes, dinosauromania, mega-bookstores

First Appearances: Pentium processor (Intel), "intelligent metal" (hardens under stress), African-American Poet Laureate (Rita Dove, 40), Nutrition Labeling and Education Act, under 3-lb. "subnotebook" computers, 1-lb. personal digital assistant (Apple, Sharp, Tandy, Casio), Video CD (Panasonic), Toys: Talking Barney, The Littlest Pet Shop, Mini Caboodles, Mighty Max Toby Terrier

1994

Newt Gingrich's "revolutionary" *Contract with America* spearheads the GOP's takeover of Congress and many state Houses. *U.S. House of Representatives.*

Facts and Figures

Economic Profile
  Dow-Jones: ↑ High 3,978
    Low 3,593
  GNP: +4.5%
  Inflation: +2.7%
  Unemployment: 6.1%
Expenditures
  Recreation: $401.7 billion
  Spectator sports: $5.3 billion
  European travel: $ 8.2
  billion
Golf courses: 13,683
Number of bowlers: 62.5
  million
Estée Lauder
  "Day of Beauty": $175
  "Perfect pedicure": $27.50
  Seaweed body wrap and
    aromatic herb wrap: $65
    (each)
"Velvet Touch Hair Removal
  Mitten": $4.95
Rejuvenal firming thigh cream:
  $34.95
Millennium makeup bag to
  chill contents (for beach
  use): $19.99
BreathAsure (sunflower,
  parsley reed): $19.95, 200
  capsules
Alpha, Glycolic Hydroxy
  complex (antiwrinkle
  cream): $79.95
Gel-filled massage shoe
  insoles: $9.95
Braun Plaque remover: $100

Deaths

Cab Calloway, Ralph Ellison,
  Erik Erikson, Burt
  Lancaster, Richard Nixon,
  Linus Pauling, Karl Popper,
  Martha Raye, Gilbert
  Roland, Jerry Rubin, "Telly"
  Savalas, Dinah Shore

In the News

EARTHQUAKE HITS L.A., 57 ARE DEAD, 9,000 INJURED . . . CLINTON ENDS TRADE EMBARGO ON VIETNAM . . . FOUR MUSLIM EXTREMISTS ARE FOUND GUILTY OF WORLD TRADE CENTER BOMBINGS . . . ICE SKATING STAR TONYA HARDING PLEADS GUILTY OF SEEKING TO INJURE RIVAL NANCY KERRIGAN . . . U.S. LEAVES SOMALIA AFTER 15 MONTHS . . . NELSON MANDELA WINS SO. AFRICAN PRESIDENCY IN FIRST ALL-RACE ELECTIONS . . . JACQUELINE KENNEDY ONASSIS, 64, DIES . . . FORMER FOOTBALL STAR O. J. SIMPSON IS ARRESTED IN L.A. FOR MURDER OF WIFE, NICOLE, AND HER FRIEND RON GOLDMAN . . . FRENCH TROOPS ENTER RWANDA TO HALT ETHNIC TRIBAL MASSACRES . . . NORTH KOREAN RULER KIM IL SUNG, 82, DIES, SON IS HEIR APPARENT . . . . TROPICAL STORM ALBERTO DEVASTATES SOUTH, CONGRESS VOTES $6.6 BILLION IN AID . . . AT WHITE HOUSE, JORDAN AND ISRAEL END STATE OF WAR . . . U.S. JETS, UNDER NATO AUSPICES, ATTACK BOSNIAN SERBS, YUGOSLAVIAN PRESIDENT MILOSEVIC BREAKS SERBIAN TIES . . . KEN STARR SUCCEEDS ROBERT FISKE AS INDEPENDENT SPECIAL PROSECUTOR OF POSSIBLE CLINTON CRIME IN 1982 WHITEWATER, ARK., LAND DEAL . . . FACING INVASION, HAITIAN MILITARY ABDICATES, CARTER, POWELL, SCHWARZKOPF ASSIST IN NEGOTIATIONS . . . 48 SOLAR TEMPLE CULT MEMBERS COMMIT SUICIDE IN SWITZERLAND . . . U.S. AND NO. KOREA RESOLVE TENSIONS OVER NUCLEAR PLANT INSPECTIONS . . . SUSAN SMITH, 22, CONFESSES TO MURDER OF TWO SONS SHE ALLEGED WERE KIDNAPPED BY BLACK, IN S.C. . . . GOP SWEEPS CONGRESS FOR FIRST TIME SINCE 1970 . . . GUNMAN KILLS 2 AT MASS. ABORTION CLINIC.

Quotes

"I have recently been told that I am one of the millions of Americans who will be afflicted with Alzheimer's Disease. . . . I now begin the journey that will lead me into the sunset of my life. I know that for America there will always be a bright dawn ahead."
—Ronald Reagan, in a letter to the nation

[On the Simpson-Goldman murder case:]
"I'm absolutely, 100 percent, not guilty" (O. J. Simpson); "If you have any information or evidence regarding the O. J. Simpson case, press 2 now. If you . . . would like to offer your services, press 3 now. . . . If you are seeking legal representation from the law offices of Robert L. Shapiro, press 4 now."
—Portion from a toll-free recording by Simpson's defense

"There is a cannibalism that's loose in our society."
—David Gergen

"Life is like a box of chocolates. You never know what you're gonna get."
—from the film *Forrest Gump*

"I'm not an Uncle Tom. . . . I'm going to be here for 40 years. For those who don't like it, get over it."
—Supreme Court Justice Clarence Thomas

"Leaders of countries called me and asked for sex. You look at any picture of a politician with some girls around him and at least three of them will be mine. . . . If I really came out and talked, I could have stopped NAFTA."
—"Hollywood madam" Heidi Fleiss

"I want a revamped feminism. Putting the vamp back means the lady must be a tramp. . . . We're still stuck with the ['nice' girl]."
—Camille Paglia, *Vamps and Tramps*

"If I could be the 'condom queen' and get every young person who is engaging in sex to use a condom in the United States, I would wear a crown on my head with a condom on it. I would!"
—Joycelyn Elders, U.S. Surgeon General

[On "whites and blacks":]
"An aggregate difference in measured intelligence is genetic instead of environmental."
—Richard J. Herrnstein and Charles Murray, *The Bell Curve*

Goldilocks
[There] lived a family of bears . . . in a little cottage as a nuclear family. They were very sorry about this, of course, since the nuclear family has traditionally served to enslave womyn . . . and imprint rigid notions of heterosexualist roles onto the next generation. [They named] their offspring the non-gender-specific "Baby."
—James Finn Garner, *Politically Correct Bedtime Stories*

"[Oliver North is a] document-shredding, Constitution-trashing, Commander-in-Chief-bashing, Congress-thrashing, uniform-shaming, Ayatollah-loving, arms-dealing, criminal-protecting, résumé-enhancing, Noriega-coddling, Social Security-threatening, public school-denigrating, Swiss-banking-law breaking, letter-faking, self-serving, election-losing, snake-oil salesman who can't tell the difference between the truth and a lie."
—Charles S. Robb, successfully campaigning against Oliver North

"The Western Canon can bring one . . . the proper use of one's own solitude . . . whose final form is one's confrontation with one's own mortality."
—Harold Bloom, *The Western Canon: The Books and School of the Ages*

Ads

TV _____

Premieres
"E.R.," George Clooney, Anthony Edwards
"Chicago Hope," Mandy Patinkin, Hector Elizondo
"My So-Called Life," Claire Danes
"Friends," Lisa Kudrow, Matt LeBlanc
"Touched by an Angel," Roma Downey, Della Reese

Top Ten (Nielsen)
"Seinfeld," "E.R.," "Home Improvement," "Grace under Fire," "NFL Monday Night Football," "60 Minutes," "NYPD Blue," "Friends," "Roseanne," "Murder, She Wrote"

Specials
"Itzhak Perlman, The Dvorak Concert from Prague: A Celebration"; "Barbra Streisand: The Concert"; "George Stevens: D-Day to Berlin"; "Irish Music and America: A Musical Migration"; "The American Experience: FDR"; "Baseball" (Ken Burns); "Bob Dylan Unplugged"; "The Oldest Living Confederate Widow Tells All"; "The Untold West"; "Vladimir Horowitz: A Reminiscence"; "I Am a Promise: The Children of Stanton Street Elementary School"; "Serving in Silence: The Margarethe Cammermeyer Story"

Emmy Awards
"Picket Fences" (drama); "Frasier" (comedy); Dennis Franz (actor, "NYPD Blue"); Sela Ward (actress,

Left: Jimmy Smits (left) joins "NYPD Blue" when acclaimed David Caruso leaves to make movies; Dennis Franz "gives new meaning to the word 'hunk,'" reports *Entertainment* magazine. Right: Morgan Freeman. The former "Electric Company" star is now a much-admired movie actor. *Movie Star News.*

"Sisters"); Kelsey Grammer (comedic actor, "Frasier"); Candice Bergen (comedic actress, "Murphy Brown"); "Late Show: David Letterman" (variety, music, or comedy series)

Of Note
Second in ratings to Oprah Winfrey's decorous talk-show is Ricki Lake's program, which introduces young audiences to subjects like "Is your boyfriend cheating with your mother?" • Millions watch O. J. Simpson's white Bronco escape on the Los Angeles freeways • A record number watch the winter Olympics from Lillehammer, Norway, particularly the skating contest between Nancy Kerrigan and Tonya Harding • $1 billion of merchandise is sold through TV home shopping • BBC's sitcom "Absolutely Fabulous" airs on the Comedy Central cable channel.

Movies _____

Openings
Forrest Gump (Robert Zemeckis), Tom Hanks, Robin Wright, Sally Field
Pulp Fiction (Quentin Tarantino), John Travolta, Bruce Willis, Uma Thurman
Four Weddings and a Funeral (Mike Newell), Hugh Grant, Andie MacDowell
Quiz Show (Robert Redford), Ralph Fiennes, Paul Scofield
The Shawshank Redemption (Frank Darabont), Morgan Freeman, Tim Robbins
Interview with the Vampire (Neil Jordan), Tom Cruise, Brad Pitt
Star Trek: Generations (David Carson), William Shatner, Patrick Stewart
Disclosure (Barry Levinson), Michael Douglas, Demi Moore
Nobody's Fool (Robert Benton), Paul Newman, Jessica Tandy
Bullets over Broadway (Woody Allen), Dianne Wiest, John Cusack, Rob Reiner
Hoop Dreams (Steve James), documentary
Thirty-Two Short Films about Glenn Gould (François Girard), Colm Feore

Clear and Present Danger (Philip Noyce), Harrison Ford, Anne Archer
True Lies (James Cameron), Arnold Schwarzenegger, Jamie Lee Curtis
Speed (John De Bont), Keanu Reeves, Sandra Bullock
Dumb and Dumber (Peter Farrelly), Jim Carrey, Jeff Daniels, Teri Garr
The Lion King (Roger Allens, Rob Minkoff), animation

Academy Awards
Best Picture: *Forrest Gump*
Best Actor: Tom Hanks, *Forrest Gump*
Best Actress: Jessica Lange, *Blue Sky*
Best Director: Robert Zemeckis, *Forrest Gump*

Top Box-Office Stars
Tom Hanks, Jim Carrey, Arnold Schwarzenegger, Tom Cruise, Harrison Ford, Tim Allen, Mel Gibson, Jodie Foster, Michael Douglas, Tommy Lee Jones

Stars of the Future
Tia Carrere, Chris O'Donnell, Elijah Wood, Sheryl Crow, Claire Danes, Tim Allen, Kirsten Dunst, Mackenzie Astin, Gil Bellows, Tara Fitzgerald

Popular Music

Hit Songs
"I'll Make Love to You"
"The Sign"
"Stay (I Missed You)"
"All for Love"
"Hero"
"Bump 'n Grind"
"Back and Forth"

Top Records

Albums: *Toni Braxton* (Toni Braxton); *12 Play* (R. Kelly); *Age Ain't Nothing but a Number* (Aaliyah); *Dookie* (Green Day); *The Division Bell* (Pink Floyd); *From the Cradle* (Eric Clapton); *Read My Mind* (Reba McEntire); *II* (Boyz II Men)

Singles: *I Swear* (All-4-1); *Whomp! (There It Is)* (Tag Team); *Cry for You* (Jodeci); *Return to Innocence* (Enigma); *I'll Remember* (Madonna); *The Sign* (Ace of Base). Country: *When Love Finds You* (Vince Gill); *Chattahoochee* (Alan Jackson)

Grammy Awards
All I Wanna Do, Sheryl Crow (record); *MTV Unplugged,* Tony Bennett (album); "Streets of Philadelphia," Bruce Springsteen (song)

Jazz and Big Bands
British "acid jazz" gains in popularity with the Brand New Heavies, Galliano, and US3. Wynton Marsalis plays the last concert with his septet. Anthony Braxton and Ornette Coleman receive the prestigious MacArthur Award. Coleman forms a new acoustic group with his son Denardo (drums), Geri Allen (piano), and Charnette Moffit (bass). Braxton, who has recorded relatively little, makes the highly successful *Duo* (London, 1993) with fellow saxophonist Evan Parker and *Trio* with Parker and trombonist Paul Rutherford. The battle line between the young and more traditional jazz performers continues. Veteran groups like the Rolling Stones (Mick Jagger, Ron Wood, Ken Richards) concertize; important popular talents also include Paul Smoker, Barry Guy, and the young, hard-bop B Sharp Jazz Quartet. The Louis Armstrong Archive is collected at Queens College, N.Y.C. Despite rain and mud, Woodstock holds its 25th anniversary festival.

Top Performers *(Downbeat):*
Joshua Redman (soloist); McCoy Tyner (big band); Charlie Haden/Quartet West (jazz acoustic group); Max Roach, Milt Jackson, Steve Lacy, James Newton, Gerry Mulligan (instrumentalists); Take 6 (vocal group); Dave Brubeck (Hall of Fame); Cassandra Wilson, Joe Williams (vocalists); Joshua Redman, *Wish* (album)

Theater

Broadway Openings

Plays
Three Tall Women (Edward Albee), Myra Carter, Marian Seldes, Jordan Baker
Broken Glass (Arthur Miller), Ron Rifkin, Amy Irving, David Dukes
Suburbia (Eric Bogosian), Tim Guinee, Steve Zahn
Twilight: Los Angeles (Anna Deavere Smith), Smith
Jackie Mason: Politically Incorrect (Jackie Mason), Mason

Musicals
Sunset Boulevard (Andrew Lloyd Webber), Glenn Close, Alan Campbell
Beauty and the Beast (Alan Menken, Howard Ashman, Tim Rice), Terrence Mann, Susan Egan
Passion (Stephen Sondheim), Marin Mazzie, Jere Shea, Donna Murphy
A Christmas Carol (Alan Menken, Lynn Ahrens), Bill Nolte, Joseph Kolinski
Jelly Roll! ("Jelly Roll" Morton), Vernel Bagneris
Show Boat (Oscar Hammerstein, Jerome Kern), John McMartin, Elaine Strich, Doug La Brecque, Joel Blum
Damn Yankees (Richard Adler, Jerry Ross), Victor Garber, Bebe Neuwirth

Classics, Revivals, and Off-Broadway Premieres
No Man's Land (Pinter), Jason Robards, Christopher Plummer; *Love! Valour! Compassion!* (Terrence McNally), John Glover, Nathan Lane; *Simpatico,* Ed Harris, Beverly D'Angelo; *Hedda Gabler,* Kelly McGillis; *Talking Pictures* (Horton Foote), Hallie Foote; *Philadelphia, Here I Come!* Pauline Flanagan, Milo O'Shea; *The Shadow Box,* Tom Courteney; *The Glass Menagerie,* Julie Harris; *The Molière Comedies,* Brian Bedford; *Carousel,* James Barbour; *Picnic,* Ashley Judd; *An Inspector Calls* (J. B. Priestley), Rosemary Harris, Kenneth Cranham

Regional
Due to financial problems, most theaters turn to revivals.

Center Theatre, Denver: *Black Elk Speaks* (Christopher Sergel)

Pulitzer Prize
Three Tall Women, Edward Albee

Tony Awards
Angels in America, Part II: Perestroika, Tony Kushner (play); *Passion,* Stephen Sondheim (musical)

Classical Music _____

Compositions
Morton Gould, *Stringmusic*
John Adams, Violin Concerto
John Harbison, Third String Quartet
Lou Harrison, *Vestiunt Silve, Triphony*
Mikel Kuehn, *Between the Lynes*

Important Events
Now 60, pianist Van Cliburn embarks on a nine-city comeback, which is not entirely successful. José Carreras, Plácido Domingo, and Luciano Pavarotti reunite for a $10 million concert of arias and popular songs at L.A.'s Dodgers Stadium; it is broadcast to over 1 billion people worldwise and sells an enormous number of recordings, although said to be poorly recorded.

Notable Performances
The Tanglewood Festival, in its new Ozawa Hall, opens with Oliver Knussen's *Fanfare*. The year's highly acclaimed performances include Dubravka Tomsic's *Emperor* with the Boston Symphony; Evgeny Kissin's *Wanderer Fantasy* (Schubert) and *Transcendental Etudes* (Liszt) in Miami; Peter Serkin's *Des canyons aux étoiles* (Messiaen) at Tanglewood; and Alfred Brendel's Beethoven, Schumann, and Brahms recital at Carnegie Hall.

New Appointments: Leonard Slatkin, National Symphony; Plácido Domingo, adviser and principal guest conductor, Los Angeles Opera; Eiji Oue, Minnesota Orchestra; Andrew Litton, Dallas Symphony

First Performances
Joan Tower, *Concerto for Orchestra* (St. Louis); John Harbison, Cello Concerto (Tanglewood); Ezra Laderman, *Eighth Symphony* (New Haven Centennial commission); Pierre Boulez, *Notations V–VIII* (Chicago); Henryk Górecki, *Miserere* (Chicago); Lukas Foss, *Piano Concerto for Left Hand* (Leon Fleischer, Tanglewood); Rodion Shchedrin, *Concerto for Trumpet* (Pittsburgh); Ned Rorem, *Concerto for English Horn* (New York); Richard Danielpour, *Concerto for Cello* (San Francisco); Donald Erb, *Evensong* (Youngstown, Ohio)

Violin virtuoso Hilary Hahn, 18, gave her first public performance at age 6. *Karen Cipolla. Sony.*

Many call Bryn Terfel the next Pavarotti. *John Stoddard. Deutsche Grammophone.*

Opera

Metropolitan: Plácido Domingo, *Otello;* Bryn Terfel (debut), Dawn Upshaw, Suzanne Mentzer, Dwayne Croft, *Marriage of Figaro;* Teresa Stratas, Upshaw, *Dialogues of the Carmelites;* Anthony Rolfe Johnson, *Death in Venice;* Mirella Freni, *Adriana Lecouvreur;* Hildegaard Behrens, *Elektra;* Maria Ewing, *Lady Macbeth of Mtsensk*

New York City: *Lakmé* (Delibes); Vladimir Grishko, *Prince Igor*

Washington, D.C.: *The Dream of Valentino* (Dominick Argento, premiere)

Chicago: Samuel Ramey, Jerry Hadley, *The Rake's Progress;* Barry Banks (debut), *Candide* (Berio, premiere)

Boston: Jane Eaglen, *Die Götterdämmerung;* Ben Heppner, *Das Lied von der Erde*

San Francisco: Premieres: Frederica von Stade, Thomas Hampson, *The Dangerous Liaisons* (Conrad Susa), *King Priam* (Michael Tippett), *Hérodiade.* Financial problems necessitate canceling part of the season.

Music Notes
Joseph Volpe fires the "temperamental" Kathleen Battle from the Met for her tardiness at rehearsals and rude behavior toward colleagues • The $9.7 million, 1,180-seat building in Tanglewood is named for Seiji Ozawa, who launched his career here in 1960 • Six Haydn piano concerti are discovered, and controversy follows regarding their authenticity • Gregorian chants gain popularity following EMI's *Chant,* recorded at a Benedictine monastery in Spain • Violin prodigies capturing world attention include Sarah Chang, Maxim Vengerov, and Leila Josefowicz • Countertenors Brian Asawa, Derek Lee Ragin, and Michael Chance gain a following • Finnish pianist Ralf Gothoni wins the largest music award, the Gilmore prize of $115,000 • The Florida Grand Opera forms.

Art

Painting

Kenneth Noland, *Flows; Blithe Spirit*

Neil Jenny, *North America Series* (1990–94)

Hughie Lee-Smith, *Parting*

Cady Noland, *Untitled 1993–94 (Wilbur Mills for President)*

Sculpture

Kiki Smith, *Lilith*

Ross Bleckner, Louise Bourgeois, Mike Kelley, Simon Leung, Lorna Simpson, Kiki Smith, Nancy Spero, *ACT UP Art Box*

Jennifer Pastor, *Untitled (Winter)*

Richard Serra, *Broad Cove Marsh II*

Chris Burden, *America's Darker Moments*

William Morris, *Suspended Artifact*

Jenny Holzer, Untitled *(Lustmord)*

Architecture

San Francisco Museum of Modern Art (Mario Botta, 62 million, largest U.S. contemporary art museum)

Andy Warhol Museum, Pittsburgh (Richard Gluckman)

Fine Arts Building, University of California, Riverside (Frank Israel)

Harrison Opera House, Norfolk, Va. (Graham Gund)

Yerba Buena Gardens, San Francisco (Fumihiko Maki, James Stewart Polshek)

American Culture Building, University of Wyoming (Antoine Predock)

Important Exhibitions

After a long tour, "A Gift to America," a collection of 54 masterworks by Titian, Goya, Van Dyck, El Greco, and others, is donated by the Kress Foundation to museums throughout the country. Traveling to several cities are Bruce Nauman, Franz Kline, and Frank Stella shows; Rauschenberg retrospective; "Weston's Westons: California and the West"; "The Age of Rubens"; "Chiseled with a Brush: Italian Sculpture, 1869–1925; "Gustave Caillebotte"; "Japanese Art after 1945"; and "Picasso and the Weeping Women: The Years of Marie-Thérèse Walter and Dora Maar." Individual shows of note include those of David Salle, Bill Owens, Fischilli Weiss, Vito Acconci, and Barbara Kruger.

Museums

New York: *Metropolitan:* The Met opens its first permanent Indian and Southeast Asian galleries. "Origins of Impressionism"; "Chinese Painting, 17th–20th Century"; "Royal Art of Benin"; Greek jewelry of the Classical world; Eakins; "Pharaoh's Gifts: Stone Vessels from Ancient Egypt"; Degas landscapes; "The Golden Age of Dutch Painting." *Museum of Modern Art:* Louise Bourgeois; Cy Twombly; "Frank Lloyd Wright: Architect"; "Masters of the Bauhaus"; Rem Koolhaas; *Whitney:* "Black Male: Representations of Masculinity"; "America's Art 1900–1940." *Morgan:* "Treasures from Heaven" (first important U.S. show of Armenian illuminated manuscripts)

Chicago: "Prince of Dreams: Odilon Redon"; "Goya, Truth, and Fantasy"

Boston, Toledo: "The Age of Rubens"; Sol LeWitt

Washington, D.C.: "The Glory of Venice: Art in the 18th Century"

Art Briefs

The debate over Andy Warhol's estate (estimated at $220–$827 million) reaches the courts. His portrait *Shot Red Marilyn* sells for a record $4.07 million at auction • The NEA comes under further attack after HIV-positive artist Ron Athey mounts a work on which he has drawn blood from himself and blotted it on towels hung above eye-level • Stanley Tigerman and Eva Maddox open a new school of architecture, Archeworks, in Chicago • Congress passes a law making theft of a museum art work a federal crime.

Dance

The Royal Ballet presents a new production of *Sleeping Beauty* at the Metropolitan. Budget problems continue at most companies; Christopher d'Amboise resigns from the Pennsylvania Ballet.

American Ballet Theatre: Julie Kent, *Echoing of Trumpets* (Anthony Tudor)

New York City Ballet: Mikhail Baryshnikov, *A Suite for Dances* (Jerome Robbins); Darci Kistler, Kyra Nichols, *Midsummer Night's Dream; The Sleeping Beauty*

Boston: Natasha Akhmarova, *Onegin; Breakers; CRWDSPCR* (Merce Cunningham)

Bill T. Jones: *Still/Here* (Jones)

Books _____

Fiction

Critic's Choice

A Frolic of His Own, William Gaddis
The Crossing, Cormac McCarthy
Snow Falling on Cedars, David
  Guterson
Brazil, John Updike
Shelter, Jayne Anne Phillips
The Collected Stories, Grace Paley
Mr. Vertigo, Paul Auster
The Alienist, Caleb Carr
Private Friendship, Harold Brodkey

Best-Sellers

The Chamber, John Grisham
The Debt of Honor, Tom Clancy
The Celestine Prophecy, James
  Redfield
The Gift, Danielle Steel
Insomnia, Stephen King
Politically Correct Bedtime Stories,
  James Finn Garner
Wings, Danielle Steel
Accident, Danielle Steel
The Bridges of Madison County,
  Robert James Waller
Disclosure, Michael Crichton

Nonfiction

Critic's Choice

*The Bell Curve: Intelligence and
  Class Structure in American Life,*
  Richard J. Herrnstein, Charles
  Murray

"I will get things done for America. . . . Faced with adversity, I will persevere," pledge Americorps volunteers for Clinton's new national service program. *Corporation for National Service.*

The Western Canon, Harold Bloom
In Europe's Name, Timothy Garton
  Ash
How We Die, Sherwin Nuland
Colored People: A Memoir, Henry
  Louis Gates
*Strange Justice: The Selling of
  Clarence Thomas,* Jane Mayer,
  Jill Abramson
Shot in the Heart, Mikal Gilmore
The Homeless, Christopher Jencks
*Sex in America: A Definitive
  Survey,* Robert T. Michael, et al.
Stories of Scottsboro, James
  Goodman
Peddling Prosperity, Paul Krugman
The Hot Zone, Richard Preston

Best-Sellers

In the Kitchen with Rosie, Rosie
  Daley
*Men Are from Mars, Women Are
  from Venus,* John Gray
Crossing the Threshold of Hope,
  John Paul II
Magic Eye I, N.E. Thing Enterprises
The Book of Virtues, William J.
  Bennett
Magic Eye II, N.E. Thing
  Enterprises

*Don't Stand Too Close to a Naked
  Man,* Tim Allen
Couplehood, Paul Reiser
Magic Eye III, N.E. Thing
  Enterprises
Dolly Parton, Dolly Parton

Poetry

A. R. Ammons, *Garbage*
Heather McHugh, *Hinge & Signs*
Carolyn Forché, *The Angel of
  History*
Rosellen Brown, *Cora Fry's Pillow
  Book*
Kenneth Koch, *One Train*

Pulitzer Prizes

The Stone Diaries, Carol Shields
  (fiction)
*No Ordinary Time: Franklin and
  Eleanor Roosevelt: The Home
  Front in World War II,* Doris
  Kearns Goodwin (U.S. history)
*The Beak of the Finch: A Story of
  Evolution in Our Time,*
  Jonathan Weiner (nonfiction)
Harriet Beecher Stowe: A Life,
  Joan D. Hedrick (biography)
The Simple Truth, Philip Levine
  (poetry)

Science and Technology _____

Paleontologists discover *Australopithecus ramidus,* the oldest known hominid by half a million years.
A new marsupial is found, a black and white kangaroo, with pandalike fur.
AZT is shown to reduce transmission of AIDS to infants by two-thirds.
Studies reveal that anger increases heart attack risk; exercise raises HDL, the good cholesterol.
For the first time in 30 years, bubonic plague is reported, in Surat, India.
A deadly strain of streptococcus is reported; it rapidly penetrates the body, and a person can lose flesh, a limb, and even life.
Researchers find that certain kinds of peptic ulcers, caused by the bacterium *Helicobacter pylori,* can be cured with antibiotics.

Laser radial keratotomy is approved for nearsightedness.
The Tokamak Fusion Test Reactor at Princeton emits 107 million watts of power, a great advance in fusion power.
Clementine travels to the moon and discovers dense polar ice.
The top quark, the 6th, one of the basic particles of matter, is identified.

Nobel Prizes

George A. Olah wins in chemistry for new methods of manipulating hydrocarbons; Clifford G. Shull in physics for improving neutron probes of atomic structure; Alfred G. Gilman and Martin Rodbell in physiology or medicine for discovering G-proteins, which help cells control fundamental life processes.

Sports

Baseball

Each league now has 3 divisions; the winners plus a "wild card" (best record) compete for the pennant.
Commissioner Bud Selig calls off play on Sept. 14, when a new labor agreement falters on the salary cap.
In April, 708 HRs are hit, 162 more than ever.
Frank Thomas (Chicago, AL) ties Lou Gehrig by hitting .300, 100 RBIs, and 100 runs in 4 seasons.
The Cy Young awards are won by Greg Maddux (Atlanta, NL, the first to win 3 in a row) and David Cone (Kansas City, AL).

Champions

Batting	Pitching
Tony Gwynn (San Diego, NL), .394	Bret Saberhagen (New York, NL), 14–4
Paul O'Neill (New York, AL), .354	Jason Bere (Chicago, AL), 12–2
	Home runs
	Matt Williams (San Francisco, NL), 43

Football

Dallas coach Jimmy Johnson resigns after a conflict with owner Jerry Jones, who says any coach could win with that team. A salary cap is implemented. Jerry Rice (San Francisco) sets the career TD record, 126.

NFC Season Leaders: Steve Young (San Francisco), passing; Barry Sanders (Detroit), rushing; Chris Carter (Minnesota), receiving, record 122 receptions

AFC Season Leaders: Dan Marino (Miami), passing; Chris Warren (Seattle), rushing; Ben Coates (New England), receiving

College All-Americans: Steve McNair (Q), Alcorn State; Ki-Jana Carter (RB), Penn State; Warren Sapp (L), Miami

Bowls (Jan. 1, 1995)
Rose: Penn State 38–Oregon 20
Orange: Nebraska 24–Miami 17
Sugar: Florida State 23–Florida 17
Cotton: USC 55–Texas 14

Basketball

Retired Michael Jordan signs with the Chicago White Sox and bats .202 for their Birmingham farm team.

NBA All-Pro First Team: Scottie Pippen (Chicago), Karl Malone (Utah), Hakeem Olajuwon (Houston), Latrell Sprewell (Golden State), John Stockton (Utah)

Olympics: At Lillehammer, Norway, winning skaters are Nancy Kerrigan, bronze; Dan Jansen, gold; Bonnie Blair, two gold. Tommy Moe wins the men's downhill.

Other Sports

Boxing: George Foreman, 45, KOs Michael Moorer for the HW title.

Hockey: Wayne Gretsky breaks Gordie Howe's career 801-goal scoring record.

Tennis: Pete Sampras wins Wimbledon and the Australian Open.

Winners

World Series	*MVP*
Not played (for the first time since 1904)	Hakeem Olajuwon, Houston
MVP	*College Basketball*
NL–Jeff Bagwell, Houston	Arkansas
AL–Frank Thomas, Chicago	*Player of the Year*
Super Bowl XXIX (Jan. 1995)	Glenn Robinson, Purdue
San Francisco 49–San Diego 26	*Stanley Cup*
MVP	New York Rangers
Steve Young (San Francisco)	*US Tennis Open*
College Football	Men: Andre Agassi
Nebraska	Women: Arantxa Sanchez Vicario
Heisman Trophy	*USGA Open*
Rashaan Salaam, Colorado	Ernie Els
NBA Championship	*Kentucky Derby*
Houston 4–New York Knicks 3	Go for Gin (Chris McCarron, jockey)

Fashion

High style and fads of dressing down—grunge and deconstruction styles—continue along with more structured clothing. Women's looser fashion is replaced by tailored pants and swingy dresses. Pants are often slimmer, skirts shortened to the thigh. Stiletto heels add to the new look. German supermodel Nadja Auermann, 23, with her long bleached white hair, red lipstick, and smoky eyeliner, 5'11" and 119 pounds, says: "I have curves, look strong, sexy, and feminine." Her sheer plastics and shiny fabrics—on the covers of four major fashion magazines—become faddish. The waif look, with slip dresses and grunged-out flannel, is moving out. Political groups organize against fur in fashion.

High-fashion notes: Versace's metallics lacquered on moiré and silk crepe; Galliano's structured-like, modified 50s-style jackets with peplum waists and sculpted bosoms.

Kaleidoscope ─────────────────────

- Newt Gingrich's "Contract with America" proposes a balanced budget amendment, term limits, orphanages for neglected children, and cutting money for the arts.
- "We are the sons and daughters of the world they saved," says President Clinton commemorating the heroes of WWII 50 years after D-Day.
- A vast TV audience meets the O. J. trial cast: Judge Lance Ito; prosecutors Marcia Clark and Chris Darden; "Dream Team" defense lawyers Johnnie Cochran, F. Lee Bailey, and Barry Scheck; "houseboy" Kato Kaelin; and LAPD Detective Mark Fuhrman.
- An Ecuadorian feminist group threatens to castrate 1,000 men if Lorena Bobbitt is sent to prison for slicing off her husband's penis.
- Lorena Bobbitt is acquitted in her husband's "malicious wounding" charge on grounds of "temporary insanity"; he makes a porn movie, *John Bobbitt Uncut.*
- Roseanne and Tom Arnold break up; she says: "I don't mind being divorced. I mind not being a widow."
- A letter written by Abraham Lincoln sells for $728,000; by George Washington, $635,000; maps of the lead Japanese pilot at Pearl Harbor, $321,000; other notable sales include Babe Ruth's 1921 bat, $63,000; Madonna's 1990 concert corset, $18,150; and Vivien Leigh's Academy Award, $563,000.
- California voters approve ballot initiative 187, barring illegal immigrants from public education and social services.
- The repaired Hubble telescope captures sharp images that range from nearby asteroids to the most distant galaxies.
- World chess champion Garry Kasparov defeats IBM supercomputer Deep Blue.
- The NIH concludes that "Gulf War Syndrome" cannot be traced to a single cause.
- Psychologists report that babies recognize their name by 4.5 months and infants begin building a vocabulary during the first months of life.
- Obesity rises 8 percent; a third of all adults are at least 20 pounds overweight.
- Rupert Murdoch's Fox Broadcasting Company pays $500 million to take over New World Communications Group; 12 CBS, NBC, and ABC affiliates join Fox.
- Debate continues on both access to and the nature of the information highway: safeguarding privacy, childproofing, and content screening.
- With the average age of cars and trucks at eight years, sales surge to about 15.3 million.
- A "parental [incest] abuse" defense leads to mistrials in the Menendezes' murder trials.
- "Repressed memory therapy"—encouraging recollection of sexual abuse—comes under professional attack.
- A few months after calling his song "I Hate Myself and Want to Die" a joke, rock star Kurt Cobain commits suicide; grieving fans at his memorial hurl burning rolls of toilet paper.
- Barbra Streisand makes her first tour in 27 years; with a $350 top, tickets for 18 concerts sell out in an hour; on tours, Pink Floyd earns $103 million; the Rolling Stones, $114 million.
- Anti-smoking forces target the Joe Camel ad; 3.1 million, aged 13–19, smoke.

- Americans protest Singapore's caning of Michael Faye, an American convicted of minor vandalism.
- The bald eagle and California gray whale are removed from the endangered species list.
- Sunflowers and delphiniums gain special attention when crossed to produce new colors.
- A Pennsylvania animal behavior clinic prescribes Prozac for depressed dogs.
- Alfonse D'Amato (R–NY) says of his $37,000 commodities trading profit: "I'm no Hillary Clinton," alluding to her $100,000 commodities' profit on $1,000.
- Richard Nixon's funeral costs the government $311,039.
- The toe tag for Lee Harvey Oswald's corpse brings $8,800 at auction.
- The Ritz-Carlton Hotel in Virginia fires a woman for refusing to shave her mustache.
- "Every time I look at Strom Thurmond [94], I'm inspired. When I see him eat a banana, I eat a banana," comments Senate leader Bob Dole, 72.
- Oprah Winfrey's personal chef publishes a best-selling cookbook.
- *Sex in America* reports that married people have more sex than single people.
- "Hollywood madam" Heidi Fleiss is sentenced to six months for pandering.
- Dick Tracy and Tess Trueheart break up over his workaholism.
- Madonna, on David Letterman's show, extols urinating for athlete's foot; Letterman recommends Desenex.
- "Sleeping with them is one thing. Liking them is another," says GOP adviser Mary Matalin of Democrats; she is married to Democratic adviser James Carville.
- Steven Spielberg, Jeffrey Katzenberg, and David Geffen form the first new major movie studio in 55 years.
- On MTV Clinton reveals that he wears boxer shorts.
- A jury awards $2.9 million to a woman scalded by McDonald's coffee.
- DNA tests on the remains of Czar Nicholas II and his wife, Alexandra, prove that Anna Anderson was not their daughter, the Grand Duchess Anastasia.
- Bryan de la Beckwith, 73, receives a life sentence for the 1963 murder of civil rights leader Medgar Evers.
- An embarrassed CIA discovers an 8-year spy in its midst, Aldrich Ames, responsible for many betrayals and 8 deaths.

Fads: Lion King paraphernalia, tattoos, Letterman's mom, cleavage, weight-losing gimmicks ("Bun Firmers," "Abs" exercisers), 35th anniversary Barbie doll, high heels, 40s-style disco, "sleaze" TV, Pan-Asian and Fusion French cuisine

New Words and Usages: information superhighway, cyberspace, Internet, e-mail, netiquette, virtual-[anything], Cyber-[anything], unplugged

First Appearances: protease inhibitors for HIV, microwave clothes dryer, World Cup soccer in U.S., synthetic odorless feces (Kimberly-Clark, to test diapers)

1995

Oklahoma City bombing. *Oklahoma City Public Information Office.*

Facts and Figures

Economic Profile
  Dow-Jones: ↑ High 5,216–
    Low 3,832
  GNP: +4.5%
  Inflation: +2.5%
  Unemployment: 5.6%
Infant mortality/1,000: 8.0
Maternal mortality/10,000:
  0.78
Physicians: 720,000
Dentists: 190,000
Hospital beds: 872,700
Rolex Cellini quartz watch,
  18k gold: $4,950–$11,450
Mont Blanc limited-edition
  Agatha Christie fountain
  pen, sterling: $650
Wellbuilt Breadmaker: $180
Krups Espresso machine: $225
Neiman Marcus
  Milk chocolate Santa, 7 oz.:
    $20
Toys 'R' Us
  Power wheels red jeep:
    $179.99
  Little Tikes' country cottage:
    $199.99
  Fisher-Price Play Desk
    (without chair): $49.99

The Hubble Space Telescope captures the birth of a star in the Eagle Nebula. *NASA.*

Deaths

Warren Burger, Howard Cosell, Jerry Garcia, Burl Ives, Mickey Mantle, Dean Martin, James Merrill, Ginger Rogers, Jonas Salk, Lana Turner

In the News

ISLAMIC SUICIDE BOMBER KILLS 19 IN ISRAEL . . . TELEVISED O. J. SIMPSON TRIAL BEGINS, ATTRACTS ENORMOUS AUDIENCE . . . CLINTON AUTHORIZES $42 BILLION LOAN TO MEXICO TO PREVENT DEFAULT . . . SARIN NERVE GAS ATTACK KILLS 11 ON JAPANESE SUBWAY, CULT IS SUSPECTED . . . CAR BOMB DEVASTATES FEDERAL OFFICE BUILDING IN OKLAHOMA CITY, MANY CHILDREN ARE FOUND AMONG OVER 150 DEAD . . . SUPREME COURT RULES THAT CONGRESSIONAL TERM LIMITS, PASSED IN 23 STATES, ARE UNCONSTITUTIONAL . . . U.S. SPACE SHUTTLE MAKES FIRST DOCKING WITH RUSSIAN SPACE STATION *MIR* . . . U.S. AND VIETNAM RESTORE DIPLOMATIC RELATIONS . . . TIMOTHY MCVEIGH AND TERRY NICHOLS, ANTI-GOVERNMENT MILITIA FANATICS, ARE ARRESTED IN OKLAHOMA CITY BOMBING . . . CHEMICAL AND CHASE MERGER CREATES LARGEST U.S. BANK . . . SENATE ETHICS COMMITTEE VOTES TO EXPEL BOB PACKWOOD (R–ORE.) FOR SEXUAL MISCONDUCT AND OBSTRUCTION OF JUSTICE . . . BLIND LEADER SHEIK OMAR ABDEL RAHMAN IS CONVICTED OF TERRORIST CONSPIRACY . . . O. J. SIMPSON IS ACQUITTED . . . JOHN SWEENEY IS ELECTED HEAD OF AFL-CIO . . . YELTSIN IS HOSPITALIZED FOR HEART ATTACK, U.S. SPECIALISTS ARE CONSULTED . . . ISRAELI PM RABIN IS ASSASSINATED BY RIGHT-WING JEWISH FANATIC . . . COLIN POWELL ANNOUNCES HE WILL NOT SEEK PRESIDENCY . . . BOSNIANS, CROATS, SERBS SIGN DAYTON PEACE ACCORD, 60,000 NATO TROOPS, INCLUDING 20,000 FROM U.S., WILL MONITOR . . . CLINTON AGAIN VETOES GOP BUDGET, CLAIMS IT WILL HURT ELDERLY, GINGRICH THREATENS GOVERNMENT SHUTDOWN . . . QUEEN PUBLICLY URGES CHARLES TO DIVORCE DIANA.

Quotes

"If the glove doesn't fit, you must acquit."
—O. J. Simpson's defense attorneys

"In the matter of the *People of the State of California v. Orenthal James Simpson.* We, the jury . . . find the defendant not guilty of murder in violation of Penal Code Section 187A."
—Jury verdict, O. J. Simpson trial

"Mend it. Don't end it."
—President Clinton, on affirmative action

"Females have biological problems staying in a ditch for 30 days because they get infections. . . . Males are biologically driven to go out and hunt giraffes."
—Newt Gingrich, on why women are not suited for combat

"I have been working in a male culture for a very long time, and I haven't met the first one who wants to go out and hunt a giraffe. I am very, very troubled by the new factual data that seems to be coming out of our new leader."
—Pat Schroeder (D–Colo.), answering Gingrich's description of gender roles

"I do have AIDS."
—American Olympics multi-gold diving champion Greg Louganis

After 20 years, Robert MacNeil retires from the acclaimed *MacNeil/Lehrer News Hour.* PBS.

"If we had God booked, and O. J. was available, we'd move God. There's nobody who wouldn't take a figure of this magnitude."
—Larry King

"Eight-, 10-, 11-year olds are using drugs because they are told it's 'cool'; little boys are calling little girls 'whore' because that's what they hear."
—C. DeLores Tucker, launching her attack against gangsta rap for its effect on African-American children

"What is this man saying about my service? Did it all mean nothing? I don't know if he did this for profit or as an old man trying to cleanse his soul, but I wish he had kept his mouth shut."
—Double amputee John Behan, on former Defense Secretary Robert McNamara's public confession that the Vietnam War was "terribly wrong"

Ads

In Rwanda, no one cries for the dead.
They don't have enough water in their bodies for tears.
(Rwanda Relief Fund)

If you don't call us
Your mother will.
(Jewish Dating Service, 542–9790)

Pearl Jam. The band displays the latest in grunge styles. *Movie Star News.*

Everybody knows the best nuts come from California.
(Sunkist California Pistachios)

Statistics show that if you grow up in Minnesota, you'll be stronger, healthier, and better looking. (Particularly if you're a tree.)
(Minnesota Forest Industries)

Someone feeds you, bathes you, and dresses you in fine garments. You're either the ruler of a small country or a baby.
(Healthtex, Inc.)

Call us when "till death do us part" starts sounding good.
(Meltzer and Kanzers, divorce attorneys at law)

Some people were born with a silver spoon. I got a fork.
(Ron De Puy, piano tuning and repair)

TV

Premieres
"Cybill" Cybill Shepherd, Christine Baranski
"The Naked Truth," Téa Leoni, Holland Taylor
"Caroline in the City," Lea Thompson
"Murder One," Daniel Benzali
"JAG," David James Elliott
"Mad about You," Paul Reiser, Helen Hunt
"The Nanny," Fran Drescher
"The Single Guy," Jonathan Silverman, Ernest Borgnine

Top Ten (Nielsen)
"E.R.," "Seinfeld," "Friends," "Caroline in the City,"
"NFL Monday Night Football," "Single Guy," "Home
Improvement," "Boston Common," "60 Minutes,"
"NYPD Blue"

Specials
Barbara Walters' interview with Christopher Reeve;
Princess Diana's BBC interview; "Sinatra: 80 Years My
Way"; "Marsalis on Music" (for children); "The
Peacekeepers: How the U.N. Failed in Bosnia" (Peter
Jennings); *A Streetcar Named Desire,"* Jessica Lange,
Alec Baldwin; "The Beatles Anthology"; "Two by Dove
(Dance in America)"; "Taxicab Confessions"; "The
U.S. Holocaust Museum Presents: One Survivor
Remembers"

Popular film stars Harrison Ford (left) and Denzel
Washington. *Movie Star News.*

Emmy Awards
"NYPD Blue" (drama); "Frasier" (comedy); Mandy
Patinkin (actor, "Chicago Hope"); Kathy Bates (actress,
"Picket Fences"); Kelsey Grammer (comedic actor,
"Frasier"); Candice Bergen (comedic actress, "Murphy
Brown"); "Joseph" (miniseries)

Of Note
TV coverage includes momentous events: the search for
survivors in the Oklahoma City bombing; Rabin's
assassination; the Simpson (trial and) verdict (57 million
viewers) • Controversy grows regarding the social value
of TV and its impact on teen sex and violence • Talk
shows like "Ricki Lake" and "Jerry Springer" focus on
guests' intimate experiences • Walt Disney buys Capital
Cities/ABC; Westinghouse, CBS; Time Warner, Ted
Turner • Rupert Murdoch is reminded of the "green book's"
stipulation that owners of 20 percent or more of the written
press cannot invest more than 15 percent in TV • Microsoft
and NBC plan a news station to challenge CNN.

Movies

Openings
Braveheart (Mel Gibson), Gibson, Sophie Marceau,
    Patrick McGoohan
Sense and Sensibility (Ang Lee), Emma Thompson,
    Hugh Grant
Apollo 13 (Ron Howard), Tom Hanks, Bill Paxton
Babe (Chris Noonan), James Cromwell
The Postman (Il Postino) (Michael Radford, Massimo
    Troisi), Troisi
Get Shorty (Barry Sonnenfeld), John Travolta, Gene
    Hackman, Rene Russo
The American President (Rob Reiner), Michael
    Douglas, Annette Bening
Clueless (Amy Heckerling), Alicia Silverstone
Smoke (Wayne Wang), Harvey Keitel, William Hurt
Leaving Las Vegas (Mike Figgis), Nicolas Cage,
    Elisabeth Shue
Seven (David Fincher), Morgan Freeman, Brad Pitt
Dead Man Walking (Tim Robbins), Susan Sarandon,
    Sean Penn
The Brothers McMullen (Edward Burns), Burns, Mike
    McGlone
The Bridges of Madison County (Clint Eastwood),
    Eastwood, Meryl Streep
Toy Story (computer-generated animation)

Mr. Holland's Opus (Stephen Herek), Richard Dreyfuss
Dolores Claiborne (Taylor Hackford), Kathy Bates

Academy Awards
Best Picture: *Braveheart*
Best Actor: Nicolas Cage, *Leaving Las Vegas*
Best Actress: Susan Sarandon, *Dead Man Walking*
Best Director: Mel Gibson, *Braveheart*

Top Box-Office Stars
Tom Hanks, Jim Carrey, Brad Pitt, Harrison Ford, Robin
Williams, Sandra Bullock, Mel Gibson, Demi Moore,
John Travolta, Kevin Costner/Michael Douglas

Stars of the Future
Alicia Silverstone, Christina Ricci, Martin Lawrence,
Carey Lowell, Elisabeth Shue, Greg Kinnear, Karen
Silas

Veteran
stars Susan
Sarandon
and Clint
Eastwood.
*Movie Star
News.*

Popular Music

Hit Songs
"One Sweet Day"
"Before You Walk Out of My Life"
"Fantasy"
"Shut Up and Kiss Me"
"Come to My Window"
"When Can I See You"

Top Records

Albums: *Daydream* (Mariah Carey); *Melloncollie and the Infinite Sadness* (Smashing Pumpkins); *Tiger Lily* (Natalie Merchant); *History of the Past, Present, and Future,* Book 1 (Michael Jackson); *The Beatles: Anthology I* (The Beatles); *The Hits* (Garth Brooks); *Cracked Rear View* (Hootie & the Blowfish)

Singles: *Can You Feel the Love Tonight* (Elton John); *Gangsta's Paradise* (Coolio); *I'll Be There for You* (Mary J. Blige/Method Man); *Dear Mama* (2 Pac); *Breathe Again* (Toni Braxton); *Baby* (Brandy); *Freak Like Me* (Adina Howard).

Country: *Any Man of Mine* (Shania Twain); *Go Rest High on That Mountain* (Vince Gill)

Grammy Awards
Kiss from a Rose, Seal (record); *Jagged Little Pill,* Alanis Morissette (album); "Kiss from a Rose," Seal (song)

Jazz and Bands
The San Francisco Bay area overtakes N.Y.C. as the nation's jazz center, with jazz and rock fusion groups, as well as hip-hop. Acid Jazz becomes increasingly popular with performers like US3, who mix jazz and hip-hop. TLC, a hip-hop group, gains mainstream popularity with *CrazySexyCool* and sells 4 million copies by midyear. Jazz vocalists Holly Cole and Cassandra Wilson gain wide interest in combining jazz interpretations with popular favorites. The Grateful Dead disbands after its leader of 30 years, Jerry Garcia, dies. Many performers release CD-ROMs with video or interactive material.

Cats, Broadway's longest running-show. *Carol Rosegg.*

The Rock & Roll Hall of Fame and Museum, designed by I. M. Pei ($92 million), opens in Cleveland.

Top Performers (*Downbeat*):
Joshua Redman (soloist); John Scofield (electric group); Roy Hargrove, John McLaughlin, Charlie Haden, Airto Moreira, Herbie Hancock, Jimmy Smith, James Newton (instrumentalists); J. J. Johnson (Hall of Fame); Joe Williams, Cassandra Wilson (vocalists); Take 6 (vocal group); Joe Lovano, Gunther Schuller, *Rush Hour* (album)

Theater

Broadway Openings

Plays
Moonlight (Harold Pinter), Jason Robards, Blythe Danner
Master Class (Terrence McNally), Zoe Caldwell
Arcadia (Tom Stoppard), Blair Brown, Victor Garber
Love! Valour! Compassion! (Terrence McNally), Nathan Lane, Anthony Heald
Rob Becker's Defending the Caveman (Rob Becker), Becker
Racing Demon (David Hare), Josef Sommer, George N. Martin
Having Our Say (Emily Mann), Mary Alice, Gloria Foster

Musicals
Victor/Victoria (Henri Mancini, Leslie Bricusse), Julie Andrews, Tony Roberts, Michael Nouri
Smokey Joe's Cafe (Jerry Leiber, Mike Stoller), Victor Trent Cook, Adrian Bailey
How to Succeed in Business without Really Trying (Frank Loesser), Matthew Broderick

Classics, Revivals, and Off-Broadway Premieres
A Month in the Country, Helen Mirren, Ron Rifkin, F. Murray Abraham; *The Young Man from Atlanta* (Horton Foote), Ralph Waite, James Pritchett; *The Cryptogram* (David Mamet), Ed Begley, Jr.; *Call Me Madame,* Tyne Daly; *After-Play* (Anne Meara), Rue McClanahan, Barbara Barrie; *Vita and Virginia,* Vanessa Redgrave, Eileen Atkins; *Hello, Dolly!* Carol Channing; *Hamlet,* Ralph Fiennes; *Cascando* and *Eh, Joe* (Beckett); *The Rose Tattoo,* Mercedes Ruehl, Anthony LaPaglia; Brooklyn Academy of Music: *Winter's Tale; Translations* (Brian Friel), Brian Dennehy; *Hapgood* (Stoppard); *Mrs. Klein,* Uta Hagen; *The Heiress,* Cherry Jones, Philip Bosco, Frances Sternhagen; *Picasso at the Lapin Agile; Sylvia* (A. R. Gurney); *Indiscretions* (Cocteau), Kathleen Turner, Roger Rees, Eileen Atkins

Pulitzer Prize
Horton Foote, *The Young Man from Atlanta*

Tony Awards
Love! Valour! Compassion! Terrence McNally (play); *Sunset Boulevard,* Andrew Lloyd Webber, Christopher Hampton, Don Black (musical)

Classical Music ———

Compositions
George Walker, *Lilacs*
Elliott Carter, Fifth Quartet, *Adagio Tenebroso*
Peter Lieberson, Variations for Violin and Piano
Brian Fennelly, *Skyscapes for Saxophone and String
    Quartet*
Leon Kushner, Music for Cello and Orchestra
Lou Harrison, Suite for Cello and Piano

Important Events
Many new recordings honor Purcell's 300th birthday;
Hindemith, Fauré, Orff, Castelnuovo, and William Grant
Still centenaries are celebrated. Also marking important
birthdays with special concerts are Pierre Boulez, Lucio
Berio, Gunther Schuller, Otto Luening, Michael Tippett,
George Perle, Earl Wild, Isaac Stern, and Itzhak Perlman.
Three U.S. orchestras—the Chicago, Pittsburgh, and St.
Louis—tour Japan.

Notable Performances
Valery Gergiev conducts the New York Philharmonic in
an all-Russian program, and Yuri Temirkanov performs
Prokofiev's score to Eisenstein's *Ivan the Terrible,* with
film scenes; at Carnegie Hall: the Cleveland's Mahler's
Eighth, and Emanuel Ax performing the two Brahms
concerti; Maurizio Pollini, the complete Beethoven
piano sonata cycle; Garrick Ohlsson, six Chopin
concerts that cover the complete solo repertory; at
Boston, an all-Tchaikovsky program, with Evgeny
Kissin performing the first piano concerto. John Adams,
collaborating with poet June Jordan, premieres *I Was
Looking at the Ceiling and Then I Saw the Sky* in N.Y.C.
The Aspen Festival performs works composed during
World War II, including *Quartet for the End of Time*
(Messiaen), Symphony no. 3 (Copland), *Concerto for
Orchestra* (Bartok), and works by Czech composers
killed at Theresienstadt.

New Appointments: Hans Vonk, St. Louis Symphony
Orchestra; Michael Tilson Thomas, San Francisco

Debuts: Helen Huang, Awadagin Pratt, Leif Ove
Andsnes

Deborah Voigt.
*Winnie Klotz.
Metropolitan
Opera.*

Evgeny Kissin. *Bette
Marshall. IMG.*

First Performances
John Adams, Violin Concerto (Minneapolis);
Christopher Rouse, Symphony no. 2 (Houston); Toru
Takemitsu, *Family Tree* (New York); Joseph Schwantner,
Percussion Concerto (New York); John Harbison, Flute
Concerto (Washington, D.C.); Oliver Knussen, Horn
Concerto (Cleveland); Peter Maxwell, Symphony no. 5
(the composer, touring and conducting his works);
Morton Feldman, *For Philip Guston* (New York); Paul
Schoenfield, *Klezmer Rondos* (New York)

Opera

Metropolitan: The company concedes to project
supertitles of foreign works on monitors, which
spectators can turn on or off. Luciano Pavarotti,
Andrea Chénier; Ben Heppner, Karita Mattila, *Die
Meistersinger;* Heppner, Denyee Graves (debut),
Carmen; Dmitri Hvorostovsky (debut), Leonie Rysanek,
Queen of Spades; Patricia Racette (debut), *La Bohème;*
Richard Margison (debut), *Madama Butterfly*

Brooklyn Academy of Music: Valery Gergiev leads
Galina Gorchakova, Vladimir Ognovenko, *The Invisible
City of Kitezh*

Houston: *Harvey Milk* (premiere, Stewart Wallace,
Michael Korie)

Chicago: Aprile Millo, Michael Sylvester (debut), *Aïda.*
Premieres: *The Guilt of Lillian Sloan* (William Neil),
The Fan (Lee Goldstein)

Music Notes
Ellen Taaffe Zwilich receives the first Carnegie Hall
Composer's Chair • Marking his retirement from the
National, Rostropovich records all the Bach cello suites
• Pavarotti lowers his high Cs in the finale of *La Fille du
régiment,* and speculations surface concerning his
"exhausted voice" • Lincoln Center for the Performing
Arts acquires the 26,000-page manuscript collection of
John Cage • The much-awaited 1984 Moscow concert of
Evgeny Kissin playing both Chopin concerti is finally
released • To attract younger audiences, "interactive
concerts" begin; at a Philadelphia Orchestra program,
audiences e-mail requests during intermission • Paul
Katz, cellist with the Cleveland Orchestra, reserves a
plane seat for his cello; finding the seat double-booked,
Robin Leach moves and asks Katz to perform en route.

Art

Painting

Frank Romero, *High Heel Shoe, Cherry Pie*

Robert Rauschenberg, *Fête (Vydock), 1995*

Larry Poons, *Amoral Cadenza*

Jasper Johns, *Mirror's Edge 2*

Philip Pearlstein, *Sepik River Triptych*

Chris Burden, *Pizza City*

Elizabeth Murray, *Rain Painting, Rescue*

Gary Simmons, *Erasure Drawings, 1995*

Sculpture

Kiki Smith, *Jersey Crows*

Sol LeWitt, *New Structures, 1995*

Jessica Stockholder, *Your Skin in This Weather*

Chakaia Booker, *Repugnant Rapunze*l *(Let Down Your Hair)*

Important Exhibitions

Traveling shows include "Discoveries of Ancient Egypt"; "Copley in America"; Monet; Kandinsky; "About Place: Recent Art of the Americas," as well as Gorky and Oldenburg shows.

Museums

New York: *Metropolitan (125th anniversary):* Goya; "Architecture of the Met, 1870–1995"; "Rembrandt— Not Rembrandt"; Horace Pippin. *Museum of Modern Art:* Mondrian retrospective; Jacob Lawrence, "Migration of the Negro"; Bruce Nauman; "Video Space: Eight Installations." *Guggenheim:* George Baselitz; Dan Flavin; "Africa: The Art of a Continent"; Felix Gonzalez-Torres. *Whitney:* Edward Hopper; Florine Stettheimer; "Beat Culture and the New America, 1950–1965"

Stanley Saitowitz, New England Holocaust Memorial, Boston

Architecture

Central Library, Denver (Michael Graves)

Cy Twombly Gallery, Houston (Renzo Piano)

"Alcatraz of the Rockies," Florence, Colorado (F. Sadeau), federal maximum security prison designed to maximize sensory deprivation and spatial disorientation (home of inmates such as John Gotti)

Arts Garden, Center for the Performing Arts, Indianapolis (Ehrenkrantz & Eckstut)

Chicago: Monet (largest exhibition ever); Bruce Goff

Boston: Landscapes of France: Monet, Renoir, Pissarro; Nolde

Washington, D.C. (National): Dutch painting; Book arts of Isfahan; Brancusi retrospective; Copley; Winslow Homer

Los Angeles: "Reconsidering the Object of Art, 1965–1975"

Art Briefs

Work continues on redesigning N.Y.C.'s Times Square area; Disney's project continues to elicit proposals from architects like Robert Venturi, Philip Johnson, Michael Graves, Cesar Pelli, Robert A. M. Stern, and Jaquelin Robertson • The art world is overwhelmed by the 74 paintings of the Hermitage's "Hidden Treasures Revealed" taken from Germany by the Soviets at the end of World War II and not seen in 50 years • Christo wraps the historic Berlin Reichstag in more than a million square feet of aluminized polypropylene fabric • A surrogate court judge awards $7.45 million to the attorney of Andy Warhol's estate, now appraised at $509.9 million • Republicans urge defunding the NEA after this year's grants; in response, the Smithsonian launches a $100 million drive that will coincide with its 150th anniversary (1996) • High-quality graphic images are transmitted on the World Wide Web as museum sites join the Web • Major sales, in millions, include Picasso's blue period *Angel Fernandez De Soto* ($29.15) and *The Mirror* ($20.02); Van Gogh's *Sous-bois* ($26.95); Miró's *La poetesse* ($4.7); and Matisse's *La pose hindoue* ($14.9).

Dance

The Kirov visits the Met. Dance companies throughout the U.S. face financial crises; the Joffrey moves from N.Y.C. to Chicago to avoid bankruptcy.

American Ballet Theatre: The exceptional Paloma Herrera is joined by Angel Corella and Vladimir Malakhov. Malakhov, *Giselle;* Malakhov, Andrew McKerrow, *Theme and Variations*

New York City Ballet: Arch Higgins, Jock Soto, Alexander Ritter, *West Side Story Suite* (Jerome Robbins); Darci Kistler, Wendy Whelan, Adams's Violin Concerto (premiere, Peter Martins); Margaret Tracey, Ethan Stiefel, *Untitled* (Martins)

San Francisco: "United We Dance Festival" (to celebrate UN 50-year charter)

Twyla Tharp: premieres: *Americans We* (various 19th-century American composers); *How near Heaven* (Benjamin Britten)

Books

Fiction

Critic's Choice
Sabbath's Theater, Philip Roth
Rule of the Bone, Russell Banks
The Wedding, Dorothy West
Moo, Jane Smiley
The Tunnel, William Gass
Painted Desert, Frederick Barthelme
RL's Dream, Walter Mosley
❧ *The First Man,* Albert Camus (posthumous)

Best-Sellers
The Rainmaker, John Grisham
The Lost World, Michael Crichton
Five Days in Paris, Danielle Steel
The Christmas Box, Richard Paul Evans
The Celestine Prophecy, James Redfield
Rose Madder, Stephen King
Silent Night, Mary Higgins Clark
Politically Correct Bedtime Stories, James Finn Garner

Nonfiction

Critic's Choice
In Retrospect, Robert S. McNamara
Lincoln, David Herbert Donald
The Secret World of American Communism, Harvey Klehr, John Earl Haynes, Fridrikh Firsov
A Civil Action, Jonathan Harr
City Life, Witold Rybczynski
Emotional Intelligence: Why It Can Matter More than IQ, Daniel Goleman
The Death of Common Sense, Philip K. Howard
Dark Sun: The Making of the Hydrogen Bomb, Richard Rhodes
The All-American Skin Game, Stanley Crouch
The De-Moralization of Society, Gertrude Himmelfarb
Walt Whitman's America, David Reynolds
The Revolt of the Elites and the Betrayal of Democracy, Christopher Lasch
Darwin's Dangerous Idea, Daniel Dennett

Best-Sellers
Men Are from Mars, Women Are from Venus, John Gray
My American Journey, Colin Powell, with Joseph Persico
Miss America, Howard Stern
The Seven Spiritual Laws of Success, Deepak Chopra
The Road Ahead, Bill Gates
Charles Kuralt's America, Charles Kuralt
To Renew America, Newt Gingrich
My Point . . . And I Do Have One, Ellen DeGeneres

Pulitzer Prize–winning Amy Tan portrays the difficulties of balancing American and Chinese cultures.

The Moral Compass, William J. Bennett

Poetry
James Merrill, *A Scattering of Salts* (posthumous)
Robert Pinsky, *The Inferno of Dante: A New Verse Translation*
William Matthews, *Time and Money*
Mark Rudman, *Rider*

Pulitzer Prizes
Independence Day, Richard Ford (fiction)
The Haunted Land: Facing Europe's Ghosts after Communism, Tina Rosenberg (nonfiction)
William Cooper's Town, Alan Taylor (U.S. history)
God: A Biography, Jack Miles (biography)
The Dream of the Unified Field, Jorie Graham (poetry)

Science and Technology

Physicists discover Einstein's predicted megaparticle, consisting of a few thousand atoms (the Bose-Einstein condensate).

Five to 10 percent of those with HIV now live more than ten years.

A vaccine for hepatitis A gains FDA approval.

Fosamax is the first nonhormonal drug for osteoporosis to gain approval.

Fish is shown to be protective against potentially fatal heart arrhythmias.

The lethal Ebola virus strikes Zaire; 244 of 315 victims die; some fear a worldwide epidemic like the 1918 influenza, but this does not occur.

Craig Venter decodes an entire genome, the bacteria *Haemophus influenzae.*

The largest dinosaur to date is found in Patagonia, a 100-ton sauropod, *Argentinosaurus.*

The frozen body of a 500-year-old Inca girl is found in the Peruvian Andes; "the mummy" was bundled in fine wool, "just lying on a hunk of ice."

Debate continues over estrogen use in women to reduce heart disease, osteoporosis, and Alzheimer's.

❧ Over 300 paintings of mammoths, woolly rhinos, bears, and other Ice Age animals are discovered near Avignon, older than those at Lascaux.

Nobel Prizes

F. Sherwood Rowland and Mario Molina in chemistry on ozone depletion; Martin L. Perl and Frederick Reines in physics for separate discoveries of subatomic particles, laptons; Edward B. Lewis and Eric F. Wieschaus in physiology or medicine for studying genetic control of human embryo development.

Sports

Baseball

Federal Judge Sonia Sotomayor ends the baseball strike by granting players' request of injunction; the season is limited to 144 games.

Cal Ripken (Baltimore, AL) breaks Lou Gehrig's record of 2,130 games played.

Greg Maddux (Atlanta, NL) is the first since Walter Johnson to win consecutive ERA titles under 1.80.

Cy Young awards go to Maddux (Atlanta, NL), a record 4th in a row, and Randy Johnson (Seattle, AL).

Champions

Batting	Pitching
Tony Gwynn (San Diego, NL), .368	Greg Maddux (Atlanta, NL), 19–2
Edgar Martinez (Seattle, AL), .356	Randy Johnson (Seattle, AL), 18–2
	Home runs
	Albert Belle (Cleveland, AL), 50

Football

Dan Marino becomes the all-time leader in passes completed, yards gained, and TDs. Deion Sanders jumps to Dallas for $35 million. This is the first season of the Bowl Alliance, which will alternate bowls matching the top two teams (Fiesta, this year).

NFC Season Leaders: Bret Favre (Green Bay), passing, 38 TDs; Emmitt Smith (Dallas), rushing; Herman Moore (Detroit), receiving, record 123 receptions

AFC Season Leaders: Jim Harbaugh (Baltimore), passing; Curtis Martin (New England), rushing; Carl Pickens (Cincinnati), receiving

College All-Americans: Danny Wuerfel (Q), Florida; Darnell Autrey (RB), Northwestern; Kevin Hardy (LB) Illinois

Bowls:

Fiesta: Nebraska 64–Florida 24
Rose: USC 41–Northwestern 32
Orange: Florida State 31–Notre Dame 26
Sugar: Virginia Tech 28–Texas 10
Cotton: Colorado 38–Oregon 6

Basketball

The UConn women's team, led by Rebecca Lobo, goes 35–0. The NBA narrowly averts a play stoppage.

NBA All-Pro First Team: Karl Malone (Utah), Scottie Pippen (Chicago), David Robinson (San Antonio), Penny Hardaway (Orlando), John Stockton (Utah)

Other Sports

Boxing: Mike Tyson returns after being paroled and beats unknown Peter McNeeley in 89 seconds; Tyson's purse is $25 million, McNeeley's $700,000.

Hockey: A 4-month lockout limits the season.

Tennis: Pete Sampras wins Wimbledon again.

Winners

World Series	*College Basketball*
Atlanta (NL) 4	UCLA
Cleveland (AL) 2	*Player of the Year*
MVP	Joe Smith, Maryland
NL–Barry Larkin, Cincinnati	*Stanley Cup*
AL–Mo Vaughn, Boston	New Jersey Devils
Super Bowl XXX (Jan. 1996)	*US Tennis Open*
Dallas 27–Pittsburgh 17	Men: Pete Sampras
MVP	Women: Steffi Graf
Bret Favre, Green Bay	*USGA Open*
College Football	Corey Pavin
Nebraska	*Kentucky Derby*
Heisman Trophy	Thunder Gulch (Gary Stevens,
Eddie George, Ohio State	jockey)

Fashion

For Women: Interest in high style wanes slightly, although designers continue their mammoth shows with supermodels like Kate Moss, Claudia Schiffer, Christy Turlington, Shalom Harlow, Cindy Crawford ($5 million a year), and Linda Evangelista (a minimum of $10,000 a day). The casual look returns; T-shirts are worn everywhere, with long and miniskirts, as well as utilitarian clothes from stores like K-Mart. Women also "cross-shop"—buying a small amount of clothing at upscale shops. Stores like Bonwit Teller close, and high-price designers like Pauline Trigère, Bob Mackie, and

Arnold Scassi retire. Bill Blass, Oscar de la Renta, Donna Karan, Calvin Klein, and Geoffrey Beene design high-fashion items within moderate prices. The pushup bra gains enormous popularity.

For Men: A preppie look returns, along with the spirit of 1940s Hollywood. Businesses introduce "casual Fridays" when employees wear jeans and sweatshirts.

High-fashion notes: Prada's finely tailored shetland coats; Gianni Versace's black and white gowns.

Kaleidoscope _____

- A government shutdown looms repeatedly when the president refuses the GOP budget plan, and the GOP withholds stopgap financing.
- While first suspicions in the Oklahoma City bombing are of foreign terrorists, two Americans are arrested (one by accident, for driving without a license); the final toll in the bombing is 169 dead, 614 injured.
- Attention focuses on the proliferation of fanatical, anti-government militias around the country, to which one Oklahoma suspect belonged.
- Through recently declassified Soviet documents, *The Secret World of American Communism* demonstrates that the American Communist Party directly served the KGB and was actively involved in atomic espionage.
- After 130 years, Mississippi lawmakers ratify the 13th Amendment abolishing slavery.
- Unexpectedly, O. J. Simpson's jury reaches a verdict in several hours, although it is not announced until the next day.
- The nation divides over Simpson's not-guilty verdict after a 372-day trial; polls indicate that whites, by 2/3, believe him guilty; blacks, by 2/3, innocent.
- Shannon Faulkner withdraws from The Citadel, its first female cadet; a T-shirt printed subsequently portrays "1,952 bulldogs and one bitch."
- "Women's rights are human rights," states Hillary Clinton at an international conference on women's rights in China.
- Colin Ferguson shoots 25 people on a Long Island commuter train, killing six.
- After much protest, Calvin Klein withdraws his ads featuring teenage models in sultry poses.
- Viking offers Simpson's prosecutor Marcia Clark a $4.2 million book advance.
- "What more do I need to say? Conservative books sell. I can't help it if liberal books don't sell," says Newt Gingrich of his $4.15 million advance.
- Despite his controversial reputation—denouncing gays, Jews, Asians, and whites—Louis Farrakhan leads a "Million Man March" in Washington, D.C.; 400,000 men gather and pledge greater social and family responsibility.
- In his last day in office, the governor of Kentucky pardons nine women for killing men who abused them; the women made a quilt that "moved the governor to tears."
- Kurt Cobain's blood-stained guitar sells for $17,000.
- John F. Kennedy, Jr. edits a new magazine, *George;* he appears frequently with Carolyn Bessette.
- Nearly 180 years since her death, Jane Austen gains new popularity through major motion pictures *Persuasion, Emma, Sense and Sensibility,* and *Clueless.*
- The "Unabomber" threatens to blow up an airplane if his manifesto is not published by a major newspaper; the *New York Times* and *Washington Post* comply; the author writes: "[Science] will conquer famine, eliminate psychological suffering, make everybody healthy and happy. . . . Yeah, sure."
- The FBI reports another sharp decline in crime rates.
- Bill Clinton's approval ratings surpass 50% for the first time.
- Worldwide attention focuses on British royalty: Prince Charles is overheard wishing he were his lover's garter, and Princess Diana admits to an affair with a former Life Guards officer James Hewitt, 37.

- A "Jenny Jones" TV guest is so distraught after being told of a male acquaintance's secret love that he kills him.
- Two of three polled oppose affirmative action; University of California regents vote to end racial considerations in hiring and admissions.
- About 55 percent of women provide half or more of household income.
- Connecticut and Utah require parenting courses for divorcing couples.
- The Centers for Disease Control report a leveling-off of teen sexual activity; 52.8 percent use condoms.
- Former singer Sonny Bono becomes a U.S. congressman.
- With the increase in lawsuits, tort reform becomes an issue.
- More than 560 die in a Chicago heatwave.
- Over 7 million people subscribe to on-line computer services, led by America Online, CompuServe, and Prodigy.
- New York becomes the 38th state to reinstate capital punishment.
- Ten hurricanes strike the Caribbean, Mexico, and Southeastern U.S.
- Coffee bars, like Starbucks, become fads, providing inexpensive, safe dating.
- The 50th anniversary of V-E Day is celebrated; controversy over Hiroshima also revives.
- For the first time, Ford sells more trucks than cars; demand for light trucks, like minivans and sports utility vehicles, increases in urban as well as rural areas.
- The export of farm products hits record heights: $54 billion (1981, a record $43.8), with Asian countries the primary markets.
- Hollywood's most expensive film, *Waterworld* ($200 million), with Kevin Costner, fails.
- Research shows that three ounces of salmon a week reduces risk of fatal heart arrhythmias by 50 percent; vitamin E reduces heart disease; and folic acid deficiency increases it.
- Researchers postulate that Emotional Intelligence (EQ) predicts success better than IQ.
- Mexican-American singer Selena, 23, is murdered by a fan club leader.
- "Yes! I know it's hard to believe," says Lisa Marie Jackson, affirming that she and Michael do "the thing."
- John Travolta's *Saturday Night Fever* polyester suit sells for $145,000.

Fads: Vietnamese, Thai, and Malaysian cuisines, shag haircut (Jennifer Aniston), netmania, rock climbing, foam dancing, "squeak-chic" (satin disco clothes), clingy T-shirts, purple, brown, and black nail polish, digital cafés, Melatonin (for sleep), pickup trucks, rock and roll memorabilia

First Appearances: blue M&Ms, reunion of Ringo and Paul, custom-made coffins (e.g., in shape of Mercedes Benz), female pilot of NASA spaceship (Eileen Collins, 38), Tagamet HB, Pepcid AC, postage stamps featuring comic strip figures, Java (computer language).

1996

Robert Dole. After nearly 30 years in the Senate, the WWII war hero resigns to spend his full time on the presidential campaign. *Institute for Public Service and Public Policy. University of Kansas.*

Facts and Figures

Economic Profile
  Dow-Jones: ↑ High 6,500–Low 5,200
  GNP: +4.4%
  Inflation: +3.3%
  Unemployment: 5.4%
Male/female ratio: 128/134
High school graduates entering college: 37%
Four-year colleges: 2,215
Public/private school: 7/1
Shirt pocket micro voice disguiser: $39.95
Money lab counterfeit detector: $59.95
Armani rainproof overcoat of Loro Piana cashmere-like fabric: $3,000–$3,500
Super Saxon merino wool sports coat: $8,500
Nautica nylon parka with fur collar: $780
Justin leather cowboy boots: $200
Buffalo Clips cowboy boots: $625
Joseph Abboud loafers (as worn by Bryant Gumbel): $200–$250
Levi-Strauss, Slates dress pants: $80
Guess, wide-leg "Bang" jeans: $68
Mercedes C320: $42,000
Cadillac Catera: $30,000
Ford Taurus: $19,000
Chevrolet Cavalier: $13,000
Saturn: $12,000

Deaths

George Balanchine, Erma Bombeck, Ella Fitzgerald, Greer Garson, Alger Hiss, Gene Kelly, Dorothy Lamour, Timothy Leary, Marcello Mastroianni, Carl Sagan

In the News

GOP AGREES TO STOPGAP SPENDING, ENDING 21-DAY GOVERNMENT SHUTDOWN . . . IRA CLAIMS LONDON BOMBING, ENDING 18-MONTH CEASEFIRE . . . SUICIDE BOMBINGS IN TEL AVIV KILL 27 . . . GEORGE BURNS DIES AT 100 . . . LONE GUNMAN IN SCOTLAND MURDERS 16 CHILDREN . . . ERIK AND LYLE MENENDEZ ARE CONVICTED OF PARENTS' MURDERS IN SECOND TRIAL . . . CHINESE MENACE TAIWANESE, U.S. SENDS WARSHIPS . . . COMMERCE SEC. RON BROWN AND 35 OTHERS DIE IN PLANE CRASH IN CROATIA . . . HARVARD GRADUATE, ONE-TIME BERKELEY MATH PROFESSOR TED KACZYNSKI IS ARRESTED AS "UNABOMBER" IN MONTANA SHACK . . . CLINTON VETOES BAN ON LATE-TERM ABORTION . . . FBI REPORTS SERIOUS CRIMES DECLINE FOR 4TH CONSECUTIVE YEAR . . . RUSSIA AND CHECHNYA SIGN PEACE AGREEMENT . . . CONSERVATIVE "BIBI" NETANYAHU WINS ISRAELI ELECTION . . . TWA FLIGHT 800 CRASHES INTO ATLANTIC SHORTLY AFTER TAKEOFF, 230 ARE KILLED, CAUSE IS UNKNOWN . . . PIPE BOMB AT ATLANTA OLYMPICS KILLS 1, INJURES MANY . . . UNEMPLOYMENT FALLS TO LOWEST IN 6 YEARS . . . GOP NOMINATES ROBERT DOLE AND JACK KEMP . . . CLINTON SIGNS BILL "ENDING WELFARE AS WE KNOW IT" . . . ROSS PEROT IS NOMINATED FOR PRESIDENT . . . MILITANT ISLAMIC GROUP, TALIBAN, GAINS CONTROL IN AFGHANISTAN . . . DOW TOPS 6,000 FOR FIRST TIME, UP NEARLY 100% IN 4 YEARS . . . CLINTON WINS PRESIDENCY WITH 49%, FIRST DEMOCRAT REELECTED SINCE FDR, GOP RETAINS CONGRESS . . . 500,000 HUTU REFUGEES BEGIN RETURN TO RWANDA . . . MADELEINE ALBRIGHT BECOMES FIRST WOMAN SEC. OF STATE . . . TUPAC AMARU GUERRILLAS SEIZE JAPANESE EMBASSY IN PERU.

Quotes _____

"After spending a year in Washington, I long for the realism and sensitivity of Hollywood."
—Former actor Sen. Fred Thompson (R–Tenn.)

"You remember the New Deal? This is the Raw Deal."
—FBI employee, working without pay during partial government shutdown

"We're the new liberals of the Republican party. Can you imagine that?"
—Barry Goldwater, (conservative) GOP candidate, 1964

"I was with some Vietnamese recently, and some of them were smoking two cigarettes at the same time. That's the kind of customers we need. Well, not exactly."
—Sen. Jesse Helms (R–N.C.), promoting North Carolina tobacco

"Where the water meets the sky, it was just fire."
—Observer of the TWA Flight 800 crash

"I was trying to do that new Democratic dance, the Macarena. I'm not going to try that anymore."
—Bob Dole, after his fall from a California platform during the campaign

Many believe that Treasury Secretary Robert Rubin's financial skills prevented a U.S. default when Congress refused stop-gap government funding. *U.S. Department of Treasury.*

"Always leave an inch of snow so it looks nice and white. Esthetics are very important in snow removal."
—Martha Stewart, "the voice of good taste"

"His favorite Scripture verse was . . . from Isaiah. 'They who wait upon the Lord shall have their strength renewed. They shall mount up with wings as eagles. They will run and not grow weary. They will walk and faint not.' Well, Ron Brown walked and ran and flew through life."
—Bill Clinton's eulogy for Commerce Secretary Brown

Ads _____

When you give the gift of love, make sure it's wrapped properly.
(Minnesota Aids Project for Condoms)

Cigarette companies should have been sponsoring hospitals, not sporting events.
(California Department of Health Services)

I'm so glad she saved herself for her wedding night.
(Hanna Dee, Acting School)

Oprah Winfrey's sensitivity, intelligence, and breadth of interest have made her talk show the highest-rated talk show in television history since its syndication in 1986, during which time she has become one of our most admired icons of talent and civility. *Victor Skrebneski.*

Courts can be hard. Get a good defense.
(Nike)

Tiptoe through the Tetons.
(Timberland [Shoe] Co.)

French mustard is a lot like French romance. The more variations you try, the better it is.
(Grey Poupon)

Something's wrong when a person gets in more trouble for violating laws than violating their child.
(National Council of Child Abuse and Family Violence)

Sandra Bullock rises swiftly to top box-office stardom. *New Line Cinema.*

TV

Premieres

"Rosie O'Donnell," talk show
"Moesha," Brandy Norwood
"Spin City," Michael J. Fox, Barry Bostwick
"Profiler," Ally Walker, Robert Davi
"The Cosby Show," Bill Cosby
"Millennium," Megan Gallagher, Lance Henrikson
"Suddenly Susan," Brooke Shields, Swoosie Kurtz
"Third Rock from the Sun," John Lithgow, Jane Curtin

Top Ten (Nielsen)

"E.R.," "Seinfeld," "Suddenly Susan," "Friends," "The Single Guy," "NFL Monday Night Football," "20/20," "Cosby," "Walker, Texas Ranger," "Home Improvement"

Specials

"Lena Horne"; "Marilyn Monroe: The Mortal Goddess"; "About Us: The Dignity of Children"; "Intimate Portrait: Bette Davis"; "America Undercover: Without Pity" (Christopher Reeve); *National Geographic*'s "Inside the White House"; "Odyssey of Life—A Nova Special"; "Truman," Gary Sinise; "Secrets of the Internet"; "Destination Mars"; "The Private Life of Plants"; "Andersonville"

Emmy Awards

"E.R." (drama); "Frasier" (comedy); Dennis Franz (actor, "NYPD Blue"); Kathy Baker (actress, "Picket Fences"); John Lithgow (comedic actor, "Third Rock from the Sun)"; Helen Hunt (comedic actress, "Mad about You"); "Rasputin" and "Gulliver's Travels" (miniseries or special)

Of Note

David Brinkley resigns as head of ABC's "This Week" • A record audience watches Hurricane Bertha and the Blizzard of '96 • Oprah Winfrey establishes a monthly segment called "Oprah's Book Club" and invites, for example, Toni Morrison to chat about her *Song of Solomon* • The government establishes a TV rating system for parents to monitor children's viewing • Jim Lehrer presides over the presidential candidate debates • Sharp TV criticism focuses on the theatricalism of the presidential campaigns and on NBC's summer Olympic coverage that "catered" to women • Cable TV takes an increasingly large audience from regular networks; it commands a 41 percent share of prime time audiences • The Administration ensures that the FCC will air at least three hours of educational TV for children each week.

Movies

The English Patient (Anthony Minghella), Kristin Scott Thomas, Ralph Fiennes
Fargo (Joel Coen), Frances McDormand, William H. Macy
Shine (Scott Hicks), Geoffrey Rush, Armin Mueller-Stahl, Noah Taylor
Jerry Maguire (Cameron Crowe), Tom Cruise, Cuba Gooding, Jr.
Secrets and Lies (Mike Leigh), Brenda Blethyn, Marianne Jean-Baptiste
Sling Blade (Billy Bob Thornton, director and writer), Thornton
Evita (Allan Parker), Madonna, Antonio Banderas, Jonathan Pryce
Breaking the Waves (Lars von Trier), Emily Watson, Stellan Skarsgård
Independence Day (Roland Emmerich), Will Smith, Jeff Goldblum
Marvin's Room (Jerry Zaks), Meryl Streep, Diane Keaton, Robert De Niro
The Nutty Professor (John Shadyac), Eddie Murphy
Hamlet (Kenneth Branagh), Branagh, Derek Jacobi, Julie Christie
Courage Under Fire (Edward Zwick), Denzel Washington, Meg Ryan
Mission Impossible (Brian De Palma), Tom Cruise, Jon Voight, Vanessa Redgrave

The First Wives Club (Hugh Wilson), Bette Midler, Goldie Hawn, Diane Keaton
101 Dalmatians (Stephen Herek), Glenn Close, Joely Richardson, Jeff Daniels
Scream (Wes Craven), Drew Barrymore, David Arquette
Michael Collins (Neil Jordan), Liam Neeson, Julia Roberts

Academy Awards

Best film: *The English Patient*
Best actor: Geoffrey Rush, *Shine*
Best actress: Frances McDormand, *Fargo*
Best director: Anthony Minghella, *The English Patient*

Top Box-Office Stars

Tom Cruise, Mel Gibson, John Travolta, Arnold Schwarzenegger, Sandra Bullock, Robin Williams, Sean Connery, Harrison Ford, Kevin Costner, Michelle Pfeiffer

Stars of the Future

Liv Tyler, Matthew McConaughey, Ray Romano, Edward Norton, Renee Zellweger, Melissa Joan Hart, Gwyneth Paltrow, Juliette Binoche, Mira Sorvino, Robert Burns

Popular Music ───────────────────────────

Hit Songs
"Macarena"
"The Crossroads"
"Twisted"
"Give Me One Reason"
"Sittin' Up in My Room"
"Count on Me"

Top Records

Albums: *The Score* (The Fugees);
Fresh Horses (Garth Brooks);
Tragic Kingdom (No Doubt);
Waiting to Exhale (Soundtrack);
New Adventures in Hi-Fi (R.E.M.);
Secrets (Toni Braxton); *New
Beginning* (Tracy Chapman)

Singles: *Because You Loved Me*
(Celine Dion); *Ironic* (Alanis
Morissette); *The Different Class*
(Pulp); *Hey Lover* (LL Cool J);

Exhale (Whitney Houston); *Fugees*
(Fugees). Country: *Time Marches
On* (Tracy Lawrence), *Blue Clear
Sky* (George Strait)

Grammy Awards
Change the World, Eric Clapton
(record); *Falling into You,* Celine
(album); "Change the World," Eric
Clapton (song). Hillary Rodham
Clinton wins a Grammy for the
best spoken-word album *It Takes a
Village.*

Jazz and Big Bands
During the Miles Davis revival,
*Miles Davis and Gil Evans: The
Complete Columbia Studio
Recordings* (6 CDs) is released.
Among the top jazz recordings are
Ornette Coleman's *Sound Museum,*
John Zom's *Masada Six,* Cassandra

Wilson's *New Moon Daughter,*
Charles Mingus's *Charles Mingus
and Friends in Concert,* Leon
Parker's *Belief,* Kenny Garrett's
Pursuance, Joe Lovano's *Quartets,*
Jerry Gonzalez and the Ford
Apache Band's *Fire Dance,* and
Joshua Redman's *Freedom in the
Groove.*

Top Performers (Downbeat):
Joe Lovano (soloist); Count Basie
(big band); Charlie Haden/Quartet
West (acoustic jazz group); Pat
Metheny (electric jazz group);
Tom Harrell, Jimmy Smith, Steve
Swallow, Eddie Daniels (instru-
mentalists); Horace Silver (Hall of
Fame); Cassandra Wilson, Mark
Murphy (vocalists); Joe Lovano,
Live at the Village Vanguard
(album)

Theater ───────────────────────────

Broadway Openings

Plays
Skylight (David Hare), Michael Gambon, Lia Williams
Seven Guitars (August Wilson), Keith David, Viola
    Davis
Taking Sides (Ronald Harwood), Daniel Massey, Ed
    Harris, Elizabeth Marvel

Musicals
Bring in 'Da Noise, Bring in 'Da Funk (George C.
    Wolfe, Savion Glover), Glover (also choreographer),
    Vincent Bingham
Rent (Jonathan Larson), Adam Pascal, Daphne Rubin-
    Vega, Idina Menzel, Anthony Rapp
Chicago (John Kander, Fred Ebb), Ann Reinking, Bebe
    Neuwirth, James Naughton, Joel Grey
A Funny Thing Happened on the Way to the Forum
    (Stephen Sondheim), Nathan Lane, Mark Linn-
    Baker, Lewis J. Stadlen
The King and I (Richard Rodgers, Oscar Hammerstein),
    Lou Diamond Phillips, Donna Murphy

Classics, Revivals, and Off-Broadway
Premieres
Gate Theater, Dublin, Lincoln Center Festival: All of
Samuel Beckett's stage works. BAM: *The Beatification
of Area Boy* (Wole Soyinka); *Antigone. Hughie* (Eugene

O'Neill), Al Pacino; *Molly Sweeney* (Brian Friel),
Jason Robards, Catherine Byrne; *A Delicate Balance,*
Rosemary Harris, George Grizzard, Elaine Stritch;
Present Laughter and *The Father,* Frank Langella;
Summer and Smoke, Harry Hamlin, Mary McDonnell;
Kingdom on Earth (Tennessee Williams); *The Waste
Land* (recitation, Fiona Shaw); *Inherit the Wind,* George
C. Scott; *Full Gallop* (Mary Louise Wilson); *An Ideal
Husband* (Oscar Wilde); *When Pigs Fly* (Howard
Crabtree)

Regional

Mark Taper Forum, Los Angeles: *Psychopathia
Sexualis* (John Patrick Shanley)

Goodman Theatre, Chicago: *A Touch of the Poet,*
Brian Dennehy, Jenny Bacon, Chris O'Neill

Alley Theatre, Houston: *Antony and Cleopatra,*
Vanessa Redgrave

Pulitzer Prize
Rent, Jonathan Larson

Tony Awards
Master Class, Terrence McNally (play); *Rent,* Jonathan
Larson (musical)

Classical Music _____

Compositions
Wynton Marsalis, *Blood on the Fields*
John Adams, *Gnarly Buttons, Music from Ceiling/Sky*
Aaron Kernis, Concerto for Violin, Guitar, and
Orchestra
Richard Danielpour, Concerto for Orchestra

Important Events
The new, multidisciplinary Lincoln Center Festival
features international ensembles and 200 performances
of 64 programs over three weeks, including 11 world
premieres and three U.S. premieres. The Pittsburgh
celebrates its centenary with an extensive U.S. tour.
Birthday celebrations include those of Yehudi Menuhin,
Virgil Thomson, Milton Babbitt, Steve Reich, and Lou
Harrison. Valery Gergiev leads the Kirov Orchestra in
official Soviet music by Shostakovich and Prokofiev.
Claudio Abbado leads the Berlin Philharmonic in four
Brahms concerts; a tribute to Fyodor Chaliapin includes
stars like Irina Arkhipova and Sergei Murzayev;
celebration of the New York Philharmonic includes
the premiere of Richard Danielpour's *Toward the
Splendid City*.

Major Recitals: Yo-Yo Ma's Philadelphia "All-American
Cello" concert, with recent work by Danielpour, Kirchner,
and Rouse; Sarah Chang's *Symphonie espagnole* (Lalo);
Vaughan Williams's *Job;* the charismatic Soviet Yuri
Bashmet's Schnittke's Viola Concerto; Yefim Bronfman
begins a series of concerts devoted to Schumann and
Prokofiev, with Isaac Stern, Lynn Harrell, Joshua Bell,
Barbara Hendricks, and Lawrence Dutton.

First Performances
Philip Glass, Cello Concerto (Pittsburgh); Ellen Taaffe
Zwilich, Triple Concerto (Minneapolis); David
Diamond, *Night Thoughts for Small Orchestra* (New
York); William Bolcom, Lyric Concerto and Three
Concertos for Left Hand (New York, Baltimore); John
Corigliano, String Quartet (Cleveland); George Perle,
Transcendental Meditations (New York); John Williams,
Concert for Trumpet (Cleveland); Peter Lieberson, *Fire*
(New York); Stanislaw Skrowaczewski, *Passacaglia
immaginaria* (Minneapolis)

Opera

Metropolitan: A seven-hour tribute to James Levine for
25 years with the company includes stars from 1,500
performances—from the younger Bryn Terfel, Roberto
Alagna, and Angela Gheorghiu to the seasoned Plácido
Domingo, Samuel Ramey, Kiri Te Kanawa, and retired
Carlo Bergonzi and Birgit Nilsson. Cecilia Bartoli (Met
debut), Carol Vaness, Jerry Hadley, *Così fan tutti;* Jane

Yo-Yo Ma, acclaimed
the greatest cellist of
this generation, whose
work extends from Bach
and contemporary
composers to jazz,
country, and the tango.
Timothy White. Sony.

Eaglen, Stanford Olsen, Thomas Hampson, *Don
Giovanni;* Bernd Weike, Catherine Malfitano, *Salome;*
Mirella Freni, Domingo, *Fedora;* Raúl Giménez (debut),
Ruth Ann Swenson, *Barber of Seville;* Sharon Sweet,
Domingo, Vladimir Chernov, *La forza del destino*

New York City: New manager-director Paul Kellogg
provokes controversy with *The Dreyfus Affair*

Los Angeles: Domingo, Veronica Villarroel, *Pagliacci;*
Sally Wolf (debut), *Norma*

St. Louis: Kristine Jepson, Horton Murray, *La clemenza
di Tito*

Chicago: *The Ring;* Eugene Grunewald (debut), *Il
tabarro;* Joyce Castle, *Suor Angelica*

Santa Fe: *Emmeline* (premiere, Tobias Picker); Bartoli,
Cenerentola

Arizona: first *Ring* cycle

Music Notes
Plácido Domingo becomes artistic director of the
Washington Opera • Completing their seasons becomes
a major concern for most orchestras, deeply affected by
NEA cuts • Carreras, Domingo, and Pavarotti travel
internationally with their three tenors concert • Three
sopranos organize their own concert: Kallen Esperian,
Cynthia Lawrence, and Kathleen Cassello • Many call
Ives's *Universe* symphony at the Microtonal festival at
Lincoln Center the year's highlight • In new
programming efforts, Kurt Mazur leads individual
concerts of composers like Ulysses Kay, Morton Gould,
Duke Ellington, and gospel singing • The onstage death
of tenor Richard Versalle occurs during the Met's *The
Makropulos Case* • Simone Young is the first woman to
conduct at the Met since Sarah Caldwell • Harvard
acquires the Haverlin/BMI collection of 16th-century
music, including Bach's Cantata no. 2 • The Library of
Congress releases unheard performances of over 60
artists like Rudolf Serkin and the Juilliard String
Quartet.

Art _____

Painting

Jim Dine, *Untitled [from Some Greeks, Some Romans], 1992–96*

Agnes Martin, *Untitled #13, 1996*

Larry Poons, *From Life's Other Side*

Leon Golub, *Breach II*

Jason Rhoades, *Uno Momento*

Sculpture

Louise Bourgeois, *Spiders (202–347–2211, Baumgartner Galleries)*

Richard Serra, *58 x 64 x 70, 1996*

Dan Flavin, *Untitled 1996*

Peter Fischil, David Weiss, *Empty Room*

Michael Helzer, *Negative Line*

Architecture

Main Public Library, San Francisco (James Ingo Freed)

Getty Center, Los Angeles (Richard Meier, first division of multi-section institution, $1 billion)

Skirball Cultural Center, Los Angeles (Moishe Safdie)

Memorial Hall restoration, Harvard University, Cambridge (Venturi, Scott, Brown)

Important Exhibitions

Traveling shows include "Possessing the Past: Treasures from the National Palace Museum, Taipei"; "Michelangelo and His Influence: Drawings from Windsor Castle"; Splendors of imperial China; Hermitage works removed from Germany during World War II; Charles Rennie Mackintosh; Winslow Homer; Corot, 1796–1875

Museums

New York: *Metropolitan:* Opening of the Egyptian Amarna and Post-Amarna gallery; "Japan's Golden Age: Momoyama"; Toulouse-Lautrec; Munch; Fabergé; "Bare Witness: Clothing and Nudity"; "Klee in Munich"; Poussin (collection of Queen Elizabeth II); "Queen Nefertiti and the Royal Women: Images of Beauty from Ancient Egypt." *Museum of Modern Art:* "Picasso and Portraiture"; Jasper Johns retrospective; Antonin Artaud; Photomontages of Hannah Höch; Roy DeCarava. *Guggenheim:* Ellsworth Kelly retrospective; "Abstraction in the Twentieth Century"; "Africa: The Art of a Continent"; "Max Beckmann in Exile." *Whitney:*

"City of Ambition: Artists and New York, 1900–1950"; Nan Goldin; "Views from Abroad, European Perspectives on American Art." *Asia Society:* "Worlds within Worlds: The Richard Rosenblum Collection of Chinese Scholars' Rocks."

Chicago: "Degas: Beyond Impressionism"; "French and British Paintings from 1600–1800"; Monet retrospective; Annette Messager

Philadelphia: Cézanne

Boston: Ancient Egyptian, Nubian, and Near Eastern Art

Washington, D.C. (National): Vermeer; "Degas as a Collector"

Atlanta, coinciding with Olympics: "Rings"; "Five Passions in World Art—7,500 Years of Civilization"

Art Briefs

National competitions continue for the design of a World War II veterans' memorial for Washington, D.C. • A number of SoHo Galleries in N.Y.C. move to Chelsea, with lower rents and more space • Women artists drawing particular attention include Nan Goldin, Jessica Stockholder, Nicole Eisenman, Diana Thater, and Ellen Gallagher • Christian de Portzamparc begins his first U.S. building, for Louis Vuitton • Dutch Rem Koolhaas also begins his first American construction, for Universal City, L.A. • Walt Disney Co. becomes the world's largest patron of architecture • In a record sale for Asian art, a 17th-century ceramic Korean dragon jar brings $8.6 million.

Dance _____

Lincoln Kirstein's death initiates numerous tributes. Ulysses Dove, 49, dies a week before the AIDS benefit "For the Love of Love."

American Ballet Theatre: Susan Jaffe, Jose Manuel Carreño, *The Sleeping Beauty* and *Apollo;* Julie Kent, *The Leaves Are Fading* (Tudor); Paloma Herrera, Wes Chapman, Amanda McKerrow, *Ballet Imperial* (Balanchine); Vladimir Malakov, Kent, *Swan Lake;* all-Tharp evening

New York City Ballet: Ethan Stiefel (debut), Miranda Weese, Tchaikovsky suite no. 3 (Balanchine); talented newcomers include Maria Kowroski and Weese.

Radio City Music Hall: *Riverdance*

Austin, Berkeley, Los Angeles: *Nur Du* (Pina Bausch)

Plácido Domingo. *Winnie Klotz. Metropolitan Opera.*

Books

Fiction

Critics' Choice

On with the Story, John Barth
Infinite Jest, David Foster Wallace
Reservation Blues, Sherman Alexie
We Were the Mulvaneys, Joyce Carol Oates
Unlocking the Air and Other Stories, Ursula K. LeGuin
The Flaming Corsage, William Kennedy
John's Wife, Robert Coover
The Manikin, Joanna Scott
Flying Home and Other Stories, Ralph Ellison (posthumous)
🐾 *The Moor's Last Sigh,* Salman Rushdie

Best-Sellers

The Celestine Prophecy, James Redfield
Primary Colors, Anonymous
The Horse Whisperer, Nicholas Evans
The Tenth Insight, James Redfield
The Runaway Jury, John Grisham
How Stella Got Her Groove Back, Terry McMillan
Executive Orders, Tom Clancy
Absolute Power, David Baldacci
Moonlight Becomes You, Mary Higgins Clark
Gods and Generals, Jeff Shaara

Nonfiction

Critics' Choice

Hitler's Willing Executioners: Ordinary Germans and the Holocaust, Daniel Jonah Goldhagen
An American Requiem: God, My Father, and the War That Came between Us, James Carroll
The Living and the Dead: Robert McNamara and Five Lives of a Lost War, Paul Hendrickson
At a Century's Ending: 1982–1995, George F. Kennan
Born to Rebel: Birth Order, Family Dynamics, and Creative Lives, Frank J. Sulloway
When Work Disappears: The World of the New Urban Poor, William Julius Wilson
This Wild Darkness: The Story of My Death, Harold Brodkey
The Temple Bombing, Melissa Faye Greene
Breaking the News: How the Media Undermine American Democracy, James Fallows
Founding Mothers and Fathers, Mary Beth Norton
Into the Wild, Jon Krakauer
The Forbidden Bestsellers of Pre-Revolutionary France, Robert Darnton

Best-Sellers

Men Are from Mars, Women Are from Venus, John Gray

The Zone, Bill Lawren
The Seven Spiritual Laws of Success, Deepak Chopra
Simple Abundance, Sarah Ban Breathnach
Emotional Intelligence, Daniel Goleman
Midnight in the Garden of Good and Evil, John Berendt
Undaunted Courage, Stephen E. Ambrose
The Dilbert Principle, Scott Adams
Rush Limbaugh Is a Big Fat Idiot, Al Franken

Poetry

Robert Pinsky, *The Figured Wheel*
Laurie Sheck, *The Willow Grove*
George Bradley, *The Fire Fetched Down*
Robert Fagles (trans.), *The Odyssey*
Hayden Carruth, *Scrambled Eggs and Whiskey*
Robert Hass, *Sun under Wood*

Pulitzer Prizes

Martin Dressler: The Tale of an American Dreamer, Steven Millhauser (fiction)
Original Meanings: Politics and Ideas in the Making of the Constitution, Jack N. Rakove (U.S. history)
Ashes to Ashes, Richard Kluger (nonfiction)
Angela's Ashes: A Memoir, Frank McCourt (biography)
Alive Together: New and Selected Poems, Lisel Mueller (poetry)

Science and Technology

A 4.5-pound meteorite 4–5 billion years old suggests evidence of bacterialike life on Mars.

The earth's inner core is mapped, a 1,500-mile wide solid rock sphere surrounded by an outer core of churning liquid iron 1,300 miles thick.

A combination of drugs can eliminate the HIV virus from the blood, but not from the body.

Aricept is found helpful to some Alzheimer's sufferers.

Biaxin, for treatment of *Heliobacter pylori,* an ulcer cause, is approved.

Dexfenfluramine (Redux) is approved as a diet pill.

Research increases on cross-species transplants (xenografts or xenotransplants) with baboon and pig brain tissue.

A new procedure for benign prostatic hyperplasia, transurethral needle ablation, reduces the prostate with fewer side effects.

Scientists discover that sperm stem cells can be frozen, stored indefinitely, and transplanted into the testes of another animal.

Nobel Prizes

Robert F. Curl, Jr., and Richard E. Smalley in chemistry for their discovery of "buckeyballs," carbon molecules shaped like geodesic spheres; David M. Lee, Douglas D. Osheroff, and Robert C. Richardson in physics for their discovery of superfluidity in helium-3.

Sports

Baseball
In the "Year of the Homer," 17 players hit over 40 HRs, 40 over 30, and 2, Brady Anderson and Mark McGwire, over 50.

Baltimore hits 257 and is 1 of 3 to break the 1961 Yankees' record of 240.

Roberto Alomar spits in umpire John Hirshbeck's face but his suspension is delayed until next season.

The Cy Young awards go to John Smoltz (Atlanta, AL) and Pat Hentgen (Toronto, AL).

Champions

Batting	Charles Nagy (Cleveland), AL,
Tony Gwynn (San Diego, NL), .357	17–5
Juan Gonzales (Texas, AL), .358	*Home runs*
Pitching	Mark McGwire (Oakland, AL),
John Smoltz (Atlanta, NL), 24–8	52

Football
Bret Favre (Green Bay) throws for a record 39 TDs.

NFC Season Leaders: Steve Young (San Francisco), passing; Barry Sanders (Detroit), rushing; Jerry Rice (San Francisco), receiving

AFC Season Leaders: John Elway (Denver), passing; Jerome Bettis (Pittsburgh), rushing; Carl Pickens (Cincinnati), receiving

College All-Americans: Peyton Manning (Q), Tennessee; Orlando Pace (OL), Ohio State

Bowls:
Rose: Ohio State 20–Arizona State 17
Orange: Nebraska 41–Virginia Tech 21
Sugar (Bowl Alliance): Florida 52–Florida St. 20
Cotton: Brigham Young 19–Kansas State 15

Basketball
NBA All-Pro First Team: Karl Malone (Utah), Scottie Pippen (Chicago), David Robinson (San Antonio), Michael Jordan (Chicago), Penny Hardaway (Orlando)

Olympics
At Atlanta, 197 countries compete. Michael Johnson wins the 200m and 400m, an Olympic first. Dan O'Brien wins the decathlon; Carl Lewis wins his 9th gold on the long jump. The U.S. wins its first team gold in gymnastics on injured Kerri Strug's last effort. Amy Van Dyken is the first American woman to win 4 gold in swimming. Beach volleyball is introduced.

Other Sports

Boxing: In a huge upset, 8–1 underdog Evander Holyfield TKOs Mike Tyson in the 11th for the HW title; Tyson gets $30 million, Holyfield $11 million.

Golf: Tiger Woods, 20, leaves Stanford, wins 2 majors; he elicits "Tigermania."

Horse Racing: Cigar ties Citation's 1950s record of 16 straight wins before losing to Dare and Go.

Winners

World Series	*MVP*
New York (AL) 4	Michael Jordan, Chicago
Atlanta (NL) 2	*College Basketball*
MVP	Kentucky
NL–Ken Caminiti, Houston	*Player of the Year*
AL–Juan Gonzales, Texas	Marcus Camby, Massachusetts
Super Bowl XXXI (Jan. 1997)	*Stanley Cup*
Green Bay 35–New England 21	Colorado
MVP	*U.S. Tennis Open*
Bret Favre, Green Bay	Men: Pete Sampras
College Football	Women: Steffi Graf
Florida	*USGA Open*
Heisman Trophy	Steve Jones
Danny Wuerfel, Florida	*Kentucky Derby*
NBA Championship	Grindstone (J. Bailey, jockey)
Chicago 4–Seattle 2	

Fashion

The "New Glamour" and classicism soften with less formal and more asymmetrical cuts—diagonals that lend a slight slouch to the look, dresses and shirts that pull off the shoulder and are held on with thin cloth straps. Chunky sweaters and baggy pants also return with skinny pants. European designers create a look of toughness and innocence by cutting traditional styles in these asymmetrical patterns, reviving high heels, and suggesting perhaps one long earring, to be worn with conventional jewelry (pearls and other chokers). Although black dresses remain "the look," they are worn with new "decadent" accessories, like pearls around the calf or upper arm. Some dresses are slashed at the arms or hem in a spiral and then held together with sheer chiffon squares or pieces of lace. Sonia Rykiel experiments with black tuxedo jackets belted with indigo denim and rhinestone-topped indigo jeans.

High-fashion notes: Ann Demeulemeester's slouchy gray suit; Sonia Rykiel's baby blue sweater with skinny pants and matching fake fur jacket.

Kaleidoscope

- Cancer mortality drops 3 percent, the first decline since the 1930s.
- In the presidential race, Dole emphasizes character and a tax cut; Clinton, the economy and education ("a bridge to the twenty-first century"); both court suburban "soccer moms."
- HMOs have 149 million subscribers (30 percent of Medicaid; 58 of Medicare).
- To prevent "drive-through" childbirth deliveries, 33 states require 48 hours of inpatient care.
- The nation is shocked when a dead newborn is left in a dumpster by two college freshmen.
- Fatal "mad cow" disease gains worldwide attention; England is forced to destroy over 1 million cows.
- Susan McDougal refuses Ken Starr's offer of immunity for testifying against the president; claiming pressure from Starr to lie, she receives 18 months for contempt.
- Newt Gingrich admits violating House ethics rules when he falsely claimed that his college course was apolitical.
- In her divorce settlement, Princess Di gains $26 million but loses the title "Royal Highness."
- Dick Morris, Clinton's presidential consultant, resigns after a tabloid exposé of his affair with a Washington, D.C., prostitute; she claims that he spoke to Clinton in her presence by phone and liked to nibble on her toes.
- The FBI publicly focuses on security guard Richard Jewell in the Olympics bombing but finally admits his innocence.
- The "Unabomber" is turned into the police by his brother, a social worker, who becomes suspicious after reading Kaczynski's 35,000-word manifesto.
- Joan Collins wins her case against Random House, which rejected her final manuscript, and is permitted to keep her $1.5 million advance.
- "MONTANA. AT LEAST THE COWS ARE SANE," reads a T-shirt sold in Montana stores during the year of the Unabomber and fanatical Montana Freemen.
- New York's crime rate, including murder, falls dramatically for the third straight year.
- A Hawaiian court rules that same-sex marriages cannot be constitutionally denied.
- Gorilla Binti-Jua saves a 3-year-old who falls into the gorilla pit; described as "people-oriented," Binti receives 1,000 letters a day.
- Kathy Lee Gifford comes under attack when her WalMart clothes are said to be made under sweatshop conditions.
- Globalization becomes a buzzword.
- Daniel Goldhagen's book claiming that "ordinary Germans" participated in the Holocaust is an international sensation.

Angela Lansbury. After 12 years, "Murder She Wrote" ends on prime time. *Movie Star News.*

- Critics of Olestra, the no-fat substitute, cite its potential intestinal effects.
- Jessica Dubroff, 7, the youngest air pilot, dies during a rainstorm near Cheyenne, Wyo.
- Carolyn Bessette, 30, marries John F. Kennedy, Jr., 36, "the world's sexiest man."
- Chicago Bulls star rebounder Dennis Rodman gains fame for his unusual hair colors, cross-dressing, body piercing (6), and tattoos (13); he wears a wedding dress while promoting his book.
- Jonathan Larson dies shortly before his hit rock-opera *Rent* opens; it retells the *La Bohème* story with poor East Village artists and AIDS.
- Oasis, a British rock quintet, arrives in the U.S. to high praise.
- Dubbed "the queen of nice," Rosie O'Donnell, 34, stars in a new TV daytime talk show; she earns $1 million a year.
- After a great deal of speculation, journalist Joe Klein, who covered the presidential campaign, admits he is the "Anonymous" author of the super-best-selling roman à clef *Primary Colors.*
- Madonna stars in *Evita* and gives birth to a daughter, Lourdes Maria, fathered by trainer-actor Carlos Leon.
- Quadriplegic "Superman" Christopher Reeve appears at the Oscars and Democratic Convention; he is also directing a film, among other activities.
- Rap star Tupac Shakur, 25, dies of gunshot wounds in Las Vegas; an East Coast–West Coast rappers' feud is suspected; his *Don Killuminati: The 7 Day Theory* sells a million copies in the next month.
- E-mail exceeds surface mail, and, for the first time, more money is spent on computers than TVs.
- Sotheby's auction of Jacqueline Kennedy Onassis's possessions brings $34.5 million, seven times the pre-sale estimate and includes JFK's rocking chair ($400,000), his golf clubs in their tattered bag ($772,500 from Arnold Schwarzenegger), and a $500 string of pearls ($211,000); the catalog sells record numbers.
- In *Bowling Alone,* Robert Putnam shows a national trend toward individual, rather than group, activity.
- A massive effort enables the recovery and reconstruction of TWA Flight 800's 747 from the ocean floor; no cause—bomb, missile, or mechanical failure—is clear.
- O. J. Simpson's civil trial for wrongful death begins late in the year; he wins custody of his children from Nicole's family.
- Michael Jackson marries L.A. nurse Debbie Rowe, 6 months pregnant.
- Seven people and their American guide are killed climbing Mt. Everest; guided climbs can cost $65,000.

Fads: female boxing, beefsteaks, martinis, cigars, conspiracy theories, macarena dance, Dilbertmania (comic strip and books), Tickle Me Elmo doll, Beavis and Butthead

First Appearances: laboratory-created antimatter, EVI (commercial electric car), web TV, home test for HIV, Arch Deluxe (McDonald's), Elph camera (Canon 420, fitting into the hand)

1997

Excitement and controversy swirl about the first cloned mammal, "Dolly."

Facts and Figures

Economic Profile
  Dow-Jones: ↑High 8,250–
    Low 6,300
  GNP: +6.2%
  Inflation: +2.5%
  Unemployment: 5.0%
Average salary: $28,200
Teacher: $38,100
Physician: $112,400
Factory worker: $31,600
New Year's Eve: N.Y.C.
  Le Cirque: $250/p.p.
  Daniel: $380/p.p.
  Lespinasse: $500/p.p.
Ultimate Vacations
  Weekend at Laguna Beach
    for 3 couples, with use of
    Mercedes SL600 roadster,
    champagne-caviar
    reception: $500,000
  Dinner party for 10,
    prepared by world chefs
    like Wolfgang Puck:
    $200,000
Lexus LX450 recreational
  vehicle: $49,999
Sports Authority rollerblades:
  $89.98–$349.99
Nash Hobie skateboard:
  $49.99

Michael Jordan. *Nike.*

Deaths

Isaiah Berlin, Willem de
Kooning, John Denver,
Victor Frankl, Allen
Ginsberg, Ben Hogan, Roy
Lichtenstein, James
Michener, Robert Mitchum,
Sviatoslav Richter, James
Stewart

In the News

BILL COSBY'S SON, ENNIS, 27, IS MURDERED, TEENAGE RUSSIAN IMMIGRANT IS ARRESTED . . . CLINTON IS INAUGURATED FOR 2ND TERM . . . O. J. SIMPSON IS FOUND LIABLE IN WRONGFUL DEATH SUIT, DAMAGES OF $33.5 MILLION ARE AWARDED GOLDMAN AND BROWN FAMILIES . . . SCOTTISH SCIENTIST CLONES FIRST MAMMAL . . . DOW TOPS 7,000 . . . CHINESE LEADER DENG XIAOPING DIES AT 93 . . . RAPPER NOTORIOUS B.I.G. IS MURDERED IN L.A. . . . 39 HEAVEN'S GATE CULT MEMBERS COMMIT SUICIDE IN SAN DIEGO MANSION TO REACH SPACESHIP ON HALE-BOPP COMET . . . HOSTAGES IN JAPANESE EMBASSY IN LIMA ARE RESCUED BY ARMY, 71 ARE SAVED, 1 DIES . . . LIGGETT ADMITS CIGARETTES ARE ADDICTIVE . . . MOBUTU FLEES ZAIREAN CAPITAL, REBELS UNDER LAURENT KABILA TAKE CITY . . . TIMOTHY MCVEIGH IS CONVICTED IN OKLAHOMA BOMBING, SENTENCED TO DEATH . . . POL POT SURRENDERS IN CAMBODIA, IS TRIED AND SENTENCED TO LIFE . . . *SOJOURNER* VEHICLE ROAMS MARS, TAKES PHOTOS . . . SERIAL KILLER "GAY GIGOLO" KILLS DESIGNER GIANNI VERSACE IN MIAMI, LATER KILLS SELF . . . ELUDING PAPARAZZI, PRINCESS DI AND BOYFRIEND DODI FAYED ARE KILLED IN PARIS AUTO ACCIDENT, THE WORLD MOURNS DIANA . . . BROOKLYN POLICE ARE CHARGED WITH BRUTAL BEATING OF HAITIAN ABNER LOUIMA . . . TEAMSTERS LEAD LARGE UPS STRIKE, CLINTON AIDS SETTLEMENT . . . MOTHER TERESA, 87, DIES IN CALCUTTA . . . DOW GAINS RECORD 337 ON DAY AFTER RECORD 554 DROP . . . SEPTUPLETS ARE BORN TO IOWA COUPLE . . . CLINTON SENDS 2ND CARRIER TO GULF, WARNS HUSSEIN THAT WEAPONS INSPECTORS MUST BE ALLOWED FREE ACCESS . . . TERRY NICHOLS IS CONVICTED AS MCVEIGH CO-CONSPIRATOR.

Secretary of State Madeleine Albright, raised as a Catholic, learns that her Jewish family was killed in Auschwitz. *U.S. State Department.*

The Mars Sojourner approaches "Yogi." *NASA.*

Quotes

"I want him to admit what he did."
—Paula Jones, accusing the president of sexual misconduct

"I have no idea what she means by that. There is no mark I remember."
—Gennifer Flowers, on Paula Jones's description of the president's anatomy

"In terms of size, shape, direction . . . the President is a normal man."
—Attorney Bob Bennett, following Clinton's medical exam

"In the future your doctor may be a nurse."
—An observer, on how managed care is changing the health professions

"[She was] the very essence of compassion, of duty, of style, of beauty."
—Earl Spencer, in eulogy to his sister, Princess Diana

"I have a feeling there wasn't a bar of gold around Europe then which didn't have at least one golden tooth . . . of a Jewish victim."
—Avraham Brug, on accusations the Swiss served as Nazi bankers in WWII

"He's Moses to our people."
—Spokesperson, on Charlton Heston's election as NRA vice-president

"He was my hero."
—Bill Cosby, on murdered son, Ennis

"The Marlboro Man is riding off into the sunset on Joe Camel."
—Florida attorney general, on suit against the tobacco industry

"Yep, I'm gay."
—Ellen DeGeneres, as herself and TV's "Ellen"

Ads

If anyone doesn't believe me, ring my bell, and you can smell my toilet.
(Vanish)

Give Your Brain As Much Attention As You Do Your Hair and You'll Be A Thousand Times Better Off.
(Public Service Ad on New York buses)

Nuclear Weapons
May They Rust in Peace.
(Public Service Ad)

WE REMEMBER OUR CUSTOMERS
(Kansas Ryder Truck Co., which rented van to Timothy McVeigh)

Let your Father's Face
Be a Lesson to You.
(Remington Lektro Blade)

Take away their uniforms, and who are they?
(Jockey)

Each culture is a transformation of nature: nature being the raw and culture being the cooked.
(Claude Lévi-Strauss, *Continue* electronics)

Ask, and ye shall receive.
(E-valuations Research Web Site, www.questions.net)

TV

Premieres
"Nothing Sacred," Kevin Anderson
"Ally McBeal," Calista Flockhart
"The Practice," Dylan McDermott
"Buffy the Vampire Slayer," Sarah Michelle Gellar
"Veronica's Closet," Kirstie Alley
"King of the Hill," prime-time cartoon

Top Ten (Neilsen)
"E.R.," "Seinfeld," "Suddenly Susan," "Friends," "Naked Truth," "Fired Up," "Monday Night Football," "Single Guy," "Home Improvement," "Touched by an Angel"

Specials
"Bette Midler: Diva Las Vegas"; "Jack Paar: As I Was Saying . . . "; "Don King"; "George Wallace"; "Lewis and Clark" (Ken Burns); "Homer's *The Odyssey";* "Stephen Hawking's Universe"; *"Cinderella,"* Brandy Norwood; "Miss Evers' Boys," Alfre Woodard, Laurence Fishburne; "American Visions," Robert Hughes; *"Horton Foote's Alone,"* Hume Cronyn; "Gotti," Armand Assante; *Rebecca,* Diana Riggs

Jerry Seinfeld announces that this will be the last season for his show "about nothing," despite a $5 million per episode offer; yada-yada-yada. *Movie Star News.*

Emmy Awards
"Law and Order" (drama); Gillian Anderson (actress, drama, "The X-Files"); Dennis Franz (actor, drama, "NYPD Blue"); "Frasier" (comedy); Helen Hunt (actor, comedy, "Mad about You"); John Lithgow (actor, comedy, "3rd Rock from the Sun"); "Prime Suspect 5: Errors of Judgement" (drama or miniseries)

Of Note
HBO receives more Emmy award nominations than any other station • *60 Minutes* produces and does not air an interview with Bill Cosby after his son's murder. Producer Don Hewitt explains: "I don't want to be part of America's soap opera" • Candice Bergen's character on "Murphy Brown" generates controversy when she uses marijuana to lessen her discomfort after chemotherapy for breast cancer • The History Channel gains popularity.

Movies

Titanic (James Cameron), Leonardo DiCaprio, Kate Winslet, Gloria Stuart
As Good as It Gets (James Brooks), Jack Nicholson, Helen Hunt, Greg Kinnear
The Full Monty (Peter Cattaneo), Robert Carlyle, Tom Wilkinson
Good Will Hunting (Gus Van Sant), Matt Damon, Robin Williams, Minnie Driver
L.A. Confidential (Curtis Hanson), Kevin Spacey, Kim Basinger, Russell Crowe, Guy Pearce
The Sweet Hereafter (Atom Egoyan), Ian Holm, Sarah Polley
Men in Black (Barry Sonnenfeld), Tommy Lee Jones, Will Smith
Air Force One (Wolfgang Peterson), Harrison Ford, Gary Oldman
The Lost World: Jurassic Park (Steven Spielberg), Jeff Goldblum, Julianne Moore
The Apostle (Robert Duvall), Duvall
Ulee's Gold (Victor Nunez), Peter Fonda

Wag the Dog (Barry Levinson), Dustin Hoffman, Robert De Niro, Anne Heche
Boogie Nights (Paul Thomas Anderson), Julianne Moore, Mark Wahlberg, Burt Reynolds
Amistad (Steven Spielberg), Anthony Hopkins, Morgan Freeman, Djimon Hounson
Deconstructing Harry (Woody Allen), Allen
My Best Friend's Wedding (P. J. Hogan), Julia Roberts, Cameron Diaz
Liar, Liar (Tom Shadyac), Jim Carrey
George of the Jungle (Sam Weisman), Brendan Fraser

Academy Awards
Best Picture: *Titanic*
Best Director: James Cameron, *Titanic*
Best Actress: Helen Hunt, *As Good as It Gets*
Best Actor: Jack Nicholson, *As Good as It Gets*

Top Box-Office Stars
Harrison Ford, Julia Roberts, Leonardo DiCaprio, Will Smith, Tom Cruise, Jack Nicholson, Jim Carrey, John Travolta, Robin Williams, Tommy Lee Jones

Stars of the Future
Matt Damon, Ben Affleck, Minnie Driver, Gillian Anderson, Lucy Lawless, Claire Forlani, Rebecca Gayheart, Jerry O'Connell, Adrian Lester, Stacy Edwards

Julia Roberts, the only woman on the Top-Ten Box Office list. *Movie Star News.*

Popular Music —————————

Hit Songs
"I'll Be Missing You"
"Don't Speak"
"You Were Meant for Me"
"MMMBop"
"Don't Let Go"
"I Believe I Can Fly"

Top Records

Albums: *Tragic Kingdom* (No Doubt); *Falling into You* (Celine Dion); *Life after Death* (The Notorious B.I.G.); *Higher Ground* (Barbra Streisand); *Secrets* (Toni Braxton); *Butterfly* (Mariah Carey)

Singles: *Candle in the Wind '97* (Elton John); *How Do I Live* (LeAnn Rimes); *Men in Black* (Will Smith); *Wannabe* (Spice Girls); *Falling in Love (Is Hard on the Knees)* (Aerosmith). Country:

Toni Braxton. *Movie Star News.*

It's Your Love (Tim McGraw); *One Night at a Time* (George Strait)

Grammy Awards
Sunny Came Home, Shawn Colvin (record); *Time Out of Mind,* Bob Dylan (album); "Sunny Came Home," Shawn Colvin (song)

Jazz and Big Bands
Wynton Marsalis wins the first Pulitzer for a jazz work, a three-hour meditation on slavery, *Blood on the Fields.* A renaissance occurs in historical collections, such as Alan Lomax's 100-volume collection of U.S., West Indian, and European music. As music of the past grows in appeal, Sean ("Puffy") Combs creates new rhythms for old hits; Cassandra Wilson continues to transform old pop songs into new jazz forms. Highly successful are Lilith's (all female) and the Rolling Stones' tours; Ornette Coleman's series at Lincoln Center. Ani DiFranco's mixture of folk and new wave attracts numerous recording offers. Among the young, novelty prevails, so tastes and fads are short-lived.

Top Performers *(Downbeat)*:
Wynton Marsalis (soloist); B. B. King (blues singer); Charlie Mingus (big band); Pat Metheny (jazz electronic group); Wayne Shorter, Sonny Rollins, Herbie Hancock (instrumentalists); Nat "King" Cole (Hall of Fame); Mark Murphy, Cassandra Wilson (vocalists); Kenny Garrett, *Pursuance* (album)

Theater —————————

Broadway Openings

Plays
The Last Night of Ballyhoo (Alfred Uhry), Jessica Hecht, Celia Weston, Dana Ivey
Barrymore (William Luce), Christopher Plummer
Stanley (Pam Gems), Antony Sher
An American Daughter (Wendy Wasserstein), Kate Nelligan, Elizabeth Marvel
The Old Neighborhood (David Mamet), Peter Riegert, Patti LuPone

Musicals
The Life (Ira Gasman, Cy Coleman), Sam Harris, Pamela Isaacs
The Lion King (Tim Rice, Elton John), John Vickery, Samuel Wright (directed by Julie Taymor)
Titanic (Maury Yeston), John Cunningham, Brian d'Arcy
The Scarlet Pimpernel (Nan Knighton, Frank Wildhorn), Douglas Sills
Jekyll & Hyde (Leslie Bricusse, Frank Wildhorn), Robert Cuccioli, Linda Eder
1776 (Sherman Edwards), Brent Spiner, Pat Hingle

Classics, Revivals, and Off-Broadway Premieres
A Doll's House, Janet McTeer; *How I Learned to Drive* (Paula Vogel), Bruce Davison, Molly Ringwald;

Candide; The Gin Game, Julie Harris, Charles Durning; *The Little Foxes; All My Sons,* John Cullum; *Bermuda Avenue Triangle,* Renee Taylor; *Psychopathia Sexualis* (John Patrick Shanley); *The Plough and the Stars,* Pauline Flanagan; *Violet; The Hairy Ape,* William Dafoe; *Gross Indecency: The Three Trials of Oscar Wilde* (Moisés Kaufman); *A View from the Bridge,* Anthony La Paglia, Allison Janney; *Ivanov,* Kevin Kline; *The Diary of Anne Frank,* Natalie Portman, George Hearn, Linda Lavin; *Pride's Crossing* (Tina Howe), Cherry Jones; *Major Barbara; The Sunshine Boys,* Jack Klugman, Tony Randall; *Jackie: An American Life* (Gil Hoppe), Margaret Colin

Regional

Goodman Theatre, Chicago: *A Young Man From Atlanta* (Horton Foote), Rip Torn, Shirley Knight

A.R.T., Cambridge: *The Old Neighborhood* (David Mamet), Patti LuPone

Pulitzer Prize
No prize is awarded.

Tony Awards
The Last Night of Ballyhoo, Alfred Uhry (drama); *Titanic,* Maury Yeston (musical)

Classical Music ───────

Compositions
Aaron Jay Kernis, String Quartet no. 2
Yehudi Wyner, Horntrio
Francis Schwartz, *Flaming June*
Mickel Kuehn, *Music through Prisms*

Important Events
Musical anniversaries include those of Brahms, Mendelssohn, Schubert, and Donizetti. Superior reviews follow Daniel Barenboim's gala Carnegie Hall opening night: Yo-Yo Ma's Elgar's Cello Concerto, Barenboim's performance with Martha Argerich of the Mozart Concerto for Two Pianos; and the 20th-century programming of the L.A. Philharmonic and the San Francisco, which includes Ruggles, Antheil, Cage, Copland, and Conlon Nancarrow. Kurt Mazur conducts new "interesting failures," like *Psyché,* by César Franck (the myth of Cupid and Psyche, as told by Cherry Jones).

Notable Performances: Awadagin Pratt's Beethoven Piano Concerto no. 1, among others, gains him comparison with the greatest pianists of the century. Successful recitals include those of Sarah Chang, Maurizio Pollini, violinist Kyung-Wha Chung (an all-Beethoven program), and Vesselina Kasarova's first N.Y. performance. Classical guitarist David Leisner concertizes after a serious 1980s injury.

New Appointments: Marriss Jansons, Pittsburgh Symphony Orchestra; Valery Gergiev, principal guest conductor, Metropolitan Opera

First Performances
Wynton Marsalis, *Blood on the Fields* (New Haven); Sofia Gubaidulina, Violin Concerto (Chicago); Eliott Carter, *Allegro Scorrevole* (Cleveland). In New York: Tan Dun, *Symphony 1997* (celebrating Hong Kong's transfer to Chinese rule); Peter Lieberson, *Fire;* Sebastian Currier, *Microsymphony;* Sheila Silver, Piano Concerto; Henri Lazarof, Oboe Concerto. In Boston: Scarlatti, *L'Affetti di Scarlatti;* Leon Kirchner, *Of Things Exactly as They Are;* Bernardo Rands, Cello Concerto

Entrance facade to Getty Center, L.A., designed by Richard Meier. *Tom Bonner,* © J. Paul Getty Trust.

Vladimir Chernov.
Winnie Klotz.
Metropolitan Opera.

Opera

Metropolitan: The Pension Gala Fund includes highly acclaimed performances by Bryn Terfel and Neil Shicoff. Mirella Freni (farewell performance), Plácido Domingo, *Fedora;* Richard Leech, Samuel Ramey, Renée Fleming, *Faust;* Domingo, Deborah Voigt, James Macurdy, *Die Walküre;* Cecilia Bartoli (after numerous cancellations), Ramón Vargas, *Cenerentola* (Rossini); Denyce Graves, *Carmen;* Carol Vaness, Anne Sofie von Otter, Heidi Grant Murphy, *La clemenza di Tito*

New York City: Lorraine Hunt, David Daniels (debuts), *Xerxes;* Laura Tucker, Adam Klein, *Marco Polo* (Tan Dun); Joyce Castle, *The Visit of the Old Lady* (Gottfried von Einem)

Lincoln Center Festival: *Palestrino* (Hans Pfitzner, premiere)

Chicago: Thomas Young, Florence Quivar, Mark S. Doss, *Amistad* (Anthony Davis, premiere); Ben Heppner, Emily Magee, *Peter Grimes;* Richard Cowan (debut), *Don Giovanni;* Vesselina Kasarova, *Idomeneo;* Leech, Malfitano, *Madama Butterfly*

Houston: *Florencia en el Amazonas* (premiere, Daniel Catán)

Boston: Lisa Saffer, *L'elisir d'amore;* Dominique Labella, *Lucia di Lammermoor; Les Mamelles de Tirésias* (Poulenc)

San Francisco: Terfel, Sylvia McNair, *Le nozze di Figaro;* Richard Margison, *Tosca*

Music Notes
Leonard Bernstein's 7'4" Bösendorfer grand piano sells at auction for $350,000; his 1961 baton, $11,000; a silver-framed *West Side Story* recording, $3,829; and conducting suit, $1,725 • David Helfgott, whose long bouts with mental illness were captured in the film *Shine,* tours the U.S. to frequently unkind reviews • Leon Fleisher resigns as director of the Tanglewood Music Center after acrimonious dealings with Seiji Ozawa • San Francisco's War Memorial Opera House opens after elaborate refurbishing and recreates the 1932 *Tosca* that originally opened the house.

Art

Painting
Jeff Koons, *Pink Bow* (1995–97)
Claes Oldenburg, *Notebook Torn in Half*
Sam Gilliam, *Cartography*
Kyle Staver, *Breakfast*
Fred Tomaselli, *Birds*
Chuck Close, *Self-Portrait*
Kenny Scarf, *Dividala*

Sculpture
Mark di Suvero, *Inner Sculpture for Euler*
Richard Serra, *Torqued Ellipses*
Tom Otterness, *Trial Scene*
Truman Lowe, *Bird Effigy*

Architecture
Neurosciences Institute, La Jolla, Calif. (Tod Williams, Billie Tsien)
Chapel of St. Ignatius, Seattle (Steven Holl)
Monona Terrace Community and Convention Center, University of Wisconsin, Madison (designed by Frank Lloyd Wright in the 1930s and modified by his successors, Taliesin Associates)
Opening in Washington, D.C., and environs: The FDR Memorial (Lawrence Halprin); Women in Military Service to America Memorial (Marian Weiss, Michael Manfredi); National Airport passenger terminal (Cesar Pelli)
Japanese Yoshio Taniguchi is selected to double the size of MoMA.

Important Exhibitions
Touring the U.S. are "New Work in China Post-1989 [since Tiananmen Square]"; "Mistress of the House, Mistress of Heaven: Women in Ancient Egypt"; "Picasso: The Early Years, 1892–1902"; "Monet and the Mediterranean"; "Exiles and Émigrés: The Flight of European Artists from Hitler"; Diebenkorn; Bill Viola

Museums

New York: *Metropolitan:* "Following the Stars: The Zodiac in Islamic Art"; "The Glory of Byzantium"; "Cartier: 1900–1939"; "School of Paris: Schoenborn Bequest"; Indian court painting; Degas; "Venetian Prints and Books in the Age of Tiepolo." *Museum of Modern Art:* "After Artaud"; "De Kooning in the Eighties"; Hannah Höch; "Objects of Desire: The Modern Still-Life"; "On the Edge"; Franz West; "Sternberg Brothers: Constructing a Revolution in Soviet Design"; "From Henri de Toulouse-Lautrec to Andy Warhol"; "Paris—The 1890s." *Guggenheim:* "Rrose is a Rrose: The Nasher Sculpture Collection"; Rauschenberg; "Gender Performance." *Whitney:* The Biennial's eclectic mix includes Matthew Barney, Vija Celmins, D. J. Spooky, and Philip Lorca di Corcia

Houston: "Splendors of Ancient Greece"; "What Do You Think? An Exhibition Lab"

Boston: Opening of permanent Oceanic, African, and Ancient American galleries; Herb Ritts; "Tales from the Land of Dragons: 1,000 Years of Chinese Painting"

Chicago: Renoir's portraits, Ivan Albright

Los Angeles: Jeff Wall (first retrospective)

Philadelphia: Robert Capa

Art Briefs
Jane Alexander resigns from the NEA because of lack of federal support for the arts • After a 20-week show at the Corcoran, "Jewels of the Romanovs: Treasures of the Imperial Court" remains for two weeks in a moving van when Russian officials blockade the show • Friedrich St. Florian wins the competition to design the WWII memorial on the Mall in Washington between the Lincoln and Washington memorials • The 1990s tendency away from neoexpressionism is typified by a variety of new techniques, like oils covered with broken crockery and new endeavors to work in 3-D reality • Frank Gehry's Guggenheim Bilbao contains a "Boat Gallery" of outstanding American sculpture • David Ross, Whitney director, explains the current obsession with the body in art as a reaction to "the Zen slap" of the AIDS crisis • Important sales include *Madame Cézanne Seated in a Yellow Chair*, $23.1 million; Toulouse-Lautrec, *Seated Dancer in Pink Stockings*, $14.5 million (highest for his work); Kiki Smith, *Ree Body*, $233,500; and a Nootka mask, $525,000.

Dance

The Hartford Ballet receives $500,000 to create a Native American *Nutcracker*. Diana Vishnyeva and Vladimir Malakhov visit the U.S. with the Kirov.

American Ballet Theatre: Martha Butler, Ethan Stiefel, *Coppélia;* Nina Ananiashvili, Julie Kent, Jose Manuel Carreño, *Othello* (Lar Lubovitch)

New York City Ballet: Miranda Weese, Albert Evans, *Concerto in Five Movements* (Prokofiev, La Fosse); *Brandenburg* (Robbins)

Houston: Carlos Acosta, *Don Quixote;* Timothy O'Keefe, *Dracula* (Ben Stevenson)

Books

Fiction

Critics' Choice

Underworld, Don DeLillo
Bear and His Daughter: Stories, Robert Stone
The Puttermesser Papers, Cynthia Ozick
Mason and Dixon, Thomas Pynchon
Echo House, Ward Just
Dreams of My Russian Summers, Andrei Makine
The Actual, Saul Bellow

Best-Sellers

The Partner, John Grisham
Cold Mountain, Charles Frazier
The Ghost, Danielle Steele
The Ranch, Danielle Steele
Special Delivery, Danielle Steele
Unnatural Exposure, Patricia Cornwell
The Best Laid Plans, Sidney Sheldon
Pretend You Don't See Her, Mary Higgins Clark
Cat & Mouse, James Patterson
Hornet's Nest, Patricia Cornwell

Nonfiction

Critics' Choice

The Undertaking: Life Studies from the Dismal Trade, Thomas Lynch
American Sphinx: The Character of Thomas Jefferson, Joseph J. Ellis
Whittaker Chambers, Sam Tanenhaus
The Kidnapping of Edgardo Mortara, David Kertzer
Big Trouble, J. Anthony Lukas
How the Mind Works, Steven Pinker
American Scripture: Making the Declaration of Independence, Pauline Maier
Civic Ideals, Rogers M. Smith
The Bible as It Was, James L. Kugel
Ernie Pyle's War: America's Eyewitness to World War II, James Tobin
The Art of Shakespeare's Sonnets, Helen Vendler
❧ *The Sense of Reality,* Isaiah Berlin

Best-Sellers

Angela's Ashes: A Memoir, Frank McCourt
Simple Abundance, Sarah Ban Breathnach
Midnight in the Garden of Good and Evil, John Berendt
The Royals, Kitty Kelley
Joy of Cooking, Irma S. Rombauer, Marion Rombauer Becker, and Ethan Becker
Diana: Her True Story, Andrew Morton
Into Thin Air: A Personal Account of the Mt. Everest Disaster, Jon Krakauer
Conversations with God, Book 1, Neale Donald Walsch
Men Are from Mars, Women Are from Venus, John Gray
Eight Weeks to Optimum Health, Andrew Weil

Poetry

William Meredith, *Effort at Speech: New and Selected Poems*
C. K. Williams, *The Vigil*
Frank Bidart, *Desire*
Marilyn Nelson, *The Fields of Praise: New and Selected Poems*
Sarah Lindsay, *Primate Behavior*
Sonia Sanchez, *Does Your House Have Lions?*

Pulitzer Prizes

American Pastoral, Philip Roth (fiction)
Summer for the Gods: The Scopes Trial and America's Continuing Debate over Science and Religion, Edward J. Larson (U.S. history)
Guns, Germs, and Steel: The Fates of Human Societies, Jared Diamond (nonfiction)
Personal History, Katharine Graham (biography)
Black Zodiac, Charles Wright (poetry)

Science and Technology

Severe asthma, common in poor urban areas, is linked to cockroaches.

The first significant decline in AIDS deaths (23 percent) is attributed to new protease inhibitors.

The widely used and FDA-approved diet pill combination "fen-phen" is removed from the market after studies reveal that it causes heart valve disease.

Trans-fatty acids, common in margarine and other hardened vegetable oils, are found to be as harmful as animal fat; diets low in fat and rich in fruits and vegetables are found to lower blood pressure.

Galileo explores new moons 500 million miles from Mars, including Europa, Ganymede, and Callisto; Europa appears to have a beautiful unfrozen ocean beneath its icy surface and the possibility of primitive life.

The Pistol Star, viewed through the Hubble telescope's new infrared camera, is 100 times as massive and 15 times as brilliant as the sun.

The Hale-Bopp comet, with three tails, is the brightest and largest comet discovered since 1872.

❧ The first adult mammal clone is created when an adult sheep cell nucleus is substituted for an egg cell nucleus and then implanted in a ewe; the ewe gives birth to a clone of the adult.

Nobel Prizes

William D. Phillips and Steven Chu in physics for development and methods to cool and trap atoms with laser light; Paul D. Boyer in chemistry for his work on cell enzyme mechanics; Stanley B. Prusiner in Physiology or Medicine for his discovery of prions, a new biological principle of infection.

Sports

Baseball

Interleague play begins (NL 117–AL 97).

Mark McGwire hits 58 HRs, 34 for Oakland (AL) and 24 for St. Louis (NL).

Seattle (AL) hits a record 264 HRs.

Tony Gwynn's 8th batting title ties Honus Wagner's NL record.

The Cy Young Awards go to Pedro Martinez (Montreal, NL) and Roger Clemens (Toronto, AL).

Champions

Batting
Tony Gwynn (San Diego, NL), .372
Frank Thomas (Chicago, AL), .347
Pitching
Denny Neagle (Atlanta, NL), 20–5

Randy Johnson (Seattle, AL), 20–4
Home runs
Ken Griffey, Jr. (Seattle, AL), 56

Football

Barry Sanders gains 2,053 yards, the 3rd player to exceed 2,000. Charles Woodson is the 1st defensive player chosen for the Heisman.

NFC Season Leaders: Steve Young (San Francisco), passing; Barry Sanders (Detroit), rushing; Herman Moore (Detroit), receiving

AFC Season Leaders: Jim Harbaugh (Indianapolis), passing; Terrell Davis (Denver), rushing; Tim Brown (Oakland), receiving

College All-Americans: Peyton Manning (Q), Tennessee; Ryan Leaf (Q), Washington State

Bowls (Jan. 1, 1998)
Rose: Michigan 21–Washington State 16
Orange: Nebraska 42–Tennessee 17
Cotton: UCLA 29–Texas A&M 23
Sugar: Florida State 31–Ohio State 14

Tiger Woods, 21, wins the Masters with a record 18 under par; he draws huge crowds and record TV ratings. *Nike.*

Basketball

Latrell Sprewell (Golden State) is banned for one year and his $32 million contract terminated when he allegedly chokes coach P. J. Carlesimo. Michael Jordan wins a record 9th scoring title. UNC coach Dean Smith retires with a record 879 victories.

All-Pro First Team: Karl Malone (Utah), Grant Hill (Detroit), Hakeem Olajuwon (Houston), Michael Jordan (Chicago), Tim Hardaway (Miami)

Other Sports

Boxing: When Mike Tyson bites off a piece of Evander Holyfield's ear in the 3rd round of their HW title fight, the fight is stopped, and he is suspended from boxing.

Tennis: Pete Sampras wins Wimbledon and the Australian Open.

Winners

World Series
Florida (NL) 4
Cleveland (AL) 3
MVP
NL–Larry Walker, Colorado
AL–Ken Griffey, Jr., Seattle
Super Bowl XXXII (Jan. 1998)
Denver 31–Green Bay 24
MVP
Bret Favre (Green Bay)
Barry Sanders (Detroit)
College Football
Michigan
Nebraska
Heisman Trophy
Charles Woodson (Michigan)
NBA Championship
Chicago 4–Utah 2

MVP
Karl Malone, Utah
College Basketball
Arizona
Player of the Year
Tim Duncan, Wake Forest
Stanley Cup
Detroit
U.S. Tennis Open
Men: Patrick Rafter
Women: Martina Hingis
USGA Open
Ernie Els
Kentucky Derby
Silver Charm (Gary Stevens, jockey)

Fashion

Evening clothes dominate fashion shows, from the understated to the extravagant: sweater and skirt, sweatshirt of black lace, designs with gold or pink lace, beads, and fur trim. Many designers focus on "romance," creating racy but unabashedly glamorous gowns. Although few black or Asian photographers work for mainstream magazines, fashion becomes global (and political): many covers, such as *Elle, Mademoiselle,* and *Vogue,* feature non-whites in Asian kimonos, chinoiserie, or Masai-inspired clothing. Most designers seek styles wearable by any woman, heavy or thin, and of every economic class.

Humble polyester provides the medium for further embellishment. Among the year's failures are the slouchy, mannish suit with bell-bottoms; the Demi Moore shaved-head military look; see-through clothes with opaque undergarments; stiletto heels; and hard-edged makeup (including blue and black nail polish for men).

High-fashion notes: Xuly Bet's hooded wrap top and hipster cargo pants; Manolo's re-embroidered and appliquéd tulle; Thierry Mugler's gown of feathers, scales, fur, and embroidered stones.

Kaleidoscope _____

- The stock market continues its dramatic rise since 1993 (over 250 percent); in the "Goldilocks" economy (neither "too hot nor too cold"), job creation continues, unemployment drops, and inflation remains low.
- A record $920 billion in mergers leads to corporations of unprecedented size.
- Princess Di's death generates more press coverage than any event of the century; millions watch her televised funeral, and millions of flowers are strewn in her honor.
- Elton John sells 32 million copies of his "Candle in the Wind '97," his elegy to Princess Di, and donates all proceeds to her favorite charities.
- Controversy arises over allegations that large contributors were invited to stay overnight in the White House Lincoln bedroom.
- Senate and House investigations of alleged Democratic campaign violations continue through much of the year.
- The Supreme Court rules 9–0 that the president cannot delay the Paula Jones sexual harassment civil suit against him until he leaves office.
- The Russian station *Mir,* with Americans aboard, encounters numerous problems, including a fire, the breakdown of its main oxygen generator, and collision with one of its modules.
- A woman claiming to be Bill Cosby's daughter allegedly tries to extort $40 million from him.
- Widespread predictions assert that the El Niño ocean warming will dramatically alter weather patterns throughout the U.S.
- Lieutenant Kelly Flinn, the first B-52 female pilot, says on "60 Minutes" that she will fight her court martial for lying about a love affair with a married, enlisted man; she receives a general discharge.
- A drill sergeant is sentenced to 25 years in jail for raping six trainees.
- Mafia-boss Vincent ("Chin") Gigante is declared sane and convicted; for decades, he has evaded prosecution because of his aberrant behavior.
- In response to public outrage, Ken Starr rescinds his resignation as independent prosecutor for a deanship at Pepperdine University.
- The Supreme Court rules that sexual offenders need not be mentally ill to be indefinitely confined.
- After an international outcry, British au pair Louise Woodward's sentence for the murder of an 8-month-old is reduced from prison to probation.
- An actor on tour with *Jesus Christ Superstar* forgets to attach the safety harness during the scene where Judas hangs himself; after five minutes someone realizes that he has died.
- Microsoft comes under antitrust scrutiny for insisting that its Internet browser is intrinsic to its extraordinarily successful Windows 95.
- Media magnate Ted Turner donates $1 billion to the UN.
- Cyberspace fills with get-rich schemes and triple X–rated material, but the Supreme Court rules that an anti-smut bill would counter the First Amendment.
- Oprah Winfrey's highly successful new Book Club encourages active reading for previous nonreaders.

- "It's highly unlikely, of course, that the actual 'Eve' made these prints, but they were made at the right time on the right continent to be hers," remarks a paleontologist on 177,000-year-old footprints found in South Africa.
- Many view Garry Kasparov's defeat by IBM's Deep Blue computer as a triumph of artificial over human intelligence; the apparently intimidated Kasparov says: "I think IBM owes me and all mankind a rematch."
- PCs drop below $1,000 (Compaq, Hewlett Packard, IBM).
- New York ticket scalpers ask $1,000 per ticket for *The Lion King.*
- Violent crime in New York City is down by 38 percent; 981 homicides are the lowest on record since 1968.
- Marv Albert, faced with life imprisonment under Virginia's anti-consensual sodomy laws and revelations of his sex habits, pleads guilty to "aggravated assault"; he admits to biting his accuser's back.
- Warning labels are attached to Cabbage Patch Snacktime dolls when their mechanical mouths injure children.
- The suicidal Heaven's Gate cult members, awaiting the Hale-Bopp spaceship, carry quarters to make phone calls from space.
- The murder of rap star Biggie Smalls, the Notorious B.I.G., inspires Sean "Puffy" Combs's "I'll be Missing You"; an East-West rapper's feud is suspected.
- The new Barbie doll has a larger waistline, smaller breasts, and more modest clothing; she also has a friend in a wheelchair.
- Children become so upset at the virtual Tamagotchi pet, which needs constant attention to stay alive, that the toys are banned by many schools; a new version can be turned off.
- Food items carrying *E. coli* bacteria now include greens like radicchio, frisée, and arugula.
- A survey of grocery owners reveals that 64 percent of their customers eat cookies, chips, or candy without buying the products.
- New York Mayor Giuliani appears in a Marilyn Monroe outfit at a press dinner.
- The president falls down a few stairs after visiting golfer Greg Norman; he badly injures a knee but recovers quickly from surgery.
- Clinton adopts "Buddy," a chocolate Labrador.

Fads: TV ads for prescription drugs, recreational vehicles, Star Wars Trilogy (rerelease). For children: Sing and Snore Ernie, *Jurassic Park* electric race set, virtual pets, Zoob (Master Builder II), Disney *Hercules* action figures, Tyco Beanie Babies

First Appearances: flavored vodka (banana, chocolate), "strip offs" (face patches to remove blemishes), digital cameras, DVD players, computers within clothing (to count calories), voice recognition software, Zyprexa (for schizophrenia), Thalidomide prescribed for leprosy, prosthetic knee joints, pill for cows that alerts owner when the cow becomes ill, Crazy Dog pet toothpaste (peanut butter flavored, $6), the *New York Times* with color photos, WNBA

1998

"I will never step aside until the last hour of the last day of my term."—Bill Clinton. *White House.*

In the News

CLINTON DENIES "SEXUAL RELATIONS" WITH 21-YEAR-OLD INTERN, MONICA LEWINSKY, AFTER "FRIEND" LINDA TRIPP REVEALS SECRET TAPES . . . CLINTON TOURS AFRICA, DECRIES WORLD'S FAILURE IN RWANDA GENOCIDE . . . NORTHERN IRELAND PEACE AGREEMENT IS REACHED . . . U.S. ALLEGES MICROSOFT ILLEGALLY SOUGHT INTERNET CONTROL . . . SENATE APPROVES CZECH REPUBLIC, POLAND, HUNGARY FOR NATO . . . DAIMLER-BENZ AND CHRYSLER MERGE . . . DOW TOPS 9,000, UNEMPLOYMENT IS LOWEST SINCE 1970 . . . INDIA AND PAKISTAN TEST NUCLEAR WEAPONS . . . JAPANESE BANKS SUFFER HUGE LOSSES, "ASIAN FLU" SPREADS . . . SERB ATTACKS ON KOSOVO ALBANIANS INCREASE . . . BOYS, 11 AND 13, SHOOT 4 IN JONESBORO, ARK., SCHOOL . . . IN CHINA, CLINTON CRITICIZES HUMAN RIGHTS POLICY ON TV . . . GUNMAN KILLS 2 POLICEMEN AT U.S. CAPITOL . . . LEWINSKY ADMITS SEXUAL INTIMACY WITH CLINTON BUT DENIES HE TOLD HER TO LIE . . . FBI TESTS LEWINSKY'S STAINED DRESS FOR CLINTON DNA . . . AMERICAN EMBASSIES IN KENYA AND TANZANIA ARE BOMBED, 257 DIE . . . AFTER GRAND JURY TESTIMONY, CLINTON ADMITS HE "MISLED" U.S. FOR 6 MONTHS . . . U.S. STRIKES AT OSAMA BIN LADEN'S TERRORIST NETWORK IN AFGHANISTAN AND SUDAN . . . RUSSIAN DEBT DEFAULT SETS OFF WORLD STOCK MARKET PLUNGE . . . HOUSE AIRS SEXUALLY GRAPHIC STARR REPORT ON INTERNET . . . CLINTON MEDIATES PALESTINIAN-ISRAELI ACCORD AT WYE, MD. . . . MOBIL AND EXXON MERGE . . . HOUSE JUDICIARY COMM. VOTES 4 ARTICLES OF IMPEACHMENT ON PARTY LINES . . . CLINTON ORDERS AIR ATTACK AFTER HUSSEIN AGAIN OBSTRUCTS UN INSPECTORS . . . HOUSE IMPEACHES CLINTON FOR PERJURY AND OBSTRUCTION ON PARTY LINES . . . CLINTON APPROVAL RATINGS RISE ABOVE 70%.

Quotes _____

[On the "Clinton-Lewinsky matter":] "I did not have sexual relations with that woman, Miss Lewinsky. I never told anybody to lie, not a single time" (President Clinton); "'Just the facts, ma'am,' Jack Webb would say" (Kenneth Starr); "I did have a relationship with Ms. Lewinsky that was not appropriate—in fact, it was wrong. . . . I misled people, including even my wife. I deeply regret that. . . . At no time did I ask anyone to lie, to hide or destroy evidence or to take any other unlawful actions" (Clinton); "The leaking . . . has reached an intolerable point" (David Kendall, the President's attorney, to Starr); "I have talked with reporters on background on some occasions" (Starr, in *Brill's Content*); "[The media are Starr's] 'lapdogs'" (Brill); "This has been a vast right-wing conspiracy against my husband since the day he announced for president" (Hillary Rodham Clinton); "Nonsense" (Starr); "What an ugly, ugly woman you are for doing such an evil thing. You are the most shameful person alive" (sent to www.lindatripp.com); "I am you, . . . an average American" (Tripp).

[From the Starr Report:] "The President maintained that there can be no sexual relationship without sexual intercourse"; "In the course of her flirting with him, she . . . showed him the straps of her thong underwear"; Lewinsky: "I have lied my entire life"; "No one ever told me to lie. No one ever promised me a job"; Tripp: "You had sex with the President" / "No, Linda. We never had sex. We just fooled around." Tripp: "The navy blue dress. . . . Put it in a Baggie, put it in a zip-lock bag, and you pack it in with your treasures." "What for?" (Lewinsky). [On the report:] "In 445 pages, [it] mentions Whitewater . . . twice. It never once mentions other issues it has been investigating for years, . . . the White House travel office and . . . FBI files. By contrast, the issue of sex is mentioned more than 500 times, in the most graphic, salacious and gratuitous manner . . . of no relevance" (Clinton's attorney).

[During the House hearings:] *Democrats:* "The President betrayed his wife. He did not betray the

Left: John Glenn, 77, returns to space; "Godspeed," says Scott Carpenter, repeating his farewell of 1962. *NASA.* Right: Steven Spielberg, along with John Huston, Billy Wilder, and Martin Scorsese, are the most cited directors of the century's 100 best American movies. *Movie Star News.*

country. God help this nation if we fail to recognize this difference"; "Beware the wrath of the American people. . . . Beware!"; "This is an Impeachment Inquiry looking for a high crime or misdemeanor." *Republicans:* "What business is more important than teaching our children right from wrong?"; "The president shall not be held above the law"; "If there is a secret policy in the White House, . . . it is like Watergate."

[On bombing Iraq:] "The President cannot be believed. Saddam Hussein knows it, and that's why he jerks [Clinton's] chain all the time" (Tom DeLay, R–Tex.). "[UN inspector Richard Butler's] . . . conclusions are . . . profoundly disturbing. . . . Hussein and the other enemies of peace may have thought that the serious [impeachment] debate . . . would distract Americans or weaken our resolve to face him down" (Clinton).

[From Articles of Impeachment Voted by House:] "Resolved that William Jefferson Clinton, President of the United States, is impeached for high crimes and misdemeanors. . . . Whereupon, William Jefferson Clinton, by such conduct, warrants impeachment and trial and removal from office and disqualification to hold and enjoy any office of honor, trust or profit under the United States."

"We damn them today. History will damn them forever" (New York *Daily News,* on the GOP impeachment).

Ads _____

TV

Left: Larry King signs a $7 million per year contract with CNN. Right: Superstar Mariah Carey. *Movie Star News.*

Premieres
"Sports Night," Peter Krause, Josh Charles
"Jesse," Christina Applegate, Bruno Campos
"The Hughleys," D.L. Hughley, Elise Neal
"That '70s Show," Topher Grace, Mila Kunis
"Felicity," Keri Russell

Top Ten (Nielsen)
"ER," "Frasier," "Friends," "Veronica's Closet," "Jesse," "NYPD Blue," "Touched by an Angel," "JAG," "60 Minutes," "Everybody Loves Raymond"

Specials
"From the Earth to the Moon" (Tom Hanks); "Merlin," Sam Neill; "[Bill] Moyers on Addiction: Close to Home"; "Oprah Winfrey Presents: *The Wedding*"; "Rear Window," Christopher Reeve; *"King Lear,"* Ian Holm; "A Paralyzing Fear: The Story of Polio in America"; "City Dump: The Story of the 1955 Basketball Scandal"; "Africans in America: America's Journey Through Slavery"; "The Temptations"; *"Lolita,"* Jeremy Irons, Dominique Swain

Emmy Awards
"The Practice" (drama); Christine Lahti (actress, drama, "Chicago Hope"); Andre Braugher (actor, drama, "Homicide"); "Frasier" (comedy); Kelsey Grammer (actor, comedy, "Frasier"); Helen Hunt (actress, comedy, "Mad About You"); "Don King: Only in America" (made-for-TV movie)

Of Note
The Bill Clinton–Monica Lewinsky story creates record numbers of "cable junkies" • Geraldo Rivera signs a 6-year contract for $30 million with CNBC • "Seinfeld" is the fourth highest rated final show in TV history • "Dateline" expands to 5 nights a week • USA's *"Moby Dick"* with Patrick Stewart draws the highest cable audience in history for any non-news show except for sporting events • Dennis Franz gains a new partner, Rick Schroder, on "NYPD Blue" after Jimmy Smits' fatal heart transplant • Jerry Springer's frequently bleeped and violent talk show rises in ratings • Jack Kevorkian demonstrates patient-assisted death on "60 Minutes" and is arrested for first-degree murder.

Movies

Openings
Shakespeare in Love (John Madden), Gwyneth Paltrow, Joseph Fiennes
Saving Private Ryan (Steven Spielberg), Tom Hanks, Matt Damon
Elizabeth (Shekhar Kapur), Cate Blanchett
Life Is Beautiful (Roberto Benigni), Benigni
The Truman Show (Peter Weir), Jim Carrey, Ed Harris
There's Something About Mary (Peter and Bobby Farrelly), Ben Stiller, Cameron Diaz, Matt Dillon
Gods and Monsters (Bill Condon), Ian McKellen, Brendan Fraser, Lynn Redgrave
Armageddon (Michael Bay), Bruce Willis, Billy Bob Thornton
Beloved (Jonathan Demme), Oprah Winfrey, Thandie Newton, Danny Glover
Deep Impact (Mimi Leder), Robert Duvall, Téa Leoni, Elijah Wood
Godzilla (Roland Emmerich), Matthew Broderick, Jean Reno
Waking Ned Devine (Kirk Jones), Ian Bannen, David Kelly
A Bug's Life (Disney-Pixar), animation
The Thin Red Line (Terrence Malick), Sean Penn, Nick Nolte
A Civil Action (Steven Zaillian), John Travolta, Robert Duvall
A Simple Plan (Sam Raimi), Bill Paxton, Billy Bob Thornton, Bridget Fonda
Out of Sight (Steven Soderbergh), George Clooney, Jennifer Lopez
The Prince of Egypt (DreamWorks), animation
Bulworth (Warren Beatty), Beatty, Oliver Platt, Halle Berry
Affliction (Paul Schrader), Nick Nolte, Sissy Spacek

Academy Awards
Best Picture: *Shakespeare in Love*
Best Director: Steven Spielberg (*Saving Private Ryan*)
Best Actress: Gwyneth Paltrow (*Shakespeare in Love*)
Best Actor: Roberto Benigni (*Life Is Beautiful*)

Top Box-Office Stars
Harrison Ford, John Travolta, Tom Hanks, Robin Williams, Leonardo DiCaprio, Sandra Bullock, Julia Roberts, Tom Cruise, Will Smith, Brad Pitt

Stars of the Future
Chloe Sevigny, Thandie Newton, Vince Vaughn, Bill Paxton, Kate Beckinsale, Jennifer Lopez, Joseph Fiennes, Christina Ricci, Catherine Zeta-Jones, Gretchen Mol

Ginger (standing, far right) leaves the Spice Girls. *Movie Star News.*

Popular Music

Hit Songs
"Too Close"
"The Boy Is Mine"
"Truly Madly Deeply"
"Nice & Slow"
"My All"

Top Records

Albums: *Titanic* (soundtrack); *Let's Talk About Love* (Celine Dion); *Backstreet Boys* (Backstreet Boys); *Come On Over* (Shania Twain); *Yourself or Someone Like You* (matchbox 20); *Savage Garden* (Savage Garden); *Spiceworld* (Spice Girls); *Sevens* (Garth Brooks)

Singles: *Together Again* (Janet); *All My Life* (K-Ci & JoJo); *How's It Going to Be* (Third Eye Blind); *Angel* (Sarah McLachlan); *You Make Me Wanna . . .* (Usher). Country: *Just to See You Smile* (Tim McGraw); *Bye* (Jo Dee Messina)

Grammy Awards
My Heart Will Go On, Celine Dion (record); *The Miseducation of Lauryn Hill*, Lauryn Hill; "My Heart Will Go On" (song)

Jazz and Big Bands
Showcases proliferate for the eclectic sounds of new bands combining old sounds with new rhythms or instrumentation—including Brazilian, Cuban, or African rhythms, minimalism, electronic music, heavy metal, hip-hop, and "trip hop." The revival of retro big bands increases, with an emphasis on earthiness, swing, or spiritualism. Revered older stars such as Oscar Peterson, Nina Simone, Pete Seeger, Mick Jagger, Hank Williams, and the Rolling Stones also gain record audiences. Classic jazz singing, where the voice is used like a solo instrument, is replaced by the new forms of Cassandra Wilson and Kevin Mahogany, which also incorporate rock, pop, and rap. On the occasion of her 80th birthday, Marian McPartland is celebrated by the greats in jazz.

Top Performers (*Downbeat*):
Nick Brignola, Sonny Rollins, Steve Swallow (instrumentalists); Mingus Big Band (jazz big band); Keith Jarrett Standard Trio (acoustic jazz group); Jerry Gonzalez, Fort Apache Band (beyond group); Bob Dylan, *Time Out of Mind* (beyond album); Cassandra Wilson (female vocalist)

Theater

Broadway Openings

Plays
Art (Yasmina Reza), Victor Garber, Alan Alda, Alfred Molina
Freak (John Leguizamo), Leguizamo
The Judas Kiss (David Hare), Liam Neeson
The Blue Room (David Hare), Nicole Kidman
Swan Lake (Matthew Bourne), all-male cast
Side Man (Warren Leight), Christian Slater
The Beauty Queen of Leenane (Martin McDonagh), Anna Manahan, Marie Mullen

Musicals
Ragtime (Lynn Ahrens, Stephen Flaherty), Brian Stokes Mitchell, Peter Friedman, Audra McDonald
Parade (Jason Robert Brown), Brent Carver

Classics, Revivals, and Off-Broadway Premieres
The Chairs, Richard Briers; *The Sound of Music*, Rebecca Luker; *Cabaret*, Natasha Richardson, Alan Cumming; *On the Town*; *Peter Pan*, Cathy Rigby; *The Ride Down Mt. Morgan* (Arthur Miller), Patrick Stewart; *The Cripple of Inishmaan* (Martin McDonagh); *Collected Stories* (Donald Margolis), Uta Hagen; *Hedwig and the Angry Inch*, John Cameron Mitchell; *R&J* (Joe Calarco); *Twelfth Night*, Helen Hunt; *The Mystery of Irma Vep* (Charles Ludlam), Everett Quinton; *This Is Our Youth* (Kenneth Lonergen), Mark Ruffalo, Missy Yager; *Killer Joe* (Tracy Letts), Scott Glenn, Amanda Plummer; *Dinah Was* (Oliver Goldstick), Yvette Freeman; *Waiting for Godot*, John Turturro, Tony Shalhoub; *Fool Moon*, Bill Irwin, David Shiner; *Wit* (Margaret Edson), Kathleen Chalfont; Moscow Art Theater: *Three Sisters*; New Royal Shakespeare: *Cymbeline, Krapp's Last Tape, Everyman*

Regional

Alliance, Atlanta: *Elaborate Lives: The Legend of Aida* (Elton John, Tim Rice)

McCarter Theatre, Princeton, N.J.: *Electra*, Zoë Wanamaker

Pulitzer Prize
Wit, Margaret Edson

Tony Awards
Art (Yasmina Reza), play; *The Lion King* (Elton John, Tom Rice), musical

Classical Music ————————

Compositions

Richard Danielpour, *Bassoon Quintet*
Joan Tower, *Tambor*
Robert Rodriguez, *Forbidden Fire*
Bright Sheng, *Spring Dreams*
Peter Lieberson, *Free and Easy Wanderer*

Important Events

Celebrations include Gershwin and Duke Ellington centennials and Elliott Carter's 90th birthday concerts. For its 150th anniversary, the N.Y. Philharmonic commissions Del Tredici's *The Spider and the Fly* and gives a five-program, all-Beethoven cycle. Carnegie presents a gala Gershwin concert with the San Francisco Symphony and soloists Al Jarreau and Audra MacDonald, the beginning of a 22-month Gershwin project. The American Composers Orchestra begins a four-year cycle of 20th-century music. Scandinavian music gains unusual attention this year—from Grieg and Sibelius to Harald Saeverud.

Notable Performances

Lauded recitals of younger or lesser-known soloists include those of Hilary Hahn, Arcadi Volodos, Evgeny Kissin, Krystian Zimerman, Leif Ove Andsnes, Stephen Hough, Olli Mustonen, Joshua Bell, Sergei Nakariakov, Vladimir Pepin, and Nigel Kennedy. Alfred Brendel receives high praise during his 25th anniversary season. Anne-Sophie Mutter performs all 10 Beethoven sonatas in three concerts (before taking them on worldwide tour); Ken Noda returns to the piano after 17 years.

First Performances

Charles Ives, *Emerson Concerto* (New York); Elliott Carter, Quintet for Piano and Strings (New York); Milton Babbitt, Piano Concerto no. 2 (New York);

Left: Husband and wife Roberto Alagna and Angela Gheorghieu. *Winnie Klotz. Metropolitan Opera.* Right: Samuel Ramey is the most recorded bass in history. *Winnie Klotz. Metropolitan Opera.*

Itzhak Perlman, premier violinist of the era. *IMG.*

Edward Elgar, Third Symphony (Philadelphia); Ellen Taaffe Zwilich, Violin Concerto (New York); Tan Dun, *Red Forest* (New York); Krzysztof Penderecki, *Credo* (Portland); Philip Glass, *Monsters of Grace* (Los Angeles); Sofia Gubaidulina, Concerto for Two Violas (New York); Brian Eno, *Music for Airports* (New York); Augusta Reed Thomas, Concerto for Saxophone Quartet (New York)

Opera

Metropolitan: Pavarotti and Domingo celebrate 30th Met anniversaries. Ben Heppner, Deborah Voigt, *Lohengrin;* Angela Gheorghiu, Roberto Alagna, *Roméo et Juliette;* Domingo, Vladimir Chernov, *Stiffelio;* Heppner, *Die Meistersinger;* Patricia Racette, Philip Langridge, *Peter Grimes;* Kiri Te Kanawa, *Capriccio;* June Anderson, Chernov, Richard Margison, *Il trovatore;* Domingo, Olga Borodina, Sergei Leiferkus, *Samson et Dalila;* Bryn Terfel, Cecilia Bartoli, Renée Fleming, *Le nozze di Figaro*

New York City: Patricia Racette, Anne-Marie Owens (debut), Curt Peterson (debut), *Emmeline* (Tobias Picker); *Paul Bunyan* (Britten, Auden)

Chicago: Maureen O'Flynn, Paul Groves, Gino Quilico, *The Pearl Fishers;* Stephen West, *Amistad* (premiere, Anthony Davis)

Los Angeles: Paula Rasmussen, Ramón Vargas, *Werther*

Music Notes

New interpretations of Mahler's 6th symphony challenge the 5th as the quintessential Mahler; some add a third hammer stroke at the conclusion, which Mahler superstitiously avoided as fate's final blow • Wynton Marsalis oversees the new jazz center built at the N.Y.C. Coliseum • Martin Bresnick wins the first Charles Ives Living Award, $225,000 over three years, the largest composer's prize • Continued interest in early music calls for the countertenor or "castrato"; John Eliot Gardiner revives Schumann on period instruments • The *New York Times* calls the Philharmonic Board, in its demand of Kurt Mazur's 2002 resignation, "out if its collective mind" • Recordings of Karol Rathaus draw attention to the little-known Holocaust victim • The New York Philharmonic tours Asia, performing in Beijing for the first time • Nine CDs of pianist William Kapell, who died in 1953 at age 31, are called a "landmark" in music history.

Art

Paintings
Robert Rauschenberg, *Georgia on My Mind*
Alex Katz, *Blue*
Chris Finley, *Drool, Sweat, Scream*
Edward Ruscha, *Clown Speaks*
Ross Bleckner, *Signaling Passion*

Sculpture
Ellsworth Kelly, *Horizontal Curve II*
Tony Smith, *Moondog* (posthumous)
Red Grooms, *Tennessee Fox Trot Carousel*
Ronald Jones, *The Bed Neil Armstrong Slept in . . .*

Important Exhibitions
"20th-Century Still-Life Paintings" from the Phillips Collection begins a three-year tour of the U.S. and Japan; other traveling shows include Dove, Rothko, Calder, Close, Monet, Charles Ray, and "Inside Out: Picasso and the War Years, 1937–1945."

Museums

New York: *Metropolitan:* Annenberg Collection of Impressionism, Post-Impressionism; "Native Paths: American Indian Art"; Klee landscapes; "The Human Figure in Transition, 1900–1945"; American sculpture; Edward Burne-Jones, Pierre-Paul Prud'hon; Korean art; Ellsworth Kelly; "Boccioni and Women." *MoMA:* Pollock; Miró; Louis Comfort Tiffany; Léger; Holzer; Bonnard; Willie Cole; Tony Smith. *Whitney:* Nevelson; Wyeth landscapes; Carrie Mae Weems; Bill Viola (first video retrospective at museum). *Guggenheim:* "China, 5,000 Years"; Masterpieces from the Pompidou and Guggenheim; "Art of the Motorcycle." *Brooklyn:* Jewels

Architecture
Monterey Bay Aquarium, Monterey, Calif. (Esherick Homsey Dodge & Davis)
Swiss Bank Center, Stamford, Conn. (Skidmore, Owings & Merrill)
POW Museum, Andersonville, Ga. (Carla McConnell)
Renovated Grand Central Terminal, N.Y.C. (Warren & Wetmore, Reed and Stem)
Alcoa Headquarters, Pittsburgh (Martin Powell, The Design Alliance Pittsburgh)

of the Romanovs. *Jewish Museum:* Chaim Soutine; Ben Shahn

Washington, D.C.: Van Gogh; Japanese art from the Imperial Collection; "Manet, Monet and the Gare St. Lazare"

Chicago: "Mary Cassatt: Modern Woman"; Whistler; Bernini's terra cottas from the Hermitage

Boston: Monet; David Hockney

Philadelphia: Van Eyck; "Delacroix: The Late Work"

Art Briefs
Debate over MoMA's Egon Schiele exhibit brings national attention to the rightful ownership of art confiscated from Holocaust victims; this includes the Met's most expensive purchase, *Wheat Fields with Cypresses* ($57 million, 1993) • "Art of the Motorcycle" is the Guggenheim's best attended show in its history, attracting many first-time museumgoers • Installation art increases in popularity: works by Robert Gober, Ann Hamilton, Robert Irwin, Ilya Kabakov, Hans Haacke, Jason Rhodes, and Robert Wilson • Scholars debate the authenticity of dozens of Van Goghs, including *Sunflowers* ($40 million, 1987) • The Whitney searches for a new mission with alternative art—e.g., Charles Ray's l'oeil sculptures of cars in wrecks • The FDR Memorial in Washington, D.C., will be amended to clearly depict the president in a wheelchair • Natasha Gelman and Betsey Roosevelt Whitney donate an estimated $600 million of art to various museums • The Met buys its first Jasper Johns painting, *White Flag,* valued at $20 million • Interesting sales of the year, in millions, include a Michelangelo print ($7.4), Andy Warhol's *Orange Marilyn* ($17.3), and Monet's *Waterlily Pond and Path by the Water* (a Monet record, $33 million, purchased in 1954 for $7,000). Intel gives the Whitney $6 million for "The American Century: Art and Culture, 1900–2000," to open April 1999.

Dance

American Ballet Theatre: *The Snow Maiden; Spring and Fall* (John Neumeier); *Without Words* (premiere, Nacho Duato); Nina Ananiashvili, Jose Manuel Carreño, *Le Corsaire; Known by Heart* (Tharp)

New York City Ballet: Merrill Ashley retires. *Stabat Mater* (Pergolesi); *Concerti Armonici* (Unico Wilhelm van Wassanaer); *Dances at a Gathering* (Chopin); *Variations on a Nursery Song; La Stravaganza* (Angelin

Preljocaj; for the company's 50th anniversary at the end of the year, 250 stars fill the stage; 100 ballets will pay tribute to Balanchine, Le Clerq, and Robbins in 1999.

Washington: *Porgy and Bess* (first full-length production); the Stanislavsky Nemirovich-Danchenko Ballet debuts landmark Vasily Vainonen *Nutcracker* (1934) and Vladimir Bourmeister *Swan Lake* (1935).

Books

Fiction

Critics' Choice
Charming Billy, Alice McDermott
A Lover's Almanac, Maureen Howard
Cloudsplitter, Russell Banks
Freedomland, Richard Price
Birds of America, Lorrie Moore
Gain, Richard Powers
Ghost Town, Robert Coover
Kaaterskill Falls, Allegra Goodman
I Married a Communist, Philip Roth
The Poisonwood Bible, Barbara
  Kingsolver
Damascus Gate, Robert Stone

Best-Sellers
The Street Lawyer, John Grisham
Rainbow Six, Tom Clancy
Bag of Bones, Stephen King
A Man in Full, Tom Wolfe
Mirror Image, Danielle Steel
Long Road Home, Danielle Steel
The Klone and I, Danielle Steel
Point of Origin, Patricia Cornwell
Paradise, Toni Morrison
All Through the Night, Mary
  Higgins Clark

Nonfiction

Critics' Choice
Slaves in the Family, Edward Ball
Titan, Ron Chernow

*Pillar of Fire: America in the King
  Years*, Taylor Branch
*Consilience: The Unity of
  Knowledge*, Edward O. Wilson
*Shakespeare: The Invention of the
  Human*, Harold Bloom
To End a War, Richard Holbrooke
The American Century, Harold
  Evans, with Gail Buckland,
  Kevin Baker
Explaining Hitler, Ron Rosenbaum
One Nation, After All, Alan Wolfe
The Nurture Assumption, Judith
  Rich Harris
Confederates in the Attic, Tony
  Horwitz
Sexual McCarthyism, Alan
  Dershowitz
*The Victors: Eisenhower and His
  Boys*, Stephen E. Ambrose
The Death of Outrage, William
  Bennett

Best-Sellers
The 9 Steps to Financial Freedom,
  Suze Orman
The Greatest Generation, Tom
  Brokaw
Sugar Busters! H. Leighton
  Steward *et al.*
Tuesdays with Morrie, Mitch Albom
The Guinness Book of Records, 1999
Talking to Heaven, James Van
  Praagh

Robert K. Shaye (left of Travolta) transforms his New Line Cinema into a major movie studio; Shaye recently implemented a screenwriting concentration at the U. of Michigan, in honor of former professors James Gindin and Donald Hall. *New Line Cinema.*

Something More, Sarah Ban
  Breathnach
In the Meantime, Iyanla Vanzant
A Pirate Looks at Fifty, Jimmy
  Buffett
*If Life Is a Game, These Are the
  Rules*, Chérie Carter-Scott

Poetry
Frederick Seidel, *Going Fast*
Donald Hall, *Without*
E. D. Hirsch, *On Love*
Gerald Stern, *This Time*

Pulitzer Prizes
The Hours, Michael Cunningham
  (fiction)
*Gotham: A History of New York
  City to 1898*, Edwin G. Burrows,
  Mike Wallace (U.S. history)
Annals of the Former World, John
  McPhee (nonfiction)
Lindbergh, A. Scott Berg (biography)
Blizzard of One, Mark Strand
  (poetry)

Science and Technology

A nearly complete 3-million-year-old skeleton (predating Lucy), the "missing link" in human evolution, is discovered; other findings indicate that early humans were apelike and tree-inhabiting.

Cloning advances include 60 mice (from three generations) and eight calves from a single cow.

Studies confirm that folic acid and B-6 supplements, potassium in foods like bananas, and an alcoholic drink a day reduce heart attack and stroke risk.

Experimental drugs cause new coronary blood vessel growth; drugs such as angiostatin may halt cancer by reducing its blood supply.

Scientists isolate human embryonic stem cells that may grow tissues to replace cells and organs lost to disease.

Herceptin is effective against a form of breast cancer by targeting mutant genes; routine PSA blood tests may greatly reduce prostate cancer deaths.

Researchers demonstrate that new brain cells can grow after birth.

The Hubble telescope reveals that the universe is expanding at an accelerating rate; Hubble photos also indicate a Dark Age 13 billion years ago, following the Big Bang.

Researchers learn that neutrinos have mass and may compose the invisible "dark matter" comprising 90 percent of the universe.

Nobel Prizes
Robert F. Furchgott, Louis J. Ignarro, and Ferid Murad in physiology for research on nitric oxide and blood vessels; Daniel C. Tsui and Robert B. Laughlin in physics for demonstrating how electrons form "quasiparticles"; Walter Kohn in chemistry for quantum work enabling calculation of complex chemical processes.

Sports

Baseball

Mark McGwire (St. Louis, NL) hits his 62nd HR in game 144, passing Roger Maris' record; Sammy Sosa (Chicago, NL) overtakes McGwire, 66–65, with three games left, but McGwire ends ahead 70 to 66.

Interest in record HR balls mounts, as the most recent one is expected to bring $1 million at auction.

New York wins an AL record 114 games, and a record 125, including the WS.

Tom Glavine (Atlanta, NL) and Roger Clemens (Toronto, AL) win the Cy Young awards; for Clemens, a record 5th.

Champions

Batting	Pitching
Larry Walker (Colorado, NL), .363	John Smoltz (Atlanta, NL), 17–3
	David Wells (New York, AL), 18–4
Bernie Williams (New York, AL), .339	*Home runs*
	Mark McGwire (St. Louis, NL), 70

Football

The NCAA sponsors the Bowl Championship Series: the top two teams play at alternating sites. Dan Marino is the first to throw for over 400 TDs. Jason Elam kicks a record-tying 63-yard FG.

NFC Season Leaders: Randall Cunningham (Minneapolis), passing; Jamal Anderson (Atlanta), rushing; Frank Sanders (Arizona), receiving

AFC Season Leaders: Vinny Testaverde (New York), passing; Terrell Davis (Denver), rushing (2,008 yds.); O. J. McDuffie (Miami), receiving

College All-Americans: Tim Couch (Q), Kentucky; Cade McNown (Q), UCLA; Michael Bishop (Q), Kansas State

Bowls (Jan. 1999)
Rose: Wisconsin 38–UCLA 31
Orange: Florida 31–Syracuse 10
Sugar: Ohio State 24–Texas A&M 14

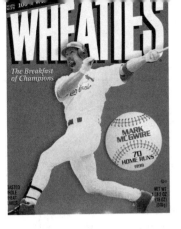

"I am in awe of myself," says the modest Mark McGwire. *General Mills.*

Cotton: Texas 38–Mississippi St. 11
Fiesta (B.C.S.): Tennessee 23–FSU 16

Basketball

Michael Jordan wins a record 10th scoring title, and Chicago wins the title for the 6th time in the decade. The NBA, trying to limit player salaries, declares a lockout for the 1998–99 season; at the end of the year, with two months of play lost, no agreement is reached.

NBA All-Pro First Team: Karl Malone (Utah), Tim Duncan (San Antonio), Shaquille O'Neal (L.A. Lakers), Michael Jordan (Chicago), Gary Payton (Seattle)

Olympics: At Nagano, Japan, Tara Lipinski, 15, defeats Michelle Kwan for the gold in figure skating; Jonny Moseley wins gold in the moguls; Picabo Street wins in the super G; and the women's team wins in hockey.

Winners

World Series	*MVP*
New York (AL)–4	Michael Jordan, Chicago
San Diego (NL)–0	*College Basketball*
MVP	Kentucky
NL–Sammy Sosa, Chicago	*Player of the Year*
AL–Juan Gonzalez, Texas	Antawn Jamison, North Carolina
Super Bowl XXXIII (Jan. 1999)	*Stanley Cup*
Denver 34–Atlanta 19	Detroit
MVP	*U.S. Tennis Open*
Terrell Davis, Denver	Men: Patrick Rafter
College Football	Women: Lindsay Davenport
Tennessee	*USGA Open*
Heisman Trophy	Lee Janzen
Ricky Williams, Texas	*Kentucky Derby*
NBA Championship	Real Quiet (Kent Desormeaux, jockey)
Chicago 4–Portland 2	

Fashion

The return of glamour, with the prevalent relaxed look, predominates—even in expensive furs such as chinchilla, sable, and lamb, designed as duffel and pea coats. Casual wear, simple sheaths, or body-binding dresses are au courant for the evening. Skirts are both mini and increasingly ankle-length. Shirts, like the popular sheer knit, are often worn braless, and backs are bared for a new sexy look, the clothing fastened with ties and strings rather than buttons or zippers. The more varied the soft tones, the more stylish the woman—with the occasional spot of red or metallic brown to enliven the outfit. At the end of the season, the long chemise, pencil-thin silhouette, and light fabrics suggest a return to 1920s styles, gray replaces black as the color of choice, and the ubiquitous suit fades from popularity. Many predict that the decade's simplicity, eclecticism, and frequent retro styles will be replaced by comfortable "postmodern" redesigns of the century's highest fashions—"deconstructions" appropriate to the millennium.

High-fashion note: Oscar de la Renta's and Mark Eisen's unadorned knee-length, sleeveless sheath in pastels.

Kaleidoscope

- "All Monica, all the time"—instant news and pundit commentary—becomes a national preoccupation, including the "60 Minutes" interview with Kathleen Willey, who alleges that Clinton "groped" her in the Oval Office, Linda Tripp's secret tapes of her young "friend" Monica's tales, Clinton's videotaped testimony, and the *Starr Report,* detailing eight alleged (oral) sexual encounters.
- Many Democrat and Republican leaders, as well as the public (via polls), express disgust with the President's behavior; Clinton's performance approval ratings remain at 60–66 percent.
- After unexpected GOP House losses in November, Speaker Newt Gingrich resigns; his nominated successor, Bob Livingston (R–La.), also resigns after admitting to several adulteries.
- "The statute of limitations has long since passed on my youthful indiscretions," says Henry Hyde (R–Ill.), House Judiciary Chair, after his five-year infidelity with a married woman is revealed.
- Welfare recipients drop below 4 percent, the lowest in 25 years; unemployment, interest rates, murders, juvenile arrests, births to unwed mothers, infant mortality, and gas prices fall to 25–35-year lows.
- AIDS deaths fall nearly 50 percent.
- Sexual discrimination suits rise to 24,728 (17,422, in 1991), including sexual harassment suits, 15,899 (6,883, in 1991); Mitsubishi settles one for a record $34 million.
- "The current economic performance, with . . . strong growth and low inflation, is as impressive as any I have [ever] witnessed," states Alan Greenspan, Federal Reserve head.
- As obesity rates reach 50 percent, so do sales of rich foods and books like *Cooking with the Two Fat Ladies;* a health food and vitamin supplement mania also grips the nation.
- Catastrophic hurricanes, heat waves, and a general alteration of weather patterns are attributed to El Niño in the world's warmest year since 1866.
- Major efforts are made to avert a catastrophic "Y2K" black-out, when computers may misread the year 2000 as 1900.
- A UC student discovers a Mark Twain manuscript, "The Great Republic's Peanut Stand," an essay on copyright in the form of a sparring match.
- The Modern Library's "100 Best Novels of the Century" list begins with *Ulysses, The Great Gatsby, A Portrait of the Artist as a Young Man, Lolita, Brave New World, The Sound and the Fury,* and *Catch-22.*
- *Citizen Kane, Casablanca, The Godfather,* and *Gone with the Wind* lead a 100 Best American Movies of the Century list.
- The IRS Reform Bill shifts the burden of proof from the taxpayer to the IRS.
- Records show that Reynolds Tobacco courted buyers as young as 14 ("tomorrow's business"); tobacco companies settle state health claims for $206 billion.
- When wrestler Jesse (the Body) Ventura is elected governor of Minnesota, he becomes Jesse (the Mind).
- Atlanta Gov. Zell Miller proposes that newborns be sent home with a recording of Mozart and Bach to stimulate brain development.
- When Oprah Winfrey defeats a Texas "beef defamation" suit over her show on Mad Cow disease, she says: "Freedom not only lives. It rocks!"

- A study proves that PMS is biological rather than psychological.
- Clinton's deposition in Paula Jones's alleged sexual harassment (1991) suit leads to the entire impeachment matter, although the Arkansas judge declares the testimony irrelevant and dismisses the suit as without merit.
- Seventeen major newspapers call for Clinton's resignation after his grand jury admissions.
- The movie *Wag the Dog* is frequently invoked after Clinton's antiterrorist actions abroad, suggesting his intent to divert attention from "Monica."
- Widespread small-town teenage school shootings stun the nation; 19 children die.
- The Atlanta Olympics and Birmingham abortion clinic bombings lead to a massive manhunt for Eric Rudolph, of "The Army of God."
- James Byrd, Jr., 49, a black salesman, is dragged to death by three racists in Jasper, Tex.; his body is dismembered.
- In Wyoming, a gay man, Matthew Shepard, dies after being beaten and impaled on a wire fence.
- KKK leader Samuel Bowers is convicted in Miss. for the 1966 murder of civil rights leader Vernon Dahmer.
- Former DA Steven Pagones wins his defamation suit against Al Sharpton and others who falsely accused him of raping Tawana Brawley in 1987.
- Ethical questions mount over induced multiple births, such as the Chukwu octuplets of Texas.
- A N.J. fertility clinic doubles its stipend to egg donors ($5,000 for a month's supply), initiating citizens' fear of a bidding war for human eggs.
- DNA evidence proves that Thomas Jefferson fathered a child with his slave-mistress Sally Hemings.
- After serving 18 months for contempt, Susan McDougal is freed; new contempt charges brought by Ken Starr are dismissed; she says: "I will not perjure myself for leniency."
- Voyager I, launched in 1977, is still transmitting from 6.5 billion miles from Earth.
- *Titanic* is the highest grossing film in history, $850 million.
- A piece of Edward VII and Wallis Simpson's wedding cake brings $29,900 at a Sotheby's auction.
- In an extensive poll, Harrison Ford is named "the sexiest man of the year"; he thinks he looks "dorky" on camera.
- Viagra, for male erectile dysfunction, sells at a record rate for $10 a pill.

First Appearances: on-line birth, Propecia, surgical glue, death under suicide-assisted law (Oregon), vaccines (for Lyme disease, pneumococcus, and childhood diarrhea), planet outside the solar system, quantum computer network, nanotubes (to replace silicon chip), "quibit," iris-scanning ID system, DNA database, female fixed-wing pilot in combat, $300-billion company (G.E.), saint-john's-wort cosmetics, the Euro (Jan. 1, 1999), "M. Lewinski" (new name, San Diego Zoo elk), drive-through cigar stores (D.C.)

Fads: Ginkgo, Titanicmania, "trance," "techno," "jungle," swing, and ballroom dancing, Internet shopping, Furby, Rugrats, Teletubbies

Name Index

Name Index

Title Index

General Index